AutoCAD Instructor

AutoCAD Instructor

James A. Leach
University of Louisville

IRWIN

Chicago • Bogota • Boston • Buenos Aires • Caracas
London • Madrid • Mexico City • Sydney • Toronto

IRWIN
Concerned About Our Environment
    In recognition of the fact that our company is a large end-user of
    fragile yet replenishable resources, we at IRWIN can assure you
that every effort is made to meet or exceed Environmental Protection Agency
(EPA) recommendations and requirements for a "greener" workplace.
To preserve these natural assets, a number of environmental policies, both
companywide and department-specific, have been implemented. From the
use of 50% recycled paper in our textbooks to the printing of promotional
materials with recycled stock and soy inks to our office paper recycling program, we are committed to reducing waste and replacing environmentally
unsafe products with safer alternatives.

Sponsoring editor:	Betsy Jones
Senior developmental editor:	Kelley Butcher
Marketing manager:	Brian Kibby
Project editor:	Beth Yates
Production manager:	Pat Frederickson
Designer:	Keith McPherson
Cover image:	Autodesk, Inc.
Art manager:	Kim Meriwether
Printer:	Wm. C. Brown

Library of Congress Cataloging-in-Publication Data

Leach, James A.
    AutoCAD instructor / James A. Leach.
        p. cm. -- (The Irwin graphics series)
        Includes index.
        ISBN 0-256-17144-0
        1. Computer graphics. 2. AutoCAD (Computer file). I. Title.
    II. Series.
    T385.L383 1994
    620'.0042'0285369--dc20   94-29190

Printed in the United States of America
1 2 3 4 5 6 7 8 9 0 WCB 1 0 9 8 7 6 5 4

"You can accomplish anything you make up your mind to..."

Norman G. Leach
to whom this book is dedicated

The Irwin Graphics Series

Providing you with the highest quality textbooks that meet your changing needs requires feedback, improvement, and revision. The team of authors and Richard D. Irwin Publishers are committed to this effort. We invite you to become part of our team by offering your wishes, suggestions, and comments for future editions and new products and texts.

Please mail or fax your comments to:

James A. Leach
c/o Richard D. Irwin Publishers
1333 Burr Ridge Parkway
Burr Ridge, IL 60521
fax: 708-789-6946

Titles in the Irwin Graphics Series include:

Engineering Graphics Communication by Bertoline, Wiebe, Miller, and Nasman, 1995

Technical Graphics Communication by Bertoline, Wiebe, Miller, and Nasman, 1995

Fundamentals of Engineering Graphics by Bertoline, Wiebe, Miller, and Nasman, 1996

Problems for Engineering Graphics Communication and Technical Graphics Communication, Workbook #1, 1995

Problems for Engineering Graphics Communication and Technical Graphics Communication, Workbook #2, 1995

Problems for Engineering Graphics Communication and Technical Graphics Communication, Workbook #3, 1995

AutoCAD Instructor by James A. Leach, 1995

The AutoCAD Companion by James A. Leach, 1995

The CADKEY Companion by John Cherng, 1995

Introduction to CADKEY by Timothy Sexton, 1995

Engineering Design and Visualization Workbook by Dennis Stevenson, 1995

PREFACE

This book was written to teach you how to use AutoCAD. The most suitable means available in a printed format for communicating the concepts, commands, and applications are used, including many "screen grabs," AutoCAD drawings, figures of AutoCAD features, and written explanations. Because the subject of this book is graphical, illustrations are used whenever possible to communicate an idea, totaling 1200 for the book. My objective is, to the best of my ability, to provide a written medium for you to learn AutoCAD, even in the case that you have no other help. This book is your AutoCAD instructor.

Release 12, the most recent release of AutoCAD at the time of this writing, is the subject of this edition of the *AutoCAD Instructor*. Commands from previous releases of AutoCAD can be found in this book since AutoCAD always keeps commands from previous releases or versions. The appearance of the user interface varies, however, from release to release.

The *AutoCAD Instructor* is for both professionals and students in the fields of engineering, architecture, design, construction, manufacturing, and any other field that has a use for AutoCAD. Applications and examples from many fields are given throughout the explanations of concepts and commands. The applications and examples used are not intended to have an inclination towards a particular field. Instead, applications to a particular field are used when they best explain an idea or use of a command.

The *AutoCAD Instructor* is presented in a logical order by delivering the fundamental concepts and commands first, then moving toward the more advanced and specialized features of AutoCAD. The writing style also follows that progression by beginning with small pieces of information explained in a simple form in short chapters and then building on that experience to deliver more complex ideas, requiring a synthesis of earlier concepts.

The exercises within each chapter follow the same progression as the topical order and writing style, beginning with a simple tutorial approach to the fundamental operations and ending with a challenging problem requiring a synthesis of earlier exercises. The exercises from chapter to chapter build in complexity yet require the least amount of busy work, which is accomplished by preparing and saving simple drawings in early chapters and using those files for more involved applications in later chapters.

The *AutoCAD Instructor* does not require that you have previous experience with AutoCAD or other CAD software packages, or with computers for that matter. However, familiarity with personal computers and the operating system interface (DOS, Windows, etc.) is helpful. The *AutoCAD Instructor* is very useful if you are an experienced AutoCAD user and want guidelines for features such as plotting or paper space, for example, or need information on advanced features, such as 3D modeling. The *AutoCAD Instructor* can also be used as a reference guide to AutoCAD. Every command is explained in simple terms and given with a "Menu Table" listing the possible methods of invoking the command. Each of the drawing and editing commands and options are illustrated, including an illustration for every dimensioning variable.

This book is written with the assumption that you do have some experience with geometry, graphical conventions, and standards for your field. In other words, it is assumed that you have in mind the type and format of the drawings, designs, or diagrams you want to create with AutoCAD. If you are a student in engineering, architecture, or design, the *AutoCAD Instructor* assumes that you are supplementing your AutoCAD course work with additional courses or reference textbooks covering standard drawing conventions and formats for your field. Appendix E in the *AutoCAD Instructor* lists the **CAD References** for *Engineering Graphics Communication* by Gary Bertoline, et al.

I predict you will have a positive learning experience with AutoCAD that leads to productive contributions in your field. Although learning AutoCAD is not a trivial endeavor, you should find it fun and interesting. It's a good feeling when the "light bulb" turns on and you say to yourself, "Oh, yeah...I see!"

James A. Leach

ABOUT THE AUTHOR

James A. Leach is assistant professor of engineering graphics and director of the AutoCAD Training Center (ATC) at the University of Louisville. James holds the B.I.D. (Industrial Design) and M.Ed. from Auburn University. He began teaching engineering graphics at Auburn in 1976 and started teaching AutoCAD Version 1.4 in early 1984. As coordinator of engineering graphics, in 1986 he established course content and facilities for AutoCAD instruction to 1200 engineering students per year. In 1989 James moved to the University of Louisville where he teaches four courses for engineering students and five courses at the ATC. The University of Louisville ATC was one of the first authorized centers, having been established in 1985.

ACKNOWLEDGMENTS

I wish to thank Steven H. Baldock for his valuable input in this work. A University of Kentucky graduate, Steve has been a helpful source of information for concepts, applications, and teaching strategies of AutoCAD during this project. Steve also created many of the figures for the **AutoCAD Instructor**. Steve is an authorized AutoCAD instructor at the University of Louisville ATC. Steve also works as a structural steel designer and has a CAD consulting firm, Infinity Computer Enterprises (ICE).

I am very grateful to my wife, Donna, for the many hours of copy editing required to produce this text.

I would also like to acknowledge Kelley Butcher at Richard D. Irwin, Inc. for her support and encouragement; Gary Bertoline for giving me a start; Robert A. Matthews and Therese Sherer for doing their jobs well and permitting me to attend to this text; Mark H. Miller, Carl Barratt, Joseph Kotowski, Cynthia L. Mahoney, Keith F. Hickman, and Kim Manner for helpful comments and suggestions during the review of this text; Charles Grantham of Contemporary Publishing Company of Raleigh, Inc. for generosity and consultation; B. J. Labate for assistance with illustrations; James B. Daily and Charles E. Skeen for miscellaneous AutoCAD goodies; and University of Louisville ATC instructors, University Center for Continuing and Professional Education staff, and Speed Scientific School Dean's Office for support and encouragement.

TRADEMARK AND COPYRIGHT ACKNOWLEDGMENTS

The object used in the Wireframe Modeling Tutorial, Chapter 35 appears courtesy of James H. Earle, *Graphics for Engineers, Third Edition*, ©1992 by Addison-Wesley Publishing Company, Inc. Reprinted by permission of the publisher.

The following drawings used for Chapter Exercises appear courtesy of James A. Leach, *Problems in Engineering Graphics Fundamentals*, Series A and Series B, ©1984 and 1985 by Contemporary Publishing Company of Raleigh, Inc.: Gasket A, Gasket B, Pulley, Holder, Angle Brace, Saddle, V-Block, Bar Guide, Cam Shaft, Bearing, Cylinder, Support Bracket, Corner Brace, and Adjustable Mount. Reprinted or redrawn by permission of the publisher.

The PUMPSOL drawing used throughout Chapter 34, 3D Display and Viewing appears courtesy of Autodesk, Inc. All sample drawings on the last page of several chapters are reprinted courtesy of Autodesk, Inc.

ADI, Advanced Modeling Extension, AME, ATC, Autodesk, AutoCAD, AutoCAD Training Center, AutoLISP, and AutoShade are registered trademarks of Autodesk, Inc.

ACAD, AutoCAD Development System, Autodesk 3D Concepts, Autodesk Device Interface, Autodesk Training Center, AutoSurf, and DXF are trademarks of Autodesk, Inc.

RenderMan is a registered trademark of Pixar used by Autodesk under license from Pixar. City Blueprint, Country Blueprint, EuroRoman, EuroRoman-oblique, PanRoman, SuperFrench, Romantic, Romantic-bold, Sans Serif, Sans Serif-bold, Sans Serif-oblique, Sans Serif-BoldOblique, Technic Technic-light, and Technic-bold are Type 1 fonts, copyright 1992 P. B. Payne.

LEGEND

The following special treatment of characters and fonts in the textual content is intended to assist you in translating the meaning of words or sentences in the **AutoCAD Instructor**.

<u>Underline</u>	Emphasis of a word or an idea
`Courier font`	An AutoCAD prompt appearing on the <u>screen</u> at the command line
Italic (Upper and Lower)	An AutoCAD command, option, menu, or dialogue box name
UPPER CASE	A file name
UPPER CASE ITALIC	An AutoCAD system variable or a drawing aid (*OSNAP*, *SNAP*, *GRID*, *ORTHO*, and *COORDS*)

Anything in **Bold** represents user input:

Bold	What you should <u>type</u> or press on the keyboard
Bold Italic	An AutoCAD <u>command</u> that you should type or <u>menu item</u> that you should select
BOLD UPPER CASE	A <u>file name</u> that you should type
BOLD UPPER CASE ITALIC	A <u>system variable</u> that you should type
PICK	Move the cursor to the indicated position on the screen and press the <u>select</u> button (button #1)

TABLE OF CONTENTS

INTRODUCTION

WHAT IS CAD?

CAD is an acronym for Computer-Aided Design or Computer-Aided Drafting. CAD allows you to accomplish design and drafting activities using a computer. A CAD software package, such as AutoCAD, enables you to create designs and generate drawings to document those designs.

Design is a broad field involving the process of making an idea into a real product or system. The design process requires repeated refinement of an idea or ideas until a solution results--a manufactured product or constructed system. Traditionally, design involves the use of sketches, drawings, renderings, 2-dimensional and 3-dimensional models, prototypes, testing, analysis, and documentation. Drafting is generally known as the production of drawings that are used to document a design for manufacturing or construction or to archive the design.

CAD is a <u>tool</u> that can be used for design and drafting activities. CAD can be used to make "rough" idea drawings, although it is more suited to creating accurate finish drawings and renderings. CAD can be used to create a 2-dimensional or 3-dimensional computer model of the product or system for further analysis and testing by other computer programs. In addition, CAD can be used to supply manufacturing equipment such as lathes, mills, laser cutters, or rapid prototyping equipment with numerical data to manufacture the product. CAD is also used to create the 2-dimensional documentation drawings for communicating and archiving the design.

The tangible result of CAD activity is usually a drawing generated by a plotter or printer, but can be a rendering of a model or numerical data for use with another software package or manufacturing device. Regardless of the purpose for using CAD, the resulting drawing or model is stored in a CAD file. The file consists of numeric data in binary form usually saved to a magnetic device such as a diskette, hard disk, or tape.

WHY SHOULD YOU USE CAD?

Although there are other methods that are used for design and drafting activities, CAD offers these advantages over other methods in many cases.

1. Accuracy
2. Productivity for repetitive operations
3. Sharing the CAD file with other software programs

Accuracy

Since CAD technology is founded on computers, it offers great accuracy compared to traditional "manual" methods of drafting and design. When you draw with a CAD system, the graphical elements, such as lines, arcs, and circles, are stored in the CAD file as numeric data. CAD systems store that numeric data with great precision. For example, AutoCAD stores values with fourteen significant digits. The value 1, for example, is stored in scientific notation as the equivalent of 1.0000000000000. This precision provides you with the ability to create designs and drawings that are 100% accurate for almost every case.

Productivity for Repetitive Operations

It may be faster to create a simple "rough" drawing, such as a sketch by hand (pencil and paper), than it would by using a CAD system. However, for larger and more complex drawings, particularly those involving similar shapes or repetitive operations, CAD methods are very efficient. Any kind of shape or operation accomplished with the CAD system can be easily duplicated since it is stored in the CAD file. In short, it may take some time to set up the first drawing and create some of the initial geometry, but any of the existing geometry or drawing setups can be easily duplicated in the current drawing or for new drawings.

Likewise, making changes to a CAD file (known as editing) is generally much faster than making changes to a traditional manual drawing. Since all the graphical elements in a CAD drawing are stored, only the affected components of the design or drawing need to be altered and the drawing can be plotted again.

As CAD and the associated technology advance and softwares become more interconnected, more productive developments are available. For example, it is possible to make a change to a 3-dimensional model that automatically causes a related change in the linked 2-dimensional engineering drawing, or changing a value in a spreadsheet can automatically cause a related change in the design drawings. One of the main advantages of these technological advances is productivity.

Sharing the CAD File with Other Software Programs

Of course CAD is not the only form of industrial activity that is making technological advances. Many industries use computer softwares to increase capability and productivity. Since softwares are written using digital information and may be written for the same or similar computer operating systems, it is possible and desirable to make software programs with the ability to share data or even interconnect, possibly appearing simultaneously on one screen.

For example, word processing programs can generate text that can be imported into a drawing file. Or a drawing can be created and imported into a text file as an illustration. (This book is a result of that capability.) A drawing created with a CAD system such as AutoCAD can be exported to a finite element analysis program that can read the computer model and compute and analyze the stresses and strains. CAD files can be dynamically "linked" to spreadsheets or databases in such a way that a changing a value in a spreadsheet or text in a database can automatically make the related change in the drawing, or vice versa.

Another advance in CAD technology is the automatic creation and interconnectivity of a 2-dimensional drawing and a 3-dimensional model in one CAD file. With this tool, you can design a 3-dimensional model and have the 2-dimensional drawings automatically generated. The resulting set has bi-directional associativity; that is, a change in either the 2-dimensional drawings or the 3-dimensional model is automatically updated in the other.

CAD, however, may not be the best tool for every design related activity. For example, CAD may help develop ideas, but probably won't replace the idea sketch, at least not with present technology. A 3-dimensional CAD model can save much time and expense for some analysis and testing, but cannot replace the "feel" of an actual model, at least not until virtual reality technology is developed and refined.

With everything considered, CAD offers us many opportunities for increased accuracy, productivity and interconnectivity. Considering the speed at which this technology is advancing, many more opportunities are rapidly obtainable. However, we need to start with the basics. Beginning by learning to create an AutoCAD drawing is a good start.

WHY USE AutoCAD?

CAD systems are available for a number of computer platforms: personal computers (PC's), workstations and mainframes. AutoCAD, offered to the public in late 1982, was one of the first PC-based CAD software products. Since that time it has grown to be the world leader in market share for <u>all</u> CAD products, including those for other platforms. At the time of this writing, Autodesk, the manufacturer of AutoCAD, is the sixth largest software producer in the world.

Learning AutoCAD offers a number of advantages to you. Since AutoCAD is the most widely used CAD software, using it gives you the highest probability of being able to share CAD files and related data and information with others.

As a student, learning AutoCAD, as opposed to learning another CAD software product, gives you a higher probability of using your skills in industry. Likewise, there are more employers who use AutoCAD than any other single CAD system. In addition, learning AutoCAD as a first CAD system gives you a good foundation for learning other CAD packages because many concepts and commands introduced by AutoCAD are utilized by other systems. In some cases, AutoCAD features become industry standards. The .DXF file format, for example, was introduced by Autodesk and has become an industry standard for CAD file conversion between systems.

As a professional, using AutoCAD gives you the highest possibility that you can share CAD files and related data with your colleagues, vendors, and clients. Compatibility of hardware and software is an important issue in industry. Maintaining compatible hardware and software allows you the highest probability for sharing data and information with others as well as offering you flexibility in experimenting with and utilizing the latest technological advancements. AutoCAD provides you with the greatest compatibility in the CAD domain.

This introduction is not intended as a selling point, but to remind you of the importance and potential of the task you are about to undertake. If you are a professional or a student, you have most likely already made up your mind that you want to learn to use AutoCAD as a design or drafting tool. If you have made up your mind, then you can accomplish anything. Let's begin.

```
■Layer 0 Snap                    7.5000,7.5000                    AutoCAD
                                                                  * * * *
                                                                  SNAP:

                                                                  ON
                                                                  OFF
                                                                  Aspect
                                                                  Rotate

                                                                  Style
                                                                   Iso
                                                                   Standrd

                                                                  DrawMode
                                                                  Dialogue
                                                                   . . .

                                                                  _LAST_
                                                                   DRAW
                                                                   EDIT



   ┌Y┐
   │W│
   └─┘────→X


Command: snap
Snap spacing or ON/OFF/Aspect/Rotate/Style <0.1250>: .5
Command:
```

CHAPTER 1

Getting Started

CHAPTER OBJECTIVES

After completing this chapter you should:

1.   understand how the X, Y, Z coordinate system is used to define the location of drawing elements in digital format in a CAD drawing file;

2.   understand why you should create drawings full size in the actual units with CAD;

3.   be able to start AutoCAD to begin drawing;

4.   recognize the areas of the AutoCAD Drawing Editor and know the function of each;

5.   be able to use the four methods of entering commands;

6.   be able to turn on and off the *SNAP*, *GRID* and *ORTHO* drawing aids.

1

BASIC CONCEPTS

Coordinate Systems

Any location in a drawing, such as the endpoint of a line, can be described in X,Y, and Z coordinate values (Cartesian coordinates).

If a line is drawn on a sheet of paper, for example, its endpoints can be charted by giving the distance over and up from the lower left corner of the sheet (Fig. 1-1).

These distances, or values, can be expressed as X and Y coordinates; X is the horizontal distance from the lower left corner (origin) and Y is the vertical distance from that origin. In a three-dimensional coordinate system the third dimension, Z, is measured from the origin in a direction perpendicular to the plane defined by X and Y.

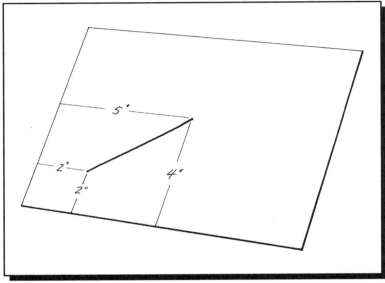

Figure 1-1

Two-dimensional (2D) and three-dimensional (3D) CAD systems use coordinate values to define the location of drawing elements such as lines and circles (called <u>entities</u> in AutoCAD).

In a 2D drawing a line is defined by the X and Y coordinate values for its two endpoints (Fig 1-2).

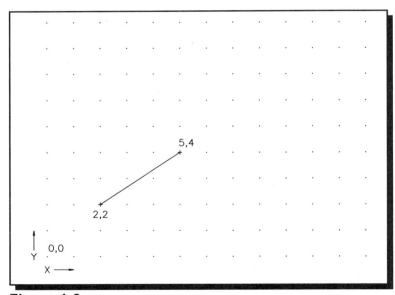

Figure 1-2

In a 3D drawing a line can be created and defined by specifying X, Y, and Z coordinate values (Fig 1-3).

Coordinate values are always expressed by the X value first and separated by a comma, then Y, then Z.

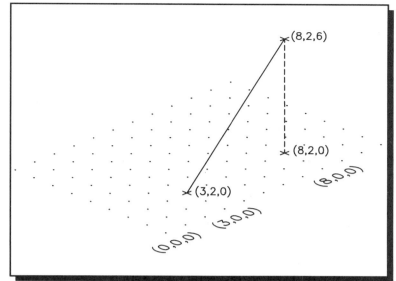

Figure 1-3

The CAD Database

A CAD (Computer-Aided Design) file, which is the electronically stored version of the drawing, keeps data in binary digital form. These digits describe coordinate values for all of the endpoints, center points, radii, vertices, etc. for all the entities composing the drawing along with another code that describes the kinds of entities (line, circle, arc, ellipse, etc.) Figure 1-4 shows part of an AutoCAD DXF (Drawing Interchange Format) file giving numeric data defining lines and other entities. Knowing that a CAD system stores drawings by keeping coordinate data helps you understand the kinds of input that are required to create entities and how to translate the meaning of prompts on the screen.

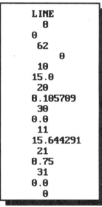

Figure 1-4

Angles in AutoCAD

Angles in AutoCAD are measured in a counter-clockwise direction. Angle 0 is positioned in a positive X direction, that is, horizontally from left to right. Therefore, 90 degrees is in a positive Y direction, or straight up; 180 degrees is in a negative X direction, or to the left; and 270 degrees is in a negative Y direction or straight down (Fig. 1-5).

The position and direction of measuring angles in AutoCAD can be changed; however, the defaults listed above are used in most cases.

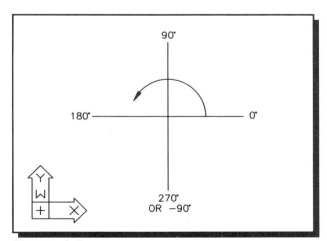

Figure 1-5

3

Draw True Size

When creating a drawing with pencil and paper tools, you must first determine a scale to use so that the drawing will be proportional to the actual object and will fit on the sheet (Fig. 1-6).

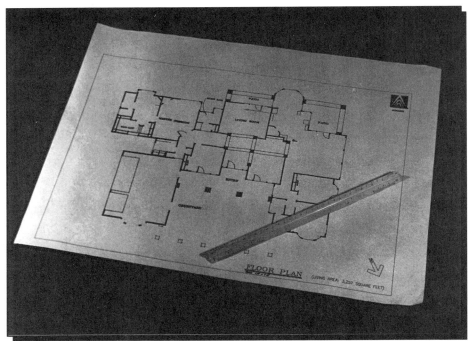

Figure 1-6

However, when creating a drawing on a CAD system, there is no fixed size drawing area. The number of drawing units that appear on the screen is variable and is assigned to fit the application.

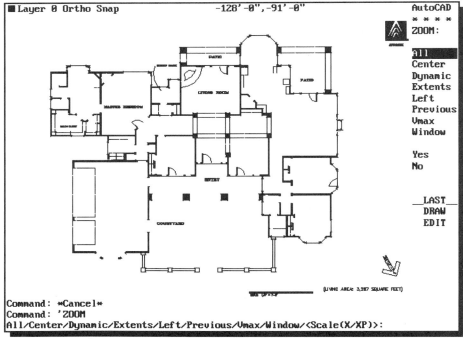

Figure 1-7 Courtesy of Autodesk, Inc.

The CAD drawing is not scaled until it is physically transferred to a fixed size sheet of paper by plotter or printer.

The rule for creating CAD drawings is that the drawing should be created <u>true size</u> using real-world units. The user specifies what units are to be used (architectural, engineering, etc.), and then specifies what size drawing area is needed (in X and Y values) to draw the necessary geometry. Whatever the specified size of the drawing area, it can be displayed on the screen in its entirety (Fig. 1-7) or as only a portion of the drawing area (Fig. 1-8).

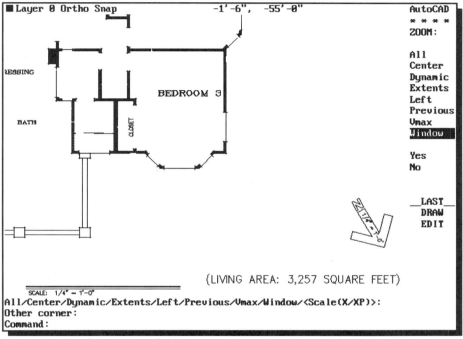

Figure 1-8 Courtesy of Autodesk, Inc.

Plot to Scale

As long as a drawing exists as a CAD file or is visible on the screen, it is considered a virtual, full-sized object. Only when the CAD drawing is transferred to paper by a plotter or printer is it converted (usually reduced) to a size that will fit on a sheet. A CAD drawing can be automatically scaled to fit on the sheet regardless of sheet size; however, this results in a plotted drawing that is not to an accepted scale (not to a regular proportion of the real object). Usually it is desirable to plot a drawing so that the resulting drawing is a proportion of the actual object size. The scale to enter as the plot scale (Fig. 1-9) is simply the proportion of the <u>plotted drawing</u> size to the <u>actual object</u>.

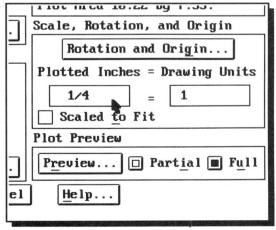

Figure 1-9

STARTING AutoCAD

Assuming that AutoCAD has been installed and configured properly for your system, you are ready to begin using AutoCAD. (See Appendix C, Installing AutoCAD.) The steps for starting AutoCAD may be slightly different on your system. The typical steps are given below.

1. If you don't have a menu system to start AutoCAD, first go to the working directory on your hard drive before starting AutoCAD. A working directory is where drawing files and temporary files are saved. You should not use the ACAD12 directory (where the AutoCAD program files are located) for your working directory. A separate working directory aids in file management and security. (See Appendix C for more information on working directories.)

    Many computer systems set up by an office or laboratory system manager have a screen menu system that appears when the computer is turned on and "boots up." If this is true for your system, making the correct selection from the menu (probably something like *AutoCAD* or *Use AutoCAD*) should set the current directory as well as start AutoCAD.

2. AutoCAD is usually started in one of three ways depending upon your system setup.

    a. Type **ACADR12**. The batch file automatically created by the AutoCAD Release 12 installation process is named ACADR12.BAT. Typing **ACADR12** runs this batch file. This batch file sets the necessary environment variables and starts AutoCAD.

    b. Type **ACAD**. This command starts the executable program file for AutoCAD, ACAD.EXE. However, only start AutoCAD by this method if the environment variables have previously been set by the AUTOEXEC.BAT or another batch file.

    c. Select **AutoCAD** from the screen menu native to your computer system (if one exists). In many offices and laboratories, menu systems are used to change to the working directory, set the environment variables, and start AutoCAD.

THE AutoCAD DRAWING EDITOR

After starting AutoCAD, the Drawing Editor appears on the screen and allows you to immediately begin drawing. There are no opening menus or other screens that appear before the Drawing Editor. The following sections give you the information you need to use the AutoCAD Drawing Editor to create and edit drawings.

Graphics Area

The large central area of the screen is the Graphics or Drawing area. It displays the lines, circles and other entities that make up the drawing (Fig. 1-10). The background color is usually black and graphics entities (lines, arcs, circles) can be a variety of colors. The default size of the graphics area is 12 units (X or horizontal) by 9 units (Y or vertical). This usable drawing area (12 x 9) is called the drawing *LIMITS* and can be changed to any size to fit the application. The <u>cursor</u> location is at the intersection of the crosshairs (vertical and horizontal lines that move with the mouse or puck movements).

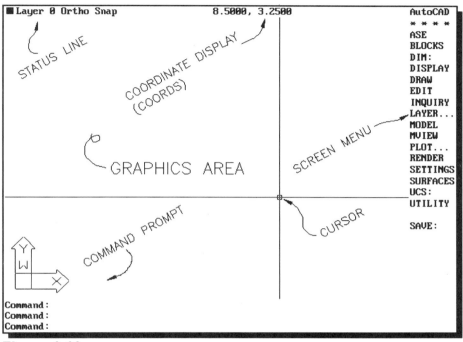

Figure 1-10

Status Line

The upper left corner of the screen has a set of informative words or symbols collectively called the Status Line (Fig. 1-10). The status line gives the status of the drawing aids and the current layer. Items that are always visible or appear periodically in the status line are:

Layer *NAME*	current layer name and color: always visible
SNAP	appears when *SNAP* is *On*
ORTHO	appears when *ORTHO* is *On*
P	appears when the cursor is in Paper Space

Coordinate Display (*COORDS*) F6

The top center area of the screen displays X and Y coordinate values of the current cursor position or the last point entered (see Fig. 1-11). The X and Y values are always separated by a comma. There are two or three formats for the coordinate display depending on whether a command is in use. The format of *COORDS* is controlled by toggling the **F6** key. The three positions are shown on the next page.

Cursor tracking

When *COORDS* is in this position, the values display the current location of the cursor.

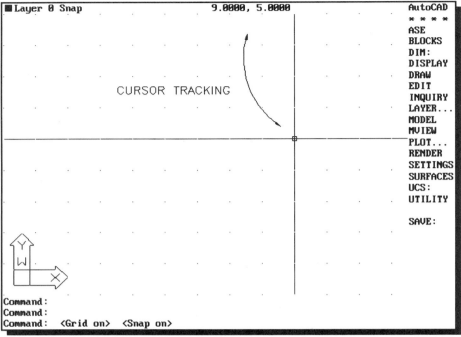

Figure 1-11

Last point

This position displays the absolute coordinate value of the last point picked.

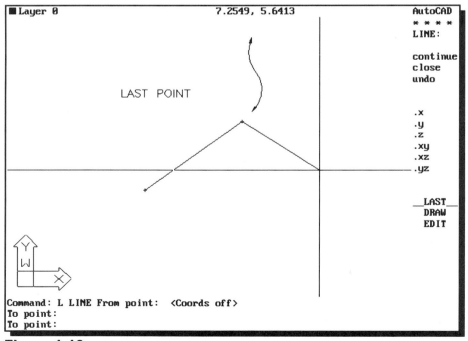

Figure 1-12

Relative polar display

This display is only possible if a draw or edit command is in use. The values give the distance and angle of the "rubberband" line from the last point established.

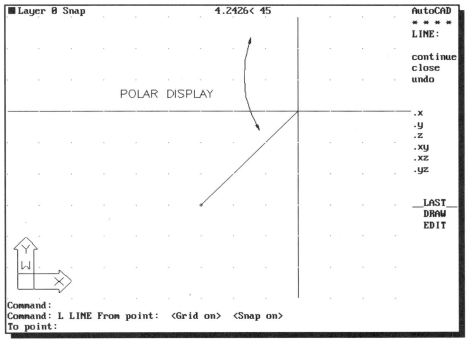

Figure 1-13

Command Line or Prompt Area

The command line or prompt area consists of the three text lines at the bottom of the screen and is the most important area other than the drawing itself (see Fig. 1-10). Any command that is entered or any prompt that AutoCAD issues for you appears here. The command line is always visible and gives the current state of drawing activity. You should develop the habit of glancing at the command line as you draw. The **F1** key (*FLIPSCREEN*) flips to a full text screen displaying more than the three lines.

Notice how the command line in the figure above, for example, indicates that the *Line* command is in use. At the last line, AutoCAD is prompting you for the `to point:`, or the end point, for the current line.

Screen Menu

All of the AutoCAD commands can be accessed through the menu system located at the right side of the screen (see Fig. 1-10). The screen menu has a tree structure; that is, other menus and commands are accessed by branching out from the root or top-level menu (Fig. 1-14). Commands (in capital letters followed by a colon) or menus (capital letters only) are selected by moving the cursor to the desired position until the word is highlighted and then pressing the PICK button. Words in capital letters followed by ellipsis (...) activate Dialogue Boxes.

Words in lower case are options within a command, requiring that the main command be selected first. The root menu is accessed from any level of the structure by selecting the word "AutoCAD" at the top of any menu. All commands in these menus (with colons) are actual command names with correct spelling that can also be typed at the keyboard. If commands are invoked by any other method, the screen menu automatically changes to the current command. The words in the screen menu are alphabetically ordered.

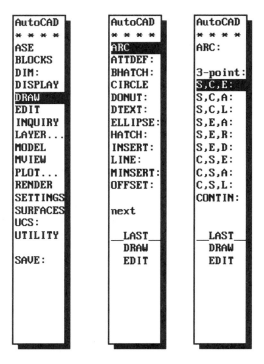

Figure 1-14

Pull-down Menus

The pull-down menu bar appears if the cursor is moved up into the top border where the Status Line and *COORDS* appear (Fig. 1-15). Selecting any of these words activates, or pulls-down, the respective menu. Selecting a word appearing with an arrow activates a cascading menu with other options. Selecting a word with ellipsis (...) activates a dialogue box (see next page). Words in the pull-down menus are not necessarily the correct command names or spellings used for typing commands, nor are they alphabetically ordered. Menus can be canceled by pressing

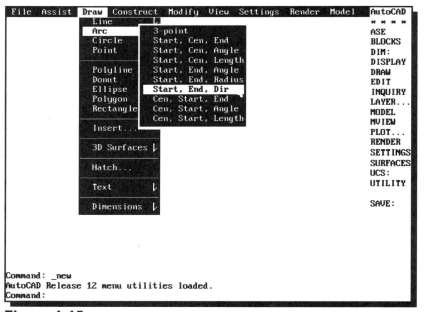

Figure 1-15

CTRL+C or PICKing in the graphics area. Double-clicking on a pull-down menu name (at the top menu bar) activates the last command and option used from that menu. The pull-down menus do <u>not</u> contain all of the AutoCAD commands.

Dialogue Boxes

Dialogue boxes provide an interface for controlling complex commands or a group of related commands. Depending on the command, the dialogue boxes allow you to choose and select among multiple options and sometimes give a preview of the effect of selections.

The *Layer Control* dialogue box gives complete control of layer colors, linetypes, and visibility.

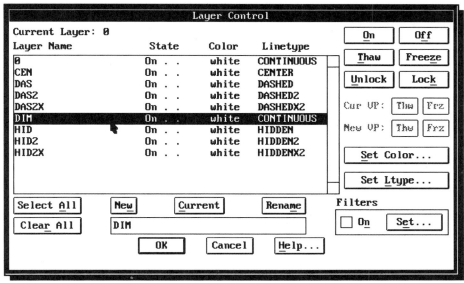

Figure 1-16

The *Plot Control* dialogue box gives complete device and plot control including plot preview.

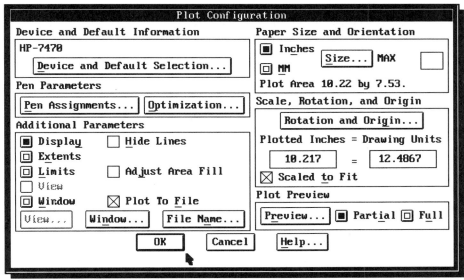

Figure 1-17

Dialogue boxes are accessible through the pull-down menus by selecting items followed by ellipsis (...). Dialogue boxes can also be invoked by typing one of several commands beginning with "*DD*". For example, *DDLMODES* is the call for the *Layer Control* dialogue box. The screen menu uses both the ellipsis (...) and the "*DD*" indicators to denote dialogue box selection.

The basic element or smallest component of a dialogue box is called a <u>tile</u>. Several types of tiles and the resulting actions of tile selection are listed below.

Button	Resembles a push button and triggers some action
Edit box	Allows entry or editing of a single line of text
Image button	A button that displays a graphical image
List box	A list of text strings from which one or more can be selected
Popup list	A text string that pops open to a list
Radio button	A group of buttons, only one of which can be turned on at a time
Slider	An indicator that drags (up or down/left or right) to some numeric value
Toggle	A check box selecting either on or off

The *DLGCOLOR* command allows you to customize the colors for your dialogue boxes. The changes made with this command can be saved (in the ACAD.CFG file) so that the next drawing session on that particular computer will display the same color combination.

New dialogue boxes can be created and customized. Programming the configuration of tiles and resulting action of tile selection requires use of Dialogue Control Language (DCL) to configure the tiles and AutoLISP programs to control the action of tile selection.

Digitizing Tablet Menu

If you have a digitizing tablet, the AutoCAD commands are available by making the desired selection from the AutoCAD digitizing table menu (Fig.1-18). The tablet is divided into areas. The open area located slightly to the right of center is called the Screen Pointing area. Locate the digitizing puck there to make the crosshairs appear on the screen. Locating the puck at any other location allows you to select a command. The commands are located in groups.

Notice the row of numbers along the top and the column of letters along the left side. In this book particular commands are referenced by giving the column and row location (number,letter). For example, the *Line* command is located at *10,J*.

COMMAND ENTRY

Four Ways to Enter Commands

There are four methods you can use to select a command in AutoCAD. Generally, <u>any one</u> of the four methods can be used to invoke a particular command.

1.	**Keyboard**	Type the command name <u>or</u> command alias at the keyboard (a command alias is a one- or two-letter short cut).
2.	**Pull-down menu**	Select the command or dialogue box from a pull-down menu.
3.	**Screen menu**	Select the command or dialogue box from the screen menu.
4.	**Tablet menu**	Select the command from the digitizing tablet menu (if available).

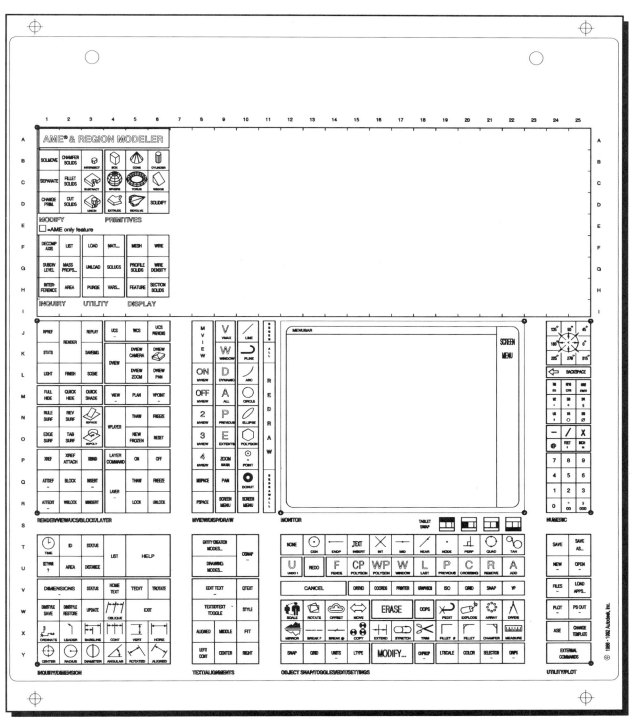

Figure 1-18 AutoCAD Release 12 Digitizing Tablet Menu

All four methods of entering commands accomplish the same goals; however, one method may offer a slightly different option or advantage to another depending on the command used. A few differences, features, and considerations are listed below.

- Commands invoked by any method automatically change the screen menu to display the same command.
- Typing commands requires that no other commands are currently in use; therefore, CTRL+C may have to be used to cancel active commands before typing. Selecting from the menus or digitizing tablet automatically cancels active commands.
- Pull-downs are easily visible and a quick way to access commands and dialogue boxes but do not contain all of the commands.
- The screen menus contain all AutoCAD commands; however, finding a particular command in the menu structure is difficult for the beginner.
- Selecting from a digitizing tablet menu allows direct access to particular commands but requires moving your eyes from the screen.
- Typing commands, particularly command aliases, are fast if you have good keyboarding skills. Typically, the left hand is kept on the keyboard (most command aliases can be entered with one hand) and the right hand is kept on the mouse or digitizing puck for cursor control.

All menus including the digitizing tablet can be customized by editing the ACAD.MNU (AutoCAD Customization Manual, p. 67), and command aliases can be added to the ACAD.PGP file (p.35) so that command selections can be designed to your preference.

How to Find a Particular Command

The following menu table is used throughout this book to show the possible methods for entering a particular command. The table gives the correct spelling for typing commands and command aliases, indicates the pull-down and screen menus where the command is located, and gives the command's location on the digitizing tablet menu (column,row). This example uses the *Copy* command.

COPY

TYPE IN:	PULL-DOWN MENU	SCREEN MENU	TABLET MENU
COPY, CP	*Construct, Copy*	*EDIT, COPY:*	*15,X*

What the menu table above means:

TYPE IN: At the keyboard, type either *COPY* or the command alias *CP* and press **Enter**.

PULL-DOWN MENU   Select the **Construct** menu at the top of the screen, then select *Copy*.

SCREEN MENU   From the Root menu, select (PICK) *EDIT*. From the next menu that appears, select *COPY:*.

TABLET MENU   The number and letter give the location of the command. The numbers appear along the top edge of the tablet menu, and the letters appear along the left edge of the tablet menu. Pick _Copy_ at location 15,X.

Special Input Device and Keyboard Functions

Mouse and Digitizing Puck Buttons

Depending on the type of mouse or digitizing puck used for cursor control, a different number of buttons are available. If a two-button mouse is used, the left button is #1 and right is #2; otherwise, button numbers are indicated on the device. In any case, the buttons perform the following tasks:

#1 **PICK**   Used to select commands or point to locations on screen.
#2 **Enter**   Performs the same action as the Enter or Return key on the keyboard (except when entering text in a drawing).
#3 **Cancel**   Cancels a command.
#4 **O**_SNAP_   Activates the cursor O_SNAP_ menu.

Button functions can also be customized to suit individual needs by editing the ACAD.MNU file (AutoCAD Customization Manual, p. 82)

Function Keys

There are six function keys that are usable with AutoCAD. They offer a quick method of turning on or off (toggling) drawing aids. Function keys are located along the top or the left side of the keyboard.

F1 _FLIPSCREEN_   Toggles between a text screen and the Drawing Editor.
F6 _COORDS_   Toggles coordinate display between cursor tracking mode and last point selected. If used transparently (during a command in operation) displays a polar coordinate format.
F7 _GRID_   Turns the _GRID On_ or _Off_ (see Drawing Aids).
F8 _ORTHO_   Turns _ORTHO On_ or _Off_ (see Drawing Aids).
F9 _SNAP_   Turns the _SNAP On_ or _Off_ (see Drawing Aids).
F10 _TABLET_   Turns the _TABLETMODE On_ or _Off_. If _TABLETMODE_ is _On_, the tablet can be used to digitize an existing paper drawing into AutoCAD.

Special Key Functions

SPACE   The Space Bar performs the same action as the Enter key or #2 button except when entering text into a drawing.
CTRL+C   Pressing the CTRL and letter C keys simultaneously cancels a command, menu, or dialogue box or interrupts processing of plotting or hatching.
Shift + #1   Simultaneously pressing Shift and the #1 button deselects (removes a highlighted object from the selection set).

Shift + #2	Simultaneously pressing Shift and the #2 button on a two-button mouse activates the O *SNAP* cursor menu.
Enter	If Enter, SPACE, or #2 button is pressed when no command is in use (the open `Command:` prompt is visible), the last command used is invoked again.

Drawing Aids

This section gives a brief introduction to AutoCAD's Drawing Aids. For a full explanation of the related commands and options, see Chapter 6.

SNAP (F9)

SNAP is a function that forces the cursor to "snap" to a regular interval (1 unit by default), which aids in drawing geometry accurate to equal interval lengths. The **Snap** command or *Drawing Aids...* dialogue box allows you to specify any value for the *SNAP* interval. In Figure 1-19, the *SNAP* is set to .125 and the *GRID* is set to 1 (note the values in the coordinate display).

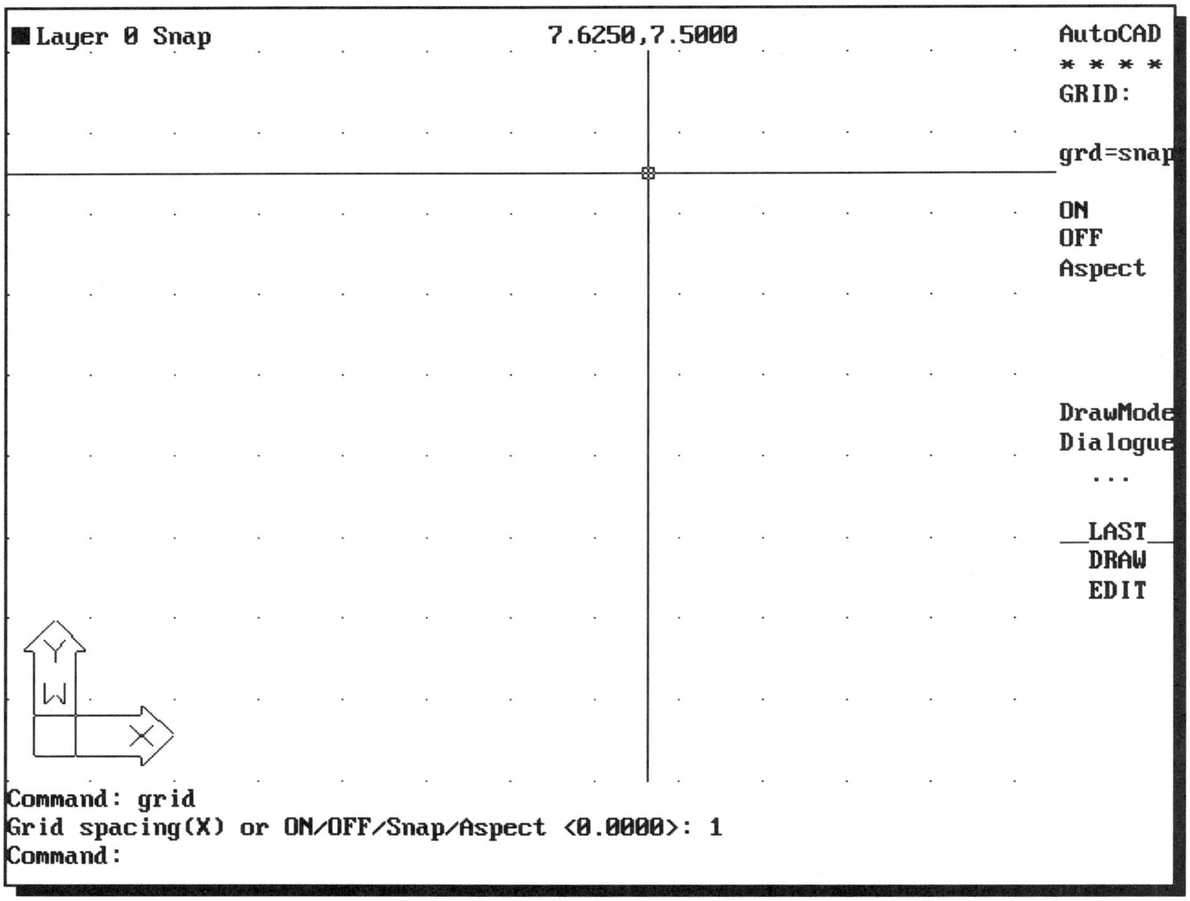

```
 Layer 0 Snap                    7.6250,7.5000                          AutoCAD
                                                                         * * * *
                                                                        GRID:

                                                                        grd=snap

                                                                        ON
                                                                        OFF
                                                                        Aspect


                                                                        DrawMode
                                                                        Dialogue
                                                                          . . .

                                                                        _LAST_
                                                                        DRAW
                                                                        EDIT




Command: grid
Grid spacing(X) or ON/OFF/Snap/Aspect <0.0000>: 1
Command:
```

Figure 1-19

GRID (F7)

A drawing aid called _GRID_ can be used to give a visual reference of units of length. The _GRID_ default value is 1 unit. The **Grid** command or _Drawing Aids..._ dialogue box allows you to change the interval to any value. The _GRID_ is not part of the geometry and is not plotted.

SNAP and _GRID_ are independent functions--they can be turned _On_ or _Off_ independently. However, you can force the _GRID_ to have the same interval as _SNAP_ by entering a _GRID_ value of **0** or you can use a proportion of _SNAP_ by entering a _GRID_ value followed by an **X**. Figure 1-20 displays a _SNAP_ of .5 and a _GRID_ of 2X (1.0).

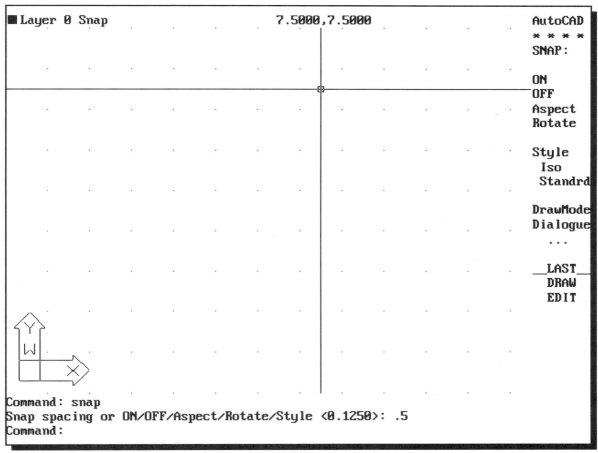

Figure 1-20

ORTHO (F8)

If _ORTHO_ is _On_, lines are forced to an orthogonal alignment (horizontal or vertical) when drawing (Figure 1-21). _ORTHO_ is often helpful since so many shapes are composed of horizontal and vertical lines.

ORTHO can only be turned *On* or *Off*.

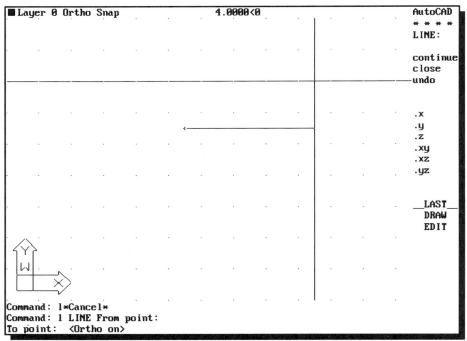

Figure 1-21

Figure 1-22 illustrates how *ORTHO* automatically aligns with *SNAP* if *SNAP* is rotated (see Chapter 6 for details on using the **Snap** command and *Rotate* option).

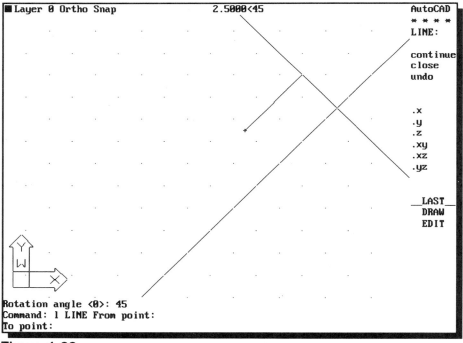

Figure 1-22

Command Entry Methods Practice

Start AutoCAD. Invoke the *LINE* command using each of the command entry methods. (When you are finished practicing, use the *Files* pull-down menu and select *Exit AutoCAD*. You can *Discard Changes*.)

1.   **Type the command**

STEPS	COMMAND PROMPT	PERFORM ACTION	COMMENTS
1.		press **CTRL + C** if another command is in use	
2.	Command:	type *Line* and press **Enter**	
3.	From point:	**PICK** any point	a "rubberband" line appears
4.	to point:	**PICK** any point	another "rubberband" line appears
5.	to point:	press **Enter**	to complete command

2.   **Type the command alias**

STEPS	COMMAND PROMPT	PERFORM ACTION	COMMENTS
1.		press **CTRL + C** if another command is in use	
2.	Command:	type *L* and press **Enter**	
3.	From point:	**PICK** any point	a "rubberband" line appears
4.	to point:	**PICK** any point	another "rubberband" line appears
5.	to point:	press **Enter**	to complete command

3. Pull-down menu

STEPS	COMMAND PROMPT	PERFORM ACTION	COMMENTS
1.	Command:	select the *Draw* menu from the menu bar on top	menu pops down
2.	Command:	select *Line* >	options cascade
3.	Command:	select *Segments*	menu disappears
4.	line From point:	**PICK** any point	a "rubberband" line appears
5.	to point:	**PICK** any point	another "rubberband" line appears
6.	to point:	press **Enter**	to complete command

4. Screen menu

STEPS	COMMAND PROMPT	PERFORM ACTION	COMMENTS
1.	Command:	select **AutoCAD** from screen menu on the side	only if menu is not at root level
2.	Command:	select *DRAW* from the root screen menu	menu changes to DRAW
3.	Command:	select *LINE:*	
4.	LINE From point:	**PICK** any point	a "rubberband" line appears
5.	to point:	**PICK** any point	another "rubberband" line appears
6.	to point:	press **Enter**	to complete command

5. Digitizing tablet menu (if available)

STEPS	COMMAND PROMPT	PERFORM ACTION	COMMENTS
1.	Command:	select *LINE*	at 10,J
2.	line From point:	**PICK** any point	a "rubberband" line appears
3.	to point:	**PICK** any point	another "rubberband" line appears
4.	to point:	press **Enter**	to complete command

CHAPTER EXERCISES

1.   Starting and Exiting AutoCAD

Start AutoCAD by whatever method is used on your computer system. Draw a _Line_.
Exit AutoCAD by selecting this option from the _Files_ pull-down menu. PICK the
Discard Changes tile. Repeat these steps until you are confident with the procedure.

2.   Using Drawing Aids

Start AutoCAD. Turn on and off each of the following modes.

> _SNAP_
> _GRID_
> _ORTHO_

3.   Understanding Coordinates

Begin drawing a _Line_ by PICKing a "`From point:`". Toggle _COORDS_ to display
each of the <u>three</u> formats. PICK several other points at the "`to point:`" prompt.
Pay particular attention to the coordinate values displayed for each point and visualize
the relationship between that point and coordinate 0,0 (absolute value) or the last point
established (relative polar value). Finish the command by pressing Enter.

4.   Using _FLIPSCREEN_

Use _FLIPSCREEN_ (**F1**) to toggle between the text screen and the graphics screen.

5.   Using the command entry methods

Invoke the _Line_ command by each of the following methods. Draw one or two _Line_
segments with each use of the command, then use **Enter** to complete the command in
each case.

> A.   type the command
> B.   type the command alias
> C.   select from the pull down menus
> D.   select from the screen menu
> E.   select from the digitizing tablet (if available)

6.   Drawing with Drawing Aids

Draw four _Lines_ using <u>each</u> Drawing Aid: _GRID, SNAP, ORTHO_. Toggle _On_ and _Off_
each of the drawing aids one at a time for each set of four _Lines_. Next, draw _Lines_
using combinations of the Drawing Aids, particularly _GRID + SNAP_ and _GRID + SNAP
+ ORTHO_.

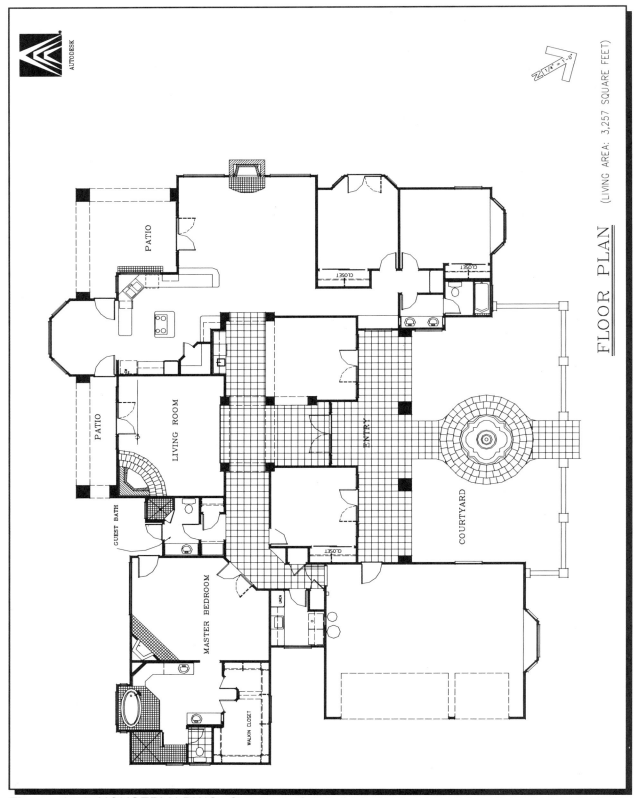

Figure 1-23 HOUSEPLN.DWG Courtesy of Autodesk, Inc.

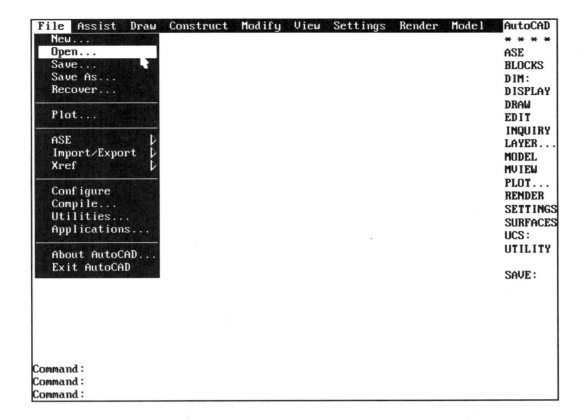

CHAPTER 2

File Commands

CHAPTER OBJECTIVES

After completing this chapter you should be able to:

1.   name drawing files;

2.   use file-related dialogue boxes;

3.   create *New* drawings;

4.   *Open* existing drawings;

5.   *Save* drawings to disk;

6.   *Exit AutoCAD*;

7.   use *File Utilities* to list, copy, rename, and delete files.

AutoCAD DRAWING FILES

Naming Drawing Files

What is a drawing file? A CAD drawing file is the electronically stored data form of a drawing visible on a screen or on a plot. The computer's hard disk is the principal magnetic storage device used for saving and restoring CAD drawing files. Diskettes are used to transport files from one computer to another, as in the case of transferring CAD files among clients, consultants or vendors in industry. The AutoCAD Commands used for saving drawings to, and restoring drawings from, files are explained in the following sections.

An AutoCAD drawing file has a name that you assign and a file extension of ".DWG." The file name you assign must be compliant with the DOS filename conventions; that is, it can only have a <u>maximum</u> of eight alphanumeric characters. Characters such as _ - $ # ( ) ^ can be used in names, but no spaces or other characters are allowed. AutoCAD automatically appends the extension of .DWG to all AutoCAD-created drawing files.

Beginning and Saving an AutoCAD Drawing

When you start AutoCAD, the drawing editor appears and allows you to begin drawing even before using any file commands. If you choose, you can assign a name for the drawing when you begin with the *New* command. As you draw, you should develop the habit of saving the drawing periodically (about every 15 or 20 minutes) using *Save*. *Save* stores the drawing in its most current state to disk. If the drawing has not yet been named, AutoCAD prompts you to assign a name for the drawing when you *Save* the first time. Upon completing the drawing, use the *Exit* option to finish your session. AutoCAD prompts you to *Save* upon *Exiting* (unless you just did). To work on that drawing at a later time, start AutoCAD and use the *Open* command to reopen it.

The typical drawing session would involve using *New* to assign a name for the drawing at the start or using *Open* to open an existing drawing. *Save* would be used periodically, and *Exit* would be used for the final save and to end the session.

AutoCAD periodically saves the current drawing automatically to a file named AUTO.SV$. To use this feature effectively, use the *SAVETIME* variable to set the time period between automatic saves.

Accessing File Commands

Although it is hard to accidentally "lose" a drawing, proper use of the file-related commands covered in this section allows you to manage your AutoCAD drawing files in a safe and efficient manner.

Although the file-related commands can be invoked by any of the four methods, they are easily accessible via the first pull-down menu option, *File* (Fig. 2-1). Most of the selections from this pull-down menu invoke dialogue boxes for selection or specification of file names.

Figure 2-1

File commands and related dialogue boxes are also available from the root screen menu (*SAVE:*) and under the *UTILITY* screen menu (Fig 2-2). Two commands from previous releases of AutoCAD, *QUIT* and *END*, are usable only by the *UTILITY* menu or by typing.

File commands can also be selected from the digitizing menu or typed at the keyboard. Generally, file commands operate the same regardless of the selection method used.

Figure 2-2

Dialogue Box Functions

There are many dialogue boxes appearing in AutoCAD that help you manage files. All of these dialogue boxes operate in the same manner. A few guidelines will help you to use them. The *Saveas* dialogue box is used as an example (Fig. 2-3).

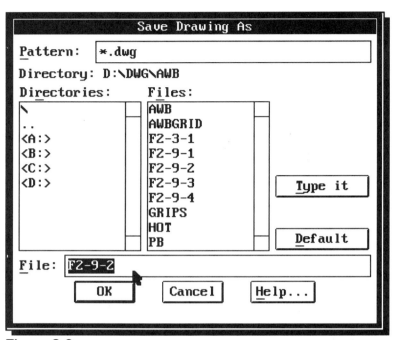

Figure 2-3

- The top of the box gives the title describing the action to be performed. It is <u>very important</u> to glance at the title before acting, especially when saving or deleting files.
- The top edit box gives the *Pattern*, or file extension. The file extension can be changed by moving the cursor to the *Pattern* edit box and PICKing, then entering the desired file extension.
- The current drive and directory (path) are listed next. Other directories can be selected by double clicking the choice under *Directories:*. PICKing the double dots (..) activates the parent directory (one level up).
- The desired file can be selected by PICKing it, then PICKing *OK*. Double clicking on the selection accomplishes the same action.
- Scroll bars with up and down arrows appear at the right of the *Directory* and/or *File* list if the list is longer than one page. PICKing the arrows pages up and down slowly or sliding the button causes paging at any rate.
- As an alternative, the file name (and path) can be typed in the bottom edit box. Make sure the blinking cursor appears in the box (move the cursor and PICK) before typing.

AutoCAD FILE COMMANDS

NEW

TYPE IN:	PULL-DOWN MENU	SCREEN MENU	TABLET MENU
NEW	_File, New..._	_UTILITY, NEW..._	_24,U_

The _New_ command should be used to assign a name to the drawing before beginning to draw or to use a specific prototype other than the default prototype. A prototype drawing is one that is used as a template, or starting point. The default prototype drawing supplied with AutoCAD is named ACAD.DWG, but other default drawings can be created and retained as the

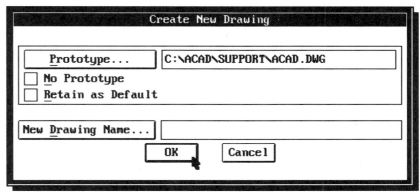

Figure 2-4

default. Keep in mind that you can draw immediately upon entering the Drawing Editor and specify a name at a later time when saving. It is not required that the drawing be named until it is saved.

The _Prototype_ option allows you to start a new drawing by using an <u>existing</u> drawing as a starting point, like a template or prototype.

Selecting the _Prototype_ tile invokes a dialogue box which shows all .DWG files in the directory where the default prototype is kept. Other directories can be selected from the _Directories:_ list. Thus, any .DWG file can be used as a prototype. As an alternative, a path and drawing name can be typed in the file edit box near the bottom.

A prototype drawing can have the initial drawing setup steps already completed, so you don't have to repeat the same steps every time you start a new drawing. A copy of the selected drawing is loaded into the Drawing Editor and used as a starting point. The original drawing on disk is not affected.

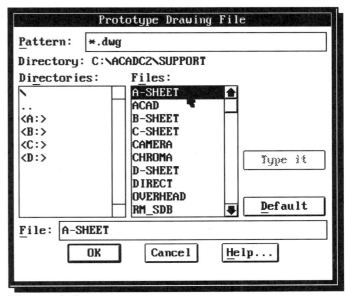

Figure 2-5

OPEN

TYPE IN:	PULL-DOWN MENU	SCREEN MENU	TABLET MENU
OPEN	*File, Open...*	*UTILITY, OPEN...*	*25,U*

This option is intended for selecting an existing drawing or a partially completed drawing that you want to load and edit or continue drawing.

The *Open Drawing* dialogue box allows selection of any drawing in the current directory (right side) or selection of another directory to list (left side). The file name of the drawing to be loaded can also be typed in the file edit box.

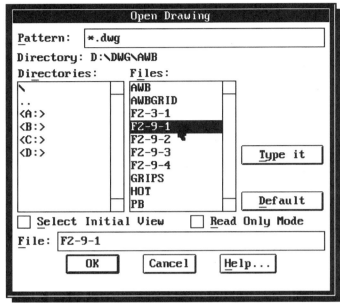

Figure 2-6

SAVE

TYPE IN:	PULL-DOWN MENU	SCREEN MENU	TABLET MENU
SAVE	*File, Save...*	*(root menu) SAVE:*	*24,T*

The *Save* command is intended to be used periodically during a drawing session (every 15 to 20 minutes is recommended). When *Save* is selected from the menus, the current version of the drawing is saved to disk without interruption to the drawing session. The first time an unnamed drawing is saved, the *Save Drawing As* dialogue box (Fig. 2-3) appears which prompts you for a drawing name. Typically, however, the drawing already has an assigned name, in which case *Save* actually performs a *Qsave* (quick save).

Typing *Save* always produces the *Save Drawing As* dialogue box. You can enter a new name and/or path to save the drawing or press Enter to keep the same name and path. Changing the name and/or path with *Save* does not reset the drawing name and/or path.

NOTE: If you want to save the drawing to a diskette in A: or B: drive, type *Save*. Enter A:NAME (where NAME is the desired name) as the drawing name. The current drawing is not reset as would be the case if you used *Saveas*.

SAVEAS

TYPE IN:	PULL-DOWN MENU	SCREEN MENU	TABLET MENU
SAVEAS	_File, Saveas..._	_UTILITY, SAVEAS:_	_25,T_

The _Saveas_ command fulfills two functions: assigns a new file name for the current drawing and saves the drawing file to disk under the assigned name. If a name has previously been assigned, _Saveas_ allows you to save the current drawing under a different name; but, beware, _Saveas_ sets the current drawing name to the last one entered. This dialogue box is shown in Figure 2-3.

A typical scenario follows. A design engineer wants to make two similar, but slightly different, design drawings. During construction of the first drawing, the engineer periodically saves under the name "DESIGN1" using _Save_. The first drawing is then completed and _Saved_. Instead of starting a _New_ drawing, _Saveas_ is used to save the current drawing under the name "DESIGN2." _Saveas_ also resets the current drawing name to "DESIGN2". The designer then has two separate but identical drawing files on disk which can be further edited to complete the specialized differences. The engineer continues to work on the current drawing "DESIGN2".

NOTE: If you want to save the drawing to a diskette in A: or B: drive, use _Save_--<u>do not</u> use _Saveas_. Since _Saveas_ resets the drawing name and path to whatever is entered in the _Save Drawing As_ dialogue box, entering A:NAME would set A: as the current drive. This could cause problems because the temporary files that AutoCAD uses would also be written to A: instead of to the hard drive.

Exit AutoCAD

TYPE IN:	PULL-DOWN MENU	SCREEN MENU	TABLET MENU
---	_File, Exit AutoCAD..._	---	---

This is the simplest method to use when you want to exit AutoCAD. This option, only available through the _File_ pull-down menu, invokes a dialogue box requiring you to _Save Changes..., Discard Changes,_ or _Cancel Command_ (Fig. 2-7). Depending upon your selection, AutoCAD actually uses _End, Quit,_ or cancel. The _Quit_ command could optionally be typed to accomplish the same action as using _Exit AutoCAD_.

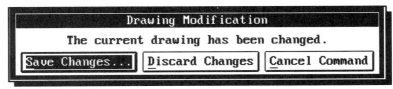

Figure 2-7

QSAVE

TYPE IN:	PULL-DOWN MENU	SCREEN MENU	TABLET MENU
QSAVE	---	---	---

Qsave (quick save) must be typed. *Qsave* saves the drawing under the previously assigned file name. No dialogue boxes appear, nor are any other inputs required. If the drawing has been named, using *Save* (from the menus) actually causes a *Qsave*. However, if the drawing has not been named when *Qsave* is invoked, the *Save Drawing As* dialogue box appears.

QUIT

TYPE IN:	PULL-DOWN MENU	SCREEN MENU	TABLET MENU
QUIT	---	*UTILITY, QUIT:*	---

The *Quit* command accomplishes the same action as *Exit AutoCAD*. *Quit* discontinues (exits) the AutoCAD session and produces the *Drawing Modification* dialogue box (Fig 2-7). If the drawing was just *Saved*, the dialogue box does not appear before exiting AutoCAD.

END

TYPE IN:	PULL-DOWN MENU	SCREEN MENU	TABLET MENU
END	---	*UTILITY, END:*	---

The *End* command ends the AutoCAD session and saves the drawing under the assigned name. If no name has been assigned, the *Saveas* dialogue box is automatically invoked. Using *End* has the same effect as selecting *Exit AutoCAD...* and *Save Changes....*

There are many file commands in AutoCAD related to saving files, principally due to evolution of new releases. However, you should not feel insecure because if *Exit AutoCAD...* is used, you are always given the opportunity to save the work and assign a name if it has not been done previously.

RECOVER

TYPE IN:	PULL-DOWN MENU	SCREEN MENU	TABLET MENU
RECOVER	*File, Recover...*	*UTILITY, RECOVER...*	---

This option is used only in the case that *Open* does not operate on a particular drawing because of damage to the file. Damage to a drawing file can occur from improper exiting of AutoCAD (such as power failure) or from damage to a diskette. *Recover* can usually reassemble the file to a useable state and load the drawing. The *Recover* dialogue box operates like the *Open Drawing* dialogue box.

FILES

TYPE IN:	PULL-DOWN MENU	SCREEN MENU	TABLET MENU
FILES	*File, Utilities...*	*UTILITY, FILES:*	*24,V*

A group of file utility commands are available for managing files. Each of the options shown in Figure 2-8 invokes a dialogue box.

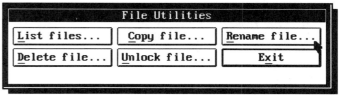

Figure 2-8

List Files...

This option invokes the dialogue box shown here. Files can only be listed and cannot be opened, saved, or have any other action performed. Any file type (other than .DWG) can be listed by entering the desired three-character extension in the *Pattern* edit box. Any drive or directory can be selected for listing by double clicking on the choice.

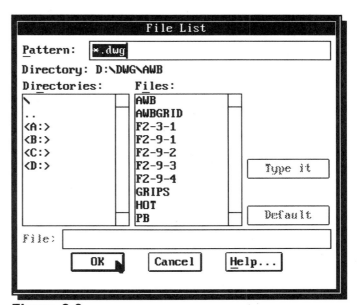

Figure 2-9

Copy Files...

This option allows you to copy the selected file to another drive or directory. Two dialogue boxes appear in sequence. The desired file is selected from the *Source File* box (Fig. 2-10). The *Destination File* box (not shown) is used to select the new directory or drive to copy to. Do not PICK an existing file name from the list in the *Destination File* dialogue box unless you want the selected file to be overwritten (a warning message appears if you do).

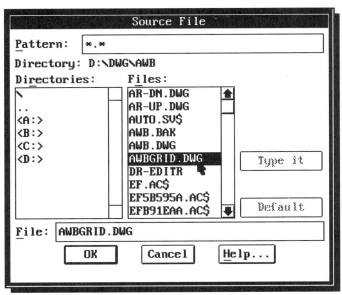

Figure 2-10

Rename Files...

This operation also has a two-dialogue box sequence. Select the desired file from the *Old File Name* dialogue box (Fig. 2-11). Type the new name in the edit box of the *New File Name* dialogue box (not shown). Make sure that the destination drive and directory are set as desired.

Do not *Rename* any files ending with .AC$ or .DWK. They are temporary files that are needed by AutoCAD and are deleted automatically when you exit AutoCAD properly (using *Exit AutoCAD*, *Quit*, or *End*).

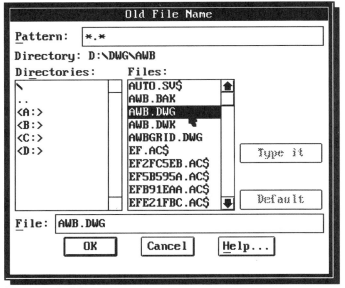

Figure 2-11

Delete Files...

Select the file to delete from the *File(s) to Delete* dialogue box. <u>Do not delete</u> any files with a .AC$ extension. They are temporary files that are needed by AutoCAD and are deleted automatically when you exit AutoCAD properly (using *Exit AutoCAD*, *Quit*, or *End*).

When a file has been selected for deletion, the verification box appears (Fig. 2-13).

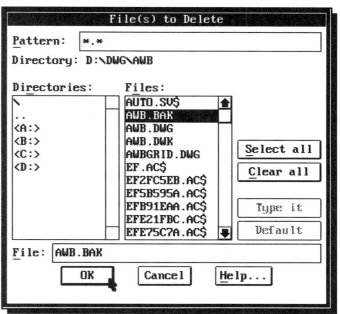

Figure 2-12

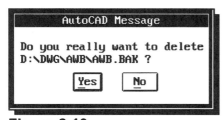

Figure 2-13

Unlock Files...

The *Unlock Files* option deletes "orphan" .DWK files. While an AutoCAD drawing is in use, a .DWK file is produced to prevent other users (on a network) from accessing the same drawing. The .DWK file is automatically deleted when the drawing is closed properly. Exiting AutoCAD improperly (power failure, etc.) causes the "orphan" .DWK file to be left on disk. Use the *Unlock Files* option to delete the .DWK file and to allow opening the "parent" drawing.

SAVETIME

SAVETIME is a variable that controls AutoCAD's automatic save feature. AutoCAD automatically saves the current drawing for you at time intervals that you specify. The default time interval is 120 (minutes)! If you want to use this feature effectively, use the *SAVETIME* variable to change the value to about 20 or 30 (minutes). A value of 0 disables this feature.

When automatic saving occurs, the current drawing is always saved in the current directory under the name AUTO.$AV. The current drawing name is not overwritten. If you want to save the drawing under the assigned name, *Save* or *Qsave* must be used, or *Saveas* should be used to save under a new name.

SHELL

TYPE IN:	PULL-DOWN MENU	SCREEN MENU	TABLET MENU
SHELL	---	*UTILITY, External Commands, SHELL:*	*25,Y*

If you are a DOS user, you can temporarily exit AutoCAD and type commands at the DOS prompt by using *Shell*. *Shell* automatically switches to the text mode while AutoCAD runs "in the background." The OS command: prompt appears and allows one operating system command before switching back to the AutoCAD command prompt. If you choose to use more than one DOS command, press **Enter** <u>twice</u> after entering *Shell*. A message appears instructing you to type **Exit** to return to AutoCAD.

Shell is very handy at times, but also very dangerous. You can perform most DOS operations like copying, deleting, or renaming files while using *Shell*. However, it is <u>very</u> important to remember that AutoCAD is running while you are "shelled out." You <u>cannot</u> turn off your computer during *Shell* because AutoCAD is still running. Two **>>** symbols appearing at the DOS prompt (for example, C:\ACAD12\DWG>>) remind you that you must type **Exit** and return to AutoCAD .

AutoCAD keeps several temporary files open while in operation. These files are only "cleaned up" if you return to AutoCAD and exit AutoCAD properly. The results of turning off the computer system while "shelled out" are the loss of the current drawing and several opened temporary files are left on disk. Do not delete any lock files (ending with *.--k extensions) or unrecognizable files (ending with *.$AC, *.$A, or *.SWR) while using *Shell*. Do not try to start AutoCAD by typing **ACAD**. Do not use the DOS command **chkdsk/f** while using *Shell*. You can use other DOS commands, but make sure that you eventually type **Exit** to return to AutoCAD. Check in the AutoCAD Reference Manual, p. 117, for other possible pitfalls and restrictions while using *Shell*.

AutoCAD Backup Files

When a drawing is saved, AutoCAD creates a file with a .DWG extension. For example, if you name the drawing PART1, using *Save* creates a file named PART1.DWG. The next time you save, AutoCAD makes a new PART1.DWG and renames the old version to PART1.BAK. One .BAK (backup) file is always kept automatically by AutoCAD (see the highlighted file name in Figure 2-12).

You cannot *Open* a .BAK file. It must be renamed to a .DWG file. Remember that you already have a .DWG file by the same name, so rename the extension <u>and</u> the filename. For example, PART1.BAK could be renamed to PART1OLD.DWG. Use the *Rename* option of *File Utilities* to rename the file if it is needed. Alternatively, you could use *Shell* and use the DOS **ren** command to rename the file.

The .BAK files can also be deleted without affecting the .DWG files. The .BAK files accumulate after time, so you should periodically delete the unneeded ones to conserve disk space.

CHAPTER EXERCISES

1. **Determine what the default or current directory is for your computer system**

   It should have a name like "C:\ACAD12\DWG" or "D:\ ACAD\FILES." The default (current) directory is used to keep AutoCAD drawing files that you create. (HINT: Use the *Saveas* command. The current directory name appears at the top of the *Saveas* dialogue box.)

2. ***Save* and name a drawing file**

   Start AutoCAD. Draw 2 vertical **Lines**. Select **Save** from the **Files** pull-down. (The *Saveas* dialogue box appears since a name has not yet been assigned.) Name the drawing "**CH2VERT**."

3. **Using *Qsave***

   Draw 2 more vertical **Lines**. Use **Save**. (Notice that the *Qsave* command appears at the command line since the drawing has already been named.)

4. **Start a *New* drawing**

   Invoke **New** from the **Files** pull-down. Enter "**CH2HORZ**" as the name for the drawing. Draw 2 horizontal **Lines**. Use **Save**. (Notice *Qsave* is actually used.) Draw 2 more horizontal **Lines**, but <u>do not</u> *Save*. Continue to exercise 5.

5. **Open an existing drawing**

   Use **Open** to open **CH2VERT**. Notice that AutoCAD forces you to *Save Changes* or *Discard Changes* to your current drawing first. **Save Changes**. CH2VERT should then open.

6. **Using *Saveas***

   Draw 2 inclined (angled) **Lines** in the CH2VERT drawing. Invoke **Saveas** to save the drawing under a new name. Enter "**CH2IN**" as the new name. (Notice the current drawing name is reset to the new name.) Draw 2 more inclined **Lines** and **Save.**

7. ***Open* an AutoCAD sample drawing**

   Open a drawing named **PVT_HGR.DWG** (Fig. 2-14, next page) usually located in the C:\ACADR12\SAMPLE directory. (Your system may have a different drive letter and directory name for the AutoCAD files, such as D:\ACAD\SAMPLE.) Use the left side of the dialogue box to change drive and directory. Do <u>not</u> *Save* the sample drawing after viewing it. Practice the **Open** command by looking at other sample drawings in the SAMPLE directory.

8. *List Files*

Use the *Utilities* option of the *Files* pull-down to list the drawings. Check for CH2VERT, CH2HORZ and CH2IN.

9. *Rename* a drawing

Use the *Rename* option from *Utilities*. Change the name of CH2IN to **CH2INCL**.

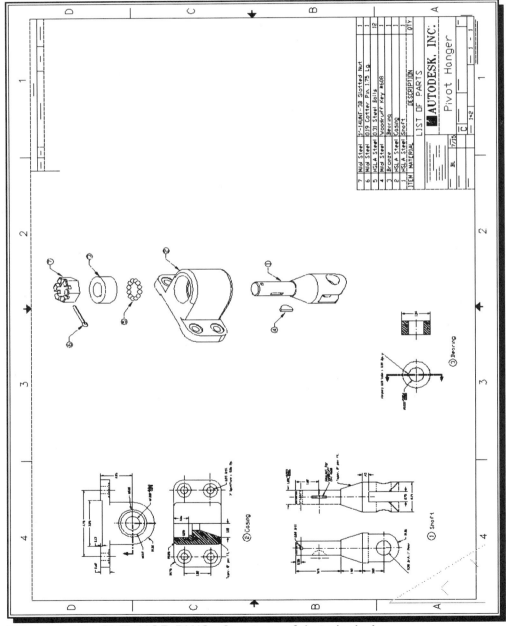

Figure 2-14 PVT_HGR.DWG Courtesy of Autodesk, Inc.

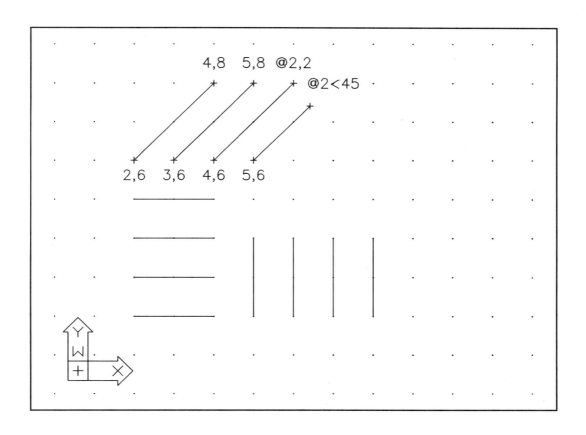

CHAPTER 3

Draw Command Basics

CHAPTER OBJECTIVES

After completing this chapter you should be able to:

1.   recognize drawing entities;

2.   draw *Lines* <u>interactively</u>;

3.   Use *SNAP*, *GRID*, and *ORTHO* while drawing *Lines* and *Circles*;

4.   create *Lines* by specifying <u>absolute</u> coordinates;

5.   create *Lines* by specifying <u>relative rectangular</u> coordinates;

6.   create *Lines* by specifying <u>relative polar</u> coordinates;

7.   create *Circles* by each of the four coordinate entry methods.

AutoCAD ENTITIES

The smallest component of a drawing in AutoCAD is called an <u>entity</u>. An example of an entity is a *Line*, an *Arc*, or a *Circle*. A rectangle created with the *Line* command would contain four entities.

Draw commands <u>create</u> entities. The draw command names are the same as the entity names.

Simple entities are *Point, Line, Arc,* and *Circle*. (These commands are covered in detail in Chapter 8.)

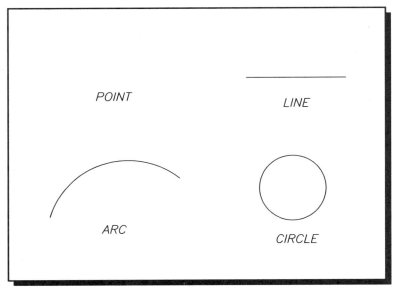

Figure 3-1

Complex entities are shapes such as *Ellipse, Polygon, Polyline,* and *Donut* which are created with one command. Even though they appear to have several segments, they are <u>treated</u> by AutoCAD as one entity. (These commands are covered in Chapter 15.)

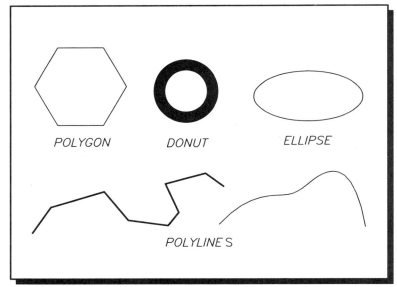

Figure 3-2

It is not always apparent whether a shape is composed of one or more entities. However, if you pick an object with the "pickbox," an entity is "highlighted," or shown in a broken line pattern (Fig. 3-3). This highlighting reveals whether the shape is composed of one or several entities.

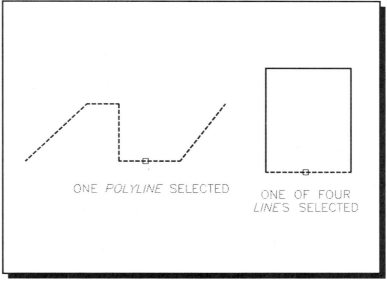

Figure 3-3

THE FOUR COORDINATE ENTRY METHODS

There are four ways to specify coordinates; that is, there are four ways to tell AutoCAD the location of points when you draw entities.

1.	**Interactive method**	**PICK**	(Use the cursor to select points on the screen.)
2.	**Absolute coordinates**	**X,Y**	(Type explicit X and Y values relative to the origin at 0,0.)
3.	**Relative rectangular coordinates**	**@X,Y**	(Type explicit X and Y values relative to the last point.)
4.	**Relative polar coordinates**	**@dist<angle**	(Type a distance value and angle value relative to the last point.)

All drawing commands prompt you to specify points, or locations, in the drawing. For example, the *Line* command prompts you to give the `From point:` and `to point:`, expecting you to specify locations for the first and second endpoints of the line. After you specify those points, AutoCAD stores the specified coordinate values to define the line. A line in AutoCAD is defined and stored in the database as two sets of X and Y values, one for each endpoint.

DRAWING *LINES* USING THE FOUR COORDINATE ENTRY METHODS

The *Line* command can be activated by any one of the methods shown in the Menu Table below.

LINE

TYPE IN:	PULL-DOWN MENU	SCREEN MENU	TABLET MENU
LINE or L	*Draw, Line > Segments*	*DRAW, LINE:*	*10,J*

Drawing Horizontal Lines

1. Draw a horizontal *Line* of 2 units length starting at point 2,2. Use the <u>interactive</u> method.

STEPS	COMMAND PROMPT	PERFORM ACTION	COMMENTS
1.		turn on *GRID* (**F7**)	Grid appears
2.		turn on *SNAP* (**F9**)	"Snap" appears on Status Line
3.	Command:	select or type **Line**	use any method
4.	From point:	**PICK** location **2,2**	watch *COORDS*
5.	to point:	**PICK** location **4,2**	watch *COORDS*
6.	to point:	press **Enter**	completes command

The preceding steps produce a *Line* as shown.

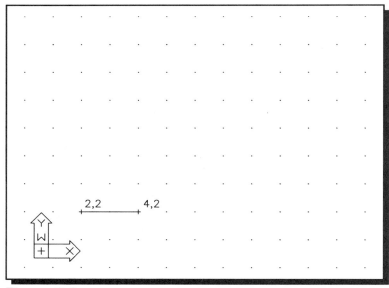

Figure 3-4

2. Draw a horizontal *Line* of 2 units length starting at point 2,3 using <u>absolute coordinates</u>.

STEPS	COMMAND PROMPT	PERFORM ACTION	COMMENTS
1.	Command:	select *Line*	use any method
2.	From point:	type **2,3** and press **Enter**	"blip" should appear
3.	to point:	type **4,3** and press **Enter**	a *Line* should appear
4.	to point:	press **Enter**	completes command

The above procedure produces the new *Line* above the first *Line* as shown.

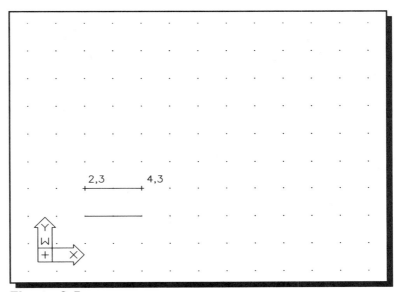

Figure 3-5

3. Draw a horizontal *Line* of 2 units length starting at point 2,4 using <u>relative rectangular coordinates</u>.

STEPS	COMMAND PROMPT	PERFORM ACTION	COMMENTS
1.	Command:	select *Line*	use any method
2.	From point:	type **2,4** and press **Enter**	"blip" should appear
3.	to point:	type **@2,0** and press **Enter**	@ means "last point"
4.	to point:	press **Enter**	completes command

The new *Line* appears above the previous two as shown here.

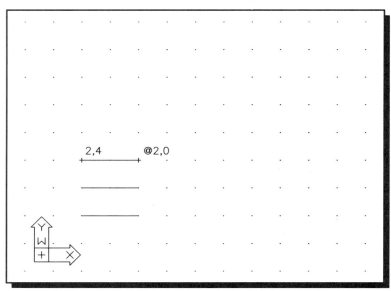

Figure 3-6

4. Draw a horizontal *Line* of 2 units length starting at point 2,5 using <u>relative polar coordinates</u>.

STEPS	COMMAND PROMPT	PERFORM ACTION	COMMENTS
1.	Command:	select *Line*	use any method
2.	From point:	type **2,5** and press **Enter**	"blip" should appear
3.	to point:	type **@2<0** and press **Enter**	@ means "last point" < means "angle of"
4.	to point:	press **Enter**	completes command

The new horizontal *Line* appears above the other three.

One of these methods may be more favorable than another in a particular situation. The interactive method is fast and easy, assuming that O*SNAP* is used (see Chapter 7) or that *SNAP* and *GRID* are used and set to appropriate values. *SNAP* and *GRID* are used successfully for small drawings where entities have regular interval lengths.

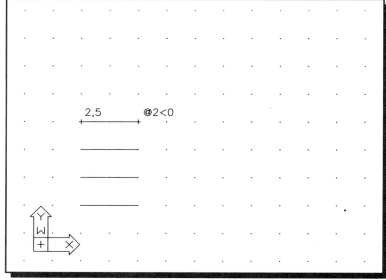

Figure 3-7

Drawing Vertical Lines

Below are listed the steps in drawing vertical lines using each of the four methods of coordinate entry. The following completed problems should look like those in Figure 3-8.

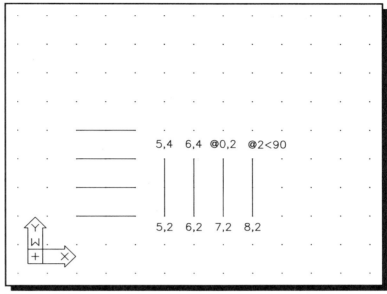

5,4   6,4   @0,2   @2<90

5,2   6,2   7,2   8,2

Figure 3-8

5.   Draw a vertical *Line* of 2 units length starting at point 5,2 using the <u>interactive</u> method.

STEPS	COMMAND PROMPT	PERFORM ACTION	COMMENTS
1.		turn on *GRID* (**F7**)	Grid appears
2.		turn on *SNAP* (**F9**)	"Snap" appears on Status Line
3.	Command:	select or type *Line*	use any method
4.	From point:	**PICK** location **5,2**	watch *COORDS*
5.	to point:	**PICK** location **5,4**	watch *COORDS*
6.	to point:	press **Enter**	completes command

6.   Draw a horizontal *Line* of 2 units length starting at point 6,2 using <u>absolute coordinates</u>.

STEPS	COMMAND PROMPT	PERFORM ACTION	COMMENTS
1.	Command:	select *Line*	use any method
2.	From point:	type **6,2** and press **Enter**	a "blip" should appear
3.	to point:	type **6,4** and press **Enter**	a *Line* should appear
4.	to point:	press **Enter**	completes command

7. Draw a vertical *Line* of 2 units length starting at point 7,2 using <u>relative rectangular coordinates</u>.

STEPS	COMMAND PROMPT	PERFORM ACTION	COMMENTS
1.	Command:	select *Line*	use any method
2.	From point:	type **7,2** and press **Enter**	a "blip" should appear
3.	to point:	type **@0,2** and press **Enter**	@ means "last point"
4.	to point:	press **Enter**	completes command

8. Draw a vertical *Line* of 2 units length starting at point 8,2 using <u>relative polar coordinates</u>.

STEPS	COMMAND PROMPT	PERFORM ACTION	COMMENTS
1.	Command:	select *Line*	use any method
2.	From point:	type **8,2** and press **Enter**	"blip" should appear
3.	to point:	type **@2<90** and press **Enter**	@ means "last point" < means "angle of"
4.	to point:	press **Enter**	completes command

The method used depends on the individual and the application. In many cases, the interactive method is the quickest, assuming that *SNAP* and *GRID* are used and set to appropriate values or *OSNAP* is used (see Chapter 7).

Drawing Inclined Lines

Following are listed the steps in drawing <u>inclined lines</u> using each of the four methods of coordinate entry. The following completed problems should look like those in this figure.

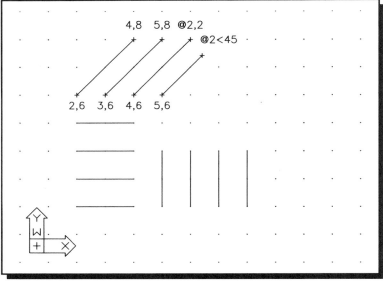

Figure 3-9

9.   Draw an inclined _Line_ of from 2,6 to 4,8. Use the <u>interactive</u> method.

STEPS	COMMAND PROMPT	PERFORM ACTION	COMMENTS
1.		turn on _GRID_ (**F7**)	Grid appears
2.		turn on _SNAP_ (**F9**)	"Snap" appears on Status Line
3.		turn off _ORTHO_ (**F8**)	in order to draw inclined _Lines_
4.	Command:	select or type _Line_	use any method
5.	From point:	**PICK** location **2,6**	watch _COORDS_
6.	to point:	**PICK** location **4,8**	watch _COORDS_
7.	to point:	press **Enter**	completes command

10.   Draw an inclined _Line_ starting at 3,6 and ending at 5,8. Use <u>absolute coordinates</u>.

STEPS	COMMAND PROMPT	PERFORM ACTION	COMMENTS
1.	Command:	select _Line_	use any method
2.	From point:	type **3,6** and press **Enter**	a "blip" should appear
3.	to point:	type **5,8** and press **Enter**	a _Line_ should appear
4.	to point:	press **Enter**	completes command

11.   Draw an inclined _Line_ starting at 4,6 and ending 2 units over (in a positive X direction and 2 units up (in a positive Y direction). Use <u>relative rectangular coordinates</u>.

STEPS	COMMAND PROMPT	PERFORM ACTION	COMMENTS
1.	Command:	select _Line_	use any method
2.	From point:	type **4,6** and press **Enter**	a "blip" should appear
3.	to point:	type **@2,2** and press **Enter**	@ means "last point"
4.	to point:	press **Enter**	completes command

12. Draw an inclined *Line* of 2 units length at a 45 degree angle and starting at 5,6. Use <u>relative polar coordinates</u>.

STEPS	COMMAND PROMPT	PERFORM ACTION	COMMENTS
1.	Command:	select *Line*	use any method
2.	From point:	type **5,6** and press **Enter**	a "blip" should appear
3.	to point:	type **@2<45** and press **Enter**	@ means "last point" < means "angle of"
4.	to point:	press **Enter**	completes command

This last method, using polar values, is preferred if you are required to draw an inclined line with an exact length and angle. Notice that each of the first three methods draws a line of 2.828 (2 * square root of 2) units length since the line is the hypotenuse of a right triangle.

DRAWING *CIRCLES* USING THE FOUR COMMAND ENTRY METHODS

Begin a *New* drawing to complete the *Circle* exercises. The *Circle* command can be invoked by any of the methods shown in the Menu Table.

CIRCLE

TYPE IN:	PULL-DOWN MENU	SCREEN MENU	TABLET MENU
CIRCLE or C	*Draw, Circle > Center, Radius*	*DRAW, CIRCLE, CEN, RAD:*	*10,M*

Below are listed the steps for drawing *Circles* using the *Center, Radius* method. The circles are to be drawn using each of the four coordinate entry methods and should look like those in this figure.

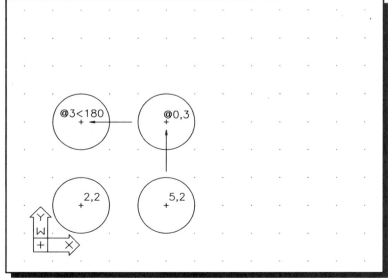

Figure 3-10

13. Draw a *Circle* of 1 unit radius with the center at point 2,2. Use the <u>interactive</u> method.

STEPS	COMMAND PROMPT	PERFORM ACTION	COMMENTS
1.		turn on *GRID* (**F7**)	Grid appears
2.		turn on *SNAP* (**F9**)	"Snap" appears on Status Line
3.		turn on *ORTHO* (**F8**)	"Ortho" appears on Status Line
4.	Command:	select or type **Circle**	use *Center, Radius* method
5.	3P/2P/TTR/<Center point>:	**PICK** location **2,2**	watch *COORDS*
6.	Diameter/<Radius>:	move 1 unit and **PICK**	watch *COORDS*

14. Draw a circle of 1 unit radius with the center at point 5,2. Use <u>absolute coordinates</u>.

STEPS	COMMAND PROMPT	PERFORM ACTION	COMMENTS
1.	Command:	select **Circle**	use *Center, Radius* method
2.	3P/2P/TTR/<Center point>:	type **5,2** and press **Enter**	a "blip" or *Circle* should appear
3.	Diameter/<Radius>:	type **1** and press **Enter**	the correct *Circle* appears

15. Draw a circle of 1 unit radius with the center 3 units above the last point (previous *Circle* center). Use <u>relative rectangular coordinates</u>.

STEPS	COMMAND PROMPT	PERFORM ACTION	COMMENTS
1.	Command:	select **Circle**	
2.	3P/2P/TTR/<Center point>:	type **@0,3** and press **Enter**	a "blip" or *Circle* should appear
3.	Diameter/<Radius>:	type **1** and press **Enter**	the correct *Circle* appears

(If the new *Circle* is not above the last, **PICK** the center of the previous *Circle* (at 5,2) when no commands are in use. The selected point becomes the last point. Then try again.)

16. Draw a circle of 1 unit radius with the center 3 units to the left of the previous *Circle*. Use <u>relative polar coordinates</u>.

STEPS	COMMAND PROMPT	PERFORM ACTION	COMMENTS
1.	Command:	select *Circle*	use *Center, Radius* method
2.	3P/2P/TTR/<Center point>:	type **@3<180** and press **Enter**	a "blip" or *Circle* should appear
3.	Diameter/<Radius>:	type **1** and press **Enter**	the *Circle* appears

CHAPTER EXERCISES

1. **Start a new drawing**

Start a *New* drawing and assign the name "**CH3EX**." Remember to *Save* often as you complete the following exercises. The completed exercise should look like Figure 3-11 on the next page.

2. **Using interactive coordinate entry**

Draw a square with sides of 2 units length. Locate the lower left corner of the square at **2,2**. Use the *Line* command with interactive coordinate entry. (HINT: Turn on *SNAP*, *GRID*, and *ORTHO*.)

3. **Using absolute coordinates**

Draw another square with 2 unit sides using the *Line* command. Enter absolute coordinates. Begin with the lower left corner of the square at **5,2**.

4. **Using relative rectangular coordinates**

Draw a third square using the *Line* command. Enter relative rectangular coordinates. Locate the lower left corner at **8,2**.

5. **Using relative polar coordinates**

Draw a fourth square beginning at a lower left corner of **2,5**. Complete the sides by drawing *Lines* with relative polar coordinates.

6. **Using relative polar coordinates**

Draw an equilateral triangle with sides of 2 units. Locate the lower left corner at **5,5**. Use relative polar coordinates (after establishing the "From point:").

7.   **Using interactive coordinate entry**

Draw a *Circle* with a 1 unit <u>radius</u>. Locate the center at **9,6**. Use the interactive method. (Turn on *SNAP* and *GRID*.)

8.   **Using relative rectangular polar or coordinates**

Draw another *Circle* with a 2 unit <u>diameter</u>. Using relative coordinates, locate the center 3 units below the previous *Circle*.

9.   ***Save* your drawing**

Use *Save*. Compare your results with Figure 3-11. When you are finished, ***Exit AutoCAD***.

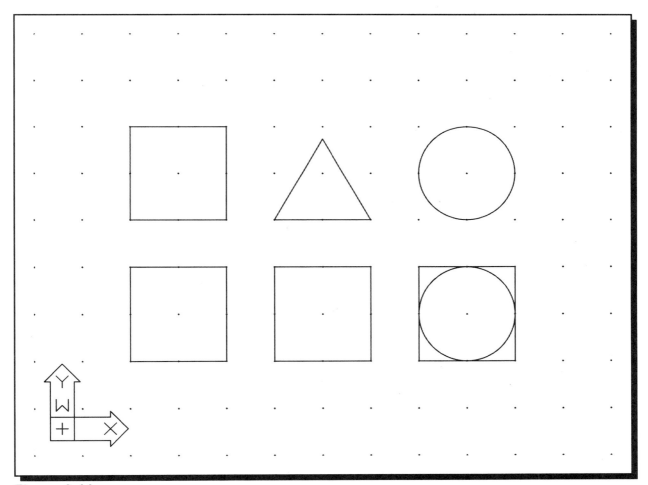

Figure 3-11

Figure 3-12 PSGLOBE.DWG Courtesy of Autodesk, Inc.

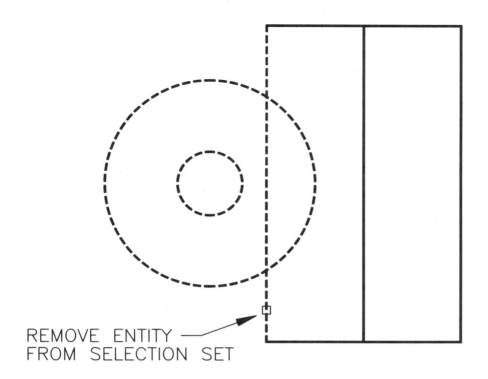

REMOVE ENTITY —
FROM SELECTION SET

CHAPTER 4

Edit Command Basics

CHAPTER OBJECTIVES

After completing this chapter you should:

1.   know where to locate edit commands in the menu systems;

2.   be able to create a selection set using each of the specification methods;

3.   be able to *Erase* entities from the drawing;

4.   be able to *Move* entities from one location to another;

5.   understand Noun/Verb and Verb/Noun order of command syntax.

EDITING ENTITIES

In AutoCAD draw commands create entities. Edit commands modify or change existing entities. An example of editing an existing entity would be to *Erase* a *Line*, *Move* a *Circle*, or *Copy* an *Arc*.

Editing commands are available by using the four command entry methods.

1.	**Type**	Typing the command name or alias
2.	**Pull-down menu**	PICKing from the pull-down menus
3.	**Screen menu**	PICKing from the screen menu
4.	**Tablet menu**	PICKing from the digitizing tablet menu

The pull-down menus have both *Modify* and *Construct* menus which contain edit commands (Fig. 4-1 and Fig. 4-2).

Figure 4-1

The *Modify* menu commands change existing entities in some way, such as *Erase* or *Move*. The *Construct* menu commands use existing entities to construct other entities; for example, *Copy* uses an existing entity but creates a new one.

Figure 4-2

All edit commands located in the Screen menu are found under *EDIT* from the root menu (Fig. 4-3).

The digitizing tablet groups all editing commands in two rows centered around *ERASE* located beneath the screen pointing area (12,W through 22,X).

For details on each command see:

Chapter 9	Modify Commands I
Chapter 10	Construct Commands I
Chapter 16	Modify Commands II
Chapter 17	Construct Commands II

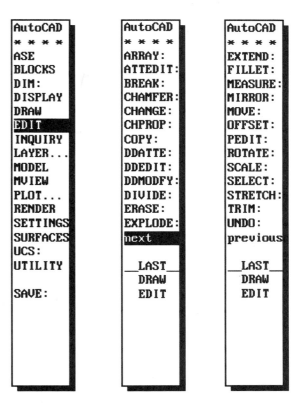

Fig. 4-3

SELECTION SETS

Since edit commands change <u>existing</u> geometry in some way, every edit command requires selection of entities as a first step. In other words, before an action is taken to change entities, you should indicate to AutoCAD which entities you want to change. This process of selecting the entity or group of entities to edit is called specifying a <u>selection set</u>. Specifying a selection set is normally the first step in using any editing command.

Generally, immediately upon invoking an editing command such as *Erase*, the Select objects: prompt is displayed at the command line and the cursor changes to a small "pickbox." You should then select the entity or group of entities for the command to act on. When you PICK the entity, it becomes highlighted (displayed as a broken line) which serves as a visual indication of the current selection set. Since AutoCAD assumes that you intend to select a group of entities, the Select objects: prompt reappears so you can select more objects if you want. The selection set is cumulative. You must press **Enter** to indicate completion of the selection set specification. The current selection set is stored in a "buffer" (selection set buffer) awaiting action from the following edit command such as *Erase* or *Move*.

Selection Set Specification

When the Select objects: prompt appears, you should select entities using the pickbox or one of a variety of other methods. Any method can be used <u>independently</u> or in <u>combination</u> to achieve the desired set of entities. The pickbox is the default option which can automatically be changed to a window or crossing window by PICKing in an open area (PICKing no entities). The other methods can be selected from the screen (Fig. 4-4) or tablet menu (14,U through 22,U) or by typing the capitalized letters shown in the option names following.

The options of specifying selection sets are described on the following pages. As you read along, try each of the options. Use an edit command (like **Erase** or **Move**). When AutoCAD prompts you to Select objects:, use the option explained and illustrated in the related figure. Press **CTRL+C** to cancel the command after using each selection option.

Figure 4-4

Selection Set Options

The options for creating selection sets (PICKing entities) are shown below and on the following pages. Two *Circles* and five *Lines* (as shown in Figure 4-5) are used for every example. If you want to follow along and practice as you read, draw *Circles* and *Lines* in a configuration similar to this.

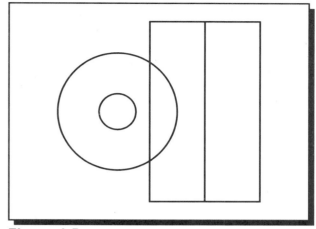

Figure 4-5

pickbox

This default option is used for selecting <u>one entity</u> at a time. Locate the pickbox so that an entity crosses through it and **PICK**.

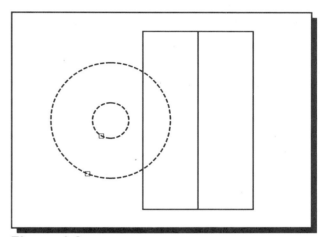

Figure 4-6

Window

All entities <u>completely within</u> the *Window* are selected. The *Window* is a solid linetype rectangular box. Select the first and second points (diagonal corners in either direction).

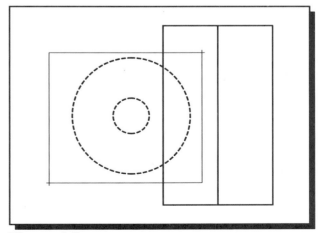

Figure 4-7

Crossing Window

All entities <u>within and crossing through</u> the window are selected. The *Crossing Window* is displayed as a broken linetype rectangular box. Select two diagonal <u>corners</u>.

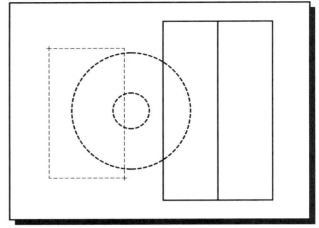

Figure 4-8

Window Polygon

The *Window Polygon* operates like a *Window*, but the box can be <u>any</u> irregular polygonal shape. You can pick any number of corners rather than just two as with the *Window* option.

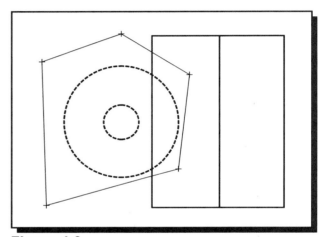

Figure 4-9

Crossing Polygon

The *Crossing Polygon* operates like a *Crossing Window*, but can have any number of corners like *Window Polygon*.

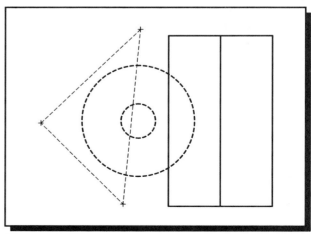

Figure 4-10

Fence

This option operates like a <u>crossing line</u>. Any entities crossing the *Fence* are selected. The *Fence* can have any number of segments.

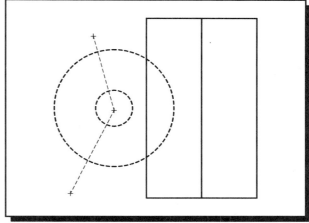

Figure 4-11

Last

This option automatically finds and selects <u>only</u> the last entity created.

Previous

Previous finds and selects the <u>previous selection set</u>, i.e., whatever was selected during the previous command (except after *Erase*). This allows you to use several editing commands on the same set of entities without having to re-specify the set.

ALL

This option selects <u>all entities</u> in the drawing except those on *Frozen* or *Locked* layers (*Layers* are covered in Chapter 12).

Remove

Selecting this option causes AutoCAD to <u>switch</u> to the `Remove objects:` mode. Any selection options used from this time on remove entities from the highlighted set (see Figure 4-12).

Add

The *Add* option switches back to the default `Select objects:` mode so additional entities can be added to the selection set.

SHIFT+ #1

Holding down the **SHIFT** key and pressing the **#1** button simultaneously <u>removes</u> entities selected from the highlighted set as shown in Figure 4-12.

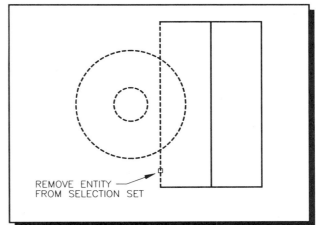

REMOVE ENTITY FROM SELECTION SET

Figure 4-12

AUto

To use this option, the pickbox must be positioned in an open area so that no entities cross through it, then **PICK** to start a window. If you drag to the right, a *Window* is created. PICK the other corner.

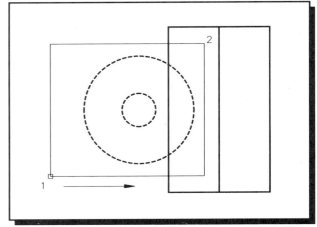

Figure 4-13

If you drag to the left instead, a *Crossing Window* forms.

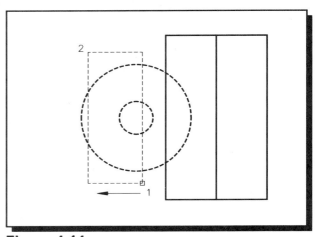

Figure 4-14

SELECT

TYPE IN:	PULL-DOWN MENU	SCREEN MENU	TABLET MENU
SELECT	---	*EDIT, SELECT:*	---

The *Select* command can be used to PICK entities to be saved in the selection set buffer for subsequent use with the *Previous* option. Any of the selection methods may be used to PICK the entities.

```
Command: select
Select objects: PICK (Use any selection option.)
Select objects: Enter (Completes the selection process.)
Command:
```

The selected entities become unhighlighted when you complete the command by pressing Enter. The entities become highlighted again and comprise the selection set if you use the *Previous* selection option in the <u>next</u> editing command.

SELECTION SETS PRACTICE

Using *Erase*

Erase is the simplest editing command. *Erase* removes entities from the drawing. The only action required is the selection of entities to be erased.

NOTE: While learning and practicing with the editing commands listed on the following pages, it is suggested that *GRIPS* be turned off. This can be accomplished by typing in **GRIPS** and setting the *GRIPS* variable to a value of **0**. The AutoCAD Release 12 default has *GRIPS* on (set to 1). *GRIPS* are covered in Chapter 23.

1.   Draw several *Lines* and *Circles*. Practice using the object selection options with the *Erase* command. The following sequence uses the pickbox, window, and crossing window.

STEPS	COMMAND PROMPT	PERFORM ACTION	COMMENTS
1.	Command:	type *E* and press **space bar**	*E* is the alias for *Erase*, space bar can be used like **Enter**
2.	Erase Select objects:	use pickbox to select entities	entities are highlighted
3.	Select objects:	type *W* or use **Select Objects** screen menu and **Window**, then select entities.	entities are highlighted
4.	Select objects:	type *C* or use **Select Objects** screen menu and **Crossing**, then select entities.	entities are highlighted
5.	Select objects:	press **Enter**	entities are erased

2. Draw several more *Lines* and *Circles*. Practice using the *Erase* command with the *AUto window* and *AUto crossing window* options as indicated below.

STEPS	COMMAND PROMPT	PERFORM ACTION	COMMENTS
1.	Command:	select the **Modify** pull-down, **Erase >** and **Select**	
2.	Erase Select objects:	use pickbox to select an open area, drag *window* to the <u>right</u> to select entities	entities are highlighted
3.	Select objects:	select an open area, drag *crossing window* to the <u>left</u> to select entities	entities are highlighted
4.	Select objects:	press **Enter**	entities are erased

Using *Move*

The *Move* command specifically prompts you to (1) select objects, (2) specify a "Base point," or point to move <u>from</u>, (3) specify a "second point of displacement," or point to move <u>to</u>.

3. Draw a *Circle* and two *Lines*. Use the *Move* command to practice selecting objects and to move one *Line* and the *Circle* as indicated below.

STEPS	COMMAND PROMPT	PERFORM ACTION	COMMENTS
1.	Command:	type **M** and press **space bar**	**M** is the command alias for *Move*
2.	Move Select objects:	use pickbox to select one *Line* and the *Circle*	entities are highlighted
3.	Select objects:	press **space bar** or **Enter**	
4.	Base point or displacement:	**PICK** near the *Circle* center	base point is the handle, or where to move <u>from</u>
5.	Second point of displacement:	**PICK** near the other *Line*	second point is where to move <u>to</u>

4. Use *Move* again to move the *Circle* back to its original position. Select the *Circle* with the *Window* option.

STEPS	COMMAND PROMPT	PERFORM ACTION	COMMENTS
1.	Command:	select the **Modify** pull-down, then **Move**	
2.	Move Select objects:	type **W** and press **space bar** or use screen menu to select **Window**	select only the circle, entity is highlighted
3.	Select objects:	press **space bar** or **Enter**	
4.	Base point or displacement:	**PICK** near the Circle center	base point is the handle, or where to move <u>from</u>
5.	Second point of displacement:	**PICK** near the original location	second point is where to move <u>to</u>

NOUN/VERB SYNTAX

Verb/Noun means to invoke a command and then select entities within the command. A command is a <u>verb</u> and an entity is a <u>noun</u>. For example, if the *Erase* command (verb) is invoked first, AutoCAD then issues the prompt to `Select Objects:`, therefore, entities (nouns) are PICKed second. In the previous examples and with previous releases of AutoCAD, only Verb/Noun order of syntax was used.

Noun/Verb syntax order means to pick entities (nouns) first, then use an editing command second (verb). If you select objects first and then immediately choose an editing command, AutoCAD recognizes the selection set and passes through the `Select objects:` prompt to the next step in the command.

Noun/Verb syntax is possible because the *AUto* object selection mode is *On* by default in Release 12. With *AUto* on, you can select objects with the pickbox, window, or crossing window methods without a command being active (the `Command:` prompt is open). The variable *PICKFIRST* (a very descriptive name) controls the availability of Noun/Verb syntax. The default setting is 1 (*On*). If *PICKFIRST* is set to 0 (*Off*), Noun/Verb syntax is disabled and the selection set can only be specified within the editing commands as with previous releases of AutoCAD. The pickbox at the intersection of the cursor crosshairs is also disabled when *PICKFIRST* and *GRIPS* are both set to 0.

Setting *PICKFIRST* to 1 provides two options: Noun/Verb and Verb/Noun. You can use <u>either</u> order you want and AutoCAD automatically understands. If objects are selected first, the selection set is passed to the next editing command used, but if no objects are selected first, the editing command automatically prompts you to select objects. See Chapter 20 for a complete explanation of *PICKFIRST* and the other selection set variables.

CHAPTER EXERCISES

Open drawing **CH3EX** that you created with the exercises in Chapter 3. Turn off _SNAP_ (**F9**) to make entity selection easier.

1.   Use the pickbox to select entities

Invoke the _Erase_ command. Select the lower left square with the pickbox (Figure 4-15). Each _Line_ must be selected individually. Press **Enter** to complete _Erase_. Then use the _Oops_ command to unerase the square. (Type _Oops_ or select it from the _Erase_ options in the _Modify_ pull-down.)

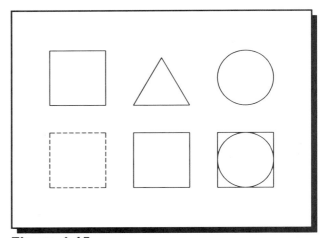

Figure 4-15

3.   Use the _AUto_ window and _Auto_ crossing window

Invoke _Erase_. Select the center square on the bottom row with the _AUto_ window and select the equilateral triangle with the _AUto_ crossing window. Press **Enter** to complete the _Erase_ as shown in Figure 4-16. Use _Oops_ to bring back the entities.

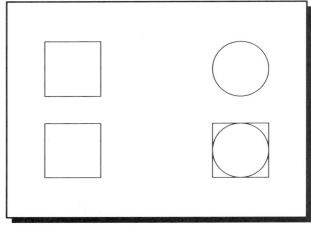

Figure 4-16

4.   Use the _Fence_ selection option

Invoke _Erase_ again. Use the _Fence_ option to select all the vertical _Lines_ and the _Circle_ from the squares on the bottom row. Complete the _Erase_ (see Figure 4-17). Use _Oops_ to unerase.

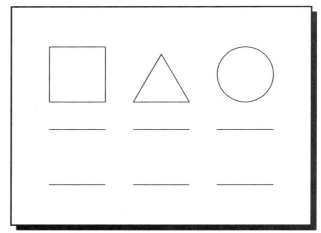

Figure 4-17

5. **Use the *ALL* option and deselect**

    Invoke *Erase*. Select all the entities with *ALL*. Remove the four *Lines* shown (highlighted) in Figure 4-18 from the set by pressing SHIFT while PICKing. Complete the *Erase* to leave only the four Lines. Finally, use *Oops*.

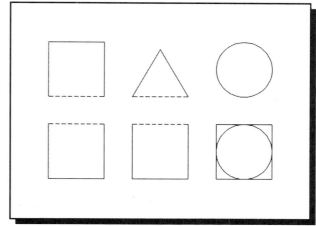

Figure 4-18

6. **Using Noun/Verb selection**

    <u>Before</u> invoking *Erase*, use the pickbox or <u>AU</u>*to* window to select the triangle. (Make sure no other commands are in use.) <u>Then</u> Invoke *Erase*. The triangle should disappear. Retrieve the triangle with *Oops*.

7. **Using *Move* with *Wpolygon***

    Invoke the *Move* command. Use the *WP* option to select only the *Lines* comprising the triangle. Turn on *SNAP* and PICK the lower left corner as the "Base point:". *Move* the triangle up 1 unit. (See Figure 4-19.)

8. **Using *Previous* with *Move***

    Invoke *Move* again. At the Select Objects: prompt, type *P* or select *Previous*. The triangle should highlight. Using the same base point, move the triangle back to its original position.

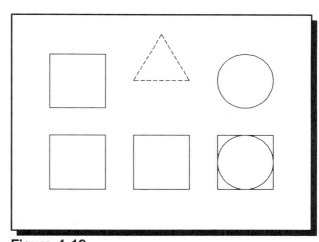

Figure 4-19

9. ***Exit AutoCAD*** and ***Discard Changes***.

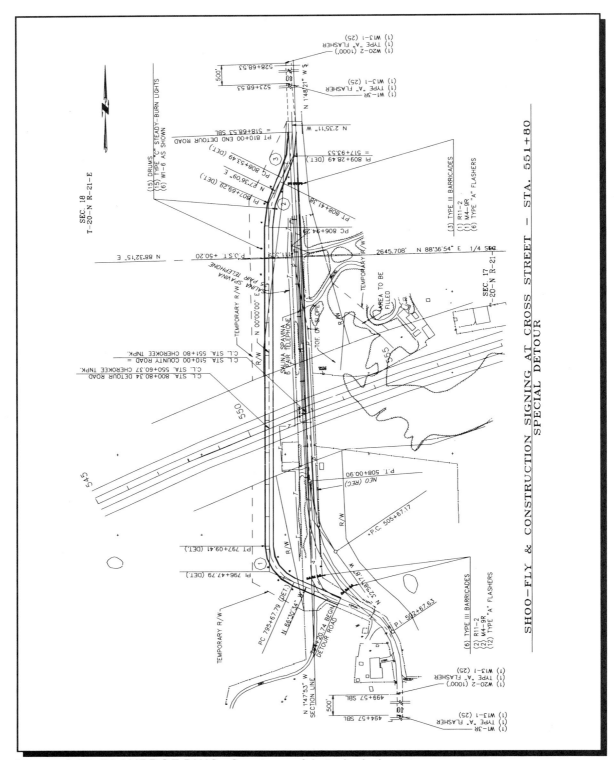

Figure 4-20 PLANPROF.DWG Courtesy of Autodesk, Inc.

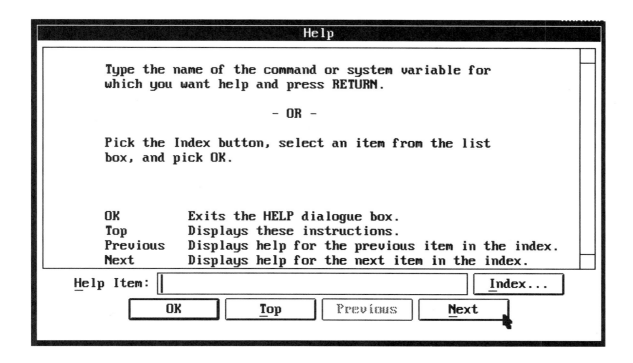

```
                                   Help
   ┌─────────────────────────────────────────────────────────────┐
   │  Type the name of the command or system variable for         │
   │  which you want help and press RETURN.                        │
   │                                                               │
   │                         - OR -                                │
   │                                                               │
   │  Pick the Index button, select an item from the list         │
   │  box, and pick OK.                                            │
   │                                                               │
   │                                                               │
   │  OK         Exits the HELP dialogue box.                      │
   │  Top        Displays these instructions.                     │
   │  Previous   Displays help for the previous item in the index.│
   │  Next       Displays help for the next item in the index.    │
   └─────────────────────────────────────────────────────────────┘
   Help Item: [                                          ]  Index...
         ┌────────┐ ┌────────┐ ┌──────────┐ ┌────────┐
         │   OK   │ │  Top   │ │ Previous │ │  Next  │
         └────────┘ └────────┘ └──────────┘ └────────┘
```

CHAPTER 5

Helpful Commands

CHAPTER OBJECTIVES

After completing this chapter you should be able to:

1. find *Help* for any command or system variable;

2. use *Oops* to unerase entities;

3. use *U* to undo one command or use *Undo* to undo multiple commands;

4. set a *Mark* and use *Undo Back* to undo all commands until the marker is encountered;

5. *Redo* commands that were undone;

6. *Redraw* the screen;

7. regenerate the drawing with *Regen*.

BASICS

There are several commands that do not draw or edit entities in AutoCAD, but are intended to assist you in using AutoCAD. The commands listed below are used by experienced AutoCAD users, and are particularly helpful to the beginner. These commands, as a group, are not located in any one menu, but are scattered about in several menus.

COMMANDS

HELP

TYPE IN:	PULL-DOWN MENU	SCREEN MENU	TABLET MENU
HELP, ?	*Assist, Help!*	*INQUIRY, HELP:*	*5,T to 6,U*

Help or **?** gives you an explanation for any AutoCAD command or system variable. *Help* displays a dialogue box which gives either an index of commands and system variables or specific information on a particular command or variable.

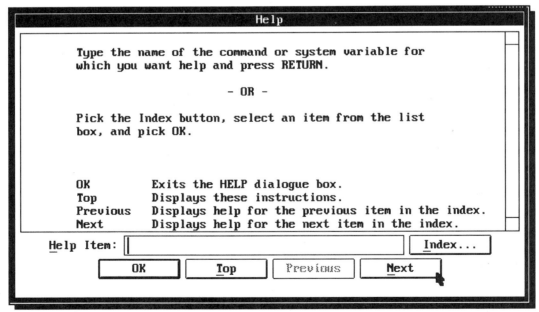

Figure 5-1

Help can be used two ways: (1) entered as a command at the open Command: prompt, or (2) used transparently while a command is currently in use.

1. If the *Help* command is entered at an open Command: prompt (when no other commands are in use), the *Help* dialogue box appears (Fig. 5-1). You can type a

command name in the edit box and page up or down through the list of commands and variables. Selecting the *Index...* tile produces another dialogue box with the complete list of AutoCAD commands and variables to PICK from (Fig. 5-2).

Figure 5-2

2. When *Help* is used transparently (when a command is in use), it is context sensitive; that is, help on the current command is given automatically (Fig. 5-3). (If typing a transparent command, a ' symbol is typed as a prefix to the command, e.g., *'HELP* or *'?*. If you PICK *Help* from the menus, it is automatically transparent.)

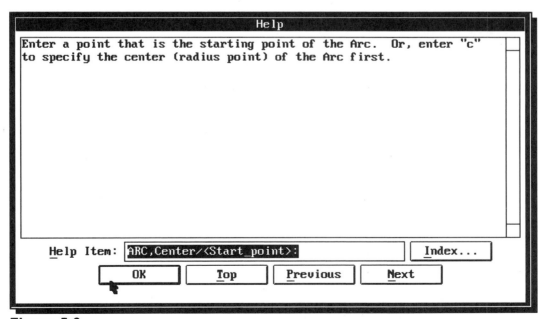

Figure 5-3

OOPS

TYPE IN:	PULL-DOWN MENU	SCREEN MENU	TABLET MENU
OOPS	*Modify, Erase > Oops*	*EDIT, ERASE:, OOPS:*	*18,W*

The *Oops* command unerases whatever was erased with the last *Erase* command. *Oops* does not have to be used immediately after the *Erase*, but can be used at any time after the *Erase*. *Oops* is typically used after an accidental erase. However, *Erase* could be used intentionally to remove something from the screen temporarily to simplify some other action. For example, you can *Erase* a *Line* to simplify PICKing a group of other entities to *Move* or *Copy*, and then use *Oops* to restore the erased *Line* after the editing action. *Oops* can be used after the *Block* or *Wblock* command to restore the original set of entities (explained in Chapter 21).

UNDO and *U*

TYPE IN:	PULL-DOWN MENU	SCREEN MENU	TABLET MENU
UNDO, U	*Assist, Undo*	*EDIT, UNDO*	*12,U*

The *U* command undoes only the last command. *U* means "undo one command." If used after *Erase*, it unerases whatever was just erased. If used after *Line*, it undoes the group of lines drawn with the last *Line* command.

The *Undo* command undoes multiple commands in reverse chronological order. For example, you can use *Undo* and enter a value of **5** to undo the last five commands that you used. Both *U* and *Undo* do not undo inquiry commands (like *Help*), the *Plot* command, or commands that cause a write-to-disk, such as *Save*.

If you type the letter *U* or select **Undo** from the pull-down menu, only the last command is undone. Typing **Undo** or selecting it from the screen menu invokes the full *Undo* command. The options are listed below.

<number>
Enter a value for the number of commands to *Undo*. This is the default option.

Mark
Sets a marker at that stage of the drawing. The marker is intended to be used by the *Back* option for future *Undo* commands.

Back
This option causes *Undo* to go back to the last marker encountered. Markers are created by the *Mark* option. If a marker is encountered, it is removed. If no marker is encountered, beware because *Undo* goes back to the beginning of the session. A warning message appears in this case.

Group

This option sets the first designator for a group of commands to be treated as one *Undo*.

End

End sets the second designator for the end of a *Group*.

Auto

If *On*, treats each command as one group; for example, several lines drawn with one *Line* command would all be undone with *U*.

Control

This option allows you to disable the *Undo* command or limit it to one undo each time it is used.

REDO

TYPE IN:	PULL-DOWN MENU	SCREEN MENU	TABLET MENU
REDO	*Assist, Redo*	*EDIT, UNDO:, REDO:*	*13,U*

The *Redo* command undoes an *Undo*. *Redo* must be used as the <u>next</u> command after the *Undo*. The result of *Redo* is as if *Undo* was never used.

REDRAW

TYPE IN:	PULL-DOWN MENU	SCREEN MENU	TABLET MENU
REDRAW, R	*View, Redraw, Redrawall*	*DISPLAY, REDRAW:, REDRALL:*	*11,L to 11,R*

Redraw refreshes the screen by redrawing all of the entities. Redraw also erases the "blips" from the screen (the tiny crosses created from an object selection or point designation, Fig. 5-4).

<u>The *Redraw* command should be used after *Erase*.</u> If two *Lines* were drawn one on top of the other and then one *Erased*, a *Redraw* would be required to display the unerased *Line* again.

Redraw refreshes the current screen. If using viewports, use *Redrawall*. (Viewports are covered in Chapters 32 and 34.)

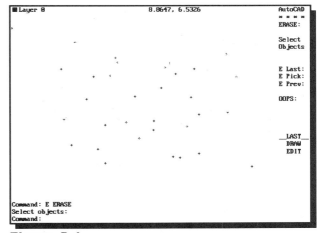

Figure 5-4

REGEN

TYPE IN:	PULL-DOWN MENU	SCREEN MENU	TABLET MENU
REGEN	---	*DISPLAY, REGEN:,* *REGENALL:*	*11,J and 11,K*

The *Regen* command reads the database and redisplays the drawing accordingly. A *Regen* is caused by some commands automatically. Occasionally the *Regen* command is required to update the drawing to display the latest changes made to some system variables. For example, if you change the form in which *Point* entities appear (displayed as a dot, an "X", or other options), you should then *Regen* in order to display the *Points* according to the new setting. (*Points* are explained in Chapter 8).

Regen regenerates only the current viewport. Usually you draw in only one viewport. Use *Regenall* to regenerate all viewports. (Viewports are helpful when creating in 3D models.)

CHAPTER EXERCISES

Begin a **New** drawing. Do not assign a name. Complete the following exercises.

1. **Use *Help***

    Enter **Help** or **?** at the command prompt to find information on the following commands. Read the text screen for each command.

    > *Line, Arc, Circle, Point*
    > *New, Open, Save, Saveas*
    > *Oops, Undo, U*

2. **Use context-sensitive *Help***

    Invoke each of the following commands. When you see the first prompt in each command, enter **'Help** or **'?** (transparently) or select **Help** from the menus. Read the explanation for each prompt.

    > *Line, Arc, Circle, Point*

3. **Using *Oops***

    Draw 3 vertical *Lines*. *Erase* one line, then use *Oops* to restore it. Next *Erase* two *Lines*, each with a separate use of the *Erase* command. Use *Oops*. Only the last *Line* is restored. *Erase* the remaining two *Lines*, but select both with a window. Now use *Oops* to restore both *Lines* (since they were *Erased* at the same time).

4. **Using delayed _Oops_**

Oops can be used at any time, not only immediately after the _Erase_. Draw several horizontal **Lines** near the bottom of the screen. Draw a **Circle** on the **Lines**. Then **Erase** the _Circle_. Use **Move**, select the _Lines_ with a window, and displace the _Lines_ to another location above. Now use **Oops** to make the _Circle_ reappear.

5. **Using _U_**

Press the letter **U** (make sure no other commands are in use). The _Circle_ should disappear (_U_ undoes the last command--_Oops_). Do this repeatedly to _Undo_ one command at a time until the _Circle_ and _Lines_ are in their original position (as when you first created them).

6. **Use _Undo_**

Use the _Undo_ command and select the _Back_ option. Answer _Yes_ to the warning message. This action should _Undo_ everything.

Draw a vertical _Line_. Next draw a square with four _Line_ segments (all drawn in the same _Line_ command). Finally, draw a second vertical _Line_. _Erase_ the first _Line_.

Now <u>type</u> **Undo** and enter a value of **3**. You should have only one _Line_ remaining. _Undo_ reversed the following three commands:

    Erase The first vertical _Line_ was unerased.
    Line   The second vertical _Line_ was removed.
    Line   The four _Lines_ comprising the square were removed.

7. **Use _Redo_**

Invoke **Redo** immediately after the _Undo_ (from the previous exercise). The 3 commands are redone. _Redo_ must be used immediately after _Undo_.

8. **Using _Redraw_**

Draw a **Line**, then draw another **Line** in the same place as the first _Line_ (one on top of the other). **Erase Last**. Both _Lines_ seem to be _Erased_. Use **Redraw** to make the first _Line_ reappear on the screen.

9. **_Exit AutoCAD_ and _Discard Changes_.**

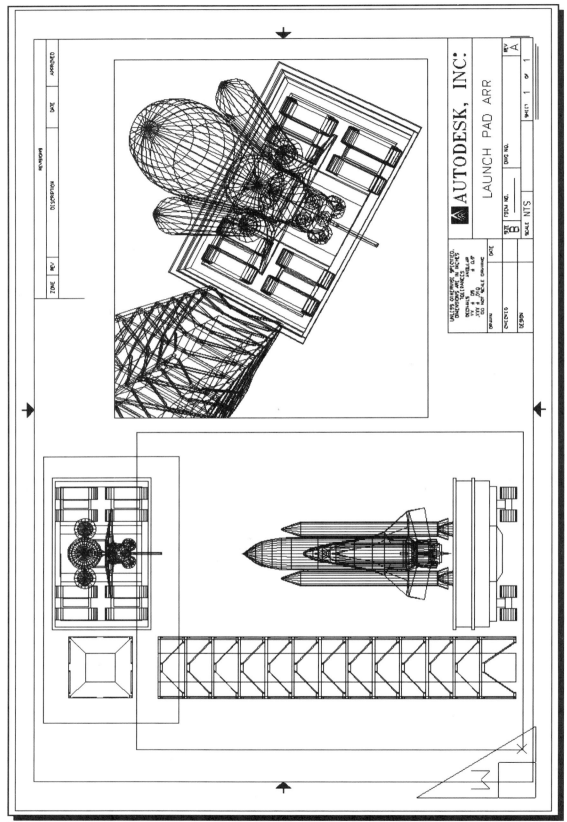

Figure 5-5 SHUTTLE.DWG Courtesy of Autodesk, Inc.

```
Report formats:        (Examples)

    1.  Scientific      1.55E+01
    2.  Decimal         15.50
    3.  Engineering     1'-3.50"
    4.  Architectural   1'-3 1/2"
    5.  Fractional      15 1/2

With the exception of Engineering and Architectural formats,
these formats can be used with any basic unit of measurement.
For example, Decimal mode is perfect for metric units as well
as decimal English units.

Enter choice, 1 to 5 <2>:
Number of digits to right of decimal point (0 to 8) <4>:
```

CHAPTER 6

Basic Drawing Setup

CHAPTER OBJECTIVES

After completing this chapter you should:

1.   know the basic steps for setting up a drawing;

2.   be able to specify the desired *Units*, *Angles* format, and *Precision* for the drawing;

3.   be able to specify the drawing *Limits*;

4.   know how to specify the *Snap* increment;

5.   know how to specify the *Grid* increment.

STEPS FOR BASIC DRAWING SETUP

Assuming the general configuration (dimensions and proportions) of the geometry to be created is known, the following steps are suggested for setting up a drawing.

1. Determine and set the _Units_ that are to be used.
2. Determine and set the drawing _Limits_, then _Zoom All_.
3. Set an appropriate _Snap_ value.
4. Set an appropriate _Grid_ value to be used.

These additional steps for drawing setup are discussed in Chapter 13, Advanced Drawing Setup.

5. Change the _Ltscale_ value based on the new _Limits_.
6. _Load Linetypes_.
7. Create the desired _Layers_ and assign appropriate _linetype_ and _color_ settings.
8. Create desired _Text Styles_ (optional).
9. Create desired _Dimstyles_ (optional).
10. Create a title block and border (optional).

SETUP COMMANDS

UNITS

TYPE IN:	PULL-DOWN MENU	SCREEN MENU	TABLET MENU
UNITS, DDUNITS	_Settings, Units..._	_SETTINGS, UNITS:_	_14,Y_

The _Units_ command allows you to specify the type and precision of linear and angular units as well as the direction and orientation of angles to be used in the drawing. The current setting of _Units_ determines the display of values by the Coordinates display (_COORDS_) and controls the format that AutoCAD uses to draw dimensional values.

You can select the _Settings_ pull-down or type _Ddunits_ to invoke the _Units Control_ dialogue box (Fig.6-1). Type _Units_ (no command alias) to produce a text screen (Fig. 6-2).

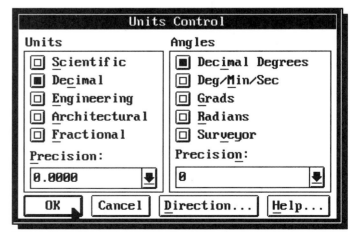

Figure 6-1

The linear and angular units options are displayed in the dialogue box format (Fig. 6-1) and in command line format (Fig. 6-2). The choices for both linear and angular *Units* are shown in the figures. Remember to use *FLIPSCREEN* (F1) to toggle back to the Drawing Editor after reading the text screens.

```
Report formats:        (Examples)

  1.  Scientific      1.55E+01
  2.  Decimal         15.50
  3.  Engineering     1'-3.50"
  4.  Architectural   1'-3 1/2"
  5.  Fractional      15 1/2

With the exception of Engineering and Architectural formats,
these formats can be used with any basic unit of measurement.
For example, Decimal mode is perfect for metric units as well
as decimal English units.

Enter choice, 1 to 5 <2>:
Number of digits to right of decimal point (0 to 8) <4>:
```

Figure 6-2

Units Format

1.	*Scientific*	1.55E+01	Generic decimal units with an exponent.
2.	*Decimal*	15.50	Generic decimal usually used for applications in metric or decimal inches.
3.	*Engineering*	1'-3.50"	Explicit feet and decimal inches with notation, one unit equals one inch.
4.	*Architectural*	1'-3 1/2"	Explicit feet and fractional inches with notation, one unit equals one inch.
5.	*Fractional*	15 1/2	Generic fractional units.

Angles

You can specify a format other than the default (decimal degrees) for expression of angles. Format options for angular display and examples of each are shown in Figure 6-1 (dialogue box format) and Figure 6-3 (command line format).

The orientation of angle **0** can be changed from the current position (3 o'clock, east) to other options by selecting the *Direction* tile in the *Units Control* dialogue box. This produces the *Direction Control* dialogue box (Fig.6-4) Alternately, the *Units* command can be typed to select these options in command line format Fig. 6-3).

```
Enter choice, 1 to 5 <2>:
Number of digits to right of decimal point (0 to 8) <4>:

Systems of angle measure:        (Examples)

   1.  Decimal degrees          45.0000
   2.  Degrees/minutes/seconds  45d0'0"
   3.  Grads                    50.0000g
   4.  Radians                  0.7854r
   5.  Surveyor's units         N 45d0'0" E

Enter choice, 1 to 5 <1>:
Number of fractional places for display of angles (0 to 8) <0>:


Direction for angle 0:
   East    3 o'clock  =   0
   North  12 o'clock  =  90
   West    9 o'clock  = 180
   South   6 o'clock  = 270
Enter direction for angle 0 <0>:

Do you want angles measured clockwise? <N>
```

Figure 6-3

The direction of angular measurement can be changed from its default of counter-clockwise to clockwise. The direction of angular measurement affects the direction of positive and negative angles used in AutoCAD commands such as *Array Polar*, *Rotate*, and dimension commands that measure angular values.

When typing angular values in a drawing, you can enter any of the following conventions for angular format if you want to specify other than the selected angular format:

    d = degrees
    ' = minutes
    " = seconds
    g = grads
    r = radians

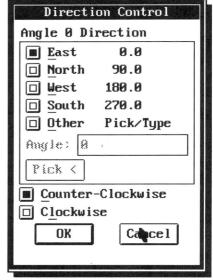

Figure 6-4

Precision

When setting *Units*, you should also set the precision. *Precision* is the number of places to the right of the decimal or the denominator of the smallest fraction to display. The precision is set by making the desired selection from the *Precision* pop-up list in the *Units Control* dialogue box (Fig. 6-5) or by keying in the desired selection in Command line format (Fig. 6-3).

Precision controls the <u>display</u> of *COORDS* and format for dimensions placed by AutoCAD. The <u>actual precision</u> of the drawing database is always the same in AutoCAD, that is, 14 significant digits.

Unfortunately, *Precision* also affects the display of dimensioning variable values in the dialogue boxes. Therefore, *Precision* should always be selected as <u>at least</u> two decimal places so the dimensioning dialogue boxes display the correct default values. If 0 places to the right of the decimal are desired for dimensions placed in the drawing, trailing zeros can be suppressed (see Chapter 29).

Figure 6-5

Keyboard Input of *Units* Values

When AutoCAD prompts for a point or a distance, you can respond by entering values at the keyboard. The values can be in any format--integer, decimal, fractional, or scientific, <u>regardless</u> of the format of *Units* selected.

If *Engineering* or *Architectural* units are in effect, you can type in explicit feet or inch values by using the ' (apostrophe) symbol after values representing feet and the " (quote) symbol after values representing inches. If no symbol is used, the values are understood by AutoCAD to be <u>inches</u>. Feet and inches input <u>cannot</u> contain a blank, so a hyphen (-) is should be typed between inches and fractions. For example with *Architectural* units, key in *6'2-1/2"* which reads "six feet two and one-half inches." The standard engineering and architectural format for dimensioning, however, places the hyphen between feet and inches (as displayed by the default setting for the *COORDS* display).

The variable *UNITMODE* if set to **1** changes the display of *COORDS* to remind you of the correct format for input of feet and inches rather than displaying the standard format (standard format, *UNITMODE* of **0**, is the default setting). If options other than *Architectural* or *Engineering* are used, values are read as generic units.

LIMITS

TYPE IN:	PULL-DOWN MENU	SCREEN MENU	TABLET MENU
LIMITS	*Settings, Drawing Limits*	*SETTINGS, LIMITS:*	---

The *Limits* command allows you to set the size of the drawing area by specifying the lower left and upper right corners in X,Y coordinate values.

The *Limits* command is invoked by any of the three methods shown in the previous Menu Table. If you are changing the *Limits* in the default ACAD.DWG drawing, the command prompt reads as follows:

Command: *limits*
ON/OFF/<Lower left corner> <0,0 or current values>: *X,Y* or *Enter* (Enter an X,Y value or accept the 0,0 default--normally use 0,0 as lower left corner.)
Upper right corner <12,9>: *X,Y* (Enter new values to change upper right corner to allow adequate drawing area.)

The default drawing supplied with AutoCAD (ACAD.DWG) has default *Limits* of 12 by 9, that is, 12 units in the X direction and 9 units in the Y direction (Fig. 6-6). The units are generic decimal units that can be used to represent inches, feet, millimeters, miles, or whatever is appropriate for the intended drawing. Typically, however, decimal units are used to represent inches or millimeters. If the default units are used to represent inches, the default drawing size would be 12 by 9 inches.

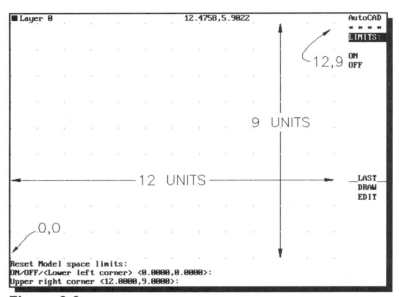

Figure 6-6

Remember that when a CAD system is used to create a drawing, the geometry should be drawn full size by specifying dimensions of entities in real world units. A completed CAD drawing or model is virtually an exact dimensional replica of the actual object. Scaling of the drawing occurs only when plotting or printing the file to a physical fixed-size sheet of paper.

Before beginning to create an AutoCAD drawing, determine the size of the drawing area needed for the intended geometry. After setting *Units*, appropriate *Limits* should be set in order to draw the object or geometry to the real world size in the actual units. There are no maximum or minimum settings for *Limits*.

The X,Y values you enter as *Limits* are understood by AutoCAD as values in the units specified by the *Units* command. For example, if you previously specified *Architectural units*, then the values entered are understood as inches unless the notation for feet (') is given (*240,180* or *20',15'* would define the same coordinate).

If you are planning to plot the drawing to scale, *Limits* should be set to a proportion of the sheet size you plan to plot on. For example, setting limits to 22 by 17 (2 times 11 by 8.5) would allow enough room for drawing an object about 20" by 15" and allow plotting at 1/2 size on the 11 x 8.5 sheet. Simply stated, set *Limits* to a proportion of the paper. (This subject is covered in detail in Chapter 14, Plotting).

ON/OFF

If the *ON* option of *Limits* is used, limits checking is activated. Limits checking prevents you from drawing entities outside of the limits by issuing an Outside-limits error. This is similar to drawing "off the paper." Limits checking is *OFF* by default.

Limits also defines the display area for *GRID* as well as the minimum area displayed when a *Zoom All* is used. *Zoom All* forces the full display of the *Limits*. *Zoom All* can be invoked by typing **Z** (command alias) and **A** for the *All* option. *(Zoom* is a display command used to increase, decrease, or otherwise change the area of the drawing displayed on the screen. See Chapter 11, Viewing Commands, for full details on *Zoom.)*

Changing *Limits* does <u>not</u> automatically change the display. As a general rule, you should make a habit of invoking a *Zoom All* <u>immediately following</u> a change in *Limits* to display the area defined by the new limits (Fig. 6-7).

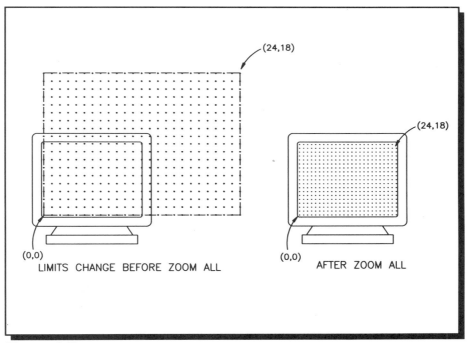

Figure 6-7

When you <u>reduce</u> *Limits* while *Grid* is *ON*, it is apparent that a change in *Limits* does not automatically change the display. In this case, the area covered by the grid is reduced in size as *Limits* are reduced, yet the display remains unchanged.

If you are already experimenting with drawing in different *Linetypes*, a change in *Limits* affects the display of the hidden and dashed lines. The *LTSCALE* variable controls the spacing of non-continuous lines. As a general rule, the *LTSCALE* should be <u>changed proportionally</u> with changes in *Limits*. (This subject is discussed in detail in Chapter 12, Layers, Linetypes and Color.)

SNAP

TYPE IN:	PULL-DOWN MENU	SCREEN MENU	TABLET MENU
SNAP, DDRMODES	*Settings, Drawing Aids*	*SETTINGS, SNAP:*	*12,Y*

The drawing *SNAP*, when activated by pressing **F9** or turning *Snap ON*, forces the cursor position to regular increments. This function can be of assistance to you by making it faster and more accurate for creating and editing entities. The *Snap* command is used to set the value for these invisible snap increments. Since *Snap* controls the cursor position, the value of *Snap* should be set to the <u>interactive</u> accuracy desired. As a general rule, you specify the *Snap* value to be that of the <u>common</u> dimensional length expected in the drawing. For example, if the common dimensional length in the drawing is 1/2", or you intend for dimensional accuracy of the drawing to be to the nearest 1/2", the *Snap* command is used to change the snap spacing to *1/2* or *.5*. In this way the cursor always "snaps" to .5 increments; however, absolute, relative, or polar coordinate values can be keyed in for lengths other than in .5 increments. *Snap* spacing can be set to any value. The default *Snap* setting in ACAD.DWG is **1**.

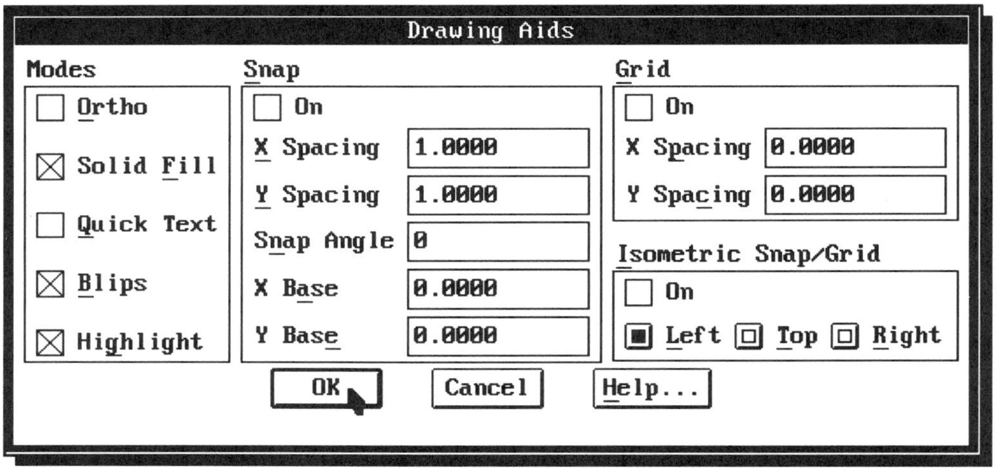

Figure 6-8

The *Snap* command is easily typed, displaying the options in command line format. The *Drawing Aids* dialogue box (Fig. 6-8) can be invoked by menu selection or typing *Ddrmodes*.

The command line format is as follows:

```
Command: snap
Snap spacing or ON/OFF/Aspect/Rotate/Style <1 or current
value>: (value or letter) (Enter a value or option.)
```

ON/OFF
Selecting *ON* or *OFF* accomplishes the same action as toggling the **F9** key. Typically *SNAP* is *ON* for drawing and editing but turned *OFF* to make object selection easier (the cursor moves smoothly to any location with *SNAP OFF*).

Aspect

The *Aspect* option allows specification of unequal X and Y spacing for *SNAP*. This action can also be accomplished in the *Drawing Aids* dialogue box by selecting different values for *X Spacing* and *Y Spacing*.

Rotate

Snap can also be *Rotate*d about any point and set to any angle. When *SNAP* has been rotated, the *GRID*, *ORTHO*, and the "cross-hairs" automatically follow this alignment (see Figure 1-22). This action facilitates creating entities oriented at the specified angle, for example, creating an auxiliary view or drawing part of a floor plan at an angle. To accomplish this, use the *R* option in command line format or set *Snap Angle* and *X Base* and *Y Base* (point to rotate about) in the dialogue box.

Style

The *Style* option allows switching between a *Standard* snap pattern (the default square or rectangular) and an *Isometric* snap pattern. If using the dialogue box, toggle *Isometric Snap/Grid On*. For creating isometric drawings, see Chapter 25.

When the *SNAP Style* or *Rotate* angle is changed, the *GRID* automatically aligns with it.

GRID

TYPE IN:	PULL-DOWN MENU	SCREEN MENU	TABLET MENU
GRID, DDRMODES	*Settings, Drawing Aids*	*SETTINGS, GRID:*	*13,Y*

GRID is visible on the screen, whereas *SNAP* is invisible. *GRID* is only a <u>visible</u> display of some regular interval. *GRID* and *SNAP* can be <u>independent</u> of each other. In other words, each can have separate spacing settings and the active state of each (*ON*, *OFF*) can be controlled independently. The *GRID* <u>follows</u> the *SNAP* if *SNAP* is rotated or changed to *Isometric Style*. Although the *GRID* spacing can be different than that of *SNAP*, it can also be forced to follow *SNAP* by using the *Snap* option. The default *GRID* setting (in ACAD.DWG) is **1**.

Grid can be accessed by command line format (shown below) or set via the *Drawing Aids* dialogue box (Fig. 6-8). The dialogue box is invoked by menu selection or typing *Ddrmodes*. The dialogue box allows only *X Spacing* and *Y Spacing* input for *Grid*.

```
Command: grid
Grid spacing(X)or ON/OFF/Snap/Aspect <current value>: (value or
letter) (Enter a value or option.)
```

Grid Spacing (X)

If you supply a value for the *Grid spacing*, *GRID* is displayed at that spacing regardless of *SNAP* spacing. If you key in an *X* as a suffix to the value (for example, *2X*), the *GRID* is displayed as that value <u>times</u> the *SNAP* spacing (for example, "2 times" *SNAP*).

ON/OFF

The *ON* and *OFF* options simply make the *GRID* visible or not (like toggling the **F7** key).

Snap

The *Snap* option of the *Grid* command forces the *GRID* spacing to equal that of *SNAP*, even if *SNAP* is subsequently changed.

Aspect

The *Aspect* option of *GRID* allows different X and Y spacing.

The *GRID* <u>cannot</u> be plotted. It is not comprised of *Point* entities and therefore is not part of the current drawing. *GRID* is only a visual aid.

CHAPTER EXERCISES

1.   A drawing is to be made to detail a mechanical part. The part is to be manufactured from sheet metal stock; therefore, only one view is needed. The overall dimensions are 18 by 10 inches, accurate to the nearest .125 inch. Complete the steps for drawing setup:

   A.   The drawing will be automatically "scaled to fit" the paper (no standard scale).

      1.   *Units* should be *Decimal*. Set the *Precision* to **0.000**.
      2.   Set *Limits* in order to draw full size. Make the lower left corner **0,0** and the upper right at **24,18**. This is a 4 by 3 proportion and should allow space for the part, a title block, border and dimensions or notes.
      3.   *Zoom All*. (Type **Z** for *Zoom*, then type **A** for *All*.)
      4.   Set the *GRID* to **1**.
      5.   Set *SNAP* to **.125**.
      6.   *Save* this drawing as **CH6EX1A** (to be used again later).
              (When plotting at a later time, "Scale to Fit" can be specified.)

   B.   The drawing will be plotted to scale on engineering "A" or "B" size paper (11" by 8.5" or 22" by 17").

      1.   *Units* should be *Decimal*. Set the *Precision* to **0.000**.
      2.   Set *Limits* to the paper size (or a proportion thereof), making the lower left corner **0,0** and the upper right at **22,17**. This allows space for drawing full size and for a title block, border, and dimensions or notes.
      3.   *Zoom All*. (Type **Z** for *Zoom*, then type **A** for *All*.)
      4.   Set the *GRID* to **1**.
      5.   Set *SNAP* to **.125**.
      6.   *Save* this drawing as **CH6EX1B** (to be used again later).
              (When plotting, a scale of 1=1 can be specified to plot on 22" by 17" paper, or a scale of 1/2=1 can be specified to plot on 11" by 8.5" paper.)

2. A drawing is to be prepared for a house plan. Set up the drawing for a floor plan that is approximately 50' by 30'. Assume the drawing is to be automatically "Scaled to Fit" the sheet (no standard scale).

- A. Set **Units** to **Architectural**. Set the **Precision** to **0'-0 1/4"**. Each unit equals 1 inch.
- B. Set **Limits** to **0,0** and **80',60'**. Use the ' (apostrophe) symbol to designate feet. Otherwise, enter **0,0** and **960,720** (size in inch units is: 80x12=960 and 60x12=720).
- C. **Zoom All**. (Type **Z** for _Zoom_, then type **A** for _All_.)
- D. Set **GRID** to **24** (2 feet).
- E. Set **SNAP** to **6** (anything smaller would be hard to PICK).
- F. **Save** this drawing as **CH6EX2**.

3. A multiview drawing of a mechanical part is to be made. The part is 125mm in width, 30mm in height, and 60mm in depth. The plot is to be made on an "A4" metric sheet size (297mm x 210mm).

- A. **Units** should be **Decimal**. Set the **Precision** to **0.00**.
- B. Calculate the space needed for three views. If **Limits** are set to the sheet size, there should be adequate space for the views. Make the lower left corner **0,0** and the upper right at **297,210**. (Since the _Limits_ are set to the sheet size, a plot can be made later at 1=1.)
- C. **Zoom All**. (Type **Z** for _Zoom_, then type **A** for _All_.)
- D. Set the **GRID** to **10**.
- E. Set **SNAP** to **2**.
- F. **Save** this drawing as **CH6EX3** (to be used again later).

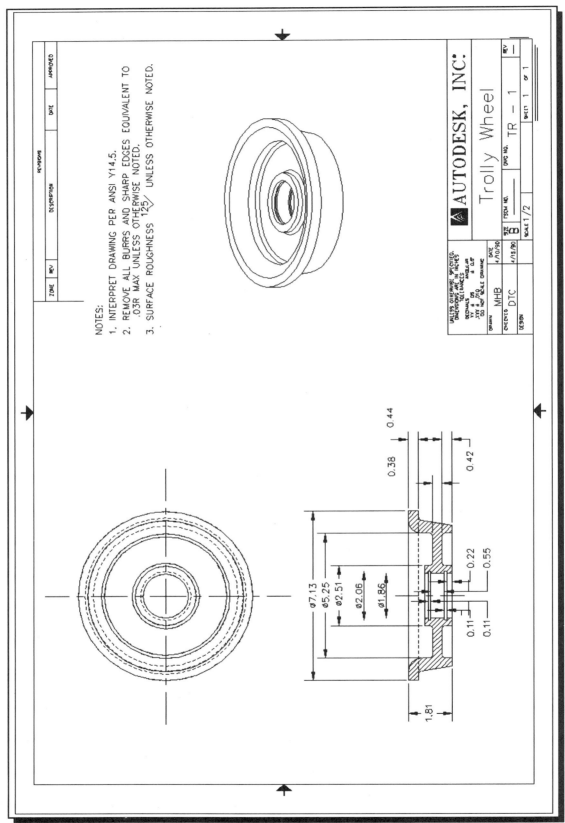

Figure 6-9 TROL1.DWG Courtesy of Autodesk, Inc.

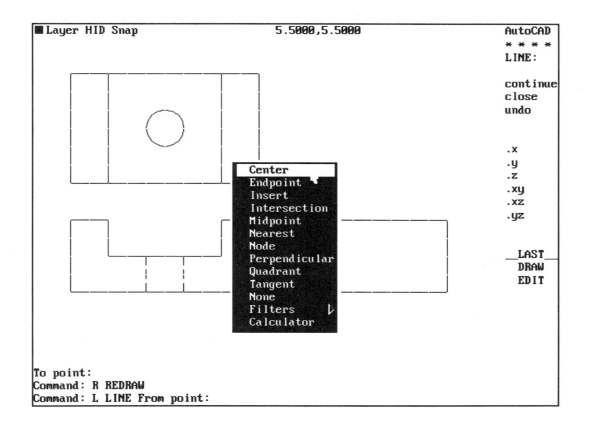

CHAPTER 7

Object Snap

CHAPTER OBJECTIVES

After completing this chapter you should:

1.   understand the importance of accuracy in CAD drawings;

2.   know the function of each of the *OSNAP* modes;

3.   be able to invoke *OSNAP*s for single point selection;

4.   be able to operate running *OSNAP* modes;

5.   be able to use *OSNAP* with fundamental <u>draw</u> commands;

6.   be able to use *OSNAP* with fundamental <u>edit</u> commands.

CAD ACCURACY

Because CAD databases store drawings as digital information with great precision (fourteen numeric places in AutoCAD), it is possible, practical, and desirable to create drawings that are 100% accurate; that is, a CAD drawing should be created as an exact dimensional replica of the actual object. For example, lines that appear to connect should actually connect by having the exact coordinate values for the matching line endpoints. Only by employing this precision can dimensions placed in a drawing automatically display the exact intended length, or can a CAD database be used to drive CNC (Computer Numerical Control) machine devices such as milling machines or lathes, or can the CAD database be used for rapid prototyping devices such as Stereo Lithography Apparatus. With CAD/CAM technology (Computer-Aided Design/Computer-Aided Manufacturing), the CAD database defines the configuration and accuracy of the finished part. Accuracy is critical. Therefore, in no case should you create CAD drawings with only visual accuracy such as one might do when sketching using the "eyeball method."

OSNAP (Object Snap)

AutoCAD provides a capability called Object Snap, or *OSNAP* for short, that enables you to "snap" to entity endpoints, midpoints, centers, and intersections, etc. When an *OSNAP* mode (*ENDpoint, MIDpoint, CENter, INTersection*, etc.) is invoked, a box, larger than the pickbox, called an "aperture," appears at the cursor crosshairs. Selecting an entity within the aperture causes AutoCAD to locate and calculate the coordinate location of the desired entity feature (endpoint or midpoint, etc.).

OSNAP Modes

AutoCAD provides the following *OSNAP* modes.

CENter

This *OSNAP* option finds the center of a *Circle*, *Arc*, or *Donut*. You must PICK the *Circle* entity, not where you think the center is.

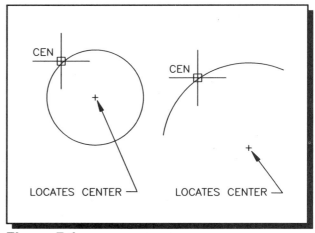

Figure 7-1

ENDpoint

The *ENDpoint* option snaps to the endpoint of a *Line*, *Pline*, or *Arc*. PICK the *Line* <u>near</u> the desired end.

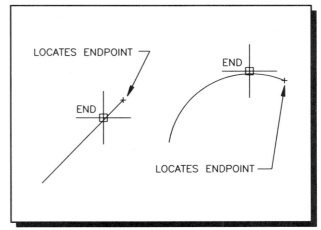

Figure 7-2

INSert

This option locates the insertion point of *Text* or a *Block*. PICK anywhere on the *Block* or line of *Text*.

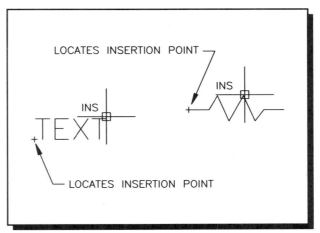

Figure 7-3

INTersection

Using this option causes AutoCAD to calculate and snap to the intersection of any two entities. Locate the aperture so that <u>both</u> entities pass through it, then PICK.

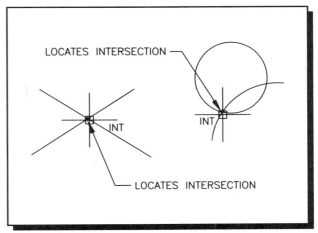

Figure 7-4

MIDpoint

The *MIDpoint* option snaps to the point of a *Line* or *Arc* that is <u>halfway</u> between the endpoints. PICK anywhere on the entity.

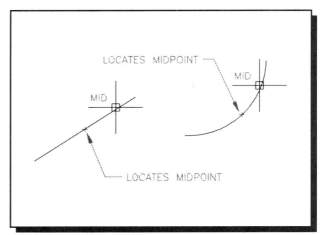

Figure 7-5

NEArest

The *NEArest* option locates the point on an entity nearest to the <u>cursor position</u>. Place the crosshair center nearest to the desired location, then PICK

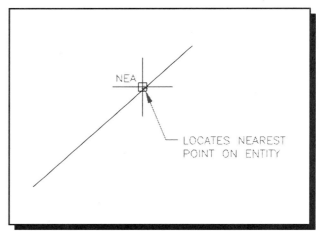

Figure 7-6

NODe

This option snaps to a *Point* entity. The *Point* must be within the aperture.

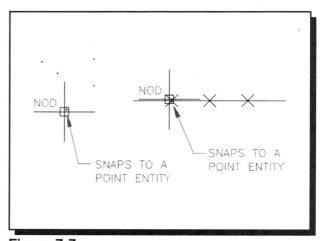

Figure 7-7

PERpendicular

Use this option to snap perpendicular to the selected entity. PICK anywhere on a *Line* or straight *Pline* segment.

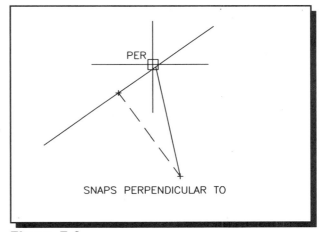

Figure 7-8

QUAdrant

The *QUAdrant* option snaps to the 0, 90, 180, or 270 degree quadrant of a *Circle*. PICK <u>nearest</u> to the desired *QUAdrant*.

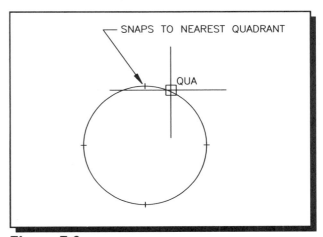

Figure 7-9

TANgent

This option calculates and snaps the entity being drawn or edited to the tangent point of an *Arc* or *Circle*. PICK the *Arc* or *Circle* as near as possible to the expected *TANgent* point.

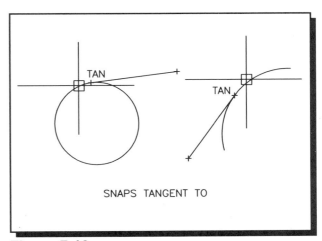

Figure 7-10

USING *OSNAP* (Single Point Selection)

TYPE IN:	PULL-DOWN MENU	SCREEN MENU	TABLET MENU
(first three letters)	*Assist, Osnap...*	****	*12,T to 22,T*

A special menu, called the <u>cursor menu,</u> is the principle method used to invoke *OSNAP* modes. The cursor menu pops up at the <u>current location</u> of the cursor and replaces the crosshairs when invoked (Fig. 7-11). This menu is activated as follows:

2-button mouse	press **SHIFT+#2**
3-button mouse	press **#3**
digitizing puck	press **#3**

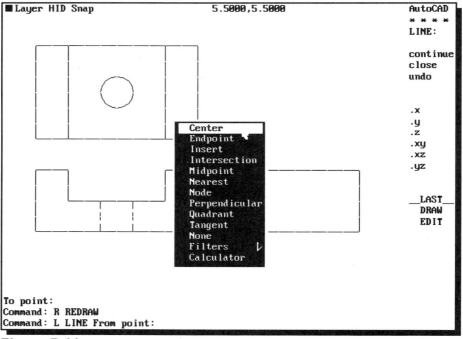

Figure 7-11

With this method, *OSNAP* modes are selected <u>transparently</u> (invoked during another command operation) immediately before selecting a point when prompted. In other words, whenever you are prompted for a point (for example, the From point: prompt of the *Line* command), select or type an *OSNAP* option. Then PICK the desired entity in the aperture. AutoCAD "snaps" to the feature of the entity and uses it for the point specification. Using *OSNAP* in this way allows the *OSNAP* mode to operate only for that <u>single point selection</u>.

For example, when using *OSNAP* during the *Line* command, the command line reads as shown on the next page.

```
Command: Line
From Point: ENDpoint of (PICK)
to point: ENDpoint of (PICK)
to point: Enter (completes the command)
```

When you are prompted for a point (From point:), type or select the desired *OSNAP* mode, then **PICK** the desired entity or location within the aperture. AutoCAD uses the *OSNAP* mode and "snaps" to the feature for the point specification. The aperture disappears after the single point selection.

The *OSNAP* modes can also be invoked by any of the four command input methods shown in the Menu Table. For example, PICKing the asterisks (****) beneath the word AutoCAD on the screen menu displays the *OSNAP* selections. If you prefer typing, only the first three letters of the *OSNAP* mode need to be typed. For example, *CEN* invokes *CENter* and *INT* invokes *INTersection*. It is a good habit to type *ENDP* for *ENDpoint* in order to prevent accidentally invoking the *END* command (which ends the AutoCAD session).

USING *OSNAP* (Running Mode)

TYPE IN:	PULL-DOWN MENU	SCREEN MENU	TABLET MENU
OSNAP, DDOSNAP	*Settings, Object Snap...*	*SETTINGS, OSNAP:*	*10,T and 10,U*

For other cases, such as when you have several *ENDpoint*s to connect, it may be desirable to turn on the *ENDpoint OSNAP* mode and leave it running during the multiple selections. This is accomplished not by transparent use as with the single point selection, but by using the *OSNAP* command, then selecting the desired mode or modes (more than one mode can be running at one time). From that time on, the aperture appears at the cursor whenever AutoCAD prompts for point selection. For running *OSNAP* with both *ENDpoint* and *INTersection* modes the command line reads:

```
Command: osnap
Object snap modes: end,int
Command:
```

The *ENDpoint* and *INTersection* modes remain on and the aperture appears for every point selection until the modes are turned off. It is critical that you turn the *OSNAP* modes off after you have used them for the application. Selecting points not associated with entities can be difficult while running *OSNAP* modes are on. Turn off the running *OSNAP* modes by removing the check toggles in the *Running Object Snap* dialogue box (Fig. 7-12) or by using the *None* option of the *OSNAP* command as follows:

```
Command: osnap
Object snap modes: none
Command:
```

One method of activating running *OSNAP* modes is to access the *Running Object Snap* dialogue box from the *Settings* pull-down menu, then the *Object Snap...* option or by typing *Ddosnap*.

Figure 7-12 illustrates tuning on the *ENDpoint* and *INTersection* running *OSNAP* modes.

The *Aperture Size* can be adjusted through this dialogue box or through the use of the *Aperture* command.

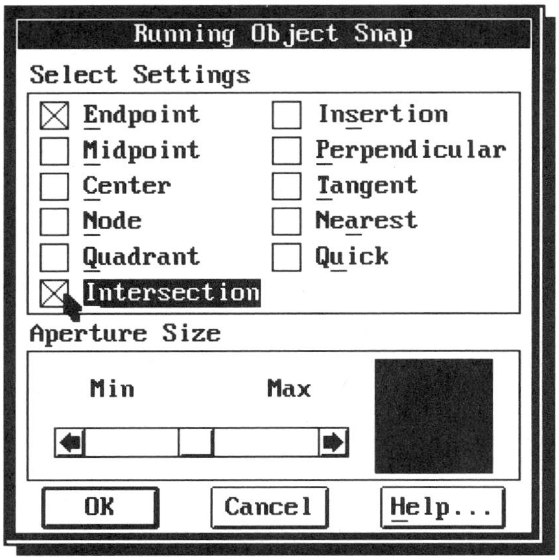

Figure 7-12

OSNAP APPLICATIONS

OSNAP can be used <u>anytime</u> AutoCAD prompts you for a point. This means that you can invoke an *OSNAP* mode during any <u>draw</u> or <u>edit</u> command as well as during many other commands. *OSNAP* provides you with the potential to create 100% accurate drawings with AutoCAD. Take advantage of this feature whenever it will improve your drawing precision. Remember, <u>anytime you are prompted for a point</u>, use *OSNAP* if it can improve your accuracy.

OSNAP PRACTICE

Single Point Selection Mode

1.   Turn off *SNAP* (F9). Draw two vertical *Lines*. Follow these steps to draw another *Line* between *ENDpoints*.

STEPS	COMMAND PROMPT	PERFORM ACTION	COMMENTS
1.	Command:	select *Line* by any method	
2.	Line From point:	type *ENDP* and press **Enter** (or space bar)	aperture appears at crosshairs
3.	endp of:	**PICK** the endpoint of an existing *Line*	rubberband line appears
4.	to point:	type *ENDP* and press **Enter** (or space bar)	aperture appears at crosshairs

| 5. | endp of: | **PICK** the endpoint of the other *Line* | *Line* is created between endpoints |
| 6. | to point: | press **Enter** | completes command |

2. Draw two **Circles**. Follow these steps to draw a *Line* between the *CENters*.

STEPS	COMMAND PROMPT	PERFORM ACTION	COMMENTS
1.	Command:	select **Line** by any method	
2.	Line From point:	invoke the cursor menu and select **Center**	aperture appears at crosshairs
3.	center of:	**PICK** a *Circle* entity	you must PICK the *Circle*, <u>not</u> where you think the center is
4.	to point:	invoke the cursor menu and select **Center**	aperture appears at crosshairs
5.	center of:	**PICK** the other *Circle*	*Line* is created between *Circle* centers
6.	to point:	press **Enter**	completes command

3. **Erase** the *Line* only from the previous exercise. Draw another **Line** anywhere, but <u>not</u> attached to the *Circles*. Follow the steps to *Move* the *Line* endpoint to the *Circle* center.

STEPS	COMMAND PROMPT	PERFORM ACTION	COMMENTS
1.	Command:	select **Move** by any method	
2.	Move Select objects:	**PICK** the *Line*	the *Line* becomes highlighted
3.	select objects:	press **Enter**	completes selection set
4.	Base point or displacement:	invoke the cursor menu and select **Endpoint**	aperture appears at crosshairs
5.	endp of	**PICK** the *Line* near an endpoint	*ENDpoint* becomes the handle for *Move*
6.	second point of displacement:	invoke the cursor menu and select **Center**	aperture appears at crosshairs
7.	center of:	**PICK** a *Circle* entity	you must PICK the *Circle*, <u>not</u> where you think the center is

Running Mode

4. Draw several *Lines* and *Circles* at random.   To draw several *Lines* to *END*point*s* and *TANgent* to the *Circles*, follow these steps.

STEPS	COMMAND PROMPT	PERFORM ACTION	COMMENTS
1.	Command:	type *Osnap*	
2.	Object snap modes:	type *END,TAN*, then press **Enter**	turns on the running *OSNAP* modes
3.	Command:	invoke the **Line** command	aperture appears
4.	From point:	**PICK** a *Line* <u>near</u> one endpoint	rubberband line appears connected to endpoint
5.	to point:	**PICK** an endpoint of another *Line*	a *Line* is created between endpoints
6.	to point:	**PICK** a *Circle* entity	a *Line* is created *TANgent* to the *Circle*
7.	to point:	**Enter**	ends *Line* command
8.	Command:	invoke the *Line* command	use any method
9.	From point:	**PICK** a *Circle*	rubberband line does NOT appear
10.	to point:	**PICK** another *Circle*	a *Line* is created tangent to the two *Circles*
11.	to point:	**Enter**	ends *Line* command

5. The running *OSNAP* modes can also be controlled (turned off or on) by the *Running Object Snap* dialogue box. Use it to turn off the running *OSNAP* modes.

STEPS	COMMAND PROMPT	PERFORM ACTION	COMMENTS
1.	Command:	select the *Settings* pull-down, then *Object Snap...*	dialogue box appears
2.	ddosnap	remove the check marks from *Tangent* and *Endpoint* boxes, then select *OK* tile	turns off the running *OSNAP* modes

CHAPTER EXERCISES

1. ***Open*** the **CH6EX1A** drawing and begin constructing the sheet metal part. Each unit in the drawing represents one inch.

A. Create four ***Circles***. All *Circles* have a radius of **1.685**. The *Circles'* centers are located at **5,5**, **5,13**, **19,5**, and **19,13**.

B. Draw four ***Lines***. The *Lines* should be drawn on the outside of the *Circles* by using the ***QUAdrant*** *OSNAP* mode as shown (highlighted) in Figure 7-13.

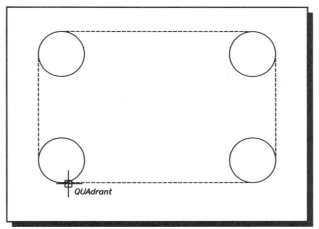

Figure 7-13

C. Draw two ***Lines*** from the ***CENter*** of the existing *Circles* to form two diagonals as shown in Figure 7-14.

D. At the ***INTersection*** of the diagonal create a ***Circle*** with a **3** unit radius.

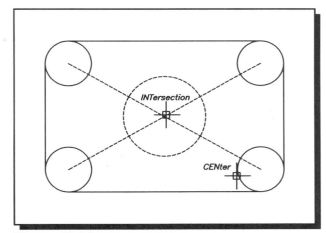

Figure 7-14

E. Draw two ***Lines***, each from the ***INTersection*** of the diagonals to the ***MIDpoint*** of the vertical *Lines* on each side. Finally, construct four new ***Circles*** with a radius of **.25**, each at the ***CENter*** of the existing ones.

F. ***Saveas*** **CH7EX1**. This drawing will be completed as another chapter exercise at a later time.

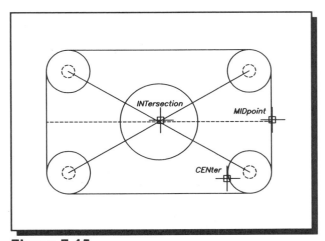

Figure 7-15

2. A multiview drawing of a mechanical part is to be constructed using the CH6EX3 drawing. All dimensions are in millimeters, so each unit in your drawing equals one millimeter.

A. *Open* **CH6EX3**. Draw a *Line* from **60,140** to **140,140**. Create two *Circles* with the centers at the **ENDpoints** of the *Line*, one *Circle* having a <u>diameter</u> of **60** and the second *Circle* having a diameter of **30**. Draw two *Lines* **TANgent** to the *Circles* as shown in Figure 7-16. *Saveas* **PIVOTARM**.

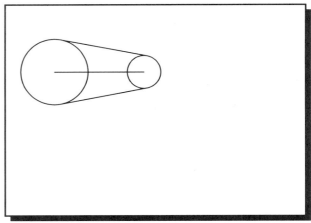

Figure 7-16

B. Draw a vertical *Line* down from the far left **QUAdrant** of the *Circle* on the left. Specify polar coordinates to make the *Line* 100 units (**@100<270**). Draw a horizontal *Line* **125** units from the last **ENDpoint** using polar coordinates. Draw another *Line* between that **ENDpoint** and the **QUAdrant** of the *Circle* on the right. Finally, draw a horizontal *Line* from point **30,70** and **PERpendicular** to the vertical *Line* on the right.

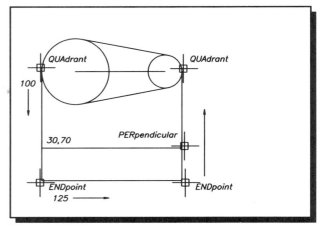

Figure 7-17

C. Draw two vertical *Lines* from the **INTersections** of the horizontal *Line* and *Circles* and **PERpendicular** to the *Line* at the bottom. Next, draw two *Circles* concentric to the previous two and with diameters of **20** and **10** as shown in Figure 7-18.

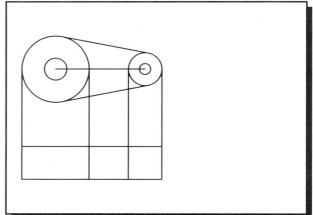

Figure 7-18

D. Draw four more vertical *Lines* as shown in Figure 7-19. Each *Line* is drawn from the new *Circles' QUAdrant* and *PERpendicular* to the bottom line. Next, draw a miter *Line* from the *INTersection* of the corner shown to *@150<45*. *Save* the drawing for completion at a later time as another chapter exercise.

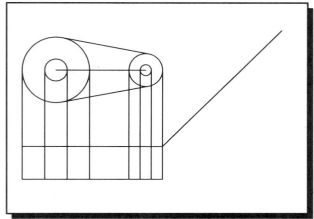

Figure 7-19

3. **Running *OSNAP***

Create a cross-sectional view of a door header composed of two 2 x 6 wooden boards and a piece of 1/2" plywood. (The dimensions of a 2 x 6 are actually 1 1/2" x 5 3/8".)

A. Begin a *New* drawing and assign the name **HEADER**. Draw four vertical lines as shown in Figure 7-20.

B. Use the *OSNAP* command or select *Object Snap...* from the *Settings* pull-down menu and turn on the *ENDpoint* and *INTersection* modes.

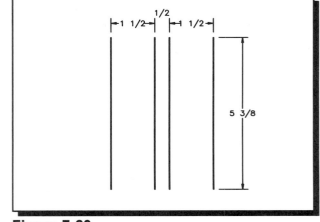

Figure 7-20

C. Draw the remaining lines as shown in Figure 7-21 to complete the header cross-section. Don't forget to turn off the running *OSNAP* modes when you are through by using the *None* option (command line format) or removing the checks (dialogue box format). *Save* the drawing.

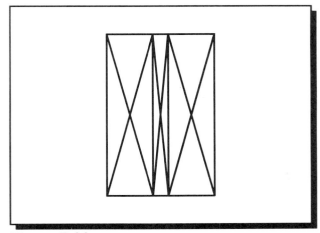

Figure 7-21

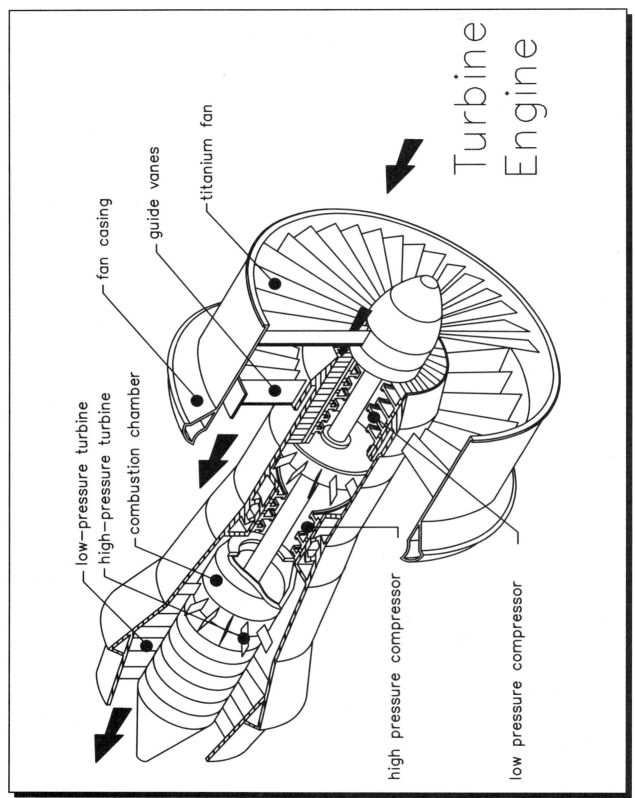

Figure 7-22 SAMPLE.DWG Courtesy of Autodesk, Inc.

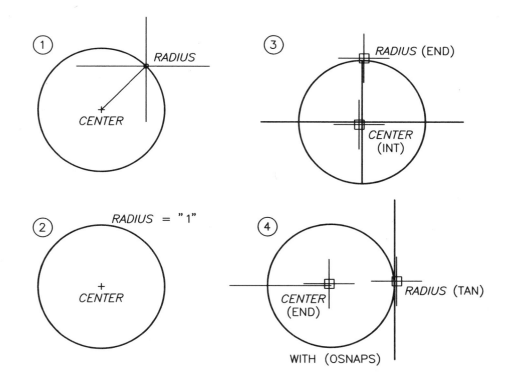

CHAPTER 8

Draw Commands I

CHAPTER OBJECTIVES

After completing this chapter you should:

1. know where to locate and how to invoke the draw commands;

2. be able to draw *Lines*;

3. be able to draw *Circles* by each of the five options;

4. be able to draw *Arcs* by each of the eleven options;

5. be able to create *Point* entities and specify the *Point Style*.

BASICS

Draw Commands--Simple and Complex

Draw commands create entities. An entity is the smallest component of a drawing. The draw commands listed immediately below create simple entities and are discussed in this chapter. Simple entities <u>appear</u> as one entity.

> *Line*
> *Circle*
> *Arc*
> *Point*

Other draw commands create more complex shapes that <u>appear</u> to be composed of several entities, but each shape is actually <u>one</u> entity. The following commands are covered in Chapter 15, Draw Commands II.

> *Pline*
> *Polygon*
> *Ellipse*
> *Dline*
> *Donut*

One draw command creates what appears to be one entity, but is actually several entities (also discussed in Chapter 15).

> *Sketch*

Coordinate Entry

When creating entities with draw commands, AutoCAD always prompts you to indicate points (such as end points, centers, radii, etc.) to describe the size and location of the entities to be drawn. An example you are familiar with is the *Line* command where AutoCAD prompts for the "`From point:`." Indication of these points, called <u>coordinate entry</u>, can be accomplished by four methods (for 2D drawings):

1.	**Interactive**	**PICK** points on screen with input device
2.	**Absolute coordinates**	**X,Y**
3.	**Relative rectangular coordinates**	**@X,Y**
4.	**Relative polar coordinates**	**@distance<angle**

Any of these methods can be used <u>whenever</u> AutoCAD prompts you to specify points. (For practice with these methods, see Chapter 3, Draw Command Basics.)

Also keep in mind that you may specify points interactively using *OSNAP* modes as discussed in Chapter 7. *OSNAP* modes can be used <u>whenever</u> AutoCAD prompts you to select points.

COMMANDS

LINE

TYPE IN:	PULL-DOWN MENU	SCREEN MENU	TABLET MENU
LINE or L	*Draw, Line > Segments*	*DRAW, LINE:*	*10,J*

This is the fundamental drawing command. The *Line* command creates straight line segments; each segment is an entity. One or several line segments can be drawn with the *Line* command.

Command: *line*
From point: **PICK** or (**coordinates**) (A point can be designated by interactively selecting with the input device or by entering coordinates. If using the input device, the *COORDS* display (at the top of the screen) can be viewed to locate the current cursor position. If entering coordinates, any format is valid.
to point: **PICK** or (**coordinates**) (Again, device input or keyboard input can be used. If using the input device to select, *ORTHO* (**F8**) can be toggled *ON* to force vertical or horizontal lines.)
To point: **PICK** or (**coordinates**) or **Enter** (Line segments can continually be drawn. Press Enter to complete the command.)
Command:

Figure 8-1 shows four examples of creating the same *Line* segments using different methods of coordinate entry. Refer to Chapter 3, Draw Command Basics, for examples of drawing vertical, horizontal and inclined lines using the four formats for coordinate entry.

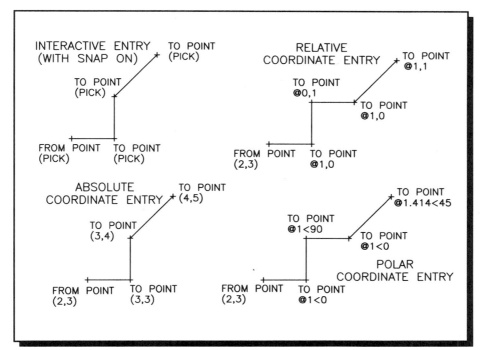

Figure 8-1

CIRCLE

TYPE IN:	PULL-DOWN MENU	SCREEN MENU	TABLET MENU
CIRCLE or C	*Draw, Circle >*	*DRAW, CIRCLE:*	*10,M*

The *Circle* command creates one entity. Depending upon the option selected, you can provide two or three points to define a *Circle*. As with all commands, the command line prompt displays the possible options:

> Command: *circle*
> 3P/2P/TTR/<Center point>:**PICK** or (**coordinates**), (**option**). (PICKing or entering coordinates designates the center point for the circle. You can enter "*3P*", "*2P*" or "*TTR*" for another option.)

As with many other commands, when typing the command, the default and other options are displayed on the command line. The default option always appears in brackets "<option>:." The other options can be invoked by typing the indicated uppercase letter(s). Explicit *Circle* command options can be selected from the menus.

The options, or methods, for drawing *Circles* are listed below. Each figure gives several possibilities for each option, with and without *OSNAPs*.

Center, Radius
Specify a center point, then a radius.

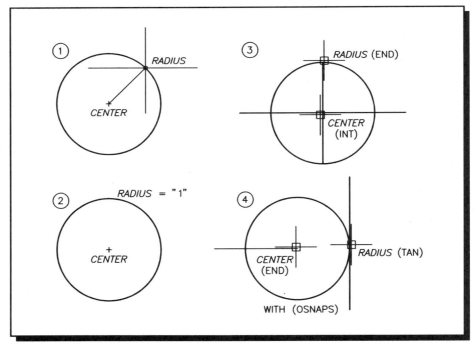

Figure 8-2

Center, Diameter
Specify the center point, then the diameter.

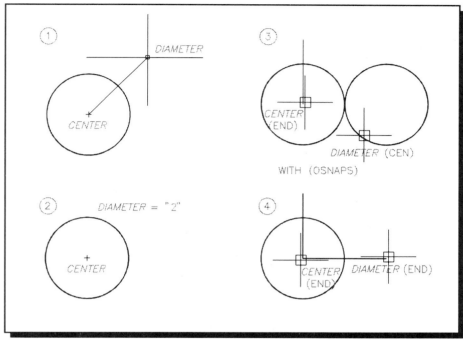

Figure 8-3

2 Points
The two points specify both the location and diameter.

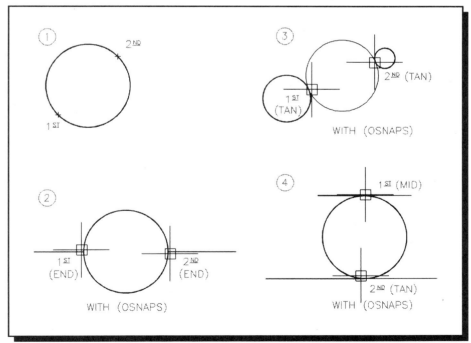

Figure 8-4

3 Points

The *Circle* passes through all three points specified.

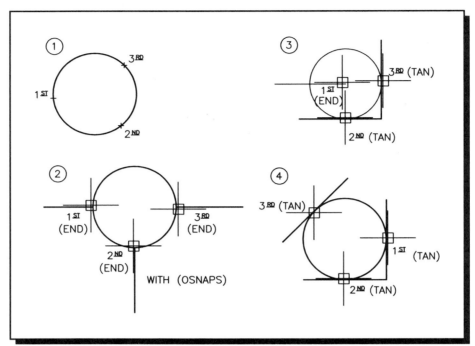

Figure 8-5

Tangent, Tangent, Radius

Specify two entities for the *Circle* to be tangent to, then specify the radius.

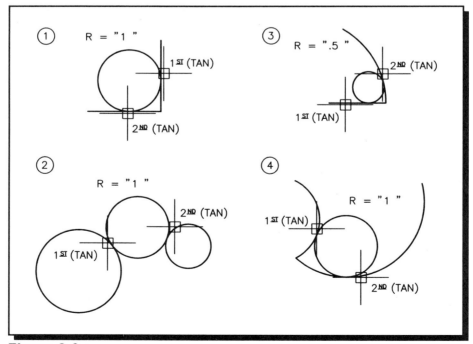

Figure 8-6

The *Radius* and *Diameter* can be specified by entering values or by indicating a length interactively (PICK two points to specify a length when prompted). As always, points can be specified by PICKing or entering coordinates. Watch *COORDS* for coordinate or distance (polar format) display. *OSNAPs* can be used for interactive point specification. For example, the *TANgent OSNAPs* can be used when selecting points with the *2 Point* and *3 Point* options as shown in Figures 8-4 and 8-5.

The *TTR* (Tangent, Tangent, Radius) method is extremely efficient and productive. The *OSNAP TANgent* modes are automatically invoked (the aperture is displayed on the cursor). This is the only draw command option that automatically calls *OSNAPs*.

ARC

TYPE IN:	PULL-DOWN MENU	SCREEN MENU	TABLET MENU
ARC or A	*Draw, Arc >*	*DRAW, ARC*	*10,L*

An arc is part of a circle; it is a regular curve of less than 360 degrees. The *Arc* command in AutoCAD provides eleven options for creating arcs. An *Arc* is one entity. *Arcs* are always drawn by default in a counter-clockwise direction. This occurrence forces you to decide in advance which points should be designated as *Start* and *End* points (for options requesting those points). The *Arc* command prompt is:

```
Command: arc
Center/<Start point>: PICK or (coordinates), or C (Interactively select or
enter coordinates in any format for the start point. Type "C" to use the Center option
instead.)
```

The prompts displayed by AutoCAD are different depending upon which option is selected.

At any time while using the command, you can select from the options listed on the command line by typing in the capitalized letter(s) for the desired option.

Alternately, to use a particular option of the *Arc* command, you can select from the pull-down menu (Fig. 8-7) or screen menus. These options require coordinate entry of points in specific order.

Figure 8-7

The *Arc* options, prompts, and comments are illustrated on the following pages.

3point (Start, Second, End)

Specify three points through which the *Arc* passes.

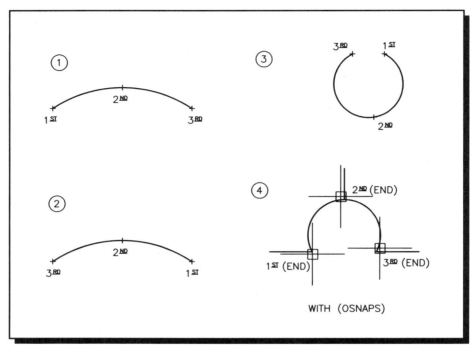

Figure 8-8

S,C,E (Start, Center, End)

The radius is defined by the first two points that you specify.

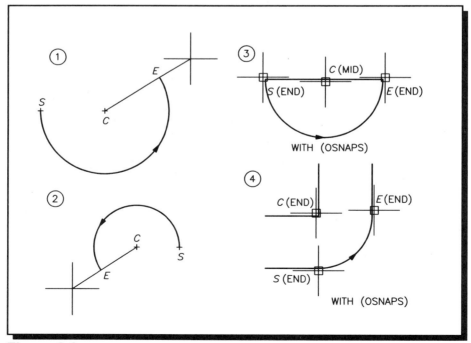

Figure 8-9

S,C,A *(Start, Center, Angle)*

The angle is the <u>included</u> angle between the sides from the center to the endpoints. A <u>negative</u> angle can be entered to generate an *Arc* in a <u>clockwise</u> direction.

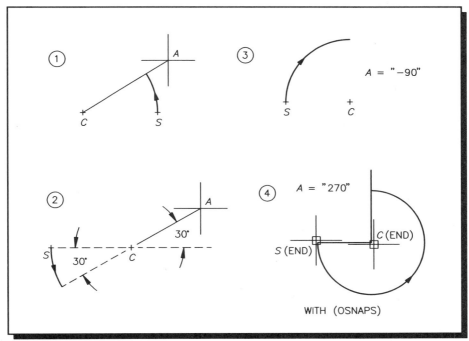

Figure 8-10

S,C,L *(Start, Center, Length of chord)*

The length of chord is between the start and the other point specified. A negative chord length can be entered to generate an *Arc* of 180+ degrees.

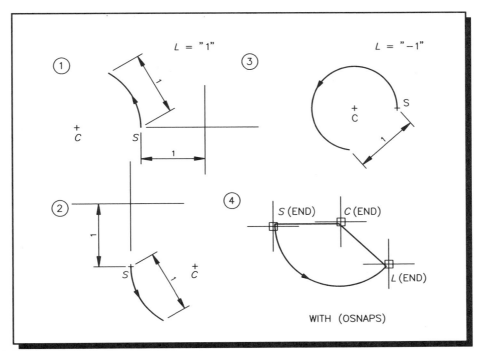

Figure 8-11

S,E,A (Start, End, Angle)

The included angle is between the sides from the center to the endpoints. Negative angles generate clockwise _Arcs_.

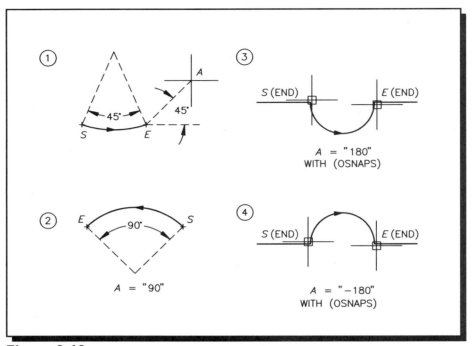

Figure 8-12

S,E,R (Start, End, Radius)

The radius can be PICKed or entered as a value. A negative radius value generates an _Arc_ of 180+ degrees.

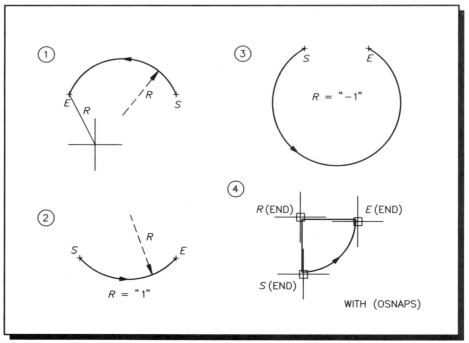

Figure 8-13

S,E,D *(Start, End, Direction)*
The direction is tangent to the start point.

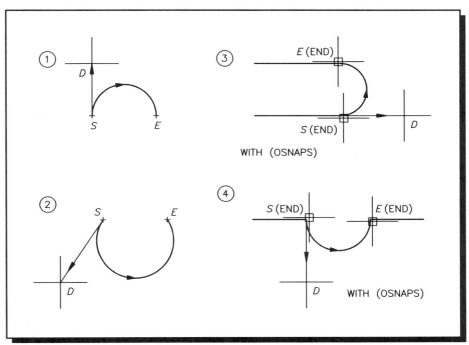

Figure 8-14

C,S,E *(Center, Start, End)*
This option is like *S,C,E* but in a different order.

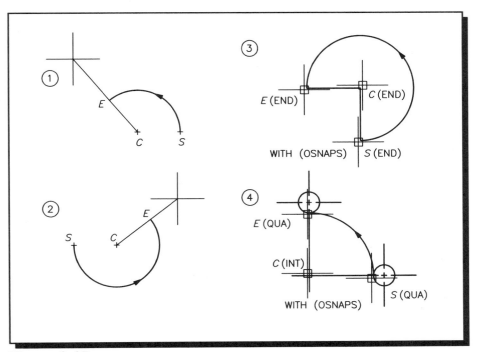

Figure 8-15

C,S,A (Center, Start, Angle)

This option is like S,C,A but in a different order.

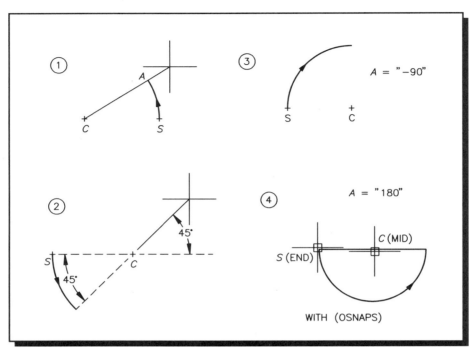

Figure 8-16

C,S,L (Center, Start, Length)

This is similar to the S,C,L option but in a different order.

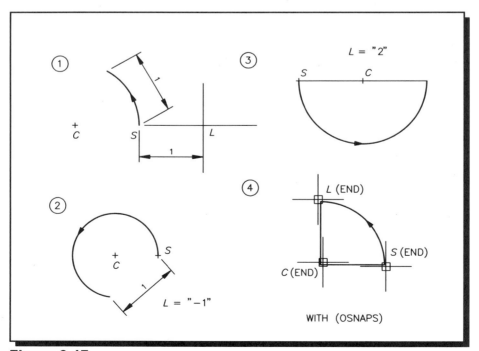

Figure 8-17

CONTIN (Continuous)

The new *Arc* continues from and is tangent to the last point. The only other point required is the endpoint of the *Arc*. This method allows drawing *Arcs* tangent to the preceding *Line* or *Arc*.

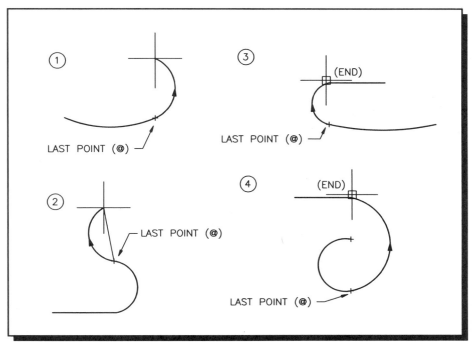

Figure 8-18

*Arc*s are always created in a <u>counter-clockwise</u> direction. This fact must be taken into consideration when using any method <u>except</u> *3-Point, S,E,D*, and *CONTIN*. The direction is explicitly specified with *S,E,D* and *CONTIN* methods, and direction is irrelevant for *3-Point* method.

As usual, points can be specified by PICKing or entering coordinates. Watch *COORDS* (at the top of the screen) to display coordinate values or distances. *OSNAP*s can be used when PICKing. The *ENDpoint, INTersection, CENter, MIDpoint,* and *QUAdrant OSNAP* options can be used with great effectiveness. The *TANgent OSNAP* option <u>cannot</u> be used effectively with most of the *Arc* options. The *Radius, Direction, Length* and *Angle* specifications can be given by entering values or by PICKing with or without *OSNAP*s.

Using *Arcs* or *Circles*

Although there are sufficient options for drawing *Arcs*, many times it is easier to use the *Circle* command followed by *Trim* to achieve the desired arc. Creating a *Circle* is generally an easier operation than using *Arc* because the counter-clockwise direction does not have to be considered. The unwanted portion of the circle can be *Trimmed* at the *INTersection* of or *TANgent* to the connecting entities using *OSNAP* (see Chapter 7, Object Snap). The *Fillet* command can also be used instead of the *Arc* command to add a fillet (arc) between two existing entities (see Chapter 17, Construct Commands II).

POINT

TYPE IN:	PULL-DOWN MENU	SCREEN MENU	TABLET MENU
POINT	_Draw, Point_	_DRAW, POINT:_	_10,P_

A _Point_ is an entity that has no dimension; it only has location. A _Point_ is specified by giving only one coordinate value or by PICKing a location on the screen.

Figure 8-19 compares _Points_ to _Line_ and _Arc_ entities.

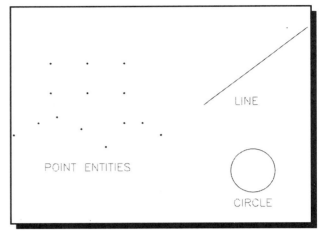

Figure 8-19

      Command: **point**
      Point: **PICK** or (**coordinates**)
      (Select a location for the _Point_ entity.)
      Command:

After creating _Points_, generally the white "blips" appear at the placement of these entities. Forcing a _Redraw_ displays the _Points_ as one-pixel dots (default display mode).

The Node OSNAP option can be used to snap to _Points_. _Points_ are useful in construction of drawings to locate points of reference for subsequent construction or locational verification.

The _Point Style..._ dialogue box (Fig. 8-20) or the _PDMODE_ variable allows you to define the format for the display of _Points_. The _Point Style_ dialogue box is accessed by the _Settings_ pull-down menu.

If you change the point style using this dialogue box or by typing the _PDMODE_ variable, the points are not automatically displayed in the new style. You must use _Regen_ to force AutoCAD to display the points in the new style.

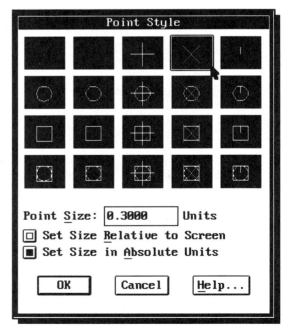

Figure 8-20

CHAPTER EXERCISES

Create a new drawing. Use default *Limits*, set *SNAP* to **.25** and *GRID* to **1**. *Save* the drawing as **CH8EX**. For each of the following problems, *Open* **CH8EX**, complete one problem, then use *Saveas* to give the drawing a new name.

1. *Open* **CH8EX**. Create the geometry shown in Figure 8-21. Start the first *Circle* center at point **4,4.5** as shown. Do not copy the dimensions. *Saveas* **LINK**. (HINT: Locate and draw the two small *Circles* first. Use *Arc, SCE* or *CSE* for the rounded ends.)

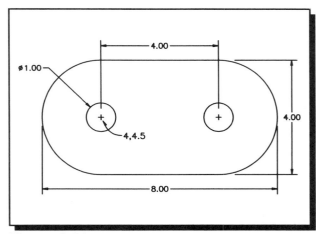

Figure 8-21

2. *Open* **CH8EX**. Create the geometry as shown in Figure 8-22. Do not copy the dimensions. Assume symmetry about the vertical axis. *Saveas* **SLOTPLAT**.

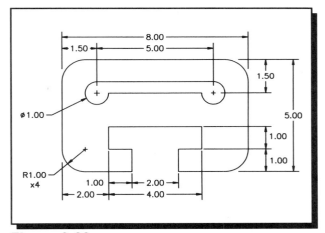

Figure 8-22

3. *Open* **CH8EX**. Create the shapes shown in Figure 8-23. Do not copy the dimensions. *Saveas* **CH8EX3**.

   Draw the *Lines* at the bottom first, starting at coordinate **1,3**. Then create *Point* entities at **5,7**, **5.4,7**, **5.8,7**, etc. Change the *Point Style* to an X and *Regen*. Use the *NODe OSNAP* mode to draw the inclined *Lines*. Create the *Arc* on top with the *Start, End, Direction* option.

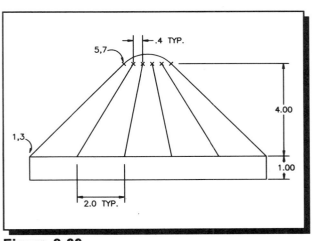

Figure 8-23

4. *Open* **CH8EX**. Create the shape shown in Figure 8-24. Draw the two horizontal *Lines* and the vertical *Line* first by specifying the endpoints as given. Then create the *Circle* and *Arcs*. *Saveas* **CH8EX4**.

(HINT: Use the *Circle 2P* method. The two upper *Arcs* can be drawn by the *Start, End, Radius* method.)

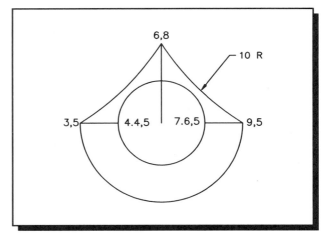

Figure 8-24

5. *Open* **CH8EX**. Draw the shape shown in Figure 8-25. Assume symmetry along a vertical axis. Start by drawing the two horizontal *Lines* at the base. Next construct the side *Arcs* by the *Start, Center, Angle* method (you can specify a negative angle). The small *Arc* can be drawn by the *3P* method. Use *OSNAP*s when needed (especially for the horizontal *Line* on top and the *Line* along the vertical axis). *Saveas* **CH8EX5**.

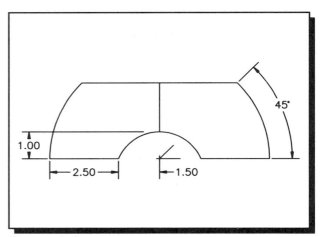

Figure 8-25

6. *Open* **CH8EX**. Complete the geometry in Figure 8-26. Use the coordinates to establish the *Lines*. Draw the *Circles* using the *Tangent, Tangent, Radius* method. *Saveas* **CH8EX6**.

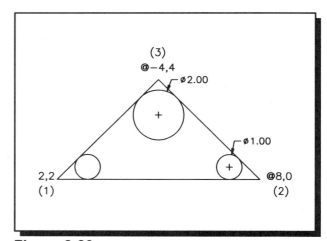

Figure 8-26

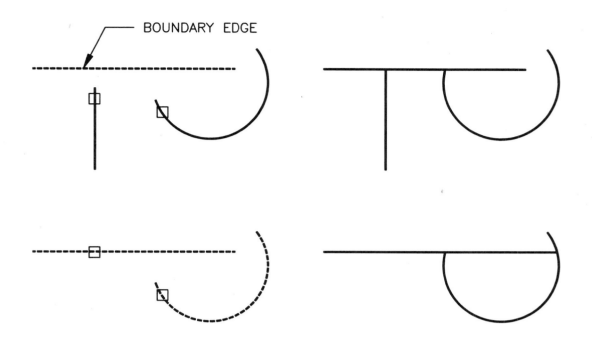

BEFORE EXTEND

AFTER EXTEND

BOUNDARY EDGE

CHAPTER 9
Modify Commands I

CHAPTER OBJECTIVES

After completing this chapter you should:

1.   know where to locate and how to invoke the fundamental modify commands;

2.   be able to *Erase* entities from the drawing;

3.   be able to *Move* entities from a base point to a second point of displacement;

4.   know how to *Rotate* entities about a base point;

5.   be able to enlarge or reduce entities with *Scale*;

6.   know how to use the three *Break* options;

7.   be able to *Trim* away parts of entities at cutting edges;

8.   be able to *Extend* entities to selected boundary edges.

BASICS

Draw commands are used to create entities, while <u>Edit</u> commands are used to <u>change</u> existing entities. Edit commands can be invoked by any one of the four command entry methods: keyboard entry, screen menu, pull-down menus and digitizing tablet menu.

There are <u>two pull-down</u> menus containing edit commands: *Construct* and *Modify*. The *Modify* menu (Fig. 9-1) contains commands that only <u>change</u> existing geometry. The *Construct* commands (Chapter 10) <u>change</u> existing geometry and also <u>create</u> new geometry.

Figure 9-1

The *EDIT* screen menu has two pages that contain all of the edit commands. The edit commands are located on the digitizing tablet menu in a group from 12,W to 22,X.

Since all Edit commands affect or use existing geometry, the first step in using any edit command is constructing a selection set (see Chapter 4). This can be done by one of two methods:

1.   Invoking the desired command and then creating the selection set in response to the `Select objects:` prompt (verb/noun syntax order).

2.   Selecting the desired set of entities with the pickbox or *AUto* window or crossing window <u>before</u> invoking the edit command (noun/verb syntax order).

The first method allows use of any of the selection options (*Last, All, WPolygon, Fence*, etc.), while the latter method allows <u>only</u> use of the pickbox and *AUto* window and crossing window.

COMMANDS

The following *Modify* commands are covered in this chapter: *Erase, Move, Rotate, Scale, Break, Trim,* and *Extend*. The other *Modify* commands are discussed in Chapter 16, Modify Commands II.

ERASE

TYPE IN:	PULL-DOWN MENU	SCREEN MENU	TABLET MENU
ERASE or E	***Modify, Erase > Select***	***EDIT, ERASE:***	***16,W and 17,W***

The *Erase* command deletes the entities you select from the drawing. Any of the object selection methods can be used to highlight the entities to *Erase*. The only other required action is for you to press *Enter* to cause the erase to take effect.

> ```
> Command: Erase
> Select objects: PICK (Use any object selection method.)
> Select objects: PICK (Continue to select desired objects.)
> Select objects: Enter (Confirms the object selection process and causes Erase
> ```
> to take effect.)

When **Enter** is pressed, all entities selected are erased from the drawing. (See Chapter 4 for practice with this command.)

It is a good habit to *Redraw after Erasing*. This action clears the drawing of "blips" and redraws any entities or parts of entities that were turned to the background color during the *Erase* (Fig. 9-2).

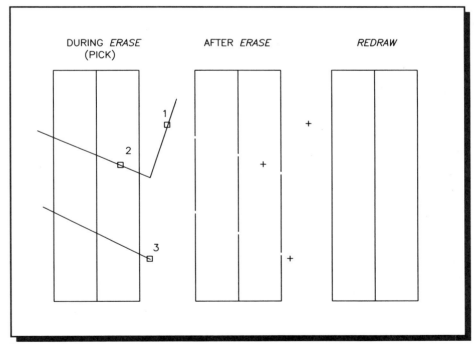

Figure 9-2

If entities are erased accidentally, *U* can be used immediately following the mistake to undo one step, or *Oops* can be used to bring back into the drawing whatever was *Erased* the last time *Erase* was used. If only part of an entity should be erased, use *Trim* or *Break*.

MOVE

TYPE IN:	PULL-DOWN MENU	SCREEN MENU	TABLET MENU
MOVE or M	*Modify, Move*	*EDIT, MOVE:*	*15,W*

Move allows you to move (or relocate) one or more entities from the existing position in the drawing to any other position you specify. After selecting the entities to *Move*, you must specify the "base point" and "second point of displacement." You can use any of the coordinate entry methods to specify these points as shown in Figure 9-3.

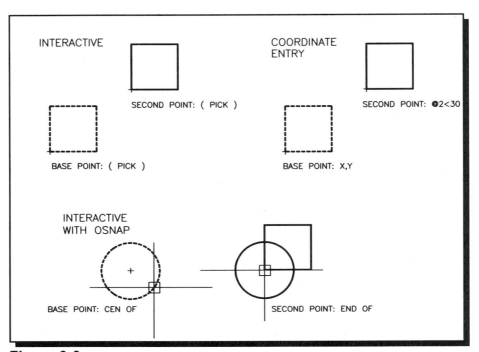

Figure 9-3

```
Command: move
Select objects: PICK (Use any of the object selection methods to select the
desired entities to move.)
Select objects: PICK (Continue to select objects until all entities to move are
highlighted.)
Select objects: Enter (Press enter to indicate selection of objects is complete.)
Base point or displacement: PICK or (coordinates) (This is the point to
move from. Select a point to use as a "handle." An ENDpoint or CENter, etc. can be
used.)
Second point of displacement: PICK or (coordinates) (This is the point to
move to. OSNAPs can also be used here.)
Command:
```

Keep in mind that *OSNAPs* can be used when PICKing any point. It is often helpful to toggle *ORTHO ON* (**F8**) to force the *Move* in a horizontal or vertical direction.

If you know a specific distance, or a distance and an angle, that the set of entities should be moved, relative rectangular or relative polar coordinates can be used. In the following sequence, relative polar coordinates are used to move entities 2 units in a 30 degree direction (see Fig. 9-3).

```
Command: move
Select objects: PICK
Select objects: PICK
Select objects: Enter
Base point or displacement: PICK
Second point of displacement: @2<30
Command:
```

ROTATE

TYPE IN:	PULL-DOWN MENU	SCREEN MENU	TABLET MENU
ROTATE	*Modify, Rotate*	*EDIT, ROTATE:*	*13,W*

Selected entities can be rotated to any position with this command. After selecting entities to *Rotate*, you select a "base point" (or point to rotate about) then specify an angle for rotation. AutoCAD rotates the selected entities by the increment specified from the original position (Fig. 9-4). For example, specifying a value of **10** would *Rotate* the selected entities 10 degrees counter-clockwise from their current position; a value of **-10** would *Rotate* the entities 10 degrees in a clockwise direction. Values of angular measurement are understood as degrees by default, although grads or radians can also be used (see *Units*, Chapter 6).

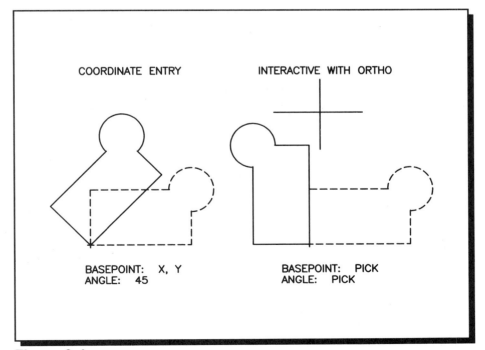

Figure 9-4

```
Command: rotate
```
Select objects: **PICK** or (**coordinates**) (Select the objects to rotate.)
Select objects: **Enter** (Indicate completion of the object selection.)
Base point: **PICK** or (**coordinates**) (Select the point to <u>rotate about</u>.)
<Rotation angle>Reference: **PICK** or (**value**) or (**coordinates**) (Enter a value
for the number of degrees to rotate, or interactively rotate the entity set.)
```
Command:
```

The base point is often selected interactively with *OSNAP*s. When specifying the angle for
rotation, a value (incremental angle) can be typed. Alternately, if you want to **PICK** an angle,
COORDS (in the polar format) displays the current angle of the rubberband line. Turning on
ORTHO forces the rotation to a 90 degree increment. The *List* command can be used to
report the angle of an existing *Line* or other entity (discussed in Chapter 18).

The **Reference** option can be used to specify a vector as the original angle before rotation
(Fig. 9-5). This vector can be indicated interactively (*OSNAP*s can be used) or entered as an
angle using keyboard entry. Angular values that you enter in response to the "New angle:"
prompt are understood by AutoCAD as <u>absolute</u> angles for the *Reference* option only.

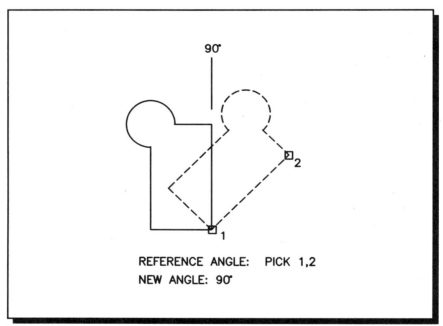

Figure 9-5

```
Command: rotate
```
Select objects: **PICK** or (**coordinates**) (Select the objects to rotate.)
Select objects: **Enter** (Indicates completion of object selection.)
Base point: **PICK** or (**coordinates**) (Select the point to rotate about.)
<Rotation angle>Reference: **R** (Indicates the *Reference* option.)
Reference angle<0>: **PICK** or (**value**) (PICK the first point of the vector.)
Second point: **PICK** (Indicates the second point defining the vector.)
New angle: **PICK** or (**value**) (Indicates the new angle value.)
```
Command:
```

SCALE

TYPE IN:	PULL-DOWN MENU	SCREEN MENU	TABLET MENU
SCALE	*Modify, Scale*	*EDIT, SCALE:*	*12,W*

The *Scale* command is used to increase or decrease the size of entities in a drawing. *Scale* does not normally have any relation to plotting a drawing to scale.

After selecting entities to *Scale*, AutoCAD prompts you to select a Base point: which is the <u>stationary point</u>. You can then scale the size of the selected entities interactively or enter a scale factor. Using interactive input, you are presented with a rubberband line connected to the base point. Making the rubberband line longer or shorter than 1 unit increases or decreases the scale of the selected entities by that proportion; for example, pulling the rubberband line to two units length increases the scale by a factor of two (Fig. 9-6).

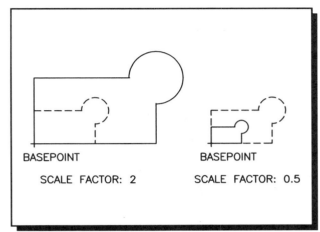

Figure 9-6

```
Command: scale
Select objects: PICK or (coordinates) (Select the objects to scale by any
object selection method.)
Select objects: Enter (Indicates completion of the object selection.)
Base point: PICK or (coordinates) (Select the stationary point.)
Scale factor<Reference>: PICK or (value) or (coordinates) (Enter a value for
the scale factor or interactively scale the set of entities.)
Command:
```

It may be desirable in some cases to use the **Reference** option to specify a value or two points to use as the reference length. This length can be indicated interactively (*OSNAP*s can be used) or entered as a value. This length is used for the subsequent reference length that the rubberband uses when interactively scaling. For example, if the reference distance is two, then the rubberband line must be stretched to a length greater than two to increase the scale of the selected entities.

Scale should <u>not</u> be used to change the scale of an entire drawing in order to plot on a specific size sheet. CAD drawings should be created <u>full size</u> in <u>actual units</u>. Only in this way can dimensioning commands automatically measure and draw the correct dimensional values or can CAD drawings be used for CNC operation or for Rapid Prototyping. Drawings are plotted to scale by entering the desired values in the *Plot Configuration* dialogue box (see Fig. 1-9). Plotting is discussed in Chapter 14.

BREAK

TYPE IN:	PULL-DOWN MENU	SCREEN MENU	TABLET MENU
BREAK	*Modify, Break >*	*EDIT, BREAK:*	*13,X and 14,X*

Break allows you to break a space in an entity or break the end off an entity. You can think of *Break* as a partial erase. If you choose to break a space in an entity, the space is created between two points that you specify (Fig. 9-7). In this case, the *Break* creates two entities from one.

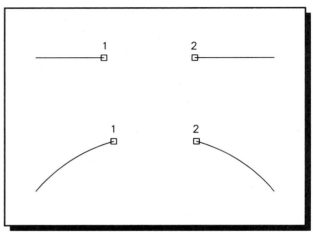

If *Break*ing a circle (Fig. 9-8), the break is in a counter-clockwise direction from the first to the second point specified.

Figure 9-7

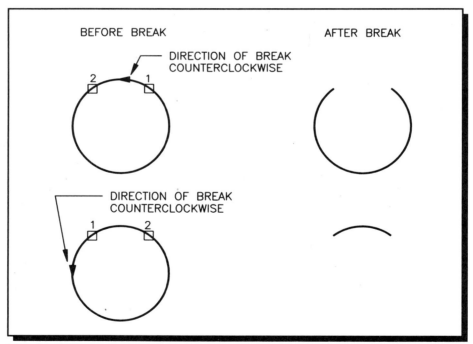

Figure 9-8

If you want to *Break* the end off of a *Line* or *Arc*, the first point should be specified at the point of the break and the second point should be <u>just off the end</u> of the *Line* or *Arc* (Fig 9-9).

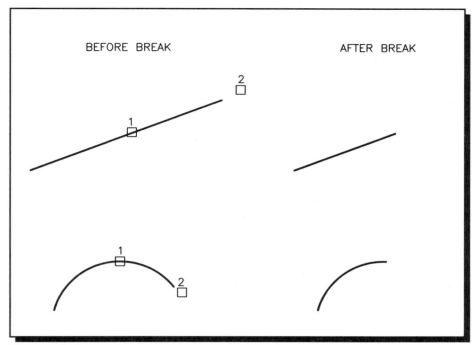

Figure 9-9

There are three ways to use *Break*: (1) select object and a second point, (2) select object and two points, and (3) break at selected point (no space). These options are available from the *Break* command in the *Modify* pull-down menu and from the screen menu. The digitizing tablet offers only the last two options. If entering commands at the keyboard, the desired option is selected by keying the letter *F* (for *First point*) or symbol @ (for "last point"). Figure 9-10 illustrates the options that are explained in detail on the next page.

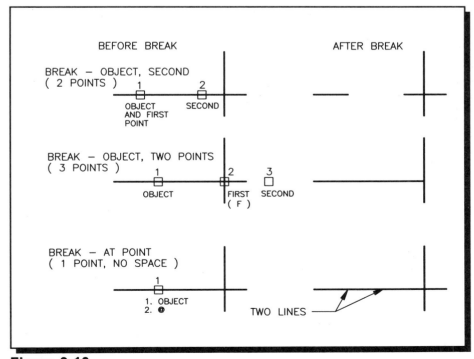

Figure 9-10

Select Object, 2nd Point

This method, the default if typing, has two steps: select the entity to break, then select the second point of the break. The first point used to select the object is <u>also</u> the first point of the break. (See Figure 9-10.)

```
Command: break
Select objects: PICK or (coordinates) (This is the first point of the break.
Normally, use the pickbox to select.)
Enter second point (or F for first point): PICK or
(coordinates) (This is the second point of the break.)
Command:
```

Select Object, Two Points

This method uses the first selection only to indicate the <u>object</u> to *Break*. You then specify the point which is the first point of the *Break*, and the next point specified is the second point of the *Break*. This option can be used with *OSNAP INTersection* to achieve the same results as *Trim*.

Selecting this option from the pull-down menu automatically sequences through the correct prompts (see Fig. 9-10). If typing, the command sequence is as follows:

```
Command: break
Select objects: PICK or (coordinates) (Select the object to break.)
Enter second point (or F for first point): F (Indicates
respecification for the first point.)
Enter first point: PICK or (coordinates) (Select the first point of the
break.)
Enter second point (or F for first point): PICK or
(coordinates) (This is the second point of the break.)
Command:
```

At selected point

This option breaks one entity into two separate entities with <u>no space</u> between. You specify only <u>one</u> point with this method. When you select the object, the point indicates the object <u>and</u> the point of the break. When prompted for the second point, the @ symbol (translated as "last point") must be specified. This second step is done automatically if selected from the pull-down menu.

Selecting this option from the pull-down menu automatically sequences through the correct prompts. If typing the command, the @ symbol ("last point") must be typed also. The command sequence is as follows:

```
Command: break
Select objects: PICK or (coordinates) (This PICKs the object and
specifies the first point of the break.)
Enter second point (or F for first point): @ (Indicates the
break to be at the last point.)
```

The resulting entity should <u>appear</u> as before; however, it has been transformed into <u>two</u> entities with matching endpoints (see Fig. 9-10).

TRIM

TYPE IN:	PULL-DOWN MENU	SCREEN MENU	TABLET MENU
TRIM	*Modify, Trim*	*EDIT, TRIM:*	*18,X*

The *Trim* command allows you to trim (or shorten) the end of an entity back to the intersection of another entity (Fig. 9-11). The middle section of an entity can also be *Trimmed* between two intersecting entities. There are two steps to this command: first, PICK one or more "cutting edges" (existing entities), then PICK the entity or entities to *Trim*. The cutting edges are highlighted after selection. Cutting edges, themselves, can be trimmed if they intersect other cutting edges but lose their highlight when trimmed.

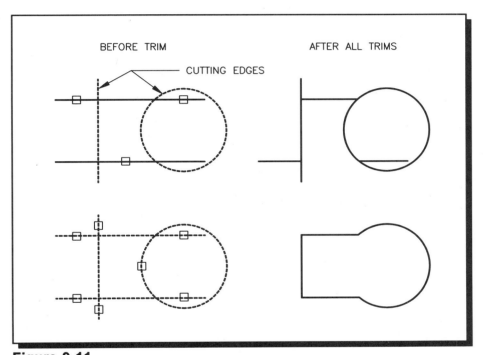

Figure 9-11

```
Command: trim
Select cutting edge(s)...
Select objects: PICK (Select an entity to use as a cutting edge.)
Select objects: PICK (Continue selecting entities to use as cutting edges.)
Select objects: Enter (Indicates completion of object selection.)
<Select object to trim>/Undo: PICK (Select the end of an entity to trim.)
<Select object to trim>/Undo: PICK (Continue selecting entities to trim.)
<Select object to trim>/Undo: Enter (Indicates completion of trimming.)
Command:
```

The *Undo* option allows you to undo the last *trim* in the case of an accidental trim.

EXTEND

TYPE IN:	PULL-DOWN MENU	SCREEN MENU	TABLET MENU
EXTEND	*Modify, Extend*	*EDIT, EXTEND:*	*16,X*

Extend can be thought of as the opposite of *Trim*. Entities such as *Lines*, *Arcs*, and *Plines* (see Chapter 15) can be *Extended* until intersecting another entity called a "boundary edge" (Fig. 9-12). The command first requires selection of <u>existing</u> entities to serve as "boundary edge(s)" which become highlighted, then the entities to extend are selected. Entities extend until, and only if, they eventually intersect a "boundary edge." An *Extend*ed entity acquires a new endpoint at the boundary edge intersection.

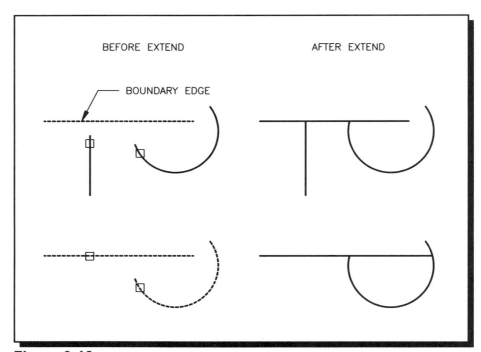

Figure 9-12

```
Command: extend
Select boundary edge(s)...
Select objects: PICK (Select an entity to use as boundary edge.)
Select objects: PICK (Continue selecting entities to use as boundary edges.)
Select objects: Enter (Indicates completion of object selection.)
<Select object to extend>/Undo: PICK (Select the end of an entity to
extend.)
<Select object to extend>/Undo: PICK (Continue selecting entities to
extend.)
<Select object to extend>/Undo: Enter (Indicates completion of trimming.)
Command:
```

CHAPTER EXERCISES

1. *Move*

Begin a **New** drawing and create the geometry in Figure 9-13, A using *Lines* and *Circles*. If desired, set **SNAP** to **.25** to make drawing easy and accurate.

For practice, turn *SNAP OFF* (**F9**). Use the **Move** command to move the *Circles* and *Lines* into the positions shown in illustration B. **OSNAP**s are required to *Move* the geometry accurately (since *SNAP* is off). Save the drawing as **CH9EX1**.

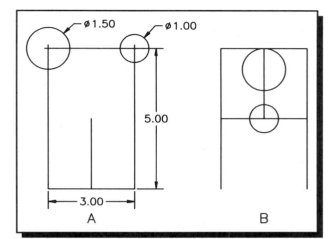

Figure 9-13

2. *Rotate*

Begin a **New** drawing and create the geometry in Figure 9-14, A.

Rotate the shape into position shown in step B. **Saveas CH9EX2B**.

Use the **Reference** option to **Rotate** the box to align with the diagonal *Line* as shown in C. **Saveas CH9EX2C**.

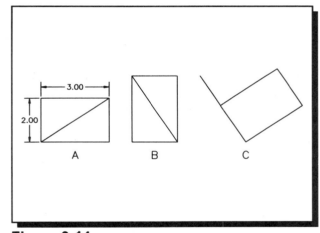

Figure 9-14

3. *Scale*

Open CH9EX2B to use the shape again shown in Figure 9-15, B (highlighted). **Scale** the shape by a factor of **1.5**.

Open CH9EX2C to use the shape again shown in C (highlighted). Use the **Reference** option of **Scale** to increase the scale of the three other *Lines* to equal the length of the original diagonal *Line* as shown. (HINT: **OSNAP**s are required to specify the **Reference length** and **New length**.

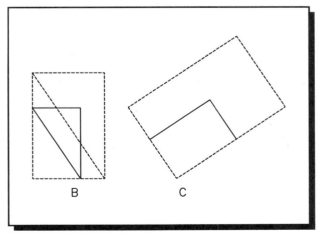

Figure 9-15

4. *Trim*

Create the shape shown in Figure 9-16, A. *Saveas* **CH9EX4A**.

Use *Trim* to alter the shape as shown in B. *Saveas* **CH9EX4B**.

Open **CH9EX4A** to create the shapes shown in C and D using *Trim*. *Saveas* **CH9EX4C** and **CH9EX4D**.

5. *Extend*

Open each of the drawings created as solutions for Figure 9-16 (**CH9EX4B**, **CH9EX4C**, and **CH9EX4D**). Use *Extend* to return each of the drawings to the original form shown in Figure 9-16, A. *Saveas* **CH9EX5B, CH9EX5C,** and **CH9EX5D**.

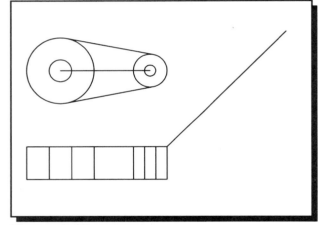

Figure 9-16

6. *Trim, Extend*

A. *Open* the **PIVOTARM** drawing from the Chapter 7 Exercises. Use *Trim* to remove the upper sections of the vertical *Lines* connecting the top and front views. Compare your work to Figure 9-17.

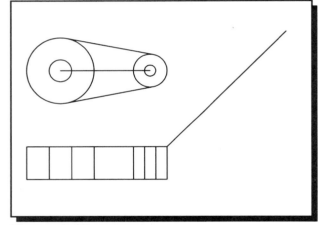

Figure 9-17

B. Next, draw a horizontal *Line* in the front view between the *MIDpoints* of the vertical *Line* on each end of the view as shown in Figure 9-18. *Erase* the horizontal *Line* in the top view between the *Circle* centers.

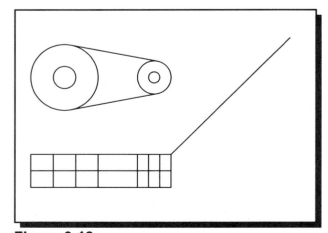

Figure 9-18

C.   Draw vertical **Lines** from the **Endpoints** of the *Line* (side of the object) in the top view down to the bottom *Line* in the front view as shown in Figure 9-19. Use the two vertical lines as **Cutting edges** for **Trimming** the *Line* in the middle of the front view as shown highlighted.

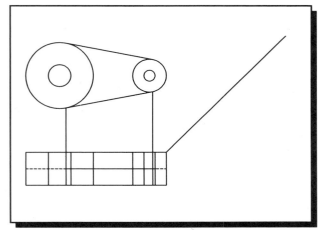

Figure 9-19

D.   Finally, **Erase** the vertical lines used for **Cutting edges** and then use **Trim** to achieve the object as shown in Figure 9-20. **Save** the drawing (again as **PIVOTARM**).

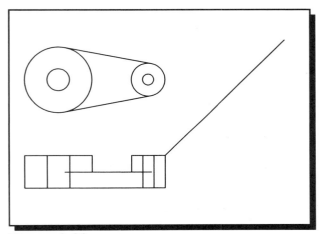

Figure 9-20

7.   **Break**

Create the shape shown in Figure 9-21, A. **Saveas CH9EX7A**.

Use **Break** to make the two breaks as shown in B. **Saveas CH9EX7B**

Open **CH9EX7A** each time to create the shapes shown in C and D with the *Break* command. **Saveas CH9EX7C** and **CH9EX7D**. (HINT: You may have to use **OSNAP**s to create the breaks at the **INTersections** or **QUAdrants** as shown.)

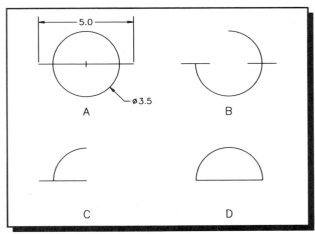

Figure 9-21

8.   GASKETA

Begin a *New* drawing and give the name **GASKETA**. Set *Limits* to **0,0** and **8,6**. Set *SNAP* and *GRID* values appropriately. Create the Gasket as shown in Figure 19-22. Construct only the gasket shape, not the dimensions or center lines. (HINT: Locate and draw the four 1/2" diameter *Circles*, then create the concentric 1/2" radius arcs as full *Circles*, then *Trim*. Make use of *OSNAPs* and *Trim* whenever applicable.)

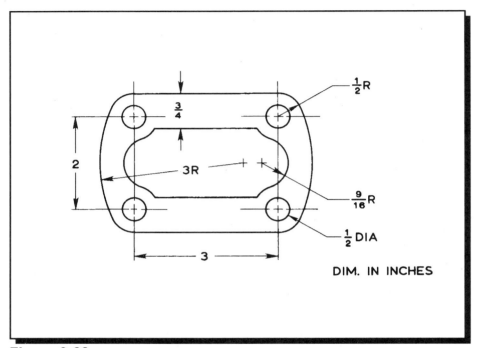

Figure 9-22

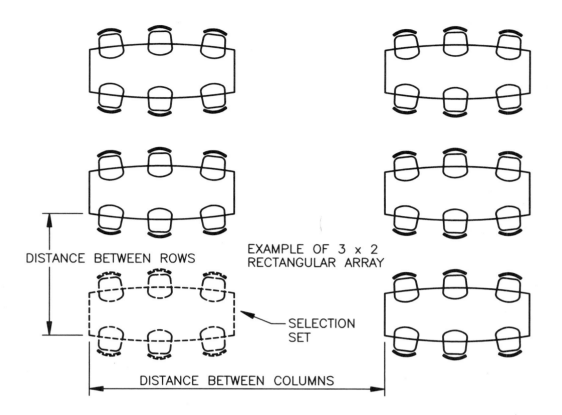

DISTANCE BETWEEN ROWS

EXAMPLE OF 3 x 2
RECTANGULAR ARRAY

SELECTION SET

DISTANCE BETWEEN COLUMNS

CHAPTER 10

Construct Commands I

CHAPTER OBJECTIVES

After completing this chapter you should:

1. know where to locate and how to invoke the fundamental *Construct* commands;

2. be able to *Copy* entities;

3. be able to make *Mirror* images of selected entities;

4. be able to make *rectangular* and *polar Arrays* of existing entities.

BASICS

Construct commands edit <u>existing</u> entities in some way but also create <u>new</u> entities in the process.

Construct commands and *Modify* commands are all considered edit commands. *Construct* and *Modify* commands have separate pull-down menus. Note the commands in the *Construct* pull-down menu (Fig 10-1).

These two types of commands are both located in the *EDIT* screen menu.

Figure 10-1

This chapter covers the following commands:

> *Copy*
> *Mirror*
> *Array*

The other *Construct* commands are discussed in Chapter 17, Construct Commands II.

COMMANDS

COPY

TYPE IN:	PULL-DOWN MENU	SCREEN MENU	TABLET MENU
COPY, CP	*Construct, Copy*	*EDIT, COPY:*	*15,X*

Copy creates a duplicate set of the selected entities and allows placement of those copies. The *Copy* operation is like the *Move* command, except with *Copy* the original set of entities remains in its original location. You specify a `Base point:` (point to copy <u>from</u>) and a `Second point of displacement:` (point to copy <u>to</u>). See Figure 10-2.

When using *Copy*, select the entity(ies), specify the `Base point:` and then the `Second point.`

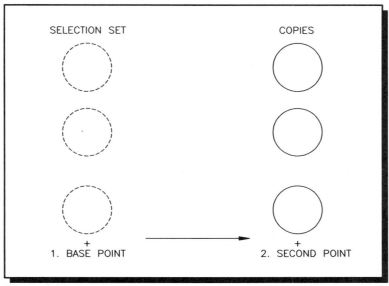

Figure 10-2

The command syntax for *Copy* is as follows.

> `Command: ` ***copy***
> `Select objects: ` **PICK** (Select entities to be copied.)
> `Select objects: ` **Enter** (Indicates completion of the selection set.)
> `<Base point or displacement>Multiple: ` **PICK** or (**coordinates**) (This is the point to copy <u>from</u>. Select a point, usually on the object, to use as a "handle" or reference point. *OSNAP*s can be used. Coordinates in any format can also be entered.)
> `Second point of displacement: ` **PICK** or (**coordinates**) (This is the point to copy <u>to</u>. Select a point. *OSNAP*s can be used. Coordinates in any format can be entered.)

In many applications it is desirable to use *OSNAP* options to **PICK** the `Base point:` and the `Second point of displacement:`.

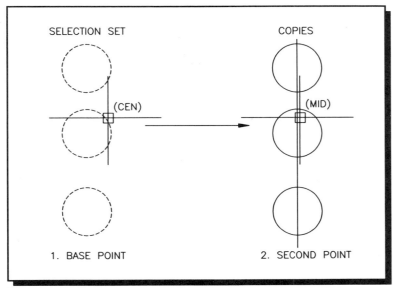

Figure 10-3

Alternately, you can PICK the `Base point:` and enter relative or polar coordinates to specify the `Second point of displacement:`.

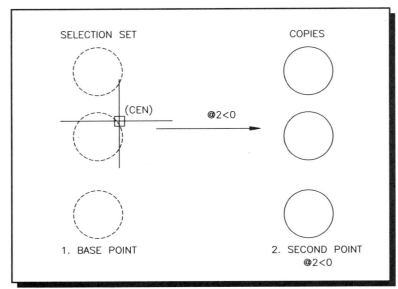

Figure 10-4

The *Copy* command has a **Multiple** option. The following command syntax is used to create *multiple* copies.

```
Command: copy
Select objects: PICK (Select entities to be copied.)
Select objects: Enter (Indicates completion of the selection set.)
<Base point or displacement>Multiple: M (Indicates multiple option.)
Base point or displacement: PICK or (coordinates) (Select a point to copy from.)
Second point of displacement: PICK or (coordinates) (Select a point to copy to.)
Second point of displacement: PICK or (coordinates) (Select another point to copy to.)
Second point of displacement: Enter (Pressing Enter ends the command.)
```

The *Multiple* option allows creating and placing multiple copies of the selection set.

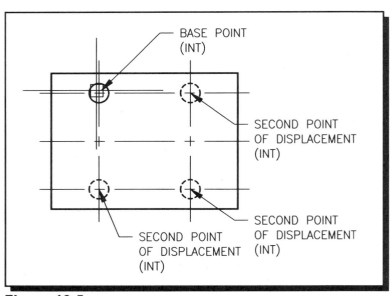

Figure 10-5

MIRROR

TYPE IN:	PULL-DOWN MENU	SCREEN MENU	TABLET MENU
MIRROR	_Construct, Mirror_	_EDIT, MIRROR:_	_12,X_

This command creates a mirror image of selected existing entities. You can retain or delete the original entities ("old objects"). After selecting entities, you create two points specifying a rubberband line, or "mirror line," about which to _Mirror_. The length of the mirror line is unimportant since it represents a vector or axis (Fig. 10-6).

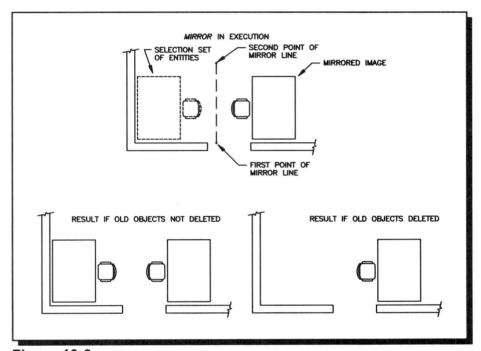

Figure 10-6

The command syntax for _Mirror_ is follows.

> Command: _**mirror**_
> Select objects: **PICK** (Select entity or group of entities to mirror.)
> Select objects: **Enter** (Press Enter to indicate completion of object selection.)
> First point of mirror line: **PICK** or (**coordinates**) (Draw first endpoint of line to represent mirror axis by PICKing or entering coordinates.)
> Second point of mirror line: **PICK** or (**coordinates**) (Select second point of mirror line by PICKing or coordinates. The rubberband line can be moved to dynamically display the mirrored objects.)
> Delete old objects? <N> **Enter** or **Y** (Press Enter to yield both sets of entities or enter Y to keep only mirrored set.)

If you want to _Mirror_ only in a vertical or horizontal direction, toggle _ORTHO_ (**F8**) _On_ before selecting the Second point of mirror line:.

Mirror can be used to draw the other half of a symmetrical object, thus saving some drawing time (Fig. 10-7).

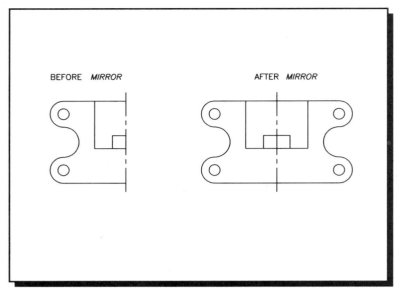

Figure 10-7

You can control whether the text is mirrored by using the _MIRRTEXT_ variable. Type _MIRRTEXT_ at the command prompt and change the value to 0 if you do <u>not</u> want the text to be reflected; otherwise, the default setting of 1 mirrors text along with other selected entities (Fig. 10-8). Dimensions are <u>not</u> affected by the _MIRRTEXT_ variable and therefore are not reflected (that is, if the dimensions are associative). Non-associative dimensions are reflected when _MIRRTEXT_ is set to 1. (See Chapter 28 for details on dimensions.)

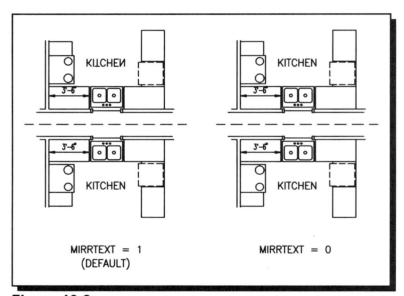

Figure 10-8

ARRAY

TYPE IN:	PULL-DOWN MENU	SCREEN MENU	TABLET MENU
ARRAY	_Construct, Array_	_EDIT, ARRAY:_	_21,W_

The _Array_ command creates either a _Rectangular_ or a _Polar_ (circular) pattern of existing entities that you select. The pattern could be created from a single entity or from a group of entities. _Array_ copies a duplicate set of entities for each "item" in the array. The command sequence for each of the two types of _Array_s is listed on the following pages.

Rectangular Array

This option creates an *Array* of the selection set in a pattern composed of <u>rows</u> and <u>columns</u>. The command syntax for a rectangular *Array* is given below.

```
Command: array
Select objects: PICK (Select entities to be arrayed.)
Select objects: Enter (Indicates completion of object selection.)
Rectangular or Polar array (R/P) <R>: R (Indicates rectangular
array.)
Number of rows (---) <1>: (value) (Enter value for number of rows.)
Number of columns (||||) <1>: (value) (Enter value for number of
columns.)
Unit cell or distance between rows (---): (value) (Enter a
value for the distance from any point on one entity to the same point on an
entity in adjacent row.  See Fig. 10-9.)
Distance between columns (||||): (value) (Enter a value for the
distance from any point on one entity to the same point on an entity in the
adjacent column.  See Fig. 10-9.)
```

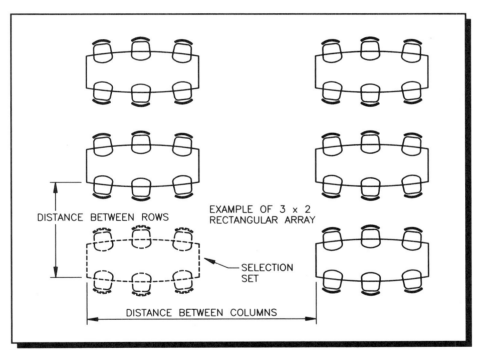

Figure 10-9

The *Array* is generated in a rectangular pattern with the original set of entities as the lower left "cornerstone." Negative values can be entered (distance between rows and columns) to generate and *Array* in a -X or -Y direction.

If you want to specify distances between cells <u>interactively</u>, use the *Unit cell* method (see Figure 10-10).

```
Unit cell or distance between rows (---): PICK (Pick point
for first point of cell.)
Other corner: PICK (Pick point for other corner of cell.)
```

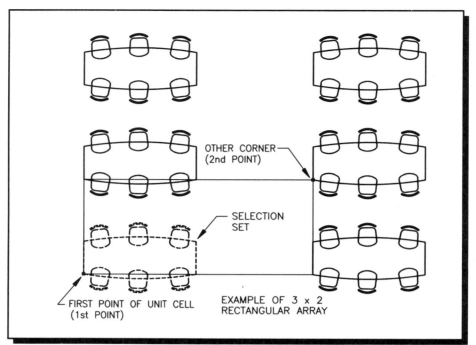

Figure 10-10

A rectangular _Array_ can be created at an angle by first rotating the _SNAP_ to the desired angle and then creating the _Array_ as shown in Figure 10-11. See Chapter 6 for information on the _Rotate_ option of the _Snap_ command.

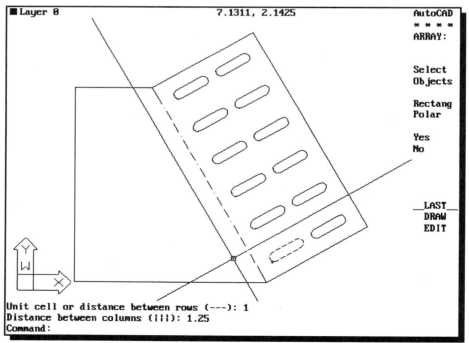

Figure 10-11

Polar Array

This option creates a <u>circular</u> pattern of the selection set with any number of copies or "items." The `Number of items:` specified <u>includes the original</u> selection set. You also specify the center of array, angle to generate the array through, and orientation of "items."

> `Command: ` ***array***
> `Select objects: ` **PICK** (Select entities to be arrayed.)
> `Select objects: ` **Enter** (Indicates object selection completed.)
> `Rectangular or Polar array (R/P) <R>: ` ***P*** (Indicates polar array.)
> `Center point of array: ` **PICK** (Select point for array to be generated around.)
> `Number of items: ` (**value**) (Enter value for number of copies <u>including</u> original selection set.)
> `Angle to fill (+=ccw, -==cw) <360>: ` **Enter** or (**value**) (Press Enter for full circular array [Fig. 10-12]; enter value for less than 360 degree array [Fig. 10-13]; enter negative value for clockwise generation of array.)
> `Rotate objects as they are copied? <Y> ` **Enter** or **N** (Press Enter for rotation of entities about center; N for keeping entities in original orientation. See Figs. 10-13, and 10-14.)

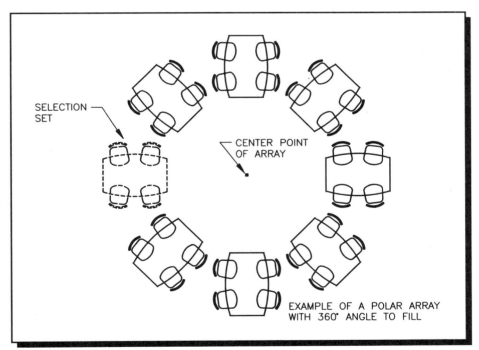

Figure 10-12

Figure 10-12 illustrates a *Polar Array* created by accepting the default values ("360" degrees and *Rotate objects as they are copied*).

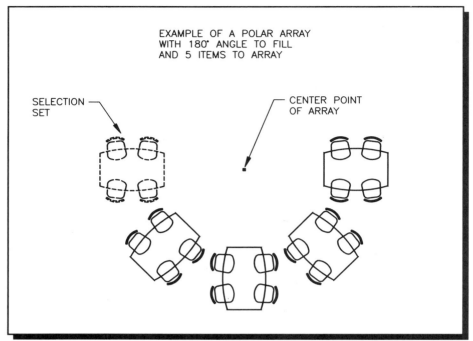

Figure 10-13

Figure 10-13 shows a _Polar Array_ through 180 degrees with objects rotated.

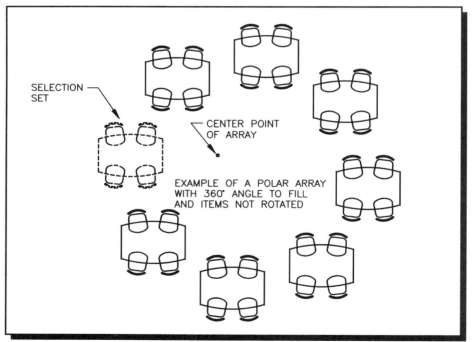

Figure 10-14

Figure 10-14 illustrates the results of answering _No_ to the prompt Rotate objects as they are rotated? Note that the orientation of the "items" remain in the same orientation (not rotated). Also notice the position of the *Array* with relation to the center point of the array.

When a *Polar Array* is created and objects are <u>not</u> rotated, the set of objects may not seem to rotate about the specified center as shown in Figure 10-14. AutoCAD uses a single reference point for the *Array*--that of the <u>last</u> entity in the selection set. If you PICK the entities one at a time (with the pickbox), the <u>last</u> one selected provides the reference point. If you use a window or other method for selection, the reference point is arbitrary. This usually creates an non-symmetric circular *Array* about the selected center point.

The solution is to create a *Point* entity in the center of the selection set and select it <u>last</u>. This will generate the selection set in a circle about the selected center. (Alternately, you can make the selection set into a *Block* and use the center of the *Block* as the *Insertion* point. See Chapter 21). This occurrence is no problem for *Polar Arrays* where the selection set is rotated.

CHAPTER EXERCISES

1.   *Copy*

Begin a *New* drawing. Set the *Limits* to **24,18**. Set *SNAP* to **.5** and *GRID* to **1**. Create the sheet metal part composed of four *Lines* and one *Circle* as shown in Figure 10-15. The lower left corner of the part is at coordinate **2,3**.

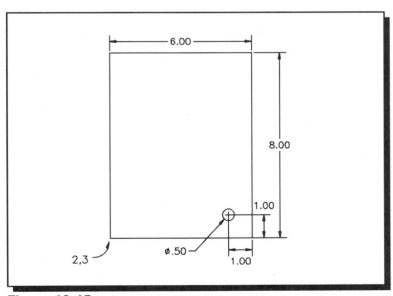

Figure 10-15

Use *Copy* to create two copies of the rectangle and hole in a side-by-side fashion shown in Figure 10-16. Allow 2 units between the sheet metal layouts. *Saveas* PLATES.

A. Use **Copy** to create the additional 3 holes equally spaced near the other corners of the part as shown in Figure 10-16, A. **Save** the drawing.

B. Use **Copy Multiple** to create the hole configuration as shown in Figure 10-16, B. **Save**.

C. Use **Copy** to create the hole placements as shown in C. Each hole <u>center</u> is **2** units at **125** degrees from the previous one (use relative polar coordinates). **Save** the drawing.

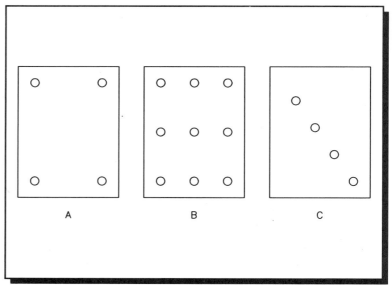

Figure 10-16

2. **Mirror**

A manufacturing cell is displayed in Figure 10-17. The view is from above showing a robot <u>centered</u> in a work station. The production line requires 4 cells. Begin by starting a **New** drawing, setting **Units** to **Engineering** and **Limits** to **40' x 30'**. It may be helpful to set *SNAP* to **6"**. Draw one cell to the dimensions indicated. Begin at the indicated coordinates of the lower left corner of the cell. **Saveas MANFCELL**.

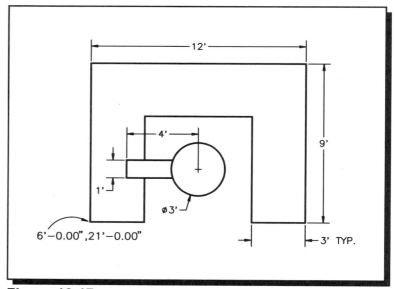

Figure 10-17

Use **Mirror** to create the other three manufacturing cells. Insure that there is sufficient space between the cells as indicated. Draw the two horizontal **Lines** representing the walkway as shown. **Save**.

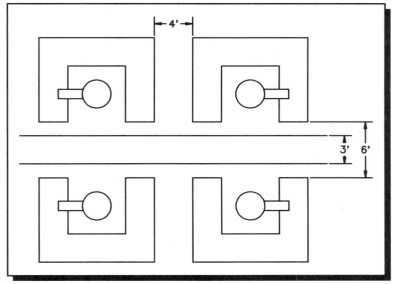

Figure 10-18

3.　　**Array, Polar**

Begin a **New** drawing. Create the starting geometry for a Flange Plate as shown in Figure 10-19. **Saveas CH10EX3**.

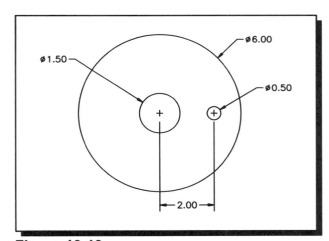

Figure 10-19

A.　　Create the **Polar Array** as shown in Figure 10-20, A. **Saveas CH10EX3A**.

B.　　**Open CH10EX3**. Create the **Polar Array** as shown in Figure 10-20, B. **Saveas CH10EX3B**. (HINT: Use a negative angle to generate the *Array* in a clockwise direction.)

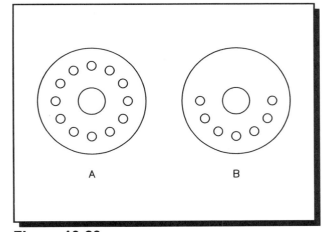

Figure 10-20

4. **_Array, Rectangular_**

Open a **New** drawing and assign the name **CH10EX4**. Create the *Array* of study carrels (desks) for the library as shown in Figure 10-21. The room size is 36' x 27' (set **Units** and **Limits** accordingly). Each carrel is **30"** x **42"**. Design your own chair. Draw the first carrel (highlighted) at the indicated coordinates. Create the **Rectangular Array** so that the carrels touch side-to-side and allow 6' isle for walking between carrels (not including chairs).

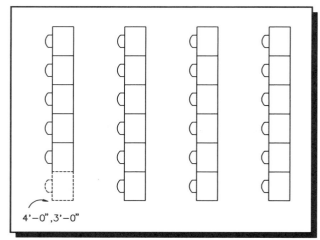

Figure 10-21

5. **_Array, Rectangular_**

Create the bolt head with one thread as shown in Figure 10-22, A. **Array** the first thread (both crest and root lines, as indicated in B) to create the schematic thread representation. There are **10** columns with **.2** units between each. Add the **Lines** around the outside to complete the fastener. **Save** as **BOLT**.

6. Create the Gasket shown in Figure 10-23. **Saveas GASKETB**.

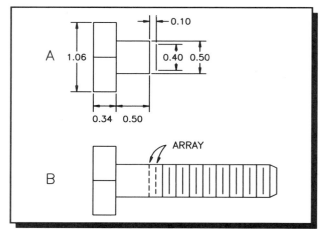

Figure 10-22

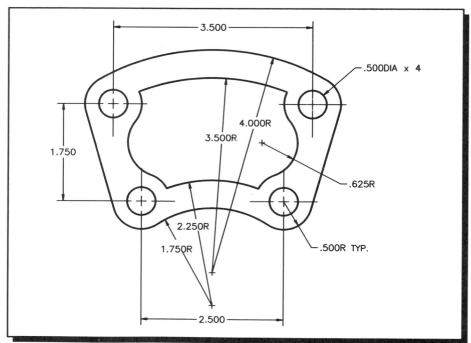

Figure 10-23

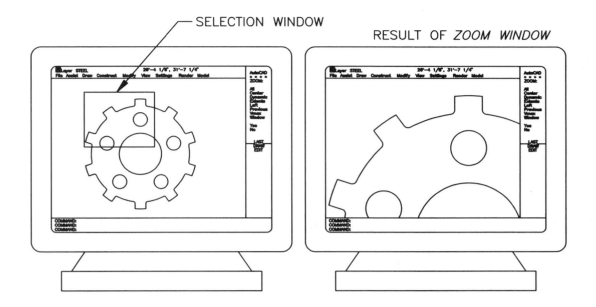

SELECTION WINDOW

RESULT OF *ZOOM WINDOW*

CHAPTER 11

Viewing Commands

CHAPTER OBJECTIVES

After completing this chapter you should:

1. understand the relationship between the drawing entities and the display of those entities;

2. be able to use all of the *Zoom* options to view areas of a drawing;

3. be able to *Pan* the display about your screen;

4. be able to *save* and *restore Views*;

5. know how to use *Viewres* to change the display resolution for curved shapes.

BASICS

The accepted CAD practice is to draw full size using actual units. Since the drawing is a virtual dimensional replica of the actual object, a drawing could represent a vast area (several hundred feet or even miles) or a small area (only millimeters). The drawing is created full size with the actual units, but it can be displayed at any size on the screen. Consider also that CAD systems provide for a very high degree of dimensional precision which permits the generation of drawings with great detail and accuracy.

Combining those two CAD capabilities (great precision and drawings representing various areas), a method is needed to view different and detailed segments of the overall drawing area. In AutoCAD the commands that facilitate viewing different areas of a drawing are *Zoom*, *Pan*, and *View*.

The Viewing commands are found in the *View* pull-down.

Zoom and *Pan* each have one-letter command aliases, Z and P.

Figure 11-1

COMMANDS

ZOOM

TYPE IN:	PULL-DOWN MENU	SCREEN MENU	TABLET MENU
ZOOM or Z	*View, Zoom >*	*DISPLAY, ZOOM:*	*9,J to 9,P*

The *Zoom* command can be invoked by any of the four command entry methods. The command alias, **Z**, can be quickly used by pressing both the letter and the space bar with the left hand. The digitizing tablet menu provides a cell for each of the *Zoom* options located in one column at 9,J through 9,P. Unlike other command entry methods (and unlike other commands on the digitizing tablet menu), a specific *Zoom* option can be selected on the tablet menu without first selecting the *Zoom* command. In other words, selecting a *Zoom* option invokes both the command and the specific option.

To *Zoom* <u>in</u> means to magnify a small segment of a drawing and to *Zoom* <u>out</u> means to display a larger area of the drawing. *Zooming* does <u>not</u> change the <u>size</u> of the drawing. *Zooming* only changes the area that is <u>displayed</u> on the screen. All entities in the drawing have the same dimensions before and after *Zooming*. Only your display of the entities changes.

The *Zoom* options described below can be selected by any menu. If typing, only the first letter is required.

Window

To *Zoom* with a *Window* is to draw a rectangular window around the desired viewing area. You PICK a first and a second corner (diagonally) to form the rectangle. The windowed area is magnified to fill the screen (Fig. 11-2). It is suggested that you draw the window with a 4 x 3 (approximate) proportion to match the screen proportion. Since *Window* is an <u>automatic</u> option, you can begin selecting the first corner of the window after issuing the *Zoom* command <u>without</u> indicating the *Window* option as a separate step.

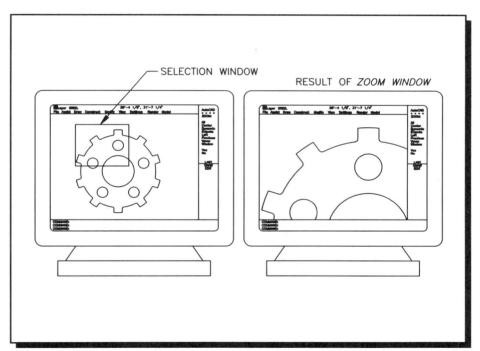

Figure 11-2

All

This option displays <u>all of the entities</u> in the drawing <u>and all of the *Limits*</u>. In Figure 11-3, notice the effects of *Zoom All* based on the drawing entities and the drawing *Limits*.

Extents

This option results in the largest possible display of <u>all of the entities</u>, <u>disregarding</u> the *Limits*. (*Zoom All* includes the *Limits*.) (See Fig. 11-3.)

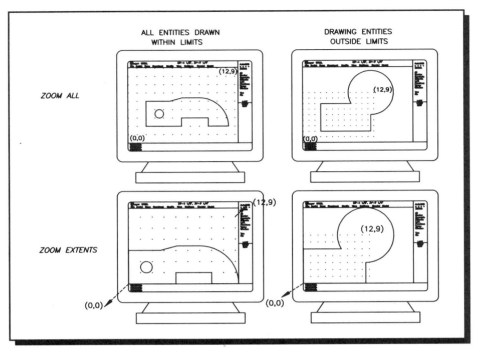

Figure 11-3

Center

First, specify a location as the center of the zoomed area, then specify either a *Magnification factor* (see *Scale X/XP*), a *Height* value for the resulting display, or PICK two points forming a vertical to indicate the height for the resulting display. In Figure 11-4, the *Center* is **PICK**ed and a *Magnification factor* of **2X** is entered.

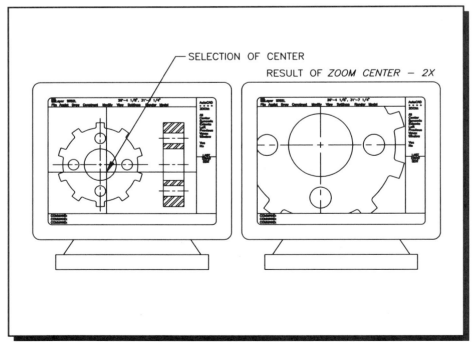

Figure 11-4

Dynamic

With this option you can change the display from one windowed area in a drawing to another without using *Zoom All* (to see the entire drawing) as an intermediate step. *Zoom Dynamic* causes the screen to display the drawing *Limits* or extents, whichever is larger, bounded by a white box. The current view or window is bounded by a green or magenta box in broken line pattern. Four red corners display the last regenerated area (called *Vmax*).

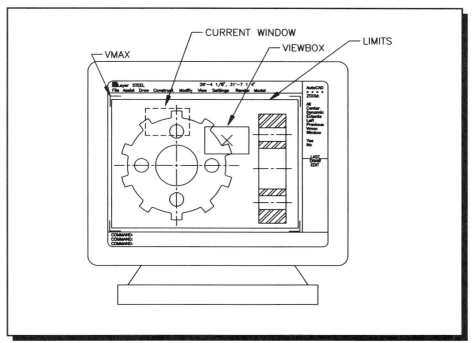

Figure 11-5

The view box is the white box with an "X" in the center which can be moved to the desired location (Fig. 11-5). The desired location is selected by pressing **Enter** (not the PICK button as you might expect). Selecting a new window outside of the red corners causes a regeneration requiring more time for the new display generation (an hour glass icon appears).

Pressing **PICK** allows you to resize the view box (displaying an arrow instead of the "X") to the desired size (Fig. 11-6). Move the mouse or puck left and right to increase and decrease the window size. Press **PICK** again to set the size and make the "X" reappear. You can then move the viewbox to select the desired viewing area.

When changing the display of a drawing from one windowed area to another, *Zoom Dynamic* is the fastest method because (1) a *Zoom All* is not required as an intermediate step and (2) the view box can be moved <u>while</u> AutoCAD is "redrawing" the display.

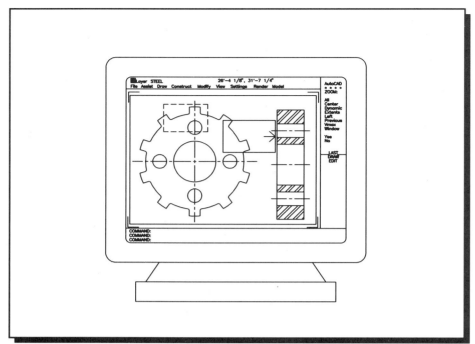

Figure 11-6

Left

This option is similar to the *Center* option except that you first PICK the lower left corner of the display window instead of the center. The *Magnification* factor or *Height* is then specified (Fig. 11-7).

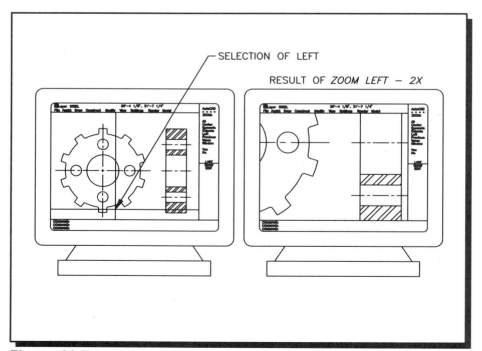

Figure 11-7

Previous

Selecting this option automatically changes to the previous display. AutoCAD saves the previous ten displays changed by *Zoom*, *Pan*, and *View*. You can successively change back through the previous ten displays with this option.

Vmax

The *Vmax* (Virtual Screen Maximum) option allows you to *Zoom* out to the maximum display without causing a regeneration. This option is helpful with large, complex drawings for achieving the maximum display without causing time-consuming regenerations.

Scale (X/XP)

This, the default, option allows you to enter a scale factor for the desired display. The value that is entered can be relative to the full view (*Limits*) or to the current display (Fig. 11-8) . A value of **1**, **2**, or **.5** causes a display that is 1, 2, or .5 times the size of the *Limits*, centered on the current display. A value of **1X**, **2X**, or **.5X** yields a display 1, 2, or .5 times the size of the <u>current display</u>. If using Paper space, a value of **1XP**, **2XP**, or **.5XP** yields a display scaled 1, 2, or .5 times paper space units.

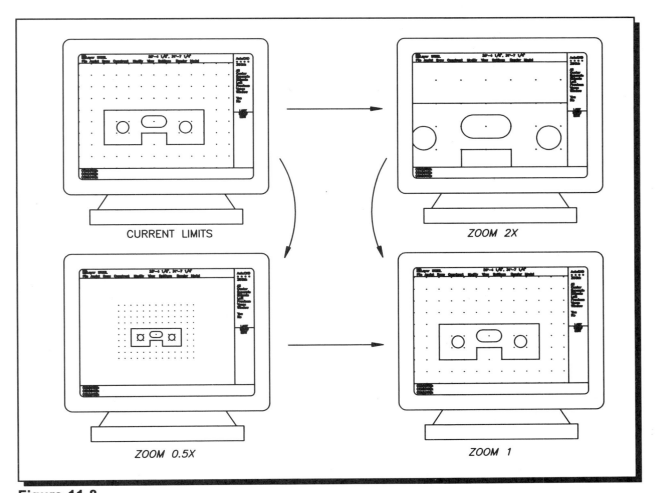

Figure 11-8

Zoom is a transparent command, meaning it can be invoked while another command is in operation. You can, for example, use the *Line* command and at the `to point:` prompt *'Zoom* with a *window* to better display the area for selecting the endpoint. This transparent feature is automatically entered if *Zoom* is invoked by the screen, pull-down, or tablet menu, but if typed it must be prefixed by the ' (apostrophe) symbol, e.g., `to point:` *'Zoom*. If *Zoom* has been invoked transparently, the **>>** symbols appear at the command prompt before the listed options as follows:

```
LINE from point: PICK
to point:'zoom
>>Center/Dynamic/Left/Previous/Vmax/Window/<Scale
(X/XP)>:
```

PAN

TYPE IN:	PULL-DOWN MENU	SCREEN MENU	TABLET MENU
PAN or P	*View, Pan*	*DISPLAY, PAN:*	*9,Q*

The *Pan* command is most useful if you want to move (pan) the display area slightly without changing the <u>size</u> of the current view window (Fig. 11-9). If *Pan* is used in this way, imagine "dragging" the drawing across the screen to view an area slightly out of view. The command syntax reads:

```
Command: pan
PAN Displacement: PICK
second point: PICK
Command:
```

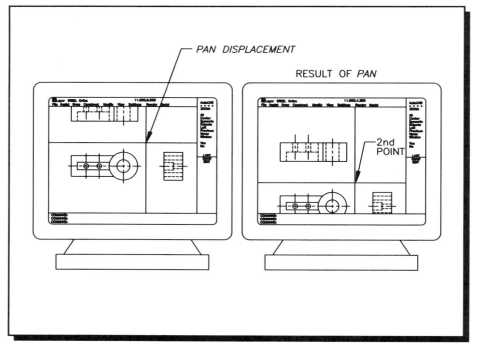

Figure 11-9

The `PAN Displacement:` can be thought of as a "handle" and `second point:` as the new location to move to.

Pan also allows coordinate values to be entered rather than interactively PICKing points with the cursor (Fig. 11-10). The command syntax for the example below is as follows.

```
Command: pan
PAN Displacement: 0,-2
second point: Enter
Command:
```

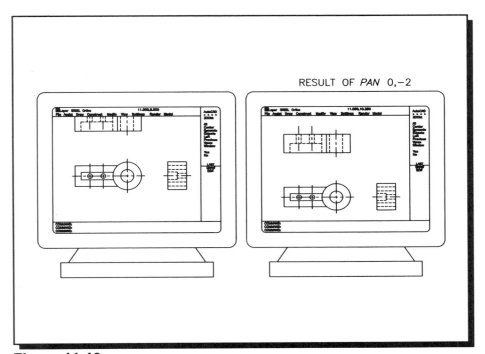

Figure 11-10

Entering coordinate values allows you to *Pan* to a location outside of the current display. If you use the interactive method (PICK points) you can only *Pan* within the range of whatever is visible on the screen.

Pan, like *Zoom*, can be used as a transparent command. The transparent feature is automatically entered if *Pan* is invoked by the screen, pull-down, or tablet menus. If you type *Pan* during another command operation; however, it must be prefixed by the ' (apostrophe) symbol.

```
Command: Line
From point: PICK
to point: 'pan
>>Displacement: PICK
>>Second point: PICK
Resuming LINE command.
To point:
```

VIEW

TYPE IN:	PULL-DOWN MENU	SCREEN MENU	TABLET MENU
VIEW	*View, Set View > Named View...*	*DISPLAY, VIEW:*	*4,M*

The *View* command provides options for you to *Save* the current display window and *Restore* it at a later time. For typical applications you would first *Zoom* in to achieve a desired display, then use *View, Save* to save that display under an assigned name. Later in the drawing session, the named *View* can be *Restored* any number of times. This method is preferred to continually *Zooming* in and out to display the same areas repeatedly. *Restoring* a named *View* requires no regeneration time. A *View* can be sent to the plotter as separate display as long as the view is named and saved.

The options of the *View* command are listed below.

?

Displays the list of named views.

Delete

Deletes one or more saved views that you enter.

Restore

Displays the named view you request.

Save

Saves the current display as a *View* with a name that you assign.

Window

Allows you to specify a window in the current display and save it as a named *View*.

To *Save* a *View*, first use *Zoom* or *Pan* to achieve the desired display, then invoke the *View* command and the *Save* option as follows:

```
Command: View
?/Delete/Restore/Save/Window: save
View name to save: name (Assign a descriptive name for the view.)
Command:
```

For assurance, check to see if the new *View* has been saved by displaying the list by using the *?* option. The *?* option causes a text screen to appear with the list of named (saved) views. Use *FLIPSCREEN* (F1) to return to the Drawing Editor after reading the list.

To *Restore* a named *View*, assuming a different area of the drawing is currently displayed, use the *Restore* option and supply the name of the desired *View*.

View can also be used transparently, but only if typed at the keyboard. Remember to preface the command with the ' (apostrophe) symbol, i.e., *'View*.

A feature of saving *Views* is that a named *View* can be plotted by toggling the *View* option in the *Plot Configuration* dialogue box (Fig. 11-11). Plotting is discussed in detail in Chapter 14.

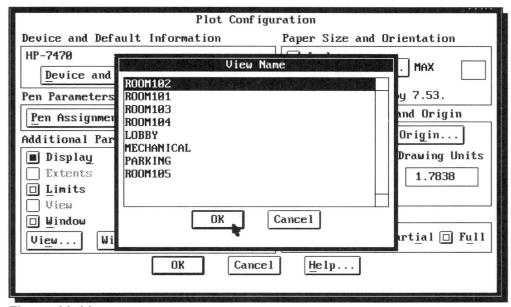

Figure 11-11

Typing the *View* command is generally quick and easy. Selecting *View* from the pull-down or tablet menus invokes the *View Control* dialogue box (Fig. 11-12), which is helpful but requires a number of steps to operate. A word of caution when selecting from the list of named views to restore: make sure that you select (1) the desired view <u>and</u> (2) the **Restore** tile, <u>then</u> (3) the *OK* tile.

The *View Control* dialogue box provides the same options that the *View* command offers. The *New* option causes the *Define New View* dialogue box to pop up giving access to the *Save* option (Fig. 11-13).

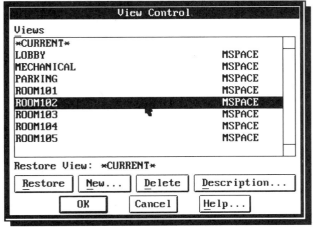

Figure 11-12

Figure 11-13

VIEWRES

TYPE IN:	PULL-DOWN MENU	SCREEN MENU	TABLET MENU
VIEWRES	---	*DISPLAY, VIEWRES:*	---

Viewres controls the resolution of curved shapes for the <u>screen display</u> only. Its purpose is to speed regeneration time by displaying curved shapes as linear approximations of curves; that is, a curved shape (such as an *Arc, Circle,* or *Ellipse*) appears as several short straight line segments (Fig. 11-14). The drawing database and a plotted drawing, however, always define a true curve. The range of *Viewres* is from 1-20,000 with 100 being the default. The higher the value (called circle zoom percentage), the more accurate the display of curves and the slower the regeneration time. The lower the value, the faster the regeneration time, but the more "jagged" the curves. A value of 500 to 1000 is suggested for most applications. The command syntax is as shown here.

```
Command: Viewres
Do you want fast zooms? <Y> Enter
Enter circle zoom percent (1-20000) <100>: 500
Command:
```

If you answer **no** to *Do you want fast zooms?*, AutoCAD causes a regeneration after every *Pan, Zoom,* or *View* command. Otherwise, regenerations occur only when *Zoom*ing extremely far in or out.

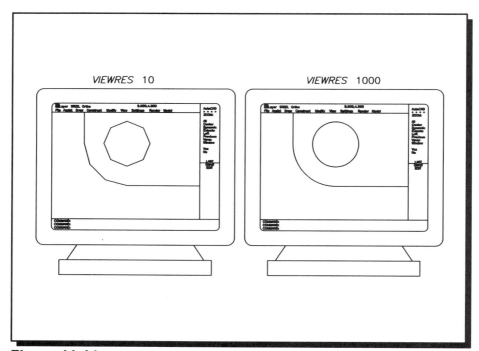

Figure 11-14

CHAPTER EXERCISES

1.   *Zoom Window, All, Previous, Center, Left*

Open the sample drawing supplied with AutoCAD called **HOUSEPLN.DWG**. It is located in the SAMPLE subdirectory. For example, if AutoCAD has been installed on your system in the C:\ACAD12 directory, you should find the sample drawings in **C:\ACAD12\SAMPLE**. The drawing shows a dimensioned house plan (Fig. 11-15).

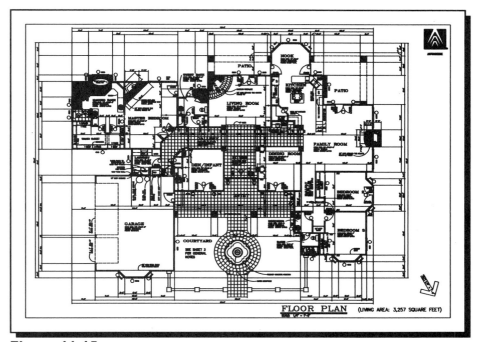

Figure 11-15

A.   Use **Zoom** with the window option to examine the Living room. Select the corners of the window to display an area as shown in Figure 11-16. What are the overall dimensions of the Living room?

B.   **Zoom All**. Now **Zoom** in to the Family room. What are the dimensions?

C.   **Zoom Previous**. Was that faster than **Zoom All**? Now **Zoom** in with a window to the Nook. What are the dimensions?

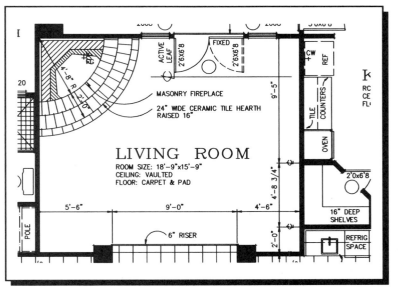

Figure 11-16

D.   You forgot to check for the type of ceiling in the Family room. *Zoom Previous* until you find the display of the Family room. What type of ceiling is designated?

E.   ***Zoom All*** to achieve a display of the entire house. Use *Zoom Center*, **PICK** the center of the Master Bath (in the upper left corner), and enter a magnification factor of **6X**. You should see a display similar to that in Figure 11-17. What are the specifications of the whirlpool tub?

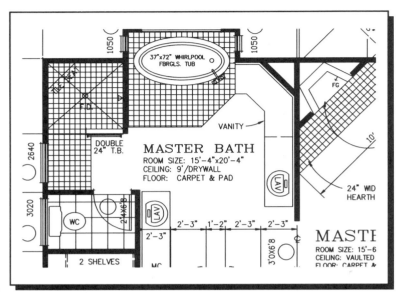

Figure 11-17

F.   Use ***Zoom Left*** and PICK a point just below and to the left of the tub. Specify a *Height* by **PICK**ing a second point just above the tub. Can you read the specifications better now?

2.   *View*

You are about to create some *Views* of the house plan. So that you don't change this drawing, use *Saveas* to save the drawing as **HOUSEPL2**. Specify the path for your working directory (for example, if your working directory is C:\DRAWINGS, pick the drive and directory from the *Saveas* dialogue box or use the edit box to enter the path and drawing name.

A.   Use the *View* command and the *Save* option to save the current view (as shown in Figure 11-18). Specify the name **TUB**.

B.   ***Zoom Previous*** until you have a display of the entire house. Use *View* with the *Window* option. Name the view **COURT**. Specify a window around the Courtyard. The display does not change. Use the *Window* option of *View* again to save a view of the Living room. Name the view **LIVING**.

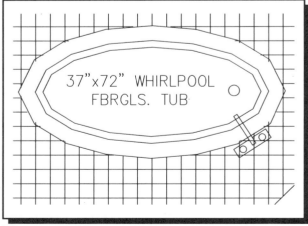

Figure 11-18

D.   Use _View, Restore_ to restore the **TUB**. Was a regeneration required? Now use _View_ again to _Restore_ **CTYARD** (use the _?_ option to check for the correct name). Now **Restore** the view **LIVING**.

3.   _Zoom Dynamic_.

A.   Invoke _Zoom Dynamic_. Notice that you can move the view box around <u>while</u> the display is regenerating. Locate the Laundry (just above the Garage). Reduce the size of the view box so it is about equal to the Laundry. _Zoom_ in. Are there any shelves? _Zoom_ with a factor of **.5X**. Now do you see any evidence of shelves?

B.   Use _Zoom Dynamic_ again to display the Den/Infant (just to the right of the Laundry). How many entrances does the room have?

C.   Use _Zoom Dynamic_ to display Bedroom 3 (lower left). How many windows do you find in this room?

4.   _Pan_

A.   Bedroom 2 is located just above Bedroom 3. Use _Pan_ to display Bedroom 2. How many windows are in this room?

B.   Notice the double doors leading outside. Use _Pan_ to determine what is just outside the doors. Is there a patio?

5.   _Viewres_

A.   Use _View Restore_ to restore the view of the **TUB**. Notice how the edges of the tub appear as straight line segments as shown in Figure 11-18 (previous page). Use _Viewres_ to increase the display resolution to **500**. After regenerating, the tub should appear as a smooth ellipse (Fig. 11-19).

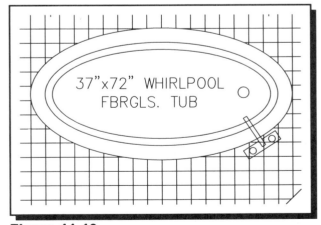

B.   Use _Zoom Dynamic_ to display the Laundry. Notice the smooth circular shapes that previously appeared as polygons.

Figure 11-19

Save the drawing. Make sure it is saved as **HOUSEPL2**.

6.   ***Zoom All, Extents***

A.   Begin a ***New*** drawing. Turn on the *GRID* (**F7**). Draw two ***Circles***, each with a **1.5** unit ***radius***. The *Circle* centers are at **3,5** and at **5,5**. See Figure 11-20.

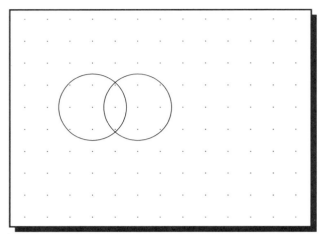

B.   Use ***Zoom All***. Does the display change? Now use ***Zoom Extents***. What happens? Now use ***Zoom All*** again. Which option <u>always</u> shows all of the *Limits*?

C.   Draw a ***Circle*** with the center at **10,10** and with a ***radius*** of **5**. Now use ***Zoom All***. Notice the GRID only

Figure 11-20

appears on the area defined by the *Limits*. Can you move the crosshairs to 0,0? Now use ***Zoom Extents***. What happens? Can you move the cross hairs to 0,0.

D.   ***Erase*** the large ***Circle***. Use ***Zoom All***. Can you move the crosshairs to 0,0? Use ***Zoom Extents***. Can you find point 0,0?

     Exit AutoCAD and ***Discard changes***.

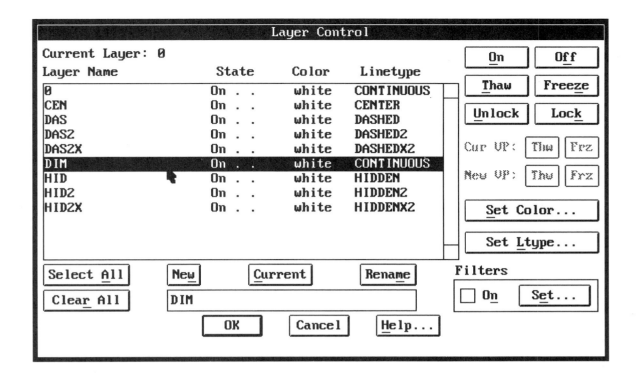

CHAPTER 12

Layers, Linetypes, and Colors

CHAPTER OBJECTIVES

After completing this chapter you should:

1. understand the strategy of grouping related geometry with *Layers*;

2. be able to create *Layers*;

3. be able to assign *Color* and *Linetype* to *Layers*;

4. be able to assign *Color* and *Linetype* to entities;

5. be able to control a Layer's *State* (*On, Off, Freeze, Thaw, Lock, Unlock*);

6. be able to *Load Linetypes* into the drawing;

7. be able to set *LTSCALE* to adjust the scale of linetypes;

8. understand that color and linetype properties can be changed with *Chprop* or *Modify*.

BASICS

In a CAD drawing layers are used to group related entities in a drawing. Entities (*Lines, Circles, Arcs*, etc.) that are created to describe one component, function, or process of a drawing are perceived as related information and, therefore, typically drawn on one layer. A single CAD drawing is generally composed of several components and, therefore, several layers. Use of layers provides you with a method of controlling visible features of the components of a drawing. For each layer, you can control its color on the screen, the linetype it will be displayed with, its visibility setting (on or off), if it is protected from being edited, or if it will or will not be plotted. Layers do <u>not necessarily</u> indicate any three-dimensional qualities such as levels of a multi-floor building.

Layers in a CAD drawing are like clear overlay sheets on a manual drawing. For example, in a CAD architectural drawing, the floor plan can be drawn on one layer, electrical layout on another, plumbing on a third layer, and HVAC (heating, ventilating, and air conditioning) on a fourth layer (Fig. 12-1). Each layer of a CAD drawing could be assigned a different color, linetype, and visibility setting similar to the way clear overlay sheets on a manual drawing can be used. Layers can be temporarily turned *OFF* or *ON* to simplify drawing and editing like overlaying or removing the clear sheets. For example, in the architectural CAD drawing, only the floor plan layer can be made visible while creating the electrical layout, but can later be cross-referenced with the HVAC layout by turning its layer on. Final plots can be made of specific layers for the subcontractors and one plot of all layers for the general contractor by controlling the layers' visibility before plotting. Simply put, only visible entities will plot.

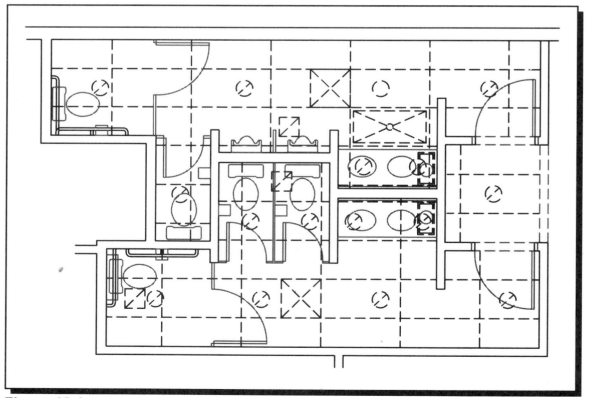

Figure 12-1

AutoCAD allows you to create an infinite number of layers. You must assign a name to each layer when you create it. The layer names should be descriptive of the information on the layer. Usually, layers are also assigned a color and a linetype so that all entities drawn on a single layer have the same color and linetype. This is called assigning color and linetype *BYLAYER*. Using the *BYLAYER* method makes it apparent which entities are related (on the same layer). It is desirable for special applications, however, to assign colors and linetypes to specific entities, overriding the layer's color and linetype setting. Using this method makes it difficult to see which layers the entities are located on. It is therefore recommended that beginners assign colors and linetypes to layers (*BYLAYER*) and use entity-specific color and linetype settings after gaining some experience.

The colors that are assigned to layers (or to entities) control the pens for plotting. In the *Plot Configuration* dialogue box, *Pen Assignments* are designated based upon the entities' color on screen (see Chapter 12). Each screen color can be assigned to use a separate pen for plotting so that all entities that appear in one color will be plotted with the same pen.

COMMANDS

LAYER

TYPE IN:	PULL-DOWN MENU	SCREEN MENU	TABLET MENU
LAYER or LA or DDLMODES	*Settings, Layer Control...*	*LAYER...*	*4,P to 6,R*

The easiest way to gain complete layer control is through the *Layer Control* dialogue box (Fig. 12-2). If typing, *Ddlmodes* invokes the dialogue box. This dialogue box allows full control for all layers. The central area lists existing layers and their *State*, *Color*, and *Linetype*. One or more layers can be selected (highlighted) from the list in order to change the layer(s) *State* (*On, Off, Freeze, Thaw, Lock, Unlock*), *Color*, or *Linetype*. Changing any of the features on the right side of the box affects all highlighted layers from the list when the *OK* tile is selected.

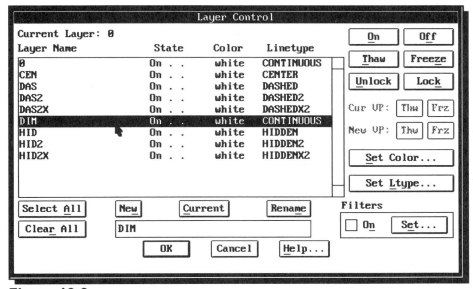

Figure 12-2

As an alternative to the dialogue box, the *Layer* command can be typed (*LA* is the command alias) in order to control layers. The command line format of *Layer* shows all of the available options:

```
Command:layer ?/Make/Set/New/ON/OFF/Color/Ltype/Freeze/
Thaw/LOck/Unlock:
```

The options are explained below.

Current, Set

To *Set* a layer as the *Current* layer is to make it the active drawing layer. Any entities created with draw commands are created on the *Current* layer. You can, however, edit entities on any layer, but can draw only on the current layer. Therefore, if you want to draw on the FLOORPLAN layer (for example), use the **Set** or **Current** option. If you want to draw with a certain *Color* or *Linetype*, set the layer with the desired *Color* and *Linetype* as the *Current* layer. Any layer can be made current, but only <u>one layer at a time</u> can be current.

To set the current layer with the *Layer Control* dialogue box (Fig. 12-2), select the desired layer from the list and then select the **Current** tile. Since only one layer can be current, it may be necessary to "deselect" highlighted layer names from the list until only one is highlighted. Alternately, if typing, use the **Set** option of the *LAYER* command to make a layer the current layer.

Layer State (*On, Off, Freeze, Thaw, Lock, Unlock*)

With the dialogue box, one or more layers can be selected from the layer name list. Any selections from the tiles on the right side of the box affect the selected layers. If you prefer typing the *Layer* command instead, activate any of the options by typing the capitalized letters of the desired option. The options are:

ON, OFF

If a layer is *ON*, it is visible. Entities on visible layers can be edited or plotted. Layers that are *OFF* are not visible even though there may be entities that exist on those layers. Entities on layers that are *OFF* will not plot and cannot be edited (unless the *ALL* selection option is used). It is not advisable to turn the current layer *OFF*.

Freeze, Thaw

Freeze and *Thaw* override *ON* and *OFF*. *Freeze* is a more protected state than *OFF*. Like being *OFF*, a frozen layer is not visible, nor can its entities be edited or plotted. Entities on a frozen layer cannot be accidentally *Erase*d with the *ALL* option. *Freezing* also prevents the layer from being considered when *Regen*s occur. *Freezing* unused layers speeds up computing time when working with large and complex drawings. *Thawing* reverses the *Freezing* state. Layers can be *Thawed* and also turned *OFF*. Frozen layers are not visible even though the word *ON* appears by the layer.

LOck, Unlock

Layers that are *LOck*ed are protected from being edited but are still visible and can be plotted. *LOck*ing a layer prevents its entities from being changed even though they are visible. Entities on *LOck*ed layers cannot be selected with the *ALL* option. Layers can be *LOck*ed and *OFF*.

Color and *Linetype* Properties

Layers have properties of *Color* and *Linetype* such that (generally) an entity that is drawn on, or changed to, a specific layer assumes the layer's linetype and color. Using this scheme enhances your ability to see what geometry is related by layer. It is also possible, however, to assign specific color and linetype to entities which will override the layer's color and linetype.

Procedures for setting one or many layers' *Color* and *Ltype* using the *Layer Control* dialogue box are similar to procedures for selecting a layer's *State*. Remember that several layers' names can be selected (highlighted) from the list for subsequent *Color* and *Ltype* setting.

Set Color

Selecting the **Set Color** tile in the *Layer Control* dialogue box causes the *Select Color* dialogue box to pop up (Fig. 12-3). The desired color can then be selected or the name or color number (called the ACI-- AutoCAD Color Index) can be typed in the edit box. Alternately, the *Color* option of the *Layer* command can be typed to enter the color name or ACI number.

The actual number of colors that are available is dependent on the type of monitor and graphics controller card that are configured. For the typical VGA configuration (Video Graphics Array standard monitor and graphics controller card) 16 colors are available as listed below. SVGA (Super VGA) setups allow 256 or more colors.

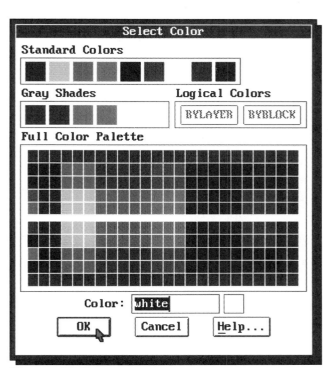

Figure 12-3

ACI	color	ACI	color
1	red	9	low intensity red
2	yellow	10	low intensity yellow
3	green	11	low intensity green
4	cyan	12	low intensity cyan
5	blue	13	low intensity blue
6	magenta	14	low intensity magenta
7	white	15	low intensity white (medium gray)
8	low intensity white (dark gray)		

The sixteenth color (not ACI 16) is black but cannot be used to draw entities since the background color is black.

Set Ltype

The default AutoCAD drawing as it is supplied by Autodesk has only one linetype available (*Continuous*). Before you can use other linetypes in a drawing, you load the linetypes from a file named ACAD.LIN or use a default drawing that has the desired linetypes already loaded (see the *LINETYPE* command).

To set a layer's linetype, select the **Set Ltype** tile of the *Layer Control* dialogue box, which in turn invokes the *Select Linetype* dialogue box. Select the desired linetype from the list. Alternately, the **Ltype** option of the *Layer* command can be typed.

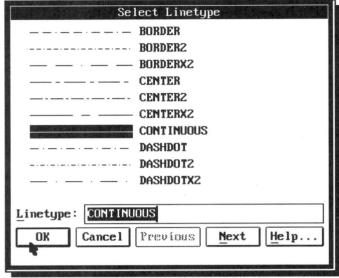

Figure 12-4

New

The *New* option allows you to make new layers. There is only one layer in the AutoCAD default drawing (ACAD.DWG) as it is provided to you "out of the box." That layer is Layer 0. Layer 0 is a part of every AutoCAD drawing because it cannot be *Purge*d, that is, erased (see Chapter 30). You can, however, change the *Ltype* and *Color* of layer 0 from the defaults (continuous ltype and color #7 white). Layer 0 is generally used as a construction layer or for geometry not intended to be included in the final draft of the drawing. Layer 0 has special properties when creating *Blocks* (Chapter 21).

You should create layers for each group of related entities and assign appropriate layer names for that geometry. Layer names can contain up to 31 characters. There is no limit to the number of layers that can be created. To create layers with the *Layer Control* dialogue box, type a layer name (or several names separated by commas) in the edit box, then select the **New** tile. The new layer name(s) then appears in the list above with the default color (white) and linetype (continuous). Colors and linetypes should be assigned as the next step.

If you want to create layers by typing, the *New* and *Make* options of the *Layer* command can be used. *New* allows creation of one or more new layers. *Make* allows creation of one layer (at a time) and sets it as the current layer.

LINETYPE

TYPE IN:	PULL-DOWN MENU	SCREEN MENU	TABLET MENU
LINETYPE or *DDEMODES*	---	*SETTINGS, LINETYP:*	*15,Y*

Linetypes can be listed ("*?*" option), *Created*, *Loaded*, or *Set* with the *Linetype* command.

Load

Linetypes cannot be loaded from within the *Layer Control* dialogue box. Linetypes are loaded with the *Linetype* command. The command is not available from Release 12 pull-down menus so it is selected elsewhere or typed.

```
Command: linetype
?/Create/Load/Set: L  (Type L for the Load option.)
Linetype(s) to load: *  (An asterisk indicates all linetypes, or type the
name of specific linetypes.)
At this point the Select Linetype File dialogue box appears.  Select the OK tile
so AutoCAD uses the ACAD.LIN file.
Linetype BORDER loaded.
...(List of 24 linetypes total appears)...
Linetype PHANTOMX2 loaded.
?/Create/Load/Set: Enter
Command:
```

Only <u>after</u> linetypes are loaded can the *Layer Control* dialogue box be used to select linetypes for specific layers. Figure 12-5 displays the linetypes provided by AutoCAD. You can also create custom linetypes like the example at the bottom of the list. (See the AutoCAD Customization Manual for creating linetypes).

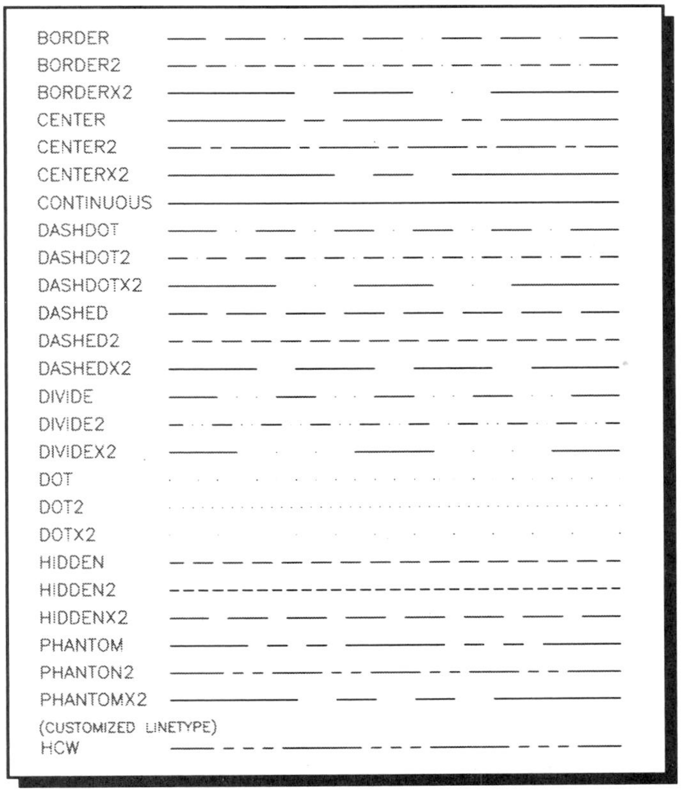

Figure 12-5

Set

The *Set* option of *Linetype* allows you to set a specific linetype for all subsequent entities <u>regardless</u> of the layer's linetype setting. Use this method only when you want an entity's linetype to override its layer linetype. Using this method of linetype designation prohibits your ability to see which entities are on which layers by their linetype appearance. However, for some applications specific linetype setting can be desirable.

```
Command: linetype
?/Create/Load/Set: s (Indicates the Set option.)
New entity linetype (or ?) <BYLAYER>: hidden (type any
linetype)
?/Create/Load/Set: Enter
Command:
```

For the example above, <u>all new</u> entities drawn have the *hidden* linetype regardless of the layers' linetype settings <u>until</u> *Linetype* is used again to *Set* another linetype or *BYLAYER* setting.

Alternately, you could select the *Settings* pull-down menu, then the *Entity Modes...* option, or type *Ddlmodes*. The *Entity Creation Modes* dialogue box appears (see Fig. 12-6) allowing specific linetype setting. Selecting the *Linetype* tile invokes the *Select Linetype* dialogue box (Fig. 12-4).

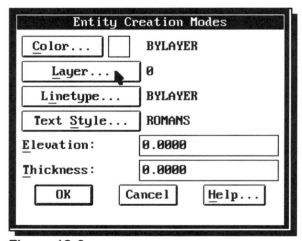

Figure 12-6

? (list)

This option is invoked by typing a question mark (?). A list of all linetypes available in the ACAD.LIN file (or another if one is available) appears in a text screen. This option is helpful if you forget the name or want to see an example among the possibilities. The command syntax is shown here.

```
Command: linetype
?/Create/Load/Set: ? (Indicates the list option.)
```
At this point the *Select Linetype File* dialogue box appears. PICK the *OK* tile to use the ACAD.LIN file.

A list appears in an AutoCAD text screen giving the information and listing the available *Linetypes* shown on the following page.

Linetypes defined in file C:\ACAD12\SUPPORT\ACAD.LIN:

```
       Name              Description
---------------    --------------------
BORDER             __ __ .  __ __ .  __ __ .  __ __ .  __ __ .  __ __ .
BORDER2            _._._._._._._._._._._._._._._._._._._._
BORDERX2           ____  ____  .  ____  .  ____  ____  ____  .  ____
CENTER             ____ _ ____ _ ____ _ ____ _ ____ _ ____
CENTER2            ____ _ ____ _ ____ _ ____ _ ____ _ ____ _

CENTERX2           _____  ____  _____  _____  ____  _____
DASHDOT            __ . __ . __ . __ . __ . __ . __ . __ . __
DASHDOT2           _._._._._._._._._._._._._._._._._._._._._
DASHDOTX2          ____  .  ____  .  ____  .  ____  .  ____  .  __
DASHED             __ __ __ __ __ __ __ __ __ __ __ __ __

DASHED2            _ _ _ _ _ _ _ _ _ _ _ _ _ _ _ _ _ _ _ _
DASHEDX2           ____ ____ ____ ____ ____ ____
DIVIDE             ____ . . ____ . . ____ . . ____ . . ____
DIVIDE2            _.._.._.._.._.._.._.._.._.._.._.
DIVIDEX2           _____ . . _____ . . _____ . .

DOT                . . . . . . . . . . . . . . . . . . .
DOT2               ........................................
DOTX2              .  .  .  .  .  .  .  .  .  .  .  .  .  .
HIDDEN             __ __ __ __ __ __ __ __ __ __ __ __ __
HIDDEN2            _ _ _ _ _ _ _ _ _ _ _ _ _ _ _ _ _ _ _

HIDDENX2           ____ ____ ____ ____ ____ ____ ____
PHANTOM            ____ __ __ ____ __ __ ____ __ __
PHANTOM2           ____ _ _ ____ _ _ ____ _ _ ____ _ _
PHANTOMX2          _____  ____  ____  _____
```

?/Create/Load/Set:

LTSCALE

TYPE IN:	PULL-DOWN MENU	SCREEN MENU	TABLET MENU
LTSCALE	---	*SETTINGS, LTSCALE:*	*19,Y*

Hidden, dashed, dotted and other linetypes that have spaces are called <u>non-continuous</u> linetypes. When drawing entities that have non-continuous linetypes (either *BYLAYER* or entity-specific linetype designations), the linetype's dashes or dots are automatically created and spaced. The *LTSCALE* variable (Linetype Scale) controls the length and spacing of the dashes and/or dots. The value that is specified for *LTSCALE* affects the drawing <u>globally and retroactively</u>. That is, all existing non-continuous lines in the drawing as well as new lines are affected by *LTSCALE*. You can therefore adjust the drawing's linetype scale for all lines at any time with this one command.

If you choose to make the dashes of non-continuous lines smaller and closer together, reduce *LTSCALE*; if you desire larger dashes, increase *LTSCALE*. The *Hidden* linetype is shown in the figure at various *LTSCALE* settings. Any value can be specified.

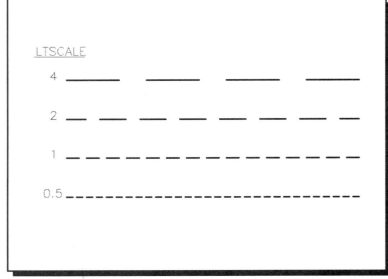

Figure 12-7

LTSCALE is always used in the command line format but can be accessed by any of the methods shown in the Menu Table shown on the previous page.

```
Command:LTSCALE
New scale factor <1 or current value>: (value) (Enter any positive
value.)
Command:
```

The *LTSCALE* scale factor set for the default drawing (ACAD.DWG) is 1. This value represents an appropriate *LTSCALE* for entities drawn within the default *Limits* of 12 x 9.

As a general rule, you should change the *LTSCALE* <u>proportionally</u> with changes in *Limits*. For example, if you increase the drawing area defined by *Limits* by a factor of 2 (to 24 x 18) from the default (12 x 9), you also change *LTSCALE* proportionally to a value of 2. Since *LTSCALE* is retroactive, it can be changed at a later time or repeatedly adjusted to display the desired spacing of linetypes.

In addition to considering the drawing *Limits*, you should also consider the size of plotting media when setting *LTSCALE*. The default value of 1 assumes an appropriate size for *Limits* of 12 x 9. For example, assume you plotted a drawing having a *LTSCALE* of 1 on an "A" size (8.5 x 11) sheet which produced the hidden line dashes at 1/4". If you then plotted the same drawing to fill a "B" size sheet (11 x 17), the dashes would be 1/2" because the plotted drawing is now twice as large. Instead, *LTSCALE* should be reduced by a factor of 2 (multiplied by .5) to achieve the same hidden line dashes of 1/4". In other words, a *LTSCALE* of 1 on an 8.5 x 11 sheet and a *LTSCALE* of .5 on an 11 x 17 sheet would yield dashes of the same plotted size (for more information, see Plotting to Scale, Chapter 14).

Even though you have some control over the size of spacing for non-continuous lines, you have almost <u>no control</u> over the <u>placement</u> of the dashes for non-continuous lines. For example, the short dashes of center lines <u>cannot</u> always be controlled to intersect at the centers of a series of circles. The spacing can only be adjusted globally (all lines in the drawing) to reach a compromise. See Chapter 24, Multiview Drawing, for further discussion and suggestions on this subject.

COLOR

TYPE IN:	PULL-DOWN MENU	SCREEN MENU	TABLET MENU
COLOR or DDEMODES	*Settings, Entity Modes...*	*SETTINGS, COLOR:*	*20,Y*

The *Color* command allows you to specify a <u>specific</u> color for all newly created entities <u>regardless</u> of the layer's color designation. This color setting <u>overrides</u> the layer color for newly created entities (unless the *BYLAYER* color is selected). Use this method only when you want an entity's color to be different than its layer color. Using this type of color designation prohibits your ability to see which entities are on which layers by their color; however, for some applications specific color setting may be desirable. You can also use this command to set the color designation back to *BYLAYER* if it has been set to a specific color.

```
Command: color
New entity color <BYLAYER>: red (Specify a color name or number.)
Command:
```

All new entities drawn will be *red* regardless of the layers' color settings until **Color** is used again to set another color or *BYLAYER* setting.

Setting entities' colors by this method is analogous to setting an entity-specific *Linetype* setting with the *Linetype* command.

Alternately, the *Entity Creation Modes* dialogue box (Fig 12-8) can be accessed by typing *Ddemodes* or using the *Settings* pull-down menu. Selecting the *Color* tile produces the *Select Color* dialogue box (see Fig. 12-3). Keep in mind that selecting a specific color by this method causes an <u>entity-specific</u> setting, not a *BYLAYER* setting.

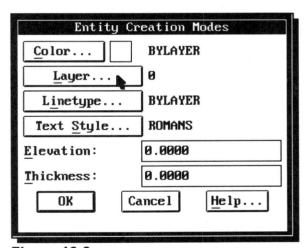

Figure 12-8

Changing *Layer*, *Linetype*, and *Color* Properties

The *Chprop* (change properties) or *Modify* commands can be used to "move" entities from one layer to another. When an entity is changed from one layer to another, it assumes the new layer's color and linetype, provided the entity was originally created with color and linetype assigned *BYLAYER*.

In other words, if an entity was created with the wrong linetype or color, or on the wrong layer, it could be "moved" to the desired layer, therefore assuming the new layer's linetype and color. A drawing strategy that can be used is to draw all entities on one layer, then use *Change* or *Modify* to "move" selected entities to the desired layers.

Chprop or *Modify* can also be used to change an entity's linetype or color designation retroactively. That is, if linetype and color are specifically assigned to one or a group of entities, *Chprop* or *Modify* can be used to change the setting to another linetype or color, or used to change the assignment to a *BYLAYER* setting.

See Chapter 17, Construct Commands II, for a full explanation of *Chprop* and *Modify*.

CHAPTER EXERCISES

1.   *Layer, Layer Control* **dialogue box**, *On, Off, Freeze, Thaw, Set Color*

    Open the sample drawing named **HOUSEPLN.DWG**. (See Chapter 11, exercise 1 for details on *Opening* this drawing.) Use *Saveas* to save the drawing <u>in your working directory</u> as **HOUSEPL3**.

A.   Invoke the *Layer* command by typing *LA*. Use the *?* option to yield the list of layers in the drawing. Notice that all the layers are *On*.

B.   Invoke the *Layer Control* dialogue box from the *Settings* pull-down menu. Turn *Off* the layer with the dimensions (**ARCDIMR**) by highlighting (PICKing) the layer and then selecting the *Off* tile. Select the *OK* tile and view the drawing. Are the dimensions displayed?

C.   Turn *Off* layers **ARCR** and **ARCMNR**. This should clean up the drawing further by not displaying the detail text. Now type *Regen* and count the number of seconds it takes for the regeneration.

D.   Use the *Layer Control* dialogue box and PICK the *Select All* tile (lower left corner). Then select the *On* tile to turn the layers back on. Now select the 3 layers again individually (**ARCDIMR, ARCR,** and **ARCMNR**) and PICK the *Freeze* tile to freeze them. Notice the *State* column says the layers are still *On*. (*Freeze* overrides *On*.) Select *OK* to return to the drawing and view the changes. Type *Regen* and count the seconds needed for the regeneration. Is a *Regen* faster with the 3 layers frozen?

E.   Select the 3 layers again from the *Layer Control* dialogue box and *Thaw* them. Since they were already *On*, they should appear when you select the *OK* tile. PICK the *Clear All* tile to unhighlight all layers. Select the 3 layers again and *Set Color* of all 3 to blue. PICK the *OK* tile. If the layers don't appear, type *Regen*.

F.   *Freeze* the three layers again and *Save* the drawing.

2. ***Linetype, Layer Control, New, Current, Set Ltype, Set Color***

A. Begin a ***New*** drawing and assign the name **CH12EX2**. Set ***Limits*** to **11** x **8.5**. Use the ***Linetype*** command and the ***Set*** option. Next invoke the **?** suboption to list the loaded linetypes. Are any linetypes already loaded? Invoke ***Linetype*** and ***Load*** all linetypes by entering the * (asterisk) wildcard. Use the ***Linetype*** command and ***Set*** option again with the list (**?**) option to make sure the load was successful.

B. Use the ***Layer Control*** dialogue box to create 3 new layers named **OBJ**, **HID** and **CEN**. Enter the names in the edit box with commas between (no spaces). Select the ***New*** tile to make the new layers appear in the list. Assign the following colors and linetypes to the layers using the ***Set Color*** and ***Set Ltype*** tiles.

OBJ red   continuous
HID yellow hidden
CEN green center

C. Make the **OBJ** layer ***Current***. PICK the ***OK*** tile. Verify the current layer by looking at the status line. Then draw the visible object lines only (not the dimensions) shown in Figure 12-9.

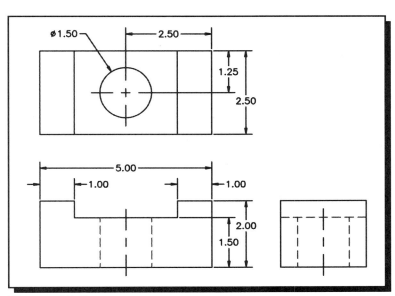

Figure 12-9

D. When you are finished drawing the visible object lines, create the necessary hidden lines by making layer **HID** the ***Current*** layer, then drawing ***Lines***. Notice that you only specify the *Line* endpoints as usual and AutoCAD creates the dashes.

E. Next, create the center lines for the holes by making layer **CEN** the ***Current*** layer and drawing ***Lines***. Save the drawing.

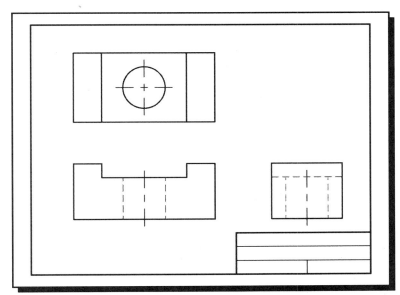

Figure 12-10

F.   As a final step, create a *New* layer named **BORDER** and draw a border and title block of your design on that layer. The final drawing should appear as that in Figure 12-10. *Save* the drawing.

3.   *LTSCALE*

A.   Begin a *New* drawing and assign the name **CH12EX3**. Create the same 4 *New* layers that you made for the previous exercise. Set the *Limits* equal to a "C" size sheet, **22 x 17**.

B.   Create the part shown in Figure 12-11. Draw on the appropriate layers to achieve the desired linetypes.

C.   Notice that the *Hidden* and *Center* linetype dashes are very small. Use **LTSCALE** to adjust the scale of the non-continuous lines. Since you changed the *Limits* by a factor of slightly more than 4, try using **4** as the **LTSCALE** factor. Notice that all the lines are affected (globally) and that the new *LTSCALE* is retroactive for existing lines as well as for new lines. This appears too large, however, because of the small hidden line segments, so it should be adjusted. Remember that you cannot control where the multiple <u>short</u> centerline dashes appear for one line segment. Try to reach a compromise.

D.   When you have the desired *LTSCALE*, *Exit AutoCAD* and *Save Changes*. Keep in mind that the *LTSCALE* may appear differently on the screen than it will on a plot. Both the plot scale and the paper size should be considered when you set *LTSCALE*. This topic will be discussed further in Chapter 13, Advanced Drawing Setup.

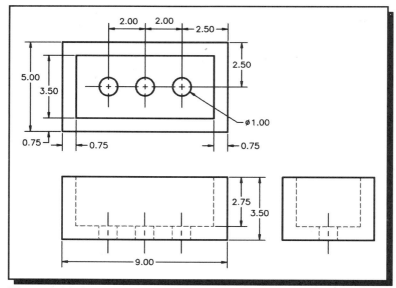

Figure 12-11

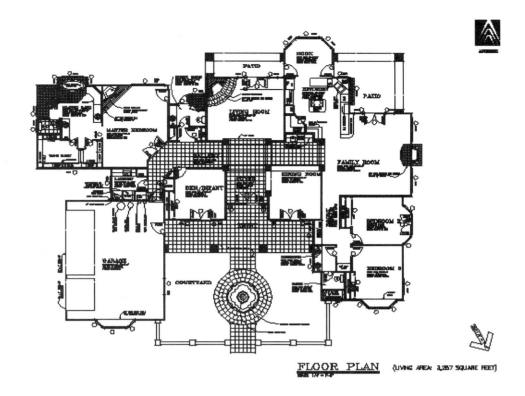

FLOOR PLAN (LIVING AREA: 3,257 SQUARE FEET)

CHAPTER 13

Advanced Drawing Setup

CHAPTER OBJECTIVES

After completing this chapter you should:

1.　know the steps for setting up a drawing;

2.　be able to determine an appropriate *Limits* setting for the drawing;

3.　be able to calculate and apply the "drawing scale factor";

4.　be able to create prototype drawings;

5.　know what setup steps can be considered for prototype drawings.

BASICS

When you begin a drawing, there are several steps that are typically performed in preparation for creating geometry such as setting *Units*, *Limits,* and creating *Layers* with *linetypes* and *colors.* Some of these basic concepts were discussed in Chapter 6, Beginning Drawing Setup. This chapter discusses setting *Limits* for correct plotting as well as other procedures such as layer creation and variables settings that help prepare a drawing for geometry creation.

Most offices produce drawings that are similar in format. The similarities may be: subject of the drawing, scale, plotting size, layering schemes, dimensioning techniques, and/or text styles. Prototype drawings can be used to prevent having to repeatedly perform the steps for drawing setup. Prototype drawing creation and use are also discussed in this chapter.

STEPS FOR DRAWING SETUP

Assuming that you have in mind the general dimensions and proportions of the drawing you want to create, and the drawing will involve using layers, dimensions, and text, the following steps are suggested for setting up a drawing.

1. Determine and set the *Units* that are to be used.
2. Determine and set the drawing *Limits*, then *Zoom All.*
3. Set an appropriate *Snap* value to be used if useful.
4. Set an appropriate *Grid* value.
5. Change the *Ltscale* value based on the new *Limits.*
6. Load *Linetypes.*
7. Create the desired *Layers* and assign appropriate *linetype* and *color* settings
8. Create desired *Text Styles.* (Optional, discussed in Chapter 19)
9. Create desired *Dimstyles.* (Optional, discussed in Chapter 29)
10. Create or *Insert* the desired title block and border. (Optional, discussed in Chapters 21 and 22)

Each of the steps for drawing setup is explained in detail here.

1. Set *Units*

This task is accomplished by using the *Units* command or the *Units Control* dialogue box. Set the linear units and precision desired. Set angular units and precision if needed. (See Chapter 6 for details on this command.)

2. Set *Limits*

Before beginning to create an AutoCAD drawing, determine the size of the drawing area needed for the intended geometry. Using the actual *Units*, appropriate *Limits* should be set in order to draw the object or geometry to the real world size. *Limits* are set with the *Limits* command by specifying the lower left and upper right corners. Always *Zoom All* after changing *Limits*. (See Chapter 6 for details on these operations.)

If you are planning to plot the drawing to scale, *Limits* should be set to a proportion of the sheet size you plan to plot on. For example, if the sheet size is 11" x 8.5", set *Limits* to 11 x 8.5 if you want to plot full size (1"=1"). Setting *Limits* to 22 x 17 (2 times 11 x 8.5) provides 2 times the drawing area and allows plotting at 1/2 size (1/2"=1") on the 11" x 8.5" sheet. Simply stated, set *Limits* to a proportion of the paper size.

Setting *Limits* to the paper size allows plotting at 1=1 scale. Setting *Limits* to a proportion of the sheet size allows plotting at the reciprocal of that proportion. For example, setting *Limits* to 2 times an 11" x 8.5" sheet allows you to plot 1/2 size on that sheet.

Drawing Scale Factor

The proportion used to increase or decrease *Limits* from the plotting sheet size to the new values sets the "drawing scale factor." This factor can be used as a general scale factor for other size-related drawing variables such as *LTSCALE, DIMSCALE* (Chapter 29), and *Hatch* pattern scales (Chapter 26).

All size-related AutoCAD drawing variables are set to 1 by default. This means that all variables (such as *LTSCALE*) that control sizing and spacing of entities are set for creating a drawing in the default *Limits* plotted full size. When *Limits* are changed, the size-related variables should also be changed proportionally. For example, if the default *Limits* (12 x 9) are changed by a factor of 2 (to 24 x 18), then 2 becomes the "drawing scale factor." Then, as a general rule, the values of variables such as *LTSCALE, DIMSCALE*, and other scales would be multiplied by a factor of 2.

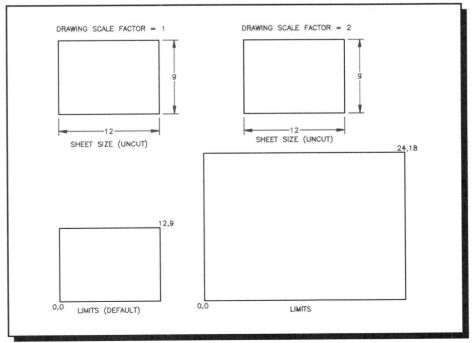

Figure 13-1

Limits should be set to a proportion of the paper size used for plotting. In many cases, "cut" paper sizes are used based on the 11" x 8.5" module. Assume you plan to plot on an 11" x 8.5" sheet. Changing the *Limits* (based on the paper size) by some multiplier makes that value the drawing scale factor. The <u>reciprocal</u> of the drawing scale factor is the scale for plotting on that sheet.

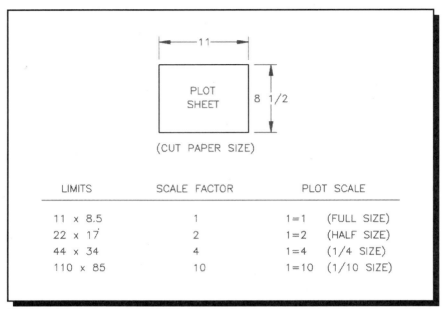

Figure 13-2

The term "drawing scale factor" is not a variable or command that can be found in AutoCAD or its official documentation. This concept has been developed by AutoCAD users and authors to describe the factor that is used to associate the variables in an AutoCAD drawing related to keeping geometry proportional and plotting drawings to a particular size.

3.   **Set *Snap***

Use the *Snap* command or *Drawing Aids* dialogue box to set an appropriate *Snap* value if it is useful. The value of *Snap* is dependent on the <u>interactive</u> drawing accuracy that is desired.

The accuracy of the drawing and the size of the *Limits* should be considered when setting the *Snap* value. On one hand, to achieve accuracy and detail, you want the *Snap* to be as small of a dimensional increment as might be used in the drawing. On the other hand, depending upon the size of the *Limits*, the *Snap* value should be large enough to make interactive selection (PICKing) fast and easy. In some drawings where the *Limits* are relatively small and the dimensional increments are relatively large, *Snap* can be set to satisfy both requirements. However, in other drawings with large *Limits* and small drawing increment lengths, or with complex geometry of irregular interval lengths, *Snap* may not be useful and can be turned *Off*. (See Chapter 6 for details on the *Snap* command.)

4. Set _Grid_

The _Grid_ value setting is usually set equal to, or proportionally larger than, that of the _Snap_ value. _Grid_ should be set to a proportion that is <u>easily visible</u>. Setting the value to a proportion of _Snap_ gives visual indication of the _Snap_ increment. For example, a _Grid_ value of **1X**, **2X**, or **5X** would give visual display of every 1, 2, or 5 _Snap_ increments, respectively. If you are not using _Snap_ because only extremely small or irregular interval lengths are needed, you may want to turn _Grid_ off. (See Chapter 6 for details on the _Grid_ command.)

5. Set the _LTSCALE_

A change in _Limits_ (then _Zoom All_) affects the display of non-continuous (hidden, dashed, dotted, etc.) lines. The _LTSCALE_ variable controls the spacing of non-continuous lines. The "drawing scale factor" can be used to determine the _LTSCALE_ setting. For example, if the default _Limits_ have been changed by a factor of 2, set the _LTSCALE_ to 2. If you prefer a _LTSCALE_ setting of other than 1 for a drawing in the default _Limits_, multiply that value by the drawing scale factor (2 in this example).

American National Standards Institute (ANSI) requires that <u>hidden lines be plotted with 1/8" dashes</u>. An AutoCAD drawing plotted full size (1 unit=1") with the default _LTSCALE_ value of 1 plots the _Hidden_ linetype with 1/4" dashes. Therefore, an <u>_LTSCALE_ of .5</u> is more appropriate for a drawing plotted full size. Multiply this value by the drawing scale factor when plotting to scale. (See Chapter 12 for details on the _LTSCALE_ variable.)

6. Load _Linetypes_

Use the _Linetype_ command to load the desired line types. You can load all of the line types or load only those that you anticipate using. (See Chapter 12 for details on loading line types with the _Linetype_ command.)

7. Create _Layers_, Assign _Linetypes_ and _Colors_

Using the _Layer_ command or the _Layer Control_ dialogue box, create the layers that you anticipate needing. Multiple layers can be created with the _New_ option. Type in several new names separated by commas. Assign a descriptive name for each layer indicating its type of geometry, part name, or function. Include a _linetype_ designator in the layer name if appropriate, for example PART1-H, PART1-V indicate hidden and visible line layers for PART1.

Once the _Layers_ have been created, assign a _Color_ and _Linetype_ to each layer. _Colors_ can be used to give visual relationships among parts of the drawing. Geometry that is intended to be plotted with different pens (pen size or color) should be drawn in different screen colors. (See Chapter 12 for details on creating _Layers_, _Linetypes_, and _Colors_.)

8.   Create *Text Styles*

AutoCAD has only one text style as part of the standard default drawing (ACAD.DWG).
If you desire other *Text Styles*, they are created using the *Style* command or the *Set Style...* option from the *Draw* pull-down menu. (See Chapter 19, Inserting and Using Text.)

If you desire engineering standard text, create a *Text Style* using the *Roman Simplex* font file.

9.   Create *Dimstyles*

If you plan to dimension your drawing, *Dimstyles* can be created at this point; however, they are generally created during the dimensioning process. *Dimstyles* are names given to groups of dimension variable settings. (See Chapter 29 for information on creating *Dimstyles*.)

Although you do not have to create *Dimstyles* until you are ready to dimension the geometry, it is very helpful to create *Dimstyles* as part of a prototype drawing. If you produce similar drawings repeatedly, your dimensioning techniques are probably similar. Much time can be saved by using a prototype drawing with previously created *Dimstyles*.

10.   Create a Title Block and Border

For 2D drawings it is helpful to insert a title block and border early in the drawing process. This action gives a visual drawing boundary as well as reserves the space occupied by the title block.

Since *Limits* are already set to facilitate drawing full size in the actual *Units*, creating a title block and border which will appear on the final plot in the appropriate size is not difficult. A simple method is to use the drawing scale factor to determine the title block size. Multiply the actual size of the title block and border by the drawing scale factor to determine their dimensions in the drawing.

One common method is to use the *Insert* command to insert a title block and border as a *Block*. If the *Block* is the actual title block and border size, simply use the drawing scale factor as the *X* and *Y scale factor* during the *Insert* command. (See Chapters 21 and 22 for information on *Block* creation and *Insertion*.)

If you are preparing prototype drawings, a title block and border can be included as part of a prototype.

CREATING PROTOTYPE DRAWINGS

Instead of going through the steps for setup <u>each time</u> you begin a new drawing, create one or more "prototype" drawings. A prototype drawing is one which has the initial setup steps (*Units, Limits, Layers, linetypes, colors*, etc.) completed and saved, but no geometry has yet been created. Prototype drawings are used as a <u>template</u> or <u>starting point</u> each time you begin a new drawing. AutoCAD actually makes a copy of the prototype you select to begin the drawing. The creation and use of prototype drawings can save many hours of preparation.

To make a prototype drawing, *Open* the default drawing (ACAD.DWG), make the initial drawing setups, and use *Saveas* to save the drawing under a different, descriptive name. Then, using DOS commands or *File Utilities*, locate the new drawing in the directory where ACAD.DWG is found (usually in the \SUPPORT subdirectory) or create another directory for multiple prototype drawings.

The *Create New Drawing* dialogue box (Fig. 13-3) is activated when the *New* command is used. This box allows you to select your new prototype drawing from a pop-up list by selecting the *Prototype...* tile. This action produces the *Prototype Drawing File* dialogue box (Figure 13-4).

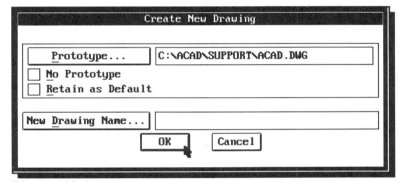

Figure 13-3

Any drawings (.DWG files) located in the directory where the default drawing (ACAD.DWG) is found are displayed for possible selection as a prototype drawing. Other directories can also be searched for drawings to be used as prototypes.

The *Create New Drawing* dialogue box (previous figure) also allows you to designate a name for a new drawing if desired. However, if no name is defined, the selected prototype drawing is <u>not</u> overwritten when the *Save* command is used. The new drawing is treated as any other new (blank) drawing. Using *Save* prompts you for a new drawing name.

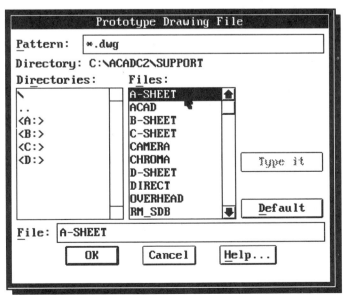

Figure 13-4

Multiple prototype drawings can be created, each for a particular situation. For example, you may want to create several prototypes, each having the setup steps completed but with different *Limits* and with the intention to plot each in a different scale or on a different size sheet. Another possibility is to create prototypes with different layering schemes. There are many possibilities, but the specific settings used depend upon your applications, typical plotting scales, or your peripheral devices.

Typical drawing steps that can be considered for developing prototype drawings are listed below.

> Set *Units*
> Set *Limits*
> Set *Snap*
> Set *Grid*
> Set *LTSCALE*
> Create *Layers* with color and linetypes assigned
> Create *Text Styles* (see Chapter 19)
> Create *Dimstyles* (see Chapter 29)
> Create or *Insert* a standard title block and border (see Chapters 21, 22)

A popular practice is to create a prototype drawing for each sheet size used for plotting. *Limits* are set to the actual sheet size, and other settings and variables (*LTSCALE*, *DIMSCALE*, text sizes) are set to the actual desired size for the finished full-size plot. Then if you want to create a new drawing and plot on a certain sheet size, start a new drawing using the appropriate prototype.

For laboratories or offices that use only one sheet size, create prototype drawings for each plot scale with the appropriate *Limits, Snap, Grid, Layers, LTSCALE, DIMSCALE*, etc.

You can also create prototypes for different plot scales <u>and</u> different sheet sizes. Make sure you assign appropriate and descriptive names to the prototype drawings.

CHAPTER EXERCISES

For the first three exercises, you will set up several drawings that will be used later for creating geometry. Follow the typical steps for setting up a drawing given in this chapter.

1. A drawing of a gasket is needed. Dimensions are in inches. The drawing will be plotted full size on an 11" x 8.5" sheet. Begin a *New* drawing and assign the name **BARGUIDE**. Follow the steps below.

    A. Set *Units* to *Fractional* and *Precision* to **1/16**.
    B. Set *Limits* to **11** x **8.5**, then *Zoom All*.
    C. Set *Snap* to **1/4** (or .250).
    D. Set *Grid* to **1/2** (or .5).
    E. Set *LTSCALE* to **.5**.

F.   *Load* the *Center* and *Hidden Linetypes*.

G.   Create the following *layers* and assign the given *Colors* and *Linetypes*:

VISIBLE	*continuous*	*red*
CONSTR	*continuous*	*white*
CENTER	*center*	*green*
HIDDEN	*hidden*	*yellow*
TITLE	*continuous*	*white*
DIM	*continuous*	*cyan*

H.   *Save* the drawing.

2.   You are to create a drawing of a wrench. The drawing will be plotted full size on an "A" size sheet and the dimensions are in millimeters. Begin a *New* drawing and assign the name **WRENCH**. Follow these steps.

A.   Set *Units* to *Decimal* and *Precision* to **0.00**.

B.   Set *Limits* to **297 x 210**, then *Zoom All*.

C.   Set *Snap* to **1**.

D.   Set *Grid* to **10**.

E.   Set *LTSCALE* to **12.5** (.5 times the scale factor of 25).

F.   *Load* the *Center Linetype*.

G.   Create the following *layers* and assign the *Colors* and *Linetypes* as shown:

WRENCH	*continuous*	*red*
CONSTR	*continuous*	*white*
CENTER	*center*	*green*
TITLE	*continuous*	*yellow*
DIM	*continuous*	*cyan*

H.   *Save* the drawing.

3.   A floorplan of an apartment has been requested. Dimensions are in feet and inches. The drawing will be plotted at 1/2"=1' scale on an 24" x 18" sheet. Begin a *New* drawing and assign the name **APARTMNT**. Continue with the steps below.

A.   Set *Units* to *Architectural* and *Precision* to **1/2**.

B.   Set *Limits* to **48' x 36'** (576" x 432"), then *Zoom All*.

C.   Set *Snap* to **1** (inch).

D.   Set *Grid* to **12** (inches).

E.   Set *LTSCALE* to **12**.

F.   Create the following *layers* and assign the *Colors*:

FLOORPLN	*red*
CONSTR	*white*
TEXT	*green*
TITLE	*yellow*
DIM	*cyan*

G.   *Save* the drawing.

4.   In this exercise you will create several "generic" prototype drawings that can be used at a later time. Creating the prototypes now will save you time later when you begin new drawings.

    A.   Create a prototype drawing for use with decimal dimensions and using standard paper "A" size format. Include the following setups.

        1.   Set *Units* to *Decimal* and *Precision* to **0.00**.
        2.   Set *Limits* to **11** x **8.5**.
        3.   *Load* all *Linetypes*.
        4.   Set *Snap* to **.25**.
        5.   Set *Grid* to **1**.
        6.   Set *LTSCALE* to **.5**.
        7.   Create the following *Layers*, assign the *Linetypes* as shown, and assign your choice of *colors* (use bright colors). Create any other layers you think you may need or any assigned by your instructor.

OBJECT	*continuous*
CONSTR	*continuous*
TEXT	*continuous*
TITLE	*continuous*
VPORTS	*continuous*
DIM	*continuous*
HIDDEN	*hidden*
CENTER	*center*
DASHED	*dashed*

        8.   Use *Saveas* and name the drawing **ASHEET**.

    B.   Using the drawing in the previous exercise (use *Open* if the drawing is not open), create a prototype for a standard engineering "B" size sheet. Set *Limits* to **17** x **11**. All other settings and layers are OK as they are. Use *Saveas* and assign the name **BSHEET**.

    C.   *Open* the **ASHEET** drawing (created in exercise A.) and create a prototype for a standard engineering "C" size sheet. Set *Limits* to **22** x **17**. Set *Snap* to **.5**. Keep all the other settings and layers as they are. Use *Saveas* and assign the name **CSHEET**.

    D.   *Open* the **ASHEET** drawing (created in exercise A.), only in this exercise create a prototype for a standard engineering "D" size sheet. Set *Limits* to **34** x **22**. All other settings and layers do not need to be changed. Use *Saveas* and assign the name **DSHEET**.

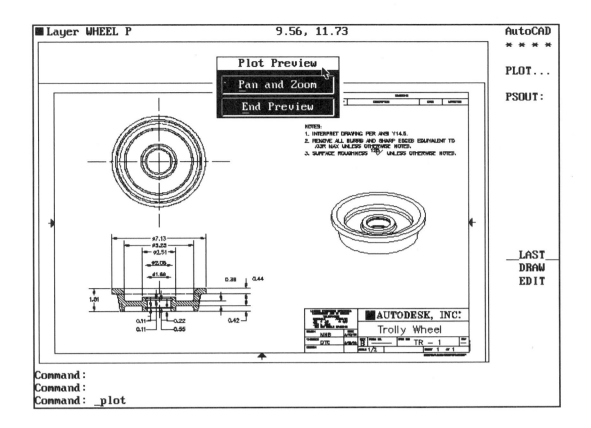

CHAPTER 14

Plotting

CHAPTER OBJECTIVES

After completing this chapter you should:

1. know the typical steps for plotting;

2. be able to invoke and use the *Plot Configuration* dialogue box;

3. be able to select from available plotting devices and set the paper size and orientation;

4. be able to specify what area of the drawing you want to plot;

5. be able to preview the plot before creating a plotted drawing;

6. be able to specify a scale for plotting a drawing;

7. know how to set up a drawing for plotting to a standard scale on a standard size sheet;

8. be able to use the Tables of Limits Settings to determine *Limits* and scale settings.

BASICS

Plotting is accomplished from within AutoCAD by invoking the *Plot* command. Using the *Plot* command by any command entry method invokes the *Plot Configuration* dialogue box (Fig. 14-1). You have complete control of plotting using the dialogue box. If desired, the command line format of the *Plot* command (Fig. 14-2) can be used for specifying the plot options by changing the *CMDDIA* variable setting. The plotting options are explained after the Typical Steps for Plotting.

TYPICAL STEPS TO PLOTTING

Assuming the CAD system has been properly configured so the peripheral devices (plotters and/or printers) are functioning, the typical basic steps to plotting using the *Plot Configuration* dialogue box are listed below.

1. Use *Save* to insure the drawing has been saved in its most recent form before plotting (just in case some problem arises while plotting).

2. Make sure the plotter is turned on, has paper and pens loaded, and is ready to accept the plot information from the computer.

3. Invoke the *Plot Configuration* dialogue box.

4. Check the upper left corner of the dialogue box to insure that the intended device has been selected. If not, select the *Device and Default Selection* tile and make the desired choice.

5. Check the upper right corner of the dialogue box to insure that the desired paper size has been selected. If not, use the *Size...* tile to do so.

6. Only when necessary, change other options such as *Rotation and Origin* and *Pen Assignments*.

7. Determine and select which area of the drawing to plot: *Display*, *Extents*, *Limits*, *Window*, or *View*.

8. Enter the desired scale for the plot. If no standard scale is needed, toggle *Scaled to Fit* (so the **X** appears in the box).

9. Always *Preview* the plot to insure that the drawing will be plotted as you expect. Select either a *Full* or *Partial* preview. If the preview does not display the plot as you intended, make the appropriate changes. Otherwise, needless time and media could be wasted.

10. If everything is OK, selecting the *OK* tile causes the drawing to be sent to the plotter for plotting.

USING THE *PLOT* COMMAND

PLOT

TYPE IN:	PULL-DOWN MENU	SCREEN MENU	TABLET MENU
PLOT	*File, Plot...*	*PLOT...*	*24,W*

Invoking *Plot* by any method normally invokes the *Plot Configuration* dialogue box (Fig. 14-1).

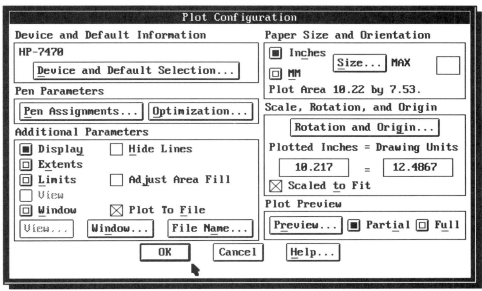

Figure 14-1

The *Plot Configuration* dialogue box can be suppressed by setting the *CMDDIA* system variable to **0**. This action displays a text screen instead and allows changing parameters by keyboard entry (Fig. 14-2). This method is used for plotting using a script file to make several plots. (See Scripts, p. 101, AutoCAD Customization Manual.)

```
Command: plot

What to plot -- Display, Extents, Limits, View, or Window <D>:

Plotter port time-out = 30 seconds
Plot device is Hewlett-Packard (HP-GL) ADI 4.2 - by Autodesk, Inc
Description: HP-7470
Plot optimization level = 4
Plot will be written to a selected file
Sizes are in Inches and the style is landscape
Plot origin is at (0.00,0.00)
Plotting area is 10.22 wide by 7.53 high (MAX size)
Plot is NOT rotated
Area fill will NOT be adjusted for pen width
Hidden lines will NOT be removed
Plot will be scaled to fit available area

Do you want to change anything? (No/Yes/File/Save) <N>:
```

Figure 14-2

Plot Configuration Dialogue Box Options

Many selections made from the *Plot Configuration* dialogue box allow you to change plotting parameters such as scale, paper size, pen assignments, rotation and origin of the drawing on the sheet. The latest changes made to plotting options are saved (in the ACAD.CFG file) so they do not have to be reentered the next time.

Device and Default Selection

Many devices (printers or plotters) can be configured for use with AutoCAD, and all configurations are saved for your selection. For example, you can have both an "A" size and a "D" size plotter as well as a laser printer, any one of which could be used to plot the current file. (All devices are first configured through AutoCAD's *Config* command. See AutoCAD Interface, Installation, and Performance Guide.)

Selecting the *Device and Default Selection* tile from the *Plot Configuration* dialogue box invokes the *Device and Default Selection* dialogue box (Fig. 14-3). Highlighted near the top is displayed the currently selected device along with the other configured choices.

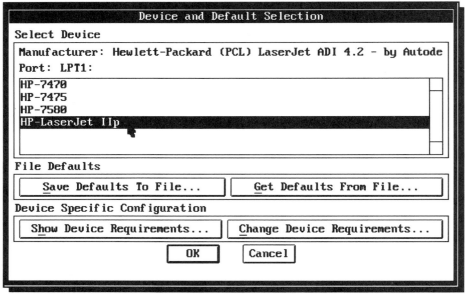

Figure 14-3

Since multiple devices can be used and there may also be several typical sets of parameters frequently used for each device (scale, pen assignments, etc.), multiple settings of plotting parameters can be saved and retrieved by using the *Save Defaults to File...* and *Get Defaults from File...* tiles in the dialogue box above. For example, several assignments for pens can be specified (possibly one for a colored felt tip carrel and one for an ink pen carrel) using the *Pen Assignment...* option (see Fig. 14-1). The *Save Defaults to File...* option produces the dialogue box shown in Figure 14-4. The settings can be saved as a .PCP (plotter configuration parameters) file and easily retrieved instead of having to make all of the selections each time you want to change parameters.

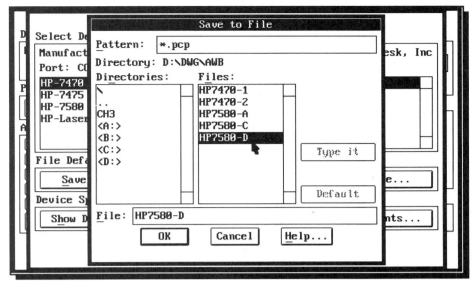

Figure 14-4

Additional Parameters (What to Plot)

You specify what part of the drawing you want to plot by selecting the desired button from the lower left corner of the dialogue box (Fig. 14-1). The choices are listed below.

Display
This option plots the current display on the screen. If using viewports, plots the current viewport display.

Extents
Plotting *Extents* is similar to *Zoom Extents*. This option plots the entire drawing (all entities) disregarding the *Limits*. Use the *Zoom Extents* command to make sure the extents have been updated before using this plot option.

Limits
This selection plots the area defined by the *Limits* command (unless plotting a 3D object from other than the plan view).

View
With this option you can plot a view previously saved using the *View* command.

Window
Window allows you to plot any portion of the drawing. You must specify the window by **PICK**ing or supplying coordinates for the lower left and upper right corners.

Hide lines
This option removes hidden lines (edges obscured from view) if you are plotting a 3D surface or solid model.

Adjust Area Fill

Using this option forces AutoCAD to adjust for solid-filled areas (*Plines, Solids*) by pulling the pen inside the filled area by one-half the pen width. Use this for critically accurate plots.

Plot to File

Choosing this option writes the plot to a file instead of making a plot. This action generally creates a .PLT file type for a plotter and .LST for printer. The format of the file depends upon the device brand and model that is configured. The plot file can be printed or plotted later <u>without</u> AutoCAD, assuming the correct interpreter for the device is available. The *File Name...* dialogue box (Fig. 14-5) is used to supply the desired name for the file to be written.

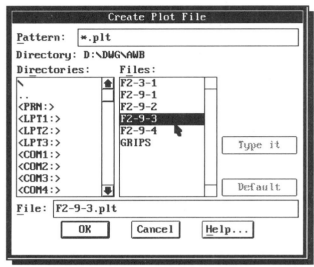

Figure 14-5

Paper Size and Orientation

Inches or *MM* should be checked to correspond to the units used in the drawing. Assuming the drawing was created using the correct units, a scale for plotting can be calculated without inch to millimeter conversion.

The *Size...* tile invokes the dialogue box shown in Figure 14-6. You can select from the list of available paper sizes handled by the configured device. User sizes within the maximum plot area can also be defined. The paper *Orientation* is indicated in the lower right (portrait is vertical, landscape is horizontal).

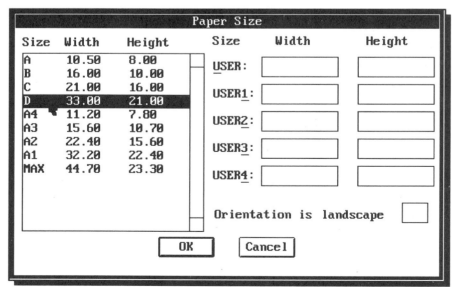

Figure 14-6

Scale, Rotation and Origin

Selecting the *Rotation and Origin...* tile invokes the dialogue box shown in Figure 14-7. The drawing can be rotated on the paper in 90 degree intervals. The origin specified indicates the location on the paper from point 0,0 (the plotter or printer's home position) from which the plot will be made. Home position for plotters is the <u>lower left</u> corner and for printers is the <u>upper left</u> corner.

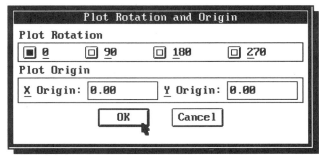

Figure 14-7

Scaled to Fit or Plot to Scale

Near the lower right corner of the *Plot Configuration* dialogue box (see Fig. 14-1) is the area where you designate the plot scale. You have two choices: scale the drawing to automatically fit on the paper or calculate and indicate a specific scale for the drawing to be plotted. By toggling the *Scaled to Fit* box, the drawing is automatically sized to fit on the sheet based on the specified area to plot (*Display, Limits, Extents,* etc.). If you want to plot the drawing to a specific scale, <u>remove the check</u> from the *Scaled to Fit* box and enter the desired ratio in the boxes under *Plotted Inches* and *Drawing Units*. Decimals or fractions can be entered. For example, to prepare for a plot of one-half size (1/2"=1"), the following ratios can be entered to achieve a plot at the desired scale: 1=2, 1/2=1, or .5=1. For guidelines on plotting a drawing to scale, see Plotting to Scale in this chapter.

Plot Preview

Selecting the *Partial* tile (see Fig. 14-1) displays the effective plotting area as shown in Figure 14-8. Use the *Partial* option of *Plot Preview* to get a quick check showing how the drawing will fit on the sheet. Two rectangles and two sets of dimensions are displayed; the "Paper size" is given and displayed in red and the "Effective area" is given and displayed in blue. The "Effective area" is based on the selection made in the *Additional Parameters* area of the plot dialogue, that is, *Display, Extents, Limits,* etc.

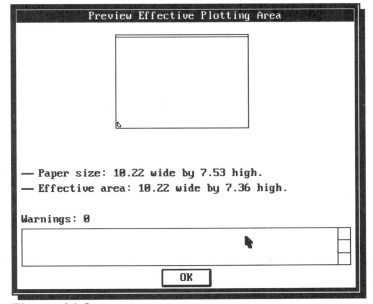

Figure 14-8

Selecting the *Full* option of *Plot Preview* displays the complete drawing as it will be plotted on the sheet (Fig. 14-9). This function is particularly helpful to insure the drawing is plotted as you expect. The white border represents the paper edge. As an additional aid, a *Pan and Zoom* option allows you to check detailed area of the drawing before making the plot. The *Pan and Zoom* option operates like the *Dynamic* option of the *Zoom* command. The *Plot Preview* pop-up can be relocated to an unobstructing location of the drawing by clicking on the title background as shown in Figure 14-9.

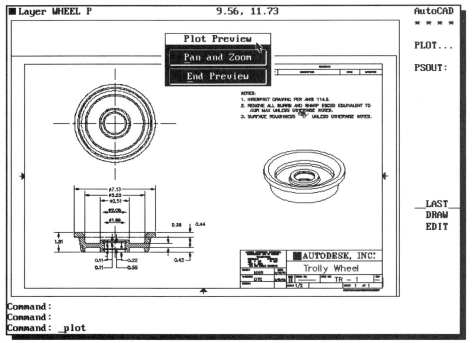

Figure 14-9

PLOTTING TO SCALE

For a full understanding of plotting to scale, let us review the ideas that were discussed in Chapter 13, Advanced Drawing Setup.

When you create a <u>manual</u> drawing, a scale is determined before you can begin drawing. The scale is determined by the proportion between paper size and the overall size (dimensions) of the object to be drawn. You then complete the drawing in that scale so that the resulting drawn object is proportionally reduced or enlarged to fit on the paper.

With a CAD drawing you are not restricted to a sheet of paper while drawing, so the geometry is created full size. Set *Limits* to provide an appropriate amount of drawing space, then the geometry can be drawn using the <u>actual dimensions</u> of the object. The resulting drawing on the CAD system is a virtual full-size dimensional replica of the actual object. Not until the CAD drawing is <u>plotted</u> on a fixed size sheet of paper, however, is it <u>scaled</u> to fit on the sheet.

Plotting an AutoCAD drawing to scale usually involves considering the intended plot scale when specifying *Limits* during the initial drawing setup. The scale for plotting is based on the proportion of the paper size to the *Limits* (the reciprocal of the "drawing scale factor").

For example, if you want to plot on an 11" x 8.5" sheet you can set the *Limits* to 22 x 17 (2 x the *Limits*). The value of **2** is then the drawing scale factor, and the plot scale (to enter in the *Plot Configuration* dialogue box) is **1/2** or **1=2** (the reciprocal of the drawing scale factor). If, in another case, the calculated drawing scale factor was **4**, then **1/4** or **1=4** would be the plot scale entered to achieve a drawing plotted at 1/4 actual size.

In order to calculate *Limits* and drawing scale factors correctly you must know the standard paper sizes.

Standard Paper Sizes

Size	Engineering (")	Architectural (")
A	8.5 x 11	9 X 12
B	11 x 17	12 x 18
C	17 x 22	18 x 24
D	22 x 34	24 x 36
E	34 x 44	36 x 48

Size	Metric (mm)
A4	210 x 297
A3	297 x 420
A2	420 x 594
A1	594 x 841
A0	841 x 1189

Guidelines for Plotting to Scale

Plotting to scale preferably begins with the appropriate initial drawing setup. Your choice for *Limits* determines the "drawing scale factor," which in turn is used to determine the plot scale. Even though *Limits* can be changed and plot scale calculated at <u>any time</u> in the drawing process, it is usually done in the first few steps. Following are suggested steps for setting up a drawing for plotting to scale.

1. Set *Units* (*Decimal, Architectural, Engineering*, etc.) and *precision* to be used in the drawing.

2. Set *Limits* to a size allowing geometry creation full size. *Limits* should be set to the sheet size used for plotting times a factor, if necessary, that provides enough area for drawing. This factor (proportion of the sheet size to the new *Limits*) becomes the

"drawing scale factor." You must also use a scale factor value that will yield a standard drawing scale (1/2"=1", 1/8"=1', 1:50, etc.), instead of a scale that is not a standard (1/3"=1", 3/5"=1', 1:23, etc.). See the Tables of Limit Settings for standard drawing scales.

3. The "drawing scale factor" is used as the scale factor (at least a starting point) for changing all size-related variables (*LTSCALE, DIMSCALE*, Hatch Pattern Scale, *Sketch Record Increment*, etc.). The reciprocal of the drawing scale factor is the plot scale to enter in the *Plot Configuration* dialogue box.

4. If the drawing is to be created using millimeter dimensions, set *Units* to *Decimal* and use metric values for the sheet size. In this way, the reciprocal of the drawing scale factor is the plot scale, the same as feet and inch drawings. However, multiply the drawing's drawing scale factor by 25.4 (25.4mm = 1") to determine the factor for changing all size-related variables (*LTSCALE, DIMSCALE,* etc.).

5. If drawing a border on the sheet, its maximum size cannot exceed the *Plot Area*. The *Plot Area* is given near the upper-right corner of the *Plot Configuration* dialogue box, but the values can be different for different devices. Since plotters do not draw all the way to the edge of the paper, the border should not be drawn outside of the *Plot Area*. Generally, approximately 1/2" offset from each edge of the paper is required. To determine the distance in from the edge of the *Limits* after new *Limits* have been set, multiply 1/2 times the "drawing scale factor." More precisely, calculate the distance based on the *Plot Area* listed for the current device and multiply by the "drawing scale factor."

The **Tables of Limit Settings** (starting on page 196) helps to illustrate this point. Sheet sizes are listed in the first column. The next series of columns from left to right indicates incremental changes in *Limits* and proportional changes in Scale Factor.

Simplifying the process of plotting to scale and calculating *Limits* and "drawing scale factor" can be accomplished by preparing prototype drawings. One method is to create a prototype for each sheet size that is used in the lab or office. In this way, the CAD operator begins the session by selecting the prototype drawing representing the sheet size and then multiples those *Limits* by some factor to achieve the desired *Limits* and drawing scale factor. Another method is to create a separate prototype drawing for each scale that you expect to use for plotting. In this way a prototype drawing can be selected with the final *Limits*, drawing scale factor, and plot scale already specified or calculated. This method requires creating a separate prototype for each expected scale and sheet size. (See Chapter 13 for help creating prototype drawings.)

Examples for Plotting to Scale

Following are several hypothetical examples of drawings that can be created using the previous steps for creating *Limits* and plotting to scale.

A. A one-view drawing of a mechanical part that is 40" in length is to be drawn requiring an area of approximately 40" x 30", and the drawing is to be plotted on an 8.5" x 11" sheet. The drawing *Limits* are set to **0,0** and **11,8.5**. (AutoCAD's default *Limits* are set to 0,0 and 12,9, which represents an uncut sheet size. Default _Limits_ of 11 x 8.5 are more practical in this case.) The expected plot scale is 1/4"=1". The following steps are used to calculate the new _Limits_.

1.   **Units** are set to **decimal**. Each unit represents 1.00 inches.
2.   Multiplying the _Limits_ of 11 x 8.5 by a factor of **4**, the new **Limits** should be set to **44 x 34**, allowing adequate space for the drawing. The "drawing scale factor" is **4**.
3.   All size-related variable default values (**LTSCALE, DIMSCALE**, etc.) are multiplied by **4**. The plot scale is entered in the **Plot Configuration** dialogue box (**Plotted inches = Drawing units**) as **1=4**, **1/4=1** or **.25=1** to achieve a plotted drawing of 1/4"=1".

B.   A floor plan of a residence will occupy 60' x 40'. The drawing is to be plotted on a "D" size architectural sheet (24" x 36"). No prepared default drawing exists, so the standard AutoCAD default drawing (12 x 9) _Limits_ are used. The expected plot scale is 1/2"=1'.

1.   **Units** are set to **Architectural**. Each unit represents 1".
2.   The floor plan size is converted to inches (60' x 40' = 720" x 480"). The sheet size of 36" x 24" (or 3' x 2') is multiplied by **24** to arrive at **Limits** of **864" x 576"** (72' x 48') allowing adequate area for the floor plan. The _Limits_ are changed to those values.
3.   All default values of size-related variables (**LTSCALE, DIMSCALE,** etc.) are multiplied by **24**, the drawing scale factor. The plot scale is entered in the **Plot Configuration** dialogue box (**Plotted inches = Drawing units**) as **1=24**, **1/2=12**, (12 units = 1') or **1/24=1** to achieve a drawing of 1/2"=1' scale.

C.   A roadway cloverleaf is to be laid out to fit in an acquired plot of land measuring 1500' x 1000'. The drawing will be plotted on "D" size engineering sheet (34" x 22"). A default drawing with _Limits_ set equal to the sheet size is used. The expected plot scale is 1"=50'.

1.   **Units** are set to **Engineering** (feet and decimal inches). Each unit represents 1.00".
2.   The sheet size of 34" x 22" (or 2.833' x 1.833') is multiplied by **600** to arrive at **Limits** of **20400" x 13200"** (1700' x 1100') allowing enough drawing area for the site. The _Limits_ are changed to **1700' x 1100'**.
3.   All default values of size-related variables (**LTSCALE, DIMSCALE**, etc.) are multiplied by **600**, the drawing scale factor. The plot scale is entered in the **Plot Configuration** dialogue box (**Plotted inches = Drawing units**) as **1=600** to achieve a drawing of 1"=50' scale.

D.   Three views of a small machine part are to be drawn and dimensioned in millimeters. An area of 480mm x 360mm is needed for the views and dimensions. The part is to be plotted on an A4 size sheet. The expected plot scale is 1:2.

1.   **Units** are set to **decimal**. Each unit represents 1.00 millimeters.
2.   Setting the _Limits_ exactly to the sheet size (297 x 210) would not allow enough area for the drawing. The sheet size is multiplied by a factor of **2** to yield **Limits** of **594 x 420** providing the necessary 480 x 360 area.

3. The plot scale entered in the ***Plot Configuration*** dialogue box (***Plotted inches = Drawing units***) is **1=2** or **1/2=1** to make a finished plot of 1:2 scale. Since this drawing is metric, the "drawing scale factor" for changing all size-related variable default values (**LTSCALE, DIMSCALE**, etc.) is multiplied by 25.4, or 2 x 25.4 = approximately **50**.

TABLES OF *LIMITS* SETTINGS

Rather than making calculations of *Limits*, drawing scale factor, and plot scale for each drawing, the Tables of Limits Settings on the following pages can be used to make calculating easier. There a four tables, one for each of the following applications:

Table	Page
Mechanical	**197**
Architectural	**198**
Metric	**199**
Civil	**200**

Each table is set up in the same configuration. The tables can be used in either of two ways:

1. **Scale**   Assuming you know the scale you want to use, look along the top row to find the desired scale that you eventually want to plot. Find the desired paper size by looking down the left column. The intersection of the row and column should yield the *Limits* settings to use to achieve the desired plot scale.

2. ***Limits***   Calculate how much space (minimum *Limits*) you require to create the drawing actual size. Look down the left column of the appropriate table to find the paper size you want to use for plotting. Look along that row to find the next larger *Limits* settings than your required area. The scale to use for the plot is located on top of that column.

MECHANICAL TABLE OF LIMITS SETTINGS
(X axis x Y axis)

Paper Size (Inches)	Drawing Scale Factor 1 / Scale 1"=1" / Plot 1=1	1.33 / 3"=4" / 3/4=1	2 / 1"=2" / 1/2=1	2.67 / 3"=8" / 3/8=1	4 / 1"=4" / 1/4=1	5.33 / 3"=16" / 3/16=1	8 / 1"=8" / 1=8
A 11 x 8.5 In	11.0 x 8.5	14.4 x 11.3	22.0 x 17.0	29.3 x 22.7	44.0 x 34.0	58.7 x 45.3	88.0 x 68.0
B 17 x 11 In	17.0 x 11.0	22.7 x 14.7	34.0 x 22.0	45.3 x 29.3	68.0 x 44.0	90.7 x 58.7	136.0 x 88.0
C 22 x 17 In	22.0 x 17.0	29.3 x 22.7	44.0 x 34.0	58.7 x 45.3	88.0 x 68.0	117.0 x 90.7	176.0 x 136.0
D 34 x 22 In	34.0 x 22.0	45.3 x 29.3	68.0 x 44.0	90.7 x 58.7	136.0 x 88.0	181.0 x 117.0	272.0 x 176.0
E 44 x 34 In	44.0 x 34.0	58.7 x 45.3	88.0 x 68.0	117.0 x 90.7	176.0 x 136.0	235.0 x 181.0	352.0 x 272.0

ARCHITECTURAL TABLE OF LIMITS SETTINGS
(X axis x Y axis)

Paper Size (Inches)		Drawing Scale Factor 12 Scale 1"=1' Plot 1=12	16 3/4"=1' 1=16	24 1/2"=1' 1=24	32 3/8"=1' 1=32	48 1/4"=1' 1=48	96 1/8"=1' 1=96
A 12 x 9	Ft	12 x 9	16.3 x 12	24 x 18	32 x 24	48 x 36	96 x 72
	In	144 x 108	192 x 144	288 x 216	384 x 288	576 x 432	1152 x 864
B 18 x 12	Ft	18 x 12	24 x 16	36 x 24	48 x 32	72 x 48	144 x 96
	In	216 x 144	288 x 192	432 x 288	576 x 384	864 x 576	1728 x 1152
C 24 x 18	Ft	24 x 18	32 x 24	48 x 36	64 x 48	96 x 72	192 x 144
	In	288 x 216	384 x 288	576 x 432	768 x 576	1152 x 864	2304 x 1728
D 36 x 24	Ft	36 x 24	48 x 32	72 x 48	96 x 64	144 x 96	288 x 192
	In	432 x 288	576 x 384	864 x 576	1152 x 768	1728 x 1152	3456 x 2304
E 48 x 36	Ft	48 x 36	64 x 48	96 x 72	128 x 96	192 x 144	384 x 288
	In	576 x 432	768 x 576	1152 x 864	1536 x 1152	2304 x 1728	4608 x 3465

METRIC TABLE OF LIMITS SETTING
(X axis x Y axis)

Paper Size (mm)		Drawing Scale Factor 25.4 — Scale 1:1 — Plot 1 = 1	50.8 — 1:2 — 1 = 2	127 — 1:5 — 1 = 5	254 — 1:10 — 1 = 10	508 — 1:20 — 1 = 20	1270 — 1:50 — 1 = 50	2540 — 1:100 — 1 = 100
A4 297 x 210	mm	297 x 210	594 x 420	1485 x 1050	2970 x 2100	5940 x 4200	14,850 x 10,500	29,700 x 21,000
	m	.297 x .210	.594 x .420	1.485 x 1.050	2.97 x 2.10	5.94 x 4.20	14.85 x 10.50	29.70 x 21.00
A3 420 x 297	mm	420 x 297	840 x 594	2100 x 1485	4200 x 2970	8400 x 5940	21,000 x 14,850	42,000 x 29,700
	m	.420 x .297	.840 x .594	2.100 x 1.485	4.20 x 2.97	8.40 x 5.94	21.00 x 14.85	42.00 x 29.70
A2 594 x 420	mm	594 x 420	1188 x 840	2970 x 2100	5940 x 4200	11,880 x 8400	29,700 x 21,000	59,400 x 42,000
	m	.594 x .420	1.188 x .840	2.970 x 2.100	5.94 x 4.20	11.88 x 8.40	29.70 x 21.00	59.40 x 42.00
A1 841 x 594	mm	841 x 594	1682 x 1188	4205 x 2970	8410 x 5940	16,820 x 11,880	42,050 x 29,700	84,100 x 59,400
	m	.841 x .594	1.682 x 1.188	4.205 x 2.970	8.41 x 5.94	16.82 x 11.88	42.05 x 29.70	84.10 x 59.40
A0 1189 x 841	mm	1189 x 841	2378 x 1682	5945 x 4205	11,890 x 8410	23,780 x 16,820	59,450 x 42,050	118,900 x 84,100
	m	1.189 x .841	2.378 x 1.682	5.945 x 4.205	11.89 x 8.41	23.78 x 16.82	59.45 x 42.05	118.9 x 84.10

CIVIL TABLE OF LIMITS SETTINGS
(X axis x Y axis)

Paper Size (Inches)		Drawing Scale Factor 120 Scale 1" = 10' Plot 1 = 120	240 1" = 20' 1 = 240	360 1" = 30' 1 = 360	480 1" = 40' 1 = 480	600 1" = 50' 1 = 600
A. 11 x 8½	In	1320 x 1020	2640 x 2040	3960 x 3060	5280 x 4080	6600 x 5100
	Ft	110 x 85	170 x 110	330 x 255	440 x 340	550 x 425
B. 17 x 11	In	2040 x 1320	4080 x 2640	6120 x 3960	8160 x 5280	10,200 x 6600
	Ft	170 x 110	340 x 220	510 x 330	680 x 440	850 x 550
C. 22 x 17	In	2640 x 2040	5280 x 4080	7920 x 6120	10,560 x 8160	13,200 x 10,200
	Ft	220 x 170	440 x 340	660 x 510	880 x 680	1100 x 850
D. 34 x 22	In	4080 x 2640	8160 x 5280	12,240 x 7920	16,320 x 10,560	20,400 x 13,200
	Ft	340 x 220	680 x 440	1020 x 660	1360 x 880	1700 x 1100
E. 44 x 34	In	5280 x 4080	10,560 x 8160	15,840 x 12,240	21,120 x 16,320	26,400 x 20,400
	Ft	440 x 340	880 x 680	1320 x 1020	1760 x 1360	2200 x 1700

CHAPTER EXERCISES

1.   **Open** the drawing you created in the exercises from Chapter 12 called **CH12EX3**.
     Check to insure that the drawing _Limits_ are set at **0,0** and **12,9**. Now, make a **Plot** on
     an 11" x 8.5" sheet. Plot the drawing **Limits**. Select the **Scaled to Fit** box. When the
     plot is finished, use a drafting scale to measure the lengths and compare them to the
     dimensions given in the Chapter 12 Exercises. Are the plotted dimensions accurate? If
     not, why? **Save** your changes.

2.   **Open** the drawing **GASKETA** that you created for the exercises after Chapters 8 and 9.
     What are the drawing _Limits_?

A.   **Plot** the drawing **Extents** on an 11" x 8.5" sheet. Select the **Scale to Fit** box.
B.   Next, **Plot** the drawing **Limits** on the same size sheet. **Scale to Fit**.
C.   Now, **Plot** the drawing **Limits** as before but plot the drawing at **1=1**. Measure the
     drawing and compare the accuracy with the dimensions given in the exercises in
     Chapters 8 and 9.
D.   Compare the three plots. What are the differences and why did they occur? (When you
     finish, there is no need to _Save Changes._)

3.   **Open** the drawing **GASKETB** that you created for an exercise after Chapter 10.

A.   **Plot** the drawing **Extents** at a **1=1** scale.
B.   When the first plot is complete, **Erase** the border and **Plot** the drawing **Extents** again at
     1=1.
C.   With the border erased, **Plot** the drawing **Limits** at **1=1**.
D.   Compare the three plots. Can you explain the differences?

4.   This exercise requires facilities for plotting an engineering "C" size sheet. **Open** drawing
     CH12EX4. Check to insure the **Limits** are set at **17 x 11**. **Plot** the **Limits** at **1=1**.
     Measure the plot for accuracy by comparing with the dimensions given for the exercise
     in Chapter 12. To refresh your memory, this exercise involved adjusting the _LTSCALE_
     factor. Does the _LTSCALE_ in the drawing yield hidden line dashes of 1/8" on the plot?
     If not, make the **LTSCALE** adjustment and plot again.

5.   For this exercise you will use a previously created prototype drawing to set up a drawing
     for plotting to scale. (The drawing will be used in later chapters for creating geometry.)
     If you know the final plot scale and sheet size, you can plan for the plot during the
     drawing setup. The _Limits_ and other scale related factors for plotting can be set at this
     phase. Follow the steps below.

     A drawing of a hammer is needed. The overall dimensions of the hammer are 12½" x
     about 5". The drawing will be plotted on an 11" x 8.5" sheet. **Open** the prototype
     ASHEET and assign the name **HAMMER**. Follow the steps on the next page.

A. Set *Units* to *Fractional* and *Precision* to **1/16**.
B. Set *Snap* to **1/8** (or .125).
C. Set *Grid* to **1/2** (or .5).
D. Since the geometry will not fit within *Limits* of 11 x 8.5, plotting at full size (1=1) will not be possible. In order to make a plot to a standard scale and show the geometry at the largest possible size on an 11" x 8.5" sheet, consult the table of Mechanical Limits Settings to determine *Limits* settings for the drawing and a scale for plotting. Find the values for setting *Limits* for a plot at **3/4=1** scale. Set *Limits* appropriately, then *Zoom All*.
E. An *LTSCALE* of .5 (previously set) creates hidden lines with the 1/8" standard dashes when plotted at 1=1. Therefore, multiply the *LTSCALE* of .5 times the scale factor indicated in the table.
F. *Save* the drawing.

6. Create a new prototype for architectural applications to plot at 1/8"=1' scale on a "D" size sheet. Open the prototype **DSHEET** and assign the name **D-8-AR**. Set *Units* to *Architectural*. Use the Architectural Table of Limits Settings to determine and set the new *Limits* for a "D" size sheet to plot at **1/8"=1'**. Multiply the existing *LTSCALE* times the scale factor shown. Turn *Snap* and *Grid* Off. *Save* the drawing.

7. Create a new prototype for metric applications to plot at 1:2 scale (1/2 size) on an "A4" size sheet. Open the prototype **ASHEET** and assign the name **A-2-M**. Use the Metric Table of Limit Settings to determine and set the new *Limits* for an "A4" size sheet to plot at **1=2**. Multiply the existing *LTSCALE*, *Snap*, and *Grid* times the scale factor shown. *Save* the drawing.

8. Create a new prototype for civil engineering applications to plot at 1"=20' scale on a "C" size sheet. Open the prototype **CSHEET** and assign the name **C-20-CV**. Set *Units* to *Engineering*. Use the Civil Table of Limits Settings to determine and set the new *Limits* for a "C" size sheet to plot at **1"=20'**. Multiply the existing *LTSCALE* times the scale factor shown. Turn *Snap* and *Grid* Off. *Save* the drawing.

9. *Open* drawing **CH10EX2**. Check to make sure that the *Limit* settings are at **0,0** and **40',30'**. Make two plots of this drawing on your plotter, according to the instructions.

A. Make one plot of the drawing using a standard architectural scale. The scale you use is your choice and should be based upon the sheet sizes available as well as the existing geometry size. *Plot* the drawing *Limits*. You may have to alter the *Limits* in order to plot the *Limits* to a standard scale. Use the Architectural Table of Limits settings for guidance.

B. Make one plot of the drawing using a standard civil engineering scale. Again, the choice of scale is yours and should be based on your available sheet sizes as well as the existing geometry. *Plot* the drawing *Limits*. You may have to alter the *Limits* for this plot also in order to plot the *Limits* to a standard scale. Use the Civil Table of Limits Settings for guidance.

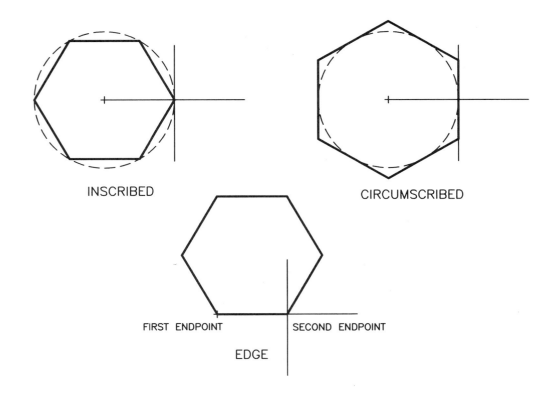

INSCRIBED

CIRCUMSCRIBED

FIRST ENDPOINT   SECOND ENDPOINT

EDGE

CHAPTER 15

Draw Commands II

CHAPTER OBJECTIVES

After completing this chapter you should:

1.   be able to create *Plines* using all of the options;

2.   be able to create *Polygons* by the *Circumscribe, Inscribe,* and *Edge* methods;

3.   be able to create *Ellipses* using the *Two Axes* method, the *Center, Axes* method, and the *Rotation* method;

4.   be able to create double lines and arcs using the *Dline* command;

5.   be able to use *Donut* to create circles with width.

6.   be able to use the *Sketch* command to create "freehand" sketch lines.

7.   be able to use the *SKPOLY* variable to create *Sketch* lines composed of one *Polyline* entity.

BASICS

The draw commands addressed in this chapter create shapes that appear to be composed of several entities, but each shape is actually treated by AutoCAD as <u>one</u> entity.

Pline, Polygon, Ellipse, Dline, Donut

The *Sketch* command creates what appears to be one entity, but is actually many short *Line* entities by default. The *SKPOLY* variable can be set to create a *Pline* instead of many *Line* entities.

COMMANDS

PLINE or POLYLINE

TYPE IN:	PULL-DOWN MENU	SCREEN MENU	TABLET MENU
PLINE or PL	*Draw, Polyline*	*DRAW, PLINE:*	*10,K*

A *Polyline* has special features that make this entity more versatile than a *Line*. There are three features that are most noticeable when first using *Pline*s:

1. A *Pline* can have a specified *width*; whereas, a *Line* has no width.

2. Several *Pline* segments created with one *Pline* command are treated by AutoCAD as <u>one</u> entity; whereas, individual line segments created with one use of the *Line* command are individual entities.

3. A *Pline* can contain arc segments.

Figure 15-1 illustrates *Pline* vs. *Line* and *Arc* comparisons.

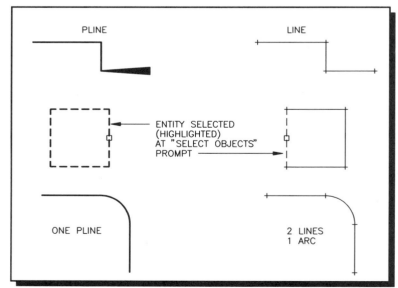

Figure 15-1

The *Pline* command begins with the same prompt as *Line*; however, <u>after</u> the "From point" is established, the *Pline* options are accessible.

> Command: ***pline***
> From point: **PICK** or (**coordinates**) (Select the first point of the *Pline* interactively or enter coordinate values in any format.)
> Arc/Close/Halfwidth/Length/Undo/Width/<Endpoint of Line>:
> **PICK** or (**coordinates**) or (**letter**) (Select the endpoint of the *Pline* interactively, or enter coordinate values in any format or select an option by entering the first letter of the option or by selecting from screen menu.)

The options and descriptions are listed below.

Width

You can use this option to specify starting and ending widths. Width is measured perpendicular to the centerline of the *Pline* segment (Fig. 15-2). *Plines* can be tapered by specifying different starting and ending widths.

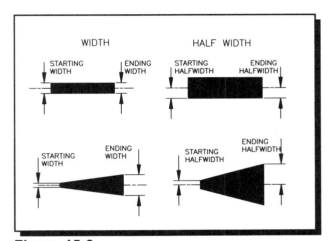

Halfwidth

This option allows specifying half of the *Pline* width. *Plines* can be tapered by specifying different starting and ending widths. (See Figure 15-2.)

Figure 15-2

Arc

This option creates an arc segment in a manner similar to the *Arc Continuous* method by default (see *ARC Contin* in Chapter 8). Any of several other methods are possible (see Polygon Arc Segments , next page).

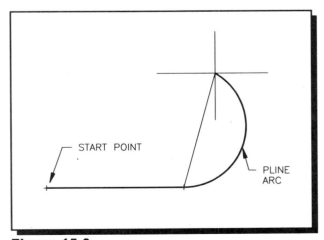

Figure 15-3

Close

The *Close* option creates the closing segment connecting the first and last points specified with the current *Pline* command as shown in Figure 15-4.

This option can also be used to close a group of *Pline* segments into one continuous *Pline* without specific start and endpoints. (A *Pline* closed by PICKing points has a specific start and end point.) A *Pline Closed* by this method has special properties if you use *Pedit* for *Pline* editing or if you use the *Fillet* command with the *Pline* option (see *Pedit* Chapter 15 and *Fillet* Chapter 16).

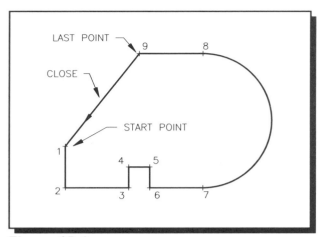

Figure 15-4

Length

Length draws a *Pline* segment at the same angle as, and connected to, the previous segment and using a length that you specify. If the previous segment was an arc, *Length* makes the current segment tangent to the ending direction. See Figure 15-5.

Undo

Using this option will *Undo* the last *Pline* segment. It can be used repeatedly to undo multiple segments.

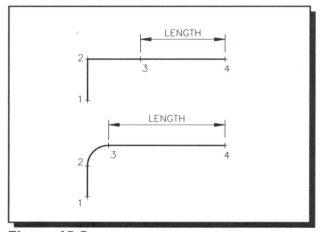

Figure 15-5

Polyline Arc Segments

When the *Arc* option of *Pline* is selected, the prompt changes to provide the various methods for construction of arcs:

```
Angle/CEnter/CLose/Direction/Halfwidth/Line/Radius/
Second pt/Undo/Width/<Endpoint of Arc>:
```

Angle

You can draw an arc segment by specifying the included angle (a negative value indicates a clockwise direction for arc generation).

CEnter

This option allows you to specify a specific center point for the arc segment.

CLose

This option closes the *Pline* group with an arc segment.

Direction

Direction allows you to specify an explicit starting direction rather than using the ending direction of the previous segment as a default.

Line

This switches back to the line options of the *Pline* command.

Radius

You can specify an arc radius using this option.

Second pt

Using this option allows specification of the 3-point arc option.

Because a shape created with one *Pline* command is <u>one entity</u>, manipulation of the shape is generally easier than with several entities. *Plines* also have other advantages over *Lines* and *Arcs* related to editing discussed later. Editing *Plines* is accomplished by using the *Pedit* command. As an alternative, *Plines* can be "broken" back down into individual entities with *Explode*. (*Pedit* and *Explode* are discussed in the next chapter).

Drawing and editing *Plines* can be somewhat involved. As an alternative you can draw a shape as you would normally with *Line*, *Circle*, *Arc*, *Trim*, etc., and then <u>convert</u> the shape to one *Pline* entity using *Pedit*. (See Chapter 16 for details.)

POLYGON

TYPE IN:	PULL-DOWN MENU	SCREEN MENU	TABLET MENU
POLYGON	*Draw, Polygon >*	*DRAW, POLYGON:*	*10,O*

The *Polygon* command creates a regular polygon (all angles are equal and all sides have equal length). A *Polygon* entity appears to be several individual entities but, like a *Pline*, is actually <u>one</u> entity. In fact, AutoCAD uses *Pline* to create a *Polygon*. There are two basic options for creating *Polygons*. You can specify an *Edge* (length of one side or specify the size of an imaginary circle for the *Polygon* to *Inscribe* or *Circumscribe*.

Edge

The command sequence for this default method follows:

```
Command: polygon
Number of sides: (value) (Enter a value for the number of sides.)
Edge/<Center of polygon>: PICK or (coordinates) or E (Select the center
point for the Polygon interactively or enter coordinate values in any format.
Inscribed in circle/Circumscribed about circle: I or C (select
inscribe or circumscribe option.)
Radius of circle: PICK or (value) or (coordinates) (Interactively PICK the
radius length and direction or enter a value for the radius. A direction can be specified
by entering relative polar or relative rectangular coordinates.)
```

The orientation of the *Polygon* and the imaginary circle is shown in Figure 15-6. A hexagon (6 sides) is used in the example. Note that the *Inscribed* option allows control of one half of the distance <u>across the flats</u>, and the *circumscribed* option allows control of one half of the distance <u>across the corners</u>.

Using *ORTHO ON* with specification of the *radius of circle* forces the *Polygon* to a 90 degree orientation.

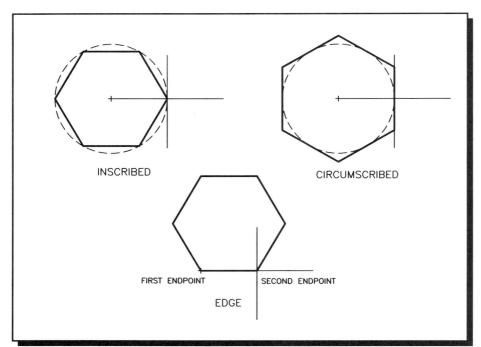

INSCRIBED

CIRCUMSCRIBED

FIRST ENDPOINT   SECOND ENDPOINT

EDGE

Figure 15-6

Edge

The *Edge* option only requires you to indicate the of number of sides desired and to specify the endpoints of one edge (Fig. 15-6).

```
Command: polygon
Number of sides: (value) (Enter a value for the number of sides.)
Edge/<Center of polygon>: E (Invokes the edge option.)
First endpoint of edge: PICK or (coordinates) (Interactively select
or enter coordinates in any format.)
Second endpoint of edge: PICK or (coordinates) (Interactively select
or enter coordinates in any format.)
```

Because *Polygons* are created as *Plines*, *Pedit* can be used to change the line width or edit the shape in some way (see *Pedit*, Chapter 16). *Polygons* can also be *Exploded* into individual entities similar to the way other *Plines* can be broken down into component entities (see *Explode*, Chapter 16).

ELLIPSE

TYPE IN:	PULL-DOWN MENU	SCREEN MENU	TABLET MENU
ELLIPSE	*Draw, Ellipse >*	*DRAW, ELLIPSE:*	*10,N*

An *Ellipse* is one entity. In fact, AutoCAD *Ellipses* are actually composed of many *Pline* segments. There are three methods of creating *Ellipses* in AutoCAD: (1) specify the length of the two axes or (2) specify the center point and the axes. Each of these two methods also permits (3) supplying a rotation angle rather than the second axis length. (The *Ellipse* command provides a method for creating isometric ellipses. This method is only available if an Isometric *SNAP* has been designated by using the *Snap* command. See Chapter 25, Pictorial Drawing, for more information on isometric ellipses.)

Command: *ellipse*
<Axis endpoint 1>/Center: **PICK** or (**coordinates**) (Select a point interactively or by entering coordinates in any format. This is the first endpoint of either the major or minor ellipse.)
Axis endpoint 2: **PICK** or (**coordinates**) (Select a point for the other axis endpoint.)
<Other axis distance>/Rotation: **PICK** or (**coordinates**) (Select a point defining the distance from the established center to the other axis endpoint. This distance is measured perpendicularly from the established axis.)

Two Axes
This default option requires PICKing three points as indicated (see the command syntax above). A few possible results of the **two axis** method are shown in Figure 15-7.

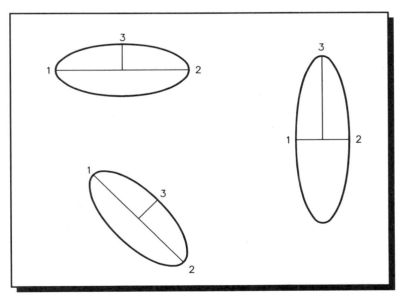

Figure 15-7

Rotation
If the **Rotation** option is used with the two axis method, the following syntax is used:

<Other axis distance>/Rotation: **R** (Invokes the rotation option.)
Rotation around major axis: **PICK** or (**value**) (Indicate the angle for rotation <u>from</u> the 90 degree (circular) position by interactive selection or by entering a value.)

Figure 15-8 illustrates using the *Rotation* option after specifying the two endpoints for axis 1 (follow the command sequence from the previous page). The specified angle is the number of degrees the shape is rotated <u>from the circular position</u>.

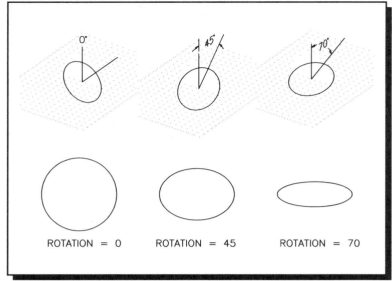

ROTATION = 0   ROTATION = 45   ROTATION = 70

Figure 15-8

Center, Axes

With many practical applications, the center point of the ellipse is known, and therefore the *Center* option should be used (Fig. 15-9).

Command: ***ellipse***
<Axis endpoint 1>/Center: **C** (Invokes *Center* option.)
Center of ellipse: **PICK** or (**coordinates**) (Select a point for the center by interactive selection or by entering coordinates.)
Axis endpoint: **PICK** or (**coordinates**) (Select a point defining the location of either axis endpoint. This point defines the endpoint of either the minor or major axis.)
<Other axis distance>/Rotation: **PICK** or (**coordinates**) (Select a point defining the distance from the established center to the other axis endpoint. This distance is measured perpendicularly from established axis.)

Figure 15-9 illustrates the *Center, Axis* option of the *Ellipse* command.

The **Rotation** option appears and can be after specifying the *Center* and first *Axis endpoint.* The results are similar to those described earlier in Figure 15-8.

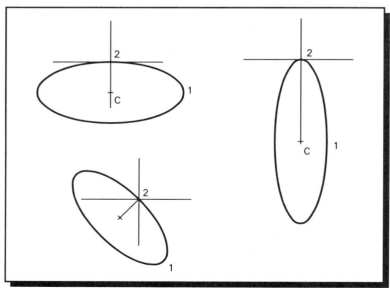

Figure 15-9

DLINE

TYPE IN:	PULL-DOWN MENU	SCREEN MENU	TABLET MENU
DLINE	_Draw, Line >_ _Double Lines_	---	---

The _Dline_ command is an AutoLISP application that allows you to draw continuous double lines using line and and arc segments. This command can be used effectively for drawing shapes requiring parallel lines indicating thickness, such as walls in a floor plan (Fig. 15-10). _Dline_ allows _Snap_ping to existing _Dlines_ without using the traditional _OSNAP_ options and automatically executes the equivalent of a _Trim_ or _Extend_ to "clean up" the intersections.

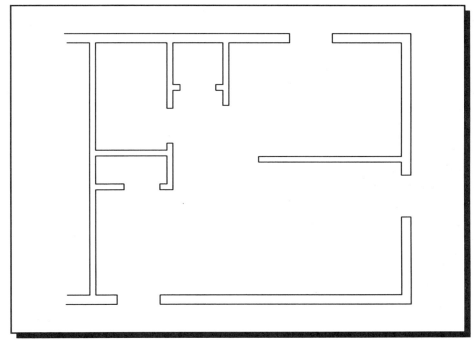

Figure 15-10

Many options are available including adjusting the width, capping the line ends, and breaking the double lines at intersections. As with all AutoCAD commands, the options appear at the command line:

```
Command: dline
Break/Caps/Dragline/Offset/Snap/Undo/Width/<Start point>:
PICK or (coordinates) or (option)
```

The options are:

Width

> This option sets the _Width_ of the _Dline_ measured perpendicular to the line center from one leg to the other. This option operates similar to the _Width_ option of _Pline_.

Dragline

By default, *Dline* uses the PICK points as the center of the *Dline*. *Dragline* allows you to offset the PICK points from the exact center of the *Dline*. The *Right* option sets the <u>PICK points</u> to the right line of the *Dline* and the *Left* option sets the <u>PICK points</u> on the left line. (Right and left are determined by looking from the start point to the end point of the *Dline*.) If you enter a positive value, the PICK points are offset to the right of center by that amount, while a negative number offsets to the left.

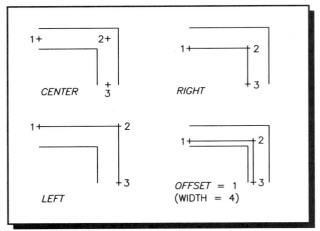

Figure 15-11

Caps

Caps determines which endcaps to draw:

```
Both/End/None/
Start/<Auto>:
```
(both ends, the last end, none, the starting end, or automatically cap all ends not snapped to other *Dlines* only).

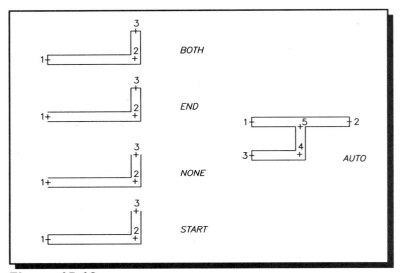

Figure 15-12

Break

This option breaks a gap at the intersection when snapping to another *Dline*. (If the *Snap* option is *On*, the specified endpoint will "snap" to another *Dline* automatically.)

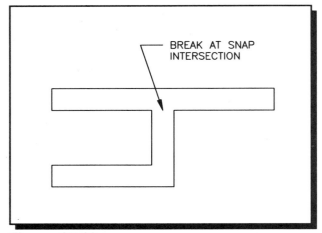

Figure 15-13

Snap

Enables or disables snapping a *Dline* to an existing entity.

```
Set snap size or On/Off
Size/OFF/<ON>:
```

The *Size* option sets the area from the crosshairs (in pixels) that is searched for entities for snapping. Figure 15-14 illustrates the effect of *Snap On*.

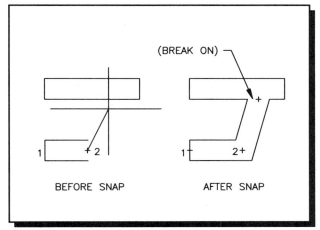

Figure 15-14

Offset

Offset allows you to locate the start of the *Dline* at a specified distance and direction from a base point. You are prompted for the base point, then the direction, and finally the distance:

```
Offset from: PICK (Select base
point)
Offset from: PICK (Select
direction)
Enter the offset distance
<current>: (value) (Enter a value)
```

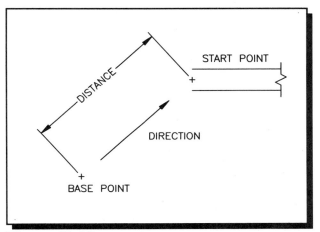

Figure 15-15

Arc

The *Arc* option appears after PICKing the *<start point>:*. Entering *A* for *Arc*, you can then draw doulble line arcs with the default 3 point method (*start point, second point, endpoint*), *CEnter* method, or *Endpoint* method. Entering *CEnter* or *Endpoint* offer several other suboptions, similar to the operation of the normal *Arc* command. Figure 15-16 displays the default (3 point) and the *CEnter* option.

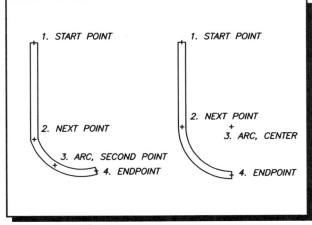

Figure 15-16

Undo

This option will *Undo* the previous *Dline* segment before it has been closed or ended.

DONUT or DOUGHNUT

TYPE IN:	PULL-DOWN MENU	SCREEN MENU	TABLET MENU
DONUT or DOUGHNUT	**Draw, Donut**	**DRAW, DONUT:**	**10,Q**

A _Donut_ is a circle with width (Fig. 15-17). Invoking the command allows changing the inside and outside diameters and creating multiple _Donuts_.

Command: **donut**
Inside diameter <current>: (**value**) or **Enter** (Enter a value for the inside diameter or press Enter to accept the default value.)
Outside diameter <current>: (**value**) or **Enter** (Enter a value for the outside diameter or press Enter to accept the default value.)
Center of doughnut: **PICK** or (**coordinates**) (Select location for donut.)
Center of doughnut: **PICK** or (**coordinates**) or **Enter** (Select location for another donut or press Enter to end command.)

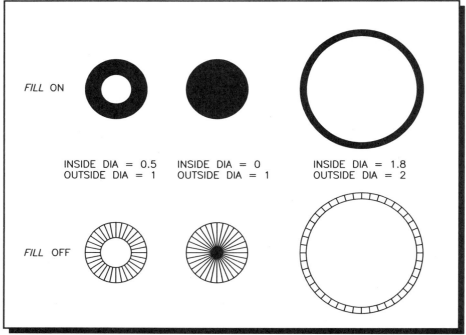

Figure 15-17

_Donut_s are actually solid filled circular _Plines_ with width. The solid fill for _Donut_s, _Plines_, and other "solid" entities can be turned off with the _Fill_ command (see Chapter 31).

SKETCH

TYPE IN:	PULL-DOWN MENU	SCREEN MENU	TABLET MENU
SKETCH	*Draw, Line > Sketch*	*DRAW, SKETCH:*	---

The *Sketch* command is unlike other draw commands. *Sketch* quickly creates many short line segments (individual entities) by following the motions of the cursor. *Sketch* is used to give the appearance of a freehand line, as used in Figure 15-18 for the tree and bushes. You do not specify individual endpoints, but rather draw a "freehand line" by placing the "pen" down, moving the cursor, and then picking up the "pen." This action creates a large number of short *Line* segments. CAUTION: *Sketch* can increase the drawing file size greatly due to the relatively large number of line segment endpoints required to define the *Sketch* "line."

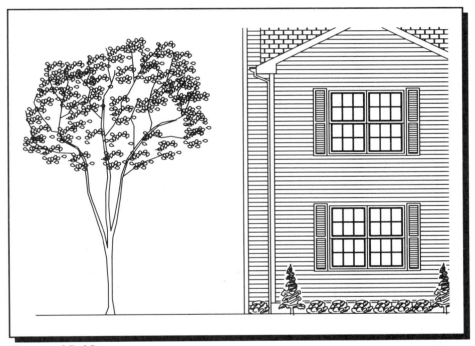

Figure 15-18

The following command prompt is displayed when using *Sketch*.

        Command: *sketch*
        Record increment <0.1000>: (value) or **Enter** (Enter a value to specify the segment increment length or press Enter to accept the default increment.)
        Sketch. Pen eXit Quit Record Erase Connect . (letter) (Enter "p" or press button #1 to put the pen down and begin drawing or enter another letter for another option. After drawing a sketch line, enter "p" or press button #1 again to pick the pen up.)

It is important to specify an *increment* length for the short line segments that are created. This *increment* controls the "resolution" of the *Sketch* line.

Too large of an *increment* makes the straight line segments apparent, while too small of an *increment* unnecessarily increases file size. The default *increment* is 0.1 (appropriate for default *Limits* of 12 x 9) and should be changed proportionally with a change in *Limits*. Generally, multiply the default *increment* of 0.1 times the "drawing scale factor" (Chapters 13, 14).

Another important rule to consider whenever using *Sketch* is to turn *SNAP* and *ORTHO OFF*, unless a "stair-step" effect is desired.

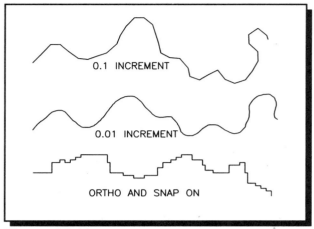

Figure 15-19

Sketch Options

Options of the *Sketch* command can be activated either by entering the corresponding letter(s) shown in uppercase at the *Sketch* command prompt or by pressing the desired mouse or puck button (described below). For example, putting the "pen" up or down can be done by entering **P** at the command line or by pressing button #1. The options of *Sketch* are as follows.

Option	Button	Function
Pen	1	Lifts and lowers the pen. Position the cursor at the desired location to begin the line. Lower the pen and draw. Raise the pen when finished with the line.
Record	2	Records all temporary lines sketched so far without changing the pen position. After recording, the lines cannot be *Erased* with the *Erase* option of *Sketch* (although the normal *Erase* command can be used).
eXit	3	Records all temporary lines entered and returns to the Command: prompt.
Quit	4	Discards all temporary lines and returns to the Command: prompt.
Erase	5	Allows selective erasing of temporary lines (before recording). To erase, move backwards from last sketch line toward the first. Press "p" to indicate the end of an erased area. This method works easily for relatively straight sections. To erase complex sketch lines, *eXit* and use the normal *Erase* command with window, crossing, or pickbox object selection.
Connect	6	Allows connection to the end of the <u>last</u> temporary sketch line (before recording). Move to the last sketch line and the pen is automatically lowered.
.(period)		Draws a straight line (using *Line*) from the last sketched line to the cursor. After adding the straight line the pen returns to the up position.

Several options are illustrated in Figure 15-20. The *Pen* option puts the pen up and down. A *period* (.) causes a straight line segment to be drawn from the last segment to the cursor location. *Erase* is accomplished by entering *E* and making a reverse motion.

As an alternative to the *erase* option of *Sketch*, the *Erase* command can be used to erase all or part of the *Sketch* lines. Using a *Window* or *Crossing Window* is suggested to make selection of all the entities easier.

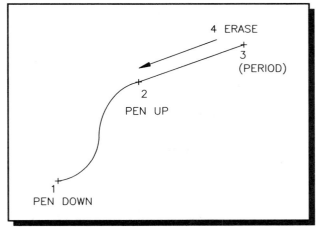

Figure 15-20

The *SKPOLY* Variable

The *SKPOLY* system variable controls whether AutoCAD creates connected *Sketch* line segments as one *Pline* (one entity) or as multiple *Line* segments (separate entities). *SKPOLY* affects newly created *Sketch* lines only.

SKPOLY=0   This setting generates *Sketch* segments as individual *Line* entities. This is the default setting.

SKPOLY=1   This setting generates connected *Sketch* segments as one *Pline* entity.

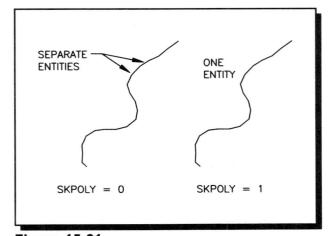

Figure 15-21

Using editing commands with *Sketch* lines can normally be tedious (when *SKPOLY* is set to the default value). In this case, editing *Sketch* lines usually requires *Zooming* in since the straight line segments are relatively small. However, changing *SKPOLY* to 1 simplifies editing such as using *Erase* or *Trim*. For example, *Sketch* lines are often used to draw break lines (Fig. 15-22) or to represent broken sections of mechanical parts, in which case use of *Trim* is very helpful. If you expect to use *Trim* or other editing commands with *Sketch* lines, change *SKPOLY* to 1 before creating the *Sketch* lines.

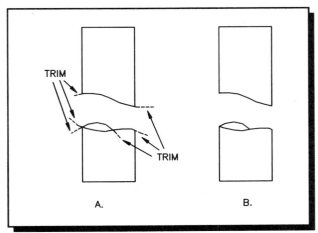

Figure 15-22

CHAPTER EXERCISES

1. *Pline*

A.   *Open* the **ASHEET** drawing. Draw a border measuring **10** x **7.5** units (starting at coordinate **.5,.5**). Construct the border from a *Pline* of **.02** *width*. Also construct a title block using a *Pline* of **.02** *width* for the outside edges and *Lines* for the inside edges. Provide space in the title block for the following text items:

> Name of company or school
> Name of drafter or designer
> Name of checker or instructor
> Name or number of project or part
> Date of completion
> Scale

The title block design can be one of your own, or you can refer to your engineering graphics or architectural drawing reference book for standard title block examples and dimensions. *Saveas* and assign the name **A-BORDER**.

B.   *Open* drawing **BSHEET** and construct a title block and border as in exercise 1A. Allow a **.5** unit margin from the *Limits* on all sides. Use a *Pline* width of **.03**. *Saveas* and assign the name **B-BORDER**.

C.   *Open* drawing **CSHEET** and construct a title block and border as in the previous exercises; however, this time use a *Pline* width of **.04**. *Saveas* and assign the name **C-BORDER**.

D.   *Open* the **DSHEET** drawing and create a tile block and border as before. Use a *Pline* *width* of **.05**. *Saveas* D-BORDER.

2. *Pline, Polygon*

Create the shape shown in Figure 15-23. Draw the outside shape with <u>one continuous</u> *Pline* (with 0.00 width). Use *Polygon* for the hexagon. When finished, *Saveas* **CH15EX2**.

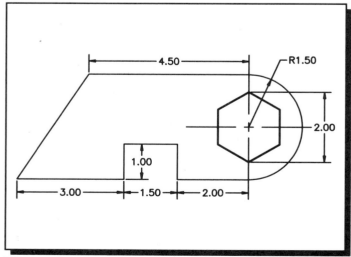

Figure 15-23

3. ***Dline, Ellipse***

    Open the **APARTMNT** drawing that you created in Chapter 13. Draw the floor plan of the efficiency apartment on layer FLOORPLAN as shown in Figure 15-24. Use ***Saveas*** to assign the name **EFF-APT**. Use ***Dline*** with 8" width for the exterior walls and 5" for interior walls. Use the ***Ellipse*** and ***Line*** commands to design and construct the kitchen sink, tub, wash basin, and toilet. ***Save*** the drawing but do not exit.

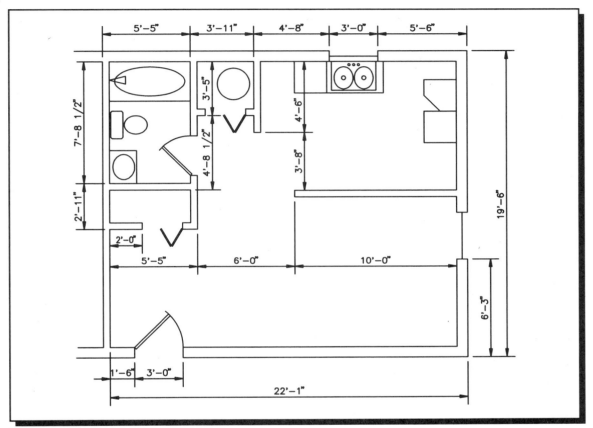

Figure 15-24

4. ***Polygon, Sketch***

    Create a plant for the efficiency apartment as shown in Figure 15-25. Locate the plant near the entry. The plant is in a hexagonal pot (use ***Polygon***) measuring 18" across the corners. Use ***Sketch*** to create 2 leaves as shown in figure A. Create a ***Polar Array*** to develop the other leaves similar to figure B. ***Save*** the **EFF-APT** drawing.

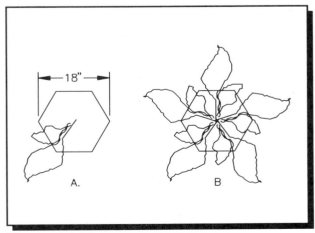

Figure 15-25

5. *Pline, Donut*

Open the **A-BORDER** drawing. Use the *Saveas* command and assign the new name of **PCB**. Construct the printed circuit board layout shown in Figure 15-26. Set *SNAP* to **.125**. Construct the layout using *Plines* with *width* of **.01** and *Donuts* with an *inside diameter* of **.01** and an *outside diameter* of **.02**. (Spacing between *Plines* is .125.)

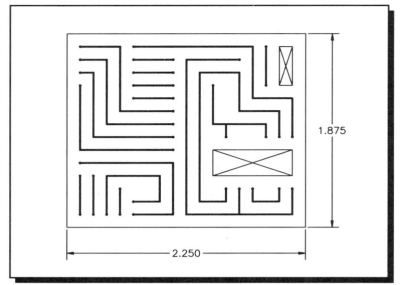

Figure 15-26

6. *Open* the drawing that you set up in Chapter 13 named **WRENCH**. Complete the construction of the Wrench shown in Figure 15-27. Center the drawing within the *Limits*. Use *Line*, *Circle*, *Arc*, *Ellipse*, *Polygon*, and *Sketch* to create the shape. Utilize *Trim*, *Rotate*, and other edit commands where necessary. HINT: Draw the wrench head in an orthogonal position, then rotate the entire shape 15°. *Save* the drawing when completed.

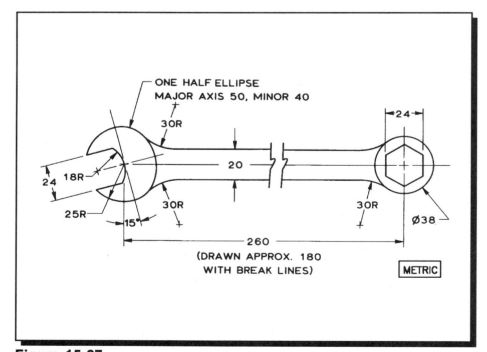

Figure 15-27

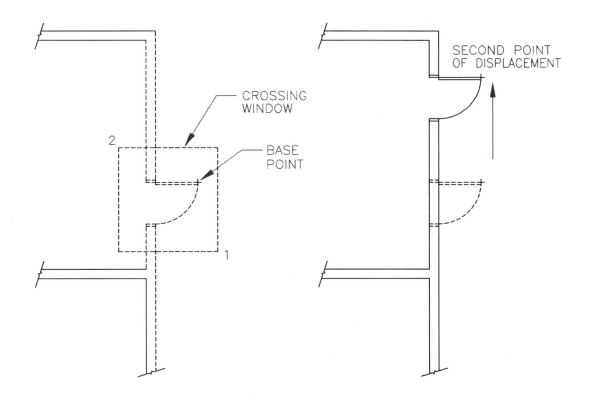

CHAPTER 16

Modify Commands II

CHAPTER OBJECTIVES

After completing this chapter you should:

1.   be able to *Stretch* selected entities;

2.   be able to *Align* entities with other entities;

3.   be able to use *Chprop* to change an entity's layer, color, and linetype properties;

4.   know how to use *Change* to change points or properties;

5.   be able to use the *Modify* dialogue box to modify any type of entity;

6.   be able to *Explode* a *Pline* or *Polygon* into its component entities and to know that *Explode* can be used with *Blocks* and other composite shapes;

7.   be able to use all the *Pedit* options to edit *Plines*;

8.   be able to convert *Lines* and *Arcs* to *Plines* using *Pedit*.

BASICS

This chapter examines commands that are used to modify existing entities. These commands are similar to, but generally more advanced and powerful than, those discussed in Chapter 9, Modify Commands I.

COMMANDS

STRETCH

TYPE IN:	PULL-DOWN MENU	SCREEN MENU	TABLET MENU
STRETCH	*Modify, Stretch*	*EDIT, STRETCH:*	*17,X*

Entities can be made longer or shorter with *Stretch*. The power of this command lies in the ability to *Stretch* groups of entities while retaining the connectivity of the group (Fig. 16-1). When *stretched*, *Lines* and *Plines* become longer or shorter and *Arcs* change radius to become longer or shorter. *Circles* do not stretch, rather they move if the center is selected within the crossing window.

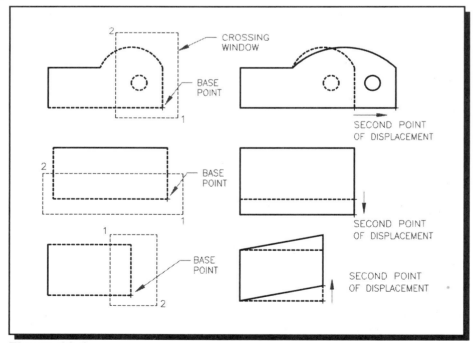

Figure 16-1

Entities to *Stretch* are not selected by the typical object selection methods but are indicated by a <u>crossing window only</u>. (If typing, you must use the *Crossing Window* option.) The *Crossing*

Window should be created so that the entities to *stretch* <u>cross</u> through the window. *Stretch* actually moves the entity endpoints that are located within the crossing window. The "base point" and "second point" of displacement can be selected interactively or by specifying coordinate values. *OSNAPs* can be used.

Following is the command sequence if *Stretch* is typed. (A *crossing window* is automatically produced if you select *Stretch* by any menu.)

> Command: **stretch**
> Select object(s) to stretch by window or polygon...
> Select objects: **C**
> First Corner: **PICK**
> Other Corner: **PICK**
> Select objects: **Enter** (Indicates completion of object selection.)
> Base point or displacement: **PICK** or **(coordinates)** (Select a point to use as the point to stretch <u>from</u>.)
> Second point or displacement: **PICK** or **(coordinates)** (Select a point to use as the point to stretch <u>to</u>.)
> Command:

If you have in mind a specific distance, or a distance and an angle, to *Stretch*, relative rectangular or relative polar coordinates can be used in response to the second point or displacement prompt. *ORTHO* (F8) can be toggled *ON* to ensure stretching in a horizontal or vertical direction.

Stretch can be used to lengthen one entity while shortening another. Application of this ability would be repositioning a door or window on a wall (Fig. 16-2).

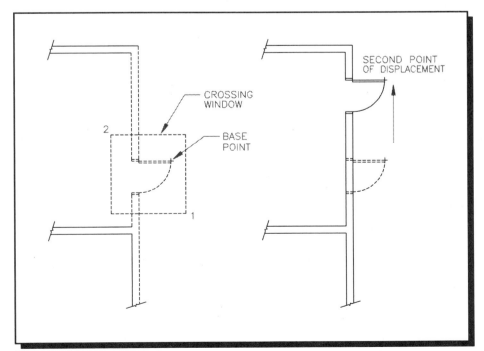

Figure 16-2

ALIGN

TYPE IN:	PULL-DOWN MENU	SCREEN MENU	TABLET MENU
ALIGN	*Modify, Align*	---	---

Unlike most other commands, *Align* is an ADS application that is initialized before using. Initialization is done automatically when typing or selecting this command from the *Modify* pull-down menu. *Align* does not appear in the screen menu or on the digitizing tablet menu.

Align provides a means of aligning one shape (an entity, a group of entities, a *Block*, a region or a 3D object) with another shape. The alignment is accomplished by connecting source points (on the shape to be moved) to destination points (on the stationary shape). You can use *OSNAP* modes to select the source and destination points, assuring accurate alignment. Either a 2D or 3D alignment can be accomplished with this command. The command syntax for alignment in a 2D drawing is as follows:

```
Command: align
Select objects: PICK
Select objects: Enter
1st source point: PICK (with OSNAP)
1st destination point: PICK (with OSNAP)
2nd source point: PICK (with OSNAP)
2nd destination point: PICK (with OSNAP)
3rd source point: Enter
<2D> or 3D transformation: Enter
```

This command performs a translation (like *Move*) and a rotation (like *Rotate*) in one motion if needed to align the points as designated (Fig. 16-3).

First, the 1st source point is connected to (actually touches) the 1st destination point (causing a translation). Next, the vector defined by the 1st and 2nd source points are aligned with the vector defined by the 1st and 2nd destination points (causing rotation).

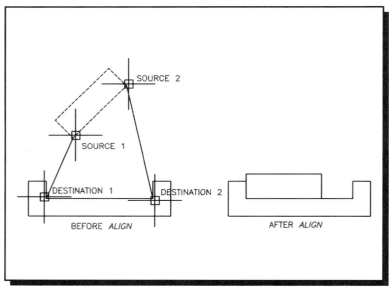

Figure 16-3

If no 3rd destination point is given (needed only for a 3D alignment), a 2D alignment is assumed and is performed on the basis of the 2 sets of points.

CHPROP

TYPE IN:	PULL-DOWN MENU	SCREEN MENU	TABLET MENU
CHPROP or DDCHPROP	Modify, Change> Properties	EDIT, CHPROP:	18,Y

The *Chprop* (Change Properties) command is a subset of the *Change* command. Typing *Ddchprop* or selecting from the pull-down menu invokes the dialogue box (Fig. 16-4).

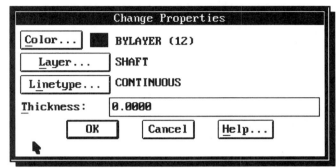

Figure 16-4

Typing *Chprop* or selecting *CHPROP:* from the screen menu produces the command line format:

```
Command: chprop
Select objects: PICK
Select objects: Enter
Change what property (Color/LAyer/LType/Thickness) ?
```

The properties of an entity that can be changed are as follows:

Layer	The layer on which the entity resides
Color	The color assigned to that entity
Linetype	The linetype in which the entity is drawn
Thickness	The three-dimensional characteristic called thickness that an entity can possess

Each option is discussed separately below.

Layer

By changing an entity's *Layer*, the entity is effectively <u>moved</u> to the designated layer. In doing so, if the entity's *Color* and *Linetype* are set to *BYLAYER*, the entity assumes the color and linetype of the layer to which it is moved.

Color

It may be desirable in some cases to assign <u>explicit</u> *Color* to an entity or entities independently of the layer on which they are drawn. The *Change Properties* command allows changing the color of an existing entity from one explicit color to another, or from *BYLAYER* assignment to an explicit color. An entity drawn with an explicit color can also be changed to *BYLAYER* with this command. (See Chapter 12 for information on *Color* assignment.)

Linetype

An entity can assume the *Linetype* assigned *BYLAYER* or can be assigned an <u>explicit</u> *Linetype*. The *Linetype* option of *Change Properties* is used to change an entity's *Linetype* to that of any layer or to any explicit linetype that has been loaded into the current drawing. There is an interesting feature of this option: if *Chprop* is <u>typed</u>, the *linetypes* that you enter are automatically loaded (even if they were not previously loaded into the current drawing) and assigned to the entity. (See Chapter 12 for information on *Linetype* assignment.)

Thickness

An entity's *Thickness* can be changed by this option. *Thickness* is a three-dimensional quality (Z dimension) assigned to a two-dimensional entity. (See Chapter 37.)

CHANGE

TYPE IN:	PULL-DOWN MENU	SCREEN MENU	TABLET MENU
CHANGE	*Modify, Change>*	*EDIT, CHANGE:*	---

The *Change* command allows changing three options: points, properties, or text. The *Change* command can be typed or selected from the *EDIT* screen menu or *Modify* pull-down menu. *Change* is not available on the digitizing menu, although *Chprop* is. The three options are:

Point

This option allows changing the endpoint of an entity or endpoints of several entities to one new position. See Figure 16-5.

```
Command: change
Select objects: PICK (Select an entity or several entities by any
selection method. OSNAPs do not need to be used.)
Select objects: Enter (Indicates selection of objects is complete.)
Properties/<Change point>: PICK (Select point to establish as new
endpoint of all entities. OSNAPs can be used.)
```

The endpoint(s) of the selected entity(ies) <u>nearest</u> the new point selected at the "Properties/<Change point>:" prompt is changed to the new point. Figure 16-5 shows examples with one and with several entities before and after using *Change Point*.

Properties

These options are discussed with the previous command. Selecting *Change* with the *Properties* option offers the same possibilities as using the *Chprop* command. The *Elevation* property (a 3D property) of an entity can also be changed with *Change*, but not with *Chprop*. (See Chapter 37 for information on *Thickness* and *Elevation*.)

```
Properties/<Change point>: p
Change what property (Color/Elev/LAyer/LType/Thickness)
?
```

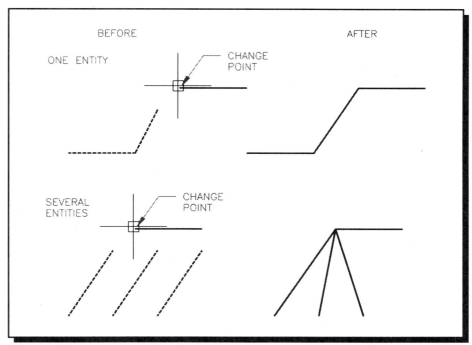

Figure 16-5

Text

Although the word "Text" does <u>not</u> appear as an option, the *Change* command recognizes text if selected and allows changing the following characteristics of text:

Text insertion point
Text style
Text height
Text rotation angle
The textual content

To change text, use the following command syntax:

Command: ***change***
Select objects: **PICK** (Select one or several lines of existing text.)
Select objects: **Enter** (Indicates selection of text is complete.)
Properties/<Change point>: **Enter** (Not wanting to change either Properties or point, pressing Enter prompts AutoCAD to respond with text change options.)
Enter text insertion point: **PICK** or **Enter** (Pick for new insertion point or press Enter for no change.)
Text Style: ROMANS (Indicates the style of the selected text.)
New style or RETURN for no change: **(text style name)** or **Enter**
New height <0.2000>: **(value)** or **Enter** (Enter a value for new height or Enter if no change.)
New rotation angle: **(value)** or **Enter** (Enter value for new angle or Enter for no change.)
New text <FILLETS AND ROUNDS .125>: **(new text)** or **Enter** (Enter the new <u>complete line</u> of text or press Enter for no change.)

DDMODIFY

TYPE IN:	PULL-DOWN MENU	SCREEN MENU	TABLET MENU
DDMODIFY	_Modify, Entity..._	_EDIT, DDMODFY:_	_16,Y and 17,Y_

The _Modify_ feature of AutoCAD is not a command name, but rather a dialogue box. It is only available through the digitizing tablet menu or by typing _Ddmodify_. The power of this feature is apparent because the configuration of the dialogue box that appears is <u>specific</u> to the <u>type</u> of entity that you select. For example, if you select a _Line_, a dialogue box appears allowing changes to any properties that a _Line_ possesses. Or, if you select a _Circle_ or some _Text_, a dialogue box appears specific to _Circle_ or _Text_ properties.

Command: **ddmodify**
Select object to
modify: **PICK** (Only one
object can be selected.
The appropriate dialogue
box appears.)
Command:

Figure 16-6 displays the dialogue box after selecting a _Line_.

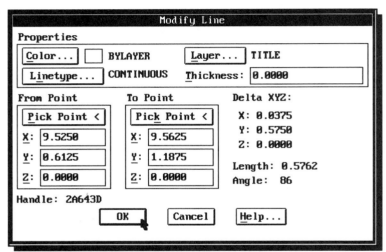

Figure 16-6

Figure 16-7 displays the dialogue box a _Pline_ selection.

The modify dialogue box series provides you with the capabilities of the _Change_ command in dialogue box form. All properties that an entity possesses, including position in the drawing, can be modified with the respective _Modify_ dialogue box.

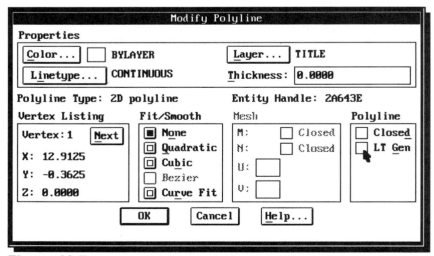

Figure 16-7

This is a very powerful and informative feature of AutoCAD. You should try using _Ddmodify_ and select different types of entities to get a sample of the possibilities. For example, selecting an _Arc_ will list its length, as well as allowing modification of any property.

EXPLODE

TYPE IN:	PULL-DOWN MENU	SCREEN MENU	TABLET MENU
EXPLODE	*Modify, Explode*	*EDIT, EXPLODE:*	*20,W*

There are many graphical shapes that can be created in AutoCAD that are made of several elements but are treated as one entity such as *Plines, Polygons, Blocks, Hatch* patterns, and dimensions. The *Explode* command provides you with a means of breaking down or "exploding" the complex shape from one entity into its many component segments (Fig. 16-8). Generally, *Explode* is used to allow subsequent editing of one or more of the component entities of a *Pline, Polygon,* or *Block,* etc. which would otherwise be impossible while the complex shape is considered as one entity.

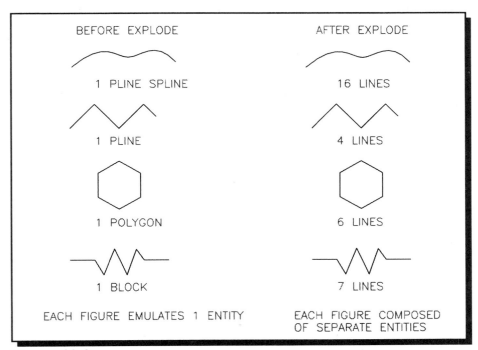

Figure 16-8

The *Explode* command has no options and is simple to use. You only need to select the objects to *Explode*.

```
Command: explode
Select objects: PICK (Select one or more Plines, Blocks, etc.)
Select objects: Enter (Indicates selection of objects is complete.)
```

The complex shape is broken into its component entities, allowing editing to any of these new entities.

When *Plines, Polygons, Blocks,* or hatch patterns are *Exploded,* they are transformed into *Line, Arc,* and *Circle* entities. *Plines* having *width* lose their width information when *Exploded* since *Line, Arc,* and *Circle* entities cannot have width.

PEDIT

TYPE IN:	PULL-DOWN MENU	SCREEN MENU	TABLET MENU
PEDIT	*Modify, Polyedit*	*EDIT, PEDIT:*	*19,W*

This command provides numerous options for editing *Polylines*. The list of options below exhibits the great flexibility possible with *Polylines*. The first step after invoking *Pedit* is to select the *Pline* to edit.

```
Command: pedit
Select polyline: PICK (Select the polyline for subsequent editing.)
Close or Open/Join/Width/Edit vertex/Fit/Spline/Decurve/
Ltype gen/Undo/eXit <X>: (option) (Select the desired option from screen
menu or entering the capitalized letter for desired option.)
```

Close

Close connects the last segment with the first segment of an existing "open" *Pline*, resulting in "closed" *Pline*. A closed *Pline* is one continuous entity having no specific start or endpoint, as opposed to one closed by PICKing points. This type of closed *Pline* reacts differently to the *Spline* option and to some commands such as *Fillet*, *Pline* option (Chapter 17).

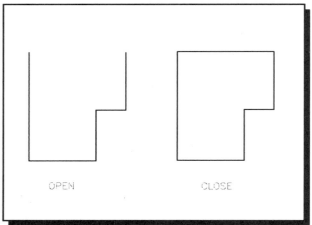

Figure 16-9

Open

Open removes the closing segment if the *Close* option was used previously.

Join

This option *Joins*, or connects, any *Plines*, *Lines*, or *Arcs* that have <u>exact</u> matching endpoints and adds them to the selected *Pline*. Previously *closed Plines* cannot be *Joined*.

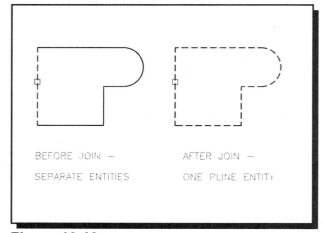

Figure 16-10

Width

Width allows specification of a uniform width for *Pline* segments. Nonuniform width can be specified with the *Edit vertex* option.

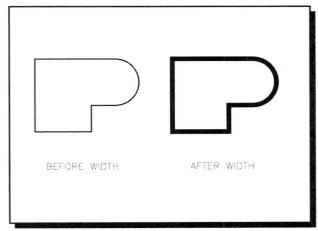

Figure 16-11

Edit vertex

This option is covered later in this chapter.

Fit

This converts the *Pline* from straight line segments to arcs. The curve consists of two arcs for each pair of vertices. The resulting curve can be radical if the original *Pline* consists of sharp angles. The resulting curve passes <u>through all</u> vertices.

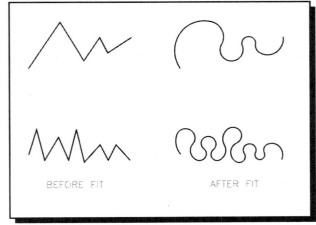

Figure 16-12

Spline

This option converts the *Pline* to a B-spline (Bezier spline). The *Pline* vertices act as "control points" affecting the shape of the curve. The resulting curve passes through <u>only the end</u> vertices.

The amount of "pull" can be changed by adding more or fewer vertices in one vicinity or by using the *SPLINETYPE* system variable to apply either a quadratic (more pull) or cubic (less pull) B-spline function. *SPLINESEGS* system variable controls the number of line segments in the curve.

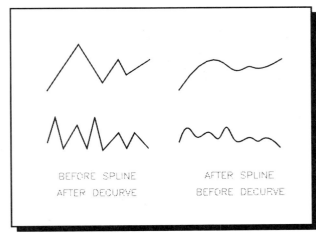

Figure 16-13

Changing the *SPLFRAME* variable to 1 causes the *Pline* frame (the original straight segments) to be displayed for *Splined* or *Fit Plines*. *Regen* must be used after changing the variable to display the original *Pline* "frame."

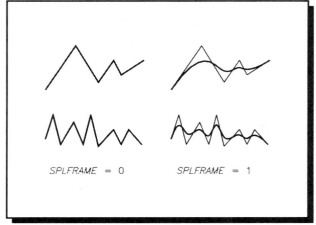

Figure 16-14

Decurve

Decurve removes the *Spline* or *Fit* curve and returns the *Pline* to its original straight line segments state.

Ltype gen

This setting controls the generation of linetypes for <u>new</u> *Plines* so as to create endpoints at, and continuing through, the *Pline* vertices. If *On*, linetypes are drawn in a consistent pattern disregarding vertices. If *Off*, non-continuous linetype dashes start and stop at each vertex. This option does <u>not retroactively</u> change *Plines* that have already been drawn. *Ltype gen* affects complex entities such as *Polygons*, *Ellipses*, and *Plines* (Fig. 16-15).

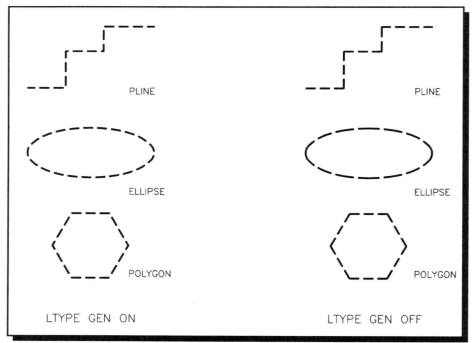

Figure 16-15

Undo

Undo reverses the most recent *Pedit* operation.

eXit

This option exits the *Pedit* options, keeps the changes and returns to the Command: prompt.

Vertex Editing

Upon selecting the *Edit Vertex* option from the *Pedit* options list, the group of suboptions is displayed on the screen menu and command line.

> Command: **pedit**
> Select polyline: **PICK** (Select the polyline for subsequent editing.)
> Close or Open/Join/Width/Edit vertex/Fit/Spline/Decurve/
> Ltype gen/Undo/eXit <X>: **E** (Invokes the Edit vertex suboptions.)
> Next/Previous/Break/Insert/Move/Regen/Straighten/Tangent/
> Width/eXit <N>:

Next

AutoCAD places an **X** marker at the first endpoint of the *Pline*. The *Next* and *Previous* options allow you to sequence the marker to the desired vertex.

Previous

See *Next* above.

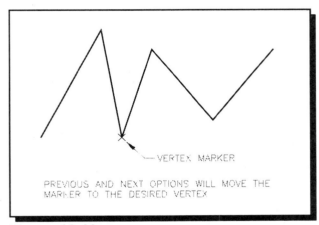
Figure 16-16

Break

This selection causes a break between the marked vertex and the next one selected by the *Next* or *Previous* option prompt:

> Next/Previous/Go/eXit <N>:

Selecting *Go* causes the break. An endpoint vertex cannot be selected.

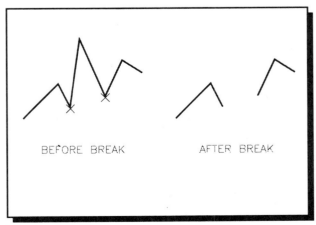
Figure 16-17

Insert

Insert allows you to insert a new vertex at any location <u>after</u> the vertex that is marked with the **X**.

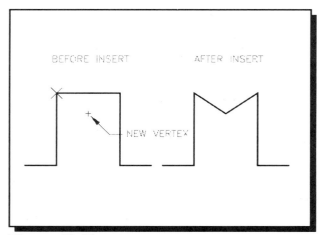

Figure 16-18

Move

You are prompted to indicate a new location to *Move* the marked vertex.

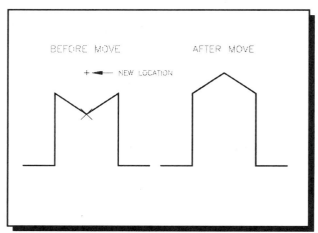

Regen

Regen should be used after the *Width* option to display the new changes.

Figure 16-19

Straighten

You can *Straighten* the *Pline* segments between the current marker and the other marker that you place by one of these options:

```
Next/Previous/Go/eXit <N>:
```

Selecting *Go* causes the straightening to occur.

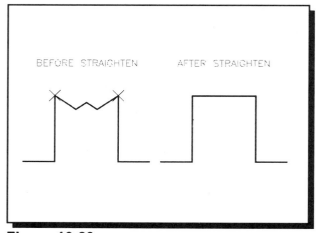

Figure 16-20

Tangent

Tangent allows you to specify the direction of tangency of the current vertex for use with curve *Fit*ting.

Width

This allows changing the *Width* of the *Pline* segment immediately following the marker, thus achieving a specific width for one segment of the *Pline*. *Width* can be specified with differing starting and ending values. *Regen* must then be used to display the changes in width after using this option.

eXit

This option exits from vertex editing, saves changes, and returns to the main *Pedit* prompt.

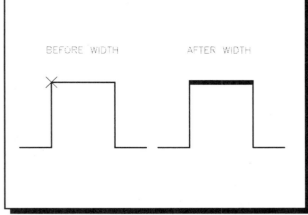

Figure 16-21

Converting *Lines* and *Arcs* to *Plines*

A very important and productive feature of *Pedit* is the ability to convert *Lines* and *Arcs* to *Plines* and closed *Pline* shapes. Potential uses of this option are converting a series of connected *Lines* and *Arcs* to a closed *Pline* for subsequent use with *Offset* or for the inquiry of the area (*Area* command) or length (*List* command) of a single shape. The only requirement for conversion of *Lines* and *Arcs* to *Plines* is that the selected entities must have <u>exact</u> matching endpoints.

To accomplish the conversion of entities to *Plines*, simply select a *Line* or *Arc* entity and request to turn it into one:

Command: ***pedit***
Select polyline: **PICK** (Select a *Line* or *Arc*.)
Entity selected is not a Pline
Do you want to turn it into one? <Y> **Enter** (Instructs AutoCAD to convert the selected entity into a *Pline*. Only <u>one</u> entity can be selected.)
Close or Open/Join/Width/Edit vertex/Fit/Spline/Decurve/
Ltype gen/Undo/eXit <X>: ***J*** (Invokes the *Join* option.)
Select objects: **PICK** (Select the entity or group of entities to join. Multiple entities can be selected.)
Select objects: **Enter** (Press Enter to indicate completion of object selection.)
(number) segments added to polyline

The resulting conversion is a closed *Polyline* shape.

Remember, it is necessary for some operations to be able to convert individual entities (*Lines, Arcs,* and other entities) into *Plines* and to join them into one *Pline*. *Pedit* and the *Join* option are used for this purpose. As the converse operation, it is very helpful to be able to break complex shapes composed of *Plines* (*Polygons, Ellipses, Blocks, Hatch* patterns) into individual entities. *Explode* is used for this operation.

CHAPTER EXERCISES

1. **Stretch**

A design change has been requested. **Open** the **SLOTPLAT** drawing and make the following changes.

A. The top of the plate (including the slot) must be moved upward. This design change will add 1" to the total height of the Slot Plate. Use **Stretch** to accomplish the change as shown in Figure 16-22. Draw the crossing window as shown.

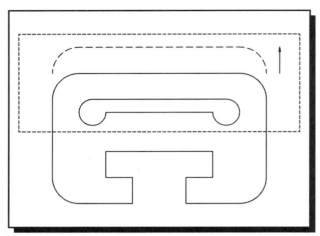

Figure 16-22

B. The notch at the bottom of the plate must be adjusted slightly by relocating it .50 units to the right as shown (highlighted) in Figure 16-23. Draw the crossing window as shown. Use **Saveas** to reassing the name to **SLOTPLT2**.

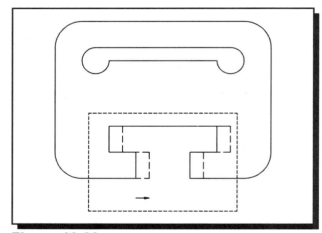

Figure 16-23

2. **Align**

Open the **PLATES** drawing. The three plates are to be stamped at one time on a single sheet of stock measuring 15" x 12". Place the three plates together to achieve the optimum nesting on the sheet stock.

A. Use **Align** to move the plate in the center (with 9 holes). Select the **1st source** and **destination points** (1S, 1D) and **2nd source** and **destination points** (2S, 2D) as shown in Figure 16-24.

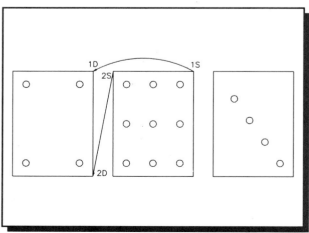

Figure 16-24

B.   After the first alignment is complete, use *Align* to move the plate on the right (with 4 diagonal holes). The *source* and *destination points* are indicated in Figure 16-25.

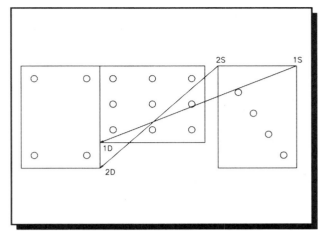

Figure 16-25

C.   Finally, draw the sheet stock outline (15" x 12") using *Line* as shown in Figure 16-26. The plates are ready for production. Use *Saveas* and assign the name **PLATNEST**.

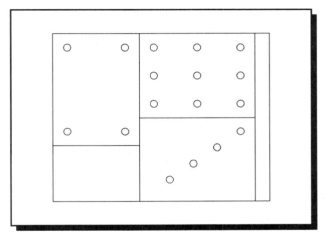

Figure 16-26

3.   *Chprop*

Open the **PIVOTARM** drawing that you worked on in Chapter 9 Exercises. *Load* the *Hidden* and *Center Linetypes*. Make two *New Layers* named **HID** and **CEN** and assign the matching linetypes. Check the *Limits* of the drawing, then calculate and set an appropriate *LTSCALE* (usually .5 times the drawing scale factor). Use *Chprop* to change the *Lines* representing the holes in the front view to the **HID** layer as shown in Figure 16-27. *Save* the drawing.

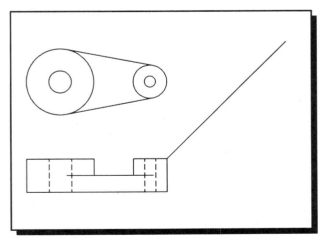

Figure 16-27

4. *Change*

Open **CH8EX3**. *Erase* the **Arc** at the top of the object. *Erase* the *Points* with a window. Invoke the **Change** command. When prompted to *Select objects*, **PICK** all of the inclined *Lines* near the top. When prompted to `<Change point>:`, enter coordinate **6,8**. The object should appear as that in Figure 16-28. Use *Saveas* and assign the name **CH16EX4**.

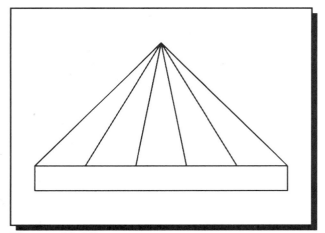

Figure 16-28

5. *Modify Entity*

A design change is required for the bolt holes in **GASKETA**. *Open* **GASKETA** and select *Entity...* (from the *Modify* pull-down menu). Change each of the four bolt holes to **7/16** diameter. *Save* the drawing.

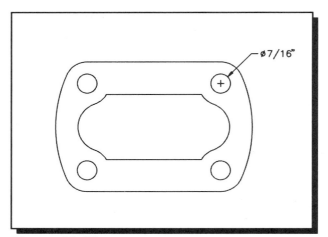

Figure 16-29

6. *Explode*

You can quickly create the shape shown (continuous lines) in Figure 16-30 by *Exploding* a *Polygon*. First, start a *New* drawing. Create a 6-sided *Polygon* with the *Center* at **6,4**. *Circumscribe* the *Polygon* about a **2** unit radius. Next *Explode* the *Polygon* and *Erase* the two *Lines* (highlighted) in Figure 16-30. Draw the bottom *Line* from the two *ENDpoints*.

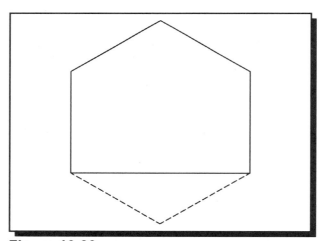

Figure 16-30

7. *Pedit*

Open the **CH15EX2** drawing that you completed in the Chapter 15 Exercises. Use ***Pedit*** with the ***Edit vertex*** options to alter the shape as shown in Figure 16-31. For the bottom notch use ***Straighten***. For the top notch use ***Insert***. Use ***Saveas*** and change the name to **CH16EX7**.

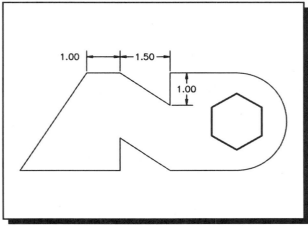

Figure 16-31

8. *Pline, Pedit*

A.   Create a line graph as shown in Figure 16-32 to illustrate the low temperatures for a week. The temperatures are as follows:

X axis	Y axis
Sunday	20
Monday	14
Tuesday	18
Wednesday	26
Thursday	34
Friday	38
Saturday	27

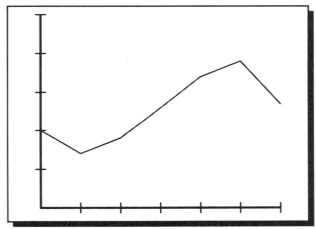

Figure 16-32

Use equal intervals along each axis. Use a ***Pline*** for the graph line. ***Save*** the drawing as **CH16EX8A**. (You will label the graph at a later time.)

B.   Use ***Pedit*** to change the *Pline* to a ***Spline***. Note that the graph line is no longer 100% accurate because it does not pass through the original vertices (see Fig. 16-33). Use the *SPLFRAME* variable to display the original "frame" (*Regen* must be used after).

Use the ***Modify Entity*** dialogue box and try the ***Cubic*** and ***Quadratic*** options. Which option causes the vertices to have more pull? Find the most accurate option. Set *SPL-FRAME* to **0** and ***Saveas* CH16EX8B**.

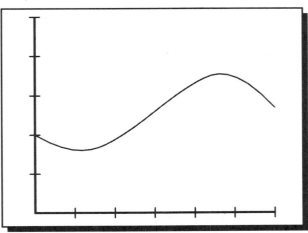

Figure 16-33

C.   Use *Pedit* to change the curve from *Pline* to *Fit Curve*. Does the graph line pass through the vertices? (Change the *SPLFRAME* setting to see the original verticies.) *Saveas* **CH16EX8C**.

9.   **Converting *Lines*, *Circles*, and *Arcs* to *Plines***

Use **ASHEET** as a prototype and assign the name **GASKETC**. Change the *Limits* for plotting on a metric A4 sheet at 2:1 (refer to the Metric Table of *Limits* Settings and set *Limits* to 1/2 x *Limits* specified for 1:1 scale). Begin, but do not complete the drawing of the Gasket shown in Figure 16-34. First, draw only the <u>inside</u> shape using *Lines* and *Circles* (with *Trim*) or *Arcs*. Then convert the *Lines* and *Arcs* to one closed *Pline* using *Pedit*. Finally, locate and draw the 3 bolt holes. *Save* the drawing. Do not draw the outside shape. The gasket will be completed in Chapter 17 Exercises.

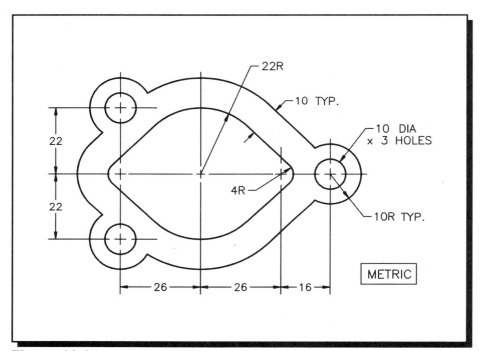

Figure 16-34

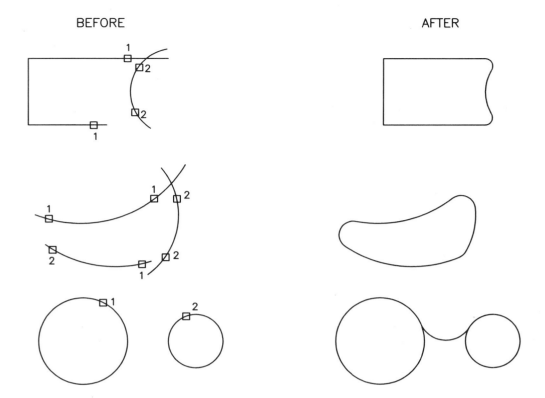

BEFORE   AFTER

CHAPTER 17
Construct Commands II

CHAPTER OBJECTIVES

After completing this chapter you should:

1.   be able to create a *Fillet* between two entities;

2.   be able to create a *Chamfer* between two entities;

3.   know how to create parallel copies of entities with *Offset*;

4.   be able to use *Divide* to add points at equal parts of an entity;

5.   be able to use *Measure* to add points at specified segment lengths along an entity.

BASICS

Construct commands <u>edit</u> existing entities in some way but also <u>create</u> new entities in the process. The fundamental *Construct* commands were covered in Chapter 10. This chapter deals with another set of somewhat more complex *Construct* commands.

COMMANDS

FILLET

TYPE IN:	PULL-DOWN MENU	SCREEN MENU	TABLET MENU
FILLET	*Construct, Fillet*	*EDIT, FILLET:*	*19,X and 20,X*

The *Fillet* command automatically rounds a sharp corner (intersection of two *Lines*, *Arcs*, *Circles*, or *Pline* vertices) with a radius. You only specify the radius and select the entities' ends to be *Filleted*. The entities to fillet do <u>not</u> have to completely intersect or can overlap. The entities are automatically extended or trimmed as necessary (Fig. 17-1).

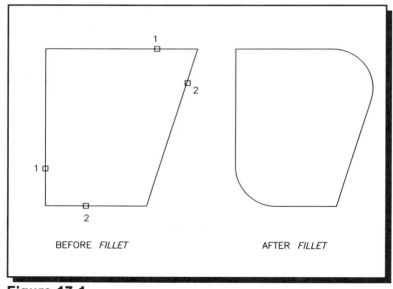

BEFORE *FILLET*   AFTER *FILLET*

Figure 17-1

The *Fillet* command must be used first to input the desired *radius* and a second time to select the objects to *Fillet*.

```
Command: fillet
Polyline/Radius/<Select first object>: r (Indicates the radius option.)
Enter fillet radius <0.0000>: (value) or PICK (Enter a value for the
desired fillet radius or select two points to interactively specify the radius.)
Command:
```

No fillet will be drawn at this time. Repeat the *Fillet* command to select objects to fillet.

Command: ***fillet***
Polyline/Distances/<Select first object>: **PICK** (Select one *Line*, *Arc*, or *Circle* near the point where fillet should be created.)
Select second object: **PICK** (Select second object to fillet near the fillet location.)

The fillet is created at the corner selected. Treatment of *Arcs* and *Circles* with *Fillet* is shown here. Note that the entities to *Fillet* do not have to intersect or can overlap.

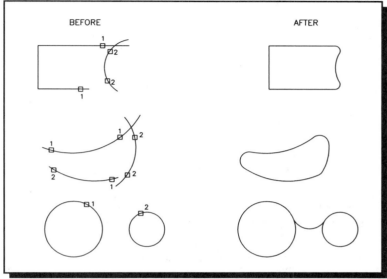

Figure 17-2

Since trimming and extending are done automatically by *Fillet* when necessary, using *Fillet* with a *radius* of *0* has particular usefulness.

Using *Fillet* with a *0 radius* creates clean, sharp corners even if the original entities overlap or do not intersect (Fig. 17-3). For example, if a drawing has been created such that endpoints do not intersect as intended, those endpoints can be corrected by using *Fillet* with *0 radius*. You use the *Fillet* command first to specify the radius and repeat the command to select entities to fillet. The *Fillet Radius 0* option is available on the digitizing tablet menu at location **19,X**.

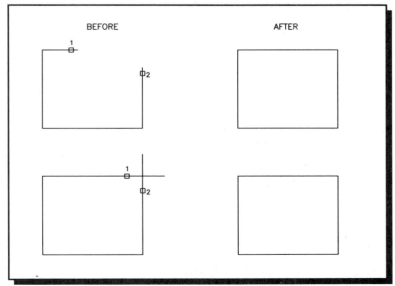

Figure 17-3

Polylines can also be used with the *Fillet* command by specifying the *Polyline* option. A fillet equal to the specified radius is added to each vertex of the *Pline* except the endpoint vertices.

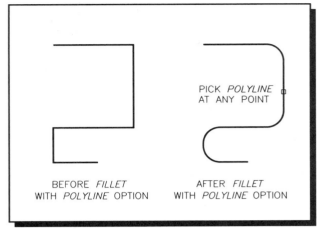

PICK *POLYLINE* AT ANY POINT

BEFORE *FILLET* WITH *POLYLINE* OPTION

AFTER *FILLET* WITH *POLYLINE* OPTION

Figure 17-4

The *Polyline* option is invoked as follows:

```
Command: fillet
Polyline/Distances/<Select first object>: P (Invokes prompts for the
Polyline option.)
Select 2D polyline: PICK (Select the desired polyline.)
```

Closed Plines created by the *Close* option of *Pedit* react differently with *Fillet* than *Plines* connected by PICKing matching end points. Figure 17-5 illustrates the effect of *Fillet Polyline* on a *Closed Pline* and on a connected *Pline*.

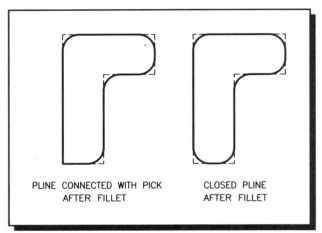

PLINE CONNECTED WITH PICK AFTER FILLET

CLOSED PLINE AFTER FILLET

Figure 17-5

CHAMFER

TYPE IN:	PULL-DOWN MENU	SCREEN MENU	TABLET MENU
CHAMFER	*Construct, Chamfer*	*EDIT, CHAMFER:*	*21,X*

Chamfering is a manufacturing process used to replace a sharp corner with an angled surface. In AutoCAD, *Chamfer* is commonly used to change the intersection of two *Lines* or *Plines* by adding an angled line.

The *Chamfer* command is similar to *Fillet*, but rather than rounding with a radius or "fillet," an angled line is automatically drawn at the distances (from the existing corner) that you specify.

The *Distances* option is used to specify the distance from the corner (intersection of two lines) to each chamfer endpoint. Use *Chamfer* once to specify *Distances* and again to draw the chamfer.

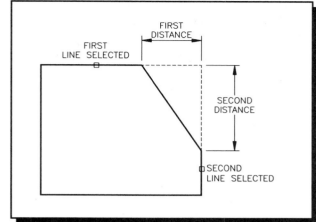

Figure 17-6

```
Command: chamfer
Polyline/Distances/<Select
first line>: D (Indicates the
distance option.)
Enter first chamfer distance <0.0000>: (value) or PICK (Enter a value
```
for the distance from the existing corner to the endpoint of chamfer on first line or select two points to interactively specify the distance.)
```
Enter second chamfer distance <value of first distance>:
```
Enter, **(value)** or **PICK** (Press Enter to use same distance as first distance, enter a value for the distance from the existing corner to an endpoint of the chamfer on the second line, or select two points to specify the distance.)
```
Command:
```

No chamfer will be drawn at this time. *Chamfer* is repeated to select lines to chamfer.

```
Command: chamfer
Polyline/Distances/<Select first line>: PICK (Select line to have first
```
distance.)
```
Select second line: PICK (Select line to have second distance.)
```

The two lines selected for chamfering do not actually have to intersect but can overlap or not connect. *Chamfer* draws the specified chamfer and automatically trims or extends as necessary (Fig.17-7).

Chamfer with a distance of 0 reacts like *Fillet* with a distance of 0; that is, overlapping corners are automatically trimmed and non-intersecting corners are automatically extended.

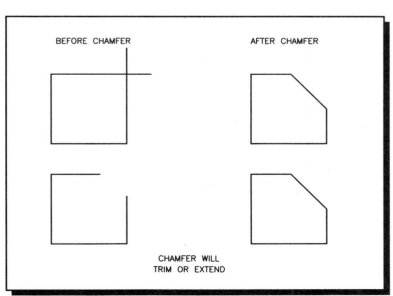

Figure 17-7

The *Polyline* option of *Chamfer* is used to create chamfers on polylines. All vertices of the *Pline* are chamfered with the supplied distances. The first end of the *Pline* that was drawn takes the first distance.

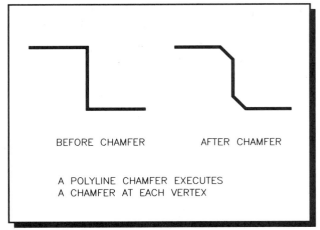

BEFORE CHAMFER   AFTER CHAMFER

A POLYLINE CHAMFER EXECUTES
A CHAMFER AT EACH VERTEX

Figure 17-8

OFFSET

TYPE IN:	PULL-DOWN MENU	SCREEN MENU	TABLET MENU
OFFSET	*Construct, Offset*	*EDIT, OFFSET*	*14,W*

Offset creates a <u>parallel copy</u> of selected entities. Selected entities can be *Line*s, *Arc*s, *Circle*s, *Pline*s or other entities. *Offset* is a very useful command that can increase productivity greatly, particularly with *Pline*s.

Depending on the entity selected, the resulting *Offset* is drawn differently (Fig. 17-9). *Offset* creates a parallel copy of a *Line* equal in length and perpendicular to the original. *Arc*s and *Circle*s have a concentric *Offset*. *Offset* closed *Pline*s result in a complete parallel shape.

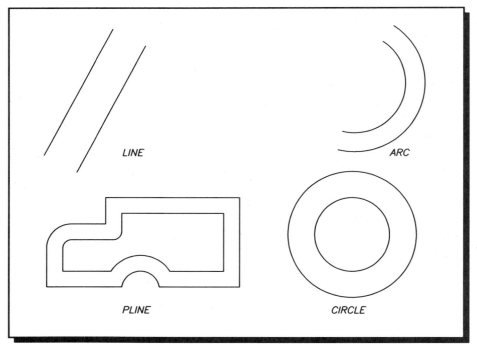

LINE   ARC

PLINE   CIRCLE

Figure 17-9

Two options are available with *Offset*: (1) *Offset* a specified *distance* and (2) *Offset through* a specified point.

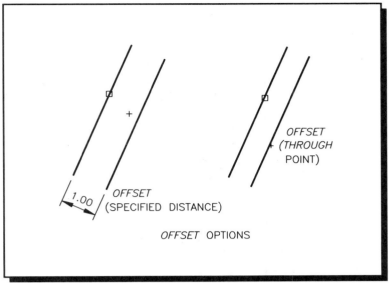

OFFSET
(THROUGH
POINT)

OFFSET
(SPECIFIED DISTANCE)

1.00

OFFSET OPTIONS

Figure 17-10

Distance

The *Distance* option command sequence is as follows:

```
Command: offset
Offset distance or Through <Through>: (value) or PICK (Indicate the
```
distance to offset by entering a value or interactively picking two points.)
`Select objects to offset:` **PICK** (Select entity to make parallel copy of.
Only one entity can be selected.)
`Side to offset?` **PICK** or (**coordinates**) (Select which side of the selected entity
for offset to be drawn. Coordinates can be entered or a point can be selected.)
`Select objects to offset:` **Enter** (*Offset* can be used repeatedly to offset at
the <u>same</u> distance as the previously specified value. Pressing Enter completes
command.)
`Command:`

Through

The command sequence for *Offset through* is as follows:

```
Command: offset
```
`Offset distance or Through <Through>:` **Enter** (Invokes the Through
option.)
`Select objects to offset:` **PICK** (Select entity to make parallel copy of.
Only one entity can be selected.)
`Through point:` **PICK** or (**coordinates**) (Select point for offset to be drawn
through. Coordinates can be entered or point can be selected with or without
OSNAPs.)
`Select objects to offset:` **Enter** (*Offset* can be used repeatedly to specify
a <u>different</u> through point. Pressing Enter completes command.)
`Command:`

Keep in mind the power of using *Offset* with closed *Pline* shapes (Fig. 17-11, next page).
Remember that any closed shape composed of *Line*s and *Arc*s can be converted to one *Pline*
entity (see *Pedit*, Chapter 16).

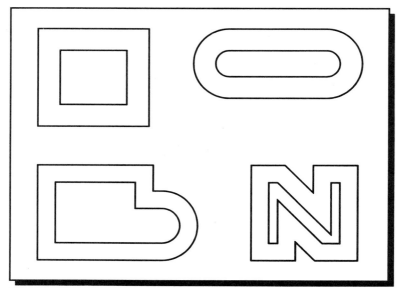

Figure 17-11

DIVIDE

TYPE IN:	PULL-DOWN MENU	SCREEN MENU	TABLET MENU
DIVIDE	*Construct, Divide*	*EDIT, DIVIDE:*	*22,W*

The *Divide* command divides an entity such as a *Line*, *Pline*, or *Arc* into an equal number of parts and adds a *Point* entity at each division.

The entity being divided is <u>not</u> actually broken into parts--it remains as <u>one</u> entity. *Point* entities are automatically added to display the "divisions."

The point entities that are added to the entity can be used for subsequent construction by providing a means for *OSNAP*ing to the equally spaced *Node*s.

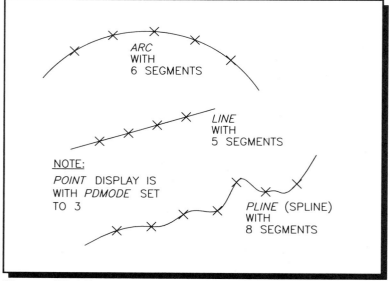

Figure 17-12

The command sequence for the *Divide* command is as follows:

```
Command: divide
Select object to divide: PICK (Only one entity can be selected.)
<Number of segments>/Block:(value) (Enter a value for number of segments.)
Command:
```

Point entities are added to divide the entity selected into the desired number of parts. Therefore, there is <u>one less</u> *Point* added than the number of segments specified.

After using the *Divide* command, the *Point* entities may not be visible unless the point style is changed with the *Point Style...* dialogue box (*Settings* pull-down) or by changing the *PDMODE* variable by command line format (see Chapter 8). A *Regen* must be invoked before the new point style will be displayed. Figures 17-12 shows *Points* displayed using a *PDMODE* of *3*.

You can request that *Block*s be inserted rather than *Point* entities along equal divisions of the selected entity. Figure 17-13 displays a generic rectangular-shaped block inserted with *Divide*, both aligned and not aligned with a *Line*, *Arc*, and *Pline*.

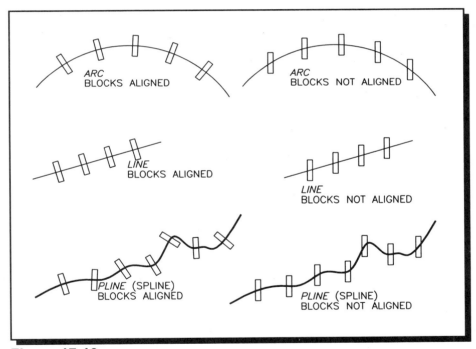

Figure 17-13

In order to insert a *Block* using the *Divide* command, the name of an <u>existing</u> *Block* is given.

```
Command: divide
Select object to divide: PICK (Only one entity can be selected.)
<Number of segments>/Block: B (Designates the Block option.)
Block name to insert: (name) (Enter name of existing block.)
Align block with object? <Y> Enter or N (Press Enter for alignment of
block along selected entity, N for insertion of block in normal orientation.)<Number of
segments>: (value) (Enter value for number of segments.)
Command:
```

MEASURE

TYPE IN:	PULL-DOWN MENU	SCREEN MENU	TABLET MENU
MEASURE	*Construct, Measure*	*EDIT, MEASURE:*	*22,X*

The *Measure* command is similar to the *Divide* command in that *Point* entities (or *Blocks*) are inserted along the selected entity. The *Measure* command, however, allows you to designate the <u>length</u> of segments rather than the <u>number</u> of segments as with the *Divide* command.

```
Command: measure
Select object to measure: PICK (Only one entity can be selected.)
<Segments length>/Block: (value) (Enter a value for length of one segment.)
Command:
```

Point entities are added to the selected entity at the designated intervals (lengths). There is one *Point* added for each interval <u>beginning at the end nearest</u> the end used for object selection. The intervals are of equal length except possibly the last segment, which is whatever length is remaining after the last *Point* entity.

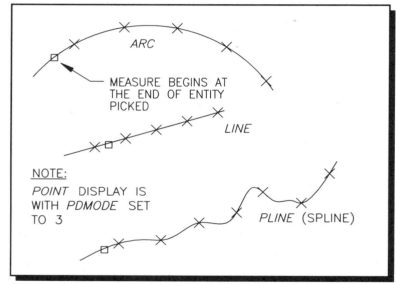

Figure 17-14

As with the *Divide* command, the *Point* entities may not be visible unless the point style is changed with the *Point Style...* dialogue box (*Settings* pull-down) or by changing the *PDMODE* variable by command line format. A *Regen* must be invoked before the new point style is displayed.

You can request that *Blocks* be inserted rather than *Point* entities at the designated intervals of the selected entity. Inserting *Blocks* with *Measure* requires that an <u>existing</u> *Block* be used.

```
Command: measure
Select object to measure: PICK (Only one entity can be selected.)
<Segments length>/Block: B (Designates the Block option.)
Block name to insert: (name) (Enter name of existing block.)
Align block with object? <Y> Enter or N (Press Enter for alignment of
block along selected entity, N for insertion of block in normal orientation.)
<Segments length>: (value) (Enter value for segment length.)
Command:
```

The named *Block*s are inserted along the selected entity at the designated intervals. Figure 17-15 displays a hypothetical block (shaped like a rectangle) inserted both aligned and not aligned with a *Line*, *Arc*, and *Pline*.

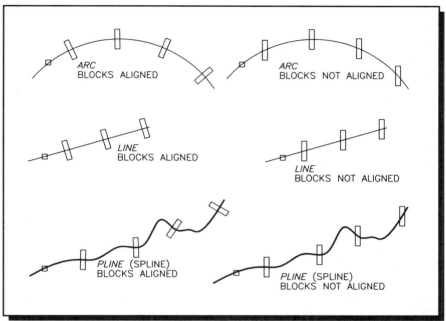

Figure 17-15

CHAPTER EXERCISES

1. *Fillet*

    Use the **ASHEET** or **A-BORDER** drawing as a prototype and create the "T" Plate shown in Figure 17-16. Use *Fillet* to create all the fillets and rounds as the last step. When finished, *Saveas* **T-PLATE** and plot the drawing at 1=1 scale.

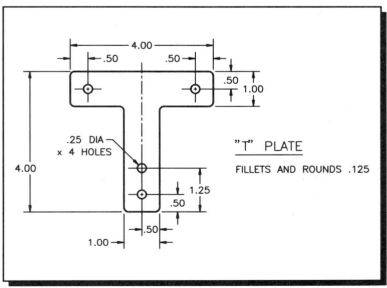

Figure 17-16

2. *Chamfer*

Use drawing **A-2-M** as a prototype drawing and assign the name **CBRACKET**. Using the Metric Table of *Limits* Settings, reset the **Limits** for plotting 1:1. Create the Catch Bracket shown in Figure 17-17. Use **Chamfer** to create the six chamfers. **Save** the drawing and create a plot to scale.

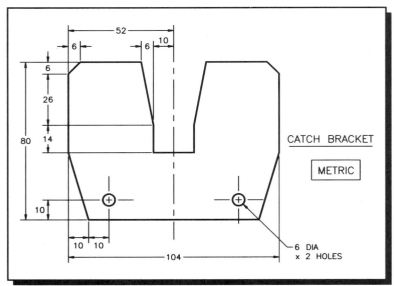

Figure 17-17

3. *Offset*

Use the **ASHEET** or **A-BORDER** drawing as a prototype and assign the name **SCHEM1**. Create the electrical schematic as shown in Figure 17-18 by drawing *Lines*, then *Offset* as needed. Because this is a schematic, you can create the symbols by approximating the dimensions. **Save** the drawing and create a plot if required.

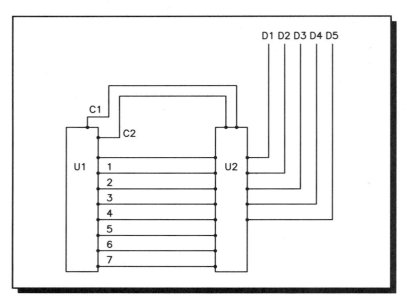

Figure 17-18

4. *Offset*

Open the **GASKETC** drawing that you began in Chapter 16 Exercises. **Offset** the existing inside shape to create the outside shape (refer to Chapter 16 Exercise 9 for dimensions). Use **Offset** to create concentric circles around the bolt holes. Use **Trim** to complete the gasket. **Save** the drawing and create a plot at 2:1 scale.

5. *Divide, Measure*

Use the **ASHEET** or **A-BORDER** drawing as a prototype and assign the name **BILLMATL**. Create the table in Figure 17-19 to be used as a bill of materials. Draw the bottom *Line* (as dimensioned) and a vertical *Line*. Use *Divide* along the bottom *Line* and *Measure* along the vertical *Line* to locate *Points* as desired. Create *Offsets Through* the Points using *NODe OSNAP*. (*ORTHO* and *Trim* may be of help.)

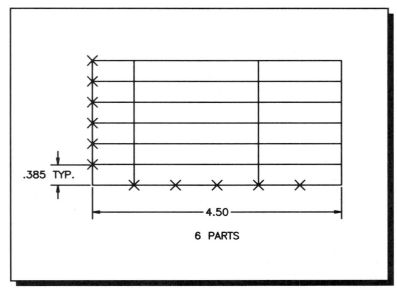

Figure 17-19

6. **HAMMER** Drawing

Open the **HAMMER** drawing that you set up in Chapter 14 Exercise 5. Create the Hammer shown in Figure 17-20. Make use of *Offset* for determining the center points for *Arc* and *Circle* radii (use the CONSTR layer for construction lines). Use *Fillet* wherever possible. When you finish, *Save* the drawing and create a plot if required.

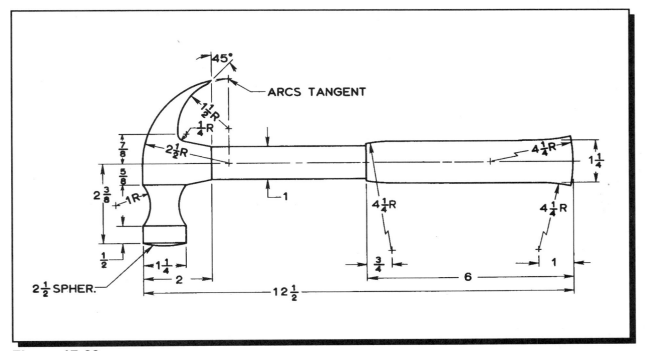

Figure 17-20

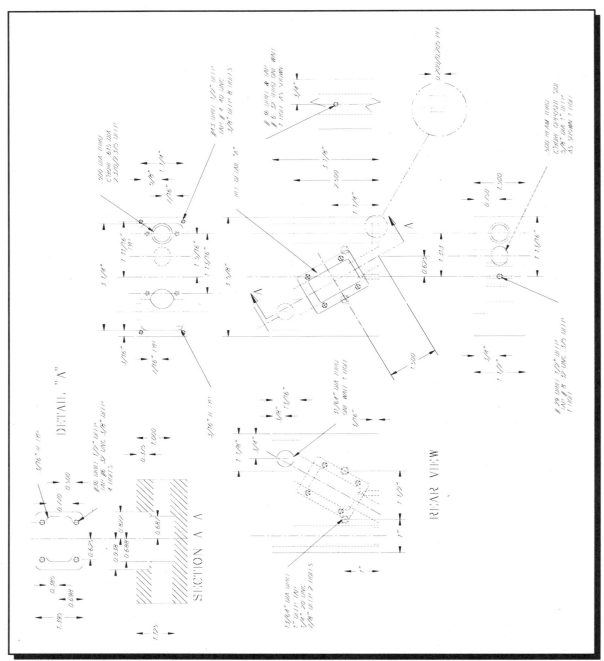

Figure 17-21 BASEPLAT.DWG Courtesy of Autodesk, Inc.

```
   LINE        Layer: 1-WALL
               Space: Model space
        Handle = 824
   from point, X=120'-2 3/8"  Y=36'-6 7/16"  Z=     0'-0"
     to point, X=120'-2 3/8"  Y=52'-5 7/16"  Z=     0'-0"
Length =  15'-11",  Angle in XY Plane =      90
        Delta X =     0'-0", Delta Y =    15'-11", Delta Z =     0'-0"


   ARC         Layer: DOOR
               Space: Model space
        Handle = C5F
  center point, X=120'-3 1/2"  Y=33'-4 7/16"  Z=     0'-0"
  radius       3'-0"
   start angle     358
     end angle      90
```

CHAPTER 18

Inquiry Commands

CHAPTER OBJECTIVES

After completing this chapter you should:

1.   be able to list the *Status* of a drawing;

2.   be able to *List* the AutoCAD database information about an entity;

3.   know how to list the entire database of all entities with *Dblist*;

4.   be able to calculate the *Area* of a closed shape with and without "islands";

5.   be able to find the *Distance* between two points;

6.   be able to report the coordinate value of a selected point using the *ID* command;

7.   know how to list the *Time* spent on a drawing or in a session.

BASICS

AutoCAD provides several commands that allow you to find out information about the current drawing status and about specific entities in the drawing. These commands as a group are known as *Inquiry* commands and are grouped together in the menu systems.

Using *Inquiry* commands, you can find out such information as the amount of time spent in the current drawing, the distance between two points, the area of a closed shape, or the database listing of properties for specific entities (coordinates of endpoints, lengths, angles, etc.) as well as other information. The *Inquiry* commands are:

Status, List, Dblist, Area, Distance, ID, Time

COMMANDS

STATUS

TYPE IN:	PULL-DOWN MENU	SCREEN MENU	TABLET MENU
STATUS	*Assist, Inquiry > Status*	*INQUIRY, STATUS:*	*3,T*

The *Status* command gives many pieces of information related to the current drawing. Typing or **PICK**ing the command from one of the menus causes a text screen to appear similar to the one shown in Figure 18-1.

```
Command:
STATUS 746 entities in D:\DWG\JAL\OFFICE2
Model space limits are X:        0'0"    Y:        0'0"    (Off)
                       X:       30'0"    Y:       20'0"
Model space uses       X:        0'0"    Y:        0'0"
                       X:       30'0"    Y:       20'0"
Display shows          X:        0'0"    Y:        0'0"
                       X: 30'1-3/4"      Y: 21'0-3/4"
Insertion base is      X:        0'0"    Y:        0'0"    Z:        0'0"
Snap resolution is     X:        0'3"    Y:        0'3"
Grid spacing is        X:        1'0"    Y:        1'0"

Current space:         Model space
Current layer:         TBLCK
Current color:         BYLAYER -- 7 (white)
Current linetype:      BYLAYER -- CONTINUOUS
Current elevation:        0'0"   thickness:        0'0"
Fill on  Grid on  Ortho off  Qtext off  Snap on  Tablet off
Object snap modes:     None
Free disk: 81332224 bytes
Virtual memory allocated to program: 3688 KB
Amount of program in physical memory/Total (virtual) program size: 63%
-- Press RETURN for more --
```

Figure 18-1

Each information item given in the *Status* text screen is described here.

> Total number of entities in the current drawing
> `Model space limits:` values set by the *Limits* command in Model Space
> `Model space uses:` area used by the entities in Model Space
> `Display shows:` current display or windowed area
> `Insertion base point:` point specified by the *Base* command or default (0,0)
> `Snap resolution:` value specified by the *Snap* command
> `Grid spacing:` value specified by the *Grid* command
> `Current space:` Paper space or Model space
> `Current layer:` name
> `Current color:` current color assignment
> `Current linetype:` current linetype assignment
> `Current elevation, thickness:` 3D properties--current height above the XY plane and Z dimension (see Chapter 37)
> `ON` or `OFF` status: *FILL, GRID, ORTHO, QTEXT, SNAP, TABLET*
> `Object Snap Modes:` Current running *OSNAP* modes
> `Free disk:` space on the current hard disk drive
> `Virtual memory allocated to program:` amount of RAM currently occupied by AutoCAD
> `Amount of program in physical memory:` the percentage of the executable AutoCAD program running in RAM
> `Total conventional memory:` lower RAM (of total 640 Kb) available
> `Total extended memory:` extended RAM available
> `Swap file size:` current size of swap (temporary) file on disk

LIST

TYPE IN:	PULL-DOWN MENU	SCREEN MENU	TABLET MENU
LIST	*Assist, Inquiry > List*	*INQUIRY, LIST:*	*4,T and 4,U*

The *List* command displays the database list of information in text screen format for one or more specified entities. The information displayed depends upon the <u>type</u> of entity selected. Invoking the *List* command causes a prompt for you to select objects.

> `Command:` *list*
> `Select objects:` **PICK**
> `Select objects:` **PICK**
> `Select objects:` **Enter**

AutoCAD then displays the list for the selected entities (see Figures 18-2, 18-3, 18-4).

A _List_ of a _Line_ and an _Arc_ is given in this figure.

For the _Line_, coordinates for the endpoints, line length and angle, current layer, and other information are given.

For an _Arc_, the center coordinate, radius, start and end angles are given. (The length of an _Arc_ can be found in the _Modify Entity_ dialogue box when an _Arc_ is PICKed.)

```
    LINE        Layer: 1-WALL
                Space: Model space
        Handle = 824
    from point, X=120'-2 3/8"  Y=36'-6 7/16"  Z=     0'-0"
      to point, X=120'-2 3/8"  Y=52'-5 7/16"  Z=     0'-0"
Length =  15'-11",  Angle in XY Plane =      90
        Delta X =    0'-0", Delta Y =   15'-11", Delta Z =     0'-0"

     ARC         Layer: DOOR
                 Space: Model space
        Handle = C5F
  center point, X=120'-3 1/2"  Y=33'-4 7/16"  Z=     0'-0"
  radius     3'-0"
  start angle    358
    end angle     90
```

Figure 18-2

The _List_ for a _Pline_ is shown in this figure. The location of each vertex is given as well as the length and area of the entire _Pline_ (area is calculated if the _Pline_ has _width_).

```
                    Space: Model space
            at point, X=   5.1440  Y=   3.2500  Z=   0.0000
    starting width    0.0200
      ending width    0.0200

            VERTEX   Layer: 0
                     Space: Model space
            at point, X=   6.5500  Y=   4.6630  Z=   0.0000
    starting width    0.0200
      ending width    0.0200

            VERTEX   Layer: 0
                     Space: Model space
            at point, X=   0.4949  Y=   4.2500  Z=   0.0000
    starting width    0.0200
-- Press RETURN for more --
      ending width    0.0200

            END SEQUENCE  Layer: 0
                     Space: Model space
        area     1.6599
      length     3.9787
```

Figure 18-3

The _List_ for an inserted _Block_ is given here. The block name, insertion point, and scale factors are shown.

```
    BLOCK REFERENCE  Layer: FURNITURE
                Space: Model space
        Handle = 1002
        DESK3
        at point, X=107'-7 15/16"  Y=48'-4 3/8"  Z=     0'-0"
        X scale factor    1.0000
        Y scale factor    1.0000
  rotation angle      0
        Z scale factor    1.0000
```

Figure 18-4

DBLIST

TYPE IN:	PULL-DOWN MENU	SCREEN MENU	TABLET MENU
DBLIST	---	_INQUIRY, DBLIST:_	---

The _Dblist_ command is similar to the _List_ command in that it displays the database listing of entities; however, _Dblist_ gives information for <u>every</u> entity in the current drawing! This command is generally used when you desire to send the list out to a printer or if there are only few entities in the drawing. If you use this command in a complex drawing, be prepared to page through many screens of information.

AREA

TYPE IN:	PULL-DOWN MENU	SCREEN MENU	TABLET MENU
AREA	_Assist, Inquiry > Area_	_INQUIRY, AREA:_	_2,U_

The _Area_ command is helpful for many applications. With this command AutoCAD calculates the area and the perimeter of any enclosed shape in a matter of milliseconds. You specify the area (shape) to consider for calculation by PICKing the _Entity_ (if it is a closed _Pline_, _Polygon_, _Circle_, or other closed entity) or by PICKing points (corners of the shape) to define the shape. The options are given below.

First Point
The command sequence for specifying the area by PICKing points is shown below. This method should only be used for shapes with <u>straight</u> sides.

```
Command: area
<First point>/Entity/Add/Subtract: PICK (Locate the first point to
designate the shape.)
Next point: PICK (Select the second point to define the shape.)
Next point: PICK (Select the third point.)
Next point: PICK (Continue selecting points until all corners have been
selected to completely define the shape.)
Next point: Enter (Indicate completion of the point selection.)
Area = xxx.xx square in.  (xxx.xx square ft.)
perimeter =    xxx.xx"
Command:
```

An example of the *Point* method (PICKing points to define the area) is shown here.

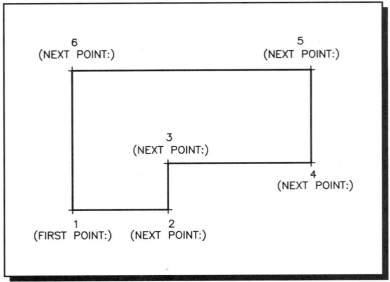

6
(NEXT POINT:)

5
(NEXT POINT:)

3
(NEXT POINT:)

4
(NEXT POINT:)

1
(FIRST POINT:)

2
(NEXT POINT:)

Figure 18-5

Entity

If the shape you want to find the area and perimeter of is a *Circle, Polygon, Ellipse,* or closed *Pline,* the *Entity* option of the *Area* command can be used. Select the shape with one PICK (since all of these shapes are considered as one entity by AutoCAD).

The ability to find the area of a closed *Pline* shape is extremely helpful. Remember that <u>any</u> closed shape, even if it includes *Arcs* and other curves, can be converted to a closed *Pline* with the *Pedit* command (as long as there are no gaps or overlaps). This method provides you with the ability to easily calculate the area of any shape, curved or straight. In short, convert the shape to a closed *Pline* and find the *Area* with the *Entity* option.

Add, Subtract

Add and *Subtract* provide you with the means to find the area of a closed shape that has islands, or negative spaces. For example, you may be required to find the surface area of a sheet of material that has several punched holes. In this case, the area of the holes is subtracted from the area defined by the perimeter shape. The *Add* and *Subtract* options are used specifically for that purpose. The following command sequence displays the process of calculating an area and subtracting the area occupied by the holes.

```
Command: area
<First point>/Entity/Add/Subtract: a (Defining the perimeter
shape is prefaced by the Add option.)
<First point>/Entity/Subtract: e (Assuming the perimeter shape
is a closed Pline or other entity.)
(Add mode)Select circle or polyline: PICK (Select the closed
Pline or Circle.)
Area = xxx.xx square in.  (xxx.xx square ft.)
perimeter =    xxx.xx" (Reports total area occupied by entity.)
```

```
(Add mode)Select circle or polyline:
```
Enter (Indicates completion of the *Add* mode.)
```
<First point>/Entity/Subtract:
```
s (Change to the *Subtract* mode.)
```
<First point>/Entity/Add:
```
e (Assuming the holes are *Circle* entities.)
```
(Subtract mode)Select circle or polyline:
```
PICK (Select first *Circle* to subtract.)
```
Area = xxx.xx square in.   (xxx.xx square ft.)
perimeter = xxx.xx"
```
(Reports total area minus last entity subtracted.)
```
(Subtract mode)Select circle or polyline:
```
PICK (Select second *Circle* to subtract.)
```
Area = xxx.xx square in.   (xxx.xx square ft.)
perimeter = xxx.xx"
```
(Reports last area minus last entity subtracted.)
```
(Subtract mode)Select circle or polyline:
```
Enter (Indicates completion of *Subtract* mode.)
```
<First point>/Entity/Add:
```
Enter (Indicates completion of *Area* command.)
```
Command:
```

Make sure that you press Enter between the *Add* and *Subtract* modes.

An example of the last command sequence used to find the area of a shape minus the holes is shown here. Notice that the entity selected in the first step is a closed *Pline* shape including an *Arc*.

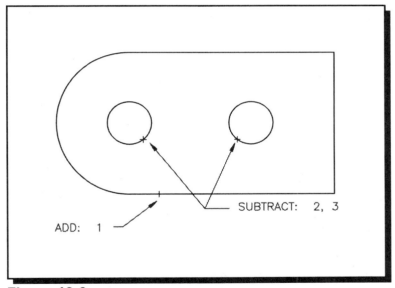

Figure 18-6

DISTANCE

TYPE IN:	PULL-DOWN MENU	SCREEN MENU	TABLET MENU
DIST	*Assist, Inquiry > Distance*	*INQUIRY, DIST:*	*3,U*

The *Distance* command reports the distance between any two points you specify. *OSNAPs* can be used to "snap" to the existing points. This command is helpful in many engineering or architectural applications, such as finding the clearance between two mechanical parts, finding the distance between columns in a building, or finding the size of an opening in a part or doorway. The command is easy to use.

```
Command: dist
First point: PICK (use OSNAPs if needed)
Second point: PICK
Distance = xxx.xx, Angle in XY Plane = xx, Angle from XY
Plane = xx
Delta X = xxx.xx, Delta Y = xxx.xx, Delta Z = xxx.xx
```

AutoCAD reports the absolute and relative distances as well as the angle of the line between the points.

ID

TYPE IN:	PULL-DOWN MENU	SCREEN MENU	TABLET MENU
ID	*Assist, Inquiry > ID Point*	*INQUIRY, ID:*	*2,T*

The *ID* command reports the coordinate value of any point you select with the cursor. If you require the location associated with a specific entity, an *OSNAP* mode (*ENDpoint, MIDpoint, CENter*, etc.) can be used.

```
Command: ID
Point: PICK or (coordinate) (Select a point or enter a coordinate.  OSNAPs can be
used.)
X = xxx.xx, Y = xxx.x, Z = xxx.x
Command:
```

NOTE: *ID* also sets AutoCAD's "last point." The last point can be referenced in commands by using the @ (at) symbol with relative rectangular or relative polar coordinates. *ID* creates a 'blip" at the location of the coordinates you enter or PICK.

TIME

TYPE IN:	PULL-DOWN MENU	SCREEN MENU	TABLET MENU
TIME	---	*INQUIRY, TIME:*	*1,T*

This command is useful for keeping track of the time spent in the current drawing session or total time spent on a particular drawing. Knowing how much time is spent on a drawing can be useful in an office situation for bidding or billing jobs. The *Time* command reports the information shown in Figure 18-7.

The *Total editing time* is automatically kept, starting from when the drawing was first created until the current time. Plotting and printing time is not included in this total, nor is the time spent in a session in which *Quit* was used to close the session.

```
Command:
TIME
Current time:             11 Aug 1993 at 16:28:15.050
Times for this drawing:
  Created:                14 Oct 1991 at 08:22:18.220
  Last updated:           16 Jun 1992 at 16:14:51.420
  Total editing time:     1 days 13:21:05.220
  Elapsed timer (on):     1 days 13:20:31.820
  Next automatic save in: 0 days 01:42:17.030

Display/ON/OFF/Reset:
```

Figure 18-7

Display

The *Display* option causes *Time* to repeat the display with the updated times.

ON/OFF/Reset

The *Elapsed timer* is a separate compilation of time controlled by the user. The *Elapsed timer* can be turned *ON* or *OFF* or can be *Reset*.

Time also reports when the next automatic save will be made. The time interval of the Automatic Save feature is controlled by the *SAVETIME* system variable (see Chapter 2). To set the interval between automatic saves, type *SAVETIME* at the command line and specify a value for time (in minutes). The default interval is 120 minutes.

CHAPTER EXERCISES

1. **Status**

A. **Open** the **PLATNEST** drawing that you completed in Chapter 16 Exercises. Check the **Status** of the drawing. How many entities are in the drawing? What is the *Snap* resolution? What is the *Grid* spacing? How much virtual memory is allocated to the program?

B. **Open** the **EFF-APT** drawing that you completed in Chapter 15 Exercises. Use the **Status** command. How many entities are in this drawing? What are the current *Limits*? What is the current *Layer*? How much virtual memory is allocated to the program?

2. **List**

A. **Open** the **PLATNEST** drawing again. Assume that a laser will be used to cut the plates and holes from the stock and you must program the coordinates. Use the **List** command to give information on the **Line**s and **Circle**s for the one plate with four holes in a diagonal orientation. Determine and write down the coordinates for the 4 corners of the plate and the centers of the 4 holes.

B.   *Open* the **EFF-APT** drawing. Use *List* to determine the area of the inside of the tub. If the tub were filled with 1' of water, could you determine the volume?

3.   **Dblist**

        Open the **PLATNEST** drawing again. Use the *Dblist* to list all the information about the entities in the drawing. Assuming you were to program the laser to cut all the plates and holes, using this method to list the coordinate data and echo to the printer would be superior to using the *List* command repeatedly.

4.   **Area**

A.   *Open* the **EFF-APT** drawing. The entry room is to be carpeted at a cost of $10.00 per square yard. Use the *Area* command (with the PICK points option) to determine the cost for carpeting the room.

B.   *Open* the **PLATNEST** drawing. Using the *Area* command, calculate the wasted material (the two pieces of stock remaining after the 3 plates have been cut or stamped).

C.   The plate with 4 holes at the corners will be painted. Using the *Add* and *Subtract* option of *Area*, calculate the surface area for painting 100 pieces, both sides. (Remember to press Enter between the *Add* and *Subtract* operations.)

5.   **Dist**

A.   *Open* the **EFF-APT** drawing.   Use the *Dist* command to determine the best location for installing a wall-mounted telephone in the apartment. Where should the telephone be located in order to provide the most equal access from all corners of the apartment? What is the farthest distance that you would have to walk to answer the phone?

B.   Using the *Dist* command, determine what length of pipe would be required to connect the kitchen sink drain to the tub drain (only that distance under the floor).

6.   **ID**

        Open the **PLATNEST** drawing once again. You have now been assigned to program the laser to cut the plate with 4 holes in the corners. Use the *ID* command (with OSNAPs) to determine the coordinates for the 4 corners and the hole centers.

7.   **Time**

        Using the *Time* command, what is the total amount of editing time you spent with the **PLATNEST** drawing? How much time have you spent in this session? How much time until the next automatic save?

TEXT FONT (STANDARD STYLE)

ROMAN SIMPLEX FONT

ROMAN COMPLEX FONT – MULTI STROKE

ROMAN DUPLEX FONT – TWO STROKE

ROMAN TRIPLEX FONT – 3 STROKE

ITALIC COMPLEX FONT –ITALICIZED, 2 STROKE

𝕲𝖔𝖙𝖍𝖎𝖈 𝕰𝖓𝖌𝖑𝖎𝖘𝖍 𝕱𝖔𝖓𝖙

𝒮𝒞𝒭𝒥𝒫𝒯 𝒮𝒥𝒨𝒫𝓛𝓔𝒳 𝒻𝒪𝒩𝒥

·ˌ♪ooo♯ ♮♭━━×♩𝄞 ℮:‖•   (MUSIC SYMBOL FONT)

⊡⊿⋀☆⊦⋈━━⬟★⊥⨯𝄞𝄞⨯⋀⌂⛋   (MAPPING SYMBOL FONT)

ΓΡΕΕΚ ΣΙΜΠΛΕΞ ΦΟΝΤ   (GREEK SIMPLEX FONT)

CHAPTER 19

Inserting and Editing Text

CHAPTER OBJECTIVES

After completing this chapter you should:

1.   be able to create text in a drawing using *Text* and *Dtext*;

2.   be able to *Justify* text using each of the methods;

3.   be able to <u>create</u> text styles with both the *Set Style...* dialogue box and the *Style* command formats;

4.   be able to <u>select</u> from created text styles with the *Style* <u>option</u> of *Text* or *Dtext*;

5.   know how to invoke the *Edit Text* dialogue box to edit an existing line of text;

6.   know that the *Modify* dialogue box can be used to modify any property of existing text;

7.   know that *Qtext* (quick text) can be used to speed text regeneration by temporarily converting lines of text to rectangles;

8.   be able to use *Asctext* to import text into a drawing from an ASCII file.

BASICS

The *Dtext and Text* commands provide you with a means of creating text in an AutoCAD drawing. "Text" in CAD drawings usually refers to sentences, words, or notes created from alphabetical or numerical characters that appear in the drawing. The numeric values that are part of specific dimensions are generally <u>not</u> considered "text," since dimensional values are a component of the dimension created automatically with the use of dimensioning commands.

Text in technical drawings is typically in the form of notes concerning information or descriptions of the objects contained in the drawing. For example, an architectural drawing might have written descriptions of rooms or spaces, special instructions for construction, or notes concerning materials or furnishings (Fig. 19-1). An engineering drawing may contain, in addition to the dimensions, manufacturing notes, bill of materials, schedules or tables (Fig. 19-2, 19-3). Technical illustrations may contain part numbers or assembly notes. Title blocks also contain text (Fig. 19-2).

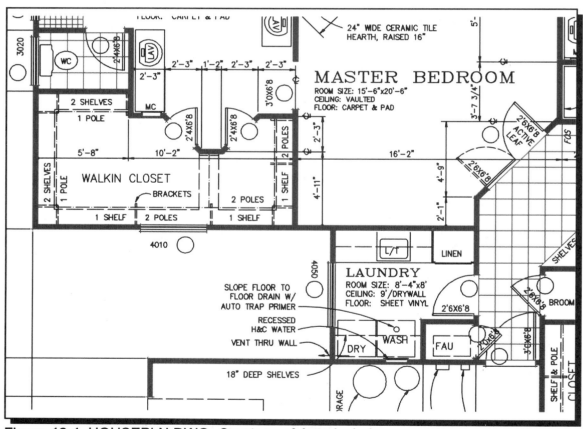

Figure 19-1 HOUSEPLN.DWG Courtesy of Autodesk, Inc.

A <u>line of text</u> in an AutoCAD drawing is treated as a entity, just like a *Line* or a *Circle*. Each line can be *Erased, Moved, Rotated* or otherwise edited as any other graphical entity. The letters themselves can be changed individually with special text editing commands. Since each line of text is treated as a graphical element, the use of many lines of text in a drawing can slow regeneration time and increase plotting time significantly.

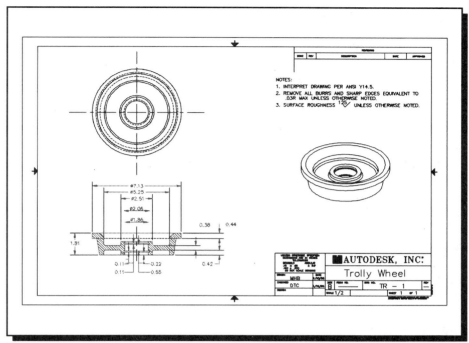

Figure 19-2 TROL1.DWG   Courtesy of Autodesk, Inc.

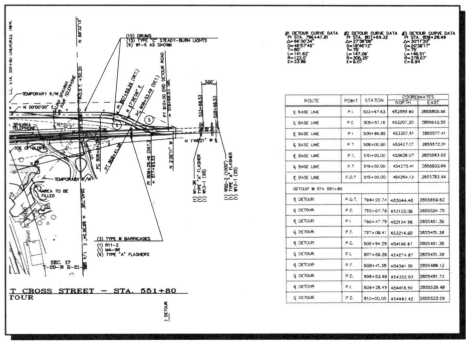

Figure 19-3 PLANPROF.DWG Courtesy of Autodesk, Inc.

The *Qtext* command (quick text) speeds regenerations and test plots by representing a line of text as a box. Text can also be imported into AutoCAD drawings from text files created in other software packages.

The *Dtext* and *Text* commands preform basically the same function; they create text in a drawing. However, *Dtext* (dynamic text) displays each character in the drawing as it is typed and allows entry of multiple lines of text; whereas, *Text* requires an **Enter** or **Return** to display each line of text. When the *Dtext* or *Text* command is used, AutoCAD accepts whatever alphanumeric characters are entered at the keyboard in response to the `Text:` prompt and enters them into the drawing at the specified "insertion point."

Many options for text justification are available for the "insertion point." *Justification* is the method of aligning the lines of text. For example, if text is right justified, the right end of the line of text is aligned at the insertion point; whereas, a line of centered text is centered about the insertion point.

The form or shape of the individual letters, is determined in AutoCAD by the text *style*. Each *style* uses an AutoCAD-supplied font. Only one *style*, called *Standard* (Fig. 19-4), has been created as part of the standard default drawing (ACAD.DWG) and uses the TXT font file. The *Standard* style is composed entirely of straight line segments (no arcs) and is therefore faster to regenerate and plot.

Standard Style

A B C D E F G H I J ... Z

a b c d e f g h i j ... z

1 2 3 4 5 6 7 8 9 10

Figure 19-4

If any other style of text is desired, it must be created with the *Style* command or *Set Style...* dialogue box. Creating a *Style* allows you to pick the font file to use and change its features if desired, e.g., the "obliquing angle" (angle of italics), width factor (compression or extension), and other options. The selection of font files is shown in the *Select Text Font* dialogue box shown in Figure 19-5.

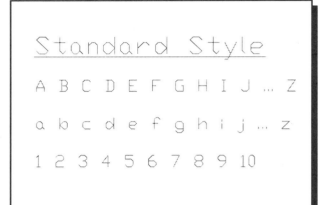

ROMAN SIMPLEX	ROMAN COMPLEX	ROMAN DUPLEX	ROMAN TRIPLEX
ABC123	ABC123	ABC123	ABC123
ITALIC COMPLEX	ITALIC TRIPLEX	SCRIPT SIMPLEX	SCRIPT COMPLEX
ABC123	*ABC123*	ABC123	ABC123
CYRILLIC ALPHABETICAL	CYRILLIC TRANSLITERAL	GREEK SIMPLEX	GREEK COMPLEX
АББ123	АБЧ123	ΣΩ	ΣΩ
GOTHIC ENGLISH	GOTHIC GERMAN	GOTHIC ITALIAN	ASTRONOMICAL SYMBOLS
ABC123	ABC123	ABC123	☉♀♀
MATHEMATICAL SYMBOLS	MUSIC SYMBOLS	MAPPING SYMBOLS	METEOROLOGICAL SYMBOLS
√≈∏	♮♯♭	▽♡✳	⊸⊗⊸

Figure 19-5

When a new *style* is created, it becomes the current one used by the *Dtext* or *Text* command. If several *styles* have been created in a drawing, a particular one can be recalled or made current by using the *style* option of the *Dtext* or *Text* command.

In summary, the *Style* command or *Set Style...* dialogue box allows you to design new styles with your choice of options, such as fonts, width factor and obliquing angle; whereas, the *style* option of *Dtext* and *Text* allow you to select from existing styles in the drawing that you previously created.

Commands related to using text in an AutoCAD drawing include:

Dtext	Places multiple lines of text in a drawing and allows you to see each letter as it is typed.
Text	Places text in a drawing one line at a time.
Style	Creates text styles from any font. This command is typed, but allows you to assign a name for each style.
Set Style...	Creates text styles from icon menu choices, but automatically assigns a style name based on the font file used.
Ddedit	Invokes a dialogue box for editing text. Allows you to edit individual characters or an entire line of text.
Change	This is a broad editing command allowing revision of many aspects of text such as height, rotation angle, insertion point, style or text itself.
Qtext	Short for quick-text, this command temporarily displays a line of text as a box instead of individual characters in order to speed up regeneration time and plot time.

TEXT INSERTION COMMANDS

DTEXT

TYPE IN:	PULL-DOWN MENU	SCREEN MENU	TABLET MENU
DTEXT	*Draw, Text > Dynamic*	*DRAW, DTEXT:*	*8,W to 10,Y*

Dtext (dynamic text) lets you insert text into an AutoCAD drawing. *Dtext* displays each character in the drawing as it is typed. You can enter multiple lines of text without exiting the *Dtext* command. The options are presented below.

```
Command: dtext
Justify/Style/<Start point>:
```

Start Point

The *Start point* for a line of text is the <u>left end</u> of the baseline for the text (Fig. 19-6). *Height* is the distance from the baseline to the top of uppercase letters. Additional lines of text are automatically spaced below and left justified. The *rotation angle* is the angle of the baseline (Fig. 19-7).

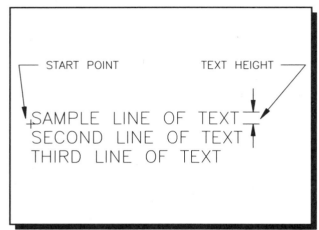

Figure 19-6

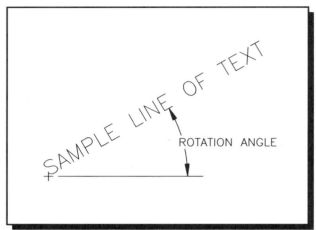

Figure 19-7

The command sequence for this option is:

Command: ***dtext***
Justify/Style/<Start point>: **PICK** or (**coordinates**) (Pick the start point.)
Height <0.20>: **Enter** or (**value**) (Press Enter to accept the default height or specify a new value.)
Rotation Angle <0>: **Enter** or (**value**) (Press Enter to accept the default rotation angle or specify a new value.)
Text: (Type the desired line of text and press **Enter**.)
Text: (Type another line of text and press **Enter**.)
Text: **Enter** (Indicates completion of the *Dtext* command.)
Command:

When the Text: prompt appears, you can also PICK a new location for the next line of text.

Justify

If you want to use one of the justification methods, invoking that option displays the choices at the prompt.

Command: ***dtext***
Justify/Style/<Start point>: ***J*** (Invokes the justification options.)
Align/Fit/Center/Middle/Right/TL/TC/TR/ML/MC/MR/BL/BC/ BR: (**choice**) (Type the capital letters of the choice.)

As an alternative, the desired justification option can be entered at the
`"Justify/Style/<Start point>:"` prompt, assuming you know which method
you want to use beforehand.

After specifying a justification option, you can enter the desired text in response to the
`"Text:"` prompt. The text is not justified until <u>after</u> pressing Enter.

Align

Aligns the line of text between
the two points specified (P1,
P2). The text height is
adjusted automatically
(Fig. 19-8).

Fit

Fits the line of text between
the two points specified (P1,
P2). The text height is drawn
as specified (Fig. 19-8).

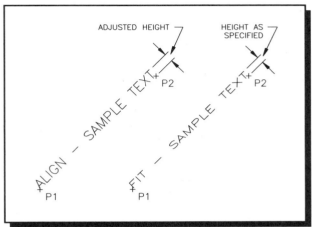

Figure 19-8

Center

Centers the baseline of the
first line of text at the specified point. Additional lines of text are centered
below the first (Fig 19-9).

Middle

Centers the first line of text both vertically and horizontally about the specified
point. Additional lines of text are centered below (Fig. 19-9).

Right

Creates text that is right justified from the specified point (Fig. 19-9).

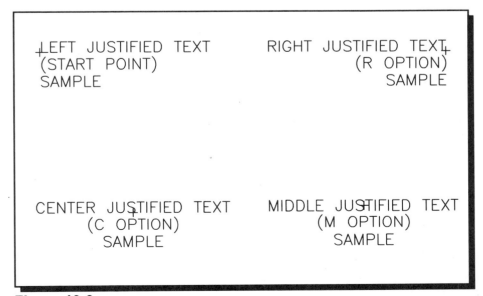

Figure 19-9

TL

> Top Left. Left justifies at the top of the text.

TC

> Top Center. Justifies at the center of the top of the line.

TR

> Top Right. Right justifies at the top right of the line.

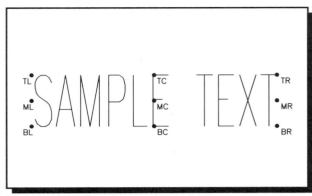

Figure 19-10

ML

> Middle Left. Left justifies at the vertical middle of the line.

MC

> Middle Center. Centers the line of text both vertically and horizontally about the specified point.

MR

> Middle Right. Right justifies at the vertical middle of the text.

BL

> Bottom Left. Left justifies text at the bottom line of the text.

BC

> Bottom Center. Centers the line of text horizontally about the bottom line.

BR

> Bottom Right. Right justifies the line of text at the bottom line.

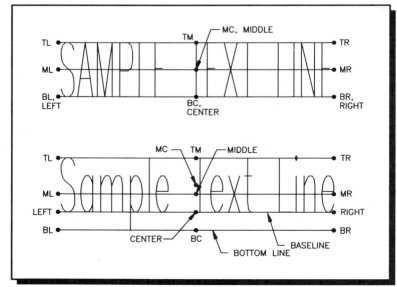

Figure 19-11

Figure 19-11 illustrates the justification points for both upper and lower case letters. Notice that when using all upper case letters, the *MC* and *Middle* points coincide and the *BL, BC, BR* and *Left, Center, Right* points coincide, respectively. If, however, a combination of upper and lower case is used, the extenders (for example, on the letter "p") cause a separate "baseline" and "bottom line"; therefore, the *MC* and *Middle* points do not coincide and the *BL, BC, BR* and *Left, Center, Right* options differ.

Style (option of *Dtext* or *Text*)

The *style* <u>option</u> of the *Dtext* or *Text* command allows you to select from the existing text styles which have been previously created as part of the current drawing. The style selected from the list becomes the current style and is used when placing text with *Dtext* or *Text* and when using dimensioning commands that automatically place numerical values in the drawing.

Since the only text *style* that is available in the default drawing (ACAD.DWG) is *Standard*, other styles must be created before the *style* option of *Text* is of any value. Various text styles are first created with the *Style* <u>command</u> or with the *Set Style...* dialogue box (this topic is discussed later).

The command prompt appears as follows:

```
Command: dtext
Justify/Style/<Start point>: s (Invokes the style option.)
Style name (or ?): (name) or ? (Enter the desired style name to use, or
press "?" to list the choices of existing styles.)
```

Listing the choices produces a text screen giving the styles created in the current drawing. An example screen is shown in Figure 19-12.

```
Text styles:

Style name: ROMANC        Font files: romanc
   Height: 0.0000  Width factor: 1.0000  Obliquing angle: 0
   Generation: Upside-down


Style name: ROMANS        Font files: romans
   Height: 0.0000  Width factor: 1.0000  Obliquing angle: 0
   Generation: Normal


Style name: STANDARD      Font files: txt
   Height: 0.0000  Width factor: 1.0000  Obliquing angle: 0
   Generation: Normal


Current text style: ROMANC
Justify/Style/<Start point>:
```

Figure 19-12

TEXT

TYPE IN:	PULL-DOWN MENU	SCREEN MENU	TABLET MENU
TEXT	---	*DRAW, DTEXT:, TEXT:*	*8,W and 10,Y*

Text is essentially the same as *Dtext* except that the text is not dynamically displayed one letter at a time as you type, but rather appears in the drawing only after pressing **Enter**. The other difference is that *Dtext* repeatedly displays the `"Text:"` prompt to allow entering multiple lines of text; whereas, *Text* requires exiting the command to enter another line. Otherwise, all the options and capabilities of *Text* are identical to *Dtext*.

If you want to type another line of text below the previous one with the *Text* command, use *Text* again, but press **Enter** at the first prompt. The *Text* command then responds with the `"Text:"` prompt, at which time you can enter the next line of text. The new line is automatically spaced below and uses the same height, justification and other options as the previous line.

The digitizing tablet menu provides the *Text/Dtext Toggle* (8,W and 9,W) which forces one or the other command to be used when the justification options are selected directly from the tablet menu (8,X through 10,Y).

STYLE

TYPE IN:	PULL-DOWN MENU	SCREEN MENU	TABLET MENU
STYLE	*Draw, Text > Set Style...*	*DRAW, DTEXT:, STYLE:*	*10,W*

Text styles can be created by using the *STYLE* command or by selecting *Set Style...* which invokes the *Select Text Font* dialogue box (Fig. 19-13). A text *Style* is created by selecting a font file as a foundation and then specifying several other parameters to define the configuration of the letters. Creating a text style involves specifying the parameters below.

Assign a style name (up to 31 characters)
Select a font file (form or shape of the characters)
Specify a fixed height (or leave it variable)
Specify a width factor (extension or compression)
Specify an obliquing angle (degree of slant or italics)
Indicate if backward text is desired (yes or no)
Indicate if text is to be upside-down (yes or no)
Indicate vertical orientation (yes or no for horizontal)

Style and *Set Style...* perform these functions with one fundamental difference: *Set Style...* automatically assigns a style name based upon the font file selected; whereas, the *Style* command allows you to assign any name. The functions are performed in command line mode with the *Style* command and in icon fashion and command line mode with *Set Style....* As a beginner, you should use the *Set Style...* icons because you can see the font options.

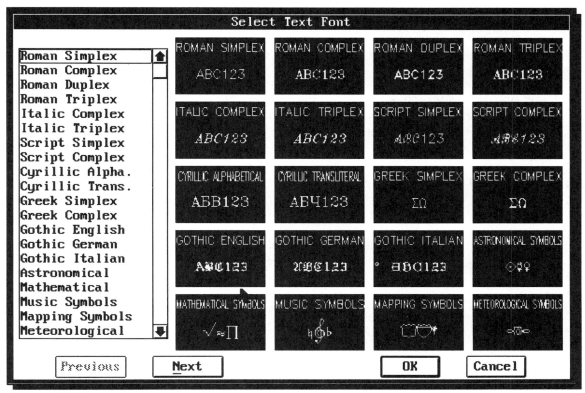

Figure 19-13

Many font files are supplied with the AutoCAD program. Each font file contains the shape description for each of the characters, numbers and symbols in that particular design (Fig. 19-14). The font files are usually located in the C:\ACAD12\ FONTS directory.

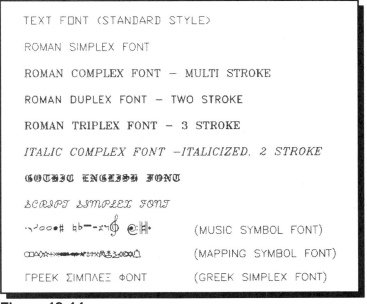

Figure 19-14

Selecting the font file is the initial step in creating a style. Selecting the font file from the icons using *Set Style...* also <u>automatically</u> assigns a style name based on the font file name. The font file selected then becomes a foundation for "designing" the new style based on your choices for the other parameters. Those parameters are presented in command line format in the following sequence.

Height <0.000>

The height should be 0.000 if you want to be prompted again for height each time the *Dtext* or *Text* command is used. In this way the height is variable for the style each time you insert text. If you want the height to be constant, enter a value other than 0. Then *Dtext* or *Text* will not prompt you for a height since it has already been specified. A specific height assignment also overrides the *DIMTXT* setting (see Chapter 29).

Width factor <1.000>

A *width factor* of 1 keeps the characters proportioned as seen in the icon. A value less than 1 compresses the width of the text (horizontal dimension) proportionally; a value of greater than 1 extends the text proportionally.

Obliquing angle <0>

An angle of 0 keeps the font file as shown in the icon. Entering an angle of 15, for example, would slant the text forward from the existing position, or entering a negative angle would cause a back-slant on a vertically oriented font (Fig. 19-15).

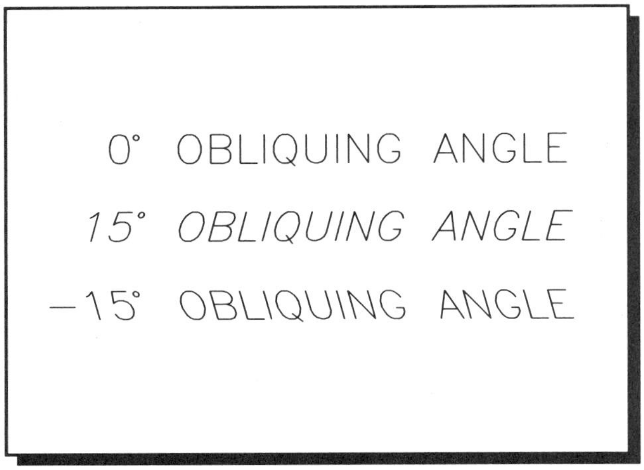

Backwards? <Y/N>

Backwards characters can be helpful for special applications, such as those in the printing industry.

Figure 19-15

Upside-down? <Y/N>

Each letter is created upside-down in the order as typed (Fig 19-16). This is different than entering a rotation angle of 180 in the *Dtext* or *Text* commands. (Turn this book 180 degrees to read the figure.)

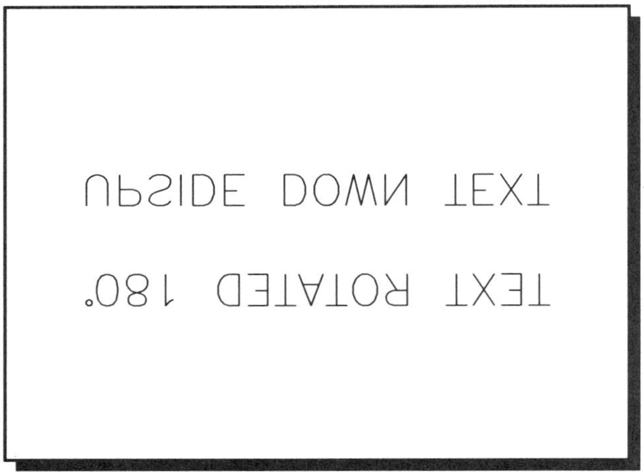

Figure 19-16

Vertical? <Y/N>

Vertical letters are shown in Figure 19-17. The normal rotation angle to enter for vertical text when using *Dtext* or *Text* is 270.

The new text style that is created automatically becomes the current style inserted when *Dtext*, *Text* or dimensioning is used.

Since specification of a font file is an initial step in creating a style, it seems logical that different styles could be created using one font but changing the other parameters. It is possible, and in many cases desirable, to do so. This can only be done by using the *Style* command because you can assign a specific name to each style; whereas, the *Set Style...* method automatically assigns the name based on the font selected. An attempt to create a second style with the same font file using *Set Style...* causes the first one to be overwritten since the names are the same. In other words, by using *Style*, multiple styles can be created from one font; whereas, by using *Set Style...* only one style can exist for each font. The relationship between fonts, styles and resulting text is shown in Figure 19-18.

Figure 19-17

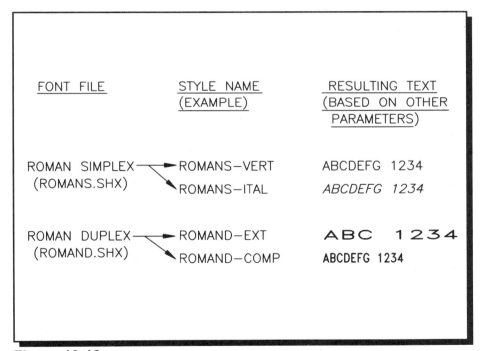

Figure 19-18

The *Style* command presents all prompts in command line format. Assigning a style name is the first step in creating a style by this method. There are no icons to use when selecting fonts, however; therefore, it is imperative that you know the name of the font file you want to use. The command syntax is shown on the next page.

```
Command: style
Text name (or ?) <current>: (Assign a descriptive name up to 31
characters.  The ? can be typed to give a list of the existing styles.)
Font file <default>: (Type the desired font file name.  The .SHX or .PFB file
extension do not need to be typed.)
Height <default>: (Enter 0 for variable height or assign another value for fixed
height.)
Width Factor <default>: (Enter a 0 for default font width, a value less than 1
for compressed text, or a value greater than 1 for extended text.)
Obliquing angle <default>: (The value entered is added to the existing slant
angle.)
Backwards? <Y/N>: (Yes or No.)
Upside-down? <Y/N>: (Yes or No.)
Vertical? <Y/N>: (Yes or No.)
(Name) is the current text style.
```

Existing text style names can be renamed with the *Rename* command (Chapter 30). The existing lines of text in the particular style assume the new text style name.

Special Text Characters

Special characters that are often used in drawings can be entered by using the "%%" symbols and a letter to designate the kind of symbol desired. The following codes are typed in response to the "Text:" prompt in the *Dtext* or *Text* command.

Code	Resulting text	Description
%%c	ø	diameter (metric)
%%d	°	degrees
%%o	‾‾‾‾	(overscored text, needed on both ends of text)
%%u	____	(underscored text, needed on both ends of text)
%%p	±	plus or minus
%%nnn	varies	ASCII text character number

For example, entering "**Chamfer 45%%d**" at the "Text:" prompt would draw the following text: **Chamfer 45°**.

Calculating Text Height for Scaled Drawings

To achieve a specific height in a drawing intended to be plotted to scale, multiply the desired text by the "drawing scale factor." (See Chapter 14, Plotting.) For example, if the drawing scale factor is 48 and the desired text height on the plotted drawing is 1/8", enter **6** (1/8 x 48) in response to the "Height:" prompt of the *Dtext* or *Text* command.

If *Limits* have already been set, use the following steps to calculate a text height to enter in response to the "Height:" prompt to achieve a specific plotted text height.

1. Determine the sheet size to be used for plotting (for example, 36" x 24").
2. Decide on the text height for the finished plot (for example, .125").
3. Check the *Limits* of the current drawing (for example, 144' x 96' or 1728" x 1152").
4. Divide the *Limits* by the sheet size to determine the drawing scale factor (1728"/36" = 48).
5. Multiply the desired text height by the drawing scale factor (.125 x 48 = 6).

TEXT EDITING COMMANDS

DDEDIT

TYPE IN:	PULL-DOWN MENU	SCREEN MENU	TABLET MENU
DDEDIT	---	*EDIT, DDEDIT:*	*8,V and 9,V*

Ddedit invokes a dialogue box for editing text. *Ddedit* allows you to edit <u>individual</u> <u>characters</u> or an entire line of text. The dialogue box displays only one line of text at a time (Fig. 19-19).

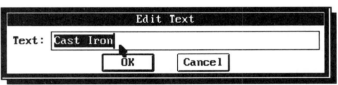

Figure 19-19

The dialogue box operates like the edit boxes that appear in other dialogue boxes. With the cursor in its default position at the end of the line, typing or pressing the **Backspace** key deletes the entire line. For editing one or two letters, place the arrow at any character location and PICK, then begin editing at that point. The **Del** or **Backspace** keys can also be used. As an alternative, a section of the line can be highlighted by holding down the button while dragging the cursor over the desired area. The **Del** or **Backspace** (depending upon the direction) can then be used to delete that section.

Ddedit also allows editing of *Block attributes*. *Attributes* are text items attached to *Blocks* (see Chapter 22). *Ddedit* can only be used to edit *Attributes* <u>before</u> they have been combined with *Blocks*.

CHANGE

TYPE IN:	PULL-DOWN MENU	SCREEN MENU	TABLET MENU
CHANGE	*Modify, Change > Points*	*EDIT, CHANGE:*	---

Change is a broad editing command allowing revision of many entities including text. (See Chapter 16 for other information on *Change*.) Even though the word "Text" does not appear as an option, *Change* can be used to edit text. You can change many aspects of text such as height, rotation angle, insertion point, style, or the text itself. The command syntax for using *Change* to edit text is as follows:

```
Command: change
Select Objects: PICK (Select the line of text to change.)
Properties/<Change point>: Enter (Press Enter to change text.  Since you
do not want to change either properties or points, give a null response--press Enter
which causes the command to pass on to the text prompts.)
Text style: (selected style)
New style or RETURN for no change: (new style name) or Enter (Type
new style name or press Enter to pass to next prompt.)
New height <current value>: (value) or Enter (Type the desired new height
or press Enter to proceed.)
New rotation angle <current value>: (value) or Enter (Type the desired
new rotation angle or press Enter to proceed.)
New Text <current text>: (Type the desired new line of text or press Enter to
complete the command.)
Command:
```

DDMODIFY

TYPE IN:	PULL-DOWN MENU	SCREEN MENU	TABLET MENU
DDMODIFY	*Modify, Entity...*	*EDIT, DDMODIFY:*	*16,Y and 17,Y*

Invoking this command prompts to select objects and causes the *Modify* dialogue box to appear. As described in Chapter 16, the dialogue box that appears is <u>specific</u> to the type of entity that is PICKed--kind of a "smart" dialogue box. If a line of text is PICKed in response to the "Select objects:" prompt, the dialogue box shown in Figure 19-20 appears.

This dialogue box allows editing of <u>all</u> aspects of text. The *Change* command allows editing <u>almost</u> all aspects of text in a command line format. *Modify* allows <u>any</u> kind of editing to text, including an *Upside down*, *Backwards*, *Width factor* and *Obliquing angle* change.

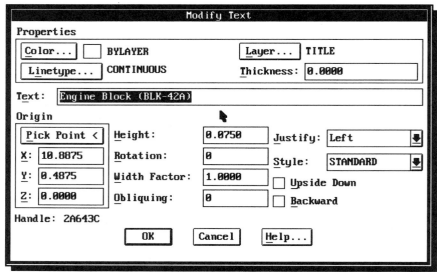

Figure 19-20

QTEXT

TYPE IN:	PULL-DOWN MENU	SCREEN MENU	TABLET MENU
QTEXT	---	*SETTINGS, QTEXT:*	*10,V*

Qtext (quick text) allows you to display a line of text as a box in order to speed up drawing and plotting times. Because lines of text are treated as graphical elements, a drawing with much text can be relatively slower for regenerations and takes considerably more time plotting than the same drawing with little or no text.

When *Qtext* is turned *ON* and the drawing is regenerated, each text line is displayed as a rectangular box (Fig. 19-21). Each box displayed represents one line of text and is approximately equal in size to the associated line of text.

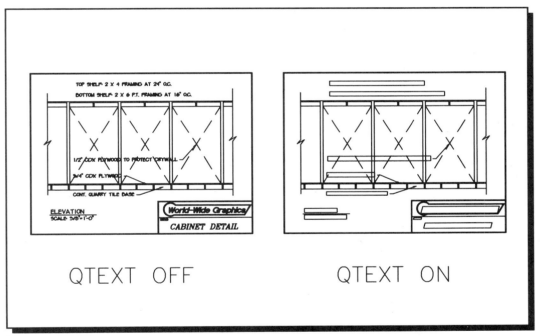

Figure 19-21

For drawings with considerable amounts of text, *Qtext ON* noticeably reduces regeneration time. For check plots (plots made during the drawing or design process used for checking progress), the drawing can be plotted with *Qtext ON*, requiring considerably less plot time. *Qtext* is then turned *OFF* and the drawing must be *Regen*erated to make the final plot.

When *Qtext* is turned *ON*, the text remains in a readable state until a *Regen* is invoked or caused. The text then changes to rectangular boxes. Newly inserted text is readable at least until the next *Regen*. When *Qtext* is turned *OFF*, the drawing must be regenerated to read the text again. Obviously, *Qtext* is *OFF* in the default drawing (ACAD.DWG).

ASCTEXT

TYPE IN:	PULL-DOWN MENU	SCREEN MENU	TABLET MENU
ASCTEXT	*Draw, Text > Import Text*	---	---

The *Asctext* command imports text from an ASCII text file. An ASCII (American Standard Code for Information Interchange) file contains only alphanumeric characters without word processing codes. Text editors and word processors in non-document mode create ASCII text files.

If you have large amounts of text to include in an AutoCAD drawing, such as a large bill of materials or a parts list, it may be more efficient to use a word processor or text editor to type the text and import it to AutoCAD using *Asctext* than to use the *Dtext* or *Text* command. As another example, existing text can be exported from a database or spreadsheet into an ASCII text file, then imported into an AutoCAD drawing using *Asctext*. This utility command can save a considerable amount of time when dealing with large amounts of text or when using existing information in alphanumeric form from another software package.

Asctext inserts text using the current text style. Invoking the command causes the *File to Read* dialogue box to appear (Fig. 19-22).

During the importation process, *Asctext* offers many options similar to the *Dtext* or *Text* commands such as insertion point, text height, and rotation angle. Several other special options are available and are explained in detail.

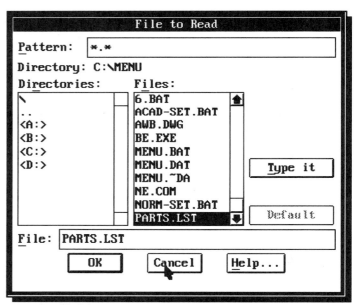

Figure 19-22

The command syntax for *Asctext* is as follows.

> Command: **asctext** (The *File to Read* dialogue box appears. Select the desired file from the list.)
> Start point or Center/Middle/Right/?: **PICK** or **(letter)** (PICK a start point or indicate the option to use. Typing the **?** displays the other justification options.)
> Height <0.2000>: **PICK** or **(value)** (PICK height or enter a value for height.)
> Change text options? <N>: **Enter** (Press enter to accept the default.)
> Command:

The text contained in the indicated file is then inserted into the AutoCAD drawing. The options that are available when answering **Y** in response to the last prompt are as follows:

`Distance between lines/<Auto>:` **PICK** or (**value**) or **Enter** (*Auto* automatically spaces between lines based on the text height specified.)
`First line to read/<1>:` (**value**) or **Enter** (This option imports beginning at the indicated line number.)
`Number of lines to read/<All>:` (**value**) or **Enter** (This specifies the number of lines to import after the previously indicated line number.)
`Underscore each line? <N>:` **Enter** or **Y**
`Overscore each line? <N>:` **Enter** or **Y**
`Change text case? Upper/Lower/<N>:` **Enter** or (**letter**) (*U* imports text as all capital letters, *L* imports text as all lower case letters.)
`Set up Columns? <N>:` **Enter** or **Y** (Responding with *Y* causes a prompt to indicate the number of, and distance between, columns.)

Figures 19-23 displays text in an ASCII file and Figure 19-24 displays the same text imported into AutoCAD (using the *Column* option) to prepare a parts list.

```
1
2
3
4
5
6
Base
Screw
Jaw
Collar
Set Screw
Bolt
1
1
1
1
1
4
Cast Iron
Mach Steel
Plate Steel
Mach Steel
Standard
Standard
```

Figure 19-23

1	Base	1	Cast Iron
2	Screw	1	Mach Steel
3	Jaw	1	Plate Steel
4	Collar	1	Mach Steel
5	Set Screw	1	Standard
6	Bolt	4	Standard

Figure 19-24

CHAPTER EXERCISES

1. **Dtext**

Open the **EFF-APT** drawing. Make **Layer** **TEXT** **Current** and use **Dtext** to label the three rooms: **KITCHEN**, **LIVING ROOM**, and **BATH**. Use the **Standard style** and the **Start point** justification option. When prompted for the **Height:**, enter a value to yield letters of 3/16" on a 1/4"=1' plot (3/16 x the drawing scale factor = text height).

2. **Set Style..., Dtext, Ddedit**

Open the drawing of the temperature graph you created as **CH16EX8C**. Use **Set Style...** to create two styles based on the **Roman Simplex** and **Roman Complex** font files (accept all defaults). Use **Dtext** with the **Center** justification option to label the days of the week and the temperatures (and degree symbols) with the **Romans** style as shown in Figure 19-25. Use a **Height** of .20. Label the axes as shown using the

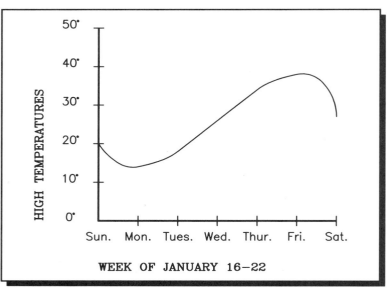

Figure 19-25

Romanc style. Use **Ddedit** for editing any mistakes. Use **Saveas** and name the drawing **TEMPGRPH**.

3. **Set Style..., Style, Dtext**

Open the **BILLMATL** drawing created in the Chapter 17 Exercises. Use **Set Style...** to create a new style using the **Roman Simplex** font. Use whatever justification methods you need to align the text information (not the titles) as shown in Figure 19-26. Next, type the **Style** command to create a new style that you name as **ROMANS-ITAL**. Use the **Romans** font file and specify a **15** degree **obliquing angle**. Use this style for the **NO.**, **PART NAME**, and **MATERIAL**. **Saveas BILLMAT2**.

NO.	PART NAME	MATERIAL
1	Base	Cast Iron
2	Centering Screw	N/A
3	Slide Bracket	Mild Steel
4	Swivel Plate	Mild Steel
5	Top Plate	Cast Iron

Figure 19-26

4. *Set Style...*

Create two new styles for each of your prototype drawings: **ASHEET**, **BSHEET**, **CSHEET**, and **DSHEET**. Use the *Roman Simplex* style with the default options for engineering applications or *City Blueprint* for architectural applications. Next, design a style of your choosing to use for larger text as in title blocks or large notes.

5. *Modify* text

Open the **EFF-APT** drawing. Create a new style using the *City Blueprint* font file. Next select *Entity...* from the *Modify* pull-down menu. Use this dialogue box to modify the text style of each the existing room names to the new style as shown in Figure 19-27. *Saveas* **EFF-APT2**.

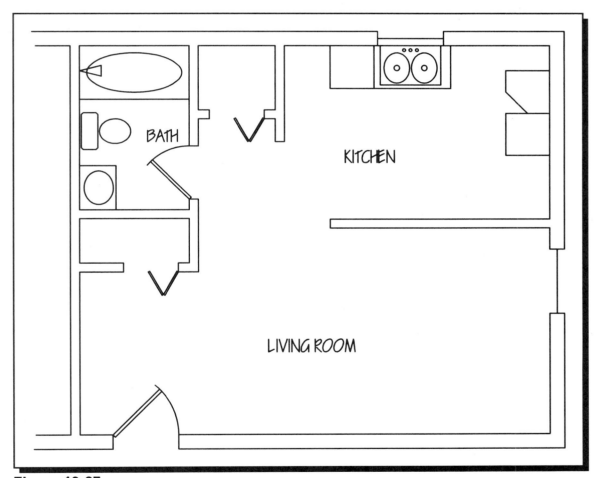

Figure 19-27

6.   *Qtext*

Open the **HOUSEPLN** (AutoCAD sample) drawing. Use *Regen* and check the time required until the *Regen* is complete. Turn **Qtext On**. Use *Regen* again and compare the time to the first *Regen*. Is a regeneration faster with *Qtext On* or *Off*? Imagine the difference in time required for plots! *Zoom* in to examine the text "boxes." Do <u>not</u> *Save* the drawing.

7.   *Import Text, Ddedit, Modify Entity...*

Use a text editor or the DOS editor to create a text file containing words similar to "Temperatures were recorded at Sanderson Field by the National Weather Service." Then *Open* the **TEMPGRPH** drawing and use *Import Text* to bring the text in the drawing as a note in the graph as shown in Figure 19-28. Use *Ddedit* to edit the text if desired or use *Modify Entity...* to change the text style or height.

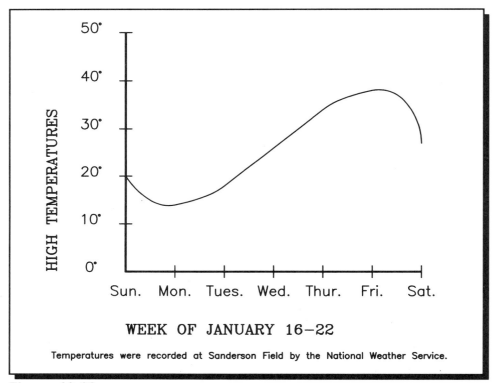

Figure 19-28

1. FIRST SELECTION SET (WINDOW)   2. NEW SELECTION SET (PICK)

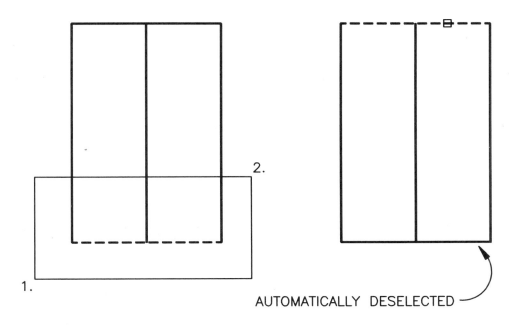

AUTOMATICALLY DESELECTED

CHAPTER 20

Selection Set Variables

CHAPTER OBJECTIVES

After completing this chapter you should:

1.   be able to set the *PICKFIRST* variable to enable or disable Noun/Verb order of editing;

2.   be able to control whether entities are added to or replace the selection set by using the *PICKADD* variable;

3.   know that the *PICKAUTO* variable enables or disables the pickbox *Auto* window/crossing window feature;

4.   be able to set the preferred window dragging style with the *PICKDRAG* variable;

5.   understand that these variable settings are saved in each computer's ACAD.CFG file and are not saved as part of the current drawing.

BASICS

There are four variables that allow you to customize the way that you select objects. Keep in mind that selecting objects occurs <u>only for editing</u> commands; therefore, the variables discussed in this chapter affect how you select objects when you <u>edit</u> AutoCAD entities. The variable names and the related action are briefly explained here.

Variable Name	Default Setting	Related Action
PICKFIRST	1	Enables and disables Noun/Verb command syntax. Noun/Verb means *PICK* entities (noun) *FIRST* and then use the edit command (verb).
PICKADD	1	Controls whether entities are *ADD*ed to the selection set when *PICK*ed, or replace the selection set when picked. Also controls whether the SHIFT key + #1 button combination (SHIFT+#1) removes or adds selected entities to the selection set.
PICKAUTO	1	Enables or disables the *PICK*box *AUTO*matic window/crossing window feature for object selection.
PICKDRAG	0	Enables or disables single *PICK* window *DRAG*ging. When *PICKDRAG* is set to 1, you start the window by pressing the *PICK* button, then draw the window by holding the button down and *DRAG*ging to specify the diagonal corner, and close the window by releasing the button. In other words, windowing is done with one PICK and one release rather than with two PICKs.

Like many system variables, the selection set variables listed above hold an integer value of either **1** or **0**. **1** (One) designates a setting of *ON* and **0** designates a setting of *OFF*. System variables that hold an integer value of either **1** or **0** "toggle" a feature *ON* or *OFF*.

Changing the Settings

Settings for the selection set variables can be changed in either of two ways: (1) the variable names can be typed, or (2) the *Entity Selection Settings* dialogue box can be called.

1. Even though these are system variables, you can type the variable name at the Command: prompt (just like an AutoCAD command) to change the setting.

2. The *Entity Selection Settings* dialogue box (Fig. 20-1) can be PICKed from the *Settings* pull-down menu or called by typing ***Ddselect***. Each of the four variables listed above can be changed in this dialogue box, but the syntax in the dialogue box is <u>not</u> the same as the variable name. A check in the checkbox by each choice does <u>not</u> necessarily mean a setting of *ON* for the related variable.

When you change any of these four selection set variables, the setting is recorded in the <u>ACAD.CFG</u> file, rather than in the current drawing file as with most variable settings. In this way, the change (which is generally personal preference of the operator) is established with the work station, not the drawing file.

The *Entity Selection Settings* dialogue box shown in Figure 20-1 displays the default settings for AutoCAD Release 12. Notice the syntax used in the dialogue box does not reflect the variables' names. To avoid confusion, it is suggested that you initially use either the variable names to change the settings in command line format or the dialogue box to change the settings, but not both.

Figure 20-1

THE VARIABLES

PICKFIRST

NOTE: If the GRIPS variable is set to **1**, entity grips are enabled and are displayed if practicing with the *PICKFIRST* variable. Entity grips do not hinder your ability to use *PICKFIRST*, but they may distract your attention from the current topic. Setting the GRIPS variable to **0** disables entity grips. You can type **GRIPS** at the command prompt to change the setting. See Chapter 23 for a full discussion of entity grips.

The **PICKFIRST** system variable enables or disables the ability to select objects <u>before</u> invoking an edit command.   If *PICKFIRST* is set to 1, or *ON*, you can select objects at the `Command:` prompt <u>before</u> a command is in use. *PICKFIRST* means that you *PICK* the entities *FIRST*, and then invoke the desired command.

How, you ask, can I select objects before the `Select Objects:` prompt is given? You can PICK entities because the pickbox and automatic windowing object selection methods are available at all times, unless you are currently using a command. Notice the small pickbox at the center of the crosshairs. At the open `Command:` prompt you can PICK entities with the pickbox and/or with the automatic window/crossing window methods.

This order of editing is called Noun/Verb; the <u>objects are the nouns</u> and the <u>command is the verb</u>. Noun/Verb editing is somewhat more intuitive because you normally imagine what objects need to be changed, then decide how (what command) you want to change them. Noun/Verb editing allows AutoCAD to operate like some other CAD systems; that is, the objects can be PICKed FIRST and then the edit command can be chosen.

The command syntax for Noun/Verb editing is given on the next page using the *Move* command as an example.

Command: **PICK** (Use the cursor pickbox, auto window/crossing window to select objects.)
Command: **PICK** (Continue selecting desired objects.)
Command: ***Move*** (Enter the desired command and AutoCAD responds with the number of entities selected.) 2 found
Base point or displacement: **PICK** or **(coordinates)**
Second point of displacement: **PICK** or **(coordinates)**
Command:

Notice that as soon as the edit command is invoked, AutoCAD reports the number of objects found and uses these as the selection set to act upon. You do not get a chance to Select objects: within the command. The selection set PICKed immediately before the command is used for the editing action. The command then passes through the Select objects: step to the next prompt in the sequence. All editing commands operate the same as with Verb/Noun syntax order with the exception that the Select objects: step is bypassed.

Only the pickbox, auto window and crossing window can be used for object selection with Noun/Verb editing. The other object selection methods (*ALL, Last, Previous, Fence, Window Polygon*, and *Crossing Polygon*) are only available when you are presented with the Select objects: prompt (when you select the command first).

You have probably noticed that until this time you invoked all commands first and then selected objects when the request was given. That syntax order is known as Verb/Noun syntax (command/objects). Since the *PICKFIRST* variable was introduced with AutoCAD Release 12, most AutoCAD users learned only Verb/Noun syntax. This syntax order is somewhat easier to learn first because the commands prompt you when it is time to select objects.

Changing the setting of *PICKFIRST* is easily accomplished in command line mode (typing). However, the *Entity Selection Settings* dialogue box can also be used to toggle the setting (20-1). The choice is titled *Noun/Verb Selection* and a check appearing in the box means that *PICKFIRST* is set to 1 (*ON*).

PICKADD

The *PICKADD* variable controls whether entities are ADDed to the selection set when they are PICKed or whether entities replace the last selection set when PICKed. This variable is *ON* (set to 1) by default. Most AutoCAD operators work in this mode.

Until you reached this section, it is probable that all PICKing you did was with *PICKADD* set to 1. In other words, every time you selected an entity that entity was added to the selection set. In this way, the selection set is cumulative; that is, each entity PICKed is added to the current set. This mode also allows you to use multiple selection methods to build the set. You can PICK with the pickbox, then with a window, then with any other method to continue selecting objects. The Select objects: process can only be ended by pressing **Enter**.

With the default option (when *PICKADD* is set to 1 or *ON*), the SHIFT+#1 key combination allows you to deselect, or remove, objects from the current selection set. This has the same result as using the _Remove_ option. Deselecting is helpful if you accidentally select objects or if it is easier in some situations to select _ALL_ and then deselect (SHIFT+#1) a few objects.

When the _PICKADD_ variable is set to 0 (_OFF_), entities that you select <u>replace</u> the last selection set. Let's say you select five entities and they become highlighted. If you then select two other entities with a window, they would become highlighted and the other five entities automatically become deselected and unhighlighted. The two new entities would replace the last five to define the new selection set. Figure 20-2 illustrates this scenario.

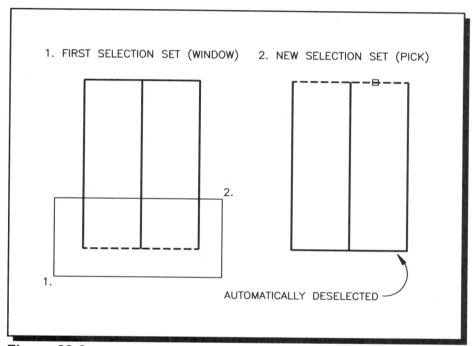

Figure 20-2

The _PICKADD_ variable also controls whether the SHIFT+#1 key combination removes from or adds to the selection set. When _PICKADD_ is set to 1 (_ON_), the SHIFT+#1 combination deselects (removes) entities from the selection set. When _PICKADD_ is set to 0 (_OFF_), the SHIFT+#1 combination toggles entities in or out of the selection set depending on the entity's current state. In other words, (when _PICKADD_ is _OFF_) if the entity is included in the set (highlighted), SHIFT+#1 deselects (unhighlights) it, or if the entity is not in the selection set, SHIFT+#1 adds it.

Changing the _PICKADD_ variable in the _Entity Selection Settings_ dialogue box is accomplished by making the desired choice in the checkbox. Changing the setting in this way is confusing because a check by _Use Shift to Add_ means that _PICKADD_ is _OFF_! Normally a check means the related variable is _ON_. To avoid confusion, use only one method (typing or dialogue box) to change the setting until you are familiar with it.

It may occur to you that you cannot imagine a practical application for using _PICKADD ON_ and that it makes perfect sense to operate AutoCAD with _PICKADD OFF_. This is true for most applications; however, if you use _GRIPS_ often, setting _PICKADD_ to _OFF_ simplifies the process of changing **warm** _Grips_ to **cold**. _Grips_ are discussed in Chapter 23.

PICKAUTO

The *PICKAUTO* variable controls automatic windowing when the `Select objects:` prompt appears. Automatic windowing is the feature that starts the first corner of a window or crossing window when the pickbox is in an open area when you **PICK**. Once the first corner is established, if the cursor is moved to the right, a window is created, and if the cursor is moved to the left, a crossing window is started. See Chapter 4 for details of this feature.

When *PICKAUTO* is set to 1 or *ON* (the default setting), the automatic window/crossing is available whenever you select objects. When *PICKAUTO* is set to 0, the automatic windowing feature is disabled. However, the *PICKAUTO* variable is overridden if GRIPS are *ON* or if the *PICKFIRST* variable is *ON*. In either of these cases, the cursor pickbox and auto windowing should be enabled so that objects can be selected at the open `Command:` prompt.

Auto windowing is a helpful feature and can be used to increase your drawing efficiency. The default setting of *PICKAUTO* is the typical setting for AutoCAD users.

PICKDRAG

This variable controls the method of drawing a selection window. *PICKDRAG* set to 1 or *ON* allows you to draw the window or crossing window by clicking at the first corner, holding down the button, dragging to the other corner, and releasing the button at the other corner (Fig. 20-3). With *PICKDRAG ON* you can specify diagonal corners of the window with one press and one release rather than with two clicks. Many GUIs (graphical user interfaces) of other softwares use this method of mouse control.

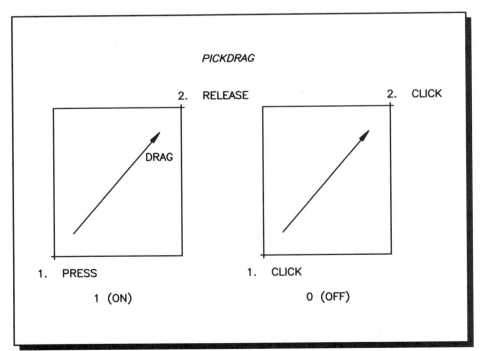

Figure 20-3

The default setting of _PICKDRAG_ is 0 or _OFF_. This method allows you to create a window by clicking at one corner and again at the other corner. Releases of AutoCAD previous to 12 use this method of window creation exclusively. Most AutoCAD users are accustomed to this style which accounts for the default setting of _PICKDRAG_ to 0 (_OFF_).

CHAPTER EXERCISES

1. _PICKFIRST_

    Check to insure that **PICKFIRST** is set to **1** (_ON_). Also make sure GRIPS are set to 0 (_OFF_) by typing **GRIPS** at the command prompt. For each of the following editing commands you use, make sure that you PICK the objects FIRST, then invoke the editing command.

A. **Open** the **PLATES** drawing that you created as an exercise in Chapter 10 (not the PLATNEST drawing). **Erase** 3 of the 4 holes from the plate on the left leaving only the one at the lower left corner (**PICK** the **Circles**, then invoke **Erase**). Create a **Rectangular Array** with **7** rows and **5** columns and **1** unit between each hole (PICK the _Circle_ before invoking _Array_). The new plate should have 35 holes as shown in Figure 20-4, plate A.

B. For the center plate, **PICK** the 3 holes on the vertical center, then invoke **Copy**. Use the **Multiple** option to create the additional 2 sets of 3 holes on each side of the center column. Your new plate should look like that in Figure 20-4, plate B. Use **Saveas** to assign a new name, **PLATES2**.

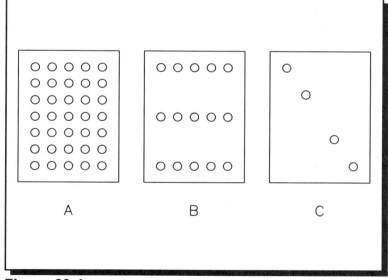

C. For the last plate (on the right), **PICK** the two top holes and **Move** them upward. Use the **CENter** of the top hole and specify

Figure 20-4

    a "_Second point of displacement_" as **1** unit from the top and left edges. Compare your results to Figure 20-4, plate C. **Save** the drawing (as **PLATES2**).

    Remember that you can leave the _PICKFIRST_ setting _ON_ always. This means that you can use both Noun/Verb or Verb/ Noun editing at any time. You always have the choice of whether you want to PICK objects first or use the command first.

2. **PICKADD**

Change **PICKADD** to **0** (**OFF**). Remember that if you want to PICK entities and add them to the existing highlighted set, hold down the **SHIFT** key, then **PICK**.

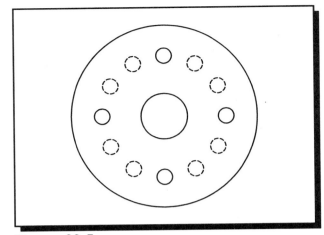

Figure 20-5

A. **Open** the **CH10EX3A** drawing. (The settings for *GRIPS* and *PICKFIRST* have not changed by *Opening* a new drawing.) **Erase** the holes (highlighted *Circles* shown in Figure 20-5) leaving only 4 holes. Use either Noun/Verb or Verb/Noun editing. **Saveas FLANGE1**.

B. **Open** drawing **CH10EX3B**. Select all the holes and **Rotate** them **180** degrees to achieve the arrangement shown in Figure 20-6. Any selection method may be used. Try several selection methods to see how *PICKADD* reacts. (The *Fence* option can be used to select all holes without having to use the SHIFT key.) **Saveas FLANGE2** and change the **PICKADD** setting back to **1** (**ON**).

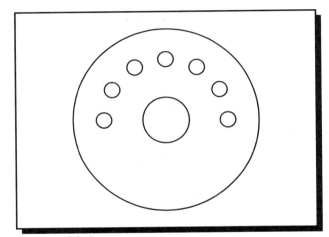

Figure 20-6

3. **PICKDRAG**

Open the **CH12EX3** drawing. Set **PICKDRAG** to **1** (**ON**). Use **Stretch** to change the front and side views to achieve the new base thickness as indicated in Figure 20-7. (Remember to hold down the PICK button when dragging the mouse or puck.) When finished, **Saveas HOLDRCUP**. Change the **PICKDRAG** setting back to **0** (**OFF**).

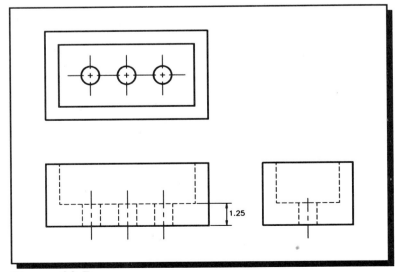

Figure 20-7

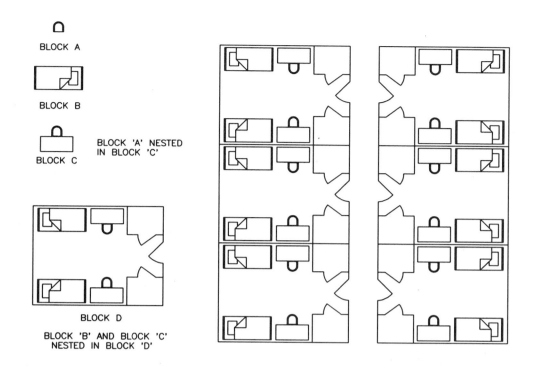

BLOCK A

BLOCK B

BLOCK C

BLOCK 'A' NESTED
IN BLOCK 'C'

BLOCK D

BLOCK 'B' AND BLOCK 'C'
NESTED IN BLOCK 'D'

CHAPTER 21

Blocks

CHAPTER OBJECTIVES

After completing this chapter you should:

1. understand the concept of creating and inserting symbols in AutoCAD drawings;

2. be able to use the *Block* command or *Bmake* program to transform a group of entities into one entity that is stored in the current drawing's block definition table;

3. be able to use the *Insert* and *Minsert* commands to bring *Blocks* into drawings;

4. know that *color* and *linetype* of *Blocks* is based on conditions when the *Block* is made;

5. be able to convert *Blocks* to individual entities with *Explode* or *Insert* with the * symbol;

6. be able to use *Wblock* to prepare .DWG files for insertion into other drawings;

7. be able to redefine and globally change previously inserted *Blocks*;

8. be able to define an insertion base point for .DWG files using *Base*.

BASICS

A *Block* is a <u>group</u> of entities that is combined into <u>one</u> entity with the *Block* command. The typical application for *Blocks* is in the use of symbols. Many drawings contain symbols, such as doors and windows for architectural drawings, capacitors and resistors for electrical schematics, or pumps and valves for piping and instrumentation drawings. In AutoCAD symbols are created first by constructing the desired geometry with entities like *Line*, *Arc*, *Circle*, etc., then transforming the set of entities comprising the symbol into a *Block*. A description of the entities comprising the *Block* is then stored in the drawing's "block definition table." The *Blocks* can then each be *Insert*ed into a drawing many times and treated as a single entity.

Figure 21-1 compares a shape composed of a set of entities and the same shape after it has been made into a *Block* and *Insert*ed back into the drawing. Notice that the original set of entities is selected (highlighted) individually for editing; whereas, the *Block* is only one entity.

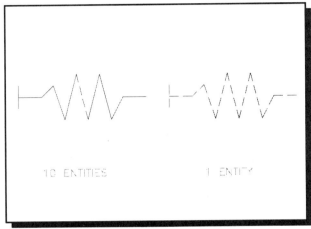

Since an inserted *Block* is one entity, it uses less file space than a set of entities that is copied with *Copy*. The *Copy* command creates a duplicate set of entities, so that if the original symbol were created with 10 entities, 3 copies would yield a total of 40 entities. If instead the original set of 10 were made into a *Block* and then *Insert*ed 3 times, the total entities would be 13 (the original 10 + 3).

Figure 21-1

Upon *Insert*ing a *Block*, its scale can be changed and rotational orientation specified without having to use the *Scale* or *Rotate* commands (Fig. 21-2). If a design change is desired in the *Blocks* that have already been *Insert*ed, the original *Block* can be redefined and the previously inserted *Blocks* are automatically updated. *Blocks* can be made to have explicit *Linetype* and *Color* regardless of the layer they are inserted onto, or they can be made to assume the *Color* and *Linetype* of the layer onto which they are *Insert*ed.

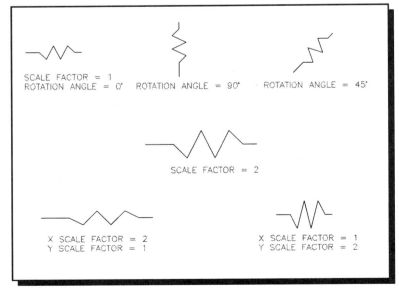

Figure 21-2

Blocks can be <u>nested</u>; that is, one *Block* can reference another *Block*. Practically, this means that the definition of *Block* "C" can contain *Block* "A" so that when *Block* "C" is inserted, *Block* "A" is also inserted as part of *Block* "C" (Fig. 21-3).

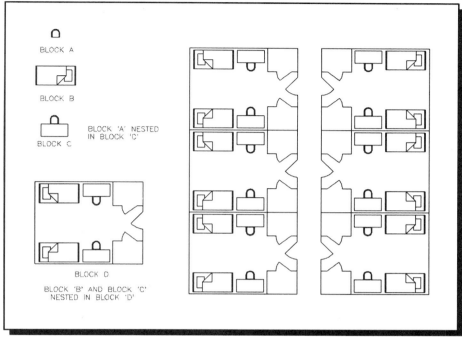

Figure 21-3

Blocks created within the current drawing can be copied to disk as complete and separate drawing files (.DWG file) by using the *Wblock* command (Write Block). This action allows you to *Insert* the *Blocks* into other drawings. Specifically, when you use the *Insert* command, AutoCAD first searches for the supplied *Block* name in the current drawing's block definition table. If the designated *Block* is not located there, AutoCAD searches the directories for a .DWG file with the designated name.

Commands related to using *Blocks* are:

Block	Creates a *Block* from individual entities
Insert	Inserts a *Block* into a drawing
Ddinsert	Invokes a dialogue box for inserting a *Block*
Minsert	Permits a multiple insert in a rectangular pattern
Insert (with *)	Inserts a *Block* as the original set of multiple entities
Explode	Breaks a *Block* into its original set of multiple entities
Wblock	Writes an existing *Block* or a set of entities to a file on disk
Base	Allows specification of insertion base point
Purge	Deletes uninserted *Blocks* from the block definition table
Rename	Allows renaming *Blocks*

Block and most of the related commands are found in the *BLOCKS* screen menu and on the digitizing tablet menu at 2,Q through 3,R. Various pull-down menus (*Draw, Construct*, and *Modify*) contain the *Block*-related commands. The command names can also be typed, but there are no defined command aliases.

COMMANDS

BLOCK

TYPE IN:	PULL-DOWN MENU	SCREEN MENU	TABLET MENU
BLOCK	*Construct, Block*	*BLOCKS, BLOCK:*	*2,Q*

After creating the desired *Lines*, *Circles*, *Arcs* and other entities comprising the geometry for the symbol, the *Block* command is used to transform the set of entities into one entity. The command prompts read as follows:

```
Command: Block
Block name (or ?): (name) (Enter a descriptive name for the Block up to 31
characters.)
Insertion base point: PICK or (coordinates) (Select a point to be used later
for insertion.)
Select objects: PICK
Select objects: PICK  (Continue selecting all desired entities.)
Select objects: Enter
```

The *Block* then <u>disappears</u> as it is stored in the current drawing's "block definition table." The *Oops* command can be used to restore the original set or "template" entities (they reappear), but the definition of the *Block* remains in the table.

Using the *?* option of the *Block* command lists the *Blocks* stored in the block definition table (Fig. 21-4).

```
Defined blocks.
   ADSH2426
   ARROW
   CNTRLINE
   D
   DBLSINK
   ELLIPSE
   FOS
   LAV
   PFAU
   PWCF
   RMNBIG
   RMNSMALL
   SCNTR
   TUB50

User       External    Dependent   Unnamed
Blocks     References   Blocks      Blocks
  14          0           0           12
```

Figure 21-4

Block Color and *Linetype* Settings

The <u>color</u> and <u>linetype</u> of an inserted *Block* are determined by one of the following settings when the *Block* is created.

1.   When a *Block* is inserted, it is drawn on its original layer with its original *Color* and *Linetype* (when the entities were <u>created</u>) regardless of the layer or *color* and *linetype* settings that are current when the *Block* is inserted (unless conditions 2. or 3. exist).

2.   If a *Block* is created on <u>Layer 0</u> (Layer 0 is current when the original entities comprising the *Block* are created), then the *Block* assumes the *color* and *linetype* of any layer that is current when it is inserted.

3.   If the *Block* is created with the special *BYBLOCK linetype* and *color* setting, the *Block* is inserted with the *Color* and *Linetype* settings that are <u>current during insertion</u>, whether the *BYLAYER* or explicit entity *Color* and *Linetype* settings are current.

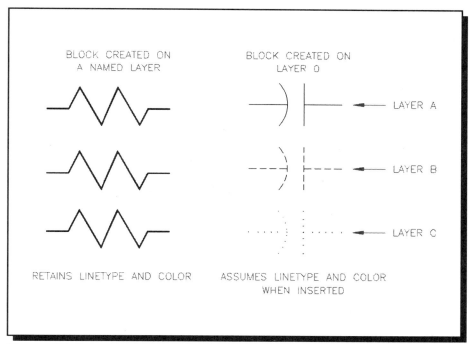

Figure 21-5

BMAKE

Bmake (Block make) is actually an AutoLISP program for making *Blocks* that is supplied with Release 12. Because it is an AutoLISP program, and because it is not located in any of the menus, it must be loaded as an initial step before you can use it. See Appendix B for instructions for loading AutoLISP programs.

Once *Bmake* is loaded, you can invoke the program by typing *Bmake* at the `Command:` prompt. Doing this produces the *Block Definition* dialogue box shown in Figure 21-6. This dialogue box provides the same functions available by using the *Block* command in command line format.

Enter the desired *Block* name in the *Block Name* box. Use the *Select Objects* tile to return to the drawing temporarily to select the entities you wish to comprise the *Block*.

The *List Block Names* tile can be chosen to select and overwrite (redefine) an existing *Block* (see Redefining Blocks).

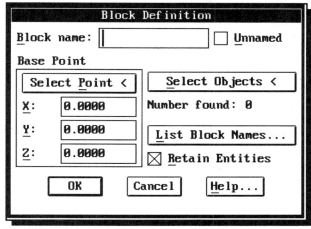

Figure 21-6

A check appearing in the *Retain Entities* check box forces AutoCAD to retain the original "template" entities, similar to using *Oops* after the *Block* command. The *Base Point* section of the dialogue box allows you to specify values or PICK a point for the base point of insertion (see *Base* in this chapter).

INSERT

TYPE IN:	PULL-DOWN MENU	SCREEN MENU	TABLET MENU
INSERT or DDINSERT	*Draw, Insert...*	*BLOCKS, INSERT:*	*3,Q*

Once the *Block* has been created, it is inserted back into the drawing at the desired location(s) with the *Insert* command. *Insert* also allows the *Blocks* to be scaled or rotated upon insertion. The command syntax is:

```
Command: Insert
Block name (or ?): name (Type the name of an existing block or .DWG file to
insert.)
Insertion point: PICK or (coordinates) (Give the desired location of the Block.)
X scale factor <1>/Corner/XYZ: PICK or (value) (Specifies the size of the
Block in the X direction.)
Y scale factor (default=X):(value) or Enter (Specifies the size in the Y
direction.)
rotation angle: PICK or (value) (Enter an angle for Block rotation.)
```

Selecting the "*X scale factor*," with the cursor specifies both X and Y factors. The rotation angle can be forced to 90 degree increments by turning *ORTHO* (F8) *On*.

The *Insert* dialogue box can be invoked by using the pull-down menu or tablet menu, or by typing *Ddinsert* (Fig 21-7). Selecting the *Block* tile causes another box to pop up listing the *Blocks* previously defined in the drawing's block definition table (see Fig 21-8). The desired *Block* is selected from the list. Selecting the *File* tile causes a box to pop up allowing selection of any drawing (.DWG files) from any accessible drive and directory for insertion.

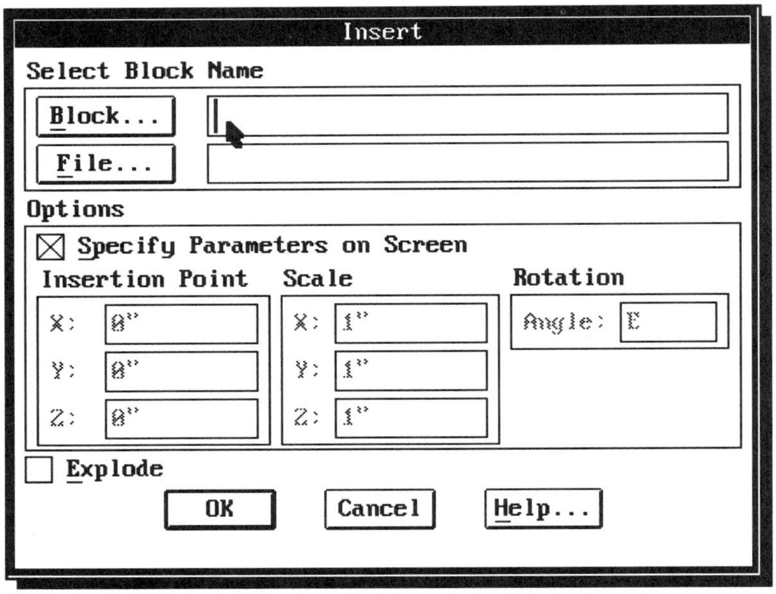

The *Insert* dialogue box provides explicit value entry of insertion point coordinates, scale, and

Figure 21-7

rotation angle. *Explode* can also be toggled, which would insert the *Block* as multiple entities (see *Insert with* *).

Selecting the *Block* tile in the *Insert* dialogue box (previous figure) causes a list of the drawing's previously defined *Blocks* to appear for selection.

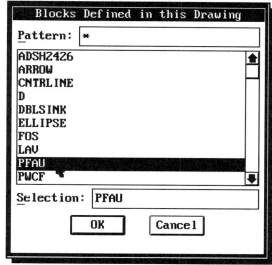

Figure 21-8

MINSERT

TYPE IN:	PULL-DOWN MENU	SCREEN MENU	TABLET MENU
MINSERT	---	*BLOCKS, MINSERT:*	*3,R*

This command allows a multiple insert in a rectangular pattern (Fig. 21-9). *Minsert* is actually a combination of the *Insert* and the *Array Rectangular* commands.

The *Blocks* inserted with *Minsert* are associated (the group is treated as one entity) and cannot be edited independently.

Examining the command syntax yields the similarity to a *Rectangular Array*.

```
Command: Minsert
Block name (or ?): name
Insertion point: PICK or
(coordinates)
```

Figure 21-9

```
X scale factor <1>/Corner/XYZ: (value) or PICK
Y scale factor (default=X): (value) or Enter
rotation angle: (value) or PICK
Number of rows (---): (value)
Number of columns (||||): (value)
```
Unit cell or distance between rows: **(value)** or **PICK** (value specifies Y distance from *Block* corner to *Block* corner; **PICK** allows drawing a unit cell rectangle.)
Distance between columns: **(value)** or **PICK** (Specifies X distance between *Block* corners.)

INSERT with *

Using the *Insert* command with the asterisk (*) allows you to insert a *Block* not as one entity, but as the original set of entities comprising the *Block*. In this way you can edit individual entities in the *Block*, otherwise impossible if the *Block* is only one entity (Fig. 21-10).

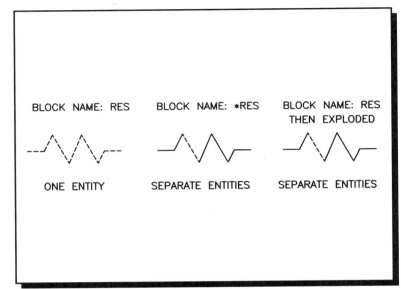

BLOCK NAME: RES   BLOCK NAME: *RES   BLOCK NAME: RES
                                                THEN EXPLODED

ONE ENTITY   SEPARATE ENTITIES   SEPARATE ENTITIES

In this case, the normal *Insert* command is used. However, when the desired <u>*Block* name</u> is entered, it is prefaced by the asterisk (*) symbol:

Figure 21-10

```
Command: INSERT
Block name (or ?): * (name) (Type the * symbol, then the name of an existing
block or .DWG file to insert.)
Command:
```

This action accomplishes the same goal as using *Insert*, then *Explode*.

EXPLODE

TYPE IN:	PULL-DOWN MENU	SCREEN MENU	TABLET MENU
EXPLODE	*Modify, Explode*	*EDIT, EXPLODE:*	*20,W*

Explode breaks a <u>previously</u> inserted *Block* back into its original set of entities (Fig. 21-10) which allows you to edit individual entities comprising the shape. *Blocks* that have been inserted with differing X and Y scale factors or *Blocks* that have been *Minsert*ed cannot be *Explode*d. There are no options for this command.

```
Command: explode
Select objects: PICK
Select objects: Enter
Command:
```

Inserting with an * (asterisk) symbol accomplishes the same goal as using *Insert* normally, then *Explode*.

WBLOCK

TYPE IN:	PULL-DOWN MENU	SCREEN MENU	TABLET MENU
WBLOCK	---	*BLOCKS, WBLOCK:*	*2,R*

The *Wblock* command writes a *Block* out to disk as a separate and complete drawing (.DWG) file. The *Block* used for writing to disk can exist in the current drawing's *Block* definition table or can be created by the *Wblock* command. Remember that the *Insert* command inserts *Blocks* (from the current drawing's block definition table) or finds and accepts .DWG files and treats them as *Blocks* upon insertion.

If you are using an existing *Block*, a copy of the *Block* is essentially transformed by the *Wblock* command to create a complete AutoCAD drawing (.DWG) file. The original block definition remains in the current drawing's block definition table. In this way *Blocks* that were originally intended for insertion into the current drawing can be inserted into other drawings.

If you want to transform a set of entities to be used as a *Block* in other drawings but not in the current one, you can use *Wblock* to transform (a copy of) the entities in the current drawing into separate .DWG file. This action does not create a *Block* in the current drawing.
As an alternative, if you want to create symbols specifically to be inserted into other drawings, each symbol could be created initially as a separate .DWG file. Figure 21-11 illustrates the relationship among a *Block*, the current drawing, and a *WBlock*.

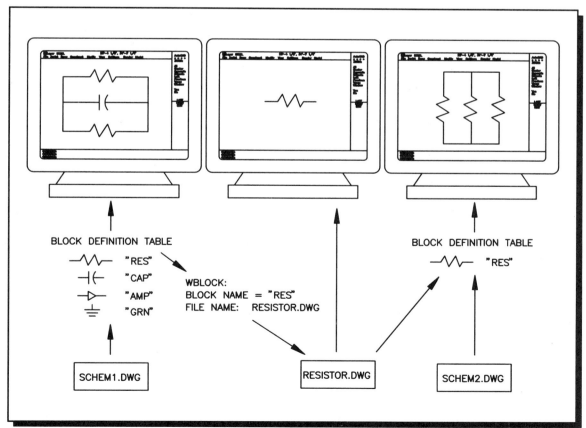

Figure 21-11

To create *Wblocks* (.DWG files) from existing *Blocks*, follow this command syntax:

> Command: **Wblock**
> (At this point, the *Create Drawing File* dialogue box appears, prompting you to supply a name for the .DWG file to be created. Typically, a new descriptive name would be typed in the edit box rather than selecting from the existing names.)
> Block name: **(name)** (Enter the name of the desired existing *Block*. If the file name given in the previous step is the same as the existing *Block* name, a "=" symbol can be entered at this prompt.)
> Command:

A copy of the existing *Block* is then created in the current or selected directory as a *Wblock* (.DWG file).

To create a *Wblock* (.DWG file) to be used as a *Block* in other drawings but not in the current drawing, follow the same steps as before, but when prompted for the "*Block name:*" press Enter or select *blank* from the screen menu. The next steps are like the *Block* command prompts.

> Command: **Wblock**
> (The *Create Drawing File* dialogue box appears, prompting you to supply a name for the .DWG file to be created)
> Block name: **(Enter)** or select **(blank)**
> Insertion base point: **PICK** or **(coordinates)** (Pick a point to be used later for insertion.)
> Select objects: **PICK**
> Select objects: **Enter** (Press Enter to complete selection.)
> Command:

When *Wblocks* are *Inserted*, the *Color* and *Linetype* settings of the *Wblock* are determined by the settings current when the original entities comprising the *Wblock* were created. The three possible settings are the same as those for *Blocks* (see the *Block* command, *Color* and *Linetype* Settings).

When a *Wblock* is *Inserted*, its parent (original) layer is also inserted into the current drawing. *Freezing* <u>either</u> the parent layer or the layer that was current during the insertion causes the *Wblock* to be frozen.

Redefining *Blocks*

If you want to change the configuration of a *Block*, even after it has been inserted, it can be accomplished by redefining the *Block*. In doing so, all of the previous *Block* insertions are automatically and globally updated (Fig. 21-12). AutoCAD stores two fundamental pieces of information for each *Block* insertion--the insertion point and the *Block* name. The actual block definition is stored in the block definition table. Redefining the *Block* involves changing that definition.

To redefine a *Block*, use the *Block* command.

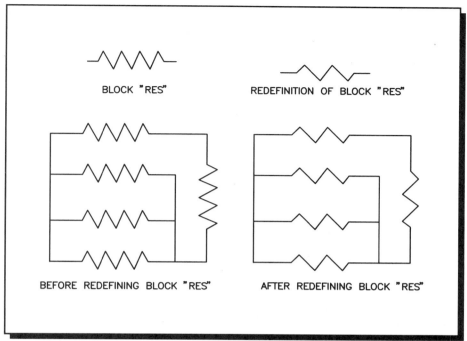

Figure 21-12

To redefine a *Block*, first draw the new geometry or change the <u>original</u> "template" set of entities. (The change cannot be made using an inserted *Block* unless it is *Exploded* because a *Block* cannot reference itself.) Next, use the *Block* command and select the new or changed geometry. The old *Block* is redefined with the new geometry as long as the <u>original *Block* name</u> is used.

```
Command: block
Block name (or ?): name (Enter the original Block name.)
Block (name) already exists.
Redefine it? <N>: Yes (Answering Y or yes causes the redefinition.)
Insertion base point: PICK or (coordinates)  (Select a point to be used later
for insertion.)
Select objects: PICK
Select objects: PICK  (Continue selecting all desired entities.)
Select objects: Enter
Command:
```

The *Block* is redefined and all insertions of the original *Block* display the new geometry.

The *Block* command can also be used to redefine *Wblocks* that have been inserted. In this case, enter the *Wblock* name (.DWG filename) at the `Block name:` prompt to redefine (actually replace) a previously inserted *Wblock*.

BASE

TYPE IN:	PULL-DOWN MENU	SCREEN MENU	TABLET MENU
BASE	---	*BLOCKS, BASE:*	---

The *Base* command allows you to specify an "insertion base point" (see the *Block* command) in the current drawing for subsequent insertions. If the *Insert* command is used to bring a .DWG file into another drawing, the insertion base point of the .DWG is 0,0 by default. The *Base* command permits you to specify another location as the insertion base point. The *Base* command is used in the symbol drawing, that is, used in the drawing to be inserted. For example, while creating separate symbol drawings (.DWGs) for subsequent insertion into other drawings, the *Base* command is used to specify an appropriate point on the symbol geometry for the *Insert* command to use as a "handle" other than point 0,0 (see Figure 21-13).

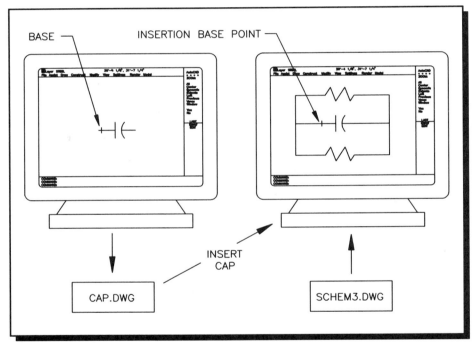

Figure 21-13

PURGE

Blocks that are part of the current drawing but are not being used (in the block definition table but not *Inserted*) can be *Purged* to minimize file size. See Miscellaneous Commands, Chapter 30.

RENAME

Blocks can be *Renamed*. See Miscellaneous Commands, Chapter 30.

CHAPTER EXERCISES

1. **_Block_**, **_Insert_**   (In the next several exercises you will create an office floor plan, then create pieces of furniture as _Blocks_ and _Insert_ them into the office. All of the block-related commands are used.)

A.   Start a **_New_** drawing and assign the name **OFF-ATT**. Set up the drawing as follows.

1.	**_Units_**	**_Architectural 1/2" Precision_**		
2.	**_Limits_**	**48' x 36'**	(1/4"=1' scale on an "A" size sheet)	
			drawing scale factor = 48	
3.	**_Snap_**	**3**		
4.	**_Grid_**	**12**		
5.	**_Layers_**	**FLOORPLAN**	**continuous**	colors of your choice, all different
		FURNITURE	**continuous**	
		ELEC-HDWR	**continuous**	
		ELEC-LINES	**hidden**	
		DIM-FLOOR	**continuous**	
		DIM-ELEC	**continuous**	
		TEXT	**continuous**	
		TITLE	**continuous**	
6.	**_Text Style_**	**_City Blueprint_**		
7.	**_LTSCALE_**	**24**		

B.   Create the floorplan shown in Figure 21-14. Center the geometry in the _Limits_. Draw on layer **FLOORPLAN**. Use any method you want for construction (e.g., _Line, Pline, Dline, Offset,_ etc.).

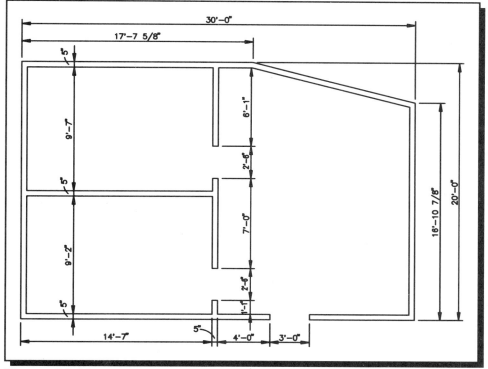

Figure 21-14

B. Create the furniture shown in Figure 21-15. Draw on layer **FURNITURE**. Locate the pieces anywhere for now. Do <u>not</u> make each piece a *Block*. **Save** the drawing (as **OFF-ATT**).

OK, now make each piece a **Block**. Use the **name** as indicated and **insertion base point** as shown by the "blip." Next, use the **Block** command again but with the **?** option to list the block definition table. Use **Saveas** and rename the drawing **OFFICE**.

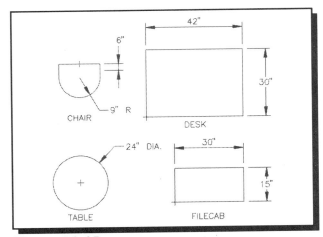

Figure 21-15

C. Use **Insert** to insert the furniture into the drawing as shown in Figure 21-16. You may use your own arrangement for the furniture, but *Insert* the same number of each piece as shown.

Save the drawing.

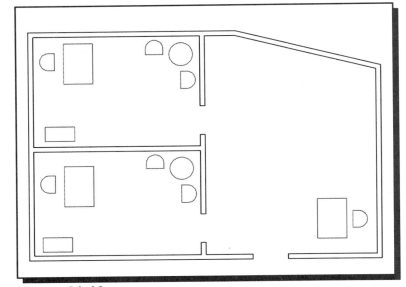

Figure 21-16

2. **Creating a .DWG file for**
    Insertion, Base

Begin a **New** drawing. Assign the name **CONFTABL**. Create the table as shown in Figure 21-17 on **Layer 0**. Since this drawing is intended for insertion into the **OFFICE** drawing, use the **Base** command to assign an insertion base point at the lower left corner of the table.

When finished, **Save** the drawing.

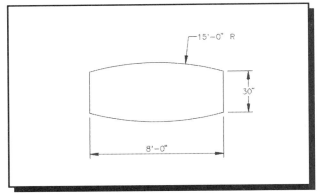

Figure 21-17

3. *Insert, Explode, Divide*

A.   ***Open*** the **OFFICE** drawing. Insure that layer **FURNITURE** is current. Use *Insert* to bring the **CONFTABL** drawing in as a *Block* in the placement shown in Figure 21-18.

        Notice that the CONFTABL assumes the linetype and color of the current layer, since it was created on layer **0**.

B.   ***Explode*** the CONFTABL. The *Exploded* CONFTABL returns to *Layer* **0**, so use ***Chprop*** to change it back to *Layer* **FURNITURE**. Then use the ***Divide*** command (with the *Block* option) to insert the **CHAIR** block as shown in Figure 21-18. Also *Insert* a **CHAIR** at each end of the table. *Save* the drawing.

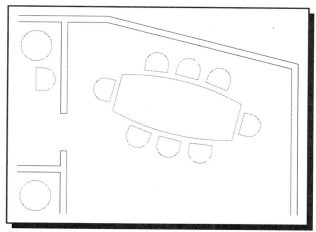

Figure 21-18

4. *Wblock, BYBLOCK setting*

A.   ***Open*** the **EFF-APT2** drawing you worked on in Chapter 19 Exercises. Use the ***Wblock*** command to transform the plant into a .DWG file. Use the name **PLANT** and *Insertion base point* as indicated in Figure 21-19. Do not save the drawing.

B.   ***Open*** the **OFFICE** drawing and *Insert* the **PLANT** into one of the three rooms. The plant probably appears in a different color than the current layer. Why? Check the *Layer* listing to see if any new layers came in with the PLANT block. *Erase* the PLANT block.

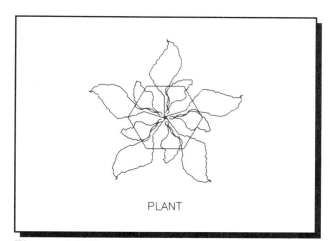

PLANT

Figure 21-19

C.   ***Open*** the **PLANT** drawing. Change the *Color* and *Linetype* setting of the plant entities to *BYBLOCK*. *Save* the drawing.

D.   ***Open*** the **OFFICE** drawing again and *Insert* the **PLANT** onto the **FURNITURE** layer. It should appear now in the current layer's *color* and *linetype*. *Insert* a **PLANT** into each of the 3 rooms. *Save* the drawing.

5.   **Redefining a *Block***

        After a successful meeting with the client, the proposed office design is accepted with one small change. The client requests a slightly larger chair than that specified.

Explode one of the **CHAIR** blocks. Use the *Scale* command to increase the size slightly or otherwise redesign the chair in some way. Use the *Block* command to redefine the **CHAIR** block. All previous insertions of the CHAIR should reflect the design change. *Save* the drawing. Your design should look similar to that shown in Figure 21-20. *Plot* to a standard scale base on your plotting capabilities.

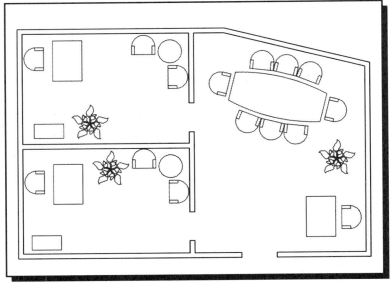

Figure 21-20

6. Create the process flow diagram shown in Figure 21-21. Create symbols (*Blocks*) for the tanks, drums, and pumps. Do not include the text in your drawing. *Save* the drawing as **PFD**.

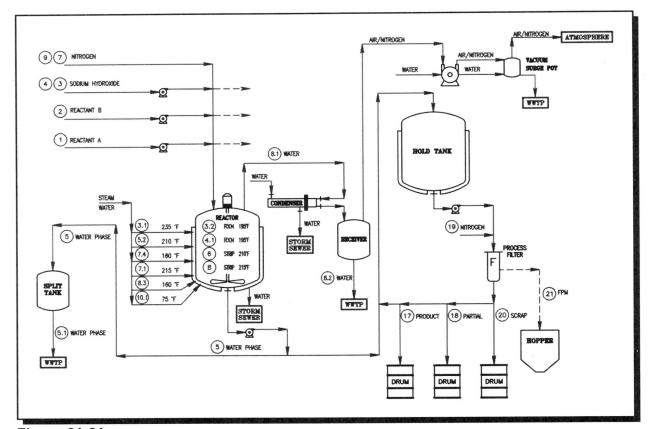

Figure 21-21

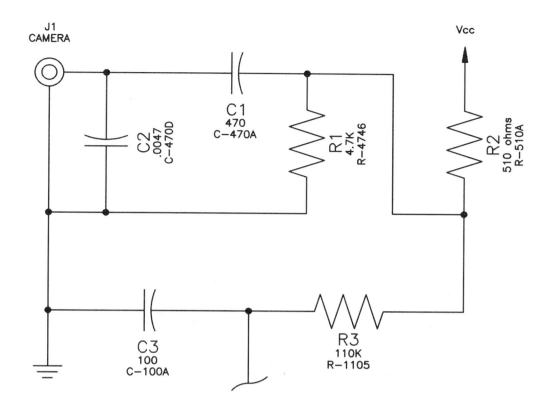

CHAPTER 22

Block Attributes

CHAPTER OBJECTIVES

After completing this chapter you should:

1. be able to define *Block* attributes using the *Attdef* command and the *Attribute Definition* dialogue box;

2. be able to specify *Invisible, Constant, Verify*, and *Preset* attribute modes.

3. be able to control the display of attributes with *Attdisp*;

4. know how to edit existing attributes with the *Edit Attributes* dialogue box;

5. be able to globally or individually edit attributes using the *Attedit* command;

6. be able to create an extract file containing a drawing's attributes in an external text file;

7. know how to create a template file in a text editor for specifying the structure of an extract file.

BASICS

A block attribute is a line of text (numbers or letters) associated with a *Block*. An attribute can be thought of as a label for a *Block*. A *Block* can have multiple attributes. The attributes are included with the drawing entities when the *Block* is defined (using the *Block* command). When the *Block* is *Inserted*, its attributes are also *Inserted*.

Since *Blocks* are typically used as symbols in a drawing, attributes are text strings that label or describe each symbol. For example, you can have a series of symbols such as transistors, resistors, capacitors, etc. prepared for creating electrical schematics. The associated attributes can give the related description of each *Block* such as ohms or wattage values, model number, part number, cost, etc. If your symbols were doors, windows and fixtures for architectural applications, attached attributes can include size, cost, manufacturer, and so on. A mechanical engineer can have a series of *Blocks* representing fasteners with attached attributes to specify fastener type, major diameter, pitch, length, etc. Attributes could even be used to automate the process of entering text into a title block, assuming the title block was *Inserted* as a *Block* or separate .DWG file.

Attributes can add another level of significance to an AutoCAD drawing. Not only can attributes automate the process of placing the text attached to a *Block*, but the inserted attribute information can be <u>extracted</u> from a drawing to form a bill of materials or used for cost analysis, for example. Extracted text can be imported to a database or spreadsheet program for further processing and analysis.

Attributes are created with the *Attdef* (attribute definition) command. *Attdef* operates similarly to *Text* or *Dtext*, prompting you for text height, placement, and justification. During attribute definition, parameters can be adjusted that determine how the attributes will appear when they are inserted.

Steps for Creating and Using Block Attributes

1. Create the entities that will comprise the *Block*. Do not use the *Block* command yet, only draw the geometry.

2. Use the *Attdef* command to create and place the desired text strings associated with the geometry comprising the proposed *Block*.

3. Use the *Block* command to convert the drawing geometry (entities) and the attributes (text) into a named *Block*. When prompted to "*Select objects:*" for the *Block*, select both the drawing entities and the text (attributes). The *Block* and attributes disappear.

4. Use *Insert* to insert the attributed *Block* into the drawing. Edit the text attributes as necessary (if parameters were set as such) during the insertion process.

This chapter discusses defining attributes, inserting attributed *Blocks*, and extracting attributes from drawings.

CREATING ATTRIBUTES

ATTDEF

TYPE IN:	PULL-DOWN MENU	SCREEN MENU	TABLET MENU
ATTDEF or DDATTDEF	*Draw, Text > Attributes > Define...*	*BLOCKS, ATTDEF*	*1,Q*

Attdef (attribute define) allows you to define attributes for future combination with a *Block*. If you are intending to associate the text attributes with drawing entities (*Line, Arc, Circle,* etc.) for the *Block*, it is usually preferred to draw the entities before using *Attdef*. In this way, the text can be located in reference to the drawing entities.

Attdef allows you to create the text and provides justification, height, and rotation options similar to the *Text* and *Dtext* commands. You can also define parameters, called Attribute Modes, specifying how the text will be inserted--*Invisible, Constant, Verify,* or *Preset*.

The *Attdef* command differs depending upon the method used to invoke it. If you select from the pull-down or tablet menu or type *Ddattdef*, the *Define Attribute* dialogue box appears (Figure 22-3). If you type *Attdef* or select it from the screen menu, the command line format is used. The command line format is presented here first.

```
Command: attdef
Attribute modes -- Invisible:N Constant:N Verify:N Preset:N
Enter (ICVP) to change, RETURN when done: Enter or (letter)
Attribute tag: Enter tag, no spaces.
Attribute prompt: Enter desired prompt, spaces allowed.
Default attribute value: Enter desired default text.
Justify/Style/<Start point>: PICK or (option)
Height <0.2000>: Enter, PICK or (value)
Rotation angle <0>: Enter, PICK or (value)
Command:
```

The first option, "attribute modes," is described later. For this example, the default attribute modes have been accepted. The next three options are defined here.

Attribute Tag

This is the descriptor for the <u>type of text</u> to be entered, such as MODEL_NO, PART_NO, NAME, etc.

Attribute Prompt

The prompt is what words <u>(prompt) you want to appear</u> when the *Block* is *Inserted* and the actual text (values) must be entered.

Default Attribute Value

This is the <u>default text</u> that appears with the *Block* when it is *Inserted*.

The other prompts are similar to those appearing when using the *Text* and *Dtext* commands.

Justify

Any of the justification methods can be selected using this option. (See Chapter 19, Inserting and Using Text, if you need help with justification.)

Style

This option allows you to select from existing text *Styles* in the drawing. Otherwise, the attribute is drawn in the current *Style*.

As an example, assume that you are using the *Attdef* command to make attributes attached to a resistor symbol to be *Blocked*. The scenario may appear as follows.

```
Command: attdef
Attribute modes -- Invisible:N Constant:N Verify:N Preset:N
Enter (ICVP) to change, RETURN when done: Enter
Attribute tag: RES_NUMBER
Attribute prompt: Enter Resistor Number:
Default attribute value: 0
Justify/Style/<Start point>: j
Align/Fit/Center/Middle/Right/TL/TC/TR/ML/MC/MR/BL/BC/BR: c
Center point: PICK
Height <0.2000>: .125
Rotation angle <0>: Enter
```

The attribute would then appear at the selected location as shown in Figure 22-1. Keep in mind that the *Lines* comprising the resistor were created before using *Attdef*. Also remember that the resistor and the attribute are not yet *Blocked*. The *Attribute Tag* only is displayed until the *Block* command is used.

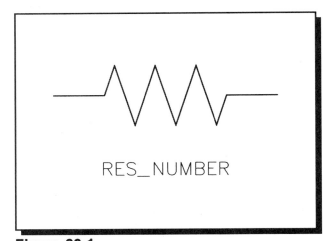

Two other attributes could be created and positioned beneath the first one by pressing **Enter** when prompted for the "*<Start point>:*". The command syntax may read like this.

Figure 22-1

```
Command: attdef
Attribute modes -- Invisible:N Constant:N Verify:N Preset:N
Enter (ICVP) to change, RETURN when done: Enter
Attribute tag: RESISTANCE
Attribute prompt: Enter Resistance:
Default attribute value: 0 ohms
Justify/Style/<Start point>: Enter
Command:
```

```
Command: attdef
Attribute modes -- Invisible:N Constant:N Verify:N Preset:N
Enter (ICVP) to change, RETURN when done: Enter
Attribute tag: PART_NO
Attribute prompt: Enter Part Number:
Default attribute value: 0-0000
Justify/Style/<Start point>: Enter
Command:
```

The resulting unblocked symbol and three attributes appear as shown in Figure 22-2. Only the _Attribute Tags_ are displayed at this point. The _Block_ command has not yet been used.

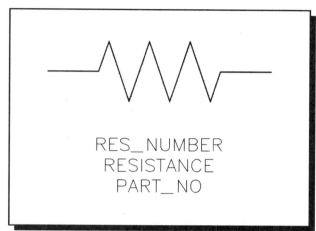

Figure 22-2

An alternative to the command line format of _Attdef_, the _Attribute Definition_ dialogue box can be used to define attributes. Making the selection from the pull-down menu, tablet menu or typing _Ddattdef_ produces the dialogue box shown in Figure 22-3.

The _Attribute Definition_ dialogue box has identical options that are found in the command line format, including justification options. Notice that this dialogue box provides the additional option of selecting from the existing _Text Styles_ to use for the attribute. The same entries have been made here to define the first attribute shown in Figure 22-1.

```
┌─────────────────────────────────────────────────────┐
│              Attribute Definition                    │
│  Mode               Attribute                        │
│  ☐ Invisible        Tag:    │RES_NUMBER         │     │
│  ☐ Constant         Prompt: │Enter Resistor Number:│  │
│  ☐ Verify           Value:  │0 ohms             │     │
│  ☐ Preset                                            │
│  Insertion Point    Text Options                     │
│  ┌─────────────┐    Justification: │Center      │▼│  │
│  │ Pick Point <│    Text Style:    │ROMANS      │▼│  │
│  X: │0.0000 │       ┌─Height <─┐  │0.125 │         │
│  Y: │0.0000 │       ┌─Rotation <┐ │0 │             │
│  Z: │0.0000 │                                        │
│  ☐ Align below previous attribute                   │
│     ┌──OK──┐  ┌─Cancel─┐  ┌─Help...─┐               │
└─────────────────────────────────────────────────────┘
```

Figure 22-3

After all attribute entries have been made, selecting the _Pick Point_ allows you to specify the text placement location. For subsequent attributes, you can check the "_Align below previous attribute_" box.

The *Attributes Modes* define the appearance or the action required when you *Insert* the attributes. The options are as follows.

Invisible

An invisible attribute is not displayed in the drawing after insertion. This option can be used to prevent unnecessary information from cluttering the drawing and slowing regeneration time. The *Attdisp* command can be used later to make these attributes visible.

Constant

This option gives the attribute a fixed value for all insertions of the *Block*. In other words, the attribute always has the same text and cannot be changed. You are not prompted for the value upon insertion.

Verify

This option forces you to verify that the attribute value is correct when the *Block* is inserted.

Preset

This option prevents you from having to enter a value during insertion. The default value is automatically used for the *Block*, although it can be changed later with the *Attedit* command.

The *Attribute Modes* are toggles (Yes or No). In command line format the options are toggled by entering the appropriate letter which reverses its current position (Y or N). For example, to create an *Invisible* attribute , type **"I"** at the prompt:

```
Command: attdef
Attribute modes -- Invisible:N Constant:N Verify:N Preset:N
Enter (ICVP) to change, RETURN when done: I
Attribute modes -- Invisible:Y Constant:N Verify:N Preset:N
Enter (ICVP) to change, RETURN when done: Enter
```

Note that the second prompt reflects the new position of the previous request.

Using our previous example, two additional attributes can be created with specific attribute modes. Either the dialogue box or command line format can be used. The following command syntax shows the creation of an *Invisible* attribute.

```
Command: attdef
Attribute modes -- Invisible:N Constant:N Verify:N Preset:N
Enter (ICVP) to change, RETURN when done: I
Attribute modes -- Invisible:Y Constant:N Verify:N  Preset:N
Enter (ICVP) to change, RETURN when done: Enter
Attribute tag: MANUFACTURER
Attribute prompt: Enter Manufacturer:
Default attribute value: Enter
Justify/Style/<Start point>: Enter
Height <0.1250>: Enter
Rotation angle <0>: Enter
Command:
```

The first attribute has been defined. Next, a second attribute is defined having _Invisible_ and _Verify_ parameters.

```
Command: attdef
Attribute modes -- Invisible:Y Constant:N Verify:N Preset:N
Enter (ICVP) to change, RETURN when done: V
Attribute modes -- Invisible:Y Constant:N Verify:Y Preset:N
Enter (ICVP) to change, RETURN when done: Enter
Attribute tag: COST
Attribute prompt: Enter Cost:
Default attribute value: 0.00
Justify/Style/<Start point>: Enter
Command:
```

Alternately, the previous attributes could have been defined using the _Attribute Definition_ dialogue box. Figure 22-4 shows the correct entries for creation of the last attribute.

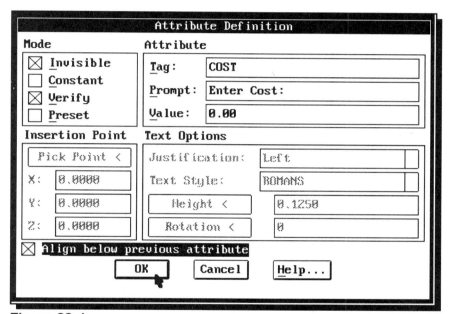

Figure 22-4

Using the _Block_ Command to Create an Attributed Block

Next, the _Block_ command is used to transform the drawing entities and the text (attributes) into an attributed block. When you are prompted to " _Select objects."_ in the _Block_ command, select the attributes <u>in the order</u> you desire their prompts to appear on insertion. In other words, the first attribute selected during the _Block_ command (RES_NUMBER) is the first attribute prompted for editing during the _Insert_ command. PICK the attributes one at a time <u>in order</u>. Then PICK the drawing entities (a window can be used). Figure 22-5 shows this sequence.

If the attributes are selected with a window, they are inserted in reverse order of creation, so you would be prompted for COST first, MANUFACTURER second, and so on.

```
Command: block
Block name (or ?): res
Insertion base point: PICK
Select objects: PICK (1)
Select objects: PICK (2)
Select objects: PICK (3)
Select objects: PICK (4)
Select objects: PICK (5)
Select objects: PICK (entities)
Select objects: Enter
Command:
```

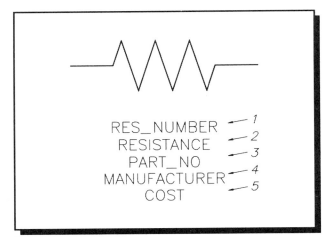

As with other *Blocks*, this one disappears
after using the *Block* command. Use the
Oops command to redisplay the original
entities if you expect to make further
changes. The RES *Block* definition remains in the block definition table.

Figure 22-5

Inserting Attributed Blocks

Use the *Insert* command to bring attributed *Blocks* into your drawing, as you would to bring
any *Block* into your drawing. After the normal *Insert* command prompts, the attribute prompts
(that you defined with *Attdef*) appear. In this step enter the desired attribute *values* for each
block insertion. The prompts appear in dialogue box fashion (*Enter Attributes* dialogue, Fig.
22-6) or in command line format depending upon the setting of the *ATTDIA* variable. (The
command line format is the default setting. *ATTDIA*=0.) See Appendix A, System Variables.

The command line format follows.

```
Command: insert
Block name (or ?): res
Insertion point: PICK
X scale factor <1> / Corner / XYZ: Enter
Y scale factor (default=X): Enter
Rotation angle <0>: Enter

Enter attribute values
Enter Resistor Number: <0>: R1
Enter Resistance: <0 ohms>: 4.7K
Enter Part Number: <0-0000>: R-4746
Enter Manufacturer: Electro Supply Co.
Enter Cost <0.00>: .37
Verify Attribute values
Enter Cost <.37> : Enter
Command:
```

Notice the prompts appearing upon insertion are those that you specified as the "*Attribute
prompt:*" with the *Attdef* command. The order of the prompts matches the order of selection
during the *Block* command. Also note the repeated prompt (*Verify*) for the COST attribute.

Entering the attribute values as indicated above yields the *Block* insertion shown in Figure 22-6. Notice the absence of the last two attributes (since they are *Invisible*).

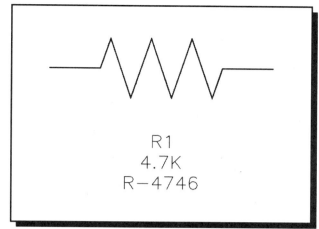

Figure 22-6

The *ATTDIA* Variable

If the *ATTDIA* system variable is set to a value of 1, the *Enter Attributes* dialogue box is invoked automatically by the *Insert* command for entering attribute values. The dialogue box, in that case, would have appeared rather than the command line format for entering attributes. The *Verify* and *Preset* Attribute Mode options have no effect on the dialogue box format of attribute value entry. The dialogue box can hold multiple screens of 10 attributes in each, all connected to 1 *Block*.

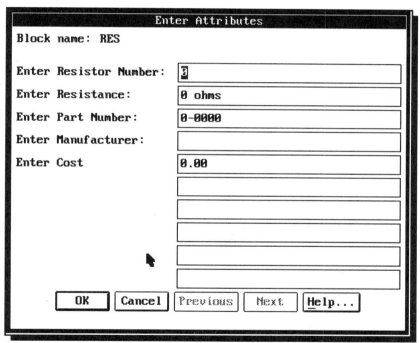

Figure 22-7

The *ATTREQ* Variable

When *Inserting Blocks* with attributes, you can force the attribute requests to be suppressed. In other words, you can disable the prompts asking for attribute values when the blocks are *Inserted*. To do this, use the *ATTREQ* (attribute request) system variable. A setting of **1** (the default) turns attribute requesting on, and a value of **0** disables the attribute value prompts.

The attribute prompts can be disabled when you want to *Insert* several *Blocks* but do not want to enter the attribute values right away. The attribute values for each *Block* can be entered at a later time using the *Attedit* or *Ddatte* commands. These attribute editing commands are discussed on the following pages.

DISPLAYING AND EDITING ATTRIBUTES

ATTDISP

TYPE IN:	PULL-DOWN MENU	SCREEN MENU	TABLET MENU
ATTDISP	---	---	---

The *Attdisp* (attribute display) command allows you to control the visibility state of all inserted attributes contained in the drawing.

```
Command: attdisp
Normal/ON/OFF <current value>: (option)
Command:
```

Attdisp has three positions. Changing the state forces a regeneration.

On

All attributes (normal and *Invisible*) in the drawing are displayed.

Off

No attributes in the drawing are displayed.

Normal

Normal attributes are displayed, *Invisible* attributes are not displayed.

Figure 22-8 illustrates the RES block example with each of the three *Attdisp* options. The last two attributes were defined with *Invisible* modes, but are displayed with the *On* state of *Attdisp*. (Since *Attdisp* affects attributes globally, it is not possible to display the three options at one time in a drawing.)

When attributes are defined using the *Invisible* mode of the *Attdef* command, the attributes are normally not displayed with the *Block* after *Insertion*. However, the *Attdisp* command allows you to override the *Invisible* mode. Turning all attributes *Off* with

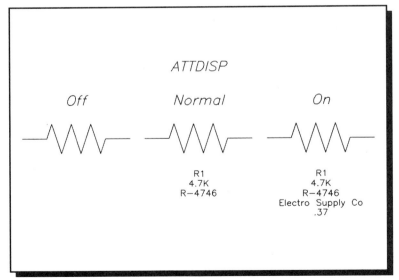

Figure 22-8

Attdisp can be useful for many applications when it is desirable to display or plot only the drawing geometry. The *Attdisp* command changes the *ATTMODE* system variable.

DDATTE

TYPE IN:	PULL-DOWN MENU	SCREEN MENU	TABLET MENU
DDATTE	*Draw, Text >* *Attributes > Edit...*	*EDIT, DDATTE:*	*1,R*

The *Ddatte* (Dialogue
Attribute Edit) command
invokes the *Edit Attributes*
dialogue box (Fig. 22-9).
This dialogue box allows you
to edit attributes of <u>existing</u>
Blocks in the drawing. The
configuration and operation
of the box is identical to the
Enter Attributes dialogue box
(Fig. 22-7).

When the *Ddatte* command
is entered, AutoCAD
requests that you select a
block. Any existing *Block*
can be selected for attribute
editing.

```
Command: ddatte
Select block:
PICK
```

```
                    ┌─────────────────────────────┐
                    │        Edit Attributes       │
                    │ Block name: RES              │
                    │                              │
                    │ Enter Resistor Number: [R1 ] │
                    │ Enter Resistance:      [4.7K]│
                    │ Enter Part Number:     [R-4746]│
                    │ Enter Manufacturer:    [Electro Supply Co]│
                    │ Enter Cost             [.37]│
                    │                              │
                    │ [ OK ] [Cancel] [Previous] [Next] [Help...]│
                    └─────────────────────────────┘
```

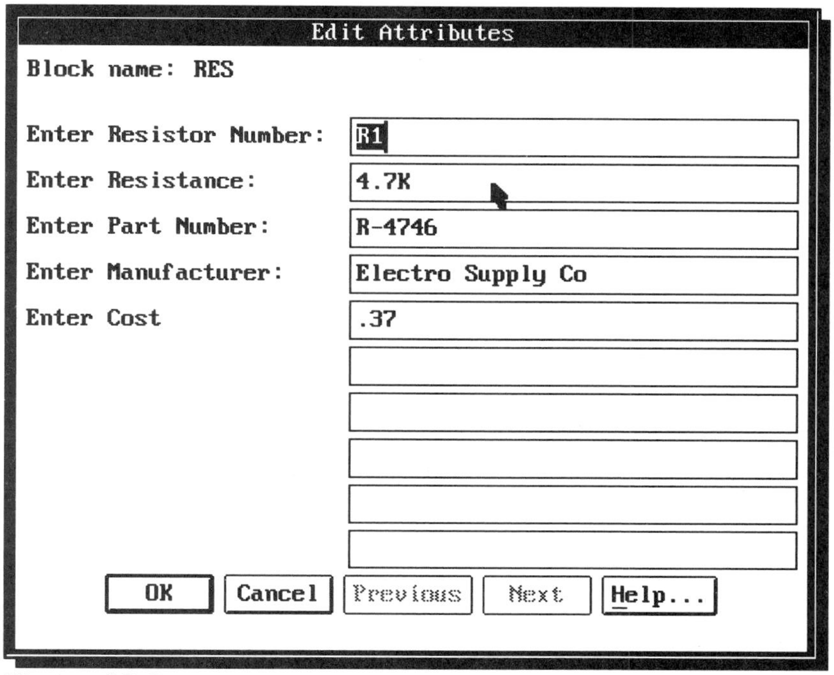

Figure 22-9

At this point the dialogue box appears. After the desired changes have been made, selecting
the *OK* tile updates the selected *Block* with the indicated changes.

MULTIPLE DDATTE

Entering the *Multiple* version of this command causes AutoCAD to repeat the *Ddatte*
command requesting multiple *Block* selections over and over until you cancel the command
with **CTRL + C**. This variant of the *Ddatte* command must be typed. (See Chapter 30 for
other uses of the *Multiple* modifier.)

```
Command: multiple ddatte
Select block: PICK
```

This form of the command can be used to query *Blocks* in an existing drawing. For example,
instead of using the *Attdisp* command to display the *Invisible* attributes, *Multiple Ddatte* can be
used on selected *Blocks* to display the *Invisible* attributes in dialogue box form. Another
example is the use of *Attdisp* to turn visibility of all attributes *Off* in a drawing, thus simplifying
the drawing appearance and speeding regenerations. The *Multiple Ddatte* command could
then be used to query the *Blocks* to display the attributes in dialogue box form.

ATTEDIT

TYPE IN:	PULL-DOWN MENU	SCREEN MENU	TABLET MENU
ATTEDIT	---	*EDIT, ATTEDIT:*	---

Attedit (Attribute Edit) is similar to *Ddatte* in that you can edit selected existing attributes. *Attedit*, however, is more powerful in that it allows many options for editing attributes, including editing of any properties of selected attributes or global editing of values for all attributes in a drawing.

```
Command: attedit
Edit attributes one at a time? <Y>
```

The following prompts depend upon your response to the first prompt.

N (No)

Indicates that you want global editing. (In other words, all attributes are selected.) Attributes can then be further filtered (selected) by *Block* name, tag, or value. Only attribute <u>values</u> can be edited using this global mode.

Y (Yes)

Allows you to PICK each attribute you want to edit. You can further filter (restrict) the selected set by *Block* name, tag, and value (see below). You can then edit <u>any property or placement</u> of the attribute.

Next, the following prompts appear which allow you to filter, or further restrict, the set of attributes for editing. You can specify the selection set to include only specific *Block* names, tags or values.

```
Block name specification <*>: Enter desired Block name(s)
Attribute tag specification <*>: Enter desired tag(s)
Attribute value specification <*>: Enter desired value(s)
```

During this portion of the selection set specification, sets of names, tags or values can be entered to only filter the set you choose. Commas and wildcard characters can be used (see Chapter 30 for information on using wildcards). Pressing **Enter** accepts the default option of all (*) selected.

Attribute values are case-sensitive. If you have entered null values (for example, if *ATTREQ* was set to **0** during block insertion), you can select all null values to be included in the selection set by using the backslash symbol (\).

The subsequent prompts depend on your previous choice of global or individual editing.

No (Global Editing--Editing Values Only)

```
Global edit of attribute values.
Edit only attributes visible on screen? <Y> Enter or (N)
```

An **N** response indicates all attributes in the selection set to this point can be edited. If your choice is *No*, you are reminded that the drawing will be regenerated after the command and the next prompt is skipped. If you select **Y**, this prompt appears.

```
Select Attributes: PICK
```

The attributes do <u>not</u> highlight <u>as you select</u> them, but highlight when you press **Enter** to complete the selection. Finally, this prompt appears.

```
String to change:
New string:
```

At this point, you can enter any string, and AutoCAD searches for it in the selected attributes and replaces all occurrences of the string with the new string. No change is made if the string is not found. The string can be any number of characters and can be embedded within an attribute text. Remember that only the attribute values can be edited with the global mode.

Yes (Individual Editing--Editing any Property)

After filtering for the *Block* name, attribute tag, and value, AutoCAD prompts:

```
Select Attributes: PICK  (The attributes do not highlight during selection.)
Value/Position/Height/Angle/Style/Layer/Color/Next <N>:
```

A marker appears at one of the attributes. Use the *Next* option to move the marker to the attribute you wish to edit. You can then select any other option. After editing the marked attribute, the change is displayed immediately and you can position the marker at another attribute to edit.

The *Value* option invokes this prompt, allowing you to change a specific string.

```
Change or Replace? <R>: C
String to change:
New string:
```

The *Replace* option responds to this prompt, providing for an entire new value.

```
New Attribute value:
```

You can also change the attribute's *Position, Height, Angle, Style, Layer,* or *Color* by selecting the appropriate option. The prompts are specific and straightforward for these options. There is a surprising amount of flexibility with these options.

Global and Individual Editing Example

Assume that the RES *Block* and a CAP *Block* were inserted several times to create the partial schematic shown in Figure 22-10. The *Attdisp* command is set to *On* to display all the attributes, including the last two for each *Block* which are normally *Invisible*. *Attedit* is used to edit the attributes of RES and CAP.

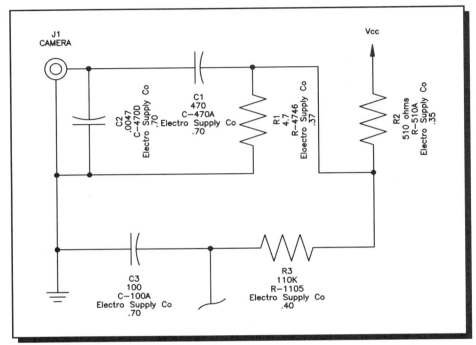

Figure 22-10

If you wish to change the <u>value</u> of one or several attributes, the global editing mode of *Attedit* would generally be used, since <u>values only</u> can be edited in global mode. For this example, assuming that the supplier changed, The MANUFACTURER attribute for all *Blocks* in the drawing is edited. The command syntax is as follows.

```
Command: attedit
Edit attributes one at a time? <Y> N
Global edit of attribute values.
Edit only attributes visible on screen? <Y> Enter
Block name specification <*>: Enter
Attribute tag specification <*>: MANUFACTURER
Attribute value specification <*>: Enter
Select Attributes: PICK (Select specifically the MANUFACTURER attributes.)
6 attributes selected.
String to change: Electro Supply Co
New string: Sparks R Us
Command:
```

All instances of the "Electro Supply Co" redisplay with the new string. Note that resistor R1 did not change because the string did not match (due to misspelling). *Ddatte* can be used to edit the value of that attribute individually.

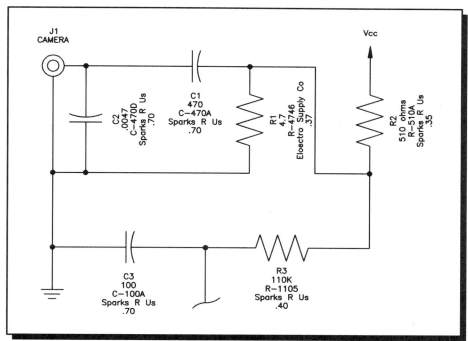

Figure 22-11

The individual editing mode of *Attedit* can be used to change the <u>height</u> of text for the RES_NUMBER and CAP_NUMBER attribute for both the RES and CAP *blocks*. The command syntax is as follows.

```
Command: attedit
Edit attributes one at a time? <Y> Enter
Block name specification <*>: Enter
Attribute tag specification <*>: Enter
Attribute value specification <*>: Enter
Select Attributes:   PICK
6 attributes selected.
Value/Position/Height/Angle/Style/Layer/Color/Next <N>: H
New height <0.1250>: .2
Value/Position/Height/Angle/Style/Layer/Color/Next <N>: Enter
Value/Position/Height/Angle/Style/Layer/Color/Next <N>: H
New height <0.1250>: .2
        etc.
```

The result of the new attribute text height for CAP and RES *Blocks* is shown in Figure 22-12. *Attdisp* has been changed to *Normal* (*Invisible* attributes do not display).

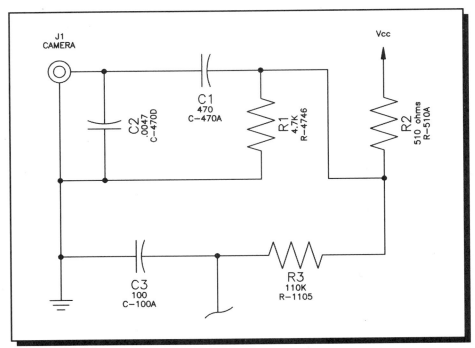

Figure 22-12

EXTRACTING ATTRIBUTES

The *Attext* (attribute extract) command and related *Ddattext* (attribute extract dialogue box) allow you to extract a list of the existing *Blocks* and text attributes from the current drawing. In other words, a list of all, or a subset, of the *Blocks* and attributes that are in a drawing can be written to a separate file (extracted) in text form. The resulting text file can be used as a report indicating a variety of information such as the name, number, location, layer and scale factor of the *Blocks*, and some or all of the *Block* attributes. If desired, the extract file can then be imported to a database or spreadsheet package for further analysis or calculations.

Steps for Creating Extract Files

1.   In AutoCAD *Insert* all desired *Blocks* and related attributes into the drawing. *Save* the drawing.

2.   With a word processor or text editor, create a <u>template</u> file. The template file specifies what information should be included in the <u>extract</u> file and the how the extract file should be structured. (A template file is not required if you specify a *DXF* format for the extract file.)

3.   In AutoCAD, use the *Attext* or *Ddattext* command to specify the name of the template file to be used and to create the extract file.

4.   Examine the extract file in the text editor or word processor or import the extract file into a database or spreadsheet package.

Creating the Template File (Step 2)

The template file is created in a text editor (such as MS-DOS Editor, Norton Editor®, or Windows Notepad®) or word processor (Microsoft Word® or WordPerfect®) in non-document mode. The template file must be in straight ASCII form (no internal word processing codes). The template file <u>must</u> be given a .TXT file extension.

Each <u>line</u> of the template file specifies a <u>column</u> of information, or field, to be written in the extract file, including the name of the column, the width of the column (number of characters or numerals), and the numerical precision. Each *Block* that matches a line in the template file creates an column in the extract file.

The possible fields that AutoCAD allows you to specify and the format that you must use for each are shown below. Use any of the fields you want to create the template file. The first two columns below must be included in the template file (*not the comments*).

```
BL:LEVEL        Nwww000     (Block nesting level)
BL:NAME         Cwww000     (Block name)
BL:X            Nwwwddd     (X coordinate of Block insertion point)
BL:Y            Nwwwddd     (Y coordinate of Block insertion point)
BL:Z            Nwwwddd     (Z coordinate of Block insertion point)
BL:NUMBER       Nwww000     (Block counter; same for all members of MINSERT)
BL:HANDLE       Cwww000     (Block handle; same for all members of MINSERT)
BL:LAYER        Cwww000     (Block insertion layer name)
BL:ORIENT       Nwwwddd     (Block rotation angle)
BL:XSCALE       Nwwwddd     (X scale factor of Block)
BL:YSCALE       Nwwwddd     (Y scale factor of Block)
BL:ZSCALE       Nwwwddd     (Z scale factor of Block)
BL:XEXTRUDE     Nwwwddd     (X component of Block's extrusion direction)
BL:YEXTRUDE     Nwwwddd     (Y component of Block's extrusion direction)
BL:ZEXTRUDE     Nwwwddd     (Z component of Block's extrusion direction)
BL:SPACE        Cwww000     (Space between fields)
Attribute Tag   Cwww000     (Attribute tag, character)
Attribute Tag   Nwwwddd     (Attribute tag, numeric)
```

All items in the first column (in `Courier` font) must be spelled exactly as shown if used. Use spaces rather than tabs or indents to separate the second column entries. In the second column, the first letter must be **N** or **C**, representing a numerical or character field. The three w's indicate digits that specify the field width (number of characters or numbers). The last three digits (0 or d) specify the number of decimal places you desire for the field (0 indicates that no decimals can be specified for that field).

The template file can specify any or all of the possible fields in any order, but should be listed in the order you wish the extract file to display. Each template file must include <u>at least one</u> attribute field. If a *Block* contains any of the specified attributes, it is listed in the extract file, otherwise it is skipped. If a *Block* contains some, but not all, of the specified attributes, the blank fields are filled with spaces or zeros.

A sample template file for the schematic drawing example in Figure 22-12 is shown here.

```
BL:NAME          C004000
BL:X             N005002
BL:Y             N005002
BL:SPACE         C002000
,RES_NUMBER      C004000
RESISTANCE       C009000
CAP_NUMBER       C004000
CAPACITANCE      C006000
PART_NO          C007000
MANUFACTURER     C012000
COST             N005002
```

Creating the Extract File (Step 3)

ATTEXT, DDATTEXT

TYPE IN:	PULL-DOWN MENU	SCREEN MENU	TABLET MENU
ATTEXT or DDATTEXT	*Draw, Text > Attributes > Extract...*	*UTILITY, ATTEXT:*	---

Once you have created a template file, you can use the *Attext* command (for command line format) or invoke the *Attribute Extraction* dialogue box by the pull-down menus or *Ddatte* command. The command line format syntax is as follows.

```
Command: attext
CDF, SDF or DXF Attribute extract (or Entities)? <C>: Enter or
(option)
```

Instead of using the *Attext* command, you may prefer to use the *Ddatte* command or the pull-down menu, both of which invoke the *Attribute Extraction* dialogue box. This dialogue box serves the same functions as the *Attext* command.

You can use the *Select Objects* option (or the *Entities* option in command line format) if you want to PICK only certain block attributes to be included in the extract file.

The *File Format* specifies the structure of the extract file. You can specify either a *SDF*, *CDF*, or *DXF* format for the extract file.

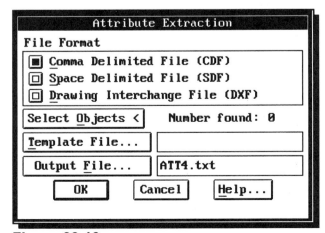

Figure 22-13

SDF

SDF (Space Delimited Format) uses spaces to separate the fields. The *SDF* format is more readable because it appears in columnar format. Numerical fields are right-justified, whereas character fields are left-justified. Therefore, it may be necessary to include a space field (BL:SPACE or BL:DUMMY) after a numeric field that would otherwise be followed immediately by a character field. This method is used in the example template file shown previously.

CDF

CDF (Comma Delimited Format) uses a character that you specify to separate the fields of the extract file. The default character for *CDF* is a comma (,). Some database packages require a *CDF* format for files to be imported.

DXF

The *DXF* format is a variation of the standard AutoCAD *DXF* (Data Interchange File format); however, it contains only *Block* and attribute information. This format contains more information than the *SDF* and *CDF* files and is generally harder to interpret. *DXF* is a standard format, and therefore does <u>not</u> request a template file.

After specifying the desired format, you must specify the *Template File* (name of previously created template file) and *Output File* (name of the extract file to create). The default extract file name is the same as the drawing name, but with the .TXT extension.

PICKing the *Template File* tile invokes the *Select Template File* dialogue box (Fig. 22-14). PICKing the *Output File* tile invokes the *Create Extract File* dialogue (Fig. 22-15). If you use the command line format (*Attext*), the dialogue boxes automatically appear.

The *Select Template File* dialogue box requests the name of the file you wish to use as a template. This file must have been previously created. The template file must have a .TXT file extension.

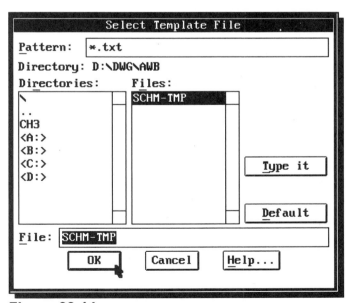

Figure 22-14

Enter the desired name for the extract file in the edit box of the *Create Extract File* dialogue box. AutoCAD uses the <u>drawing</u> name as the default extract file name and appends the .TXT file extension.

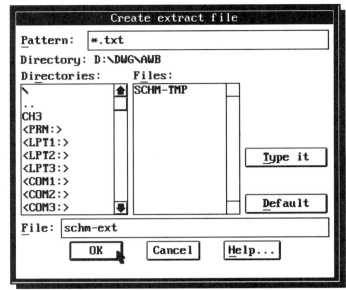

Figure 22-15

If the *FILEDIA* variable is set to 0 (file dialogue boxes turned off), the dialogue boxes do not appear, and requests for template and extract file names appear in command line format as follows.

```
Template file <default>: Enter name of template file with .TXT extension.
Extract filename <drawing name>: Enter desired name of extract file.
```

Finally, AutoCAD then creates the extract file based upon the specified parameters, displaying a message similar to the following.

```
6 records in extract file.
Command:
```

If you receive an error message, check the format of your template file. An error can occur if, for example, you have a BL:NAME field with a width of 10 characters, but a *Block* in the drawing has a name 12 characters long.

Below is the sample extract file that is created using the electrical schematic drawing and the previous example template file.

Sample Extract File

```
RES   7.25 5.75  R1   4.7                   R-4746 Sparks R Us   0.37
RES  10.00 5.75  R2   510 ohms              R-510A Sparks R Us   0.35
CAP   6.00 7.00            C1   470  C-470A Sparks R Us   0.70
CAP   3.75 5.75            C2   .0047 C-470D Sparks R Us   0.70
CAP   4.50 2.75            C3   100  C-100A Sparks R Us   0.70
RES   8.00 2.75  R3   110K                   R-1105 Sparks R Us   0.40
```

This extract file lists the *Block* name, X and Y location of the *Block*, resistor number, resistance value, capacitor number, capacitance value, manufacturer, and cost. Compare the resulting extract file with the matching template file shown below. Remember that each <u>line</u> in the template file creates a <u>column</u> in the extract file.

Sample (Matching) Template File

```
BL:NAME        C004000
BL:X           N005002
BL:Y           N005002
BL:SPACE       C002000
RES_NUMBER     C004000
RESISTANCE     C009000
CAP_NUMBER     C004000
CAPACITANCE    C006000
PART_NO        C007000
MANUFACTURER   C012000
COST           N005002
```

The extract file below was created from the template file shown above using the *CDF* option.

```
'RES', 7.25, 5.75,'','R1','4.7K','','','R-4746','Sparks R Us',
0.37
'RES',10.00, 5.75,'','R2','510 ohms','','','R-510A','Sparks R
Us', 0.35
'CAP', 6.00, 7.00,'','','','C1','470','C-470A','Sparks R Us',
0.70
'CAP', 3.75, 5.75,'','','','C2','.0047','C-470D','Sparks R Us',
0.70
'CAP', 4.50, 2.75,'','','','C3','100','C-100A','Sparks R Us',
0.70
'RES', 8.00, 2.75,'','R3','110K','','','R-1105','Sparks R Us',
0.40
```

CHAPTER EXERCISES

1.   Create an Attributed Title Block

A.   Begin a *New* drawing and assign the name **TBLOCK**. Create the title block as shown in Figure 22-16 or design your own allowing space for 8 text entries. The dimensions are set for an A size sheet. Draw on *Layer* **0**. Use a *Pline* with **.02** *width* for the boundary and *Lines* for the interior divisions. (No *Lines* are needed on the right side and bottom because the title block will fit against the border lines.)

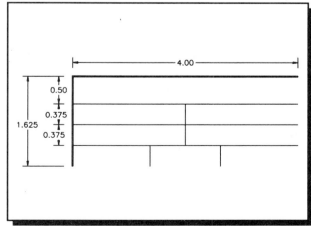

Figure 22-16

B. Create 2 text *Styles* using *Roman Simplex* and *Roman Complex* font files. Define the attributes as described below.

Tag	Prompt	Value	Mode
COMPANY		CADD Design Co.	const
PROJ_TITLE	Enter Project Title	PROJ-	
SCALE	Enter Scale	1"=1"	
DES_NAME		Des.- B. R. Smith	const
CHK_NAME	Enter Checker Name	Ch.-	
COMP_DATE	Enter Completion Date	1/1/94	
CHK_DATE	Enter Check Date	1/1/94	
PROJ_NO	Enter Project Number	PROJ	verify

The completed attributes should be defined as shown in Figure 22-17. *Save* the drawing.

C. Use the *Base* command to assign the *Insertion base point*. **PICK** the lower right corner (shown in Figure 22-17 by the "blip") as the *Insertion base point*.

Since the entire TBLOCK drawing will be inserted as a *Block*, you do not have to use the *Block* command to define the attributed block. *Save* the drawing (as **TBLOCK**).

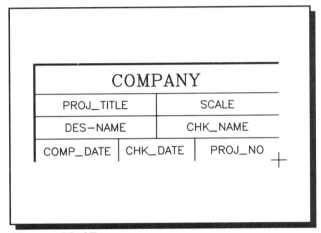

Figure 22-17

D. Begin a *New* drawing and use the **ASHEET** drawing as a *Prototype*. Set the **TITLE** layer *current* and draw a border with a *Pline* of .02 *width*. Set the *ATTDIA* variable to 1 (*On*). Use the *Insert* command to bring the **TBLOCK** drawing in as a *Block*. The *Enter Attributes* dialogue box should appear. Enter the attributes to complete the title block similar to that shown in Figure 22-18. Do not *Save* the drawing.

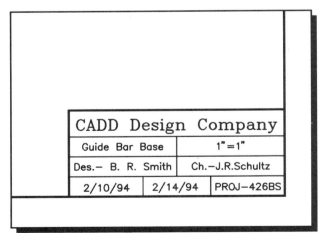

Figure 22-18

2. Create Attributed *Blocks* for the OFF-ATT Drawing

A. *Open* the **OFF-ATT** drawing that you prepared in Chapter 21 Exercises. The drawing should have the office floor plan completed and the geometry drawn for the furniture

Blocks. The furniture has not yet been transformed to _Blocks_. You are ready to create attributes for the furniture as shown in Figure 22-19.

Include the information below for the proposed _Blocks_. Use the same tag, prompt, and mode for each proposed _Block_. The values are different depending on the furniture item.

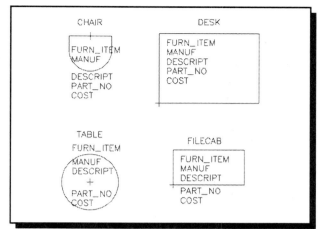

Figure 22-19

<u>Tag</u>	<u>Prompt</u>	
FURN_ITEM	Enter furniture item	
MANUF	Enter manufacturer	
DESCRIPT	Enter model or size	
PART_NO	Enter part number	Invisible
COST	Enter dealer cost	Invisible

<u>Values</u>

CHAIR	DESK	TABLE	FILE CABINET
WELLTON	KERSEY	KERSEY	STEELMAN
SWIVEL	50" x 30"	ROUND 2'	28 x 3
C-143	KER-29	KER-13	3-28-L
79.99	249.95	42.50	129.99

B. Next, use the **Block** command to make each attributed _Block_. Use the **Block names** shown (Figure 22-19). Select the attributes <u>in the order</u> you want them to appear upon insertion, then select the geometry. Use the **Insertion base points** as shown. **Save** the drawing.

C. Set the _ATTDIA_ variable to 0 (**Off**). **Insert** the **Blocks** into the office and accept the default values. Create an arrangement similar to that shown in Figure 22-20.

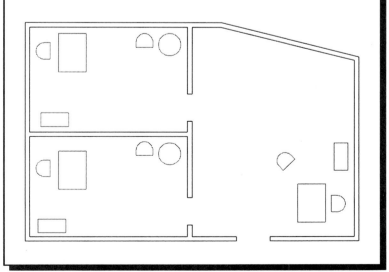

Figure 22-20

D.   Use the ***ATTDISP*** variable and change the setting to ***Off***. Do the attributes disappear?

E.   A price change has been reported for all KERSEY furniture items. Your buyer has negotiated an additional 10% off the current dealer cost. Type in the ***Multiple Ddatte*** command and select each block one at a time to view the attributes. Make the COST changes as necessary. Use ***Saveas*** and assign the new name **OFF-ATT2**.

F.   Change the ***ATTDISP*** setting back to ***Normal***. It would be helpful to increase the ***Height*** of the FURN_ITEM attribute (CHAIR, TABLE, etc.). Use the ***Attedit*** command, and answer ***Yes*** to "*Edit attributes one at a time?*" Enter **FURN_ITEM** in response to "*Attribute tag specification*" and accept the default for the other two prompts. Select all the FURN_ITEM attributes (no highlighting occurs at this time). Increase the ***Height*** to **3"** for each. If everything looks correct, ***Save*** the drawing.

3.   Extract Attributes

A.   A cost analysis of the office design is required to check against the $3400.00 budget allocated for furnishings. This can be accomplished by extracting the attributes into a report. Use a text editor or word processor (in ASCII or non-document mode) to generate the template file below. (Insure that you have no extra spaces or lines.) Name the file **OFF-TMPL.TXT**.

```
BL:NAME         C008000
BL:X            N008002
BL:Y            N008002
BL:SPACE        C002000
FUR_ITEM        C014000
MANUF           C012000
COST            N006002
```

B.   Use the ***Ddattext*** command (or select ***Extract...*** from the pull-down menu). Select **SDF** format. Specify **OFF-EXT.TXT** for the extract file name. The resulting extract file should appear similar to that below.

```
DESK      165.00   348.00   DESK            KERSEY      224.95
DESK      165.00   228.00   DESK            KERSEY      224.95
DESK      405.00   174.00   DESK            KERSEY      224.95
CHAIR     156.00   327.00   CHAIR           WELLTON      79.99
CHAIR     153.00   204.00   CHAIR           WELLTON      79.99
CHAIR     249.00   336.00   CHAIR           WELLTON      79.99
CHAIR     249.00   216.00   CHAIR           WELLTON      79.99
CHAIR     447.00   153.00   CHAIR           WELLTON      79.99
CHAIR     387.00   189.00   CHAIR           WELLTON      79.99
TABLE     276.00   204.00   TABLE           KERSEY       38.25
TABLE     276.00   327.00   TABLE           KERSEY       38.25
FILECAB   450.00   225.00   FILE  CABINET   STEELMAN    129.99
FILECAB   135.00   132.00   FILE  CABINET   STEELMAN    129.99
FILECAB   135.00   249.00   FILE  CABINET   STEELMAN    129.99
```

C.   Total the COST column to acquire the total furnishings cost so far for the job. If you purchase the $880 conference table and 8 more chairs, how much money will be left in the budget to purchase plants and wall decorations?

4.   Create the electrical schematic illustrated in Figure 22-21. Use *Blocks* for the symbols. The text associated with the symbols should be created as attributes. Use the following *Block* names and tags.

Block Names: RES
                     CAP
                     GRD
                     AMP

Attibute Tags: PART_NUM
                     MANUF_NUM
                     RESISTANCE
                     CAPACITANCE

(Only the RES and CAP *Blocks* have values for resistance or capacitance.) When you are finished with the drawing, create an extract file reporting information for all attribute tags (X and Y coordinate data is not needed). Save the drawing as **SCHEM2**.

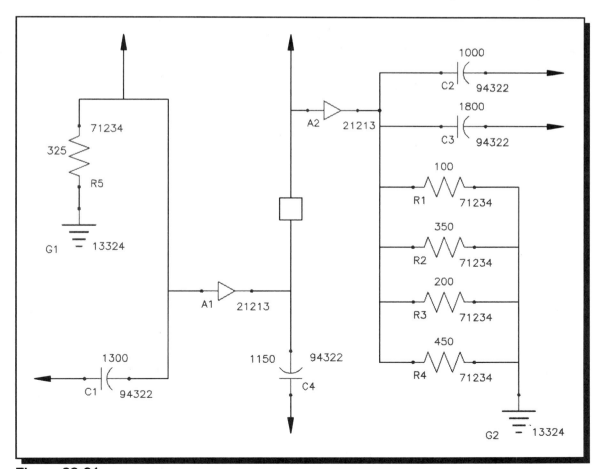

Figure 22-21

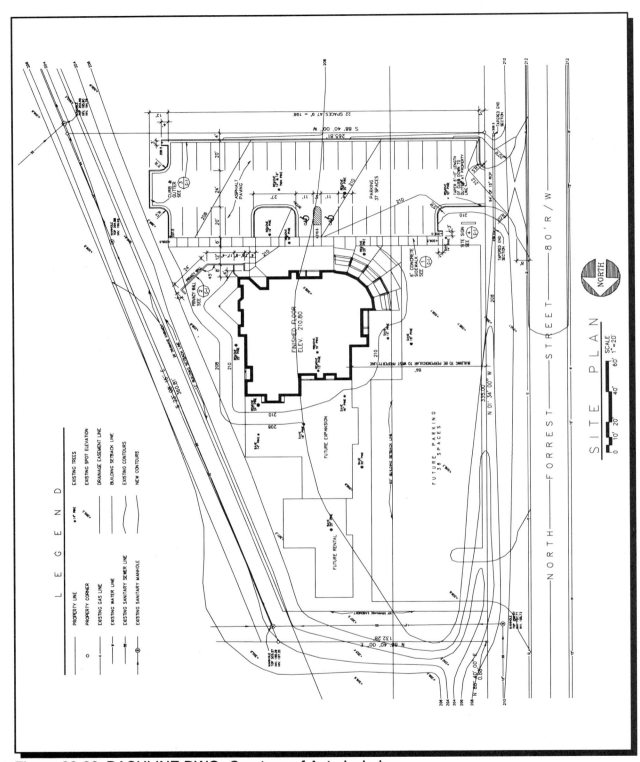

Figure 22-22 DASHLINE.DWG Courtesy of Autodesk, Inc.

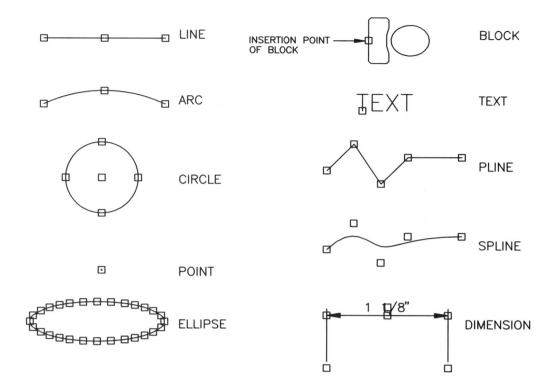

CHAPTER 23

Grip Editing

CHAPTER OBJECTIVES

After completing this chapter you should:

1. be able to use the *GRIPS* variable to enable or disable entity grips;

2. be able to activate the grips on any entity;

3. be able to make an entity's grips warm, hot or cold;

4. be able to use each of the grip editing options, namely, Stretch, Move, Rotate, Scale, and Mirror;

5. be able to use the Copy and the Base suboptions;

6. be able to use the auxiliary grid that is automatically created when the Copy suboption is used;

7. be able to change grip variable settings using the *Grips* dialogue box or the command line format.

BASICS

Grips provide an alternative method of editing AutoCAD entities. The entity grips are available for use by setting the *GRIPS* variable to **1**. Entity grips are small squares appearing on selected entities at endpoints, midpoints, or centers, etc. The entity grips are activated (made visible) by **PICK**ing entities with the cursor pickbox only <u>when no commands are in use</u> (at the open `Command:` prompt). Grips are like small, magnetic *OSNAPs* (*ENDpoint, MIDpoint, CENter, QUAdrant,* etc.) that can be used for snapping one entity to another, for example. If the cursor is moved within the small square, it is automatically "snapped" to the grip. Grips can replace the use of *OSNAP* for many applications. The grip option allows you to `STRETCH`, `MOVE`, `ROTATE`, `SCALE`, `Mirror`, or `Copy` entities without invoking the normal editing commands or *OSNAPs*.

As an example, the endpoint of a *Line* could be "snapped" to the endpoint of an *Arc* (shown in Figure 23-1) by the following steps:

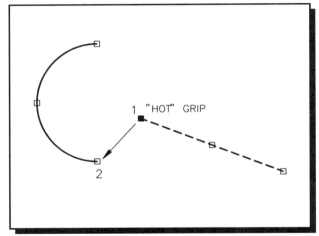

1. Activate the grips by selecting both entities. Selection is done when no commands are in use (during the open `Command:` prompt).
2. Select the grip at the endpoint of the *Line* (1). The grip turns **hot** (red).
3. The `** STRETCH **` option appears in place of the `Command:` prompt.
4. `STRETCH` the *Line* to the endpoint grip on the *Arc* (2). **PICK** when the cursor "snaps" to the grip.

Figure 23-1

5. The *Line* and the *Arc* should then have connecting endpoints. The `Command:` prompt reappears. Press CTRL-C twice to cancel (deactivate) the grips.

GRIP FEATURES

The *GRIPS* Variable

Grips are enabled or disabled by changing the setting of the system variable, *GRIPS*. A setting of **1** enables or turns *ON GRIPS* and a setting of **0** disables or turns *OFF GRIPS*. This variable can be typed at the `Command:` prompt, or the *Grips* dialogue box can be invoked from the *Settings* pull-down menu or by typing *Ddgrips* (Fig. 23-2). Using the dialogue box, toggle *Enable Grips* to turn *GRIPS ON*. The default setting in AutoCAD Release 12 for the *GRIPS* variable is **1** (*ON*).

The *GRIPS* variable is saved in the ACAD.CFG file rather than in the current drawing as with most other system variables. Variables saved in the ACAD.CFG file are effective for any drawing session on that <u>particular computer</u>, no matter which drawing is current. The reasoning is that grip-related variables (and selection set-related variables) are a matter of personal preference and therefore should remain constant for a particular CAD station.

When *GRIPS* have been enabled, a small pickbox (3 pixels is the default size) appears at the center of the cursor crosshairs. (The pickbox also appears if the *PICKFIRST* system variable is set to 1. (See Chapter 20.) This pickbox operates in the same manner as the pickbox appearing during the `Select objects:` prompt. <u>Only</u> the pickbox, *AUto window*, or *AUto crossing window* methods can be used for selecting objects to activate the grips. (These three options are the only options available for Noun/Verb entity selection as well.)

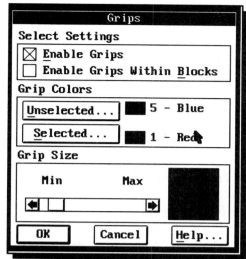

Figure 23-2

Activating Grips on Entities

The grips on entities are activated by selecting desired entities with the crosshair pickbox, window or crossing window. This action is done when no commands are in use (at the open `Command:` prompt). When an entity has been selected, two things happen: the grips appear and the entity is highlighted. The grips are the small blue (default color) boxes appearing at the endpoints, midpoint, center, quadrants, vertices, insertion point, or other locations depending upon the entity type (Fig. 23-3). Highlighting indicates that the entity is included in the selection set.

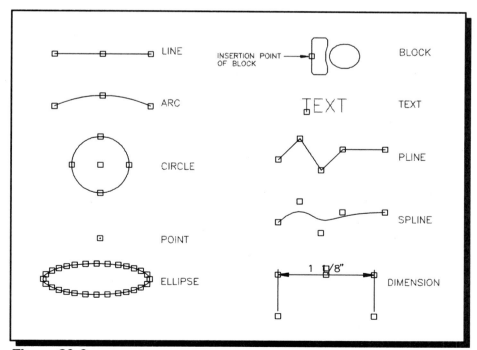

Figure 23-3

Warm, Hot, and Cold Grips

Grips can have three states: **warm, hot,** or **cold** (Fig. 23-4).

A grip is always **warm** first. When an entity is selected, it is **warm**--its grips are displayed in blue (default color) and the entity is highlighted. The grips can then be made **hot** or **cold**. **Cold** grips are also blue, but the entity becomes <u>unhighlighted</u>.

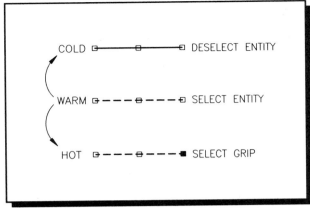

Figure 23-4

Cold grips are created by <u>deselecting</u> a highlighted <u>entity</u> that has **warm** grips. In other words, removing the **warm** grip entity from the selection set with SHIFT+#1, or using the *Remove* mode, makes its grips **cold**. A **cold** grip can be used as a point to snap <u>to</u>. A **cold** grip's entity is not in the selection set and therefore is not affected by the MOVE, ROTATE, or other editing action. Pressing CTRL-C <u>once</u> changes all **warm** grips to **cold** and clears the selection set. Pressing CTRL-C again deactivates all grips. (In short, press CTRL-C <u>twice</u> to cancel grips entirely.)

A **hot** grip is red (by default) and its entity is almost always highlighted. Any grip can be changed to **hot** by selecting the grip itself. A **hot** grip is the default base point used for the editing action such as MOVE, ROTATE, SCALE, or MIRROR, or is the stretch point for STRETCH. When a **hot** grip exists, a new series of prompts appear in place of the Command: prompt that displays the various grip editing options. <u>**A grip must be changed to**</u> <u>**hot before the editing options appear.**</u> A grip can be transformed from **cold** to **hot** but the entity is not highlighted (included in the selection set). Two or more grips can be made **hot** simultaneously by pressing SHIFT while selecting <u>each</u> grip.

The three states of grips can be summarized as follows:

Cold grips base	blue grips unhighlighted entity	The entity is not part of the selection set, but cold can be used to "snap" to or used as an alternate point.
Warm	blue grips highlighted entity	The entity is included in selection set and is affected by the entity action.
Hot	red grips highlighted entity	The base point or control point for the editing action, depending on which option is used. The entity is included in selection set.

Grip Editing Options

When a **hot grip** has been activated, the grip editing options are available. The Command: prompt is replaced by the STRETCH, MOVE, ROTATE, SCALE, or MIRROR grip editing options. You can sequentially cycle through the options by pressing the SPACE bar. The editing options are displayed in the following figures.

```
** STRETCH **
<Stretch to point>/Base point/Copy/Undo/eXit:
```

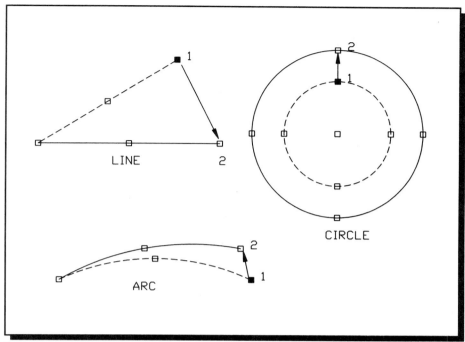

Figure 23-5

```
** MOVE **
<Move to point>/Base point/Copy/Undo/eXit:
```

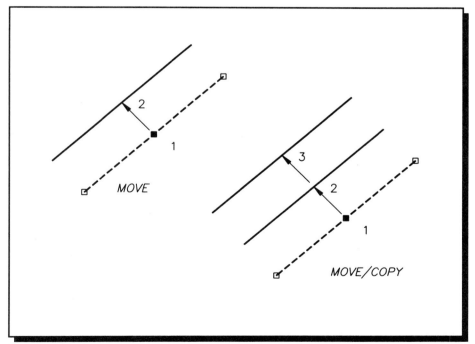

Figure 23-6

```
** ROTATE **
<Rotate angle>/Base point/Copy/Undo/Reference/eXit:
```

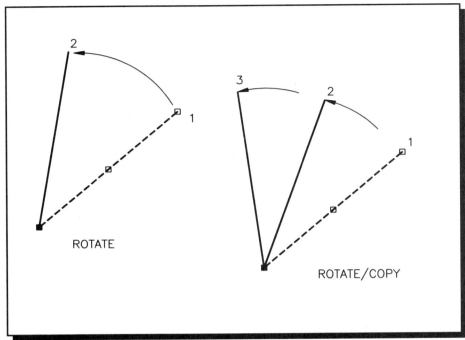

Figure 23-7

```
** SCALE **
<Scale factor>/Base point/Copy/Undo/Reference/eXit:
```

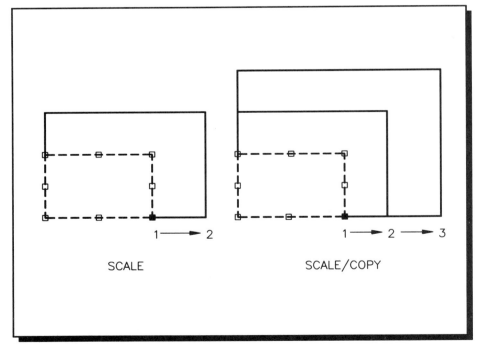

Figure 23-8

```
** MIRROR **
<Second point>/Base point/Copy/Undo/eXit:
```

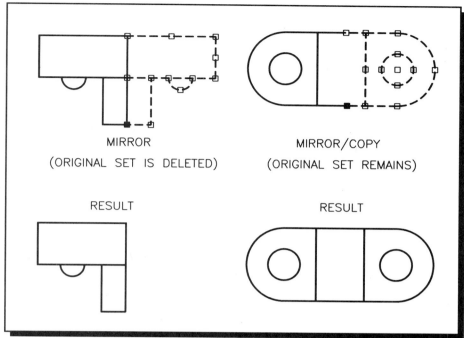

Figure 23-9

The *Grip* options are easy to understand and use. Each option operates like the full AutoCAD command by the same name. Generally, the editing option used (except for STRETCH) affects all highlighted entities. The **hot** grip is the base point for each operation. The suboptions, Base and Copy, are explained below.

NOTE: The STRETCH option differs from other options in two ways. First, STRETCH affects <u>only</u> the entity that is attached to the **hot** grip rather than affecting all highlighted entities. Second, STRETCH is not available when a **cold** grip has been changed directly to a **hot** because its entity is not in the selection set and therefore cannot be stretched.

Base

The Base suboption appears with all of the main grip editing options (Stretch, Move, etc.). Base allows using any other grip as the base point instead of the **hot** grip. The letter *B* is typed to invoke this suboption.

Copy

Copy is a suboption of every main choice. Activating this suboption by typing the letter *C* invokes a Multiple copy mode, such that whatever set of entities are STRETCHed, MOVEd, ROTATEd, etc. becomes the first of an unlimited number of copies (see the previous five figures). The Multiple mode remains active until eXiting back to the Command prompt.

Undo

The Undo option, invoked by typing the letter *U*, will undo the last Copy or the last Basepoint selection. Undo <u>only</u> functions after a Base or Copy operation.

Auxiliary Grid

An auxiliary grid is <u>automatically</u> established upon creating the first Copy (Fig. 23-10). The grid is activated by pressing SHIFT while placing the subsequent copies. The subsequent copies are then "snapped" to the grid in the same manner that *SNAP* functions. The spacing of this auxiliary grid is determined by the location of the first Copy, that is, the X and Y intervals between the base point and the second point.

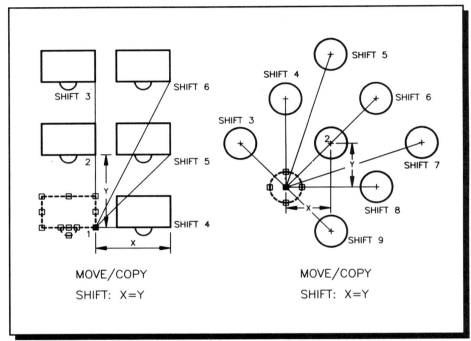

Figure 23-10

For example, a "polar array" can be simulated with grips by using ROTATE with the Copy suboption (Fig. 23-11).

The "array" can be constructed in one of 2 ways: (1) about an <u>existing</u> circle using the auxiliary grid or the grips at the quadrants or (2) by making one Copy, then using the auxiliary grid to achieve equal angular spacing.

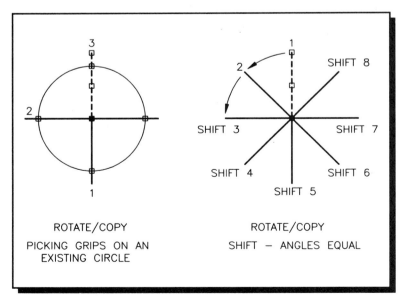

Figure 23-11

The steps for creating a "polar array" are as follows:

1.   Select the entities to array and the circle to array about. Deselect the circle to make its grips **cold**.

2.   Select a grip on the set of entities to array. Cycle to the ROTATE option by pressing the Space bar.

3.   Type **C** and **Enter** to invoke the Copy suboption. Then type **B** and **Enter** to invoke the Base point option. Select the center grip of the circle as the new base point.

4.   Make the copies in a circular fashion in one of two ways:
      a.   Select each quadrant grip of the circle.
      b.   After making the first copy at any desired location, activate the auxiliary circular grid by holding down SHIFT while making the other copies.

5.   Cancel the grips or select another command from the menus.

Editing Dimensions

One of the most effective applications of grips is as a dimension editor. Because grips exist at the dimension's extension line origins, arrowhead end points, and dimensional value, a dimension can by changed in many ways and still retain its associativity (Fig. 23-12). See Chapter 28, Dimensioning, for further information about dimensions, associativity, and editing dimensions with *Grips*.

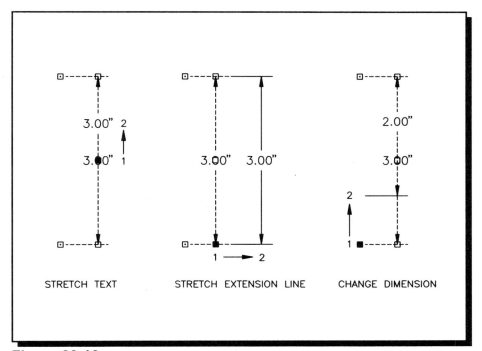

Figure 23-12

Guidelines for Using Grips

Although there are many ways to use grips based upon the existing entities and the desired application, a general set of guidelines for using grips is given here.

1. Create the entities to edit.

2. Select **warm** and **cold** grips first. This is usually accomplished by selecting <u>all</u> grips first (**warm** state), then <u>deselecting</u> entities to establish the desired **cold** grips.

3. Select the desired **hot** grip(s). The *Grip* options should appear in place of the Command: line.

4. Press SPACE to cycle to the desired editing option (STRETCH, MOVE, ROTATE, SCALE, MIRROR).

5. Select the desired suboptions, if any. If the Copy suboption is needed or the Base point needs to be re-specified, do so at this time. Base or Copy can be selected in either order.

6. Make the desired STRETCH, MOVE, ROTATE, SCALE, or MIRROR.

7. Cancel the grips by pressing CTRL-C twice or selecting a command from a menu.

Variables that Control Grips

Following is a list of variables that control the way grips appear or operate. The variables can be changed by typing in the variable name at the command prompt or by invoking the *Grips* dialogue box (Fig. 23-13).

<u>Variable</u>	<u>Dialogue Option</u>	<u>Default</u>	<u>Action</u>
GRIPS	*Enable Grips*	1 (*ON*)	Enables or disables *GRIPS*.
GRIPBLOCK	*Enable Within Blocks*	0 (*OFF*)	If set to 0, only one grip at the *Block's* insertion point is visible. If set to 1, all grips on all entities contained in the *Block* are visible and functional (however, individual entities in the *Block* cannot be edited independently).
GRIPCOLOR	*Grip Colors Unselected*	5 (blue)	Specifies the color of **warm** and **cold** grips.
GRIPHOT	*Grip Colors Selected*	1 (red)	Specifies the color of **hot** grips.
GRIPSIZE	*Grip Size*	3	Specifies the size of grips in pixels.

All *Grip*-related variables are accessible from within the *Grips* dialogue box (Fig. 23-13). All *Grip*-related variables are saved in the ACAD.CFG file rather than in the current drawing file. This generally means that changes in these variables remain with the computer, not the drawing being used.

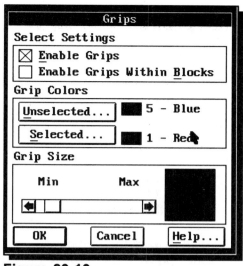

Figure 23-13

Point Specification Precedence

When you select a point with the input device, AutoCAD uses a point specification precedence to determine which location on the drawing to find. The hierarchy is listed here.

1. Object Snap (*OSNAP*)
2. Explicit coordinate entry (absolute, relative, or polar coordinates)
3. *ORTHO*
4. Point filters (XY filters)
5. *Grips* auxiliary grid (rectangular and circular)
6. *Grips* (on entities)
7. *SNAP* (F9 grid snap)
8. Digitizing a point location

Practically, this means that *OSNAP* has priority over any other point selection mode. As far as *Grips* are concerned, *ORTHO* overrides *Grips*, so turn off *ORTHO* if you want to snap to *Grips*. *Grips*, however, overrides *SNAP* (F9) so *SNAP* can be active while using *Grips*.

CHAPTER EXERCISES

1. *Open* the **CH16EX8B** drawing. It was learned that there was a mistake in reporting the temperatures for that week. Thursday's low must be changed to 38 degrees and Friday's to 34 degrees. Use grips to make the change. **PICK** the *Splined Pline* to activate **warm** grips. Make Thursday's grip **hot** as shown in Figure 23-14. Use the **STRETCH** option to stretch it **4** units above. **Cancel** the grips. Repeat the steps to stretch Friday's grip down **4** units. *Save* the drawing as **CH23EX1**.

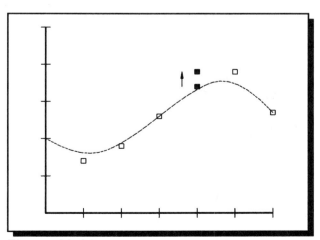

Figure 23-14

2. ***Open*** **CH16EX4** drawing. Activate **grips** on the *Line* to the far right. Make the top grip **hot**. Use the STRETCH option to stretch the top grip to the right to create a vertical *Line*. **Cancel** the grips.

Next, activate the **grips** for all the *Lines* (including the vertical one on the right), then make the vertical *Line* grips **cold** as shown in Figure 23-15. STRETCH the top of all inclined *Lines* to the top of the vertical *Line* by making the common top grips **hot**, then stretching to the cold **grip** of the vertical *Line*. ***Save*** the drawing as **CH23EX2**.

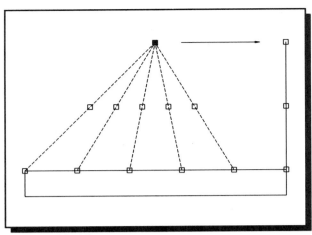

Figure 23-15

3. This exercise will involve all the options of grip editing to create a Space Plate. Begin a ***New*** drawing or use the **ASHEET** *Prototype* and use *Saveas* to assign the name **SPACEPLT**.

A. Set the ***Snap*** value to **.125**. Draw the geometry shown in Figure 23-16 using the ***Line*** and ***Circle*** commands.

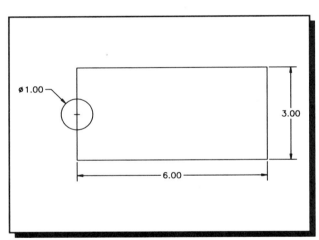

Figure 23-16

B. Activate the **grips** on the *Circle*. Make the center grip **hot**. Cycle to the MOVE option. Enter **C** for the Copy option. you should then get the prompt for MOVE (multiple). Make two copies as shown in Figure 23-17. The new *Circles* should be spaced evenly, with the one at the far right in the center of the rectangle. If the spacing is off, use **grips** with the STRETCH option to make the correction.

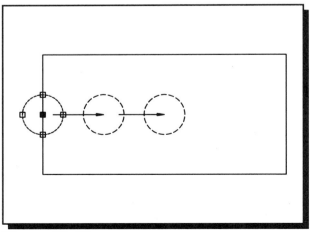

Figure 23-17

C. Activate the **grips** on the number 2 *Circle* (from the left) to make them **warm**. Also activate the **grips** on the bottom horizontal *Line*, but make them **cold**. Make the center *Circle* grip **hot** and cycle to the MIRROR option. Enter *C* for the Copy option. (You'll see the MIRROR(multiple) prompt.) Then enter *B* to specify a new basepoint as indicated in Figure 23-18. Turn *On ORTHO* and specify the mirror axis as shown to create the new *Circle* (shown in Figure 23-18 in hidden linetype).

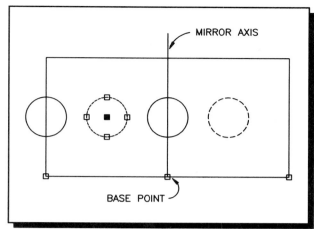

Figure 23-18

D. Use *Trim* to trim away the outer half of the *Circle* and the interior portion of the vertical *Line* on the left side of the Space Plate. Activate the **grips** on the two vertical *Lines* and the new *Arc*. Make the common grip **hot** (on the *Arc* and *Line* as shown in Figure 23-19) and STRETCH it downward .5 units. (Note how you can affect multiple entities by selecting a common grip.) Stretch the upper end of the *Arc* upward .5 units.

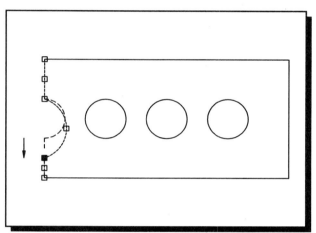

Figure 23-19

E. *Erase* the *Line* on the right side of the Space Plate. Use the same method that you used in step C. to MIRROR the *Lines* and *Arc* to the right side of the plate (as shown in Figure 23-20).

(REMINDER: Make sure that you make the grips on the bottom *Line* **cold**. After you select the **hot** grip, use the Copy option <u>and</u> the Basepoint option. Use *ORTHO*.)

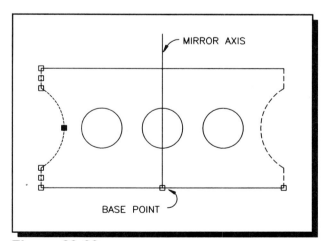

Figure 23-20

F.   In this step you will **STRETCH** the top edge upward one unit and the bottom edge downward one unit by selecting <u>multiple</u> **hot** grips.

Select the desired horizontal <u>and</u> attached vertical *Lines*. Hold down SHIFT while selecting <u>each</u> of the endpoint grips as shown in Figure 23-21. Although they appear **hot**, you must select one of the two again to activate the **STRETCH** option.

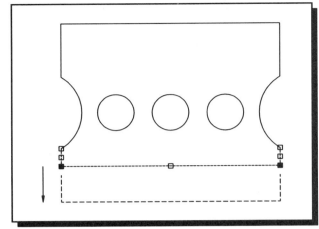

Figure 23-21

G.   In this step two more *Circles* are created by the **ROTATE** option (see Figure 23-22). Select the three existing *Circles* to make the grips **warm**. PICK the center grip to make it **hot**. Cycle to the **ROTATE** option. Enter *C* for the **Copy** option. Make sure *ORTHO* is *On* and create the new *Circles*.

H.   Select the center *Circle* and make the center grip **hot** (Fig. 23-23). Cycle to the **SCALE** option. The scale factor is **1.5**. Since the *Circle* is a 1 unit diameter, it can be interactively scaled (watch the *COORDS* display), or you can enter the value. The drawing is complete. *Save* the drawing as **SPACEPLT**.

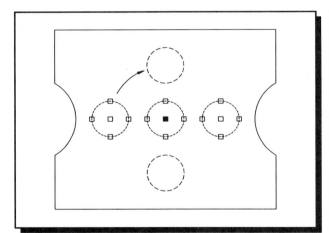

Figure 23-22

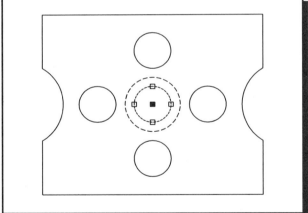

Figure 23-23

4.   *Open* the **OFF-ATT2** drawing that you worked on in Chapter 22 Exercises. Use grips to **STRETCH**, **MOVE**, **ROTATE**, **SCALE**, **MIRROR**, and **Copy** the furniture *Blocks*. Experiment with each option. Notice that each attribute has a grip. The attributes can be **STRETCH**ed independently of the *Blocks*. Change the *GRIPBLOCK* variable to enable all the grips on the *Blocks* for some of the editing. *Save* any changes that you like.

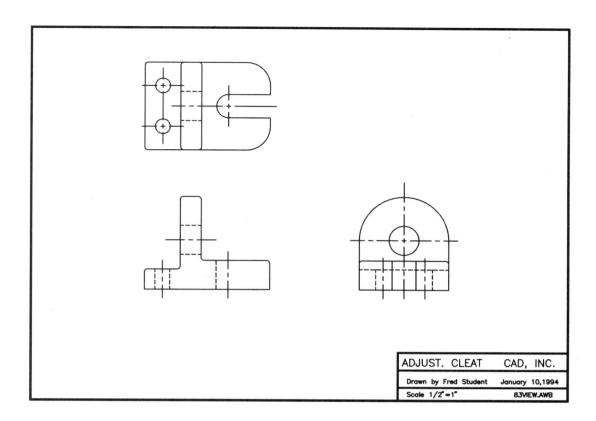

ADJUST. CLEAT	CAD, INC.
Drawn by Fred Student	January 10,1994
Scale 1/2"=1"	83VIEW.AWB

CHAPTER 24

Multiview Drawing

CHAPTER OBJECTIVES

After completing this chapter you should:

1.   know how to use the crosshairs for checking alignment of views;

2.   be able to draw projection lines using *ORTHO* and *SNAP*;

3.   be able to use point filters for alignment of lines and views;

4.   be able to use construction layers for managing construction lines and notes;

5.   be able to use linetypes and layers to draw and manage ANSI standard linetypes;

6.   know how to create fillets, rounds, and runouts;

7.   know the typical guidelines for creating a two-view multiview drawing;

8.   know the typical guidelines for creating a three-view multiview drawing.

BASICS

Multiview drawings are used to represent 3D objects on 2D media. The standards and conventions related to multiview drawings have been developed over years of using and optimizing a system of representing real objects on paper. Now that our technology has developed to a point that we can create 3D models, some of the methods we use to generate multiview drawings have changed, but the standards and conventions have been retained so that we can continue to have a universally understood method of communication.

This chapter illustrates methods of creating 2D multiview drawings with AutoCAD (without a 3D model) while complying with most industry standards. (The use of 3D models to generate 2D drawings is addressed in Chapter 46.) There are many techniques that can be used to construct multiview drawings with AutoCAD because AutoCAD is such a versatile tool. The methods shown in this chapter are the more common methods because they are derived from traditional manual techniques. Other methods are possible.

PROJECTION AND ALIGNMENT OF VIEWS

Projection theory and conventions of multiview drawing dictate that the views be aligned with each other and oriented in a particular relationship. AutoCAD has particular features, such as horizontal/vertical crosshairs, *SNAP*, *ORTHO*, Object Snap, and point filters, that can be used effectively for facilitating projection and the alignment of views. Each feature is illustrated below and on the following pages.

Using the Crosshairs for Checking Alignment of Views

The crosshairs are arranged in a perpendicular fashion and can be used for a "visual" check for alignment of views and object features. For example, Figure 24-1 illustrates the use of the crosshairs to check the alignment of a hole center.

In Figure 24-1 the crosshairs are located at the center of the circular view of the hole. Following the vertical and horizontal elements of the crosshairs reveals that the hole is located correctly in the top view but appears to be aligned <u>incorrectly</u> in the right side view.

Keep in mind that in some cases the crosshairs can only be used as a "visual" check for alignment. <u>Only</u> in cases where all of the geometry elements are at *SNAP* increments and *SNAP* is *ON* are the crosshairs be 100% accurate for inspecting alignment. In Figure 24-2 all dimensions of the object are at 1/8 increments. Since *SNAP* is set to a value of .125 and is *ON*, the crosshairs can be used as a valid alignment check. In this case, both views have <u>correct</u> alignment.

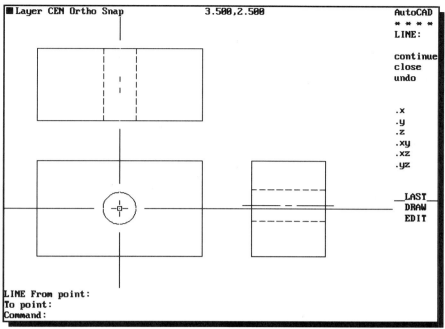

Figure 24-1

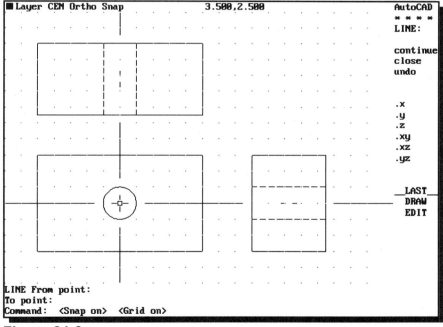

Figure 24-2

Using *ORTHO* and *OSNAP* for Drawing Projection Lines

ORTHO (F8) can be used effectively in concert with *OSNAP* to draw projection lines during construction of multiview drawings. For example, drawing a *Line* interactively with *ORTHO* *ON* forces the *Line* to be drawn in either a horizontal or vertical direction.

Figure 24-3 simulates this feature while drawing projection *Lines* from the right side view up to a 45 degree miter line (intended for transfer of dimensions to the top view). The `From point:` of the *Line* originated from the *ENDpoint* of the *Line* on the side view.

Figure 24-4 illustrates the next step. The horizontal projection *Line* is drawn from the *INTersection* of the 45 degree line and the last projection line. *ORTHO* forces the *Line* to the correct horizontal alignment with the top view.

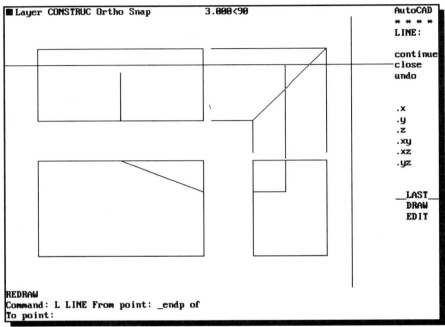

Figure 24-3

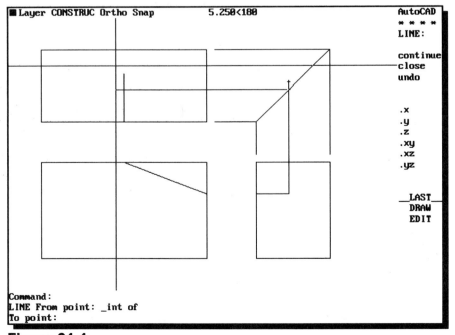

Figure 24-4

Remember that any draw <u>or</u> edit command that requires PICKing is a candidate for *ORTHO* and/or *OSNAP*. NOTE: *OSNAP* overrides *ORTHO*. If *ORTHO* is *ON* and you are using an *OSNAP* mode to PICK the `to point:` of a *Line*, the *OSNAP* mode has priority and therefore may not result in an orthogonal *Line*. (See Point Specification Precedence, Chapter 23.)

Using *Offset* for Construction of Views

An alternative to using the traditional miter line method for construction of a view by projection, the *Offset* command can be used to transfer distances from one view and construct another. The *Distance* option of *Offset* provides this alternative.

For example, assume that the top view was completed and you need to construct a side view (Fig. 24-5). First create a vertical line as the inner edge of the side view (shown highlighted) by *Offset* or other method. To create the outer edge of the side view (shown as hidden), use *Offset* and PICK points (1) and (2) to specify the *distance*. Select the existing line (3) as the "*Object to Offset:*," then the "*Side to offset?*" at the current crosshairs position.

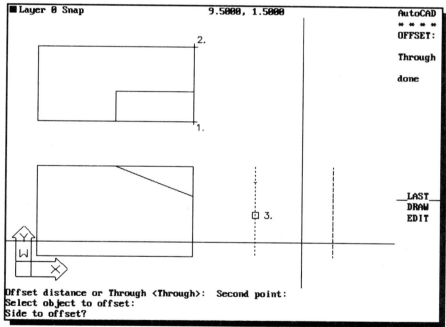

Figure 24-5

Realignment of Views Using *ORTHO* and *SNAP*

Another application of *ORTHO* and *OSNAP* is with the use of *Move* to change the location of an entire view. For example, assume that the views of the multiview in Figure 24-6 are complete and ready for dimensioning, however, there is not enough room between the front and side views. You can invoke the *Move* command, select the entire view with a *window* or other option, and "slide" the entire view outward. *ORTHO* assures the proper alignment. Make sure *SNAP* is *ON* during the *Move* (if *SNAP* was used in the original construction). This action assures that the final position of the view is on a *SNAP* point and that the entities retain their orientation with respect to the *SNAP*.

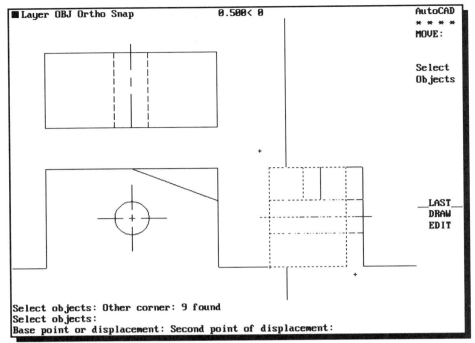

Figure 24-6

An alternative to *Moving* the view interactively is through the use of coordinate specification (absolute, relative rectangular, or relative polar).

Using Point Filters for Alignment

If you want to draw a *Line* so that it ends or begins in alignment with another entity or view, X or Y point filters can be used. For example, Figure 24-7 shows the construction of a *Line* in the top view. It is desired to end the *Line* in alignment with the X position (directly above) of the left side of the front view. An *.X* point filter is used to accomplish this action. *ORTHO is On*.

The following command syntax is used for the construction.

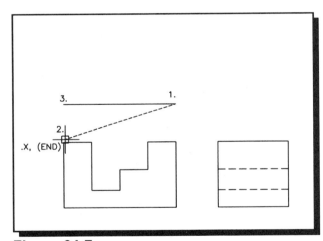

Figure 24-7

```
Command: line
From point: PICK (1.)
To point: .X (Type ".X", then press Enter.)
of ENDpoint of PICK (2.) (AutoCAD uses only the X value of the point selected.)
(need YZ): PICK (anywhere near 3. AutoCAD uses the Y and Z points selected.)
To point: Enter
Command:
```

Another possibility is the use of a .Y point filter for construction in alignment with the Y value (height) of existing entities. In this case, enter a **.Y** in response to the "*to point:*" prompt and press Enter. The point you PICK (2) supplies only the Y value. AutoCAD responds with "*(need XZ)*". PICK again near (3) to supply the X value. Make sure *ORTHO* is *On*.

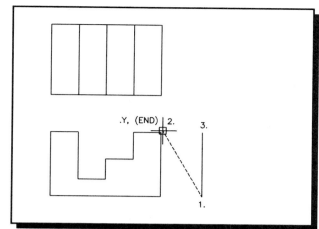

Figure 24-8

X and Y point filters can be used anytime AutoCAD requires point selection. For example, alignment of the side view (highlighted) can be corrected by invoking the *Move* command, entering a Y point filter and selecting the *ENDpoint* of the front view (2) as the Second point of displacement. The X coordinate can be supplied by PICKing (3) with *ORTHO On*. The resulting position of the side view is aligned with the front.

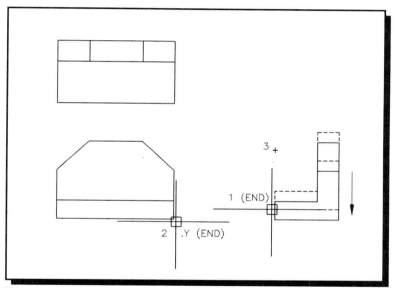

Figure 24-9

USING CONSTRUCTION LAYERS

The use of layers for isolating construction lines can make drawing and editing faster and easier. The creation of multiview drawings can involve construction lines, reference points, or notes that are not intended for the final plot. Rather than *Erasing* these construction lines, points, or notes before plotting, they can be created on a separate layer and turned *Off* or made *Frozen* before running the final plot. If design changes are required, as they often are, the construction layers can be turned *On*, rather than having to recreate the construction.

There are two strategies for creating construction entities on separate layers.

1. Use Layer 0 for construction lines, reference points, and notes. This method can be used for fast, simple drawings.

2.   <u>Create</u> a <u>new</u> layer for construction lines, reference points, and notes. Use this method for more complex drawings, drawings intended to be used as an Xreference (see Chapter 31), or drawings involving use of *Blocks* on Layer 0.

For example, consider the drawing during construction in Figure 24-10. A separate layer has been created for the construction lines, notes, and reference points.

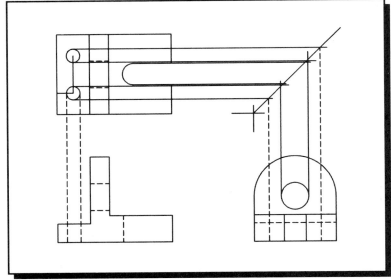

Figure 24-10

In Figure 24-11, the same drawing is shown ready for making the final plot. Notice that the construction Layer has been *Frozen*.

If you are plotting the *Limits*, and the construction layer has entities <u>outside</u> the *Limits*, the construction layer should be *Frozen*, rather than being turned *Off*.

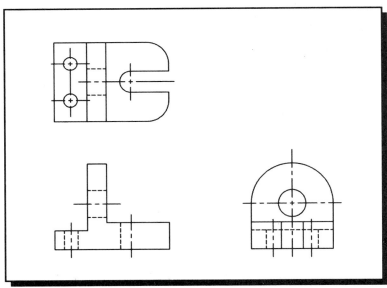

Figure 24-11

USING LINETYPES

Different types of lines are used to represent different features of a multiview drawing. Linetypes in AutoCAD are accessed by the *Linetype* command or by selection in the *Layer Control* dialogue box. *Linetypes* can be changed retroactively by the *Change Properties* or the *Modify* dialogue boxes. *Linetypes* can be assigned to individual entities specifically or to layers (*BYLAYER*). See Chapter 12 for a full discussion on this topic.

AutoCAD complies with the ANSI standard for linetypes. The principal AutoCAD linetypes used in multiview drawings and the associated names are shown in Figure 24-12.

Many other linetypes are provided in AutoCAD. Refer to Chapter 12 for the full list and illustration of the linetypes.

Other ANSI standard lines are created by AutoCAD automatically. For example, dimension lines can be automatically drawn when using dimensioning commands (Chapter 28) and section lines

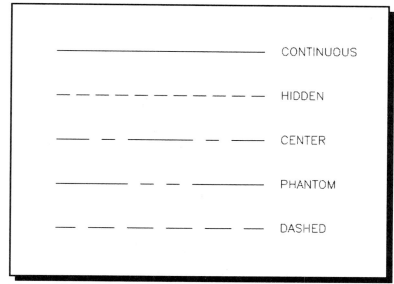

Figure 24-12

can be automatically drawn when using the _Hatch_ command (Chapter 26).

AutoCAD linetypes do not have a specified thickness, but can be created by either creating _Plines_ and specifying _Width_ or by plotting with specific width pens. (See Chapter 15 for information on _Plines_ and Chapter 14 for information on plotting.)

Drawing Hidden and Center Lines

Although AutoCAD supplies ANSI standard linetypes, the application of those linetypes does not always follow ANSI standards. For example, you do not have control over the placement of the individual dashes of center lines and hidden lines. (You have control of only the endpoints of the lines and the _LTSCALE_.) Therefore, the short dashes of center lines may not cross exactly at the circle centers, or the dashes of hidden lines may or may not always intersect as desired.

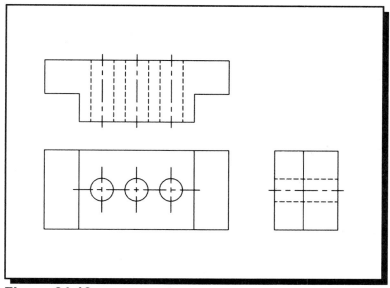

Figure 24-13

Figure 24-13 illustrates a typical application of AutoCAD _Hidden_ and _Center_ linetypes. Notice that the horizontal center line in the front view does not automatically locate the short dashes correctly, and the hidden lines line in the right side view incorrectly intersect the center vertical line.

You do, however, have control of the endpoints of the lines. Draw lines with the *Center* linetype such that the endpoints are symmetric about the circle or group of circles. This action assures that the short dash occurs at the center of the circle (if an odd number of dashes are generated). Figure 24-14 illustrates correct and incorrect technique.

You can also control the relative size of non-continuous linetypes with the *LTSCALE* variable. <u>In some cases</u> the variable can be adjusted to achieve the desired results.

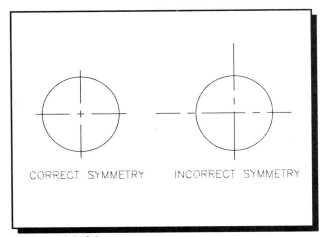

Figure 24-14

For example, Figure 24-15 demonstrates the use of *LTSCALE* to adjust the center line dashes to the correct spacing. However, since *LTSCALE* adjusts linetypes <u>globally</u> (all linetypes across the drawing), a compromise is necessary in most cases.

The *Center* command (a dimensioning command) can be used to draw center lines automatically with correct symmetry and spacing (see Chapter 28). The CL.LSP AutoLISP routine can also be used to automatically draw center lines (see Appendix B for loading LISP routines).

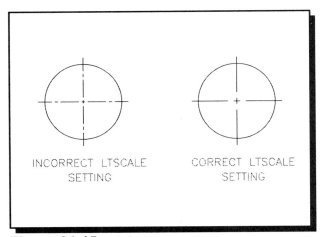

Figure 24-15

Managing Linetypes

Once the linetypes have been loaded (using the *Linetype* command), the linetypes can be selected and assigned to layers using the *Ltype* option in the *Layer Control* dialogue box (for *BYLAYER* assignment). Figure 24-16 displays the *Select Linetype* dialogue box.

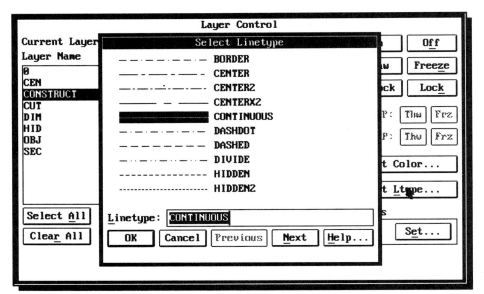

Figure 24-16

After you assign *Linetypes* to specific layers, you simply set the layer (with the desired linetype) as the *Current* layer and draw on that layer in order to draw entities in a specific linetype (see Fig. 24-17).

A default drawing for creating typical multiview drawings could be set up with the layer and linetype assignments similar to that shown in Figure 24-17. Notice the layer names, associated colors and the assigned *Ltypes*.

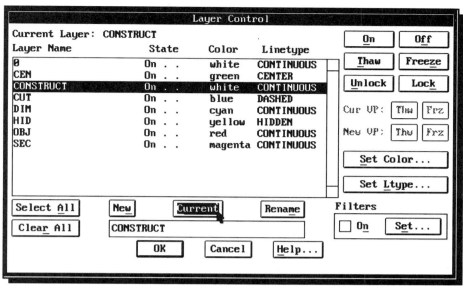

Figure 24-17

Using this strategy (*BYLAYER Linetype* and *Color* assignment) gives you flexibility. You can control the linetype visibility by controlling the layer visibility. You can control the associated plotting pen for each linetype (in the *Plot Control* dialogue box) if each linetype is assigned a specific color. You can also <u>retroactively</u> change the linetype and color of an existing entity by changing the entity's *Layer* property with the *Change Properties* or the *Modify* dialogue box. Entities changed to a different layer assume the *color* and *linetype* of the new layer.

Another strategy for multiview drawings involving several parts, such as an assembly, is to create layers for each linetype <u>specific to each part</u> as shown in Figure 24-18. With this strategy, each part has the complete set of linetypes, but only one color per part in order to distinguish the part from others in the display.

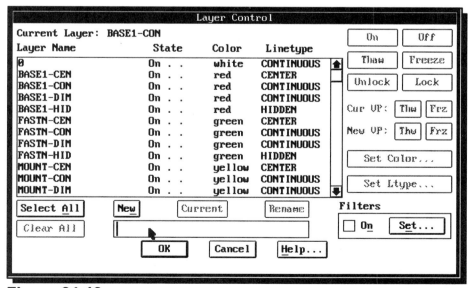

Figure 24-18

Related layer <u>groups</u> can be selected within the dialogue box using the *Filters* dialogue box. If the *Layer* command is used instead, wildcards can be typed for layer selection (see Chapter 30). For example, entering "?????-HID" selects all of the layers with hidden lines, or entering "MOUNT*" would select all of the layers associated with the "MOUNT" part.

The strategy shown here for using linetypes is to assign linetypes to specific layers (*BYLAYER Ltype*). The *Linetype* command can also be used to assign linetypes to be used for subsequent drawing commands (for entity-specific *Linetype* assignment).

CREATING FILLETS, ROUNDS, AND RUNOUTS

Many mechanical metal or plastic parts manufactured from a molding process have slightly rounded corners. The otherwise sharp corners are rounded because of limitations in the molding process or for safety. A convex corner is called a <u>round</u> and a concave corner is called a <u>fillet</u>. These fillets and rounds are created easily in AutoCAD by using the *Fillet* command.

The example in Figure 24-19 shows a multiview drawing of a part with sharp corners before the fillets and rounds are drawn.

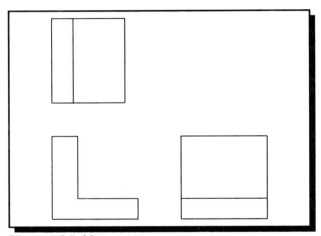

Figure 24-19

The corners are rounded using the *Fillet* command. First, use *Fillet* to specify the *Radius*. Once the *Radius* is specified, just select the desired lines to *Fillet* near the end to round.

If the *Fillet* is in the middle portion of a *Line* instead of the end, *Extend* can be used to reconnect the part of the *Line* automatically trimmed by *Fillet*.

The finish marks ("V" shaped symbols) indicate machined surfaces. Finished surfaces have sharp corners.

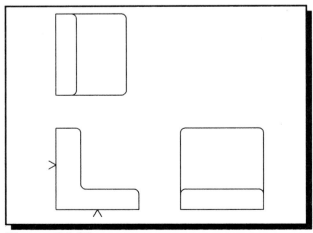

Figure 24-20

When two filleted edges intersect at less than a 90 degree angle, a <u>runout</u> should be drawn as shown in the top view of the multiview drawing. A runout is a visual representation of the complex fillet that would actually exist on the part.

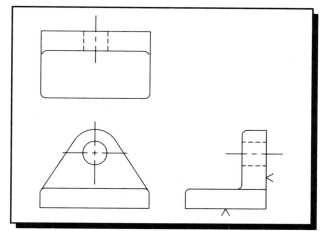

Figure 24-21

A close-up of the runouts is shown in Figure 24-22. There is no AutoCAD command provided for this specific function. The *3point* option of the *Arc* command can be used to create the runouts, although other options can be used. Alternately, the *Circle TTR* option can be used with *Trim* to achieve the desired effect. As a general rule, use the same radius or slightly larger than that given for the fillets and rounds, but draw it less than 90 degrees.

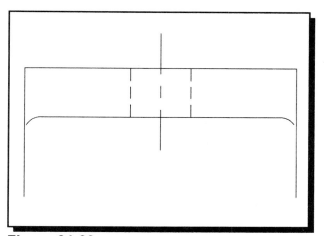

Figure 24-22

GUIDELINES FOR CREATING A TYPICAL TWO-VIEW DRAWING

Some guidelines for creating the two-view drawing in Figure 24-23 are given here. Dimensions are shown if you want to create the multiview drawing as an exercise.

1.   Drawing Setup

      Units are set to *Decimal* with 2 places of *Precision*.
      Limits of 11 x 8.5 are set to allow enough drawing space for both views. The finished
              drawing can be plotted on an "A" size sheet at a scale of 1"=1".
      Snap is set to an increment of .125.
      Grid is set to an increment of .5.
      Layers are created (OBJ, HID, CEN, and CONSTR) with appropriate *Ltypes* and
              Colors assigned.

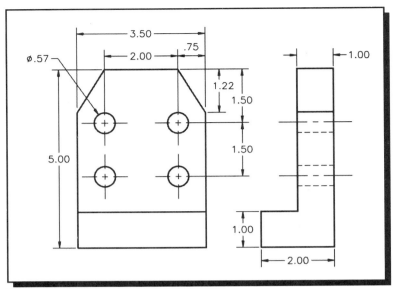

Figure 24-23

2. Each view is "blocked in" by drawing the appropriate *Lines* on the OBJ layer. This action can be accomplished interactively if *SNAP* is *On*. *ORTHO* assists in drawing horizontal and vertical *Lines*. Insure that the views align horizontally.

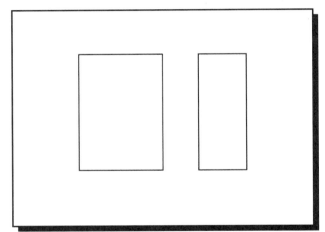

Figure 24-24

3. Additional *Lines* are drawn adding details to the views. Insure that the horizontal lines align. Two original *Lines* in the side view are *Trimmed* (highlighted).

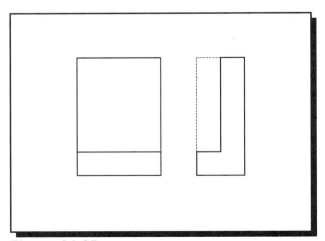

Figure 24-25

4. Use *Circle* to construct two holes in the prescribed location. *Mirror* or *Copy* can be used to create the other two holes (highlighted).

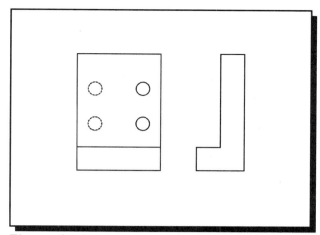

Figure 24-26

5. *Chamfer* can be used to create the inclined edges of the object in the front view. The highlighted lines are automatically trimmed.

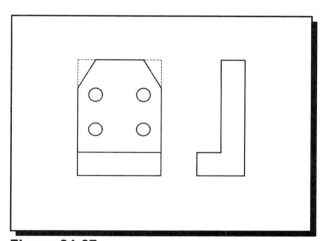

Figure 24-27

6. Project (draw a *Line*) from the *ENDpoint* of the inclined *Line* in the front view through the side view. *Trim* the extending ends of the new *Line* (highlighted).

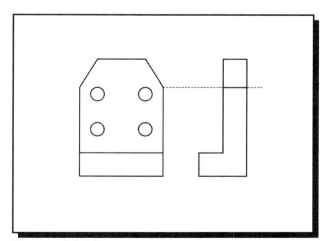

Figure 24-28

7. Make layer HID the *Current* layer. Draw the correct hidden *Lines* in the side view by projecting from the *Circles* in the front view. Use *QUAdrant* or *TANgent OSNAP* <u>and</u> *ORTHO* to draw the horizontal Lines. *Trim* the portions of the hidden lines extending from the side view.

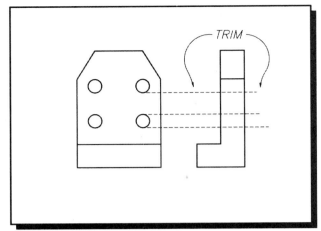

Figure 24-29

8. Set layer CEN *Current*. Draw the two center *Lines* in the side view. Draw the center lines in the front view. Insure that the center lines are symmetrical about the holes. Adjust the value of *LTSCALE* as necessary.

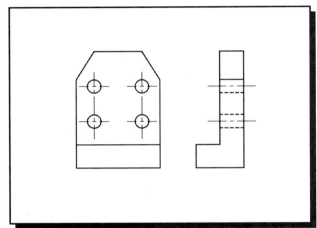

Figure 24-30

9. If desired, draw a border on a separate layer with a *Pline* (width of .02 or .03). Draw or *Insert* the title block.

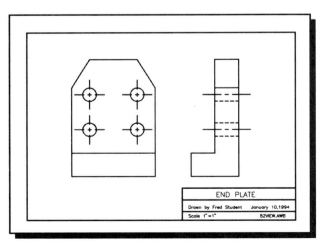

Figure 24-31

GUIDELINES FOR CREATING A TYPICAL THREE-VIEW DRAWING

Following are some guidelines for creating the three-view drawing in Figure 24-32. This object is used only as an example. The steps or particular construction procedure may vary depending upon the specific object drawn. Dimensions are shown in the figure so you can create the multiview drawing as an exercise.

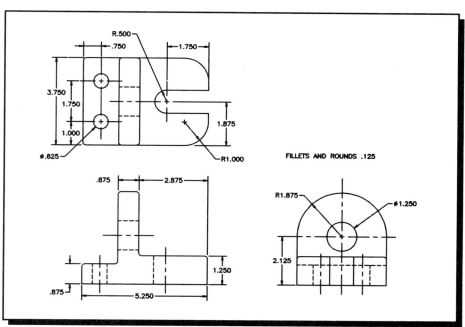

Figure 24-32

1.   Drawing Setup

Units are set to *Decimal* with 3 places of *Precision*.
Limits of 22 x 17 are set to allow enough drawing space for both views. The finished
      drawing can be plotted on a "B" size sheet at a scale of 1"=1" or on an "A" size
      sheet at a scale of 1/2"=1".
Snap is set to an increment of .125.
Grid is set to an increment of .5.
LTSCALE is not changed from the default of 1.
Layers are created (OBJ, HID, CEN, DIM, BORDER, and CONSTR) with appropriate
      Ltypes and *Colors* assigned.

2.   An outline of each view is "blocked in" by drawing the appropriate *Lines* and *Circles* on
      the OBJ layer similar to that shown in Figure 24-33. The interactive method can be
      used. Insure that *SNAP* is *ON*. *ORTHO* should be turned *ON* when appropriate. Use
      the crosshairs to insure that the views align horizontally and vertically. Note that the
      top edge of the front view was determined by projecting from the *Circle* in the right side
      view.

3. This drawing requires some projection between the top and side views. The CONSTR layer is set as *Current*. Two *Lines* are drawn from the inside edges of the two views (using *OSNAP* and *ORTHO* for alignment). A 45 degree miter line is constructed for the projection lines to "make the turn."

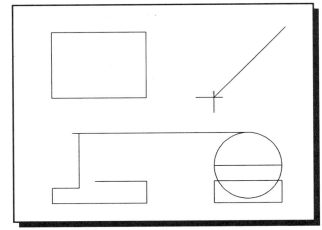

Figure 24-33

4. Details are added to the front and top views. The projection line from the side view to the front view (previous figure) is *Trimmed*. A *Circle* representing the hole is drawn in the side view and projected up and over to the top view and to the front view. The object lines are drawn on layer OBJ and some projection lines are drawn on layer CONSTR. The horizontal projection lines from the 45 degree miter line are drawn on layer HID awaiting *Trimming*. Alternately, those two projection lines could be drawn on layer CONSTR and changed to the appropriate layer with *Change Properties* after *Trimming*.

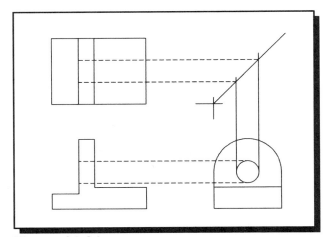

Figure 24-34

5. The hidden lines used for projection to the top view and front view (previous figure) are *Trimmed*. The slot is created in the top view with a *Circle* and projected to the side and front views. It is usually faster and easier to draw round object features in their circular view first, then project to the other views. Make sure you use the correct layers (OBJ, CONSTR, HID) for the appropriate features. If you do not, *Change Properties* can be used retroactively.

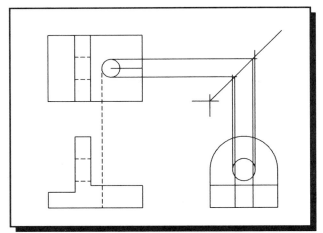

Figure 24-35

6. The hidden lines (shown in the previous figure as projection lines) and features used for construction of the slot are *Trimmed* or *Erased*. The holes in the top view are drawn on layer OBJ and projected to the other views. The projection lines and hidden lines are drawn on their respective layers.

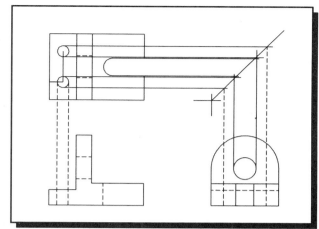

Figure 24-36

7. *Trim* the appropriate hidden lines. *Freeze* layer CONSTR. On layer OBJ, use *Fillet* to create the rounded corners in the top view. Draw the correct center lines for the holes on layer CEN. The value for *LTSCALE* should be adjusted to achieve the optimum center line spacing.

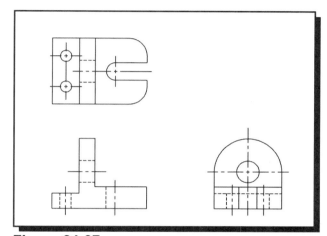

Figure 24-37

8. Fillets and rounds are added using the *Fillet* command. The runouts are created by drawing a *3point Arc* and *Trimming* or *Extending* the *Line* ends as necessary. Use *Zoom* for this detail work.

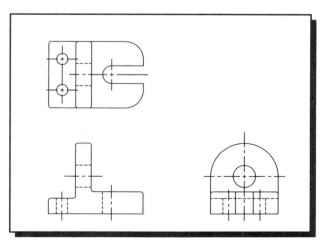

Figure 24-38

9.   Add a border and a title block using *Pline*. Include the part name, company, draftsperson, scale, date, and drawing file name in the title block (see Chapters 21 and 22 for information on creating a title block).

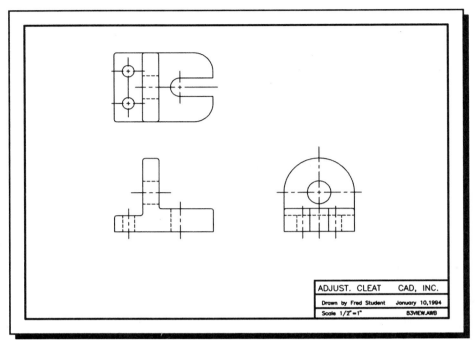

Figure 24-39

CHAPTER EXERCISES

1.   *Open* the **PIVOTARM** drawing that you last edited in Chapter 16 Exercises.

A.   Create the right side view. Use **OSNAP** and **ORTHO** to create construction lines to the miter line and down to the right side view as shown in Figure 24-40. **Offset** may be used effectively for this purpose instead. Use **Extend** or **Offset** to create the projection lines from the front view to the right side view.

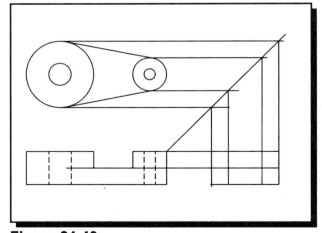

Figure 24-40

B.   ***Trim*** or ***Erase*** the unwanted projection lines, as shown in Figure 24-41.   Draw a ***Line*** from the ***ENDpoint*** of the diagonal *Line* in the top view down to the front to supply the boundary edge for ***Trimming*** the horizontal *Line* in the front view as shown.

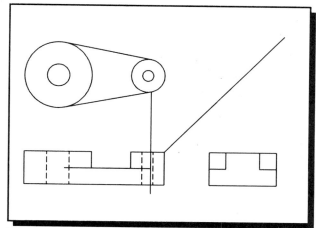

Figure 24-41

C.   Next, create the hidden lines for the holes by the same fashion as before. Make use of previously created ***Layers*** for achieving the desired ***Linetypes***. Complete the side view by adding the horizontal hidden ***Line*** in the center of the view.

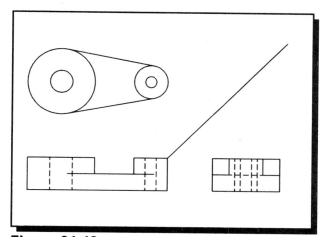

Figure 24-42

D.   Another hole for a set screw must be added to the small end of the Pivot Arm. Construct a ***Circle*** of **4mm** diameter located **8mm** from the top edge in the side view as shown in Figure 24-43. Project the set screw hole to the other views.

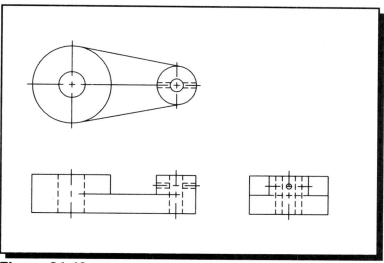

Figure 24-43

E.   Make new layers **CONSTR**, **OBJ**, and **TITLE** and change entities to the appropriate layers with *Change Properties*. *Freeze* layer **CONSTR**. Add center lines on the **CEN** layer as shown in Figure 24-43. Change the *LTSCALE* to **18**. To complete the PIVOTARM drawing, draw a *Pline* border (*width* .02 x scale factor) and *Insert* the **TBLOCK** drawing that you created in Chapter 22 Exercises.

For exercises 2 through 6, construct and plot the multiview drawings as instructed. Use an appropriate *prototype* drawing for each exercise unless instructed otherwise. Use conventional practices for *layers* and *linetypes*. Draw a *Pline* border with the correct *width* and *Insert* your **TBLOCK** drawing.

2.   Construct a two-view multiview drawing of the Camshaft shown in Figure 24-44. *Save* the drawing as **CAMSHAFT**. Plot the drawing full size (**1=1**).

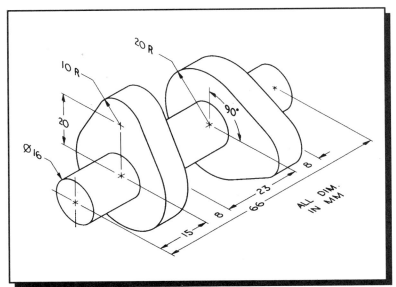

Figure 24-44

3.   Make a two-view multiview drawing of the Clip. Since the Clip is so small, *Plot* the drawing 2 times size (**2=1**). Use the **ASHEET** prototype drawing, modify the *Limits* and other size related features to achieve the desired plot scale. *Save* the drawing as **CLIP**.

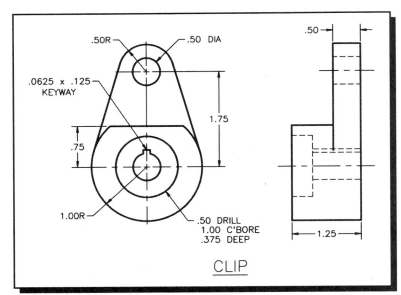

Figure 24-45

4. Make a three-view multiview drawing of the Bar Guide and *Plot* it **1=1**. Use the **BARGUIDE** drawing you set up in Chapter 13 Exercises. Note that a partial *Ellipse* will appear in one of the views.

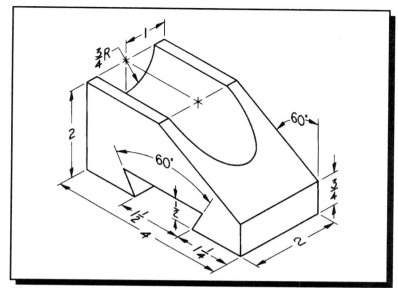

Figure 24-46

5. Construct a multiview drawing of the Saddle. Three views are needed. The channel along the bottom of the part intersects with the saddle on top to create a slotted hole visible in the top view. *Plot* the drawing at **1=1**. *Save* as **SADDLE**.

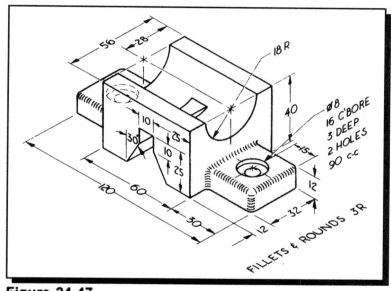

Figure 24-47

6. Draw a multiview of the Adjustable Mount shown in Figure 24-48. Determine an appropriate prototype drawing to use and scale for plotting based on your plotter capabilities. *Plot* the drawing to an accepted scale. *Save* the drawing as **ADJMOUNT**.

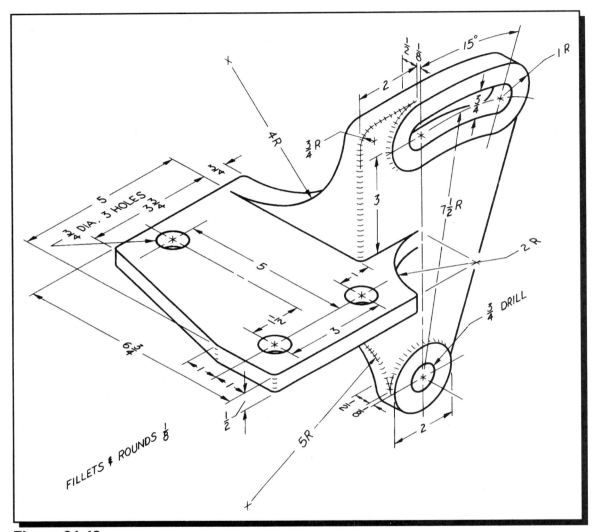

Figure 24-48

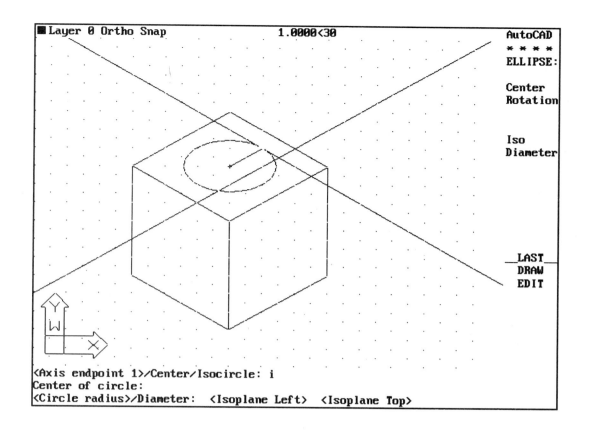

```
■ Layer 0 Ortho Snap                1.0000<30              AutoCAD
                                                           * * * *
                                                           ELLIPSE:

                                                           Center
                                                           Rotation

                                                           Iso
                                                           Diameter




                                                           __LAST__
                                                           DRAW
                                                           EDIT



<Axis endpoint 1>/Center/Isocircle: i
Center of circle:
<Circle radius>/Diameter:   <Isoplane Left>   <Isoplane Top>
```

CHAPTER 25

Pictorial Drawings

CHAPTER OBJECTIVES

After completing this chapter you should:

1. know the characteristics of Isometric, Dimetric, Trimetric, and Oblique pictorial drawings;

2. be able to activate the *Isometric Style* of *Snap* for creating isometric drawings;

3. be able to draw on the three isometric planes by toggling *Isoplane* using CTRL+E;

4. be able to create isometric ellipses with the *Isocircle* option of *Ellipse*;

5. be able to construct an isometric drawing in AutoCAD;

6. know that a 3D model can be viewed from Isometric, Dimetric, and Trimetric *Viewpoints*;

7. be able to create Oblique Cavalier and Cabinet drawings in AutoCAD.

BASICS

Isometric drawings and oblique drawings are pictorial drawings. Pictorial drawings show three principal faces of the object in one view. A pictorial drawing is a drawing of a 3D object as if you were positioned to see (typically) some of the front, some of the top, and some of the side of the object. All three dimensions of the object (width, height, and depth) are visible in a pictorial drawing.

Multiview drawings differ from pictorial drawings because a multiview only shows two dimensions in each view, so two or more views are needed to see all three dimensions of the object. A pictorial drawing shows all dimensions in the one view. Pictorial drawings depict the object similar to the way you are accustomed to viewing objects in everyday life, that is, seeing all three dimensions. Figure 25-1 and Figure 25-2 show the same object in multiview and in pictorial representation, respectively.

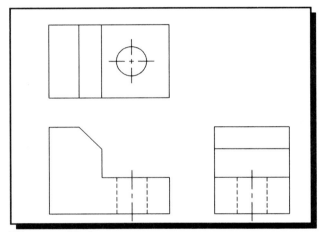

Figure 25-1   **Figure 25-2**

Types of Pictorial Drawings

Pictorial drawings are classified as follows.

1.   Axonometric drawings
        a.   Isometric drawings
        b.   Dimetric drawings
        c.   Trimetric drawings

2.   Oblique drawings

Each of the drawing types are illustrated and explained on the following pages.

Axonometric drawings are characterized by how the angle of the edges or axes (axon-) are measured (-metric) with respect to each other.

Isometric drawings are drawn so that each of the axes have equal angular measurement (isometric means equal measurement). The Isometric axes are drawn at 120 degree increments. All rectilinear lines on the object (not inclined or oblique) are drawn on the isometric axes.

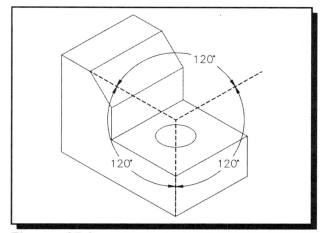

Figure 25-3

Dimetric drawings are made so that the angle of two of the three axes are equal.

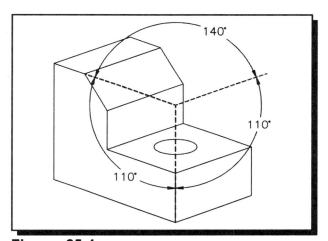

Figure 25-4

Trimetric drawings have three unequal angles between the axes.

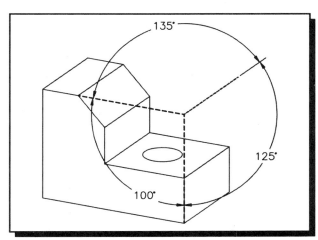

Figure 25-5

Oblique drawings are characterized by a vertical axis and horizontal axis for the two dimensions of the front face and a third (receding) axis of either 30, 45 or 60 degrees.

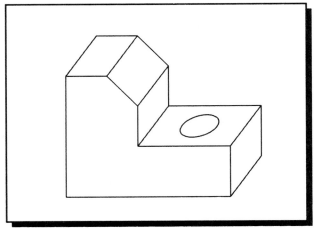

Figure 25-6

Pictorial Drawings Are 2D Drawings

Isometric, Dimetric, Trimetric and Oblique drawings are <u>2D drawings</u> whether created with AutoCAD or otherwise. Pictorial drawing was invented before the existence of CAD, and therefore was intended to simulate a 3D object on a 2D plane (the plane of the paper). If AutoCAD is used to create the pictorial, the geometry lies on a 2D plane, the XY plane. All coordinates defining entities have X and Y values with a Z value of 0. When the *Isometric* style of *Snap* is activated, an isometrically structured *SNAP* and *GRID* appear on the XY plane.

This figure illustrates the 2D nature of an isometric drawing created in AutoCAD. Isometric Lines are created on the XY plane. The *Isometric SNAP* and *GRID* are also on the 2D plane. (The *Vpoint* command was used to give other than a *Plan* view of the drawing in Figure 25-7.)

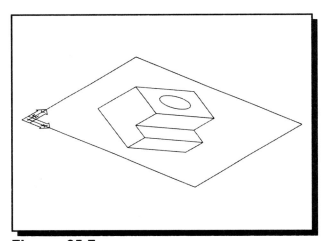

Figure 25-7

ISOMETRIC DRAWING IN AutoCAD

AutoCAD provides the capability for construction of isometric drawings. An isometric *SNAP* and *GRID* are available as well as a utility for creation of isometrically correct ellipses. Isometric lines are created with the *Line* command. There are no special options of *Line* for isometric drawing, but the use of the isometric *SNAP* and *GRID* are used to force *Lines* to an isometric orientation. Begin creating an isometric drawing in AutoCAD by activating the *Isometric Style* option of the *Snap* command. This action can be done using any of the options listed in the following Menu Table.

SNAP

TYPE IN:	PULL-DOWN MENU	SCREEN MENU	TABLET MENU
SNAP	*Settings, Drawing Aids...*	*SETTINGS,*	*12,Y*

```
Command: snap
Snap spacing or ON/OFF/Aspect/Rotate/Style <1.0000>: S
Standard/Isometric <S>: I
Vertical spacing <1.0000>: Enter
Command:
```

Alternately, toggling the indicated checkbox in the lower right corner of the *Drawing Aids* dialogue box activates the Isometric *SNAP* and *GRID*.

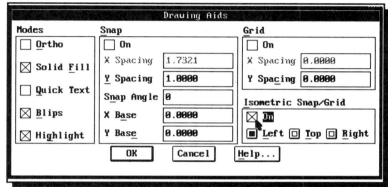

Figure 25-8

Figure 25-9 illustrates the effect of setting the Isometric *SNAP* and *GRID*. Notice the new position of the crosshairs.

Using CTRL+E (pressing the CTRL key and the letter E simultaneously), or 19,V on the digitizing tablet, toggles the crosshairs to one of three possible *Isoplanes* (AutoCAD's term for the three faces of the isometric pictorial). If *ORTHO* is *ON*, only isometric lines are drawn; that is, you can only draw *Lines* aligned with the isometric axes. *Lines* can be drawn on

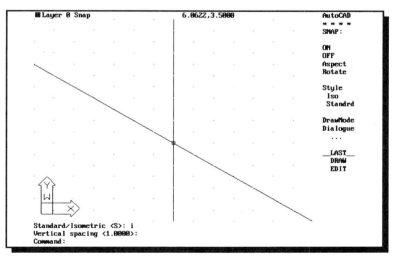

Figure 25-9

only two axes for each isoplane. CTRL-E allows drawing on the two axes aligned with another face of the object. *ORTHO* is *OFF* in order to draw inclined or oblique lines (not on the isometric axis). The functions of *GRID* (F7) and *SNAP* (F9) remain unchanged.

With *SNAP ON*, toggle *COORDS* (F6) several times and examine the read-out as you move the cursor. The absolute coordinate format is of no particular assistance while drawing in isometric because of the configuration of the *GRID*. The <u>relative polar</u> format, however, is very helpful. Use relative polar format for *COORDS* while drawing in isometric.

The effects of changing the *Isoplane* are shown in the following figures. Press CTRL+E to change *Isoplane*.

With *ORTHO ON*, drawing a *Line* is limited to the two axes of the current *Isoplane*. Only one side of a cube, for example, can be drawn on the current *Isoplane*. Watch *COORDS* (in a polar format) to give the length of the current *Line* as you draw.

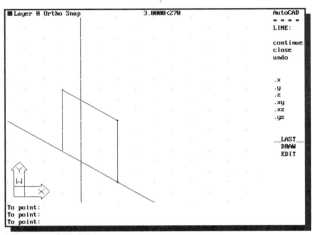

Figure 25-10

Toggling CTRL+E switches the crosshairs and the effect of *ORTHO* to another *Isoplane*. One other side of a cube can be constructed on this *Isoplane*.

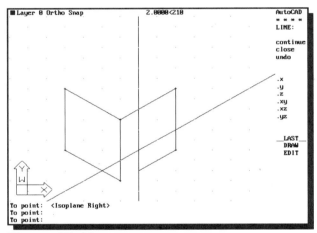

Figure 25-11

Toggling CTRL+E again forces the crosshairs and the effect of *ORTHO* to the third *Isoplane*. The third side of the cube can be constructed.

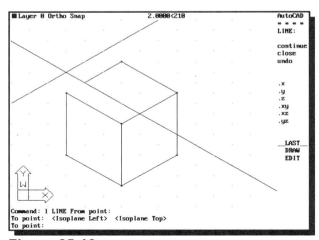

Figure 25-12

Isometric Ellipses

Isometric ellipses are easily drawn in AutoCAD by using the *Isocircle* option of the *Ellipse* command. This option <u>only</u> appears when the isometric *SNAP* is *ON*.

ELLIPSE

TYPE IN:	PULL-DOWN MENU	SCREEN MENU	TABLET MENU
ELLIPSE, I	*Draw, Ellipse > Axis, Eccentricity*	*DRAW, ELLIPSE: ISO*	*10,N*

Although the *Isocircle* option does not appear in the pull-down or digitizing tablet menus, it can be invoked as an option of the *Ellipse* command. The command syntax is as follows.

```
Command: ellipse
<Axis endpoint 1>/Center/Isocircle: I
Center of circle: PICK or (coordinates)
<Circle radius>/Diameter: PICK or (coordinates)
```

After selecting the center point of the *Isocircle*, the isometrically correct ellipse appears on the screen on the current *Isoplane*. Use CTRL+E to toggle the ellipse to the correct orientation. When defining the radius interactively, use *ORTHO* to force the rubberband line to an isometric axis.

Since isometric angles are equal, all isometric ellipses have the same proportion (major to minor axis). The only differences in isometric ellipses are the size and the orientation.

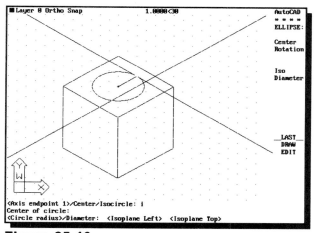

Figure 25-13

Figure 25-14 shows 3 ellipses correctly oriented on their respective faces. Use CTRL+E to toggle the correct *Isoplane* orientation: *Isoplane Top, Isoplane Left,* or *Isoplane Right.*

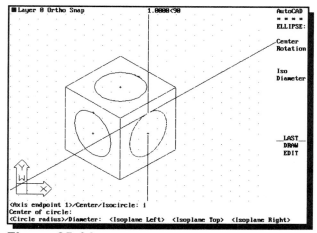

Figure 25-14

When defining the radius or diameter of an ellipse, it should always be measured in an isometric direction. In other words, an isometric ellipse is always measured on the two isometric axes (or center lines) parallel with the plane of the ellipse.

If you define the radius or diameter interactively, use _ORTHO ON_. If you enter a value, AutoCAD automatically applies the value to the correct isometric axes.

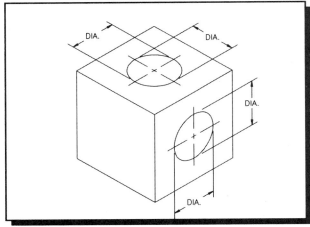

Figure 25-15

Creating an Isometric Drawing

In this exercise, the object in Figure 25-16 is drawn in isometric.

The initial steps to creating an isometric drawing begin with the typical setup (see Chapter 6, Drawing Setup).

1. Set the desired _Units_.
2. Set appropriate _Limits_.
3. Set the _Isometric Style_ of _Snap_ and specify an appropriate value for spacing.

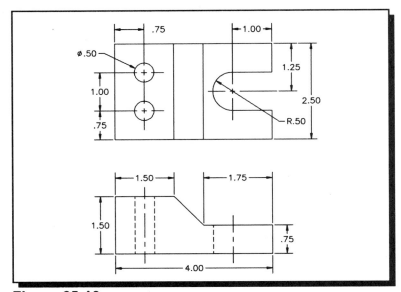

Figure 25-16

4. The next step involves creating an isometric framework of the desired object. In other words, draw an isometric box equal to the overall dimensions of the object. Using dimensions given in the previous figure, create the encompassing isometric box with the _Line_ command.

    Use _ORTHO_ to force isometric _Lines_. Watch the _COORDS_ display (in a relative polar format) to give the current lengths as you draw.

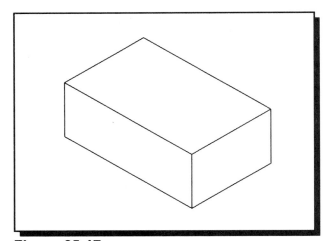

Figure 25-17

5. Add the lines defining the lower surface. Define the needed edge of the upper isometric surface as shown.

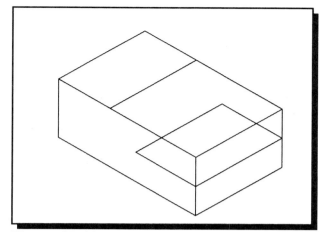

Figure 25-18

6. The <u>inclined</u> edges of the inclined surface can only be drawn (with *Line*) when *ORTHO* is *OFF*. <u>Inclined</u> lines in isometric cannot be drawn by transferring the lengths of the lines, but only by defining the <u>ends</u> of the inclined lines on <u>isometric</u> lines, then connecting the endpoints. Next, *Trim* or *Erase* the necessary *Lines*.

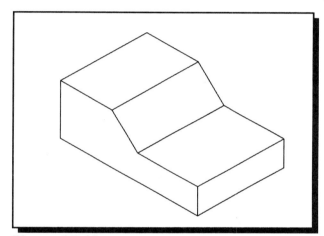

Figure 25-19

7. Draw the slot by constructing an *Ellipse* with the *Isocircle* option. Draw the two *Lines* connecting the circle to the right edge. *Trim* the unwanted part of the *Ellipse* (highlighted) using the *Lines* as cutting edges.

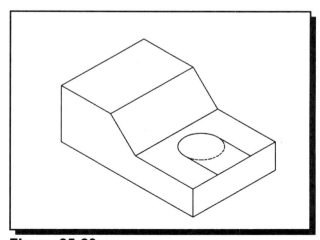

Figure 25-20

8.   *Copy* the far *Line* and the *Ellipse* down to the bottom surface. Add two vertical *Lines* at the end of the slot.

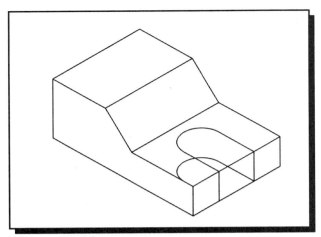

Figure 25-21

9.   Use *Trim* to remove the part of the *Ellipse* that would normally be hidden from view. *Trim* the *Lines* along the right edge at the opening of the slot.

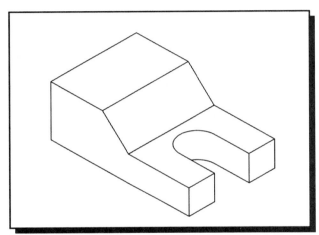

Figure 25-22

10.   Add the two holes on the top with *Ellipse, Isocircle* option. Use *ORTHO ON* when defining the radius. *Copy* can also be used to create the second *Ellipse* from the first.

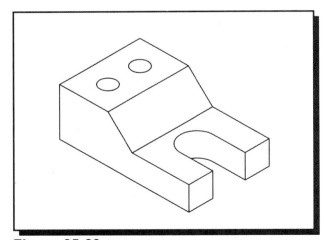

Figure 25-23

Creating an Isometric Drawing with an Oblique Plane

In this exercise, the object in Figure 25-24 is to be drawn in isometric.

The initial steps for creating an isometric drawing like the figure above begin with the typical setup.

1. Set the desired *Units*.
2. Set appropriate *Limits*.
3. Set the *Isometric Style* of *SNAP* and specify an appropriate value for spacing.

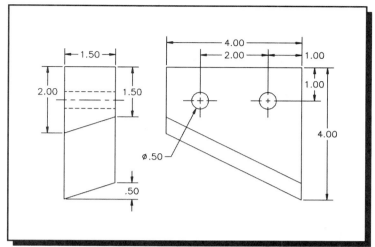

Figure 25-24

4. Draw an isometric box encompassing the overall shape of the object. Use the overall dimensions from the previous figure.

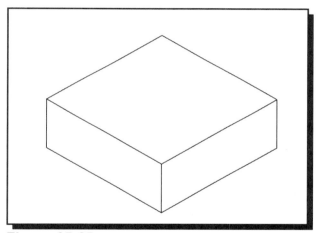

Figure 25-25

5. Draw the inclined *Lines* on the top and bottom surfaces representing the edges of the oblique plane. The measurements are made on the isometric axes to the <u>endpoints</u> of the inclined lines. You cannot transfer the length of an inclined line directly. It is helpful to make some short reference *Lines* at the measuring points.

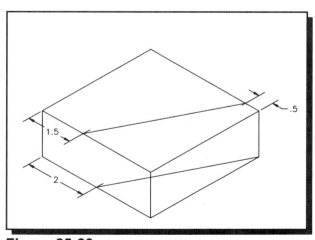

Figure 25-26

6.   Connect the last inclined *Lines* with two other inclined *Lines* defining the other edges of the oblique surface.

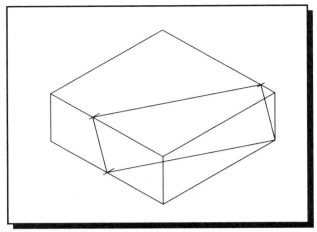

Figure 25-27

7.   *Erase* the reference marks (*Lines*) and *Erase* or *Trim* the unwanted parts of the object. Add two *Ellipses* (*Isocircles*) at the correct location.

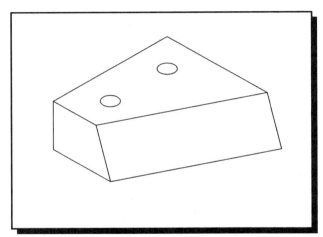

Figure 25-28

Dimensioning Isometric Drawings in AutoCAD

Refer to Chapter 28, Dimensioning, for details on how to dimension isometric drawings.

CREATING ISOMETRIC, DIMETRIC, AND TRIMETRIC VIEWPOINTS OF 3D MODELS

Assuming that your 3D model is at least partially complete, an isometric-type of a viewpoint can be easily achieved. This is done by using the *Vpoint* command or the *Viewpoints Presets* dialogue box (see Chapter 34, 3D Display and Viewing).

Keep in mind that a true isometric drawing is a 2D drawing made to show three sides of an object. This section discusses viewing 3D drawings (wireframe, surface or solid models) from viewpoints that simulate isometric, dimetric, or trimetric views.

Isometric *Viewpoints*

To achieve an isometric-type of a viewpoint, use the *Vpoint* command with either the *Rotate* option or enter coordinates. The correct settings are as follows:

Rotate

In response to the prompts Enter angle in XY plane from X axis and Enter angle from XY plane, enter values of **315** and **35.27**.

coordinates

In response to Viewpoint <0,0,1>: enter **1,-1,1**.

Either method should give an isometric-type *Viewpoint* of your 3D model, as shown in the figure. The resulting display shows an equal portion of the front, top, and right side of the object. Note that a perfect isometric *Viewpoint* of a <u>cube</u> (shown in wireframe representation) aligns the far corner directly behind the near corner.

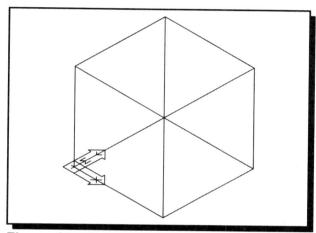

Figure 25-29

Actually, any combination of **45**, **135**, **225**, or **315** entered as the "angle in the XY plane" and either **35.27** or **-35.27** as the "angle from the XY plane" yields an isometric-type *Vpoint*. Alternatively, any combination of positive or negative **1**'s (ones) as coordinate entry gives some type of an isometric *Vpoint*.

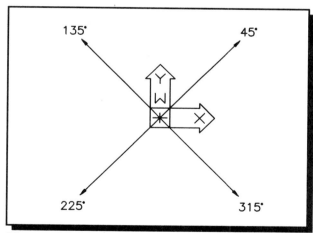

Figure 25-30

Dimetric *Viewpoints*

A dimetric-type of a Viewpoint can be attained most easily by using the *Rotate* option of *Vpoint*. Although there are many possible viewing angles considered dimetric, the correct settings for a typical dimetric viewing angle are as follows:

Rotate

In response to the prompts `Enter angle in XY plane from X axis` and `Enter angle from XY plane`, enter values of **315** and **15.54**, respectively.

A wireframe model of a cube given the previous *Viewpoint* angles appears as shown in this figure. This *Viewpoint* is a typical dimetric-type orientation with two axes at 15 degrees from horizontal.

Alternately, a dimetric *Viewpoint* (two angles equal) can be achieved by entering an angle shown in Figure 25-30 (previous page) as the "angle in the XY plane from the X axis." Any value can be entered as the "angle from the XY plane" since only two of the three angles between axes are equal.

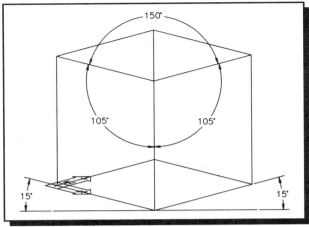

Figure 25-31

Trimetric *Viewpoints*

The definition of a trimetric drawing requires that the angles between the axes be unequal. Therefore, <u>any</u> viewpoint other that an isometric or dimetric falls into this category. However, a typical combination of angles can be approximated by entering the following values with the *Rotate* option of the *Vpoint* command.

`Angle in the XY plane from the X axis:` **294.55**
`Angle from the XY plane:` **22.7**

These angles result in the viewpoint shown in Figure 25-32. Angles between the axes for this typical trimetric orientation are shown.

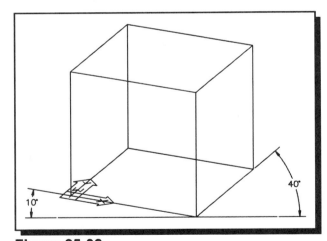

Figure 25-32

CREATING OBLIQUE DRAWINGS IN AutoCAD

Oblique drawings are characterized by having two axes at a 90 degree orientation. Typically, you should locate the <u>front face</u> of the object along these two axes. Since the object's characteristic shape is seen in the front view, an oblique drawing allows you to create all shapes parallel to the front face true size and shape as you would in a multiview drawing. Circles on or parallel to the front face can be drawn as circles.

The third axis, the receding axis, can be drawn at a choice of angles, 30, 45 or 60 degrees, depending on whether you want to show more of the top or the side of the object.

Figure 25-33 illustrates the axes orientation of an oblique drawing, including the choice of angles for the receding axis.

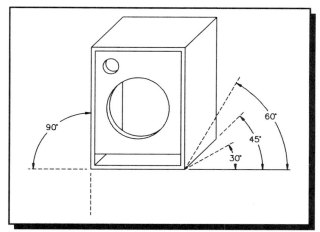

Figure 25-33

Another option allowed with oblique drawings is the measurement used for the receding axis. Using the full depth of the object along the receding axis is called <u>Cavalier</u> oblique drawing. This method depicts the object (a cube with a hole in this case) as having an elongated depth.

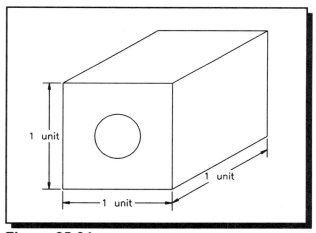

Figure 25-34

Using 1/2 or 3/4 of the true depth along the receding axis gives a more realistic pictorial representation of the object. This is called a <u>Cabinet</u> oblique.

There are no functions or commands in AutoCAD that are intended specifically for oblique drawing. However, *SNAP* and *GRID* can be aligned with the receding axis using the *Rotate* option of the *Snap* command to simplify the construction of edges of the object along that axis. The steps for creating a typical oblique drawing are given on this and the following pages.

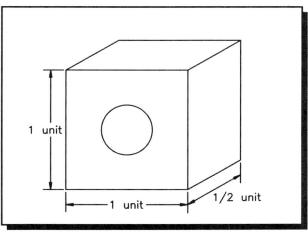

Figure 25-35

The object in Figure 25-36 is used for the example. From the dimensions given in the multiview, create a cabinet oblique with the receding axis at 45 degrees.

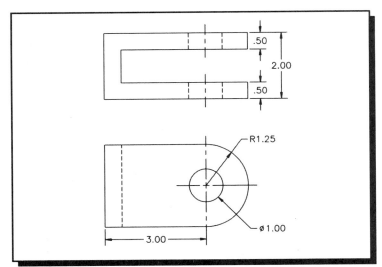

Figure 25-36

1. Create the characteristic shape of the front face of the object as shown in the front view.

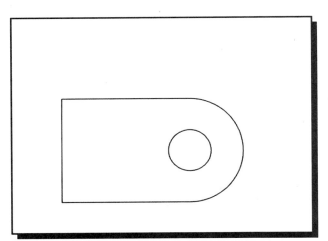

Figure 25-37

2. Use *Copy* with the *Multiple* option to copy the front face back on the receding axis. Polar coordinates can be entered as the "second point of displacement." For example, the first *Copy* should be located at **@.25<45** relative to the "Base point." (Remember to calculate 1/2 of the actual depth.) As an alternative, a *Line* can be drawn at 45 degrees and *Divided* to place *Points* at .25 increments. *Multiple Copies* of the front face can be *OSNAP*ed with the *NODe* option.

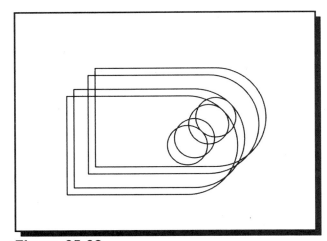

Figure 25-38

3. Draw the *Line* representing the edge on the upper left of the object along the receding axis. Use *ENDpoint OSNAP* to connect the *Lines*. Make a *Copy* of the *Line* or draw another *Line* .5 units to the right. Drop a vertical *Line* from the *INTersection* as shown.

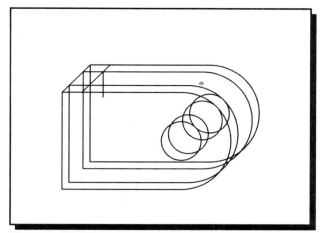

Figure 25-39

4. Use *Trim* and *Erase* to remove the unwanted parts of the *Lines* and *Circles* (those edges that are normally obscured).

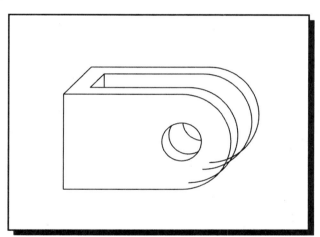

Figure 25-40

5. *Zoom* with a *window* to the lower right corner of the drawing. Draw a *Line* *TANgent* to the edges of the arcs to define the limiting elements along the receding axis. *Trim* the unwanted segments of the arcs.

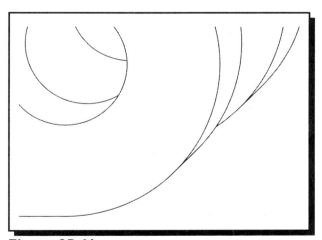

Figure 25-41

6.   The resulting cabinet oblique drawing should appear as that in Figure 25-42.

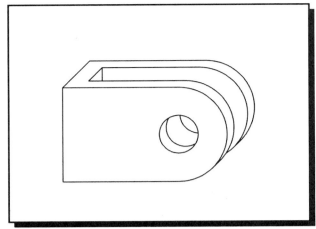

Figure 25-42

CHAPTER EXERCISES

Isometric Drawing

For exercises 1, 2, and 3 create an isometric drawing as instructed. To begin, use an appropriate prototype drawing and draw a *Pline* border and insert the **TBLOCK**.

1.   Create an isometric drawing of the cylinder shown in Figure 25-43. *Save* the drawing as **CYLINDER** and *Plot* so the drawing is *Scaled to Fit* on an A size sheet.

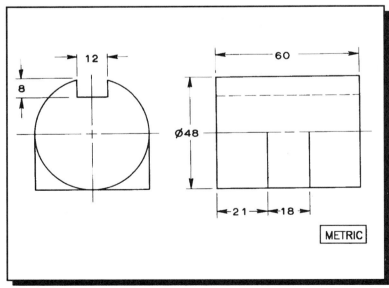

Figure 25-43

2. Make an isometric drawing of the Corner Brace shown in Figure 25-44. *Save* the drawing as **CRNBRACE**. *Plot* at **1=1** scale on an A size sheet.

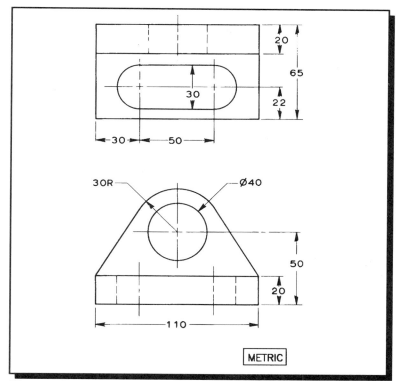

Figure 25-44

3. Draw the Support Bracket (Fig. 25-45) in isometric. The drawing can be *Plotted* at **1=1** scale on an A size sheet. *Save* the drawing and assign the name **SBRACKET**.

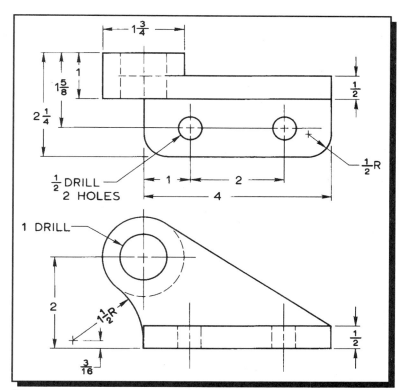

Figure 25-45

Oblique Drawing

For exercises 4 and 5 on the following page, create an oblique drawing as instructed. To begin, use an appropriate prototype drawing and draw a _Pline_ border and _Insert_ the **TBLOCK**.

4. Make an oblique cabinet projection of the Bearing shown in Figure 25-46. Construct all dimensions on the receding axis 1/2 of the actual length. Select the optimum angle for the receding axis to be able to view the 15 x 15 slot. _Plot_ at **1=1** scale on an A size sheet. _Save_ the drawing as **BEARING**.

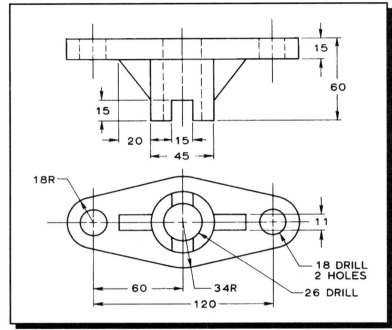

Figure 25-46

5. Construct a Cavalier oblique drawing of the Pulley showing the circular view true size and shape. The illustration in Figure 25-47 gives only the side view. All vertical dimensions in the figure are diameters. _Save_ the drawing as **PULLEY** and make a _Plot_ on an A size sheet at **1=1**.

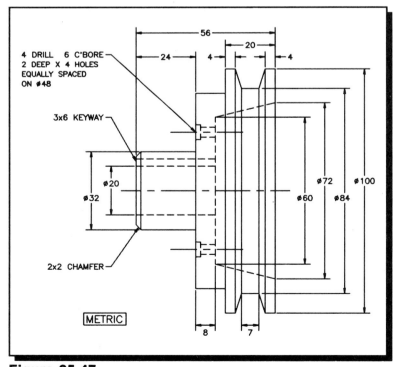

Figure 25-47

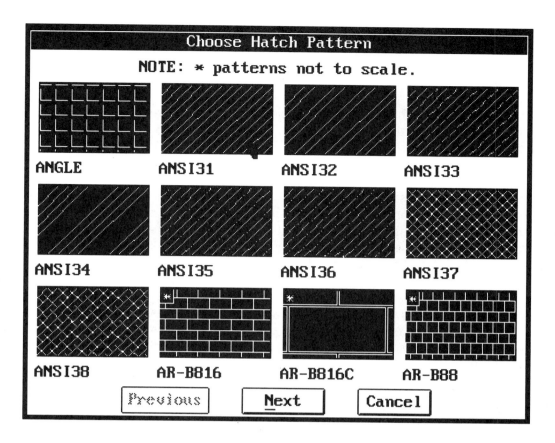

CHAPTER 26

Section Views

CHAPTER OBJECTIVES

After completing this chapter you should:

1.   be able to use the *Bhatch* command to select hatch patterns from the icon menu;

2.   be able to specify a *Scale* and *Angle* for hatch lines;

3.   know how to define a boundary for hatching using the *Pick Points* (ray-casting) method;

4.   be able to *Preview* the hatch and make necessary adjustments, then *Apply* the hatch pattern.

5.   know how to create boundary *Plines* with the *Bpoly* command.

6.   know how to define the boundary set using the *Select Objects* method of the *Hatch* command.

7.   be able to create cutting plane lines for a section view.

BASICS

A section view is a view of the interior of an object after it has been imaginarily cut open to reveal the object's inner details. A section view is only one of two or more views of a multiview drawing describing the object. For example, a multiview drawing of a machine part may contain three views, one of which is a section view.

Hatch lines (also known as section lines) are drawn in the section view to indicate the solid material that has been cut through. ANSI (American National Standards Institute) has published standard configurations for types and combinations of section lines. Each combination of section lines is called a hatch pattern and each pattern is used to represent a specific material. In full and half section views, hidden lines are omitted since the inside of the object is visible.

A cutting plane line is drawn in an adjacent view to the section view to indicate the plane that imaginarily cuts through the object. Arrows on each end of the cutting plane line indicate the line of sight for the section view. ANSI dictates that a dashed thick line be used as the standard cutting plane line.

This chapter discusses the AutoCAD methods used to draw hatch lines for section views and related cutting plane lines. Creating sectional views in AutoCAD (for 2D drawings) is a semi-automatic process. The *Bhatch* (boundary hatch) command allows you to select an enclosed area and select the hatch pattern and the parameters for the appearance of the hatch pattern; then, AutoCAD automatically draws the hatch (section) lines. Because there is a preview option, you can make adjustments to the hatch parameters until you have just the display you want before applying the hatch lines. Cutting plane lines are created in AutoCAD by using a dashed linetype. The line itself should be created with the *Pline* command to achieve line width.

Figure 26-1 shows a typical mechanical part drawing including a section view. This drawing is used as an example for describing the use of the hatching commands and options as well as for the creation of cutting plane lines.

DEFINING HATCH PATTERNS AND HATCH BOUNDARIES

A hatch pattern is composed of many lines that have a particular linetype, spacing, and angle. Many ANSI standard hatch patterns, as well as others, are provided by AutoCAD for your selection. Rather than having to draw each section line individually, you are required only to specify the area to be hatched and AutoCAD fills the designated area with the selected hatch pattern.

An AutoCAD hatch pattern is inserted as one entity. For example, you can *Erase* the inserted hatch pattern by selecting only one line in the pattern and the entire pattern in the area is *Erased*. Similar to a *Block*, individual lines in an inserted pattern can only be edited after you *Explode* the pattern or by requesting the pattern to be pre-exploded upon insertion.

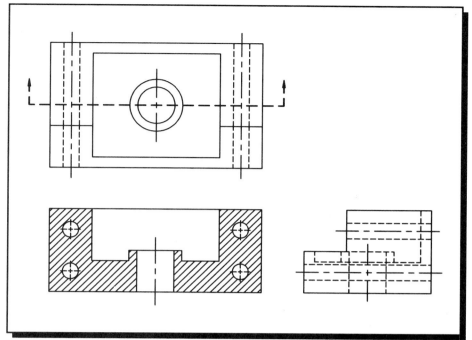

Figure 26-1

In a typical section view (Fig. 26-1), the hatch pattern completely fills the area representing the material that has been cut through. With the *Bhatch* command you can define the boundary of an area to be hatched simply by pointing inside of an enclosed area. Alternately, you can select each entity comprising the boundary or use a combination of the two selection methods.

The *Bhatch* command uses a ray-casting technique to cast rays outward from the selected point to determine the nearest entity, then follows the shape around in a counter-clockwise direction until the entire boundary of the enclosed area has been located (Fig 26-2). The resulting boundary determines the hatch fill area.

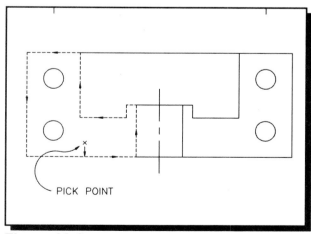

Figure 26-2

Both the *Hatch* and the *Bhatch* commands fill a specified area with a selected hatch pattern. *Hatch* requires that you select <u>each entity</u> defining the boundary; whereas, the *Bhatch* command finds the boundary automatically (by ray-casting) when you point inside it. Additionally, *Hatch* operates in command line format; whereas, *Bhatch* operates in dialogue box fashion.

Steps for Creating a Section View Using the *Bhatch* Command

1. Create the view that contains the area to be hatched using typical draw commands such as *Line, Arc, Circle, Pline*, etc. If you intend to have text inside the area to be hatched, add the text before hatching.

2. Invoke the *Bhatch* command. The *Boundary Hatch* dialogue box appears.

3. Specify the hatch pattern to use. Select the *Hatch Options...* tile and then the *Pattern...* tile to invoke the set of icon boxes displaying hatch patterns. Select the desired pattern.

4. Specify the *Scale, Angle*, and *Hatching Style*, from the *Hatch Options* dialogue box.

5. Define the area to be hatched by PICKing an internal point (AutoCAD automatically traces the boundary), or by individually selecting the entities, or by using a combination of both methods.

6. *Preview* the hatch to make sure everything is as expected. Adjust hatching parameters as necessary and *Preview* again.

7. *Apply* the hatch. The hatch pattern is automatically drawn and becomes an entity in the drawing.

8. If other areas are to be hatched, additional internal points or objects can be selected to define the new area for hatching. The parameters previously used are again applied to the new hatch area by default.

9. Draw a cutting plane line in a view adjacent to the section view. The *Pline* command with a *Dashed* or *Phantom* linetype is used. Arrows at the ends of the cutting plane line indicate the line of sight for the section view.

The *Bhatch* and *Hatch* commands with all dialogue boxes and options are explained in detail on the following pages.

BHATCH

TYPE IN:	PULL-DOWN MENU	SCREEN MENU	TABLET MENU
BHATCH	*Draw, Hatch...*	*DRAW, BHATCH:*	---

Bhatch allows you to create hatch lines for a section view (or for other purposes) by simply PICKing inside a closed boundary. A closed boundary refers to an area completely enclosed by entities. *Bhatch* locates the closed boundary automatically by creating a temporary *Pline* that follows the outline found by the ray-casting technique, fills the area with hatch lines, and then deletes the boundary (default option) after hatching is completed. *Bhatch* ignores all entities or parts of entities that are not part of the boundary.

Any method of invoking *Bhatch* yields the *Boundary Hatch* dialogue box (Fig. 26-3). Operation of this dialogue box is the first and last step of hatching with *Bhatch*. Several levels of dialogue boxes are accessed through this main one. Typically, the first step in the *Boundary Hatch* dialogue box is the selection of a hatch pattern. Select the *Hatch Options* tile as shown in the figure.

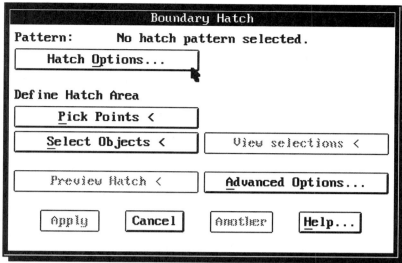

Figure 26-3

Hatch Options

Pattern Type--Stored Hatch Patterns

When you select the *Hatch Options* tile the *Hatch Options* dialogue box is displayed. This dialogue box allows you to specify the type and configuration of the hatch pattern.

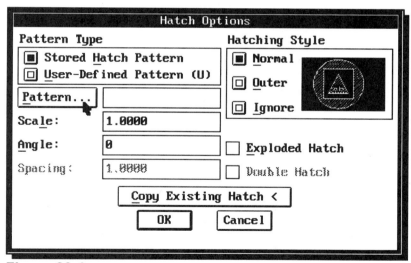

Figure 26-4

Pattern...

To use an AutoCAD-defined hatch pattern, make sure the *Stored Hatch Pattern* button is selected. Then select the *Pattern* tile as shown in Figure 26-4. (If you know the pattern name, you can enter it in the edit box instead.)

Selecting the *Pattern...* tile invokes a series of dialogue boxes titled *Choose Hatch Pattern* in which the patterns are listed in alphabetical order. This dialogue box (Fig. 26-5) is the first of the series and contains the ANSI patterns. Select the desired pattern by PICKing the icon. The pattern names are listed below. The *Next* tile invokes the next box in the series. A total of 53 pre-defined patterns are available from 5 dialogue boxes.

The list of AutoCAD pre-defined patterns is shown below. The patterns are defined and stored in the ACAD.PAT file.

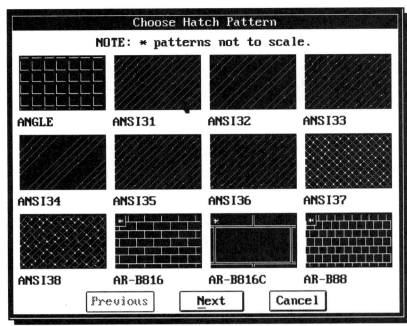

Figure 26-5

Pattern Name	Description
ANGLE	- Angle steel
ANSI31	- ANSI Iron, Brick, Stone masonry
ANSI32	- ANSI Steel
ANSI33	- ANSI Bronze, Brass, Copper
ANSI34	- ANSI Plastic, Rubber
ANSI35	- ANSI Fire brick, Refractory material
ANSI36	- ANSI Marble, Slate, Glass
ANSI37	- ANSI Lead, Zinc, Magnesium, Sound/Heat/Elec Insulation
ANSI38	- ANSI Aluminum
AR-B816	- 8x16 Block elevation stretcher bond
AR-B816C	- 8x16 Block elevation stretcher bond with mortar joints
AR-B88	- 8x8 Block elevation stretcher bond
AR-BRELM	- Standard brick elevation english bond with mortar joints
AR-BRSTD	- Standard brick elevation stretcher bond
AR-CONC	- Random dot and stone pattern
AR-HBONE	- Standard brick herringbone pattern @ 45 degrees
AR-PARQ1	- 2x12 Parquet flooring: pattern of 12x12
AR-RROOF	- Roof shingle texture
AR-RSHKE	- Roof wood shake texture
AR-SAND	- Random dot pattern
BOX	- Box steel
BRASS	- Brass material
BRICK	- Brick or masonry-type surface
BRSTONE	- Brick and stone
CLAY	- Clay material
CORK	- Cork material
CROSS	- A series of crosses

DASH	-	Dashed lines
DOLMIT	-	Geological rock layering
DOTS	-	A series of dots
EARTH	-	Earth or ground (subterranean)
ESCHER	-	Escher pattern
FLEX	-	Flexible material
GRASS	-	Grass area
GRATE	-	Grated area
HEX	-	Hexagons
HONEY	-	Honeycomb pattern
HOUND	-	Houndstooth check
INSUL	-	Insulation material
LINE	-	Parallel horizontal lines
MUDST	-	Mud and sand
NET	-	Horizontal/vertical grid
NET3	-	Network pattern 0-60-120
PLAST	-	Plastic material
PLASTI	-	Plastic material
SACNCR	-	Concrete
SQUARE	-	Small aligned squares
STARS	-	Star of David
STEEL	-	Steel material
SWAMP	-	Swampy area
TRANS	-	Heat transfer material
TRIANG	-	Equilateral triangles
ZIGZAG	-	Staircase effect

Since hatch patterns have their own linetype, the *Continuous* linetype or a layer with the *Continuous* linetype <u>should be current</u> when hatching. (The previous list of patterns can be displayed in a text screen with the *Hatch* command. See *Hatch* later in this section.)

After you select a pattern, AutoCAD then returns to the *Hatch Options* dialogue box. The selected pattern appears in the *Pattern* edit box (ANSI31, in this example). You should then specify the desired *Scale* and *Angle* of the pattern.

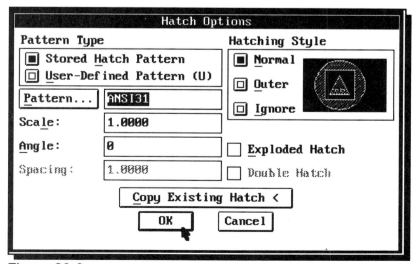

Figure 26-6

Angle

The *Angle* specification determines the angle (slant) of the hatch lines. The default angle of 0 represents whatever angle is displayed in the pattern's icon. Any value entered deflects the existing pattern by the specified value (in degrees). The value entered in this box is held in the *HPANG* system variable.

Scale

The value entered in this edit box is a scale factor that is applied to the existing selected pattern. Normally, this scale factor should be changed proportionally with changes in the drawing *Limits*. Like many other scale factors (*LTSCALE, DIMSCALE*), AutoCAD defaults are set to a value of 1 which is appropriate for the default *Limits* of 12 x 9. If you have figured the drawing scale factor, it can be applied here (see Chapter 13). In the example, *Limits* are set to 22 x 17, so a *Scale* of 1.8 is used. The *Scale* value is stored in the *HPSCALE* system variable.

Pattern Type--User-Defined Patterns (U)

To define a simple hatch pattern "on the fly," select the *User-Defined Pattern (U)* button in the upper left corner of the *Hatch Options* dialogue box (Fig. 26-6). This causes the *Pattern* and *Scale* options to be disabled and the *Angle, Spacing*, and *Double Hatch* options to be enabled. The options that apply to user-defined patterns are explained below.

Angle

This represents the true angle (relative to the X axis) for the hatch lines to be drawn. Enter the desired angle in the edit box.

Spacing

This value specifies the spacing between hatch lines. The value is stored in the *HPSPACE* system variable.

Double Hatch

Checking this box causes a second set of lines to be drawn at a 90 degree angle to the original set. If checked, the *HPDOUBLE* system variable is set to 1.

Hatching Style

The upper right corner of the *Hatch Options* dialogue box allows you to specify how the hatch pattern is drawn when the area inside the defined boundary contains text or closed areas (islands). Selecting the buttons automatically changes the display in the dialogue box to reflect the selected option. These options are applicable <u>only</u> when interior objects (inside of a selected outer boundary) have been included in the selection set (considered for hatching). Otherwise, if only the outer shape is included in the selection set, the results are identical to the *Outer* option.

Normal

This should be used for most applications of *Bhatch*. Text or closed shapes within the outer border are considered in such cases. Hatching will begin at the outer boundary and move inward alternating between applying and not applying the pattern as interior shapes or text are encountered (Fig. 26-7).

Outer

This option causes AutoCAD to hatch only the outer closed shape. Hatching is turned off for any interior closed shapes (Fig. 26-7).

Ignore

Ignore draws the hatch pattern from the outer boundary inward ignoring any interior shapes. The resulting hatch pattern is drawn through the interior shapes (Fig. 26-7).

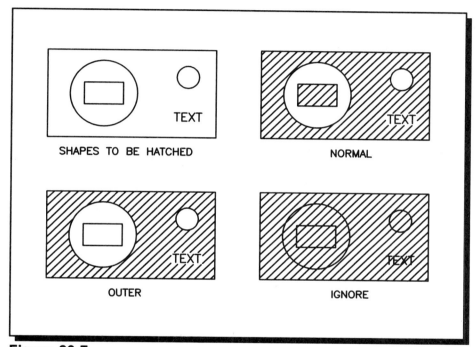

Figure 26-7

Other *Hatch Options*

Exploded Hatch

Bhatch normally draws a hatch pattern as one entity, similar to a *Block*. Checking this box causes the hatch patterns to be pre-exploded when inserted . (This is similar to *Inserting* a *Block* with an asterisk (*) prefixing the *Block* name.) Exploded hatch patterns allow you to edit the hatch lines individually.

Copy Existing Hatch

This option allows you to select a hatch pattern from one existing in the drawing. Selecting this box causes the dialogue box to disappear and the following prompt is displayed.

```
Select objects: PICK (an existing hatch pattern)
Select objects: Enter
```

The _Hatch Options_ dialogue box reappears and the selected hatch pattern name is automatically entered in the _Pattern..._ edit box. The selected pattern becomes the current pattern.

Now that the hatch pattern has been selected, you must indicate to AutoCAD what area(s) should be hatched. Either the _Pick Points_ method, _Select Objects_ method, or a combination of both can be used to accomplish this.

Other _Boundary Hatch_ Dialogue Box Options

Pick Points

This tile should be selected (from the _Boundary Hatch_ dialogue box) if you wish AutoCAD to automatically determine the boundaries for hatching using the ray-tracing technique. You must only select a point inside the area you wish to hatch. When the _Pick Points_ tile is selected, AutoCAD gives the following prompts.

```
Select internal point PICK
Selecting everything...
Selecting everything visible...
Analyzing the selected data...
Select internal point PICK another area or Enter
```

When an internal point is PICKed, AutoCAD traces and highlights the boundary. Multiple boundaries can be designated by selecting multiple internal points. Type _U_ to undo the last one if necessary.

By default AutoCAD finds the nearest entity to the internal point selected. Therefore, you must PICK a point nearest to the desired boundary. (The direction of the ray-casting can be changed using _Advanced Options_.)

For the example section view, three internal points are selected as shown in Figure 26-8. Point 1 specifies the outer boundary and points 2 and 3 specify the "islands." The order of selection is not critical. However, the points must be PICKed nearest the expected boundary.

(Note that center lines have not yet been added to the circles because those lines should not be considered when AutoCAD determines the boundary for hatching. Center lines would cause an incorrect boundary to be found.)

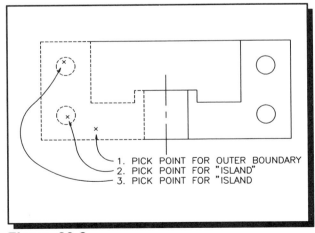

Figure 26-8

If the point PICKed is nearer to another entity than the one you want, AutoCAD traces the nearest boundary. If the selected point is outside of the detected boundary, a _Boundary Definition Error_ box appears (Fig. 26-9). The _Look at it_ option highlights the detected boundary.

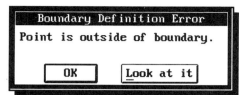

Figure 26-9

For example, if the first point selected is nearer to and outside one of the islands, AutoCAD traces the island, determines that the selected point is outside and displays the error box.

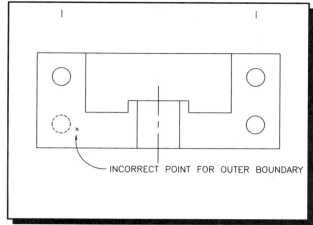

Figure 26-10

Select Objects

Alternately, you can designate the boundary with the *Select Objects* method. This method works well only if the objects are closed entity shapes or text. If you select objects that do not comprise a <u>closed</u> boundary, or if parts of the entities are not included in the boundary, problems will occur when hatching. This method works well for selecting closed objects (such as *Circles*, closed *Plines*, or text) inside of an outer boundary previously determined by the *Pick Points* method. For the example, the outer boundary could be determined by the ray-casting method (*Pick Points*) as in Figure 26-8, point 1. The *Select Objects* method could be used to select the *Circles* as in Figure 26-8, points 2 and 3.

View Selections

Clicking the *View Selections* tile causes AutoCAD to highlight all selected boundaries. This can be used as a check to insure the desired areas are selected.

Preview Hatch

You should always use the *Preview Hatch* option after specifying the hatch options and selecting boundaries, but before you *Apply* the hatch. This option allows you to temporarily look at the hatch pattern with the current settings applied to your drawing and allows you to adjust the settings if necessary before using *Apply*. After viewing the drawing, pressing **Enter** redisplays the *Boundary Hatch* dialogue box allowing you to make adjustments.

Advanced Options...

This tile invokes the *Advanced Options* dialogue box as shown in Figure 26-11.

Define Boundary Set

By default, AutoCAD examines all entities in the drawing when determining the boundaries by the ray-casting method. (The *From Everything on Screen* button is depressed by default when you begin the *Bhatch* command.) For complex drawings this can take some time. In that case, you may want to specify a smaller boundary set for AutoCAD to consider. Clicking the *Make New Boundary Set* tile clears the dialogue boxes and permits you to select objects as normal to define the new set. If you have already specified an area to hatch by either the *Pick Points* or the *Select Objects* method, the *From Existing Boundary Set* button is depressed.

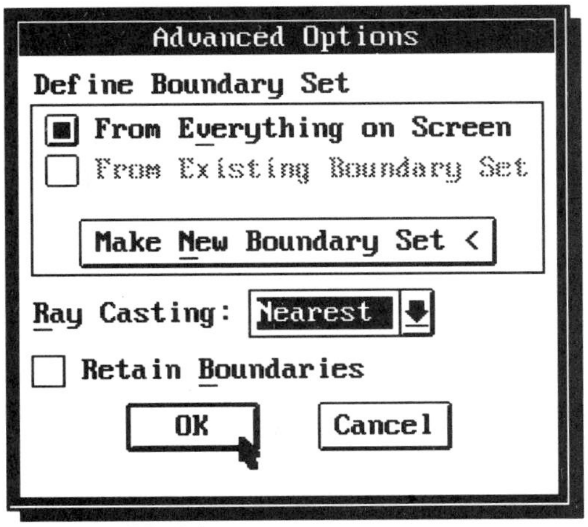

Ray Casting

The default ray-casting option (when using the *Pick Points* method) is *Nearest*, meaning that AutoCAD locates the nearest entity to the selected point, then traces the boundary in a counter-clockwise direction until a closed area is found. You can select a specific X or Y direction for ray-casting by clicking the popup list. The options are as follows.

Figure 26-11

Nearest   AutoCAD casts out to locate the nearest entity, then turns left to trace the boundary.

+X   The ray is cast in a positive X direction until a traceable entity is located, then the boundary is traced counter-clockwise.

-X   The ray is cast in a negative X direction for boundary tracing.

+Y   The ray is cast in a positive Y direction for boundary tracing.

-Y   The ray is cast in a negative Y direction for boundary tracing.

Retain Boundaries

When AutoCAD uses the ray-tracing method to locate a boundary for hatching, a temporary *Pline* is created for hatching, then discarded after the hatching process. Checking this box forces AutoCAD to <u>keep</u> the boundary *Pline*. When the box is checked, *Bhatch* creates two entities--the hatch pattern and the boundary *Pline*.

After using *Bhatch*, the *Pline* can be used for other purposes. To test this, complete a *Bhatch* with the *Retain Boundaries* box checked, then use *Move* (make sure you select the boundary) to reveal the new *Pline*.

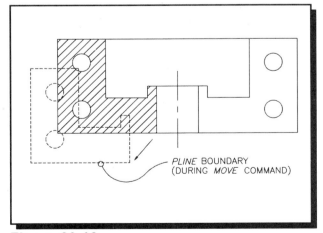

Figure 26-12

Apply

This is typically the last step to the hatching process with *Bhatch*. Selecting *Apply* causes AutoCAD to create the hatch as specified and pass on to the Command: prompt for further drawing and editing.

Another

This button makes the *Boundary Hatch* dialogue box reappear after the hatching process is complete. This option allows you to perform multiple hatching operations.

In the drawing example (see Figure 26-13), after applying the hatch to the area on the left half of the section view, the *Another* option could be used to hatch the right half. However, it would also be possible to complete the hatch for both sides with one use of the *Bhatch* command by selecting both areas with the *Pick Points* option as before.

The drawing including the completed section view should appear as shown in Figure 26-13. *Center* lines are added to the view <u>after</u> hatching.

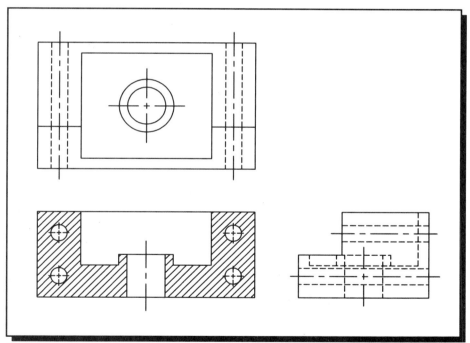

Figure 26-13

BPOLY

TYPE IN:	PULL-DOWN MENU	SCREEN MENU	TABLET MENU
BPOLY	---	---	---

The *Bpoly* (Boundary Polyline) command uses the ray-casting technique to generate a *Pline* boundary. Although this command is not necessarily related to creating section views or hatching, it uses the same procedure and similar dialogue box interface that are used for hatching by the *Pick Points* (ray-casting) method of *Bhatch*. The main difference is that *Bpoly* does not create hatch lines. The resulting *Pline* boundary that is automatically generated with *Bpoly* (or with *Bhatch*, for that matter) can be used for many purposes, such as a simple substitute for outlining and copying a shape or finding the perimeter of a shape for area calculation. See Figure 26-12 for an example of retaining the boundary found with *Bhatch*.

Typing the *Bpoly* command causes AutoCAD to display the *Polyline Creation* dialogue box shown in Figure 26-14. The *Define Boundary Set* section and the *Ray Casting* section of this dialogue box are identical to those found in the *Advanced Options* dialogue box (of the *Bhatch* command). When using *Bpoly*, however, the *Retain Boundary* check box is permanently enabled since retaining the boundaries is the only option.

Notice the similarity between the *Polyline Creation* dialogue box and the *Advanced Options* dialogue box shown in Figure 26-11. Selecting the *Pick Points* tile redisplays the drawing so you can select an internal point. When the boundary is found, AutoCAD creates a *Pline* around the boundary. You can continue to select multiple internal points and AutoCAD creates the related *Plines*. Press Enter to discontinue the command.

Selecting a point outside of a closed area results in display of the *Boundary Definition Error* dialogue box (see Fig. 26-9).

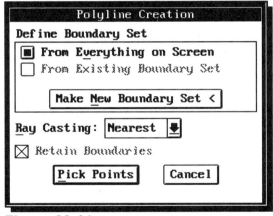

Figure 26-14

HATCH

TYPE IN:	PULL-DOWN MENU	SCREEN MENU	TABLET MENU
HATCH	---	*DRAW, HATCH:*	---

Using the *Hatch* command, you can create hatch (section) lines as you can with *Bhatch*; however, *Hatch* operates differently in two basic ways. First, *Hatch* only operates in command line format. There are no dialogue boxes. Second, *Hatch* does not find boundaries automatically by the ray-casting (*Pick Points*) method, but only provides the normal object selection method of determining hatching boundaries.

The command syntax typically reads like this.

```
Command: hatch
Pattern (? or name/U,style): ? or (name) or U or N,O,I
Scale for pattern <1.0000>: (value)
Angle for pattern <0>: (value)
Select objects: PICK
Select objects: Enter
Command:
```

The following options are valid.

?

Generates a text screen list of all stored hatch patterns (see *BHATCH, Pattern Type-- Stored Hatch Patterns*.

(name)

Enter any valid stored hatch pattern name (see *BHATCH, Pattern Type--Stored Hatch Patterns*.

U

Indicates that you wish to create a User-defined hatch pattern. See *BHATCH, Pattern Type--User-Defined Pattern*.

N

Creates the hatched area using the *Normal* style (see *BHATCH, Hatching Style*).

O

Creates the hatched area using the *Outermost* style (see *BHATCH, Hatching Style*).

I

Creates the hatched area using the *Ignore* style (see *BHATCH, Hatching Style*).

Scale for pattern <1.0000>

This prompt permits you to specify a value to determine the scale of the pattern. The value entered should be based upon the drawing *Limits* (see *BHATCH*). The drawing scale factor can be used as the scale value (see Chapter 13).

Angle for pattern <0>

This prompt allows you to specify a value for the angle of the lines. This angle represents a deflection from the angle of the lines as they appear in their default position. (The patterns can be viewed in their default position by inspecting the *Bhatch* hatch pattern icons.)

Select Objects

Selecting the objects for the boundary using the *Hatch* command is usually a more difficult process than for the *Bhatch* command. When you use *Hatch*, only the *Select Objects* method is available and not the *Pick Points* (ray-casting) method. With the select objects method, the entities selected for the boundary must connect at the endpoints. In other words, if any part of the boundary entities extend past the boundary, problems will result. For many applications, the select object method requires the use of *Trim*, *Break*, or *Erase*.

For the section view example, the select objects method would yield the indicated (highlighted) boundary definition. The resulting hatch pattern application would incorrectly include the parts of the entities outside of the desired closed area.

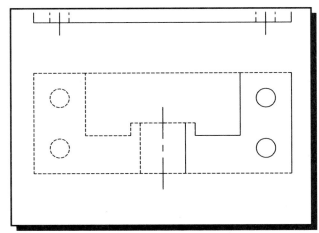

Figure 26-15

Trim (or *Break*) must used to remove the parts of the entities extending past the desired closed area as shown in Figure 26-16. *Hatch* requires a discrete and contiguous boundary. After hatching, new *Lines* should be created to replace those that were *Trimmed*. Alternately, *Break* could be used to break the extending parts into separate entities.

For most applications *Bhatch* is preferred to *Hatch* since *Bhatch* automatically defines boundaries by the ray-casting method.

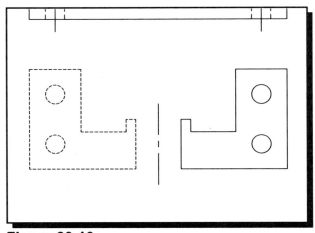

Figure 26-16

Exploded hatch patterns can be created with *Hatch* by using an asterisk (*) as a prefix to the pattern name. For example, if you wished to used the ANSI31 hatch pattern but wanted it pre-exploded, this command syntax would be used.

```
Command: hatch
Pattern (? or name/U,style): *ansi31
Scale for pattern <1.0000>: 1.8
Angle for pattern <0>: Enter
Select objects: PICK
Select objects: Enter
Command:
```

The resulting hatch pattern would be inserted as it normally would with the exception that individual lines could be *Erased*, *Trimmed*, or otherwise edited.

DRAWING CUTTING PLANE LINES

Most section views (full, half, and offset sections) require a cutting plane line to indicate the plane on which the object is cut. The cutting plane line is drawn in a view <u>adjacent</u> to the section view because the line indicates the plane of the cut from its edge view. (In the section view, the cutting plane is perpendicular to the line of sight, therefore, not visible as a line.)

ANSI standards provide two optional line types for cutting plane lines. In AutoCAD, the two linetypes are *Dashed* and *Phantom* as shown in Figure 26-17.

The linetypes can be created using either the *BYLAYER* or entity-specific assignment. Creating a separate layer for cutting plane lines and assigning the *Dashed* or *Phantom* linetypes *BYLAYER* provides the most control. Arrows at the ends of the cutting plane line indicate the line-of-sight for the section view.

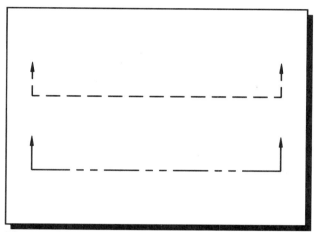

Figure 26-17

ANSI standards also dictate that cutting plane lines be drawn or plotted in a <u>heavy</u> line weight. This is accomplished in AutoCAD by using the *Pline* command to draw the cutting plane line having width assigned using the *Width* option. For potting full size, a width of .02 for small plots (8.5 x 11, or 17 x 22) to .03 for large plots is recommended. (Keep in mind that *Pline Width* is affected by the drawing *Limits*; and therefore *Width* should be increased or decreased by that proportion. For example, if you changed the *Limits*, multiply .02 times the drawing scale factor. (See Chapter 13 for information on drawing scale factor.)

For the example section view, a cutting plane line is created in the top view to indicate the plane on which the object is cut and the line of sight for the section view (Fig. 26-19, next page). (The cutting plane could be drawn in the side view, but the top would be much clearer.) First, a *New* layer named CUT is created and the *Dashed linetype* is assigned to the layer. The layer is *Set* as the *Current* layer. Next, construct a *Pline* with the desired *Width* to represent the cutting plane line.

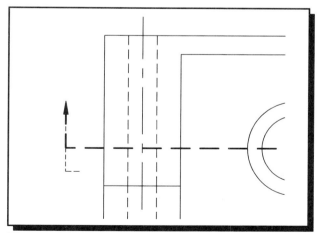

Figure 26-18

The resulting cutting plane line appears as shown in Figure 26-19 (next page) but without the arrowheads. The horizontal center line for the hole (top view) was *Erased* before creating the cutting plane line.

The last step is to add arrowheads to the ends of the cutting plane line. This can be accomplished by either using the _Solid_ command to draw a filled triangle or "stealing" an arrowhead from a dimension _Leader_. In the example, a _Leader_ is drawn, and the leader line and shoulder (highlighted) are _Erased_ to leave only the arrowhead (see Fig. 26-18, previous page). The arrowhead can be _Scaled_ or _Rotated_ if necessary, then _Copied_ to the other end of the cutting plane line. See Chapter 28, Dimensioning, for details on the _Leader_ command.

The resulting multiview drawing with section view is complete and ready for dimensioning, drawing a border, and inserting a title block.

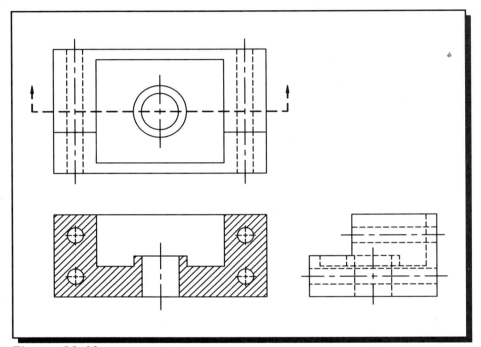

Figure 26-19

CHAPTER EXERCISES

For the following exercises, create the section views as instructed. Use an appropriate prototype drawing for each unless instructed otherwise. Include a border and title block for each drawing.

1.　　_**Open**_ the **SADDLE** drawing that you created in Chapter 24 Exercise 5. Convert the front view to a full section. _**Save**_ the drawing as **SADL-SEC**. _**Plot**_ the drawing at **1=1** scale.

2. Make a multiview drawing of the Bearing shown in Figure 26-20. Convert the front view to a full section view. Add the necessary cutting plane line in the top view. *Save* the drawing as **BEAR-SEC**. Make a *Plot* at full size.

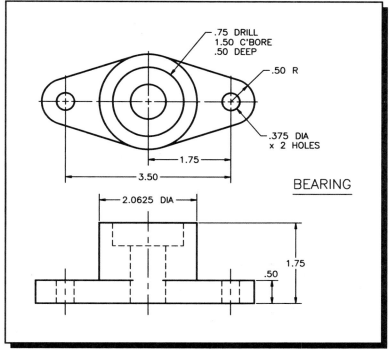

Figure 26-20

3. Create a multiview drawing of the Clip shown in Figure 26-21. Include a side view as a full section view. You can use the **CLIP** drawing you created in Chapter 24 and convert the side view to a section view. Add the necessary cutting plane line in the front view. *Plot* the finished drawing at **1=1** scale and *Save* as **CLIP-SEC**.

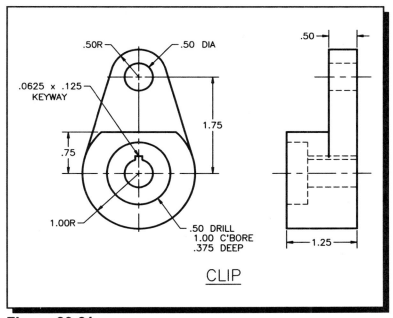

Figure 26-21

4. Create a multiview drawing including two full sections of the Stop Block as shown in Figure 26-22. Section B-B' should replace the side view shown in the figure. *Save* the drawing as **SPBK-SEC**. *Plot* the drawing to at **1=2** scale.

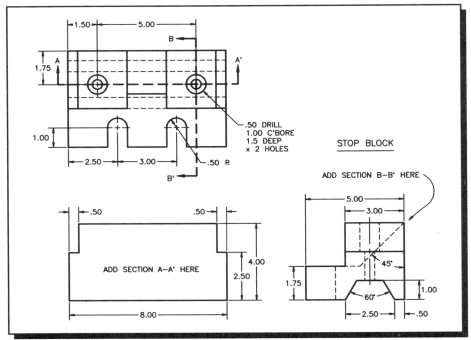

Figure 26-22

5. Make a multiview drawing including a half section of the Pulley (the same object that you created as an oblique drawing in Chapter 25 Exercise 5). Two views (including the half section) are sufficient to describe the part. Add the necessary cutting plane line. *Save* the drawing as **PUL-SEC** and make a *Plot* at **1=1** scale.

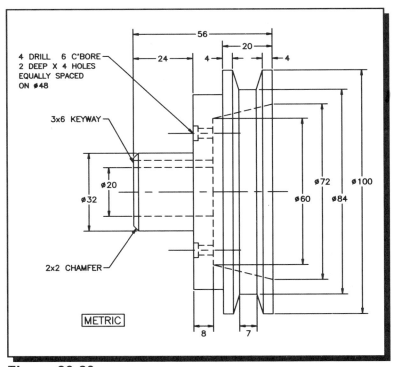

Figure 26-23

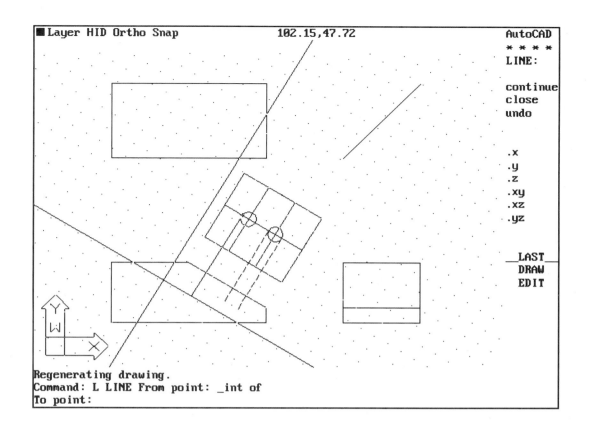

```
■Layer HID Ortho Snap          102.15,47.72          AutoCAD
                                                     * * * *
                                                     LINE:

                                                     continue
                                                     close
                                                     undo


                                                     .x
                                                     .y
                                                     .z
                                                     .xy
                                                     .xz
                                                     .yz

                                                     _LAST_
                                                      DRAW
                                                      EDIT




Regenerating drawing.
Command: L LINE From point: _int of
To point:
```

CHAPTER 27

Auxiliary Views

CHAPTER OBJECTIVES

After completing this chapter you should:

1.   be able to use the *Rotate* option of *Snap* to change the angle of the *SNAP*, *GRID*, and *ORTHO*;

2.   know how to use the *Offset* command to create parallel line copies;

3.   know how to create auxiliary views in AutoCAD using the two features discussed in this chapter (*Snap Rotate* and *Offset*).

BASICS

AutoCAD provides no features explicitly for the creation of auxiliary views in a 2D drawing. No new commands are discussed in this chapter. There are, however, two particular features that have been discussed earlier that can assist you in construction of auxiliary views. Those features are *SNAP* rotation and the *Offset* command. As a reminder, the *SNAP* and *GRID* can be rotated to any angle. In conjunction with *ORTHO*, these features simplify the task of drawing parallel and perpendicular lines with respect to any given angle. The *Offset* command can be used to create parallel line copies at any distance or through specified points.

An auxiliary view is a supplementary view among a series of multiviews. The auxiliary view is drawn in addition to the typical views that are mutually perpendicular (top, front, side). An auxiliary view is one that is normal to (the line-of-sight is perpendicular to) an inclined surface of the object. Therefore, the auxiliary view is constructed by projecting in a 90 degree direction from the edge view of an inclined surface in order to show the true size and shape of the inclined surface. The edge view of the inclined surface could be at any angle (depending on the object), so lines are typically drawn parallel and perpendicular relative to that edge view. Hence, the *SNAP* rotation feature and the *Offset* command can provide assistance in this task.

An example auxiliary view is used for the application of these AutoCAD features related to auxiliary view construction. Assume the given object shown in Figure 27-1. As you can see, there is an inclined surface that contains two drilled holes. To describe this object adequately, an auxiliary view should be created to show the true size and shape of the inclined surface.

This chapter explains the construction of the auxiliary view for the example object.

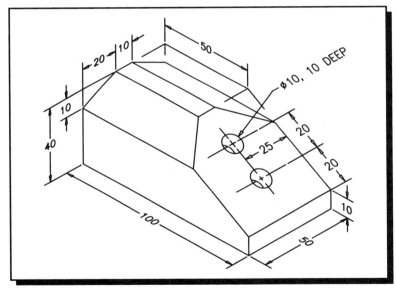

Figure 27-1

CONSTRUCTING AN AUXILIARY VIEW

Setting Up the Principal Views

To begin this drawing, the typical steps are followed for drawing setup (Chapter 13). Because the dimensions are in millimeters, *Limits* should be set accordingly. For example, to provide enough space to draw the views full size and to plot full size on an A4 sheet, *Limits* of 297 x 210 are specified.

416

In preparation of the auxiliary view, the principal views are "blocked in" as shown in Figure 27-2. The purpose of this step is to insure that the desired views fit and are optimally spaced within the allocated _Limits_. If there is too little or too much room, adjustments can be made to the _Limits_.

Notice that space has been allotted between the views for a partial auxiliary view to be projected from the front view.

Before additional construction on the principle views is undertaken, initial steps in the construction of

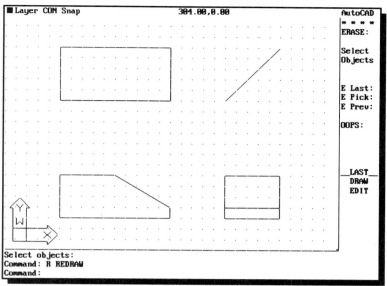

Figure 27-2

the partial auxiliary view should be performed. The projection of the auxiliary view requires drawing lines perpendicular and parallel to the inclined surface. One of two alternatives (explained next) can be used.

Using _Snap Rotate_

One possibility is to use the _Snap_ command with the _Rotate_ option. This permits you to rotate the _SNAP_ to any angle about a specified base point. The _GRID_ automatically follows the _SNAP_. Turning _ORTHO ON_ forces _Lines_ to be drawn orthogonally with respect to the rotated _SNAP_ and _GRID_.

Figure 27-3 displays the _SNAP_ and _GRID_ after rotation. The command syntax is given below.

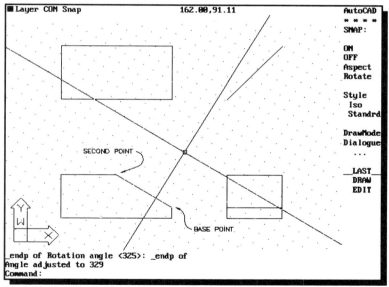

Figure 27-3

```
Command: snap
Snap spacing or ON/OFF/Aspect/Rotate/Style <current>: r
Base point <0.00,0.00>: PICK or (coordinates) (Starts a rubberband line.)
Rotation angle <0>: PICK or (value) (PICK to specify the second point to
define the angle.)
Command:
```

PICK (or specify coordinates for) the endpoint of the _Line_ representing the inclined surface as the `Base point`. At the `Rotation angle:` prompt, a value can be entered or another point (the other end of the inclined _Line_) can be PICKed. Use _OSNAP_ when PICKing the _ENDpoints_. If you want to enter a value but don't know what angle to rotate to, use _List_ to display the angle of the inclined _Line_. The _GRID_ and _SNAP_ should align as shown in Figure 27-3.

After rotating the _SNAP_ and _GRID_, the partial auxiliary view can be "blocked in" as displayed in Figure 27-4. Begin by projecting _Lines_ up from and perpendicular to the inclined surface. (Make sure _ORTHO_ is _ON_.) Next, two _Lines_ representing the depth of the view should be constructed parallel to the inclined surface and perpendicular to the previous two projection lines. The depth dimension of the object in the auxiliary view is equal to the depth dimension in the top or right view. _Trim_ as necessary.

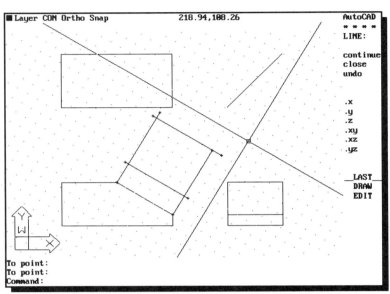

Figure 27-4

Using the _Offset_ Command

Another possibility, and an alternative to the _SNAP_ rotation, is to use _Offset_ to make parallel _Lines_. This can be particularly useful for construction of the "blocked in" partial auxiliary view because it is not necessary to rotate the _SNAP_ and _GRID_.

Invoke the _Offset_ command and specify a distance. The first distance is arbitrary. Specify an appropriate value between the front view inclined plane and the nearest edge of the auxiliary view (20 for the example). _Offset_ the new _Line_ at a distance of 50 or PICK two points (equal to the depth of the view). Note that the _Offset_ lines have equal length to the original and therefore do not require additional editing. Next, draw two _Lines_ connected to the existing _ENDpoints_ as shown in Figure 27-5.

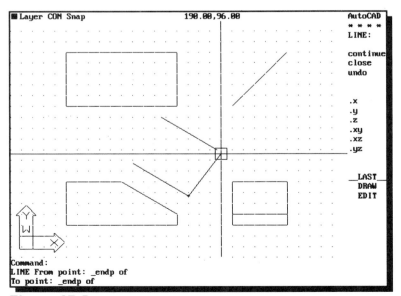

Figure 27-5

Even though the *Offset* method did not require *SNAP* and *GRID* rotation, the complete construction of the auxiliary view would be simplified using the rotated *SNAP* and *GRID*. The following steps illustrate the creation of the holes in the auxiliary view.

Locate the centers of the holes in the auxiliary view and construct two *Circles*. It is generally preferred to construct circular shapes in the view in which they appear as circles, then project to the other views. That is particularly true for this type of auxiliary since the other views contain ellipses. The centers can be located by projection from the front view or by *Offsetting Lines* from the view outline.

Next, project lines from the *Circles* and their centers back to the inclined surface. Use of a hidden line layer can be helpful here. While the *SNAP* and *GRID*

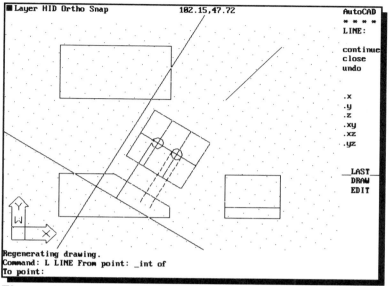

Figure 27-6

are rotated, construct the *Lines* representing the bottom of the holes in the front view. (Alternately, *Offset* could be used to copy the inclined edge down to the hole bottoms, then *Trim* the unwanted portions of the *Lines*.)

Rotating *SNAP* Back to the Original Position

Before details can be added to the other views, the *SNAP* and *GRID* should be rotated back to the original position. It is very important to rotate back using the <u>same basepoint</u>. Fortunately, AutoCAD remembers the original basepoint so you can accept the default for the prompt. Next, enter a value of **0** when rotating back to the original position. (When using the *Snap Rotate* option, the value entered for the angle of rotation is absolute, not relative to the current position. For example if the *Snap* was rotated to 45 degrees, rotate back to 0 degrees, not -45.)

```
Command: snap
Snap spacing or ON/OFF/Aspect/Rotate/Style <2.00>: r
Base point <150.00,40.00>: Enter (AutoCAD remembers the previous
basepoint.)
Rotation angle <329>: 0
Command:
```

Construction of multiview drawings with auxiliaries typically involves repeated rotation of the *SNAP* and *GRID* to the angle of the inclined surface and back again as needed.

With the *SNAP* and *GRID* in the original position, details can be added to the other views as shown in Figure 27-7. Since the two circles appear as ellipses in the top and right side views, project lines from the inclined surface from the circles' centers and limiting elements. Locate centers for the two *Ellipses* to be drawn in the top and right side views.

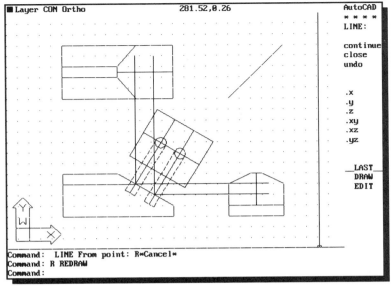

Figure 27-7

Use the *Ellipse* command to construct the ellipses in the top and right side views. Using the *Center* option of *Ellipse*, specify the center by PICKing with the *INTersection OSNAP* mode. *OSNAP* to the appropriate construction line *INTersection* for the first axis endpoint. For the second axis endpoint (as shown), use the actual circle diameter, since that dimension is not foreshortened.

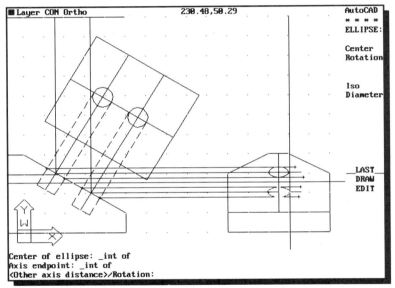

Figure 27-8

The remaining steps for completing the drawing involve finalizing the perimeter shape of the partial auxiliary view and *Copying* the *Ellipses* to the bottom of the hole positions. The *SNAP* and *GRID* should be rotated back to project the new edges found in the front view. Depth distances can the same as in the other (top and right side) views. See Figure 27-9.

At this point, the multiview drawing with auxiliary view is ready for center lines, dimensioning, and construction or insertion of a border and title block.

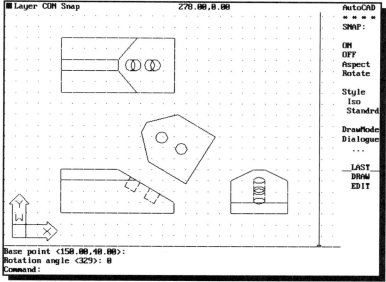

Figure 27-9

Constructing Full Auxiliary Views

The construction of a full auxiliary view begins with the partial view. After initial construction of the partial view, begin the construction of the full auxiliary by projecting the other edges and features of the object (other than the inclined plane) to the existing auxiliary view.

The procedure for constructing full auxiliary views in AutoCAD is essentially the same as that for partial auxiliary views. Use of the *Offset* command and *SNAP* and *GRID* rotation should be used as illustrated for the partial auxiliary view example. Because a full auxiliary view is projected at the same angle as a partial, the same rotation angle and basepoint would be used for the *SNAP*.

CHAPTER EXERCISES

For the following exercises, create the multiview drawing including the partial or full auxiliary view as indicated. Use the appropriate prototype drawing based on the given dimensions and indicated plot scale.

1.   Make a multiview drawing with a partial auxiliary view of the example used in this chapter. Refer to Figure 27-1 for dimensions. *Save* the drawing as **CH27EX1**. *Plot* on an A size sheet at **1=1** scale.

2. Recreate the views given in Figure 27-10 and add a partial auxiliary view. *Save* the drawing as **CH27EX2** and *Plot* on an A size sheet at **2=1** scale.

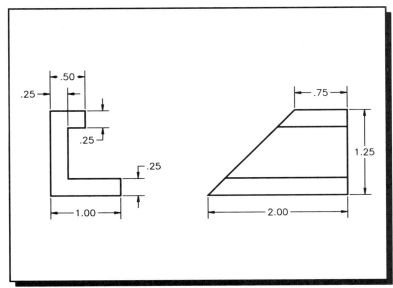

Figure 27-10

3. Recreate the views shown in Figure 27-11 and add a partial auxiliary view. *Save* the drawing as **CH27EX3**. Make a *Plot* on an A size sheet at **1=1** scale.

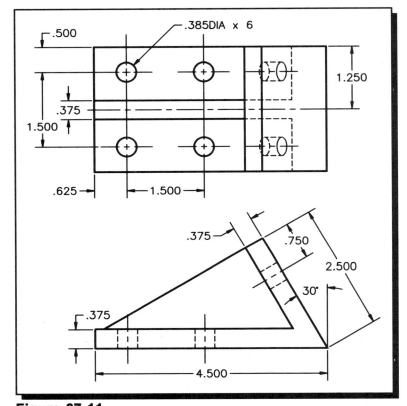

Figure 27-11

4. Make a multiview drawing of the given views. Add a full auxiliary view. *Save* the drawing as **CH27EX4**. *Plot* the drawing at an appropriate scale on an A size sheet.

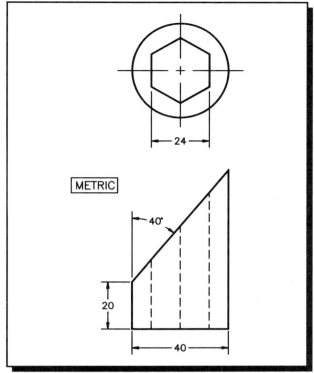

Figure 27-12

5. Draw the front, top, and a partial auxiliary view of the Holder. Make a *Plot* full size. Save the drawing as **HOLDER**.

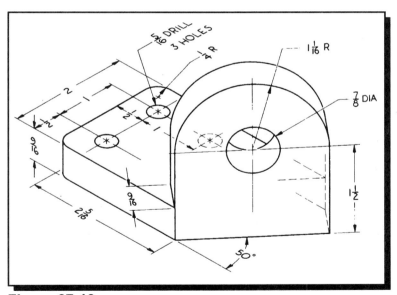

Figure 27-13

6. Draw three principal views and a full auxiliary view of the V-block shown in Figure 27-14. *Save* the drawing as **VBLOCK**. *Plot* to an accepted scale.

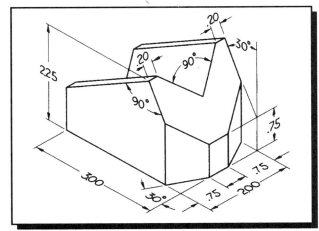

Figure 27-14

7. Draw two principal views and a partial auxiliary of the Angle Brace. *Save* as **ANGLBRAC**. Make a plot to an accepted scale on an A or B size sheet.

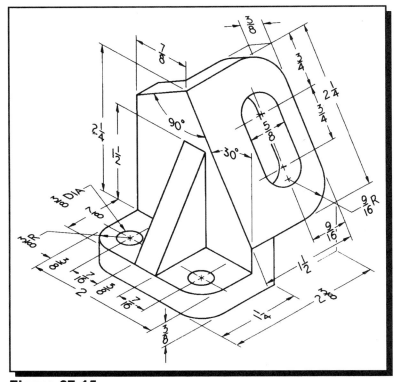

Figure 27-15

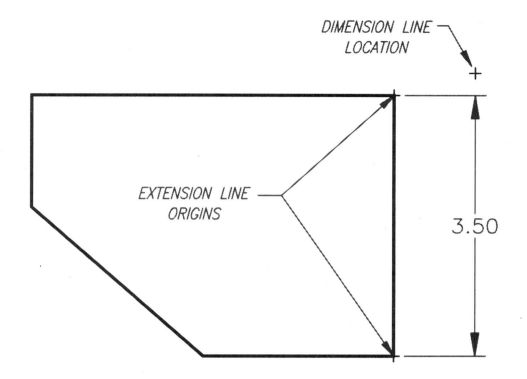

DIMENSION LINE
LOCATION

EXTENSION LINE
ORIGINS

3.50

CHAPTER 28

Dimensioning

CHAPTER OBJECTIVES

After completing this chapter you should:

1. be able to create linear dimensions: *Horizontal, Vertical, Aligned,* and *Rotated*;

2. be able to append *Continue* and *Baseline* dimensions to existing dimensions;

3. be able to create *Angular, Diameter* and *Radius* dimensions;

4. know how to affix notes to drawings with *Leaders*;

5. be able to dimension a part with *Ordinate* dimensioning;

6. know the possible methods for editing associative dimensions;

7. be able to use all of the methods for editing dimensioning text;

8. know how to dimension isometric drawings.

BASICS

As you know, drawings created with CAD systems are in the actual dimensions and units as the real-world objects they represent. The importance of this practice is evident when you begin applying dimensions to the drawing geometry in AutoCAD. The features of the drawn object that you specify for dimensioning are automatically measured and those values are used for the dimensioning text. If the geometry has been drawn accurately, the dimensions will be created correctly.

The main features of a dimension are:

1.   dimension line
2.   extension lines
3.   dimension text (usually a numeric value)
4.   arrow heads or tick marks

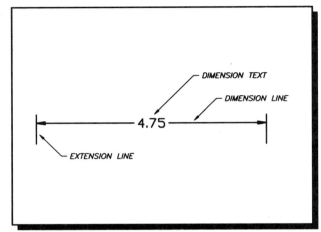

AutoCAD dimensioning is <u>semi-automatic</u>. When you invoke a command to create a linear dimension, AutoCAD only requires that you PICK an entity or specify the extension line origins (where you want the extension lines to begin) and PICK the location of the dimension line (distance from the object). AutoCAD then measures the feature and

Figure 28-1

draws the extension lines, dimension line, arrow heads, and dimension text. The dimension text is drawn using the current text *Style*, *Units*, and *Precision* settings.

Dimensioning in AutoCAD is <u>associative</u> (by default). Because the extension line origins are "associated" with the geometry, the dimension text automatically updates if the geometry is *Stretched*, *Rotated*, *Scaled*, or likewise edited using grips.

Because dimensioning is semi-automatic, <u>dimensioning variables</u> are used to control the way dimensions are created. Dimensioning variables can be used to control features such as associativity, text or arrow size, direction of the leader arrow for radial or diametrical dimensions, format of the text, and many other possible options. Groups of variable settings can be named and saved as <u>Dimension Styles</u>. Dimensioning variables and dimension styles are discussed in Chapter 29.

Dimension commands can be invoked from any menu or can be typed. If you wish to type the dimensioning command, you must first type "**Dim**" to enter the dimensioning mode (AutoCAD assumes that you will use many dimensioning commands once you are ready to dimension the completed object). The `Dim:` prompt replaces the `Command:` prompt.

DIM

TYPE IN:	PULL-DOWN MENU	SCREEN MENU	TABLET MENU
DIM	*Draw, Dimensions > any command*	*DIM:*	*any dimensioning command*

The *Dim* command is used to begin dimensioning. Entering this command activates the `Dim:` prompt which replaces the `Command:` prompt and allows you to enter any dimensioning command.

> `Command:` **Dim**
> `Dim:`

If you select any dimensioning command from the pull-down or tablet menus, the `Dim:` prompt <u>automatically</u> appears before the selected dimensioning command. When you select a drawing or editing command from the menus, the `Dim:` mode is automatically exited. If you prefer typing, you must type *Exit* or cancel (CTRL+C) to reactivate the `Command:` prompt to allow other than dimensioning commands to be used. (*Units, Style* [text style] and system variables are exceptions and can be typed at the `Dim:` prompt.)

DIM1

TYPE IN:	PULL-DOWN MENU	SCREEN MENU	TABLET MENU
DIM1	---	---	---

Type this command if you wish to use only <u>one</u> dimensioning command and then return to the `Command:` prompt without having to type *Exit* or cancel (CTRL+C). This command is useful only if you prefer typing.

DIMENSION DRAWING COMMANDS

HORIZ

TYPE IN:	PULL-DOWN MENU	SCREEN MENU	TABLET MENU
HORIZ	*Draw, Dimensions > Linear > Horizontal*	*DIM:, Horizntl*	*6,X*

The *Horiz* command creates a horizontally oriented dimension line. Generally, you should PICK the corners of the geometry that you want to dimension as the extension line origins (Fig. 28-2).

It is <u>very important</u> to PICK the <u>entities</u> if the dimensions are to be truly associative (associated with the geometry). _OSNAP_ must be used to find the entity's _ENDpoint_, _INTersection_, etc., unless that part of the geometry is located at a _SNAP_ point.

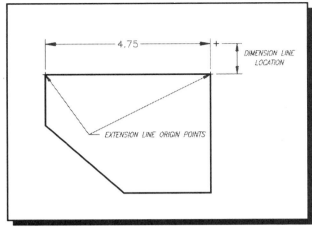

Figure 28-2

The command syntax to produce the _Horiz_ dimension in Figure 28-2 is as follows:

```
Dim: horiz
First extension line origin or RETURN to select: PICK or
(coordinates)
Second extension line origin: PICK or (coordinates)
Dimension line location (Text/Angle): PICK
Dimension text <4.75>: Enter or specify new text
Dim:
```

If you press **Enter** in response to `First extension line origin...` AutoCAD prompts you to select an entity. This method is easier to use because you do not have to PICK each extension line origin.

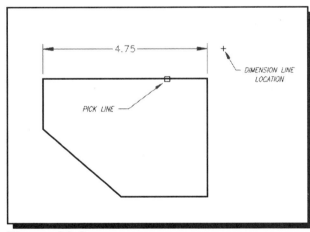

Figure 28-3

The command syntax to produce the dimension shown in Figure 28-3 follows.

```
Dim: horiz
First extension line origin or RETURN to select: Enter
Select line, arc, or circle: PICK
Dimension line location (Text/Angle): PICK
Dimension text <4.75>: Enter
Dim:
```

If you wish to specify dimension text other than that offered by AutoCAD (shown in brackets; e.g., <4.75>) you can enter any value or text. This practice should be discouraged, however. If the geometry is accurate, the dimensional value is accurate and should not have to be changed. If you specify explicit dimension text, the text is <u>not</u> updated in the event of _Stretching_, _Rotating_, or otherwise editing the associative dimension. You can add additional text to the AutoCAD-supplied value using the _DIMPOST_ variable (see Chapter 29).

You can <u>preview</u> text that you specify or rotate as you PICK the dimension line location by using the *Text/Angle* option. Pressing **T** allows you to enter text which is used for the dimension. Alternatively, you can enter **A** to specify an angle for rotating the text. In either case, the new text is shown as you PICK the dimension line location.

The *Horiz* command creates a horizontal dimension, regardless of the angle of the geometry that is measured. For example, if a diagonal *Line* is selected for dimensioning, the resulting dimension line is horizontal and the extension lines are automatically drawn to extend as needed.

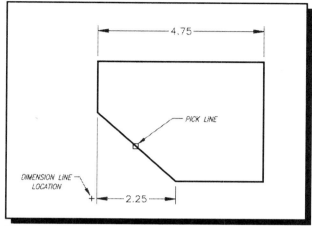

Figure 28-4

VERT

TYPE IN:	PULL-DOWN MENU	SCREEN MENU	TABLET MENU
VERT	*Draw, Dimensions >* *Linear > Vertical*	*DIM:, Vertical*	*5,X*

The *Vert* command creates a vertically measured and oriented dimension. This command operates identically to *Horiz* with the exception that the resulting dimension is vertical. The command syntax follows.

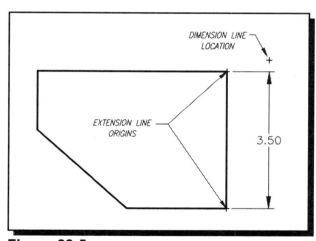

Figure 28-5

```
Dim: vert
First extension line origin or RETURN to select: PICK or
(coordinates)
Second extension line origin: PICK or (coordinates)
Dimension line location (Text/Angle): PICK or (coordinates)
Dimension text <3.50>: Enter
Dim:
```

As with a *Horiz* dimension, you can press **Enter** in response to First extension line origin... and AutoCAD prompts you to select an <u>entity</u>. This method is an efficient alternative to PICKing each extension line origin.

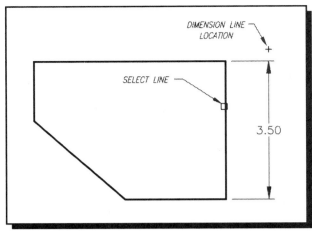

Figure 28-6

The command syntax used to produce the dimension shown in Figure 28-6 is given here.

```
Dim: vert
First extension line origin or RETURN to select: Enter
Select line, arc, or circle: PICK
Dimension line location (Text/Angle): PICK
Dimension text <3.50>: Enter
Dim:
```

Like a *Horiz* dimension, if you wish to specify dimension text other than that offered by AutoCAD, you can enter any value or text. The dimension text that you specify explicitly remains even in the event of *Stretching*, *Rotating*, or otherwise editing the associative dimension.

You can <u>preview</u> text that you specify or rotate as you PICK the dimension line location by using the *Text/Angle* option. Pressing *T* allows you to enter new text and/or pressing *A* allows you to specify an angle for rotating the text. In either case, the new text is shown as you PICK the dimension line location.

The *Vert* command creates a vertical dimension line no matter what the angle of the selected entity or the angle between extension line origins is. As shown in Figure 28-7, if a diagonal line is selected for dimensioning, the resulting dimension is vertical.

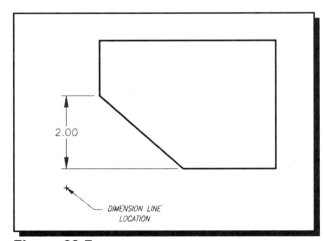

Figure 28-7

ALIGNED

TYPE IN:	PULL-DOWN MENU	SCREEN MENU	TABLET MENU
ALI	*Draw, Dimensions >* *Linear > Aligned*	*DIM:, Aligned*	*6,Y*

An *Aligned* dimension is aligned with (at the same angle as) the selected entity or the extension line origins. For example, when *Aligned* is used to dimension the angled entity shown in Figure 28-8, the resulting dimension aligns with the *Line*. This holds true for either option--PICKing the entity or the extension line origins.

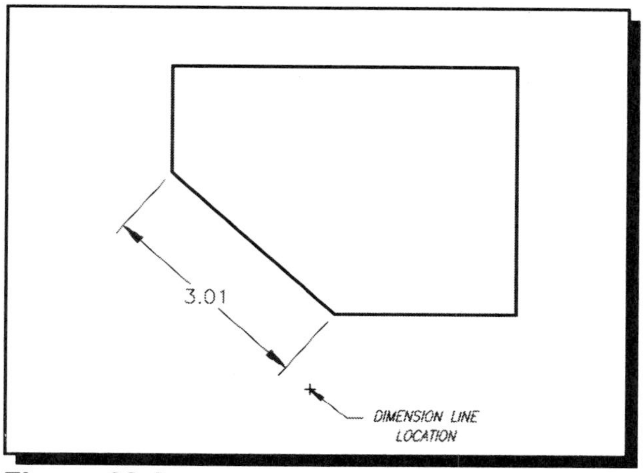

Figure 28-8

The command syntax for the *Aligned* command accepting the defaults is:

```
Dim: aligned
First extension line
origin or RETURN to select: PICK
Second extension line origin: PICK
Dimension line location (Text/Angle): PICK
Dimension text <3.01>: Enter
Dim:
```

The options and features available for the *Aligned* command are the same as those for *Horiz* and *Vert*. Specifically those are:

The extension line origins can be specified individually or an entity (*Line*, *Arc*, or *Circle*) can be PICKed. If an entity is PICKed, the dimension is aligned with the end points of a *Line* or *Arc*. If a *Circle* is PICKed, the dimension line is aligned with the selected point on the *Circle* and its center.

If you wish to specify dimension text other than that offered by AutoCAD, you can enter any value or text at the `Dimension text <xxx.xx>:` prompt. (Remember that if the geometry has been drawn accurately, the AutoCAD-supplied value is correct and there is no need to change the text.)

You can <u>preview</u> text that you specify or rotate as you PICK the dimension line location by using the *Text/Angle* option.

The typical application for *Aligned* is for dimensioning an angled, but <u>straight</u> feature of an object as shown in Figure 28-8. *Aligned* should not be used to dimension an object feature that contains "steps" as shown in Figure 28-9. *Aligned* always draws extension lines of equal length.

Be careful not to use *Aligned* to create a dimension when the geometry has "steps" as shown in Figure 28-9. *Aligned* is <u>inappropriate</u> in this case because the resulting dimension line is not parallel to the object feature. The dimension shown gives no valuable information and should <u>not</u> be used as a standard practice. Using the option to PICK an entity results in one extension line overlapping an object line, which should also be avoided.

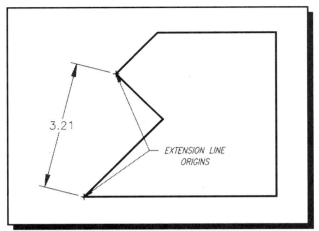

Figure 28-9

ROTATED

TYPE IN:	PULL-DOWN MENU	SCREEN MENU	TABLET MENU
ROT	*Draw, Dimensions > Linear > Rotated*	*DIM:, Rotated*	*5,Y*

A *Rotated* dimension is an angled dimension (similar to *Aligned*) except that you are prompted for an explicit angle for the dimension line to be drawn. This feature alleviates the problem illustrated in Figure 28-9. A *Rotated* dimension should be used when the geometry has "steps" or any time the desired dimension line angle is different than the dimensioned feature (when you need extension lines of different lengths).

Figure 28-10 illustrates the result of using a *Rotated* dimension to give the correct dimension line angle and extension line origins for the given object. In this case, the extension line origins were explicitly PICKed.

The feature of *Rotated* that makes it unique is that you specify the <u>angle</u> that the dimension line will be drawn. The command syntax for creation of the *Rotated* dimension in Figure 28-10 follows.

Figure 28-10

```
Dim: rotated
Dimension line angle <0>:
45
First extension line origin or RETURN to select: PICK
Second extension line origin: PICK
Dimension line location (Text/Angle): PICK
Dimension text <2.88>: Enter
Dim:
```

All the options available and explained with the previous dimensioning commands are valid for the *Rotated* command, i.e; an entity (*Line*, *Arc* or *Circle*) can be PICKed, any value or text can be entered at the `Dimension text <value>:` prompt, and you can <u>preview</u> or rotate text using the *Text/Angle* option.

BASELINE

TYPE IN:	PULL-DOWN MENU	SCREEN MENU	TABLET MENU
BASE	*Draw, Dimensions >* *Linear > Baseline*	*DIM:, Baseline*	*3,X*

Baseline allows you to create a dimension that uses an extension line origin from a previously created dimension. Successive *Baseline* dimensions can be used to create the style of dimensioning shown in Figure 28-11.

A *Baseline* dimension must be connected to an existing dimension. If *Baseline* is invoked immediately after another dimensioning command, you are required only to specify the second extension line origin since AutoCAD knows to use the previous dimension's first extension line origin.

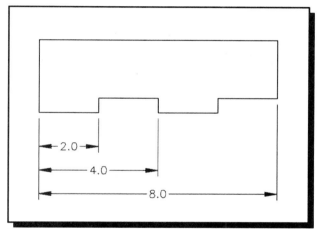

Figure 28-11

```
Dim: base
Second extension line origin or RETURN to select: PICK
Dimension text <4.0>: Enter
Dim:
```

The previous dimension's first extension line is used also for the *Baseline* dimension. Therefore, you only specify the second extension line origin. Note that you are not required to specify the `Dimension line location.` AutoCAD spaces the new dimension line automatically based on the setting of the dimension line increment variable (Chapter 29).

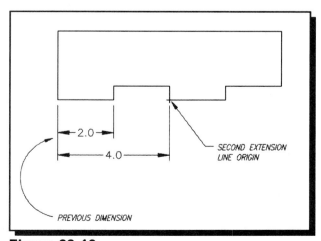

Figure 28-12

If you wish to create a *Baseline* dimension using a dimension other than the one created immediately preceding, use the `Return to select` option.

```
Dim: base
Second extension line origin or RETURN to select: Enter
Select base dimension: PICK an extension line
Second extension line origin or RETURN to select: PICK
Dimension text <2.5>: Enter
Dim:
```

The extension line selected as the `base dimension` becomes the first extension line for the new *Baseline* dimension (Figure 28-13).

As with other dimensioning commands, you can enter any text other than the AutoCAD measured value. There are no options for previewing or rotating the dimension text within the *Baseline* command.

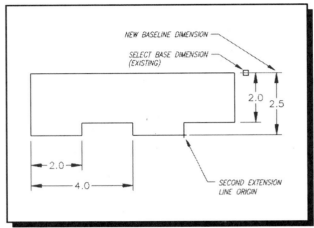

Figure 28-13

CONTINUE

TYPE IN:	PULL-DOWN MENU	SCREEN MENU	TABLET MENU
CONT	*Draw, Dimensions > Linear > Continue*	*DIM:, Continue*	*4,X*

Continue dimensions continue in a line from a previously created dimension. *Continue* dimension lines are attached to, and drawn the same distance from, the object as an existing dimension.

Continue is similar to *Baseline* except that an existing dimension's <u>second</u> extension line is used to begin the new dimension. In other words, the new dimension is connected to the <u>second</u> extension line, rather than to the <u>first</u> as with a *Baseline* dimension.

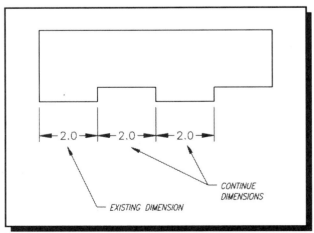

Figure 28-14

The command syntax is as follows.

```
Dim: cont
Second extension line origin or RETURN to select: PICK
Dimension text <2.0>: Enter
Dim:
```

Assuming a dimension was just specified, _Continue_ could be used to place the next dimension as shown in Figure 28-15.

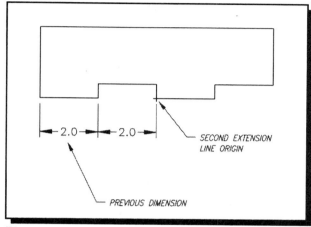

Figure 28-15

If you want to create a _Continue_ dimension and attach it to an extension line other than the previous dimension's second extension line, you can RETURN to select. This option allows you to continue from any existing dimension by selecting it.

```
Dim: cont
Second extension line origin or RETURN to select: Enter
Select continued dimension: PICK an existing extension line
Second extension line origin or RETURN to select: PICK the
second extension line origin for the new dimension.
Dimension text <0.5>: Enter
Dim:
```

Figure 28-16 illustrates the option of attaching a _Continue_ dimension to an existing dimension (that was not created immediately preceding the new dimension).

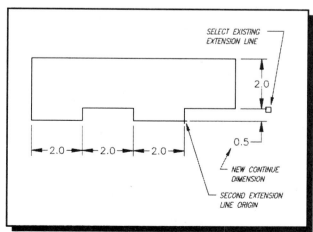

Figure 28-16

DIAMETER

TYPE IN:	PULL-DOWN MENU	SCREEN MENU	TABLET MENU
DIA	*Draw, Dimensions > Radial > Diameter*	*DIM:, Diameter*	*3,Y*

The *Diameter* command creates a radial dimension by selecting any *Circle*. *Diameter* dimensions should be used only for full 360 degree *Circles*, not for *Arcs* (less than 360 degrees).

The point at which the *Circle* is selected determines the angle of the dimension line. Try to select the *Circle* at a location that will produce a 45, 60, or a 90 degree dimension line. As with other dimensioning commands, you have the option of entering specific text other than what AutoCAD measures.

A typical correct *Diameter* dimension appears as the example in Figure 28-17. According to ANSI standards, a *Diameter* dimension line and arrow should point inward (toward the center) unless the dimension line and text are completely within the *Circle* (as shown in the next figure). Although it is possible to create a *Diameter* dimension with the arrow pointing outward, the variables that control these features are set by default to generate the dimension as shown.

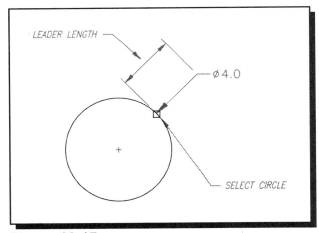

The command syntax to create the *Diameter* dimension like that in Figure 28-17 is as follows:

Figure 28-17

```
Dim: dia
Select arc or circle: PICK at the desired arrow location.
Dimension text <4.0>: Enter
Enter leader length for text: PICK
Dim:
```

Notice in the previous figure that AutoCAD automatically created the phi symbol (Ø) placed before the dimension value. This symbol is generally used to represent metric diameters. If you prefer instead for the letters "DIA" to appear after the dimension value, it can be accomplished by setting the *DIMPOST* variable to "<> DIA" (see Chapter 29, Dimensioning Variables and Dimension Styles).

Notice also that the *Diameter* command creates center marks at the *Circle's* center. Center marks can also be drawn by the *Center* command (discussed later in this chapter). AutoCAD uses the center and the point selected on the *Circle* to maintain its associativity.

Another accepted ANSI standard for dimensioning large *Circles* is illustrated in Figure 28-18. Dimensioning variables must be changed from the defaults in order to force the dimension line and text inside.

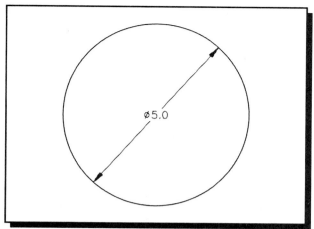

Figure 28-18

RADIUS

TYPE IN:	PULL-DOWN MENU	SCREEN MENU	TABLET MENU
RAD	*Draw, Dimensions >* *Radial > Radius*	*DIM:, Radius*	*2,Y*

A *Radius* dimension is used to create a dimension for an *Arc* (anything less than a full 360 degree *Circle*). ANSI standards dictate that a *Radius* leader should point outward (from the *Arc's* center. The text can be located inside the *Arc* (if sufficient room exists) or outside of the *Arc* on a leader.

Unfortunately, the dimensioning variables that control the placement of dimensioning text and direction of the arrow affect both the *Diameter* command and the *Radius* command. The *DIMTOFL* variable should be reset to force the dimension line inside in order to create ANSI standard *Radius* dimensions (see Chapter 29). Alternately, the leader can be dynamically dragged inside while placing the dimension.

Assuming the variable is set to force the dimension line inside, a *Radius* dimension should appear as shown in Figure 28-19.

The command syntax for creating a *Radius* dimension as in Figure 28-19 is given here.

```
Dim: rad
Select arc or circle: PICK
Dimension text <2.0>: Enter
Dim:
```

The point on the *Arc* that is selected determines the angle for the leader to be drawn. Leaders should be drawn at 45, 30, or 60 degrees.

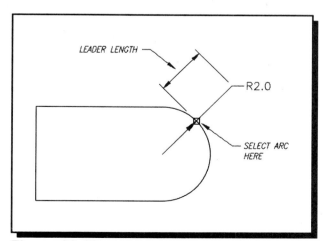

Figure 28-19

If the dimension variable is set to force the text inside, the *Radius* dimension is created as shown in Figure 28-20. This method is preferred for large radii. (See Chapter 29, *DIMTIX*.)

Notice that the *Radius* command does not automatically create center marks at the *Arc's* center when either the text or the dimension line is forced inside (*DIMTOFL* or *DIMTIX* is set to 1 or *ON*). Center marks can be created using the *Center* command (discussed next).

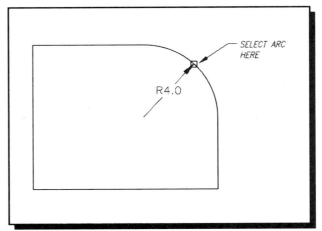

Figure 28-20

The default settings for the dimension variables controlling the placement of the dimension line and dimension text create a leader pointing inward toward the center with the text on the outside. These settings are appropriate for very small radii (if there is insufficient room for the dimension line and text to fit inside the *Arc*) as shown in Figure 28-21. (The default settings are also appropriate for most *Diameter* dimensioning.)

AutoCAD automatically inserts the letter "R" before the numerical text whenever a *Radius* dimension is created. This is the correct notation for both metric and feet and inch dimensions. Placement of the "R" can be changed to appear after the numerical value by setting the *DIMPOST* variable to "<> R". (See Chapter 29.)

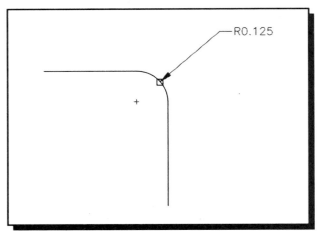

Figure 28-21

CENTER

TYPE IN:	PULL-DOWN MENU	SCREEN MENU	TABLET MENU
CENTER	*Draw, Dimensions >* *Radial > Center Mark*	*DIM:, Center*	*1,Y*

The *Center* command draws a center mark on any selected *Arc* or *Circle*. As shown earlier, the *Diameter* command and the *Radius* command usually create the center marks automatically.

The command only requires you to select the desired *Circle* or *Arc* to acquire the center marks.

```
Dim: center
Select arc or circle: PICK
Dim:
```

No matter if the center mark is created by the *Center* command or by the *Diameter* or *Radius* commands, the center mark can be either a small cross or complete center lines extending past the *Circle* or *Arc*. The type of center mark drawn is controlled by the *DIMCEN* variable. (See Chapter 29 for a complete explanation of the *DIMCEN* variable.)

A positive value for *DIMCEN* draws short marks and a negative value draws complete center lines.

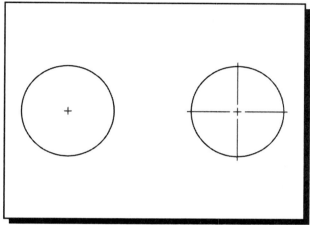

Figure 28-22

When dimensioning, short center marks should be used for *Arcs* of less than 180 degrees and full center lines should be drawn for *Circles* and for *Arcs* of 180 degrees or more.

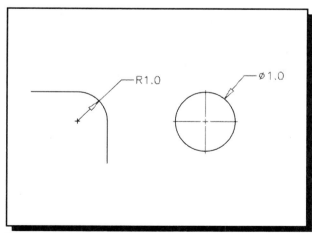

Figure 28-23

NOTE: Since the center marks created with the *Center* command are not associative, they may be *Trimmed, Erased,* or otherwise edited as shown in Figure 28-24. The center marks created with the *Radius* or *Diameter* commands are associative and cannot be edited.

The lines comprising the center marks created with *Center* can be *Erased* or otherwise edited. In the case of a 180 degree *Arc*, two center mark lines can be shortened using *Break* and one line can be *Erased* to achieve center lines as shown in Figure 28-24.

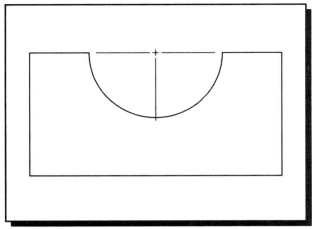

Figure 28-24

ANGULAR

TYPE IN:	PULL-DOWN MENU	SCREEN MENU	TABLET MENU
ANG	*Draw, Dimensions > Angular*	*DIM:, Angular*	*4,Y*

The *Angular* command provides many possible methods of creating an angular dimension.

A typical angular dimension is created between two *Lines* that form an angle (of other than 90 degrees). The dimension line for an *Angular* dimension is radiused with its center at the vertex of the angle (Figure 28-25). An *Angular* dimension automatically adds the degree symbol (°) to the dimension text. The dimension text format is controlled by the current settings for *Angles*, *Precision* (*Units Control...*), and *Text Style* settings.

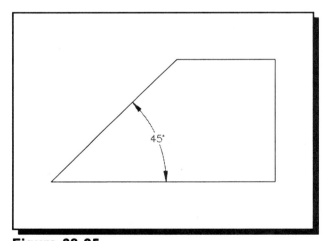

Figure 28-25

AutoCAD automates the process of creating this type of dimension by offering options within the command syntax. The default options create a dimension as shown here.

```
Dim: ang
Select arc, circle, line, or RETURN: PICK the first line.
Second line: PICK the second line.
Dimension arc line location (Text/Angle): PICK (the desired
location of the radiused dimension line).
Dimension text <45>: Enter
Enter text location (or RETURN): Enter
```

As with many other dimensioning commands, any other desired text can be entered in response to the `Dimension text <value>:` prompt. User-supplied text is static and is not automatically updated if the associative dimension is edited.

In addition, the text can be rotated or user-supplied text can be previewed by typing *T* or *A* in response to the `Dimension arc line location (Text/Angle):` prompt. The altered text appears when you dynamically select the dimension arc line location.

Angular dimensioning offers some very useful and easy-to-use options for placing the desired dimension line and text location.

At the `Dimension arc line location (Text/Angle):` prompt, you can move the cursor around the vertex to dynamically display possible placements available for the dimension. The dimension can be placed in any of four positions as well as any distance from the vertex (Figure 28-26). Extension lines are automatically created as needed.

When the dimension arc line location is positioned, you can select any location for the dimension text when presented with the `Enter text location (or RETURN):` prompt. Pressing **Enter** positions the text at the midpoint of the dimension arc.

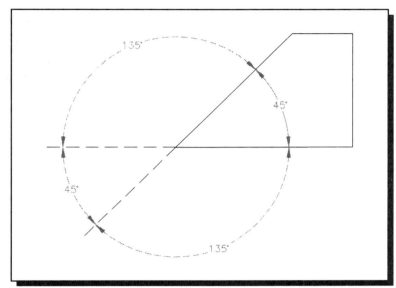

Figure 28-26

The *Angular* command offers other options including dimensioning angles for *Arcs*, *Circles*, or allowing selection of any three points.

If you select an *Arc* in response to the `Select arc, circle, line or RETURN:` prompt, AutoCAD uses the *Arc's* center as the vertex and the *Arc* endpoints to generate the extension lines. You can select either angle of the *Arc* to dimension (Figure 28-27).

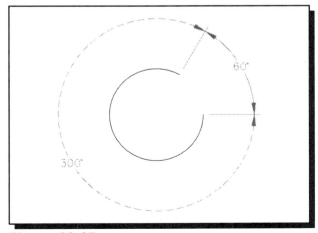

Figure 28-27

If you select a *Circle*, AutoCAD uses the PICK point as the first extension line origin (use *QUAdrant OSNAP*). The second extension line origin does not have to be on the *Circle*, as shown in this figure.

If you press **Enter** in response to the `Select arc, circle, line or RETURN:` prompt, AutoCAD responds with the following.

> `Angle vertex:` **PICK**
> `First angle endpoint:` **PICK**
> `Second angle endpoint:` **PICK**

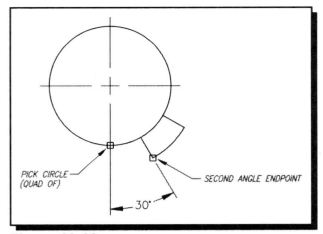

Figure 28-28

This option allows you to apply an *Angular* dimension to a variety of shapes.

LEADER

TYPE IN:	PULL-DOWN MENU	SCREEN MENU	TABLET MENU
LEA	*Draw, Dimensions > Leader*	*DIM:, Leader*	*2,X*

The *Leader* command allows you to create a leader similar to that created with the *Diameter* command. The *Leader* command is intended to be used for giving dimensional notes such as manufacturing or construction specifications such as those shown here.

> `Dim:` ***lea***
> `Leader start:` **PICK**
> `To point:` **PICK**
> `To point:` **Enter**
> `Dimension text <0>:` **CASE HARDEN**
> `Dim:`

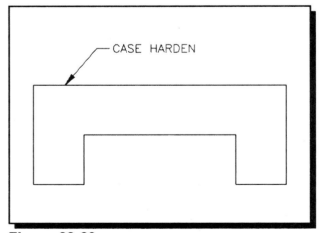

Figure 28-29

At the `Leader start:` prompt, select the desired location for the arrow. You should use *SNAP* or an *OSNAP* option (such as *NEArest*, in this case) to insure the arrow touches the desired entity.

A short horizontal line segment called the "shoulder" is automatically added to the last line segment drawn. Note that command syntax for the *Leader* in Figure 28-29 indicates only one line segment was PICKed.

A *Leader* can have as many segments as you desire. A *Leader* with 2 segments is illustrated here (Figure 28-30).

The `To point:` prompt reappears after each PICK made (similar to the *Line* command). Pressing **Enter** ends the series and causes the `Dimension text:` prompt to appear.

A *Leader*, unlike other dimension drawing commands, is <u>not</u> an associative dimension. There are no two points that are designated for AutoCAD to measure (as with a *Horiz, Vert, Radius*, or other dimensions). As a result, the default dimension text is whatever value was measured from the previous associative dimension, or <0>.

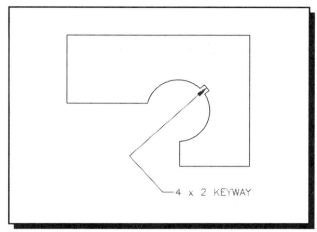

Figure 28-30

ORDINATE

TYPE IN:	PULL-DOWN MENU	SCREEN MENU	TABLET MENU
ORD	*Draw, Dimensions > Ordinate > Automatic*	*DIM: Ordinate*	*1,X*

Ordinate dimensioning is a specialized method of dimensioning used in the manufacturing of flat components such as those in the sheet metal industry. Because the thickness (depth) of the parts is uniform, only the width and height dimensions are specified as Xdatum and Ydatum dimensions.

Thus, *Ordinate* dimensions give an Xdatum or a Ydatum distance between object "features" and a reference point on the geometry treated as the origin, usually the lower left corner of the part. This method of dimensioning is relatively simple to create and easy to understand. Each dimension is composed only of one leader line and the aligned numerical value.

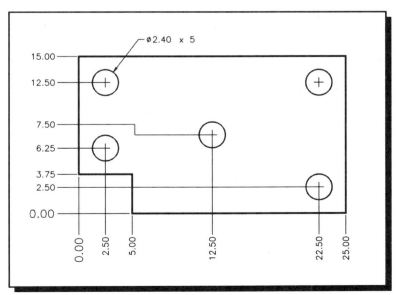

Figure 28-31

To create *Ordinate* dimensions in AutoCAD, the *UCS* command should be used first to establish a new 0,0 point. *UCS*, which stands for User Coordinate System, allows you to establish a new coordinate system with the origin and the orientation of the axes anywhere in 3D space (see Chapters 33 and 36 for complete details). In this case, we need only to change the location of the origin and leave the orientation of the axes as is. Type **UCS** and use the **Origin** option to PICK a new origin as shown.

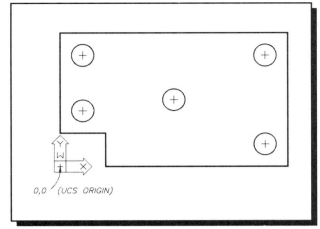

Figure 28-32

When you create an *Ordinate* dimension, AutoCAD only requires you to (1) PICK the object feature and then (2) specify the other end of the leader line. The dimension text is automatically aligned with the leader line.

It is not necessary in most cases to indicate whether you are creating an Xdatum or a Ydatum. Using the default (*Automatic*) option of *Ordinate*, AutoCAD makes the determination based on the direction of the leader you specify (step 2). If the leader is <u>more perpendicular</u> to the X axis than the Y, an Xdatum is created. If the leader is <u>more perpendicular</u> to the Y axis than the X, a Ydatum is created. The command syntax for an *Automatic Ordinate* dimension is this.

```
Dim: ord
Select Feature: PICK
Leader endpoint (Xdatum/Ydatum): PICK
Dimension text <6.25>: Enter
Dim:
```

An *Ordinate* dimension is created in Figure 28-33 by PICKing the object feature and the leader endpoint. That's all there is to it. The dimension is a Ydatum, yet AutoCAD automatically makes that determination since the leader is perpendicular to the Y axis.

It is a good practice to turn *ORTHO ON* in order to insure the leader lines are drawn horizontally or vertically.

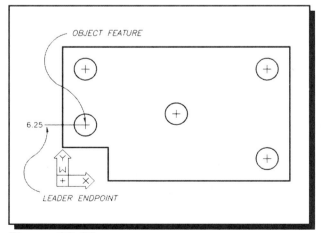

Figure 28-33

An Xdatum *Ordinate* dimension is created in the same manner. Just PICK the object feature and the other end of the leader line (Figure 28-34). The leader is perpendicular to the X axis, therefore an Xdatum dimension is created.

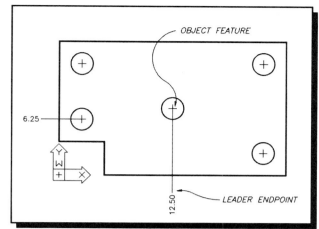

Figure 28-34

The leader line does not have to be purely horizontal or vertical. In some cases, where the dimension text may be crowded, it is desirable to select that end of the leader so that sufficient room is provided for the dimension text. In other words, draw the leader line at an angle. (*ORTHO* must be turned *Off* to specify an offset leader line.) AutoCAD automatically creates an offset in the leader as shown in the 7.50 Ydatum dimension in Figure 28-35. As long as the leader is more perpendicular to the X axis, an X datum is drawn, and vice versa.

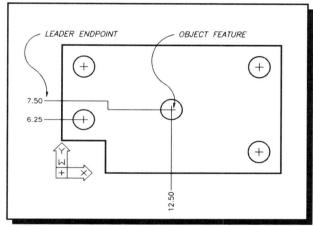

Figure 28-35

The *Xdatum* or *Ydatum* options are used to specify one of these dimensions explicitly. This is necessary in case the leader line that you specify is <u>not</u> more perpendicular to the axis you wish to measure along. The command syntax would be as follows.

```
Dim: ord
Select Feature: PICK
Leader endpoint (Xdatum/Ydatum): X
Leader endpoint: PICK
Dimension text <12.50>: Enter
Dim:
```

Customizing Dimensioning Text

You can specify dimensioning text other than what AutoCAD measures and supplies as the default text during the `Dimension text <xxx.xx>:` prompt. You can change the numerical value and/or add prefixes and suffixes. Changing the numerical value results in static text which does <u>not</u> update when the associative dimension is modified (by *Stretching*, *Scaling*, etc. the geometry).

For example, if you change the dimension text at the following prompt:

```
Dimension text <10.000>: 9.00
```

the resulting dimension displays the "9.00" even if the geometry is later modified. However, the *Newtext* command can be used to restore the measured text.

You can add prefixes and suffixes by using the <> symbols to designate placement of the default text at the `Dimension Text <xxx.xx>:` prompt. For example, if you want the dimension to read "Maximum 10.000 Drill," enter the following.

```
Dimension text <10.000>: Maximum <> Drill
```

(Remember to include spaces on each side of the "<>.") The numerical value can be automatically updated if the dimension is modified and the suffix and prefix are retained.

You can also enter special characters by using the "%%" symbols and a letter to designate the character desired. The following codes can be entered in response to the `Dimension Text <xxx.xx>:` prompt.

Code	Resulting text	Description
%%c	ø	diameter (metric)
%%d	°	degrees
%%o	‾‾‾	(overscored text, required on each end of text within a string)
%%u	___	(underscored text, use on each end)
%%p	±	plus or minus
%%nnn	varies	ASCII character number

For example, to specify a note on a *Leader* reading "HEAT TREAT TO 1450°," enter:

```
Dimension text <10.000>: HEAT TREAT TO 1450%%d
```

EDITING DIMENSIONS

Associative Dimensions

AutoCAD creates associative dimensions by default. Associative dimensions contain "definition points" that define points in the dimensions such as extension line origins, placement of dimension line, the selected points of *Circles* and *Arcs*, and the centers of those *Circles* and *Arcs*. If the geometry is modified by certain editing commands (more specifically, if the definition points are changed), the dimension components including the numerical value automatically update. When you create the first associative dimension, AutoCAD automatically creates a new layer called DEFPOINTS that contains all the definition points. The layer should be kept in a *Frozen* state. If you alter the points on this layer, existing dimensions lose their associativity and you eliminate the possibility of automatic editing.

All of the dimensioning commands are associative by default (except *Leader*) and the resulting dimensions would be affected by the editing commands listed below. The *DIMASO* variable can be changed to make the new dimensions <u>unassociative</u> if you desire (see Chapter 29). The commands that affect associative dimensions are:

> *Extend, Mirror, Rotate, Scale, Stretch, Trim* (linear dimensions only), *Array* (if rotated in a *Polar* array), grip editing options

These commands cause the changed dimension to adjust to the changed angle or length and automatically update to the current *Units* settings, *Text Style*, and dimension variable settings.

For example, if *Scale* were used to increase the size of some geometry, the attached associative dimensions would automatically adapt. The dimensions (definition points, specifically) <u>must be included</u> in the selection set to be affected by the editing command.

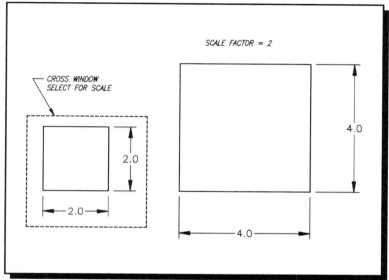

Figure 28-36

If you use *Stretch* to change some geometry with associative dimensions, the numerical values and extension lines automatically update as the related geometry changes. Remember to use a <u>crossing window</u> for selection and to include the extension line <u>origin</u> (definition point) in the selection set.

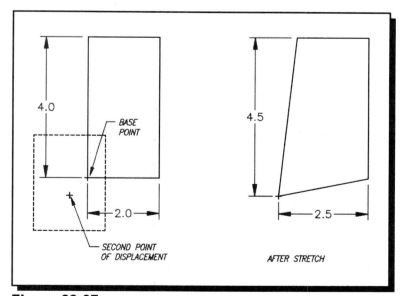

Figure 28-37

Trim and *Extend* can also be used with associative dimensions. However, the `cutting edge` or `boundary edge` should be perpendicular to the imaginary line between the extension line origin points. As long as orthogonal lines and dimensions are used, no problems occur. Otherwise, the action can produce undesirable results. *Stretch* can be used as an alternative in these cases.
In Figure 28-38, the *Horizontal* dimension and *Line* are selected for trimming.

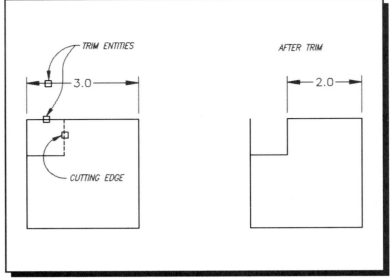

Figure 28-38

Grip Editing Dimensions

Grips can be used effectively for editing dimensions. Any of the grip options (`Stretch`, `Move`, `Rotate`, `Scale` and `Mirror`) are applicable. Depending upon the type of dimension (linear, radial, angular, etc.) grips appear at several locations on the dimension when you activate the grips by selecting the dimension at the `Command:` prompt. Associative dimensions offer the most powerful editing possibilities, although non-associative dimension components can also be edited with grips. There are many ways in which the grips can be used to alter the measured value and configuration of dimensions. Some possibilities are discussed and illustrated here.

Figure 28-39 shows the grips for each type of associative dimension. Linear dimensions (*Horizontal, Vertical, Aligned,* and *Rotated*) and *Angular* dimensions have grips at each extension line origin, the dimension line position, and a grip at the text. A *Diameter* dimension has grips defining two points on the diameter as well as one defining the leader length. The *Radius* dimension has center and radius grips as well as a leader grip.

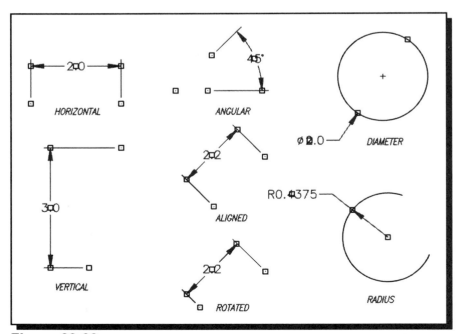

Figure 28-39

With dimension grips, a wide variety of editing options are possible. Any of the grips can be PICKed to make them **hot** grips. All grip options are valid methods for editing dimensions.

For example, a _Horizontal_ dimension value can be increased by stretching an extension line origin grip in a horizontal direction. A vertical direction movement changes the length of the extension line. The dimension line placement is changed by stretching its grips. The dimension text can be stretched to any position.

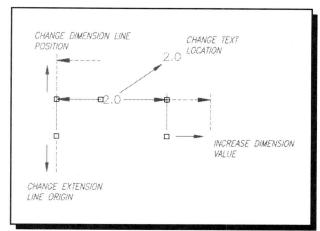

Figure 28-40

An _Angular_ dimension can be increased by stretching the extension line origin grip. The numerical value automatically updates.

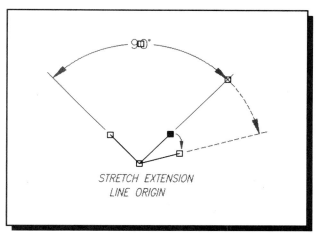

Figure 28-41

Stretching a _Rotated_ dimension's extension line origin allows changing the length of the dimension as well as the length of the extension line. An _Aligned_ dimension's extension line origin grip also allows you to change the aligned angle of the dimension.

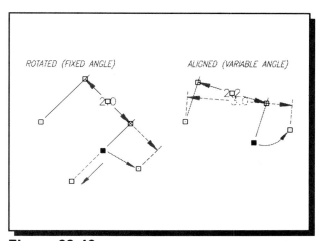

Figure 28-42

Rotating the center grip of a *Radius* dimension (with the ROTATE option) allows you to reposition the location of the dimension around the *Arc*. Note that the text remains in its original horizontal orientation.

Many other possibilities exist for editing dimensions using grips. Experiment on your own to discover some of the possibilities that are not shown here.

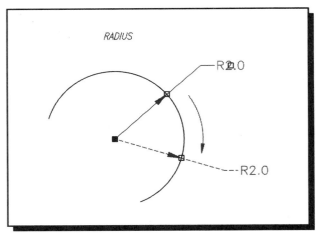

Figure 28-43

Exploding Associative Dimensions

Associative dimensions can also be edited using *Explode*. Associative dimensions are treated as one entity. If *Erase* is used with an associative dimension, the entire dimension (dimension line, extension lines, arrows and text) are selected and *Erased*.

Since a *Leader* is not an associative dimension, it is composed of individual entities (arrow, line segments, and text); whereas, an associative dimension is treated as one entity. This fact is evident when a dimension and a *Leader* are selected for editing.

Explode can be used to break an associative dimension into its component parts. The individual components can then be edited. For example, after *Exploding*, an extension line can be *Erased* or text can be *Moved*.

There are two main drawbacks to *Exploding* associative dimensions. First, the associative property is lost. Editing commands or *Grips* cannot be used to change the entire dimension but affect only the component entities. Secondly, the dimension is *Exploded* onto Layer 0 and loses its *color* and *linetype* properties. This can include additional work to reestablish the desired layer, *color*, and *linetype*. An alternative to *Exploding* is to use the XPLODE.LSP program available in the SAMPLE directory. This AutoLISP program allows you to reestablish the original layer, *color*, and *linetype*. (See the Release 12 AutoCAD Extras Manual.)

Dimension Editing Commands

Several commands are provided to facilitate easy editing of existing dimensions in a drawing. Most of these commands are intended to allow variations in the appearance of dimension <u>text</u>. These editing commands operate <u>only</u> with <u>associative</u> dimensions.

Since these commands edit existing dimensions, they are located in the *Modify* pull-down menu. The screen and tablet menus locate these commands with the other dimension (creation) commands.

TEDIT

TYPE IN:	PULL-DOWN MENU	SCREEN MENU	TABLET MENU
TEDIT	*Modify, Edit Dimension> Dimension Text > Move Text*	*DIM:, Edit, Tedit*	*5,V*

Tedit (text edit) allows you to change the position or orientation of the text for a single associative dimension. To move the position of text, this command syntax is used.

```
Dim: tedit
Select dimension: PICK
Enter text location (Left/Right/Home/Angle): PICK
```

At the Enter text location prompt, drag the text to the desired location. AutoCAD corrects the break in the dimension line to adapt to the new text location. The selected text can be changed to any position, while the text retains its associativity.

The text can be restored to its original (default) position or rotation angle with the *Home* option. The *Home* option is identical to the effect of the *Hometext* command.

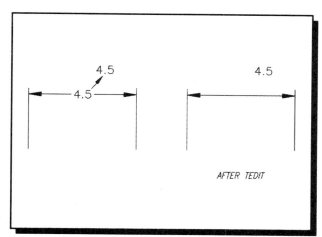

Figure 28-44

The **Angle** option works with any *Horizontal, Vertical, Aligned, Rotated, Radius*, or *Diameter* dimensions. You are prompted for the new text angle.

```
Dim: tedit
Select dimension: PICK
Enter text location
(Left/Right/Home/Angle): a
Enter text angle: 45
Dim:
```

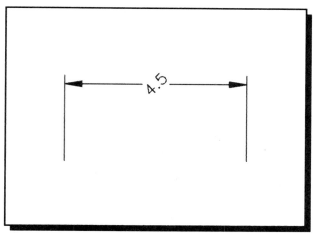

Figure 28-45

The **Right** and **Left** options automatically justify the dimension text at the extreme right and left ends, respectively, of the dimension line. The arrow and a short section of the dimension line, however, remain between the text and closest extension line.

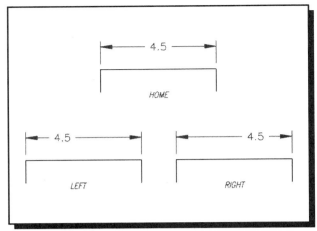

Figure 28-46

TROTATE

TYPE IN:	PULL-DOWN MENU	SCREEN MENU	TABLET MENU
TROTATE	_Modify, Edit Dimension> Dimension Text > Rotate Text_	_DIM:, Edit, TRotate_	_6,V_

TRotate rotates the dimension text to the angle you specify. This command is identical to the _Rotate_ option of _Tedit_ (see Figure 28-45). If you prefer typing, _TR_ can be entered to invoke the _TRotate_ command.

```
Dim: tr
Enter text angle: 45
Select objects: PICK
Select objects: Enter
Dim:
```

NEWTEXT

TYPE IN:	PULL-DOWN MENU	SCREEN MENU	TABLET MENU
NEWTEXT	_Modify, Edit Dimension> Dimension Text_	_DIM:, Edit, Newtext_	---

Newtext is the command to use if you wish to change the dimension text string. Any alphanumeric characters can be used. AutoCAD replaces the existing text of the dimension with the new text specified.

```
Dim: newtext
Enter new dimension text: 5.0
Select objects: PICK
Select objects: Enter
Dim:
```

NOTE: If you enter a null response (press **Enter**) to the `Enter new dimension text:` prompt, AutoCAD restores the default text (the actual dimension measurement). A prefix and/or suffix can be added to the text using the <> symbols (see Customizing Dimensioning Text in this chapter).

HOMETEXT

TYPE IN:	PULL-DOWN MENU	SCREEN MENU	TABLET MENU
HOMETEXT	*Modify, Edit Dimension> Dimension Text > Home Position*	*DIM:, Edit, Hometext*	*4,V*

Hometext restores the text of an associative dimension to its original position if it has been moved or rotated. *Hometext* does not restore the text characters if they have been changed from the default. *Newtext* can be used to change the characters.

OBLIQUE

TYPE IN:	PULL-DOWN MENU	SCREEN MENU	TABLET MENU
OBLIQUE	*Modify, Edit Dimension> Oblique Dimension*	*DIM:, Edit, Oblique*	*4,W*

The *Oblique* command affects the angle of the extension lines for <u>existing</u> dimensions. Since the default extension lines for linear dimensions are normally perpendicular to the direction of the dimension line, it is desirable in some situations to set an oblique angle for the extension lines. Using *Oblique* can be helpful when dimensions are crowded and hard to read as in Figure 28-47.

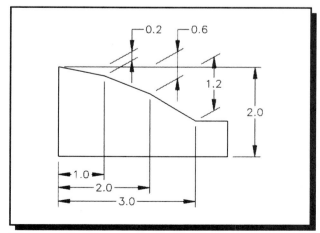

Figure 28-47

453

To use *Oblique*, PICK the existing dimension and enter the obliquing angle.

```
Dim: oblique
Select objects: PICK
Select objects: Enter
Enter obliquing angle (RETURN for none): 30
```

Pressing **Enter** at the Enter obliquing angle (RETURN for none): prompt restores a previously obliqued dimension to its default position. Oblique dimensions are used for dimensioning isometric or other pictorial drawings. See Dimensioning Isometric Drawings.

UPDATE

TYPE IN:	PULL-DOWN MENU	SCREEN MENU	TABLET MENU
UPDATE	*Modify, Edit Dimension> Update Dimension*	*DIM:, Edit, Update*	*3,W*

This command is used to *Update* the selected existing dimension(s) with the <u>current</u> *Units* setting, *Text Style*, and dimension variables settings. If Dimension Styles are used in the drawing, the selected dimension acquires the dimension variable settings of the current Dimension Style. This command is discussed in Chapter 29, Dimensioning Variables and Dimension Styles.

DIMENSIONING ISOMETRIC DRAWINGS

Dimensioning Isometric drawings in AutoCAD is accomplished using *Aligned* dimensions and then adjusting the angle of the extension lines with *Oblique*. The technique follows two basic steps.

1. Use *Aligned* or *Vertical* to place a dimension along one edge of the isometric face. Isometric dimensions should be drawn on the isometric axes lines (vertical or at a 30° increment).

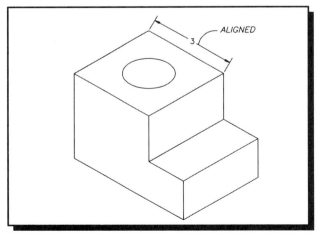

Figure 28-48

2. Use the *Oblique* dimensioning option and select the dimension just created. When prompted to `Enter obliquing angle`, enter the desired value (**30** in this case) or PICK two points designating the desired angle. The extension lines should change to the designated angle. In AutoCAD, the possible obliquing angles for isometric dimensions are **30**, **150**, **210**, or **330**.

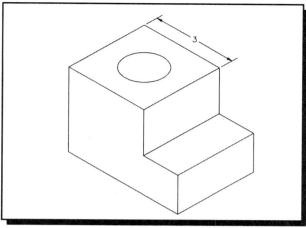

Figure 28-49

Place isometric dimensions so that they align with the face of the particular feature. <u>Unidirectional</u> dimensioning (all values read from the bottom) is preferred since there is no provision for drawing the numerical values in an isometric plane automatically. However, three text *Styles* could be created with the correct obliquing angles, one for each isoplane.

Dimensioning the object in the previous illustrations would continue as follows.

Create a *Vertical* dimension along a vertical edge.

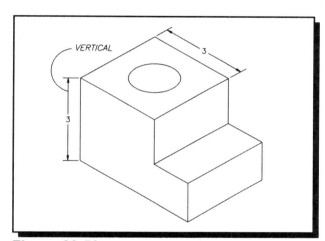

Figure 28-50

Use *Oblique* to force the dimension to an isometric axis orientation. Enter a value of **150** or PICK two points in response to the `Enter obliquing angle` prompt.

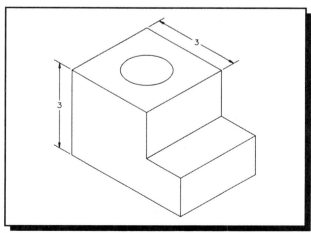

Figure 28-51

For isometric dimensioning, the extension line origin points <u>must</u> be aligned with the isometric axes. If not, the dimension is not properly oriented. This is important when dimensioning an isometric ellipse (such as this case) or an inclined or oblique edge. One solution to insure that the extension line origins are aligned with the isometric axes is to extend a *Line* (a center *Line* in this case) to *OSNAP* the extension line origin to.

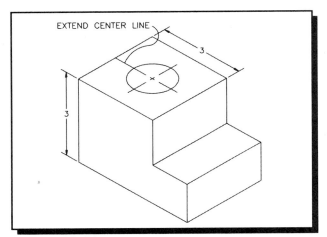

Figure 28-52

After the center line extension has been made, the *Aligned* dimension is correctly oriented. Use *Oblique* to reorient the angle of the extension lines.

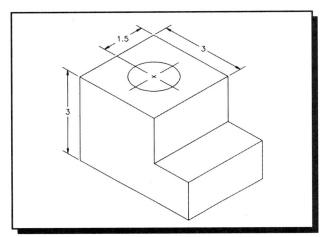

Figure 28-53

Using the same technique, other appropriate *Vertical* or *Aligned* dimensions are placed and reoriented with *Oblique*. Use a *Leader* to dimension a diameter of an *Isocircle* since *Diameter* cannot be used for an ellipse.

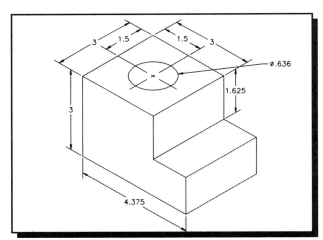

Figure 28-54

CHAPTER EXERCISES

Only four exercises are offered in this chapter to give you a start with the dimensioning commands. Many other dimensioning exercises are given at the end of Chapter 29, Dimensioning Variables and Dimension Styles. Since most dimensioning practices in AutoCAD require the use of dimensioning variables and dimension styles, that information should be discussed before you can begin dimensioning effectively.

1.   *Open* the **PLATES** drawing that you created in Chapter 10 Exercises. *Erase* the plate on the right. Use *Move* to move the remaining two plates apart allowing 5 units between. Create a *New* layer called **DIM** and make it *Current*. Create a *Text Style* using *Roman Simplex* font. Set *Units* to *Decimal* with **0.00** *Precision*. Dimension the two plates as shown in Figure 28-55. *Save* the drawing as **PLATES-D**.

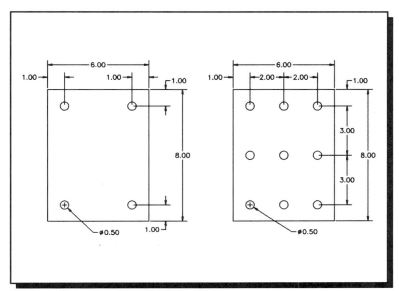

Figure 28-55

2.   *Open* the **CH16EX7** drawing. Create a *New* layer called **DIM** and make it *Current*. Create a *Text Style* using *Roman Simplex* font. Set *Units* to *Fractional* with **1/32** *Precision*. Dimension the part as shown in Figure 28-56. *Save* the drawing as **CH28EX2**. Draw a *Pline* border of **.02** *width* and *Insert* **TBLOCK**. *Plot* on an A size sheet using *Scale to Fit*.

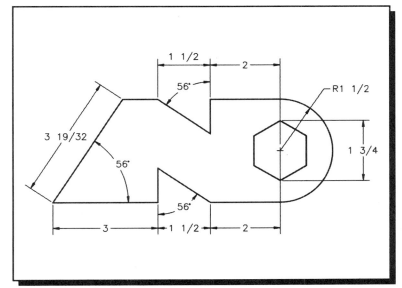

Figure 28-56

3. ***Open*** the **GASKETA** drawing that you created in Chapter 9 Exercises. Create a ***New*** layer called **DIM** and make it ***Current***. Create a ***Text Style*** using ***Roman Simplex*** font. Set ***Units*** to ***Fractional*** with **1/4 *Precision***. Dimension the part as shown in Figure 28-57. ***Save*** the drawing as **GASKETD**. NOTE: The *Radius* dimensions will point inward toward the center by default. You can dynamically drag the leader inside, or adjust it after reading Chapter 29.

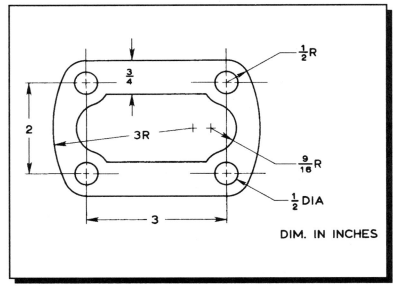

Figure 28-57

Draw a ***Pline*** border with **.02 *width*** and ***Insert*** **TBLOCK** with an **8/11** scale factor. ***Plot*** the drawing ***Scaled to Fit*** on an A size sheet.

4. ***Open*** the **BARGUIDE** multiview drawing that you created in Chapter 24 Exercises. Create the dimensions on the **DIM** layer using the ***Units*** and ***Precision*** as shown in Figure 28-58. Keep in mind that you have more possibilities for placement of dimensions than are shown in the pictorial. NOTE: The 3/4 *Radius* dimension will point inward toward the center by default. You can drag the leader inside or adjust it after reading Chapter 29. ***Save*** the drawing as **BARGD-DM**.

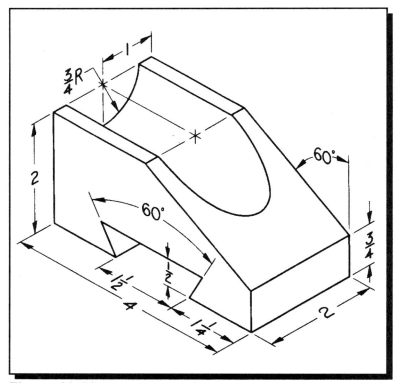

Figure 28-58

```
┌─────────────────────────────────────────────────────────────┐
│         Dimension Styles and Variables                       │
│  Dimension Styles          Dimension Variables               │
│  ┌──────────────────────┐  ┌─────────────────────────────┐   │
│  │*UNNAMED            │▓│  │   ┌───────────────────────┐ │   │
│  │                    │ │  │   │   Dimension Line...   │ │   │
│  │                    │ │  │   └───────────────────────┘ │   │
│  │                    │ │  │   ┌───────────────────────┐ │   │
│  │                    │ │  │   │   Extension Lines...  │ │   │
│  │                    │ │  │   └───────────────────────┘ │   │
│  │                    │ │  │   ┌───────────────────────┐ │   │
│  │                    │ │  │   │      Arrows...        │ │   │
│  │                    │ │  │   └───────────────────────┘ │   │
│  │                    │ │  │   ┌───────────────────────┐ │   │
│  │                    │ │  │   │   Text Location...    │ │   │
│  │                    │ │  │   └───────────────────────┘ │   │
│  │                    │ │  │   ┌───────────────────────┐ │   │
│  │                    │ │  │   │   Text Format...      │ │   │
│  │                    │ │  │   └───────────────────────┘ │   │
│  │                    │ │  │   ┌───────────────────────┐ │   │
│  │                    │ │  │   │     Features...       │ │   │
│  │                    │▓│  │   └───────────────────────┘ │   │
│  └──────────────────────┘  │   ┌───────────────────────┐ │   │
│                            │   │      Colors...        │ │   │
│  Dimension Style:          │   └───────────────────────┘ │   │
│  ┌──────────────────────────────────────────────────────┐   │
│  │                                                      │   │
│  └──────────────────────────────────────────────────────┘   │
│       ┌──────────┐   ┌──────────┐   ┌──────────┐             │
│       │    OK    │   │  Cancel  │   │  Help... │             │
│       └──────────┘   └──────────┘   └──────────┘             │
└─────────────────────────────────────────────────────────────┘
```

CHAPTER 29

Dimensioning Variables and Dimension Styles

CHAPTER OBJECTIVES

After completing this chapter you should:

1. understand the function of each dimensioning variable;

2. be able to use this chapter as reference to find dimension variable names, default settings, and application settings;

3. be able to control dimension variable settings at the Dim: prompt;

4. be able to control dimension variable settings using the *Dimension Styles and Variables* dialogue box;

5. be able to create and use Dimension Styles for particular applications;

6. be able to make final adjustments to dimensions using *Dimstyles*, *Update*, and *Override*;

7. know the guidelines for dimensioning.

BASICS

Since a large part of AutoCAD's dimensioning capabilities are automatic, some method must be provided for you to control the way dimensions are drawn. A set of <u>dimensioning variables</u> allows you to affect the way dimensions are drawn by controlling on/off switches, scales, distances, extension and dimension line parameters, and dimension text formats.

Changes to dimensioning variables do <u>not</u> affect the <u>existing</u> dimensions. Changes to dimensioning variables only affect <u>newly created</u> dimensions. The variables are <u>not</u> <u>retroactive</u> like *Ltscale*, which can be continually modified to adjust the spacing of existing non-continuous lines. Generally, dimensioning variables should be set <u>before</u> creating the desired dimensions. (The *Update* command, however, allows you to update existing dimensions with the current variable settings.)

There are two basic ways to control dimensioning variables:

1.   using the command line format;
2.   using the *Dimension Styles and Variables* dialogue box series.

The command line format uses the dimensioning variable names while the dialogue box uses a different, more "user friendly" terminology and selection.

There is an advantage to learning the dimensioning variable names even though it may be more "user-friendly" to use dialogue boxes. The dimensioning variable <u>names</u> remain constant throughout the development of new releases of AutoCAD; whereas, the dialogue boxes (or other graphic interface devices) have a history of changing with new releases. Therefore, exposure to the dimension variables by name is treated first in this chapter.

If you use many dimensioning variables in one drawing or use the same variable settings in different drawings, it is desirable to save and use <u>Dimension Styles</u>. A Dimension Style is a group of dimensioning variable <u>settings</u> that has been saved under a name you assign.

In this chapter the dimensioning variables are explained first. Secondly, changing variables using the *Dimension Styles and Variables* dialogue box series are discussed. Lastly, creation and use of dimensioning styles are covered.

STATUS

TYPE IN:	PULL-DOWN MENU	SCREEN MENU	TABLET MENU
STATUS	---	---	*3,V*

This utility command is provided for you to list the current settings, or status, of all of the dimensioning variables. If you are typing, *Status* must be entered at the `Dim:` prompt rather than the `Command:` prompt. The following list is printed to the screen. In <u>this</u> example, *Status* shows the default settings (no variables have been changed from the default position or value).

```
Dim: status

DIMALT     Off         Alternate units selected
DIMALTD    2           Alternate unit decimal places
DIMALTF    25.4000     Alternate unit scale factor
DIMAPOST               Suffix for alternate text
DIMASO     On          Create associative dimensions
DIMASZ     0.1800      Arrow size
DIMBLK                 Arrow block name
DIMBLK1                First arrow block name
DIMBLK2                Second arrow block name
DIMCEN     0.0900      Center mark size
DIMCLRD    BYBLOCK     Dimension line color
DIMCLRE    BYBLOCK     Extension line & leader color
DIMCLRT    BYBLOCK     Dimension text color
DIMDLE     0.0000      Dimension line extension
DIMDLI     0.3800      Dimension line increment for continuation
DIMEXE     0.1800      Extension above dimension line
DIMEXO     0.0625      Extension line origin offset
DIMGAP     0.0900      Gap from dimension line to text
DIMLFAC    1.0000      Linear unit scale factor
DIMLIM     Off         Generate dimension limits
DIMPOST                Default suffix for dimension text
DIMRND     0.0000      Rounding value
DIMSAH     Off         Separate arrow blocks
DIMSCALE   1.0000      Overall scale factor
DIMSE1     Off         Suppress the first extension line
DIMSE2     Off         Suppress the second extension line
DIMSHO     On          Update dimensions while dragging
DIMSOXD    Off         Suppress outside extension dimension
DIMSTYLE   *UNNAMED    Current dimension style (read-only)
DIMTAD     Off         Place text above the dimension line
DIMTFAC    1.0000      Tolerance text height scaling factor
DIMTIH     On          Text inside extensions is horizontal
DIMTIX     Off         Place text inside extensions
DIMTM      0.0000      Minus tolerance
DIMTOFL    Off         Force line inside extension lines
DIMTOH     On          Text outside extensions is horizontal
DIMTOL     Off         Generate dimension tolerances
DIMTP      0.0000      Plus tolerance
DIMTSZ     0.0000      Tick size
DIMTVP     0.0000      Text vertical position
DIMTXT     0.1800      Text height
DIMZIN     0           Zero suppression

Dim:
```

DIMENSIONING VARIABLES

(*VARIABLE NAME*)

TYPE IN:	PULL-DOWN MENU	SCREEN MENU	TABLET MENU
(variable name)	*Settings, Dimension Styles..*	*DIM:, Dim Vars, (variable name)*	*1,V or 2,V*

There are two fundamentally different methods for controlling dimensioning variables--command line format or dialogue boxes. Typing or the using screen menus results in a command line format, while the pull down menu and the tablet menu access the dialogue boxes. The dialogue box can also be invoked by typing *DDIM*.

There is a noticeable difference in the two methods--the *Dimension Styles and Variables* dialogue box uses a <u>different nomenclature</u> than the actual dimensioning variable names used in command line format. That is, the dialogue boxes use descriptive terms that, if selected, make the appropriate change to the dimensioning variable. The actual dimensioning variable names, however, all begin with the letters *DIM*, are limited to eight characters, and can be accessed <u>directly</u> by typing or selection from the screen menu.

The following section of this chapter, Dimensioning Variables Illustrated, explains and illustrates the dimensioning variables by their formal <u>names</u>. In order to access and change a variable's setting by name, simply type the variable name at the Dim: prompt or select it from the screen menu under *DIM:*, then *Dim Vars*. For dimension variables that require distances, you can enter the distance (in any format accepted by the current *Units* settings) or you can designate (PICKing) two points.

For example, to change the value of the *DIMSCALE* to **.5**, this command syntax is used.

```
Dim: dimscale
Current value <1.0000> New value: .5
Dim:
```

Dimensioning Variables Illustrated

This section explains each of the dimensioning variables. An illustration showing the effect of the variable settings accompanies each variable. The dimensioning variables are listed in alphabetical order beginning on the next page.

DIMALT (Alternate Units)

If *On*, enables alternate units dimensioning. The alternate units are displayed next to the primary units in brackets [ ]. Millimeters are the default alternate units. See also *DIMALTF*, *DIMAPOST*, and *DIMALTD*.

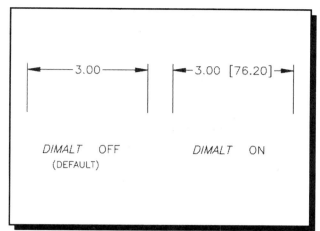

Figure 29-1

DIMALTD (Alternate Unit Decimal Places)

DIMALTD controls the number of decimal places displayed in the alternate measurement (if the *DIMALT* variable is *On*). The number of decimal places is independent of that set in *Units*.

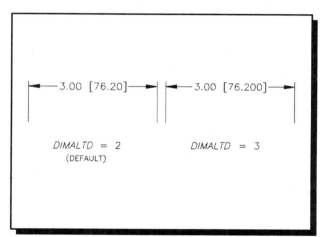

Figure 29-2

DIMALTF (Alternate Unit Scale Factor)

If the associated *DIMALT* variable is *On*, all measured linear dimensions are multiplied by this factor to produce a value in any alternate system of measurement. The default *DIMALT* value is 25.4.

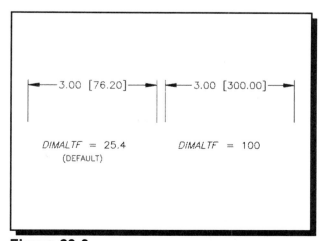

Figure 29-3

DIMAPOST (Alternate Unit Suffix)

This variable allows you to specify a character string that is displayed following an _alternate_ dimensioning value. (_DIMALT_ must be _On._) To disable the established suffix, set it to a single period (.). _DIMAPOST_ does not affect angular dimensions.

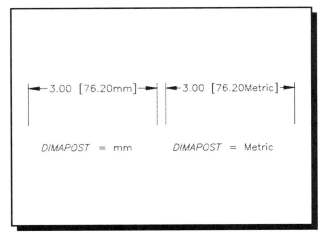

Figure 29-4

DIMASO (Associative Dimensioning)

This switch toggles creation of associative dimension entities _On_ or _Off_. When _DIMASO_ is _Off_, the dimension lines, extension lines, arrows, and text are drawn as separate entities. When it is _On_, the elements of the dimension are created as a single entity that remains associated with the geometry used to define it. The _DIMASO_ value cannot be stored in a dimension style.

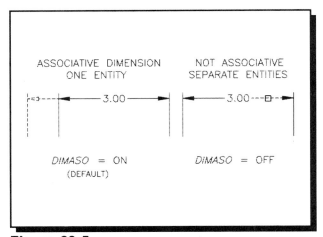

Figure 29-5

DIMASZ (Arrow Size)

This variable allows you to control the size of the dimension line arrows. (The arrow size can affect whether dimension lines and text fit between the extension lines.) If another symbol is used instead of an arrow (set by the _DIMBLK_ variable), _DIMASZ_ controls its scale. _DIMASZ_ does _not_ affect tick mark size if ticks are used instead of arrows. This variable, like other size-related variables, is automatically multiplied times _DIMSCALE_.

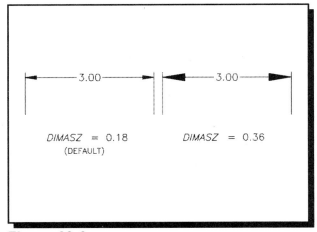

Figure 29-6

DIMBLK (Arrow Block)

By using this variable, any <u>user-made</u> *Block* can be drawn instead of the normal arrow at the ends of the dimension line. The *Block* must be <u>previously created</u> and its name specified as the *DIMBLK*. (Make the *Blocks* to be used as the *DIMBLK* one unit in size.) To disable a block name and reset the arrow, set *DIMBLK* to a single period (.).

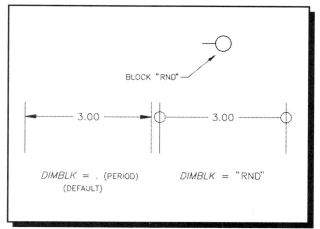

Figure 29-7

DIMBLK1, DIMBLK2 (Arrow Block 1, 2)

DIMBLK1 and *DIMBLK2* specify user-defined blocks for the first and second ends of the dimension line. (*DIMSAH* must be *On*.) These variables contain the names of previously created blocks (like that used for *DIMBLK*). To disable an established block name and reset the arrow, set it to a single period (.). First and second ends of the dimension line are determined by the PICK order.

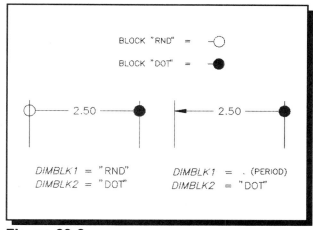

Figure 29-8

DIMCEN (Center Mark)
DIMCEN controls the center marks and center lines created by the *Center*, *Diameter* and *Radius* commands. The value entered has this effect:

0 = do not draw center mark
positive = size of short cross
negative = draw long lines, size of
       short cross

For *Radius* and *Diameter*, the center mark is drawn only if the dimension line is placed <u>outside</u> the *Circle* or *Arc*.

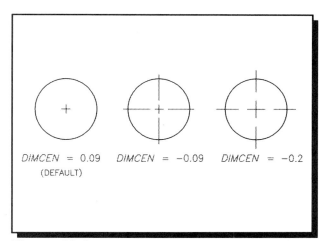

Figure 29-9

DIMCLRD (Color of Dimension Lines)

This variable allows you to assign a specific color to <u>dimension</u> lines and arrows. Use any valid color number, name, or _BYBLOCK_ or _BYLAYER_ color. Assigning a separate color lets you control the pen that is used for plotting dimension lines. For example, you may want the dimension lines to plot in a thin, thick, or special color pen.

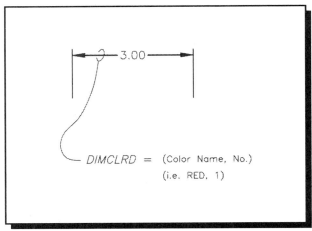

Figure 29-10

DIMCLRE (Color of Extension Lines)

This variable controls the color assigned to dimension extension lines. It can take on any valid color number or the special color labels _BYBLOCK_ or _BYLAYER_. (See the earlier description of _DIMCLRD._) Often _DIMCLRD_ and _DIMCLRE_ are set to the same color and plotted in a thin line weight pen.

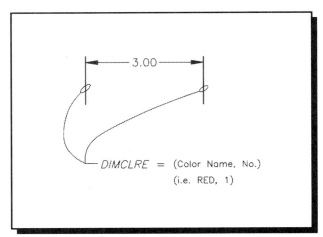

Figure 29-11

DIMCLRT (Color of Text)

DIMCLRT controls the color assigned to dimension <u>text</u>. The variable can be assigned any valid color number, name, or the special color labels _BYBLOCK_ or _BYLAYER_. (See the earlier description of _DIMCLRD_ and _DIMCLRE._) Dimension text color is often set to plot in a dark or thick pen.

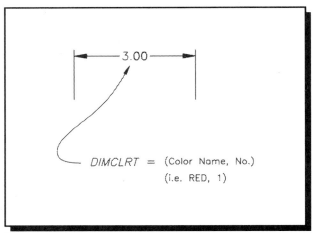

Figure 29-12

DIMDLE (Dimension Line Extension for ticks)

When tick marks are drawn instead of arrows, this value sets the distance that the <u>dimension line</u> <u>extends</u> <u>past</u> the extension line. (*DIMTSZ* must have some nonzero value for ticks to be drawn.)

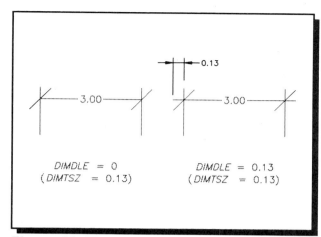

Figure 29-13

DIMDLI (Dimension Line Increment)

This variable allows you to set the distance between successive dimension lines when *Baseline* dimensions are used. The value (as well as other size-related variables) is automatically multiplied by *DIMSCALE*. The default value is .38.

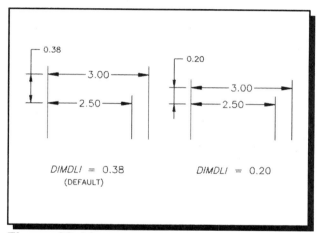

Figure 29-14

DIMEXE (Extension Line Extension)

This variable lets you specify how far the extension line should extend beyond the dimension line. The default is .18. This value is automatically multiplied times *DIMSCALE*.

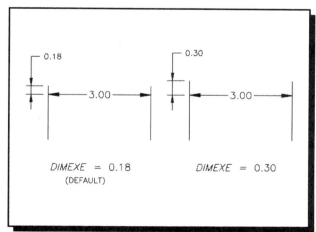

Figure 29-15

DIMEXO (Extension Line Offset)

The extension lines are offset from the object (or from the origin points you specify) by this amount. Therefore, you can PICK the corners of an object to be dimensioned but the extension lines will be offset by the value of *DIMEXO*. The default distance is .0625. This value is also automatically multiplied by *DIMSCALE*.

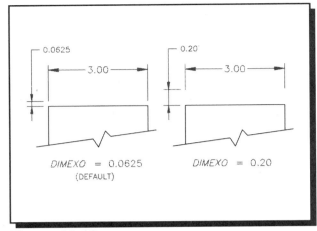

Figure 29-16

DIMGAP (Dimension Line Gap)

This is the distance maintained around the dimension text which serves to break the dimension line to accommodate the text. *DIMGAP* is like an invisible box around the text. The *DIMGAP* value is also used as the minimum length for the dimension lines; if the dimension lines are less than the *DIMGAP* value, the text or the dimension line or both may be forced outside.

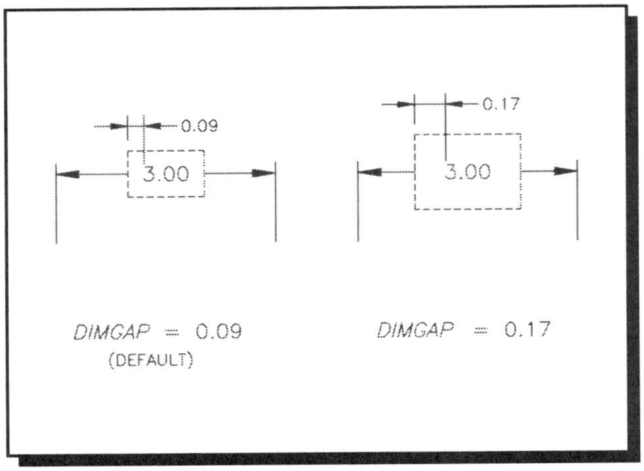

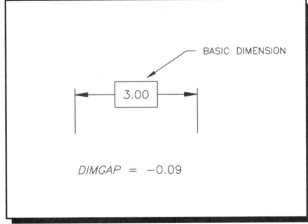

Figure 29-17

DIMGAP also allows you to create a <u>basic dimension</u> as used with limit dimensioning, geometric dimensioning, and tolerancing. A basic dimension is text with a box drawn around its full extents. This is accomplished by entering a <u>negative</u> *DIMGAP* value, which in effect makes the invisible box visible.

Figure 29-18

DIMLFAC (Length Factor)

This serves as a global scale factor for linear dimensioning measurements. All measured linear dimensions are multiplied by the value of *DIMLFAC* when AutoCAD draws the dimension text. *DIMLFAC* affects only the <u>numerical value</u> of the default text. *DIMLFAC* is useful for scaling a drawing for the purpose of making a detail. *DIMLFAC* has a special meaning when in Paper Space (See Chapter 32).

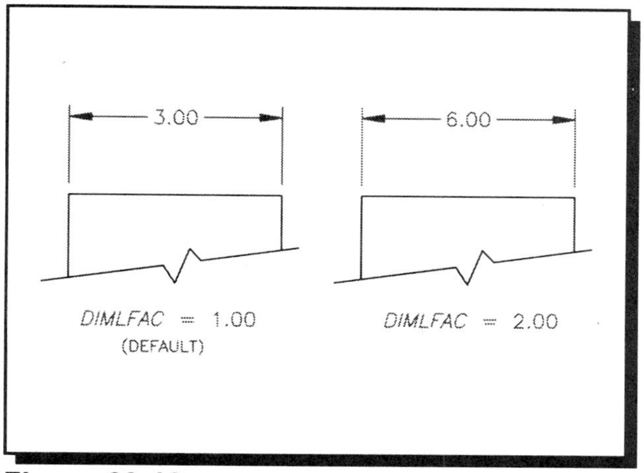

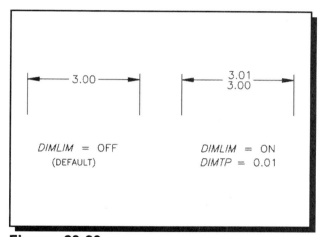

Figure 29-19

DIMLIM (Limit Dimensions)

DIMLIM toggles limit dimensions *On* or *Off*. Limit dimensions consist of an upper and a lower limit for a part to be manufactured. The upper and lower limit values are specified with *DIMTP* and *DIMTM*. If no upper and lower limits have been specified, two of the same measured dimensions appear. Setting *DIMLIM On* forces *DIMTOL* (tolerance dimensions) to be *Off*.

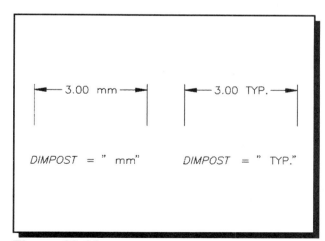

Figure 29-20

DIMPOST (Dimension Suffix)

This variable allows you to specify a <u>prefix or suffix</u> to the measured dimension value. Any letters or numbers specified for *DIMPOST* are applied to the measured dimension.

Figure 29-21

To create a <u>prefix</u> before the dimension value with *DIMPOST*, enter a prefix followed by the <> symbols. Don't forget to use a space before the <> symbols. (The <> symbols are not required for a suffix only. However, if you want both a prefix and a suffix, you must enter the <> characters). To disable a prefix or suffix, set the *DIMPOST* value to a single period (.).

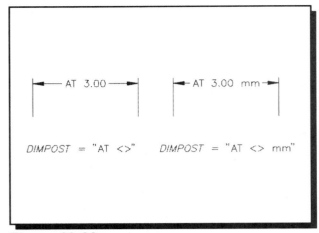

Figure 29-22

When you create a prefix with *DIMPOST*, it overrides any default prefixes such as those used in *Diameter* (ø) and *Radius* (R) dimensions. The <> symbols must be used to make a null prefix. For example, "<> DIA" would disable the "ø" and place "DIA" after the numerical value. (Don't forget the space.) This makes it easy to use the "R" or letters "DIA" <u>after</u> the dimensional value if you prefer.

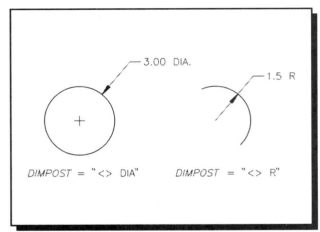

Figure 29-23

DIMRND (Rounding Value)

This variable allows you to control the increment to which all measured dimensions are rounded. For example, setting *DIMRND* to 0.25 forces all distances to be rounded to the nearest 0.25 unit. A *DIMRND* value of 0 (default) disables rounding. The number of places to the right of the decimal is controlled by *Units* and has precedence. *DIMRND* does not apply to *Angular* dimensions.

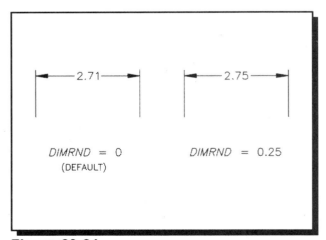

Figure 29-24

DIMSAH (Separate Arrow Heads)

DIMSAH turns *On* or *Off* the use of *DIMBLK1* and *DIMBLK2*. With *DIMSAH On*, the user-defined arrow blocks are drawn at the end(s) of the dimension line if one or both have been defined. Set *DIMSAH* to a period (.) to disable *DIMBLK1* and *DIMBLK2* and restore the arrows. *DIMSAH* has no effect on *DIMBLK*.

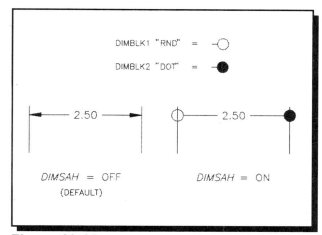

Figure 29-25

DIMSCALE (Dimensioning Scale Factor)

This is the <u>overall scale factor</u> applied to all dimensioning variables that specify sizes, distances, or offsets. The default *DIMSCALE* is 1. The factor that you specify for *DIMSCALE* is used as a <u>multiplier for all other size-related variables</u>. It is *not* applied to tolerances or to measured lengths, coordinates, or angles. To change the overall sizes of all dimensional elements proportionally, use *DIMSCALE*.

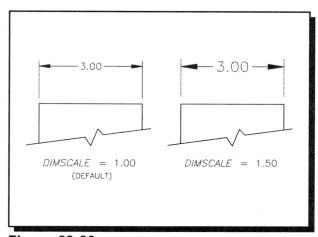

Figure 29-26

DIMSE1 (Suppress Extension Line 1)

DIMSE1 allows you to suppress (prevent drawing of) the first extension line. The first extension line is the first one PICKed. Set this variable to *On* to suppress the first extension line. The default is *Off* (suppression is *Off*). This feature is useful for preventing double extension lines (one "on top of" another) or for dimensioning to object lines, in which case extension line(s) are not needed.

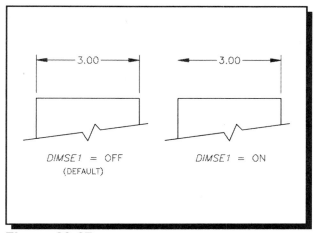

Figure 29-27

DIMSE2 (Suppress Extension Line 2)

> If *On*, suppresses drawing the second extension line PICKed. This is similar to *DIMSE1*. Setting *DIMSE1* and *DIMSE2 On* suppresses both extension lines.

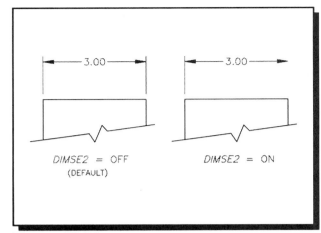

Figure 29-28

DIMSHO (Show Dragging)

> If *On*, the dimensional values of associative dimensions show as they increase or decrease dynamically while dragging (during a *Stretch* or other editing action). If *Off*, the new values do not display until after the editing action. Dynamic dragging is displayed during *Radius* and *Diameter* leader length input regardless of *DIMSHO*. *DIMSHO* is *On* by default. Turn *DIMSHO Off* for computers that are too slow to update the display while dragging. The *DIMSHO* value is not stored in a dimension style.

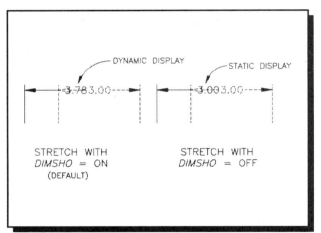

Figure 29-29

DIMSOXD (Suppress Outside Dimension Lines)

> When there is not enough room for the text and arrows, AutoCAD draws the dimension lines outside of the extension lines. *DIMSOXD* prevents AutoCAD from drawing dimension lines outside the extension lines. However, *DIMTIX* (Text Inside eXtension) <u>must also be On</u> for *DIMSOXD* to have an effect.

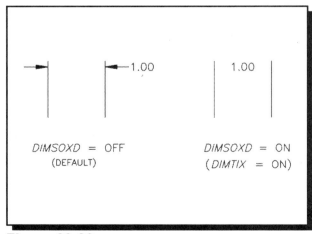

Figure 29-30

DIMSTYLE (Dimension Style)

> Returns the name of the current dimension style. (No figure.)

DIMTAD (Text Above Dimension Line)

When *DIMTAD* is *On*, the text is placed above the dimension line and a single solid dimension line is drawn beneath it. *DIMTAD* takes effect whenever dimension text is drawn between the extension lines and at the same angle as the dimension line, or when the dimension text is placed outside of the extension lines. If *DIMTAD* is *Off*, *DIMTVP* (if assigned a nonzero value) controls the text vertical placement.

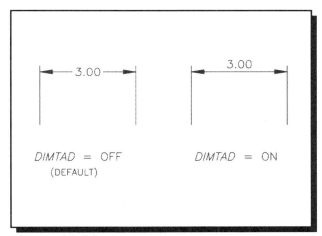

Figure 29-31

When *DIMTAD* is *On*, a single solid dimension line is drawn beneath the dimension except in the case that (1) you are creating a small dimension and (2) *DIMTOFL* is *Off*. In this case, the interior dimension line is drawn outside the extension lines. For large dimensions, the dimension line is always drawn inside, as shown in Figure 29-31.

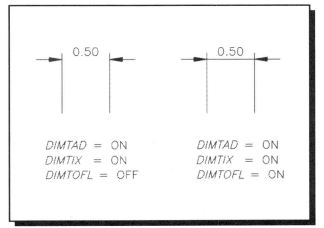

Figure 29-32

DIMTFAC (Tolerance Text Scale Factor)

DIMTFAC is the proportion of text height of tolerance values to the dimension text height. For example, if *DIMTFAC* is set to .75, the text height of tolerances is three-fourths the size of dimension text. The value of *DIMTFAC* is multiplied times the *DIMTXT* value. *DIMTFAC* is used for plus and minus tolerance strings when either *DIMTOL* or *DIMLIM* is *On*.

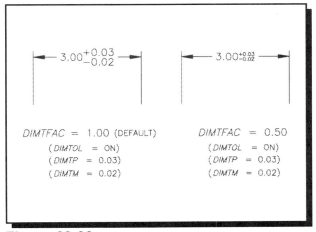

Figure 29-33

DIMTIH (Text Inside Horizontal)

If *DIMTIH* is *On*, the text is always drawn horizontally. If *Off*, the text is aligned with angle of the dimension line. *DIMTIH* affects text for all *Linear*, *Radius*, and *Diameter* dimensions where the text fits between the extension lines.

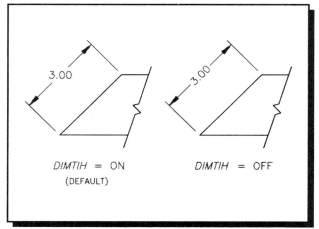

Figure 29-34

DIMTIX (Text Inside Extension Lines)

If *DIMTIX* is turned *On*, the dimension text is forced between the extension lines even when AutoCAD would normally force text outside the lines. If it is *Off* (the default), AutoCAD places the text inside the extension lines <u>only</u> if there is sufficient room for *Linear* and *Angular* dimensions. For *Radius* and *Diameter* dimensions, the text is always outside the *Circle* or *Arc* unless *DIMTIX* is *On*.

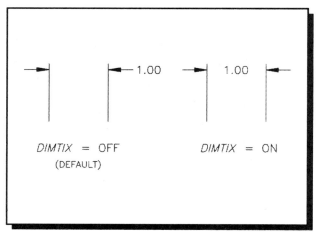

Figure 29-35

DIMTM (Tolerance Minus Value)
DIMTP (Tolerance Plus Value)

These variables hold the dimension values for tolerance or limit dimensioning (when either *DIMTOL* or *DIMLIM* is *On*). *DIMTP* specifies the <u>plus</u> tolerance and *DIMTM* specifies the <u>minus</u> tolerance. If limit dimensioning is used (*DIMLIM* is *On*), the plus tolerance is added to the measured dimension to achieve the upper limit and the minus tolerance is subtracted to achieve the lower limit. AutoCAD accepts negative or positive values for *DIMTP* and *DIMTM*.

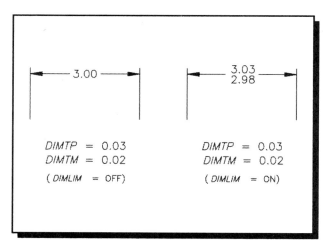

Figure 29-36

When tolerance dimensions are used (*DIMTOL* is *On*), *DIMTP* specifies the plus tolerance and *DIMTM* specifies the minus tolerance. If they are set to the same value, AutoCAD draws both + and - symbols followed by the tolerance value.

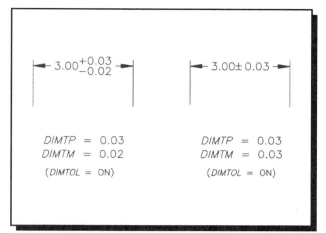

Figure 29-37

DIMTOFL (Text Outside, Force Line Inside)

When there is insufficient room for text and arrows, AutoCAD normally places the text and dimension line outside of the extension lines. If *DIMTOFL* is turned *On*, the dimension <u>line</u> is forced between the extension lines while the text remains outside the extension lines. The arrows are forced inside also if there is room. *DIMTOFL* has no effect on normal dimensions (when text and dimension lines are both inside).

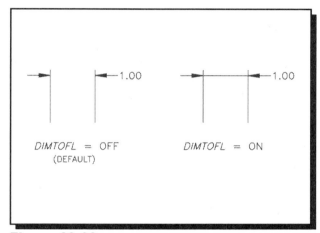

Figure 29-38

For *Radius* and *Diameter* dimensions, setting *DIMTOFL On* causes the leader line and arrowheads to be drawn inside the *Circle* or *Arc*, while the text and leader are drawn outside. *DIMTOFL On* is preferred for *Radius* dimensions. If *DIMTOFL On* is used with *DIMTIX On* (text inside extensions), both text and leaders are drawn inside.

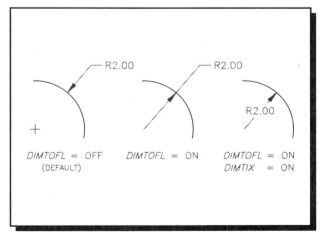

Figure 29-39

DIMTOH (Text Outside Horizontal)

Text is normally drawn horizontally, even when it is outside the extension lines because *DIMTOH* is *On* by default. Turn *DIMTOH Off* to force the text that is drawn outside to be aligned with the dimension line. *DIMTOH* works similarly to *DIMTIH* (Text Inside Horizontal) except that it controls text drawn outside the extension lines.

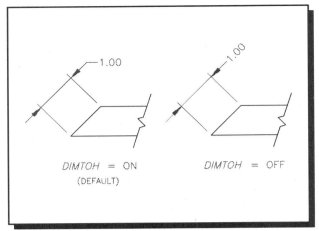

Figure 29-40

DIMTOL (Tolerance Dimensions)

DIMTOL, when turned *On*, creates dimension tolerances to appear after the measured dimension text. *DIMTOL* draws a tolerance of + or -0 unless values are entered for plus (*DIMTP*) and minus (*DIMTM*) tolerances. Setting *DIMTOL On* forces limits (*DIMLIM*) to be *Off*.

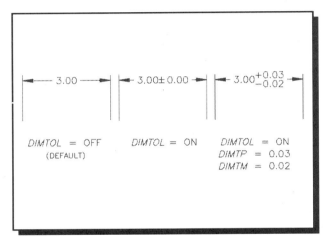

Figure 29-41

DIMTSZ (Tick Size)

This variable forces tick marks to be drawn instead of arrows and specifies the size of the ticks. The *DIMTSZ* variable holds a value. If the value is 0, arrows are drawn. If *DIMTSZ* is larger than 0, ticks are drawn. The size of the ticks are *DIMTSZ* times *DIMSCALE*. The *DIMTSZ* value (like *DIMASZ*) affects whether dimension lines and text will fit between extension lines.

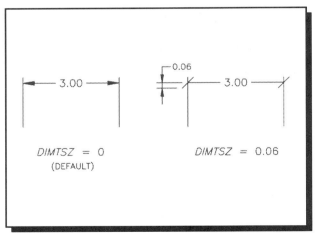

Figure 29-42

DIMTVP (Text Vertical Position)

DIMTVP allows you to specify the vertical position of the text above or below the dimension line. The value of DIMTVP is multiplied times the text height to achieve the vertical offset. For example, setting DIMTVP to .8 (or -.8) places the text .8 times the text height above (or below) the dimension line. DIMTVP must be at least .7 (or -.7) to be completely above (or below). Setting DIMTVP to 1 is the same as turning DIMTAD On. DIMTAD (text above dimension line), if On, overrides DIMTVP.

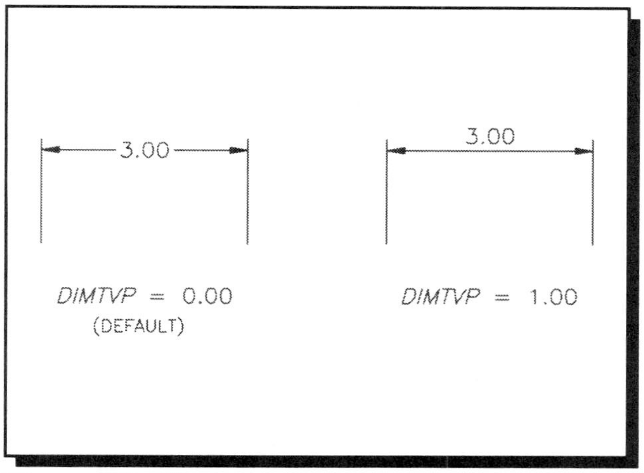

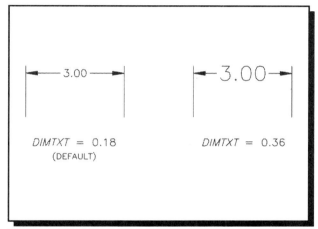

Figure 29-43

DIMTXT (Text Height)

DIMTXT allows you to specify the height of the dimension text. DIMTXT is multiplied times DIMSCALE to achieve the actual height. If the current text style (when dimensions are created) has a fixed height, DIMTXT is overridden.

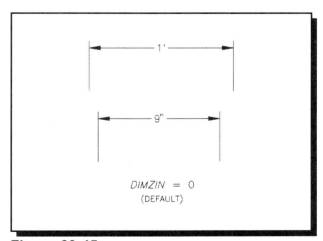

Figure 29-44

DIMZIN (Zero Inch Suppression)

DIMZIN provides options for suppressing a 0 value for inches or feet when it would otherwise appear. DIMZIN can be set to values 0-3 to control zero feet and inch suppression. This and the following figures explain the result of each option, assuming that Units have been set to Engineering with no places to the right of the decimal.

The default DIMZIN setting is 0, which suppresses 0 feet and 0 inches.

Figure 29-45

If *DIMZIN* is set to 1, neither zero values for feet nor inches are suppressed.

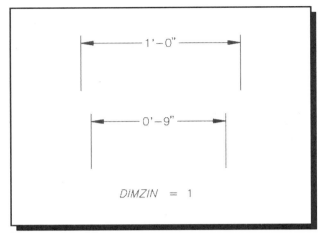

Figure 29-46

If *DIMZIN* is set to 2, zero values for inches only are suppressed, while 0 feet values are displayed.

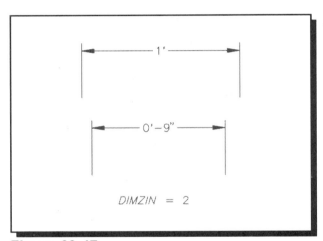

Figure 29-47

A *DIMZIN* setting of 3 suppresses 0 values for feet but displays 0 inches.

When fractional inches are used and the measurement is more than 1 foot, the number of inches is included even if zero, no matter how *DIMZIN* is set. For example, a dimension like 1'-3/4" never occurs; it would be displayed as 1'-0 3/4".

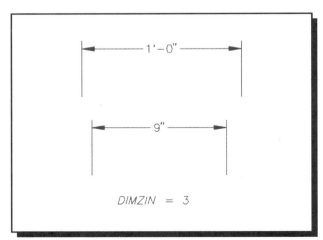

Figure 29-48

DIMZIN values 0-3 affect <u>feet-and-inch</u> dimensions only. To control leading and trailing zeroes in all <u>decimal</u> dimensions, the values 4, 8, and 12 are used as shown in this and the following figures. These examples assume a decimal *Precision* of 2 places.

A *DIMZIN* setting of 4 suppresses leading zeros in decimal dimensions as shown in Figure 29-49).

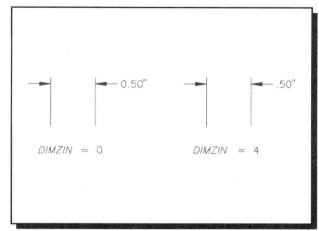

Figure 29-49

If *DIMZIN* is set to 8, all trailing zeros but not leading zeros are suppressed.

A *DIMZIN* setting of 12 suppresses both leading and trailing zeros for decimal dimensions.

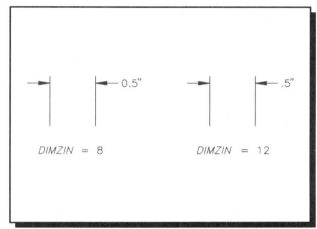

Figure 29-50

The values used to control feet and inch zeros (0-3) can be added to the values used to control decimal leading and trailing zeros (4, 8, 12). For example 1 + 12 = 13 would be used to display 0 feet (1) but suppress leading and trailing zeros (12), giving a display of 0'-.5" (for the example in Figure 29-50).

DIMENSIONING VARIABLES TABLE

This table is a summary of the dimensioning variables. Each variable has a brief description, the type of variable it is, and its <u>default setting</u>. (Reprinted from the AutoCAD Reference Manual, pages 473 and 474.)

Name	Description	Type	Default
DIMALT	Alternate Units	Switch	Off
DIMALTD	Alternate Units Decimal Places	Integer	2
DIMALTF	Alternate Units Scale Factor	Scale	25.4
DIMAPOST	Alternate Units Text Suffix	String	None
DIMASO	Associative Dimensioning	Switch	On
DIMASZ	Arrow Size	Distance	0.18
DIMBLK	Arrow Block	String	None
DIMBLK1	Separate Arrow Block 1	String	None
DIMBLK2	Separate Arrow Block 2	String	None
DIMCEN	Center Mark Size	Distance	0.09
DIMCLRD	Dimension Line Color	Color number	BYBLOCK
DIMCLRE	Extension Line Color	Color number	BYBLOCK
DIMCLRT	Dimension Text Color	Color number	BYBLOCK
DIMDLE	Dimension Line Extension	Distance	0.0
DIMDLI	Dimension Line Increment	Distance	0.38
DIMEXE	Extension Line Extension	Distance	0.18
DIMEXO	Extension Line Offset	Distance	0.0625
DIMGAP	Dimension Line Gap and Reference Dimensioning	Distance	0.09
DIMLFAC	Length Factor	Scale	1.0
DIMLIM	Limits Dimensioning	Switch	Off
DIMPOST	Dimension Text Prefix, Suffix, or both	String	None
DIMRND	Rounding Value	Scaled distance	0.0
DIMSAH	Separate Arrow Blocks	Switch	Off

Name	Description	Type	Default
DIMSCALE	Dimension Feature Scale Factor	Scale	1.0
DIMSE1	Suppress Extension Line 1	Switch	Off
DIMSE2	Suppress Extension Line 2	Switch	Off
DIMSHO	Show Dragged Dimension	Switch	On
DIMSOXD	Suppress Outside Dimension Lines	Switch	Off
DIMSTYLE	Dimension Style	Name	*UNNAMED
DIMTAD	Text Above Dimension Line	Switch	Off
DIMTFAC	Tolerance Text Scale Factor	Scale	1.0
DIMTIH	Text Inside Horizontal	Switch	On
DIMTIX	Text Inside Extension Lines	Switch	Off
DIMTM	Minus Tolerance Value	Scaled distance	0.0
DIMTP	Plus Tolerance Value	Scaled distance	0.0
DIMTOFL	Text Outside, Force Line Inside	Switch	Off
DIMTOH	Text Outside Horizontal	Switch	On
DIMTOL	Tolerance Dimensioning	Switch	Off
DIMTSZ	Tick Size	Distance	0.0
DIMTVP	Text Vertical Position	Scale	0.0
DIMTXT	Text Size	Distance	0.18
DIMZIN	Zero Suppression	Integer	0

CHANGING DIMENSIONING VARIABLES WITH *DIMENSION STYLES AND VARIABLES* DIALOGUE BOXES

As mentioned earlier in this chapter, the two fundamental methods of controlling dimensioning variables are by command line format (typing or selecting from the screen menu) or by using the *Dimensioning Styles and Variables* and related dialogue boxes (selected from the pull-down or tablet menu or entering *DDIM*). This section explains the use of the dialogue boxes to control dimension variables.

The *Dimensioning Styles and Variables* and related dialogue boxes use longer, descriptive terms instead of giving the formal variable names. Making a selection in a dialogue box, however, results in a change to the related variable. In other words, using the dialogue boxes is a somewhat more descriptive, but indirect method of controlling dimensioning variables than using the command line format.

The *Dimensioning Styles and Variables* dialogue box (Figure 29-51) is the top-level, or first, of a series of dialogue boxes. Making a selection from the options on the right side of the box invokes another dialogue box that controls dimensioning variables related to a particular feature. For example, selecting *Dimension Line...* invokes the *Dimension Line* dialogue box providing control of variables related to dimension lines. Making a selection in this dialogue box automatically makes the appropriate change to the related variable, such as *DIMDLI* (dimension line increment) or *DIMGAP* (dimension line gap), for example. The left side of the *Dimensioning Styles and Variables* dialogue box is intended for use with Dimension Styles, which are discussed in the next section.

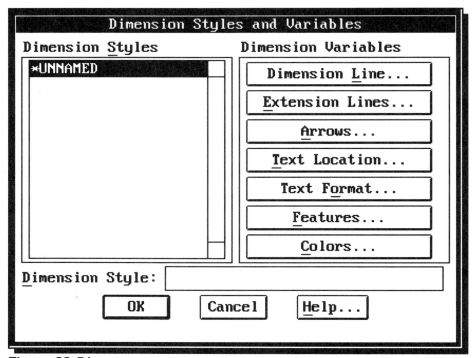

Figure 29-51

The selections on the right side of the *Dimensioning Styles and Variables* dialogue box are descriptively titled and invoke other dialogue boxes providing control of the specific features. The *Features...* selection, however, is a combination and duplication of the other selections, all in one large dialogue box.

This section discusses the options in each dimensioning variable dialogue box. The information serves as a "translator" between the dialogue box selections and the related variables explained and illustrated in the previous section, Dimensioning Variables Illustrated.

IMPORTANT NOTE: The values displayed in these dialogue boxes are affected by *Precision* set in the *Units* command or dialogue box. *Units Precision* should be set to a minimum of 2 places to the right of the decimal (0.00) in order to display most of the default settings for the dimensioning variables.

Dimension Line...

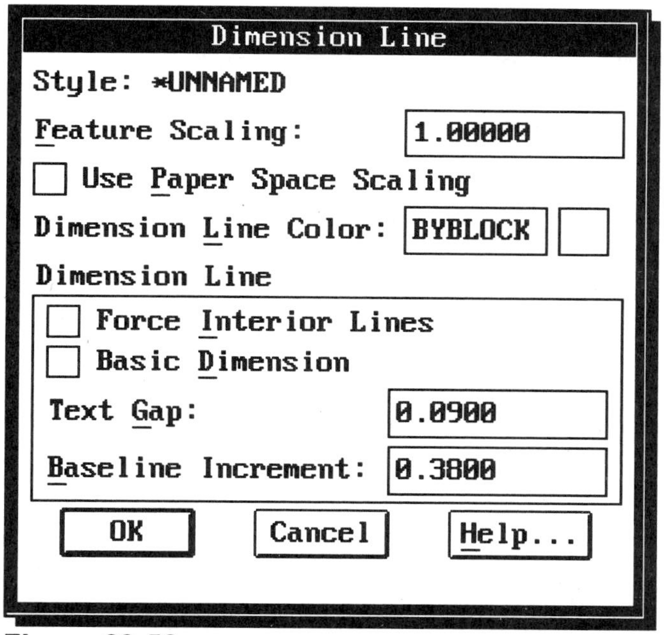

Figure 29-52

Feature Scaling

This option appears in each dimensioning dialogue box. The value entered here is the *DIMSCALE*, the overall dimensioning scale factor. The value for *DIMSCALE* is used as a multiplier for all other size-related variables. Increasing or decreasing this one variable increases or decreases all of the size-related features proportionally, such as text height, arrow size, dimension line increment, etc. Using this one variable is preferred to changing each of the size-related variables individually (*DIMTXT, DIMASZ, DIMLI*, etc.).

It is recommended that this variable be changed <u>first</u> to size the dimensions appropriately according to the drawing *Limits* (see Dimensioning Guidelines, this chapter). The new *DIMSCALE* setting is then included in the "template" used for creating other dimension styles.

Paper Space Scaling

Use this option if you are dimensioning in Paper Space. A check in this box enters a value of 0 in the *DIMSCALE* variable. A 0 (zero) value causes AutoCAD to compute a scale factor based on the Paper Space *Limits* and the current modelspace viewport *Zoom XP* factor. See Chapter 32, Paper Space.

Dimension Line Color

PICK the square to the right of the color name to invoke a color pallet to select the desired color. The selection made (color number) is stored in the *DIMCLRD* variable.

Force Interior Lines

A check in this box turns *DIMTOFL On*. This forces dimension lines inside the *Circle* or *Arc* for *Diameter* and *Radius* dimensions. When linear dimensions are used, the dimension line is forced inside the extension lines even when the text is forced outside. This option is <u>recommended</u> for dimensioning an *Arc* with the *Radius* command.

Reference Dimension

This option creates a <u>basic dimension</u> by drawing a box around the dimension text. This is identical to entering a negative *DIMGAP* value.

Text Gap

The value entered is the *DIMGAP* value. The value controls the distance maintained around the text used for computing the break in the dimension line.

Baseline Increment

When creating *Baseline* dimensions, AutoCAD uses this value to determine the distance to "stack" the dimension line above or below the previous one. The value is held in the *DIMDLI* (Dimension Line Increment) variable.

Extension Lines...

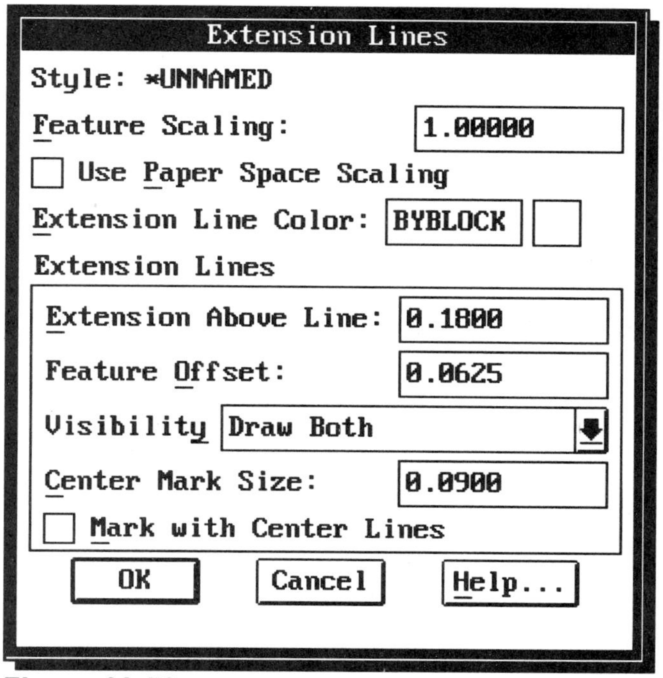

Figure 29-53

The first three options in this dialogue box are similar to those in the previous dialogue boxes. See *Dimension Line...* for information on *Feature Scaling* and *Use Paper Space Scaling*. The *Extension Line Color* is stored in the *DIMCLRE* variable.

Extension Above Line

This value is stored in the *DIMEXE* variable. It sets the distance that the extension line extends above the dimension line.

Feature Offset

This value specifies the distance between the origin points that you specify and the extension lines. This gap allows you to PICK the object corners, yet the extension lines stop short of the object. The value is stored in the *DIMEXO* variable.

Visibility

The extension line suppression is controlled by this selection. PICK this tile to invoke a popup list revealing the following four options. The affected variables are *DIMSE1* and *DIMSE2*.

Draw Both   Draws both extension lines. *DIMSE1* and *DIMSE2* are *Off.*

Suppress First	Suppresses the first extension line PICKed. Sets _DIMSE1_ to _Off_.
Suppress Second	Suppresses the second extension line PICKed. Sets _DIMSE2_ to _Off_.
Suppress Both	Both extension lines are suppressed. _DIMSE1_ and _DIMSE2_ are turned _On_.

Center Mark Size

The value entered controls the size of the short dashes of the center marks that are drawn when _Center, Diameter_, or _Radius_ are used. A value of 0 disables the center marks. The value is stored in the _DIMCEN_ variable.

Mark with Center Lines

AutoCAD draws center lines extending past the _Circle_ or _Arc_ if this is checked. This effectively enters a negative value in the _DIMCEN_ variable.

Arrows...

Figure 29-54

The options on the top section of this dialogue box are identical to those in the *Dimension Lines* dialogue box. See *Dimension Lines...* for information on *Feature Scaling*, *Use Paper Space Scaling*, and *Dimension Line Color*.

Arrow

This causes arrows to be drawn at dimension line ends. The size of the arrow is held in the *DIMASZ* variable. Keep in mind that this value, as well as other size-related variables, are multiplied by the *Feature Scaling* (*DIMSCALE*) value. If you wish to increase arrows and text, etc. proportionally, use *Feature Scaling* (*DIMSCALE*).

Tick

This radio button causes tick marks to be drawn instead of arrows. *DIMASZ* is set to 0 and the default arrow size value (.18) is stored in *DIMTSZ*, which effectively turns on ticks.

Dot

This option causes AutoCAD to use a block named "DOT" to be stored in the *DIMBLK* variable.

User

Press this radio button and supply the name of any defined *Block* in the *User Arrow* box to cause AutoCAD to draw the *Block* instead of arrows. The *Block* name is stored in the *DIMBLK* variable.

Separate Arrows

This option allows you to use two different arrows, one for each dimension line end. The *User* button must be selected. Then check the *Separate Arrows* box. The *Block* names must be entered in the *First Arrow* and *Second Arrow* edit boxes. This is the same as turning *DIMSAH On* and entering the *Block* names in *DIMBLK1* and *DIMBLK2*.

Tick Extension

This option allows you to specify the distance you want the dimension lines to extend past the extension line when ticks are used instead of arrows. When the *Tick* radio button is depressed, you can enter the tick size in the *Tick Extension* edit box. The value is kept in the *DIMDLE* (Dimension Line Extension) variable.

Text Location...

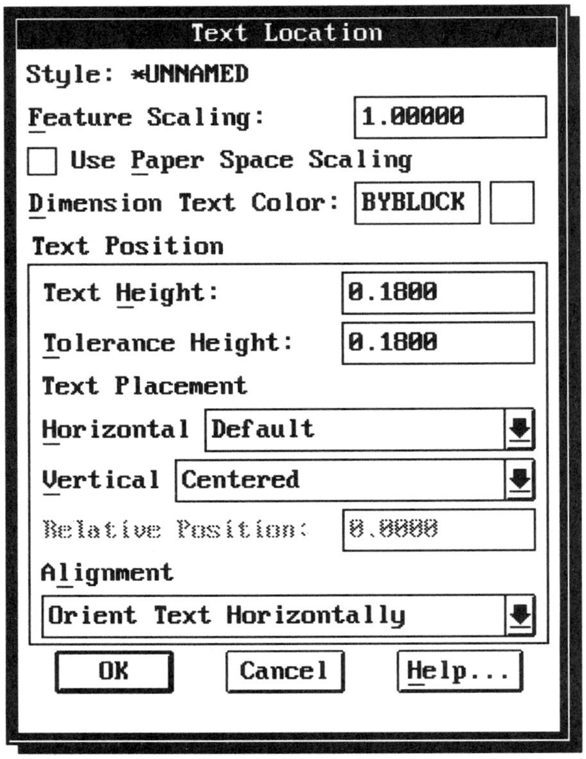

Figure 29-55

The first three options in this dialogue box (*Feature Scaling, Paper Space Scaling*, and *Dimension Text Color*) are similar to those discussed on the preceding pages. *Dimension Text Color* is stored in the *DIMCLRT* variable.

Text Height

You can specify the text height by entering the value in this edit box (if the current *Text Style* is not a fixed height). The related variable is *DIMTXT*. Keep in mind that this value, as well as other size-related variables, are multiplied by the *Feature Scaling* (*DIMSCALE*) value. If you want to change the size of text, arrows, and other dimensioning features proportionally, use *Feature Scaling* (*DIMSCALE*).

Tolerance Height

The value entered here is the proportion of the *Text Height* that tolerances are drawn. The related variable is *DIMTFAC*.

Horizontal

These options control the placement of the text with respect to the extension lines (not necessarily a horizontal placement). PICKing the tile invokes a popup list with the following options.

Default	Places text inside the extension lines unless there is insufficient room, in which case it is forced outside. _Radius_ and _Diameter_ dimension text is placed outside in all cases. This setting turns _DIMTIX_ and _DIMSOXD Off._
Force Text Inside	Forces the text inside the extension lines. _DIMTIX_ is turned _On_ with _DIMSOXD Off._
Text, Arrows Inside	Forces text and arrows inside. Identical to turning _DIMTIX_ and _DIMSOXD On._

Vertical

Select this popup list to control the vertical placement of text. The options are given here.

Centered	This is the default position. Text is vertically centered on the dimension line.
Above	Uses the text height value as the distance to place the text above the dimension line. _DIMTAD_ is _On._
Relative	Uses the value entered in the _Relative Position_ edit box to determine the distance from the center. This turns _DIMTAD Off._

Relative Position

To use this edit box, _Relative_ must be selected from the _Vertical_ options. The value entered is the <u>actual</u> displacement distance from the center line. This is <u>not</u> the same as the _DIMTVP_ value. (The _DIMTVP_ value is multiplied times the text height to achieve the vertical placement.) In this case, the value entered in the _Relative Position_ edit box is <u>divided</u> by the text height to achieve the _DIMTVP_ value.

Alignment

Selecting the _Alignment_ popup list reveals the options.

Orient Text Horizontally	Draws text horizontally in all cases. _DIMTIH_ and _DIMTOH_ are _On._
Align With Dimension Line	Aligns the text with the dimension line. Turns _Off DIMTIH_ and _DIMTOH._

Aligned When Inside Only   Aligns text inside with the dimension line. Text outside is horizontal. *DIMTIH* is *On* and *DIMTOH* is *Off.*

Aligned When Outside Only Aligns text outside with the dimension line. Text inside is horizontal. *DIMTIH* is *Off* and *DIMTOH* is *On.*

Text Format...

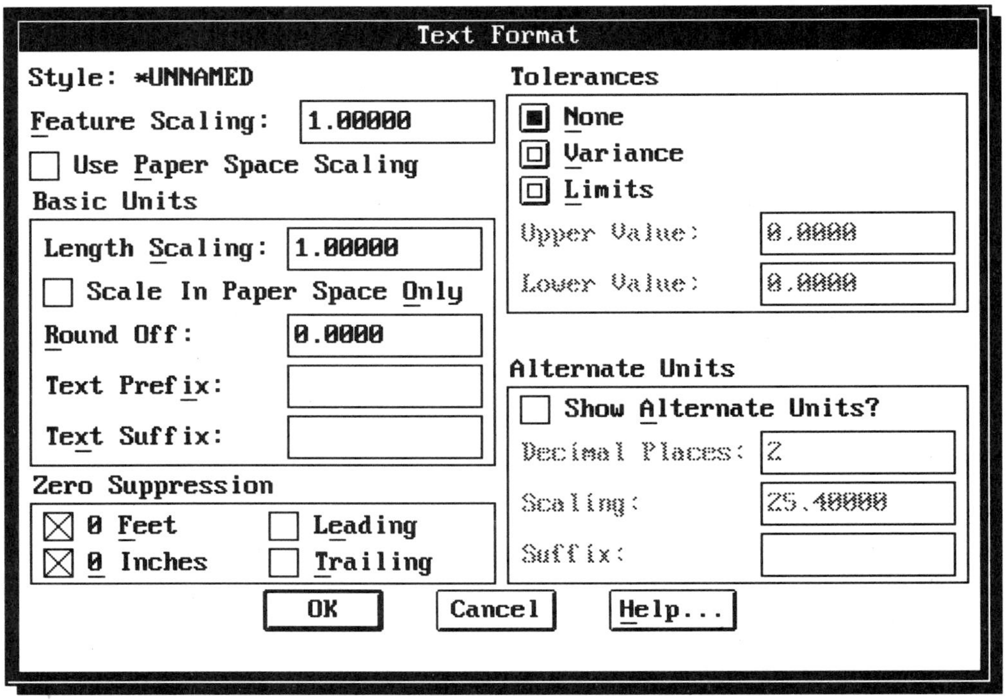

```
┌──────────────────────────────────────────────────────────┐
│                       Text Format                        │
│  Style: *UNNAMED                Tolerances               │
│  Feature Scaling: [1.00000]     [■] None                 │
│  [ ] Use Paper Space Scaling    [□] Variance             │
│  Basic Units                    [□] Limits               │
│  ┌────────────────────────────┐ Upper Value:  [0.0000]   │
│  │ Length Scaling: [1.00000]  │ Lower Value:  [0.0000]   │
│  │ [ ] Scale In Paper Space Only│                         │
│  │ Round Off:  [0.0000]       │ Alternate Units          │
│  │ Text Prefix: [        ]    │ [ ] Show Alternate Units?│
│  │ Text Suffix: [        ]    │ Decimal Places: [2]      │
│  └────────────────────────────┘ Scaling: [25.40000]      │
│  Zero Suppression               Suffix: [        ]       │
│  [X] 0 Feet    [ ] Leading                               │
│  [X] 0 Inches  [ ] Trailing                              │
│         [ OK ]   [ Cancel ]   [ Help... ]                │
└──────────────────────────────────────────────────────────┘
```

Figure 29-56

The first two options in the *Text Format* dialogue box (*Feature Scaling* and *Use Paper Space*) are identical to those in other dimension variables dialogue boxes. See *Dimension Lines...* for details.

Length Scaling

Values entered into this edit box are stored in the *DIMLFAC* variable. *DIMLFAC* is a global scale factor used as a multiplier for all measured lengths. Thus, this option affects the measured dimension text, not the width factor of the text.

Scale in Paper Space Only

Use this option if you are placing dimensions in paper space. Checking this box applies the value entered in the *Length Scaling* edit box to paper space. This is the same as entering a negative value in the *DIMLFAC* variable. This option does not automatically calculate and set *DIMLFAC* to the model space *Zoom XP* factor, as does the *DIMLFAC Viewport* option. See Chapter 32, Paper Space.

Round off

> The value entered is stored in the *DIMRND* variable. AutoCAD rounds all values to the increment entered. For example, if .5 were entered, all measured dimensional values would be rounded to a .5 increment. (The number of displayed zeros is determined by the *Units Precision* setting.)

Text Prefix

> Entered numbers or text are added to the measured dimension value. Any prefix overrides default prefixes, such as the Ø symbol or the R entered before the *Diameter* or *Radius* dimensions. The string is stored in the *DIMPOST* variable. Alternately, the *DIMPOST* variable can be used with the <> symbols to establish a prefix.

Text Suffix

> Any letters or numbers entered in this box are reflected as a suffix to the measured dimension text. The string is stored in the *DIMPOST* variable.

> It is recommend to use the letters "DIA" after a non-metric *Diameter* dimension rather than using the default Ø symbol. The suffix can be entered with this dialogue box; however, the default prefix (Ø) is not overridden unless a space (press Space Bar) is entered as a prefix. You must use the *DIMPOST* variable with the <> mechanism to suppress the default prefix without a space.

Zero Suppression

> The *0'* check suppresses a zero appearing in a zero feet dimension (5 1/2" rather than 0'-5 1/2").

> The *0"* check suppresses a zero appearing in a zero inch dimension (14' rather than 14'-0").

> Suppressing *Trailing* and *Leading* zeros applies to decimal dimensions.

> The *Zero Suppression* settings are stored as one of the *DIMZIN* integers.

> NOTE: If you desire decimal dimensions to appear with less than 2 places to the right of the decimals, use this option to suppress trailing zeros rather than setting *Units Precision* to less than 2 places. A *Units* setting of a minimum of 2 places is required for AutoCAD to display most default dimension variable settings in the dialogue box series. Alternately, *DIMRND* can be set to limit decimal places.

Tolerances

> The options in this section (*Variance, Limits, Upper Value*, and *Lower Value*) are as follows.

Variance	Tolerances are displayed if this radio button is depressed. This turns *DIMTOL On*. The values entered in the *Upper Value* and *Lower Value* are appended to the measured dimension. See *DIMTP* and *DIMTM* for details on how the same and different upper and lower values appear.
Limits	AutoCAD creates limit dimensions when this radio button is depressed. The value specified as the *Upper Value* is added to the measured dimension and the value specified as the *Lower Value* is subtracted from the measured length. Positive and negative values are accepted. For details, see *DIMLIM*, *DIMTP*, and *DIMTM*.

Alternate Units

Checking the *Show Alternate Units?* box enables the other options in this section. If only this box is checked, the default alternate units (millimeters) are appended to the measured dimension with 2 decimal places. This turns the *DIMALT* variable *On*.

Decimal Places	This option sets the number of places to the right of the decimal for the alternate units. The value is stored in the *DIMALTD* variable.
Scaling	Any value can be entered here. The default is set to the millimeter conversion factor (25.4). The value is stored in the *DIMALTF* variable.
Suffix	This option allows a suffix to be added to the alternate units. For example, a string of "mm" would cause "mm" to appear after the default millimeter units. The string is stored in the *DIMAPOST* variable.

Colors...

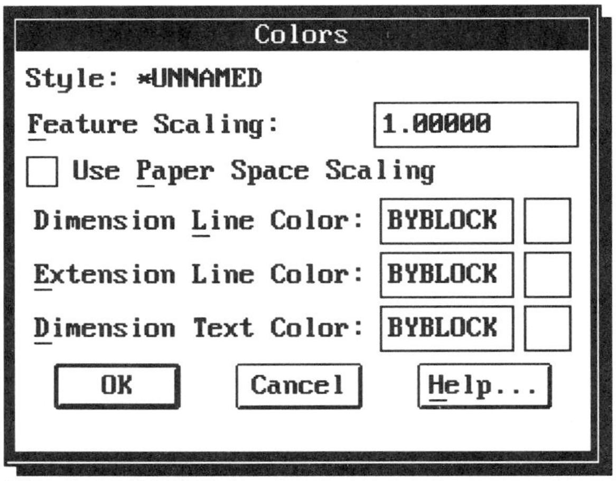

Figure 29-57

The first two options in the *Colors* dialogue box (*Feature Scaling* and *Use Paper Space*) are identical to those in other dimension variables dialogue boxes. See *Dimension Lines...* for details.

The colors section of this dialogue box provides you with control of the colors for all the individual features of dimensions. To change a color, select the square at the right of each option to invoke a color pallet. These options are identical to the options appearing in the *Dimension Line*, *Extension Line*, and *Text Location* dialogue boxes. These settings are stored in the *DIMCLRD*, *DIMCLRE*, and *DIMCLRT* variables.

Features...

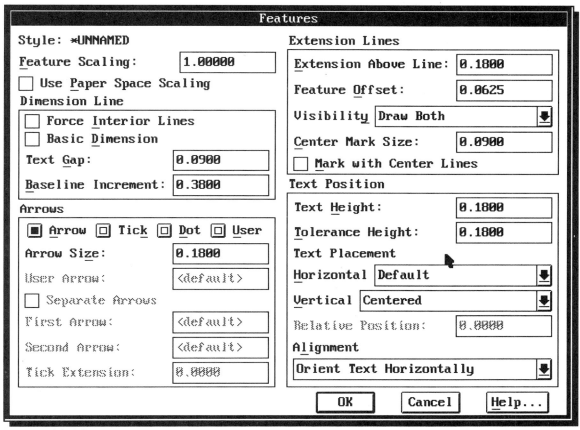

Figure 29-58

The options in this dialogue box are a duplication of the other dialogue boxes explained earlier. This dialogue box is intended to give an overview of the current settings or settings for a particular *Dimstyle*. See the previous pages in this section for an explanation of these options.

DIMENSION STYLES

After reading through the previous pages in this chapter, it should be apparent that managing dimensioning variables can be a large task. However, using Dimension Styles, or *Dimstyles* for short, can simplify the task of managing dimensioning variables.

Assume that you are dimensioning a complex drawing that requires changing many dimensioning variables, but the work is done without the use of *Dimstyles*. In order to create limit dimensions, for example, you would change the desired variable settings, then create the dimensions that used those particular settings. To create *Radius* dimensions, the previous variables would have to be reset and changes made to other variables in order to place the *Radius* dimensions as you prefer. This same process would be repeated each time you want to create a new type of dimension. If you needed to add another limit or *Radius* dimension, you would have to reset the same variables as before.

To simplify this process, you can create *Dimstyles*, then *Save* and *Restore* them. A *Dimstyle* is a name given to a particular combination of variable settings. A *Dimstyle* could contain all the default settings, or the defaults plus only one or two variable changes, or a large number of dimensioning variable changes.

When you *Save* a *Dimstyle*, AutoCAD remembers the current settings for all of the dimensioning variables and allows you to specify a name for that particular combination. You can *Save* as many *Dimstyles* as you want. When you *Restore* a *Dimstyle*, AutoCAD remembers and resets all of the dimensioning variable settings for that particular combination.

Therefore, you could create a *Dimstyle* that contained all the desired settings for your limit dimensions, called LIMITS for example, another for all of your *Radius* dimensions called RADIUS-1, and others containing any combination of variable settings that you want. To create a limit dimension at any time, simply *Restore* LIMITS and place the dimension. You can even change one or more existing dimensions to take on the variable settings of another *Dimstyle* by making the desired *Dimstyle* current and then using the *Update* command on the dimensions. *Update* renews the selected dimension to the current variable settings.

Changes made to dimensioning variables are saved to the *UNNAMED *Dimstyle* by default. When a new drawing is created, the *UNNAMED style is active. Unless you create a new *Dimstyle*, any variable changes you make (in command line format or through dialogue boxes) are saved to the *UNNAMED style. AutoCAD provides no previously created *Dimstyles*.

As with the dimensioning variables, *Dimstyles* can be created, *Saved* and *Restored* using either the command line format or the *Dimension Styles and Variables* dialogue box (Fig. 29-51). This section discusses the Dimension Style commands in "command line" format first, then the dialogue box *Dimstyle* functions.

Dimension Style Commands

Like other dimensioning commands, the `Dim:` prompt must appear at the command line in order to use the following Dimension Style commands.

DIMSTYLE

TYPE IN:	PULL-DOWN MENU	SCREEN MENU	TABLET MENU
DIMSTYLE	---	*DIM:, Dim Styl. Dimstyle*	---

The *Dimstyle* command only returns the <u>name</u> of the current *Dimstyle*. There are no options. For example, if the current *Dimstyle* was "LIMITS-1," the command line would read as follows.

```
Dim: dimstyle
DIMSTYLE = "LIMITS-1"
Dim:
```

SAVE

TYPE IN:	PULL-DOWN MENU	SCREEN MENU	TABLET MENU
SAVE	---	*DIM:, Dim Styl, Save*	*1,W*

Save entered at the `DIM:` prompt saves the <u>current</u> dimensioning variable settings to a name that you assign for that particular combination. (If the `Command:` prompt is active, the *Save* command saves the drawing to disk!) To create a *Dimstyle*, make the desired dimensioning variable settings, then use *Save*.

```
Dim: save
?/Name for new dimension style: limits-1
Dim:
```

You can assign any name for the *Dimstyle*. Use a descriptive name. The **?** option lists any or all of the previously created *Dimstyles* in the drawing. AutoCAD provides no previously created *Dimstyles*.

```
Dim: save
?/Name for new dimension style: ?
Dimension style(s) to list <*>: Enter (to list all)
Named dimension styles:
   DEFAULTS
   LIMITS-1
   SHOW-MM
 Dim:
```

RESTORE

TYPE IN:	PULL-DOWN MENU	SCREEN MENU	TABLET MENU
RESTORE	---	*DIM:, Dim Styl, Restore*	*2,W*

Restore makes the selected *Dimstyle* current. This action causes AutoCAD to remember and restore the settings for all the variables for that particular *Dimstyle*. At that point you can create new dimensions or *Update* existing dimensions to exhibit the features dictated by the variable settings.

```
Dim: restore
Current dimension style: SHOW-MM
?/Enter dimension style name or RETURN to select dimension:
(name) or Enter to PICK
Dim:
```

Restore displays the current *Dimstyle*. At the `?/Enter dimension style name or RETURN to select dimension:` prompt, enter the name of the style to restore. Alternatively, you can PICK any existing dimension to *Restore* its *Dimstyle*.

UPDATE

TYPE IN:	PULL-DOWN MENU	SCREEN MENU	TABLET MENU
UPDATE	*Modify, Edit Dimension> Update*	*DIM:, Edit, Update*	*3,W*

This command is intended for editing <u>existing</u> dimensions. The *Update* command allows you to revise one or more existing dimensions with the <u>current</u> variable settings. The selected dimensions also assume the current *Units* settings and current *Text Style*.

For example, assume that your drawing was complete, however, a design change required a particular dimension to be called out with limit dimensions. You might *Erase* the dimension, *Restore* the LIMITS-1 *Dimstyle* (assuming this *Dimstyle* existed), and then create a new dimension. Alternately, *Restore* the LIMITS-1 *Dimstyle* and use *Update* to change the existing dimension. Using *Update* would cause any selected dimension(s) to take on all of the features dictated by the current *Dimstyle* variable settings.

```
Dim: update
Select objects: PICK
Select objects: Enter
Dim:
```

All selected dimensions are updated with the current variable settings. Any number of dimensions can be selected. The entire drawing can be selected, but only the dimensions are highlighted.

CAUTION: Using _Update_ causes the selected dimensions to take on the current dimension variable settings as well as the current _Units_ settings and current _Text Style_. This can cause unexpected surprises if the _Units_ settings or the _Text Style_ has been changed since the dimensions were created.

VARIABLES

TYPE IN:	PULL-DOWN MENU	SCREEN MENU	TABLET MENU
VARIABLES	---	_DIM:, Dim Styl, Variable_	---

The _Variables_ command displays the settings for every variable for the selected or named _Dimstyle_. This command displays a text screen identical to that of the _Status_ command. The _Status_ command shows the <u>current</u> settings only. However, by using the _Variables_ command, you can enter any _Dimstyle_ name or PICK from existing dimensions to show the settings for that style.

```
Dim: variables
Current dimension style: LIMITS-1
?/Enter dimension style name or RETURN to select dimension:
limits-1

Status of LIMITS-1:
DIMALT    Off                  Alternate units selected
DIMALTD   2                    Alternate unit decimal places
DIMALTF   25.40                Alternate unit scale factor
DIMAPOST                       Suffix for alternate text
DIMASO    On                   Create associative dimensions
     (etc.)
Dim:
```

This is only part of the list displayed by the _Variables_ command. See _Status_ for the full list of variables.

~stylename

This option is not a full command, but can be entered in response to the _Variables_ or _Restore_ commands. Entering a _Dimstyle_ name preceded by the tilde symbol (~) displays the <u>differences between the named style and the current _Dimstyle_</u>.

For example, assume that you created a _Dimstyle_ called DEFAULTS. This _Dimstyle_ was saved <u>before making any changes</u> to the default variable settings. (By the way, saving the default settings to a _Dimstyle_ is a good practice.) To display the <u>differences</u> between DEFAULTS and any other _Dimstyle_ (LIMITS-1, for example), first make DEFAULTS current, then use _Variables_ with the ~ symbol. (The ~ symbol is used as a wildcard to mean "all but.")

```
Dim: variables
Current dimension style: DEFAULTS
```

```
?/Enter dimension style name or RETURN to select dimension:
~limits-1
Differences between LIMITS-1 and current settings:

          LIMITS-1                Current Setting

DIMLIM    On                      Off
DIMTFAC   0.75                    1.00
DIMTIX    On                      Off
DIMTM     0.03                    0.00
DIMTP     0.05                    0.00

?/Enter dimension style name or RETURN to select dimension:
*Cancel*
Dim:
```

This is useful for keeping track of your _Dimstyles_ and variable settings.

OVERRIDE

TYPE IN:	PULL-DOWN MENU	SCREEN MENU	TABLET MENU
OVERRIDE	---	_DIM:, Dim Styl, Override_	---

Override is a very powerful and useful command, but is overlooked by many users because it does not appear on the pull-down menu, tablet menu, or dialogue boxes. _Override_ might be better named _"SuperUpdate"_ because it allows you to (1) change dimension variable settings, (2) then update any existing dimension(s), (3) then update (or not update) the dimension's _Dimstyle_ with the new variable setting(s)--all in one command! The term "_Override_" is based on the ability to update a dimension, but override the _Dimstyle_ settings for that variable.

A good application is globally updating dimensions (changing all existing dimensions) with a new variable setting. For example, assume a drawing was complete, but you decided to plot it on a smaller sheet, requiring a larger _DIMSCALE_ in order to read the dimensions adequately. _Override_ would allow you to make the variable change, _Update_ the dimensions, and modify (or not) the _Dimstyles_.

```
Dim: override
Dimension variable to override: dimscale
Current value <1.00> New value: 1.5
Dimension variable to override: Enter
Select objects: Other corner: PICK with a window to select all
dimensions
Select objects: Enter
Modify dimension style "TEXT-IN"? <N> y
Modify dimension style "SHOW-MM"? <N> y
Modify dimension style "RADIUS-1"? <N> y
Modify dimension style "DEFAULTS"? <N> n
Dim:
```

This action would cause all dimensions to be *Updated* to the new *DIMSCALE* setting. Answering **Y** to the `Modify dimension style:` prompt causes that style to be changed. Notice the DEFAULTS *Dimstyle* was not updated by entering **N** or pressing **Enter**.

Use *Override* to change any dimensioning variable setting. Only one, a few, or all dimensions can be updated with the new setting. <u>Only the *Dimstyles* associated with the selected dimensions are prompted for "Modifying."</u>

Using Dimstyles with the *Dimension Styles and Variables* Dialogue Box

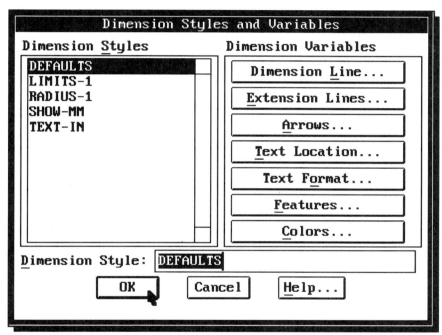

Figure 29-59

The *Dimension Styles and Variables* dialogue box can be invoked by selecting from the *Settings* pull-down menu or typing *"DDIM."* The left side of this dialogue box is used for listing and selecting the desired *Dimstyles*.

<u>Whenever</u> you change variables using the *Dimension Styles and Variables* dialogue box series, the <u>current</u> *Dimstyle* is <u>automatically updated</u>. If no *Dimstyles* have been created, any changes to variable settings through the dialogue box series are saved to the *UNNAMED style. In contrast, using command line format (typing), variable changes are <u>only</u> saved to the *UNNAMED style unless you use *Save* to create a new or modify an existing named style. When a new drawing is created, a temporary *Dimstyle* called *UNNAMED is active. Unless you create another named *Dimstyle*, changes made to variables through the dialogue boxes are saved to the *UNNAMED style. This style is automatically used as a template when you create your first *Dimstyle*.

NOTE: With the exception of the variables *DIMASO* and *DIMSHO*, AutoCAD stores the value of each dimension variable with each dimension style.

Creating a new *Dimstyle* using the *Dimension Styles and Variables* Dialogue Box

1. Select an existing style from the list on the left to use as a template. Whatever *Dimstyle* appears in the edit box is used as a template. The new style contains all of the variable settings of the template plus any changes you make before exiting the dialogue box series by checking the *OK* tiles. If only the *UNNAMED style exists, it is automatically used as a template.

2. Type over or modify the name in the edit box to assign the new *Dimstyle* name.

3. Select any option from the right side of the dialogue box (*Dimension Variables*) to make the desired variable changes for the new *Dimstyle*. Select the *OK* tile in each of these boxes to keep your changes.

4. After the changes have been made you are returned to the main (*Dimension Styles and Variables*) dialogue box. To *Save* the variable changes to the new *Dimstyle*, you must select the *OK* tile. *Cancel* cancels the creation of the new *Dimstyle*.

Restoring a *Dimstyle* using the *Dimension Styles and Variables* Dialogue Box

1. Select the desired style from the list on the left. The style should then appear in the edit box. Select the *OK* tile.

2. The selected *Dimstyle* becomes the current style and remains so until another is made current. Any dimensions created while the style is current contain the features dictated by the style's variable settings.

Modifying a *Dimstyle* and *Updating* Dimensions using the Dialogue Boxes

1. Select the desired style from the list on the left of the *Dimension Styles and Variables* dialogue box. The style should then appear in the edit box. The selected *Dimstyle* becomes the current style.

2. Select any option from the right side of the dialogue box (*Dimension Variables*) to make the desired variable changes for the current *Dimstyle*. Select the *OK* tile in each of these boxes to keep your changes. When you select the *OK* tile in the main dialogue box the current *Dimstyle* is updated.

3. As you exit the dialogue box, you will notice some activity in the Drawing Editor. All dimensions originally created with the *Dimstyle* are <u>automatically</u> *Updated*. There is no switch to disable the automatic *Update* when using the dialogue boxes.

Saving the Default Settings to a named *Dimstyle*

Since AutoCAD provides no mechanism for saving the default settings of dimensioning variables, using dimensioning variables and *Dimstyles* can be frustrating at first. In other words, when you change variable settings, there is no way to automatically *Restore* the default settings. As an alternative to having to reset each variable individually to the default settings, you should <u>create a *Dimstyle* containing the default settings</u>.

Upon entering a new drawing, or at least before any dimensioning variables have been changed, use the command line format or *Dimension Styles and Variables* dialogue box to create a named *Dimstyle* containing the default settings as follows.

Using command line format:

> At the `Dim:` prompt, type *Save*. Enter the name DEFAULTS, ORIGINAL, or any other descriptive name. The default settings are saved under DEFAULTS (or other assigned name).

Using the *Dimension Styles and Variables* dialogue box:

> Invoke the dialogue box. Enter the name DEFAULTS (or other descriptive name) in the edit box. Select the *OK* tile and <u>exit the dialogue box</u>. You <u>must</u> exit the dialogue box to save the *Dimstyle*. If you wish to immediately create another *Dimstyle*, you still must exit the dialogue box to save DEFAULTS.

There are two advantages to this strategy. First, if you want to establish the default settings for all of the dimension variables, simply *Restore* the DEFAULTS *Dimstyle*. Secondly, DEFAULTS can be used as a template when creating new *Dimstyles*. When you create a new *Dimstyle*, the current style is used as a template. Unless you restore the default settings, the new styles are cumulative (contain all of the settings from the previous *Dimstyle* plus the new changes.)

GUIDELINES FOR DIMENSIONING IN AutoCAD

Listed below are some guidelines to use for dimensioning a drawing using Dimensioning Variables and Dimension Styles. Although there are other strategies for dimensioning, two strategies are offered here as a framework so you can begin developing an organized approach to dimensioning.

In almost every case, dimensioning is one of the last steps in creating a drawing, since the geometry must exist in order to dimension it. You may need to review the steps for drawing setup, including the concept of "drawing scale factor" (Chapter 13).

Strategy 1.   Dimensioning a Single Drawing

This method assumes that the fundamental steps have been taken to set up the drawing and create the geometry. Assume this has been accomplished:

- Drawing setup is completed: *Units, Limits, Snap, Grid, Ltscale, Layers*, border and title block.
- The drawing geometry (entities comprising the subject of the drawing) has been created.

Now you are ready to dimension the object (subject of the multiview drawing, pictorial drawing, floor plan, or whatever type of drawing).

1. Create a *Layer* (named DIM, or similar) for dimensioning, if one has not already been created. Set *Continuous* linetype and appropriate color. Make it the *current* layer.

2. Set the *DIMSCALE* accounting for drawing *Limits* and expected plotting size.

    For dimension text of 3/16":

    > Multiply *DIMSCALE* times the "drawing scale factor." The default *DIMSCALE* is set to 1, which creates dimensioning text of approximately 3/16" (default *DIMTXT* =.18) when plotted full size. All other size-related dimensioning variables' defaults are set appropriately.

    For dimension text of 1/8":

    > Multiply *DIMSCALE* times the "drawing scale factor," <u>times .7</u>. Since the *DIMSCALE* times the scale factor produces dimensioning text of .18, then .18 x .7 = .126 or approximately 1/8". (See Optional Method for Fixed Dimension Text Height.)

3. Before changing any other variables, save a *DIMSTYLE* named "DEFAULTS." Because AutoCAD provides no utility to automatically restore all of the default settings for dimensioning variables, this step allows you to do so by *Restoring* "DEFAULTS."

    Since the DEFAULTS dimension style has the default settings (except *DIMSCALE*), it should be used as a template when you create most new dimension styles. The *DIMSCALE* is already set appropriately for new dimension styles in the drawing. If you use the *Dimension Styles and Variables* dialogue box to do this, remember that you must select the **OK** tile and exit the dialogue box in order to save the *Dimstyle*.

4. Create all the relatively simple dimensions first. These are dimensions that are easy and fast and require <u>no dimension variable changes</u>. Begin with linear dimensions, then progress to the other types of dimensions.

5. Create the special dimensions last. These are dimensions that require variable changes. There are two possibilities here.

    a. For relatively simple drawings, make the dimensioning variable changes as needed but do not save them as *Dimstyles*. Restore the DEFAULTS *Dimstyle* as needed to reset the default settings.

    b. For more complex drawings that require many dimension variable changes, create appropriate *Dimstyles*. They can be created "on the fly" or as a group before dimensioning. Use DEFAULTS as a template when appropriate.

6.   Make the final adjustments. *Restore* the appropriate *Dimstyles* and *Update* existing dimensions where necessary. Remember that *Override* allows you to apply variable changes to existing dimensions and update each affected *Dimstyle* if you choose.

Strategy 2. Creating *Dimstyles* as Part of Prototype Drawings

1.   *Open* a *New* drawing or an existing *Prototype*. Assign a descriptive name.

2.   Create a DIM *Layer* for dimensioning with *continuous* linetype and appropriate color (if one has not already been created).

3.   Set the *DIMSCALE* accounting for the drawing *Limits* and expected plotting size. Use the guidelines given in Strategy 1., step 2.

4.   Before changing any other variables, save a *DIMSTYLE* named "DEFAULTS." This can be used to restore the default settings of the dimensioning variables and should be used as a template when you create most new dimension styles. The *DIMSCALE* is already set appropriately for new dimension styles in the drawing.

5.   Create the appropriate *Dimstyles* for expected drawing geometry. (See Dimension Style Examples for possible *Dimstyles* to create.) Use DEFAULTS *Dimstyle* as a template when appropriate.

6.   *Save* and *Exit* the newly created prototype drawing.

7.   Use this prototype in the future for creating new drawings. *Restore* the desired *Dimstyles* to create the appropriate dimensions.

Using a prototype drawing with *Saved Dimstyles* is a preferred alternative to repeatedly creating the same *Dimstyles* for each new drawing.

Optional Method for Fixed Dimension Text Height in Prototype Drawings

To summarize Strategy 1., step 2., the default *DIMSCALE* (1) times the default *DIMTXT* (.18) produces dimensioning text of approximately 3/16" when plotted to 1=1. To create 1/8" text, multiply *DIMSCALE* times .7 (.18 x .7 = .126). As an alternative to this method, try the following.

For 1/8" dimensions, for example, multiply the default values of the size related variables by .7, namely:

DIMTXT	text height	.18 x .7 = .126
DIMASZ	arrow size	.18 x .7 = .126
DIMEXE	extension line extension	.18 x .7 = .126
DIMDLI	dimension line increment	.38 x .7 = .266

Save these settings in your prototype drawing(s). When you are ready to dimension, simply multiply _DIMSCALE_ (1) times the "drawing scale factor."

Although this may seem complex, drawing setup for individual drawings is simplified. For example, assume your prototype drawing contained preset _Limits_ to the paper size, say 11 x 8.5. In addition, the previously mentioned dimension variables were set to produce 1/8" (or whatever) dimensions when plotted full size. Other variables such as _LTSCALE_ could be appropriately set. Then, when you wish to plot a drawing to 1=1, everything is preset. If you wish to plot to 1=2, simply multiply all the size-related system variables (_LIMITS, DIMSCALE, LTSCALE,_ etc.) times 2!

CHAPTER EXERCISES

For each of the following exercises, use the existing drawings as instructed. Create dimensions on the DIM (or other) appropriate layer. Follow the Guidelines for Dimensioning given in the chapter including setting an appropriate _DIMSCALE_ based on the drawing scale factor. Use dimension variables and create and use _Dimstyles_ when needed.

1. **Dimensioning a Multiview**

   Open the **SADDLE** drawing that you created in Chapter 24 Exercises. Set the appropriate ***Units*** and ***Precision***. Add the dimensions as shown. Because the illustration in Figure 29-60 is in isometric, placement of the dimensions can be improved for your multiview. Use optimum placement for the dimensions. ***Save*** the drawing as **SADDL-DM** and make a ***Plot*** to scale.

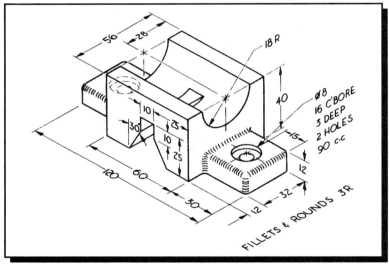

Figure 29-60

2. **Dimensioning a Multiview**

   Open the **ADJMOUNT** drawing that you completed in Chapter 25. Add the dimensions shown in Figure 29-61. Set appropriate ***Units*** and ***Precision*** (if not already set). Calculate and set an appropriate ***DIMSCALE***. Use the Guidelines for Dimensioning given in this chapter. Save the drawing as **ADJM-DIM** and make a ***Plot*** to an accepted scale.

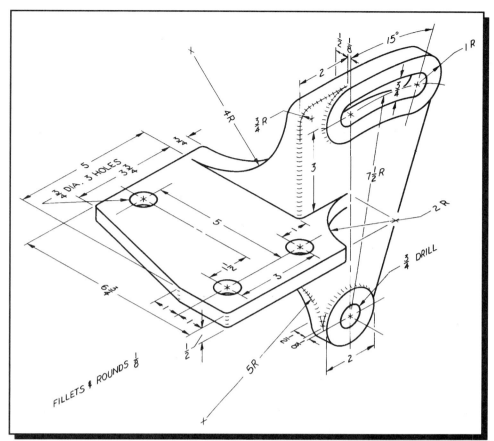

Figure 29-61

3. **Dimensioning an Auxiliary**

Open the **ANGLBRAC** drawing that you created in Chapter 27. Dimension as shown in Figure 29-62 but convert the dimensions to *Decimal*. Use the Guidelines for Dimensioning. Dimension the slot width as a *Limit* dimension--**.6248/.6255**. *Save* the drawing as **ANGL-DIM** and *Plot* to an accepted scale.

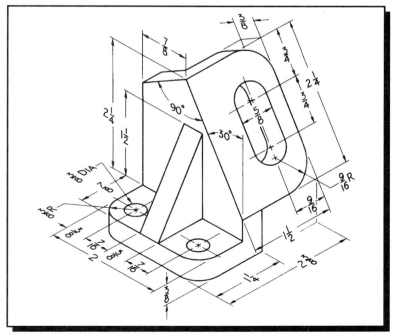

Figure 29-62

4.   Architectural Dimensioning

Open the **OFFICE** drawing that you completed in Chapter 21. Dimension the floor plan as shown in Figure 21-14. Add *Text* to name the rooms. *Save* the drawing as **OFF-DIM** and make a *Plot* to an accepted scale and sheet size based on your plotter capabilities.

5.   Isometric Dimensioning

Dimension the Support Bracket that you created as an isometric drawing named **SBRACKET** in the Chapter 25 Exercises. Convert the dimensions to *Decimal*. All of the dimensions shown in Figure 29-63 should appear on your drawing in the optimum placement. *Save* the drawing as **SBRCK-DM** and *Plot* to **1=1** on and A size sheet.

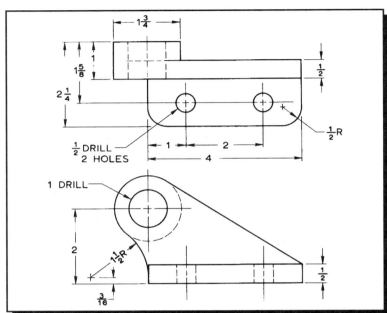

Figure 29-63

6.   Ordinate Dimensioning

Open the **PLATES** drawing that you created in Chapter 10 Exercises. *Erase* the plate located on the left, then *Move* the two remaining plates so their lower-left corners are located at coordinates **4,5** and **15,5** as shown in Figure 29-64. If the coordinate icon does not appear in your drawing by default, type *UCSICON* and turn the icon *On*. Also use the *ORigin* option to locate the icon at 0,0. Next type *UCS*, use

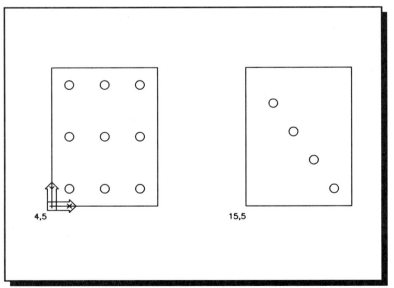

Figure 29-64

the *Origin* option, and **PICK** coordinate **4,5**. The icon should appear as shown in Figure 29-64. Use *Ordinate* dimensioning to create dimensions for the plate on the left. Use *UCS* with the *Origin* option again to relocate the icon to coordinate **15,5**. Dimension the second plate with *Ordinate* dimensions. *Save* as **PL-ORDIM.**

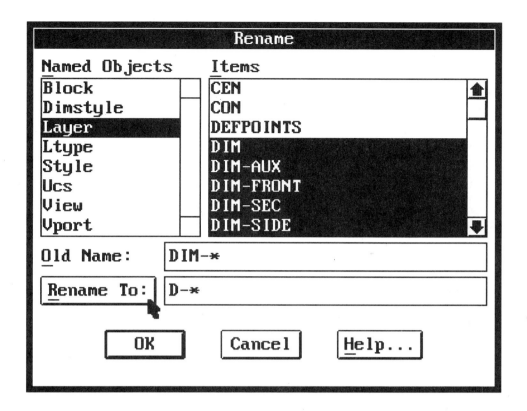

CHAPTER 30

Miscellaneous Commands

CHAPTER OBJECTIVES

After completing this chapter you should:

1. be able to use Wildcards when specifying named objects or files;

2. be able to *Rename* any named object in a drawing;

3. know when *Regenall, Redrawall*, and *Regenauto* are useful;

4. be able to set *BLIPMODE* to control "blip" markers and *DRAGMODE* to control dynamic dragging;

5. be able to turn *Fill Off* and *On* to speed regenerations and test plots;

6. be able to reinitialize devices and I/O ports using *Reinit;*

7. know how to use the *Multiple* modifier to automatically repeat commands;

8. be able to check the current drawing for errors using *Audit.*

BASICS

This chapter discusses several commands that are helpful intermediate-level features of AutoCAD. The following miscellaneous commands, variables, and wildcards are covered in this chapter.

Wildcards	*BLIPMODE*
Rename	*DRAGMODE*
Purge	*Fill*
Redrawall	*Reinit*
Regenall	*Multiple*
Regenauto	*Audit*

Named Objects

There are objects other than entities that AutoCAD may keep as part of a drawing file called Named Objects. The named objects are:

Blocks
Dimension Styles
Layers
Linetypes
Text Styles
User Coordinate Systems
Views
Viewport configurations

Wildcard characters, the *Rename* command, and the *Purge* command can be used to access or alter named objects.

MISCELLANEOUS COMMANDS, VARIABLES, AND WILDCARDS

Using Wildcards

Whenever AutoCAD prompts for a list of names, such as File names, system variables, *Block* names, *Layer* names, or other named objects, any of the wildcards in the following wildcard list can be used to access those names. These wildcards help you specify a specific group of named objects from a long list without having to repeatedly type or enter the complete spelling for each name in the list.

For example, the asterisk (*) is a common wildcard that is used to represent any alphanumeric string (group of letters or numbers). You may choose to specify a list of layers all beginning with the letters "DIM" and ending with any string. Using the *Layer* command and entering "DIM*" in response to the ? option would yield a list of only the layer names beginning with DIM.

Commands that Accept Wildcards

There are several AutoCAD commands that prompt you for a name or list of names or display a list of names to match your specification. Any command that has a ? option provides a list. Wildcards can be used with any of these commands.

Attedit
Block
Insert
Layer
Linetype
Load
Rename
Setvar
Style
UCS
View
Vplayer
Xref

Valid Wildcards for Use with AutoCAD

The following list defines valid wildcard characters that can be used with AutoCAD. The list below and the following list of examples is reprinted from the AutoCAD Reference Manual, Release 12, pages 122 and 123.

Character	Definition
# (Pound)	Matches any numeric digit
@ (At)	Matches any alpha character
. (Period)	Matches any nonalphanumeric character
* (Asterisk)	Matches any string, including the null string. It can be used anywhere in the search pattern: at the beginning, middle or end of the string
? (Question mark)	Matches any single character
~ (Tilde)	Matches anything but the pattern
[...]	Matches any one of the characters enclosed
[~...]	Matches any character not enclosed
- (Hyphen)	Used with brackets to specify a range for a one character
' (Reverse quote)	Escapes special characters (reads next character literally)

Below are listed one or more examples for each application of wildcard patterns.

Pattern	Will match or include . . .	But not . . .
ABC	Only ABC	
~ABC	Anything but ABC	
A?C	Any 3-character sequence beginning with A and ending with C	AC, ABCD, AXXC or XABC
AB?	ABA, AB3, ABZ, etc.	AB, ABCE or XAB
?BC	ABC, 3BC, XBC, etc.	AB, ABCD, BC or XXBC
A*C	AAC, AC, ABC, AX3C, etc.	XA or ABCD
A*	Anything starting with A	XAAA
*AB	Anything ending with AB	ABX
AB	AB anywhere in string	AXB
~*AB*	All strings without AB	AB, ABX, XAB or XABX
'*AB	*AB	AB, XAB or *ABC
[AB]C	AC or BC	ABC or XAC
[~AB]C	XC or YC	AC, BC or XXC
[A-J]C	AC, BC, JC, etc.	ABC, AJC or MC
[~A-J]C	Any character not in the range A-J, followed by C	AC, BC or JC

Wildcard Examples

For example, assume that you have a drawing of a 2-story residential floor plan with the following *Layers* and related settings.

```
   Layer name          State          Color          Linetype
-------------------   ---------   --------------   -------------
0                      On          7 (white)        CONTINUOUS
1-ELEC-DIM             On          7 (white)        CONTINUOUS
1-ELEC-LAY             On          7 (white)        CONTINUOUS
1-ELEC-TXT             On          7 (white)        CONTINUOUS
1-FLPN-DIM             On          7 (white)        CONTINUOUS
1-FLPN-LAY             On          7 (white)        CONTINUOUS
```

```
1-FLPN-TXT          On          7 (white)     CONTINUOUS
1-HVAC-DIM          On          7 (white)     CONTINUOUS
1-HVAC-LAY          On          7 (white)     CONTINUOUS
1-HVAC-TXT          On          7 (white)     CONTINUOUS
2-ELEC-DIM          On          7 (white)     CONTINUOUS
2-ELEC-LAY          On          7 (white)     CONTINUOUS
2-ELEC-TXT          On          7 (white)     CONTINUOUS
2-FLPN-DIM          On          7 (white)     CONTINUOUS
2-FLPN-LAY          On          7 (white)     CONTINUOUS
2-FLPN-TXT          On          7 (white)     CONTINUOUS
2-HVAC-DIM          On          7 (white)     CONTINUOUS
2-HVAC-LAY          On          7 (white)     CONTINUOUS
2-HVAC-TXT          On          7 (white)     CONTINUOUS
```

If you wanted to turn *Off* all the layers related to the second floor (names beginning with "2"), you can use the asterisk (*) wildcard as follows:

```
Command: Layer
?/Make/Set/New/ON/OFF/Color/Ltype/Freeze/Thaw/LOck/Unlock: off
Layer name(s) to turn Off: 2*
?/Make/Set/New/ON/OFF/Color/Ltype/Freeze/Thaw/LOck/Unlock: ?
Layer name(s) to list <*>:
```

Layer name	State	Color	Linetype
0	On	7 (white)	CONTINUOUS
1-ELEC-DIM	On	7 (white)	CONTINUOUS
1-ELEC-LAY	On	7 (white)	CONTINUOUS
1-ELEC-TXT	On	7 (white)	CONTINUOUS
1-FLPN-DIM	On	7 (white)	CONTINUOUS
1-FLPN-LAY	On	7 (white)	CONTINUOUS
1-FLPN-TXT	On	7 (white)	CONTINUOUS
1-HVAC-DIM	On	7 (white)	CONTINUOUS
1-HVAC-LAY	On	7 (white)	CONTINUOUS
1-HVAC-TXT	On	7 (white)	CONTINUOUS
2-ELEC-DIM	Off	7 (white)	CONTINUOUS
2-ELEC-LAY	Off	7 (white)	CONTINUOUS
2-ELEC-TXT	Off	7 (white)	CONTINUOUS
2-FLPN-DIM	Off	7 (white)	CONTINUOUS
2-FLPN-LAY	Off	7 (white)	CONTINUOUS
2-FLPN-TXT	Off	7 (white)	CONTINUOUS
2-HVAC-DIM	Off	7 (white)	CONTINUOUS
2-HVAC-LAY	Off	7 (white)	CONTINUOUS
2-HVAC-TXT	Off	7 (white)	CONTINUOUS

You may want to *Freeze* all layers (both floors) related to the electrical layout (having ELEC in the layer name). (Assume all the layers are *On* again.) You could use the question mark (?) to represent any floor and asterisk (*) for any string after ELEC as follows.

```
Command: Layer
?/Make/Set/New/ON/OFF/Color/Ltype/Freeze/Thaw/LOck/Unlock: fr
Layer name(s) to Freeze: ?-elec*
?/Make/Set/New/ON/OFF/Color/Ltype/Freeze/Thaw/LOck/Unlock: ?
Layer name(s) to list <*>:
```

Layer name	State	Color	Linetype
0	On	7 (white)	CONTINUOUS
1-ELEC-DIM	Frozen	7 (white)	CONTINUOUS
1-ELEC-LAY	Frozen	7 (white)	CONTINUOUS
1-ELEC-TXT	Frozen	7 (white)	CONTINUOUS
1-FLPN-DIM	On	7 (white)	CONTINUOUS
1-FLPN-LAY	On	7 (white)	CONTINUOUS
1-FLPN-TXT	On	7 (white)	CONTINUOUS
1-HVAC-DIM	On	7 (white)	CONTINUOUS
1-HVAC-LAY	On	7 (white)	CONTINUOUS
1-HVAC-TXT	On	7 (white)	CONTINUOUS
2-ELEC-DIM	Frozen	7 (white)	CONTINUOUS
2-ELEC-LAY	Frozen	7 (white)	CONTINUOUS
2-ELEC-TXT	Frozen	7 (white)	CONTINUOUS
2-FLPN-DIM	On	7 (white)	CONTINUOUS
2-FLPN-LAY	On	7 (white)	CONTINUOUS
2-FLPN-TXT	On	7 (white)	CONTINUOUS
2-HVAC-DIM	On	7 (white)	CONTINUOUS
2-HVAC-LAY	On	7 (white)	CONTINUOUS
2-HVAC-TXT	On	7 (white)	CONTINUOUS

You may want to use only the layout layers (names ending with LAY) and _Freeze_ all the other layers. (Assume all layers are _On_ and _Thawed_.) The tilde (~) character can be used to match anything but the pattern given. The tilde (~) character is translated as "anything except."

```
Command: layer
?/Make/Set/New/ON/OFF/Color/Ltype/Freeze/Thaw/LOck/Unlock: fr
Layer name(s) to Freeze: ~*lay
?/Make/Set/New/ON/OFF/Color/Ltype/Freeze/Thaw/LOck/Unlock: ?
Layer name(s) to list <*>:
```

Layer name	State	Color	Linetype
0	On	7 (white)	CONTINUOUS
1-ELEC-DIM	Frozen	7 (white)	CONTINUOUS
1-ELEC-LAY	On	7 (white)	CONTINUOUS
1-ELEC-TXT	Frozen	7 (white)	CONTINUOUS
1-FLPN-DIM	Frozen	7 (white)	CONTINUOUS
1-FLPN-LAY	On	7 (white)	CONTINUOUS
1-FLPN-TXT	Frozen	7 (white)	CONTINUOUS
1-HVAC-DIM	Frozen	7 (white)	CONTINUOUS
1-HVAC-LAY	On	7 (white)	CONTINUOUS
1-HVAC-TXT	Frozen	7 (white)	CONTINUOUS
2-ELEC-DIM	Frozen	7 (white)	CONTINUOUS
2-ELEC-LAY	On	7 (white)	CONTINUOUS

```
2-ELEC-TXT           Frozen       7  (white)     CONTINUOUS
2-FLPN-DIM           Frozen       7  (white)     CONTINUOUS
2-FLPN-LAY           On           7  (white)     CONTINUOUS
2-FLPN-TXT           Frozen       7  (white)     CONTINUOUS
2-HVAC-DIM           Frozen       7  (white)     CONTINUOUS
2-HVAC-LAY           On           7  (white)     CONTINUOUS
2-HVAC-TXT           Frozen       7  (white)     CONTINUOUS
```

Remember that wildcards can be used with many AutoCAD commands. For example, you may want to load a certain set of _Linetypes_, perhaps all the HIDDEN variations. The following sequence could be used.

```
Command: linetype
?/Create/Load/Set: l
Linetype(s) to load: hid*

Linetype HIDDEN loaded.
Linetype HIDDEN2 loaded.
Linetype HIDDENX2 loaded.
```

Or, you may want to load all of the linetypes except the "X2" variations. This syntax could be used:

```
Command: linetype
?/Create/Load/Set: l
Linetype(s) to load: ~*x2

Linetype BORDER loaded.
Linetype BORDER2 loaded.
Linetype CENTER loaded.
Linetype CENTER2 loaded.
Linetype DASHDOT loaded.
Linetype DASHDOT2 loaded.
Linetype DASHED loaded.
Linetype DASHED2 loaded.
etc.
```

RENAME and DDRENAME

TYPE IN:	PULL-DOWN MENU	SCREEN MENU	TABLET MENU
RENAME or DDRENAME	---	UTILITY, RENAME:, Rename Dialogue...	---

These utility commands allow you to rename any named object that is part of the current drawing. _Rename_ does not have the same function as the _Rename File_ option of the _File_

Utilities, which only renames file names. *Rename* and the related dialogue box accessed by the *Ddrename* command allow you to rename the <u>named objects</u> listed at the beginning of this chapter, namely:

> *Blocks, Dimension Styles, Layers, Linetypes, Text Styles, User Coordinate Systems, Views*, and *Viewport* configurations.

The *Rename* command can be used to rename objects one at a time. For example, the command sequence might be as follows.

```
Command: rename
Block/Dimstyle/LAyer/LType/Style/Ucs/VIew/VPort: la (use the
Layer option)
Old layer name: dim-sec
New layer name: d-sec
Command:
```

Wildcard characters are not allowed with the *Rename* command, only with the dialogue box.

Optionally, if you prefer to use dialogue boxes, you may type *Ddrename* or select *Rename Dialogue...* to access the dialogue box shown in Figure 30-1.

You may select from the *Named Objects* list to display the related objects existing in the drawing. Then select or type the old name so it appears in the *Old Name* edit box. Specify the new name in the *Rename To:* edit box. You must then PICK the *Rename To:* tile and the new names will appear in the list. Then select the *OK* tile to confirm.

The *Rename* dialogue box can be used with wildcard characters to specify a list of named object for renaming. For

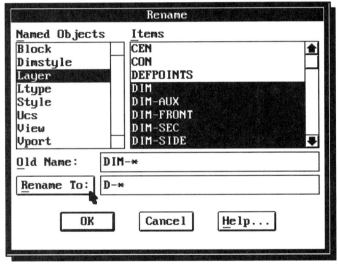

Figure 30-1

example, if you desired to rename all the "DIM-*" layers so that the letters "DIM" were replaced with only the letter "D", the following sequence would be used.

1.   In the *Old Name* edit box, enter "DIM-*" and press Enter. All of the layers beginning with "DIM-" are highlighted.

2.   In the *Rename To:* edit box, enter "D-*." Next, the *Rename To:* tile must be PICKed. Finally PICK the OK tile to confirm the change.

PURGE

TYPE IN:	PULL-DOWN MENU	SCREEN MENU	TABLET MENU
PURGE	---	*UTILITY, PURGE:*	---

Purge allows you to selectively delete any named object that is not referenced in the drawing. In other words, if the drawing has any named objects defined but not appearing in the drawing, they can be deleted with *Purge*. Examples of unreferenced named objects are:

> *Blocks* that have been defined but not *Inserted*;
> *Layers* that exist without entities residing on the layers;
> *Dimstyles* that have been defined, yet no dimensions created in the style;
> *Linetypes* that were loaded but not used;
> *Shapes* that were loaded but not used;
> *Text Styles* that have been defined, yet no text has been created in the *Style*.

Since these named objects occupy a small amount of space in the drawing, using *Purge* to delete unused named objects can reduce the file size. This may be helpful when drawings are created using prototype drawings that contain many unused named objects or when other drawings are inserted that contain many unused *Layers* or *Blocks*, etc.

There is one catch to using *Purge*; the command must be invoked <u>before</u> any entities are created or edited (before the database has been changed) in a particular drawing session. Usually this means the drawing should be *Saved* (or *Exited*), then *Purge* should be invoked immediately (or after *Opening* the drawing again). The command options are listed here.

```
Command: purge
Purge unused Blocks/Dimstyles/LAyers/LTypes/SHapes/
STyles/All:
```

You can select one type of object to be *Purged*, or select *All* to have all named objects listed. AutoCAD lists all named objects matching the type selected. For example, if you specified *LAyers* to purge, AutoCAD responds with a list of <u>unused</u> layers that may look something like this:

```
Purge layer HID? <N>
Purge layer CON? <N>
Purge layer CEN? <N>
Purge layer HIGH? <N>
Purge layer TEXT? <N>
Purge layer DOT? <N>
Purge layer DEFPOINTS? <N>
Purge layer DIM? <N>
Command:
```

Answering with a "Y" causes the deletion of the named object. The other named object options operate similarly.

REDRAWALL

TYPE IN:	PULL-DOWN MENU	SCREEN MENU	TABLET MENU
REDRAWALL	*View, Redraw All*	*DISPLAY, REDRAWALL:*	*11,Q and 11,R*

As you know, the *Redraw* command cleans up the screen of all "blips" and redraws entities that have been partly removed by *Erasing* other objects. The *Redraw* command redraws the entire screen if you are not using viewports or redraws <u>only the current viewport</u> if you are using viewports.

The *Redrawall* command redraws the screen for <u>all viewports</u>. Viewports are separate areas of the screen that can be controlled to display a particular part or view of the geometry. Viewports are of two types: paper space viewports created with the *Mview* command (Chapter 32) and tiled viewports created with the *Vports* command (Chapter 34).

REGENALL

TYPE IN:	PULL-DOWN MENU	SCREEN MENU	TABLET MENU
REGENALL	---	*DISPLAY, REGENALL*	*11,K*

In most cases when changes are made to a drawing that affect the appearance of the entities on the screen, the drawing is automatically regenerated. In a few cases when changes are made to system variables, such as a new *PDMODE* (*Point* type), the *Regen* or *Regenall* command should be used to display the effect of the new setting.

The *Regen* command causes a regeneration of the entire drawing; however, if you are using viewports, *Regen* will only redraw the <u>current viewport</u>. The *Regenall* command should be used if you are using viewports (paper space or tiled viewports) and want to regenerate <u>all viewports</u>. See Chapter 32 and Chapter 34 for information on using paper space viewports and tiled viewports, respectively.

REGENAUTO

TYPE IN:	PULL-DOWN MENU	SCREEN MENU	TABLET MENU
REGENAUTO	---	*DISPLAY, RGNAUTO:*	---

When changes are made to a drawing that affect the appearance of the entities on the screen, the drawing is generally regenerated automatically. A regeneration can be somewhat time-consuming if you are working on an extremely complex drawing or are using a relatively slow computer. In some cases you may be performing several operations that cause regenerations between intermediate steps that you feel are unnecessary.

Regenauto allows you to control whether automatic regenerations are performed. *Regenauto* is *On* by default, but for special situations you may want to turn the automatic regenerations *Off* temporarily.

If *Regenauto* is *Off* and a regeneration is needed, AutoCAD prompts:

```
About to regen--proceed? <Y>
```

If you prompt with a *No* response, the regeneration will be aborted.

BLIPMODE

TYPE IN:	PULL-DOWN MENU	SCREEN MENU	TABLET MENU
BLIPMODE	*Settings, Drawing Aids... Blips*	*SETTINGS, BLIPS:*	---

"Blips" are the small white markers that appear on the screen whenever you PICK a point. The blips are automatically erased upon a *Redraw* or *Regen*.

The *BLIPMODE* system variable allows you to control the generation of the temporary marker blips. The *BLIPMODE* is *On* by default. When *BLIPMODE* is *Off*, no marker blips appear. The command format is this.

```
Command: blipmode
ON/OFF <ON>: (option)
```

The setting is saved with the drawing file in the *BLIPMODE* system variable. The variable can also be accessed using the *Setvar* command (see Appendix A).

DRAGMODE

TYPE IN:	PULL-DOWN MENU	SCREEN MENU	TABLET MENU
DRAGMODE	---	*SETTINGS, DRAGMODE:*	---

AutoCAD dynamically displays some entities such as *Circles, Blocks, Polygons*, etc. as you draw or insert them. This dynamic feature is called "dragging." If you are using a slow computer or for certain operations, you may wish to turn dragging off.

The *DRAGMODE* system variable provides three positions for the dynamic dragging feature. The command format is as follows.

```
Command: dragmode
ON/OFF/Auto <Auto>: (option)
```

By default, *DRAGMODE* is set to *Auto*. In this position, dragging is automatically displayed whenever possible, based upon the ability of the command in use to support it. Commands that support this feature issue a request for dragging when the command is used. This request is automatically filled when *DRAGMODE* is in the *Auto* position.

When *DRAGMODE* is *On*, you must enter **drag** at the command prompt when the request is issued by selected commands if you want to enable dragging. If *DRAGMODE* is *Off*, dragging is not displayed and all requests are automatically ignored.

The *DRAGMODE* variable setting is stored with the current drawing file.

FILL

TYPE IN:	PULL-DOWN MENU	SCREEN MENU	TABLET MENU
FILL	*Settings, Drawing Aids... Solid Fill*	---	---

The *Fill* command controls the display of entities that are filled with solid color. Commands that create solid filled entities are *Donut*, *Solid*, and *Pline* (*width*). *Fill* can be toggled *On* or *Off* to display or plot the entities with or without solid color. The command format produces this prompt.

```
Command: fill
ON/OFF <On>: (option)
Command:
```

The default position for the *Fill* command is *On*. If *Fill* is changed, the drawing must be regenerated to display the effects of the change. The setting for *Fill* is stored in the *FILLMODE* system variable.

Figure 30-2 displays several entities with *Fill On* and *Off*.

Since solid filling may be time consuming to regenerate a drawing with many wide *Plines*, *Donuts* and *Solids*, it may be useful to turn *Fill Off* temporarily. *Fill Off* would be <u>especially</u> helpful for speeding up test plots.

Figure 30-2

REINIT

TYPE IN:	PULL-DOWN MENU	SCREEN MENU	TABLET MENU
REINIT	---	---	---

The *Reinit* command reinitializes the input/output ports of the computer (to the digitizer and plotter); reinitializes the communications link to the peripheral devices, such as the digitizer and monitor; and reinitializes the AutoCAD Program Parameters (ACAD.PGP) file.

Reinitialization may be necessary if you physically switch the port cable from the plotter to the printer and back, or if the digitizer loses power temporarily. Occasionally, the monitor may lose alignment and have to be reinitialized.

Many software programs would require you to exit and restart the program in order for reinitialization to be performed. AutoCAD provides the *Reinit* command to prevent having to exit AutoCAD to accomplish this task.

Typing the *Reinit* command causes the *Re-initialization* dialogue box to appear (Fig. 30-3). You may check one or several of the boxes. PICKing the *OK* tile causes an immediate reinitialization.

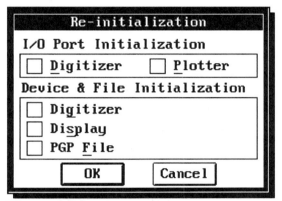

Figure 30-3

MULTIPLE

TYPE IN:	PULL-DOWN MENU	SCREEN MENU	TABLET MENU
MULTIPLE	---	---	---

Multiple is actually called a command modifier (or adjective) since it affects another command. Entering "*multiple*" at the Command: prompt as a prefix to any command (except *Plot*) causes the command to automatically repeat until you stop the sequence with the CTRL+C key sequence. For example, if you wanted to use the *Insert* command repetitively, you enter the following.

     Command: ***multiple insert***

The *insert* command would repeat until you stop it with CTRL+C.

The multiple modifier repeats only the command, not the command options. For example, if you wanted to repeatedly use *Circle* with the *Tangent, Tangent, Radius* option, the *TTR* would have to be entered each time the *Circle* command was automatically repeated.

AUDIT

TYPE IN:	PULL-DOWN MENU	SCREEN MENU	TABLET MENU
AUDIT	---	*UTILITY, AUDIT:*	---

The *Audit* command is AutoCAD's diagnostic utility for checking drawing files and correcting errors. *Audit* will examine the current drawing. You can decide whether or not AutoCAD should fix any errors if they are found. The command may yield a display something like this.

```
Command: audit
Fix any errors detected? <N> y
10      Blocks audited
20      Blocks audited
23      Blocks audited
Pass 1 100      entities audited
Pass 1 200      entities audited
Pass 1 300      entities audited
Pass 1 400      entities audited
Pass 1 483      entities audited
Pass 2 100      entities audited
Pass 2 200      entities audited
Pass 2 300      entities audited
Pass 2 400      entities audited
Pass 2 483      entities audited

Total errors found 0 fixed 0

Command:
```

If errors are detected and you requested for them to be fixed, the last line of the report indicates the number of errors found and the number fixed. If *Audit* cannot fix the errors, try the *Recover* command (see Chapter 2).

You can create an ASCII report file by changing the *AUDITCTL* system variable to 1. In this case, when the *Audit* command is used, AutoCAD automatically writes the report out to disk in the current directory using the current drawing file name and an .ADT file extension. The default setting for *AUDITCTL* is 0 (off).

CHAPTER EXERCISES

1.   Wildcards

In this exercise you will use wildcards to manage layers for a complex drawing. ***Open*** the AutoCAD **HOUSEPLN** drawing that is located in the **SAMPLE** directory. Use the ***Layer Control*** dialogue box to view the layers. Examine the layer names, then ***Cancel***.

A.   Type the *Layer* command. *Freeze* all of the layers whose names begin with the letters **ARC**. (Hint: enter **ARC*** at the `Layer name(s) to Freeze:` prompt.) Do you notice the change in the drawing? Use the *Layer Control* dialogue box or list the layers using the *?* option to view the *State* of the layers.

B.   *Thaw* all layers (use the asterisk *). Now *Freeze* all of the layers <u>except</u> the wall layers (those beginning with **WAL**). (Hint: enter **~WAL*** at the `Layer name(s) to Freeze:` prompt.) Do only the walls appear in the drawing now? Examine the list of layers and their *State*. *Thaw* all layers again.

C.   Next, *Freeze* all of the layers except the dimensioning layer (layer names having a DIM string). (Hint: enter **~*DIM*** at the `Layer name(s) to Freeze:` prompt.) Do only the dimensions appear in the drawing now? Examine the list of layers and their *State*. *(Layer 0 cannot be Frozen* because it is the Current layer.) *Thaw* all layers again and do <u>not</u> *Save* changes.

2.   *Rename*

        Open the **OFF-ATT2** drawing that you last worked on in Chapter 22. Enter *Ddrename* (or select from the *UTILITY* screen menu) to produce the *Rename* dialogue box. *Rename* the *Blocks* as follows:

New Name	Old Name
DSK	**DESK**
CHR	**CHAIR**
TBL	**TABLE**
FLC	**FILECAB**

        Next, use the *Rename* dialogue box again to rename the *Layers* as indicated below.

New Name	Old Name
FLOORPLN-DIM	**DIM-FLOOR**
ELEC-DIM	**DIM-ELEC**

        Use the *Rename* dialogue box again to change the *Text Style* name as follows.

New Name	Old Name
ARCH-FONT	**CITY BLUEPRINT**

        Save the drawing.

3.   *Purge*

        With the OFF-ATT2 drawing open, use the *Purge* command. The command is probably invalid at this point. *Save* the drawing and *Exit AutoCAD*. While in DOS, list the directory (type **DIR**) to check the file size (of OFF-ATT2.DWG). Now, *Open* **OFF-ATT2** and try *Purge* again. Since you will not need any of the **ELEC** layers, *Purge* all of those layers beginning with **ELEC**. *Exit AutoCAD* and *Save Changes*. Check the file size again. Is the file size slightly smaller?

4.   *Multiple* modifier

Open the **OFF-ATT2** drawing again and prepare to *Insert* several more furniture *Blocks* into the office. Type *Multiple* at the Command: prompt, then a space, then *Insert* and return. Proceed to *Insert* the *Blocks*. Notice that you do not have to repeatedly enter the *Insert* command. Now try the *Multiple* modifier with the *Line* command. Remember this for use with other repetitive commands. (Do not *Save* the drawing.)

5.   *Audit*

With the OFF-ATT2 drawing open, use the *Audit* command to report any errors. If errors exist, use *Audit* again to fix the errors.

6.   *BLIPMODE, DRAGMODE*

A.   Begin a *New* drawing using your **ASHEET** prototype. Turn *BLIPMODE Off*. Experiment with this setting by drawing a few *Lines* and *Circles*. Use *Erase*. Notice that you do not have to *Redraw* as often as you did when *BLIPMODE* was *On*.

B.   Now change the setting of *DRAGMODE* to *Off*. Draw a few *Circles*, a *Polygon*, an *Ellipse*, and then **dimension** your figures. Do you prefer *DRAGMODE On* or *Off*?

C.   Since the *BLIPMODE* and *DRAGMODE* system variables are saved with the drawing file, you can make the settings in the prototype drawings so they will preset to your preference when you begin a *New* drawing (if you prefer other than the default settings). If you prefer *BLIPMODE* or *DRAGMODE Off*, *Exit* the **ASHEET** and *Discard Changes*. Use *Open* to open each of the prototype drawings (**ASHEET, BSHEET, CSHEET**, and **DSHEET**), change the desired setting, and *Save*.

7.   *Fill*

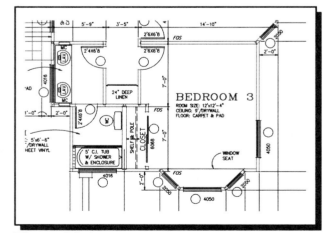

Figure 30-4

Open the **HOUSEPLN** sample drawing. *Zoom* in to the lower right corner of the drawing to view "Bedroom 3" as shown in Figure 30-4. Make a test *Plot* of the *Display*, *Scaled to Fit*, and time the plot.

Now turn *Fill Off*. The walls should appear as in Figure 30-4. Also turn *Qtext On*. Make another *Plot* as before and check the time. Was there much improvement? If you do not have a plotter, you can check the time required for regenerations. *Fill* and *Qtext* can be set to save time for test plots or *Regens*. (Do <u>not</u> *Save* the changes to HOUSEPLN.)

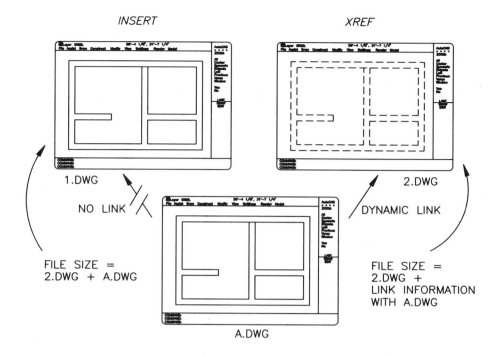

INSERT

XREF

1.DWG

NO LINK

FILE SIZE =
2.DWG + A.DWG

A.DWG

2.DWG

DYNAMIC LINK

FILE SIZE =
2.DWG +
LINK INFORMATION
WITH A.DWG

CHAPTER 31

Xreferences

CHAPTER OBJECTIVES

After completing this chapter you should:

1.   know the difference between an *Xrefed* drawing and an *Inserted* drawing;

2.   be able to *Attach* an externally referenced drawing to the current drawing;

3.   be able to *Reload* an *Xrefed* drawing while in a drawing session;

4.   be able to *Detach* an externally referenced drawing;

5.   know the naming scheme for dependent objects (*Blocks, Layers, Text Styles*, etc.);

6.   be able to *Bind* an entire *Xrefed* drawing and *Xbind* individual named objects;

7.   be able to use the *VISRETAIN* variable to retain dependent layer visibility settings;

8.   know how to control the creation of *Xref* log files (.XLG) with the *XREFCTL* variable.

BASICS

AutoCAD's Xreference (external reference) feature enables you to view another drawing from within your current drawing. The externally referenced drawing (Xref) is visible in the same screen as the current drawing; however, you cannot draw in or edit the Xref drawing.

Similar to the *Insert* command's ability to bring another drawing into the current drawing as a *Block*, the *Xref* command can bring any drawing (or *WBlock*) into the current drawing but not as a permanent part of the current drawing. Comparisons between the *Insert* and the *Xref* commands are outlined below.

INSERT

- The drawing comes in as a *Block*.

- The *Block* drawing is a permanent part of the current drawing.

- The current drawing file size increases approximately equal to the *Block* drawing size.

- The *Inserted Block* drawing is static. It never changes.

- If the original drawing that was *Inserted* is changed, the drawing *Block* must be redefined to reflect the new changes in the current drawing.

- Entities of the *Inserted* drawing cannot be changed unless *Exploded*.

- The visibility of the *Inserted* drawing's individual layers can be controlled in the current drawing.

- Any drawing can be *Inserted* as a *Block*.

- The current drawing can contain multiple *Block*s.

- *Block*s can be nested.

XREF

- The drawing comes in as an *Xref*.

- The *Xref* is not permanent, only "attached."

- The current drawing increases only by a few bytes (enough to store the *Xref* name and path).

- Each time the current drawing is opened, it loads the most current version of the *Xref* drawing.

- If the original *Xref* drawing is changed, the changes are automatically reflected when the current drawing is *Opened*.

- The *Xref* cannot be changed in the current drawing. (Changes are typically made in the original drawing.)

- The visibility of the *Xref* drawing's individual layers can be controlled in the current drawing.

- Any drawing can be *Xrefed*.

- The current drawing can contain multiple *Xrefs*.

- *Xrefs* can be nested.

INSERT (cont.)

- A *Block* drawing cannot be converted to an *Xref*.

- When the current drawing is plotted, the *Inserted Block* is also plotted.

XREF (cont.)

- An *Xref* can be converted to a *Block*. The *Bind* option makes it a permanent part of the current drawing, like a *Block*.

- When the current drawing is plotted, *Xref* drawings can be plotted also (if their layers are *On*).

As you can see, an *Xrefed* drawing has many similarities and some differences to an *Inserted* drawing. The following figures illustrate both the differences and similarities between an *Xrefed* drawing and an *Inserted* one.

The main differences are Illustrated in Figure 31-1. The relationship between the current drawing and a drawing that has been *Inserted* and one that has been Xreferenced is illustrated here. The current drawing is thought of as the "parent" drawing. The *Inserted* drawing becomes a permanent part of the current drawing. No link exists between the parent drawing and the original *Inserted* drawing. In contrast, the *Xrefed* drawing is not a permanent part of the parent drawing. The *Xref* is a dynamic link between the two drawings. In this way, when the original *Xrefed* drawing is edited, the changes are reflected in the parent drawing (if a *Reload* is invoked or when the parent drawing is *Opened* next). The file size of the parent drawing for the *Inserted* case is the sum of both the drawings; whereas, the file size of the parent drawing for the *Xref* case is only the original size plus the link information.

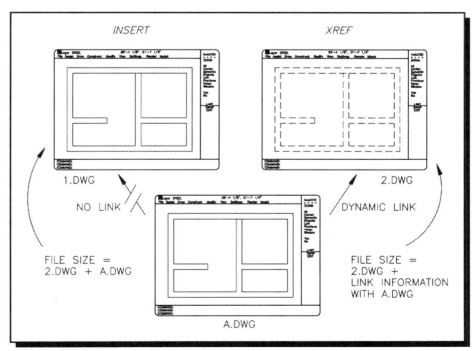

Figure 31-1

Some of the similarities between Xreferenced drawings and *Inserted* drawings are shown in the following figures.

Any number of drawings can be *Xrefed* into the current drawings as shown in Figure 31-2. For example, component parts can be *Xrefed* to compile an assembly drawing.

The capability of a drawing to contain multiple *Xrefs* is similar to the ability of a drawing to contain an unlimited number of *Blocks*.

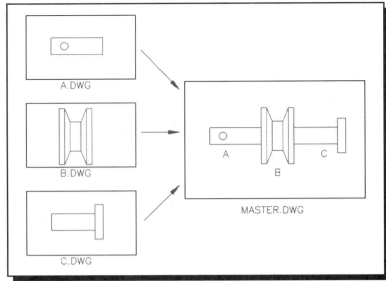

Figure 31-2

The current drawing can contain nested *Xrefs*. This feature is also similar to *Blocks*.

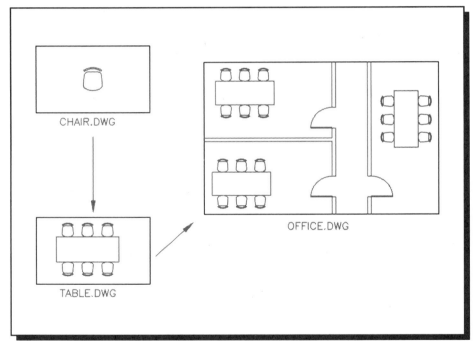

Figure 31-3

One of the main features and purposes of an *Xref* drawing is that it cannot be edited. In other words, you cannot draw or edit any geometry on any of its layers. You do, however, have complete control over the visibility of the *Xref* drawing's layers. The *State* of the layers (*On*, *Off*, *Freeze*, and *Thaw*) of the *Xref* drawing can be controlled.

The named objects (*Layers, Text styles, Blocks,* Views, etc.) that may be part of a *Xref* drawing become dependent objects when they are *Xrefed*. These dependent objects cannot be renamed, changed, or used in the parent drawing. They can, however, be converted individually into the parent drawing with the *Xbind* command.

Xref drawings have many applications. Xrefs are particularly useful in a networked office or laboratory environment. For example, several people may be working on one project; each person constructing individual components of the project. The components may be mechanical parts of an assembly, or electrical, plumbing, and HVAC layouts for a construction project, or several areas of a plant layout. In any case, each person can *Xref* another person's drawing as an external reference without fear of the original drawing being edited. The entire team can access (*Xref*) the same master layout, such as a floorplan, assembly drawing, or topographic map. The project coordinator could *Open* a new drawing, *Xref* all components, analyze the relationships among components, and plot the compilation of the components. The master drawing may not even contain any entities other than *Xrefs*, yet each time it is *Opened*, it would contain the most up-to-date component drawings.

The simplicity of using Xrefs is that one command, *Xref*, controls almost all of the external referencing features. Several options permit you to create, sever, or change the link between the current (parent) drawing and the *Xref* (externally referenced) drawing.

XREF AND RELATED COMMANDS AND VARIABLES

XREF

TYPE IN:	PULL-DOWN MENU	SCREEN MENU	TABLET MENU
XREF	*Files, Xref >*	*BlockS, XREF:*	*1,P and 2,P*

The *Xref* command provides you with control of externally referenced drawings. The options allow you to *Attach, Detach, Reload*, and *Bind* an Xref. The command syntax to *Attach* (create the link between) the current drawing and the *Xref* drawing is as follows.

```
Command: xref
?/Bind/Detach/Path/Reload/<Attach>: Enter
Xref to Attach: (Enter the drawing name)
Attach Xref (NAME): (NAME)
(NAME) loaded.
Insertion point: PICK or (coordinates)
X scale factor <1> / Corner / XYZ: Enter or (value) or (option)
Y scale factor (default=X): Enter or (value)
Rotation angle <0>: Enter or (value)
Command:
```

The *Attach* option creates a link between the current drawing and the *Xref* drawing. This action causes the specified drawing to appear in the current drawing similar to the way a drawing appears when it is *Inserted* as a *Block*. Notice the similarity of the last four prompts to the *Insert* command. Similar to the action of *Insert*, the base point of the *Xref* drawing is its 0,0 point unless a different base point has been previously defined with the *Base* command.

The X scale factor:, Y scale factor:, and Rotation angle: prompts operate identically to the _Insert_ command.

For example, assume that you are an interior designer in an architectural firm. Your job is to design the interior layout comprised of desks, tables, chairs and office equipment for an office complex. Your current drawing is only an outline of the office space, but it contains _Blocks_ of each chair, desk, etc. as shown in Figure 31-4.

The INTERIOR.DWG contains only the perimeter of the office space and the following _Block_ definitions:

CHAIR, CONCHAIR,
DESK, TABLE, FILECAB,
CONTABLE.

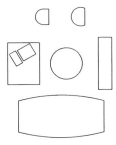

Figure 31-4

Next, use _Xref_ to _Attach_ the architect's finished floor plan drawing, OFFICEX.DWG. The OFFICEX drawing is inserted at the desired location. The _Xrefed_ drawing is visible; however, it cannot be altered.

The visibility of the individual dependent layers can be controlled with the _Layer_ command or _Layer Control_ dialogue box.

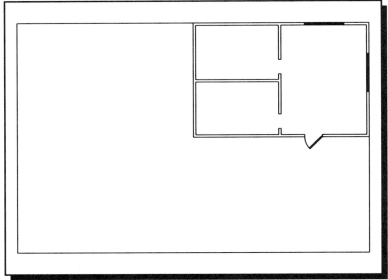

Figure 31-5

The next step is to draw entities in the current drawing, or in this case _Insert_ the office furniture and equipment _Blocks_ that are defined in the current drawing (INTERIOR.DWG).

The resulting drawing would display a complete layout of the office floorplan and the furniture as if it were one drawing (see Figure 31-6).

If a change in the floorplan design were required, the architect would notify you after the redesign so you could *Reload* the FLOORPLAN drawing. The *Reload* would display the latest version of the office floorplan. The appropriate changes could easily be made to the interior as needed. In contrast, if the OFFICEX drawing had originally been *Inserted* as a *Block*, the design changes would not be apparent, unless the *Block* were *Erased*, *Purged*, and the new drawing *Inserted*.

The CHAIR, CONCHAIR, DESK, TABLE, CONTABLE and FILECAB *Block*s could be *Inserted* or any other entities drawn in the parent drawing. The *Xrefed* OFFICEX floorplan drawing is used as a guide.

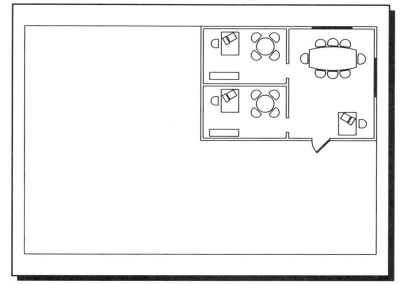

Figure 31-6

Any changes subsequently made to the OFFICEX drawing, such as the relocation of the door, would be displayed after a *Reload* (as shown). The appropriate changes would then be made to the INTERIOR drawing.

When all parts of the office complex are completed, the INTERIOR (parent) drawing could be plotted. The resulting plot would include the parent and the *Xref* drawing.

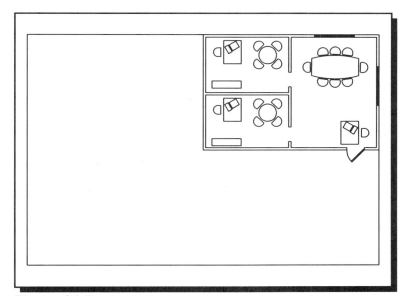

Figure 31-7

The complete list of options of the *Xref* command (`?/Bind/Detach/Path/Reload/<Attach>:`) are explained on the following page.

Attach

This option <u>creates</u> an external reference <u>link</u> between two drawings. Only the <u>name</u> of the reference drawing and its directory <u>path</u> become a permanent part of the current drawing. Each time the current drawing is *Opened*, the *Attached* drawing is loaded as an *Xref*. You must specify the *Insertion point, Scale factors*, and *Rotation angle*. More than one reference drawing can be *Attached* to the current drawing. A single reference drawing can be *Attached* to any number of insertion points in the current drawing. The dependent objects in the reference drawing (*Block*s, *Text styles*, etc.) are assigned new names, "external drawing|old name" (See Dependent Objects and Names).

Bind

The *Bind* option <u>converts</u> the <u>*Xref*</u> drawing to a <u>*Block*</u> in the current drawing, then terminates the external reference partnership. The names of the dependent objects in the external drawing are changed to avoid possible conflicts. If you want to only bind selected named objects, use the *Xbind* command.

Detach

Detach severs the link between the parent drawing and the *Xref*. When the parent drawing is *Opened*, the previously *Attached* drawing is <u>no longer</u> loaded as an *Xref*.

?

This option lists all existing external references in the current drawing.

Path

You can respecify the directory location of the external drawing using the *Path* option. This is necessary if an *Xrefed* drawing has been relocated to another directory on the disk, computer hard drive, or network drives.

Reload

This option forces a *Reload* of the external drawing at any time while the current drawing is in the drawing editor. This ensures that the current drawing contains the <u>most recent version</u> of the external drawing. In a networking environment you cannot *Attach, Bind*, or *Reload* an external drawing which is in an editing session because the external drawing is locked (a .DWK file exists).

Dependent Objects and Names

The <u>named objects</u> that have been created as part of a drawing become <u>dependent objects</u> when the drawing is *Xrefed*. The named objects of an *Xref* drawing are listed here.

*Block*s
Dimension Styles
Linetypes
Layers
Text Styles
User Coordinate Systems
Views
Viewport Configurations

These dependent objects <u>cannot</u> be renamed or changed in the parent drawing. Dependent text or dimension styles cannot be used in the parent drawing. You cannot draw on dependent layers; you can only control the visibility of the dependent layers. You <u>can</u>, however, *Bind* the entire *Xref* and the dependent named objects, or you can bind individual dependent objects with the *Xbind* command. *Xbind* converts an individual dependent object into a permanent part of the parent drawing. (See *Xbind.*)

When an *Xref* contains named objects, the names of the dependent objects are changed. The original names are prefixed by the *Xref* drawing name and separated by a pipe (|) symbol. For example, if the OFFICEX.DWG was *Xrefed* and contained a FLOORPLAN layer, it would be renamed in the parent drawing to OFFICEX|FLOORPLAN. Likewise, if the *Xrefed* drawing contained the *Block* named DOOR, it would be renamed in the parent drawing to OFFICEX|DOOR. This naming scheme prevents conflicts in the case that the *Xref* drawing and the parent drawing both contained *Layers* or *Blocks*, etc. with the same names.

For the example parent drawing (INTERIOR), the *Layer Control* dialogue box displays the original layers as well as the dependent layers (prefixed with "OFFICEX|").

Likewise, listing the *Blocks* would yield a display showing both the original *Blocks* in INTERIOR drawing and the dependent *Blocks* from OFFICEX drawing. Note that the *Xref* is also listed. The same naming scheme operates with all named objects--*Dimstyles, Text styles, Views*, etc.

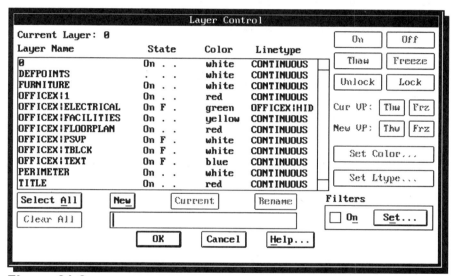

Figure 31-8

```
Command: block
Block name (or ?): ?
Block(s) to list <*>: Enter
Defined Blocks.
     CHAIR
     CONCHAIR
     CONTABLE
     DESK
     FILECAB
     OFFICEX                 Xref: resolved
     OFFICEX|DOOR            Xdep: OFFICEX
     OFFICEX|WINDOW          Xdep: OFFICEX
     TABLE
User        External       Dependent      Unnamed
Blocks      References      Blocks         Blocks
  6            1              2              0
```

Notice the *Block*s (originally named DOOR and WINDOW) in the dependent drawing are prefixed with OFFICEX|. If you wanted to bind the *Xref* drawing using the *Bind* option, the link is severed and the *Xref* drawing becomes a *Block* in the parent drawing. In this case, the dependent objects are renamed. The pipe (|) character is replaced with three characters: a "$", a number, and another "$". For example, layer OFFICEX|FLOORPLAN would be renamed to OFFICEXnFLOORPLAN. Since the layers become a permanent part of the parent drawing, the *Rename* command could then be used to change the names if desired. For Xrefs that have been converted to a *Block* with *Bind*, *Explode* would then be required to enable editing individual entities of the *Block* drawing.

VISRETAIN

This variable controls dependent layer *State*. Remember that you cannot draw or edit on a dependent layer; however, you can change the layer's *State* (*On, Off, Freeze, Thaw*) with the *Layer* command or *Layer Control* dialogue box. The setting of *VISRETAIN* determines if the visibility settings that have been made are retained when the *Xref* is reloaded.

When *VISRETAIN* is set to 1 in the parent drawing, all the global layer settings (*Freeze, Thaw,* and *On, Off*) are retained for the Xreferenced dependent layers. When you *End* or *Save*, the current visibility for dependent layers is saved with the <u>current</u> (parent) drawing regardless of whether the visibility has changed in the externally referenced drawing itself. In other words, if *VISRETAIN*=1, the parent drawing's *Layer State* settings override the Xref drawing settings.

If *VISRETAIN* is set to 0, then dependent layer visibility at the start of a drawing session is determined by the state in which they were left when the <u>external</u> drawing was last saved.

XBIND

TYPE IN:	PULL-DOWN MENU	SCREEN MENU	TABLET MENU
XBIND	---	*Blocks, XBIND:*	*3,P*

The *Xbind* command is a separate command; it is not an option of the *Xref* command as most other Xreference controls. *Xbind* is similar to *Bind*, except that *Xbind* binds an <u>individual</u> dependent object; whereas, *Bind* converts the <u>entire</u> *Xref* drawing to a *Block*. Any of the listed dependent named objects (see Dependent Objects and Names) that exist in an drawing can be converted to a permanent and usable part of the current drawing with *Xbind*.

For example, if you want to *Xbind* the DOOR *Block* from the OFFICEX drawing, the command syntax would be as follows.

```
Command: xbind
Block/Dimstyle/LAyer/LType/Style: b
Dependent Block name(s): OFFICEX|DOOR
    Scanning...
1 Block(s) bound.
Command:
```

The name given in response to the "*Dependent (option) Name(s):*" must be the full name as it appears in the current (parent) drawing, including the pipe (|) character. The name of the object (*Block, Layer*, etc.) which was the subject of the *Xbind* is changed using the same naming scheme as used with the *Bind* option of *Xref*. The pipe (|) character is changed to n. In the example, the *Block* name would be changed to OFFICEX0DOOR. The listing of *Block*s in the INTERIOR drawing (using *Block*, ?) would now yield the list below.

```
Command: block
Block name (or ?): ?
Block(s) to list <*>: Enter
Defined Blocks.
      CHAIR
      CONCHAIR
      CONTABLE
      DESK
      FILECAB
      OFFICEX                    Xref: resolved
      OFFICEX$0$DOOR
      OFFICEX|WINDOW             Xdep: OFFICEX
      TABLE

User        External      Dependent    Unnamed
Blocks      References    Blocks       Blocks
  7             1            1            0
Command:
```

The name(s) of permanent *Block*s could be subsequently changed with the *Rename* command if desired.

When the *Block* is bound, it can be *Inserted* like any normal *Block*. *Xbinding* other dependent objects makes them a permanent part of the current drawing and available to be used in the drawing. *Xbinding* a *Layer* allows you to draw and edit on the previously dependent *Layer*. *Xbind* also makes *Text styles, Linetypes*, and *Dimstyles* usable in the current drawing.

Xref Log Files

AutoCAD has a tracking mechanism for the Xref activity for a particular drawing. It is an external ASCII log file which is maintained on each drawing which contains information on external references. Creation of the log file is controlled with the *XREFCTL* variable.

If *XREFCTL* is set to 1, a log file registers each *Attach, Bind, Detach*, and *Reload* of each external reference for the current drawing. This file has the same name as the current drawing and a file extension ".XLG". The log file is always placed in the same directory as the current drawing. Whenever the drawing is *Opened* again and the *Xref* command is used, the activity is appended to an existing log. XLG files have <u>no direct connection</u> to the drawing and can be deleted if desired without consequences to the related drawing file.

If *XREFCTL* is set to 0 (the default), no log file is created or appended. The *XREFCTL* variable is saved in the ACAD.CFG file.

An example .XLG file is shown here. This file lists the activity from the previous example when the OFFICEX drawing was *Xrefed* to the INTERIOR drawing.

```
================================
Drawing: C:\ACAD\DWG\INTERIOR
Date/Time: 01/05/94 16:03:51
Operation: Attach Xref
================================

Attach Xref OFFICEX: office1

    Update Block symbol table:
     Appending symbol: OFFICEX|DOOR
     Appending symbol: OFFICEX|WINDOW
    Block update complete.

    Update Ltype symbol table:
     Appending symbol: OFFICEX|BORDER
     Appending symbol: OFFICEX|BORDER2
     Appending symbol: OFFICEX|BORDERX2
     Appending symbol: OFFICEX|CENTER
     Appending symbol: OFFICEX|CENTER2
     Appending symbol: OFFICEX|CENTERX2
     Appending symbol: OFFICEX|DASHDOT
     Appending symbol: OFFICEX|DASHDOT2
     Appending symbol: OFFICEX|DASHDOTX2
     Appending symbol: OFFICEX|DASHED
     Appending symbol: OFFICEX|DASHED2
     Appending symbol: OFFICEX|DASHEDX2
     Appending symbol: OFFICEX|DIVIDE
     Appending symbol: OFFICEX|DIVIDE2
     Appending symbol: OFFICEX|DIVIDEX2
     Appending symbol: OFFICEX|DOT
     Appending symbol: OFFICEX|DOT2
     Appending symbol: OFFICEX|DOTX2
     Appending symbol: OFFICEX|HIDDEN
     Appending symbol: OFFICEX|HIDDEN2
     Appending symbol: OFFICEX|HIDDENX2
     Appending symbol: OFFICEX|PHANTOM
     Appending symbol: OFFICEX|PHANTOM2
     Appending symbol: OFFICEX|PHANTOMX2
    Ltype update complete.

    Update Layer symbol table:
     Appending symbol: OFFICEX|FLOORPLAN
     Appending symbol: OFFICEX|FACILITIES
     Appending symbol: OFFICEX|ELECTRICAL
     Appending symbol: OFFICEX|TEXT
     Appending symbol: DEFPOINTS
     Appending symbol: OFFICEX|PSVP
     Appending symbol: OFFICEX|TBLCK
     Appending symbol: OFFICEX|1
    Layer update complete.
```

```
        Update Style symbol table:
          Appending symbol: OFFICEX|STANDARD
          Appending symbol: OFFICEX|ROMANS
          Appending symbol: OFFICEX|COMPLEX
          Appending symbol: OFFICEX|SIMPLEX
        Style update complete.

        Update Appid symbol table:
        Appid update complete.

        Update Dimstyle symbol table:
          Appending symbol: OFFICEX|ST1
          Appending symbol: OFFICEX|ST2
        Dimstyle update complete.
   OFFICEX loaded.
```

Managing *Xref* Drawings

Because of the external reference feature, the contents of a drawing can now be stored in multiple drawing files and directories. In other words, if a drawing has *Xrefs*, the drawing is actually composed of several drawings, each possibly located in a different directory. This means that special procedures to handle drawings linked in external reference partnerships should be considered when drawings are to be backed up or sent to clients. Three possible solutions to consider are listed here.

1. Modify the current drawing's path to the external reference drawing so they are both stored in the same directory, then archive them together.

2. Archive the directory of the external reference drawing along with the drawing which references it. Tape backup machines do this automatically. The DOS XCOPY command or BACKUP command can help with this.

3. Make the external reference drawing a permanent part of the current drawing with the *Bind* option of the *Xref* command prior to archiving. This option is preferred when a finished drawing set is sent to a client.

CHAPTER EXERCISES

1. *Open* the **SLOTPLT2** drawing that you modified last (with *Stretch*) in Chapter 16 Exercises. The Slot Plate is to be manufactured by a stamping process. Your job is to nest as many pieces as possible within the largest stock sheet size of 30" x 20" that the press will handle.

A. While in the SLOTPLT2 drawing, use the **Base** command to specify a base point at the plate's lower left corner. **Save** the drawing.

Begin a *New* drawing using the **DSHEET** prototype and assign the name **SLOTNEST**. Draw the boundary of the stock sheet (30" x 20"). *Xref* the **SLOTPLT2** into the sheet drawing multiple times as shown in Figure 31-9 to determine the optimum nesting pattern for the Slot Plate and to minimize wasted material. The Slot Plate can be rotated to any angle but cannot be scaled. Can you fit 12 pieces within the sheet stock? *Save* the drawing.

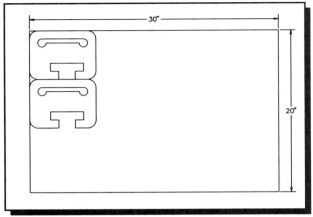

Figure 31-9

B. In the final test of the piece it was determined that a symmetrical orientation of the "T" slot in the bottom would allow for a simplified assembly. *Open* the **SLOTPLT2** drawing and use *Stretch* to center the "T" slot about the vertical axis as shown in Figure 31-10. *Save* the new change.

C. *Open* the **SLOTNEST** drawing. Is the design change reflected in the nested pieces?

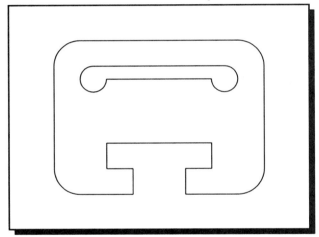

Figure 31-10

2. As the interior design consultant for an architectural firm, you are required to place furniture in an efficiency apartment. You can use some of the furniture drawings (*Blocks*) that you specified for a previous job, the office drawing, and *Insert* them into the apartment along with some new *Blocks* that you create.

A. Use the **CSHEET** as a *prototype* and set *Architectural Units* and set *Limits* of **48'** x **36'**. (Scale factor is 24 and plot scale is 1/2"=1' or 1=24). Assign the name **INTERIOR**. *Xref* the **OFFICE** drawing that you created in Chapter 21 Exercises. Examine the layers (using the *Layer Control* dialogue box) and list (*?*) the *Blocks*. *Freeze* the **TEXT** layer. Use *Xbind* to bring the **CHAIR**, **DESK**, and **TABLE** *Blocks* and the **FURNITURE** *Layer* into the INTERIOR drawing. *Detach* the **OFFICE** drawing. Then *Rename* the new *Blocks* and the new *Layer* to the original names (without the **OFFICE0-** prefix). In the INTERIOR drawing, create a new *Block* called **BED**. Use measurements for a Queen size (60" x 80"). *Save* the INTERIOR drawing.

B. *Xref* the **EFF-APT2** drawing (that you last worked on in Chapter 30 Exercises). Change the *Layer* visibility to turn *Off* the **EFF-APT2|TEXT** layer. *Insert* the furniture *Blocks* as you wish into the apartment (on *Layer* **FURNITURE**).

Lay out the apartment as you choose; however, your design should include at least one Insertion of each of the furniture *Blocks* as shown in Figure 31-11. When you are finished with the design, *Save* the INTERIOR drawing.

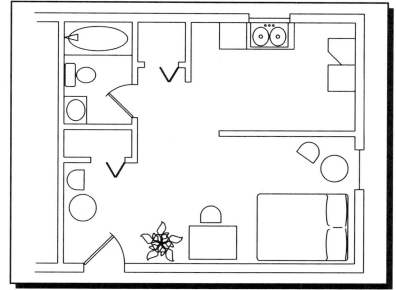

Figure 31-11

C. Assuming that you are now the architect, a design change is requested by the client. In order to meet the fire code, the entry doorway must be moved further from the end of the hall within the row of several apartments. *Open* the **EFF-APT2** drawing and use *Stretch* to relocate the entrance **8'** to the right as shown in Figure 31-12. *Save* the EFF-APT2 drawing.

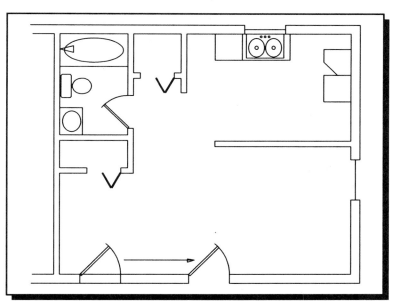

Figure 31-12

D. Next (as the interior design consultant), *Open* the **INTERIOR** drawing. Notice that the design change made by the architect is reflected in your INTERIOR drawing. Does the text appear in the drawing? *Freeze* the **TEXT** layer again, but this time change the **VISRETAIN** variable to **1**. Make the necessary alterations to the interior layout to accommodate the new entry location. *Save* the INTERIOR drawing.

3. As project manager for a mechanical engineering team you are responsible for coordinating an assembly composed of 5 parts. The parts are being designed by several people on the team. You are to create a new drawing and Xref each part, check for correct construction and assembly of the parts, and make the final plot.

A.   The first step is to create two new parts (as <u>separate</u> drawings) named **SLEEVE** and **SHAFT** as shown in Figure 31-13. Use appropriate drawing set up and layering techniques. In each case, draw the two views on <u>separate layer setups</u> (so that appearance of each view can be controlled by layer visibility). Use the **Base** command to specify an insertion point at the right end of the rectangular views at the center line.

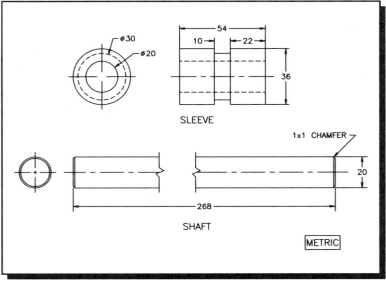

Figure 31-13

B.   You will eventually **Xref** the drawings **SHAFT**, **SLEEVE**, **PUL-SEC** (from Chapter 27 Exercises), **SADDLE** (from Chapter 25 Exercises), and **BOLT** (from Chapter 10 Exercises) to achieve the assembly as shown in Figure 31-14. Before creating the assembly, **Open** each of the drawings and use **Chprop** to move the desired view (with all related geometry, no dimensions) to a new layer. You may also want to set a **Base** point for each drawing. Finally, begin a **New** drawing (or use a **Prototype**) and assign the name **ASSY**. Set appropriate **Limits**. Make a **Layer** called **Xref** and set it **Current**. **Xref** the drawings to complete the assembly. The **BOLT** drawing must be scaled to acquire a diameter of **6mm**. Use the **Layer Control** dialogue box to achieve the desired visibility for the Xrefs. Set **VISRETAIN** to **1**. **Bind** the Xrefs and make a **Plot** to scale. **Save** the **ASSY** drawing.

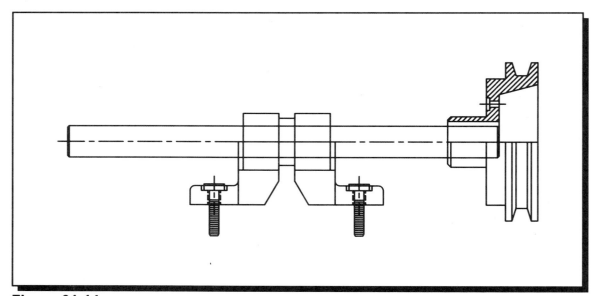

Figure 31-14

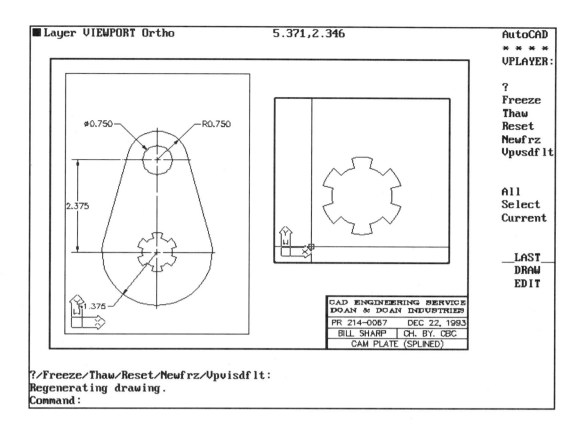

CHAPTER 32

Paper Space

CHAPTER OBJECTIVES

After completing this chapter you should:

1.   know the suggested guidelines for using paper space;

2.   be able to use paper space to display multiple viewports of one drawing and to display viewports of several *Xrefed* drawings;

3.   know the difference between tiled viewports and paper space viewports and the purpose of the *TILEMODE* variable;

4.   be able to use the options of *Mview* to create paper space viewports;

5.   be able to use *Vplayer* or the *Layer Control* dialogue box to control viewport-specific layer visibility;

6.   know how to use *Zoom XP*, *DIMSCALE*, *DIMLFAC* and *PSLTSCALE* to scale viewport geometry, dimensions, and linetypes;

7.   be able to use *Mvsetup* for viewport creation and title block insertion in paper space.

BASICS

AutoCAD allows you to work on your drawing in two separate spaces, model space and paper space. The space that you have been drawing in up to this time is called model space. The Drawing Editor begins a drawing in model space by default. The model geometry (entities that represent the object or subject of the drawing) is almost always drawn in model space. Dimensioning is also accomplished in model space because it is associative--directly associated to the model geometry. Usually the model geometry is completed before using paper space.

Paper space represents the <u>paper that you plot or print on</u>. When you enter paper space for the first time, you see a blank "sheet." In order to see any model geometry, paper space viewports must be created (like cutting rectangular holes) in paper space so you can "see" into model space. Any number or size of rectangular shaped viewports can be created in paper space. Since there is only one model space in a drawing, you see the same model space geometry in each viewport. You can, however, control which layers are *Frozen* and *Thawed* and the scale of the geometry displayed <u>in each viewport</u>. Since paper space represents the actual paper used for plotting, plot from paper space at a scale of 1=1.

Consider this brief example to explain the basics of using paper space. In order to keep this example simple, only one viewport is created to set up a drawing for plotting.

First, the part geometry is created in model space as usual. The geometry may have associative dimensions. This step is the same method that you would have normally used to create a drawing.

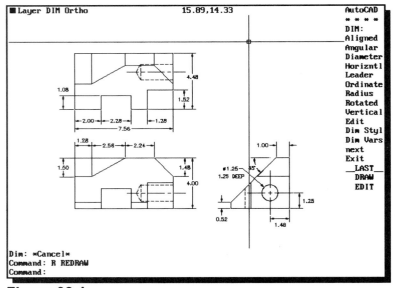

Figure 32-1

To use paper space, change the setting of a variable called *TILEMODE* (explained in detail later). The default setting of *TILEMODE* is 1, which is the setting you have always used if you have never used paper space. Paper space is automatically enabled by changing the *TILEMODE* variable to 0. "*TILEMODE*" can be typed at the command prompt.

By setting the *TILEMODE* variable to 0, you are automatically switched to paper space. When you enable paper space for the first time in a drawing, a "blank sheet" appears. The *Limits* command is used to set the paper space *Limits* to the sheet size intended for plotting.

Next, entities such as a title block and border are created <u>in paper space</u>. See Figure 32-2.

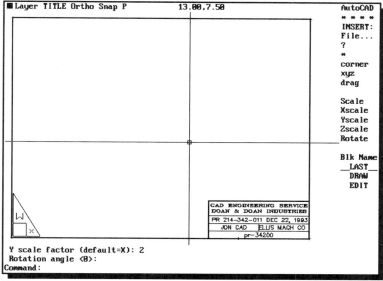

Figure 32-2

A viewport must be created in the "paper" with the *Mview* command in order for you to peer into model space. The model geometry in the drawing appears in the viewport. At this point, there is no specific scale relation between paper space units and the size of the geometry in the viewport (see Fig. 32-3).

You can control the scale and what part of model space geometry you want to see in a viewport. Two methods are used to control the geometry that is visible in a particular viewport.

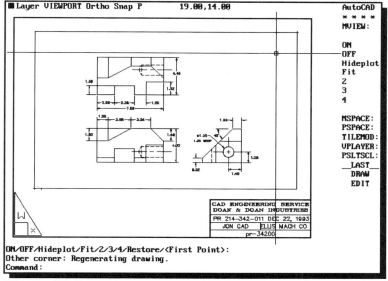

Figure 32-3

1. **Display commands**

   The *Zoom, Pan, View, Vpoint* and other display commands allow you to specify the part of model space you want to see in a viewport. There is even a *Zoom XP* option used to <u>scale</u> the geometry in model space units "times paper space" (*XP*) units. *Zoom XP* is the method used to define the <u>scale</u> of model geometry for the final plot.

2. **Viewport-specific layer visibility control** (used for multiple viewports)

   You can control what layers are visible in specific viewports. This function is used for displaying different model space geometry in separate viewports. The *Vplayer* (Viewport layer) command or the *Cur VP* and *New VP* options in the *Layer Control* dialogue box are for this purpose.

For example, the *Zoom* command could be used in model space to display a detail of the model geometry in a viewport. In this case, the model geometry is scaled to 3/4 size by using *Zoom 3/4XP*.

While in a drawing session with paper space enabled, the *Mspace* (Model Space) and *Pspace* (Paper Space) commands allow you to switch between and draw or edit in either space. Commands that are used will affect the entities or display of the current space. An entity <u>cannot be in both spaces</u>. You can, however, draw in paper space and <u>*OSNAP* to entities in model space</u>. When drawing is completed, activate paper space and plot at 1=1 since paper space *Limits* are set to the <u>actual paper size</u>.

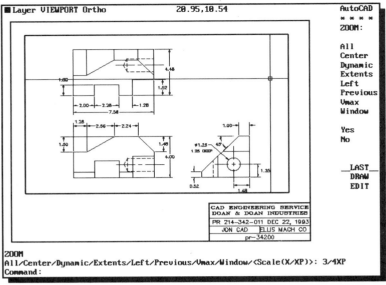

Figure 32-4

PAPER SPACE APPLICATIONS

Paper space is intended as an aid to plotting. Since paper space represents a sheet of paper, it provides you with a means of preparing specific plotting applications.

If you are creating a typical 2D drawing, you don't have to use paper space. The methods used otherwise for creating drawings and plots are still valid and are used for most cases. Paper space can be used for the typical 2D drawing, however, by creating the model geometry as you normally would but using paper space for the border, title block, tables or other annotations (like the previous example). More importantly, paper space can be used to prepare plots with <u>multiple views</u> or <u>multiple drawings</u> as listed here.

1. Use paper space to plot several views of the same drawing on one sheet, possibly in different scales, such as a main view and a detail.

2. Use paper space to plot several drawings on one sheet. This action is accomplished by using *Xref* to bring several drawings into model space and by using layer visibility control to display individual drawings in separate viewports.

3. Use paper space to plot different views (e.g., top, front, side) of a 3D model on one sheet.

Examples of the applications are given on the following pages along with the basic concepts, commands, and related system variables.

GUIDELINES FOR USING PAPER SPACE

Although there are other alternatives, the typical steps using paper space to set up a drawing for plotting are listed below.

1.   Create the part geometry in model space. Associative dimensions are also created in model space.

2.   Switch to paper space by changing *TILEMODE* to 0.

3.   Set up paper space using the following steps.

   A.   Set *Limits* in paper space equal to the sheet size used for plotting. (Paper space has its own *Limits, Snap*, and *Grid* settings.)
   B.   *Zoom All* in paper space.
   C.   Set the desired *Snap* and *Grid* for paper space.
   D.   Make a layer named BORDER or TITLE and *Set* that layer as current.
   E.   Draw, *Insert*, or *Xref* a border and a title block.

4.   Make paper space viewports.

   A.   Make a layer named VIEWPORT (or other descriptive name) and set it as the *Current* layer (it can be turned *Off* later if you do not want the viewport entities to appear in the plot).
   B.   Use the *Mview* command to make viewports. Each viewport contains a view of model space geometry.

5.   Control the display of model space graphics in each viewport. Complete these steps for each viewport.

   A.   Use the *Mspace* (*MS*) command to activate model space. Move the crosshairs and PICK (or use CTRL+V) to activate the desired viewport.
   B.   Use *Zoom XP* to scale the display of the model units to paper space units. This action dictates the plot scale for the model space graphics. The *Zoom XP* factor is the same as the plot scale factor that would otherwise be used (reciprocal of the "drawing scale factor"). For example: *Zoom Center .5XP* or *Zoom Left 1/2XP* would scale the model geometry at 1/2 times paper space units.
   C.   Use the *Vplayer* command or the *Cur VP* and *New VP* options in the *Layer Control* dialogue box to control the layer visibility for each viewport.

6.   Plot from paper space at a scale of 1=1.

   A.   Use the *Pspace* (*PS*) command to switch to paper space.
   B.   If desired, turn *Off* the VIEWPORT layer so the viewport entities do not plot.
   C.   Plot the drawing from paper space at a plot scale of 1=1 since paper space is set to the actual paper size. The paper space geometry will plot full size and the resulting model space geometry will be plotted to the same <u>scale</u> as the *Zoom XP* factor.

PAPER SPACE VIEWPORTS FOR DIFFERENT VIEWS OF ONE DRAWING

Below is a simple example of using paper space viewports to display two views of one drawing. In this case, a full view of the part is displayed in one viewport and a detail of the part is displayed in a different scale in a second viewport.

1. Create the part geometry in model space.

Begin AutoCAD and create the part geometry as you normally would (model space is enabled by default when you enter the Drawing Editor). Associative dimensions are placed on the part in model space.

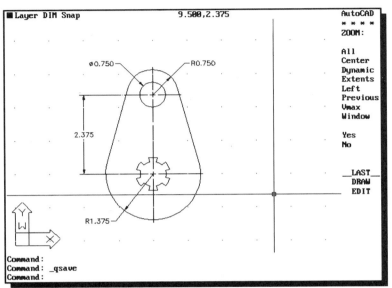

Figure 32-5

2. Switch to paper space by changing *TILEMODE* to 0.

When *TILEMODE* is set to **0**, you are automatically switched from model space to paper space. To remind you that paper space is enabled, the letter **P** appears on the status line and the coordinate system icon (in the lower left corner of the Drawing Editor) changes to a drafting triangle as shown in Figure 32-6.

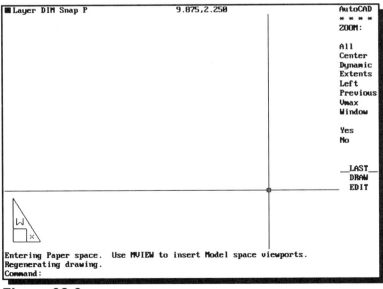

Figure 32-6

3. Set up paper space to mimic the plot sheet.

Paper space can have *Limits*, *Snap*, and *Grid* settings independent of those settings in model space. Set paper space *Limits* equal to the paper size. *Snap* and *Grid* spacing can be set to an appropriate value.

Make a new layer called BORDER or TITLE for the title block and border. Draw, *Insert*, or *Xref* the title block and border on the new layer.

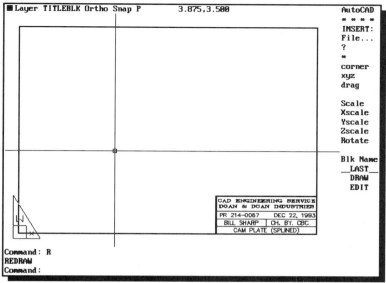

Figure 32-7

4. Make paper space viewports.

Make a layer named VIEWPORT and set it as the *Current* layer. Next, draw viewport entities with the *Mview* command while in paper space in order to see part geometry created in model space. Paper space viewports are windows into model space.

Paper space viewports created with *Mview* are actually <u>entities</u> drawn on the current layer. Because they are entities, they are affected by *Move, Copy, Array, Scale*, and *Erase* and can overlap one another.

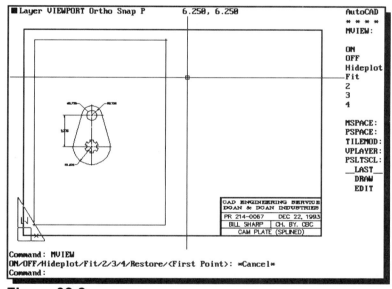

Figure 32-8

Subsequent viewports can be created by *Copying* or *Arraying* existing viewports or by using the *Mview* command. There are options of the *Mview* command that allow you to make *2, 3* or *4* viewports or to *Fit* multiple viewports into a window. (See *Mview.*)

When several paper space viewports exist, you see the same display of model space in each viewport by default. Remember that there is <u>only one model space</u>, so you will see it in each viewport (see Figure 32-9). You can, however, control the part of model space you wish to see in each viewport by using display or *Vplayer* commands.

A second viewport, such as that shown, is created by the *Mview* command or other commands (like *Copy* and *Stretch*, for example). The new viewport is also a window into model space. By default, the display is the same geometry as in the first viewport.

You can switch between drawing in paper space and model space by using *Pspace* (*PS* is the command alias) and *Mspace* (or *MS*) commands. A letter "P" is displayed on the status line when in paper space. If you are in model space, the crosshairs are only visible <u>within</u> the viewport as

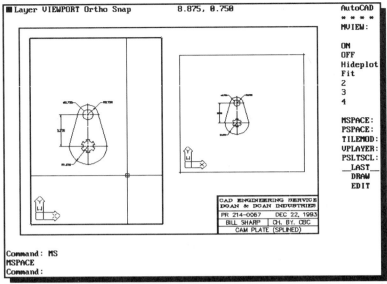

Figure 32-9

shown in Figure 32-9. When in paper space, the crosshairs extend <u>completely across</u> the screen as shown in Figure 32-8. The current viewport is highlighted by a thick border. You can make a different viewport current by PICKing a point inside it or by pressing CTRL-V.

5. Control the display of model space graphics in each viewport with display and layer visibility controls.

Use the *Mspace* (*MS*) command to activate model space. Move the crosshairs and PICK (or use CTRL+V) to activate the desired viewport. Use *Zoom XP* to scale the display of the model units to paper space units. In this case, *Zoom 1XP* would be used to scale the model geometry in the left viewport to 1 times paper space units. The geometry in the right viewport is scaled to 2 times paper space units by using *Zoom 2XP*.

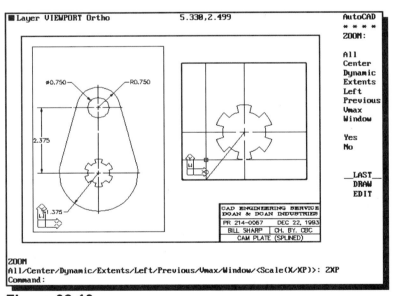

Figure 32-10

When switched to model space, display commands that are invoked affect the display of the <u>current viewport</u> only. Draw and edit commands, however, affect the <u>model geometry</u>, so these effects are potentially visible in all viewports.

Next, set the viewport-specific layer visibility. Use the *Vplayer* command or the *Cur VP* and *New VP* options in the *Layer Control* dialogue box to control which layers are visible in which viewports. The desired layer(s) can be *Frozen* or *Thawed* for each viewport. For example, the dimension layer could be frozen for the right viewport only to yield a display as shown in Figure 32-11. (See *Vplayer.*)

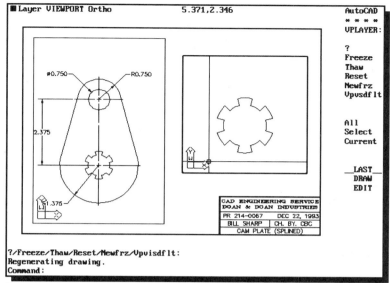

Figure 32-11

6. Make the final adjustments in paper space and plot at a scale of 1=1.

Use the *Pspace* (*PS*) command to switch to paper space. Annotations can be added to the drawing in paper space (such as the "Detail A" notes in Figure 32-12).

Because the viewports are on a separate layer, you can control the display of the rectangular viewport borders (entities) by controlling the layer's visibility. Turning the VIEWPORT layer (or whatever name is assigned) *Off*

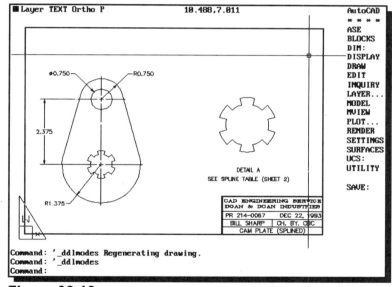

Figure 32-12

prevents the viewport entities from displaying. This is useful when the drawing is ready for plotting.

Plot the drawing from paper space at a plot scale of 1=1. Since paper space is set to the actual paper size, the paper space geometry plots full size and the model space geometry plots at the scale determined by the *Zoom XP* factor.

PAPER SPACE COMMANDS AND VARIABLES

TILEMODE

There are two types of viewports in AutoCAD, tiled viewports and paper space viewports. Tiled viewports divide the screen into several areas that fit together like <u>tiles</u>. Tiled viewports are manipulated by the *Vports* command. Each tiled viewport can show a different area of model space by using display commands--especially helpful for 3D models. Tiled viewports, however, <u>cannot</u> be used with paper space viewports. Tiled viewports were introduced with AutoCAD Release 10 and are discussed in Chapter 34. This chapter addresses only paper space viewports.

When paper space viewports were introduced with Release 11, a new system variable called *TILEMODE* was also introduced. Since only <u>one</u> type of viewport can be used at a time, the *TILEMODE* system variable is used to enable one or the other type of viewports.

When *TILEMODE* is set to 1 (the default setting for the AutoCAD prototype drawing ACAD.DWG), only tiled viewports are available. The viewports must then be created, however, with the *Vports* command (Chapter 34).

If *TILEMODE* is set to 0, paper space style viewports are available. Paper space viewports must be created with the *Mview* command. Therefore, setting *TILEMODE* to 0 disables tiled viewports and automatically enables paper space.

Whether or not viewports of any kind have been created with either the *Vports* or the *Mview* commands, the setting of *TILEMODE* displays the following.

<u>*TILEMODE* setting</u>	<u>Resulting display</u>
1	model space only
0	paper space (Model space is visible only if *Mview* viewports have been created.)

Switching spaces via *TILEMODE* does not affect anything you have drawn except change its visibility on the display.

MVIEW

TYPE IN:	PULL-DOWN MENU	SCREEN MENU	TABLET MENU
MVIEW	*View, Mview >*	*MVIEW, MVIEW:*	*8,J to 8,P*

Mview provides several options for creating paper space viewport entities. The *Mview* command only operates when paper space has been enabled (*TILEMODE* is 0). If you have switched to model space, invoking *Mview* automatically and temporarily switches back to paper space. There is no limit to the number of paper space viewports that can be created in a drawing. The command syntax to create one viewport (the default option) is as follows.

```
Command: mview
ON/OFF/Hideplot/Fit/2/3/4/Restore/<First Point>: PICK or
(coordinates)
Other corner: PICK or (coordinates)
Regenerating drawing.
Command:
```

This action creates one rectangular viewport between the diagonal corners specified. The other options are described briefly.

ON

Turns on the display of model space geometry in the selected viewport. Select the desired viewport to turn on.

OFF

Turns off the display of model space geometry in the selected viewport. Select the desired viewport to turn off.

Hideplot

Causes hidden line removal in the selected viewport during a <u>plot</u>. This is used for 3D surface or solid models. Select the desired viewport.

Fit

Creates a new viewport and fits it to the size of the current display. If you are *Zoomed* in paper space, the resulting viewport is the size of the *Zoomed* area. The new viewport becomes the current viewport.

Restore

Creates new viewports in the same relative shape as a named tiled viewport configuration (see Chapter 34 for the *Vports* command).

2/3/4

Creates a number of viewports within a rectangular area that you specify. The *2* option allows you to arrange 2 viewports either *Vertically* or *Horizontally*. The *4* option automatically divides the specified area into 4 equal viewports.

Figure 32-13 displays the possible configurations using the *3* option. Using this option yields the following prompt.

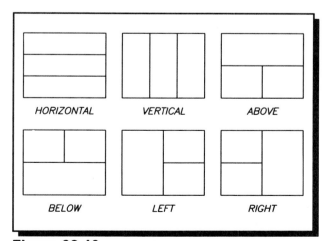

Figure 32-13

```
Horizontal/Vertical/Above/
Below/Left/<Right>:
```

After making the desired selection, AutoCAD prompts: `Fit/<First Point>:`. The *Fit* option automatically fills the current display with the specified number of viewport configurations (similar to the *Fit* option described earlier).

Paper space viewports created with *Mview* are treated by AutoCAD as <u>entities</u>. Like other entities, *Mview* viewports can be affected by most editing commands. For example, you could use *Mview* to create one viewport, then use *Copy* or *Array* to create other viewports. You could edit the size of viewports with *Stretch* or *Scale*. Additionally, you can use *Move* (Fig. 32-14) to relocate the position of viewports. Delete a viewport using *Erase*. You must be in paper space to PICK the viewport entities (borders).

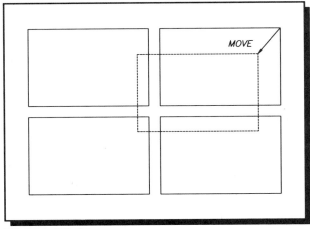

Figure 32-14

Paper space viewports can also overlap (Fig. 32-14). This feature makes it possible for geometry appearing in different viewports to occupy the same area on the screen or on a plot. You should avoid creating one viewport completely within another's border because visibility and selection problems may result.

The viewports created by *Mview* or other editing methods are always rectangular and have a vertical and horizontal orientation (they cannot be *Rotated*).

PSPACE

TYPE IN:	PULL-DOWN MENU	SCREEN MENU	TABLET MENU
PSPACE or PS	*View, Paper Space*	*MVIEW, PSPACE:*	*8,R*

The *Pspace* command switches from model space to paper space. There are no options. The crosshairs are displayed across the entire screen when in paper space.

```
Command: pspace
Command:
```

MSPACE

TYPE IN:	PULL-DOWN MENU	SCREEN MENU	TABLET MENU
MSPACE or MS	*View, Model Space*	*MVIEW, MSPACE:*	*8,Q*

The *Mspace* command switches from paper space to model space. There must be at least one paper space viewport and it must be *On* (not turned *Off* by the *Mview* command) or AutoCAD cancels the command. If paper space viewports exist in the drawing, you are switched to the last active viewport. The crosshairs appear only <u>in</u> that viewport. The current viewport displays a heavy border. You can switch to another viewport (make another current) by toggling CTRL+V or PICKing in it.

VPLAYER

TYPE IN:	PULL-DOWN MENU	SCREEN MENU	TABLET MENU
VPLAYER	*View, Mview >* *Vplayer*	*MVIEW, VPLAYER:*	*4,N to 6,O*

The *Vplayer* (Viewport Layer) command provides options for control of the layers you want to see in each viewport (viewport-specific layer visibility control). With *Vplayer* you can specify the *State* (*Freeze/Thaw* and *Off/On*) of the drawing layers in any existing or new viewport. You do <u>not</u> have to make the desired viewport current before using *Vplayer*.

The *Layer* command allows you to *Freeze/Thaw* layers <u>globally</u>; whereas, *Vplayer* allows you to *Freeze/Thaw* layers that are <u>viewport-specific</u>. The *TILEMODE* variable must be set to 0 for the *Vplayer* command to operate and a layer's global (*Layer*) settings must be *On* and *Thawed* to be affected by the *Vplayer* settings.

For example, you may have two paper space viewports set up such as in Figure 32-15. In order to control the visibility of the DIM (dimensioning) layer for a specific viewport, the command syntax shown below would be used. In this case, the DIM layer is *Frozen* in the right viewport.

Notice (in the command sequence below) that if model space is active, AutoCAD automatically switches to paper space to allow the selection.

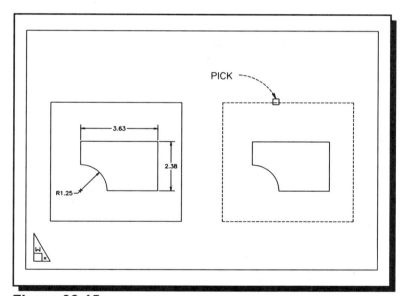

Figure 32-15

```
Command: vplayer
?/Freeze/Thaw/Reset/Newfrz/Vpvisdflt: freeze
Layer(s) to Freeze: dim
All/Select/<Current>:  S (Use the Select option.)
Switching to Paper space.
Select objects: PICK (Select the desired viewport entity.  See Fig 32-15.)
Select objects: Enter
Switching to Model space.
?/Freeze/Thaw/Reset/Newfrz/Vpvisdflt: Enter
Regenerating drawing.
Command:
```

The *Vplayer* **Current** option automatically selects the current viewport. The *All* option automatically selects all viewports. Note that the *Select* option switches to paper space so that the viewport entities (borders) can be selected. The *Freeze* or *Thaw* does not take place until the command is completed and the drawing is automatically regenerated. All of the options are explained briefly here.

?

> This option <u>lists the frozen layers</u> in the current viewport or a selected viewport. AutoCAD automatically switches to paper space if you are in model space to allow you to select the viewport entity.

Freeze

> This option controls the visibility of specified layers in the current or <u>selected viewports</u>. You are prompted for layer(s) to *Freeze*, then to select which viewports for the *Freeze* to affect.

Thaw

> This option turns the visibility control back to the global settings of *On/Off/Freeze/Thaw* in the <u>*Layer*</u> command. The procedure for specification of layers and viewports is identical to the *Freeze* option procedure.

Reset

> This option returns the layer visibility status to the <u>default</u> if one was specified with *Vpvisdflt*, which is described below. You are prompted for "*Layer(s) to Reset*" and viewports to select by "*All/Select/<Current>:*".

Newfrz

> This option <u>creates new layers</u>. The new layers are frozen in all viewports. This is a short cut when you want to create a new layer that is visible only in the current viewport. Use *Newfrz* to create the new layer, then use *Vplayer Thaw* to make it visible only in that (or other selected) viewport(s). You are prompted for "*New viewport frozen layer name(s):*" You may enter one name or several separated by commas.

Vpvisdflt

> This option allows you to set up <u>layer visibility</u> for <u>new</u> viewports. This is handy when you want to create new viewports, but do not want any of the <u>existing</u> layers to be visible in the new viewports. This option is particularly helpful for *Xrefs*. For example, suppose you created a viewport and *Xrefed* a drawing "into" the viewport. Before creating new viewports and *Xrefing* other drawings "into" them, use *Vpvisdflt* to set the default layer visibility to *Off* for the <u>existing</u> *Xrefed* layers in new viewports. (See the following application example.) You are prompted for a list of layers and whether they should be *Thawed* or *Frozen*.

Layer Control Dialogue Box

As an alternative to the *Vplayer* command, the *Layer Control* dialogue box (Figure 32-16) can be used to *Freeze/Thaw* current or new viewports. The *Cur VP* and *New VP* tiles on the right side of the dialogue box control viewport-specific layer visibility.

The *Cur VP* and *New VP* tiles in the *Layer Control* dialogue box are grayed out when *TILEMODE* is set to 1. If paper space is enabled (*TILEMODE*=0) and a viewport is active (the crosshairs are in a viewport), the *Layer Control* dialogue box that appears gives the *State* of layers <u>specific</u> to that <u>current viewport</u>. In other words, the *State* column may display <u>different</u> information depending upon which viewport is current. If you are in paper space (the crosshairs are in paper space), the *Freeze/Thaw* tiles affect the selected layer's *State* in paper space, but not in the viewports. The tiles perform the following functions.

Cur VP

Sets the *Freeze/Thaw* state for the selected layer(s) in the current viewport.

New VP

Sets the *Freeze/Thaw* state for the selected layer(s) in new viewports (any viewports that are subsequently created).

For example, the *Cur VP* tile could have been used as an alternative to the *Vplayer* command to control layer visibility of the DIM layer of the drawing as illustrated in Figure 32-15. The procedure in this case is to switch to model space (*MS*), make the right viewport active, and then invoke the *Layer Control* dialogue box. In the dialogue box (Figure 32-16), select the desired layer (DIM) and select the *Frz* tile for the *Cur VP*. The letter "C" appears in the *State* column to indicate the DIM layer is *Frozen* in the current viewport. Note also that the DIM layer has been *Frozen* for new layers indicated by the letter "N".

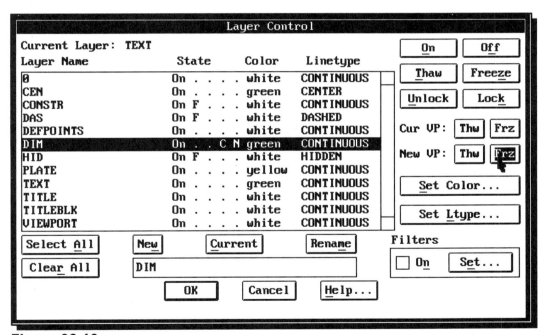

Figure 32-16

The *Layer Control* dialogue box is helpful for listing the viewport-specific layer visibility, but only for the <u>current</u> viewport. Keep in mind that the dialogue box requires that the <u>specific</u> viewport be current; whereas, the *Vplayer* command provides viewport-specific layer visibility control for <u>any</u> viewport, current or otherwise.

Zoom XP Factors

Paper space entities such as title block and border should correspond to the paper on a 1=1 scale. Paper space is intended to represent the plotting sheet. *Limits* in paper space should be set to the exact paper size, and the finished drawing is plotted from paper space to a scale of 1=1. The model space geometry, however, should be true scale in real world units, and *Limits* in model space are generally set to accommodate that geometry.

When model space geometry appears in a viewport in paper space, the size of the displayed geometry can be controlled so that it appears and plots in the correct scale. This action is accomplished with the *XP* option of the *Zoom* command. *XP* means "times paper space." Thus, model space geometry is *Zoomed* to some factor "times paper space."

Since paper space is actual size, the *Zoom XP* factor that should be used for a viewport is equivalent to the plot scale that would otherwise be used for plotting that geometry in model space. The *Zoom XP* factor is the reciprocal of the "drawing scale factor" (Chapter 13). *Zoom XP* only while you are "in" the desired model space viewport. Fractions or decimals are accepted.

For example, if the model space geometry would normally be plotted at 1/2"=1" or 1:2, the *Zoom* factor would be .5*XP* or 1/2*XP*. If a drawing would normally be plotted at 1/4"=1', the *Zoom* factor would be 1/48*XP*. Other examples are given below.

1:5	*Zoom .2XP* or 1/5 XP	3"=1'	*Zoom 1/4XP*
1:10	*Zoom .1XP* or 1/10XP	1"=1'	*Zoom 1/12XP*
1:20	*Zoom .05XP* or 1/20XP	3/4'=1'	*Zoom 1/16XP*
1/2"=1"	*Zoom 1/2XP*	1/2"=1'	*Zoom 1/24XP*
3/8"=1"	*Zoom 3/8XP*	3/8"=1'	*Zoom 1/32XP*
1/4"=1"	*Zoom 1/4XP*	1/4"=1'	*Zoom 1/48XP*
1/8"=1"	*Zoom 1/8XP*	1/8"=1'	*Zoom 1/96XP*

DIMSCALE

The *DIMSCALE* variable has a special meaning when you dimension in paper space. As you know, this variable allows you to control the size of the dimensioning features (arrows, text, etc.) *DIMSCALE* can be set to insure that dimensions appearing in different viewports of different *Zoom XP* factors have the same text sizes, arrow sizes, etc.

If *DIMSCALE* is set to 0, AutoCAD computes a value based on the scaling between the current viewport and paper space. In other words, a *DIMSCALE* of 0 leads to dimension text sizes, arrow sizes, and other scaled distances to plot at their original face values by counteracting the effects of the viewport's *Zoom* factor. If you are in paper space, AutoCAD uses a scale factor of 1.0.

For example, assume that you have completed the model geometry for a part with associative dimensions in model space as you would normally. Next, enable paper space and create two viewports to display two views as shown in Figure 32-17. *Zoom XP* factors have been applied to model geometry in each viewport as follows.

Left- *Zoom 1XP*
Right- *Zoom 2XP*

Notice how the dimension sizes are displayed according to the *Zoom XP* values.

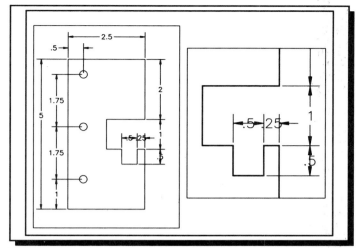

Figure 32-17

In order to force the dimensions to appear the same size in each viewport, switch to paper space and set *DIMSCALE* to 0. This forces the viewport-specific *DIMSCALE* to be divided by the *Zoom* factor.

Next, switch to model space, activate the desired viewport, and *Update* the three existing dimensions as shown in Figure 32-18. Notice that dimensions appearing in both viewports can only be displayed in one size (there is only one model space geometry).

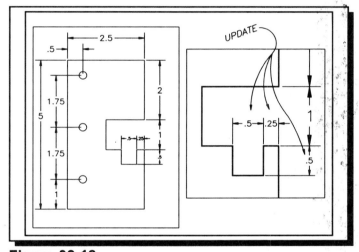

Figure 32-18

An alternative is to create dimensions on separate layers for each viewport (or use *Change Properties* to change layers for existing dimensions). In this way you can have viewport-specific layer visibility for dimensions and avoid the problem of having dimensions appearing in both viewports.

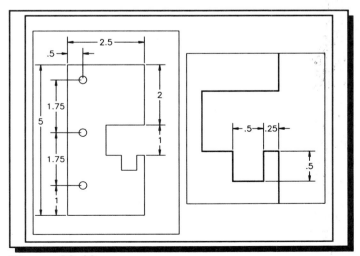

Figure 32-19

DIMLFAC

DIMLFAC has a special meaning when placing <u>dimensions in paper space</u> related to geometry in model space. If *DIMLFAC* is set to a negative value and you are creating a dimension in paper space, the distance measured is multiplied by the absolute value of *DIMLFAC*. A negative *DIMLFAC* value equal to the *Zoom* factor of the viewport generates a measured length (dimension text value) relative to the model space units instead of paper space units. If you are creating a dimension in model space, negative values are ignored and the value of 1.0 is used instead.

AutoCAD computes a value of *DIMLFAC* for you if you change *DIMLFAC* from the `Dim:` prompt while in paper space and you select the **Viewport** option. You must be in <u>paper space</u> and invoke *DIMLFAC* from the `Dim:` prompt (not the `Command:` prompt) to enable the *Viewport* option.

```
Dim:  dimlfac
Current value <1.0000> New value (Viewport): v
Select viewport to set scale: PICK the desired viewport entity.
Dimlfac set to -xxx.xx
Dim:
```

AutoCAD calculates the scaling of model space to paper space and assigns the negative of this value to *DIMLFAC*. Setting the *DIMLFAC* variable with the *Viewport* option causes the measured value to be calculated relative to the model space geometry rather than indicating the actual paper space measurement.

For example, suppose an additional dimension is required for the detailed view and you want to create the dimension in paper space. First, switch to paper space, then create the associative dimension in paper space (see Fig 32-20, above the right viewport). *OSNAP* can be used to snap to the model space geometry.

When dimensioning in paper space using the <u>default</u> *DIMLFAC* setting, the dimensional value as measured by AutoCAD appears in <u>paper space units</u> as in Figure 32-20. Obviously this is an incorrect value for the model space geometry.

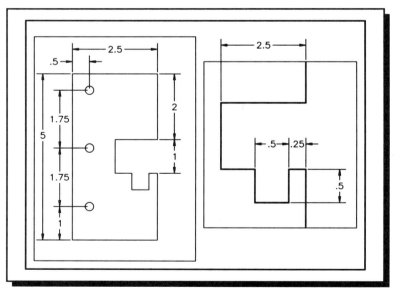

Figure 32-20

DIMLFAC should be set for paper space using the *Viewport* option (at the `Dim:` prompt). Select the viewport entity (border). *Update* must be used, however, to update an existing dimension to the new *DIMLFAC* setting. The resulting dimension is displayed relative to model space units as shown in Figure 32-21.

Alternatively, *DIMLFAC* could be set before creating the dimension. Either procedure should produce the correct measured value.

The VIEWPORT layer can be *Frozen* with the *Layer Control* dialogue box to prepare the drawing for plotting as shown in Figure 32-21.

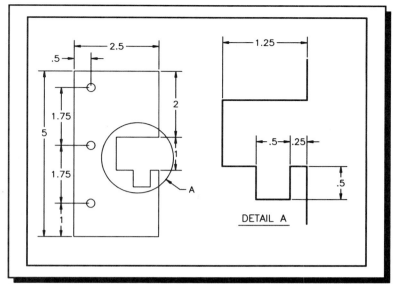

Figure 32-21

PSLTSCALE

LTSCALE controls linetype scaling <u>globally</u> for the drawing; whereas, the *PSLTSCALE* variable controls the linetype scaling for non-continuous lines only in <u>paper space</u>. A *PSLTSCALE* setting of 1 (the default setting) displays all non-continuous lines relative to paper space units so that all lines in both spaces and in different viewports appear the same regardless of viewport *Zoom* values. *LTSCALE* can still be used to change linetype scaling globally regardless of the *PSLTSCALE* setting.

If *PSLTSCALE* is set to 0, linetype spacing is controlled by the *LTSCALE* variable and based on the drawing units in the space the entities are created in (paper or model). In other words, if *PSLTSCALE* is 0, the linetypes appear different lengths if the units in paper and model spaces are scaled differently or if different viewports are scaled differently as in Figure 32-22.

If *PSLTSCALE* is changed, a *Regenall* must be used to display the effects of the new setting.

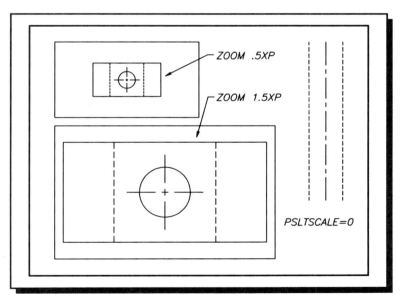

Figure 32-22

If *PSLTSCALE* is set to 1 (and *TILEMODE* is 0), the linetype scales for both spaces are <u>scaled to paper space units</u> so that all dashed lines appear equal. The model geometry in viewports can have different *Zoom XP* factors yet the linetypes display the same (as shown in Figure 32-23).

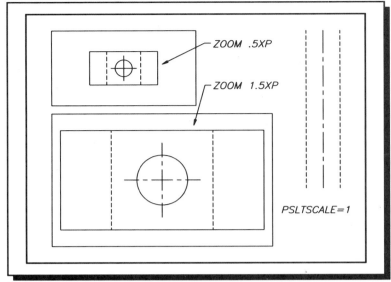

Figure 32-23

PAPER SPACE VIEWPORTS FOR *XREFED* DRAWINGS

In the following example multiple viewports are created. The drawing also contains several *Xrefs*, each *Xref* appearing in a separate viewport. Viewport-specific layer visibility control is important for this application to insure that <u>only one *Xref*</u> is displayed in <u>each viewport</u>. This example to describes a typical procedure. Slightly different applications may require different procedures.

First, a *New* drawing is begun and *Units* are set to *Architectural*. Paper space is enabled immediately by setting *TILEMODE* to 0, then setting *Limits* in paper space equal to a "D" size sheet (36 x 24). After doing a *Zoom All*, the XREF, VIEWPORT, and TITLE layers are created. These layers are necessary for visibility control of the viewport entities that are created and the Xref information that is attached.

Next, a *Pline* border is drawn and a title block is drawn, *Inserted*, or *Xrefed* on layer TITLE.

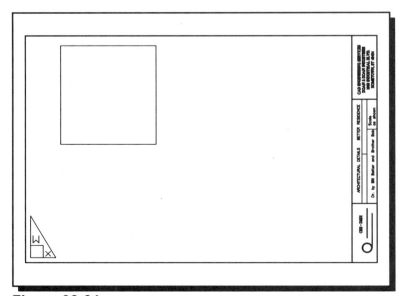

Figure 32-24

Then the VIEWPORT layer is set as the current layer and *Mview* is used to create a viewport. The drawing at this point should appear as that in Figure 32-24.

The *MS* (*Mspace*) command is used to activate model space so the *Xrefed* drawings will come into model space. The current layer is then set to XREF. The *Xref* command with the *Attach* option is used to bring in the first drawing--a door detail named DOOR.DWG. Accepting all the defaults, the drawing may not appear until *Zoom Extents* is used to make the geometry visible in the viewport.

In order to make the drawing appear in the viewport and plot to the correct scale, a *Zoom XP* factor should be used. The original door drawing was created

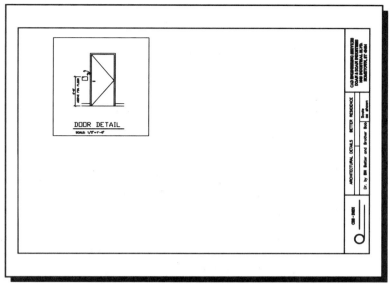

Figure 32-25

full size and would normally be plotted on a D size sheet at a scale of 3/4"=1'. Since paper space is set to the actual paper size, the drawing is scaled proportionally by using a *Zoom* factor of *1/16XP*. (3/4"=12" is equal to 1/16.) *Pan* is used to center the door in the viewport. The resulting drawing appears in Figure 32-25. Note that it is unnecessary to set model space *Limits* in this case since all model geometry has been previously created in separate *Xrefed* drawings.

Before creating another viewport, *PS* is used to activate paper space and the current layer is set to VIEWPORT. A second viewport is created with the *Mview* or *Copy* command.

The current layer is set again to XREF and model space is activated with *MS*. Another detail drawing, STAIR, is *Attached* with *Xref*. The intended plot scale for the STAIR drawing is 3/8"=1', so the drawing is scaled in the viewport by using a *Zoom* factor of 1/32*XP* (3/8"=12" is equal to 1/32). The drawing at this point appears as that in Figure 32-26.

Note that both drawings appear in each viewport. They have each been *Xrefed* into (the same) model space. Viewport-specific layer control must be exercised to display only one *Xref* per viewport.

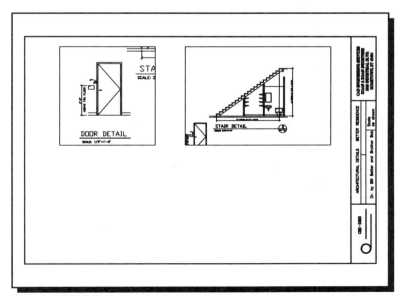

Figure 32-26

Using the *Layer Control* dialogue box, the visibility of dependent layers can be controlled for each viewport. With the right viewport active (stair detail), all the DOOR drawing layers are selected and frozen for the current viewport by PICKing the *Frz* tile for *Cur VP* and for *New VP* as shown in Figure 32-27. Confirming the dialogue box (PICK *OK*) regenerates the new display.

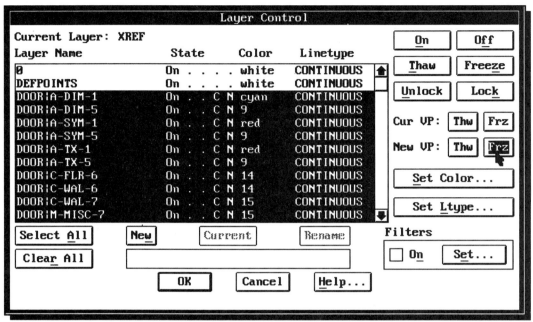

Figure 32-27

Next, visibility for the left viewport must be specified. The left viewport is made active and the dialogue box invoked again. Remember that the *Layer Control* dialogue box displays settings specific to the <u>active</u> viewport. All of the STAIR drawing dependent layers are set to *Frz* for the *Cur VP* and for *New VP*. The correct layer visibility appears in Figure 32-28. The dependent STAIR and DOOR layers do not appear in any new viewports.

Alternatively, the *Vplayer* command could be used to accomplish the viewport-specific layer visibility as shown here. (See the alternate method at the end of this section.)

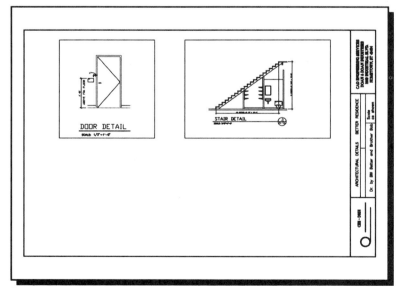

Figure 32-28

Next, paper space is activated (with *PS*) and the current layer is set to VIEWPORT. Two more viewports are created with *Mview*. Model space is activated and the lower left viewport is made current. Layer XREF is set current. *Xref* is used to *Attach* the WALL detail drawing and is scaled to 3"=1' by using *Zoom 1/4XP* as shown in Figure 32-29.

The same procedure is followed to make a fourth viewport and *Xref* the SECTION drawing. It is *Zoomed* to *1/16XP* to achieve a scale of 3/4"=1'.

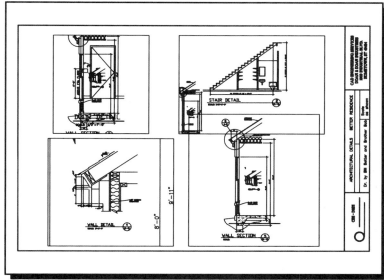

Figure 32-29

Notice that even though the DOOR and STAIR layers appear only in the appropriate viewports, all of the SECTION dependent layers and the WALL dependent layers appear in all viewports.

Figure 32-30 illustrates the results of the following action to *Freeze* the WALL* layers in the other three viewports. The SECTION drawing, however, appears in all viewports.

The *Vplayer* command can be used to control layer visibility as an alternative to the *Layer Control* dialogue box. *Vplayer* can be used to set a default visibility setting for specific layers with the *Freeze* option. *Vplayer* can be invoked from paper space or model space. The asterisk (*) is used to specify all WALL layers as shown in the following command sequence.

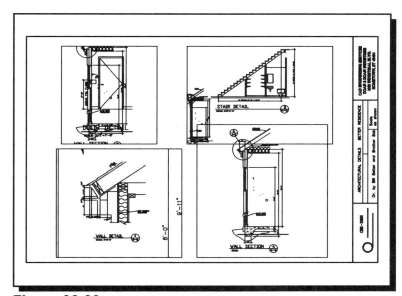

Figure 32-30

```
Command: vplayer
?/Freeze/Thaw/Reset/Newfrz/Vpvisdflt: f
Layer(s) to Freeze: WALL*
All/Select/<Current>: S (use the Select option)
Select objects: PICK (upper left viewport entity)
Select objects: PICK (upper right viewport entity)
Select objects: PICK (lower right viewport entity)
Select objects: Enter
```

```
?/Freeze/Thaw/Reset/Newfrz/Vpvisdflt: Enter
Regenerating drawing.
Command:
```

The *Vplayer* command is used again as in the previous procedure to *Freeze* the SECTION* layers in the other three viewports.

Lastly, the VIEWPORT layer is *Frozen* so the viewport borders do not appear. The resulting drawing as shown in Figure 32-31 is ready for plotting.

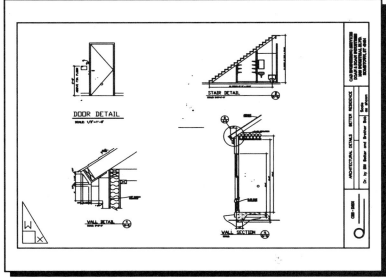

Figure 32-31 Detail drawings courtesy of Autodesk, Inc.

Alternate Method

As an alternative method of layer control for the previous example, the *Vpvisdflt* option of *Vplayer* can be used to set the default visibility settings for new viewports. The procedure is as follows.

1. Create the first viewport and *Xref* the DOOR drawing as before.

2. Invoke the *Vplayer* command with the *Vpvisdflt* option as listed below.

```
Command: vplayer
?/Freeze/Thaw/Reset/Newfrz/Vpvisdflt: V
Layer name(s) to change default viewport visibility: DOOR*
Change default viewport visibility to Frozen/<Thawed>: f
?/Freeze/Thaw/Reset/Newfrz/Vpvisdflt: Enter
Command:
```

The DOOR layers are frozen for any <u>new</u> viewports that are created.

3. Create the second viewport and *Xref* the STAIR drawing as before.

4. Invoke *Vplayer* and use the *Vpvisdflt* option to freeze the STAIR* layers for <u>new</u> viewports.

5. Invoke *Vplayer* and use the *Freeze* option to freeze the STAIR* layers for the first viewport.

6. Continue this sequence for the other two viewports.

USING *MVSETUP* FOR 2D DRAWINGS

Mvsetup is an AutoLISP program supplied with AutoCAD that enables you to automatically create viewports and insert title blocks for 2D model geometry. Several ANSI (American National Standards Institute) and ISO (International Standards Organization) title blocks and borders are available for insertion. This application is discussed on the following pages.

Mvsetup can also be used to create, scale, and align viewports in paper space. The popular application for these options of *Mvsetup* is displaying 3D objects in a typical multiview-type viewport configuration. *Mvsetup* is discussed for this purpose in Chapter 46.

MVSETUP

TYPE IN:	PULL-DOWN MENU	SCREEN MENU	TABLET MENU
MVSETUP	*View, Layout >* *MV Setup*	---	---

The *Mvsetup* (Mview setup) command is actually an AutoLISP routine that is accessible either through the *View* pull-down menu or by typing *Mvsetup*. One application of *Mvsetup* with paper space (*TILEMODE* is 0) is for the setup of paper space viewports and insertion of title blocks for 2D drawings. The typical steps for using *Mvsetup* for this application are as follows.

1.   Create the 2D drawing in model space.

2.   Load *Mvsetup* and use *Options* to set the preferences for title block insertion and to specify the units to be used.

3.   Use *Title block* to *Insert* or *Xref* one of many AutoCAD-supplied or user-supplied borders and title blocks.

4.   Use the *Create* option to make one or an array of paper space viewports. (The "*Std. Engineering*" option is intended for 3D drawings.)

5.   Use *Scale viewports* to set the scale factor (*Zoom XP* factor) for the geometry displayed in the viewports.

Mvsetup can be used with *TILEMODE* at either setting (1 or 0). If paper space has not been enabled (*TILEMODE* = 1), *Mvsetup* enables it for you. For *TILEMODE* set to 0, the command syntax is listed here. The options are explained. The *Align* and *Scale* options are explained as applied to 3D models in Chapter 46.

```
Command: mvsetup
Initializing... MVSETUP loaded.
MVSetup, Version 1.15, (c) 1990-1993 by Autodesk, Inc.
Align/Create/Scale viewports/Options/Title block/Undo:
```

Create

Displays the following prompt: `Delete objects/Undo/<Create viewports>:`

Create viewports

`Available Mview viewport layout options:`

```
0.   None
1.   Single
2.   Std. Engineering
3.   Array of Viewports
```

1. Single

This option prompts for a first and other point to define the viewport.

2. Std. Engineering

This option is for 3D drawings and is discussed in Chapter 46.

3. Array of Viewports

Selecting this option prompts for a bounding box and a number of viewports along the X and Y axes. You can also specify a distance between viewports. The resulting viewports are of equal size.

Delete objects

This option allows you to delete existing viewports.

Undo

Undoes the previous *Mvsetup* operation.

Options

Set Layer

This selection allows you to specify a layer on which to insert a title block. The layer can be existing or you can make a new one.

Limits

If desired, this option resets the *Limits* after inserting the title block and border to the drawing extents defined by the border.

Units

You may specify inch or millimeter units for use in paper space.

Title block

Delete Objects

This option allows you to delete (erase) objects from paper space without having to leave the *Mvsetup* routine. It operates like the *Erase* command.

Origin

You can relocate the plotter origin point for the sheet with this option. You are prompted to PICK a point.

Undo

Undoes the last *Mvsetup* operation.

Insert title block

Provides the following options and title blocks with borders for insertion.

```
Available title block options:

0:                          None
1:                          ISO A4 Size(mm)
2:                          ISO A3 Size(mm)
3:                          ISO A2 Size(mm)
4:                          ISO A1 Size(mm)
5:                          ISO A0 Size(mm)
6:                          ANSI-V Size(in)     (Vertical A size)
7:                          ANSI-A Size(in)
8:                          ANSI-B Size(in)
9:                          ANSI-C Size(in)
10:                         ANSI-D Size(in)
11:                         ANSI-E Size(in)
12:                         Arch/Engineering (24 x 36in)
13:                         Generic D size Sheet (24 x 36in)

Add/Delete/Redisplay/<Number of entry to load>:
```

Entering a number causes the appropriate size border and title block to be created. Custom borders can be created and inserted instead of the AutoCAD-supplied ones by using the *Add* option. The *Add* option allows you to add title block options to the list shown above. *Delete* will delete options from the list.

Using *Mvsetup* to Create a Single Viewport in Paper Space

Following is a simple example of using *Mvsetup* to create a paper space viewport and insert a title and border for a completed 2D drawing.

Assume that you have just completed the drawing shown in Figure 32-32. The geometry is created in model space.

Normally, the next step is to set *TILEMODE* to 0 which enables paper space. This step is not required when using *Mvsetup* because the program automatically enables paper space if necessary.

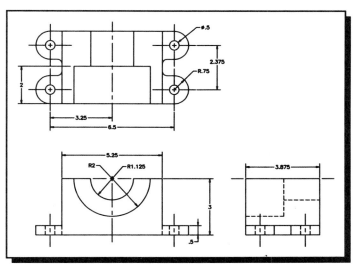

Figure 32-32

Invoke *Mvsetup*. From the first prompt, select *Options*. Use *Set Layer* to define an existing layer or create a new layer (named TITLE or similar descriptive name) for title block and border insertion.

The *Limits* option can be used to automatically set paper space *Limits* equal to the paper space extents after the border and title block are inserted (the drawing *Extents* is equal the border size).

Next, use the *Title block* option and then *Insert title block*. Since this drawing is intended to be plotted on a B size sheet, option *8. ANSI-B size* is selected. The resulting title block appears in paper space as Figure 32-33.

Then layer VIEWPORT must be created and made current for the viewport entities.

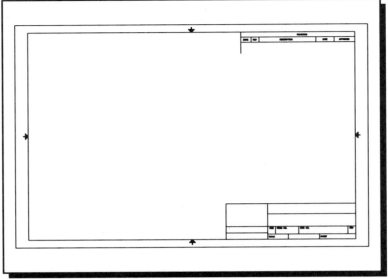

Figure 32-33

To make the viewports, the *Create* option of the *Mvsetup* command is invoked. Then *Create viewports* is selected. From the list of available viewport layouts, *1. Single* is designated. PICK the *First point* and the *Other corner* to define the viewport size. By default, the model geometry is displayed in the viewport at maximum size (AutoCAD causes a *Zoom Extents*) as shown in Figure 32-34.

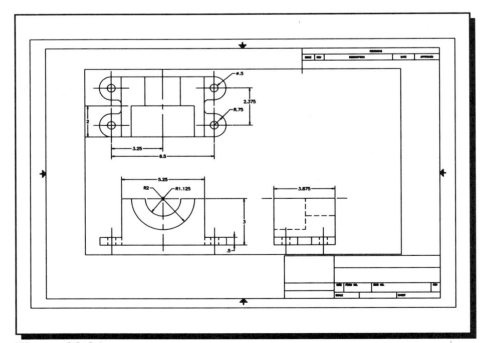

Figure 32-34

In order to display the model geometry to scale, the *Scale viewports* option from the main prompt is invoked. AutoCAD requires you to enter the ratio of model space units to paper space units. This ratio is essentially the same as the *Zoom XP* factor; for example, 2 model space unit to 1 paper space units is the same as *Zoom 1/2XP*.

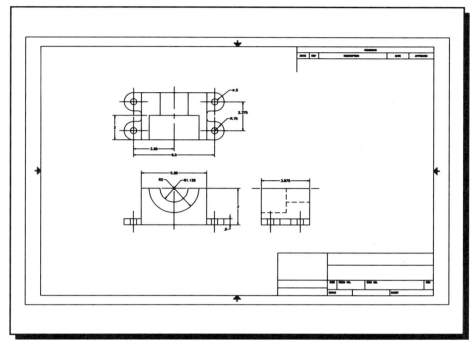

Figure 32-35

The resulting drawing should appear as shown in Figure 32-35. Enter the desired text into the title block. If desired, *Freeze* the VIEWPORT layer. The drawing is ready for plotting.

The *Mvsetup* command is an AutoLISP program that can be used to automate the process of setting up paper space viewports. It can save time and effort compared to the previous methods discussed in which the steps are not as automated. See Chapter 46 for using *Mvsetup* and other methods to create 2D (paper space) drawings from 3D models.

CHAPTER EXERCISES

1. In this exercise you will enable paper space, draw a border and insert a title block, and show a drawing in viewport.

A. ***Open*** the **ASSY** drawing that you created in the Chapter 31 Exercises. Set **TILEMODE** to **0**. Set *Limits* in paper space to the paper size that you intend to plot on. Set paper space *Snap* and *Grid* to an appropriate size (**.250"** or **6mm**).

B.   Make a *New Layer* named **TITLE** and set it as the *Current* layer. Draw a border and draw, *Insert*, or *Xref* a title block (in paper space).

C.   Make a *New Layer* called **VIEWPORT** or **VPORT** and set it as *Current*. Next, use *Mview* to create one viewport. Make the viewport as large as possible while staying within the confines of the title block and border. Type **MS** to activate model space in the viewport and use *Zoom XP* to scale the model geometry times paper space (remember that the geometry is in millimeter units). Enter the scale in the title block (scale=XP factor).

D.   Turn *Off* the **VIEWPORT** layer and *Save* the drawing as **ASSY2**. *Plot* the drawing <u>from paper space</u> at **1=1**. Your drawing should appear as Figure 32-36.

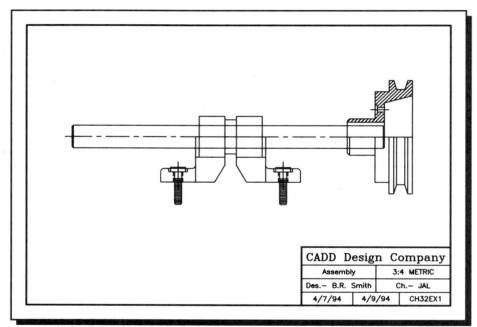

CADD Design Company		
Assembly		3:4 METRIC
Des.— B.R. Smith		Ch.— JAL
4/7/94	4/9/94	CH32EX1

Figure 32-36

2.   In this exercise you will use paper space with 3 viewports to show an overall view of a drawing and two details in different scales. *DIMSCALE* will be set to 0 to produce dimension features appearing equal in size.

A.   *Open* the **EFF-APT2** drawing that you worked on in Chapter 31 Exercises. *Erase* the plant. Create a text *Style* using *Roman Simplex* font. Create **dimensions** for the interior of each room on the **DIM** layer. *Zoom* in, and on another *New Layer* named **DIM2** give the dimensions for the wash basin in the Bath, and the counter for the Kitchen sink.

B.   Change *TILEMODE* to **0**. Set *Limits* to the paper size for plotting. Set appropriate *Snap* and *Grid* increments. Set *Layer* **TITLE** *Current*. Draw, *Insert*, or *Xref* a border and title block.

C.   Make a *New Layer* named **VIEWPORT** and set it as the *Current* layer. Use *Mview* to make one viewport occupying approximately 2/3 of the right half of the page. Use *Mview* again to make two smaller viewports in the remaining space on the left.

D.   Activate the large viewport (in *MS*) and *Zoom XP* to achieve the largest possible display of the apartment to an <u>accepted scale</u>. In the top left viewport use display controls (including *Zoom XP*) to produce a scaled detail of the Bath. Produce a <u>scaled</u> detail of the kitchen sink in the lower left viewport.

E.   Use the *Layer Control* dialogue to *Freeze* layer **DIM2** in the large viewport and *Freeze* layer **DIM** in the two small viewports. Change to *PS*. Set *DIMSCALE* to **0**. Return to *MS* and *Update* the dimensions in the small viewports so that the dimensions appear the same size in all viewports.

F.   Return to paper space and turn *Off Layer* **VIEWPORT**. Use *Text* (in paper space) to label the detail views and give the scale for each. *Save* the drawing as **EFF-APT3** and *Plot* from paper space at **1=1**. The final plot should look similar to Figure 32-37.

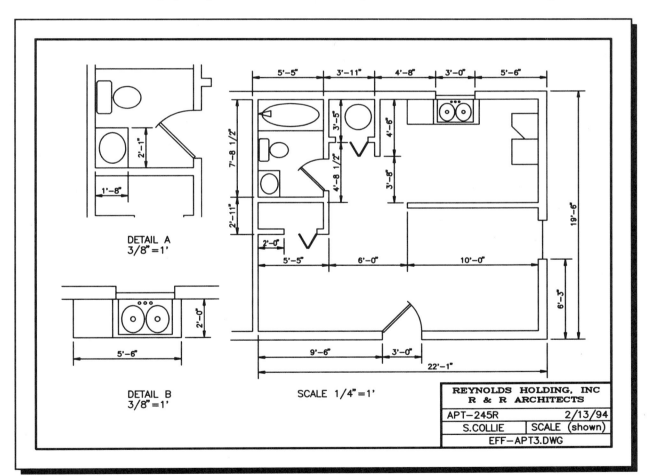

Figure 32-37

3. In this exercise you will create three paper space viewports and display three _Xrefed_ drawings, one in each viewport. Viewport-specific layer visibility control will be exercised to produce the desired display.

A. Begin a **New** drawing using a **Prototype** to correspond to the sheet size you intend to plot on. Create **New Layers** named **TITLE**, **XREF**, and **VIEWPORT**. Set **TILEMODE** to **0** and prepare paper space with **Limits**, **Snap**, **Grid**, a border, and title block. On the **VIEWPORT** layer, use **Mview** to create a viewport occupying about 1/2 of the page on the right side.

B. Make the **XREF** layer **Current**. Change to **MS**. In the viewport, **Xref GASKETD** drawing. Use **Zoom** with an **XP** value to scale it to paper space. Use the **Layer Control** dialogue box to **Freeze** the **GASKETD|DIM** layer and to **Freeze** all **GASKETD*** layers for **New VP**.

C. Option 1. Change to **PS** and create two more viewports on **Layer VIEWPORT** equal in size to the first. Set **Layer XREF Current** and **Xref** the **GASKETB** and the **GASKETC** drawings. Change to **MS** and use the **Layer Control** dialogue box or **Vplayer** to constrain only one gasket to appear in each viewport.

Option 2. Change to **PS** and create one more viewports on **Layer VIEWPORT** equal in size to the first. Set **Layer XREF Current** and **Xref** only the **GASKETB** drawing. Change to **MS** and use the **Layer Control** dialogue box or **Vplayer** to set the **GASKETB** visibility for the existing and new viewports. Repeat these steps for **GASKETC**.

D. Use **Zoom XP** values to produce a scaled view of each new gasket. Change to **PS** and **Freeze** layer **VIEWPORT**. Use **Text** to label the gaskets. **Plot** the drawing to scale. Your plot should look similar to Figure 32-38. **Save** the drawing as **GASKETS**.

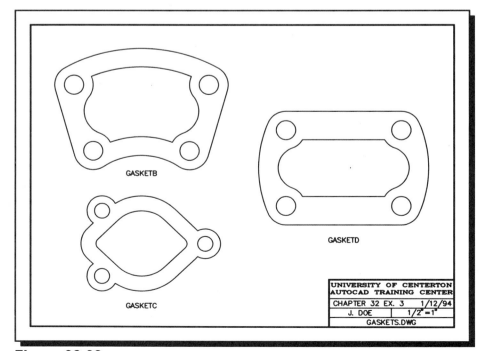

Figure 32-38

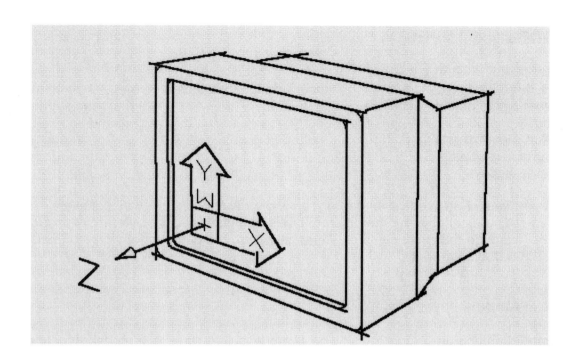

CHAPTER 33

3D Modeling Basics

CHAPTER OBJECTIVES

After completing this chapter you should:

1.   know the characteristics of wireframe, surface, and solid models;

2.   know the five formats for 3D coordinate entry;

3.   understand the application of point filters;

4.   understand the orientation of the World Coordinate System (WCS);

5.   know the purpose of a User Coordinate System (UCS);

6.   be able to recognize and know the purpose of the Coordinate System Icon;

7.   be able to use the right-hand rule for orientation of the X, Y, and Z axes and for determining positive and negative rotation about an axis.

3D MODELING TYPES

There are three basic types of 3D (three-dimensional) models created by CAD systems used to represent actual objects. They are:

1.   Wireframe models
2.   Surface models
3.   Solid models

These three types of 3D models range from a simple description to a very complete description of an actual object. The different types of models require different construction techniques, although many concepts of 3D modeling are the same for any type of model or any type of CAD system.

Wireframe Models

"Wireframe" is a good descriptor of this type of modeling. A wireframe model of a cube is like a model constructed of 12 coat hanger wires. Each wire represents an <u>edge</u> of the actual object. The <u>surfaces</u> of the object are <u>not</u> defined, only the boundaries of surfaces are represented by edges. No wires exist where edges do not exist. The model is see-through since it has no surfaces to obscure the back edges. A wireframe model has complete dimensional information but contains no volume. Examples of wireframe models are shown in Figures 33-1 and 33-2.

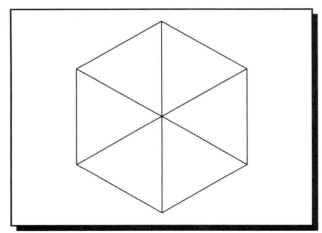

Figure 33-1

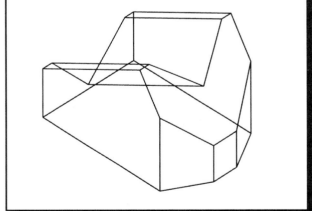

Figure 33-2

Wireframe models are relatively easy and quick to construct; however, they are not very useful for visualization purposes because of their "transparency." For example, does Figure 33-1 display the cube as if you are looking towards a top front edge or looking toward a bottom back edge? Wireframe models tend to have an optical illusion effect allowing you to visualize the object from two opposite directions unless another visual clue such as perspective is given.

With AutoCAD a wireframe model is constructed by creating 2D entities in 3D space. The *Line, Circle, Arc,* and other 2D draw and edit commands are used to create the "wires," but 3D coordinates must be specified. The cube in Figure 33-1 was created with 12 *Line* segments. AutoCAD provides all the necessary tools to easily construct, edit and view wireframe models.

A wireframe model offers many advantages over a 2D engineering drawing. Wireframe models are useful in industry for providing a computerized replica of an actual object. A wireframe model is dimensionally complete and accurate for all three dimensions. Visualization of a wireframe is generally better than a 2D drawing because the model can be viewed from any position or a perspective can be easily attained. The 3D database can be used to test and analyze the object <u>3 dimensionally</u>. The sheet metal industry, for example, uses wireframe models to calculate flat patterns complete with bending allowances. A wireframe model can also be used as a foundation for construction of a surface model.

Surface Models

Surface models provide a better description of an object than a wireframe, principally because the surfaces as well as the edges are defined. A surface model of a cube is like a cardboard box--all the surfaces and edges are defined, but there is nothing inside. Therefore, a surface model has volume but no mass. A surface model provides an excellent visual representation of an actual 3D object because the front surfaces obscure the back surfaces and edges from view. Figure 33-3 shows a surface model of a cube and Figure 33-4 displays a surface model of a somewhat more complex shape. Notice that a surface model leaves no question as to which side of the object you are viewing.

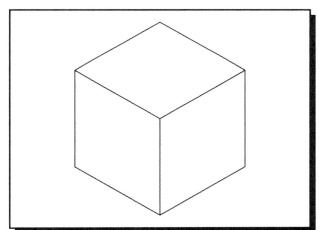

Figure 33-3

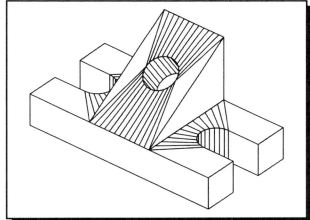

Figure 33-4

Surface models require a relatively tedious construction process. Each surface must be constructed individually. Each surface must be created in, or moved to, the correct orientation with respect to the other surfaces of the object. In AutoCAD, a surface is constructed by defining its edges. Often, wireframe models are used as a framework to build and attach surfaces. The complexity of the construction process of a surface is related to the number and shape of its edges. AutoCAD Release 12 is not a complete surface modeler. The tools provided allow construction of simple planar and single curved surfaces, but there are few capabilities for construction of double curved or other complex surfaces. No NURBS (Non-Uniform Rational B-Splines) capabilities exist in Release 12, although these capabilities are available in another Autodesk product called AutoSurf™.

Most CAD systems, including AutoCAD, can display surface and solid models in both wireframe and "hidden" representation. Figure 33-4 shows the object "hidden" (with the *Hide* command). Figure 33-5 displays the same object in "wireframe" (the default) representation. Surface modeling systems use wireframe representation during the construction and editing process to speed computing time. The user activates the "hidden" representation after completing the model to enhance visibility. With our technology, a reasonable amount of computing time is required to calculate the surface model "visibility." That is, the process required to determine which surfaces would obscure other surfaces for every position of the model would require noticeable computing time, so wireframe display is used during the model construction process.

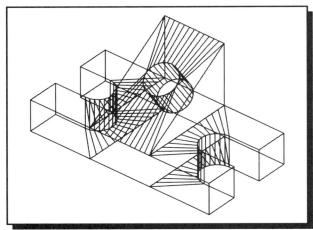

Figure 33-5

Solid Models

Solid modeling is the most complete and descriptive type of 3D modeling. A solid model is a complete computerized replica of the actual object. A solid model contains the complete surface and edge definition as well as description of the interior features of the object. If a solid model is cut in half (sectioned), the interior features are visible. Since a solid model is "solid," it can be assigned material characteristics and is considered to have mass. Because solid models have volume and mass, most solid modeling systems include capabilities to automatically calculate volumetric and mass properties.

Solid model construction techniques are generally much simpler (and much more fun) than those of surface models. AutoCAD's solid modeler, called AME (Advanced Modeling Extension), is a <u>hybrid</u> modeler. That is, AME is a combination CSG (Constructive Solid Geometry) and B-Rep (Boundary Representation) modeler. CSG is characterized by its simple and straight-forward construction techniques of combining primitive shapes (boxes, cylinders, wedges, etc.) utilizing Boolean operations (*Union*, *Subtraction*, and *Intersection*, etc.). Boundary Representation modeling defines a model in terms of its edges and surfaces (boundaries) and determines the solid model based on which side of the surfaces the model lies. The user interface and construction techniques used in AME (primitive shapes combined by Boolean operations) are CSG-based; whereas, the B-Rep capabilities are invoked automatically to display models in mesh representation and are somewhat transparent to the user. Figure 33-6 displays a solid model constructed of simple primitive shapes combined by Boolean operations.

The CSG modeling techniques offer you the advantage of complete and relatively simple editing. CSG construction typically begins by specifying dimensions for simple primitive shapes such as boxes or cylinders, then combining the primitives using Boolean operations to create a "composite" solid. Other primitives and/or composite solids can be combined by the same process. Several repetitions of this process can be continued until finally achieving the desired solid model. The individual steps of construction are recorded by the modeling software in a "CSG

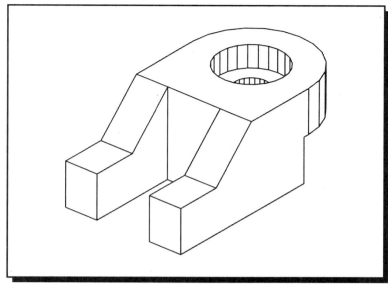

Figure 33-6

tree." When design changes must be made after the model is complete, only the individual primitive or Boolean operation needs to be changed by the user, and the model is "reevaluated" or recreated automatically by the modeling software by repeating the construction process recorded in the CSG tree. CSG techniques are discussed in detail in Chapters 42 and 43.

Solid models provide the same visualization characteristics as surface models with the additional capability of displaying sectional views (Fig. 33-7). Solid models, like surface models, are capable of either wireframe or "hidden" display. Generally, wireframe display is used during construction and meshed and hidden representation is used to display the finished model.

Although there are distinct differences between wireframe and surface models and their related construction and editing techniques, AutoCAD does not make an obvious difference in the

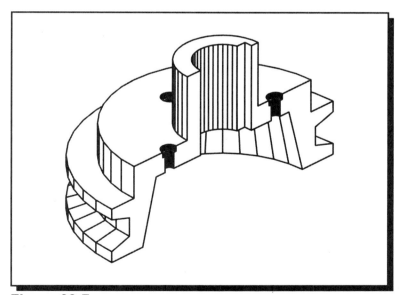

Figure 33-7

menu structure or command syntax for either of these concepts. The commands related to AME solid modeling, however, all begin with the letters *SOL* and are all located in the *Model* pull-down menu.

3D COORDINATE ENTRY

When creating a model in three-dimensional drawing space, the concept of the X and Y coordinate system, which is used for two-dimensional drawing, must be expanded to include the third dimension, Z, which is measured from the origin in a direction perpendicular to the plane defined by X and Y. Remember that two-dimensional CAD systems use X and Y coordinate values to define and store the location of drawing elements such as *Lines* and *Circles*. Likewise, a three-dimensional CAD system keeps a database of X, Y, and Z coordinate values to define locations and sizes of two- and three-dimensional elements. For example, a *Line* is a two-dimensional entity, yet the location of its endpoints in three-dimensional space must be specified and stored in the database using X, Y, and Z coordinates (Fig. 33-8). The X, Y, and Z coordinates are always defined in that order delineated by commas. The AutoCAD Coordinate Display (*COORDS*), however, only displays X and Y values even though a three-dimensional model can be displayed in the Drawing Editor.

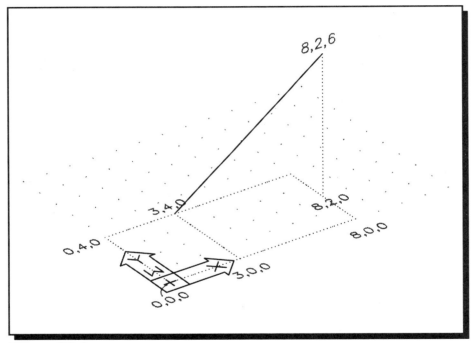

Figure 33-8

The icon that appears in the lower left corner of the AutoCAD drawing editor is called the Coordinate System Icon (Fig. 33-9). The Coordinate System Icon displays the directions for the X and the Y axes, the orientation of the XY plane, and can be made to locate itself at the origin, 0,0. The X coordinate values increase going to the right along the X axis and the Y values increase going upward along the Y axis. The Z axis is not indicated by the Coordinate System Icon but is assumed to be in a direction <u>perpendicular</u> to the XY plane. In other words, in the default orientation (when you begin a new drawing) the XY plane is <u>parallel</u> with the screen and the Z axis is <u>perpendicular</u> to the screen (Fig. 33-10).

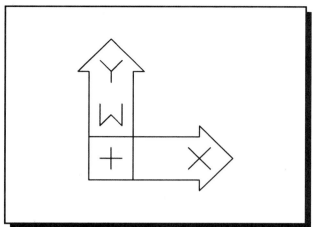

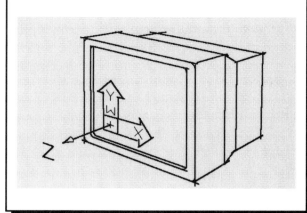

Figure 33-9   **Figure 33-10**

3D Coordinate Entry Formats

Because construction in three dimensions requires the definition of X, Y, <u>and</u> Z values, the methods of coordinate entry used for 2D construction must be expanded to include the Z value. The four methods of command entry used for 2D construction are valid for 3D coordinates with the addition of a Z value specification. Relative polar coordinate specification (@dist<angle) is expanded to form two other coordinate entry methods available explicitly for 3D coordinate entry. The five methods of coordinate entry for 3D construction follow.

1.	**Interactive coordinates**	**PICK**	Use the cursor to select points on the screen. *OSNAP* or point filters must be used to select a point in 3D space, otherwise points selected are on the XY plane.
2.	**Absolute coordinates**	**X,Y,Z**	Enter explicit X,Y and Z values relative to point 0,0.
3.	**Relative rectangular coordinates**	**@X,Y,Z**	Enter explicit X,Y and Z values relative to the last point.
4.	**Cylindrical coordinates (relative)**	**@dist<angle,Z**	Enter a distance value, an angle in the XY plane value, and a Z value, all relative to the last point.
5.	**Spherical coordinates (relative)**	**@dist<angle<angle**	Enter a distance value, an angle <u>in</u> the XY plane value, and an angle <u>from</u> the XY plane value, all relative to the last point.

Cylindrical and spherical coordinates can be given <u>without</u> the @ symbol, in which case the location specified is relative to point 0,0,0 (the origin). This method is useful if you are creating geometry centered around the origin. Otherwise, the @ symbol is used to establish points in space relative to the last point.

Examples of each of the five 3D coordinate entry methods are illustrated in the following section. In the illustrations, the orientation of the observer has been changed from the default plan view in order to enable the visibility of the three dimensions.

Interactive Coordinate Specification

Figure 33-11 illustrates using the interactive method to PICK a location in 3D space. *OSNAP* must be used in order to PICK in 3D space. Any point PICKed with the input device without *OSNAP* will result in a location on the XY plane. In this example, the *ENDpoint OSNAP* mode is used to establish the to point: of a second *Line* by snapping to the end of an existing *Line* at 8,2,6.

```
Command: Line
From point: ENDpoint of
PICK
to point:
```

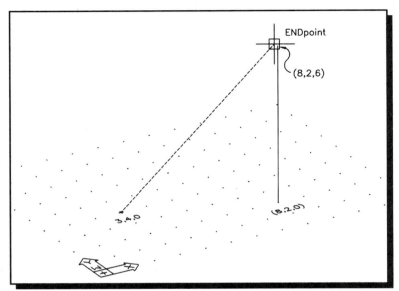

Figure 33-11

Absolute Coordinates

Figure 33-12 illustrates the absolute coordinate entry to draw the *Line*. The endpoints of the *Line* are given as explicit X,Y,Z coordinates.

```
Command: Line
From point: 3,4,0
To point: 8,2,6
Command:
```

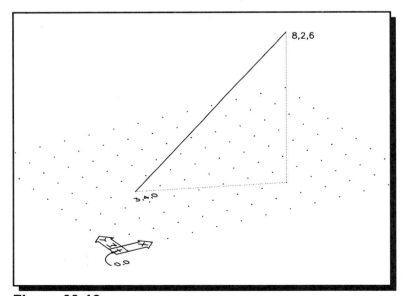

Figure 33-12

Relative Rectangular Coordinates

Relative rectangular coordinate
entry is displayed in Figure
33-13. The `From point:` of
the **Line** is given in absolute
coordinates and the `to point:`
end of the *Line* is given as X,Y,Z
values <u>relative</u> to the last point.

`Command:` **Line**
`From point:` **3,4,0**
`to point:` **@5,-2,6**
`Command:`

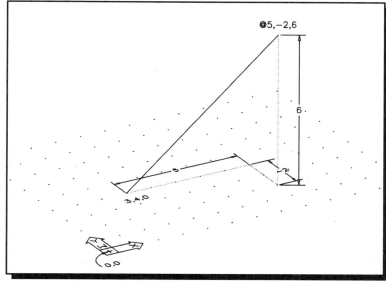

Figure 33-13

Cylindrical and spherical coordinates are an extension of polar coordinates with a provision for
the third dimension.

Cylindrical Coordinates (Relative)

Relative cylindrical coordinates give the distance <u>in</u> the XY plane, angle <u>in</u> the XY plane, and
Z dimension, and can be relative to the last point by prefixing the @ symbol. The *Line* in
Figure 33-14 is drawn with absolute and relative cylindrical coordinates. (The *Line* established
is approximately the same *Line* as in the previous figures.)

`Command:` **Line**
`From point:` **3,4,0**
`to point:` **@5<-22,6**
`Command:`

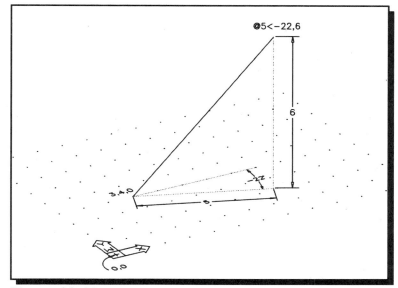

Figure 33-14

Spherical Coordinates (Relative)

Spherical coordinates are also an extension of polar coordinates with a provision for specifying the third dimension in angular format. Spherical coordinates specify a distance, angle <u>in</u> the XY plane, and an angle <u>from</u> the XY plane, and can be relative to the last point by prefixing the @ symbol. The distance specified is a <u>3D distance</u>, not a distance in the XY plane. Figure 33-15 illustrates the creation of approximately the same line as in the previous figures using absolute and relative spherical coordinates.

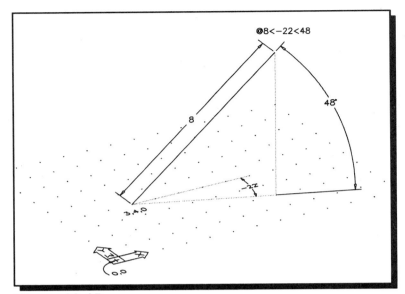

Figure 33-15

```
Command: Line
From point: 3,4,0
to point: @8<-22<48
Command:
```

Point Filters

Point filters are used to filter X and/or Y and/or Z coordinate values from a location PICKed with the pointing device. Point filtering makes it possible to build an X,Y,Z coordinate specification from a combination of point(s) selected on the screen and point(s) entered at the keyboard. A .XY (read "point XY") filter would extract, or filter, the X and Y coordinate value from the location PICKed and then prompt you to enter a Z value. Valid point filters are listed below.

.X	Filters (finds) the X component of the location PICKed with the pointing device.
.Y	Filters the Y component of the location PICKed.
.Z	Filters the Z component of the location PICKed.
.XY	Filters the X and Y components of the location PICKed.
.XZ	Filters the X and Z components of the location PICKed.
.YZ	Filters the Y and Z components of the location PICKed.

The .XY filter is the most commonly used point filter for 3D construction and editing. Because 3D construction often begins on the XY plane of the current coordinate system, elements in Z space are easily constructed by selecting existing points on the XY plane using .XY filters and then entering the Z component of the desired 3D coordinate specification by keyboard. For example, in order to draw a line in Z space two units above an existing line on the XY plane, the .XY filter can be used in combination with *ENDpoint OSNAP* to supply the XY component for the new line. See Figure 33-16 for illustration of the following command sequence.

```
Command: Line
From point: .XY of
```
END of **PICK** (Select one *ENDpoint* of the existing line on the XY plane.)
```
(need Z) 2
to point: .XY of
```
END of **PICK** (Select the other *ENDpoint* of the existing line.)
```
(need Z) 2
Command:
```

Typing **.XY** and pressing **Enter** cause AutoCAD to respond with "of" similar to the way "of" appears after typing an *OSNAP* mode. When a location is specified using an .XY filter, AutoCAD responds with "(need Z)" and, likewise when other filters are used, AutoCAD prompts for the missing component(s).

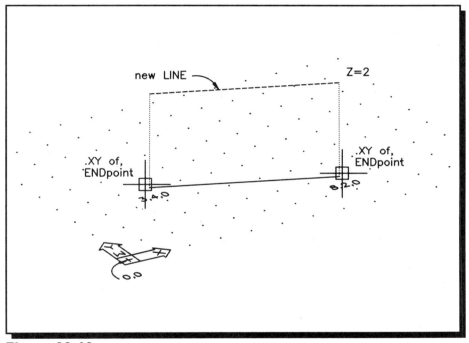

Figure 33-16

COORDINATE SYSTEMS

In AutoCAD two kinds of coordinate systems can exist, the <u>World Coordinate System</u> (WCS) and one or more <u>User Coordinate Systems</u> (UCS). The World Coordinate System <u>always</u> exists in any drawing and cannot be deleted. The user can also create and save multiple User Coordinate Systems to make construction of a particular 3D geometry easier. Only <u>one</u> coordinate system can be active at any one time, either the WCS or one of the user-created UCS's.

The World Coordinate System (WCS) and WCS Icon

The World Coordinate System (WCS) is the default coordinate system in AutoCAD for defining the position of drawing entities in 2D or 3D space. The WCS is always available and cannot be erased or removed, but is deactivated temporarily when utilizing another coordinate system created by the user called a User Coordinate System (UCS). The icon that appears (by default) at the lower left corner of the Drawing Editor (Fig. 33-9) indicates the orientation of the WCS. The coordinate system icon indicates only X and Y directions, so Z is assumed to be perpendicular to the XY plane. The icon, whose appearance (*ON, OFF*) is controlled by the *UCSICON* command, appears for the WCS and for any UCS. However, the letter "W" appears in the icon slightly above the origin only when the WCS is active.

The orientation of the WCS with respect to the Earth may be different among CAD systems. In AutoCAD the WCS has an architectural orientation such that the XY plane is a horizontal plane with respect to the Earth, making Z the height dimension. A 2D drawing (X and Y coordinates only) is thought of as being viewed from above, sometimes called a plan view. Therefore, in a 3D AutoCAD drawing, X is the width dimension, Y is the depth dimension, and Z is height. This default orientation is like viewing a floor plan--from above (Fig. 33-17).

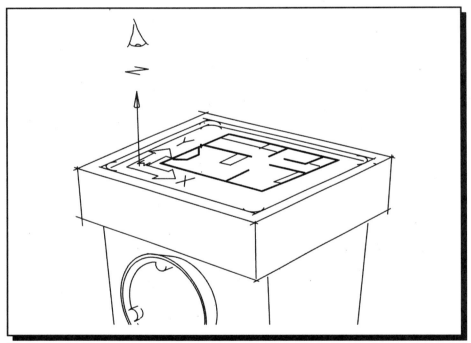

Figure 33-17

Some CAD systems that have a mechanical engineering orientation align their World Coordinate Systems such that the XY plane is a vertical plane intended for drawing a front view. In other words, some mechanical engineering oriented CAD systems define X as the width dimension, Y as height, and Z as depth.

User Coordinate Systems (UCS) and Icons

There are no User Coordinate Systems that exist as part of the AutoCAD default drawing (ACAD.DWG) as it comes "out of the box." UCS's are created to suit the 3D model when and where they are needed.

Creating geometry is relatively simple when having only to deal with X and Y coordinates such as in creating a 2D drawing or when creating simple 3D geometry with uniform Z dimensions. However, 3D models containing complex shapes on planes not parallel with the XY plane are good candidates for UCS's (Fig. 33-18).

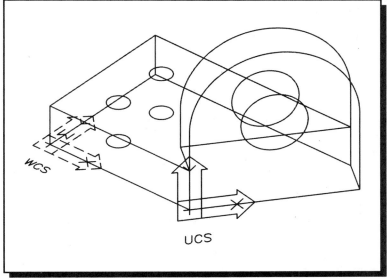

Figure 33-18

A User Coordinate System is thought of as a construction plane created to simplify creation of geometry on a specific plane or surface of the object. The user creates the UCS aligning its XY plane with a surface of the object, such as along an inclined plane, with the UCS origin typically at a corner or center of the surface (Fig. 33-19).

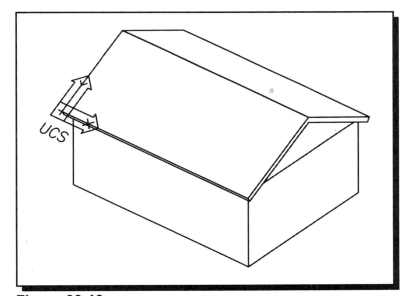

Figure 33-19

The user can then create geometry aligned with that plane by defining only X and Y coordinate values of the current UCS (Fig. 33-20). The *SNAP* and *GRID* automatically align with the current coordinate system providing *SNAP* points and enhancing visualization of the construction plane. Practically speaking, it is easier in some cases to specify only X and Y coordinates with respect to a specific plane on the object rather than calculating X, Y, and Z values with respect to the World Coordinate System.

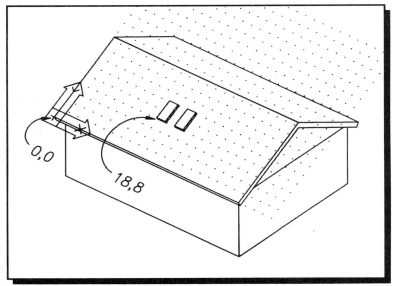

Figure 33-20

User Coordinate Systems can be created by any of several options of the *UCS* command. Once a UCS has been created, it becomes the current coordinate system. Only one coordinate system can be active; therefore, it is suggested that UCS's be saved (by using the *Save* option of *UCS*) for possible future geometry creation or editing.

When a UCS is created, the icon at the lower left corner of the screen can be made to automatically align itself with the UCS along with *SNAP* and *GRID*. The letter "W", however, only appears on the icon when the WCS is active (when the WCS is the current coordinate system). When creating 3D geometry, it is recommended that the *ORigin* option of the *UCSICON* command be used to place the icon always at the origin of the current UCS, rather than in the lower left corner of the screen. Since the origin of the UCS is typically specified as a corner or center of the construction plane, aligning the Coordinate System Icon with the current origin aids the user's visualization of the UCS orientation. The Coordinate Display (*COORDS*) in the Status Line always displays only the X and Y values of the current coordinate system, whether it is WCS or UCS.

It is important for you to have some experience creating and viewing 3D models before UCS's can be effectively learned. Therefore, User Coordinate Systems are introduced in Chapter 35, Wireframe Modeling, and discussed in detail in Chapter 36, User Coordinate Systems.

THE RIGHT-HAND RULE

AutoCAD complies with the right-hand rule for defining the orientation of the X, Y, and Z axes. The right-hand rule states that if your right hand is held partially open, the thumb, first and middle fingers define positive X, Y, and Z directions, respectively, and positive rotation about any axis is like screwing in a light bulb.

More precisely, if the thumb and first two fingers are held out so as to be mutually perpendicular, the thumb points in the positive X direction, the first finger points in the positive Y direction, and the middle finger points in the positive Z direction.

In this position, looking toward your hand from the tip of your middle finger is like the default AutoCAD viewing orientation--positive X is to the right, positive Y is up, and positive Z is toward you.

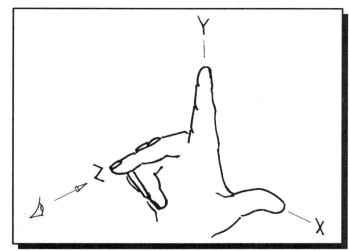

Figure 33-21

Positive rotation about any axis is <u>counter-clockwise looking toward the origin</u>.

For example, viewing your right hand, positive rotation about the X axis is as if you look down your thumb toward the hand (origin) and twisting counter-clockwise.

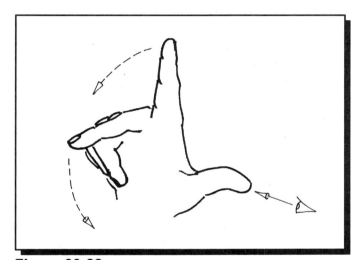

Figure 33-22

Figure 33-23 shows the Coordinate System Icon in a +90 degree rotation about the X axis (like the previous figure). This orientation is typical for setting up a <u>front</u> view UCS for drawing on a plane parallel with the front surface of an object.

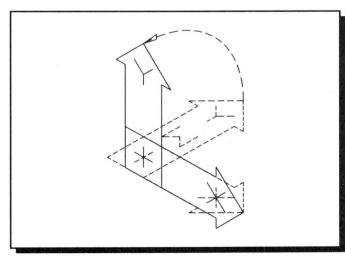

Figure 33-23

Positive rotation about the Y axis would be as if looking down your first finger toward the hand (origin) and twisting counter-clockwise (Fig. 33-24).

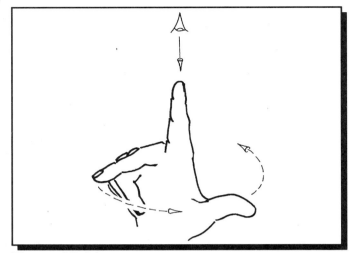

Figure 33-24

Figure 33-25 illustrates the Coordinate System Icon with a +90 degree rotation about the Y axis (like the previous figure).

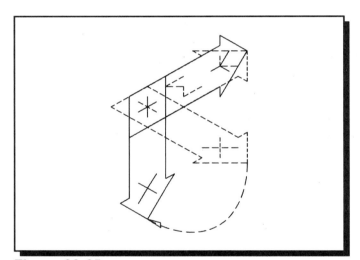

Figure 33-25

Positive rotation about the Z axis would be as if looking toward your hand from the end of your middle finger and twisting counter-clockwise.

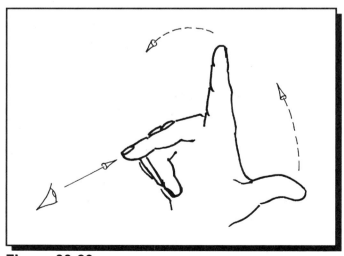

Figure 33-26

Figure 33-27 shows the Coordinate System Icon with a +90 degree rotation about the Z axis (like the previous figure).

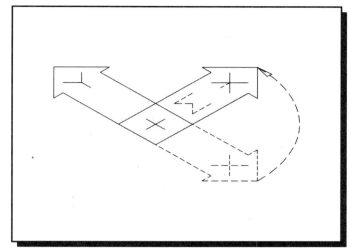

Figure 33-27

CHAPTER EXERCISES

1. What are the three types of 3D models?

2. What characterizes each of the three types of 3D models?

3. What similarities do the three types of 3D modeling systems have?

4. What kind of modeling techniques does AutoCAD's AME solid modeling system use?

5. What are the five formats for 3D coordinate specification?

6. Examine the 3D geometry shown in Figure 33-28. Specify the designated coordinates in the specified formats below.

A. Give the coordinate of corner D in absolute format.

B. Give the coordinate of corner F in absolute format.

C. Give the coordinate of corner H in absolute format.

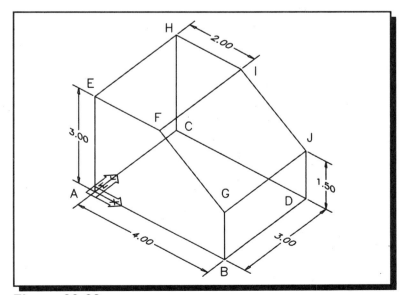

Figure 33-28

D.   Give the coordinate of corner J in absolute format.

E.   What are the coordinates of the line that defines edge F-I?

F.   What are the coordinates of the line that defines edge J-I?

G.   Assume point E is the "last point." Give the coordinates of point I in relative rectangular format.

H.   Point I is now the last point. Give the coordinates of point J in relative rectangular format.

I.   Point J is now the last point. Give the coordinates of point A in relative rectangular format.

J.   What are the coordinates of corner G in cylindrical format (from the origin)?

K.   If E is the "last point, what are the coordinates of corner C in relative cylindrical format?

7.   Using the model in Figure 33-28, assume a UCS was created by rotating about the X axis 90 degrees from the existing orientation (World Coordinate System).

A.   What would the absolute coordinates of corner F be?

B.   What would the absolute coordinates of corner H be?

C.   What would the absolute coordinates of corner J be?

8.   Using the model in Figure 33-28, assume a UCS was created by rotating about the X axis 90 degrees from the existing orientation (WCS) and then rotating 90 degrees about the (new) Y.

A.   What would the absolute coordinates of corner F be?

B.   What would the absolute coordinates of corner H be?

C.   What would the absolute coordinates of corner J be?

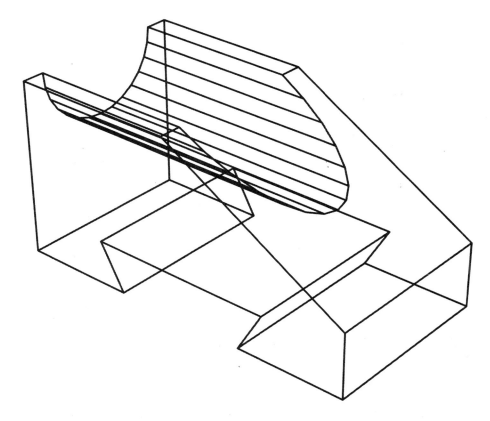

CHAPTER 34

3D Viewing and Display

CHAPTER OBJECTIVES

After completing this chapter you should:

1.   be able to recognize a 3D model in wireframe, perspective, *Hide, Shade*, and *Render* display representations;

2.   be able to use *Vpoint* to view a 3D model from various viewpoints such as isometric, top, front, and side;

3.   be able to use the *Coordinates, Axes*, and *Rotate* options of *Vpoint*;

4.   be able to use *Dview* to specify a *TArget* and *CAmera* point and to generate a perspective with the *Distance* option;

5.   be able to use the *PAn, Zoom, TWist, CLip*, and *Hide* options of *Dview*;

6.   be able to create several configurations of tiled viewports with the *Vports* command;

7.   be able to suppress "hidden lines" of a surface or solid model with the *Hide* command.

AutoCAD'S 3D VIEWING AND DISPLAY CAPABILITIES

Viewing Commands

These commands allow you to change the direction from which you view a 3D model or otherwise affect the view of the 3D model.

Vpoint   *Vpoint* allows you to change your viewpoint of a 3D model. The object remains stationary while the viewpoint of the observer changes. Three options are provided: *Coordinates*, *Axes*, and *Rotate*.

Plan   The *Plan* command automatically gives the observer a plan (top) view of the object. The plan view can be with respect to the WCS (World Coordinate System) or an existing UCS (User Coordinate System).

Dview   This command allows you to dynamically (interactively) rotate the viewpoint of the observer about 3D objects. *Dview* also allows generation of perspective views. *PAn*, Zoom, *TWist*, and *Clip* can also be generated from within *Dview*.

Zoom   Although *Zoom* operates in 3D just as in 2D, the *Zoom Previous* option will restore the previous 3D viewpoint.

View   The *View* command can be used with 3D viewing to *Save* and *Restore* 3D viewpoints.

Vports   The *Vports* command creates tiled viewports. *Vports* does not actually change the viewpoint of the model, but divides the screen into several viewports and allows you to display several viewpoints or sizes of the model on one screen.

Display Commands

Once the desired viewpoint has been attained, these commands can change the appearance of a 3D surface or solid model from the default wireframe representation by displaying the surfaces.

Hide   This command removes normally "hidden" edges and surfaces from a solid or surface model making it appear as an opaque rather than a transparent object.

Shade   The *Shade* command fills the surfaces with the object's color and calculates light reflection by applying gradient shading (variable gray values) to the surfaces. (This command and related variables are covered in detail in Chapter 45.)

Render   Part of AutoCAD's Advanced Visualization Extension (AVE), *Render* allows you to create and place lights in 3D space, adjust the light intensity, and assign color and reflective qualities (finishes) to the surfaces. This is the most sophisticated of the visualization capabilities offered with AutoCAD. (This feature is covered in detail in Chapter 45.)

A brief understanding of most of the viewing and display commands can be gained from the following figures.

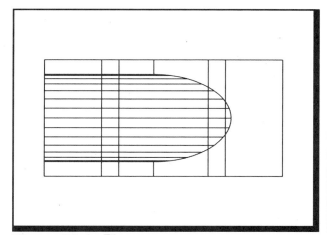

Figure 34-1 *Plan*

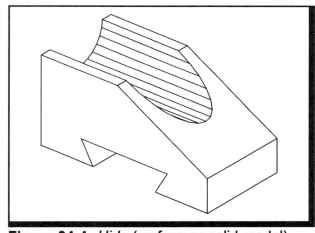

Figure 34-2 *Vpoint* (wireframe representation)

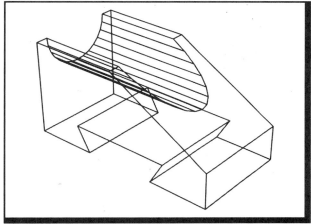

Figure 34-3 *Dview, Distance* (perspective)

Figure 34-4 *Hide* (surface or solid model)

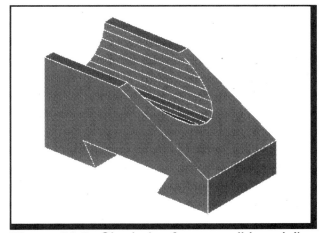

Figure 34-5 *Shade* (surface or solid model)

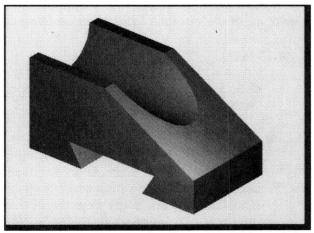

Figure 34-6 *Render* (surface or solid model)

3D VIEWING COMMANDS

In order to construct 3D geometry, you must be able to see other than a plan view. If you display only the plan (top) view, the Z (height) dimension is not visible because it is perpendicular to the screen. The *Vpoint* (viewpoint), *Dview* (dynamic view), and *Plan* commands are used to change the direction from which you view the geometry. *Zoom Previous* will generate the previous viewpoint. The *Vports* command allows you to divide the screen into several viewports such that each can then be made to display a different viewpoint of the geometry.

When using the viewing commands *Vpoint*, *Dview*, and *Plan*, it is important to imagine that the observer moves about the object, rather than imagining that the object rotates. The object and the coordinate system (and icon) always remain stationary and always keep the same orientation with respect to the Earth. Since the observer moves and not the geometry, the entities' coordinate values retain their integrity; whereas, if the geometry rotated within the coordinate system, all coordinate values of the entities would have to change as the object rotated. The *Vpoint*, *Dview*, and *Plan* commands change only the viewpoint of the observer.

As the 3D viewing commands are discussed, it would be helpful if you opened a 3D drawing that could be used to practice the viewing commands. *Open* the **PUMPSOL** drawing located in the ACAD12\SAMPLE directory. When the drawing comes up, it is displayed with four paper space viewports. Type **TILEMODE** and change the value to **1**. This action causes a display of only one view, the plan view.

VPOINT

TYPE IN:	PULL-DOWN MENU	SCREEN MENU	TABLET MENU
VPOINT	*View, Set view > Viewpoint > Set Vpoint*	*DISPLAY, VPOINT:*	*6,M*

The *Vpoint* command (short for viewpoint) allows you three options for changing your viewpoint of the geometry displayed in the drawing editor. They are:

Coordinates
    Enter X, Y, and Z coordinates. The coordinate values define a vector specifying the direction of viewing with respect to the WCS. The observer is positioned along the vector looking toward the origin.

Rotate
    The name of this option is somewhat misleading because the object is not rotated. The *Rotate* option prompts for two angles in the WCS (by default) which specify a vector indicating the direction of viewing. The two angles are (1) the angle in the XY plane and (2) the angle from the XY plane (similar to spherical coordinates). The observer is positioned along the vector looking toward the origin.

Axes

This option displays a three-pole axes system which rotates dynamically on the screen as the cursor is moved within a "globe." The axes represent the X, Y, and Z axes of the WCS. When you PICK the desired viewing position, the geometry is displayed in that orientation.

Bring up the PUMPSOL drawing and change the settings as explained in the previous section. Your display should appear as that in Figure 34-7.

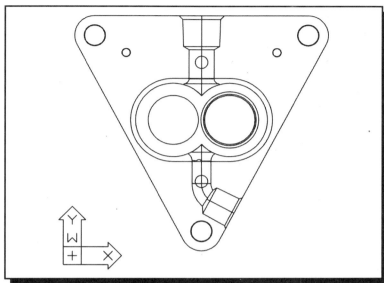

Figure 34-7

Rotate

Invoke the *Vpoint* command. Type **R** to invoke the *Rotate* option. The command syntax to enter is as follows:

```
Command: Vpoint
Rotate <View point><0,0,1>: R
Enter angle in XY plane from X axis <270>: 315
Enter angle from XY plane <90>: 35
Command:
```

The first angle is the angle in the XY plane at which the observer is positioned looking toward the origin. This angle is just like specifying an angle in 2D. The second angle is the angle that the observer is positioned <u>up or down</u> from the XY plane. The two angles are given with respect to the WCS.

If using the *Viewpoint Presets* dialogue box, the angles can be specified relative to the current UCS. The *Viewpoint Presets* dialogue box is accessible through the *View* pull-down menu, then *Set View* and *Vpoint*.

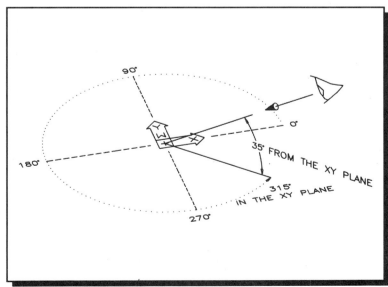

Figure 34-8

The resulting display of the PUMPSOL drawing should look like that in Figure 34-9. Solid models are shown in wireframe representation during the construction process.

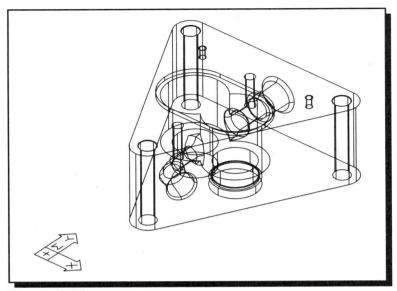

Figure 34-9

Angles of **315** and **35** specified in response to the *Rotate* option display an almost <u>perfect</u> <u>isometric</u> viewing angle. An isometric drawing often displays some of the top, front, and right sides of the object. For some regularly proportioned objects, perfect isometric viewing angles can cause visualization difficulties, while a slightly different angle can display the object more clearly. Figure 34-10 and Figure 34-11 display a cube from a perfect isometric viewing angle (**315** and **35**) and from a slightly different viewing angle (**310** and **40**), respectively.

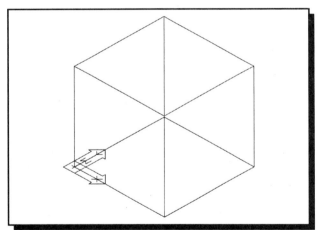

Figure 34-10

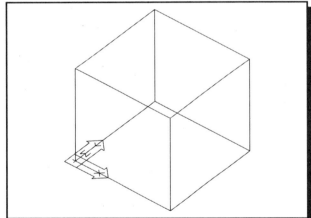

Figure 34-11

The *Vpoint* command displays a parallel projection rather than a perspective projection. In a parallel projection all visual rays from the observer to the object are parallel as if the observer were (theoretically) an infinite distance from the object. The resulting display shows all parallel edges of the object as being parallel in the display. This projection differs from a perspective projection, where parts of the object that are further from the observer appear smaller and parallel edges converge to a point on the horizon.

The PUMPSOL model could be viewed from the back side by entering appropriate angles in response to the *Rotate* option. The following command sequence allows the observer to view the model from above the back and right side. This *Vpoint* is shown in Figure 34-12.

```
Command: Vpoint
Rotate <View point><0,0,1>: R
Enter angle in XY plane from X
axis <270>: 45
Enter angle from XY plane <90>:
40
Command:
```

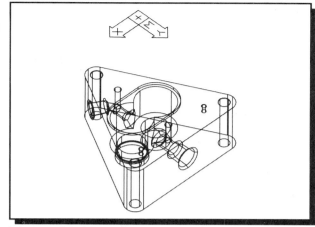

Figure 34-12

The *Vpoint Rotate* option can be used to display 3D objects from a front, top, or side view. Figure 34-13 displays the model as if viewing from <u>slightly</u> above the front side, achieved by using *Rotate* angles of 270, 10. *Rotate* angles for three principal views are:

Top	270, 90
Front	270, 0
Right side	0,0

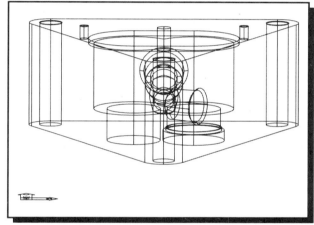

Figure 34-13

Figure 34-14 displays the top view using angles of 270, 90, and Figure 34-15 displays a right side view achieved by viewing angles of 0, 0.

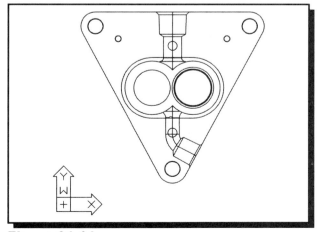

Figure 34-14

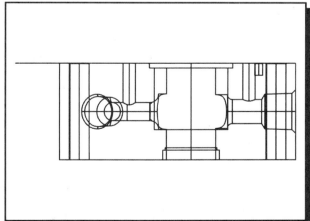

Figure 34-15

Coordinates

Another option of the *Vpoint* command is to enter X,Y,Z coordinate values. The coordinate values indicate the position in 3D space at which the observer is located. The coordinate values do not specify an absolute position, but rather specify a <u>vector</u> passing through the coordinate position and the origin. In other words, the observer is located at <u>any point along the vector looking toward the origin</u>.

Because the *Vpoint* command generates a parallel projection, and since parallel projection does not consider a distance (which is only considered in perspective projection), the magnitude of the coordinate <u>values</u> are of no importance, only the relationship among the values. Values of 1,-1,1 would generate the same display as 2,-2,2.

The command syntax for specifying a perfect isometric viewing angle is as follows:

```
Command: Vpoint
Rotate <View point><0,0,1>: 1,-1,1
Command:
```

Coordinates of 1,-1,1 generate a display from a perfect isometric viewing angle.

Figure 34-16 illustrates positioning the observer in space using coordinates of 1,-1,1. Using *Vpoint* coordinates of 1,-1,1 generates a display identical to *Rotate* angles of 315, 35. Coordinates of 1,-1,1 would generate a display of the PUMPSOL identical to Figure 34-9.

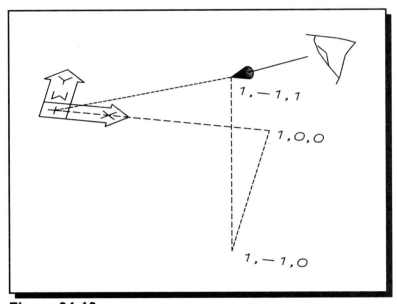

Figure 34-16

Other typical views of an object can be easily achieved by entering coordinates at the *Vpoint* command. Consider the following coordinate values and the resulting displays.

<u>Coordinates</u>	<u>Display</u>	<u>Figures</u>
0,0,1	top view	Figs. 34-17, 34-18
0,-1,0	front view	Figs. 34-19, 34-20
1,0,0	right side view	Figs. 34-21, 34-22

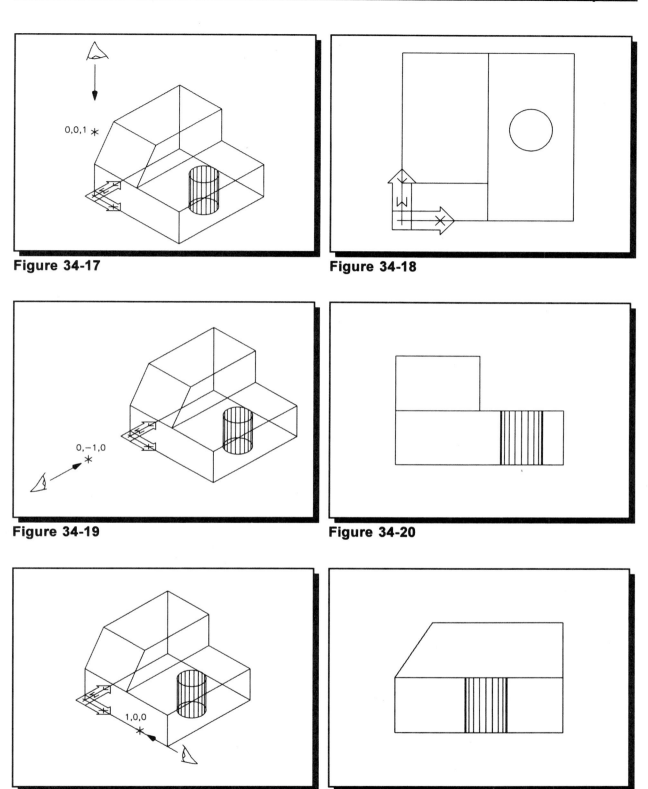

Figure 34-17

Figure 34-18

Figure 34-19

Figure 34-20

Figure 34-21

Figure 34-22

Practice using the *Vpoint* command with coordinate values to generate the views of the PUMPSOL drawing.

Axes

This option allows you to quickly and easily generate a view of an object. Because the viewing direction is specified by PICKing a point, it is difficult to specify an exact viewpoint.

The *Axes* option does not appear on the command line as one of the possible *Vpoint* methods. This option must be invoked by pressing **Enter** at the `Rotate<Viewpoint <(coordinates)>:` prompt, or by selecting the word *Axes* from one of the menus. When the *Axes* method is invoked, the current drawing temporarily disappears and a three-pole axes system appears at the center of the screen. The axes are dynamically rotated by moving the cursor (a small cross) in a small "globe" at the upper right of the screen (Fig. 34-23).

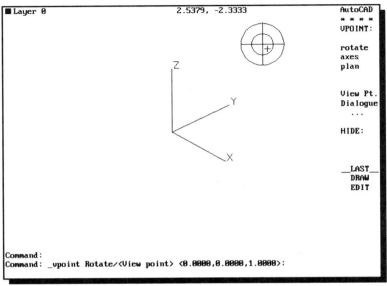

Figure 34-23

The three-pole axes indicate the orientation of the X, Y, and Z axes for the new *Vpoint*. The center of the "globe" represents the North Pole, so moving the cursor to that location generates a plan, or top, view. The small circle of the globe represents the Equator, so moving the cursor to any location on the Equator generates an elevation view (front, side, back, etc.). The outside circle represents the South Pole, so locating the cursor there shows a bottom view. When you **PICK**, the axes disappear and the current drawing is displayed from the new viewpoint. The command syntax for using the *Axes* method is as follows.

```
Command: Vpoint
Rotate <Viewpoint><(current coordinates)>: Enter (axes appear)
PICK (Select desired cursor location.)
Regenerating drawing. (Current drawing appears showing the new viewpoint.)
```

Using the *Axes* method of *Vpoint* is quick and easy. Because no exact *Vpoint* can be given, it is difficult to achieve the exact *Vpoint* twice. Therefore, if you are working with a complex drawing that requires a <u>specific</u> viewpoint of a 3D model, use another option of *Vpoint* or save the desired *Vpoint* as a named *View*.

Using *Zoom .9X* with *Vpoint*

In the PUMPSOL drawing, the Coordinate System Icon was previously turned *ON* and forced to appear at the *ORigin*. This action was accomplished by the *UCSICON* command (see *UCSICON*, Chapter 36). The icon does not <u>always</u> appear at the origin after using the *Vpoint* command. This is because *Vpoint* causes a *Zoom Extents*, forcing the geometry against the border of the graphics screen area. This sometimes prevents the icon from aligning with the origin since the origin can also be against the border of the graphics screen area. In order to cause the icon to appear at the origin, try using **Zoom** with a **.9X** magnification factor. This action usually brings the geometry slightly away from the border and allows the icon to "pop" into place at the origin.

PLAN

TYPE IN:	PULL-DOWN MENU	SCREEN MENU	TABLET MENU
PLAN	*View, Set View >* *Plan View >*	*DISPLAY, PLAN:*	*5,M*

This command is useful to quickly display a plan view of any UCS.

```
Command: plan
<Current UCS>/Ucs/World: (letter) or Enter
```

Responding by pressing Enter causes AutoCAD to display the plan (top) view of the current UCS. Typing **W** causes the display to show the plan view of the World Coordinate System. The World option does <u>not</u> cause the WCS to become the active coordinate system, but only displays its plan view. Invoking the *UCS* option displays the following prompt:

```
?/Name of UCS:
```

The *?* displays a list of existing UCS's. Entering the name of an existing UCS displays a plan view of that UCS.

DVIEW

TYPE IN:	PULL-DOWN MENU	SCREEN MENU	TABLET MENU
DVIEW	*View > Set View >* *Dview*	*DISPLAY, DVIEW:*	*4,K to 6,L*

Dview (Dynamic View) has many capabilities for displaying a 3D model. It can be used like *Vpoint* to specify different viewpoints of an object. *Dview* can be used to change the *TArget* (point to look <u>at</u>) and the *CAmera* (point to view <u>from</u>) as well as to *Zoom*, *PAn*, and establish clipping planes. *Dview* is commonly used to generate perspective projections of the current drawing. The *Dview* options are described here briefly and in detail on the following pages.

CAmera
> The *CAmera* point is the observer's location. It is analogous to *Vpoint*.

TArget
> This is a point specifying the focus of viewing, i.e., the *TArget* point of the *CAmera*.

Distance
> This option is used for generating a perspective. A perspective takes into account the distance the observer (*CAmera*) is from the object (*TArget*).

POints

The *POints* option allows you to specify both the *CAmera* and the *TArget* points.

PAn

This is a dynamic, 3D *PAn*.

Zoom

The effect is identical to the *Zoom* command. In this context it is dynamic and only changes the <u>size</u> of the display without affecting the <u>amount</u> of perspective (*Distance*).

TWist

The user can rotate (*TWist*) the object about the *TArget* point dynamically.

CLip

This option allows you to establish *Front* or *Back* clipping planes. The clipping planes prevent portions of the geometry from being displayed.

Hide

Like the *Hide* command, this option removes normally hidden edges of an object from the display.

OFF

This option turns perspective mode off, but keeps all of the other parameters that affect the display valid.

Undo

A typical *Undo* option, selecting this choice undoes the last action.

eXit

Exits the *Dview* command and displays the 3D model in the new position.

Because *Dview* dynamically displays rotation or other movement of objects on the screen, you are first given the chance to select objects for this action. If your 3D drawing is large and complex, select only the "framework" of the set of entities; otherwise, select all entities for dynamic action. If too many entities are selected, the dynamic motion is slow and difficult to see. As an alternative, if a null selection set is used (**Enter** is pressed in response to the `Select objects:` prompt), the DVIEWBLK house appears, which is used temporarily for dynamic

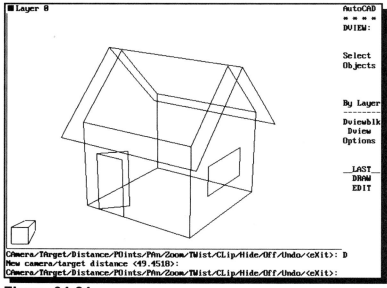

Figure 34-24

movement (Fig. 34-24). When the dynamic action of the command is completed, your entire 3D object reappears on the screen in the new position. The command syntax for *Dview* is:

Command: ***dview***
Select objects: **PICK** or **Enter** (Select entities for dynamic action or press Enter for the DVIEWBLK house.)
Select objects: **Enter** (If you selected objects instead of Enter in the previous step, press Enter to complete the selection process.)
CAmera/TArget/Distance/POints/PAn/Zoom/TWist/CLip/Hide/Off/
Undo/<eXit>:**(letters)** Enter choice.

The *Dview* options are given here in the best order for understanding related concepts.

eXit

This option should be used to save the resulting *Dview* display after using any of the other options to generate the desired view or perspective of the 3D model. *Dview* must be exited before any other AutoCAD commands can be used. Using the *Dview eXit* option saves the current display and returns to the Command: prompt. Remember to enter an **X**, not an *E*.

CAmera

This option allows you to specify a point representing the observer's location, like the *Vpoint* command, only *Dview CAmera* is <u>dynamic</u>. Although it appears that the object is being dynamically rotated, imagine that the <u>observer</u> is changing position. When **PICK** is used to indicate the desired position, AutoCAD records a coordinate value representing the *CAmera* position. (The *CAmera* position can be specified by entering coordinate values when using the *POints* option rather than the *CAmera* option.)

Upon selecting the *CAmera* option, the selected objects appear to rotate with movement of the crosshairs. If the crosshairs are positioned at the center of the screen, the objects are viewed from the positive X axis (or from angles 0, 0). Moving the crosshairs to the upper left displays the objects from a viewing angle similar to an isometric viewpoint (angles 315, 35). Figure 34-25 displays the PUMPSOL drawing in this position. Vertical cursor movement causes rotation about the vertical axis and horizontal cursor movement causes

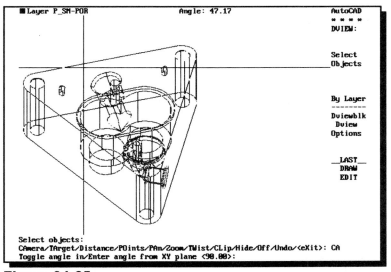

Figure 34-25

horizontal rotation. Since *Dview* displays a wireframe image, it may be difficult to see which "side" of the object you are viewing. The Coordinate System Icon reappears only after **PICK**ing a *CAmera* position. Use the PUMPSOL drawing to experiment with *Dview CAmera*.

Rather than PICKing a *CAmera* position interactively, you can specify angles in the XY plane and from the XY plane. This method is like the *Vpoint* command except the angles are given in the <u>reverse order</u>; first specify the angle <u>from</u> the XY plane, then the angle <u>in</u> the XY plane.

```
Command: dview
Select objects: PICK or Enter (Select entities for dynamic action or press Enter
for the DVIEWBLK house.)
Select objects: Enter (If you selected objects instead of Enter in the previous
step, press Enter to complete the selection process.)
CAmera/TArget/Distance/POints/PAn/Zoom/TWist/CLip/Hide/Off/
Undo/<eXit>:ca
Toggle angle in/Enter angle from XY plane<0.00>:(value) (Enter
angle from XY plane.)
Toggle angle from/Enter angle in XY plane from XY
axis<0.00>:(value) (Enter angle in XY plane.)
```

TArget

The *TArget* is the point that the *CAmera* (observer position) is focused on (looking toward). For comparison, when using the *Vpoint* command, the observer always looks toward the <u>origin</u>. The default *TArget* used with the *Dview* command is automatically calculated approximately at the <u>center of the selected geometry</u>. The *TArget* option allows you to specify any position to focus on. This is accomplished with the *TArget* option either interactively or by specifying angles. The interactive method operates like the *CAmera* option.

Selecting a *TArget* position can also be accomplished by specifying angles <u>from</u> the XY plane and <u>in</u> the XY plane. The current *TArget* angles are always <u>opposite</u> the current *CAmera* angles. Another method for specifying the *TArget* is the *POints* option (see *POints*).

The *TArget* option is useful for viewing specific areas of a large 3D model such as an architectural plan. For example, the *CAmera* (observer) can be stationed in the middle of a room and a separate display of each end of the room can be generated by specifying two *TArget*s, one at each end of the room (Fig. 34-26 and 34-27).

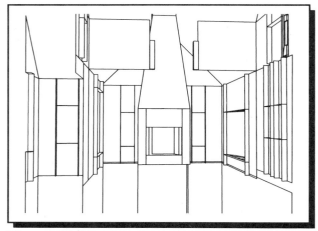

Figure 34-26

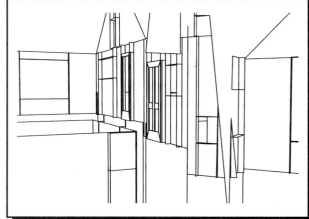

Figure 34-27

POints

Another method for specifying the _TArget_ and/or the _CAmera_ is the _POints_ option. This option allows specification of the _CAmera_ and/or _TArget_ points <u>either</u> by specifying coordinate values or by interactive selection. Typing exact coordinate values is the preferred method for designating an <u>exact</u> _TArget_ position (assuming you are familiar with the coordinate geometry of the 3D model). The interactive method is useful for PICKing 3D points on the geometry with _OSNAP_. The _POints_ option can also be used to display the current _TArget_ position established automatically by AutoCAD (unless you previously specified a _TArget_).

```
CAmera/TArget/Distance/POints/PAn/Zoom/TWist/CLip/Hide/Off/
Undo/<eXit>:po
Enter target point<(current coordinates)>:(coordinates) or (PICK)
Enter camera point<(current coordinates)>:(coordinates) or (PICK)
```

Distance

The distance option of _Dview_ generates <u>perspective</u> projections. _Distance_ takes into account the distance that the _CAmera_ is from the _TArget_; whereas, all other _Dview_ options use a vector between the _CAmera_ and _TArget_ to generate <u>parallel</u> projections.

Distance uses a slide bar along the top of the screen to allow you to interactively adjust the amount of perspective (distance) for the display. The default value (1X on the slide bar) represents the previously specified distance between the _CAmera_ and _TArget_ points.

A default distance of 1 is used unless you previously specified the points in response to the _Vpoint_ command or entered values in response to the _POints_ option of _Dview_. Otherwise, the default distance is usually too small, and the slide bar must be adjusted to a greater value. The _Distance_ option can be used repeatedly, or a value entered, in order to generate a distance greater than 16X.

Figure 34-28 shows the _Distance_ option using the DVIEWBLK house.

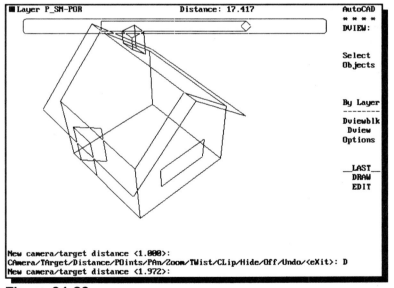

Figure 34-28

Distance is used to adjust the <u>amount</u> of perspective, not the <u>size</u> of the display. Disregard the size of the display as you use _Distance_. The size of the display can be adjusted <u>later</u> with the _Zoom_ option of _Dview_.

Use *Dview Distance* with the PUMPSOL drawing to generate a perspective. Figure 34-29 shows the PUMPSOL drawing using *Distance*.

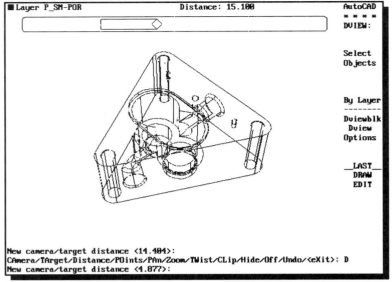

Figure 34-29

Off

Once a perspective projection of a drawing has been generated (*Dview Distance* used), draw and edit commands <u>cannot</u> be used. Perspective drawings in AutoCAD are intended for display and output only. The drawing <u>can</u> be plotted and rendered, and slides can be made while perspective is in effect. When the perspective mode is active, a small icon representing a perspective box is displayed in the lower left corner of the screen.

The *Off* option of *Dview* turns off <u>perspective</u> mode only and allows further editing and drawing with the existing geometry. When *Off* is used, a parallel projection of the geometry is generated but all other changes to the display of the geometry made with *Dview* remain in effect. Figures 34-30 and 34-31 show the PUMPSOL drawing in perspective (*Distance* used) and parallel projection (*Off* used).

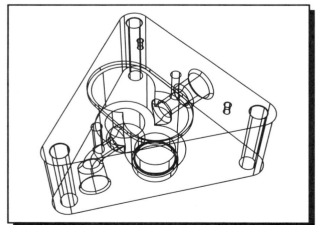

Figure 34-30

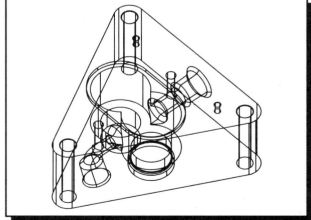

Figure 34-31

There is <u>not</u> an _On_ option of _Dview_; therefore, in order to change back to perspective mode, the _Distance_ option must again be used. Accepting the defaults generates the previous perspective.

Zoom

The _Zoom_ option of _Dview_ changes the size of the 3D objects with respect to the screen display. Zoom does <u>not</u> affect the amount of perspective.

Zoom allows you to use the slider bar for interactive adjustment or to enter a camera lens size at the keyboard. The "lens length" represents that of a 35mm camera, with 50mm being the default length (zoom factor of 1X). The status line dynamically displays the lens length as the slider bar is moved.

```
CAmera/TArget/Distance/POints/PAn/Zoom/TWist/CLip/Hide/Off/
Undo/<eXit>:z
Adjust lens length<50.000mm>:PICK or (value) (Use slider bar or enter a
value for the lens length.)
CAmera/TArget/Distance/POints/PAn/Zoom/TWist/CLip/Hide/Off/
Undo/<eXit>:
```

Typically the _Zoom_ option must be used after the _Distance_ option to adjust the size of the geometry so that it is visible and appropriately sized on the screen. _Distance_ often makes the geometry too large or too small so that it must be adjusted with _Zoom_.

PAn

The _PAn_ option of _Dview_ operates similarly to the full _PAn_ command. _Dview PAn_, however, is <u>dynamic</u> and fully 3D. As you use _Dview PAn_, you can watch the 3D model as it is moved and see the 3D features of the object adjust in real-time as your viewpoint of the object changes. _Dview PAn_ allows panning both vertically and horizontally. The command syntax is similar to the full _PAn_ command.

```
CAmera/TArget/Distance/POints/PAn/Zoom/TWist/CLip/Hide/Off/
Undo/<eXit>: pa (PA must be typed to distinguish this option from POints.)
Displacement base point: PICK or (coordinates) (Usually PAn is used
interactively rather than entering coordinates.)
second point of displacement: move and PICK (moving the cursor
dynamically pans the geometry about the screen.  PICK the desired new location.)
CAmera/TArget/Distance/POints/PAn/Zoom/TWist/CLip/Hide/Off/
Undo/<eXit>:
```

PAn is generally used to center the geometry on the screen after _Distance_ and _Zoom_ are used. The three _Dview_ options, _Distance, Zoom_, and _PAn_, can be used as a related group of commands to generate perspective projections and to size and center the 3D model appropriately on the screen.

TWist

TWist is used to rotate the 3D geometry on the screen. The 3D model twists (rotates) about the line of sight (between *CAmera* point and *TArget* point). *TWist* operates interactively so that you can see the position of the 3D model as you move the cursor. As an alternative, an angle can be entered at the keyboard. The *TWist* angle is measured counter-clockwise starting at the 0 degree angle in X positive direction. *TWist* is typically used to tilt the 3D model for a particular effect. The status line displays the current twist angle interactively. Figure 34-32 displays the PUMPSOL drawing during a *TWist*.

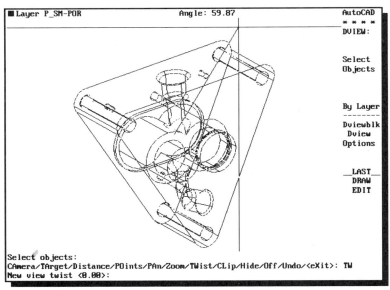

Figure 34-32

```
CAmera/TArget/Distance/POints/PAn/Zoom/TWist/CLip/Hide/Off/
Undo/<eXit>: tw (TW must be typed to distinguish this option from TArget.)
New view twist<0.000>: move and PICK or (value) (Twist interactively or
enter a value for degrees.)
CAmera/TArget/Distance/POints/PAn/Zoom/TWist/CLip/Hide/Off/
Undo/<eXit>:
```

CLip

In many applications it is desirable to display only a part of a 3D model. For example, an architect may wish to display a view of a room in a house but not include the roof in the display.

The *CLip* option of *Dview* is used to establish a *Front* or *Back* clipping plane in a 3D model. Any geometry <u>behind</u> a *Back* clipping plane or any geometry in <u>front</u> of a *Front* clipping plane are <u>not</u> displayed. In the architectural example, a *Front* clipping plane could be established just below the roof of the model. Everything in front of (between the *CAmera* and) the clipping plane would not be included in the resulting display. A view of the room's interior would then be visible from above without being obscured by the roof. Likewise, a *Back* clipping plane could be established in a model to eliminate portions of the model that can distract the viewer's attention from the focus of the display.

The *Front* and *Back* clipping planes are like invisible walls perpendicular to the line of sight between the *CAmera* and the *TArget*. Like the other options of *Dview*, *CLip* is dynamic and uses slider bars, so you can move clipping planes dynamically forward and backward. As an alternative, you can enter a distance from the *TArget* (for *Back* clipping planes) or from the

CAmera (for *Front* clipping planes). Clipping planes can be used in a parallel or perspective projection. The command syntax for creating a *Front* clipping plane is as follows.

```
CAmera/TArget/Distance/POints/PAn/Zoom/TWist/CLip/Hide/Off/
Undo/<eXit>: cl (CL must be typed to distinguish this option from CAmera.)
Front/Back/<Off>:f (Invokes the Front option.)
Eye/On/Off<Distance from target><1.0000>: move and PICK or (value)
```
(Dynamically move the clipping plane or enter a value for a distance from the *TArget*.)

Establishing a clipping plane distance automatically turns it *On*. *Off* can be used to disable an established clipping plane.

Figure 34-33 displays the PUMPSOL drawing in wireframe representation with a front clipping plane established.

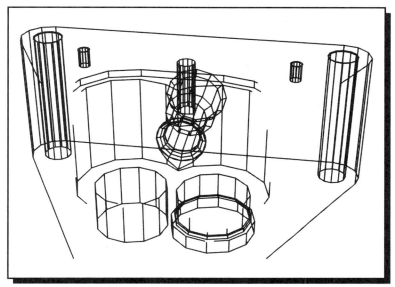

Figure 34-33

Figure 34-34 displays the PUMPSOL drawing after using *Render*. Clipping planes can be used in this manner to create section views of a solid model.

(Solid models that are rendered must be meshed before *Render* or *Hide* affects their visibility.)

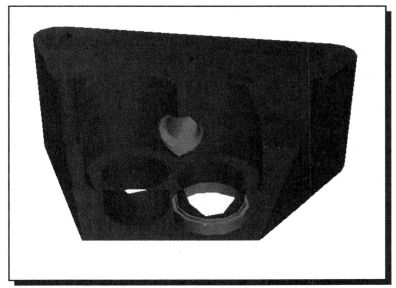

Figure 34-34

Hide

The *Hide* option of *Dview* removes hidden lines from a surface or solid model. (A solid model must be meshed with the *Solmesh* command before *Hide* has an effect on the display.) *Hide* causes all edges and surfaces that would normally be obscured by other surfaces or edges to be removed so that the model appears solid rather than "see through." There are no options of *Hide*. *Hide* remains active only for the current display. If another option of *Dview* is used, or if *Dview* is exited, hidden lines reappear. Figures 34-35 and 34-36 display the PUMPSOL drawing before and after *Hide* has been performed.

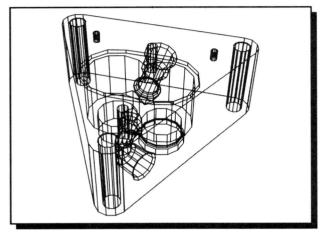

Figure 34-35

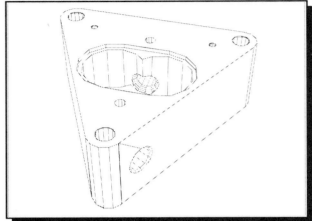

Figure 34-36

Undo

Undo reverses the effect of the last *Dview* option. Multiple *Undo*s can be performed to step backward through the *Dview* operations.

ZOOM

The *Zoom* command can be used effectively with 3D models just as with 2D drawings. There are, however, two options of *Zoom* that are particularly applicable to 3D work: *Previous* and *<magnification factor>*.

Previous
> This option of *Zoom* restores the previous display. When you are using *Vpoint, Dview,* and *Plan* for viewing a 3D model, *Zoom Previous* will display the previous viewpoint.

<magnification factor>
> When a *Vpoint* is specified, AutoCAD automatically causes a *Zoom Extents* which leaves the 3D model against the borders of the screen. If you are using the *UCSICON* with the *ORigin* option, invoking a *Zoom* **.9X** or **.8X** usually allows room for the icon to "pop" back to the origin position.

VIEW

The *View* command can also be used effectively for 3D modeling. When a desirable viewpoint is achieved by the *Vpoint* or *Dview* commands, the viewpoint can be saved with the *Save* option of *View*. *Restoring* the *View* is often easier than using *Vpoint* or *Dview* again.

VPORTS

TYPE IN:	PULL-DOWN MENU	SCREEN MENU	TABLET MENU
Vports	*View, Layout >* *Tiled Viewports*	*SETTINGS, VPORTS:*	---

The *Vports* command allows <u>tiled</u> viewports to be created on the screen. *Vports* allows the screen to be divided into several areas. Tiled viewports are different than paper space viewports. *Vports* (tiled viewports) are available only when the *TILEMODE* variable is set to **1**. (See Chapter 32, Paper Space, for a complete explanation.) Tiled *Vports* affect <u>only the screen display</u>. The viewport configuration <u>cannot be plotted</u>. If the *Plot* command is used, only the <u>current</u> viewport display is plotted. *Vports* can be used in command line format or in dialogue box format. Figure 34-37 displays the AutoCAD drawing editor after the *Vports* command was used to divide the screen into tiled viewports.

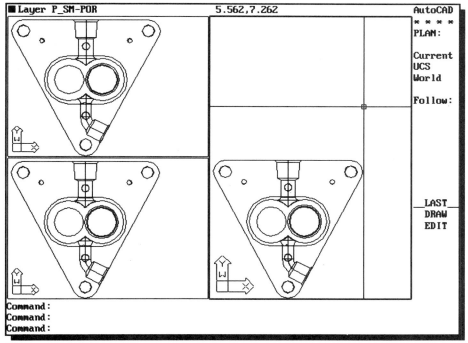

Figure 34-37

Vports creates <u>tiled</u> viewports. Tiled viewports always fit together like tiles. The shape and location of the viewports is not flexible as with paper space viewports.

```
Command: vports
Save/Restore/Delete/Join/SIngle/?/2/<3>/4: Enter or (option)
Horizontal/Vertical/Above/Below/Left/<Right>: Enter or (option)
Regenerating drawing.
Command:
```

Save

Allows you to assign a name to and save the current viewport configuration. The configuration is the arrangement of viewports and the viewpoint settings of the model in each viewport. Up to 31 characters can be used when assigning a name. The configuration can be *Restored* at a later time.

Restore

Redisplays a previously *Saved* viewport configuration. AutoCAD prompts for the assigned name.

Delete

Deletes a named viewport configuration. AutoCAD prompts for the assigned name.

Join

This option allows you to combine (join) two adjacent viewports. For example, if four viewports were displayed, two of the four could be joined to produce a total of three viewports. You must select a *dominant* viewport. The *dominant* viewport determines the display to be used for the new viewport.

SIngle

Changes back to a single screen display using the current viewport's display.

?

Displays the identification numbers and screen positions of named (saved) and active viewport configurations. The screen positions are relative to the lower left corner of the screen (0,0) and the upper right (1,1).

2, 3, 4

These options are for determining how many and in what configuration you choose. The possibilities are illustrated if you use the *Tiled Viewport Layout* dialogue box.

Optionally, the *View* pull-down menu can be used to display the *Tiled Viewport Layout* dialogue box (Fig. 34-38). This dialogue box allows you to PICK the icon representing the layout that you want.

After you select the desired layout, the previous display appears in <u>each</u> of the viewports. For example, if a plan view of the 3D model was displayed when you used the *Vports* command or the related dialogue box, the resulting display in each of the viewports would be the plan view (see Fig. 34-37). It is up to you then to use viewing commands (*Vpoint, Dview, Plan, Zoom,* etc.) to specify what viewpoints or areas of the model you want to see in each viewport. There is no automatic viewpoint configuration option with *Vports*.

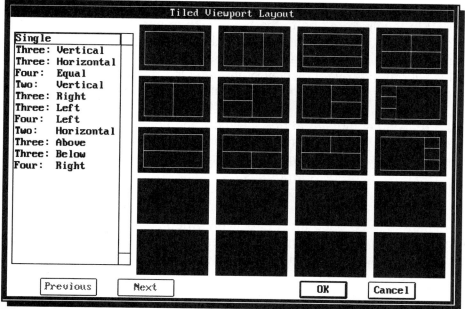

Figure 34-38

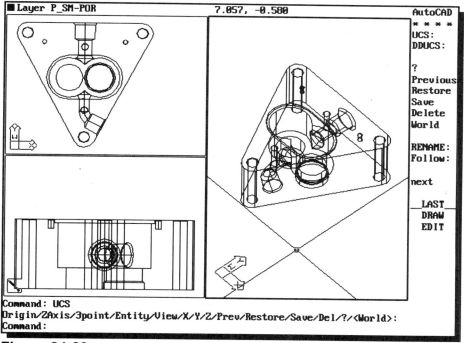

Figure 34-39

A popular arrangement of viewpoints for construction and editing of 3D models is a combination of principal views (top, front, side, etc.) and an isometric or other pictorial type of viewpoint (Fig. 34-39). You can use *Zoom* with magnification factors to size the model in each viewport and use *PAn* to "align" the views. There is, however, <u>no automatic method</u> of alignment of views to achieve a true orthogonal projection. You cannot draw or project from one viewport to another.

A viewport is made active by PICKing a point in it (like using paper space viewports) or by pressing CTRL+V to toggle from one to the next. Like paper space viewports, any display commands (*Zoom, Vpoint, Redraw*, etc.) used and drawing aids (*SNAP, GRID, ORTHO*) affect only the current viewport. Draw and edit commands that affect the model are potentially apparent in all viewports (for every display of the affected part of the model). *Redrawall* and *Regenall* can be used to redraw and regenerate all viewports.

You can begin a drawing command in one viewport and finish in another. In other words, you may toggle viewports within a command. For example, you can use the *Line* command to PICK the From point: in one viewport, then make another viewport current to PICK the to point:. The advantage of viewports is having several viewpoints of a 3D model during construction.

The *Vports* command can be used most effectively when constructing and editing 3D geometry; whereas, paper space viewports are generally used when the model is complete and ready to prepare a plot. *Vports* is typically used to display a different _Vpoint_ of the 3D model in each viewport, as in Figure 34-37. In this way, you can create 3D geometry and view the construction from different *Vpoint*s in order to enhance your visibility in all three dimensions.

3D DISPLAY COMMANDS

Commands that are used for changing the appearance of a surface or solid model in AutoCAD are *Hide, Shade*, and *Render*. By default, surface and solid models are shown in wireframe representation in order to speed computing time during construction. As you know, wireframe representation can somewhat hinder your visualization of a model because it presents the model as transparent. To display surfaces and solid models as opaque and to remove the normally obscured edges, *Hide, Shade*, or *Render* can be used.

Wireframe models are not affected by these commands since they do not contain surfaces. Wireframe models can only be displayed in wireframe representation.

HIDE

TYPE IN:	PULL-DOWN MENU	SCREEN MENU	TABLET MENU
HIDE	*Render, Hide*	*RENDER, HIDE:*	*1,M*

The *Hide* command suppresses the hidden lines (lines that would normally be obscured from view by opaque surfaces) for the current display or viewport.

        Command: *hide*

There are no options for the command. The current display may go blank for a period of time depending upon the complexity of the model(s), then the new display with hidden lines removed temporarily appears.

The hidden line display is only maintained for the current display. Once a regeneration occurs, the model is displayed in wireframe representation again. You cannot *Plot* the display generated by *Hide*. Instead, use the *Hide Lines* option of the *Plot Configuration* Dialogue box (or *Hideplot* option of *Mview* for paper space viewports).

Figure 34-40 displays the PUMPSOL model in the default wireframe representation and Figure 34-41 illustrates the use of *Hide* (after using *Solmesh*) with the same drawing.

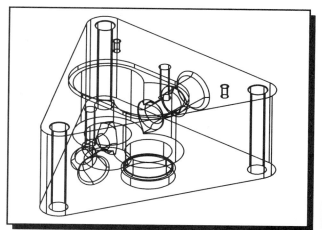

Figure 34-40

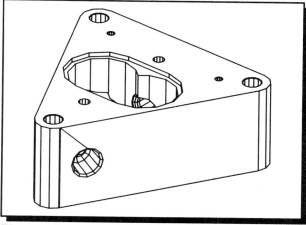

Figure 34-41

If you are using *Hide* with a solid model the *Solmesh* command (or *Mesh* from the *Model* pull-down menu) must be used on the model before *Hide* will have any effect. A surface model requires no preparation before using *Hide* or *Shade*.

The *Hide* option of *Dview* is used for the same purpose as *Hide*. If you have a large drawing with multiple models you can use *Dview Hide* to select only some of the entities (models) for hiding.

SHADE

The *Shade* command fills the surfaces with the object's color and calculates light reflection by applying gradient shading (variable gray values) to the surfaces. This command and related variables are covered in Chapter 45.

RENDER

Render is only one of several commands included in AutoCAD's Advanced Visualization Extension (AVE). With AVE you can create and place lights in 3D space, adjust the light intensity, and assign color and reflective qualities (called finishes) to the surfaces or solids. AVE is a sophisticated visualization feature included with AutoCAD. Chapter 45 is devoted to Shading and Rendering.

CHAPTER EXERCISES

1. In this exercise you will use an AutoCAD sample drawing to practice with *Vpoint*. *Open* the **SITE-3D** drawing from the **SAMPLE** directory. (If AutoCAD is installed in the C:\ACADR12 directory, then the sample drawings are found in C:\ACADR12\SAMPLE. When the drawing generates, change *TILEMODE* to **1**.

A. Use the *Plan* command to display the view of the house and property from above. Examine the view and notice the coordinate system icon. Assume that north is in a positive Y direction and east is a positive X direction.

B. Use *Vpoint* with the *Axes* option to view the house looking from the southeast direction and from slightly above. (HINT: PICK the lower-right quadrant inside the small circle.) Use *Vpoint* with the *Axes* option to view the house looking from the southwest and slightly above. View an elevation of the house again from the north side (PICK on the "equator" at the top of the small circle).

C. Use the *Plan* command again to view from above. Now use the *Vpoint* command with the *Rotate* option to display the house looking directly from the east and 30 degrees above level (the XY plane). (HINT: enter angles of 0, 30.) Use *Vpoint Rotate* again to view the house and land from the southeast at 45 degrees above level. Now view it from the northwest.

D. Assuming the house faces south, view the house from the front at elevation 0. Use *coordinates* to specify the *Vpoint*. Use coordinates to specify a viewpoint from the southeast and above the house. Next specify *coordinates* to view the house directly from the back (north). Finally enter coordinates to view the house directly from the east.

E. Experiment and practice more if you want. Do <u>not</u> *Save* the drawing.

2. *Open* a *New* drawing to practice with *Dview*. You do not have to assign a name. Immediately invoke the *Dview* command. When prompted to `Select objects:`, press **Enter**. The DVIEWBLK house should appear as you view from above.

A. Use the *Zoom* option of *Dview* to make the house smaller by moving the slider bar or entering a scale factor of **.5**. Now use the *CAmera* option. Place the crosshairs slightly to the upper left of center of the screen and PICK. Use the *Hide* option of *Dview* to remove hidden edges.

B. Next, invoke the *DIstance* option. Since the default distance is so small, you can enter a value of **35** or use *Distance* with the slider bar to the maximum position twice. Note the perspective generation. To compare to a parallel projection, use the *Off* option. To turn the perspective on again, use the *Distance* option and accept the default value.

C. Now use the *CLip* option and set up a *Front* clipping plane. Slide the plane into the house slowly until the roof begins to disappear, then **PICK**. Turn the front clipping plane *Off*, then use a *Back* clipping plane in the same manner.

D. Use the *TWist* option. *TWist* the house around approximately 90 degrees. Use *TWist* again to bring the house to its normal position.

E. Experiment more if you like. Do <u>not</u> *Save* the drawing.

3. *Open* the **SHUTTLE** drawing from the **SAMPLE** directory. Change *TILEMODE* to **1**.

A. Use *Vports* or the *Tiled Viewports Layout* dialogue box to generate **4** viewports. The SHUTTLE drawing should appear in an isometric-like viewpoint in all viewports.

B. Use the *Vpoint* command with either the *Rotate* or *coordinates* option to create a specific *Vpoint* for each viewport as shown below.

> Upper left   plan view
> Lower left   front view
> Lower right   right side view
> Upper right   isometric-type view

Zoom at a .9X magnification factor in each viewport.

C. Use the *Vports* command to *Save* the viewport configuration as **TFRI** (Top, Front. Right, Iso). (This naming scheme will help you determine the number and configuration of the viewports from a list of configurations.) Use *Saveas* and give the name **SHUTTLE2**. Make sure you save the drawing in <u>your working directory</u>.

4. *Open* the **SITE-3D** drawing again. Change the *TILEMODE* setting to **1**. *Freeze* the **LAND**, **ROAD**, and **RETWALL** layers.

A. *Zoom* in to view the house. Use the *Hide* command to remove hidden edges.

B. Use *Vpoint* or *Dview* to generate another view of the house from the front. Use *Hide* again.

C. Use *Vpoint* and enter coordinates of **1,-1,1**. Now use *Dview* with the *DIstance* option and enter a distance of **50'**.

D. Use the *DIstance* option again and specify a value of **25'**. Invoke the *CAmera* option and place the crosshairs slightly above and to the left of the center of the screen. Move the crosshairs to view the main room. Move the crosshairs to view the front stairs. Now view the small gazebo building to the east side of the house.

E. If you can manipulate the *CAmera* option without difficulty, try setting a new *TArget* so you can view other parts inside the house. If you get lost you can *Undo*. If you really get lost, *Open* the drawing again and use the default *TArget* point again.

F. Have fun, but do <u>not</u> *Save* the drawing unless you use *Saveas* to rename it.

Figure 34-42 SITE-3D.DWG Courtesy of Autodesk, Inc.

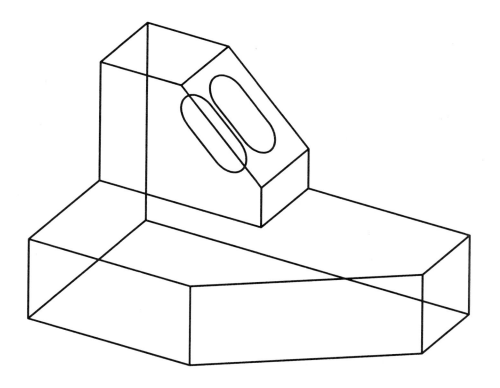

CHAPTER 35

Wireframe Modeling

CHAPTER OBJECTIVES

After completing this chapter you should:

1. understand how normal 2D draw and edit commands are used to create 3D wireframe models by specifying 3D coordinates;

2. gain experience in specification of 3D coordinates;

3. gain experience with 3D viewing commands;

4. be able to apply point filters to 3D model construction;

5. gain fundamental experience with creating, *Saving*, and *Restoring* User Coordinate Systems;

6. be able to create, *Save*, and *Restore* tiled viewport configurations;

7. be able to manipulate the Coordinate System Icon.

BASICS

Wireframe models are created in AutoCAD by using common draw commands that create 2D entities. When draw commands are used with X ,Y, and Z coordinate specification, geometry is created in 3D space. A true wireframe model is simply a combination of 2D elements in 3D space.

A *Line*, for example, can be drawn in 3D space by specifying 3D coordinates in response to the From point: and to point: prompts (Fig. 35-1).

```
Command: line
From point: 3,2,0
to point: 8,2,6
Command:
```

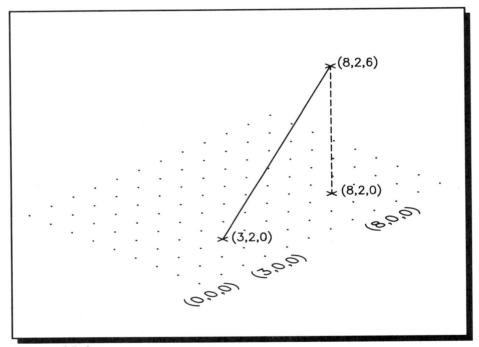

Figure 35-1

The same procedure of entering 3D coordinate values can be applied to other draw commands such as *Arc, Circle,* etc. These 2D entities are combined in 3D space to create wireframe models. There are no draw commands that are used specifically for creating wireframe models (with the exception of *3Dpoly*), only the draw commands that are also used for 2D geometry. It is the use of 3D viewing and display, User Coordinate Systems (UCS), and 3D coordinate entry that are the principal features of AutoCAD, along with the usual 2D entity creation commands that allow you to create wireframe models. Specification of 3D coordinate values (Chapter 33), 3D display and viewing (Chapter 34), and use of UCS's (Chapter 36) aid in creating wireframe models as well as surface and solid models. The *3Dpoly* command is discussed at the end of this chapter.

WIREFRAME MODELING TUTORIAL

Because you are experienced in 2D geometry creation, it can be efficient to apply your experience, combined with the concepts already given in the previous two chapters, to create a wireframe model in order to learn fundamental modeling techniques. Using the tutorial in this chapter, you create the wireframe model shown in Figure 35-2 in a step-by-step fashion. The Wireframe Modeling Tutorial employs the following fundamental modeling techniques.

> 3D coordinate entry
> Point filters
> *Vports*
> An introduction to User Coordinate Systems
> *Ucsicon* manipulation

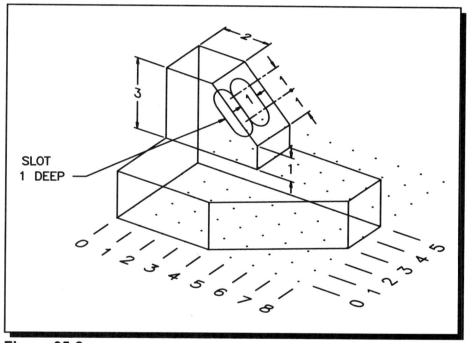

Figure 35-2

It is suggested that you follow along on your computer as you read and work through the pages of this tutorial. The Wireframe Modeling Tutorial has 22 steps. The steps give written instructions with illustrations.

Tutorial Hints

Additional hints, such as explicit coordinate values and menus that can be used to access the commands, are given on pages immediately following the tutorial (beginning on page 630). Try to complete the wireframe modeling tutorial without looking at the hints given on the following pages. Refer to the Tutorial Hints only if you need assistance.

1.   Set up your drawing.

    A.   Start AutoCAD. Begin a **New** drawing and name the drawing **WIREFRAM**.

    B.   Examine the figure on the previous page showing the completed wireframe model. Notice that all of the dimensions are to the nearest unit. For this exercise, assume generic units.

    C.   Keep the default **Decimal Units**. Set **Units Precision .00** (two places to the right of the decimal).

    D.   Keep the default *Limits* (assuming they are already set to 0,0 and 12,9 or close to those values). It appears from Figure 35-2 that the drawing space needed is a minimum of 8 units by 5 units on the XY plane.

    E.   Turn on the *SNAP*.

    F.   Turn on the *GRID*.

    G.   Make a layer named **MODEL**. Set it as the **Current** layer. Set a **Color** if desired.

2.   Draw the base of the part on the XY plane.

    A.   Use **Line**. Begin at the origin (0,0,0) and draw the shape of the base of the Stop Plate. Use *SNAP* as you draw and watch the *COORDS* display. See Figure 35-3.

    B.   Change your **Vpoint** with the **Rotate** option. Specify angles of **305**, **30**. Next, **Zoom .9X**.

    C.   Turn the **Ucsicon ON** and force it to the **ORigin**. See Figure 35-4 to see if you have the correct *Vpoint*.

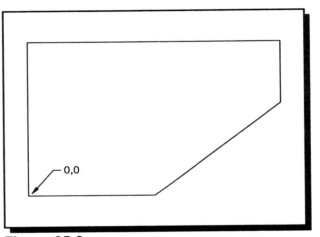

Figure 35-3

3.   Begin drawing the lines bounding the top "surface" of the base by using absolute coordinates and .XY filters.

    A.   Draw the first two *Lines* as shown in Figure 35-4 by entering <u>absolute</u> coordinates. You cannot PICK points interactively (without *OSNAP*) since it results in selections only <u>on the XY plane</u> of the current coordinate system. Do not exit the *Line* command when you finish.

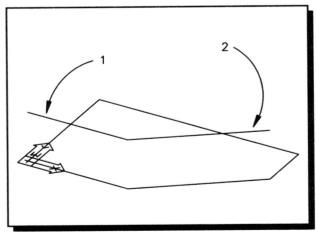

Figure 35-4

B.   Draw *Lines* 3 and 4 using **.XY** point filters (Figure 35-5). Do not exit the *Line* command.

C.   Complete the shape defining the top surface (*Line* 5) by using the **Close** option. The completed shape should look like Figure 35-5.

4.   There is an easier way to construct the top "surface," that is, use *Copy* to create the top "surface" from the bottom "surface."

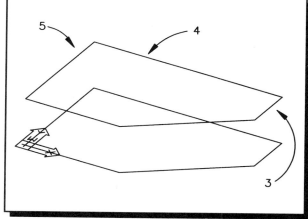

Figure 35-5

A.   *Erase* the 5 lines defining the top shape.

B.   Use **Copy** and select the 5 lines defining the bottom shape. You can PICK **0,0,0** as the "Base Point." The "second point of displacement" can be specified by entering absolute coordinates or relative coordinates, or by using an .XY filter. Compare your results with Figure 35-5.

5.   Check your work and *Save* it to disk.

A.   Use **Plan** to see if all of the *Lines* defining the top shape appear to be aligned with those on the bottom. The correct results at this point should look like Figure 35-3 since the top shape is directly above the bottom.

B.   Use **Zoom Previous** to display the previous view (same as *Vpoint, Rotate*, 305,30.)

C.   If you have errors, correct them. You can use *Undo*, or *Erase* the incorrect *Lines* and redraw them. See Tutorial Hints for further assistance. You may have to use *OSNAP* or enter absolute coordinates to begin a new *Line* at an existing *ENDpoint*.

D.   *Save* your drawing. Since you already defined a name, *Qsave* is automatically invoked when you use *Save*.

6.   Draw the vertical *Lines* between the base and top "surfaces" using the following methods.

A.   Enter absolute coordinates (X, Y, and Z values) to draw the first two vertical *Lines* shown in Figure 35-6 (1., 2.).

B.   Use another method (interactive coordinate entry) to draw the remaining three *Lines* (3., 4., 5.) You have learned that if you PICK a point, with or without *SNAP*, the selected point is on the <u>XY</u>

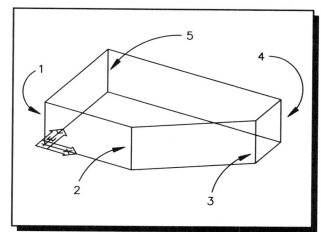

Figure 35-6

plane of the current coordinate system. *OSNAP*, however, allows you to PICK points in 3D space. Begin each of the three *Lines* ("From point:") by using *SNAP* and picking the appropriate point on the XY plane. The second point of each *Line* ("to point:") can only be specified by using *OSNAP* (use *END*point).

C.   Once again, there is an easier method. *Erase* four lines and leave one. You can use *Copy* with the *Multiple* option to copy the one vertical *Line* around to the other positions. Make sure you select the *Multiple* option. In response to the "Base point or displacement:" prompt, select the base of the remaining *Line* (on the XY plane) with *SNAP ON*. In response to "second point of displacement:" make the multiple copies.

D.   Use a *Plan* view to check your work. *Zoom Previous*. Correct your work if necessary.

7.   Draw two *Lines* defining a vertical plane. Often in the process of beginning a 3D model (when geometry has not yet been created in some positions), it may be necessary to use absolute coordinates. This is one of those cases.

A.   Use absolute coordinates to draw the two *Lines* shown in Figure 35-7. Refer to Figure 35-2 for the dimensions.

B.   *Zoom Extents* and then *Zoom .9X* so that the coordinate system icon appears at the origin. Your screen should appear as Figure 35-7.

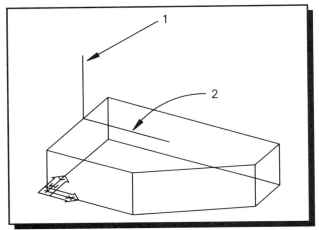

Figure 35-7

8.   Rather than drawing the next entities by defining absolute coordinates, you can establish a vertical construction plane and just PICK points with *SNAP* and *GRID* on the construction plane.

A.   This can be done by creating a new UCS (User Coordinate System). Invoke the *UCS* command by typing *UCS* or by selecting it from the screen menu. Use the *3point* option and select the line *END*points in the order indicated (Figure 35-8) to define the origin, point on X axis, and point on Y axis.

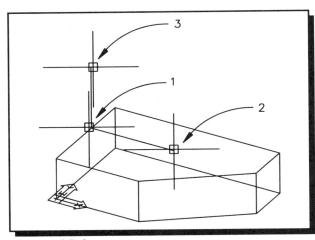

Figure 35-8

B. The Coordinate System Icon should appear in the position shown in Figure 35-9. Notice that the *GRID* and *SNAP* have followed the new UCS. Move the cursor and note the orientation of the crosshairs. You can now draw on this vertical construction plane simply by PICKing points on the XY plane of the new UCS!

If your UCS does not appear like that in the figure, *UNDO* and try again.

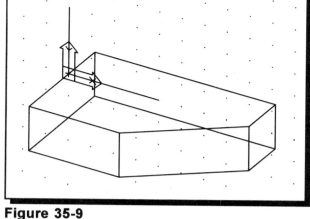

Figure 35-9

C. Draw the *Lines* to complete the geometry on the XY plane of the UCS. Refer to Figure 35-2 for the dimensions. The Stop Plate should look like that in Figure 35-10.

9. Check your work; save the drawing and the newly created UCS.

A. View your drawing from a plan view of the UCS. Invoke *Plan* and accept the default option "*<current UCS>*." If your work appears to be correct, use *Zoom Previous*.

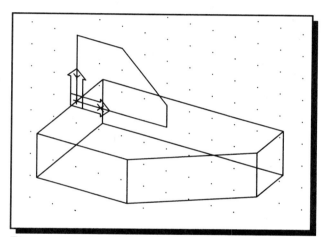

Figure 35-10

B. Save your new UCS. Invoke the *UCS* command as before. Use the *Save* option and assign the name **FRONT**.

10. Create a second vertical surface behind the first with *Copy* (Fig. 35-11). You can give coordinates relative to the (new) current UCS.

A. Invoke *Copy*. Select the four lines (highlighted) comprising the vertical plane (on the current UCS). Do <u>not</u> select the bottom line defining the plane. Specify **0,0** as the "Base point:" and give either absolute or relative coordinates (with respect to

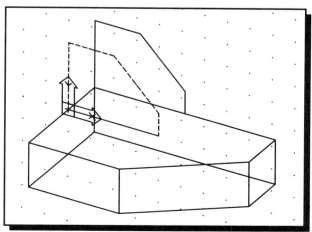

Figure 35-11

the current UCS) as the "second point of displacement." Note that the direction to *Copy* is <u>negative</u> Z.

B.   Alternately, using *Copy* with *OSNAP* would be valid here since you can PICK (with *OSNAP*) the back corner.

11.   Draw the horizontal lines between the two vertical "surfaces" using one of several possible methods.

A.   Use the **Line** command to connect the two vertical surfaces with four horizontal edges as shown in Figure 35-12. With *SNAP* on, you can **PICK** points on the XY plane of the UCS. Use *OSNAP* to **PICK** the **ENDpoints** of the lines on the back vertical plane.

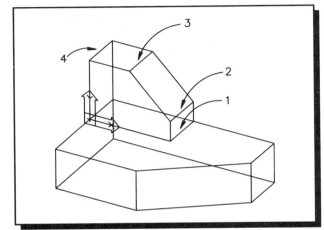

Figure 35-12

B.   As another possibility, you could draw only one **Line** by the previous method and **Copy** it with the **Multiple** option to the other three locations. In this case, **PICK** the "Base point" on the XY plane (with *SNAP ON*). Specifying the "second point(s) of displacement" is easily done (also at *SNAP* points).

12.   A wireframe model uses 2D entities to define the bounding edges of "surfaces." There should be no entities that do not fulfill this purpose. If you examine Figure 35-13, you notice two lines that should be removed (highlighted). These lines do not define edges since they each exist between coplanar "surfaces." Remove these lines with *Trim*. There is one catch when using *Trim* with 2D entities in 3D space--you cannot *trim* on a plane perpendicular to the XY plane of the current coordinate system. In other words, the entities you select for cutting edges and for

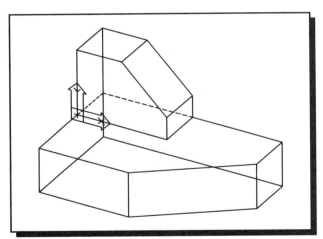

Figure 35-13

trimming should be parallel to the XY plane of the current UCS or WCS.

(Remember to check the Tutorial Hints <u>if</u> you need additional help.)

A. Use **Trim** and select the vertical *Line* (highlighted) as the *cutting edge* and *Trim* the horizontal Line. *Trim* does not function if the adjacent horizontal line is selected as the *cutting edge*. The lines should lie parallel to the UCS.

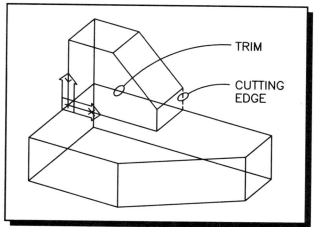

Figure 35-14

B. The other line to *Trim* lies perpendicular to the current UCS; therefore, in order to *Trim* it, the WCS must be made current. Invoke **UCS**, make the **World** coordinate system current, and **Trim** the second *Line*. (Make sure you select a *Line* as a *cutting edge* that is parallel with the WCS.)

13. Check your work and *Save* your drawing.

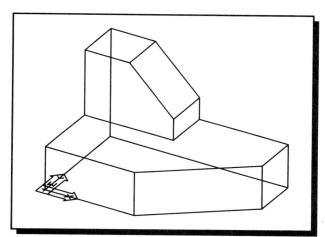

Figure 35-15

A. Make sure your wireframe model looks like that in Figure 35-15.

B. Use **Save** to secure your drawing.

14. It may be wise to examine your model from other viewpoints. As an additional check of your work and as a review of 3D viewing, follow these steps.

A. Invoke **UCS** and **Restore** the UCS you saved called **FRONT**. Now, use **Plan** with the **Current UCS** option. This view represents a front view and should allow you to visualize the alignment of the two vertical planes constructed in the last several steps.

B. Next, use **UCS** and restore the **World** Coordinate System. Then use **Plan** again with the **Current UCS** option. Check your model from this viewing angle.

C. Finally, Use **Vpoint Rotate** and enter angles of **305** and **30**. This should return to your original viewpoint.

15. Instead of constantly changing *Vpoints*, it would be convenient to have several *Vpoints* of your model visible on the screen <u>at one time</u>. This can be done with the *Vports* (Viewports) command. In order to enhance visualization of your model for the

following constructions, divide your screen into four sections or viewports with *Vports* and then set a different *Vpoint* in each viewport.

A. The first step is to type **Vports** or select from the **View** pull-down **Layout..., Tiled Viewports**. Specify **4** (four) viewports. Your screen should appear as that in Figure 35-16. Move your cursor around in the viewports. The crosshairs only appear in the <u>current</u> viewport. Only <u>one</u> viewport can be current at a time. Any change you make to the model appears in all viewports. You cannot draw <u>between</u> view-ports; however, you can begin a draw or edit command in one viewport and finish in another. Experiment by drawing and *Erasing* a **Line**.

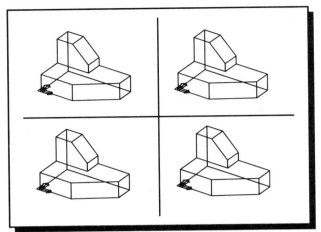

Figure 35-16

B. Now configure the upper left viewport with a top view. Make the upper left the current viewport. To produce a top view, use the **Plan** command. Next, use **Zoom** with a **.9X** magnification factor to bring the edges of the model slightly away from the viewport borders.

C. Now make the lower left viewport current. In order to configure this for a front view, use the **Vpoint** command with the **Rotate** option. The angle *in the XY plane* to enter is **270**. The angle *from the XY plane* is **0**. Next, **Zoom .9x** in this viewport. Use the **UCSICON** command with the **All** option to make the icon appear at the origin for all viewports. Check your results with Figure 35-17.

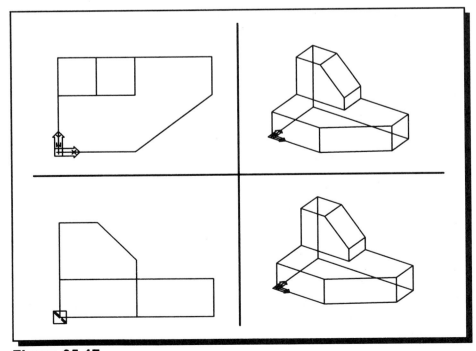

Figure 35-17

Note that by using viewports you can achieve multiple views of the model; however, only <u>one coordinate system</u> can be current at a time. The Coordinate System icon appears in all viewports indicating the current coordinate system orientation. The *Ucsicon ORigin* and *All* settings force the icons to appear at the origin in all viewports. Since the XY plane of the coordinate system is not visible in the lower left viewport, a different symbol appears in place of the Coordinate System Icon. This icon, a broken pencil, indicates that it is not a good idea to draw from the viewpoint because you cannot see the XY plane.

16. The next construction you add to the Stop Plate is the slot milled into the inclined surface. Because the slot is represented by geometry parallel with the inclined surface, a UCS should be created on the surface to facilitate the construction.

  A. Make the lower right viewport current. Use the **UCS 3point** option. Select the three points indicated in Figure 35-18 for (1) the "Origin," (2) "Point on the positive X axis," and (3) "Point on the positive Y axis portion on the XY plane." Make sure you *OSNAP* with the **ENDpoint** option.

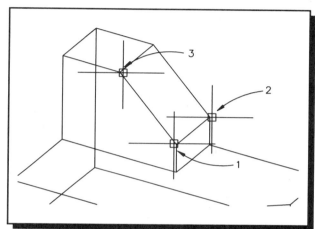
Figure 35-18

  B. The icon should move to the new UCS origin. Its orientation should appear as that in Figure 35-19. Notice that the new coordinate system is current in all viewports.

  C. Save this new UCS by using the **UCS** command with the **Save** option. Assign the name **AUX** (short for auxiliary view).

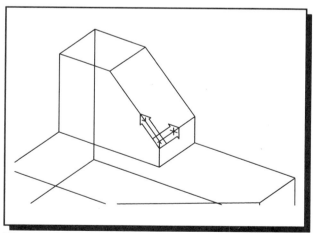
Figure 35-19

(Remember to check the Tutorial Hints <u>if</u> you have trouble.)

17. To enhance your visualization of the inclined surface, change your viewpoint for the lower right viewport.

A. Make sure that the lower right viewport is current. Use the **Plan** command and accept the default **<Current UCS>**. This action should yield a view normal to the inclined surface-- an auxiliary view.

B. It would also be helpful to **Zoom** in with a window to only the inclined surface. Do so. Your results (for that viewport) should look like Figure 35-20.

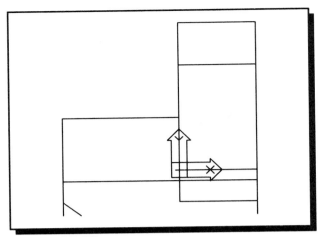

Figure 35-20

18. The next several steps guide you through the construction of the slot. Refer to Figure 35-2 for the dimensions of the slot.

A. Turn on the *SNAP* and *GRID* for the viewport.

B. Draw two **Circles** with a .5 radius. The center of the lower circle is at coordinate **1,1** (of the UCS). The other circle center is one unit above.

C. Draw two vertical **Lines** connecting the circles. Use **TANgent** or **QUAdrant** *OSNAP*.

D. Use **Trim** to remove the inner halves of the *Circles* (highlighted). Notice that changes made in one viewport are reflected in the other viewports.

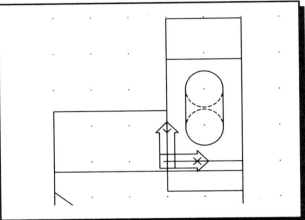

Figure 35-21

19. The slot has a depth of 1 unit. Create the bottom of the slot by *Copy*ing the shape created on the top "surface."

A. With the current UCS the direction of the *Copy* is in a negative Z direction. Use **Copy** and select the two *Arcs* and two *Lines* comprising the slot. Use the **CENter** of an *Arc* or the origin of the UCS as the "base point." The "second point of displacement" can be specified using absolute or relative coordinates.

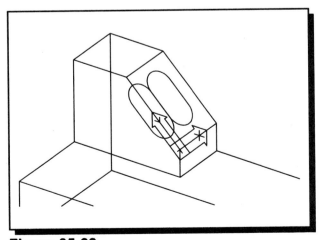

Figure 35-22

B.   Check to insure that the copy has been made correctly. Compare your work to that in Figure 35-22. No other lines are needed to define the slot. The "surface" on the inside of the slot has a smooth transition from curved to straight, so no additional edges (represented by lines) exist.

20.   The geometry defining the Stop Plate is complete at this point. There are no other edges needed to define the "surfaces." However, you may be called on to make a design change to this part in the future. Before you change your display back to a _Single_ viewport and save your work, it is helpful to _Save_ the viewport configuration so that it can be recalled in some future session. Unless you save the current viewport configuration, you have to respecify the _Vpoints_ for each viewport.

A.   Use the **Vports** command and the **Save** option (not the _SAVE_ command). You can specify any name for the viewport configuration. A descriptive name for this configuration is **FTIA** (short for Front, Top, Isometric, and Auxiliary). Using this convention tells you how many viewports (by the number of letters in the name) and the viewpoints of each viewport when searching through a list of named viewports.

B.   When changing back to a single viewport, the <u>current</u> viewport becomes the single viewport. Make the upper right viewport (isometric-type viewpoint) current. Invoke the **Vports** command and the **Single** option. The resulting screen should display only the isometric-type viewpoint (like Figure 35-23). If needed, the viewport configuration can be recalled in the future by using the **Restore** option of **Vports**.

C.   Before saving your drawing, you should make the WCS current by using the **UCS** command. Notice that changing display options (like _Vpoint_ or _Vports_) has no effect on the UCS. UCS controls are independent from display controls (unless the _UCSFOLLOW_ variable is set to 1).

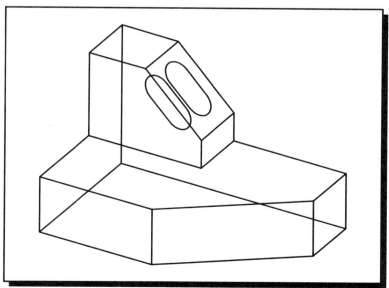

Figure 35-23

21.   **Save** your drawing. Use this drawing for practicing with display commands covered in the previous chapter, 3D Viewing and Display. The Stop Plate is especially good for practicing with *Dview*. The Stop Plate is very helpful for learning the commands to be presented in the next chapter, User Coordinate Systems.

22.   When you are finished experimenting with display and view commands, **Exit AutoCAD** and **Discard Changes**.

Tutorial Hints

H1.   A.   Type **ACAD** (or the name of the batch file used on your system to start AutoCAD) at the DOS prompt.
             Select the **File** pull-down menu, **New...**.
       B.   (no help needed)
       C.   **Settings** pull-down menu, **Units Control...**
       D.   (no help needed)
       E.   Press **F9**. Make sure the word **Snap** appears on the status line (upper right).
       F.   Press **F7**. The *GRID* should be visible.
       G.   **Settings** pull-down menu, **Layer Control...**, type **MODEL** in the edit box, select **Current** and **OK**.

H2.   A.   **Draw** pull-down menu, **Line >**, **Segments**. The entire shape can be drawn with one *Line* command or with several separate *Lines*. Make sure *SNAP* is *ON*. The *COORDS* (coordinate display, top center) helps you keep track of the line lengths as you draw. You may have to press **F6** until *COORDS* will display cursor tracking or polar display.
       B.   Type **Vpoint**. Type **r**. Enter **305** for the first angle and **30** for the second. Type **Z** (for Zoom). Enter **.9X**
       C.   **Settings** pull-down, **UCS >**, **Icon >**, **On**. Do it again for the **Origin** option.

H3.   A.   Line 1   From point: **0,0,2**
                       to point: **4,0,2**
             Line 2   to point: **8,3,2**
                       to point: do not press **Enter** yet

       B.   If you happened to exit the *Line* command you can use **Line** again and attach to the last endpoint by entering a "@" in response to the "From point:" prompt. If that does not work, use *OSNAP* **ENDpoint** to locate the end of the last *Line*.

             Using point filters: At the "From point:" or "to point:" prompt, type **.XY** and press **Enter**. AutoCAD responds with "of." **PICK** a point on the XY plane directly below the desired location for the *Line* end (Fig 35-24). AutoCAD responds with "(need Z)." Enter a value of **2**. The resulting *Line* end coordinate has the X and Y values of the point you PICKed and the Z value of 2. In other words, since you can only PICK points on the XY plane, using the .XY point filter locates only the X and Y coordinates of the selected point and allows you to specify the Z coordinate separately.

C.   Enter the letter **C** in response to the "to point:" prompt. AutoCAD *closes* the first and last *Line* segments created in one use of the *Line* command. If you used the *Line* command two or more times to complete the shape defining the top "surface," this option does not work. In that case, use absolute coordinates, .XY filters, or *OSNAP ENDpoint*.

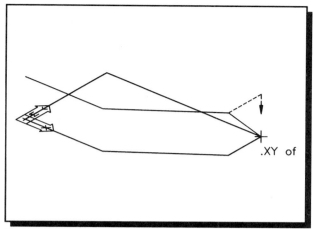

Figure 35-24

H4.   A.   Type **E** for *Erase* or use the **Modify** pull-down, **Erase >, Select**.

B.   Type **CP** for *Copy* or use the **Construct** pull-down, **Copy**. Select the 5 Lines in response to "Select objects:." PICK or enter **0,0,0** as the "Base point or displacement." Enter either **0,0,2** (absolute coordinates) or **@0,0,2** (relative coordinates) in response to "second point of displacement:."

H5.   A.   Type **Plan** and then the **W** option or select **View** pull-down, **Set View >, Plan View >, World**.

B.   Type **Z** for *Zoom* and type **P** for *Previous*.

C.   If you have mistakes, correct them by first *Erasing* the incorrect *Lines*. Begin redrawing at the last correct *Line ENDpoint*. You have to use absolute coordinates, .XY filters, or *OSNAP ENDpoint* to attach the new *Line* to the old.

D.   Type **Save**, or select **File** pull-down, **Save**.

H6.   A.   Line 1 From point: **0,0,0**
              to point: **0,0,2**
       Line 2 From point: **4,0,0**
              to point: **4,0,2**

B.   Line 3 From point:
              PICK point a.
              to point:
              ENDpoint of, **PICK** point b.
       Line 4 From point:
              PICK point c.
              to point:
              ENDpoint of, **PICK** point d.
       Line 5 From point:
              PICK point e.
              to point:
              ENDpoint of, **PICK** point f.

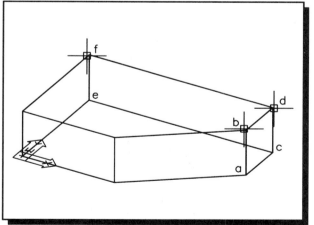

Figure 35-25

C. Type *E* for *Erase*. *Erase* the last four vertical lines, leaving the first. Type *CP* for *Copy*. Select the remaining vertical line. At the next prompt, type *M* for *Multiple*. When asked for the "Base Point:" select the bottom of the line (on the XY plane). At the "second point of displacement:" prompt, pick the other locations for the new lines.

D. *View* pull-down, *Set View >*, *Plan View >*, *World*. Examine your work. Type *Z* for *Zoom*. Type *P* for *Previous*.

H7. A. Line 1 From point: **0,3,2** to point: **0,3,5**
Line 2 From point: **0,3,2** to point: **4,3,2**

B. Type *Z*. Type *E* for *Extents*. Press *Enter* to invoke the last command (*Zoom*). type **.9X**.

H8. A. Type *UCS*. Type **3** for *3point*. When prompted for the first point ("Origin"), invoke the cursor (*OSNAP*) menu and select *ENDpoint*. PICK point 1 (Fig. 35-8). When prompted for the second point ("Point on positive portion of the X-axis"), again use *ENDpoint* and PICK point 2. Repeat for the third point ("Point on positive Y portion of the UCS XY plane").

B. If you are having trouble establishing this UCS, you can type the letter *U* to undo one step. Repeat until the icon is returned to the origin of the WCS orientation. If that does not work for you, type *UCS*, and use the *World* option. Repeat the steps given in the previous instructions. Make sure you are using *OSNAP* correctly to PICK the indicated *ENDpoint*s.

C. When constructing the *Lines* representing the vertical plane, insure that *SNAP* (F9) and *GRID* (F7) are *ON*. Notice how you can only PICK points on the XY plane of the UCS with the cursor. This makes drawing entities on the plane very easy. Use the *Line* command to draw the remaining edges defining the vertical "surface."

H9. A. *View* pull-down menu, *Set View >*, *Plan View >*, *World*. Check your work. Then type *Z*, then *P*. Correct your work if necessary.

B. Type *UCS*. Type *S* for the *Save* option. Enter the name **FRONT**.

H10. A. Type *CP* or select *Copy* from the *Construct* pull-down menu. Select the indicated four *Lines* (Figure 35-11). For the basepoint, enter or PICK **0,0**. For the second point of displacement, enter **0,0,-2**.

B. Alternately, perform the same sequence except when prompted for the "second point of displacement:", select *ENDpoint* from the *OSNAP* menu and PICK the corner indicated in Figure 35-26.

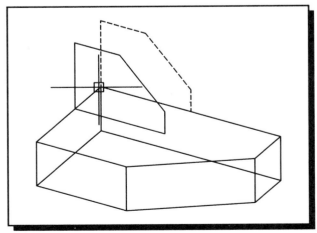

Figure 35-26

H11.　A.　Type *L* for *Line*. At the "From point:" prompt **PICK** point A on the UCS XY plane (Fig. 35-27). You should be able to *SNAP* to the point. At the "to point:" prompt, select the ***ENDpoint OSNAP*** option and **PICK** point B. Repeat the steps for the other 3 *Lines*.

　　　B.　Alternately, draw only the first *Line* (line 1, Figure 35-12). Type *CP* for *Copy*. Select the first *Line*. Type *M* for *Multiple*. At the "Base point:" prompt, **PICK** point A (Fig. 35-27). Since this point is on the XY

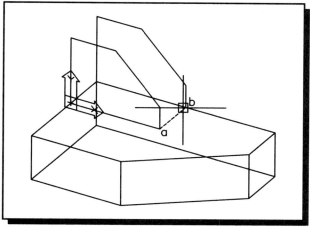

Figure 35-27

plane, PICK (with *SNAP ON*). For the second points of displacement, **PICK** the other corners of the vertical surface on the XY plane (with *SNAP ON*).

H12.　A.　***Modify*** pull-down, ***Trim.*** Remember that all *cutting edges* and entities to *Trim* should lie <u>parallel</u> with the current XY plane. If you are having trouble with this, insure that the FRONT UCS is current and that you are selecting the *Lines* indicated in Figure 35-14.

　　　B.　Type *UCS*, then *W* for *World*. The WCS icon should appear at the origin (Fig. 35-28). Now invoke *Trim* as before. Select the *Line* indicated as the "cutting edge" (this is the only possibility since it should be parallel to the XY plane). *Trim* the indicated *Line*.

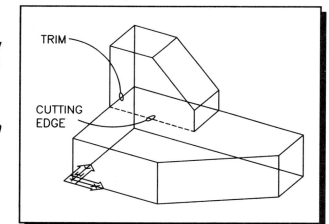

H13.　A.　If your wireframe model is not correct, make the necessary changes before the next step.

　　　B.　*File* pull-down, *Save*.

Figure 35-28

H14.　A.　***Settings*** pull-down, *UCS >*, ***Named UCS....*** In the *UCS Control* dialogue box, select **FRONT**. **PICK** the ***Current*** tile, then *OK*. Make sure you PICK <u>**Current**</u>. Then, from the *View* pull-down, select *Set View >*, *Plan View >*, *Current UCS*. Examine your figure from this viewpoint.

　　　B.　Invoke the *UCS Control* dialogue box again and set *World* as *Current*. Next, use the *View* pull-down menu again to see a *Plan View* of the *World* coordinate system.

　　　C.　Type *Vpoint*, then *R* for the *Rotate* option. Enter **305** for the "angle in the XY plane from the X axis." Enter **30** for the "angle from the XY plane."

H15. A. No help needed for creating viewports. To experiment with creating and erasing *Lines*, invoke the **Line** command and **PICK** points in the current viewport (wherever the crosshairs appear). Now, use **Line** again and **PICK** only the "From point:." Move your cursor to another viewport and make it current (**PICK**). **PICK** the "to point:" in the new viewport. Notice that you can change the current viewport <u>within</u> a command to facilitate using the same draw command (or edit command) in multiple viewports. **Erase** the experimental *Lines*.

    B. **PICK** the top left viewport to make it current. Viewing commands that you use affect only the current viewport. Select **View** (pull-down), **Set View >**, **Plan View >**, **World**. Type **Z** for *Zoom*, then **.9X**.

    C. **PICK** the lower left viewport. Type **Vpoint**, then **R**. Enter angles as indicated. Next, type **Z**, then **.9X**. Type **Ucsicon**, then **A** for the *All* option.

H16. A. **PICK** the lower right viewport. Type **UCS**, then **3**. When prompted for the "Origin," select **ENDpoint** from the *OSNAP* menu and **PICK** point 1 (see Figure 35-18). Use **ENDpoint** *OSNAP* to select the other two points.

    B. No help needed.

    C. Select the **Settings** pull-down menu, **UCS >**, **Named UCS...**. When the *UCS Control* dialogue appears, **PICK** the current UCS "***No Name***." In the edit box, type over the *No Name* with the name **AUX**. **PICK** *OK*.

H17. A. **PICK** the lower right viewport. Select **View** pull-down, **Set View >**, **Plan View >**, **Current UCS**.

    B. Type **Z**. Make a window around the entire inclined surface.

H18. A. Check to see if *SNAP* and *GRID* are *ON*. If not, press **F9** (*SNAP*) or **F7** (*GRID*).

    B. Select the **Draw** pull-down menu, then **Circle >** with the **Center, Radius** option. For the center, **PICK** point **1,1** (watch the *COORDS* display). Enter a value of **.5** for the radius. Repeat this for the second *Circle*, but the center is at **1,2**.

    C. Type **L** for *Line*. At the "From point:" prompt, select the **QUAdrant** *OSNAP* mode and **PICK** point A (Fig. 35-29). At the "to point:" prompt use **QUAdrant** again and **PICK** point B.

    D. **Modify** pull-down, **Trim**. Select the two *Lines* as *Cutting edges* and *Trim* the inner halves of the circles as shown in Figure 35-21.

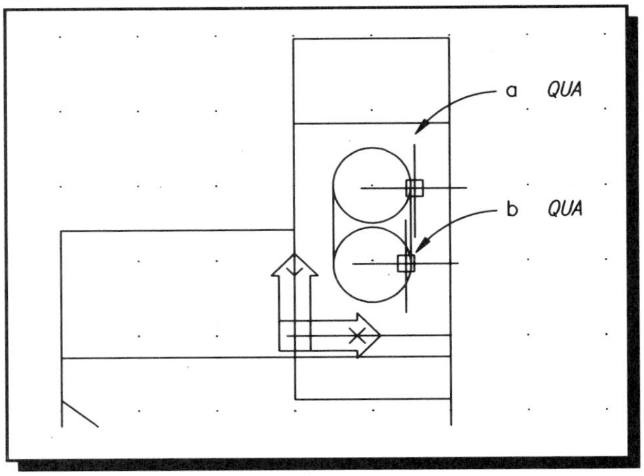

Figure 35-29

H19. A. Type **CP**. Select the two arcs and two lines comprising the slot. At the "Base point or displacement:" prompt, Enter **0,0,0**. At the "second point of displacement:" prompt, enter **0,0,-1**.

    B. No help needed.

H20.   A.   Type **Vports**, then **S** for **Save**. At the "Name for new viewport configuration prompt," enter **FTIA**.

   B.   **PICK** the upper right viewport. Type **Vports**. Type **S** for the *Single* option. Activate **Vports** again. Type **?** to display a list of viewports. The name FTIA should appear. Type **Vports** again. This time type **R** for *Restore*. Give the name **TFIA**. Finally, type **U** to undo the last action.

   C.   Select the **Settings** pull-down menu and then **UCS >**, **Named UCS...**. **PICK** **World** from the list and make it **Current**.

H21.   **File** pull-down, **Save**.

H22.   **File** pull-down, **Exit AutoCAD**.

COMMANDS

The draw and edit commands that operate for 2D drawings are used to create 3D elements by entering X,Y,Z values, or by using UCS's. *Pline* cannot be used with 3D coordinate entry. Instead, the *3Dpoly* command is used especially for creating 3D polylines.

3DPOLY

TYPE IN:	PULL-DOWN MENU	SCREEN MENU	TABLET MENU
3DPOLY	---	*SURFACES: 3DPOLY:*	*3,O*

A line created by *3Dpoly* is a *Pline* with 3D coordinates. The *Pline* command only allows 2D coordinate entry. *3Dpoly* allows you to create only straight polyline segments in 3D space by specifying 3D coordinates. A *3Dpoly* line has the "single entity" characteristic of normal *Plines*; that is, several *3Dpoly* line segments created with one *3Dpoly* command are treated as one entity by AutoCAD. A *3Dpoly* line is especially useful for creating 3D B-splines using the *Spline* option of the *Pedit* command.

```
Command: 3dpoly
From point: PICK or (X,Y,Z coordinates)
Close/Undo/<Endpoint of line>: PICK or (X,Y,Z coordinates) or (option)
```

If you PICK points or specify coordinate values, AutoCAD simply connects the endpoints with straight polyline segments.

Close

This option closes the last point to the first point entered in the command sequence.

Undo

This option deletes the last segment and allows you to specify another point for the new segment.

A *3Dpoly* does <u>not</u> have the other features or options of a *Pline* such as *Arc* segments and line *Width*. *Lines* and *Arcs* cannot be converted to *3Dpolys* using *Pedit*. Remember that you can also create *Plines* on the XY plane of any UCS. These *Plines* can have *Arc* segments. You can also convert *Lines* and *Arcs* to *Plines* if they lie on the XY plane of the current UCS.

CHAPTER EXERCISES

1.-4. Introduction to Wireframes

Create a wireframe model of each of the objects in Figures 35-30 through 35-33. Use each dimension marker in the figure to equal one unit in AutoCAD. Begin with the lower left corner of the model located at 0,0,0. Assign the names **WFEX1**, **WFEX2**, **WFEX3**, and **WFEX4**. Additional exercises for more complex wireframe models are given in Chapter 36 Exercises after more experience with UCS's.

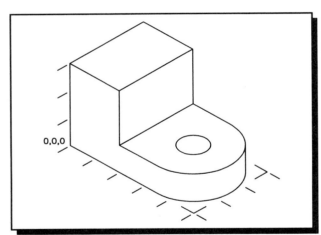

1. Figure 35-30

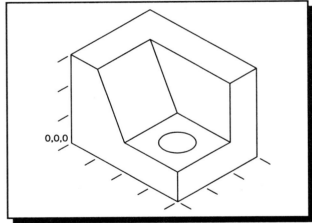

2. Figure 35-31

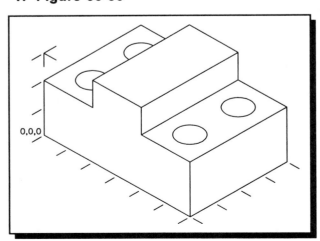

3. Figure 35-32

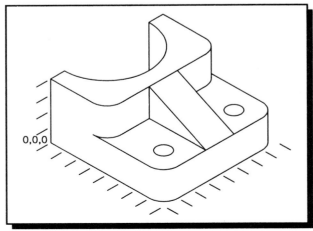

4. Figure 35-33

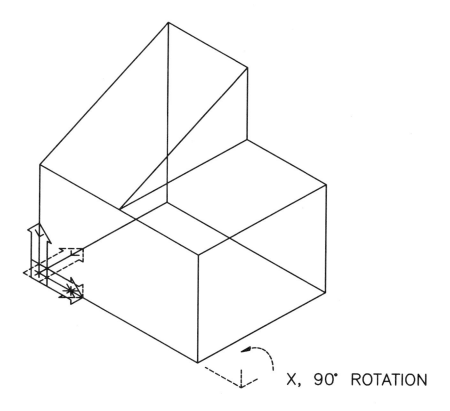

X, 90° ROTATION

CHAPTER 36

User Coordinate Systems

CHAPTER OBJECTIVES

After completing this chapter you should:

1.   be able to control the appearance and positioning of the Coordinate System Icon with the *Ucsicon* command;

2.   be able to create, *Save*, *Restore*, and *Delete* User Coordinate Systems;

3.   be able to create UCS's by the *Origin*, *Zaxis*, *3point*, *Entity*, *View*, *X*, *Y*, or *Z* methods;

4.   be able to use the *UCS Control* dialogue box to *List*, *Delete*, *Rename*, and set *Current* UCS's;

5.   know that changing the *UCSFOLLOW* variable to **1** causes the plan view of a UCS to be displayed when the UCS is made *Current*.

BASICS

The WCS (World Coordinate System) is the only coordinate system supplied with the standard AutoCAD default drawing (ACAD.DWG). The WCS is always available and cannot be deleted. An unlimited number of UCS's (User Coordinate Systems) can be created to simplify construction in 3D space. Rather than always dealing with coordinate values and constructing geometry in relation to the WCS, UCS's can be created and aligned with existing or intended geometry in order to simplify construction and coordinate input. UCS's can be saved as part of the current drawing file.

When the WCS is active, the *SNAP* and *GRID* are on the XY plane, so it is easy to interactively PICK and create geometry aligned with the XY plane. When a UCS is created, the *SNAP* and *GRID* automatically align with the current UCS, so creation of geometry aligned with the XY plane of the UCS is quick and easy--at least easier than specifying coordinate values, rotation angles, directions, etc. with relation to the WCS. Entities are extruded in the direction of the Z axis of the current UCS. For example, if a series of holes must be drilled into an inclined surface, it would be easier to create a UCS aligned with the inclined surface and then create the circular or cylindrical shapes by PICKing points on the UCS rather than specifying WCS coordinates. This is apparent in creation of the object in the Wireframe Tutorial in Chapter 35.

If you are using viewports, several viewpoints of a 3D model can be possible, a different one for each viewport. However, only one coordinate system can be current at a time. If another UCS is created or restored, that coordinate system is current in all viewports.

When a new UCS becomes the current coordinate system, AutoCAD does not cause a change in the display (unless the *UCSFOLLOW* variable is set to 1). Likewise, display commands (*Vpoint, Plan, Dview, Vports*) do not cause a change in the current coordinate system.

UCS COMMANDS AND VARIABLES

UCSICON

TYPE IN:	PULL-DOWN MENU	SCREEN MENU	TABLET MENU
UCSICON	*Settings, UCS > Icon*	*SETTINGS, UCSICON:*	---

The *Ucsicon* command controls the appearance and positioning of the Coordinate System Icon. In order to aid your visualization of the current UCS or the WCS, it is highly recommended that the Coordinate System Icon be turned *ON* and positioned at the *ORigin*.

```
Command: ucsicon
ON/OFF/All/Noorigin/ORigin<ON>: on
Command:
```

The _Ucsicon_ command must be invoked again to use the _ORigin_ option.

```
Command: ucsicon
ON/OFF/All/Noorigin/ORigin<ON>: or
Command:
```

This setting causes the icon to appear at the origin of the current coordinate system. The results of _Ucsicon On_ and _Ucsicon, ORigin_ are displayed in Figures 36-1 and 36-2, respectively.

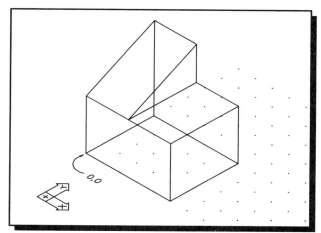

Figure 36-1

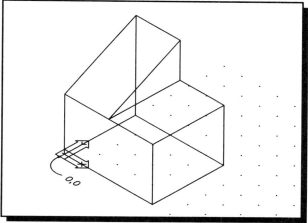

Figure 36-2

The icon does not <u>always</u> appear at the origin after using the _Vpoint_ command. This is because _Vpoint_ causes a _Zoom Extents_, forcing the geometry against the border of the graphics screen (or viewport) area. This sometimes prevents the icon from aligning with the origin. In order to cause the icon to appear at the origin, try using _Zoom_ with a **.9X** magnification factor. This action usually brings the geometry slightly in from the border and allows the icon to align itself with the origin.

Options of the _UCSICON_ command are:

ON
  Turns the Coordinate System Icon on.

OFF
  Turns the Coordinate System Icon off.

All
  Causes the _Ucsicon_ settings to be effective for all viewports.

Noorigin
  Causes the icon to appear always in the lower left corner of the screen.

ORigin
  Forces the placement and orientation of the icon to align with the origin of the current coordinate system.

UCS

TYPE IN:	PULL-DOWN MENU	SCREEN MENU	TABLET MENU
UCS	*Settings, UCS*	*UCS:*	*4,J and 6,J*

The *UCS* command allows you to create, save, restore, and delete UCS's. The options allow creation of UCS's. There are many possibilities for creating UCS's to align with any geometry.

```
Command: ucs
Origin/ZAxis/3point/Entity/View/X/Y/Z/Previous/Save/Restore
/Delete/?<World>: (letter) (Enter capitalized letters of desired option.)
```

When you create UCS's, AutoCAD prompts for points. These points can be entered as coordinate values at the keyboard, or points on existing geometry can be PICKed. *OSNAP*s should be used to PICK points in 3D space. Understanding the right-hand rule is imperative when creating UCS's. You may wish to review the directions for axis rotation (see Right-Hand Rule in Chapter 33).

Origin

This option defines a new UCS by specifying a new X,Y,Z location for the origin. The <u>orientation</u> of the UCS (direction of X,Y,Z axes) remains the same, only the location of the origin changes. AutoCAD prompts:

```
Origin point<0,0,0>:
```

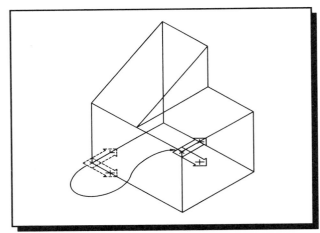

Figure 36-3

ZAxis

You can define a new UCS by specifying an <u>origin</u> and a direction for the <u>Z axis</u>. The X <u>or</u> Y axis generally remains parallel with the current UCS XY plane, depending upon how the Z axis is tilted. AutoCAD prompts:

```
Origin point <0,0,0>:
Point on positive portion
of the Z axis <default>:
```

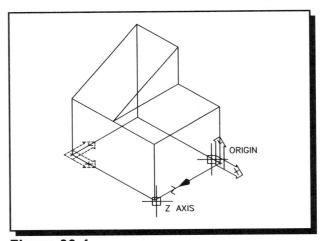

Figure 36-4

3point

The new UCS is defined by (1) the origin, (2) a point on the X axis (positive direction), and (3) a point on the Y axis (positive direction) or XY plane (positive Y). This is the most universal of all the UCS options (works for most cases). It helps if you have geometry established that can be PICKed with *OSNAP* to establish the points. The prompts are:

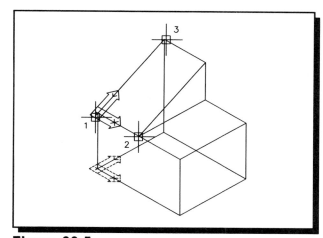

Figure 36-5

```
Origin point <0,0,0>:
Point on positive portion
of the X axis <default>:
Point on positive-Y portion of the UCS XY plane <default>:
```

Entity

This option creates a new UCS aligned with the selected entity. The orientation of the new UCS is based on the type of entity selected and the XY plane that was current when the entity was created (see UCS Entity Table below). AutoCAD prompts:

```
Select object to align
UCS:
```

The following list gives the orientation of the UCS using the *Entity* option for each type of entity.

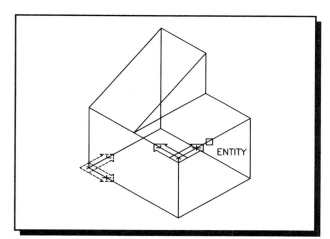

Figure 36-6

Entity	Orientation of New UCS
Line	The end nearest the point PICKed becomes the new UCS origin. The new X axis aligns with the *Line*.
Circle	The center becomes the new UCS origin, with the X axis passing through the PICK point.
Arc	The center becomes the new UCS origin. The X axis passes through the endpoint of the *Arc* that is closest to the pick point.
Point	The new UCS origin is at the *Point*. The X axis is derived by an arbitrary but consistent algorithm. (See the *AutoCAD Customization Manual*.)
2D *Pline*	The *Pline* start point is the new UCS origin, with the X axis extending from the start point to the next vertex.

Solid	The first point of the *Solid* determines the new UCS origin. The new X axis lies along the line between the first two points.
Dimension	The new UCS origin is the middle point of the dimension text. The direction of the new X axis is parallel to the X axis of the UCS that was current when the dimension was drawn.
3Dface	The new UCS origin is the first point of the *3Dface*, the X axis aligns with the first two points, and the Y positive side is on that of the first and fourth points. (See Chapter 37, Surface Modeling, *3Dface*.)
Text, Insertion, or *Attribute*	The new UCS origin is the insertion point of the entity, while the new X axis is defined by the rotation of the entity around its extrusion direction. Thus, the entity you PICK to establish a new UCS will have a rotation angle of 0 in the new UCS.

View

This *UCS* option creates a UCS parallel with the screen (perpendicular to the viewing angle). The UCS origin remains unchanged. This option is handy if you wish to use the current viewpoint and include a border, title, or other annotation. There are no options or prompts.

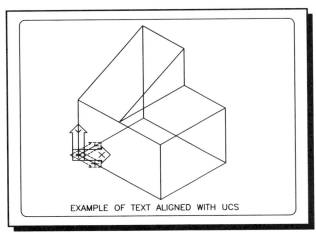

EXAMPLE OF TEXT ALIGNED WITH UCS

Figure 36-7

X/Y/Z

Each of these options rotates the UCS about the indicated axis according to the right-hand rule. The command prompt is:

```
Rotation angle about n
axis:
```

The angle can be entered by PICKing two points or by entering a value. This option can be repeated or combined with other options to achieve the desired location of the UCS.

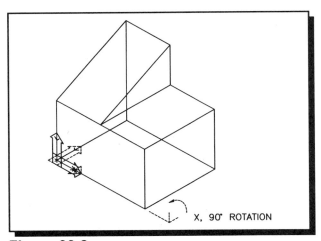

X, 90° ROTATION

Figure 36-8

Previous

Use this option to restore the previous UCS. AutoCAD remembers the ten previous UCS's used. *Previous* can be used repeatedly to step back through the UCS's.

Save

Invoking this option prompts for a name for saving the current UCS. Up to 31 characters can be used in the name. The prompt is as follows:

```
?/Desired UCS name:
```

Entering a name causes AutoCAD to save the current UCS. The *?* option lists all previously saved UCS's.

Restore

Any *Saved* UCS can be restored with this option. The *Restored* UCS becomes the <u>current</u> UCS. AutoCAD prompts:

```
?/Name of UCS to restore:
```

The ? lists the previously saved UCS's.

Delete

You can remove a *Saved* UCS with this option. The AutoCAD prompt is:

```
UCS name(s) to delete <none>:
```

Entering the name of an existing UCS causes AutoCAD to delete it.

?

This option lists the origin and X, Y, and Z axes for any saved UCS you specify. Invoking this option causes AutoCAD to respond with:

```
UCS name(s) to list <*>:
```

World

Using this option makes the WCS (World Coordinate System) the current coordinate system.

It is important to remember that changing to another UCS does <u>not</u> change the display (unless *UCSFOLLOW* is activated). Only <u>one</u> coordinate system (WCS or a UCS) can be current at a time. If you are using viewports, several *Viewpoints* can be displayed, but only <u>one</u> UCS can be current and it appears in all viewports.

DDUCS

TYPE IN:	PULL-DOWN MENU	SCREEN MENU	TABLET MENU
DDUCS	*Settings, UCS > Named UCS*	*UCS:, DDUCS:*	*3J*

The *DDUCS* command invokes the *UCS Control* Dialogue box (Fig. 36-9). By using this tool, named UCS's (those that have been previously *Saved*) can be made the current UCS by highlighting the desired name from the list and checking the *Current* tile. This performs the same action as *UCS, Restore*. Named UCS's can also be *Renamed, Deleted,* or *Listed* from this dialogue box.

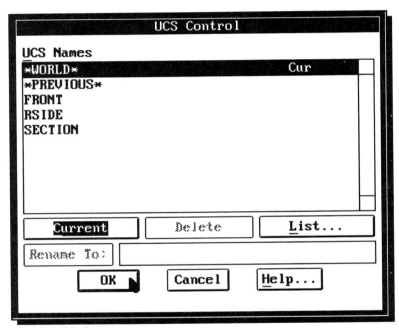

Figure 36-9

UCSFOLLOW

The *UCSFOLLOW* system variable, if set to 1 (*On*), causes the plan view of a UCS to be displayed automatically <u>when a UCS is restored</u>. The default setting for *UCSFOLLOW* is 0 (*Off*). *UCSFOLLOW* can be set separately for each viewport.

This is the only variable or command that directly links a change in UCS to an automatic change in viewpoint. Normally, changing to a different current UCS does not change the display, except in this case (when *UCSFOLLOW* is set to 1). On the other hand, making a change in viewpoint <u>never</u> causes a change in UCS.

SOLUCS

TYPE IN:	PULL-DOWN MENU	SCREEN MENU	TABLET MENU
SOLUCS or SU	_Model, Utility >_ _SolUCS_	_MODEL, UTILITY,_ _SOLUCS_	_4,G_

SOLUCS aligns the UCS with an AME solid face or edge. This command is only useful with AME solid models. This is similar to aligning a UCS with the _Entity_ option of _UCS_; however, the _UCS Entity_ option is intended for use with wireframe and surface models and _SOLUCS_ operates only for AME solids or regions.

```
Command: solucs
Edge/<Face>: (option)
Pick an Face: (or Pick an Edge:)
```

Edge

You are prompted to PICK and edge of a solid or region. The origin of the new UCS is generally at the midpoint of the edge with the UCS Z axis along the edge length. The X and Y axes point outward from the solid faces.

Face

This option aligns the UCS with the selected face (surface). You "pick" the face by entering "N" or pressing Enter to the "Next/<OK>:" prompt. Since you can only PICK an edge, AutoCAD highlights the faces defined by the selected edge and allows you to toggle from one to the next by using the "Next/<OK>:" prompt. The UCS generally aligns its XY plane on the face and the X axis along the long edge of the face.

CHAPTER EXERCISES

1. **Open** the **WIREFRAM** drawing that you created in the Wireframe Modeling Tutorial in Chapter 35. Practice the **UCS** command by creating a new UCS for every position shown in Figure 36-10.

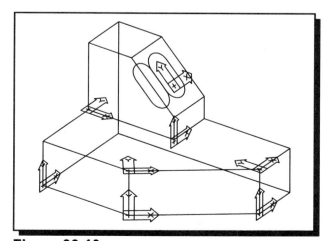

Figure 36-10

2. Create a wireframe model of the Corner Brace shown in Figure 36-11. *Save* the drawing as **CBRAC-WF**.

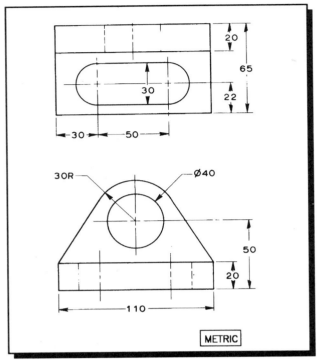

Figure 36-11

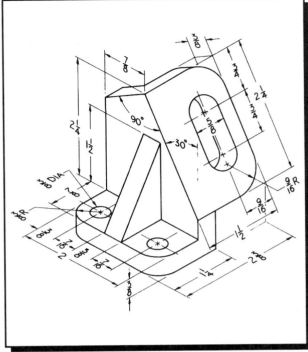

Figure 36-12

3. Make a wireframe model of the Bar Guide (Figure 36-13 <u>below</u>). *Save* as **BGUID-WF**.

4. Make a wireframe model of the V-block (Figure 36-14 <u>below</u>). *Save* as **VBLCK-WF**.

5. Make a wireframe model of the Angle Brace (Figure 36-12 <u>above</u>). *Save* as **ANGLB-WF**.

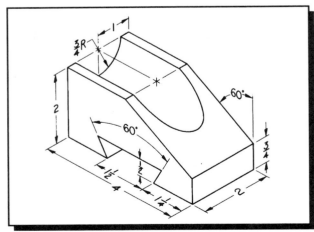

Figure 36-13

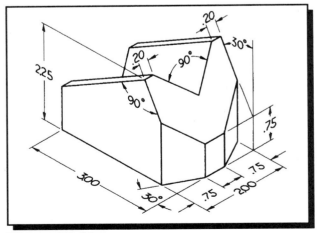

Figure 36-14

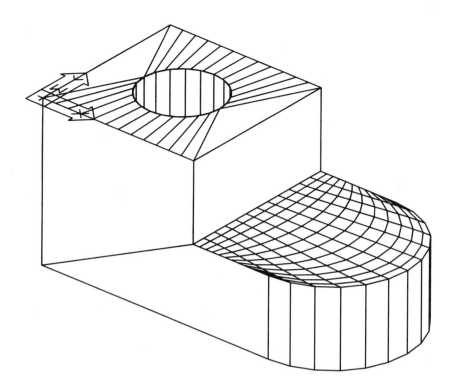

CHAPTER 37

Surface Modeling

CHAPTER OBJECTIVES

After completing this chapter you should:

1. be able to create planar surfaces bounded by straight edges using *3Dface* and to edit *3Dfaces* using Grips;

2. be able to create meshed surfaces bounded by straight sides using *3Dmesh*;

3. be able to create geometrically defined meshed surfaces using *Rulesurf*, *Tabsurf*, *Revsurf*, and *Edgesurf*;

4. be able to edit polygon meshes (*3Dmesh*, *Rulesurf*, *Tabsurf*, *Revsurf*, and *Edgesurf*) using *Pedit*, *Explode*, and Grips;

5. be able to use surface modeling primitives (*3D Objects*) to aid in construction of complex surface models;

6. be able to use *Thickness* and *Elevation* to create surfaces from 2D draw commands.

BASICS

A surface model is more sophisticated than a wireframe model because it contains the description of surfaces as well as the description of edges. Surface models may contain descriptions of complex curves; whereas, surfaces on a wireframe are assumed to be planar or single curved. Surface models are superior to wireframe models in that they provide better visualization cues. The surface information describes how the surfaces appear and gives the model a "solid" look since surfaces that are nearer to the observer naturally obscure the surfaces and edges that are behind.

Surface modeling is similar to wireframe modeling in that 3D coordinate values must be used for the creation and editing of the geometry. However, the construction and editing process of surface modeling is complex and somewhat tedious compared to wireframe modeling. Each surface must be defined by describing the edges that bound the surface. Each surface must be constructed individually in location or moved into location with respect to other surfaces that comprise the 3D model.

Surface modeling is the type of 3D modeling that is best suited for efficiently defining complex curved shapes such as automobile bodies, aircraft fuselages, and ship hulls. Thus, surface modeling is a necessity for 3D modeling in many industries.

The surface modeling capabilities of AutoCAD Release 12 provide solutions for about 30% of the possible applications. At the time of this writing, AutoCAD does not utilize NURBS (Non-Rational B-Spline) technique, which is the current preferred surface modeling technology. NURBS technology is utilized, however, in Autodesk's AutoSurf™ product line.

The categories of surfaces and commands that AutoCAD Release 12 provides to create surface models are as follows:

Surfaces with straight edges (usually planar)

    3Dface   A surface defined by 3 or 4 straight edges

Meshed surfaces (Polygon meshes)

    3Dmesh   A planar, curved, or complex surface defined by a mesh
    Pface   A surface with any number of vertices and faces

Geometrically defined meshed surfaces (Polygon meshes)

    Edgesurf   A surface defined by "patching" together 4 straight or curved edges
    Rulesurf   A surface created between 2 straight or curved edges
    Revsurf   A surface revolved from any 2D shape about an axis
    Tabsurf   A surface created by sweeping a 2D shape in the direction specified by a vector

Surface model primitives

3D Objects... A menu of complete 3D primitive surface models (box, cone, wedge, sphere, etc.) is available. These simple 3D shapes can be used as a basis for construction of more complex shapes.

Thickness, Solid

AutoCAD's early methods for creation of planar "extrusions" of 2D shapes are discussed briefly.

AutoCAD also includes a Region Modeler which creates planar surfaces. The Region Modeler utilizes Boolean operations which makes creation of surfaces with holes and/or complex outlines relatively easy. The Region Modeler is the subject of Chapter 38.

A visualization enhancement for surfaces is provided by the *Hide* command. Normally during construction, surfaces are displayed by default in <u>wireframe</u> representation. *Hide* causes a regeneration of the display showing surfaces as <u>opaque</u>, therefore obscuring other surfaces or entities behind them. *Hide* operates only for the current display. (See Chapter 34, 3D Viewing and Display.)

The surfacing commands are discussed first in this chapter. Application of the surfacing commands to a complete 3D model are then discussed.

SURFACES WITH STRAIGHT EDGES

3DFACE

TYPE IN:	PULL-DOWN MENU	SCREEN MENU	TABLET MENU
3DFACE	*Draw, 3D Surfaces > 3D Face*	*DRAW, 3DFACE:*	*3,N*

3Dface creates a surface bounded by three or four straight edges. The three or four sided surface can be connected to other *3Dfaces* within the same *3Dface* command sequence similar to the way several *Line* segments created in one command sequence are connected. Beware, there is no *Undo* option for *3Dface*. The command sequence is:

```
Command: 3dface
First Point: PICK or (coordinates)
Second point: PICK or (coordinates)
Third point: PICK or (coordinates)
Fourth point: PICK or (coordinates)
Third point: PICK or (coordinates)
Fourth point: PICK or (coordinates)
Third point: Enter (Indicates completion of the 3Dface sequence.)
```

After completing four points, AutoCAD connects the next point (Third point:) to the previous fourth point. The next fourth point is connected to the previous third point, and so on. Figure 37-1 shows the sequence for attaching several *3Dface* segments in one command sequence.

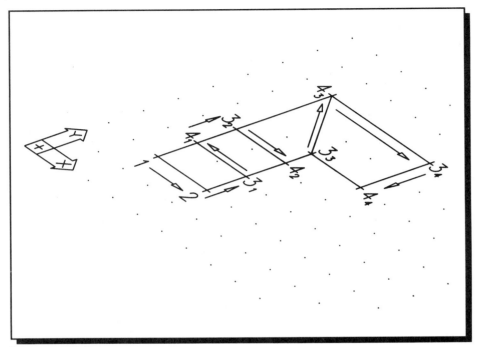

Figure 37-1

In the example above, each edge of the *3Dface* is <u>coplanar</u> as is the entire sequence of *3Dfaces* (the Z value of every point on each edge is 0). The edges must be <u>straight</u>, but not necessarily coplanar. Entering specific coordinate values, using point filters, or using *OSNAP* in 3D space allows you to create geometry with *3Dface* that is not on a plane. The following command sequence creates a *3Dface* as a complex curve by entering a different Z value for the fourth point (Fig. 37-2).

```
Command: 3dface
First Point: PICK
Second point: PICK
Third point: PICK
Fourth point: .XY
of PICK
(need Z): 2
Third point: Enter
Command:
```

Although it is possible to use *3Dface* to create complex curved surfaces, the surface curve is not visible as it would be if a mesh were used. A *3Dmesh* provides superior visibility and flexibility and is recommended for such a surface.

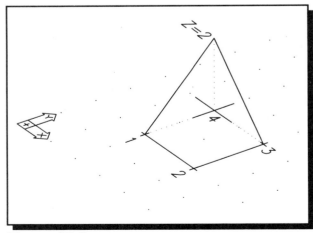

Figure 37-2

Figure 37-3 displays a possibility for creating nonplanar geometry in one command sequence. .XY Filters can be used to PICK points, or absolute X,Y,Z values can be entered.

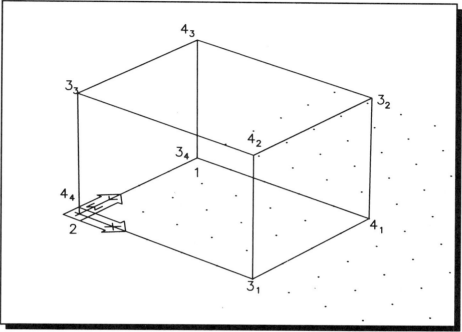

Figure 37-3

The lines between *3Dface* segments in Figure 37-1 are visible even though the segments are coplanar. AutoCAD provides two methods for making invisible edges. The first method requires that you enter the letter "*I*" immediately before the <u>first</u> of the two points that define an invisible edge. For the shape below, enter the letter "*I*" <u>before</u> points 3_1, 3_2, and 3_3.

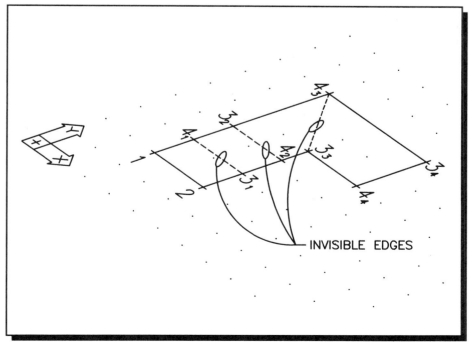

Figure 37-4

The command sequence for creating the shape in Figure 37-4 is as follows:

```
Command: 3dface
First Point: PICK
Second point: PICK
Third point: / Enter PICK
Fourth point: PICK
Third point: / Enter PICK
Fourth point: PICK
Third point: / Enter PICK
Fourth point: PICK
Third point: Enter
Command:
```

The first method for creating invisible edges described above takes careful planning. The same action shown in Figure 37-4 can be accomplished much more easily and retroactively by the second method. AutoCAD provides an AutoLISP program called EDGE.LSP to create invisible edges after the fact. This AutoLISP program must first be loaded. (For information about loading AutoLISP programs, see Appendix B). EDGE.LSP is located in the SAMPLE subdirectory. After loading, the EDGE.LSP command is invoked by typing *Edge*. The command prompt is:

```
Display<select edge>: PICK
```

Selecting edges converts visible edges to invisible edges. <u>Any</u> edges on the *3Dface* can be made invisible by this method. The *Display* option causes selected invisible edges to become visible again.

Applications of *3Dface*

3Dface is used to construct 3D surface models by creating individual (planar) faces or connected faces. For relatively simple models, the faces are placed in space as they are constructed. A construction strategy to use for more complex models is to first construct a wireframe model and then attach surfaces (*3Dfaces* or other surfaces) to the wireframe. The wireframe geometry can be constructed on a separate layer, then the layer can be turned off after the surfacing is complete.

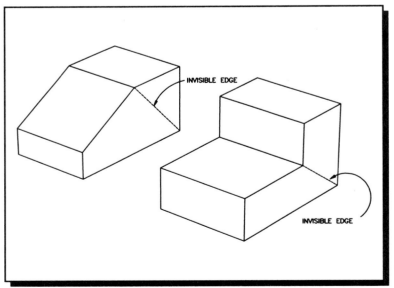

Figure 37-5

Figures 37-5 and 37-6 show some applications of *3Dface* for construction of surface models. Remember, *3Dface* can be used <u>only</u> for construction of surfaces with straight edges.

(*Hide* has been used in these figures to enhance visualization. Invisible edges are displayed in a hidden linetype. You may want to use *Hide* periodically to enhance the visibility of surfaces.

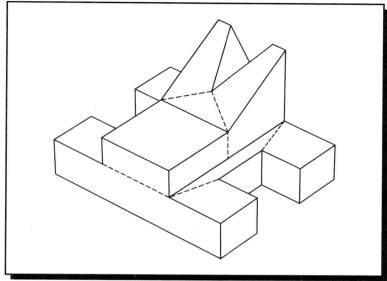

Figure 37-6

Editing *3Dfaces*

Grips can be used to edit *3Dfaces*. Each *3Dface* has 3 or 4 grips (one for each corner). By activating grips (PICKing the *3Dface* at the open Command: prompt), the individual *3Dface* surface becomes highlighted and displays its **warm** grips. If you then make one of the 3 or 4 grips **hot**, all of the normal grip editing options are available; i.e., STRETCH, MOVE, ROTATE, SCALE, and MIRROR. The single activated *3Dface* surface can then be edited. MOVE, for example, could be used to move the single activated surface to another location.

The STRETCH option, however, is generally the most useful grip editing option, since all of the other options change the entire surface. The STRETCH option allows you to change one (or more) corner of the *3Dface* (rather than the entire surface, as with the other options). For example, Figure 37-7 shows four *3Dfaces* connected to form a four-sided box. One corner of the box could be relocated by activating the grips on two of the *3Dfaces*. Two grips (common to one intersection) can be made **hot** simultaneously by holding down SHIFT while PICKing the **hot** grip. When the STRETCH option appears at the command line, stretch the common **hot** grips to the new location as shown (highlighted) in the figure.

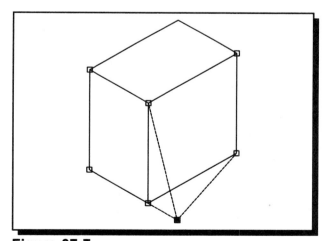

Figure 37-7

Explode or *Pedit* cannot be used to edit *3Dfaces*.

CREATING MESHED SURFACES

3DMESH

TYPE IN:	PULL-DOWN MENU	SCREEN MENU	TABLET MENU
3DMESH	*Draw, 3D Surfaces >* *3D Objects... Mesh*	*SURFACES, 3Dmesh:*	---

3Dmesh is a versatile method for generating a surface. *3Dmesh* can be used to create a simple planar surface bounded by four straight edges (Fig. 37-8), or it can be used to create a complex surface defining an irregular shape bound by four sides (Fig. 37-9). *Pedit* can be used to edit the *3Dmesh* (see *Editing Polygon Meshes*, this chapter).

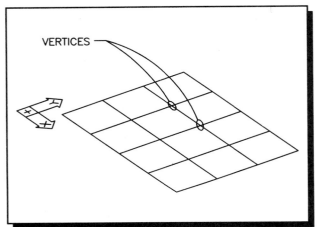

Figure 37-8

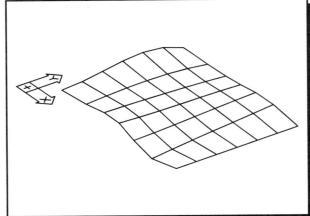

Figure 37-9

The surface created with *3Dmesh* differs from a *3Dface* because the surface is defined by a "mesh." A mesh is a series of vertices (sometimes called nodes) arranged in rows and columns connected by lines.

In AutoCAD Release 12, the vertices of a *3Dmesh* are defined differently depending upon how the command is <u>invoked</u>. Utilizing the pull-down menus and selecting the *Mesh* icon from the *3D Objects...* icon box allows you to quickly create a *3Dmesh* defined by straight edges, like the example in Figure 37-8. Invoking *3Dmesh* by typing or from the screen menu activates prompts for entering coordinate values for the placement of <u>each</u> vertex, allowing you to create a variety of shapes, like the surface in Figure 37-9. Using the <u>pull-down</u> menu causes:

```
Command: ai_mesh (Mesh selected from the Pull-down menu.)
First corner: PICK or (coordinates)
Second corner: PICK or (coordinates)
Third corner: PICK or (coordinates)
Fourth corner: PICK or (coordinates)
Mesh M size: (value) (Enter a value for the number of vertices in the M
direction.)
Mesh N size: (value) (Enter a value for the number of vertices in the N direction.)
Command:
```

Invoking *3Dmesh* from the pull-down menu prompts you for four corners of the mesh. The number of vertices along each side are defined by the *M* size and the *N* size. The *M* direction is perpendicular to the first side specified and the *N* direction is perpendicular to the second side specified (Fig. 37-10).

The values specified for the *M* size and *N* size include the vertices along the edges of the surface. The *M* and *N* sizes could be considered the number of rows and columns of vertices (density of the mesh).

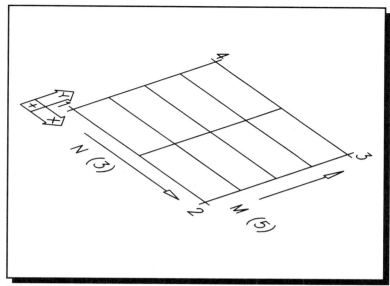

Figure 37-10

3Dmesh invoked by the same method (pull-down menu) can quickly generate a complex curved surface with straight edges by specifying nonplanar coordinates for the corners. The following command sequence is used to generate the surface shown in Figure 37-11.

```
Command: ai_mesh (Mesh selected from the pull-down menu.)
First corner: 1,1,0
Second corner: 5,1,0
Third corner: 5,5,0
Fourth corner: 1,5,2
Mesh M size: 4
Mesh N size: 6
Command:
```

3Dmesh visually defines the curvature of a surface better than *3Dface* because of the mesh lines.

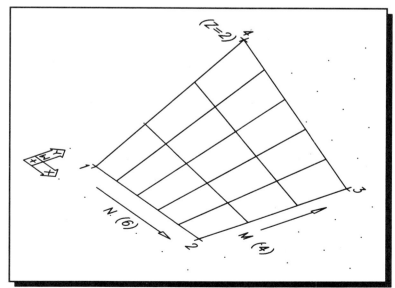

Figure 37-11

Figure 37-12 illustrates an application for a nonplanar *3Dmesh*.

If <u>typed</u> or selected from the <u>screen menu</u>, the *3Dmesh* command responds with a different series of prompts. These prompts allow you to develop complex shapes similar to that shown in Figure 37-9. This method requires the specification of coordinate values for <u>each vertex</u>. A numbering scheme is used to label each vertex. The first vertex in the <u>first</u> row in the M direction is labeled *0,0*, and the second in the first row is labeled *0,1*, and so on. The first vertex in the <u>second</u> row is labeled *1,0*, and the second in that row is *1,1*, and so on.

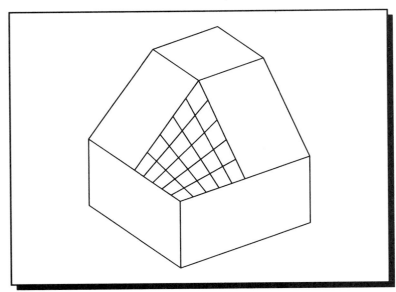

Figure 37-12

Since each vertex can be given explicit coordinates, a surface can be created with any shape. An example is shown in Figure 37-13.

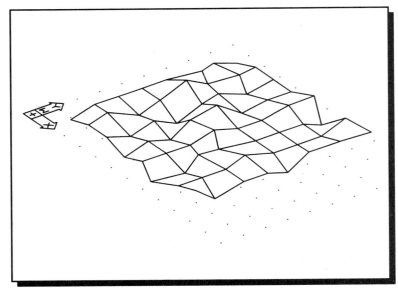

The command syntax for this method of defining a *3Dmesh* is as follows.

Figure 37-13

```
Command: 3dmesh (Type or select from the screen menu.)
M size: (value) (Enter a value for the number of vertices in the M direction.)
N size: (value) (Enter a value for the number of vertices in the N direction.)
Vertex (0,0): PICK or (coordinates)
Vertex (0,1): PICK or (coordinates)
Vertex (0,2): PICK or (coordinates)
(continues sequence for all vertices in the row)
Vertex (1,0): PICK or (coordinates)
Vertex (1,1): PICK or (coordinates)
Vertex (1,2): PICK or (coordinates)
```

```
(continues sequence for all vertices in the row)
Vertex (2,0): PICK or (coordinates)
Vertex (2,1): PICK or (coordinates)
Vertex (2,2): PICK or (coordinates)
(continues sequence for all vertices in the row)
(sequence continues for all rows)
Command:
```

Obviously, using *3Dmesh* by the latter method (entering coordinates for each vertex) is very tedious. For complex shapes such as topographical maps, an AutoLISP program can be written to read coordinate data from an external file to generate the mesh.

PFACE

TYPE IN:	PULL-DOWN MENU	SCREEN MENU	TABLET MENU
PFACE	---	*SURFACES, PFACE:*	---

The *Pface* (polyface mesh) command can be used to create a polygon mesh of virtually any topology. *Pface* is the most versatile of any of the 3D mesh commands. It allows creation of any shape, any number of vertices, and even entities that are not physically connected yet are considered as the same object. The *Pface* command, however, is designed primarily for use by applications that run with AutoCAD and for use by other software developers. *Pedit* <u>cannot</u> be used to edit *Pface*s.

The procedure for creation of geometry with *Pface* is tedious and somewhat like the previous procedure for *3Dmesh*. There are two basic steps to *Pface*. AutoCAD first prompts for the coordinate location for each vertex. Any number of vertices can be defined.

```
Command: Pface
Vertex 1: (coordinates)
Vertex 2: (coordinates)
(the sequence continues until pressing Enter)
```

Secondly, AutoCAD prompts for the vertices to be assigned to each face. A face can be attached to any set of vertices.

```
Face 1, vertex 1: (number) (Enter number of vertex for face to be attached.)
Face 1, vertex 2: (number) (Press Enter to complete face.)
Face 2, vertex 1: (number)
Face 2, vertex 2: (number) (Press Enter twice to complete command.)
Command:
```

Specifying a *Pface* mesh of any size can be tedious. The geometrically defined mesh commands (*Rulesurf, Tabsurf, Revsurf,* and *Edgesurf*) are more convenient to use for most applications.

CREATING GEOMETRICALLY DEFINED MESHES

Geometrically defined meshes are meshed surfaces that are created by "attaching" a surface to existing geometry. In other words, geometrically defined meshed surfaces <u>require</u> existing geometry to define them. *Edgesurf, Rulesurf, Tabsurf,* and *Revsurf* are the commands that create these meshes. The geometry used may differ for the application, but always consists of either 2 or 4 entities (*Lines, Circles, Arcs,* or *Plines*).

Controlling the Mesh Density

Geometrically defined mesh commands (*Edgesurf, Rulesurf, Revsurf,* and *Tabsurf*) do not prompt the user for the number of vertices in the *M* and *N* direction. Instead, the number of vertices is determined by the settings of the *SURFTAB1* and *SURFTAB2* variables. The number of vertices includes the endpoints of the edge.

```
Command: surftab1
New value for SURFTAB1 <6>: (value)
Command:
```

SURFTAB1 and *SURFTAB2* must be set <u>before</u> using *Edgesurf, Rulesurf, Revsurf,* and *Tabsurf*. These variables are <u>not</u> retroactive for previously created surface meshes.

The individual surfaces (1 by 1 meshes between vertices) created by geometrically defined meshes are composed of a series of <u>straight</u> edges connecting the vertices. These edges do not curve, only change direction between vertices. The higher the settings of *SURFTAB1* and *SURFTAB2*, the more closely these straight edges match the curved defining edges.

Notice that the defining edges of geometrically defined mesh <u>do not become part</u> of the surface; they remain as separate entities. Therefore, you can construct surface models by utilizing existing wireframe model entities as the defining edges. If the wireframe model is on a separate layer, that layer can be turned off after constructing the surfaces since the defining edges are not part of the surfaces.

EDGESURF

TYPE IN:	PULL-DOWN MENU	SCREEN MENU	TABLET MENU
EDGESURF	*Draw, 3D Surfaces >* *Edge Defined Patch*	*SURFACES,* *EDGSURF:*	*1,0*

An *Edgesurf* is a meshed surface generated between <u>four existing</u> edges. The four edges can be of any shape as long as they have connecting end points (no gaps, no overlaps). The four edges can be *Lines, Arcs,* or *Plines*. The four edges can be selected in any order. The surface that is generated between the edges is sometimes called a Coon's surface patch. *Edgesurf* interpolates the edges and generates a smooth transitional mesh, or patch, between the four shapes.

The command syntax is as follows:

```
Command: edgesurf
Select first defining curve: PICK
Select second defining curve: PICK
Select third defining curve: PICK
Select fourth defining curve: PICK
Command:
```

Figure 37-14 displays an *Edgesurf* generated from four planar edges. Settings for *SURFTAB1* and *SURFTAB2* are *6* and *8*.

The relation of *SURFTAB1* and SURFTAB2 for any *Edgesurf* are given here.

SURFTAB1   1st edge picked (*M* direction)

SURFTAB2   2nd edge picked (*N* direction)

Figure 37-14

Edges used to define an *Edgesurf* may be <u>non</u>planar, resulting in a smooth, nonplanar surface as displayed in Figure 37-15. Remember, the edges may be any *Pline* shape in 3D space.

Use *Hide* to enhance your visibility of nonplanar surfaces.

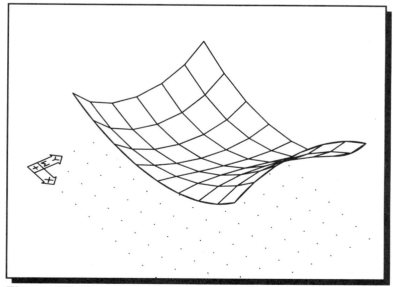

Figure 37-15

RULESURF

TYPE IN:	PULL-DOWN MENU	SCREEN MENU	TABLET MENU
RULESURF	*Draw, 3D Surfaces > Ruled Surface*	*SURFACES, RULSURF:*	*1,N*

A *Rulesurf* is a polygon meshed surface created between <u>two edges</u>. The edges can be *Lines*, *Arcs*, or *Plines*. The command syntax only asks for the two "defining curves." The two defining edges must <u>both</u> be open or closed.

Figure 37-16 displays two planar *Rulesurfs*.

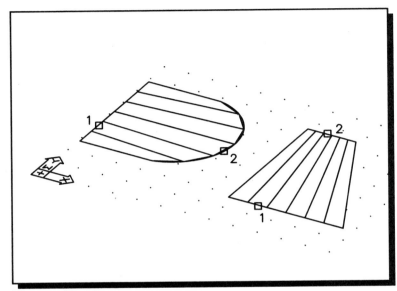

Figure 37-16

Figure 37-17 displays possibilities for creating *Rulesurfs* between two edges that are nonplanar.

Figure 37-17

The command syntax for *Rulesurf* is as follows:

```
Command: rulesurf
Select first defining curve: PICK
Select second defining curve: PICK
Command:
```

A cylinder can be created with *Rulesurf* by utilizing two *Circle*s lying on different planes as the defining edges. A cone can be created by creating a *Rulesurf* between a *Circle* and a *Point* (Fig. 37-18). Or, a complex shape can be created using two identical closed *Pline* shapes (Fig. 37-18).

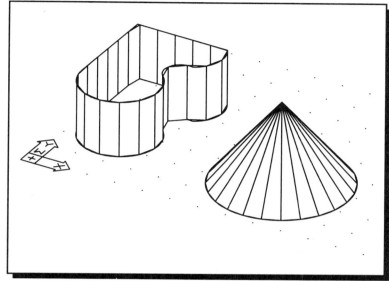

Figure 37-18

For open defining edges (not *Circles* or closed *Plines*), the *Rulesurf* is generated connecting the two <u>selected</u> ends of the defining edges. Figure 37-19 illustrates the two possibilities for generating a *Rulesurf* between two straight nonplanar *Lines* based upon the endpoints selected.

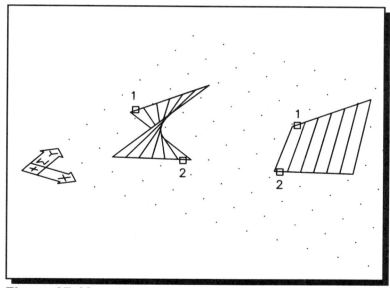

Figure 37-19

Since the curve is stretched between only two edges, the number of vertices along the *defining curve* is determined only by the value previously specified for *SURFTAB1*.

SURFTAB1	*defining curve*	*N* direction
SURFTAB2	not used	*M* direction

TABSURF

TYPE IN:	PULL-DOWN MENU	SCREEN MENU	TABLET MENU
TABSURF	*Draw, 3D Surfaces > Tabulated Surface*	*SURFACES, TABSURF:*	*2,O*

A *Tabsurf* is generated by an existing *path curve* and a *direction vector*. The *curve path* (generatrix) is extruded in the direction of, and equal in length to, the *direction vector* (directrix) to create a swept surface. The path curve can be a *Line, Arc, Circle, 2D Polyline,* or *3D Polyline*. The direction vector can be a *Line* or an open 2D *Pline*. If a curved *Pline* is used, the surface is generated in a direction connecting the two end vertices of the *Pline*.

A *Circle* can be swept with *Tabsurf* to generate a cylinder. The *Tabsurf* has only *N* direction; therefore, the current setting of *SURFTAB1* controls the number of vertices along the *path curve*.

The relation of *SURFTAB1* and SURFTAB2 for *Tabsurf* are:

SURFTAB1	*Path curve* *N* direction
SURFTAB2	not used *M* direction

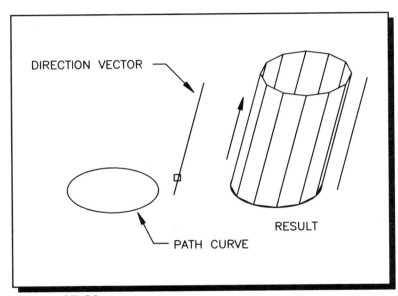

Figure 37-20

The *Tabsurf* is generated in the direction <u>opposite</u> the end of the direction vector that is selected. This is evident in both Figures 37-20 and 37-21.

The command sequence is:

```
Command: tabsurf
Select path curve: PICK
Select direction
vector: PICK
```

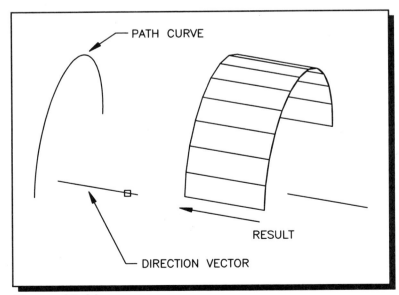

Figure 37-21

REVSURF

TYPE IN:	PULL-DOWN MENU	SCREEN MENU	TABLET MENU
REVSURF	*Draw, 3D Surfaces >* *Surface of Revolution*	*SURFACES,* *REVSURF:*	*2,N*

This command creates a surface of revolution by revolving an existing *path curve* around an *axis*. The path curve can be a *Line, Arc, Circle*, 2D or 3D *Pline*. The *axis* can be a *Line* or open *Pline*. If a curved *Pline* is used as the *axis*, only the endpoint vertices are considered for the axis of revolution.

```
Command: revsurf
Select path curve: PICK
Select axis of revolution: PICK
Start angle<0>: PICK or (value)
Included angle (+=ccw, -=cw)<Full circle>: PICK or (value)
Command:
```

The structure of the command allows many variables. The *path curve* can be open or closed. The *axis* can be in any plane. The *start angle* and *included angle* allow for complete (closed) or partial (open) revolutions of the surface in any orientation. Figures 37-22 and 37-23 show possible *Revsurfs* created with *path curves* generated through 360 degrees.

The wine glass was created with an open *path curve* generated through 360 degrees.

The number of vertices in the direction of revolution is controlled by the setting of *SURFTAB2*. The *SURFTAB1* setting controls the number of vertices along the length of the *path curve*.

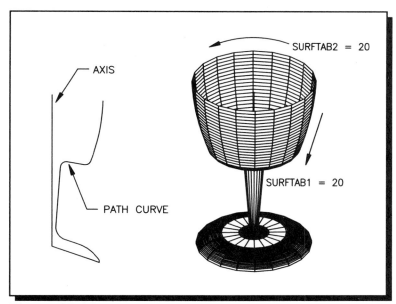

Figure 37-22

The relation of *SURFTAB1* and SURFTAB2 for *Revsurf* are given here.

SURFTAB1	*Axis of revolution*	*M* direction
SURFTAB2	*Path curve*	*N* direction

A torus can be created by using a closed *path curve* generated through 360 degrees. In this case, the surface begins at the *path curve* and is revolved all the way around the axis and closes on itself.

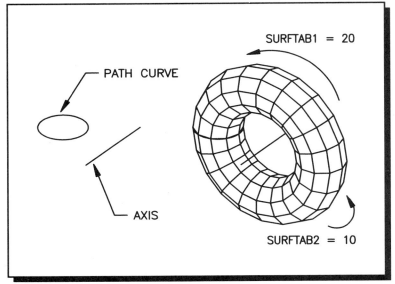

Figure 37-23

When generating a curve path through <u>less than</u> 360 degrees, the included angle must be specified. Entering a positive angle specifies a counter-clockwise direction of revolution and a negative angle specification causes a clockwise revolution. As an alternative, you can pick different points on the *axis of revolution*. The end of the line PICKed represents the end nearest the origin for positive rotation using the Right-Hand Rule.

Figure 37-24 displays a *Revsurf* generated through 90 degrees. The end of the *axis of revolution* PICKed specifies the direction of positive rotation.

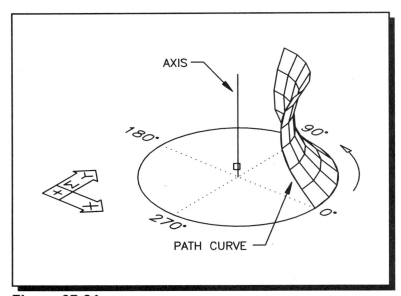

Figure 37-24

Figure 37-25 displays a *Revsurf* generated in a negative revolution direction accomplished by specifying a negative angle or by PICKing a point specifying an inverted origin (of the Right-Hand Rule) for rotation.

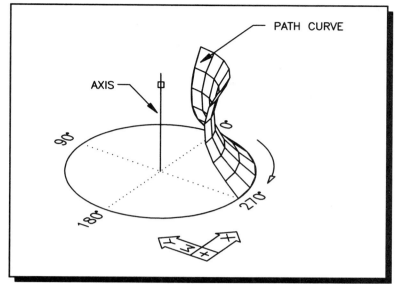

Figure 37-25

EDITING POLYGON MESHES

There are several ways that existing AutoCAD polygon meshed surfaces (*3Dmesh, Rulesurf, Tabsurf, Revsurf,* and *Edgesurf*) can be changed. The use of *Pedit, Grips,* and *Explode* each provide special capabilities.

PEDIT with Polygon Meshes

One of the options of *Pedit* is *Edit vertex,* which allows editing of individual vertices of a *Pline*. Vertex editing can also be accomplished with *3Dmeshes, Revsurfs, Edgesurfs, Tabsurfs,* and *Rulesurfs*. *Pedit* does not allow editing of *3Dfaces*.

```
Command: Pedit
Select objects: PICK (Select the surface.)
Select objects: Enter (Indicate completion of the object selection process.)
Edit vertex/Smooth surface/Desmooth/Mclose/Nclose/Undo
/eXit<X>:
```

Each *Pedit* option for editing Polygon Meshes is explained and illustrated here.

Edit Vertex
Invoking this option causes the display of another set of options at the command prompt which allows you to locate the vertex that you wish to edit.

```
Vertex(0,0).Next/Previous/Left/Right/Up/Down/Move/
REgen/eXit<N>:
```

Pressing Enter locates the marker (X) at the next vertex. Selecting *Left/Right* or *Up/Down* controls the direction of the movement in the *N* and *M* directions (as specified by *SURFTAB1* and *SURFTAB2* when the surfaces were created) (Fig. 37-26).

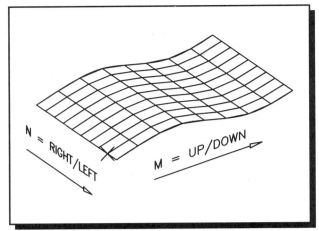

Figure 37-26

Once the vertex has been located, use the *Move* option to move the vertex to any location in 3D space (Fig. 37-27).

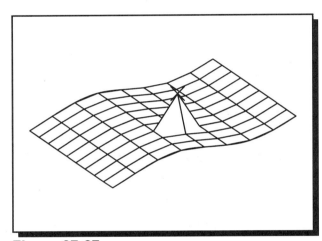

Figure 37-27

Smooth surface

Invoking this option causes the surface to be smoothed using the current setting of *SURFTYPE* (described later) (Fig. 37-28).

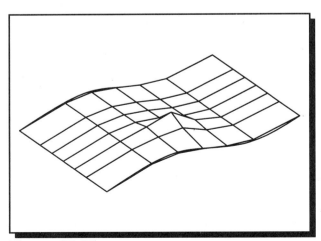

Figure 37-28

Desmooth

The *Desmooth* option reverses the effect of *Smooth*.

Mclose/Nclose

The *Mclose* and *Nclose* options cause the surface to close in either the *M* or *N* directions. The last and first set of vertices automatically connect. Figure 37-29 displays a half-cylindrical surface closed with *Nclose*.

Undo

Undo reverses the last operation with *Pedit*.

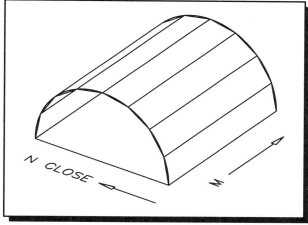

Figure 37-29

eXit

This option is used to keep the editing changes, exit the *Pedit* command, and return to the Command: prompt.

Variables Affecting Polygon Meshes

SURFTYPE

This variable affects the degree of smoothing of a surface when using the *Smooth* option of *Pedit*. The command prompt syntax is shown here.

```
Command: Surftype
New value for Surftype<6>: (value)
```

The values allowed are **5**, **6**, and **8**. The options are illustrated in the following figures.

Original polygon mesh (Fig. 37-30)

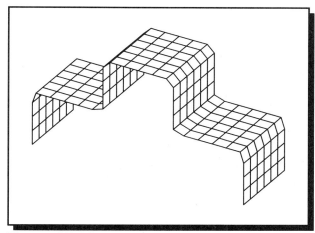

Figure 37-30

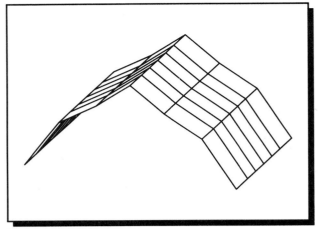

Figure 37-31

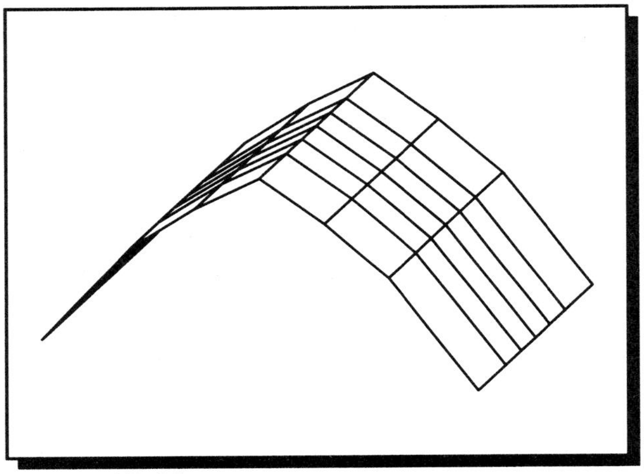

5

Quadratic B-spline surface (Fig. 37-31)

6

Cubic B-Spline surface (Fig. 37-32)

8

Bezier surface (Fig. 37-33)

Figure 37-32

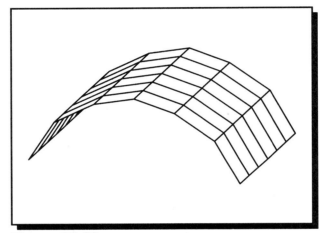

Figure 37-33

SPLFRAME

The *SPLFRAME* (spline frame) variable causes the original polygon mesh to be displayed along with the smoothed version of the surface. The values allowed are **0** for off and **1** for on. *SPLFRAME* can also be used with 2D polylines when using the *Spline* option.

SPLFRAME is set to **1** in Figure 37-34 to display the original polygon mesh.

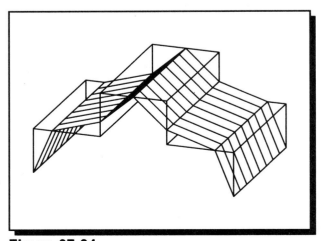

Figure 37-34

Editing Polygon Meshes with Grips

Grips can be used to edit the individual vertices of a polygon mesh (*3Dmesh*, *Edgesurf*, *Rulesurf*, *Tabsurf*, and *Revsurf*). Normally the STRETCH option of grip editing would be used to stretch (move) the location of a single vertex grip. The other grip editing options (MOVE, SCALE, ROTATE, MIRROR) affect the entire polygon mesh. Selecting the mesh at the open Command: prompt activates all of the grips (one for each vertex) and makes them **warm**. Selecting one of the individual grips again makes that one **hot** and able to be relocated with the STRETCH option.

For example, a *3Dmesh* could be generated to define a surface with a rough texture, such as a chipped stone.

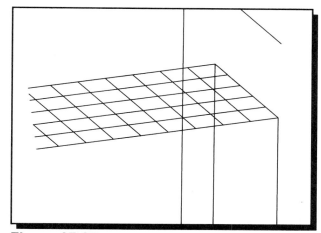

Figure 37-35

Grip editing STRETCH option could be used to relocate individual vertices of the mesh. The result is a surface with a rough or bumpy surface such as that shown in this figure.

Although the concept is simple, some care should be taken to assure that the individual vertices are moved in the desired plane. Since grip editing is interactive, any points PICKed are on the <u>current XY plane</u>. Careful use of UCS's can insure that the vertices are STRETCHed in the desired XY plane.

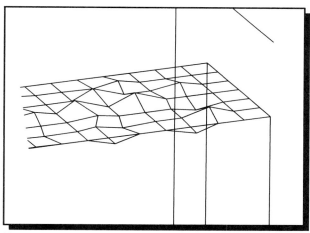

Figure 37-36

Editing Polygon Meshes with *Explode*

The *Explode* command can be used to allow editing *3Dmeshes*, geometrically defined meshes (*Edgesurf, Revsurf*, etc.), 3D primitives (*3D Objects...*), and Regions.

When used with other AutoCAD entities, *Explode* will "break down" the entity group into a lower level of entities; for example, a *Pline* can be broken into its individual segments with *Explode*. Likewise, *Explode* will "break down" a 3D polygon mesh, for example, into individual 1 by 1 meshes (in effect, *3Dfaces*). *Explode* will affect any polygon meshes (*3Dmesh, Edgesurf, Revsurf, Tabsurf, Rulesurf*).

Explode converts a polygon mesh into its individual 1 by 1 meshes (*3Dfaces*) (Fig. 37-37).

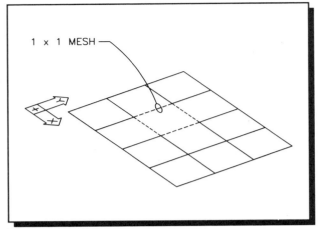

Figure 37-37

CONSTRUCTION TECHNIQUES FOR POLYGON MESHES AND *3DFACES*

Surfaces are created individually and combined to form a complete surface model. The surfaces can be created and moved into place in order to "assemble" the complete model, or surfaces can be created <u>in place</u> to form the finished model. Because polygon meshes require existing geometry to define the surfaces, the construction technique generally used is:

1. Construct a wireframe model (or partial wireframe) defining the edges of the surfaces on a separate layer.
2. Attach polygon mesh and other surfaces to the wireframe using another layer.

The creation of UCS's greatly assists in constructing 3D elements in 3D space during construction of the wireframe and surfaces. The sequence in the creation of a complete surface model is given here as an example surface modeling strategy.

Surface Model Example 1

Consider the object in Figure 37-38. To create a surface model of this object, first create a partial wireframe.

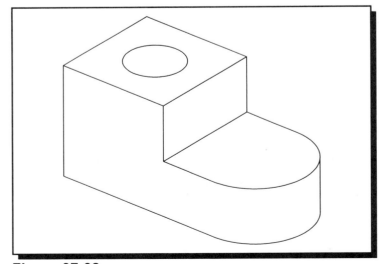

Figure 37-38

1. Create part of a wireframe model using *Line* and *Circle* elements. Create the wireframe on a separate layer. Begin the geometry at the origin. Use *Vpoint* to enable visualization of three dimensions.

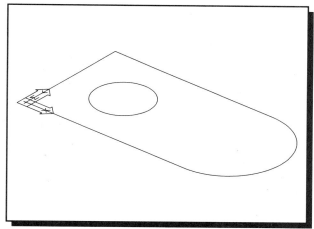

Figure 37-39

2. *Copy* the usable entities to the top plane by specifying a Z dimension at the "second point of displacement" prompt.

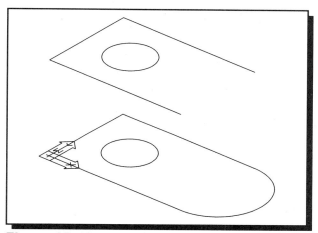

Figure 37-40

3. Create a UCS on this new plane using the *Origin* option. *OSNAP* the *Origin* to the existing geometry. Draw the connecting *Line* and *Trim* the extensions.

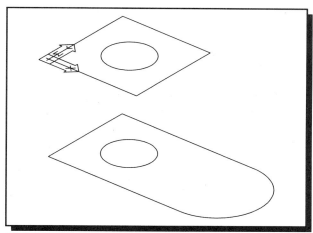

Figure 37-41

4. *Copy* the *Arc* and two attached *Lines* specifying a Z dimension for the "second point of displacement." *Copy* the *Line* drawn last (on the top plane) specifying a negative Z dimension. *Trim* the extending *Line* ends. A new *UCS* is not necessary on this plane.

   This is not a complete wireframe, but it includes all the edges that are necessary to begin attaching surfaces.

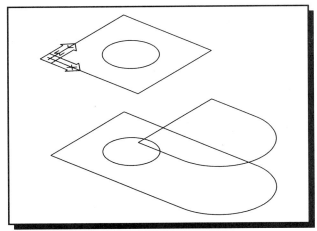

Figure 37-42

5. On a new layer, a 2-segment *3Dface* is created by PICKing the *ENDpoints* of the wireframe entities in the order indicated. Remember that *3Dface* segments connect at the 3rd and 4th points. (*Hide* is used in this figure to provide visibility of the *3Dface*.)

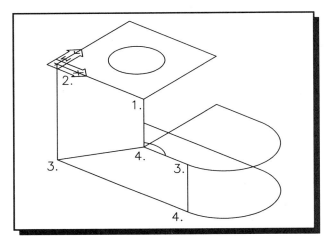

Figure 37-43

6. The *3Dface* is *Copied* to the opposite side of the model. A vertical *3Dface* is created between the top and the intermediate plane. Another vertical *3Dface* is created on the back (not visible). (*Hide* is used again in this figure. Notice how the *Circle* is treated.)

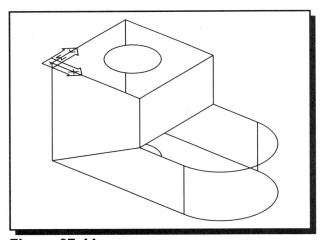

Figure 37-44

7.   *Rulesurf* is used to create the rounded surface shown between the two *Arcs*. The *SURFTAB1* and *SURFTAB2* variables were previously set to 12.

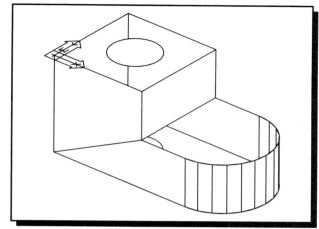

Figure 37-45

8.   Next, a *Rulesurf* is used to create the cylindrical hole surface between the *Circles* on the top and bottom planes. The wireframe layer was *Frozen* before *Hide* was used for this figure.

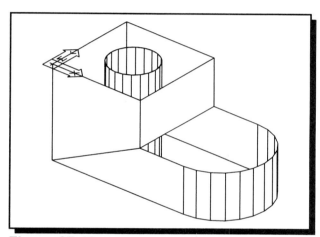

Figure 37-46

9.   The surface connecting the *Arc* and three *Lines* is created by *Edgesurf*.

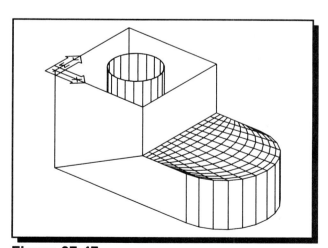

10. The only remaining surfaces to create are the top and bottom. <u>There is no</u> polygon mesh, *3Dface*, or *3Dmesh* that can be generated to create a simple surface configuration such as that on top--a surface with a hole! It must be accomplished by creating several adjoining surfaces.

Figure 37-47

There are several possible methods for construction of a surface with a hole. (The top surface has been isolated here for simplicity.) Probably the simplest is shown in this figure. First, the *Circle* must be <u>replaced</u> by two 180 degree *Arcs*. Next a *Rulesurf* is created between one *Arc* and one edge as shown.

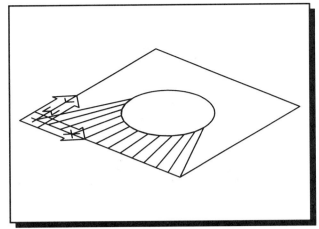

Figure 37-48

11. The top plane is completed by creating another *Rulesurf* and two triangular *3Dfaces* adjoining the *Rulesurfs*. (Wireframe elements are <u>not</u> required for the *3Dface*.)

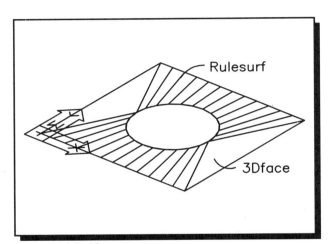

Figure 37-49

12. The surface model is shown in this figure. The bottom surface (not visible here) was created by *Copying* the top plane surfaces and the intermediate plane *Edgesurf*. The layer containing the wireframe elements has been *Frozen* and *Hide* used to enhance visibility.

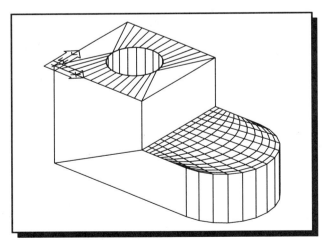

Figure 37-50

13. The mesh lines shown in Figure 37-51 (above) are not visible when a *Render* is performed. This figure illustrates the completed model after using *Render*. *Shade* also provides options to display or to hide the edge and mesh lines.

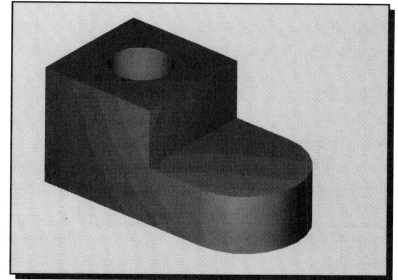

Figure 37-51

APPLICATIONS AND LIMITATIONS OF POLYGON MESHES AND *3DFACE*

From the previous example of the creation of a relatively simple 3D surface model, you can see how construction of some shapes with *3Dface* or polygon meshes can be somewhat involved. The particular characteristics of a surface that cause some difficulty in creation are the surfaces that embody many edges or that have holes, slots, or other "islands." Examine the surfaces shown in the following figures. Although some of these shapes are fairly common, the construction techniques using *3Dfaces* and polygon meshes could be very involved.

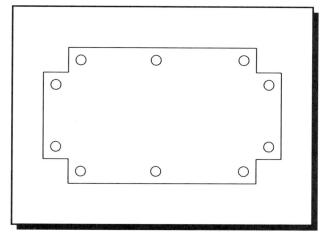

Figure 37-52

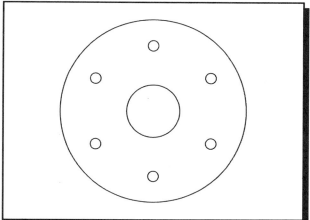

Figure 37-53

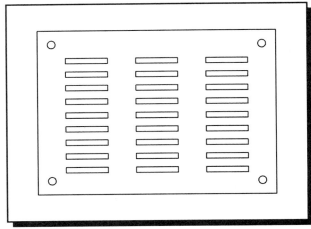

Figure 37-54

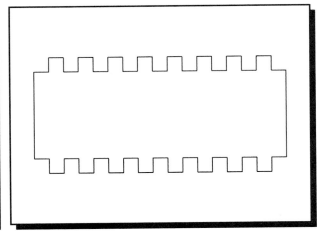

Figure 37-55

3Dface and polygon meshes would <u>not</u> be an efficient construction technique to use in the creation of shapes such as these. AutoCAD has provided a feature in Release 12 that makes construction of such shapes relatively simple. That feature is called Region Modeling. Region modeling is an extension of Constructive Solid Modeling (CSG) technique facilitated by AutoCAD's AME (Advanced Modeling Extension). Technically, Region Modeling allows you to create "2D solids." Region models can be combined with _3Dfaces_, polygon meshes, and other surfacing techniques to create surface models. (See Chapter 38.)

SURFACE MODELING PRIMITIVES

3D Objects...

TYPE IN:	PULL-DOWN MENU	SCREEN MENU	TABLET MENU
---	_Draw, 3D Surfaces >_ _3D Objects..._	_SURFACES, 3d objects..._	---

This command allows you to create 3D <u>primitives</u>. A primitive is a simple 3D geometric shape such as a _box, cylinder, wedge, torus, cone, dome, sphere_, or _dish_ (the mesh is a _3Dmesh_, discussed earlier). These primitives are pre-created shapes composed of _3Dfaces_ or polygon meshes. The primitives in the _3D Objects_ icon menu are surface models (Figure 37-56).

When a primitive is selected from the icon menu, AutoCAD prompts you for the dimensions of the primitive. Depending upon the type of primitive chosen, the prompts differ. The prompts for a _cube_ are given below.

```
Command: ai-box
Corner of box: PICK or (value)
Cube<Width>: PICK or (value)
Height: PICK or (value)
Rotation angle about Z axis: PICK or (value)
```

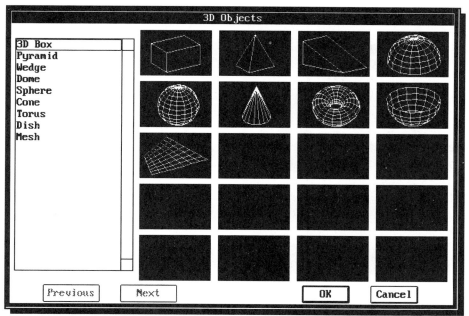

Figure 37-56

These primitives are composed of AutoCAD surfaces. The 3D primitives (*3D Objects*) are provided in order to simplify the process of creating complex surface models. Generally, the primitives have to be edited and combined with other surfaces to build the complex model you need for a particular application. In this case, editing commands (*Pedit, Explode*, Grip editing, etc.) as discussed in this chapter can be used along with other surfacing capabilities (*3Dmesh, 3Dface, Revsurf, Edgesurf*, Regions, etc.). The editing commands used differ depending on the type of surface. *Pedit, Explode*, and Grip editing can be used with any polygon mesh (*torus, sphere, dome, dish*). *Pedit* <u>cannot</u> be used with *3Dfaces* (*box, wedge*); however, *Explode* and Grip editing can be used. See Editing Polygon Meshes and Editing *3Dfaces* in this chapter.

For example, the *3D Box* can be *exploded* into its individual *3Dfaces*. Figure 37-57 exhibits the box in its original form. Figure 37-58 illustrates the *box* after it has been *Exploded* and the top *3Dface* removed to reveal the inside. (*Hide* has been performed in these figures to enhance visualization.)

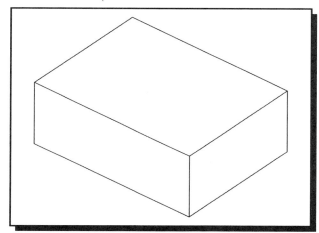

Figure 37-57

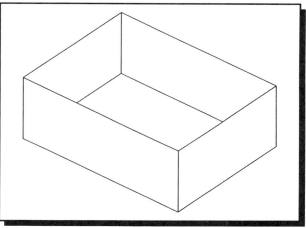

Figure 37-58

Surface Model Example 2

The following example is given as an example of surface model construction strategy utilizing *3D Objects* combined with *3Dfaces* and polygon meshes.

In this example the object in Figure 37-59 is constructed from 3D Primitives (*3D Objects*), edited, and combined with other surfaces.

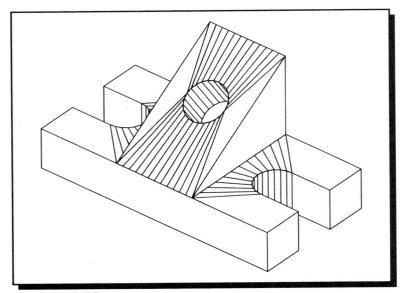

Figure 37-59

1. The drawing is set up by creating a layer for the surface model and setting the *Ucsicon ON* and at the *Origin*. The construction begins by selecting a *3D Box* from the *3D Objects* dialogue box.

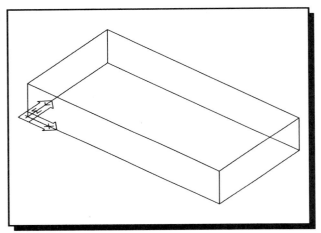

Figure 37-60

2. The *3D Box* is *exploded* and the top and side faces are *erased*.

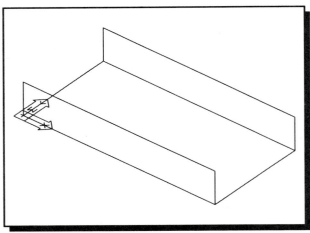

Figure 37-61

3. A *UCS* is created with the *origin* option with its location (using *OSNAP*) on the top plane.

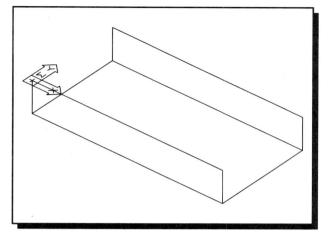

Figure 37-62

4. A new *Layer* is created for a wireframe. Wireframe elements (*Line, Arc*) are added to prepare for creating *3Dfaces* and polygon meshes.

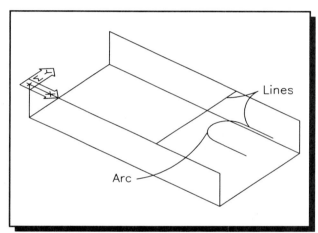

Figure 37-63

5. *SURFTAB1* and *SURFTAB2* are set to 12. *Rulesurf* and *3Dface* are used to create part of the top surface. (*Hide* is used in this figure to portray the surfaces.)

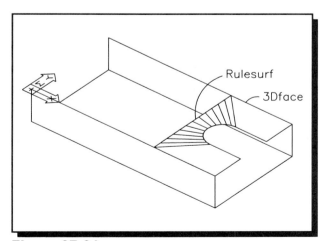

Figure 37-64

6. The bottom surface (part of the original *3D Box*) is erased. The new surfaces and wireframe elements are *copied* to the bottom plane.

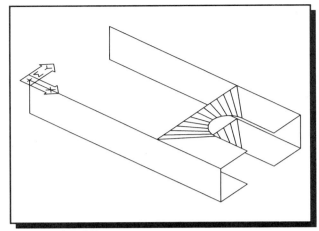

Figure 37-65

7. A *Rulesurf* and four *3Dfaces* are created connecting the top and bottom surfaces. Use of layers is critical but somewhat laborious at this point. Only the wireframe elements can be selected as the defining edges for *Rulesurf*; therefore, turning the surface model layer *off* is required to allow selection of the wireframe elements.

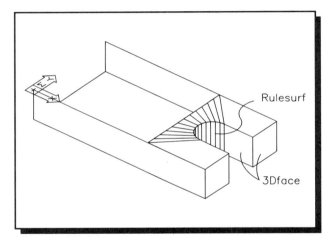

Figure 37-66

8. Next, the eleven surfaces are mirrored to the other side. *Mirror3D* is used with the *YZ* option and PICKing the *MIDpoint* of the long surface across the front as the "point on YZ plane." A *3Dface* is created to fill the opening on the bottom surface.

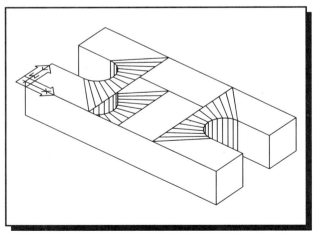

Figure 37-67

9. The *3D Objects* dialogue box is used again to select a *Wedge*. The *Wedge* is placed in the center of the top surface.

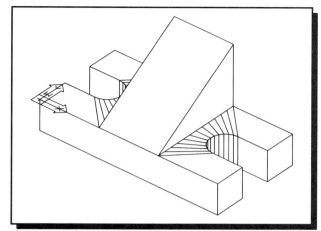

Figure 37-68

10. *Explode* breaks the *Wedge* into its individual *3Dfaces*. The inclined plane is *Erased*.

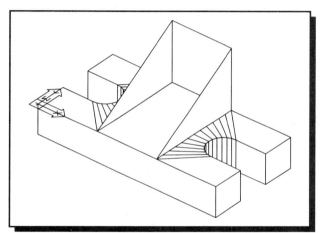

Figure 37-69

11. A new *UCS* is created to enable the construction of a new inclined surface with the hole. The *3point* option would be effective in this case.

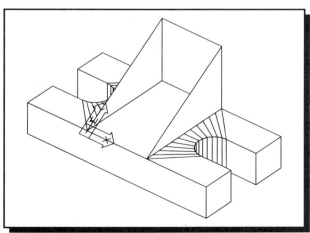

Figure 37-70

12. Wireframe elements (four *Arcs* and two *Lines*) are created on the wireframe layer as a foundation for construction of the new inclined surface and hole.

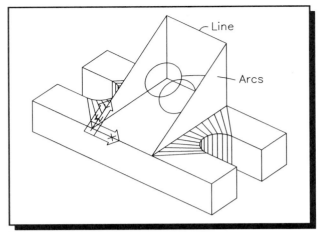

Figure 37-71

13. An inclined surface and hole are created on the surface model layer by applying the technique used in Surface Model Example 1. (Wireframe elements are not required for *3Dfaces*.)

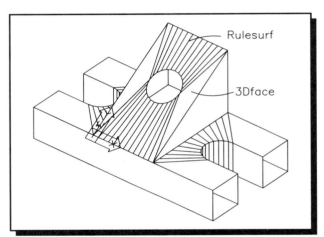

Figure 37-72

14. The model is completed by using *Rulesurf* to create the hole surface (sides) and a *Circle* establishes the bottom of the hole. Keep in mind that the *Rulesurf* must be defined by the original *Arcs*, not by the previous *Rulesurf* of the inclined plane.

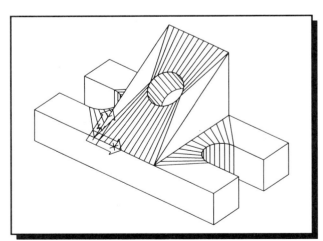

Figure 37-73

15. Figure 37-74 illustrates the completed surface model in *rendered* representation.

Figure 37-74

USING *THICKNESS* AND *ELEVATION*

THICKNESS and *ELEVATION*

TYPE IN:	PULL-DOWN MENU	SCREEN MENU	TABLET MENU
THICKNESS or ELEVATION	*Settings, Entity Modes*	*SETTINGS, ELEV:*	---

Thickness and *Elevation* were introduced with Version 2.1 (1985) as AutoCAD's first capability for creating 3D entities. *Thickness* and *Elevation* are still useful for creating simple surfaces. Any 2D entity (*Line, Circle, Arc, Pline,* etc.) can be assigned a *Thickness* or *Elevation* property. *Thickness* and *Elevation* are usually assigned before using a 2D command.

Thickness is a value representing a Z dimension for (normally) a 2D entity. The new entity is created using the typical draw command (*Line, Circle, Arc,* etc.), but the resulting entity has a uniform Z dimension as assigned. For example, a 2 unit high cylinder can be created by setting *Thickness* to 2 and then using the *Circle* command (Fig. 37-75).

Thickness is always perpendicular to the XY plane. Until recent versions of AutoCAD, this posed a major limitation with the use of *Thickness*. This limited cylinders, for example, to being oriented vertically only, no cylinders could be created with a horizontal

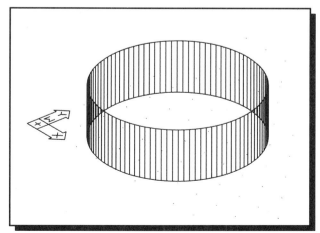

Figure 37-75

orientation. The term "2½-D" was used to describe this capability of CAD packages during this phase of development.

Today, with the ability to create User Coordinate Systems (UCS), *Thickness* can be used to create surfaces in any orientation. Therefore, the effectiveness of *Thickness* and *Elevation* commands is increased. Figure 37-76 displays a cylinder oriented horizontally, achieved by creating a UCS having a vertical XY plane and a horizontal Z dimension. UCS's can be created to achieve any orientation for using *Thickness*.

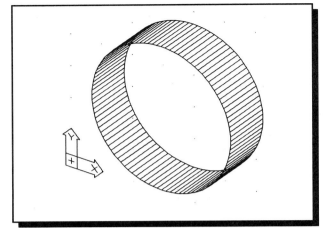

Figure 37-76

With a *Thickness* set to a value greater than 0, commands normally used to create 2D entities can be used to create 3D surfaces having a uniform Z dimension perpendicular to the current XY plane. Figure 37-77 shows a *Line, Arc,* and *Point* possessing *Thickness* property. Note that a *Point* entity with *Thickness* creates a line perpendicular to the current XY plane.

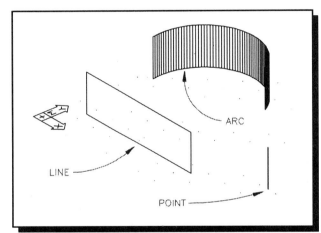

Figure 37-77

The ability to create *Plines* with *Thickness* offers many possibilities for developing complex surface models (Fig. 37-78). (Keep in mind that 2D shapes created with *Line* and *Arc* entities can be converted to *Plines* with *Pedit*.)

Figure 37-78

Using the *Hide* command with surfaces created with *Thickness* enhances your visibility. Figures 37-78 and 37-79 show examples of *Hide*. Notice that *Circles* created with *Thickness* have a "top." Other closed shapes created with *Line* or *Pline* do not have a "top."

Assigning a value for *Thickness* causes all subsequently created entities to have the assigned *Thickness* property. *Thickness* must be set back to **0** to create normal 2D entities.

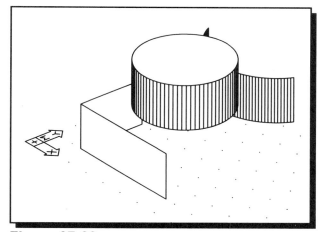

Figure 37-79

Elevation controls the Z dimension for the "base plane" for subsequently created entities. Normally, unless an explicit Z value is given, 2D entities (with or without *Thickness*) are created on the XY plane or at an *Elevation* of **0**. Changing the value of the *Elevation* changes the "base plane," or the elevation, of the construction plane for newly created objects.

Figure 37-80 displays the same objects as in the previous figure except the *Circle* has an *Elevation* of **2** (level with the top edges of the other entities). It may be necessary to use *Hide* or several *Vpoints* to "see" the relationship of objects with differing *Elevations*.

Like *Thickness, Elevation* should be set back to 0 to create geometry normally with relation to the 0 XY plane.

Figure 37-80

Changing *Thickness* and *Elevation*

Because *Thickness* and *Elevation* are properties that 2D entities may possess (like *Color* and *Linetype*), they can be changed or assigned <u>retroactively</u>. *Elevation* can only be changed retroactively using the *Change* command with the *Properties* option (see Chapter 16). *Thickness* can be changed using the *Modify* dialogue box.

Modify Entity

TYPE IN:	PULL-DOWN MENU	SCREEN MENU	TABLET MENU
DDMODIFY	*Modify, Entity*	*EDIT, DDMODFY:*	*16,Y and 17,Y*

Invoking this dialogue box provides you with the ability to change the *Thickness* of existing entities. The dialogue box is shown in Figure 37-81.

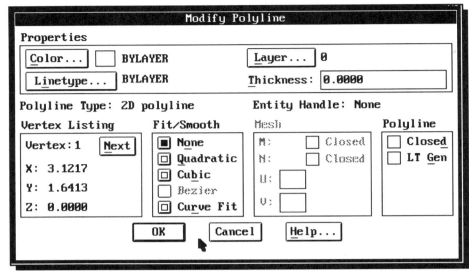

Figure 37-81

As an alternative to setting *Thickness* before creating surfaces, the 2D geometry can first be created and then changed to 3D surfaces by using this dialogue box to retroactively set *Thickness*.

Figure 37-82 displays a 2D *Pline* shape. The *Modify* dialogue box can be used to change the *Thickness* of the shape to create a 3D surface model.

Figure 37-83 shows the same *Pline* shape as in the previous figure after the *Thickness* property was changed to generate the 3D surface model.

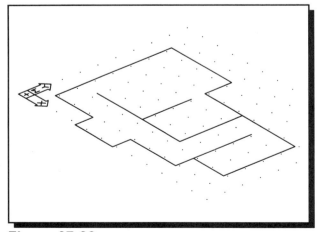

Figure 37-82

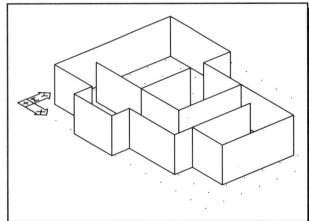

Figure 37-83

CHAPTER EXERCISES

1-4. Create a surface model of each of the objects in Figures 37-84 through 37-87. These are the same objects you worked with in Chapter 35, Wireframe Modeling. You can use each of the Chapter 35 Exercises wireframes (**WFEX1**, **WFEX2**, etc.) as a "skeleton" on which to attach surfaces. Make sure you create a **New Layer** for the surfaces. Use each dimension marker in the figure to equal one unit in AutoCAD. Locate the lower left corner of the model at coordinate **0,0,0**. Assign the names **SURFEX1**, **SURFEX2**, and so on. Make a plot of each model with hidden lines removed.

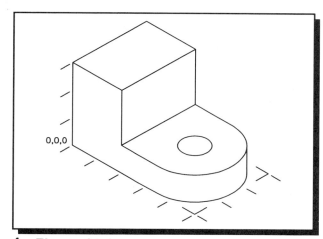

1. Figure 37-84

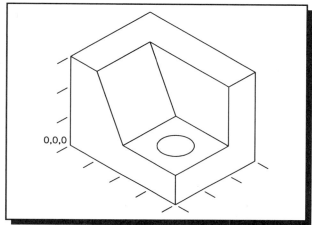

2. Figure 37-85

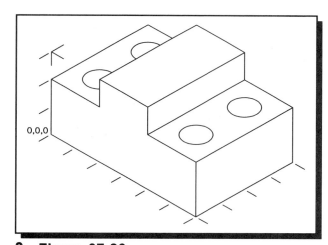

3. Figure 37-86

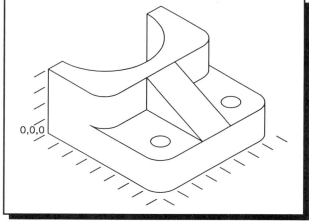

4. Figure 37-87

5. Create a surface model of the Bar Guide shown in Figure 37-88. You may want to use the **BGUID-WF** drawing that you created in Chapter 36 Exercises as a wireframe foundation. Make a **New Layer** for the surface model. Align a **UCS** with the **View** and create a title block and border. **Plot** the model with hidden lines removed. **Save** the surface model as **BGD-SURF**.

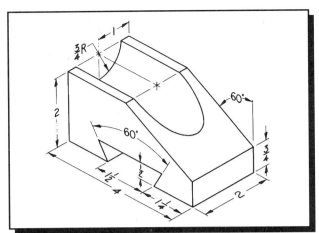

Figure 37-88

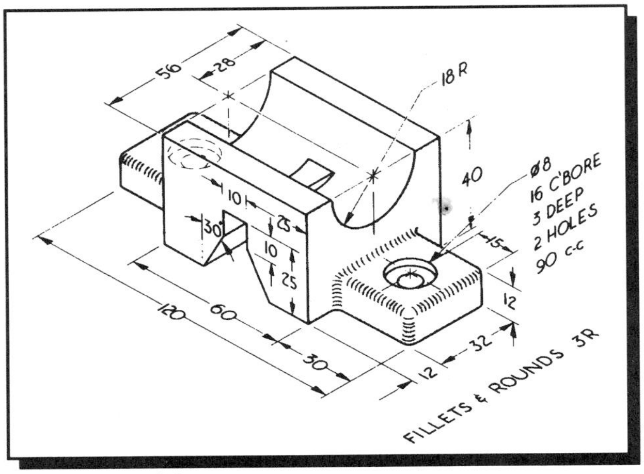

Figure 37-89

6. Create a surface model of the Saddle in Figure 37-89. There is no previously created wireframe model, so you must begin a *New* drawing or use a *Prototype*. The fillets and rounds should be created using *Rulesurf* or *Tabsurf*. *Revsurf* must be used to create the complex fillets and rounds at the corners. Align a *UCS* with the *View* and create a title block and border. Plot the drawing with hidden lines removed. *Save* the drawing as **SDL-SURF**.

7. Begin a *New* drawing (or use a *Prototype*) for the Pulley shown in Figure 37-90. This is the same object that you worked with in Chapter 25 Exercises. As a reminder, the vertical dimensions are diameters. Use *Revsurf* to create the curved (cylindrical) surfaces, but do not create the vertical circular faces that would appear on the front and back (the surfaces containing the 4 counterbored holes or the keyway). Consider methods for creating the surfaces using commands learned in Chapter 37. *Save* the drawing as **PUL-SURF**. You will complete this drawing in Chapter 38 Exercises using the Region Modeler.

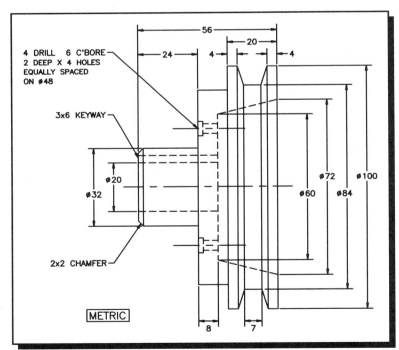

Figure 37-90

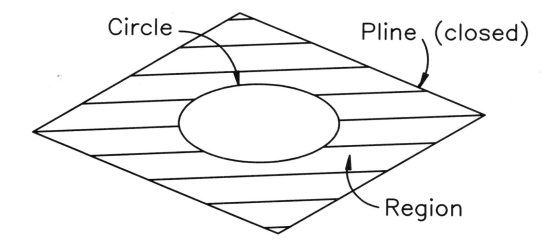

Circle

Pline (closed)

Region

CHAPTER 38

Region Modeling

CHAPTER OBJECTIVES

After completing this chapter you should:

1. understand the relationship of surface models, region models, and solid models;

2. be able to create regions by applying Boolean operations (*Union*, *Subtraction*, *Intersection*) to closed 2D entities (*Plines, Circles, Polygons, Ellipses*);

3. be able to convert a closed 2D entity to a region with *Solidify*;

4. be able to edit region primitives (the original closed 2D shapes) with *Solchpr*;

5. be able to control the region mesh density with *SOLWDENS*;

6. be able to use *Solmesh* to mesh regions and prepare for use with *Hide, Shade*, or *Render*;

7. know how to control the hatch pattern appearance for regions with the *SOLHPAT*, *SOLHANGL*, and *SOLHSIZE* variables.

BASICS

Region modeling is defined in the AutoCAD documentation as "2D solid modeling," not "surface modeling." This is because region modeling applies solid modeling techniques, namely, Boolean operations, to 2D closed entities. Practically, however, regions can be considered surfaces.

AutoCAD's Region Modeler allows you to utilize the Boolean operations *Union*, *Subtraction*, and *Intersection*. A region is created by applying the commands *Union*, *Subtraction*, *Intersection* or *Solidify* to closed 2D entities such as *Plines*, *Circles*, *Ellipses*, and *Polygons*. In the process of performing the Boolean operation, the 2D entities are converted to a surface. The resulting shape is called a region and is visually designated by widely spaced cross-hatch lines across the surface (by default). Composite regions can be constructed by combining multiple 2D shapes with other shapes or regions using Boolean operations. Regions are always planar. These surfaces can then be combined with other surfaces (regions, *3Dfaces*, or polygon meshes) on other planes to create complex surface models.

AutoCAD Release 12 is shipped with the Region Modeler. The AutoCAD Advanced Modeling Extension (AME) is not required for region modeling. However, the Region Modeler must be loaded before use. One method of loading can be accomplished by typing:

Command: **(xload "region")**

The Region Modeler can also be loaded by selecting *Utility* and *Load Modeler* from the *Model* pull-down menu. However, typing the commands *Solunion, Solsub,* or *Solint* at the command prompt or selecting them from the *Model* pull-down causes AutoCAD to prompt you to load the Region Modeler or AME. Do so by pressing **Enter**.

BOOLEAN OPERATIONS

Because *Union*, *Subtraction*, and *Intersection* are principally AME commands, the formal name for each AME command begins with **SOL**. The formal command names for the Boolean commands in AutoCAD are *Solunion, Solsub,* and *Solint*. However, command aliases have been defined for these commands and are listed in the respective menu tables. A digitizing tablet menu insert for AME & Region Modeler is available inside the back cover of the "Advanced Modeling Extension Reference Manual."

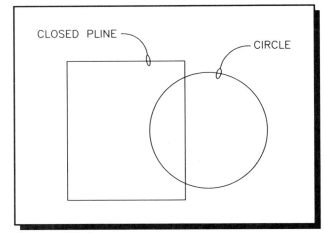

Figure 38-1

Assume that you have drawn the two shapes (a closed *Pline* and a *Circle*) shown in Figure 38-1. The results of *Solunion*, *Solsub*, and *Solint* are each illustrated in the following figures.

SOLUNION

TYPE IN:	PULL-DOWN MENU	SCREEN MENU	TABLET MENU
Union or SOLUNION	*Model, Union*	*MODEL, SOLUNION:*	*3,D*

Invoking *Union* causes AutoCAD to prompt you to select objects. Select two or more closed *Plines*, *Circles*, *Polygons*, or *Ellipses*.

```
Command: solunion
Select objects: PICK (Pline)
Select objects: PICK (Circle)
Select objects: Enter
2 regions unioned.
```

The shapes are combined into one region (Fig. 38-2).

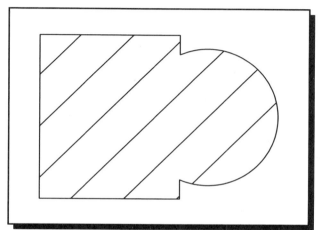

Figure 38-2

SOLSUB

TYPE IN:	PULL-DOWN MENU	SCREEN MENU	TABLET MENU
SUB or SOLSUB	*Model, Subtract*	*MODEL, SOLSUB:*	*3,C*

Solsub requires that you PICK source objects and objects to subtract from them (or it).

```
Command: solsub
Source objects...
Select objects: PICK (closed Pline)
Objects to subtract from
them...
Select objects: PICK (Circle)
```

The source object(s) is the one or more shapes that you desire to keep (most of, anyway). Entities you select to subtract are removed. The result should be similar to Figure 38-3.

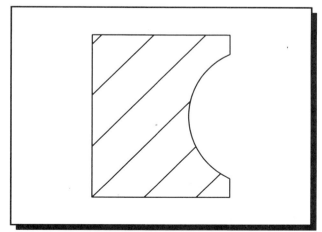

Figure 38-3

SOLINT

TYPE IN:	PULL-DOWN MENU	SCREEN MENU	TABLET MENU
SOLINT	_Model, Intersection_	_MODEL, SOLINT:_	_3,B_

Solint creates an intersection of the selected shapes. Two or more shapes can be selected.

```
Command: solint
Select objects: PICK (Pline)
Select objects: PICK (Circle)
Select objects: Enter
2 regions intersected
```

The resulting region is whatever area is common to both (or all) the selected shapes.

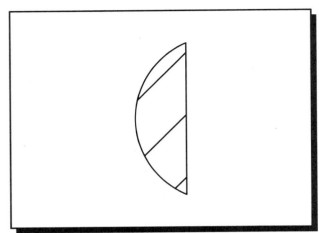

Figure 38-4

SOLIDIFY

TYPE IN:	PULL-DOWN MENU	SCREEN MENU	TABLET MENU
SOLIDIFY	_Model, Solidify_	_MODEL, SOLIDIFY:_	_6,D_

Because the Region Modeler uses AME CSG (Constructive Solid Geometry) techniques, some of those features (other than the Boolean operations discussed above) are available with the Region Modeler. The _Solidify_ command (not a Boolean operation) can be used to transform a single 2D closed entity into a region.

Solidify transforms a closed 2D entity into a region without having to perform a Boolean operation. The Boolean operations (_Solunion, Solsub, Solint_) also convert closed 2D shapes into regions, but combine multiple shapes into one region.

```
Command: solidify
Select objects: PICK
Select objects: Enter
```

Figure 38-5 shows a closed _Pline_ before and after _Solidify_ has been used to convert it to a region. The resulting region can be used in the construction of a complete surface model.

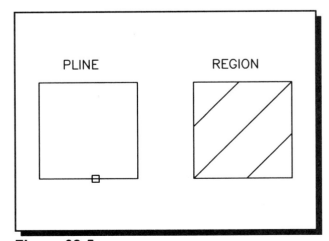

Figure 38-5

EDITING REGIONS

The following commands can be used to edit regions.

Explode   *Explode* breaks composite regions into primitive regions and breaks primitive regions back into individual entities. *Explode* does <u>not</u> reverse the effects of a Boolean operation.

Solchp   Available for use only with regions (and solids), *Solchp* (Change Primitive) allows you to change features of any primitive of a composite region (or solid).

EXPLODE

Explode is commonly used to "break down" composite entities (*Blocks*, *Hatch* patterns, *Plines*, dimensions, etc.) into the component entities. For example, a *Hatch* pattern is normally treated as one entity by AutoCAD, but can be *Exploded* into individual *Lines*. Likewise, *Explode* can be used with regions to break a region into its component parts. *Explode* does <u>not</u> reverse the effects of a Boolean operation. *Explode* affects the region <u>as it is</u> by breaking it into a subset of entities.

Consider a region constructed of a *Circle* and a closed *Pline* combined into a region with *Union*. The first time *Explode* is applied, the region appears to be unaffected, but in fact is converted to two entities--the outer shape and the interior hatch lines (Fig. 38-6).

Explode can be used a second time to break down the shapes further. A second application of *Explode* converts the outer shape to five *Lines* and one *Arc* (the outer shape) and several diagonal *Lines* (the hatch pattern lines).

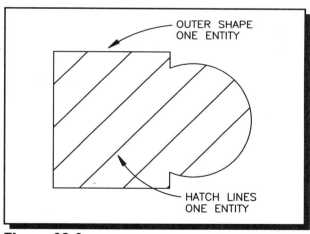

Figure 38-6

SOLCHP

TYPE IN:	PULL-DOWN MENU	SCREEN MENU	TABLET MENU
SOLCHPR	*Model, Modify > Change Primitives*	*MODEL, MODIFY, SOLCHP:*	*1,D*

Another feature of the Region Modeler which is principally an AME CSG (Constructive Solid Geometry) technique is the ability to change primitives with *Solchp*. Used with the Region Modeler, the *Solchp* command can be used to change features of any "primitive" that is part of a composite region. "Region primitives" are the original closed 2D shapes from which the regions were created. The options are listed in the command prompt:

```
Command: solchp
Color/Delete/Evaluate/Instance/Move/Next/Pick/Replace/Size
/eXit<N>:
```

The *Next* and *Pick* options highlight the primitive you intend to change (Fig. 38-7).

Next

This option cycles through (highlighting) the primitives one at a time.

Pick

This option allows you to **PICK** the desired primitive.

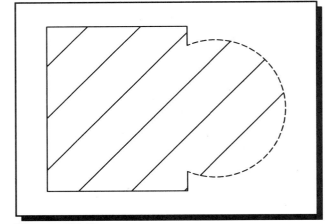

Figure 38-7

Size

The dimensions of any primitive can be changed with this option. AutoCAD prompts for the appropriate dimensions for the selected primitive if a *Circle, Ellipse*, or *Polygon* is selected (Fig. 38-8). *Solchp* must be exited before the change is displayed. If a *Pline* shape is selected, you must exit *Solchp*, change the newly created *Pline* copy, then use *Solchp* again with the *Replace* option. The *Size* option can invoke the MCS (movable coordinate system) icon.

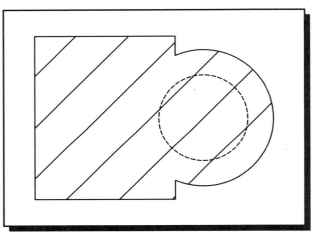

Figure 38-8

Replace

This option is used to replace the selected entity with another. Make sure that the new entity is located in the <u>desired</u> position before you use *Replace*. *Solchp* must be exited before the change is displayed.

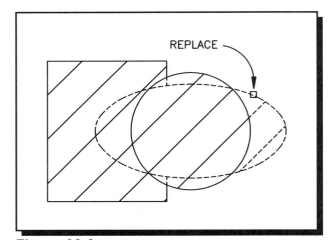

Figure 38-9

Move

The selected primitive can be moved to another position with this option. Just like the *Move* command, you are prompted for a "Base point" and a "second point of displacement." *Solchp* must be exited before the change is displayed.

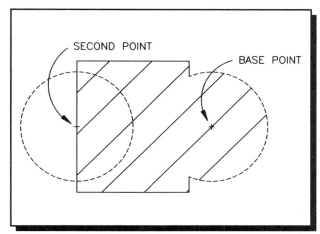

Figure 38-10

Instance

An *Instance* is a copy. This option creates a duplicate region from the selected primitive. The new copy is positioned at the <u>same</u> location as the original primitive. *Move* can be used to reposition the new primitive. After exiting *Solchp*, use *Redraw* to display the new copy.

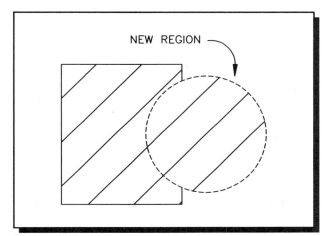

Figure 38-11

Delete

Delete removes the selected primitive from the composite region (Figure 38-12). *Delete* does not perform a *Solsub*--the remaining composite primitive is configured as if the *Delete*d primitive never existed. *Solchp* must be exited before the change is visible.

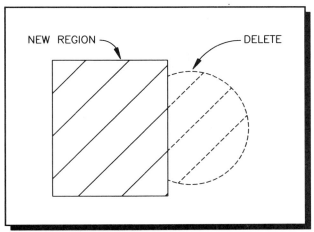

Color

The color of the primitive can be assigned independently of the composite region with this option. Only the <u>outline</u> of the primitive is

Figure 38-12

displayed in the assigned color. Depending upon the application, this feature is useful for bringing attention to primitives that possess special features or functions.

Evaluate

This option forces a reevaluation of the composite region. This is necessary when you have made many changes to the structure of the region that need to be displayed.

THE CSG TREE

The *Solchp* command functions for any region created with the Region Modeler or solid model created with AME. AutoCAD can make changes to any region or solid using *Solchp* only because a record is kept of every primitive and every Boolean and modeling operation used. This record is called the <u>CSG tree</u> (Fig. 38-13). For this reason, when a change is made to a region or solid with *Solchp*, AutoCAD reconstructs (reevaluates) the composite region or model based upon the record kept in the CSG tree. AutoCAD stores the primitive information on an automatically created layer named AME_FRZ. Altering this layer results in losing the ability to use *Solchp*.

The ability to change individual primitives of a composite region or solid is of primary importance to you, the user. This feature makes region modeling and solid modeling very flexible for practical applications. Change is an essential characteristic of the design process, permitting continual design, testing, and improvement cycles to be applied to the development of products and systems.

Surface modeling with polygon meshes (*3Dmesh, Rulesurf, Edgesurf, Revsurf,* and *Tabsurf*) and *3Dface*s is not only a relatively tedious process, but does not allow using *Solchpr* with these surfaces. Each polygon mesh surface affected by a desired change must be edited individually or deleted and reconstructed.

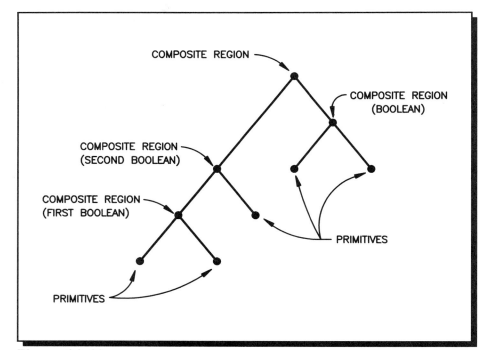

Figure 38-13

REGION MODELING APPLICATIONS

Region modeling allows the creation of regions that can be combined with polygon mesh surfaces to construct a complete surface model. Region modeling solves the problem of creating relatively simple surfaces that are not easily accomplished with the polygon mesh commands such as *3Dmesh*, *Rulesurf*, *Revsurf*, *Tabsurf*, and *Edgesurf*. Region modeling makes creation of surfaces with islands (holes) especially easy. Additionally, *Solchpr* offers editing options for regions that are nonexistent with *3Dface* and polygon meshes.

For example, consider the creation of a rectangular surface with a circular hole. This problem is addressed in the Surface Model Example 1 in Chapter 37. Using the polygon mesh commands (Figure 38-14), this relatively simple surface requires four *Lines*, two *Arcs* as a wireframe structure, then two *Rulesurfs* and two *3Dfaces* to complete the surface.

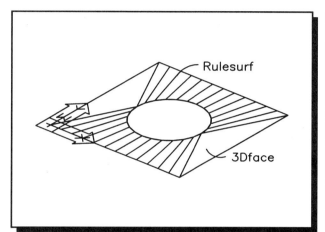

Figure 38-14

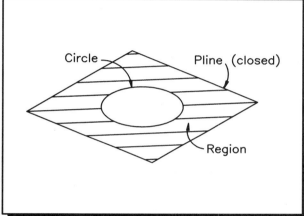

Figure 38-15

With the Region Modeler, the same surface can be created as a region with one *Circle*, one closed *Pline*, and one Boolean *Subtraction* (Figure 38-15).

Consider the surfaces shown in Figure 38-16. Imagine the amount of work involved in creating the surfaces using commands such as *3Dface*, *3Dmesh*, *Rulesurf*, *Revsurf*, *Tabsurf*, and *Edgesurf*.

Next, consider the work involved to create these shapes as regions. Surfaces such as these are very common for mechanical applications for surface models.

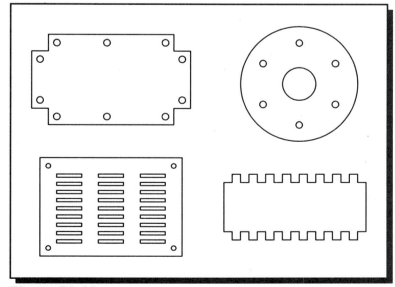

Figure 38-16

USING REGIONS WITH SURFACE MODELS

Regions can easily be combined with surfaces created by *3Dface*, *3Dmesh*, *Rulesurf*, *Revsurf*, *Tabsurf*, and *Edgesurf*. There are, however, a few features of regions that should be controlled in order to do so.

Regions must be meshed with *Solmesh* before using *Hide*, *Shade*, or *Render*. In addition, the mesh density (*Wire Density*) of the region affects the accuracy of curved surfaces and the density of the invisible mesh, and should be set <u>before</u> meshing regions. Although the *Solmesh* command causes the hatch lines on a region to disappear, the hatching parameters may optionally be set to control the display of regions if you do not intend to use *Solmesh*, *Hide*, *Shade*, or *Render*.

Using the *Solmesh* Command

Since regions are considered AME 2D solids, the features and related variables of solids apply to regions. Specifically, a region must be *meshed* before *Hide*, *Shade*, or *Render* will treat the region as an opaque surface. Using *Hide* on a region without meshing it results in a "transparent" surface as shown on the left in Figure 38-18. *Shade* and *Render* are covered in Chapter 45.

SOLMESH

TYPE IN:	PULL-DOWN MENU	SCREEN MENU	TABLET MENU
SOLMESH, *MESH*	*Model, Display>* *Mesh*	*MODEL, DISPLAY,* *SOLMESH:*	*5,F*

The *Solmesh* or *Mesh* command can be typed (assuming the Region Modeler has been loaded) or can be selected from the menus. There are no options.

```
Command: solmesh
Select objects: PICK
Select objects: Enter
1 region selected.
Command:
```

After using *Solmesh*, an invisible mesh is applied to the region and the region will be treated as an opaque surface by the *Hide*, *Shade*, or *Render* commands.

Figure 38-17 displays a region before (left) and after (right) using *Solmesh*. (The region on the right is meshed with a *Wire Density* of 1.)

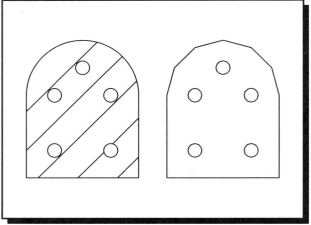

Figure 38-17

Using *Solmesh* causes AutoCAD to convert the region to a meshed surface (right), although the vertices and mesh lines are not visible. You may notice that curved surfaces take on the faceted effect (multiple straight segments) typical of meshed surfaces and solids. The number of facets is controlled by the *Wire Density* (*SOLWDENS* variable). This variable is discussed later.

Using the *Solmesh* command also causes the hatch lines on a region to disappear. For this reason it is not necessary to control the hatching parameters for a region if you eventually plan to mesh it (see *Hatch* Parameters).

You must mesh a region before using the *Hide* command if you want the regions to appear opaque. Figure 38-18 displays the two regions from the previous figure after using *Hide*. Notice that the region on the left does not *Hide* correctly since it was not meshed first. If *Hide* is used to display a non-meshed region, *Circles* (that may actually be holes) appear filled. (The *Vpoint* has been changed to help you visualize the 3D properties of the example.)

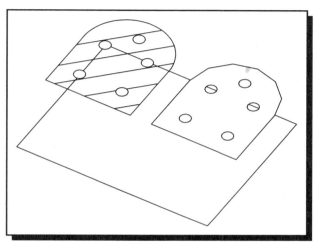

Figure 38-18

SOLWIRE

TYPE IN:	PULL-DOWN MENU	SCREEN MENU	TABLET MENU
SOLWIRE, *WIRE*	*Model, Display>* *Wireframe*	*MODEL, DISPLAY,* *SOLWIRE:*	*6,F*

The *Solwire* command reverses the effect of *Solmesh*. *Solwire* converts a meshed region into a "wireframe" region. The hatch lines generally appear on a region that has been converted back to a "wireframe," just like one that has not been meshed.

```
Command: solwire
Select objects: PICK
Select objects: Enter
1 region selected.
Command:
```

You do not have to convert a region to a "wireframe" before performing another Boolean operation. Performing a Boolean operation on a meshed region will automatically return the new composite region to an unmeshed region.

SOLWDENS

The *SOLWDENS* variable controls the wire density (mesh density) for regions and AME solids. The default setting is 1, the lowest possible value. The maximum setting of 12 creates curved surfaces (and mesh density) with the highest accuracy. *SOLWDENS* is <u>not</u> retroactive; therefore, the desired setting should be made <u>before</u> using *Solmesh*.

A high setting (10-12) for *SOLWDENS* is preferred if very accurate and smooth curves are desired. The higher the value, however, the larger the file size and the more time required for regenerations. A lower setting (2-4) is desired for small curves or for large and complex drawings with many regions or AME solids. A medium setting (5-6) is best for most applications.

Figure 38-19 displays the same region as in the previous examples with the maximum value for *SOLWDENS* (12) on the left and the minimum setting (1) on the right.

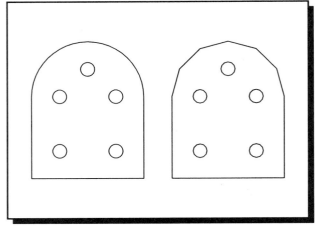

Figure 38-19

Setting *Hatch* Parameters

The AME variables that control the hatch parameters (*SOLHPAT*, *SOLHANGLE*, and *SOLHSIZE*) should be set as desired <u>before</u> creating regions. The variables control the appearance of hatch patterns for newly created regions and are not retroactive. Keep in mind that application of the *Solmesh* command for regions causes the hatch patterns to disappear.

SOLHPAT

SOLHPAT is an AME variable that controls the <u>hatch pattern</u> used when regions are drawn or when solid models are sectioned with *Solsect*. Use this to change the pattern to any desired available pattern name. If no hatch patterns are desired, enter the name **none**. Changing this variable does not affect existing regions or sections unless they are reevaluated.

SOLHANGLE

This AME variable controls the <u>angle</u> of hatch patterns drawn on regions or sectioned solid models. Enter an angle in degrees (deflection from the pattern's normal lines, as shown in the *Hatch* options dialogue box). The variable affects only newly created regions or sections.

SOLHSIZE

The size (scale) of the hatch pattern is controlled by this variable. This is similar to the *scale factor* for the *Hatch* command.

CHAPTER EXERCISES

1. Create a gear using region modeling. Begin a *New* drawing and assign the name **GEARREGN**.

A. Set *Limits* at **8** x **6** and *Zoom All*. Create a *Circle* of **1** unit *diameter* with the center at **4,3**. Create a second concentric *Circle* with a *radius* of **1.557**. Create a closed *Pline* by entering the following coordinates:

From point:	**5.571,2.9191**
to point:	**@.17<160**
to point:	**@.0228<94**
to point:	**@.0228<86**
to point:	**@.17<20**
to point:	**c**

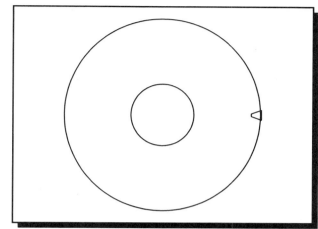
Figure 38-20

The gear at this stage should look like that in Figure 38-20.

B. *Array* the closed *Pline* in a *Polar* array about the center of the gear. There are **40** items that are rotated as they are copied. This action should create the teeth of the gear.

C. Finally, *Subtract* the small *Circle* and all of the *Plines* (teeth) from the large *Circle*. Use the *Fence* option to select the *Plines*. The resulting gear should resemble Figure 38-21. *Save* the drawing.

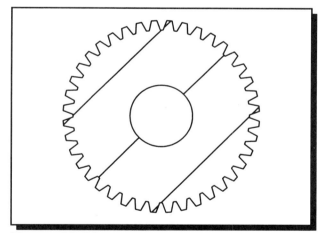
Figure 38-21

D. Consider the steps involved if you were to create the gear (as an alternative) by using *Trim* to remove 40 small sections of the large *Circle* and all unwanted parts of the teeth. Region modeling is clearly easier in this case.

2. Create the Wrench using region modeling. Begin a *New* drawing or use a *Prototype* for a metric A4 size sheet. Assign the name **REGWRNCH**.

A. Set *Limits* to **396,280** to prepare the drawing for plotting at 3:4 (the drawing scale factor is 33.87). Set the *GRID* to **10**. Change the *SOLHSIZE* to **34**.

B.   Draw a *Circle* and an *Ellipse* as shown on the left in Figure 38-22. The center of each shape is located at **70,150**. *Trim* half of each shape as shown (highlighted). Use *Pedit* to convert and *Join* the shapes to a closed *Pline*. Use *Solidify* to convert the shape into a region as shown on the right of Figure 38-22.

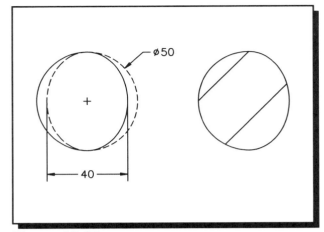

Figure 38-22

C.   Next, create a *Circle* with the center at **120,150** and a diameter as shown in Figure 38-23. Then draw a closed *Pline* in a rectangular shape as shown. The height of the rectangle must be drawn as specified. The width of the rectangle should be drawn <u>approximately</u> as shown on the left. Finally, use *Intersection* to create the region as shown on the right side of the figure.

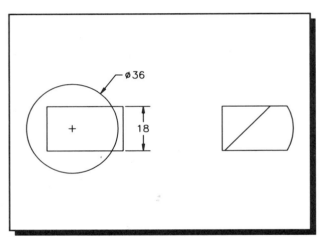

Figure 38-23

D.   *Move* the rectangular-shaped region **68** units to the left to overlap the first region as shown in Figure 38-24. Use *Subtraction* to create the composite region on the right representing the head of the wrench.

E.   Complete the construction of the wrench in the manner used in the previous steps. Refer to Chapter 15 Exercises, Figure 15-27, for dimensions of the Wrench. Complete the wrench as one region. *Save* the drawing as **REGWRNCH**.

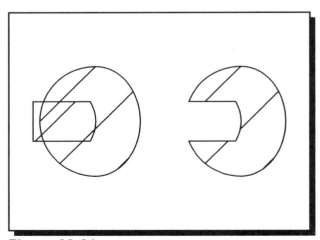

Figure 38-24

3. Complete the pulley drawing (**PUL-SURF**) that you began in Chapter 37 Exercises. The surface model should be lacking only a few circular faces (the vertical faces containing the holes and keyway, appearing in edge view in Figure 37-90). Set an appropriate **SOLWDENS** and create the surfaces as regions. Display the completed surface model from a pictorial **Vpoint**. Align a **UCS** with the **View** and create a border and title block. **Save** the drawing as **PUL-REG**. **Mesh** the regions and **Plot** the model with the **Hide Lines** option.

4. **Open** the **WFEX4** drawing that you created in Chapter 35 Exercises. **Saveas REGNEX4**. For this exercise, create a surface model using a combination of regions and polygon meshes. Use the existing wireframe geometry. Convert the *Lines*, *Arcs* and *Circles* representing <u>planar</u> surfaces to closed **Plines**, then to regions. Use polygon meshes for the curved surfaces. **Save** the drawing. Generate a pictorial **Vpoint** and align a **UCS** with the **View**. **Plot** the drawing with hidden lines removed.

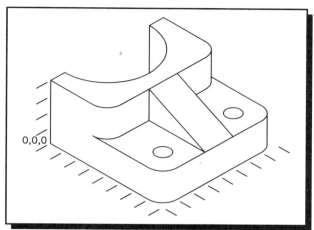
0,0,0

Figure 38-25

5. Create a surface model of the Support Bracket shown in Figure 38-26. Assign the name **SUPBRK-R**. Use a combination of regions and polygon meshes to construct the model. Create *UCS*'s as necessary.

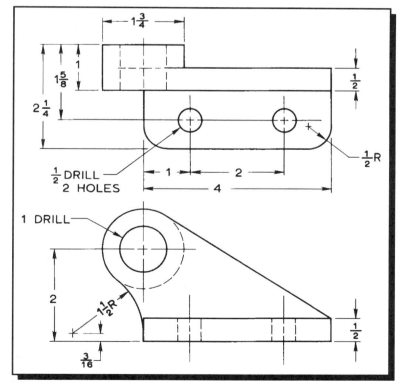

Figure 38-26

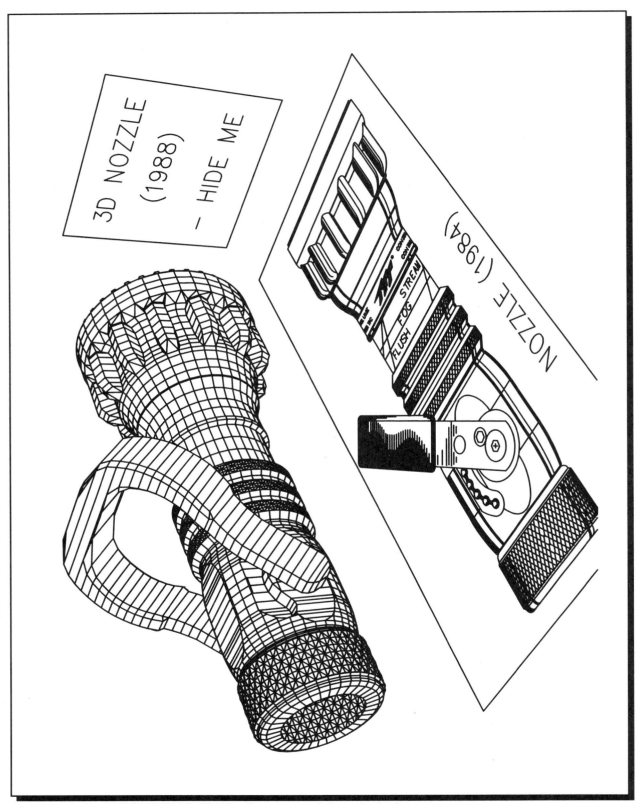

Figure 38-27 REGNDEMO.DWG Courtesy of Autodesk, Inc.

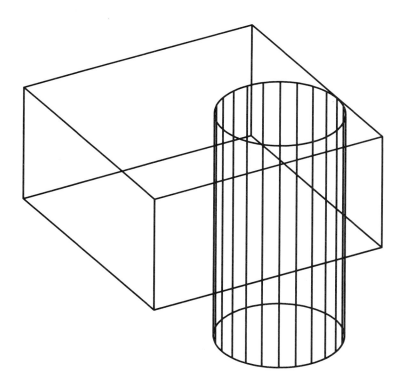

CHAPTER 39

Solid Modeling Basics

CHAPTER OBJECTIVES

After completing this chapter you should:

1.   know the three basic steps for creating most AME solid models--creating primitives, moving primitives, and using Boolean operations to construct composite solids;

2.   understand that AME is a hybrid modeler that uses Constructive Solid Geometry techniques and that keeps a Boundary Representation file;

3.   know the solid primitives that are used for construction of composite solid models;

4.   know the Boolean operations that are used to create composite solids;

5.   understand that a chronological record of primitives and Boolean operations is saved in the CSG tree;

6.   know the options for creating temporary UCS's with the *Baseplane* and *Construction Plane* options of any AME primitive creation command.

7.   understand the purpose of the *Solmesh* and the *Solwire* commands.

BASICS

The techniques used with AME for construction of many solid models follow three general steps:

1.   Construct simple 3D <u>primitive</u> solids, or create 2D shapes and convert them to 3D solids by extruding or revolving.

2.   Create the primitives <u>in location</u> relative to the associated primitives, or <u>move</u> the primitives into the desired location relative to the associated primitives.

3.   Use <u>Boolean operations</u> (such as *Union*, *Subtraction*, or *Intersection*) to combine the primitives to form a <u>composite solid</u>.

The following chapters deal with each of those steps: Solid Model Primitives (Chapter 40), Moving Solids (Chapter 41), and Boolean Operations (Chapter 42).   The extension of AutoCAD that provides the solid modeling capability is called the Advanced Modeling Extension.

The Advanced Modeling Extension (AME) is an optional add-on module for AutoCAD Release 12.   With AME you can create complex 3D parts and assemblies using Boolean operations to combine simple shapes, called *primitives*.   This modeling technique is often referred to as CSG or Constructive Solid Geometry modeling.   AME also provides a means for editing, analyzing, and sectioning the geometry of the models (Chapter 43).

A solid model is an informationally complete representation of the shape of a physical object.   Solid modeling differs from wireframe or surface modeling in two fundamental ways: (1) the information is more complete in a solid model and (2) the method of construction of the model itself is relatively easy to construct and edit.

The AME solid modeler is called a <u>hybrid modeler</u> because it maintains two principal types of data describing a model--geometric spatial data and topology data.   The geometric spatial data is a record of what primitive shapes and Boolean operators were used to create the solid. This geometric spatial record is called the <u>CSG tree</u> and provides the essential data required for editing.   The topological data, or the <u>boundary representation</u> (B-rep), is responsible for the display capabilities necessary for meshing, hiding, and rendering.

BOUNDARY REPRESENTATION

The boundary-representation activity in AME is almost transparent to the user.   A Boundary Representation (or B-Rep) model represents the solid model in terms of its spatial boundary, usually the enclosed surface with some method of defining on which side of the surface the solid lies.   The solid is represented by combinations of faces, bound by edges, which are bound by vertices.   A B-Rep model stores the mathematical data of the surface geometry on which the faces lie, the curve geometry on which the edges lie, and the point coordinates of the vertices.   AutoCAD keeps a B-rep file with the model even though CSG techniques are used to create the solids.

CONSTRUCTIVE SOLID GEOMETRY

AME uses Constructive Solid Geometry (or CSG) techniques for construction of solid models. CSG is characterized by primitives combined by Boolean operations to form composite solids. The CSG tree keeps a record of the primitives and Boolean operations that are used to build the models. The CSG technique is a relatively fast and natural way of modeling that imitates the manufacturing process. One common problem with CSG modelers is limited support of surfaces. Therefore, AME also stores a boundary file or a B-file. Because the B-file is stored, it is necessary for the modeler to re-compute boundaries whenever the solids get loaded. When the composite model is complete, the *Solmesh* command updates the B-file and enables display capabilities such as *Hide, Shade*, and *Render.*

AutoCAD AME (Advanced Modeling Extension) is considered a hybrid modeler in that it uses CSG techniques of modeling and stores boundary information as well.

Primitives

Solid primitives are the basic building blocks that make up more complex solid models. They are the simplest elements of the CSG tree. The AME primitives are:

SOLBOX	Creates a solid box or cube
SOLCONE	Creates a solid cone with a circular or elliptical base
SOLCYL	Creates a solid cylinder with a circular or elliptical base
SOLEXT	Creates a solid by extruding (adding a Z dimension to) a closed 2D object (*Pline, Circle*, Region)
SOLIDIFY	Creates a solid from closed entities created with *Thickness*
SOLREV	Creates a solid by revolving a shape about an axis
SOLSHPERE	Creates a solid sphere
SOLTORUS	Creates a solid torus
SOLWEDGE	Creates a solid wedge

Primitives can be created by entering the command name or by selecting from the menus. Accessing the *Primitives...* option of the *Model* pull-down yields the icon menu shown in Figure 39-1.

3D Primitives...

TYPE IN:	PULL-DOWN MENU	SCREEN MENU	TABLET MENU
DDSOLPRIM	*Model, Primitives...*	*MODEL, PRIMS.*	*4,B and 6,C*

The solid modeling primitives are available through the *AME Primitives* dialogue box icon menu (Fig. 39-1). The desired primitive can be selected, which activates the associated command. For example, selecting the "box" icon invokes the *Solbox* command.

Selecting one of the primitives icons from the *AME Primitives* dialogue box causes the associated command to appear at the command line. Each primitive command prompts for dimensions to define the primitive you want to create.

You can locate the primitive at the origin, specify or PICK coordinates, or use the *Baseplane* or *Construction Plane* options to set up a temporary UCS just for the creation of the primitive. Depressing the *Baseplane* radio button in the dialogue box causes the selected *Baseplane* mode to appear at the command line before you specify the primitive's dimensions (see Baseplanes and Construction Planes, this chapter).

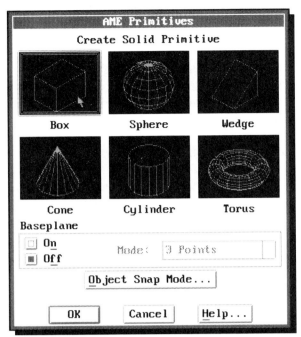

Figure 39-1

Boolean Operations

Primitives are combined to create complex solids by using Boolean operations. The AME Boolean operators are listed below. The first four operators are also available for use with the Region Modeler. The Boolean commands are explained in detail in Chapter 42; however, an illustration for each of the commands below is given on the following pages.

SOLUNION   Unions (joins) selected solids (Figure 39-3).

SOLSUB   Subtracts one set of solids from another (Figure 39-4).

SOLINT   Creates a solid of intersection (common volume) from the selected solids (Figure 39-5).

SOLSEP   Undoes the last Boolean operation. The CSG tree can be broken down several levels by successive use of the command (Figure 39-6).

SOLCHAM   Chamfers the edge of a solid.

SOLFILL   Fillets the edges of a solid. To obtain the desired results it may be necessary to perform all the fillets at once or perform a sequence of fillet commands.

Primitives are created at the desired location, or are moved into the desired location, before using a Boolean operator. In other words, two or more primitives can occupy the same space (or part of the same space), yet are separate solids. When a Boolean operation is performed, the solids are combined (except in the case of *Solsep*) or altered in some way to create one solid. AME takes care of deleting or adding the necessary geometry and displays the new composite solid complete with the correct configuration and lines of intersection.

Consider the two solids shown in Figure 39-2. When solids are created, they can occupy the same physical space. A Boolean operation is used to combine the solids into a composite solid and interprets the resulting utilization of space.

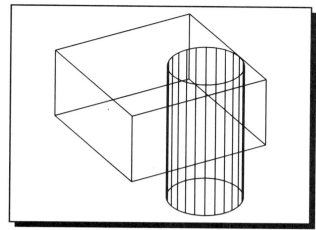

Figure 39-2

SOLUNION (Union)

Solunion creates a union of the two solids into one composite solid (Fig. 39-3). The lines of intersection between the two shapes are calculated and displayed by AME. (The solid is displayed in the figure after performing a *Hide*.)

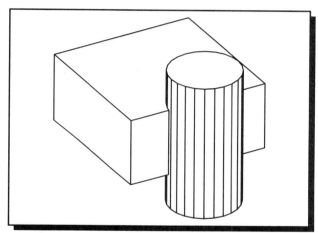

Figure 39-3

SOLSUB (Subtraction)

Solsub subtracts one or more solids from another solid. AME calculates the resulting composite solid. The term "difference" is sometimes used rather than "subtract." In Figure 39-4 the cylinder has been subtracted from the box.

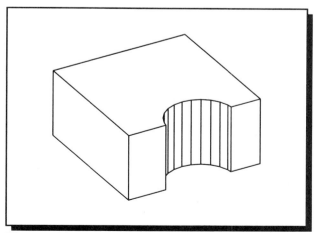

Figure 39-4

SOLINT (Intersection)

> *Solint* calculates the intersection between two or more solids. When *Solint* is used with Regions (2D surfaces), it determines the shared <u>area</u>. Used with solids, as in Figure 39-5, *Solint* creates a solid comprised of the shared <u>volume</u> of the cylinder and the box. In other words, the result of *Solint* is a solid that has only the volume which is part of both (or all) of the selected solids.

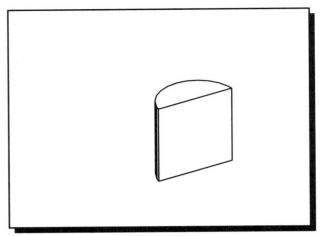

Figure 39-5

SOLSEP (Separation)

> *Solsep* breaks down the <u>last</u> Boolean operation. Solsep is similar to an *Undo* for Boolean operators. If *Solsep* were applied to any of the composite solids in Figures 39-3 (after a *Solunion*), 39-4 (after a *Solsub*), or 39-5 (after a *Solint*), the resulting solids would be those shapes shown in Figure 39-6. The resulting shapes are identical to the original shapes before the last Boolean.

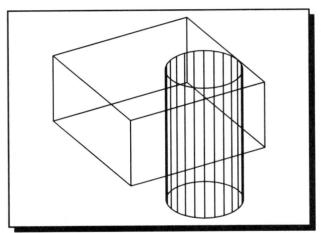

Figure 39-6

CSG Tree

AutoCAD's AME solid modeler keeps a record of each primitive and each Boolean operation used to construct a composite solid model. This chronological sequence of construction is stored in the <u>CSG Tree</u>.

The existence of the CSG Tree enables a powerful and versatile editing capability, *Solchp* (Solid Change Primitive), which allows you to change an individual primitive and forces AME to reconstruct (reevaluate) the composite solid according to the original sequence of operations. *Solchp* and other methods of editing solids are discussed in Chapter 43, Solids Editing, Analyzing, and Sectioning.

AutoCAD automatically creates a frozen layer (named AME_FRZ) in association with the CSG Tree which contains the primitives data. This layer is intended for use only by AME such that altering the layer results in your inability to edit the composite solid.

Figure 39-7 illustrates a schematic representation of the CSG Tree including the primitives and the operations used to construct a composite solid model.

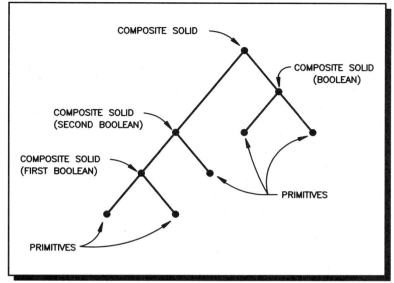

Figure 39-7

BASEPLANES AND CONSTRUCTION PLANES

When you are creating 3D models, it is usually necessary to create UCS's to simplify the construction of geometry that may not have the same orientation as the WCS. With AME you can create <u>temporary</u> UCS's <u>within</u> an AME primitive creation command. These temporary UCS's cannot be named or saved. You can use either the *Baseplane* or the *CP* option to do this. The fundamental difference between the *Baseplane* option and the *CP* option is that *Baseplane* operates for the <u>duration of the command</u> while *CP* is only active for input of <u>one point</u>. Generally, the *Baseplane* option is preferred for creation of geometry since it remains active throughout the command.

Baseplane

AME primitive creation commands offer a *Baseplane* option. Invoking this option gives you the opportunity to set up a temporary unnamed UCS for the duration of the command. The Coordinate System Icon and crosshair tracking align with the *Baseplane* orientation to enhance your visualization and aid construction. The new *Baseplane* is only active for the <u>duration of the command</u> and automatically reverts back to the previous coordinate system after completing the command.

CP (Construction Planes)

As an alternative, any time you are prompted for the location of a <u>point</u>, you can transparently enter the Construction Plane (*'CP*) option that lets you temporarily set a construction plane (change the location and orientation of the XY plane). The UCS icon is reoriented and displayed at the CP origin and the crosshairs track in its XY plane. Once a point is located, the construction plane and icon automatically return to the location and orientation of the UCS XY plane. This feature lets you locate points on different planes within any AME command. The *CP* option is <u>not</u> listed with the regular options of a command. It is understood as a general AME option (like the AutoCAD XYZ point filters). To create a temporary construction plane, enter *cp* or *'cp* whenever you are prompted for a point.

Baseplane and *CP* Orientations

Possible methods for orienting a plane for construction (*Baseplane* or *CP*) are identical for both the *Baseplane* and *CP* options and are similar to those for creating a new UCS.

```
Entity/Last/Zaxis/View/XY/YZ/ZX/<3points>:
```

In the following discussion, the term "construction plane" is used to describe that for either the *Baseplane* or *CP* option.

Entity

This option aligns the construction plane with a *Circle*, *Arc*, or 2D *Pline* segment.

```
Pick a circle, arc or 2D-Pline segment: PICK
```

The construction plane is aligned with the plane of the selected entity. If a *Circle* or *Arc* is selected, the construction plane is located in the plane of the *Circle* or *Arc* with the origin at the center. If you select a 2D *Pline*, the construction plane is aligned with the plane of the *Pline* with the origin of the construction plane located at the endpoint of the segment closest to the PICK point. In both cases the X and Y axes of the construction plane are oriented according to the "arbitrary axis algorithm," which generally means that the X axis is in the direction of the X axis when the entity was created.

Last

This option aligns the construction plane to the plane last used by any *CP* or *Baseplane* option. If there is no previous plane, a message to that effect is displayed.

Zaxis

With this option, you define the construction plane by locating its origin point and a point on the *Z* axis (perpendicular to the XY plane). The positive *Z* axis is from the first point through the second point. The X and Y axes of the construction plane are oriented according to the arbitrary axis algorithm (generally, the X axis is in the direction of the X axis of the previous coordinate system).

```
Point on plane: PICK
Point on Z-axis (normal) of the plane: PICK
```

View

This option aligns the construction plane perpendicular to the line of sight (parallel with the screen). The origin of the construction plane is located by selecting a point. The positive X axis of the construction plane is horizontal and to the right with respect to the screen.

```
            Point on view plane <0,0,0>: PICK
```

XY

This option is similar to the *Origin* option of the AutoCAD *UCS* command. It aligns the construction plane with the *XY* plane of the current UCS, but a new origin point can be selected.

```
            Point on XY plane <0,0,0>: PICK
```

YZ

The *YZ* option aligns the new <u>XY</u> construction plane with the <u>YZ</u> plane of the current UCS. The X, Y, and Z axes of the construction are parallel to Y, Z, and X of the current coordinate system, respectively. The origin of the construction plane is located by PICKing a point.

```
            Point on YZ plane <0,0,0>: PICK
```

ZX

This option is similar to the previous two, but aligns the new <u>XY</u> construction plane with the <u>ZX</u> plane of the current UCS. This option is similar to rotating the UCS 90 degrees about the X axis except the X and Y axis are reversed. The origin of the construction plane is located by a point.

```
            Point on ZX plane <0,0,0>: PICK
```

3points

This, the default, option allows you to locate three points that define the construction plane. The first point locates the origin of the construction plane, the second point determines the positive direction of the X axis, and the third point determines the positive Y axis portion of the plane.

```
            1st point on plane: PICK
            2nd point on plane: PICK
            3rd point on plane: PICK
```

NOTE: If you use a pointing device to PICK points, use *OSNAP* when possible to PICK points in 3D space. If you do not use *OSNAP*, the selected points are located on the current XY construction plane, so the true distance may not be obvious. It is recommended that you use *OSNAP* or enter values.

CP Shortcuts

You can bypass the prompt for *CP* options and go directly to the option you want by entering the option's minimum abbreviation at the same time you enter *'CP*. For example, you can go directly to the *CP Last* option by entering *'CPL* at any point input prompt. The shortcuts for the *CP* option are listed on the following page. There are no shortcuts for the *Baseplane* option.

CP Shortcut	*CP* Option
CPE	*Entity*
CPL	*Last*
CPZ	*Zaxis*
CPV	*View*
CPXY	*XY*
CPYZ	*YZ*
CPZX	*ZX*
CP3	*3point*

DISPLAYING SOLIDS

AME solid models are displayed in wireframe representation by default. Wireframe representation requires less computation time and less complex file structure, so your drawing time can be spent more efficiently. AME solid models must be meshed (using the *Solmesh* command) before they can be displayed with hidden lines removed (using the *Hide* command) or as a shaded image (using the *Shade* command). Using *Hide* or *Shade* can increase your visualization of solid models because the model is displayed with "opaque" surfaces instead of being "transparent" as with the wireframe representation. Meshed solids can be displayed again as wireframe solids by using the *Solwire* command. *Solmesh* and *Solwire* perform opposite functions. The *SOLDISPLAY* variable controls the setting for the initial representation of AME solids with *wireframe* as the default.

SOLMESH

TYPE IN:	PULL-DOWN MENU	SCREEN MENU	TABLET MENU
SOLMESH, *MESH*	*Model, Display>* *Mesh*	*MODEL, DISPLAY,* *SOLMESH:*	*5,F*

Solmesh displays solids as meshed entities. *Solmesh* converts a solid from a wireframe to a meshed solid. A meshed solid appears as a transparent object similar to a wireframe solid, but only a meshed solid can be displayed as being "solid" (opaque) by the *Hide* or *Shade* commands. Curved surfaces of a meshed solid appear as faceted planar surfaces rather than a smooth curve as with wireframe solids. The number of facets, or tessellation lines, is determined by the *wire density* controlled by the *SOLWDENS* variable setting.

Figure 39-9 displays an AME solid in meshed representation. Notice the faceted appearance of the curved surfaces. Using *Solmesh* causes normally curved surfaces to become polygons.

When *Solmesh* is used, AutoCAD actually creates the meshed solid and displays it, while the wireframe display is saved but frozen on the AME_FRZ layer. Using *Solwire* displays the wireframe representation and places the meshed display on layer AME_FRZ. The *Solpurge* command can be used to purge the drawing of the mesh information to conserve file space (See Chapter 43).

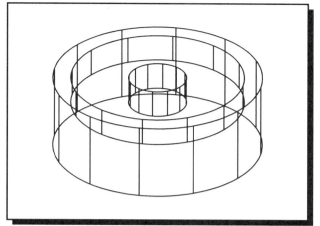

Figure 39-8 Wireframe Representation

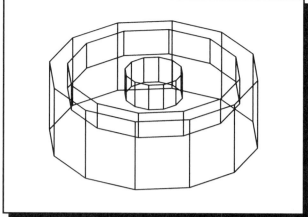

Figure 39-9 Meshed Representation

SOLWIRE

TYPE IN:	PULL-DOWN MENU	SCREEN MENU	TABLET MENU
SOLWIRE, WIRE	*Model, Display>* *Wireframe*	*MODEL, DISPLAY,* *SOLWIRE:*	*6,F*

Solwire performs the opposite function of *Solmesh*. *Solwire* converts a meshed solid into a wireframe representation (Fig. 39-8). Since wireframe representation is the default initial form of an AME solid, *Solwire* is used if you want to change a meshed solid back to wireframe representation. The faceted (planar) surfaces of a meshed solid representing curves are converted to smooth curved surfaces by the *Solwire* command. This can be useful if you want to use some *OSNAP* options that function only for radiused shapes, such as *QUAdrant*, *TANgent* or *CENter*. These *OSNAP* options do not operate for meshed solids since they do not contain radiused shapes.

CHAPTER EXERCISES

1.   What are the typical three steps for creating composite solids?

2.   Why is AME called a hybrid modeler?

3.   What is the CSG tree and why is it important (helpful) to the user?

4.   What is layer AME_FRZ and what should you do with this layer?

5.   Consider the two solids in Figure 39-10. They are two extruded hexagons that are overlapping (occupying the same 3D space).

A. Sketch the resulting composite solid if you performed a *Solunion* on the two solids.

B. Sketch the resulting composite solid if you performed a *Solint* on the two solids.

C. Sketch the resulting composite solid if you performed a *Solsub* on the two solids.

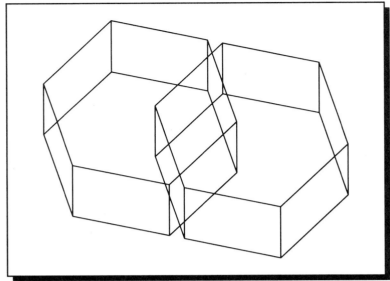

Figure 39-10

6. Examine the object shown in Figure 39-11. Assume that the *Baseplane* or *CP* methods are used to set up temporary construction planes as shown. Also assume that the process used to construct the model is not known (which could affect possibilities for the *Entity* option).

A. What is the only method that could be used to set up the construction plane indicated by coordinate system icon A?

B. List two options that could be used to set up the construction plane indicated by coordinate system icon B.

C. List three options that could be used to set up the construction plane indicated by coordinate system icon C.

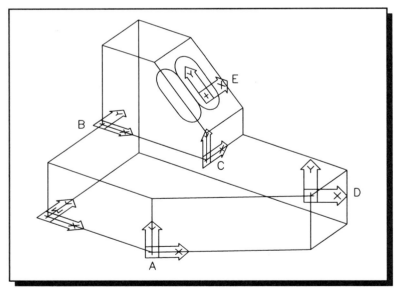

Figure 39-11

D. What is the only option that can be used to set up a temporary construction plane indicated by coordinate system icon D?

E. There are possibly two methods that could be used to set up the temporary construction plane indicated by coordinate system icon E depending upon the type of model (wireframe, surface, or solid) and the construction process used. What are the two likely methods?

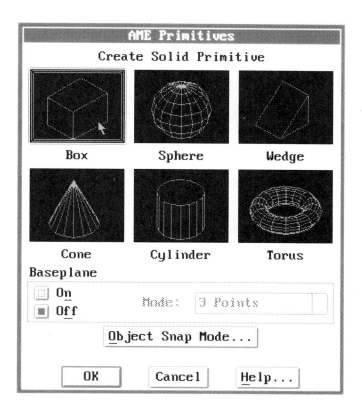

CHAPTER 40

Solid Model Primitives

CHAPTER OBJECTIVES

After completing this chapter you should:

1.　be able to create solid model primitives using the following commands:　*Solbox*, *Solwedge*, *Solcone*, *Solcyl*, *Soltorus*, and *Solsphere*.

2.　be able to create swept solids from existing 2D shapes using the *Solext* and *Solrev* commands;

3.　be able to convert a 2D entity with *Thickness* into a solid model using *Solidify*;

4.　be able to use the *CP* and *Baseplane* options within the primitive creation commands.

BASICS

This chapter explains the commands that allow you to create primitives used for construction of composite solid models. The commands allow you to specify the dimensions and the orientation of the solids. Once primitives are created, they can be moved to a specific position or orientation and then combined with other solids using Boolean operations to form composite solids. Commands for moving solids and performing Boolean operations are discussed in the next two chapters.

As you read through these pages, it will be helpful to follow along on your computer using each command discussed. When creating solid models, you can enhance your visualization to set a *Vpoint* other than the default plan view. If you need help with this, refer to Chapter 34, 3D Viewing and Display.

Solid models in the figures in this chapter are shown with a *SOLWDENS* of **6**. *SOLWDENS* is a solid modeling variable that controls the mesh density for newly created solids. The mesh density is only apparent by examining the number of contour lines on curved surfaces. The default setting for *SOLWDENS* is **1**. (See AME Variables and Sample Programs, Chapter 44.)

Many of the solid primitives creation commands can be invoked using the *AME Primitives* dialogue/icon box (see chapter title page or Figure 39-1) by typing **DDSOLPRM** or selecting ***Primitives...*** from the *Model* pull-down menu.

SOLID PRIMITIVES CREATION COMMANDS

SOLBOX

TYPE IN:	PULL-DOWN MENU	SCREEN MENU	TABLET MENU
SOLBOX or BOX or DDSOLPRM	*Model, Primitives..., Box*	*MODEL, PRIMS., SOLBOX*	*4,B*

Solbox creates a solid box primitive to your dimensional specifications. You can specify dimensions of the box by PICKing or by entering values. The box can be defined by (1) giving the corners of the base, then height, (2) by locating the center and height, or (3) by giving each of the three dimensions.

Options are provided for the location and orientation of the box. Normally the box is oriented parallel to the current XY plane, or the *Baseplane* option allows you to specify another orientation for the base of the box.

```
Command: solbox
Baseplane/Center/<Corner of box><0,0,0>: PICK or (coordinates) or
(letter) or Enter
```

Options for the *Solbox* command are listed as follows.

Corner of box

Pressing **Enter** begins the corner of a box at 0,0,0 of the current coordinate system. In this case, the box can be moved into its desired location later. As an alternative, a coordinate position can be entered or **PICK**ed as the starting corner of the box. AutoCAD responds with:

```
Cube/Length/<Other corner>:
```

The other corner can be PICKed or specified by coordinates. The *Cube* option requires only one dimension to define the cube. The *Length* option prompts you for the three dimensions of the box in the order of X, Y, and Z. (NOTE: The *Length* option prompts for the box *Length, Width*, and *Height*. AutoCAD really means *Width, Depth*, and *Height*, since the term "Length" actually refers to <u>any</u> generic measurement.)

Figure 40-1 shows a box created at 0,0,0 with width, depth, and height dimensions of 5, 4, and 3.

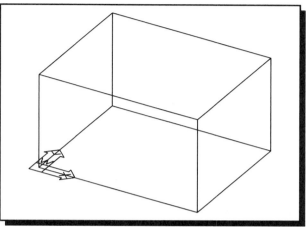

Figure 40-1

Baseplane

This option allows you specify the origin as well as the orientation of the box. The following set of options appears:

```
Baseplane by Entity/Last/Zaxis/View/XY/YZ/ZX/<3points>:
```

These options are similar to the *'CP* option (see Baseplanes and Construction Planes, Chapter 39). The *Baseplane* option is used most often for creating solid geometry because you can specify a temporary construction plan that remains in effect <u>throughout</u> the command. The *'CP* option retains the construction plane orientation only for <u>one</u> point specification. In this case, *'CP* is good only for the *Corner of box* specification, while the *Baseplane* option retains the construction plane for all dimensional specifications of the box.

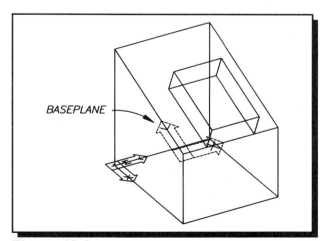

Figure 40-2

Figure 40-2 shows a box created using the *3points* option of *Baseplane* to define its orientation.

Center

With this option, you first locate the center of the box, then specify the three dimensions of the box. AutoCAD prompts:

```
Center of box: PICK or
(coordinates)
```

Figure 40-3 illustrates a box created with the *Center* option using *OSNAP* to snap to the *CENter* of the top of the cylinder. Note that the center of the box is the <u>volumetric</u> center, not the center of the base.

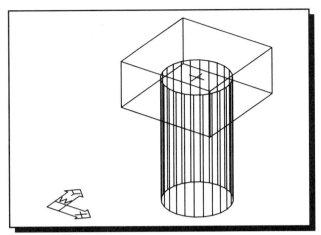

Figure 40-3

SOLCONE

TYPE IN:	PULL-DOWN MENU	SCREEN MENU	TABLET MENU
SOLCONE or CONE or DDSOLPRM	*Model, Primitives..., Cone*	*MODEL, PRIMS., SOLCONE:*	*5,B*

Solcone creates a right circular or elliptical solid cone ("right" means the axis forms a right angle with the base). You can specify the center location, radius (or diameter), and height. By default, the orientation of the cylinder is determined by the current UCS so that the base lies on the XY plane and height is perpendicular (in a Z direction). The *Baseplane* option allows you to realign the orientation of the cone within the *Solcone* command without creating another UCS. Alternately, the orientation can be defined by using the *Apex* option.

Using the defaults (center at 0,0,0, PICK a radius, enter a value for height), the cone is generated in the orientation shown in Figure 40-4. The cone here may differ in detail (number of contour lines) depending on the current setting of the *SOLWDENS* variable. The default prompts are shown on the next page.

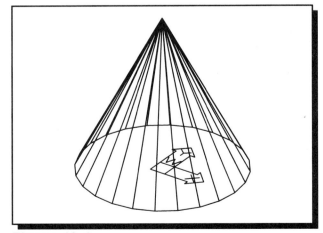

Figure 40-4

```
Command:  solcone
Baseplane/Elliptical/<Center point><0,0,0>:  PICK or (coordinates)
Diameter/<Radius>:  PICK or (coordinates)
Apex/<Height>:  PICK or (value)
Command:
```

Invoking the **Baseplane** option displays the following prompt:

```
Baseplane by Entity/Last/Zaxis/View/XY/YZ/ZX/<3points>:
```

These options allow you to specify an orientation for the cone other than with the base parallel to the current XY plane and height in the current Z direction. The baseplane options are explained in detail in Chapter 39. Figure 40-5 shows a *Solcone* created using the *YZ* option of *Baseplane*.

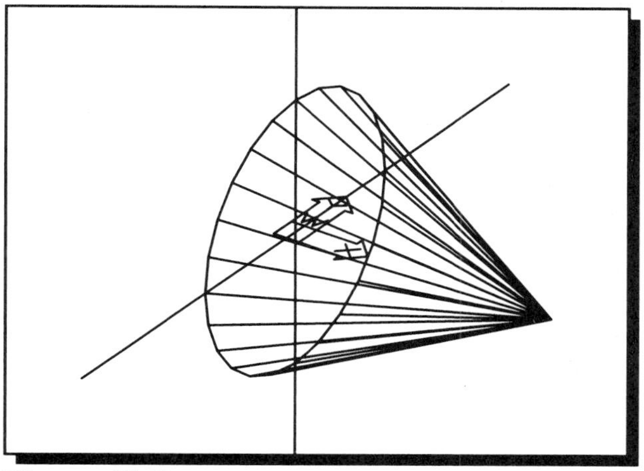

Invoking the **Apex** option (after *Center point* of the base and *Radius* or *Diameter* have been specified) displays the following prompt:

```
Apex:  PICK or (coordinates)
```

Locating a point for the apex defines the height and orientation of the cone. The axis

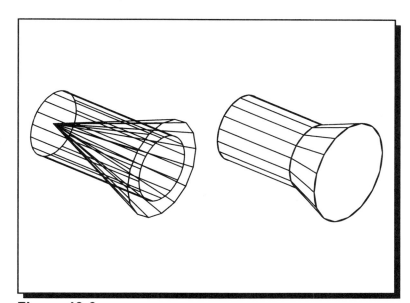

Figure 40-5

of the cone is aligned with the line between the specified center point and the *Apex* point, and the height is equal to the distance between the two points.

The solid model in Figure 40-6 was created by a *Solcone* and a *Solcyl*. The cylinder was created first, then the cone was created using the *Apex* option of *Solcone*. The orientation of the *Solcone* was generated by PICKing the *CENter* of one end of the cylinder for the *Center point* of the base of the cone and the *CENter* of the cylinder's other end for the *Apex*. *Solunion* created the composite model.

Figure 40-6

SOLCYL

TYPE IN:	PULL-DOWN MENU	SCREEN MENU	TABLET MENU
SOLCYL or CYL or DDSOLPRM	*Model, Primitives..., Cylinder*	*MODEL, PRIMS., SOLCYL:*	*6,B*

Solcyl creates a cylinder with an elliptical or circular base with a center location, diameter and height you specify. Default orientation of the cylinder is determined by the current UCS, such that the circular plane is coplanar with XY plane and height is in a Z direction. However, the orientation can be defined otherwise by either the *Baseplane* option or the *Center of other end* option. The default options are as follows:

```
Command: solcyl
Baseplane/Elliptical/<Center point><0,0,0>: PICK or (coordinates)
or Enter
Diameter/<Radius>: PICK or (coordinates)
Center other end/<Height>: Pick or (coordinates)
```

The default options create a cylinder in the orientation shown in Figure 40-7.

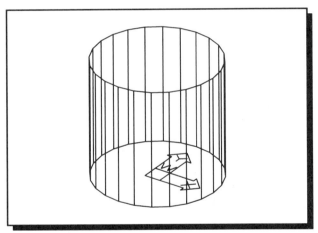

Figure 40-7

The orientation of the cylinder can be controlled "on the fly" (during the command) by using the **Baseplane** option. Figure 40-8 displays two drill holes created by using the *Baseplane 3point* option within *Solcyl* and entering a negative value for *Height*.

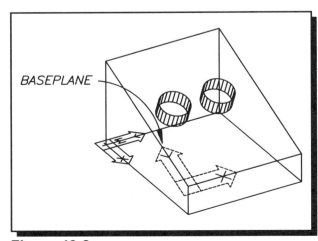

Figure 40-8

The **Center other end** option of *Solcyl* is similar to *Solcone Apex* option in that the height and orientation are defined by the *Center point* and the *Center other end*. In Figure 40-9, a hole is created in the *Solbox* by using *Center other end* option and *OSNAP*ing to the diagonal lines' *MIDpoints*.

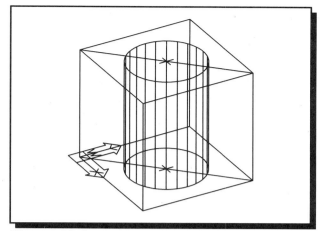

Figure 40-9

SOLWEDGE

TYPE IN:	PULL-DOWN MENU	SCREEN MENU	TABLET MENU
SOLWEDGE or WEDGE or DDSOLPRM	**Model, Primitives..., Wedge**	**MODEL, PRIMS., SOLWEGE:**	**6,C**

Solwedge creates a wedge solid primitive. By default, the base of the wedge is parallel to the current UCS and the <u>slope of the wedge is parallel to the X axis</u>.

```
Command: solwedge
Baseplane/<Corner of wedge><0,0,0>: PICK or (coordinates)
Length/<other corner>: PICK or (coordinates)
Height:
```

Accepting all the defaults, a *Solwedge* can be created as shown in Figure 40-10 with the slope along the X axis.

Invoking the **Length** option prompts you for the *Length, Width*, and *Depth*. AutoCAD really means Width (X dimension), Depth (Y dimension), and Height (Z dimension).

Figure 40-10

With the ***Baseplane*** option of *Solwedge*, the orientation of the wedge can be controlled without having to create a UCS beforehand. Figure 40-11 displays a *Solwedge* aligned with the existing block using the *Baseplane 3point* option and *OSNAP*s.

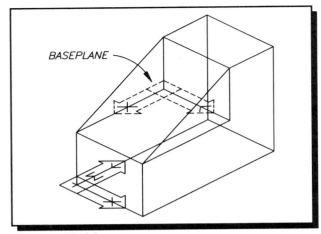

Figure 40-11

SOLSPHERE

TYPE IN:	PULL-DOWN MENU	SCREEN MENU	TABLET MENU
SOLSPHERE or SPHERE or DDSOLPRM	*Model, Primitives..., Sphere*	*MODEL, PRIMS., SOLSPH:*	*4,C*

Solsphere allows you to create a solid sphere by defining its center point and radius or diameter.

```
Command:  solsphere
Baseplane/<Center point><0,0,0>:  PICK or (coordinates)
Diameter/<radius>:  PICK or (coordinates)
Command:
```

Creating a *Solsphere* with the default options would yield a sphere similar to that in Figure 40-12.

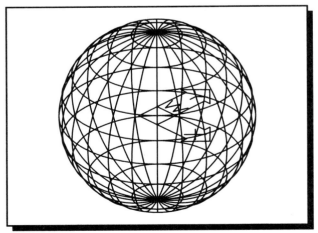

Figure 40-12

The **Baseplane** option is available in the
Solsphere command. However, a sphere
needs no specific orientation since it has a
uniform dimension; therefore, the importance
of that option is limited. *Baseplane* can be
used effectively to locate the center of the
sphere relative to existing geometry. Figure
40-13 illustrates a case where *Baseplane*
can be used to specify coordinates relative to
an inclined surface.

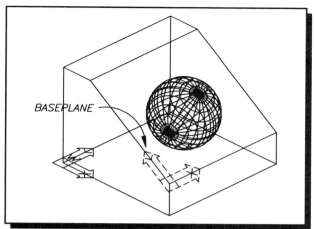

Figure 40-13

SOLTORUS

TYPE IN:	PULL-DOWN MENU	SCREEN MENU	TABLET MENU
SOLTORUS or TORUS or DDSOLPRM	**Model, Primitives..., Torus**	**MODEL, PRIMS., SOLTORS:**	**5,C**

Soltorus creates a torus (donut shaped) solid primitive using the dimensions you specify. Two
dimensions are specified: (1) the radius or diameter of the tube and (2) the radius or diameter
from the axis of the torus to the center of the tube. AutoCAD prompts:

```
Command: soltorus
Baseplane/<Center of torus><0,0,0>: PICK or (coordinates) or Enter
Diameter/<radius> of torus: PICK or (coordinates)
Diameter/<radius> of tube: PICK or (coordinates)
Command:
```

Figure 40-14 shows a *Soltorus* created using
the default orientation with the axis of the
tube aligned with the Z axis of the UCS and
the center of the torus at 0,0,0.

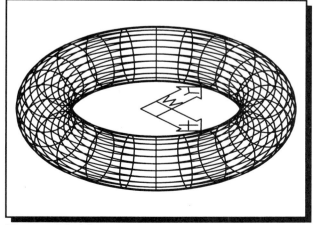

Figure 40-14

A self-intersecting torus is allowed with the *Soltorus* command. A self-intersecting torus is created by specifying a torus radius less than the tube radius. Figure 40-15 illustrates a torus with a torus radius of 3 and a tube radius of 4.

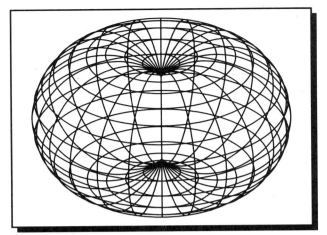

Figure 40-15

A negative value for the torus radius is specified to generate a shape similar to that in Figure 40-16 (also a self-intersecting torus). In this case, a torus radius of **-1** and a tube radius of **4** was designated. (If a negative torus radius is given, the tube radius must be positive and be greater than the absolute value of the torus radius).

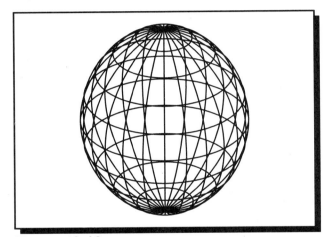

Figure 40-16

The **Baseplane** option can be used to position the *Soltorus* in the desired orientation. Given a cylinder (Fig. 40-17 A), a torus could be unioned to its end to create a rounded edge (B). The *Baseplane Zaxis* option is used to align the axis of the torus with that of the cylinder.

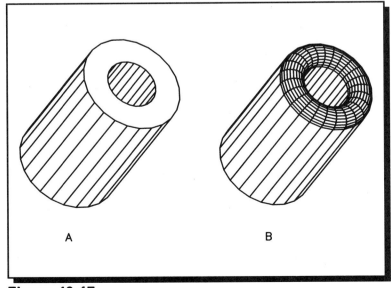

Figure 40-17

Both *Solext* and *Solrev* create swept solids. Each of these commands use <u>existing</u> 2D entities and generate a sweeping operation to create a solid. These two commands have surprising versatility and important features (see Design Efficiency in Chapter 42 for more information on the *Solext* command).

SOLEXT

TYPE IN:	PULL-DOWN MENU	SCREEN MENU	TABLET MENU
SOLEXT or EXT	*Model, Extrude*	*MODEL, SOLEXT:*	*4,D*

Solext extrudes an existing 2D shape such as a *Circle*, *Pline*, *Polygon*, *Ellipse*, or Region. Extrude means to generate a Z dimension (height). The selected 2D shape is extruded perpendicular to the plane of the shape <u>regardless</u> of the current UCS orientation. There is no *Baseplane* option of *Solext* because the extrusion direction is always perpendicular to the plane of the existing 2D shape.

If the *Pline* entity selected for extrusion is not closed, *Solext* closes it (connects the first and last point) as it extrudes. The versatility of this command lies in the fact that <u>any shape</u> that can be created by *Pline* can be transformed into a solid. Create the 2D shape in the desired orientation and invoke *Solext*.

```
Command: solext
Select objects: PICK
Select objects: Enter (Indicates completion of selection.)
Extrusion height: (value) or PICK
Taper angle<0>: Enter or (value)
Command:
```

Figure 40-18 shows a *Pline* before and after using *Solext*.

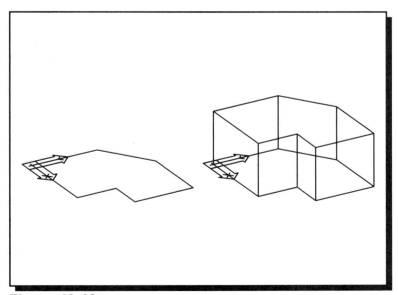

Figure 40-18

An open *Pline* selected for *Solext* is automatically closed while extruded as shown in Figure 40-19.

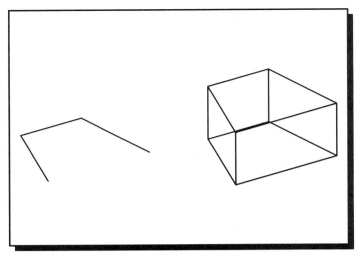

Figure 40-19

A taper angle can be specified for the extrusion. The resulting solid has sides extruded inward at the specified angle (Fig. 40-20). This is helpful for developing parts for molds that require a slight draft angle to facilitate easy removal of the part from the mold.

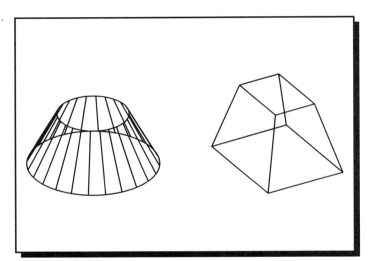

Figure 40-20

Figure 40-21 illustrates two other possibilities for *Solext*. Remember that the extrusion direction is determined by the plane of the 2D shape. If a horizontal extrusion is desired, for example, create the 2D shape on a vertical UCS.

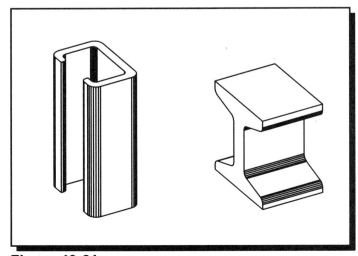

Figure 40-21

SOLREV

TYPE IN:	PULL-DOWN MENU	SCREEN MENU	TABLET MENU
SOLREV or REV	*Model, Revolve*	*MODEL, SOLREV:*	*5,D*

Solrev creates a swept solid. *Solrev* creates a solid by revolving a 2D shape about a selected axis. The 2D shape to revolve can be a *Pline, Polygon, Circle, Ellipse,* or a Region entity. Only one entity at a time can be revolved. If an open *Pline* is selected, it is closed automatically upon revolving. The command syntax for *Solrev* (accepting the defaults) is:

```
Command: solrev
Select Region, polyline or circle for revolution . . .
Select objects: PICK
Select objects: Enter (Indicates completion of selection process.)
Axis of revolution - Entity/X/Y/<Start point of axis>: PICK
End point of axis: PICK
Included angle <full circle>: (value) or Enter
Command:
```

Figure 40-22 illustrates a possibility for an existing *Pline* shape and the resulting *Solrev* generated through a full circle.

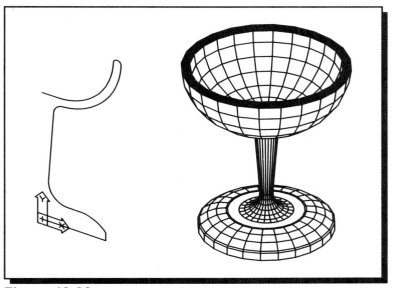

Figure 40-22

There is no *Baseplane* option for *Solrev*. Because *Solrev* acts upon an existing entity, the 2D shape intended for revolution should be created in the desired orientation. There are multiple options for selecting an axis of revolution.

Entity

A *Line* or single segment *Pline* can be selected for an axis. The positive axis direction is from the closest endpoint PICKed to the farthest.

X or Y

Uses the positive *X* or *Y* axis of the current UCS as the positive axis direction.

Start point of axis

Defines two points in the drawing to use as an axis (length is irrelevant). The two points do not have to be coplanar with the 2D shape.

If the *Entity* or *Start point* options are used, the selected entity or the two indicated points do not have to be coplanar with the 2D shape. The axis of revolution used is always on the plane of the 2D shape to revolve and is aligned with the direction of the entity or selected points.

Figure 40-23 demonstrates a possible use of the *Entity* option of *Solrev*. In this case, a *Pline* square is revolved about a *Line* entity. Note that the *Line* used for the axis is not on the same plane as the *Pline*. *Solrev* uses an axis on the plane of the revolved shape aligned with the direction of the selected axis. In this case, the endpoints of the *Line* are 0,-1,-1 and 0,1,1 so the shape is revolved about the X axis.

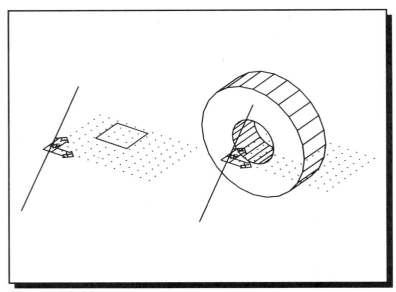

Figure 40-23

After defining the axis of revolution, *Solrev* requests the number of degrees for the object to be revolved. Any angle can be entered.

Another possibility for revolving a 2D shape is shown in Figure 40-24. The *Solrev* is generated through 270 degrees.

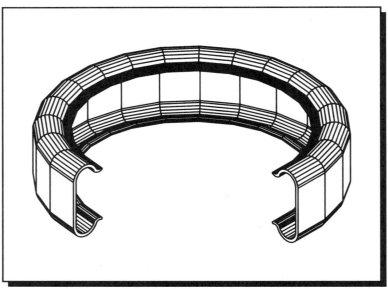

Figure 40-24

SOLIDIFY

TYPE IN:	PULL-DOWN MENU	SCREEN MENU	TABLET MENU
SOLIDIFY or SOL	*Model, Solidify*	*MODEL, SOLIDIFY*	*6,D*

Solidify transforms many previously created entities that have *Thickness* into an AME solid. *Thickness* is a property that many 2D entities can possess (see Chapter 37, Surface Modeling). Entities having *Thickness* that can be *Solidified* are *Pline, Polygon, Circle, Ellipse, Trace, Donut,* and *Solid* (the old 2D *Solid* command). If *Plines* with *Thickness* are not closed, they will be closed upon using *Solidify*. Lines with *Thickness*, *3Dlines*, *3Dfaces*, or 3D polygon meshes <u>cannot</u> be used with *Solidify*. *Solidify* can also be used to convert 2D entities (not having *Thickness*) to Regions (see Chapter 38).

```
Command: solidify
Select objects: PICK
```

It may not be immediately apparent that the selected shape has been transformed into an AME solid if the objects are shown in wireframe representation. Figure 40-25 displays a closed *Pline* with thickness before (A) and after (B) using *Solidify*.

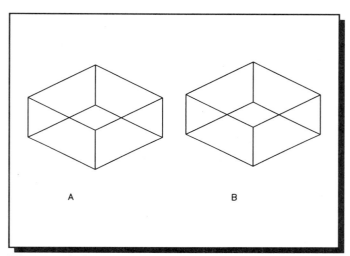

Figure 40-25

If *Hide* or *Shade* are used, the properties of the *Pline* with *Thickness* and the solid are visible. (The AME solid must be transformed from a wireframe to a meshed representation with *Solmesh* before *Hide* or *Shade* has an effect.) The *Pline* (A) is clearly a surface model, while the AME model has a top surface and appears "solid."

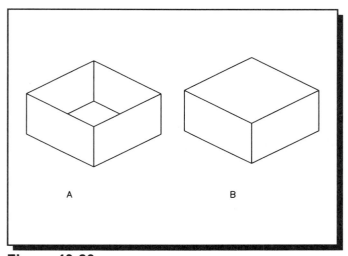

Figure 40-26

If a *Donut* is created with *Thickness*, it appears as shown in Figure 40-27 (A). Using *Solidify* transforms the *Donut* into an AME solid (B). The *Donut* loses its wall diameter when it is *Solidified*. The resulting diameter is the average between the inside and outside diameters of the *Donut*.

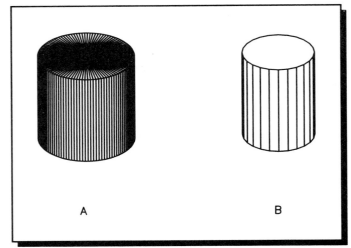

A   B

Figure 40-27

When a *Solid* (2D solid command) is created with *Thickness*, it appears as if it has "solid" properties; however, it is actually a surface model. The *Solid* can be *Exploded* into individual surfaces. When the *Solid* is transformed with *Solidify*, it becomes an AME solid model.

If you wish, the original entity selected for solidification can be retained in the drawing along with the AME solid. The *SOLDELENT* variable controls whether the selected objects are deleted or retained after they are solidified. The default is set to delete the original selected objects. (See Chapter 44, AME Variables and Sample Programs.)

It is possible to have 2D objects with *Thickness* automatically solidified when encountered by an AME command by setting the *SOLSOLIDIFY* variable to 3. (See Chapter 44, AME Sample Programs and Variables.)

CHAPTER EXERCISES

For the following exercises, use a *Prototype* drawing or begin a *New* drawing. Turn *On* the *UCSICON* and set it to the *Origin*. Set the *Vpoint* with the *Rotate* option to angles of **310**, **30**. Set *SOLWDENS* to **6**.

1.   Open a drawing and assign the name **CH40EX1**.

A.   Create a *box* (*Solbox*) with the lower left corner at **0,0,0**. The *Lengths* are **5**, **4**, and **3**.

B.   Create a second *box* at a *Baseplane* located above the WCS as shown in Figure 40-28 (use the *XY* option). The *box* dimensions are **2 x 4 x 2**.

C. Create a **cylinder** (*Solcyl*). Establish the same **Baseplane** as in the previous step. The *cylinder* **Center** is at **3.5,2** (of the *Baseplane*), the **Diameter** is **1.5**, and the **Height** is **-2**.

D. **Save** the drawing.

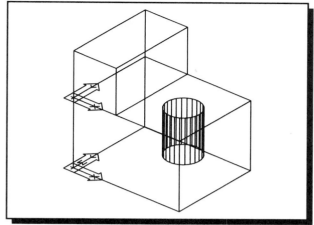

Figure 40-28

2. Open a drawing and assign the name **CH40EX2**.

A. Create a **wedge** (*Solwedge*) at point **0,0,0** with the **Lengths** of **5**, **4**, **3**.

B. Create a **cone** (*Solcone*) using the **3point Baseplane** option with an orientation indicated in Figure 40-29. The *cone* **Center** is at **2,3** (of the *Baseplane*) and has a **Diameter** of **2** and a **Height** of **-4**.

C. **Save** the drawing.

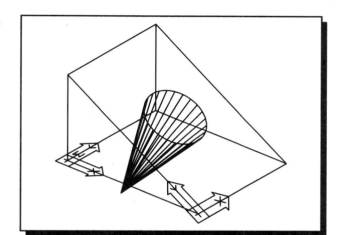

Figure 40-29

3. Open a drawing and assign the name **CH40EX3**. Display a **Plan** view.

A. Create 2 **Circles** as shown in Figure 40-30 with dimensions and locations as specified. Use **Pline** to construct the rectangular shape. Combine the 3 shapes into a Region by using the **Solunion** command.

B. Change the display to an isometric-type **Vpoint**. **Extrude** (*Solext*) the Region with a **Height** of **3** (no *taper angle*).

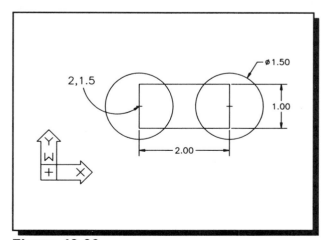

Figure 40-30

C. Create a **box** (*Solbox*) with the lower left corner at **0,0**. The **Lengths** of the box are **6**, **3**, **3**.

D. Your solid primitives should look like those in Figure 40-31. **Save** the drawing.

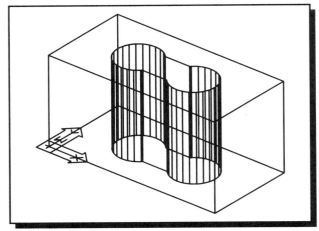

Figure 40-31

4. Open a drawing and assign the name **CH40EX4**. Display a **Plan** view.

A. Set **Thickness** to a value of **2**. Create the geometry as shown Figure 40-32 with dimensions as specified. Use **Pline** to construct the shape or use **Lines** and **Arc** or **Circle**, then convert to one **Pline** with **Pedit**.

B. Change the display with **Vpoint Rotate** and specify angles of **285,45**. Use **Hide** to display the "surface" quality of *Thickness*. Next, use **Solidify** to convert the 2D shape with *Thickness* to an AME solid. Now

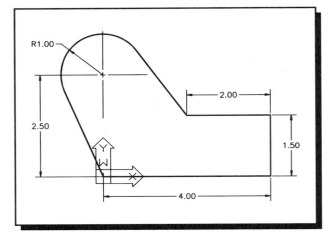

Figure 40-32

mesh the shape (with **Solmesh**) and use **Hide** again. The model should appear "solid."

C Regenerate the drawing and then **Save** it. Create a **cylinder** (*Solcyl*) concentric with the arc. Specify a **Diameter** of **1** and a **Height** of **2**.

D. Create a second **cylinder** using the **Baseplane 3point** option as shown in Figure 40-33. The new *cylinder* **center** is at **3,1** and has a **Diameter** of **.5** and a **Height** of **-1.5**.

E. The solid primitives should appear as those in Figure 40-33. **Save** the drawing.

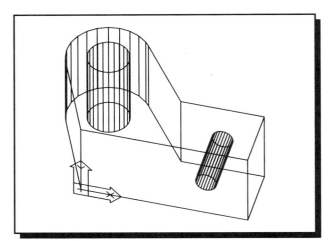

Figure 40-33

5.   Open a drawing and assign the name **CH40EX5**. Display a *Plan* view.

A.   Create a closed *Pline* shape symmetrical about the X axis with the locational and dimensional specifications given in Figure 40-34.

B.   Change to an isometric-type *Vpoint*. Set the *SOLWDENS* to **8**. Use *Solrev* to generale a complete circular shape from the closed *Pline*. Revolve about the **Y** axis.

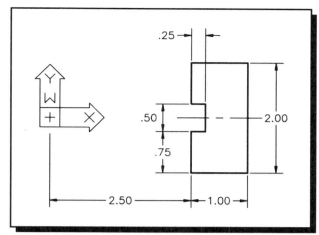

Figure 40-34

C.   Create a *torus* (*Soltorus*) with the *Center* at **0,0**. The *Radius of torus* is **3** and the *Radius of tube* is **.5**. The two shapes should intersect as shown in Figure 40-35.

D.   (Optional) If you have a fast computer, you can mesh the two solid primitives (with *Solmesh*), then use *Hide* to generate a display like Figure 40-35.

E.   Create a *cylinder* (*Solcyl*) with the *Center* at **0,0,0**, a *Radius* of **3**, and a *Height* of **8**.

F.   *Save* your drawing. These shapes will be combined into a composite solid in another chapter exercise.

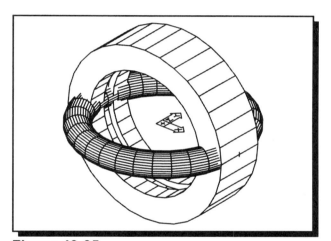

Figure 40-35

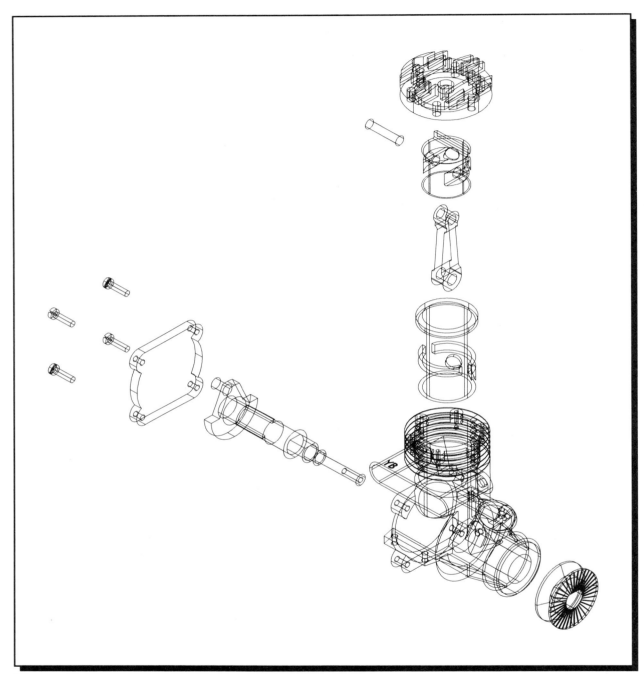

Figure 40-36 ENGINE.DWG Courtesy of Autodesk, Inc.

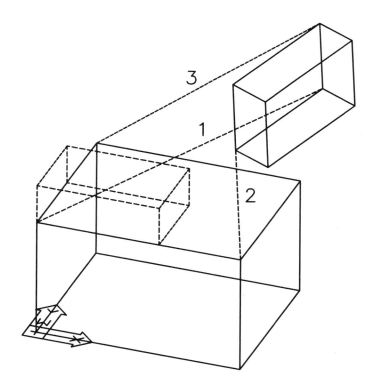

CHAPTER 41

Moving Solids

CHAPTER OBJECTIVES

After completing this chapter you should:

1.   be able to use the *Move* command to move solids in 3D space;

2.   know how to use *Solmove* to translate and rotate solids in 3D space;

3.   be able to attach the *Solmove* MCS icon at a solid edge or face, or at the WCS or UCS origin;

4.   be able to align the *Solmove* MCS icon and attached solid to another edge or face, or to the WCS or UCS;

5.   know how to assemble a solid to another solid in 3D space using *Align*;

6.   be able to rotate a solid about any axis in 3D space with *Rotate3D*;

7.   be able to mirror a solid about any axis in 3D space with *Mirror3D*.

BASICS

When you create the desired primitives, Boolean operations are used to construct the composite solids. However, the primitives must be in the correct position and orientation with respect to each other before Boolean operations can be performed. You can either create the primitives in the desired position during construction (by using UCS's or by using the *Baseplane* or *CP* option) or move the primitives into position after their creation. Several methods that allow you to move solid primitives are explained in this chapter.

COMMANDS FOR MOVING SOLIDS

MOVE

The *Move* command that you use for moving 2D entities in 2D drawings can also be used to move 3D primitives. Generally *Move* is used to change the position of an entity in one plane (translation), which is typical of 2D drawings. *Move* can be also be used to move an AME primitive in 3D space <u>if</u> *OSNAP*s are used.

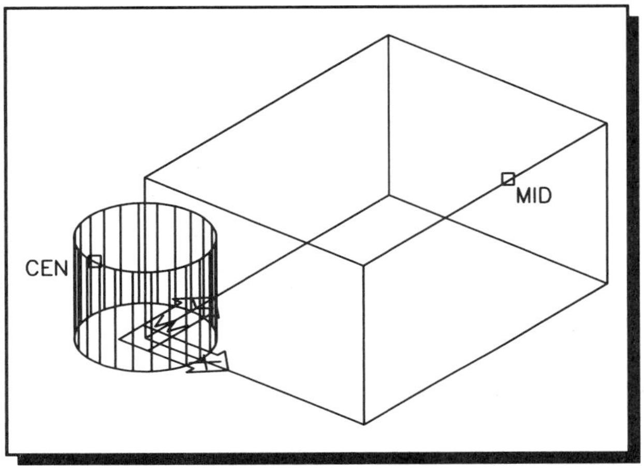

Figure 41-1 depicts a *cylinder* primitive moved by using *Move* with the *CENter OSNAP* to snap to the center of a primitive in response to the "Basepoint or displacement:" prompt. The *MIDpoint* of an edge of the *box* is selected in response to the "Second point of displacement:" prompt. Even though solid primitives are considered entities, an edge, corner, or center can be selected.

Figure 41-1

Figure 41-2 shows the result of the *Move* with *OSNAP*s. The primitives are in the desired position and ready for the Boolean operation.

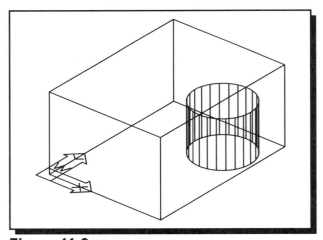

Figure 41-2

The result of the Boolean operation, _Solsub_ (subtract), is shown in Figure 41-3. The cylinder primitive has been subtracted from the box to create a composite solid.

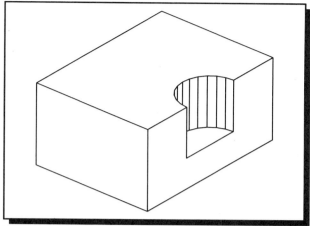

Figure 41-3

SOLMOVE

TYPE IN:	PULL-DOWN MENU	SCREEN MENU	TABLET MENU
SOLMOVE or _MOV_	_Model, Modify >_ _Move Object_	_MODEL, MODIFY,_ _SOLMOVE:_	_1,B_

With _Solmove_, you can move primitives by rotation and translation, or align faces or edges with other faces, edges, the WCS, or a UCS. A large green Motion Coordinate System (MCS) icon appears to assist you in visualizing the orientation and previewing the movement of the objects you select.

Translation is movement in a plane. You can specify X, Y, or Z translation. You can translate in any direction by using UCS's. Rotation is also permitted about the X, Y, or Z axis. Combinations of rotation and translation are possible with one _Solmove_.

When you select the 3D objects you wish to move, the MCS icon appears giving the X direction (one tip), Y direction (two tips) and Z direction (three tips).

Next, you define the _motion description_. _Motion description_ specifies the translation, rotation, and/or alignment that you desire. The command syntax follows.

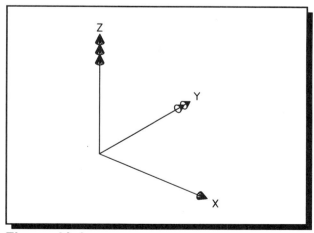

Figure 41-4

```
Command: solmove
Select objects: PICK (Select the solids you want to move.  Only AME solids or
regions can be selected.)
Select objects: Enter (Indicates completion of the selection set.)
?/<Motion description>: (Enter description of desired motion.)
?/<Motion description>: Enter (Press Enter to complete command.)
Command:
```

Notice that the "?/Motion description:" prompt reappears after each use. With many applications, several steps are required to position the solid objects in the expected location and orientation. The options for motion description are:

e	(edge)	Places the MCS at the selected edge of a solid.
f	(face)	Places the MCS at the selected face of a solid.
u	(UCS)	Places the MCS at the UCS origin.
w	(WCS)	Places the MCS at the WCS origin.
ae	(Align to edge)	Moves the MCS and selected solid so that it aligns with an edge.
af	(Align to face)	Moves the MCS and selected solid so that it aligns with a face.
au	(Align with UCS)	Moves the MCS and selected solid so that it aligns with the UCS.
aw	(Align with WCS)	Moves the MCS and selected solid so that it aligns with the WCS.
rx	(Rotate X)	Rotates about the X axis.
ry	(Rotate Y)	Rotates about the Y axis.
rz	(Rotate Z)	Rotates about the Z axis.
tx	(Translate X)	Translates in the X direction.
ty	(Translate Y)	Translates in the Y direction.
tz	(Translate Z)	Translates in the Z direction.
o	(original)	Restores the objects to their original position and orientation.
?	(list)	Gives the list of Motion Description options.

AutoCAD uses lower case characters to represent the options for *Solmove*. Upper or lower case letters can be used. In the following discussion, upper case is used for consistency with other commands.

A rotation and/or translation or *original* can be accomplished in <u>one</u> step. Using *e, f, u, w,* and the alignment options usually requires <u>two or more</u> steps: first, place the MCS in the desired position, and then translate, rotate, or align it and the selected object with another object. Applications of most of the options are illustrated on the next several pages.

Translate

These first two figures demonstrate the translation of a cylinder to the center of the box. Translation is required in the X and Y directions. This situation assumes that the two primitives were created at the default location and orientation at 0,0,0.

The first motion description is *TX5*, meaning "translate in the X direction 5 units" (Fig. 41-5).

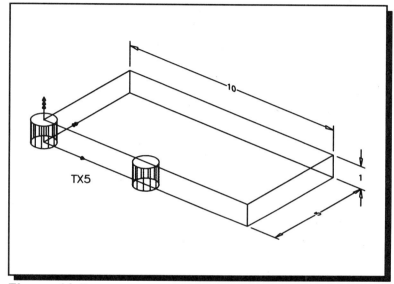

Figure 41-5

Next, the cylinder must be moved in the Y direction 2.5 units. The motion description is *TY2.5*.

When using the *Solmove* command with the translate option, notice the MCS remains in its original position aligned with the WCS or UCS. It changes position when using the alignment options.

As an alternative, both the X and Y translations can be given in one motion description delineated by

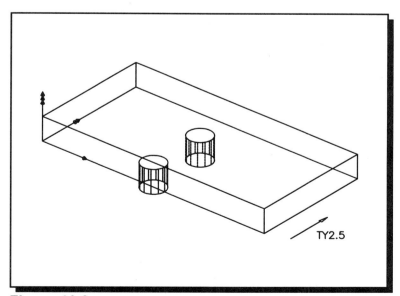

Figure 41-6

a comma. Entering ***TX5,TY2.5*** would accomplish the same action as that shown in the previous two figures.

If you wanted to move the cylinder to the top center of the box, three translations would be required: one in the X direction, one in the Y direction, and one in the Z direction.

Figure 41-7 illustrates the translation in three planes required to position the cylinder. All three movements can be accomplished in <u>one</u> step. The motion description to enter is *TX5,TY2.5,TZ1*.

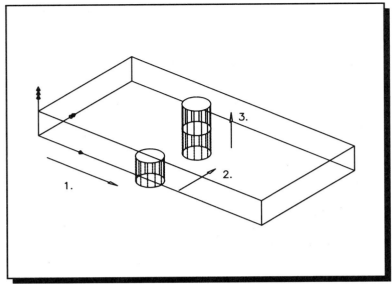

Figure 41-7

Rotate

Rotation is accomplished only about the X, Y, and/or Z axes of the <u>MCS</u>. The MCS originally appears at the current WCS or UCS. In this case, rotation of a solid coincides with that of the X, Y, or Z axis of the WCS or UCS (Fig. 41-8). However, the MCS can be placed at the edge or face of an AME solid using the *e* or *f* option. In this case, rotation occurs in relation to the MCS aligned with the solid (Fig. 41-9).

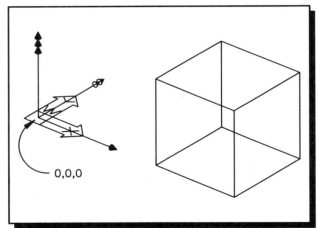

Figure 41-8

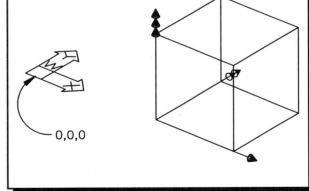

Figure 41-9

Rotation about any axis is a simple process, especially when the solid object and the MCS are located at the origin of the current UCS, as shown in the following figure. A motion description could be entered as a single rotation or multiple rotations in one step.

Figure 41-10 pictures a box rotated -20 degrees (negative value= clockwise) about the Y axis of the MCS by entering the motion description as *RY-20*.

Rotation about the X and Z axes would be accomplished similarly.

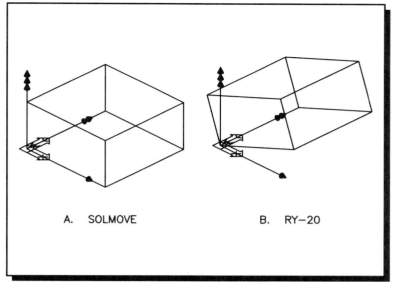

A. SOLMOVE   B. RY−20

Figure 41-10

When a solid is <u>not</u> located at the origin of the current UCS, rotation still occurs about the current X, Y, or Z axis <u>unless</u> the MCS is placed at an *edge* or *face* of the solid. The *e* or *f* option places the MCS at the desired edge or face so that rotation can occur with respect to the MCS <u>at</u> the edge or face.

Figure 41-11 (A.) illustrates the process of placing the MCS at the selected face by entering *f* at the "<Motion Description>:" prompt. Next, enter *RZ20* to cause a rotation of 20 degrees about the MCS Z axis.

When using the *f* (face) option to align the MCS with the solid, select any edge and the MCS will be placed at one of the two faces defined by the edge. You are prompted for "next/<OK>:" allowing you to select the desired

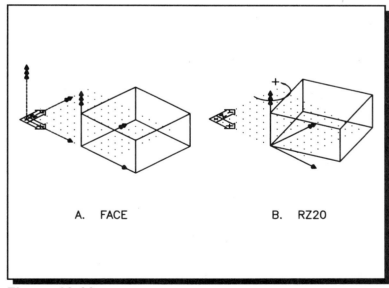

A. FACE   B. RZ20

Figure 41-11

adjacent face. (You can only select edges in wireframe representation because no surfaces are visible; therefore, this mechanism is used to define the desired face.)

When you select the *e* (edge) option, the MCS is oriented at the <u>midpoint</u> of the edge. Only one orientation of the MCS is possible for the edge coordinate system.

Translate and *Rotate*

Since it is possible to translate and rotate in one *Solmove* command and rotation can be accomplished by the two previously described strategies, an example is shown here to illustrate two alternatives.

Assume a cylinder and box primitive have been created at the origin (Fig. 41-12 A). The desired composite solid is shown in (B).

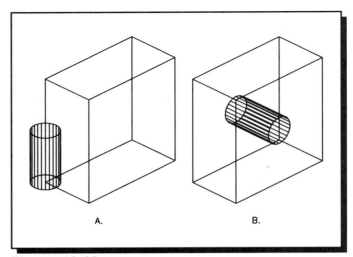

A.   B.

Figure 41-12

One possibility is to rotate the cylinder at the origin, then translate it into position.

The *Motion Descriptions* to enter are **RY90** to rotate the selected cylinder 90 degrees about the Y axis (Fig 41-13 A), then enter **TY2,TZ2** in order to translate in both the Y and Z directions 2 units each.

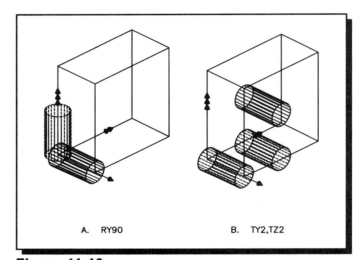

A.   RY90   B.   TY2,TZ2

Figure 41-13

An alternative method to accomplish the desired orientation of the cylinder would be to translate in the Y and Z directions first, then place the MCS along the face of the cylinder and rotate on the MCS Y axis.

This method actually involves three steps. First, enter **TY2,TZ2** (A). Second, use the *f* (face option) to place the MCS icon at the <u>bottom</u> face of the cylinder. (You may have to use "Next" to

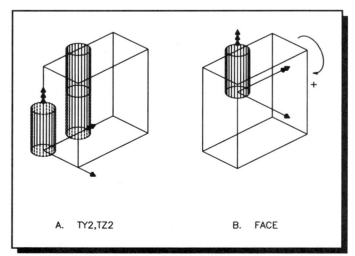

A.   TY2,TZ2   B.   FACE

Figure 41-14

orient the MCS as shown.) The third step is to enter **RY90** to rotate the cylinder to the desired orientation.

The previous alternatives were intended to provide an understanding of _Solmove_. Given the example composite solid, an alternative construction method would be to create the box first, then create the cylinder using the _Baseplane_ option to place it in the correct location and orientation.

e (Edge)

The edge option positions the MCS at the selected edge of an AME solid. The new orientation of the MCS is at the midpoint of the edge (similar to _OSNAP MIDpoint_). The Y axis of the MCS always aligns along the selected edge, with the X and Y axes perpendicular to the edge, facing away from the adjacent faces.

Two possibilities for aligning the MCS to the edge of a box are shown in Figure 41-15.

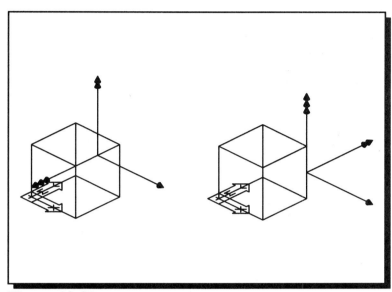

Figure 41-15

Aligning the MCS to the edge of a cylinder yields the orientation as shown. The Z axis is always parallel with the axis of the cylinder and the X and Y axes lie along the face of the selected edge.

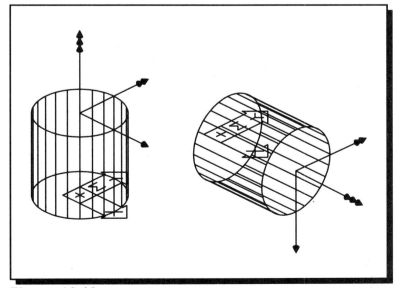

Figure 41-16

f (Face)

Using the *f* (face) option aligns the MCS to the selected face. Because you cannot PICK a face and you must PICK an edge (surfaces are not visible in wireframe representation), *Solmove* prompts you for "Next/<OK>:." Entering an **N** for the *Next* option displays the MCS orientation on the other face (only two faces are connected by the selected edge). AutoCAD orients the MCS with the XY plane on the face and the Z axis perpendicular to the face.

The *f* option places the MCS in one of the two positions. The *Next* option is used to toggle from one to the other. Use the *o* (restore original orientation) option to move the MCS back to the origin.

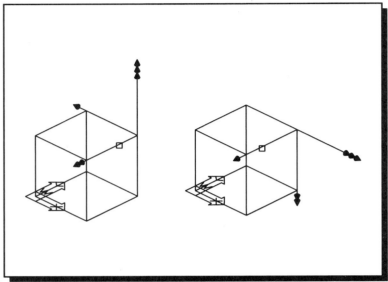

Figure 41-17

Using the *f* option with a cylinder orients the MCS as shown. The Z axis is always parallel with the axis of the cylinder (like the *edge* option). The two possibilities are available by using *Next*.

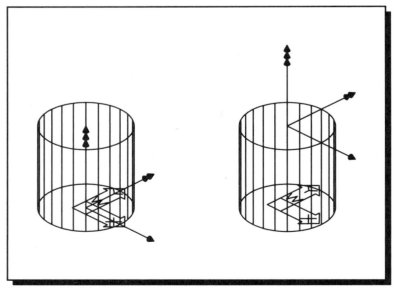

Figure 41-18

ae (Align to Edge)

Align to Edge and Align to Face options align the MCS <u>and</u> the selected solids to the edge or face of another solid. These two options of *Solmove* usually require two steps to position selected objects in the desired orientation. The first step involves using the *e* (edge) or *f* (face) option to position the MCS on the desired solid object.

Assume that the two boxes have been created at the origin (Fig 41-19). The design requires a notch (small box) to be removed from the long upper edge of the larger box. The following illustrations indicate the steps involved in positioning the two boxes correctly in preparation for the Boolean operation.

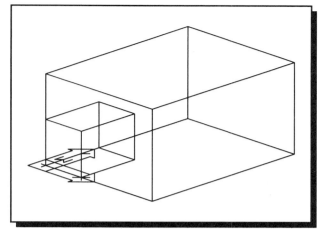

Figure 41-19

The first step is to use the *e* (edge) option in response to the "Motion Description:" prompt of *Solmove* to position the MCS on the small box. The motion description is *e*. PICK the indicated edge.

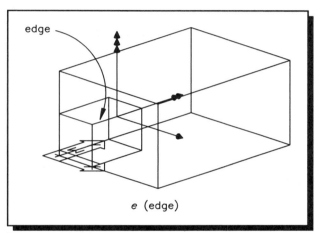

Figure 41-20

Next use *ae* (align to edge) to align the MCS with the long upper edge of the large box as shown. In so doing, a <u>second</u> MCS temporarily appears prompting for your approval. Press **Enter** in response to the "No/<Yes>:" prompt.

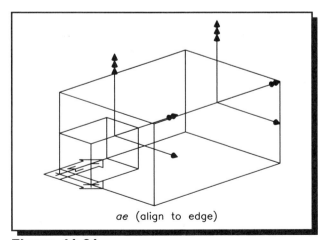

Figure 41-21

The result of the alignment should be as shown. The two primitives are ready for you to perform the *Solsub* (subtract) Boolean operation. Complete the command by pressing **Enter**.

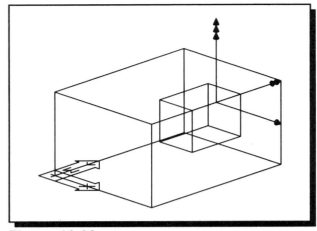

Figure 41-22

af (Align to Face)

Similar to *ae* (Align to Edge), this option of *Solmove* is generally used in conjunction with the *e* (edge) or *f* (face) option first. Thus, two steps are required.

The following example uses a wedge subtracted from a box. Assume the box and wedge have been created at the origin. Invoking *Solmove* causes the MCS to appear.

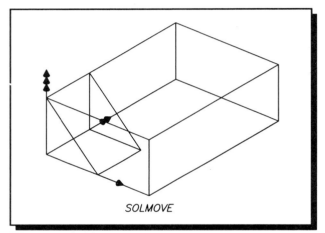

Figure 41-23

Use the *f* (face) option to attach the MCS to the bottom face of the wedge. Select an edge on the bottom face of the wedge as shown. Use the *Next* option to flip the MCS between the two adjacent faces to the desired position.

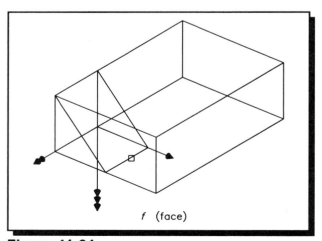

Figure 41-24

Next, use *af* (Align with Face) and select the top edge of the box as shown. A second MCS should be oriented with the selected face. Use the *Next* option to achieve the desired position.

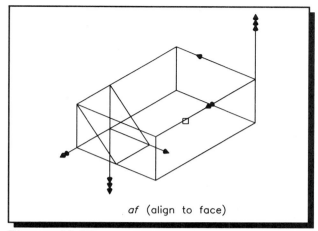

af (align to face)

Figure 41-25

Press Enter to accept the indicated alignment. The wedge should change position as illustrated. If you need to start over, use the **o** (restore original position) option. Otherwise, press Enter to end the command.

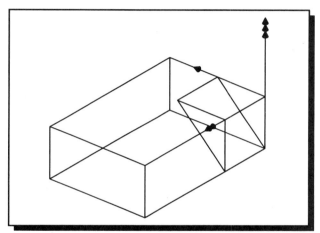

Figure 41-26

Using *Solsub* to subtract the wedge from the box yields the composite solid.

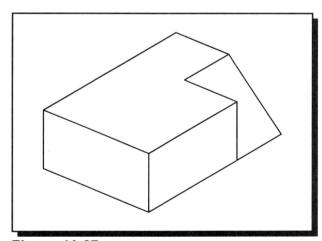

Figure 41-27

au (Align to UCS)

This option moves the selected objects <u>and</u> the MCS to align with the current UCS. This action is useful when you want to move an object from some position in 3D space to the origin of the UCS.

The cylinder is moved back to the origin of the UCS by first using the *e* (edge) option to align the MCS with the solid (A) Then the *au* option relocates the MCS and the cylinder back at the UCS origin.

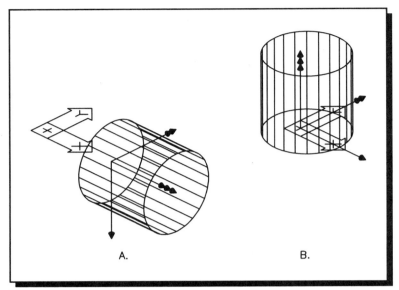

Figure 41-28

aw (Align to WCS)

The *aw* option moves the selected objects and the MCS to align with the WCS. In cases when you wish to move an AME solid to the WCS orientation, use this option. An AME primitive created at the origin could be relocated in a different orientation also at the origin as shown in the following figure.

The *e* (edge) option can be used to position the MCS at the indicated edge. Then the *aw* option aligns the selected solid and the MCS with the WCS in the new orientation.

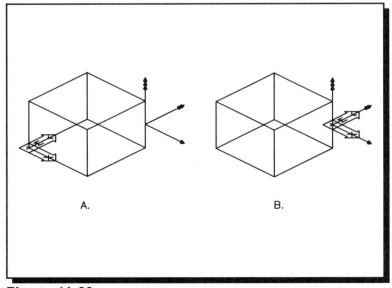

Figure 41-29

ALIGN

TYPE IN:	PULL-DOWN MENU	SCREEN MENU	TABLET MENU
ALIGN	_Modify, Align_	---	---

Align is not an AME command. It is an ADS application and is loaded automatically when typing or selecting this command from the _Modify_ pull-down menu. _Align_ does not appear in the screen menu or on the digitizing tablet menu. _Align_ is discussed in Chapter 16 but only in terms of 2D alignment.

Align is, however, a very powerful 3D command because it automatically performs 3D translation and rotation. _Align_ is more intuitive and in many situations is easier to use than _Solmove_. All you have to do is select the points on two 3D objects that you want to align (connect).

Align provides a means of aligning one shape (an entity, a group of entities, a block, a region, or a 3D solid) with another shape. The alignment is accomplished by connecting source points (on the shape to be moved) to destination points (on the stationary shape). You can use _OSNAP_ modes to select the source and destination points, assuring accurate alignment. Either a 2D or 3D alignment can be accomplished with this command. The command syntax for 3D alignment is as follows:

```
Command: align
Select objects: PICK (Select object to move.)
Select objects: Enter
1st source point: PICK (use OSNAP)
1st destination point: PICK (use OSNAP)
2nd source point: PICK (use OSNAP)
2nd destination point: PICK (use OSNAP)
3rd source point: PICK (use OSNAP)
3rd destination point: PICK (use OSNAP)
```

After the source and destination points have been designated, lines connecting those points temporarily remain until _Align_ performs the action. _Align_ performs a translation (like _Move_) and two rotations (like _Rotate_) each in separate planes to align the points as designated. The motion automatically performed by _Align_ is actually done in three steps.

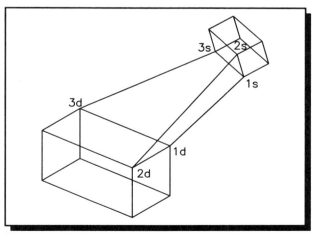

Figure 41-30

Initially, the first source point is connected to the first destination point (translation). These two points are the only set that physically <u>touch</u>.

Next, the vector defined by the first and second source points are aligned with the vector defined by the first and second destination points. The length of the segments between the first and second points on each object is of no consequence because AutoCAD only considers the <u>vector direction</u>. This second motion is a rotation along one axis.

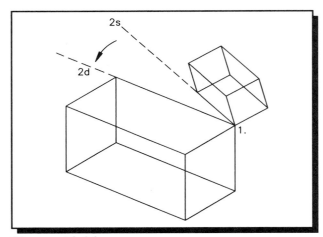

Figure 41-31

Finally, the third set of points are aligned similarly.

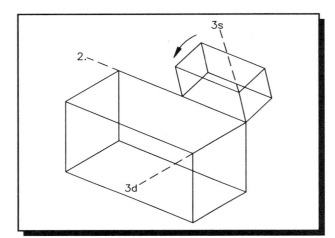

Figure 41-32

This third motion is a rotation along the other axis, completing the alignment.

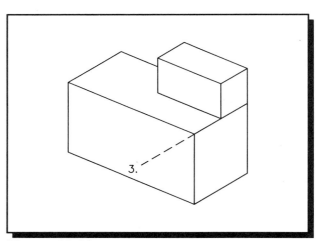

Figure 41-33

ROTATE3D

TYPE IN:	PULL-DOWN MENU	SCREEN MENU	TABLET MENU
ROTATE3D	*Modify, Rotate 3D*	*EDIT, ROTATE:, 3D ROTATE:*	---

Rotate3D is not an AME command, therefore is not located in the *Model* menus. *Rotate3D* is very useful for any type of 3D modeling, particularly with AME where primitives must be moved, rotated, or otherwise aligned with other primitives before Boolean operations can be performed.

Rotate3D allows you to rotate a 3D object about any axis in 3D space. Many alternatives are available for defining the desired rotational axis. Following is the command sequence for rotating a 3D object using the default (*2points*) option.

```
Command: rotate3d
Select Objects: PICK
Select Objects: Enter (Indicates completion of selection process.)
Axis by Entity/Last/View/Xaxis/Yaxis/Zaxis/<2points>: PICK or
(coordinates) (Select first point to define the rotational axis.)
2nd point on axis: PICK or (coordinates) (Select second point to define
rotational axis.)
<Rotation angle>/Reference: PICK or (value) (Select two points to define
the rotation angle or enter a value. If two points are PICKed, the angle between the
points in the XY plane of the current UCS determine the angle of rotation.)
```

The options are explained below and on the following pages.

2points

The power of *Rotate3D* (over *Rotate*) is that any points or entities in <u>3D space</u> can be used to define the axis for rotation. When using the default (*2points* option, remember that you can use *OSNAP* to select points on existing 3D objects. Figure 41-34 illustrates the *2points* option used to select 2 points with *OSNAP* on the solid object selected for rotating.

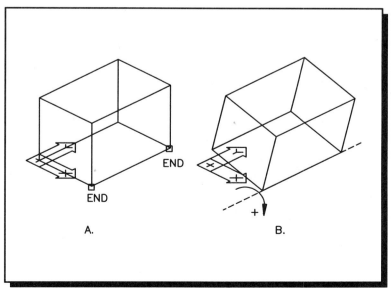

Figure 41-34

Another possible application of the *2points* option of *Rotate3D* is depicted in Figure 41-35. Here, a primitive is rotated about an axis established by *OSNAP*ing to another primitive's *MIDpoint*s.

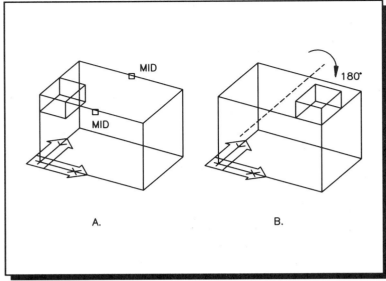

Figure 41-35

Entity

This option allows you to rotate about a selected entity. You can select a *Line*, *Circle*, *Arc,* or 2D *Pline* segment. The rotational axis is aligned with the selected *Line* or *Pline* segment. Positive rotation is determined by the right-hand rule and the "arbitrary axis algorithm." When selecting *Arc* or *Circle* entities, the rotational axis is perpendicular to the plane of the *Arc* or *Circle* passing through the center (Fig. 41-36).

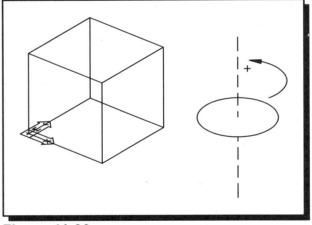

Figure 41-36

Even though the prompts for the *Entity* option do not indicate so, you can select an edge of an AME solid as an entity (Fig. 41-37). This capability provides many simple but versatile possibilities.

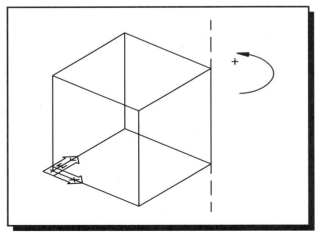

Figure 41-37

Last

Rotates about the axis used for the last rotation.

View

Allows you to pick a point on the screen and rotates the selected entity(s) about an axis perpendicular to the screen and passing through the selected point (Fig. 41-38).

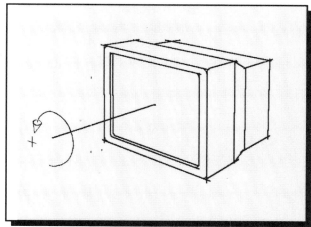

Figure 41-38

Xaxis

With this option you can rotate the selected objects about the X axis of the current UCS or any axis <u>parallel</u> <u>to</u> the X axis of the current UCS. You are prompted to pick a point on the X axis. The point selected defines an axis for rotation parallel to the current X axis passing through the selected point. You can use *OSNAP* to select points on existing 3D objects (Fig. 41-39). The current X axis can be used if the point you select is on the X axis.

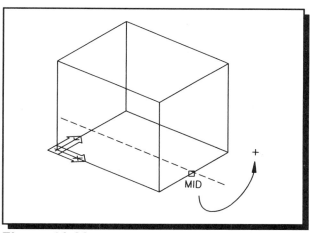

Figure 41-39

Yaxis

This option allows you to use the Y axis of the current UCS or any axis <u>parallel to</u> the Y axis of the current UCS as the axis of rotation. The point you select defines a rotational axis parallel to the current Y axis passing through the point. *OSNAP* can be used to snap to existing geometry (Fig. 41-40).

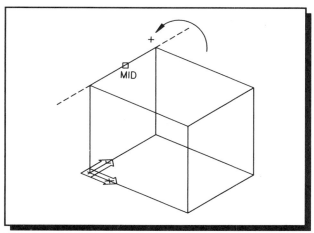

Figure 41-40

Zaxis

With this option you can use the Z axis of the current UCS or any axis <u>parallel to</u> the Z axis of the current UCS as the axis of rotation. The point you select defines a rotational axis parallel to the current Z axis passing through the point. Figure 41-41 indicates the use of the *MIDpoint OSNAP* to establish a vertical (parallel to Z axis) rotational axis.

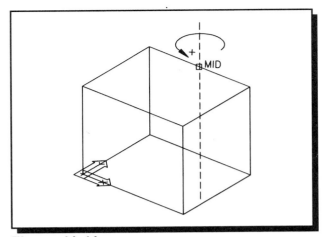

Figure 41-41

Reference

After you have specified the axis for rotation, you must specify the rotation angle. You are presented with the following prompt.

```
<Rotation angle>/Reference: r (Indicates the Reference option.)
Reference angle: PICK or (value) (PICK two points; OSNAPs can be
used. You can enter a value.)
New angle: PICK or (value) (Specify the new angle by either method.)
```

The angle you specify for the reference (relative) is used instead of angle 0 (absolute) for the starting position. You can enter either a value or PICK two points to specify the angle. You then specify a new angle (position). The *Reference* angle you select is rotated to the absolute angle position you specify as the *New angle*.

Figure 41-42 illustrates how *ENDpoint OSNAPs* are used to select a *Reference* angle. The *New angle* is specified as **90**. AutoCAD rotates the reference angle to the 90 degree position.

Combining this capability with the other options provides endless capabilities for rotating AME or other models in 3D space.

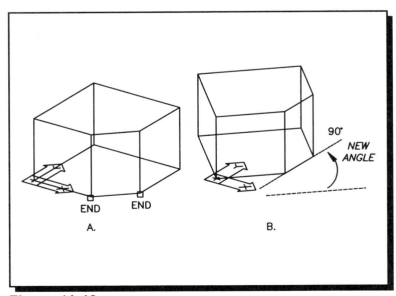

Figure 41-42

MIRROR3D

TYPE IN:	PULL-DOWN MENU	SCREEN MENU	TABLET MENU
MIRROR3D	*Construct, Mirror 3D*	*EDIT, MIRROR:, MIRROR3D:*	---

Mirror3D provides you with the capability to mirror an entity about any axis in 3D space. This command, like *Rotate3D*, is not an AME command, so it is not found in the *Model* menus. However, *Mirror3D* is especially useful for any type of 3D modeling, especially solid modeling with AME.

Mirror3D operates similarly to the 2D version of the command *Mirror*, in that mirrored replicas of selected objects are created. With *Mirror* (2D) the selected objects are mirrored about an axis. The axis is defined by a vector lying in the XY plane. With *Mirror3D*, selected objects are mirrored about a <u>plane</u>. *Mirror3D* provides multiple options for specifying the plane to mirror about.

```
Command: mirror3d
Select objects: PICK (Select one or multiple objects to mirror.)
Select objects: Enter (Indicate completion of the selection process.)
Plane by Entity/Last/Zaxis/View/XY/YZ/ZX/<3points>: PICK or
(letters) (PICK points for the default option or enter a letter(s) to designate option.)
```

The options are listed and explained below. The Coordinate System icon does <u>not</u> appear in the orientation of the mirror plane when you use this command. A phantom icon is shown <u>only</u> in the figures below to aid in your visualization of the mirroring plane.

3points

The *3points* option mirrors selected objects about the plane you specify by selecting three points to define the plane. You can PICK points (with or without *OSNAP*) or give coordinates. *MIDpoint OSNAP* is used to define the 3 points in Figure 41-43 (A) to achieve the result in (B).

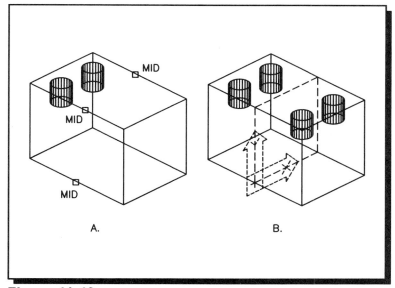

Figure 41-43

Entity

Using this option establishes a mirroring plane with the plane of the entity. Selecting an *Arc* or *Circle* automatically mirrors selected objects using the plane in which the *Arc* or *Circle* lies. The plane defined by a *Pline* segment is the XY plane of the *Pline* when the *Pline* segment was created. Figure 41-44 shows a box mirrored about the plane of the circles. Using *Solsub* produces the result shown in (B). Using a *Line* entity or edge of an AME solid is not allowed.

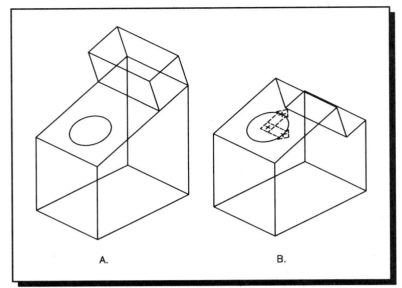

Figure 41-44

Last

Selecting this option uses the plane that was last used for mirroring.

Zaxis

With this option the mirror plane is the XY plane perpendicular to a Z vector you specify. The first point you specify on the Z axis establishes the location of the XY plane origin (a point through which the plane passes). The second point establishes the Z axis and the orientation of the XY plane (perpendicular to the Z axis). Figure 41-45 illustrates this concept. Note that this option only requires two PICK points.

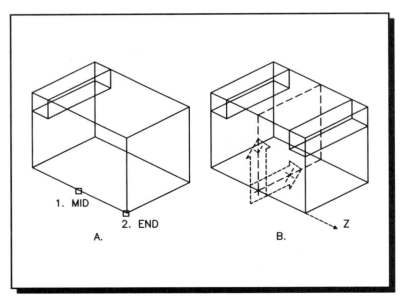

Figure 41-45

View

The *View* option of *Rotate3D* uses a mirroring plane <u>parallel</u> with the screen and perpendicular to your line of sight based on your current viewpoint. You are required to select a point on the plane. Accepting the default (0,0,0) establishes the mirroring plane passing through the current origin. Any other point can be selected. You should change *Vpoint* to "see" the mirrored objects (Fig. 41-46).

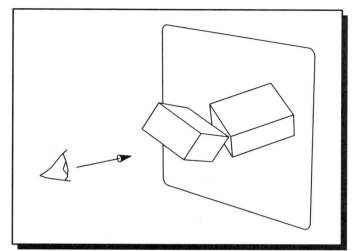

Figure 41-46

XY

This option situates a mirroring plane parallel with the current XY plane. You can specify a point through which the mirroring plane passes. Figure 41-47 represents a plane established by selecting a point by *OSNAP*ing to the *CENter* of an existing solid.

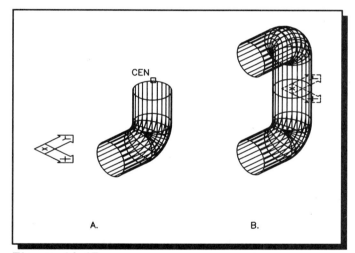

Figure 41-47

YZ

Using the *YZ* option constructs a plane to mirror about that is parallel with the current YZ plane. Any point can be selected through which the plane will pass.

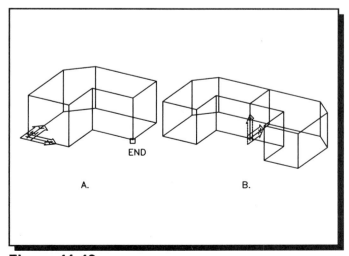

Figure 41-48

ZX

This option uses a plane parallel with the current ZX plane for mirroring. Figure 41-49 shows a point selected on the *MIDpoint* of an existing edge to mirror two holes.

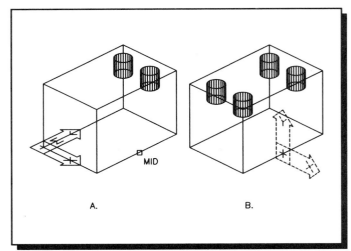

Figure 41-49

CHAPTER EXERCISES

1. Create two **boxes** (*Solbox*), each with the lower-left corner at point **0,0,0**. Dimensions (**Lengths**) for the large box are **5**, **4**, and **3**, and for the small box are **3**, **2**, and **1**. Display an appropriate **Vpoint**. Save the drawing as **CH41EX1**.

A. Move the small box to the position shown highlighted in Figure 41-50 (**MIDpoint** of the upper right edge) using the **Move** command. Do not *Save* the drawing.

B. **Undo** (or **Open CH41EX1** again). Move the small box as before, only this time use **Solmove** with the *Translate* options (**TX, TY, TZ**). Do not *Save*.

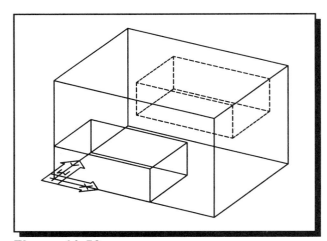

Figure 41-50

C. **Undo** (or **Open CH41EX1** again). Move the small box again with **Solmove**. This time use the **e** (Edge) and **ae** (Align to Edge) methods. Do not *Save*.

D. **Undo** (or **Open CH41EX1** again). Now move the small box to the upper, far right corner (opposite corner) of the large box (not the same as shown highlighted in Figure 41-50). Use **Solmove** with the **f** (Face) and **af** (Align to Face) options. Do not *Save* the drawing.

2.   ***Open*** the **CH40EX5** drawing that you worked on in Chapter 40 Exercises.

A.   Use ***Solmove*** with the ***Rotate*** option to rotate the vertically oriented shape **90** degrees (the *Pline* shape that was previously converted to a solid by *Solrev*--not the torus). Next, move the shape up (positive Z) **6** units with ***Solmove***.

B.   Move the torus up **4** units with ***Solmove***.

C.   The solid primitives should appear as those in Figure 41-52. (*Hide* has been used for the figure.) ***Save*** the drawing as **CH41EX2**.

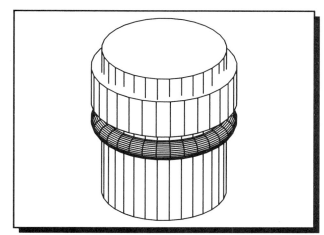

Figure 41-51

3.   ***Open*** the **CH41EX1** drawing. Create a ***UCS*** on the vertical face on the right side as shown in Figure 41-52.

A.   Use ***Solmove*** with the ***f*** (Face) and ***au*** (Align with UCS) options to move the small box into the position shown highlighted in Figure 41-52.

B.   ***Save*** the drawing as **CH41EX3**.

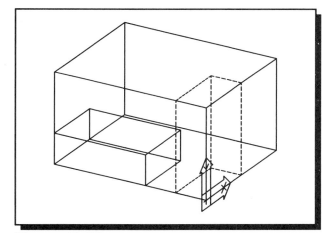

Figure 41-52

4.   ***Open*** the **CH41EX1** drawing. ***Erase*** the small box.

A.   Set an appropriate ***SOLWDENS***. Create a ***cylinder*** (*Solcyl*) at **0,0,0** with a ***Diameter*** of **.5** and a ***Height*** of **5**.

B.   Use ***Rotate3D*** to orient the cylinder, ***Solmove*** to translate the cylinder, and ***Mirror3D*** to produce the other three cylinders as shown in Figure 41-53. Each cylinder center is 1 unit from the nearest edges. (HINT: Use the ***XY*** and ***ZX*** mirroring planes and ***OSNAP*** to the box edge ***MIDpoints***.) ***Save*** the drawing as **CH41EX4**.

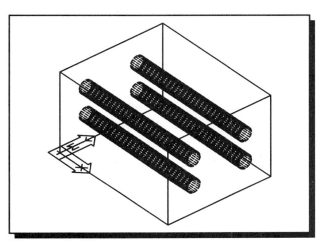

Figure 41-53

5. *Open* the **CH41EX1** drawing. In this exercise, you will move the small box to an unusual orientation in 3D space, then use *Align* to align it to the large box.

A. Use *Solmove* and translate the small box **8** units in the *X* direction. Then use any method to rotate the small box **30** degrees (absolute) about the *X* axis. Finally, rotate the box **-45** degrees (absolute) about the *Y* axis to achieve the position shown in Figure 41-54.

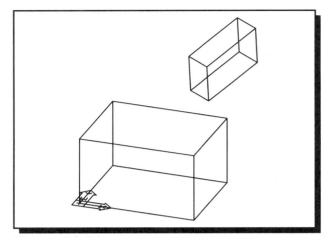

Figure 41-54

B. Use *Align* to align the small box on top of the large box as shown (highlighted) in Figure 41-55. *Save* the drawing as **CH41EX5**.

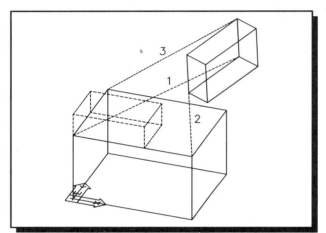

6. Begin a *New* drawing and assign the name **CH41EX6**.

A. Set an appropriate *SOLWDENS*. Create a the following primitives to the given specifications:

Figure 41-55

Box	*Lengths*	5, 4, 3
Box	*Lengths*	4, 2, 2
Cone	*Diameter*	2
	Height	4
Cyl	*Diameter*	.5
	Height	1.5
Wedge	*Lengths*	2, 2, 1

Use appropriate methods to move, translate, rotate, mirror, or otherwise place the primitives in the orientations shown in Figure 41-56. Assume symmetry for locational placement of the primitives. *Save* the drawing.

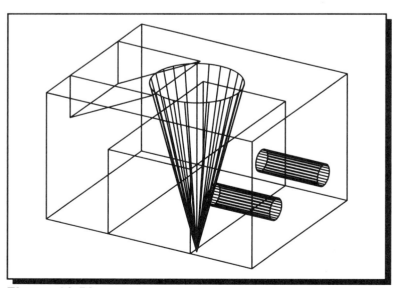

Figure 41-56

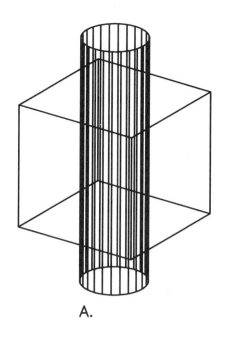

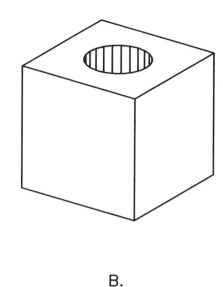

A.

B.

CHAPTER 42

Boolean Operations

CHAPTER OBJECTIVES

After completing this chapter you should:

1. be able to use *Solunion* to combine multiple primitives into one composite solid;

2. be able to subtract one or a set of primitives from another using *Solsub*;

3. be able to produce one solid from the intersecting volumes of several primitives using *Solint*;

4. know that *Solsep* can be used to reverse the action of the previous Boolean operation;

5. know how to create beveled edges (chamfers) on solids with *Solcham*;

6. know the methods for creating rounded corners (fillets) on solids using *Solfill*;

7. know the strategies for making composite solid designs more efficient in order to reduce computation time, file complexity, and file size.

BASICS

Once the individual 3D primitives have been created and moved into place, you are ready to put together the parts. The primitives can be "assembled" or combined by Boolean operations to create composite solids. All of the Boolean operations found in AME are listed in this chapter: *Solunion, Solsub, Solint, Solsep, Solcham,* and *Solfill.*

BOOLEAN OPERATION COMMANDS

SOLUNION

TYPE IN:	PULL-DOWN MENU	SCREEN MENU	TABLET MENU
Solunion or UNI	*Model, Union*	*MODEL, Solunion:*	*3,D*

Solunion unions (joins) selected primitives or composite solids to form one composite solid. Usually the selected solids occupy portions of the same space, yet are separate solids. *Solunion* creates one solid comprised of the total encompassing volume of the selected solids. (You can union solids even if the solids do not overlap.) All lines of intersections (surface boundaries) are calculated and displayed by AME. Multiple solid objects can be unioned with one *Solunion* command.

```
Command: solunion
Select objects: PICK (Select two or more solids.)
Select objects: Enter (Indicate completion of the selection process.)
x solids selected.
Command:
```

Two solid boxes are combined into one composite solid with *Solunion* (Fig 42-1). The original two solids (A) occupy the same physical space. The resulting union (B) contains the total contained volume. The new lines of intersection are automatically calculated and displayed. *Hide* was used to enhance visualization in (B).

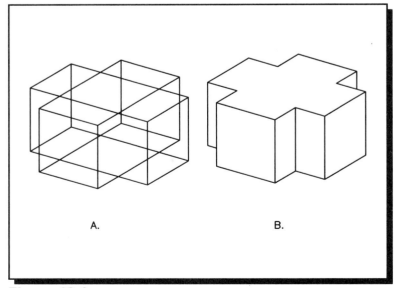

A.   B.

Figure 42-1

Because the volume occupied by any one of the primitives is included in the resulting composite solid, any redundant volumes are immaterial. The two primitives in Figure 42-2 (A) yield the same common volume as the composite solid (B).

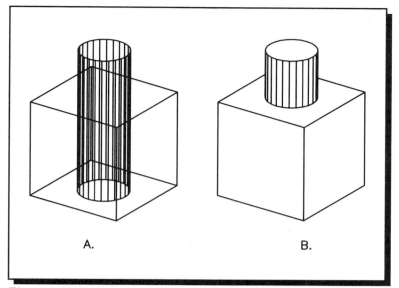

A.   B.

Figure 42-2

Two primitives that have coincident faces (touching sides) can be joined with *Solunion*. Several "blocks" can be put together to form a composite solid.

Multiple objects can be selected in response to the *Solunion* "Select objects:" prompt. It is not necessary, nor is it efficient, to use several successive Boolean operations if one or two can accomplish the same result.

Figure 42-3 illustrates how several primitives having coincident faces (A) can be combined into a composite solid (B). Only one *Solunion* is required to yield the composite solid.

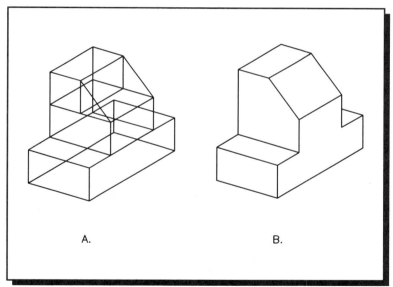

A.   B.

Figure 42-3

Even though it seems simple and intuitive to build composite solids by creating "blocks" and joining them with *Solunion*, it may not be the most efficient method. The solid in Figure 42-3 could be created more efficiently by extruding (*Solext*) the outline shape (as a closed *Pline*) as seen from the right side and then removing a wedge to create the inclined surface (using *Solcham*).

Because each primitive and each Boolean has a "cost" related to computation time, CSG tree complexity, and file size, it is important to design CSG solid models as efficiently as possible by planning for the minimum number of primitives and Boolean operations.

The two possible combinations in Figure 42-4 result in the same composite solid as that shown in Figure 42-1 (A); however, there is a difference in "cost." The "cost" is file complexity--increased number of levels of the CSG tree and increased computer computation time, resulting in increased file size. Figure 42-4 (A) has 5 primitives; whereas, (B) is a more efficient solution since it contains only 2 primitives.

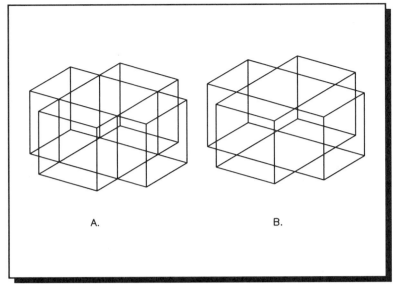

A.   B.

Figure 42-4

SOLSUB

TYPE IN:	PULL-DOWN MENU	SCREEN MENU	TABLET MENU
Solsub or SUB	*Model, Subtract*	*MODEL, Solsub:*	*3,C*

Solsub subtracts (or takes the difference of) one set of solids from another. *Solsub* operates with regions as well as solids. When using solids, *Solsub* subtracts the volume of one set of solids from another set of solids. Either set can contain only one or several solids. *Solsub* requires that you first select the set of solids that will remain (the "source objects") and secondly select the set you want to subtract from the first.

```
Command: solsub
Source objects...
Select objects: PICK
Select objects: Enter (Indicate completion of the selection.)
Objects to subtract from them...
Select objects: PICK
Select objects: Enter (Indicate completion of the selection.)
Command:
```

The entire volume of the solid or set of solids that is subtracted is completely removed, leaving the remaining volume of the source set.

Because you can select more than one object for the "source objects" and the "objects to subtract from them," many possible construction techniques are possible. *Solsub* also allows you to use a composite solid or a set of composites as the "source objects" and the "objects to subtract from them."

To create a box with a hole, a cylinder is located in the same 3D space as the box (see Figure 42-5). *Solsub* is used to subtract the entire volume of the cylinder ("Objects to subtract from them...") from the box ("Source objects..."). Note that the cylinder can have any height, as long as it is at least equal in height to the box.

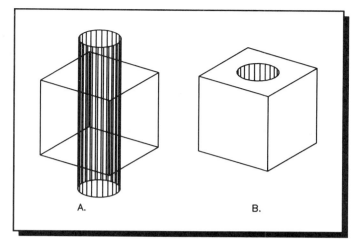

Figure 42-5

Figure 42-6 illustrates a method of creating a bearing race in a block by subtracting from the block either (1) a cylinder and a torus or (2) a composite solid of the unioned cylinder and torus. In terms of efficiency, it is preferred to subtract the torus and the cylinder with one *Solsub* rather than using *Solunion* to join the torus with the cylinder first and then using *Solsub* to subtract the composite shape from the block.

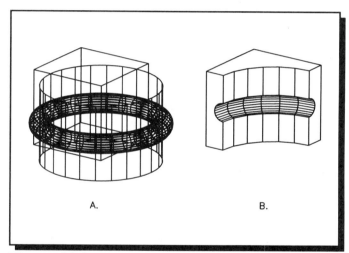

Figure 42-6

If you select multiple solids in response to the select "Source objects..." prompt, they are <u>automatically</u> unioned. This is known as an *n*-way Boolean operation. Using *Solsub* in this manner is very efficient and fast.

Figure 42-7 illustrates an *n*-way Boolean. The two boxes (A) are selected in response to the select "Source objects..." prompt. The cylinder is selected as the "objects to subtract from them...". *Solsub* joins the source objects (identical to a *Solunion*) and subtracts the cylinder. The resulting composite solid is shown in (B).

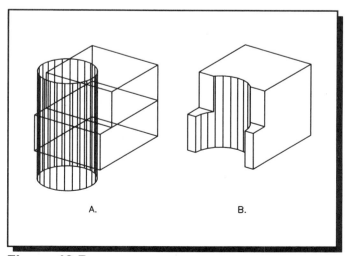

Figure 42-7

SOLINT

TYPE IN:	PULL-DOWN MENU	SCREEN MENU	TABLET MENU
Solint	*Model, Intersect*	*MODEL, Solint:*	*3,B*

Solint creates composite solids by calculating the intersection of two or more solids. The intersection is the common volume shared by the selected objects. Only the 3D space that is <u>part of all</u> of the selected objects is included in the resulting composite solid. *Solint* requires only that you select the solids from which the intersection is to be calculated.

```
Command: solint
Select objects: PICK (Select all desired solids.)
Select objects: Enter (Indicate completion of the selection process.)
n solids selected.
Command:
```

An example of *Solint* is shown in Figure 42-8. The cylinder and the box share common 3D space (A). The result of the *Solint* is a composite solid that represents that common space (B).

Solint can be very effective when used in conjunction with *Solext*. A technique known as <u>reverse drafting</u> can be used to create composite solids that may otherwise require several primitives and several Boolean operations. Consider the composite solid shown in Figure 42-3. Using *Solunion*, the composite shape requires five primitives.

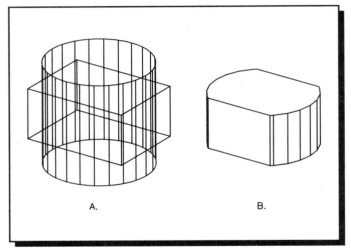

Figure 42-8

A more efficient technique than unioning several box primitives is to create two *Pline* shapes on vertical planes (Fig. 42-9). Each *Pline* shape represents the outline of the desired shape from its respective view, in this case, the front and the side views. The *Pline* shapes are intended to be extruded to occupy the same space. It is apparent from this illustration why this technique is called reverse drafting.

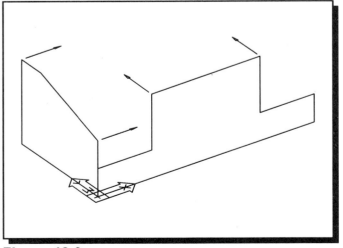

Figure 42-9

The two *Pline* "views" are extruded with *Solext* to comprise the total volume of the desired solid (Fig. 42-10, A). Finally, *Solint* is used to calculate the common volume and create the composite solid (B.).

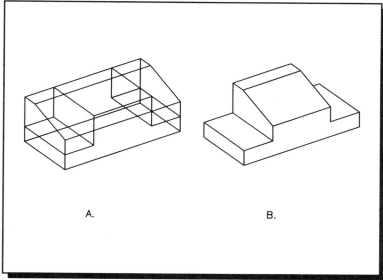

A.   B.

Figure 42-10

SOLSEP

TYPE IN:	PULL-DOWN MENU	SCREEN MENU	TABLET MENU
SOLSEP or SEP	*Model, Modify >* *Separate*	*MODEL, MODIFY* *SOLSEP:*	*1,C*

Solsep separates composite solids created by *Solunion*, *Solsub*, or *Solint*. This command is considered a Boolean operation because it changes the configuration of composite solids. It may be more accurate to consider *Solsep* as a reverse Boolean, or *Undo*. *Solsep* reverses, or undoes, the last Boolean operation that was performed by separating the composite solid into the previous individual composites or primitives.

Solsep reverses only the last Boolean operation. In other words, *Solsep* breaks down one level of the CSG tree. If three primitives were joined with one use of *Solunion*, *Solsep* would reverse the effect of the union and restore all three of the solids that were joined to their original primitive state. You can use *Solsep* successively to completely break down a composite solid (and the CSG tree) one step at a time into its individual primitives.

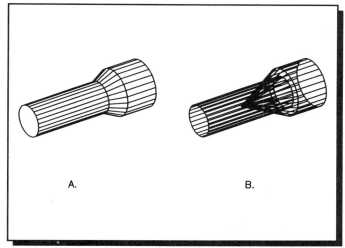

A.   B.

Figure 42-11

Consider the composite solid in Figure 42-11 (A). *Solsep* reverses the effect of the *Solunion* that was used to join the three primitives (B).

Keep in mind that *Solsep* restores the original primitives. Figure 42-12 shows a composite solid created by intersecting extrusions. *Solint* was used to combine the two extrusions (A). *Solsep* breaks down the CSG tree one level and restores the original primitives (B). *Solsep* <u>cannot</u> be used again in this case to break the extrusions into the original *Plines*. *Solsep* <u>only</u> undoes a *Solunion*, *Solsub*, or *Solint*.

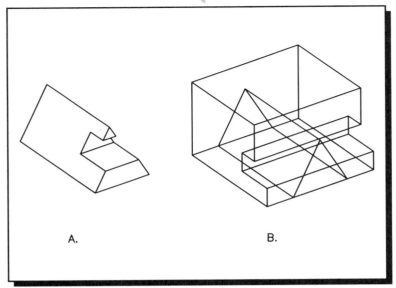

A.   B.

Figure 42-12

SOLCHAM

TYPE IN:	PULL-DOWN MENU	SCREEN MENU	TABLET MENU
SOLCHAM or CHAM	*Model, Modify > Chamfer Solids*	*MODEL, MODIFY, SOLCHAM:*	*2,A*

Chamfering is a machining operation that bevels a sharp corner. *Solcham* chamfers selected edges of an AME solid. The 2D equivalent command is *Chamfer*. *Solcham* performs two operations by first creating a wedge primitive and then adding it to or subtracting it from the selected solid. When using *Solcham*, you must select both the "base surface" and indicate which edge(s) on that surface you wish to chamfer. The command syntax "Next/<OK>:" is the AutoCAD convention used to allow you to highlight the desired surface for chamfering.

```
Command: solcham
Select base surface: PICK
Next/<OK>: Enter or N (Pressing N causes AutoCAD to highlight the next
```
connected surface.)
```
Pick edges of this face to chamfer (Press ENTER when done):
```
PICK (Multiple edges can be chamfered.)
```
Enter distance along base surface <size>: PICK or (value) (Enter
```
the distance from the edge to the new edge of the bevel along the selected surface.)
```
Enter distance along adjacent surface <size>: PICK or (value)
```
(Enter the distance from the edge to the new edge of the bevel along other surface.)

When AutoCAD prompts to select the "base surface," only an edge can be selected since the solids are displayed in wireframe. When you select an edge, AutoCAD highlights one of the two surfaces connected to the selected edge. Therefore, you must use the "Next/<OK>:" option to indicate which of the two surfaces you want to chamfer (Fig. 42-13 A).

Like *Chamfer*, *Solcham* requires two distances. A distance is from the selected edge to a newly created edge of the bevel. The first distance is applied to the base surface and the second distance is applied to the adjacent surface (Fig. 42-13 B).

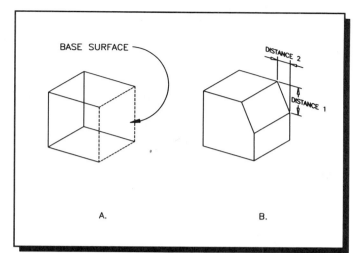

Figure 42-13

It is possible to chamfer multiple edges bounding the selected "base surface" with *Solcham* (Fig. 42-14, A) If the base surface is adjacent to cylindrical edges, the bevel follows the curved shape (B). *Solcham* also chamfers an edge defined by a *Pline*, but you must select each "edge to be chamfered" one face at a time.

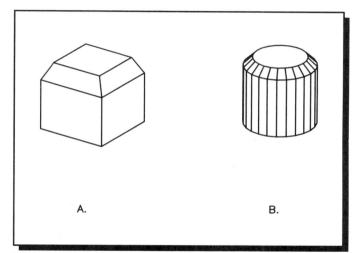

Figure 42-14

Solcham always connects the base surface with the selected adjoining surface(s), no matter the orientation. Figure 42-15 illustrates bevels created by *Solcham* automatically adding one wedge and subtracting another.

A *Solcham* operation would be stored in the CSG tree the same as if you created a wedge primitive and used *Solunion* or *Solsub* to combine it with the model. This is evident when you use *Solchp* (Change Primitives) and highlight the wedge primitives. The "distances" specified with *Solcham* can be changed on the wedge primitives with *Solcham*.

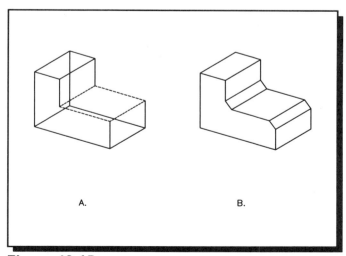

Figure 42-15

SOLFILL

TYPE IN:	PULL-DOWN MENU	SCREEN MENU	TABLET MENU
SOLFILL or FIL	*Model, Modify >* *Fillet Solids*	*MODEL, MODIFY,* *SOLFILL:*	*2,C*

Solfill rounds (fillets) the edge of selected solids. *Solfill* is the 3D equivalent to a 2D *Fillet*. *Solfill* creates a rounded primitive and automatically performs the Boolean needed to add or subtract it from the selected solids. *Solfill* creates fillets (concave corners) or rounds (convex corners). After selecting the edges to fillet, you must specify either a diameter or radius.

```
Command: solfill
Select edges to be filleted (Press ENTER when done): PICK
Diameter/<Radius>of fillet<current>: PICK or (value) or D or Enter
Command:
```

When selecting edges to fillet, the edges must be PICKed individually. The window options cannot be used.

Figure 42-16 depicts concave and convex fillets created with *Solfill*. The selected edges are highlighted.

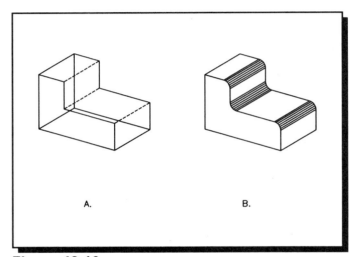

Figure 42-16

Curved surfaces can be treated with *Solfill* as shown in Figure 42-17. Only the end (circular shape) of the cylinder can be filleted with *Solfill*. *Solfill* can <u>not</u> be used to fillet the longitudinal elements of a cylindrical shape (other priimitives and Boolean operations must be used in that case).

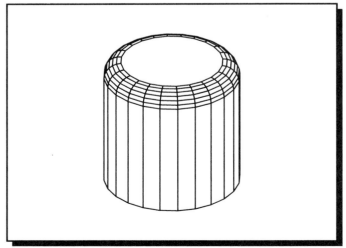

Figure 42-17

If you want to fillet three intersecting concave or convex edges, *Solfill* handles your request providing that you specify all edges in <u>one</u> use of the command. Figure 42-18 (A) highlights the edges selected in response to the "Select edges of solids to be filleted" prompt. The resulting solid is shown in (B). Make sure you select <u>all</u> edges together (in one *Solfill* command).

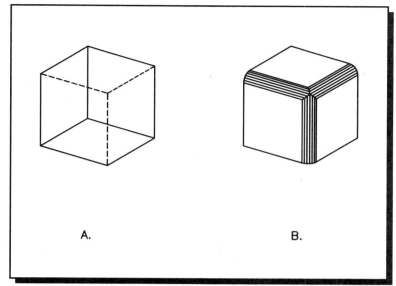

A.   B.

Figure 42-18

Solfill correctly fillets all intersecting convex edges as exemplified in Figure 42-19.

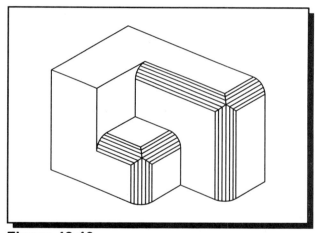

Figure 42-19

Solfill allows you to fillet intersecting concave edges as shown in Figure 42-20. The edges must all be selected for filleting with one use of the command.

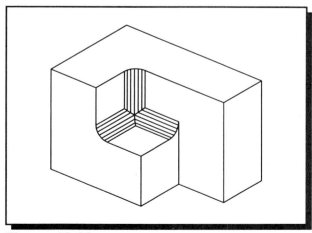

Figure 42-20

Concave <u>and</u> convex edges can be filleted with one use of _Solfill_ as long as the concave and convex edges do not intersect, as shown in Figure 42-21.

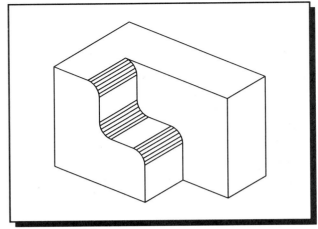

Figure 42-21

A combination of concave and convex edges can present some complex intersections for filleting. _Solfill_ correctly fillets complex intersections providing the correct procedure is used. However, in this example, if all edges are selected together, _Solfill_ does <u>not</u> fillet intersecting concave and convex fillets correctly. Results can be similar to Figure 42-22.

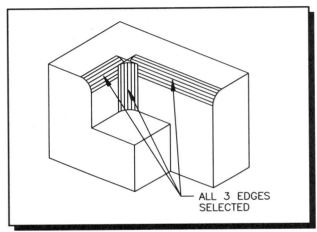

Figure 42-22

When using _Solfill_ to fillet an intersection of concave and convex edges, fillet the <u>odd</u> edge first. Then, invoke _Solfill_ again and fillet the other edges <u>including</u> the newly created arc. Figure 42-23 illustrates this point.

After you have created a fillet with _Solfill_, you can change its radius with the _Size_ option of _Solchp_ (see Chapter 43).

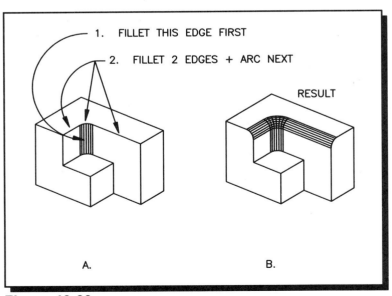

Figure 42-23

DESIGN EFFICIENCY

Now that you know the complete sequence for creating composite solid models, you can work toward improving design efficiency. The typical construction sequence is: (1) create primitives, (2) insure the primitives are in place by using UCS's, _Baseplanes_, or any of several move and rotate options, and (3) combine the primitives into a composite solid using Boolean operations. The typical step-by-step, "building-block" strategy, however, may not lead to the most efficient design.

Each Boolean operation requires computer computation time and creates an additional level of information stored in the CSG tree. In order to minimize computation time, CSG tree complexity, and the resulting file size, you should minimize the number of Boolean operations and, if possible, the number of primitives that you use.

For any composite solid, there are usually several strategies that could be used to construct the geometry. You should plan your designs ahead of time striving to minimize primitives and Boolean operations.

For example, consider the procedure shown in Figure 42-3. As discussed, it is more efficient to accomplish all unions with one _Solunion_, rather than each union as a separate step. Even better, create a closed _Pline_ shape of the profile, then use _Solext_. Figure 42-4 is another example of design efficiency based on using only 2 primitives and one _Solunion_ rather than multiple primitives, each unioned as a separate step. Figure 42-7 illustrates an N-way Boolean. Multiple solids can be unioned automatically by selecting them at the select "Source objects" prompt of _Solsub_. Also consider the strategy of reverse drafting as shown in Figure 42-9. Using _Solext_ in concert with _Solint_ can minimize file complexity and size tremendously.

In order to create efficient designs and minimize Boolean operations and primitives, keep these strategies in mind:

- Execute as many subtractions, unions, or intersections as possible within one _Solsub_, _Solunion_, or _Solint_ command. This action results in fewer levels of the CSG tree.

- Use n-way Booleans with _Solsub_. Combine solids (union) automatically by selecting multiple "Source objects" and then subtract solids from them.

- Make use of _Plines_ or regions for complex profile geometry, then extrude the profile shape with _Solext_. This is almost always more efficient for complex curved profile creation than using multiple Boolean operations.

- Make use of reverse drafting by extruding the "view" profiles (_Plines_ or regions) with _Solext_, then finding the common volume with _Solint_.

CHAPTER EXERCISES

1. ***Open*** the **CH40EX2** drawing. Use ***Solsub*** to subtract the cone from the wedge. The resulting composite solid should resemble that in Figure 42-24. Use ***Saveas*** and assign the name **CH42EX1**.

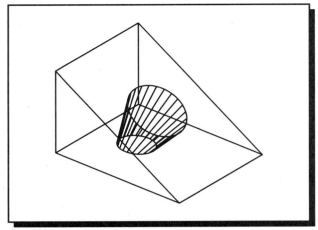

Figure 42-24

2. ***Open*** **CH40EX1**.

A. Perform a ***Solunion*** to combine the two boxes. Next, use ***Solsub*** to subtract the cylinder to create a hole. The resulting composite solid should look like that in Figure 42-25. Use ***Saveas*** and assign the name **CH42EX2A**.

B. ***Open*** **CH40EX1** again. This time perform an n-way Boolean with ***Solsub***. (When AutoCAD prompts for "Source objects," select both boxes.) Use ***Saveas*** and assign the name **CH42EX2B**. List the directory and compare the file size with CH42EX2A.

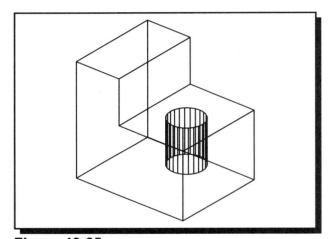

Figure 42-25

3. ***Open*** the **CH41EX2** drawing. Use ***Solsub*** <u>once</u> to subtract both revolved shapes from the cylinder. Use ***Solmesh*** to mesh the composite solid, then use ***Hide***. The solid should resemble that in Figure 42-26. ***Save*** the drawing as **CH42EX3**.

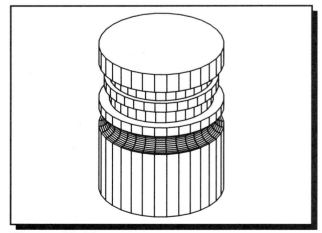

Figure 42-26

4. ***Open*** **CH41EX6**. Perform the necessary operations to establish the composite solid shown in Figure 42-27. Use ***Saveas*** and assign the name **CH42EX4**.

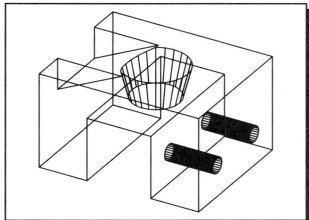

5. Begin a ***New*** drawing or use a ***Prototype***. Assign the name **FAUCET**.

Figure 42-27

A. Draw 3 closed ***Pline*** shapes as shown in Figure 42-28. Assume symmetry about the longitudinal axis. Use the WCS and create two new ***UCS***'s for the geometry. Use ***3point Arcs*** for the "front" profile.

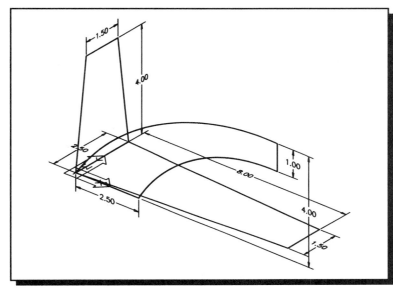

B. Use ***Solext*** to extrude each of the 3 profiles into the same space. Make sure you specify the correct positive or negative ***Height*** value.

Figure 42-28

C. Check the ***SOLWDENS*** setting. Set it to **6** or **8** if not already set. Finally, use ***Solint*** to create the composite solid of the Faucet. ***Save*** the drawing.

D. (Optional) Create a nozzle extending down from the small end. Then create a channel for the water to flow (through the inside) and subtract it from the faucet.

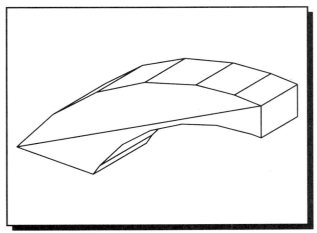

Figure 42-29

6. Construct a solid model of the Bar Guide in Figure 42-30. Strive for the most efficient design. It is possible to construct this object with one *Solext* and one *Solsub*. Save the model as **BGUID-SL**.

7. Make a solid model of the V-block shown in Figure 42-31. There are several strategies that could be used for construction of this object. Strive for the most efficient design. Plan your approach by sketching a few possibilities. Save the model as **VBLOK-SL**.

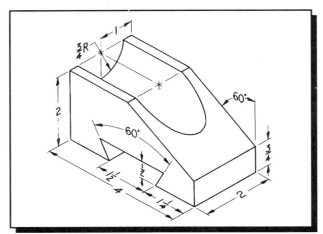

Figure 42-30

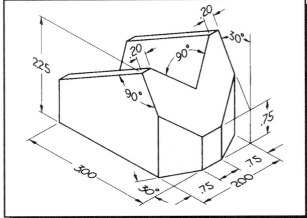

Figure 42-31

8. Construct a composite solid model of the Support Bracket using efficient techniques. Save the model as **SUPBK-SL**.

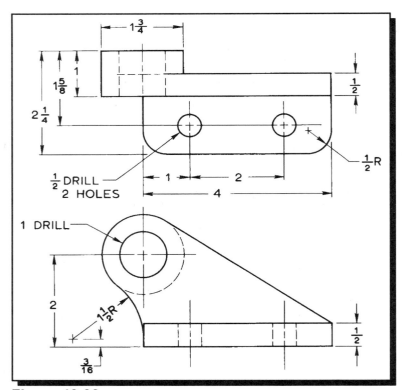

Figure 42-32

9. Construct a solid model of the Angle Brace shown in Figure 42-33. Use efficient design techniques. Save the drawing as **AGLBR-SL**.

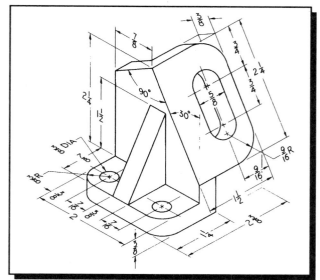

Figure 42-33

10. Construct a solid model of the Saddle shown in Figure 42-34. An efficient design can be utilized by creating *Pline* profiles of the top "view" and the front "view" as shown in Figure 42-35. Use *Solext* and *Solint* to produce a composite solid. Additional Boolean operations are required to complete the part. The finished model should look like Figure 42-36 (with *Hide* performed). Save the drawing as **SADL-SL**.

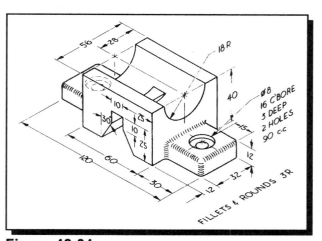

Figure 42-34

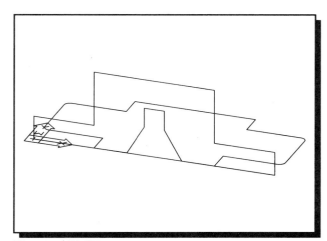

Figure 42-35

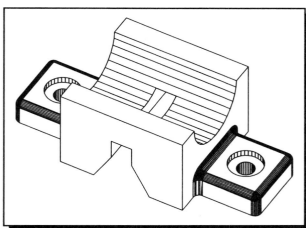

Figure 42-36

11. Create a solid model of the Pulley. All vertical dimensions are diameters. Orientation of primitives is critical in the construction of this model. Try creating the circular shapes on the XY plane (circular axis aligns with Z axis of the WCS). Then use **Rotate3D** or **Solmove** to align the circular axis of the composite solid with the Y axis of the WCS. **Save** the drawing as **PULLY-SL**.

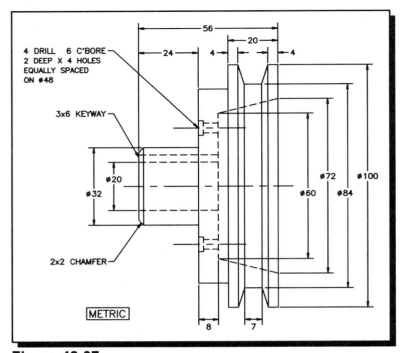

Figure 42-37

12. Create a composite solid model of the Adjustable Mount (Fig. 42-38). Use of efficient design techniques is extremely important with a model of this complexity. Save your model in wireframe represen-tation (before using *Solmesh*) to conserve file size. Assign the name **ADJMT-SL**.

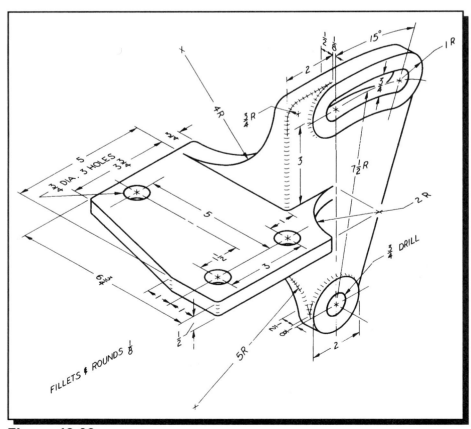

Figure 42-38

```
┌─────────────────────────────────────────────────────────────────┐
│                        Materials Browser                          │
├─────────────────────────────────────────────────────────────────┤
│                                                                   │
│   ┌──────┐            ┌─────────────────────────────────────┐    │
│   │File..│ acad.mat   │ Current Material:                   │    │
│   └──────┘            │ MILD_STEEL                          │    │
│                       │                                     │    │
│                       └─────────────────────────────────────┘    │
│                                                                   │
│   Materials in File    ┌─────────┐  Materials in Drawing         │
│   ┌──────────────────┐ │ New...  │  ┌────────────────────────┐   │
│   │ALUMINUM         │ └─────────┘  │MILD_STEEL             │ │   │
│   │BRASS            │ ┌─────────┐  │                        │ │   │
│   │BRONZE           │ │ Load >  │  │                        │ │   │
│   │COPPER           │ └─────────┘  │                        │ │   │
│   │GLASS            │ ┌─────────┐  │                        │ │   │
│   │HSLA_STL         │ │ < Save  │  │                        │ │   │
│   │LEAD             │ └─────────┘  │                        │ │   │
│   │MILD_STEEL       │ ┌─────────┐  │                        │ │   │
│   │NICU             │ │ Remove  │  │                        │ │   │
│   │STAINLESS_STL    │ └─────────┘  │                        │ │   │
│   └──────────────────┘ ┌─────────┐  └────────────────────────┘   │
│                        │  Set    │                               │
│                        └─────────┘                               │
│                        ┌─────────┐                               │
│                        │ Edit... │                               │
│                        └─────────┘                               │
│                        ┌─────────┐                               │
│                        │ Change  │                               │
│                        └─────────┘                               │
│                                                                   │
│            ┌────────┐  ┌────────┐  ┌─────────┐                    │
│            │   OK   │  │ Cancel │  │ Help... │                    │
│            └────────┘  └────────┘  └─────────┘                    │
│                                                                   │
└─────────────────────────────────────────────────────────────────┘
```

CHAPTER 43

Solids Editing, Analyzing, and Sectioning

CHAPTER OBJECTIVES

After completing this chapter you should:

1. be able to use *Solchp* to modify any primitive of an AME composite solid, including changing color or size, replacing, copying, moving, or deleting the primitive;

2. be able to free up memory and reduce drawing file size with *Solpurge*;

3. know how to list information about a specific solid with *Sollist*;

4. be able to calculate mass properties of an AME solid using *Solmassp*;

5. know how to use *Solmat* to set, edit, create new, and save material properties;

6. be able to check for interferences between solids with *Solinterf*;

7. be able to create cross sections with *Solsect* and extract features with *Solfeat*;

8. know how to cut an AME solid or create a mold with *Solcut*.

EDITING AME SOLID MODELS

The *Solchp* command allows you to change any complex solid model created with AME. *Solchp* accesses the CSG tree and highlights the original primitives that were used in the construction of the AME model. You have the freedom to change dimensions of the original primitives, move primitives, replace primitives, and perform other operations. When your change has been made, AutoCAD reconstructs (reevaluates) the composite solid based upon the record of primitives and Boolean operations kept in the CSG tree. The *Solpurge* command can be used to conserve file space by removing unwanted information from an AME model.

SOLCHP

TYPE IN:	PULL-DOWN MENU	SCREEN MENU	TABLET MENU
SOLCHP or SCHP	*Model, Modify > Change Primitives*	*MODEL, MODIFY, SOLCHP:*	*1,D*

One of the most powerful and versatile features of AME CSG (Constructive Solid Geometry) modeling is the ability to change primitives with *Solchp*. *Solchp* can be used to change the features of any primitive that is part of a composite solid. *Solchp* operates with solids similarly to its function with the Region Modeler. The changes that can be made are listed in the command prompt:

```
Command: solchp
Color/Delete/Evaluate/Instance/Move/Next/Pick/Replace/Size
/eXit<N>:
```

Each of the options of *Solchp* are described and illustrated below.

Next and *Change* are the two options that allow you to select (highlight) the primitive you want to change (Fig. 43-1).

Next

    This option cycles through (highlighting) the primitives one at a time.

Pick

    This option allows you to **PICK** the desired primitive.

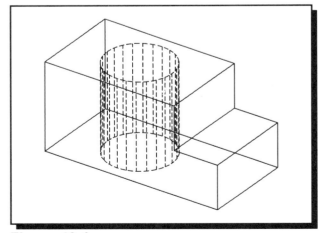

Figure 43-1

Size

The dimensions of any primitive can be changed with this option. Invoking this option causes the MCS icon to appear. AutoCAD prompts you for the appropriate dimensions for the selected primitive. For example, if a cylinder is selected, you can change the radius along the X or Y axis or height along the Z axis. *Solchp* must be exited before the change is displayed.

Figure 43-2 illustrates using *Size* to change the radius of the hole in the composite solid. First, select the primitive (A). Next, specify the new dimensions. Exit *Solchp* to see the change (B).

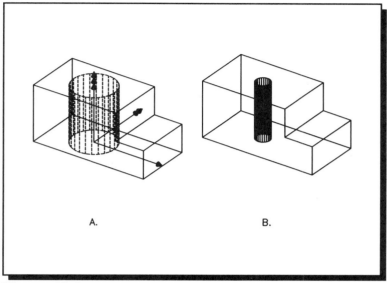

Figure 43-2

The *Size* option allows you to change the following dimensions listed for each type of primitive.

Solbox	Length along X, length along Y, length along Z.
Solcone	Radius along X, radius along Y, length along Z (height).
Solcyl	Radius along X, radius along Y, length along Z (height).
Solwedge	Distance along first surface, distance along second surface.
Solsphere	Radius.
Soltorus	Radius of torus, radius of tube.
Solcham	Length along X, length along Y, length along Z.
Solfil	Radius.
Solext	Height. If you desire to change the *Pline* shape, a new 2D *Pline* is created. You must exit *Solchp*, edit the *Pline* shape, and use the *Replace* option.
Solrev	Angle of revolution. If you desire to change the axis of revolution or shape of *Pline* shape, another *Pline* shape is created for you to edit after you exit *Solchp*. Then use the *Replace* option.

Replace

This option is used to replace the selected primitive with another. First create the new primitive, then position it in the desired position <u>before</u> you invoke *Solchp* with *Replace*. The *Replace* option simply asks you to select the primitive (old) and the solid to replace the primitive (new). You can discard or retain the old primitive. *Solchp* must be exited before the change is displayed.

Make sure the new primitive (cone) is in position before using *Replace*. Figure 43-3 (A) displays both the old (cylinder) and new primitive. *Solchp* must be exited before the change is visible (B).

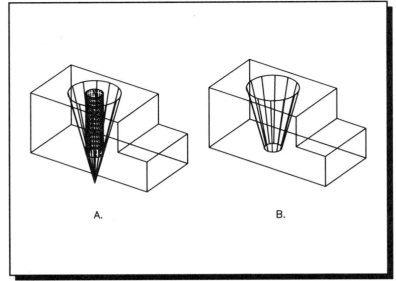

Figure 43-3

Move

The selected primitive can be moved to another position with this option. Just like the *Move* command, you are prompted for a "Base point" and a "second point of displacement."

In Figure 43-4 (A) *OSNAP* is used to specify the basepoint of the highlighted primitive. The primitive is moved to the second point of displacement (B). *Solchp* must be exited before the change is displayed.

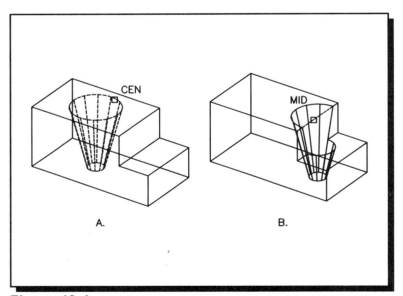

Figure 43-4

Instance

An *Instance* is a copy. This option creates a duplicate primitive from the selected primitive. The original primitive is not changed or removed from the model. The new copy is positioned at the <u>same</u> location as the original primitive and on the current layer. *Solchp move*, *Solmove*, or *Move* can be used to reposition the new primitive. After using a move option, *Redraw* to display the change. The newly created *Instance* is <u>not</u> part of the composite solid and requires a Boolean operation to make it so.

Figure 43-5 (A) shows the selected primitive (highlighted) for creating an *instance*. Because the *instance* is created in the <u>same space</u> as the original primitive, there appears to be no change in the model. You should move the newly created primitive. If you use the *Move* option while still in the *Solchp* command, the <u>original</u> primitive is automatically selected for the move. Results should appear as in (B) after exiting *Solchp* and causing a *Redraw*.

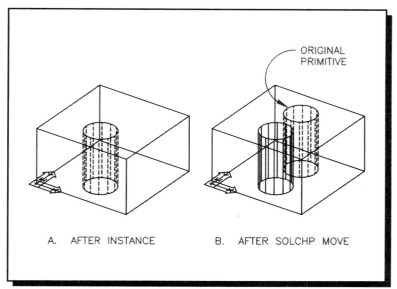

A. AFTER INSTANCE   B. AFTER SOLCHP MOVE

ORIGINAL PRIMITIVE

Figure 43-5

The other alternatives are to use the *Move* or the *Solmove* command to reposition the new copy. In either case, using the *last* option to select objects automatically finds the <u>newly created primitive</u>, not the original (Fig. 43-6). Don't forget to *Redraw* after the move.

In any case, a Boolean operation (*Solsub* in this case) must be performed next to make the newly created, and moved, primitive part of the composite solid.

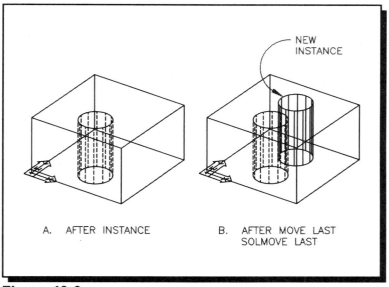

A. AFTER INSTANCE   B. AFTER MOVE LAST
                              SOLMOVE LAST

NEW INSTANCE

Figure 43-6

Delete

Delete removes the selected primitive from its composite solid. You can choose whether or not to retain the deleted primitive. If you choose <u>not</u> to retain the selected primitive (the default option), the resulting composite solid is as if the *Delete*d primitive never existed. In other words, the selected primitive is detached (like undoing the related Boolean operation) and erased from the drawing. If you choose to <u>retain</u> the deleted primitive, it is only detached from the composite solid but remains in place. This action is similar to *Solsep*, assuming the selected primitive was the subject of the last Boolean operation.

Figure 43-7 (A) displays a composite solid composed of two box primitives with the smaller subtracted from the larger. (This figure is shown in meshed representation with the *Hide* command performed.)

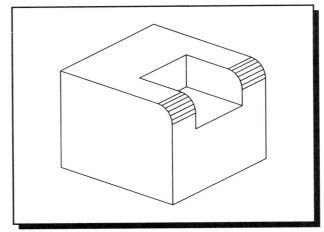

Figure 43-7

Figure 43-8 simulates using the *Delete* option of *Solchp* with the small box, accepting the default option <u>not</u> to retain the detached primitive.

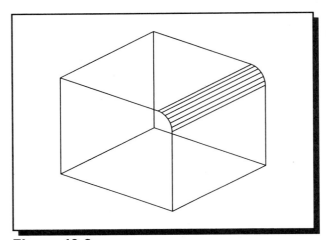

Figure 43-8

Figure 43-9 depicts the result of <u>retaining</u> the detached primitive. The small box is not part of the composite solid but occupies some of the same space.

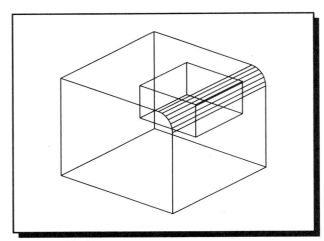

Figure 43-9

Color

When creating composite solid models with AME, different colors within one model can be achieved by first creating primitives of different colors and combining them into a composite model using Boolean operations. If *Shade* is used, edges and faces of the resulting composite model acquire the color of the primitives defining the particular edge or face.

NOTE: If the *SOLRENDER* variable has been changed from the default option of *CSG* to *Uniform*, the composite solids are always shown in uniform color (see Chapter 44).

The *Color* option of *Solchp* allows you to <u>retroactively</u> assign colors to the individual primitives of the composite solid. Only the <u>outline</u> of the primitive is displayed in the assigned color if the model is displayed in wireframe representation. The assigned color is used to fill the surfaces if *Shade* or *Render* is used. Depending on the application, this feature is useful for bringing attention to primitives that possess special features or functions.

The *Color* option is simple to use. Just select the desired primitive(s) and assign an ACI number (AutoCAD Color Index) or name for the color (for example, green or red). The change is displayed immediately.

Evaluate

This option forces a reevaluation of the composite solid. This is necessary when you have made changes to the structure of the composite solid that need to be displayed but you are not ready to *eXit* the *Solchp* command.

eXit

This option <u>must</u> be used to keep the changes made within *Solchp*. The *eXit* option terminates the *Solchp* command and returns to the `Command:` prompt. The CSG tree is automatically reevaluated upon exiting.

SOLPURGE

TYPE IN:	PULL-DOWN MENU	SCREEN MENU	TABLET MENU
SOLPURGE	*Model, Utility >* *Purge Objects*	*MODEL, UTILITY,* *SOLPURG:*	*3,H*

Solpurge is a utility command intended for reducing file size and conserving memory. When creating and editing solids, AME stores various information for possible future use and reserves some memory for individual solid entities and primitives. *Solpurge* frees memory and information related to AME solids and regions but <u>does not erase</u> any solids or regions from the drawing. *Solpurge* allows you to free memory and file contents (depending on the selected option); however, there may be a time penalty in some cases where AME may have to reconstruct information by evaluating the CSG tree.

```
Command: solpurge
Memory/2dtree/Bfile/Pmesh/<Erased>: option
```

The options are explained here.

Memory

This option frees up memory reserved for solids and regions but does not erase the entities. The record of the creation of the entities is still stored in the CSG tree which can be reevaluated if needed. There are two suboptions.

All   This suboption releases memory associated with all solids and regions. No solids or regions are erased, only the part of memory reserved for them.

\<Select\>   This suboption allows you to select which solids or regions should have the associated memory purged. This is helpful when one solid is completed and you want to work on another solid in the same drawing.

2dtree

This minimizes the CSG tree for <u>regions only</u>. The size and complexity of the tree is reduced without changing any region entities in the drawing.

Bfile

This option can reduce the size of the AutoCAD <u>drawing file</u> up to <u>50 percent</u>. This option purges selected solids' B-rep files from your drawing. The solid entities are not erased or changed in any way. However, if related solids are selected for use in an AME command, time will be required to reevaluate the solids (reconstruct from the CSG tree record). This option is useful if you have completed some solids and want to create more or edit other solids.

Pmesh

Similar to the *Bfile* option, this option can reduce file size. *Pmesh* removes file information related to the selected *Pmeshes* (created when a solid is meshed). If a solid in meshed representation is selected, it is changed to wireframe representation, then the mesh information is removed.

Erased

If you *Erase* a composite solid from your drawing, even though it may seem that the solid is completely removed, some information related to the primitives used to construct the composite still exists in the drawing. This option removes all information and memory related to <u>previously</u> erased composite solids. The result is reduced file size. The file can be reduced further by *Opening* it and *Saving* it again.

ANALYZING AME SOLID MODELS

Several commands in AME allow you to inquire about and analyze the solid geometry. Because AME solids have a material assigned (MILD_STEEL is the default), they possess material characteristics; therefore, mass property calculations can be easily generated. You can also request area calculations, request specific database information for a solid, and check for interferences between solids.

788

Solarea calculates the surface area encompassing a solid model. _Sollist_ lists the _Edge, Face, Tree,_ or _Object_ information for a selected AME solid. _Solmassp_ calculates a variety of properties for the selected AME solid model. These commands are easy to use because AutoCAD does the calculation and lists the information in screen or text box format. The data can be saved to a file for future exportation to a report document or an analysis package. The _Solmat_ command allows you to specify the current material for newly created solids as well as providing a utility for listing and editing specific material characteristics. The _Solinterf_ command finds the interference of two or more solids and highlights the overlapping features so you can make necessary alterations.

SOLAREA

TYPE IN:	PULL-DOWN MENU	SCREEN MENU	TABLET MENU
SOLAREA or SA	_Model, Inquiry > Area Calc._	_MODEL, INQUIRY, SOLAREA:_	_2,H_

The _Solarea_ command automatically calculates the surface area of one or more solids. Solids can be in wireframe or meshed display. Multiple solids can be selected to be included in the area calculation. AutoCAD responds with a single total for all selected solids. The command format follows.

```
Command: solarea
Select objects: PICK
Select objects: PICK or Enter
Updating object...
Done.
1 solid selected.
Surface area of solids is 106.5841 sq cm
```

Solarea calculates the surface area using the current units setting. The _SOLAREAU_ variable is used to set the units for area calculations (see Chapter 44). _Sq cm_ is the default setting. Accepted units for area calculations are the square of any length unit such as in, m, cm, mm, etc. Available units for length, area, or otherwise are listed in the ACAD.UNT file.

SOLLIST

TYPE IN:	PULL-DOWN MENU	SCREEN MENU	TABLET MENU
SOLLIST or SL	_Model, Inquiry > List Solids_	_MODEL, INQUIRY, SOLLIST_	_2,F_

The _Sollist_ command lists a variety of information for selected AME solids. You can inquire about coordinate information for a _Face_ or an _Edge,_ or you can get a list of information defining the solid (_Object_ option). Additionally, _Sollist_ provides an option for listing information about the CSG _Tree_ for a selected solid. The command prompt displays the options.

```
Command: sollist
Edge/Face/Tree/<Object>: option
```

The options are listed and explained with example text read-outs. In these examples, a simple solid composed of a cylinder *Subtracted* from a box (Fig. 43-10) is used as the solid for listing information.

Object

This option lists information about the top tree level of the selected solid. Using this option for the example solid (Fig. 43-10) yields the display shown.

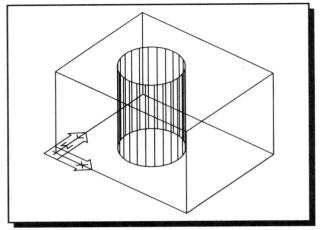

Figure 43-10

```
Command: sollist
Edge/Face/Tree/<Object>: Enter
Select objects: PICK
Select objects: Enter
1 solid selected.

Object type = SUBTRACTION      Handle = 4E
   Component handles:   15 and 21
   Area = 106.584115    Material = MILD_STEEL
   Representation = WIREFRAME    Render type = CSG
Rigid motion:
      +1.000000    +0.000000    +0.000000    +0.000000
      +0.000000    +1.000000    +0.000000    +0.000000
      +0.000000    +0.000000    +1.000000    +0.000000
      +0.000000    +0.000000    +0.000000    +1.000000
```

Information included in the text screen for this example includes the following items.

Object type	This is the Boolean operation used to create this (the highest) level of the CSG tree for the solid.
Handle	This is the handle for the object in the top level.
Component handles	Handles for the objects of the next lower level that make up the composite solid are given.
Area	Surface area for the solid is given. The value only appears if the *Solarea* or *Solmesh* command have been previously used for the solid.
Material	The material assigned to the solid is listed.
Representation	This is the current display type (mesh or wireframe).

Render type	Render type is either _CSG_ or _Uniform_ as set by the _SOLRENDER_ variable (See Chapter 44).
Rigid motion	The translation and rotation that have been used on the solid are given in coordinate format. The first three columns represent the X, Y, and Z axis rotation, respectively. The fourth column specifies the translation vector.

Edge

This option of _Sollist_ gives length and/or coordinate data for the selected edge. Selecting the top right edge of the solid in Figure 43-10 yields the following information.

```
Command: sollist
Edge/Face/Tree/<Object>: e
Pick an edge: PICK
Updating object...
Done.
Straight edge, length = 4.
coordinates: (5, 4, 3) to (5, 0, 3)
```

Face

This option displays information about the selected face. For the example in Figure 43-10, PICKing the top face results in information that gives the direction for outward normal and a point on the plane. The outward normal direction may be helpful when rendering (See Chapter 45, _Rpref_ command).

```
Command: sollist
Edge/Face/Tree/<Object>: f
Pick a face: PICK
Next/<OK>: Enter
Planar face, outward normal is (0 0 1).
point on plane: (5 4 3).
```

Tree

This option of _Sollist_ lists the CSG tree information for the selected solid. Selecting the object in Figure 43-10 displays the following information.

```
Command: sollist
Edge/Face/Tree/<Object>: t
Select objects: PICK
Select objects: Enter

Object type = SUBTRACTION      Handle = 4E
   Component handles:  15 and 21
   Area = 106.584115   Material = MILD_STEEL
   Representation = WIREFRAME    Render type = CSG

Object type = BOX (5.000000, 4.000000, 3.000000) Handle
             = 15
   Area not computed   Material = MILD_STEEL
   Representation = WIREFRAME    Render type = CSG
   Node level = 1
```

```
Object type = CYLINDER (1.000000, 1.000000, 4.000000)
        Handle = 21
Area not computed    Material = MILD_STEEL
Representation = WIREFRAME   Render type = CSG
Node level = 1
```

The first paragraph of information _Tree_ lists is related to the top level of the CSG tree and is identical to that displayed by the _Object_ option. The other information groups (_Object type_) relate to the next lower level of the CSG tree, specifically, the nodes (primitives) that comprise the composite solid.

SOLMASSP

TYPE IN:	PULL-DOWN MENU	SCREEN MENU	TABLET MENU
SOLMASSP or MP	_Model, Inquiry > Mass Property..._	_MODEL, INQUIRY, SOLMASSP:_	2,G

Since solid models define a complete description of the geometry and have material characteristics, they are ideal for mass properties and area analysis. The _Solmassp_ command automatically computes a variety of mass properties such as mass, volume, bounding box, centroid, moments and product of inertia, radii of gyration and principal moments. The material assigned to a solid is specified by the _Solmat_ command (discussed later).

Mass and area properties are useful for a variety of applications. The data generated by the _Solmassp_ command can be saved to a file for future exportation in order to develop bills of material, stress analysis, kinematics studies, and dynamics analysis.

Solmassp calculates the mass properties using the current units settings. The units used in the calculations are specified by the variables _SOLMASS_, _SOLVOLUME_, _SOLAREAU_, and _SOLLENGTH_ (see Chapters 43, 44).

Two other variables affect the results of the mass properties calculations. _SOLSUBDIV_ sets the subdivision level and _SOLDECOMP_ sets the direction for decomposition.

Applying the _Solmassp_ command to the solid model shown in Figure 43-1 produces the _Mass Properties_ dialogue box (Fig. 43-11). The top portion of the dialogue box displays the following list of calculations (accessed by the slider bar).

```
Ray projection along X axis, level of subdivision: 3.
Mass:                    383.0361 gm
Volume:                  48.73233 cu cm   (Err: 1.250226)
Bounding box:      X: 0  --   5 cm
                   Y: 0  --   4 cm
                   Z: 0  --   3 cm
Centroid:          X: 2.59637   cm      (Err: 0.05130993)
                   Y: 1.917915  cm      (Err: 0.1692455)
                   Z: 1.502979  cm      (Err: 0.118843)
```

```
Moments of inertia:  X: 3093.668   gm sq cm (Err: 292.7818)
                     Y: 4639.083   gm sq cm (Err: 151.8174)
                     Z: 5431.041   gm sq cm (Err: 275.8292)
Products of inertia: XY: 1907.991  gm sq cm (Err: 160.4677)
                     YZ: 1085.97   gm sq cm (Err: 131.3106)
                     ZX: 1492.802  gm sq cm (Err: 114.5131)
Radii of gyration:   X: 2.841954  cm
                     Y: 3.480136  cm
                     Z: 3.768957  cm
Principal moments(gm sq cm) and X-Y-Z directions about
centroid:
        I: 819.4339 along [0.9999936 0.00181111 -0.003090469]
        J: 1451.26 along [0.0029565 0.06981054 0.9975559]
        K: 1190.457 along [0.002022431 -0.9975586 0.06980474]
```

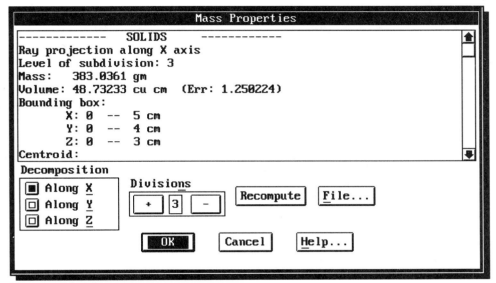

Figure 43-11

A brief explanation of mass properties is given below:

Mass: Mass is a measure of the weight of a solid. Mass is also considered a measure of a solid's resistance to linear acceleration (overcoming inertia).

Volume: This value specifies the amount of space occupied by the solid.

Bounding Box: These lengths specify the extreme width, depth, and height of the selected solid.

Centroid: This is the center of mass. The solid theoretically can be balanced when supported only at this point. The centroid is also considered the geometrical center.

Moments of Inertia: Moments convey how the mass is distributed around the X, Y, and Z axes of the current coordinate system. These values are a measure of a solid's resistance to <u>angular</u> acceleration (mass is a measure of a solid's resistance to <u>linear</u> acceleration). Moments of inertia are helpful for stress computations.

Products of Inertia: These values specify the solid's resistance to <u>angular</u> acceleration with respect to two axes at a time (XY, YZ, or ZX). Products of inertia are also useful for stress analysis.

Radii of Gyration: If the object were a concentrated solid mass without holes or other features, the radii of gyration represent these theoretical dimensions (radius about each axis) such that the same moments of inertia would be computed.

Principle Moments and X, Y, Z Directions: In structural mechanics, it is sometimes important to determine the orientation of the axes about which the moments of inertia are at a maximum. When the moments of inertia about centroidal axes become a maximum, the products of inertia become zero. These particular axes are called the principal axes and the corresponding moments of inertia with respect to these axes are the principal moments (about the centroid).

The *Mass Properties* dialogue box (Fig. 43-11) also provides other options listed here.

Decomposition

AME uses a ray-casting method to calculate mass properties. This option specifies the direction (along the X, Y, or Z axes of the current coordinate system) that the "rays" are sent. You should specify that the rays be fired along the longest axis of the solid in order to improve the accuracy of computations. The direction can also be set by the system variable *SOLDECOMP*.

Divisions

You can set the number of divisions from 1 to 8. The higher the value, the more accurate the calculations but the more time that is required. With the ray-casting method, the solid is broken down into a number of subdivisions. Rays are fired on each subdivision and the volumes of all subdivisions are added up to give the total for calculations. The subdivision level can also be controlled by setting the system variable *SOLSUBDIV*.

Recompute

Use this option to force AME to recompute mass properties if you made changes to *Decomposition* or *Divisions*.

File...

This option allows you to specify a file to which the mass properties calculations are written. A file dialogue box appears (not shown). The mass properties are written to an ASCII file with an .MPR (Mass Properties) extension.

SOLMAT

TYPE IN:	PULL-DOWN MENU	SCREEN MENU	TABLET MENU
SOLMAT or MAT or DDSOLMAT	*Model, Utility > Material*	*MODEL, UTILITY, SOLMAT*	*4,F*

Solmat is the command that you use to specify the type of material to be assigned to solids as you create them. *Solmat* also provides a number of utilities that allow you to list, edit, change, load, remove, save, and create new material properties. When mass properties are generated using the *Solmassp* command, AME uses only the <u>density</u> material characteristic specified for the assigned material.

Solmat operates in command line or dialogue box format. The command line format is shown below. Wild cards are not supported for *Solmat*.

```
Command: solmat
Change/Edit/LIst/LOad/New/Remove/SAve/SEt/?/<eXit>:
```

Selecting *Material...* from the *Utility >* option in the *Model* pull down menu or typing *Ddsolmat* produces the *Materials Browser* dialogue box providing access to all options (Fig. 43-12). The options for both formats are explained below.

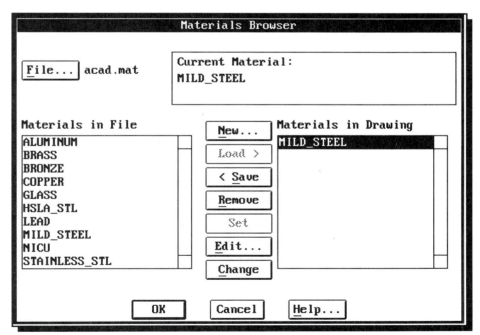

Figure 43-12

Set

This is the option you use to set the default material that is used for newly created solids. Combining solids of different materials by Boolean operations will cause them all to have this default material.

Change

Use this option to change the material assigned to an existing solid in your drawing.

?

(This option is for command line format only.) The *?* option displays the list of materials in the drawing and in an external file. ACAD.MAT is the default file used for storing materials. The list is the same as that shown in the *Materials Browser* dialogue box.

Load

This option loads a material definition from an external file (ACAD.MAT) into your drawing. Using the dialogue box, first select the material from the *Materials in File* list on the left, then PICK the *Load >* tile. If you use command line format, you are prompted for a material.

Remove

Use this option to remove a material definition from your drawing. If you use the dialogue box, select the material from the *Materials in Drawing* list on the right, then PICK the *Remove* tile. If you use command format, you are prompted for the material name to remove.

Edit

This utility allows you to redefine specific material characteristics for any material. The material must already be loaded into your drawing. If you use the dialogue box format, the *Material Properties* dialogue box appears (Fig. 43-13). Highlight a specific property and enter the new value in the *Value* edit box. The changes are updated to the material in the drawing but not in the ACAD.MAT file. If you use command line format, you are prompted to save the changes to the materials file.

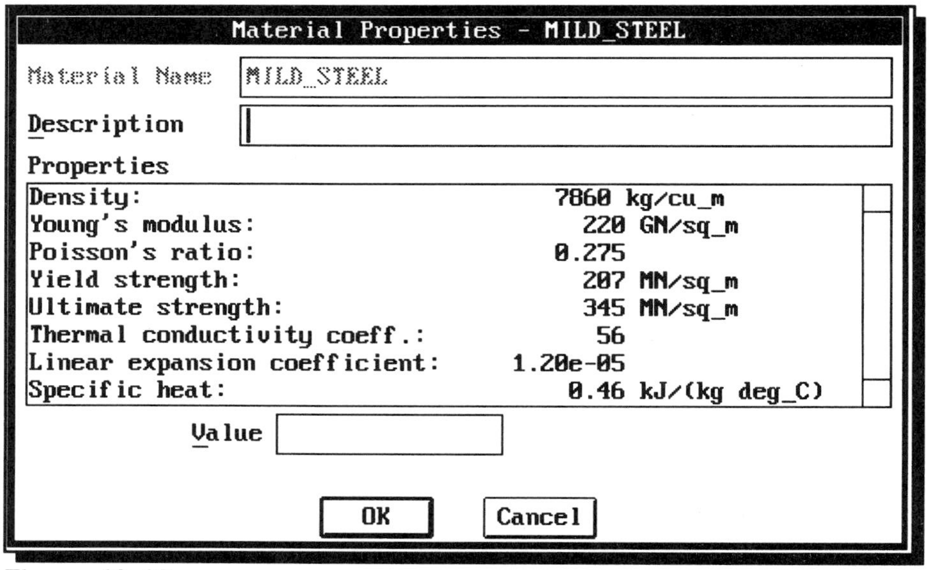

```
┌──────────────────────────────────────────────────────────────┐
│              Material Properties - MILD_STEEL                  │
│  Material Name    │MILD_STEEL                              │    │
│                                                                │
│  Description      │                                        │    │
│  Properties                                                    │
│ ┌────────────────────────────────────────────────────────┐    │
│ │Density:                          7860 kg/cu_m          │█│   │
│ │Young's modulus:                   220 GN/sq_m          │ │   │
│ │Poisson's ratio:                 0.275                  │ │   │
│ │Yield strength:                    207 MN/sq_m          │ │   │
│ │Ultimate strength:                 345 MN/sq_m          │ │   │
│ │Thermal conductivity coeff.:        56                  │ │   │
│ │Linear expansion coefficient:   1.20e-05                │ │   │
│ │Specific heat:                    0.46 kJ/(kg deg_C)    │█│   │
│ └────────────────────────────────────────────────────────┘    │
│            Value  │                              │              │
│                                                                │
│                 ┌──────────┐    ┌──────────┐                   │
│                 │    OK    │    │  Cancel  │                   │
│                 └──────────┘    └──────────┘                   │
└──────────────────────────────────────────────────────────────┘
```

Figure 43-13

Save

This option allows you to save a material definition from your drawing to the ACAD.MAT file or other external file. This is helpful if you used *Edit* in dialogue box format and want to save the changes to a file.

List

(Command line format only) This option lists the material properties identical to those that appear in the *Material Properties* dialogue box text window.

New

This option allows you to define a new material. *New* is similar to *Edit* in that you specify new values for the material properties. However, *New* requires that you assign a name for the material as well as a value for <u>each</u> of the material properties. The *Material Properties - New* dialogue box (Fig. 43-14) operates like the *Edit* dialogue box. If you invoke *New* from command line format you are presented with a numbered list of material properties. Typing a number allows you to specify that value.

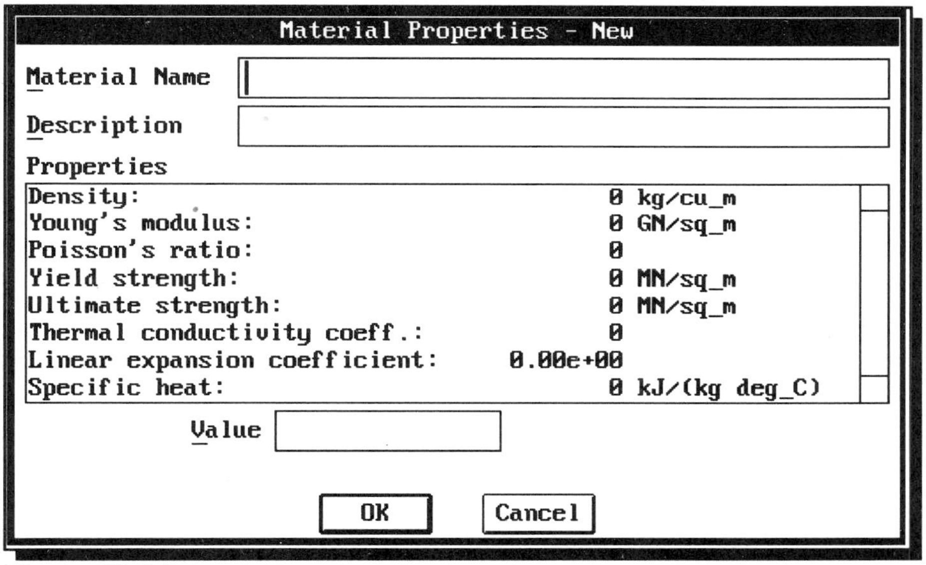

```
┌─────────────────────────────────────────────────────────┐
│              Material Properties - New                   │
│  Material Name  │                                      │ │
│                                                          │
│  Description    │                                      │ │
│                                                          │
│  Properties                                              │
│  │Density:                        0 kg/cu_m          │   │
│  │Young's modulus:                0 GN/sq_m          │   │
│  │Poisson's ratio:                0                  │   │
│  │Yield strength:                 0 MN/sq_m          │   │
│  │Ultimate strength:              0 MN/sq_m          │   │
│  │Thermal conductivity coeff.:    0                  │   │
│  │Linear expansion coefficient:   0.00e+00           │   │
│  │Specific heat:                  0 kJ/(kg deg_C)    │   │
│                                                          │
│           Value  │                          │            │
│                                                          │
│              ┌──────┐   ┌────────┐                       │
│              │  OK  │   │ Cancel │                       │
│              └──────┘   └────────┘                       │
└─────────────────────────────────────────────────────────┘
```

Figure 43-14

File

The *File* tile (available only in the *Materials Browser* dialogue box, Fig. 43-13) allows you to specify the file you want to use whenever a material is accessed or saved. ACAD.MAT is the default file and the only file AutoCAD provides. You may wish to create other files with other materials you create.

Material Properties

Following is a brief explanation of material properties. Remember that density is the only property that AME uses (when mass properties are generated).

Density   This characteristic defines the mass per unit of volume for the material.

Young's modulus	Also known as the Modulus of Elasticity, this property is a ratio of stress and strain.
Poisson's ratio	This property measures strain as a ratio of compression and extension.
Yield strength	This is the force at which the elasticity is exceeded and the material bends.
Ultimate strength	This is the maximum tensile force the material can withstand before breaking.
Thermal conductivity coefficient	The material's ability to conduct heat is measured by this coefficient.
Linear expansion coefficient	This value is a ratio of expansion per unit of temperature.
Specific heat	This is the amount of heat required to raise one unit of mass by one unit of temperature.

SOLINTERF

TYPE IN:	PULL-DOWN MENU	SCREEN MENU	TABLET MENU
SOLINTERF or INTERF	_Model, Inquiry > Interference_	_MODEL, INQUIRY, INTERF:_	_1,H_

In AutoCAD, unlike real life, it is possible to create two solids that occupy the same physical space. _Solinterf_ checks solids to determine whether or not they interfere (occupy the same space). If there is interference, _Solinterf_ highlights the portions of the solids that overlap. You can even create a new solid from the interfering volume if you desire.

Solinterf operates only in command line format. Normally you specify two sets of solids for AME to check against each other.

```
Command: solinterf
Select the first set of solids...
Select objects: PICK
Select objects: Enter
1 solid selected.

Select the second set of solids...
Select objects: PICK
Select objects: Enter
1 solid selected.
```

AME then compares the two sets for interference. If interference occurs, it is reported. AME asks if you want to create a separate solid from the interfering volume.

```
Comparing 1 solid against 1 solid.
Interfering solids (first  set): 1
                   (second set): 1
Interfering pairs           : 1
Create interference solids? <N>: y
Command:
```

The newly created solid could then be used to determine the exact size and volume of the interference. The original sets are not changed in any way.

You can compare <u>more than two</u> solids against each other with *Solinterf*. This is accomplished by selecting all desired solids at the first prompt and none at the second.

```
Select the first set of solids... PICK
Select the second set of solids... Enter
```

AME then compares all solids in the first set against each other. If more than one interference is found, AutoCAD highlights intersecting solids, one pair at a time.

For an example of using *Solinterf*, consider the two solids shown in Figure 43-15. (The parts are displayed in wireframe representation.) The two shapes fit together as an assembly. The locating pin on the part on the right should fit in the hole in the left part.

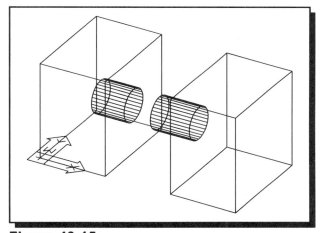

Figure 43-15

Sliding the parts together until the two vertical faces meet produces the assembly shown in Figure 43-16. There appears to be some inconsistency in the assembly of the hole and the pin. Either the pin extends beyond the hole (interference) or the hole is deeper than necessary (no interference).

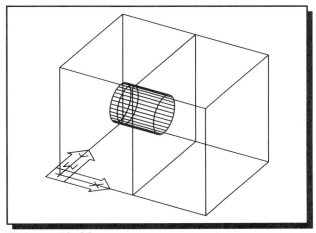

Figure 43-16

Solinterf is used to make the determination. *Solinterf* is invoked and the two components of the assembly are selected as the first and second sets. *Solinterf* reports that an interference exists and <u>highlights</u> the volume of interference as shown in Figure 43-17.

If no interference is found, AutoCAD reports "Solids do not interfere."

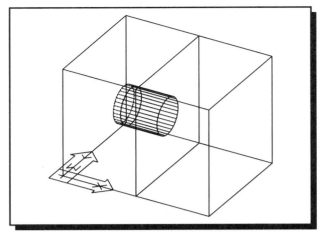

Figure 43-17

CREATING SOLID SECTIONS AND COPYING FEATURES

Two AME commands are intended for creating sections from solid models. *Solsect* creates a 2D projection and *Solcut* cuts a solid into two parts. Another drafting feature, *Solfeat*, will extract 2D features (edges or faces) from an AME solid.

Solsect is a drafting feature that creates a 2D "section view." The cross section is determined by specifying a cutting plane. A cross section view, complete with hatch lines, is automatically created based on the solid geometry that intersects the cutting plane. The original solid is not affected by the action of *Solsect*.

Solcut actually cuts the solid at the specified cutting plane. *Solcut* therefore creates two solids from the original one and offers the possibility to retain both halves or only one. Many options are available for placement of the cutting plane.

Solfeat creates a new, duplicate entity or set of entities from a selected edge or face. The new features can be extracted from the solid for subsequent editing without affecting the original solid.

SOLSECT

TYPE IN:	PULL-DOWN MENU	SCREEN MENU	TABLET MENU
SOLSECT or SECT	*Model, Display > Section Solids*	*MODEL, DISPLAY, SOLSECT:*	*6,H*

Solsect creates a 2D cross section of a solid or set of solids. The cross section created by *Solsect* is considered a traditional 2D section view. The cross section is defined by a cutting plane and the resulting section is determined by any solid material that passes through the cutting plane. The cutting plane can be specified by a variety of methods. The options for establishing the cutting plane are listed in the command prompt.

```
Command: solsect
Select objects: PICK
Select objects: Enter
Sectioning plane by
        Entity/Last/Zaxis/View/XY/YZ/ZX/<3points>:
```

These options are the same as those available when creating a new UCS (Chapter 36) or an AME solid by the *Baseplane* or *CP* methods (Chapter 39).

For example, assume a cross section is desired for the geometry shown in Figure 43-18. To create the section you must define the cutting plane.

For this case, the *ZX* option is used and the requested point is defined to establish the position of the plane as shown in Figure 43-19. The cross section will be created on this plane.

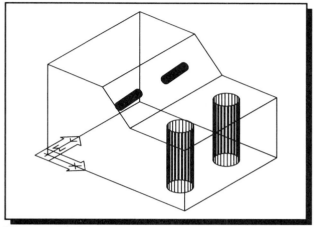

Figure 43-18

Once the cutting plane is established, a cross section, complete with hatch lines, is automatically created by *Solsect*. The resulting geometry is created on the <u>current</u> layer. It is composed of 2D entities on the cutting plane.

By default, the resulting cross section is automatically filled with a cross hatch pattern as shown in Figure 43-19. The hatching is governed by the current settings of three variables explained next.

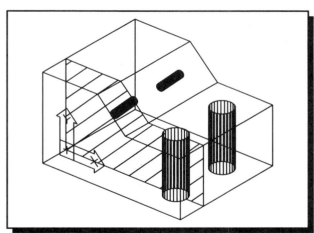

Figure 43-19

SOLHPAT   This variable determines the hatch pattern that is applied by *Solsect*. Set this variable to any valid pattern name. The default pattern name is U.

SOLHSIZE   This controls the scale factor of the hatch pattern. The default is 1.

SOLHANGLE The angle of the hatch pattern lines is set by this variable. The actual angle is dependent on the hatch pattern used (see Chapter 26). The default setting is 45. Entering a value rotates the specified hatch lines by that amount.

Using the default settings produces the cross section shown in the previous figure. However, the size and angle of the hatch pattern should be modified as explained next.

In the example, *SOLHANGLE* is set to 75 to create hatch lines that are not parallel or perpendicular to features of the solid. *SOLHSIZE* is reduced which results in closer spacing between hatch lines.

The first cross section is *Erased* and a new *Solsect* is created to reflect the new variable settings (Fig. 43-20).

The cross section created by *Solsect* has no permanent connection to the solid and can be *Moved, Copied, Erased*, or otherwise edited without consequence to the original solid. The cross section as shown in Figure 43-20 has been *Moved*.

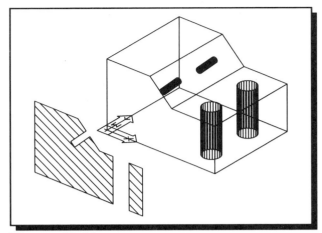

Figure 43-20

Note that *Solsect* only creates lines where the geometry intersects the cutting plane. For the example, additional lines (for the top and bottoms of the holes) should be added to convert this to a complete section view.

The cross section can be generated by *Solsect* as one of three types of entities depending on the setting of the *SOLSECTYPE* variable:

SOLSECTYPE setting	Result of *Solsect*
1	*Solsect* creates a *Block* containing *Lines, Arcs*, and *Circles*.
2	*Solsect* creates a *Block* containing *Plines*.
3	*Solsect* creates a *Region*.

SOLSECTYPE must be set before using *Solsect*. The default setting is 1. Thus, the cross section geometry displayed in Figure 43-20 is composed of two entities, the hatch pattern and one *Block* comprising the outlines.

SOLCUT

TYPE IN:	PULL-DOWN MENU	SCREEN MENU	TABLET MENU
SOLCUT or CUT	*Model, Modify > Cut Solids*	*MODEL, MODIFY, SOLCUT:*	*2,D*

Solcut creates a true solid section. *Solcut* cuts an AME solid or set of solids on a specified cutting plane. The original solid(s) are converted to two (sets of) solids. You have the option to keep both halves or only the half that you specify. Examine the following command syntax used to create the sectioned solid shown in Figure 43-21.

```
Command: solcut
Select objects: PICK
Select objects: Enter
Updating object...  Done.
1 solid selected.
Cutting plane by
      Entity/Last/Zaxis/View/XY/YZ/ZX/<3points>: ZX
Point on XY plane <0,0,0>: PICK
Both sides/<Point on desired side of the plane>: _endp of
PICK
Phase I - Boundary evaluation begins. (etc.)
Command:
```

Entering **B** at the "Both sides/<Point on desired side of plane>:" prompt retains the solids on both sides of the cutting plane. Otherwise, you can pick a point on either side of the plane to specify which half to <u>keep</u>.

For example, using the solid model shown previously in Figure 43-18, *Solcut* is used to create a new sectioned solid shown here. The *ZX* method is used to define the cutting plane (note the coordinate system icon). Next, the new solid to retain was specified by PICKing a point on that geometry. The resulting sectioned solid is shown in Figure 43-21. Note that the solid on the near side of the cutting plane was not retained.

Solcut can also be used to create molds for cast pieces. The method used to create molds is as follows.

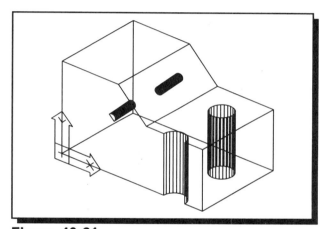
Figure 43-21

1.	Create the part geometry.
2.	Create a solid box around the part representing the mold. *Subtract* the part geometry.
3.	Use *Solcut* to create the two mold halves.

The first step is to create the part geometry with AME. For example, the part shown in Figure 43-22 is to be cast (hidden lines have been removed for better visibility in this figure).

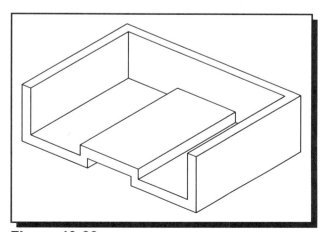
Figure 43-22

Next, create a box equal in shape and size to the mold. The box and the part geometry should be oriented in the same configuration as desired in the final mold. Use a Boolean *Subtract* to create the mold cavity as shown in Figure 43-23.

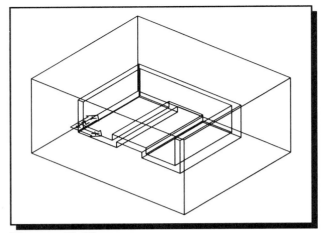

Figure 43-23

Use *Solcut* to create the two mold halves. Specify the parting line by creating the cutting plane at the desired location (see the icon in the previous figure). Retain both halves. The top half of the mold in Figure 43-24 has been rotated to reveal the interior features.

The final step is to create the sprues (for injection of molten material), attachments, and fixtures for securing the mold to the parent machine.

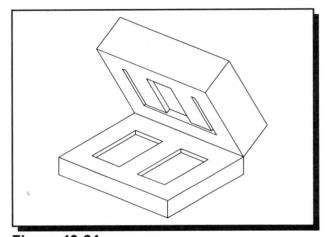

Figure 43-24

SOLFEAT

TYPE IN:	PULL-DOWN MENU	SCREEN MENU	TABLET MENU
SOLFEAT or FEAT	*Model, Display > Copy Feature*	*MODEL, DISPLAY, SOLFEAT:*	*5,H*

Solfeat allows you to extract features (faces or edges) from an existing AME solid. Similar to *Solsect*, *Solfeat* creates new entities on the plane of the edge or feature selected. The resulting geometry is a *Block* created on the current layer. The new feature is not connected to the solid and may be *Moved*, *Copied*, or otherwise edited.

```
Command: solfeat
Edge/<Face>: f
All/<Select>: Enter
Pick a face: PICK
Updating object...  Done.
Next/<OK>: Enter
```

The procedure to create a face feature is shown in the previous command syntax. The "Next/<OK>:" option allows you to designate between the two faces adjoining the edge that you select.

Using the command sequence above, a feature is created from the solid illustrated in Figure 43-25. When the face is selected (only the pickbox can be used with *Solfeat*), it is highlighted as shown.

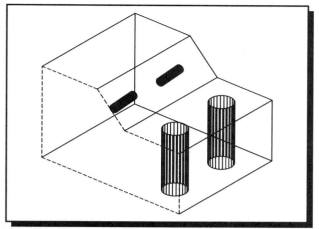

Figure 43-25

The new feature is not connected in any way to the original geometry and can therefore be edited. Figure 43-26 shows the feature *Moved* away from the object for examination.

Typically, *Solfeat* is used to extract shapes from existing solids as a beginning point for creating new solids.

Multiple faces can be selected with one use of the *Solfeat* command. This is made possible by the repeated prompt for you to "Pick a Face:."

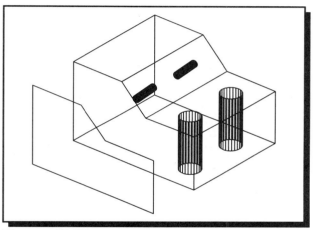

Figure 43-26

The *Edge* option allows you to extract any number of edges from the existing model. Any edge feature of the solid can be selected. The *All* option causes AME to create a new entity for each edge on the selected solid. Using the *All* option creates a complete, duplicate model, except it is a <u>wireframe</u>. When you use the "<Select>:" option, AutoCAD continues to prompt for you to select multiple edges.

```
Command: solfeat
Edge/<Face>: e
All/<Select> : Enter
Pick an edge: PICK
Pick an edge: PICK
Pick an edge: Enter
Command:
```

Solfeat can be used to extract multiple edges from an existing solid. In Figure 43-27, several edges have been selected--the three edges of the near corner and tops of the two large holes. Then, the newly created edges (*Blocks*) are *Moved* to the right in this figure. The original solid is unaffected by the use of *Solfeat*.

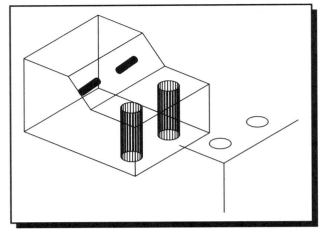

Figure 43-27

CHAPTER EXERCISES

1. *Open* the **CH42EX1** drawing. Construct a *cylinder* (*Solcyl*) in the same location and orientation as the cone. The cylinder *Diameter* is **2** and the *Height* is **-3**. Use *Solchp* with the *Replace* option to make the switch. Remember to *eXit Solchp*. The new composite solid should look like Figure 43-28. *Saveas* **CH43EX1**.

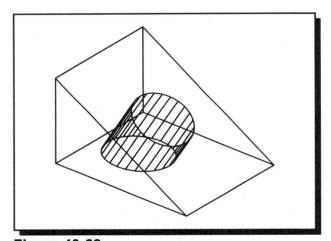

Figure 43-28

2. *Open* the **CH42EX3** drawing. Use *Solpurge* to conserve file space in the drawing. Use the *Bfile* and the *Pmesh* options. If you *Erased* any primitives during the construction of the model, use the *Erased* option of *Solpurge*. *Save* the drawing as **CH43EX2**. *Shell* from AutoCAD or otherwise list the directory where the files are stored to compare the file sizes of CH42EX3 and CH43EX2. How may bytes did you save?

3. Find **ADJMT-SL.DWG** in the list of files (that you created in Chapter 42 Exercises) and check the file size. Return to **AutoCAD** and *Open* the **ADJMT-SL** drawing. Use the appropriate options of *Solpurge* to reduce the file size. *Save* the drawing. How many bytes did you save?

4.   *Open* the **CH42EX4** drawing. A design change requires the composite solid to be modified as follows:

The channel in the bottom must be widened from 2 to **2.5** units.

The hole *Radii* must be changed from .25 to **.38** units.

Use the *Size* option of *Solchp* to make the changes. The finished geometry should compare to Figure 43-29. *Saveas* **CH43EX4**.

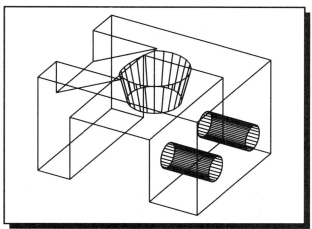

Figure 43-29

5.   *Open* the **SADL-SL** drawing that you created in Chapter 42 Exercises. Open the *Material Browser* dialogue box and *Load Aluminum* into the drawing. Use the *Set* option to set *Aluminum* as the current material, then use the *Change* option to change the material assigned to the Saddle. Next invoke *Sollist* to list the *Object* to insure *Aluminum* is listed as the assigned material.

Activate the *AME System Variables* dialogue box and set the *Length Units* to *mm*. Check the *Consistent Units* box. Next, calculate *Mass Properties* for the Saddle. Write the report out to a file named **SADL-SL.MPR**. Use a text editor or the DOS TYPE command to examine the file.

6.   *Open* the **BGUID-SL** model that you created in Chapter 42 Exercises. Create a *New Layer* named **WIREFRAM** and set it *Current*. Use the *Solfeat* command with the *Edge* option to create edges for *All* of the edges of the model. Now *Freeze* the layer that the solid model geometry is on. Do you see a new wireframe model of the Bar Guide? *Save* the drawing.

7.   *Open* the **SADL-SL** drawing again. Use *Solcut* to cut the model in half longitudinally. Use an appropriate method to establish the *Cutting plane* in order to achieve the resulting model as shown in Figure 43-30. Use *Saveas* and assign the name **SADL-CUT**.

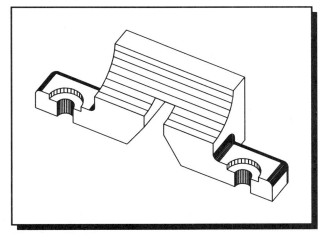

Figure 43-30

8. ***Open*** the **PULLY-SL** drawing that you created in Chapter 42 Exercises. Set the following variables:

SOLHPAT	ANSI31
SOLHANGLE	0
SOLHSIZE	20
SOLSECTYPE	3

    Next, make a ***New Layer*** named **SECTION** and set it ***Current***. Then use the ***Solsect*** command to create a full section "view" of the pulley. Establish a vertical cutting plane through the center of the model. Remove the section view entity (region) with the ***Solmove*** command, translating **100** units in the **X** direction. The model and the new section view should appear as in Figure 43-31 (*Hide* was performed on the Pulley to enhance visualization). Complete the view by establishing a ***UCS*** at the section view, then adding the necessary ***Lines***. ***Saveas*** **PULLY-SC**.

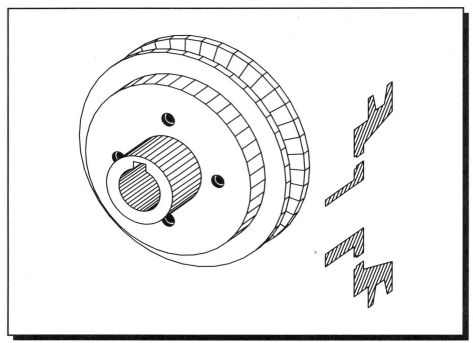

Figure 43-31

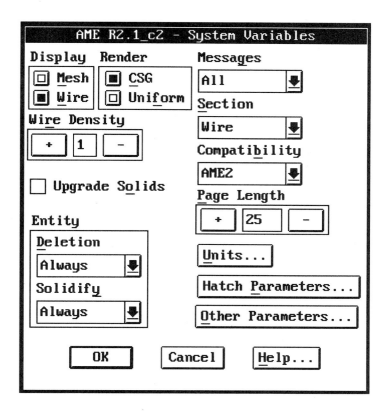

CHAPTER 44

AME Variables and Sample Programs

CHAPTER OBJECTIVES

After completing this chapter you should:

1.   be able to set AME system variables to achieve the desired solid modeling characteristics;

2.   be able to update existing solids with new variable settings with *Solupdate*;

3.   know how to create countersunk and counterbored holes with the *Hole* command;

4.   know to use *Wblksol* and *Insrtsol* for creating and inserting AME models as *Blocks*;

5.   be able to assemble solids using the *Solcontact* and *Solalign* commands;

6.   be able to create solid shafts, wheels, gears, bearing brackets, bolts, and nuts using the options provided by DESIGN.EXP;

7.   be able to use the *Soldrill* command to create drilled holes in AME solids.

AME VARIABLES

AME system variables are used to control the way in which solid models and regions are created or edited. The complete list of variables with a brief explanation, possible settings, and default settings is given here.

You can set the value of a variable in any of three ways:

1   Type the variable name at the Command: prompt.
2.   Use the *Solvar* command (similar to the AutoCAD *Setvar* command).
3.   Use the *AME R2.1 System Variable* dialogue box.

If you want to type the variable name at the command prompt, the whole name must be entered. If AME is not yet loaded, AutoCAD will ask if you want to load it.

If you want to use the *Solvar* command instead of typing the name at the command prompt, the command syntax is as follows.

```
Command: solvar
Variable name or ?:
```

Enter any AME variable name. You do not have to enter the leading *SOL* at the beginning of variable names if you use *Solvar*. If you enter a question mark (?), AutoCAD displays a list of the variables and their current settings as well as a brief description.

If you select the *Model* pull-down menu, then *Setup >*, then *Variables...*, the *AME R2.1 System Variables* dialogue box appears (Fig. 44-1). All AME variables are accessible from this dialogue box.

The table on the next two pages gives the AME variable names and AME System Variables dialogue box choices along with functions, and default settings.

Remember that variables can be changed and saved in the default (ACAD.DWG) drawing or in other prototype drawings.

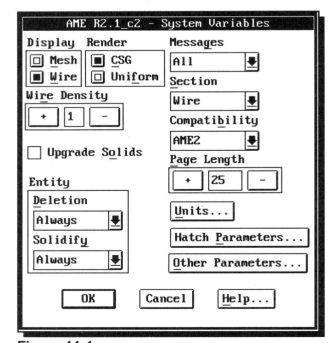

Figure 44-1

Variable Name	Dialogue Box Choice	Function: Possible Settings	Default Setting
SOLAMECOMP	Compatibility	Determines what release AME commands and scripts operate with: AME R1 or AME R2	AME2
SOLAMEVER	(Listed on box title)	Displays the AME release number (read only)	R2.1
SOLAREAU	Units..., Area	Assigns the units for area calculations: use any valid length unit*	sq cm
SOLAXCOL	Other Parameters..., Axis color	Assigns the color number (ACI) of the MCS icon: 1-256	3
SOLDECOMP	Other Parameters..., Decomposition	Sets the direction for decomposition for mass properties calculation: X, Y, or Z	X
SOLDELENT	Deletion	Determines whether the 2D objects are automatically deleted by AME after use by *Solidify*, *Extrude*, or *Revolve*: 1=never 2=ask 3=never	3
SOLDISPLAY	Display	Sets the display mode for solids and regions: Wire or Mesh	Wire
SOLHANGLE	Hatch Parameters..., Angle	Sets the hatch pattern angle used for regions and *Solsect*: any value between 360 and -360	45.0000
SOLHPAT	Hatch Parameters..., Name	Sets the hatch pattern name used for regions and *Solsect*: any valid pattern name	U
SOLHSIZE	Hatch Parameters..., Size	Sets the hatch pattern scale factor used for regions *Solsect*: any positive value	1.0000
SOLLENGTH	Units..., Length	Sets the units used for length calculations: any valid length unit*	cm
SOLMASS	Units..., Mass	Sets the units used for mass calculations: any valid mass unit*	gm

Variable Name	Dialogue Box Choice	Function: Possible Settings	Default Setting
SOLMATCURR	*Other Parameters..., Material*	Reports the current material setting (Use the *Solmat* command to set the current material)	MILD_ STEEL
SOLPAGELEN	*Page Length*	Sets the length of the text screen page: 0=scroll 1-1000=number of lines	25
SOLRENDER	*Render*	Determines color display for composite solids: Uniform=uses color of top-level solid CSG=uses colors of individual solids	CSG
SOLSECTYPE	*Section*	Determines the type of objects created by *Solsect* command: 1= wireframe 2= polyline 3= region	1
SOLSERVMSG	*Messages*	Sets level of message reporting: 0=none 1=errors only 2=errors and computation 3=all	3
SOLSOLIDIFY	*Solidify*	Determines if selected 2D objects (*Plines, Polygons, Circles, Ellipses, Donuts*) should be automatically solidified when selected by an AME command: 1=never 2=ask 3=always	3
SOLSUBDIV	*Other Parameters..., Divisions*	Sets the accuracy of mass properties calculations: 1-8	3
SOLUPGRADE	*Upgrade Solids*	Sets automatic upgrade of solids from single-precision solids to double-precision: 0=off 1=on	0
SOLVOLUME	*Units..., Volume*	Sets the units used to calculate volume: any valid volumetric unit*	cu cm
SOLWDENS	*Wire Density*	Determines the wire density of newly created objects: 1-12	1

*Valid units are listed in the ACAD.UNT file.

AME SAMPLE PROGRAMS

AutoCAD supplies a variety of sample programs that increase the capabilities and potential applications of AME. These programs are shipped with AME and have probably been installed on your system; however, they must be loaded before you can use them.

The AME sample programs are written either in AutoLISP or in C programming language. The programs written in C are called AutoCAD Development System (ADS) applications that use API (AutoCAD Programming Interface). AutoLISP programs have a file extension of .LSP and API programs have file extensions of .EXP (.EXE for AutoCAD for Windows).

The sample AutoLISP programs and ADS/API programs provided for use with AME are:

HOLE.LSP	Creates countersink and counterbore holes.
SOLMAINT.LSP	Can be used to update AME models with new variables settings and reduce file size for AME R1 models.
STLSUP.LSP	Creates a support structure for stereolithography applications.
WBLKSOL.LSP	Used for creating and retrieving solids in *Block* form.
AMELINK.EXP, .EXE	Creates output files for other solid modeling packages.
ASM.EXP, .EXE	Lets you assemble parts by axis or edge alignment.
DESIGN.EXP, EXE	Creates solid shafts, gears, bolts, nuts, etc.
DRILL.EXP, .EXE	Drills holes of specific diameter and depth.
LAYOUT.EXP, .EXE	Determines nesting for sheet metal applications.
OFFSOL.EXP, .EXE	Creates offsets for machining and milling.
SOLSTLOUT	Converts a AME solid to an .STL file for use with rapid prototyping technology.
SOLVIEW.EXP, .EXE	Automatically lays out paper space viewports and draws 2D views from a solid model.
SYMMETRY.EXP, .EXE	Finds symmetrical axes for regions.
TUTOR.EXP, .EXE	Is a tutor for basic API programming functions.

Loading AutoLISP and ADS Programs

The AME sample programs described here must be loaded using the *Load AutoLISP and ADS Files* dialogue box or using the *Load* or *Xload* commands. See Appendix B, Loading AutoLISP and ADS Programs. (AutoCAD uses other AutoLISP and ADS programs that are <u>automatically</u> loaded when you invoke the commands from the menus, such as *Dline, Modify Entity, Asctext, Mvsetup,* and others.)

Assuming that your system has AutoCAD installed on C: drive in the ACAD12 directory, the AutoLISP programs are found in the C:\ACAD12\SAMPLE subdirectory or the C:\ACAD12\API\SAMPLE subdirectory.

HOLE.LSP

HOLE.LSP is the AutoLISP program that must be loaded before using the *Hole* command at the command prompt. *Hole* automatically creates a counterbore or countersink on an <u>existing</u> <u>hole</u> in an AME solid. The hole must be circular and the side of the hole for the countersink or counterbore must lie on a planar face.

```
Command: hole
CSink/<CBore>: cb
Select planar face with hole to CBore: PICK
Updating object...Done.
Next/<OK>: Enter
Select edge of hole to CBore: PICK
Diameter of selected hole is 1.5
Radius or <Diameter> of CBore <2.25>: Enter
Depth of CBore:<1.0> Enter
1 solid subtracted from 1 solid
Command:
```

For example, assume you have created the simple solid model by *Subtracting* a cylinder from a box to achieve the hole as shown in Figure 44-2.

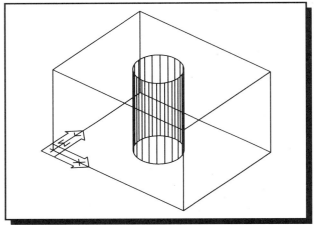

Figure 44-2

Hole can be then used to create the counterbore or countersink in the existing hole. The *CB* option of *Hole* was used to create the counterbore for the model shown in Figure 44-3. See the command syntax above.

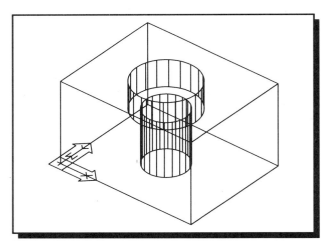

Figure 44-3

Hole can also be used to create a countersink in an existing hole. Using the *CS* option of *Hole*, the countersink is created in the solid model shown in Figure 44-4. The command syntax is similar to that for a counterbore.

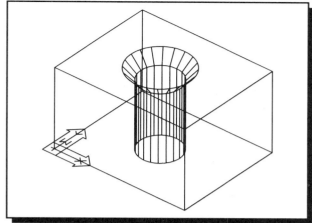

Figure 44-4

SOLMAINT.LSP

SOLMAINT has two commands that can be used with AME: *Solmaint* and *Solupdate*. SOLMAINT is an AutoLISP program and <u>must</u> be loaded before using.

SOLMAINT

If you have created solid models with AME R1, *Solmaint* removes all unneeded intermediate wireframes created by AME R1, resulting in memory and disk space savings and increased performance. AME R2 (or later) does not need the intermediate wireframes created by AME R1. If you load an AME R1 solid into AME R2.1, it is maintained automatically.

```
Command:  solmaint
Delete primitive wireframes/meshes?  <Y>:
```

Entering **yes** deletes the intermediate wireframes and meshes of R1 solids.

SOLUPDATE

This command updates selected AME models according to new variable settings that you may have made since creating the model. This is very helpful because changing some AME variables does not automatically update the existing solid models, even if you *Regen*.

For example, changing the *SOLWDENS* (wireframe density) variable does not automatically update the model. Using a Boolean operation after changing *SOLWDENS*, however, updates the entire model. If the model is complete and you wish to change *SOLWDENS*, *Solupdate* must be used to display the new setting.

```
Command: solupdate
Select object: PICK
Updating object...  Done.
Command:
```

For example, assume that you created the simple composite solid shown in Figure 44-5. The default *SOLWDENS* setting of 1 was used when the model was created as characterized by the small number of tessellation lines as shown. After using the *Subtract* Boolean operation, you realize that *SOLWDENS* should be increased.

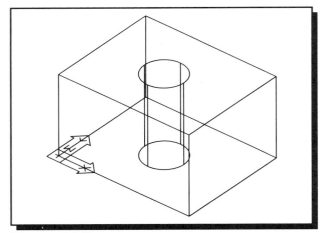

Figure 44-5

Change *SOLWDENS* to the desired setting (5 in this case), then use *Solupdate* (after loading SOLMAINT) and select the model. The model should reflect the new variable setting as shown in Figure 44-6.

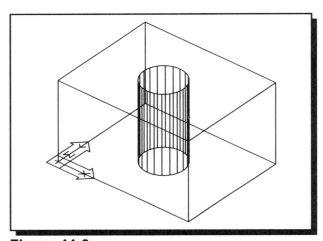

Figure 44-6

STLSUP.LSP

If you want to create a prototype part with a Stereolithography Apparatus (SLA) from an AME solid model, the *Solstlout* command can be used to convert the solid model drawing file from a .DWG to a .STL file for import to the SLA. (See *Solstlout* in this chapter.)

The STLSUP.LSP program allows you to create a support structure for the parts being created by the SLA. When prototypes are created using SLA, the solid must be supported by a structure made of several thin walls. *Stlsup* creates a *star* or *eggcrate* support.

Since STLSUP.LSP is an AutoLISP program, it must be loaded before you can use the *Stlsup* command at the command prompt. AME must also be loaded for this application to work.

```
Command: stlsup
Star/<Eggcrate>:
```

Selecting an option causes AutoCAD to prompt for dimensions. The support structure is automatically created based on the parameters you specify.

In Figure 44-7 a *Star* support structure is created using *Stlsup* and placed under the solid model.

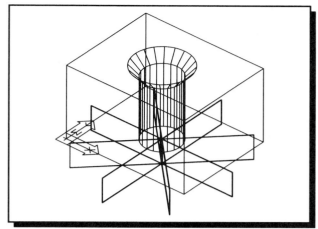

Figure 44-7

WBLKSOL.LSP

The WBLKSOL AutoLISP program provides two commands for storing AME solids or regions as blocks and inserting them again. WBLKSOL must be loaded before using the two commands explained below.

WBLKSOL

The *Wblksol* command should be used instead of the *Wblock* command if you want to create *Blocks* on disk from an AME solid model. The *Wblock* command does not write the composite solid's <u>component</u> parts to disk with the parent block because they reside on the AME_FRZ layer. *Wblksol* uses the AutoCAD *Wblock* command, but it retains the solid's handles and component parts that AME requires to maintain the structure of a composite model.

INSRTSOL

The *Insrtsol* command is used instead of *Insert* to retrieve blocks containing solids or regions into your drawing. You can use *Insrtsol* to retrieve blocks either from the block table in the current drawing or from a block stored on disk.

AMELINK.EXP

Use this program if you want to export AME solid models to other solid modeling and analysis packages. The AMELINK.EXP program must be loaded before using the *Amelink* command. *Amelink* writes the solid model to an ASCII CSIGES file format. The CSIGES file is a variation of the IGES file format specifically for AME solid models. For more information, see the AutoCAD Advanced Modeling Extension Reference Manual, page 179.

ASM.EXP

ASM.EXP provides a utility for moving solids into position relative to other solids. It is useful for putting together several solids that comprise an assembly, hence the name ASM (short for assembly). ASM.EXP is an ADS application that you must load before you can use the associated commands. ASM.EXP makes two commands available at for use at the command prompt.

SOLCONTACT

This command lets you move a solid so that a planar face that you specify aligns with (touches) a planar face on another solid. You must specify a base point (point of contact and axis of alignment) and a reference point (for correct alignment between the two parts) for each face. An XY axis icon aligns with these selected points.

```
Command: solcontact
Select objects: PICK
Select objects: Enter
Select old contact face: PICK
Next/<OK>: Enter
Old base point <0,0,0>: PICK (OSNAPs may be used)
Old reference point <Axial Symmetry>: PICK
Select new contact face: PICK
Next/<OK>: Enter
New base point <0,0,0>: PICK
New reference point <Axial Symmetry>: PICK
Ok to move the objects, No/<Yes>: Enter
```

The solids in Figure 44-8 are displayed after both faces, base points, and reference points have been specified. Note the XY icon that locates its origin at the base points and the X axes (single arrow) along the edge pointing to the specified reference point.

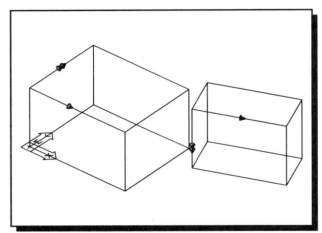

Figure 44-8

If the assembly appears OK, answer *Yes* to the "OK to move objects" prompt. AutoCAD automatically performs the necessary rotations and translations to assemble the parts as shown in Figure 44-9.

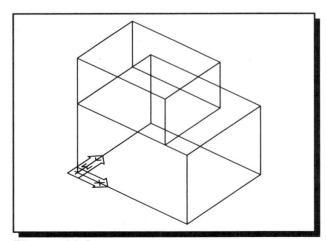

Figure 44-9

SOLALIGN

Solalign aligns a set of solids based on two axes that you specify. You specify a base point on the axis and the other end of the axis for both objects, then specify a reference point for rotational alignment about the axes. If the selected objects are axially symmetric (like a cylinder), the reference points can be automatically aligned.

```
Command: solalign
Select objects: PICK
Select objects: Enter
Base point of old axis <0,0,0>: PICK
End point of old axis <0,0,1>: PICK
Old reference point <Axial Symmetry>: Enter
Base point of new axis <0,0,0>: PICK
End point of new axis <0,0,1>: PICK
New reference point <Axial Symmetry>: Enter
Ok to move the objects, No/<Yes>: Enter
Command:
```

Figure 44-10 illustrates two cylinders in different orientations. *Solalign* is invoked and the base points and other axes endpoints are specified. The origin of the XY axis icon indicates the selected base point and axes directions.

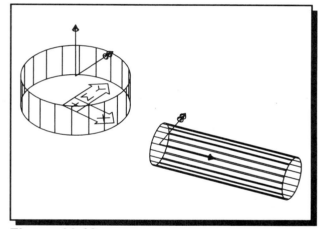

Figure 44-10

Answering *Yes* to the "OK to move objects" prompt automatically aligns the axes of the solids.

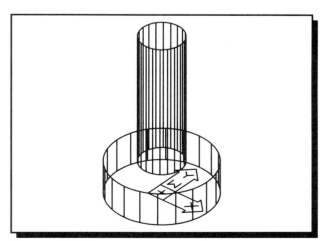

Figure 44-11

DESIGN.EXP

DESIGN.EXP is an ADS application. After loading this program you can use six commands at the command prompt to create common mechanical parts. This method of creating parts is very easy because all you have to do is specify the dimensions and AME automatically creates the parts. Each command is explained briefly below. For these examples only the defaults are shown in the command syntax.

SOLSHAFT

Solshaft automatically creates a cylindrical shaft with a keyway using dimensions that you specify. The shaft is parallel to the Z axis of the current coordinate system.

```
Command: solshaft
Insertion base point <0,0,0>:  Enter or (value)
Enter shaft diameter <1.0>:  Enter or (value)
Enter shaft length <5.0>:  Enter or (value)
Enter keyway depth <0.3>:  Enter or (value)
Enter keyway width <0.4>:  Enter or (value)
Enter keyway length <2.0>:  Enter or (value)
Phase I - Boundary evaluation begins. etc.
Command:
```

The shaft shown in Figure 44-12 was created using the command syntax above and entering specific dimensions for each prompt. The "Base point" is the center of one end of the shaft. Notice the keyway is automatically created to the specified dimensions.

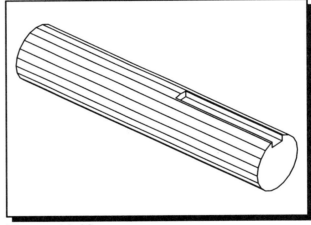

Figure 44-12

SOLWHEEL

This command creates a flywheel. The plane of the flywheel is parallel to the current XY plane and centered on the base point. The flywheel also has a hub of dimensions you specify.

```
Command: solwheel
Insertion base point <0,0,0>:  Enter or (value)
Enter wheel diameter <5.0>:  Enter or (value)
Enter wheel thickness <1.0>:  Enter or (value)
Enter hub diameter <3.0>:  Enter or (value)
Enter hub extrusion thickness <0.25>:  Enter or (value)
Enter hole diameter <1.0>:  Enter or (value)
Enter keyway depth <0.2>:  Enter or (value)
```

```
Enter keyway width <0.4>:   Enter or (value)
Phase I - Boundary evaluation begins.  etc.
Command:
```

The flywheel is centered symmetrically at the specified base point and parallel to the current XY plane as shown in Figure 44-13.

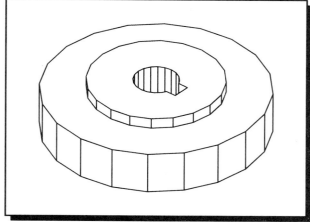

Figure 44-13

SOLGEAR

Solgear automatically creates a spur gear to your specifications. The gear lies parallel to the current XY plane. You must specify the pitch diameter and pressure angle as well as other parameters. The command syntax follows.

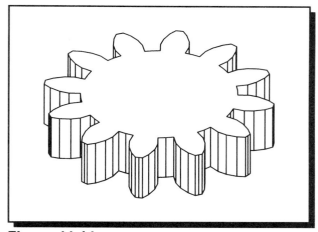

Figure 44-14

```
Command: solgear
Insertion base point <0,0,0>:   Enter or (value)
Enter pitch circle diameter <4.0>:   Enter or (value)
Enter number of teeth <12>:   Enter or (value)
Enter gear thickness <1.0>:   Enter or (value)
Enter pressure angle <25 degrees>:   Enter or (value)
Working...
Command:
```

SOLBEAR

Solbear automatically creates a bearing bracket. As with the *Solwheel*, the bracket is created lying parallel to the XY plane of the current coordinate system and its base is centered on the specified base point.

```
Command: solbear
Insertion base point <0,0,0>:  Enter or (value)
Enter bearing diameter <5.0>:  Enter or (value)
Enter bearing thickness <3.0>:  Enter or (value)
Enter hole diameter <2.0>:  Enter or (value)
Enter distance from base to center of hole <5.0>:  Enter
or (value)
Enter base height <1.0>:  Enter or (value)
Enter base width <6.0>:  Enter or (value)
Phase I - Boundary evaluation begins.  etc.
```

Figure 44-15 displays a bearing bracket created with *Solbear*. In this case all of the default dimensions were accepted.

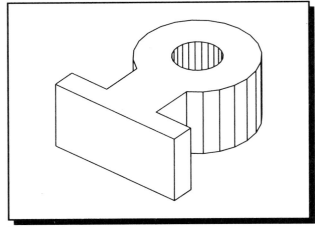

Figure 44-15

SOLBOLT

This command automatically creates a bolt with a hexagonal head. The shaft of the bolt (like *Solshaft*) is created along the Z axis of the current coordinate system. The base point specifies the location for the center of the hex-head. As you can see in Figure 44-16, the bolt has no threads.

See the command syntax following for the specific dimensions required. This example was created accepting all the defaults.

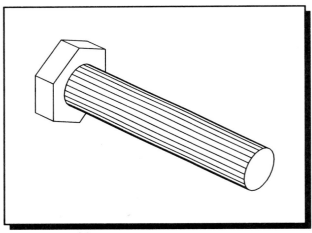

Figure 44-16

```
Command: solbolt
Insertion base point <0,0,0>:  Enter or (value)
Enter head diameter <2.0>:  Enter or (value)
Enter head height <0.5>:  Enter or (value)
Enter screw diameter <1.0>:  Enter or (value)
Enter screw length <5.0>:  Enter or (value)
Phase I - Boundary evaluation begins.  etc.
Command:
```

SOLNUT

The *Solnut* command creates a hexagonal nut. The nut is created lying parallel to the XY plane (with the cylindrical axis along the Z axis) of the current coordinate system. The nut is centered on the base point that you specify. The completed nut has no threads. This example uses the command syntax given below accepting all the defaults.

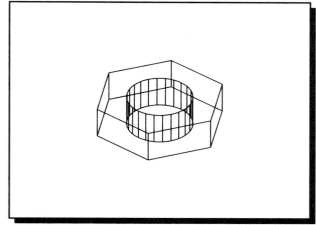

Figure 44-17

```
Command: solnut
Insertion base point <0,0,0>:
Enter nut diameter <2.0>:
Enter nut height <0.5>:
Enter hole diameter <1.0>:
Phase I - Boundary evaluation begins.  etc.
Command:
```

DRILL.EXP

DRILL.EXP is an ADS application that, when loaded, allows you to use the *Soldrill* command. The *Soldrill* command automatically creates a drilled hole of the diameter and depth that you specify into an AME solid. You must PICK a planar face into which the hole will be drilled.

Figure 44-18 shows a box in wireframe representation. The command sequence shown below was used to create the drilled hole. Essentially, *Soldrill* creates a cylinder to the specified dimensions and *Subtracts* it from the solid.

Figure 44-18

```
Command: soldrill
Select a planar face to drill
the hole: PICK
Next/<OK>:   N or Enter
Center <0,0,0>:   Enter or (value)
Diameter <1.0>:   Enter or (value)
Depth <through>:   Enter or (value)
Phase I - Boundary evaluation begins. etc.
Command:
```

LAYOUT.EXP

LAYOUT.EXP is an ADS application that defines three commands for automating sheet metal layouts. LAYOUT.EXP must be loaded before you can use the *Gear, Sheet*, and *Layout* commands at the command prompt.

GEAR

Gear creates a gear-shaped <u>region</u> according to the pitch circle diameter, number of teeth, and pressure angle that you specify. This command is similar to the *Solgear* command, except the resulting shape is a 2D region instead of an AME solid. The region is created parallel to the XY plane of the current coordinate system and centered on the insertion point (not shown).

SHEET

The *Sheet* command simply creates a rectangular region that represents a sheet of stock material. The resulting region is intended to be used with the *Layout* command (see below). You specify the width and depth. The sheet is created parallel to the XY plane and is centered about the specified base point.

LAYOUT

The *Layout* command automatically nests any region that you specify within the *Sheet* or other specified region. You only have to PICK the sheet, the region you want to nest, and the angle for the orientation of the region. AME then copies the region onto the sheet and lays it out to the closest possible fit. *Layout* then reports the total number of parts that fit on the sheet and the percentage of material utilization. You should, however, try several angles until you find the optimum material utilization.

OFFSOL.EXP

OFFSOL.EXP is an ADS program that assists in calculating 2D cutting tool paths for machining and milling operations. Tool paths are determined first by offsetting one-half of the tool diameter from the desired milled or machined shape. Several offsets are combined to generate a path (series of movements) that the cutting tool makes in order to realize the finished part.

The OFFSOL program loads two commands, *Soloff* and *Solmac*, that are used to create *Polylines* representing cutting tool paths. *Soloff* and *Solmac* create tool paths only for closed, straight, 2D *Plines*. They cannot be used to calculate tool paths for AME solids.

SOLOFF

The *Soloff* command creates one closed *Pline* at a specified distance from the selected closed *Pline*. The *Pline* shape must have only straight segments.

SOLMAC

The *Solmac* command creates multiple *Pline* tool paths until the entire 2D solid is milled off. It uses the *Soloff* command repeatedly to create the concentric tool path *Plines*.

SOLSTLOUT

The *Solstlout* <u>command</u> is not an ADS application or an AutoLISP command and therefore does not have to be loaded before use. AME must be loaded, however. *Solstlout* writes an ASCII or binary .STL file from an AME solid model.

Use *Soltlout* if you want to use an AME solid and create a prototype part using stereo-lithography or sintering technology. This technology reads the CAD data and creates a part by using a laser to solidify micro-thin layers of plastic or wax polymer or powder. A complex 3D prototype can be created from a CAD drawing in a matter of hours. See the AutoCAD Advanced Modeling Extension Reference Manual, page 172, for detailed information.

SOLVIEW.EXP

SOLVIEW.EXP is an ADS program that allows you to automatically generate a 2D drawing from a 3D AME model. The process has two steps; first, use the *Solview* command, then use *Soldraw*. *Solview* creates paper space viewports for the views of the model that you specify. *Soldraw* projects the 3D models onto 2D planes (optional) and automatically creates layers for dimensioning with correct visibility settings. Because of the importance of this program for engineering, it is discussed in detail in Chapter 46.

SYMMETRY.EXP

The SYMMETRY ADS application makes possible the use of the *Symmetry* command at the command prompt. *Symmetry* determines whether or not a region is symmetric. Symmetry reports if the region is circularly (radially) symmetric, symmetric with respect to its X axis or Y axis, or symmetric to both axes.

TUTOR.EXP

TUTOR.EXP is an ADS application intended to be used as a tutorial for those interested in learning to program using the AutoCAD Programming Interface. This tutorial program shows the fundamental concepts, data structure, and 3D solid modeling power of API. If you are interested in API programming, see the AutoCAD Advanced Modeling Extension Reference Manual, page 163, for more information.

CHAPTER EXERCISES

1. ***Open*** the **CH43EX4** drawing. Check the value for ***SOLWDENS*** by any method (*AME Variables* dialogue box or typing the variable name). It should be set to 6 or 8. Change the setting to **3**. Notice that no change is made to the composite solid. Load SOLMAINT.EXP. Next, use the ***Solupdate*** command to update the solid with the new wire density setting. The display should appear with fewer tessellation lines, as shown in Figure 44-19. Do not exit the drawing.

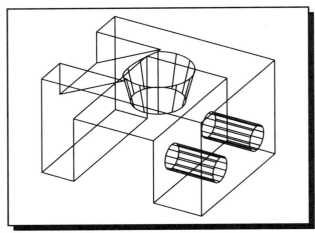

Figure 44-19

2. Load HOLE.LSP (using the same drawing as the previous exercise). Use ***Hole*** with the ***CS*** option to create a countersink on the nearest hole. Use the default settings. Create a counterbore (with the ***CB*** option) on the other hole using the default diameter and a depth of **.5** Compare your results to Figure 44-20. ***Saveas*** **CH44EX2**.

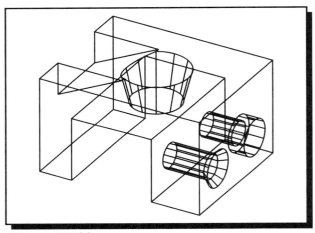

Figure 44-20

3. Begin a ***New*** drawing (or use a ***Prototype***) and assign the name **ASSEMBLY**. Create ***New Layers*** named **SHAFT**, **BEARING**, **PULLEY**, and **BOLTS**. Set **SHAFT** as the ***Current*** layer. Set ***SOLWDENS*** to 6. Load **DESIGN.EXP** and use the ***Solshaft*** command. Create a shaft using the following dimensions:

```
Command: solshaft
Insertion base point <0,0,0>: Enter
Enter shaft diameter <1.0>: 20
Enter shaft length <5.0>: 200
Enter keyway depth <0.3>: 4
Enter keyway width <0.4>: 6
Enter keyway length <2.0>: 40
```

Next, set **BEARING** as the ***Current*** layer and use ***Solbear*** to create a bearing bracket with the following dimensions:

```
Command: solbear
Insertion base point <0,0,0>: Enter
Enter bearing diameter <5.0>: 40
Enter bearing thickness <3.0>: 28
Enter hole diameter <2.0>: 20
Enter distance from base to center of hole <5.0>: 60
Enter base height <1.0>: 12
Enter base width <6.0>: 100
```

Save the drawing but do not Exit.

4. Use **Solmove** or **Rotate3D** to set the bearing bracket upright (90 degrees on X axis) and to rotate the shaft similarly. **Load DRILL.EXP** and use **Soldrill** to drill two holes through the bearing bracket base. Select the top plane of the base. The hole *Centers* are at **-14,20** and **-14,-40** with **Diameters** of **7**. The drawing should look like Figure 44-21 at this stage.

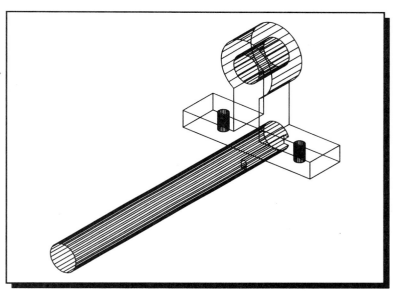

Figure 44-21

Set the **Current Layer** to **BOLTS** and create one bolt and a matching nut using **Solbolt** and **Solnut**. Specifications are as follows:

```
Command: solbolt
Insertion base point <0,0,0>: Enter
Enter head diameter <2.0>: 11
Enter head height <0.5>: 4
Enter screw diameter <1.0>: 6
Enter screw length <5.0>: 30

Command: solnut
Insertion base point <0,0,0>: Enter
Enter nut diameter <2.0>: 11
Enter nut height <0.5>: 5
Enter hole diameter <1.0>: 6
```

5. *Load* **ASM.EXP** and use the *Solalign* command to align the axes of the shaft and bearing bracket, then the nut and bolt with the hole. (HINT: Use *CENter* of the circular shapes to align the matching axes.) You should also use *Solmove* to slide the shapes along the axes. Use *Copy* or *Mirror* to create the other nut and bolt. *Save* the drawing. Compare with the assembly shown in Figure 44-22.

6. *Open* the **PULLY-SL** drawing you created in Chapter 42 Exercises. *Load* **WBLKSOL** and convert the Pulley into a *Wblock*. Assign the name **PUL-BLK**. Do <u>not</u> *Save* the PULLY-SL drawing.

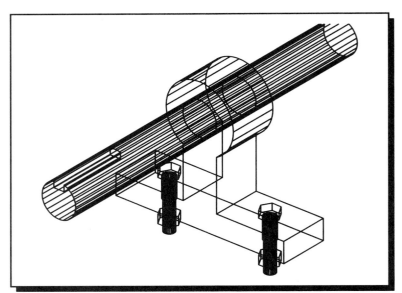

7. *Open* the **ASSEMBLY** drawing and *Load* **WBLKSOL**. Use *Insrtsol* to insert the **PUL-BLK** drawing. Use any method you want to align the Pulley on the end of the shaft. Compare your work to Figure 44-23. *Save* the drawing.

Figure 44-22

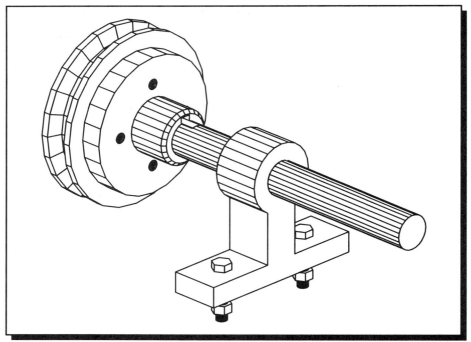

Figure 44-23

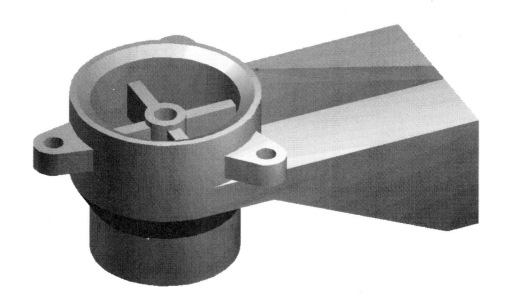

CHAPTER 45

Shading and Rendering

CHAPTER OBJECTIVES

After completing this chapter you should:

1.   know how to use *Shade* to create a quick, shaded display of a surface or solid model;

2.   be able to adjust the shaded display with the *SHADEDIF* and *SHADEDGE* variables;

3.   know the typical steps for rendering a surface or solid model using AVE;

4.   understand and be able to create the three types of lights: *Ambient*, *Diffuse*, and *Distant*;

5.   understand and be able to assign the three types of finish reflections: *Ambient*, *Diffuse*, and *Specular*;

6.   know how to use *Rpref* to specify parameters for rendering;

7.   be able to use *Saveimg* to save and *Replay* to replay rendered images.

BASICS

AutoCAD provides the ability to enhance the visualization of a <u>surface</u> or a <u>solid</u> model with the *Shade* and the *Render* commands. Because the default representation for surface and solid models is wireframe representation, it is difficult for the viewer to sense the three dimensional properties of the model in this mode. Hidden line removal (using *Hide*) and perspective generations (using *Dview*) certainly improve visualization capabilities, but *Shade* and *Render* add another level of realism to surface and solid models.

Shading and rendering involve the use of *Light* sources and the application of a surface *Finish* for the 3D model. Both *Shade* and *Render* allow you to control the viewpoint (using *Vpoint* or *View*) from which you envision the model. *Shade* and *Render* differ in the level of complexity and user control of light source(s) and finishes.

Shade is a simple and quick method that uses a default light location and fills the surfaces of the 3D model with the entity color. You have control of only two variables, *SHADEDIF* and *SHADEDGE*, that affect the results of the shaded model.

Render, on the other hand, provides control of type, intensity, and positioning of lights, as well as surface reflective qualities and colors. The *Render* capabilities are accessible from within AutoCAD as an ADS application named AVERENDR.EXP. AVE stands for the AutoCAD Visualization Extension, sometimes referred to as AutoCAD Render.

Both *Shade* and *Render* are intended as visualization tools for 3D models. Visualization of a design before it has been constructed or manufactured can be of significant value. Presentation of a model with light sources, color, and reflectivity can reveal aspects of a design that may otherwise only be possible after construction or manufacturing. For example, a rendered architectural setting may give the designer and client previews of color, lighting, or spacial relationships. Or a rendered model may allow the engineer to preview the functional relationship of mechanical parts in a manner otherwise impossible with wireframe representation. Thus, this "realistic" presentation, made possible by *Shade* or *Render*, can shorten the design feedback cycle and improve communication between designers, engineers, architects, contractors, and clients.

SHADING

SHADE

TYPE IN:	PULL-DOWN MENU	SCREEN MENU	TABLET MENU
SHADE	*Render, Shade*	*DISPLAY, SHADE*	*3,M*

The *Shade* command allows you to shade the model in a full screen display or in the current viewport. This command is sufficient to get a quick image of your model and can be saved using the *Mslide* command. *Shade* automatically positions one light in space and sets a default intensity. The light location is always over your right shoulder. Several options allow you to fill the model surfaces and/or edges with the entity color.

Two system variables control how the shade appears: *SHADEDGE* and *SHADEDIF*. *SHADEDGE* controls how the surfaces and edges are shaded. The only lighting control is a percentage of diffuse and ambient light adjusted by *SHADEDIF*.

Steps for Creating a Shaded Model

1. Create a solid or surface model using the desired color assigned to the layer or entities.

2. Use the *Vpoint* command or the *Dview* command to arrange the desired viewing position. Perspectives displays generated by *Dview* are allowed. The display position can be saved to a named view using the *View* command if desired.

3. Use *Solmesh* to convert the model to meshed representation.

4. Activate the *Shade* command to automatically create a shaded image of the model on the screen or in the current viewport.

5. If you want to alter the appearance of the shaded image, adjust the ratio of diffused and ambient light with the *SHADEDIF* variable. The *SHADEDGE* variable can be used to vary the use of the background or the entity color for the edges and the solid filled surfaces.

6. Use *Shade* again to display the new changes.

7. If desired, save the shaded image to an .SLD file using the *Mslide* command.

To illustrate a typical approach to using *Shade*, the following figures are provided.

The first step is to create or *Open* a surface or solid model drawing. For this example, assume the Intake Housing in Figure 45-1 has been created in AutoCAD as a solid model. In this display, it appears in wireframe representation. This viewpoint is of the top (plan) view.

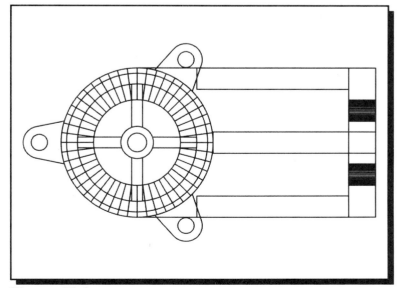

Figure 45-1

The second step is to use the *Vpoint* or *Dview* command to achieve the desired viewing position. Generally the viewpoint should show the most descriptive orientation or show the object in its functioning position. You can save the display using *View* with the *Save* option if you need to do some further editing to the geometry. The *Restore* option of *View* returns the named display.

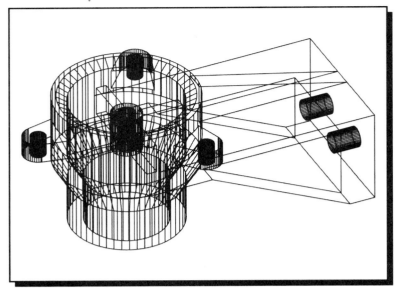

Figure 45-2

Next, use the *Shade* command. A light source is automatically assigned and located over your right shoulder. The default setting for *SHADEDGE* (3) causes the surfaces to be filled with the entity color and the edges to have the background color. (This display has been reversed and converted to gray scale. Your screen probably shows colors on a black background.)

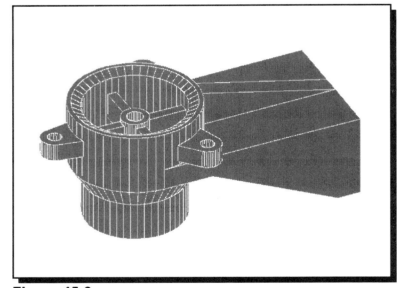

Figure 45-3

The *SHADEDGE* and *SHADEDIF* variables can be adjusted to yield a different display of the model. Possible settings for these variables are explained in the following sections. Any changes made to the *SHADEDGE* variable are displayed on the next use of the *Shade* command.

Shade creates the image only for the current screen display. You can think of the shaded display as being projected in front of the current drawing. You cannot draw or edit the drawing while a shaded image is displayed. If you want to view or edit the original drawing again, use *Regen*.

NOTE: You cannot select entities in a shaded image. You must use *Regen* to regenerate the original drawing.

SHADEDGE

The _SHADEDGE_ variable controls how the edges of surfaces are displayed and if the surfaces are filled with solid color, filled with gradient shading, or not filled. The variable can be changed by typing in _SHADEDGE_ at the command prompt and entering the desired integer or by using the screen menu to select the _SHADE:_ command and selecting the desired descriptor. The four possible settings are given here listing the integer values and descriptors as they appear in the screen menu.

0, 256-col

This option causes the object surfaces to be shaded in gradient values of the entity color. The object's visible edges are not highlighted. This option requires 256 color display capabilities on the monitor and video card. (Keep in mind that these figures have been reversed and converted to gray scale. Your screen probably shows colors on a black background.)

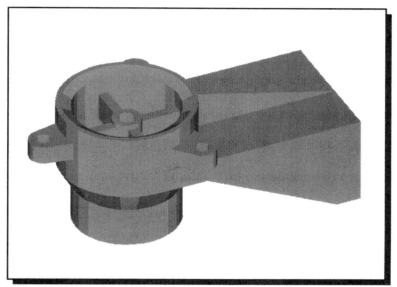

Figure 45-4

1, 256-edg

This option shades the surfaces in gradient values of the entity color and highlights the visible edges in the background color. This option also requires a 256 color display.

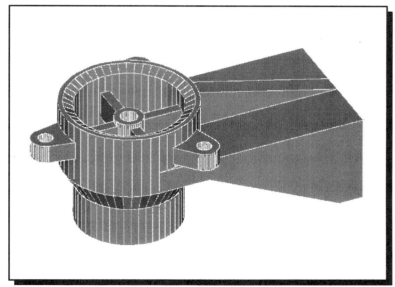

Figure 45-5

2, *hidden*

This option simulates hidden line removal. The resulting display is identical to using the *Hide* command. All surfaces are painted in the background color and the visible edges have the entity color. This display works well for display capabilities of less than 256 colors or for monochrome displays.

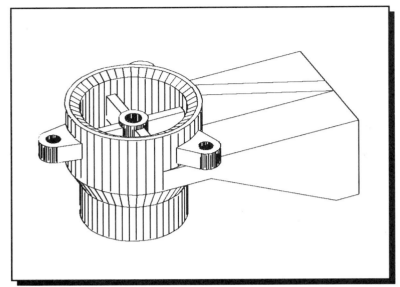

Figure 45-6

3, *filled*

The surfaces are filled by the entity's color <u>without</u> gradient shading when this option is used. The visible edges are drawn in the background color. This display also works well for display capabilities of less than 256 colors and for monochrome displays.

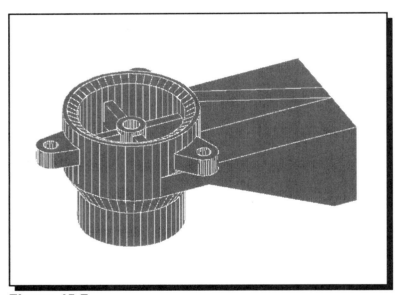

Figure 45-7

SHADEDIF

When you set *SHADEDGE* to 0 or 1, the object is shaded with different values (from light to dark) in the entity color. *SHADEDIF* controls the contrast of those values. Two kinds of lights are used with *Shade*: <u>ambient</u> and <u>diffuse</u>. The ambient light is all around and illuminates all surfaces equally. Diffuse light is reflected off the surfaces of the object from a light source located behind the observer. With diffuse light, surfaces that are perpendicular to the line of sight are lighter and surfaces that are angled to the line of sight are darker.

The *SHADEDIF* variable controls the amount of diffuse reflection of light versus the overall (ambient) light. The default setting of 70 specifies 70% diffuse and 30% ambient light. The higher the *SHADEDIF* setting, the greater the reflected light and the greater the contrast of surfaces on the object. The lower the *SHADEDIF* setting, the lower the contrast and the more all surfaces are lighted equally.

The *SHADEDIF* setting may be changed by typing the variable name at the command prompt or by selecting from the screen menu. The range is from 1 to 100. The value entered represents the percentage of diffuse light.

The following examples illustrate different *SHADEDIF* settings. The brightness of the shaded image is also affected by the color of the object.

SHADEDIF low (**40-50**)

The display in Figure 45-8 illustrates a low setting for *SHADEDIF*. There is little contrast because all surfaces are lighted almost equally by the ambient light. Since *SHADEDIF* is a ratio of diffuse to ambient light, a low diffuse percentage causes a high ambient setting. (The *SHADEDGE* setting for this and the next display is *1, 256-edg.*)

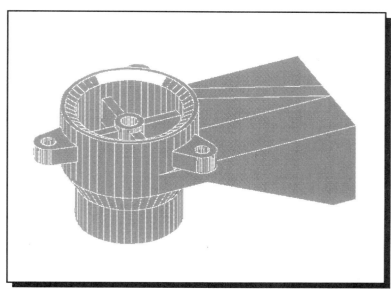

Figure 45-8

SHADEDIF high (**80-100**)

With a high diffuse setting, *Shade* creates a greater contrast among surfaces. Since the light source is behind you, surfaces that are perpendicular to the line of sight reflect light more than surfaces that are angled to the line of sight.

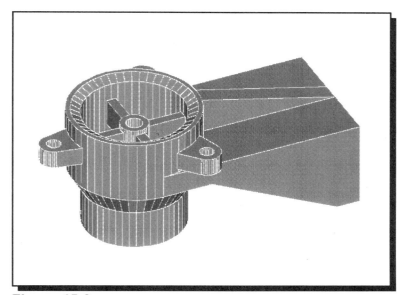

Figure 45-9

If you enjoy using *Shade*, you will certainly be excited by the capabilities that AutoCAD Render provides. Although Render is more complicated, the results are well worth it.

RENDERING

AutoCAD Visualization Extension

The AutoCAD Visualization Extension (AVE), sometimes called AutoCAD Render, is a rendering application that gives you control over *Light* parameters and defining *Finishes* for your model. You can place *Point Lights* and *Distant Lights*. These different light sources can be adjusted for intensity. *Point Lights* can also be adjusted for light fall-off. No light sources in AVE cast shadows. *Finish* parameters can be adjusted for color and reflective qualities. 3D Models do <u>not</u> have to be meshed with *Solmesh* before using AVE.

AutoCAD Render renders to a viewport or to the whole screen as a separate rendering display. The *Render* command uses the *Lights* and *Finishes* you assign and calculates the display based on the parameters that you specified. If no *Lights* or *Finishes* are created for the drawing, a default light and finish are used to render the current viewport. If you have created several *Lights*, *Finishes*, and *Views*, you can use the *Scene* option to specify a particular named *View*, a *Finish,* and a combination of *Lights*.

The rendered screen image created with the *Render* command may be saved as a TIFF, TGA, RND, and/or a GIF file and replayed at a later time. You may also save a hard copy of the rendered image as an EPS file. The *Rendering Preferences* dialogue box provides control for format and quality of the rendered image.

AVE commands can easily be accessed by the *RENDER* option from the top-level screen menu or the *Render* pull-down menu (Fig. 45-10). Optionally, the digitizing menu has the area from 1J through 3L specified for commands related to AVE. Of course, AVE commands may also be typed at the command prompt.

Figure 45-10

Typical Steps for Using AVE

1.　As with using *Shade*, you must first create or open an existing 3D model. Both surface and solid models can be rendered.

2.　Use *Vpoint* or *Dview* to specify the desired viewing position. Perspective generations (created with *Dview Distance*) are allowed. If you want to create several renderings from different viewpoints use the *Save* option of *View* to save each display to a named view so it can be *Restored* at a later time.

3.　Use the *Lights* dialogue box series to create one or more lights. Parameters such as light type, intensity, and location (position in space) can be specified.

4.　Use the *Finishes* dialogue box series to define the desired finish properties. The properties involve specification of color and the desired reflective qualities for the surfaces. You can *Preview* the finish as you adjust the parameters.

5.　If you have created several *Views*, *Finishes*, and *Lights*, use the *Scenes* dialogue box to select the specific combination of lights and the desired *View* for the rendered scene.

6.　Specify the desired format and quality for the rendering by way of the *Rendering Preferences* dialogue box. If you are creating a preliminary or a test rendering, a *Quick Render* is usually performed.

7.　Use the *Render* command to create the rendered image on the screen.

8.　Because rendering normally involves a process of continual adjustment to *Light* and *Finish* parameters, any or all of steps 3 through 7 may be repeated to make the desired adjustments. Don't expect to achieve exactly what you want the first time.

9.　When the final adjustments have been made, use the *Rendering Preferences* dialogue box to create a *Full Render* to achieve the highest quality image.

10.　Use the *Render* command again to calculate the rendered display or hard copy. Usually you should render to the screen until you have just the image you want, then save to a file or hard copy if desired.

11.　If you rendered to the framebuffer (screen), you can then save the rendered image to a .TIF, .GIF, .TGA, or .RND file using the *Save Image* dialogue box. An .EPS file can be created using the PSOUT command.

Now that you know the general procedure for creating a rendered image, the lighting and finish concepts and commands are presented next. Examples of the dialogue boxes used to achieve the desired effects are included in the following information.

Lights

AutoCAD recognizes three types of light: *Ambient Light, Point Light*, and *Distant Light. Point Lights* and *Distant Lights* can be positioned anywhere in space and adjusted for intensity. *Distant Lights* can be set to shine in a specific direction; whereas, *Point Lights* shine in all directions. *Ambient Light* has no location and affects all surfaces equally. *Ambient Light* can only be controlled for intensity. No lights cast shadows. All light passes unobstructed through surfaces.

Ambient Light

Ambient Light is the overall lighting of surfaces. Each surface is illuminated with an equal amount of ambient light, regardless of the surface's position. Thus, you would not be able to distinguish the adjoining faces of a box if this was the only type of light in the model. Figure 45-11 illustrates the rendering of a box with only ambient light. Adjusting ambient light would be like using a dimmer switch to darken or lighten a room, except that the light has no source or direction. Ambient light is the most unrealistic type of light, but it is needed to display surfaces that may not be illuminated by point or distant lights. You do not create or position an *Ambient Light* in the model; it is ever-present unless its intensity has been set to zero.

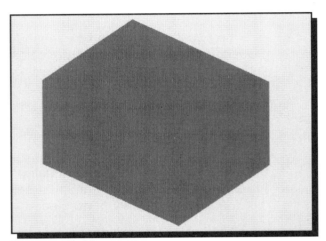

Figure 45-11

Distant Light

A *Distant Light* shines in one direction and has parallel rays. It is used to simulate sunlight. Distant light is inserted with a *Target* point and a light *Location*. The vector between the *Target* and *Location* determines the direction of the parallel beams of light which extend to infinity. The light intensity of distant lights does not fall off as the distance between the location and the surface increases. Figure 45-12 illustrates a box illuminated by only one *Distant Light* located above and to the right. Notice how each surface is illuminated differently because of the angle of the surface to the direction vector, yet each individual surface is illuminated evenly across the entire surface.

Figure 45-12

Point Light

A *Point Light* is inserted at the location you specify, but no direction vector is needed since this light shines in all directions. Point light would be typical of the light emitted from a light bulb. Point light <u>falls off</u> as the distance between the light source and surface increases, so surfaces close to the light are brighter than those at a distance. The box in Figure 45-13 is illuminated by only one *Point Light* above and to the right side. Notice how the light falls off the further the surfaces are from the light source.

Figure 45-13

For *Point* and *Distant Lights*, the brightness of a rendered surface depends on the following parameters.

1. The intensity of the light can be specified. The brighter the light, the brighter the rendered surfaces appear.

2. The angle between the light source and the surface affects the brightness of the surface. A surface that shines the brightest is one in which the light is shining perpendicular to the surface. The more angled the surface is from perpendicular, the darker it appears.

3. The distance between the light and the surface affect brightness (*Point Lights* only).

Now that you understand the types of lights and the effects of each type on the rendered object, here is how you insert and control the lights.

LIGHT

TYPE IN:	PULL-DOWN MENU	SCREEN MENU	TABLET MENU
LIGHT	*Render, Lights...*	*RENDER, LIGHT...*	*1,L*

When you invoke the *Light* command by any method, the *Lights* dialogue box appears as shown in Figure 45-14. The *Lights* dialogue is where the <u>global</u> *Ambient Light* is set with the slider bar or entered numerically in the edit box. *Point Light Fall-off* is set here as well. *Point Light Fall-off* means that the further from the light, the darker the rendered surface will be. *Point Light Fall-off* has three options.

None

This option forces the light emitted from a point light to keep full intensity no matter how far the rendered surfaces are from the source. This is similar to a distant light.

Inverse Linear

This option sets a linear inverse relation between the distance and the illumination. The brightness of a rendered surface is inversely proportional to the distance from the source. Put another way, there is a 1 to 1 relationship between distance and darkness.

Inverse Square

This is the greatest degree of fall-off. The light falls off in an inverse proportion to the square of the distance. In other words, if the rendered surfaces are 2, 3, and 4 units from the light source, the illumination for each will be $1/2^2$, $1/3^2$, and $1/4^2$ (1/4, 1/9, and 1/16) as strong. This option simulates the physical law explaining light fall-off in real life.

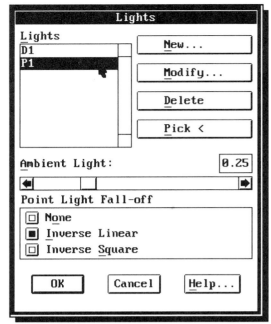

Figure 45-14

Generally, *Inverse Linear* fall-off is the easiest to work with and appears realistic for most AutoCAD renderings.

To insert lights in your drawing, select *New...* from the *Lights* dialogue box (Fig 45-14). The *New Light Type* dialogue pops up (Fig. 45-15) and allows you to select a *Point Light* or a *Distant Light* (*Spotlights* are only available if you are using AutoShade with RenderMan). Once you choose the light type you want and select *OK*, the light is automatically placed in the drawing. In this example, a *Point Light* is selected. AutoCAD calculates a default *Location* for the light (and *Target* for distant lights).

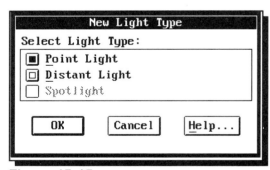

Figure 45-15

Once the *Point* or *Distant Light* is placed, the *New Point* (or *Distant*) *Light* dialogue appears (see Fig. 45-16). You must assign a name for the light before proceeding. In this example "P2" is assigned as the name for a new point light. The intensity can be set with the slider bar or by entering a value in the edit box. Selecting the *Show* tile displays the default *Location* of the light (and *Target* for Distant lights) as shown in Figure 45-17. The *Location* is the position of the light itself and the *Target* is the point at which distant lights are directed. You can change the position by selecting the *Modify* tile, then entering the desired coordinates for the new light position or target position in command line format. It is recommended that you enter coordinate values or use point filters if you PICK a position.

New Point Light

Light **N**ame: P2

Intensity: 22.71

◄| |►

Position

| **M**odify < | **S**how... |

| Modify Light Color... |

Depth Map Size: 0

| OK | Cancel | **H**elp... |

Figure 45-16

Show Light Position

Location	Target
X = 2.8958	X =
Y = 1.1476	Y =
Z = 0.5736	Z =

| OK | **H**elp... |

Figure 45-17

Once you have selected *OK*, the *Lights* dialogue box appears again with the name of your light in the light list box. The same procedure is used to insert additional lights.

Icons representing the light type and location appear in the drawing at the light positions as shown in Figure 45-18. These icons are actually *Block* insertions and will appear in a plot. You can use the *Move* command to reposition the lights; however, moving a *Direct Light* position will also move the *Target* position. Generally, it is safe to *Move Point Lights*, but for *Distant Lights* use the dialogue box series. A light can be deleted by *Erasing* its icon or by using the *Delete* option in the *Lights* dialogue box (Fig. 45-14).

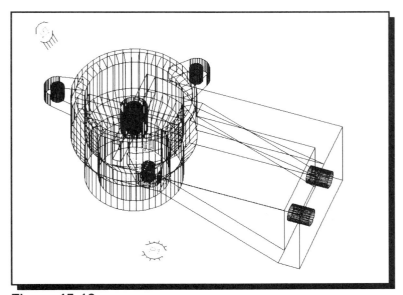

Figure 45-18

When the lights have been inserted and adjusted for position and intensity, you are ready to assign a *Finish* and attach it to the model. Multiple *Finishes* can be created and attached to different components of the model.

Finishes

The reflective qualities and colors of surfaces are defined as *Finishes*. You create a finish by using the *Finish* command and the related dialogue boxes to specify several properties that define the finish. The *Finish* is then *Attached* to AutoCAD entities or assigned to an AutoCAD Color Index number. AVE allows you to control five parameters that define a surface finish.

Ambient reflection, *Diffuse* reflection, *Specular* reflection, *Roughness*, and *Color*

Ambient reflection

Ambient <u>light</u> is background light that provides constant illumination to all surfaces. The amount of ambient light that is emitted for the model is set in the *Lights* dialogue box as described earlier.

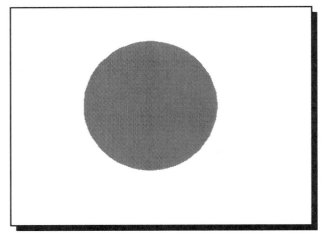

Ambient <u>reflection</u> assigned to a surface determines how much ambient light is reflected by that particular surface. *Ambient* reflection is a function of the surface's ambient setting and the global setting in the *Light* dialogue box. With <u>only</u> ambient light, there is no contrast as shown on the ball in Figure 45-19.

Figure 45-19

Diffuse reflection

Surfaces such as blotting paper or matte-painted walls exhibit diffuse reflection. Light hitting diffuse surfaces is dispersed equally in all directions. No matter where your viewpoint is, the reflection of the surface is the same for a particular light.

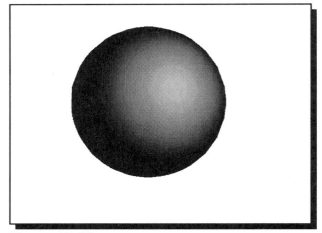

Diffuse reflection only considers the relationship of the surface to the light source; that is, the reflection is determined only by the distance and the angle of the surface to the light. *Diffuse* reflection does not consider the position of your viewpoint. With

Figure 45-20

<u>only</u> *Diffuse* reflection (as shown in Figure 45-20) there is contrast as a result of distance and angle, but there are no highlights.

Specular reflection

Specular reflection reflects light in a narrow cone. A beam of light striking a perfectly specular surface, like a mirror, reflects light in one direction only. Therefore, specular reflection considers the light location and the viewpoint since the reflected beam is visible only from a viewpoint where the angle of incidence is equal to the angle of reflection.

Specular reflection is that type of reflection that accounts for highlights such as the shiny spot on a ball. If you move around the ball, the point of reflection, the highlight, changes to

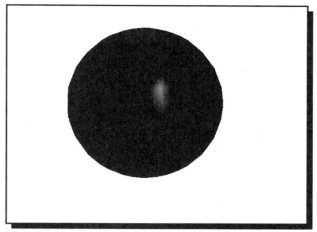

Figure 45-21

mirror your viewpoint. With <u>only</u> *Specular* reflection, the image displays highlights but is very dark (Fig. 45-21).

Roughness

AVE lets you control the <u>size</u> of the cone of specular refection using the *Roughness* factor. If a surface has roughness, its specular reflection is spread in a less perfect, larger cone. The larger the roughness factor, the larger the cone of reflection and the larger the highlight.

Roughness does not affect the amount of highlight, only the <u>size</u> of the highlight. The ball in Figure 45-22 has the same amount of *Specular* reflection as that in the previous figure but a higher roughness factor.

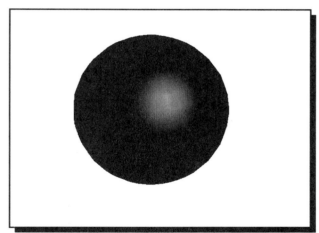

Figure 45-22

Generally, the most realistic renderings involve a combination of all reflective qualities. The particular qualities should be varied to simulate the type of surface desired for the rendering.

Color

The color associated with a finish may be assigned by one of several methods. You can use the original entity (or *BYLAYER*) color, select from the ACI pallet, or create a color using a color wheel or *RGB* slider bars. The dialogue box series guides you through the procedure.

To create a finish with these properties, use the *Finish* command described next.

FINISH

TYPE IN:	PULL-DOWN MENU	SCREEN MENU	TABLET MENU
FINISH	*Render, Finishes...*	*RENDER, FINISH:*	*2L*

Invoking the *Finish* command invokes the *Finishes* dialogue box (Fig. 45-23). When you create a *Finish* for the first time in a drawing, no finishes appear in the *Finishes* list box, only an AutoCAD-supplied default or **GLOBAL** finish. Select the *New...* tile to create a new finish. The *New Finish* dialogue box appears (see Figure 45-24).

If finishes exist and appear in the list box, you can select *Modify...* to change the settings for the selected finish. The *Modify Finish* dialogue is the same as the *New Finish* dialogue box shown in the next figure (Fig. 45-24).

Alternately, you can *Import...* a pre-defined finish supplied by AutoCAD (see Other *Finish* Options). Once a *Finish* has been created or imported, you will be returned to this dialogue box. If finishes already exist, you can use the other options in this dialogue, which are explained later.

Figure 45-23

The *New Finish* and *Modify Finish* dialogue boxes are where you name the finish and set the reflective parameters. A name for the finish must be assigned (in the upper right corner edit box) before you can proceed.

The *Ambient, Diffuse, Specular,* and *Roughness* factors can be set by the slider bars or by entering values in the edit boxes. Next (the best part of this dialogue box), you can select *Preview Finish* to render a sphere using the default color with the combination of reflective factors you set. This allows you to change settings and immediately see the results without having to perform a *Render*. (AVE must be configured to "render to a viewport" in order to use the *Preview Finish* option.)

You can base the finish on the entity color by selecting *Use Entity Color* or select *Set Color...* to specify the color of the finish. Set color invokes the *Color* dialogue box shown in Figure 45-25.

Figure 45-24

Once you set the *Ambient, Diffuse, Specular,* and *Roughness* factors, assign a color for the *Finish.* Three methods are available. You can use the *RGB/HLS* system on the left side of the dialogue box, you can use the color wheel (assuming your monitor has sufficient colors needed to display it), or you can PICK *Select from ACI...* to display another dialogue box with the 256-color ACI palette.

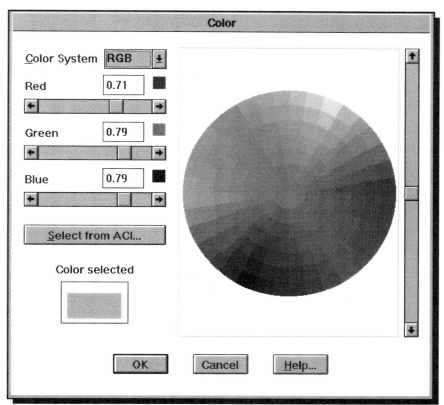

Figure 45-25

Color Wheel

This method is fast and easy. Just select the desired color from the wheel. The slider bar on the right changes the values (lightness) of the colors in the wheel. The selected color appears in the *Color Selected* swatch.

Color System

RGB   Make sure *RGB* is selected. Move the slider bars or enter values and watch the mix of colors appear in the *Color Selected* swatch. Pure red, green or blue hues can be achieved by moving <u>only</u> that color to the right. Moving all of the *Red, Green,* and *Blue* color bars to the left produces black and moving to the right produces white.

HLS   You must select *HLS* from the pop-down edit box. The slider bars adjust the *Hue, Lightness,* and *Saturation* visible in the small boxes. The mix of *HLS* appears in the *Color Selected* swatch.

Hue	Controls the color (red, blue, yellow, etc.)
Lightness	Controls the value (white to black). White is all the way to the right or a value of 1.0 and black is to the left or 0.
Saturation	Controls the purity of the color (mix of *Hue* and *Lightness*). Pure color is to the right or a value of 1.0 and pure gray scale is to the left or 0.

A pure hue is achieved by a *Lightness* of .5 and *Saturation* of 1.

Select from ACI...

Selecting this option invokes the 256-color ACI (AutoCAD Color Index) palette (Fig. 45-26). Select the desired color from the palette or enter the name or number in the edit box. If your monitor or video card only supports 16 colors, you can only select from the *Standard Colors* and *Gray Shades*.

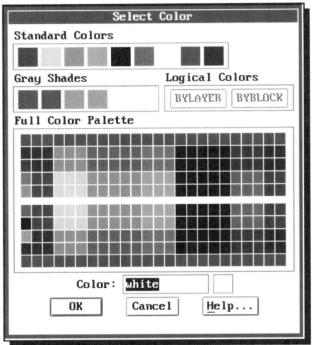

Attaching Finishes

Figure 45-26

Once the reflective factors and color have been specified for the *Finish,* you are automatically returned to the *New Finish* or *Modify Finish* dialogue box. Here you can further adjust the settings if desired. When you select the *OK* tile to exit the box, AutoCAD prompts you (at the command line) to place the finish icon in the drawing.

```
Enter New Finish location <current>: PICK or Enter to accept 0,0.
```

AutoCAD then redisplays the *Finishes* dialogue box. The last step is to *Attach* the finish to an entity or to an ACI number. This step is accomplished by selecting the *Entities<* tile or the *ACI...* tile from the bottom of the box (see Figure 45-27). If you choose to attach the finish to an *Entity*, a prompt similar to the one described below is given.

```
Select objects to attach "F2" to: PICK
Select objects: Enter
Updating drawing...done.
Command:
```

If you select the *ACI...* method of attaching finishes, the *Attach AutoCAD Color Index* dialogue box appears (not shown). Enter the ACI number or select from the list.

Other *Finish* Options

When the *Finish* has been *Attached*, you are ready to render. However, AutoCAD returns to the *Finishes* dialogue for further action if desired. For example, you may want to create other finishes for other objects or use the other options in the *Finishes* dialogue box described here.

The newly created finish appears in the list with any other finishes. A number appearing after the finish is the ACI number to which it is attached. A period (.) after the finish means it is not attached to an ACI.

Any highlighted finish from the list can be deleted by using *Delete*.

The *Pick>* tile allows you to PICK a finish (icon) from the drawing for subsequent action such as *Export, Modify*, etc.

You can also *Import...* or *Export* finishes from this box.

Figure 45-27

Selecting the *Import...* tile from the *Finishes* dialogue box allows you to use pre-defined finishes that AutoCAD supplies. The selection of preset finishes available in the *Import Preset Finish* dialogue box is shown in Figure 45-28. The *Preview Finish* option operates like those in the *New Finish* or *Modify Finish* dialogue boxes.

The *Ambient, Diffuse*, and *Specular* finishes have "pure" reflective factors and appear much the same as those illustrated in Figures 45-19, 45-20, and 45-21, respectively. These finishes are stored in a file kept by AutoCAD named NULLSURF.SP3.

A finish that you create or modify can be saved and used in other drawings by highlighting it in the *Finishes* dialogue box and selecting the *Export* option. The finish is saved in the NULLSURF.SP3 file with the preset finishes. The *Import* dialogue box lists all finishes saved in this file.

Figure 45-28

When the *Lights* have been inserted and *Finishes* have been attached, you can use the *Render* command to calculate the rendered view and display it in the viewport or in the rendering screen (whichever is configured). If no *Scene* has been specified, AutoCAD renders all objects in the current view and uses all lights. However, you may choose to use *Scene* to specify a particular view or lighting combination.

Using *Scenes*

SCENE

TYPE IN:	PULL-DOWN MENU	SCREEN MENU	TABLET MENU
SCENE	*Render, Scenes...*	*RENDER, SCENE...*	*3,L*

If you wish to render the object(s) from one of several named *Views* or use different light combinations for a viewpoint, you can use the *Scene* command to select the *View* and *Light* combinations for each render. You can save particular *Views* and lighting configurations to a *Scene* as a name that you assign. This action allows you to create multiple renderings without having to recreate the configuration each time. *Scenes* do not have icons that are inserted into the drawing like *Light* or *Finish* icons.

Invoking the *Scene* command by any method displays the *Scenes* dialogue box (Fig. 45-29).

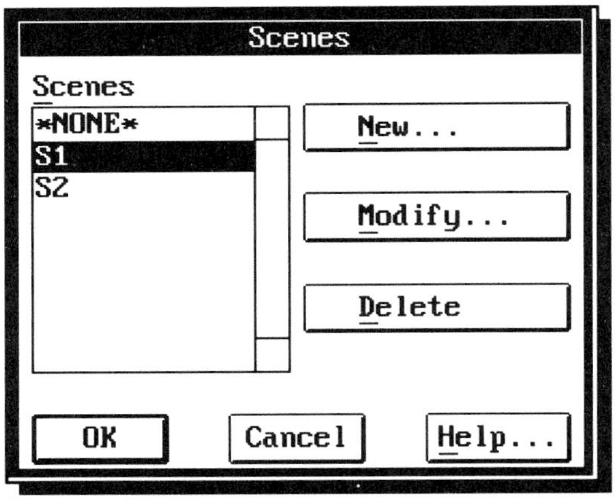

The **NONE** entry is the default. Selecting it will render the current viewpoint and use all lights inserted in the drawing. If no lights are inserted, AutoCAD uses one from over the shoulder like the one used for *Shade*.

Selecting the *New...* option allows you to create a new *Scene* for the drawing and produces the *New Scene* dialogue box (Fig. 45-30).

Selecting the *Modify...* option produces the *Modify Scene* dialogue box where you can modify existing *Scenes*. This dialogue box is the same as the *New Scene* dialogue.

Figure 45-29

Delete will delete the highlighted scene from the drawing.

The *New Scene* and the *Modify Scene* dialogue boxes allow you to select from a list of existing named *Views* and inserted *Lights*.

The first step is to assign the desired name for the scene by entering it in the edit box in the upper right of the *New Scene* dialogue box (see Fig. 45-30). The name is limited to eight characters.

The *Views* column lists all the previously created views. The **CURRENT** view can be selected if no *Views* have been previously assigned. You can only have <u>one</u> *View* in a

Scene. Selecting an existing view makes it the current view as well as that used for the subsequent *Render.*

You can also select *Lights* from the list to be included for the rendering of the scene. Any number of lights can be selected for a scene. Highlighted lights are included in the scene. Selecting a non-highlighted light adds it to the scene. There is no limit to the number of *Scenes* that can be created.

Before creating the first rendering, rendering preferences are set in the *Rendering Preferences* dialogue box. Normally the first rendering is set to use *Quick Render.*

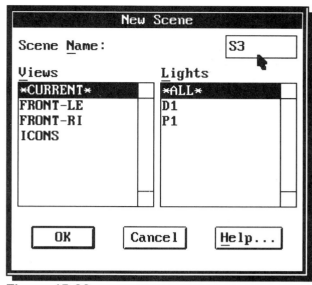

Figure 45-30

Specifying Rendering *Preferences*

RPREF

TYPE IN:	PULL-DOWN MENU	SCREEN MENU	TABLET MENU
RPREF	*Render, Preferences...*	*RENDER, RPREF...*	*1,J*

The *Rpref* command invokes the *Rendering Preferences* dialogue box (Fig. 45-31). This box lets you specify options that are used when you render the view or scene. It is a good habit to determine or check the settings in this dialogue box immediately before using the *Render* command. Since rendering takes time, taking a minute to make sure the desired options are set beforehand can save wasted rendering time. The options are described here.

Rendering Type

Full Render This options gives the highest quality rendering but normally takes more time than *Quick Render. Full Render* applies *Finishes, Smooth Shading,* and checks the drawing for overlapping edges and faces. It calculates a color for each pixel and uses the Gouraud shading method.

      When two different colors have a common edge, use *Full Render.* When you want to produce hard copy output or render to high resolution displays, use *Full Render.*

Quick This option uses scanline rendering by calculating a color for each
Render vertex, then blending between vertices. Thus, the smoothness of the render is a function of the mesh density.

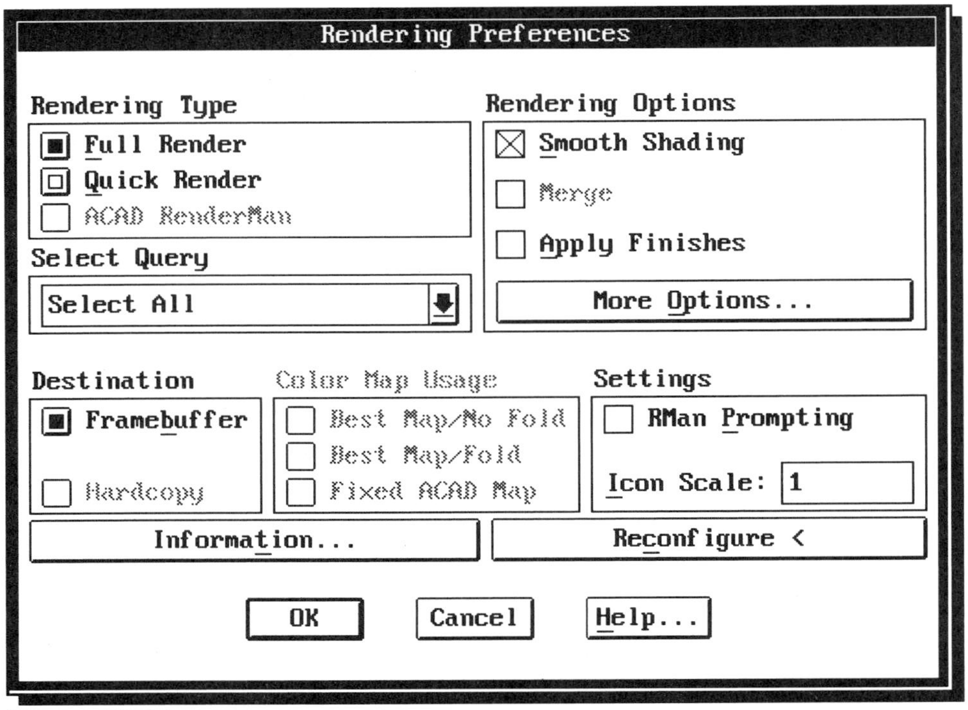

Figure 45-31

Rendering Options

Smooth Shading	If *Smooth Shading* is checked, AVE automatically smooths out the multifaceted appearance of polygon meshes. With *Smooth Shading* off, the mesh edges appear in the final rendering. If an edge forms a corner of 135 degrees or less, it will not be affected by *Smooth Shading.*
Merge	This option is only available with *Full Render* and for 24-bit color devices (16 million colors). *Merge* allows you to merge a smaller rendered object with the rendering in the framebuffer (previous rendered screen). In other words, first render a scene or *Replay* an existing rendering to fill the framebuffer, then render a smaller object or area and *Merge* will combine the most recent rendering with (in front of) the contents of the framebuffer. This is helpful if you want to re-render a small part of the previous rendering or combine a new image with an existing saved rendering.
Apply Finishes	This option applies your surface finishes when the rendering is calculated. If *Apply Finishes* is not checked, AVE uses the ambient, diffuse, and specular settings for the default *GLOBAL* finish for the next rendering.

Select Query

This option specifies how the selection set will be determined the next time you render.

| *Select All* | When you render, AVE automatically selects everything for the render. |
| *Make Selection* | When you render, you are prompted to specify a selection set. |

More Options...

Selecting this tile produces a dialogue box with advanced options related to the current rendering type, *Full Render* or *Quick Render*. See *More Options...* at the end of this section.

Destination

| *Framebuffer* | The framebuffer is the screen that is currently configured (a window, viewport, or single-screen display). If this option is checked, AVE calculates the rendering and displays it in the framebuffer. |
| *Hardcopy* | This option sends the rendering to the configured hard copy device that you specified when configuring AVE. If this option is checked, the rendering is calculated and written to the file or device, but is not displayed. |

Color Map Usage

These options control how colors are mapped if AVE is configured to render in 256 colors to a viewport, otherwise the options are grayed out.

Best Map/ No Fold	This option uses the best color map available for your system for the rendering viewport and for drawing vectors in other viewports. The vectors in other viewports may change colors somewhat after the rendering (called color flashing).
Best Map/ Fold	When you render in a viewport, this setting folds the colors in the non-rendered viewports to the standard eight colors. There is no color flashing in the non-rendering viewports.
Fixed ACAD Map	This option uses the AutoCAD 256-color map for both renderings and drawing vectors. There is no color flashing.

Settings

| *RMan Prompting* | Use this option if you are using AutoShade Version 2 with RenderMan and want to use spotlights, colored lights and shadows. |
| *Icon Scale* | Enter a value to scale the *Light* and *Finish* icons that are inserted into the drawing. |

Information

This tile produces an informational dialogue box giving your current configuration and AVE version.

Reconfigure

This option allows you to reconfigure the display and hard copy devices for AVE. This action can also be performed by using the *Rconfig* command. See *Rconfig*.

More Options...

Selecting this tile produces a dialogue box with advanced options related to the current rendering type, *Full Render* or *Quick Render*. Figure 45-32 displays the *Full Render Options* dialogue box.

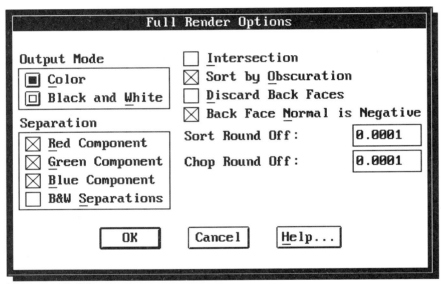

Figure 45-32

Settings in this dialogue box are for the advanced user of AVE. A brief explanation of the options is given below. For complete details, refer to the AutoCAD Render Reference Manual, pages 124 through 128.

Output Mode This option simply toggles a *Color* or *Black and White* render.

Intersection Unlike objects in real world, it is possible in AutoCAD to have two or more solids occupying the same 3D space. In most cases, models do not contain intersections. Turning *Intersection* on forces AVE to check for (and render correctly) intersecting solids. This check takes considerably more rendering time.

Sort by Obscuration By default, AVE checks to see which objects are in front of (obscure) others. With this option off, AVE renders more quickly, but the results may be inaccurate.

Discard Back Faces	This setting forces AVE to read the back faces of surfaces when rendering, which can save considerable time but may not display important geometry, such as the back of a cylinder normally visible from an open end.

Back Face Normal is Negative — Turning this setting off reverses which faces AVE considers as back faces. This setting affects the results of the previous option.

Sort Round Off — This option sets the accuracy of the round off error. A low setting can create jagged edges on an object's boundary. A high setting produces more accurate results but takes more time.

Chop Round Off — Similar to the previous setting, this value specifies a round off error accuracy. This value is used only when the *Intersection* option is on.

Separation — These options are used to create separate color displays if you want to make the separations for printing plates or transparencies.

B&W Separations — This option is used to convert the color separations to gray scale. They can then be used to project through color filters to display a full color image on a screen.

Finally, after inserting *Lights*, attaching *Finish*(s), and setting the *Rendering Preferences*, you are ready to create the rendering. Using the *Render* command is the easiest step in creating a rendering because AVE does the work.

Creating the Rendering

RENDER

TYPE IN:	PULL-DOWN MENU	SCREEN MENU	TABLET MENU
RENDER	*Render, Render*	*RENDER, RENDER:*	*2,J and 2,K*

Using this command causes AVE to calculate and display the rendered scene to the configured device. The rendering will be rendered according to the settings in the *Rendering Preferences* dialogue box. AVE uses the *Lights* and *View* selected in the *Scene* dialogue. If no *Scene* has been created, AVE renders the current view with all *Lights*.

There are no options or any other action that is required of you except to wait for the rendering to be displayed (or written to the hard copy device). However, if the *Make Selection* option is checked, you are prompted for the objects to render. Rendering can take considerable time, depending on the complexity of the scene, your computer system capabilities, and the settings in the *Rendering Preferences* dialogue box.

If you specified that AVE make a hard copy (in the *Rendering Preferences* dialogue box), the rendering is calculated and written to the specified file or device but is not displayed on the screen (see *Rconfig*). Alternately, if the framebuffer is the rendering *Destination*, and you decide to save the rendered screen display to a file, you can use *Saveimg* (see *Saveimg*).

Rendering Example

The Intake Housing used for the previous *Shade* examples is used again here as an example for inserting *Lights*, creating a *Finish*, and creating a rendering (refer to Typical Steps for Using AVE).

After the geometry is completed, *Dview* or *Vpoint* is used to provide an appropriate viewing orientation for the rendering. If desired, the viewpoint can be saved to a named *View* to be used later for defining *Scenes*.

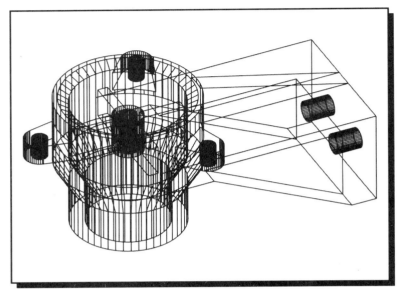

Figure 45-33

Next, the *Lights* dialogue box series is used to insert a light in the drawing. For this example, the first light is a *Point* light positioned to the upper right. Generating a *Quick Render* displays the results of the light position and intensity. You can make several adjustments to position and intensity settings, then generate *Quick Renderings* until the desired effect is obtained (Fig. 45-34).

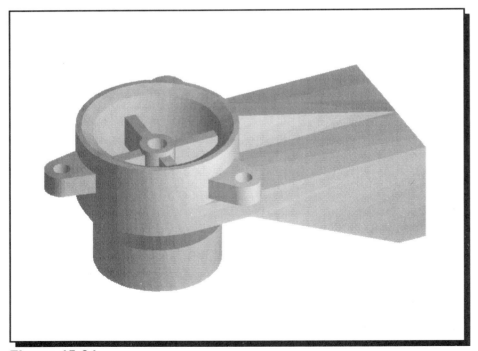

Figure 45-34

This light position in Figure 45-34 illuminates the front, top, and right sides of the Intake Housing. Notice how the point light illumination falls off; that is, the top and right side surfaces appear brighter than other surfaces in the model.

A rendering with only one point light may create drastic contrast from one side of the model to the other. Therefore, a second *Light* is inserted into the drawing to provide more even and realistic illumination over the surfaces of the model. This second light is a *Distant* light positioned on the left side and having a *Target* location at the base of the cylindrical element.

Figure 45-35

A *Quick Render* reveals the initial settings (Fig. 45-35). The new light compensates for the previously dark left side of the model. *Intensity* is adjusted to provide slightly less illumination than the *Point* light. Make several *Intensity* and *Position* adjustments if necessary to achieve the desired effects.

With the desired lighting set, the *Finish* should then be considered. The model at this stage appears to have the surface properties of a matte finish. The surfaces seem to reflect light evenly like a soft material.

In order for the observer to perceive the model as a hard metal such as machined cast iron, a *Finish* is attached with the appropriate reflective qualities specified. A low *Ambient* setting and a high *Diffuse* factor intensify the contrast of the light reflection between surfaces and amplifies the cylindrical shape. A high *Specular* factor, coupled with low *Roughness*, creates the highlights generated by hard, shiny, metallic surfaces.

The resulting rendering is evenly illuminated, yet has enough contrast and highlighting to yield a realistic and interesting image (see Fig. 45-36).

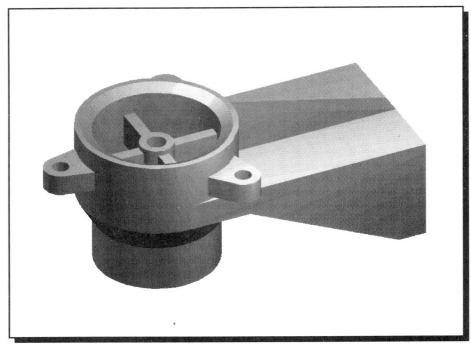

Figure 45-36

Saving and Replaying Renderings

SAVEIMG

TYPE IN:	PULL-DOWN MENU	SCREEN MENU	TABLET MENU
SAVEIMG	*Render, Files >* *Save Image...*	*RENDER, SAVEIMG.*	*3,K*

The *Saveimg* command allows you to save the rendered image in the framebuffer (the rendering screen or viewport) to a GIF, TIFF, TGA, or RND file format. The image can be displayed at a later time with the *Replay* command. No matter how long it took for AVE to calculate and display the original rendering, when it is saved to a GIF, TIFF, TGA, or RND file, it can be *Replayed* in a matter of seconds.

The *Saveimg* command can also save the <u>drawing screen</u> (any drawing, not only renderings) with or without the menus and the command line to the raster file type you specify. This can be useful if you want to import the screen image to a word processor to include in a document.

If you want to create a rendering and save it to a file directly (without first rendering to the screen), you can select *Hardcopy* as the *Destination* in the *Rendering Preferences* dialogue box. A hard copy device must be configured to use this option. Depending on the configured device, many file formats are available (see *Rconfig*).

The *Saveimg* command invoked by any method produces the *Save Image* dialogue box where you can select the file format and the portion of the image you wish to save. There are two forms of the dialogue box based on your current configuration--set either to render to a separate rendering screen (Fig. 45-37) or to render to a viewport (Fig. 45-38).

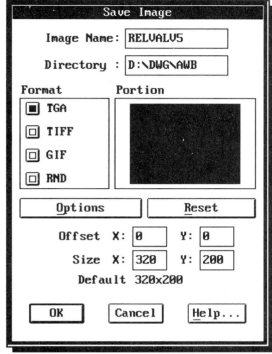

Figure 45-37

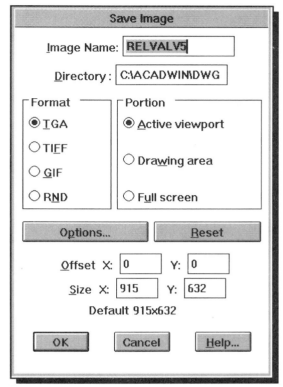

Figure 45-38

Format

GIF | This is the CompuServe image format (.GIF file extension). The _Size_ and _Offset_ options let you save a portion of the image.

TGA | This is the Truevision v2.0 format (.TGA file extension). It is a 32-bit format (16 million colors), although 8-, 16-, or 24-bit images can be saved to this format. A partial image can be saved with the _Size_ and _Offset_ options.

TIFF | Also a 32-bit format, this option is a Tagged Image File Format (.TIF file extension). A partial image can be saved with the _Size_ and _Offset_ options.

RND | This is the AutoCAD scanline format (.RND file extension). You cannot save a partial image in this format.

Options

Depending on the type of file (TIF and TGA only), file compression is available.

Offset

Sets the lower left corner for the image to save. The X and Y values are in screen pixels.

Size

Sets the upper right corner for the image in pixels.

Reset

Resets the *Offset* and *Size* values to 0,0.

Portion

The *Portion* option lets you save part of the image if you are saving to a TIFF, GIF, or TGA format. The methods of determining the portion you want to save differ based on the current configuration, either set to render to a viewport (Fig. 45-38) or set to render to a separate rendering screen (Fig. 45-37).

Portion	This image tile selector allows you to PICK the lower left and upper right corners of the image to save, or you can enter a X,Y values in the *Offset* and *Size* edit boxes.
Active Viewport	Saves the image in the active viewport.
Drawing Area	Saves the display in the drawing area without menus or command line.
Full Screen	Saves the drawing area, menus, and command line.

REPLAY

TYPE IN:	PULL-DOWN MENU	SCREEN MENU	TABLET MENU
REPLAY	*Render, Files>* *Replay Image...*	*RENDER, REPLAY...*	*3,J*

The *Replay* command calls the *Replay* dialogue box (Fig. 45-39) where you specify the file you want to replay. You can replay any TIFF, GIF, TGA, or RND files. Enter the desired file format to replay in the *Pattern:* edit box to make the existing files appear in the *Files:* list.

After you select the file to replay, the *Image Specifications* dialogue box (Fig 45-40) appears.

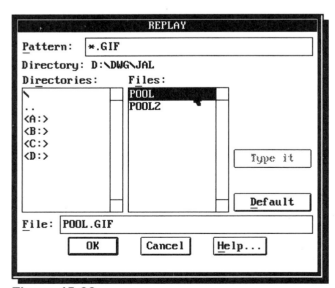

Figure 45-39

In the *Image Specifications* dialogue box (Fig 45-40) you can specify that the entire image or a portion of the image be displayed. You can also offset the image in the screen area.

The *IMAGE* area of the dialogue box displays the full image size (listed below in the *Image Size* edit boxes). You can display the full image or PICK the lower left and upper right corners in this box to define a portion of the image to display. Optionally, you can enter the lower left corner X,Y values (in pixels) in the *Image Offset* edit box and the image size (in pixels) in the *Image Size* edit box.

The *SCREEN* image box allows you to PICK the location on the screen for the image to be replayed. Just PICK a location in this image tile to specify the new location for the <u>center</u> of the image. Alternately, the lower left corner position can be specified by entering X,Y values (in pixels) in the *Screen Offset* edit boxes.

When AutoCAD displays the image, the size is limited to the size (in pixels) of the window in which it is displayed.

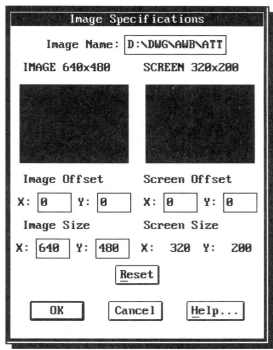

Figure 45-40

RCONFIG

TYPE IN:	PULL-DOWN MENU	SCREEN MENU	TABLET MENU
RCONFIG	*Render, Preferences, Reconfigure...*	*RENDER, RPREF..., Reconfigure...*	----

When you use an AVE command for the first time after installation, you must configure the type of display driver and hard copy device you want to use. The *Rconfig* command allows you to <u>re</u>configure your AVE setup during a rendering session.

The destination for the render (next time you use the *Render* command) is determined by the *Destination* setting in the *Rendering Preferences* dialogue box. You can select *Framebuffer* (screen) or *Hardcopy*. If a hard copy device has not yet been configured, the choice is grayed out.

When you invoke *Rconfig*, AutoCAD displays the current configuration for the display driver and hard copy device which may look something like the following text display.

```
Command: rconfig
Current AVE_RENDER configuration

    Rendering:  AutoCAD's configured P386 ADI combined
    display/rendering driver

    Hard copy:  None(Null Rendering device)

Press RETURN to continue: Enter

Configuration menu

0.  Exit to drawing editor
1.  Show current configuration

2.  Configure rendering device
3.  Configure hard copy rendering device

Enter selection <0>:
```

At this point you may select either of choices 2. or 3. to allow reconfiguration. After reconfiguration, select 0. to exit and save your changes.

Rendering Device

The rendering device possibilities are limited by your monitor capabilities and video card. The capabilities usually range from 640 x 480 pixels (horizontal x vertical picture elements or "dots") with 16 colors to 1280 x 1024 pixels with 16 million colors or higher. If you have a typical SVGA (Super VGA) high resolution monitor and matching video card, your display should be capable of 1024 x 768 pixels and 256 colors or 65,000 colors. Generally the pixel resolution is based on your monitor capabilities, while the number of colors can be increased by adding RAM on the video card.

AVE uses a display driver as the communication link between AVE and the video card and monitor. For a typical high resolution monitor, one of several possible display driver configurations can be selected. AutoCAD provides some generic display drivers with the AutoCAD software. Assuming AutoCAD is installed on your system in the C:\ACAD12 directory, the driver files are located in the C:\ACAD12\DRV directory. The display driver file names for Release 12 begin with RC and have an .EXP extension; for example, AutoCAD's supplied generic SVGA display driver is RCPSVADI.EXP. Many video card manufacturers also provide a display driver for AutoCAD with the video card software.

If you wish to configure a new display driver, you should first read the section on configuring AutoCAD in the AutoCAD Interface, Installation, and Performance Guide as well as the documentation that is supplied with your monitor and video card.

Depending on your monitor and video card capabilities, you may be able to use the currently configured display driver, but you can reconfigure AVE to render to a viewport or to a separate rendering screen. This is accomplished by selecting option **2.** from the AVE configuration menu. Depending on your current driver, the syntax would be something like the following.

```
Configuration menu

0.   Exit to drawing editor
1.   Show current configuration

2.   Configure rendering device
3.   Configure hard copy rendering device

Enter selection <0>: 2

Your current Rendering display is:
AutoCAD's configured P386 ADI combined display/rendering
driver
Do you want to select a different one? <N>   Enter

Select mode to run display/rendering combined driver:

1.   Render to display viewport
2.   Render to rendering screen

Rendering mode <1>:   Enter choice
```

At this point you will be asked to save or not to save the changes. The configuration for AVE is saved in the file named AVE.CFG.

Keep in mind that the current rendering mode affects the _New Finish_ and _Modify Finish_ dialogue box preview feature and the contents of the _Save Image_ dialogue box. AVE must be configured to <u>render to a viewport</u> to use the _Finish_ preview feature.

Hard Copy Device

The configured hard copy device capabilities are dependent on the device itself. If you wish to configure a hard copy device, read the section on Configuring AutoCAD in the AutoCAD Interface, Installation, and Performance Guide as well as the documentation that is supplied with your hard copy device.

RHEXPORT.EXP

Even if you don't have a hard copy device connected to your system, you can write AVE renderings to a raster file format instead of rendering to the framebuffer. This is accomplished by configuring an AutoCAD-supplied rendering driver called RHEXPORT.EXP (Rendering Hardcopy Export), then toggling the _Destination_ in _Rendering Preferences_ to _Hardcopy_. The RHEXPORT.EXP file is located with the other drivers in the DRV directory. This driver offers a variety of common raster file formats, each with a variety of resolutions.

For example, if you have configured RHEXPORT.EXP as the AVE hard copy device, and _Hardcopy_ is toggled in the _Rendering Preferences_, the following screens are displayed when you next use the _Render_ command (Fig. 45-41).

```
------------ AUTODESK RENDERING FILE DRIVER CONFIGURATION ----------

Please specify the size of the image that you wish to render:

                     Resolution           Image size      Aspect ratio
        -----------------------------     ----------      ------------
1    -   320 x 200    (CGA/MCGA Color)     (320x200)        0.8333
2    -   320 x 200                         (320x200)        1.0000
3    -   640 x 200    (CGA Monochrome)     (640x480)        0.4166
4    -   640 x 350    (EGA)                (640x350)        0.8203
5    -   640 x 400                         (640x400)        0.8333
6    -   640 x 480    (VGA)                (640x480)        1.0000
7    -   720 x 540                         (720x540)        1.0000
8    -   792 x 612    (PostScript A)       (792x612)        1.0000
9    -   800 x 600                         (800x600)        1.0000
10   -  1024 x 768                         (1024x768)       1.0000
11   -  1152 x 900    (Sun standard)       (1152x900)       1.0000
12   -  1600 x 1280   (Sun hi-res)         (1600x1280)      1.0000
13   -  Custom                             ( ? x ? )        ???


Enter the desired resolution, 1 to 13 <2>:
```

Figure 45-41

Enter a selection to display the file format options shown in Figure 45-42.

```
        1.   TGA (TrueVision Format)
        2.   GIF (CompuServe Graphics Interchange Format)
        3.   TIFF (Tag Image File Format)
        4.   PCX (Z-Soft Format)
        5.   BMP (Microsoft Windows Device-independent Bitmap)
        6.   PostScript image
        7.   Sun (Rasterfile)
        8.   FAX (Group 3 Image Encoding)
        9.   XWD (X Windows Dump)
        10.  PBM (Jef Poskanzer's Portable Bitmap Toolkit Formats)
        11.  FITS (Flexible Image Transfer System)
        12.  IFF/ILBM (Amiga Format)

In which format would you like to export the file, 1 to 12 <1>: 5

You can write the file using any of the following color gamuts.
Usually, the more colors you use, the larger the file will be.


        1.   Monochrome (black & white)
        2.   Grayscale (256 shades of gray)
        3.   8-bit (256 colors)

Enter the color format you wish to use, 1 to 3 <3>:
```

Figure 45-42

To configure RHEXPORT as the hard copy rendering driver, use *Rconfig*. At the AVE configuration menu prompt, the command syntax would be as shown. (This example assumes you have installed AutoCAD in a directory called C:\ACAD12.)

```
Configuration menu

0.  Exit to drawing editor
1.  Show current configuration

2.  Configure rendering device
3.  Configure hard copy rendering device

Enter selection <0>: 3

Your current Rendering display is:
None (Null rendering device)
Do you want to select a different one? <N> Y


Select rendering hard copy device:

1.   None (null rendering device)
2.   P386 Autodesk Device Interface rendering driver
3.   Rendering file (256 color map)
4.   Rendering file (continuous color)

Rendering hard copy selection <1>: 2

Cannot find ADI P386 rendering hard copy driver
adirndhc.exp
Enter ADI driver name: C:\ACAD12\DRV\RHEXPORT.EXP
```

This configuration allows you to export renderings to any of the raster file formats listed in Figure 45-42.

CHAPTER EXERCISES

1. Open the **BGUID-SL** drawing that you created as a solid modeling exercise in Chapter 42 Exercises. Use the **Shade** command, accepting all the defaults. Do you see a shaded model? Probably not. You must first use **Solmesh** to convert an AME solid to meshed representation before shading. Do so.

    Now try it again. Any success? Try each of the settings for **SHADEDGE** to see which works best for your video display. If you can shade with 256 colors, set **SHADEDGE** to **256-edg**. Try several settings for **SHADEDIF**. Make sure you try a high diffused light percentage (**90-95**).

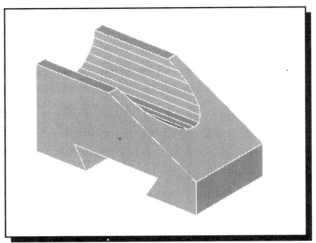

Figure 45-43

2. **Open** one of the surface models that you created as an exercise in Chapter 37 or 38. Experiment with the **SHADEDIF** and **SHADEDGE** settings to achieve the best display.

3. **Open** the **PULLY-SL** drawing that you created in Chapter 42 Exercises. Refer to the "Typical Steps for Using AVE" in this chapter to create a rendering. As an aid, follow these brief suggestions.

    Create a **Vpoint** showing the best view of the Pulley. Create a **Distant Light** located to the left side and slightly above the Pulley. Create a **Point Light** located to the right side and above. Define and **Attach** a **Finish** having **high Specular** and **low Roughness** reflective qualities to appear as metal. Perform several **Quick Renderings** and adjust the **Light** positions and intensity until you find the desired results. Experiment also with the **Finish** properties. When

Figure 45-44

you have the best settings, perform a *Full Render*. Finally use *Saveimg* to save the rendering as a .GIF file. Use *Replay* to insure the image is saved. *Save* the drawing.

4.　　*Open* the SADL-SL model that you created in Chapter 42 Exercises. For this rendering, use *Dview* to generate a useful viewpoint and a small amount of perspective (*Distance*). Set up two lights--a *Distant Light* to the left and above and a *Point Light* to the right and nearer to the *Camera* location. Create a *Finish* to represent metal--high *Specular* (.70-75) with low *Roughness* (.01-.03).

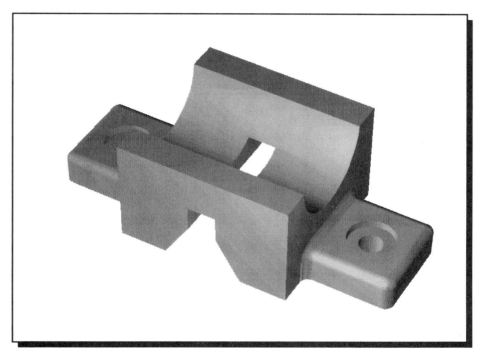

Figure 45-45

Create several *Quick Renderings* to adjust the light intensities. The *Point Light* should provide slightly more light (at the near end of the model) and the *Distant Light* should provide slightly less (on the far side). This effect gives the impression of distance. Also make necessary adjustments to the *Finish* parameters. When you have a good combination, compare your image to Figure 45-45 and create a *Full Render*. Save the rendering to a .GIF file by the same file name. *Save* the drawing.

5.　　*Open* the ASSEMBLY drawing that you created as an exercise in Chapter 44. Use *Dview* to achieve a small amount of perspective and a viewpoint that shows as many features of the assembly as possible. (Keep in mind that too much perspective makes the objects appear large. A great amount of perspective (small *Distance*) is good for displaying architectural models, but not for small mechanical parts.

Create and position at least two lights. Create a *Point Light* near the closer end of the model and adjust the intensity to be slightly brighter than the other lights. Use at least one *Distant light* to produce more even lighting near the far end of the model.

Create a *Finish* for each component of the assembly, however, assume that each piece is metal. Each component should have a high *Specular* and low *Roughness* factor, but can be slightly different *Colors*.

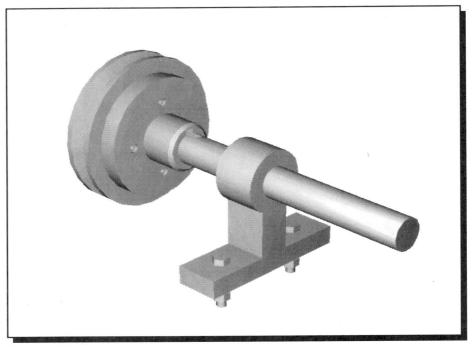

Figure 45-46

Make sure that you use only *Quick Render* while you adjust the lighting and finish parameters. Create two or three *Scenes*, using a different lighting combination for each. Finally, use *Full Render* and create a rendering of each *Scene*. Try to *Render* one *Scene* to appear similar to that in Figure 45-46. Save each rendering to a .GIF (or other) file specifying the names **ASSEMBL1**, **ASSEMBL2**, and so on. *Save* the drawing.

6.   *Open* the **ADJMT-SL** or other solid or surface model that you would like to render. There are several good possibilities with the AutoCAD sample drawings (in the SAMPLE subdirectory). Achieving skill with AVE requires time and experimentation. Experiment with different *Lights*, *Finishes*, and *Scenes*. Have fun.

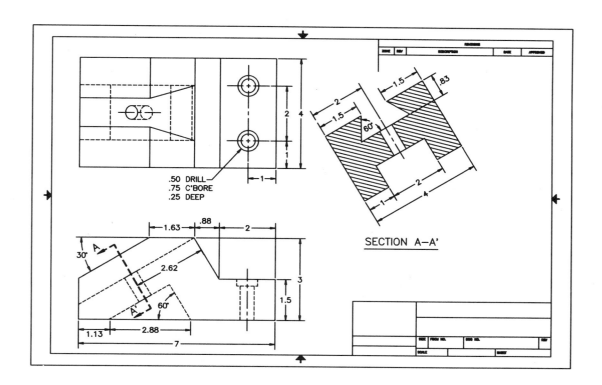

CHAPTER 46

Creating 2D Drawings from 3D Models

CHAPTER OBJECTIVES

After completing this chapter you should:

1. be able to use *Project* to project 2D views from an existing wireframe model;

2. be able to use *Solprof* to create a 2D or a 3D profile from an AME solid model;

3. be able to use *Mvsetup* to create viewports showing the standard engineering "views" of an existing 3D model;

4. be able to use *Solprof* in conjunction with *Mvsetup* to create a 2D drawing from an AME solid model;

5. be able to use *Solview* to create viewports and layers for use with *Soldraw*;

5. be able to use *Soldraw* to project 3D geometry onto 2D planes, complete with hidden and visible lines;

6. be able to use layers created by *Soldraw* to complete a dimensioned 2D multiview drawing.

BASICS

This chapter discusses the use of several AutoCAD features that provide a means for creating a 2D drawing from a 3D model. The features are *Project*, *Solprof*, *Mvsetup*, and *Solview*.

Project is an AutoLISP program that projects a <u>wireframe</u> model onto a 2D plane. The resulting projected geometry can be converted to *Blocks* or *Wblocks* and *Inserted* to create the principal views of an engineering drawing. Additional editing work is required to convert the projected geometry into conventional views with hidden and visible lines.

Solprof creates a profile of AME <u>solid</u> models. The profiled geometry can be used as a wireframe or projected onto a 2D plane. *Solprof* creates new layers for the profile geometry, complete with correct hidden lines. *Solprof* can be used in conjunction with *Mvsetup* to create standard engineering views.

Mvsetup is an AutoLISP routine that can be invoked by selection from the pull-down menus or by typing at the command prompt. It operates with <u>any type</u> of 3D model. This routine automatically sets up paper space viewports. It also has a series of options that allow you alternative arrangements for the viewports. If you use the *Standard Engineering* option, *Mvsetup* creates the viewports and automatically places the 3D model correctly with a top, front, right side, and isometric view. Although the viewports are set up and the 3D geometry is arranged for you, other operations may be required if you want to project the model to a 2D plane with *Solprof* or create dimensions with correct visibility within viewports, for example.

The SOLVIEW.EXP program is an ADS application that is far more automated and powerful than the other features listed. This program is the best alternative for creating 2D drawings from AME solid models. Since SOLVIEW.EXP is an ADS application, it must be loaded before it can be used. SOLVIEW.EXP provides two commands that are entered at the command prompt, *Solview* and *Soldraw*. *Solview* is similar to *Mvsetup* in that it automatically sets up the views in paper space viewports (*Solview* or *Mvsetup* will operate for any type of 3D model.) It differs from *Mvsetup*, however, because you can select the desired views and their placement, including section and auxiliary views. *Solview* also creates layers for use with *Soldraw*. The *Soldraw* command projects the geometry (of AME solid models only) onto a 2D plane (optional) and automatically uses the newly created layering scheme for creating the 2D geometry. Dimensions can be created as an additional "manual" step on layers provided by *Solview*, complete with correct viewport-specific visibility.

In summary, SOLVIEW.EXP is the superior method for creating 2D drawings from AME solid models. It is the most universal and accomplishes the most for you automatically, including setting up layers for dimensioning. *Mvsetup* does a good job of semi-automatically setting up standard engineering views, but does not project onto a 2D plane. *Solprof* can be used with *Mvsetup* to create the 2D views of solid models with hidden and visible lines. *Project* projects wireframes to a 2D plane. The topics are discussed in the following order.

> *Project*
> *Mvsetup*
> *Solprof*
> *Solview*

USING *PROJECT* WITH WIREFRAMES

PROJECT.LSP is an AutoLISP program that projects 3D <u>wireframe</u> models onto a 2D plane. It operates for models constructed of *Lines*, *Plines*, *Circles*, and *Arcs*, but does not work for surface models or for AME solids.

Because PROJECT.LSP is a sample AutoLISP program, it must be loaded (from the SAMPLE directory) before you can use the *Project* command at the Command: prompt. See Appendix B for details on loading AutoLISP and ADS programs. Once PROJECT.LSP has been loaded, you can use three commands at the command prompt:

Project	This command allows you to select either type of projection. A thorough explanation of each type of projection (*Project1* and *Project2*) is given in a text screen when you invoke this command.
Project1	This command projects the 3D model onto the current UCS. New 2D entities are created. The original 3D model is left intact.
Project2	This command projects entities existing on the current UCS to another construction plane that you define.

Using *Project1*

For the purpose of projecting a wireframe model onto a 2D plane, the *Project1* command is used.

```
Command: project1
Layer name <0>: (Enter name of an existing layer to create projected entities
on.)
Select objects: PICK
Select objects: Enter
Projecting . . .      please wait
Project another entity? Y/N <N>: Enter
Make into block? <N>: Enter
Write to disk as DWG file? <N>: Enter
Command:
```

Note that *Project1* optionally creates a *Block* or a *Wblock* of the new 2D geometry. A separate 2D drawing can be created by creating *Wblocks* for each view, then *Inserting* them into another drawing in the appropriate arrangement to comprise a multiview drawing. Another strategy is to create the projected geometry on separate layers, then use paper space viewports to display one view in each viewport by controlling layer visibility.

Before using *Project1*, these preparations can be made.

1. Create a UCS perpendicular to the line of sight for <u>each</u> of the desired views.
2. Create layers for the TOP, FRONT, SIDE, and/or other desired views if you do not want to create *Wblocks*.

Remember that *Project1* projects the geometry onto the current UCS. Before using *Project1*, insure that you have set the desired UCS current.

As an example, assume that you have created the wireframe model as shown in Figure 46-1. If a front view is desired, a UCS should be created perpendicular to the line of sight for the front view as shown in the figure.

(Keep in mind that the geometry may appear incomplete for some wireframe models. In this case, the limiting elements for the curved surfaces seem to be missing. Because limiting element lines change depending on your viewpoint, they are usually not included. This is a complete wireframe.)

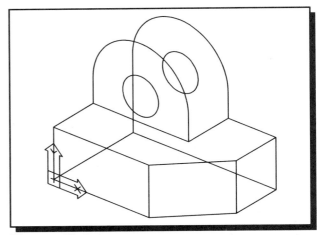

Figure 46-1

Invoke *Project1*. Enter FRONT as the layer name for new 2D entities. Select all entities for projection. The new 2D geometry is projected onto the current UCS in a *Continuous* linetype as shown in Figure 46-2. No changes are made to the original wireframe model by *Project1*.

If you desire to create a separate .DWG file from the projection, use the option to "Write to disk as a .DWG file" (a *Wblock* is created). The projection does not appear in the current drawing, but rather is written to disk.

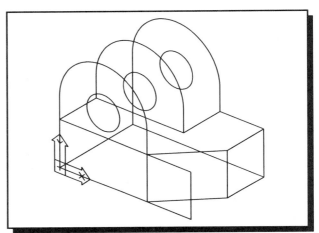

Figure 46-2

The same procedure is followed to create projections for the other views. Remember to set the desired UCS as current <u>before</u> invoking *Project1*.

The top view, for example, is created by setting the World Coordinate System active and using *Project1* to make a 2D view on a layer named TOP. Alternately, the projection could be written to disk as a .DWG file, in which case the new 2D geometry does not appear in the current drawing.

This procedure is followed for any other views desired.

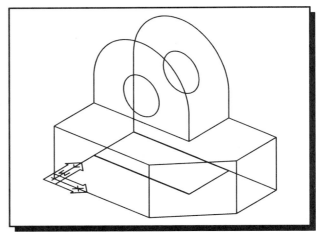

Figure 46-3

Strategies for Creating a Multiview Drawing from a Wireframe Using *Project1*

1.　　Create a separate *Wblock* for each view, then insert each into a new drawing in the correct arrangement.

2.　　Create paper space viewports and use *Vpoint* to set the correct viewpoint for each view. *(Mvsetup* can be used to automatically set up the viewports and *Vpoints* for standard engineering layouts.) Create a layer for the projected geometry for each view. Then use *Project1* to create 2D geometry for each view on the appropriate layer. Set the viewport-specific layer visibility such that only the 2D geometry for the TOP layer is visible in the top viewport, and so on.

In either case, additional steps must be taken to add or convert some of the 2D lines to the *Hidden* linetype in order to produce a complete and correct multiview drawing.

Strategy 1

To create a new multiview drawing from separate *Wblocks*, the *Wblocks* must be *Inserted* into the new drawing with the correct position and rotation angle. For the previous examples, the drawing might be created from the related *Wblocks* as shown in Figure 46-4. Obviously, additional steps are necessary to produce a complete and correct multiview drawing, namely, addition of some visible and all hidden lines.

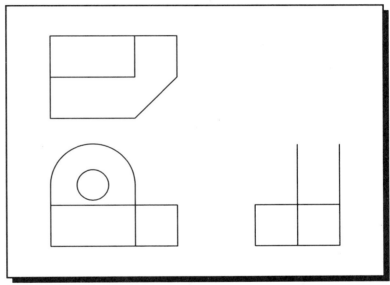

Figure 46-4

Strategy 2

Creating multiview drawings from wireframe models using *Project1* involves the use of paper space viewports. *Mvsetup* or *Solview* can be used to do some of the initial work setting up the views. *Project1* is used to project the 3D geometry onto 2D planes.

1.　　Assuming the wireframe model is complete, use *Mvsetup* or *Solview* to set up the paper space viewports and *Vpoints*.

2.　　Create new layers for the projections, such as TOP, FRONT, and SIDE. It is necessary to have the geometry on separate layers for future viewport visibility control.

3.　　With the coordinate system current for a top view projection, invoke *Project1* to create the new 2D geometry. Specify that the geometry is created on layer TOP.

4.　　This procedure is repeated to project each of the desired views. Each view has its own layer and uses a different UCS.

5.	When projection is complete using *Project1*, set *TILEMODE* back to 0. Use the *Layer* command or the *Layer Control* dialogue box to *Freeze* the MODEL layer and set the layer visibility for each viewport. (The TOP layer is the only layer visible in the top viewport, etc.)

6.	The resulting drawing should appear as that in Figure 46-4. Additional work is still required to create some visible lines and all of the hidden lines.

For the previous strategies, the procedure for creating a 2D drawing from a 3D wireframe model can be tedious and time-consuming. Keep in mind that creating AME solid models and using SOLVIEW.EXP may satisfy your needs with less work on your part.

USING *MVSETUP* FOR STANDARD ENGINEERING DRAWINGS

MVSETUP

TYPE IN:	PULL-DOWN MENU	SCREEN MENU	TABLET MENU
MVSETUP	*View, Layout >* *MV Setup*	---	---

This section discusses the use of *Mvsetup* using the *Standard Engineering* option, that is, for creating engineering drawings from 3D models. This option of *Mvsetup* operates with any type of 3D model. It automatically creates four viewports and displays the model from four *Vpoints* (front, top, side, and isometric views).

The fundamental concepts and details of all other options of *Mvsetup* are discussed in Chapter 32. Refer to Chapter 32 if you need more information on *Mvsetup* since only the *Standard Engineering* option is discussed in this chapter.

The *Mvsetup* (Mview setup) command is actually an AutoLISP routine that is accessible either through the *View* pull-down menu or by typing *Mvsetup*. For the application of *Mvsetup* for creating standard engineering paper space viewports, the sequence is as follows.

1.	Create the 3D part geometry in model space.

2.	Invoke *Mvsetup* and use *Options* to set the *Mvsetup* preferences.

3.	Use *Title block* to *Insert* or *Xref* one of many AutoCAD-supplied or user-supplied borders and title blocks.

4.	Use the *Create* option to make the paper space viewports. Select the *Standard Engineering* option from the list.

5.	Use *Scale viewports* to set the scale factor (*Zoom XP* factor) for the model geometry displayed in the viewports.

6.	The model geometry that appears in each viewport must then be aligned with the display in adjacent viewports using the *Align* option.

7.　From this point, other AutoCAD commands would be used if you wanted to create dimensions for the views or project the geometry to a 2D plane (*Project* for wireframe models or *Solprof* for AME solid models).

Mvsetup Example

To illustrate these steps, the Adjustable Slide (AME solid model) is used as an example.

1.　Create the 3D part geometry in model space.　The Adjustable Slide is shown here as it exists in model space.　It is shown from an isometric-type *Vpoint* in wireframe representation in order to reveal the internal features.

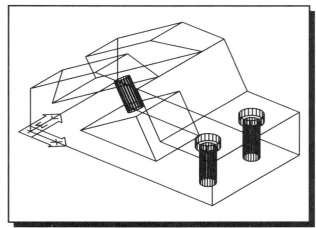

2.　Invoke *Mvsetup* and use *Options* to set the *Mvsetup* preferences.　For the example, the *Layer* option is used to specify the layer for title block. Additionally, the *Limits* option is used to automatically set paper space *Limits* to the border extents.

Figure 46-5

```
Command: mvsetup
Paperspace/Modelspace is disabled.  The pre-R11 setup
will be invoked unless it is enabled.  Enable
Paper/Modelspace?  <Y>: Enter
Entering Paper space.
Mvsetup, Version 1.15, (c) 1990-1993 by Autodesk, Inc.

Align/Create/Scale viewprts/Options/Title block/Undo: o
Set Layer/LImits/Units/Xref: L
Layer name for title block or . for current layer: title
Set Layer/LImits/Units/Xref: Li
Set drawing limits? <N>: y
Set Layer/LImits/Units/Xref: Enter
Align/Create/Scale viewports/Options/Title block/Undo:
```

3.　The *Title* block option is used to insert a title block and border in paper space.

```
Align/Create/Scale viewprts/Options/Title block/Undo: t
Delete objects/Origin/Undo/<Insert title block>: Enter
Available title block options:
0:          None
1:          ISO A4 Size(mm)
2:          ISO A3 Size(mm)
(13 title block options are displayed here.)
Add/Delete/Redisplay/<Number of entry to load>: 8
Create a drawing named ansi-b.dwg? <Y>: n
Align/Create/Scale viewports/Options/Title block/Undo:
```

The previously selected options produce a title block and border appearing in paper space as shown in Figure 46-6. The 3D model is not visible because no viewports have yet been created.

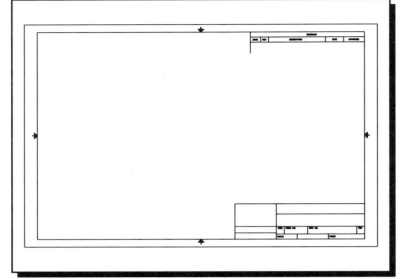

Figure 46-6

4.   Use the *Create* option of *Mvsetup* to create the desired viewport configuration.

```
Align/Create/Scale viewprts/Options/Title block/Undo: c
Delete objects/Undo/<Create viewports>: Enter
Available Mview viewport layout options:
       0:          None
       1:          Single
       2:          Std. Engineering
       3:          Array of Viewports
Redisplay/<Number of entry to load>: 2
Bounding area for viewports.  First point: PICK
Other point: PICK
Distance between viewports in X. <0>: Enter
Distance between viewports in Y. <0>: Enter
```

Select the "2: *Std. Engineering*" option. PICK two corners to define the bounding area for the four new viewports. The action produces four new viewports and automatically defines a *Vpoint* for each viewport. The resulting drawing displays the standard engineering front, top, and right side views of the 3D model in addition to an isometric-type view, as shown in Figure 46-7.

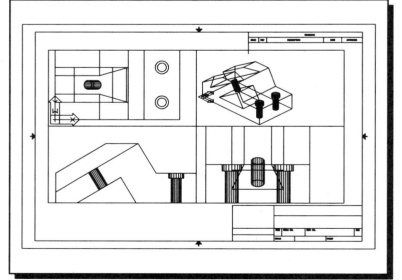

Figure 46-7

5. Notice in Figure 46-7 that the geometry in each viewport is displayed in its maximum size, as if a *Zoom Extents* were used. The *Scale viewports* option is used to set a scale for the geometry in each viewport.

```
Align/Create/Scale viewprts/Options/Title block/Undo: s
Select the viewports to scale:
Select objects: PICK the viewport entities
Select objects: Enter
Set zoom scale factors for viewports.
Interactively/<Uniform>: u
Enter the ratio of paper space units to model space
      units...
Number of paper space units.  <1.0>: Enter or (value)
Number of model space units.  <1.0>: Enter or (value)
Align/Create/Scale viewprts/Options/Title block/Undo:
```

Make sure you select the viewport entities (borders) at the "Select viewports to scale" prompt. The *Uniform* option insures that the 3D model will be scaled to the same proportion in each viewport. The ratio of paper space units to model space units is like a *Zoom XP* factor; for example, a ratio of 1 paper space unit to 2 model space units is equivalent to a *Zoom 1/2XP*.

The above action produces the scaling of the 3D model space units relative to paper space units, as shown in Figure 46-8.

There is still one major problem in the resulting drawing. The views are not orthogonally aligned exactly as they should be. Examine the front and the right side view and notice that they do not align horizontally.

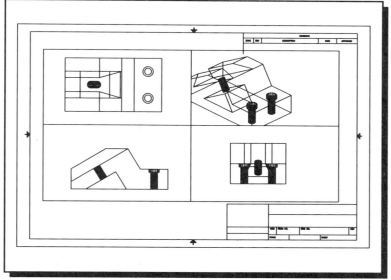

Figure 46-8

6. Use the *Align* option of *Mvsetup* to orthogonally align the views. In this case the right side view is aligned with the front using the *Horizontal* option and the top is aligned with the front view using the *Vertical* option.

```
Align/Create/Scale viewprts/Options/Title block/Undo: a
Angled/Horizntal/Vertical alignment/Rotate view/Undo? h
Basepoint: ENDp of PICK
Other point: ENDp of PICK
Angled/Horizntal/Vertical alignment/Rotate view/Undo? v
Basepoint: ENDp of PICK
```

```
Other point: ENDp of PICK
Angled/Horizontal/Vertical alignment/Rotate view/Undo?
Align/Create/Scale viewprts/Options/Title block/Undo:
```

Since the front view is used in this case for aligning the other views to it, the front view establishes the "Basepoint." Select the bottom right edge of the front view as the "Basepoint" as shown. Notice that it is important to use an *OSNAP* option for the PICK. When prompted for the "Other point," the right side viewport must be activated before PICKing its geometry. The "Other point" is a bottom edge on the right side view.

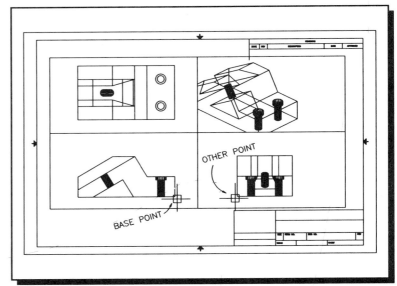

Figure 46-9

The *Vertical* option is used to select model geometry for alignment of the top view to the front. The resulting drawing appears as shown in Figure 46-10.

An additional step is required for this example in order to display the isometric view completely within the viewport. *Zoom Center* and *Zoom XP* can be used to locate and size the model appropriately.

Finally, the VPORTS layer created for inserting the viewports can be turned *Off* or *Frozen* to display the views without the viewport borders, as shown in Figure 46-10.

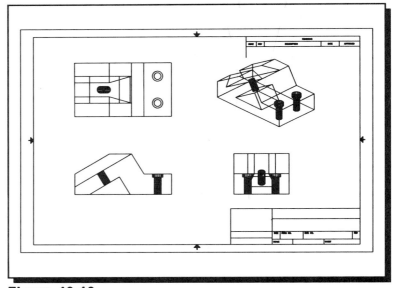

Figure 46-10

This is as far as *Mvsetup* goes. As you notice, the result is not a complete conventional multiview drawing because there are no hidden lines representing the invisible edges of the object. Since the views are actually different *Vpoints* of a 3D model, hidden lines are not possible for solid models using *Mvsetup*. It is possible, however, to project a 3D model onto 2D planes to achieve the correct 2D views. This can be done with PROJECT.LSP for wireframe models or with *Solprof* for AME solid models.

USING *SOLPROF* WITH AME SOLID MODELS

SOLPROF

TYPE IN:	PULL-DOWN MENU	SCREEN MENU	TABLET MENU
SOLPROF	*Model, Display> Profile Solids*	*MODEL, DISPLAY, SOLPROF:*	*5,G*

Solprof is an AME command that creates a profile of AME solids. *Solprof* generates a separate profile containing only edges of straight and curved surfaces of a solid as seen from a particular viewpoint (parallel projection only--not perspective). The "profile" can be projected to a plane (similar to *Project*) or can be generated as a wireframe model. The profile is generated on two new layers that are <u>automatically created</u>, one with hidden and one with visible lines. *Solprof* determines which profile edges should be projected as hidden or as visible lines and draws them on the appropriate layer. *Solprof* can be used in conjunction with *Mvsetup* to create standard engineering 2D drawings.

Solprof must be run <u>within a paperspace viewport</u>. Set *TILEMODE* to 0, make a paperspace viewport with *Mview*, and activate model space with the *MS* command. Then use *Solprof* and select the solids that you want profiled.

```
Command: solprof
Select objects: PICK (Select the solid or solids that you want profiled.)
Select objects: Enter
Display hidden profiles lines on separate layer? <Y>:
Project profile lines onto a plane? <Y>:
Delete tangential edges? <Y>:
```

Accepting the *Yes* default for "Display hidden profiles on a separate layer?" prompt causes *Solprof* to create two *Blocks*, one with hidden lines and one with the linetype of the existing solid. Two new layers are created for the *Block* insertions:

PV-(viewport handle)	Visible profile layer
PH-(viewport handle)	Hidden profile layer

The *Hidden* linetype must be loaded into the drawing before *Solprof* can use it. The viewport handle is a number and letter AutoCAD assigns to the viewports. (You can *List* the viewport entity to display its handle.)

Answering **No** to the "Display hidden profiles on a separate layer?" prompt causes *Solprof* to create one *Block* drawn as visible lines with the linetype of the existing solid.

The next prompt, "Project profile lines onto a plane? <Y>:," allows you to create a 3D wireframe or a 2D profile. Answering **Yes** causes AutoCAD to project the profile onto a plane parallel to the screen, similar to the *UCS View* option. In other words, the solid as it appears from the current viewpoint is transformed to a 2D projection. This option is particularly useful for creating a 2D "view" from a solid model *Vpoint*.

The last prompt allows you to delete "tangential edges." These edges are lines between two tangent faces. Answering _No_ to this prompt creates a line between a planar surface and a tangent curved surface. Tangential edges <u>should</u> be deleted for most applications.

When _Solprof_ has been used, the new entities may not be visible because _Solprof_ does not change the layer visibility. To see the new _Solprof_ layers, use the _Layer Control_ dialogue box or _Layer_ command to _Freeze_ the model layers. The new _Solprof_ layers can then be viewed and edited if you choose.

Solprof Example

As an example, consider the solid model shown in Figure 46-11. In this case, the model has been completed and is displayed in model space. Also assume that the _Hidden_ linetype has been loaded into the drawing.

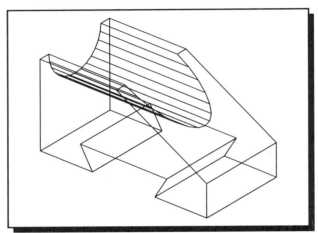

First, change _TILEMODE_ to 0 to activate paper space. Use _Mview_ to create a paper space viewport.

Next, type _MS_ to activate model space and use _Vpoint_ to achieve the desired view of the model. In this case, an isometric-type viewpoint is desired.

Figure 46-11

Invoke _Solprof_ while model space is active (the crosshairs are <u>in</u> the viewport) and select the solid. All of the defaults are accepted. The resulting new layers are created as shown.

PH-1DD	_Hidden_ linetype
PV-1DD	_Continuous_ linetype

Layer visibility is _automatically_ set to display the profile geometry only in the specific viewport (_Frozen for New_ viewports).

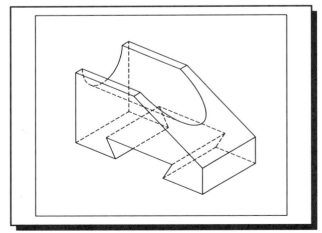

Using the _Layer_ command, the model layer is _Frozen_ to reveal the two profile layers. The resulting profile geometry is displayed in its paper space viewport in Figure 46-12.

This procedure can be used to generate a 2D drawing from an AME solid model. The procedure involves creating paper space viewports (with _Mview_) for each desired "view"--top, front, side, etc. Next, _Solprof_ is used to create the views, complete with hidden and visible lines, for each viewport.

Figure 46-12

Using *Solprof* with *Mvsetup*

The procedure for creating 2D drawings from AME solid models using *Solprof* can be automated by using *Mvsetup* in conjunction with *Solprof*. *Mvsetup* is a LISP routine that automatically creates paperspace viewports with standard engineering views (*Vpoints* of the model). *Solprof* is then used to create the hidden and visible lines for each "view."

For example, consider the case used earlier to illustrate *Mvsetup*. *Mvsetup* was used to create the paper space viewports and "standard engineering" viewpoints. The drawing at this point (as far a *Mvsetup* goes) displays 4 *Vpoints* of the same solid model.

Solprof can be used next. The *MS* (model space) command is used to activate any viewport. Invoke *Solprof* and select the geometry in the current viewport to profile.

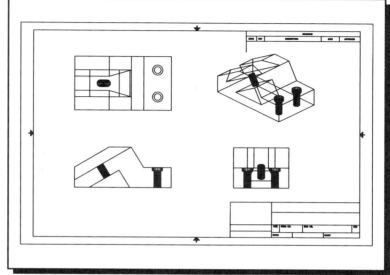

Figure 46-13

```
Command: solprof
Select objects: PICK (Select the solid or solids that you want profiled.)
Select objects: Enter
Display hidden profiles lines on separate layer? <Y>:
Project profile lines onto a plane? <Y>:
Delete tangential edges? <Y>:
```

This procedure is followed for each viewport. *Solprof* creates the profiles for each viewport. Remember that *Solprof* creates two layers for <u>each profile</u> (or for each viewport), one for hidden lines and one for visible lines. For this example, the following layers exist after the profile geometry is created. (PH-* and PV-* are created by *Solprof*.)

Layer name	State			Color	Linetype
0	On			7 (white)	CONTINUOUS
AME_FRZ	On			7 (white)	CONTINUOUS
MODEL	On			7 (white)	CONTINUOUS
PH-A61	On	C	N	7 (white)	HIDDEN
PH-A62	On	C	N	7 (white)	HIDDEN
PH-A63	On	C	N	7 (white)	HIDDEN
PH-A64	On	C	N	7 (white)	HIDDEN
PV-A61	On	C	N	7 (white)	CONTINUOUS
PV-A62	On	C	N	7 (white)	CONTINUOUS
PV-A63	On	C	N	7 (white)	CONTINUOUS
PV-A64	On	C	N	7 (white)	CONTINUOUS
TITLE	On			7 (white)	CONTINUOUS
VPORTS	Frozen			7 (white)	CONTINUOUS

Notice that *Solprof* automatically determines the viewport-specific layer visibility. Each of the profile layers (PV-* and PH-*) are *Frozen* for the *Current* and *New* viewports. In other words, only the front view profile is visible in the front viewport, only the top view profile is visible in the top viewport, and so on.

Freezing the MODEL layer reveals the profile geometry (PV-* and PH-* layers). Figure 46-14 displays the drawing after *Solprof* has been used in each viewport and the MODEL layer has been *Frozen*. The drawing is now ready for dimensioning.

If you want to dimension a drawing, such as that in Figure 46-14, it is possible to do so by using the normal dimensioning commands. However, some additional work is required to create layers for dimensions so that they appear only in the top, front, and side views. The top, front, and side view dimensions

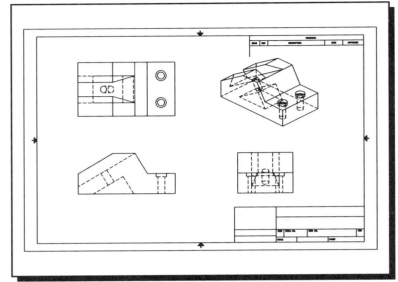

Figure 46-14

must each have their <u>own</u> layers. Next, viewport-specific visibility must be set for each viewport. In other words, only the dimensions related to the top view can be visible in the top viewport, and only dimensions related to the front view can be visible in the front viewport, and so on. This can be quite a chore, but SOLVIEW.EXP creates viewport-specific dimensioning layers automatically!

USING SOLVIEW.EXP TO CREATE MULTIVIEW DRAWINGS

Since SOLVIEW.EXP is an AME/ADS sample program, it must be loaded before it can be used. See Appendix B for details on loading ADS applications. SOLVIEW.EXP operates for AME solid models only.

Once the SOLVIEW.EXP program is loaded, two commands are available for use at the command prompt. The *Solview* command creates new layers and new views in paper space viewports for the existing 3D model space geometry. The *Soldraw* command creates new 2D entities on the new layers. *Soldraw* projects the model geometry onto a 2D plane with the appropriate continuous or hidden linetype. *Soldraw* can only operate with viewports that have been created with *Solview* (not with those created with *Mvsetup*).

The typical steps for using *Solview* and *Soldraw* to create a 2D drawing from a 3D model are described.

Typical Steps for Using *Solview* and *Soldraw*

1. Create the part geometry in model space. Set up a UCS parallel to the desired profile (front) view of the object.

2. Enable paper space (change *TILEMODE* to 0) and set up paper space *Limits* to the paper size. Set paper space *Snap* and *Grid* if desired.

3. Load SOLVIEW.EXP. Then type the *Solview* command at the command prompt.

4. Use the *UCS* option to create the profile (front) view. You can select the location and scale for the view.

5. Use the *Ortho* option to create the other principal orthographic views. Usually a top and/or side view is needed.

6. If a section or auxiliary view is desired, use the *Section* or *Auxiliary* option to create the view in the desired location.

7. Invoke *Soldraw* at the command prompt.

8. Use *Soldraw* to project the "views" to a 2D plane, thus creating new 2D geometry on the appropriate layers (created by *Solview*).

9. To display the new 2D geometry, *Freeze* the MODEL layer and VPORTS layer using the *Layer* command or *Layer Control* dialogue box.

10. You can then create dimensions for the 2D drawing on layers prepared by *Solview*. Use the normal commands for creating and editing dimensions.

11. Create a new layer named TITLE and draw, *Insert*, or *Xref* a titleblock and border in paper space.

SOLVIEW

Solview creates paper space viewports and automatically specifies the correct viewing angle (*Vpoint*) for each *viewport*. You select which views you want and the location for each. *Solview* also prepares new layers for subsequent use with the *Soldraw* command.

```
Command: solview
Ucs/Ortho/Auxiliary/Section/<eXit>:
```

Ucs

The *Ucs* option creates a profile <u>view</u> normal (perpendicular) to a User Coordinate System. The *Ucs* option is generally the best way to create the first viewport from which other viewports can be created. All other *Solview* options require an existing viewport. You can select and readjust the view's location. You can also specify the size of the viewport.

Ortho

This option creates a principal orthographic view (top, side, bottom) from an existing viewport. New *Ortho* viewports are created by selecting the <u>edge</u> of the viewport entity to project from. You can select and readjust the view's location and PICK the size of the viewport.

Auxiliary

This option is used to create an auxiliary view from an existing view. You are switched to model space to PICK two points to define the inclined plane used for the auxiliary projection. *OSNAP*s may be used for selection.

Section

This option creates a section view. *Solview* uses *Solcut* to create the section at the cutting plane that you define. The 3D geometry behind the cutting plane remains visible. Similar to the *Auxiliary* option, you PICK two points to define a cutting plane.

Solview creates the layers that *Soldraw* uses to place the visible lines, hidden lines, and section hatching for <u>each view</u>. *Solview* also creates layers for dimensioning that are set for visibility per viewport. Because of the possible complexity of the drawing, *Solview* places the visible lines, hidden lines, dimensions, and section hatching for each view on <u>separate layers</u>. This provides you with complete visibility control. The following naming convention is used for the layering scheme.

Layer Name	Entity Type
view name--VIS	Visible lines
view name--HID	Hidden lines
view name--DIM	Dimensions
view name--HAT	Hatch patterns

(The *view name* is the original name that you specified for the view when it was created.)

Solview also creates a layer called VPORTS for the viewport entities. This layer should be reserved exclusively for the use of *Solview* and *Soldraw*. Do not draw or alter information on this layer.

SOLDRAW

The *Soldraw* command uses the 3D model in each viewport created by the *Solview* command and projects the profiles onto a 2D plane. (*Solview* actually uses the *Solprof* command.) New 2D entities are created for the profiles and sections in the viewports. The new 2D entities are drawn in the appropriate *Continuous* or *Hidden* linetypes. If sectional views are included, hatch patterns are drawn using the current values of the *SOLHPAT*, *SOLHSIZE*, and *SOLHANGLE* variables. You can only use *Soldraw* with previously created *Solview* viewports.

Soldraw is very easy to use because all you have to do is select the viewports that you want to be affected by *Soldraw*. There are no options for *Soldraw*.

```
Command: soldraw
Viewports to draw...
Select objects: PICK viewport entities
Command:
```

Solview and *Soldraw* Example

As the steps (given previously) for using *Solview* and *Soldraw* are explained here, an example AME solid model is used to illustrate the process. The AME solid model is the Adjustable Slide shown in previous figures.

1.   The first step in the use of *Solview*
      and *Soldraw* is to create a 3D model.
      When the geometry is complete,
      create a UCS parallel to the desired
      front view of your model, as shown in
      Figure 46-15.

      Your first view selected using *Solview*
      should be the profile (front) view.

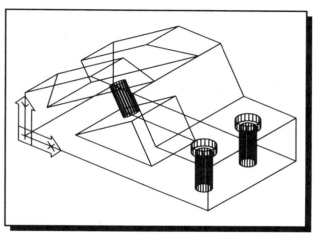

2.   The second step is to enable paper
      space and set *Limits* to the intended
      plotting paper size. If desired, also
      set *Snap* and *Grid* increments for
      paper space.

Figure 46-15

3.   Load SOLVIEW.EXP. The *Solview* command is available only after SOLVIEW.EXP
      has been loaded. Invoke *Solview* at the Command: prompt.

4.   The *Current UCS* option is used to create a paper space viewport displaying the profile
      (front) view (see Figure 46-16). The *UCS* option creates a view normal (perpendicular)
      to the current UCS.

```
Command: solview
Ucs/Ortho/Auxiliary/<eXit>: UCS
Named/World/?/<Current>: Enter (to use current UCS)
Enter view scale<1>: Enter or (value)
View center: PICK
View center: PICK (to readjust if necessary)
View center: Enter
Clip first corner: PICK
Clip other corner: PICK
View name: front
Ucs/Ortho/Auxiliary/Section/<eXit>:
```

The "Enter view scale<1>:" value is the same value as a *Zoom XP* factor. That is, enter the proportion of paper space units to model geometry units.

PICK the desired "View Center" to specify the desired location of the view. The model geometry appears <u>after</u> PICKing the view center. The "View Center" can be readjusted if necessary.

At the "Clip first corner:" and "Clip other corner:" prompts, select the desired paper space viewport corners as indicated in Figure 46-16. Make sure you allow sufficient room for dimensions or other drawing entities you may

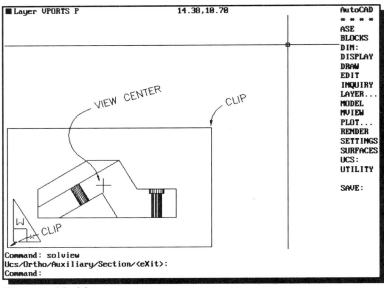

Figure 46-16

want to include later. (It is OK if the viewports overlap.) Finally, you must name the view. In this case, "FRONT" is used as the name of the new viewport.

5. After the front view is created, you can create other views with the *Ortho* option. This option creates a new viewport orthographically aligned with the <u>edge</u> of the viewport entity that you PICK.

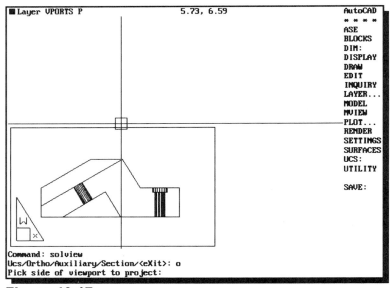

Figure 46-17

```
Ucs/Ortho/Auxiliary/Section/<eXit>: o
Pick side of viewport to project: PICK the desired edge of viewport
View center: PICK
View center: PICK (to adjust if necessary)
View center: Enter
Clip first corner: PICK
Clip other corner: PICK
View name: top
Ucs/Ortho/Auxiliary/Section/<eXit>:
```

As shown in Figure 46-17, PICK the edge of the viewport entity representing the viewing direction for the new *Ortho* viewport. In other words, PICK the top edge of the front viewport to produce a top view. Next, PICK the view center for the top view as before (when the front viewport was established).

The new view then appears. Clip the corners to specify the size for the viewport. Assign a name for this viewport such as "TOP."

You can continue creating viewports with the *Ortho* option until the necessary principal views are established. For example, a right side view could be created by using the *Ortho* option, then PICKing the right edge of the front viewport entity.

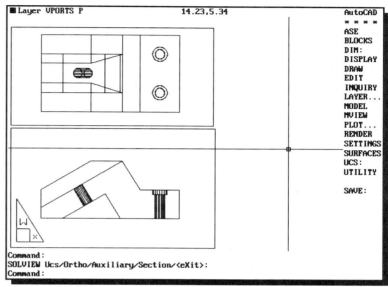

Figure 46-18

6. In this example, an auxiliary section view is required to provide the necessary visual and dimensional information for the drawing. *Solview* is used with the *Section* option to create the viewport.

For this procedure you must select two points to define the cutting plane. You are automatically switched to model space for PICKing the cutting plane's first and second points (*OSNAPs* may be used). For the example, the cutting plane is established passing through hole as shown in Figure 46-19.

Next, PICK a point to define which side of the cutting plane to view the object from.

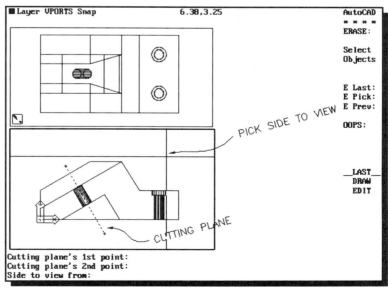

Figure 46-19

See the following command syntax.

```
Ucs/Ortho/Auxiliary/Section/<eXit>: s
Cutting plane's 1st point: PICK
Cutting plane's 2nd point: PICK
Side to view from: PICK (on desired side of cutting plane)
Enter view scale<1>: Enter or (value)
View center: PICK
View center: Enter
Clip first corner: PICK
Clip other corner: PICK
View name: section
Ucs/Ortho/Auxiliary/Section/<eXit>:
```

The resulting viewport with section view is shown in Figure 46-20. Notice that _Solview_ does not create hatch lines that are conventional for section views. The hatch pattern lines are created when _Soldraw_ is used.

The model geometry visible in the viewports is the existing 3D model. The model has not been changed in any way by _Solview_. However, besides the viewports that are new, _Solview_ creates new layers complete with viewport-specific layer visibility.

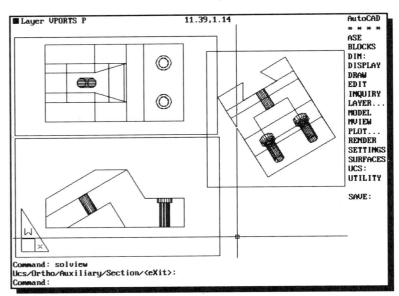

Figure 46-20

For our example, listing the layers reveals the work that was done by _Soldraw_. The following list shows <u>all</u> and <u>only</u> layers created by the previous options of _Soldraw_.

Layer name	State	Color	Linetype
FRONT-DIM	On	7 (white)	CONTINUOUS
FRONT-HID	On	7 (white)	HIDDEN
FRONT-VIS	On	7 (white)	CONTINUOUS
SECTION-DIM	On	7 (white)	CONTINUOUS
SECTION-HAT	On	7 (white)	CONTINUOUS
SECTION-HID	On	7 (white)	HIDDEN
SECTION-VIS	On	7 (white)	CONTINUOUS
TOP-DIM	On	7 (white)	CONTINUOUS
TOP-HID	On	7 (white)	HIDDEN
TOP-VIS	On	7 (white)	CONTINUOUS
VPORTS	On	7 (white)	CONTINUOUS

```
Current layer: VPORTS
```

Solview uses the name that you specify for the views as prefixes for the layer names. The layer visibility has automatically been set so that layers are only visible in the related viewports (TOP-* layers are only visible in the top view, for example).

7. Invoke the *Soldraw* command. Now that the views have been established by the *Solview* command, the model geometry is ready for projection onto a 2D plane.

8. The viewport entities are PICKed in response to the "Viewports to draw..." prompt. Normally you would select all viewports. PICK the viewport entities (borders) with the pickbox, as shown in Figure 46-21.

    Because there is much computation involved, *Soldraw* takes time. Depending on the complexity of the model and the speed of your computer system, you should expect to wait several minutes until the computation is complete.

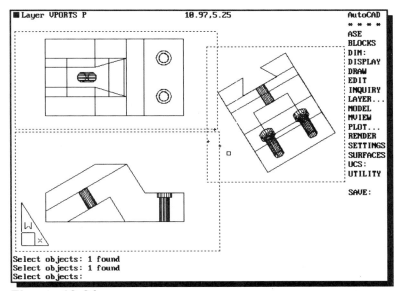

Figure 46-21

    When *Soldraw* has finished, the results may not be apparent. This is due to the fact that even though the layering scheme is set up correctly all of the layers are still visible including the 3D model.

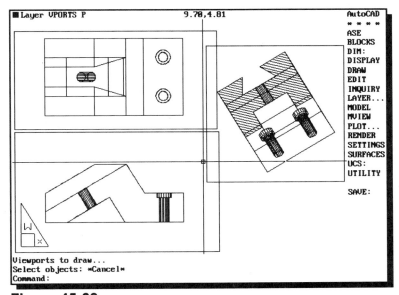

Figure 45-22

9. Use the *Layer* command or the *Layer Control* dialogue box to control the visibility of the layers.

Freeze the MODEL layer (or whatever layer you used for the model geometry). Also, *Freeze* the VPORTS layer to prevent the viewport borders from displaying as shown in Figure 46-23.

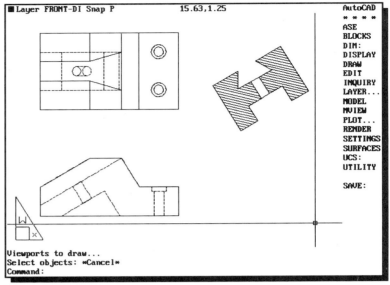

Figure 46-23

10. If you want to create dimensions for the new 2D views, use the normal dimensioning commands. This process is not as "automatic" as using *Solview* and *Soldraw*; however, all the layers for dimensions have been created and viewport-specific visibility is preset by *Solview*. Set the appropriate layers *Current* and create the related associated dimensions in model space. For our example, the dimensions would appear as shown in Figure 46-24.

11. To complete the drawing, create a new layer (called TITLE or BORDER, for example) and draw, *Insert*, or *Xref* a titleblock and border in paper space.

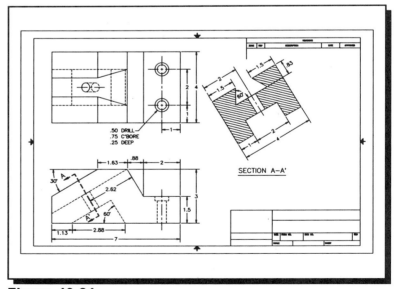

Figure 46-24

CHAPTER EXERCISES

1   *Open* the **VBLCK-WF** drawing that you created in Chapter 36. Use *Project1* to make four *Wblocks*. Make a *Wblock* for the front view (named **VB-FRONT**), for the top view (**VB-TOP**), for the right side view (**VB-RIGHT**), and for the auxiliary view (**VB-AUX**). Remember to create the appropriate *UCS* before using *Project1* for each "view."

Begin a *New* drawing or *Prototype*. Assign the name **VBLK-PRJ**. *Insert* each of the *Wblocks* you created for each "view." Make sure you assign a suitable *insertion point* and *rotation angle* for each. It may be helpful to use a construction line to *OSNAP* to when inserting the **VB-AUX** "view" as shown in Figure 46-25.

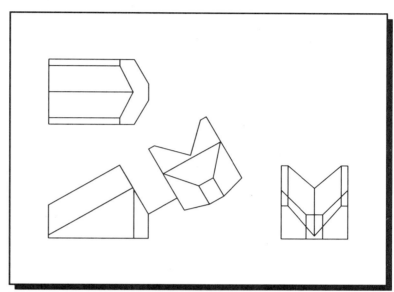

Explode the views and make the corrections for hidden and visible lines. Create or *Insert* a title block and border.

Figure 46-25

Dimension the drawing on the **DIM** layer. *Save* the drawing.

2.   *Open* the **BGUID-SL** drawing that you created in Chapter 42 Exercises. Use *Saveas* to assign a new name, **BGUD-MVS**. Use *Mvsetup* with the following *Options*: *Layer*, *Limits*, and *Title*. Insert the **B-size** sheet title block. Then use the *Create* option for *Standard Engineering* set up. *Scale* the geometry in each viewport *Uniformly* to a factor of **1**. The drawing should look like Figure 46-26. *Save* the drawing as **BGUD-MVS**. Continue this drawing in Exercise 3.

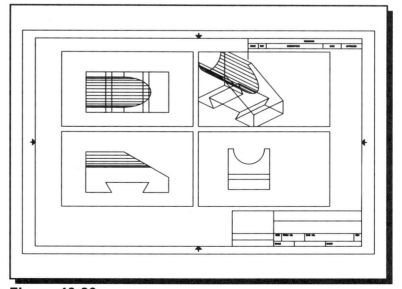

Figure 46-26

3. Note that the "views" do not line up correctly in the previous figure (Fig. 46-26). Use the *Align* option of *Mvsetup* for both *Vertical* and *Horizontal* alignment. Use *Zoom* to *Center* and size the isometric view properly.

Next use *Solprof* to create the profile geometry (make sure the *Hidden Linetype* is *Loaded* first). Finally, *Freeze* the **MODEL** *Layer* and compare to Figure 46-27. Use *Saveas* to save the drawing as

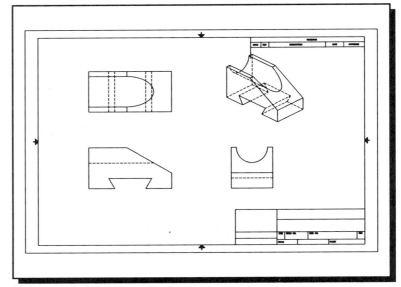

Figure 46-27

BGUD-SLP and make a *Plot* to scale. (Do not dimension the drawing since it is easier to use *Solview* for dimension layer creation.)

4. *Open* the **SADL-SL** drawing from the Chapter 42 Exercises. Change *TILEMODE* to **0** and set *Limits* in paper space to a metric A-size (**297,210**). Next, make sure the *Hidden Linetype* is loaded. Use *Saveas* to give the name **SDL-SVW**.

Set up a *UCS* to create the front view as shown in Figure 46-28. Use *Solview* with the *UCS* option to create the **FRONT** view. A *Scale* factor of **1** can be used. Use the *Ortho* option for

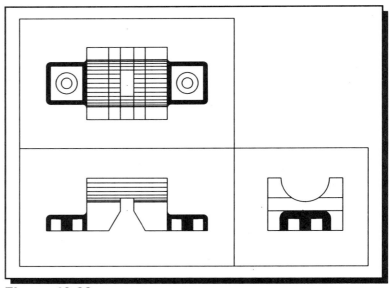

Figure 46-28

the **TOP** and **RIGHT** views. Your results should appear like Figure 46-28. *Save* the drawing (as **SDL-SVW**.)

Next, use *Soldraw* to create the visible and hidden line geometry. When finished, *Freeze* the layer that the solid model is on. The drawing should appear like Figure 46-29 (next page). Use *Saveas* and change the name to **SDL-SDR**.

Next, dimension the drawing and add center lines. Remember to use the layers that *Solview* created for the dimensions (one for each viewport). **Save** the drawing when you are finished (as **SADL-SDR**). Make a **Plot** to scale.

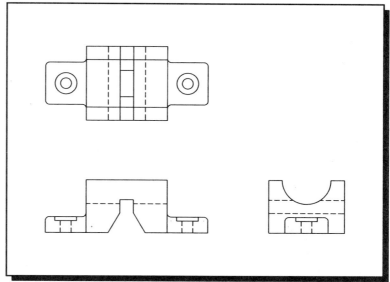

Figure 46-29

5. Create a multiview drawing from the solid model you created of the Angle Brace (**AGLBR-SL** drawing from Chapter 42). Use **Solview** and **Soldraw** to create the multiviews. Use the **Auxiliary** option to create an auxiliary view. Create the dimensions on the **DIM** layers. **Save** the drawing as **AGLBR-SV**.

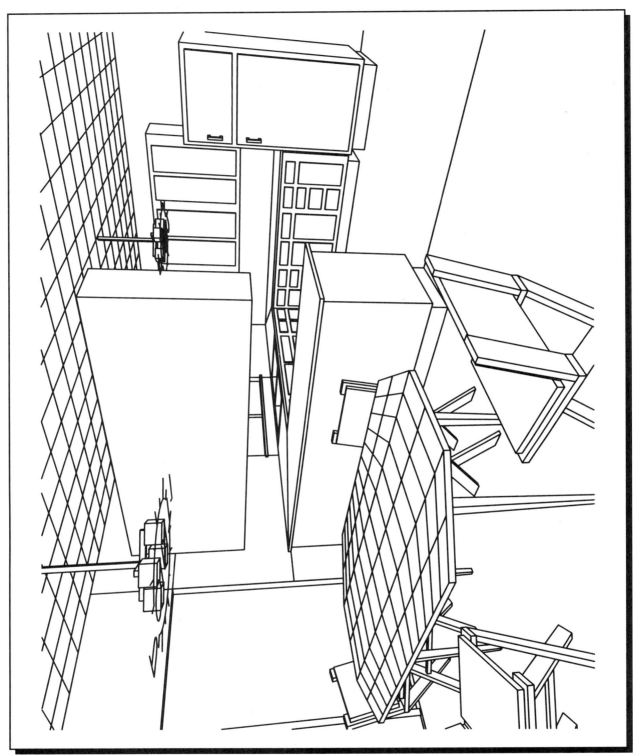

Figure 46-30 KITCHEN2.DWG Courtesy of Autodesk, Inc.

APPENDICES

CONTENTS

SYSTEM VARIABLES

This complete list of AutoCAD system variables is reprinted from the AutoCAD Reference Manual for Release 12. These variables can be examined and changed (unless they are read-only) at the `Command:` prompt by typing the variable name or by using the _Setvar_ command. Most of the system variables are saved in the drawing itself, while others are saved in the AutoCAD general configuration file, ACAD.CFG.

Variable name	Type	Saved in	Meaning
ACADPREFIX	String		The directory path, if any, specified by the ACAD environment variable with path separators appended if necessary (read-only).
ACADVER	String		This is the AutoCAD version number, which can have values like "12" or "12a" (read-only). Note that this differs from the DXF file $ACADVER header variable, which contains the drawing database level number.
AFLAGS	Integer		Attribute flags bit-code for ATTDEF command (sum of the following): 0 = No Attribute mode selected 1 = Invisible 2 = Constant 4 = Verify 8 = Preset
ANGBASE	Real	Drawing	Angle 0 direction (with respect to the current UCS)
ANGDIR	Integer	Drawing	1 = clockwise angles, 0 = counterclockwise (with respect to the current UCS)
APERTURE	Integer	Config	Object snap target height, in pixels (default value = 10)
AREA	Real		Last area computed by AREA, LIST, or DBLIST (read-only)
ATTDIA	Integer	Drawing	1 causes the Insert command to use a dialogue box for entry of Attribute values; 0 to issue prompts.
ATTMODE	Integer	Drawing	Attribute display mode (0 = off, 1 = normal, 2 = on)
ATTREQ	Integer	Drawing	0 assumes defaults for the values of all Attributes during Insert of Blocks; 1 enables prompts (or dialogue box) for Attribute values, as selected by ATTDIA

Variable name	Type	Saved in	Meaning
AUDITCTL	Integer	Config	Controls whether an .adt log file (audit report file) is created: 0 = Disables (or prevents) the writing of .adt log files 1 = Enables the writing of .adt log files by the AUDIT command
AUNITS	Integer	Drawing	Angular units mode (0 = decimal degrees, 1 = degrees/minutes/seconds, 2 = grads, 3 = radians, 4 = surveyor's units)
AUPREC	Integer	Drawing	Angular units decimal places
BACKZ	Real	Drawing	Back clipping plane offset from the target plane for the current viewport, in drawing units. Meaningful only if the Back clipping bit in VIEWMODE is on. The distance of the back clipping plane from the camera point can be found by subtracting BACKZ from the camera-to-target distance (read-only).
BLIPMODE	Integer	Drawing	Marker blips on if 1, off if 0
CDATE	Real		Calendar date/time (read-only) (special format)
CECOLOR	String	Drawing	Sets the color for new entities
CELTYPE	String	Drawing	Sets the linetype for new entities
CHAMFERA	Real	Drawing	Sets the first chamfer distance
CHAMFERB	Real	Drawing	Sets the second chamfer distance
CIRCLERAD	Real		Sets the default circle radius. To specify no default, enter 0 (zero).
CLAYER	String	Drawing	Sets the current layer.
CMDACTIVE	Integer		Bit-code that indicates whether an ordinary command, transparent command, script, or dialogue box is active (read-only). It is the sum of the following: 1 = Ordinary command is active 2 = Ordinary command and a transparent command are active 4 = Script is active 8 = Dialogue box is active
CMDDIA	Integer	Config	1 = Use dialogue boxes for PLOT command; 0 = don't use dialogue boxes for PLOT command

Variable name	Type	Saved in	Meaning
CMDECHO	Integer		When the AutoLISP (command) function is used, prompts and input are echoed if this variable is 1, but not if it is 0.
CMDNAMES	String		Displays in English the name of the command (and transparent command) that is currently active. For example: LINE'ZOOM indicates that the ZOOM command is being used transparently during the LINE command
COORDS	Integer	Drawing	If 0, coordinate display is updated on point picks only. If 1, display of absolute coordinates is continuously updated. If 2, distance and angle from last point are displayed when a distance or angle is requested.
CVPORT	Integer	Drawing	The identification number of the current viewport
DATE	Real		Julian date/time (read-only) (special format)
DBMOD	Integer		Bit-code that indicates the drawing modification status (read-only). It is the sum of the following: 1 = Entity database modified 2 = Symbol table modified 4 = Database variable modified 8 = Window modified 16 = View modified
DIASTAT	Integer		Dialogue box exit status. If 0, the most recent dialogue box was exited via "CANCEL." If 1, the most recent dialogue box was exited via "OK" (read-only).
DIMxxx	Assorted	Drawing	All the dimensioning variables are also accessible as system variables.
DISTANCE	Real		Distance computed by DIST command (read-only)
DONUTID	Real		Default donut inside diameter, can be zero.
DONUTOD	Real		Default donut outside diameter. Must be nonzero. If DONUTID is larger than DONUTOD, the two values are swapped by the next command.
DRAGMODE	Integer	Drawing	0 = no dragging, 1 = on if requested, 2 = auto

Variable name	Type	Saved in	Meaning
DRAGP1	Integer	Config	Regen-drag input sampling rate (default value = 10)
DRAGP2	Integer	Config	Fast-drag input sampling rate (default value = 25)
DWGCODEPAGE	String	Drawing	Drawing code page. This variable is set to the system code page when a new drawing is created, but otherwise AutoCAD doesn't maintain it. It should reflect the code page of the drawing and you can set it to any of the values used by the SYSCODEPAGE system variable or "undefined." It is saved in the header.
DWGNAME	String		Drawing name as entered by the user. If the drawing hasn't been named yet, DWGNAME reports that it is "unnamed." If the user specified a drive/directory prefix, it is included as well (read-only).
DWGPREFIX	String		Drive/directory prefix for drawing (read-only).
DWGTITLED	Integer		Bit-code that indicates whether the current drawing has been named (read-only): 0 = The drawing hasn't been named 1 = The drawing has been named
DWGWRITE	Integer		Controls the initial state of the read-only toggle in the OPEN command's "Open Drawing" standard file dialogue box: 0 = Opens the drawing for reading only 1 = Opens the drawing for reading and writing. The default is 1.
ELEVATION	Real	Drawing	Current 3D elevation, relative to the current UCS for the current space
ERRNO	Integer		Code for errors caused by on-line programs such as AutoLISP and ADS applications (see *ADS Programmer's Reference Manual*)

Variable name	Type	Saved in	Meaning
EXPERT	Integer		Controls the issuance of certain "Are you sure?" prompts, as indicated next: 0 = Issues all prompts normally 1 = Suppresses "About to regen, proceed?" and "Really want to turn the current layer off?" 2 = Suppresses the preceding prompts and BLOCK's "Block already defined. Redefine it?" and SAVE/WBLOCK's "A drawing with this name already exists. Overwrite it?" 3 = Suppresses the preceding prompts and those issued by LINETYPE if you try to load a linetype that's already loaded or create a new linetype in a file that already defines it. 4 = Suppresses the preceding prompts and those issued by "UCS SAVE" and "VPORTS Save" if the name you supply already exists. 5 = Suppresses the preceding prompts and those issued by "DIM SAVE" and "DIM OVERRIDE" if the dimension style name you supply already exists (the entries are redefined). When a prompt is suppressed by EXPERT, the operation in question is performed as though you had responded Y to the prompt. In the future, values greater than 5 may be used to suppress additional safety prompts. The setting of EXPERT can affect scripts, menu macros, AutoLISP, and the command functions. The default value is 0.
EXTMAX	3D point	Drawing	Upper-right point of drawing extents. Expands outward as new objects are drawn, shrinks only by ZOOM All or ZOOM Extents. Reported in World coordinates for the current space (read-only).
EXTMIN	3D point	Drawing	Lower-left point of drawing extents. Expands outward as new objects are drawn, shrinks only by ZOOM All or ZOOM Extents. Reported in World coordinates for the current space (read-only).
FILEDIA	Integer	Config	1 = Use file dialogue boxes if possible; 0 = don't use file dialogue boxes unless requested via ~ (tilde).
FILLETRAD	Real	Drawing	Fillet radius
FILLMODE	Integer	Drawing	Fill mode on if 1, off if 0

Variable name	Type	Saved in	Meaning
FRONTZ	Real	Drawing	Front clipping plane offset from the target plane for the current viewport, in drawing units. Meaningful only if the front clipping bit in VIEWMODE is On and the Front clip not at eye bit is also On. The distance of the front clipping plane from the camera point can be found by subtracting FRONTZ from the camera-to-target distance (read-only)
GRIDMODE	Integer	Drawing	1 = grid on for current viewport; 0 = grid off
GRIDUNIT	2D point	Drawing	Grid spacing for current viewport, X and Y
GRIPBLOCK	Integer	Config	Controls the assignment of grips in blocks: 0 = Assigns grip only to the insertion point of the block. The default value is 0. 1 = Assigns grips to entities within the block.
GRIPCOLOR	Integer (1-255)	Config	Color of nonselected grips; drawn as a box outline. Its default value is 5.
GRIPHOT	Integer (1-255)	Config	Color of selected grips; drawn as a filled box. The default value is 1.
GRIPS	Integer	Config	Allows the use of selection set grips for the Stretch, Move, Rotate, Scale, and Mirror modes: 0 = Disables grips. 1 = Enables grips. The default value is 1. To adjust the size of the grips, use the GRIPSIZE variable. To adjust the effective pick area used by the graphics cursor when you snap to a grip, use the GRIPSIZE system variable.
GRIPSIZE	Integer (1-255)	Config	The size in pixels of the box drawn to display the grip. The default value is 3.
HANDLES	Integer	Drawing	If 0, entity handles are disabled. If 1, handles are on (read-only).
HIGHLIGHT	Integer		Object selection highlighting on if 1, off if 0. HIGHLIGHT does not affect objects selected with grips.
HPANG	Real		Default hatch pattern angle
HPDOUBLE	Integer		Default hatch pattern doubling for "U" user-defined patterns: 0 = Disables doubling 1 = Enables doubling

Variable name	Type	Saved in	Meaning
HPNAME	String		Default hatch pattern name. Up to 34 characters, no spaces allowed. Returns "" if there is no default. Enter . (period) to set no default.
HPSCALE	Real		Default hatch pattern scale factor. Must be nonzero.
HPSPACE	Real		Default hatch pattern line spacing for "U" user-defined simple patterns. Must be nonzero.
INSBASE	3D point	Drawing	Insertion base point (set by BASE command) expressed in UCS coordinates for the current space.
INSNAME	String		Default block name for DDINSERT or INSERT. The name must conform to symbol naming conventions. Returns "" if there is no default. Enter . (period) to set no default.
LASTANGLE	Real		The end angle of the last arc entered, relative to the XY plane of the current UCS for the current space (read-only).
LASTPOINT	3D point		The last point entered, expressed in UCS coordinates for the current space. Referenced by @ during keyboard entry.
LENSLENGTH	Real	Drawing	Length of the lens (in millimeters) used in perspective viewing, for the current viewport (read-only).
LIMCHECK	Integer	Drawing	Limits checking for the current space. On if 1, off if 0.
LIMMAX	2D point	Drawing	Upper-right drawing limits for the current space, expressed in World coordinates
LIMMIN	2D point	Drawing	Lower-left drawing limits for the current space, expressed in World coordinates
LOGINNAME	String		Displays the user's name as configured or input when AutoCAD is loaded (read-only).
LTSCALE	Real	Drawing	Global linetype scale factor
LUNITS	Integer	Drawing	Linear units mode (1 = scientific, 2 = decimal, 3 = engineering, 4 = architectural, 5 = fractional)
LUPREC	Integer	Drawing	Linear units decimal places or denominator

Variable name	Type	Saved in	Meaning
MACROTRACE	Integer		Debugging tool for DIESEL expressions (see the *AutoCAD Customization Manual* for details). 0 = Disables MACROTRACE. Default is 0. 1 = Displays an evaluation of all DIESEL expressions in the command line area, including an evaluation of expressions used in menus and the status line.
MAXACTVP	Integer		Maximum number of viewports to regenerate at one time
MAXSORT	Integer	Config	Maximum number of symbol/file names to be sorted by listing commands. If the total number of items exceeds this number, then none of the items are sorted (default value = 200).
MENUCTL	Integer	Config	Controls the page switching of the screen menu: 0 = Screen menu doesn't switch pages in response to keyboard command entry. 1 = Screen menu switches pages in response to keyboard command entry. The default value is 1.
MENUECHO	Integer		Menu echo/prompt control bits (sum of the following): 1 = Suppresses echo of menu items (^P in a menu item toggles echoing) 2 = Suppresses printing of system prompts during menu 4 = Disables ^P toggle of menu echoing 8 = Debugging aid for DIESEL macros. Prints input/output strings. The default value is 0 (all menu items and system prompts are displayed).
MENUNAME	String	Drawing	The name of the currently loaded menu file. Includes a drive/path prefix if you entered it (read-only).
MIRRTEXT	Integer	Drawing	MIRROR command reflects text if nonzero; retains text direction if 0.

Variable name	Type	Saved in	Meaning
MODEMACRO	String		Allows you to display a text string in the status line, such as the name of the current drawing, time/date stamp, or special modes. You can use MODEMACRO to display a simple string of text, or use special text strings written in the DIESEL macro language to have AutoCAD evaluate the macro from time to time and base the status line on user-selected conditions. See the *AutoCAD Customization Manual* for details.
OFFSETDIST	Real		Sets the default distance. If you enter a negative value, it defaults to Through mode.
ORTHOMODE	Integer	Drawing	Ortho mode on if 1, off if 0
OSMODE	Integer	Drawing	Sets object snap modes using the following bit codes. To specify more than one osnap, enter the sum of their values. For example, entering 3 specifies the Endpoint (1) and Midpoint (2) osnaps. 0 = None 1 = Endpoint 2 = Midpoint 4 = Center 8 = Node 16 = Quadrant 32 = Intersection 64 = Insertion 128 = Perpendicular 256 = Tangent 512 = Nearest 1024 = Quick
PDMODE	Integer	Drawing	Point entity display mode
PDSIZE	Real	Drawing	Point entity display size
PERIMETER	Real		Perimeter computed by AREA, LIST, or DBLIST (read-only).
PFACEVMAX	Integer		Maximum number of vertices per face (read-only)

Variable name	Type	Saved in	Meaning
PICKADD	Integer	Config	Controls additive selection of entities: 0 = Disables PICKADD. The most recently selected entities, either by an individual pick or windowing, become the selection set. Previously selected entities are removed from the selection set. You can add more entities to the selection set, however, by holding down the Shift key while selecting. 1 = Enables PICKADD. Each entity you select, either individually or by windowing, is added to the current selection set. To remove entities from the selection set, hold down the Shift key while selecting. The default value of PICKADD is 1.
PICKAUTO	Integer	Config	Controls automatic windowing when the Select objects: prompt appears: 0 = Disables PICKAUTO. 1 = Allows you to draw a selection window (both window and crossing window) automatically at the Select objects: prompt. The default is 1.
PICKBOX	Integer	Config	Object selection target height, in pixels
PICKDRAG	Integer	Config	Controls the method of drawing a selection window: 0 = You draw the selection window by clicking the mouse at one corner, and then at the other corner. The default value is 0. 1 = You draw the selection window by clicking at one corner, holding down the mouse button, dragging, and releasing the mouse button at the other corner.
PICKFIRST	Integer	Config	Controls the method of entity selection so that you can select objects first, and then use an edit/inquiry command: 0 = Disables PICKFIRST 1 = Enables PICKFIRST. The default value is 1.
PLATFORM	String		Read-only message that indicates which version of AutoCAD is in use. This is a string such as one of the following: Microsoft Windows 386 DOS Extender Apple Macintosh Sun4/SPARCstation DECstation Silicon Graphics Iris Indigo

Variable name	Type	Saved in	Meaning
PLINEGEN	Integer	Drawing	Sets the linetype pattern generation around the vertices of a 2D Polyline. When set to 1, PLINEGEN causes the linetype to be generated in a continuous pattern around the vertices of the Polyline. When set to 0, Polylines are generated with the linetype to start and end with a dash at each vertex. PLINEGEN doesn't apply to Polylines with tapered segments.
PLINEWID	Real	Drawing	Default polyline width. It can be zero.
PLOTID	String	Config	Changes the default plotter, based on its assigned description.
PLOTTER	Integer	Config	Changes the default plotter, based on its assigned integer (0-maximum configured). You can create up to 29 configurations.
POLYSIDES	Integer		Default number of sides for the POLYGON command. The range is 3-1024.
POPUPS	Integer		1 if the currently configured display driver supports dialogue boxes, the menu bar, pull-down menus and icon menus. 0 if these features are not available (read-only).
PSLTSCALE	Integer	Drawing	Controls paper space linetype scaling: 0 = No special linetype scaling 1 = Viewport scaling governs linetype scaling
PSPROLOG	String	Config	Assigns a name for a prologue section to be read from the *acad.psf* file when using the PSOUT command. See the *AutoCAD Customization Manual* for details.
PSQUALITY	Integer	Config	Controls the rendering quality of PostScript images and whether they are drawn as filled objects or as outlines. A zero setting disables PostScript image generation and a nonzero setting enables PostScript generation. Positive setting: Sets the number of pixels per AutoCAD drawing unit for the PostScript resolution. Negative setting: Still sets the number of pixels per drawing unit, but uses the absolute value. Causes AutoCAD to show the PostScript paths as outlines and doesn't fill them.
QTEXTMODE	Integer	Drawing	Quick text mode on if 1, off if 0

Variable name	Type	Saved in	Meaning
REGENMODE	Integer	Drawing	REGENAUTO on if 1, off if 0
RE-INIT	Integer		Reinitializes the I/O ports, digitizer, display, plotter, and _acad.pgp_ file using the following bit codes. To specify more than one reinitialization, enter the sum of their values, for example, 3 to specify both digitizer port (1) and plotter port (2) reinitialization: 1 = Digitizer port reinitialization 2 = Plotter port reinitialization 4 = Digitizer reinitialization 8 = Display reinitialization 16 = PGP file reinitialization (reload)
SAVEFILE	String	Config	Current auto-save filename (read-only)
SAVENAME	String		The filename you save the drawing to (read-only)
SAVETIME	Integer	Config	Automatic save interval, in minutes (or 0 to disable automatic saves). The SAVETIME timer starts as soon as you make a change to a drawing and is reset and restarts by a manual SAVE, SAVEAS, or QSAVE. The current drawing is saved to _auto.sv$_.
SCREENBOXES	Integer	Config	The number of boxes in the screen menu area of the graphics area. If the screen menu is disabled (configured off), SCREENBOXES is zero. On platforms that permit the AutoCAD graphics window to be resized or the screen menu to be reconfigured during an editing session, the value of this variable might change during the editing session (read-only).
SCREENMODE	Integer	Config	A (read-only) bit code indicating the graphics/text state of the AutoCAD display. It is the sum of the following bit values: 0 = text screen is displayed 1 = graphics mode is displayed 2 = dual-screen display configuration
SCREENSIZE	2D point		Current viewport size in pixels, X and Y (read-only)
SHADEDGE	Integer	Drawing	0 = faces shaded, edges not highlighted 1 = faces shaded, edges drawn in background color 2 = faces not filled, edges in entity color 3 = faces in entity color, edges in background color

Variable name	Type	Saved in	Meaning
SHADEDIF	Integer	Drawing	Ratio of diffuse reflective light to ambient light (in percent of diffuse reflective light)
SHPNAME	String		Default shape name. Must conform to symbol naming conventions. If no default is set, it returns a "". Enter . (period) to set no default.
SKETCHINC	Real	Drawing	SKETCH record increment
SKPOLY	Integer	Drawing	SKETCH generates lines if 0, Polylines if 1
SNAPANG	Real	Drawing	Snap/grid rotation angle (UCS-relative) for the current viewport
SNAPBASE	2D point	Drawing	Snap/grid origin point for the current viewport (in UCS X,Y coordinates)
SNAPISOPAIR	Integer	Drawing	Current isometric plane (0 = left, 1 = top, 2 = right) for the current viewport
SNAPMODE	Integer	Drawing	1 = snap on for current viewport; 0 = snap off
SNAPSTYL	Integer	Drawing	Snap style for current viewport (0 = standard, 1 = isometric)
SNAPUNIT	2D point	Drawing	Snap spacing for current viewport, X and Y
SORTENTS	Integer	Config	Controls the display of entity sort order operations using the following codes. To select more than one, enter the sum of their codes, for example, enter 3 to specify codes 1 and 2. The default, 96, specifies sort operations for plotting and PostScript output: 0 = Displays SORTENTS 1 = Sort for object selection 2 = Sort for object snap 4 = Sort for redraws 8 = Sort for MSLIDE slide creation 16 = Sort for REGENs 32 = Sort for plotting 64 = Sort for PostScript output

Variable name	Type	Saved in	Meaning
SLPFRAME	Integer	Drawing	If = 1: · The control polygon for spline fit Polylines is to be displayed · Only the defining mesh of a surface fit polygon mesh is displayed (the fit surface is not displayed) · Invisible edges of 3D Faces are displayed If = 0: · Does not display the control polygon for spline fit Polylines · Displays the fit surface of a polygon mesh, not the defining mesh · Does not display the invisible edges of 3D Faces
SPLINESEGS	Integer	Drawing	The number of line segments to be generated for each spline patch
SPLINETYPE	Integer	Drawing	Type of spline curve to be generated by PEDIT Spline. The valid values are: 5 = quadratic B-spline 6 = cubic B-spline
SURFTAB1	Integer	Drawing	Number of tabulations to be generated for RULESURF and TABSURF. Also mesh density in the M direction for REVSURF and EDGESURF
SURFTAB2	Integer	Drawing	Mesh density in the N direction for REVSURF and EDGESURF
SURFTYPE	Integer	Drawing	Type of surface fitting to be performed by PEDIT Smooth. The valid values are: 5 = quadratic B-spline surface 6 = cubic B-spline surface 8 = Bezier surface
SURFU	Integer	Drawing	Surface density in the M direction
SURFV	Integer	Drawing	Surface density in the N direction

Variable name	Type	Saved in	Meaning
SYSCODEPAGE	String	Drawing	Indicates the system code page specified in *acad.xmf* (read-only). Codes are as follows: ascii dos932 dos437 iso8859-1 dos850 iso8859-2 dos852 iso8859-3 dos855 iso8859-4 dos857 iso8859-5 dos860 iso8859-6 dos861 iso8859-7 dos863 iso8859-8 dos864 iso8859-9 dos865 mac-roman dos869
TABMODE	Integer		Controls the use of tablet mode: 0 = Disables tablet mode 1 = Enables tablet mode
TARGET	3D point	Drawing	Location (in UCS coordinates) of the target (look-at) point for the current viewport (read-only)
TDCREATE	Real	Drawing	Time and date of drawing creation (read-only)
TDINDWG	Real	Drawing	Total editing time (read-only)
TDUPDATE	Real	Drawing	Time and date of last update/save (read-only)
TDSRTIMER	Real	Drawing	User elapsed timer (read-only)
TEMPPREFIX	String		This variable contains the directory name (if any) configured for placement of temporary files with a path separator appended if necessary (read-only).
TEXTEVAL	Integer		If = 0, all responses to prompts for text strings and attribute values are taken literally. If = 1, text starting with "(" or "!" is evaluated as an AutoLISP expression, as for nontextual input. Note: The DTEXT command takes all input literally, regardless of the setting of TEXTEVAL.
TEXTSIZE	Real	Drawing	The default height for new Text entities drawn with the current text style (meaningless if the style has a fixed height).
TEXTSTYLE	String	Drawing	Contains the name of the current text style
THICKNESS	Real	Drawing	Current 3D thickness

Variable name	Type	Saved in	Meaning
TILEMODE	Integer	Drawing	1 = Release 10 compatibility mode (uses VPORTS) 0 = Enables paper space and Viewport entities (uses MVIEW)
TRACEWID	Real	Drawing	Default trace width
TREEDEPTH	Integer	Drawing	A 4-digit (maximum) code that specifies the number of times the tree-structured spatial index may divide into branches, hence affecting the speed in which AutoCAD searches the database before completing an action. The first two digits refer to the depth of the model space nodes, and the second two digits refer to the depth of paper space nodes. Use a positive setting for 3D drawings and a negative setting for 2D drawings.
UCSFOLLOW	Integer	Drawing	If = 1, any UCS change causes an automatic change to plan view of the new UCS (in the current viewport). If = 0, a UCS change doesn't affect the view. The setting of UCSFOLLOW is maintained separately for both spaces and can be accessed in either space, but the setting is ignored while in paper space (it is always treated as if set to 0).
UCSICON	Integer	Drawing	The coordinate system icon bit-code for the current viewport (sum of the following): 1 = On - icon display enabled 2 = Origin - if icon display is enabled, the icon floats to the UCS origin if possible
UCSNAME	String	Drawing	Name of the current coordinate system for the current space. Returns a null string if the current UCS is unnamed (read-only)
UCSORG	3D point	Drawing	The origin point of the current coordinate system for the current space. This value is always returned in World coordinates (read-only)
UCSXDIR	3D point	Drawing	The X-direction of the current UCS for the current space (read-only)
UCSYDIR	3D point	Drawing	The Y-direction of the current UCS for the current space (read-only)

Variable name	Type	Saved in	Meaning
UNDOCTL	Integer		A (read-only) code indicating the state of the UNDO feature. It is the sum of the following values: 1 = set if UNDO is enabled 2 = set if only one command can be undone 4 = set if Auto-group mode is enabled 8 = set if a group is currently active
UNDOMARKS	Integer		The (read-only) number of marks that have been placed in the UNDO control stream by the UNDO command's Mark option. The Mark and Back options are unavailable if a group is currently active
UNITMODE	Integer	Drawing	0 = Displays fractional, feet and inches, and surveyor's angles as previously set 1 = Displays fractional, feet and inches, and surveyor's angles in input format
USERI1-5	Integer	Drawing	Five variables for storage and retrieval of integer values. Intended for use by third-party developers.
USERR1-5	Real	Drawing	Five variables for storage and retrieval of real numbers. Intended for use by third-party developers.
USERS1-5	String		Five variables for storage and retrieval of text string data. Accepts strings with embedded blanks. To discard the existing text string, enter ".". The maximum string length is platform-dependent, and can be as low as 460 characters. Intended for use by third-party developers.
VIEWCTR	2D point	Drawing	Center of view in current viewport, expressed in UCS coordinates (read-only)
VIEWDIR	3D vector	Drawing	The current viewport's viewing direction expressed in UCS coordinates. This describes the camera point as a 3D offset from the TARGET point (read-only).

Variable name	Type	Saved in	Meaning
VIEWMODE	Integer	Drawing	Viewing mode bit-code for the current viewport (read-only). The value is the sum of the following: 1 = perspective view active 2 = front clipping on 4 = back clipping on 8 = UCS follow mode on 16 = Front clip not at eye. If On, the front clip distance (FRONTZ) determines the front clipping plane. If Off, FRONTZ is ignored and the front clipping plane is set to pass through the camera point (i.e., vectors behind the camera are not displayed). This flag is ignored if the front clipping bit (2) is off.
VIEWSIZE	Real	Drawing	Height of view in current viewport, expressed in drawing units (read-only)
VIEWTWIST	Real	Drawing	View twist angle for the current viewport (read-only)
VISRETAIN	Integer	Drawing	If = 0, the current drawing's On/Off, Freeze/Thaw, color, and linetype settings for Xref-dependent layers take precedence over the Xref's layer definition. If = 1 (the default value), these settings don't take precedence.
VSMAX	3D point		The upper-right corner of the current viewport's virtual screen, expressed in UCS coordinates (read-only)
VSMIN	3D point		The lower-left corner of the current viewport's virtual screen, expressed in UCS coordinates (read-only)
WORLDUCS	Integer		If = 1, the current UCS is the same as the World Coordinate System. If = 0, it is not (read-only).
WORLDVIEW	Integer	Drawing	DVIEW and VPOINT command input is relative to the current UCS. If this variable is set to 1, the current UCS is changed to the WCS for the duration of a DVIEW or VPOINT command. Default value = 1.
XREFCTL	Integer	Config	Controls whether .xlg files (external reference log files) are written: 0 = Xref log (.xlg) files not written 1 = Xref log (.xlg) files written

LOADING AutoLISP AND ADS PROGRAMS

One way to load an AutoLISP or ADS program is to use the *Applications...* option in the *File* pull-down menu. Selecting this option produces the *Load AutoLISP and ADS Files* dialogue box (Fig. B-1).

The first time you use this dialogue box, no files appear in the *Files to Load* list. Generally, the first step is to use the *File...* tile to find the desired files (AutoLISP or ADS programs) to load. The options are briefly explained below Figure B-1.

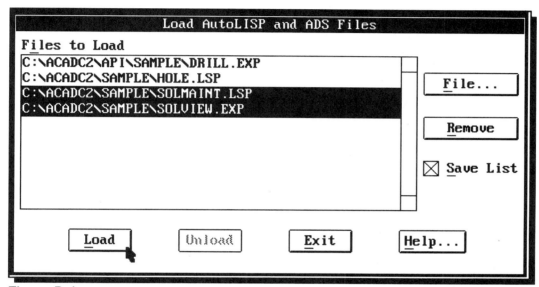

Figure B-1

File...

This option allows you to search for and select files to add to the list box shown above. When you select this option, the standard format file selection dialogue box appears (Fig B-2). Any files selected via the file selection dialogue are added to the list box above.

Remove

This option removes the highlighted selection(s) from the list box in the *Load AutoLISP and ADS Files* dialogue box.

Load

This option loads the ADS and AutoLISP applications that are highlighted. PICK one or more files in the list and select the *Load* tile. The applications can then be started in AutoCAD like any other AutoCAD command by typing the command name at the command prompt.

Save List

> If this box contains a check, the list of files is saved for the next time you use AutoCAD. In this way, you do not have to search for the files again. The list is saved in a file called APPLOAD.DFS. The file names and their paths are saved, but the files are not automatically loaded the next time you start AutoCAD.

The standard file dialogue box (Fig. B-2) appears when you select the _File..._ option from the _Load AutoLISP and ADS Files_ dialogue box.

Assuming that AutoCAD was installed on your system with the default directory and sub-directory names, the AutoCAD sample programs are located in the ACAD12/SUPPORT, ACAD12/SAMPLE, or ACAD12/API/SAMPLE subdirectories.

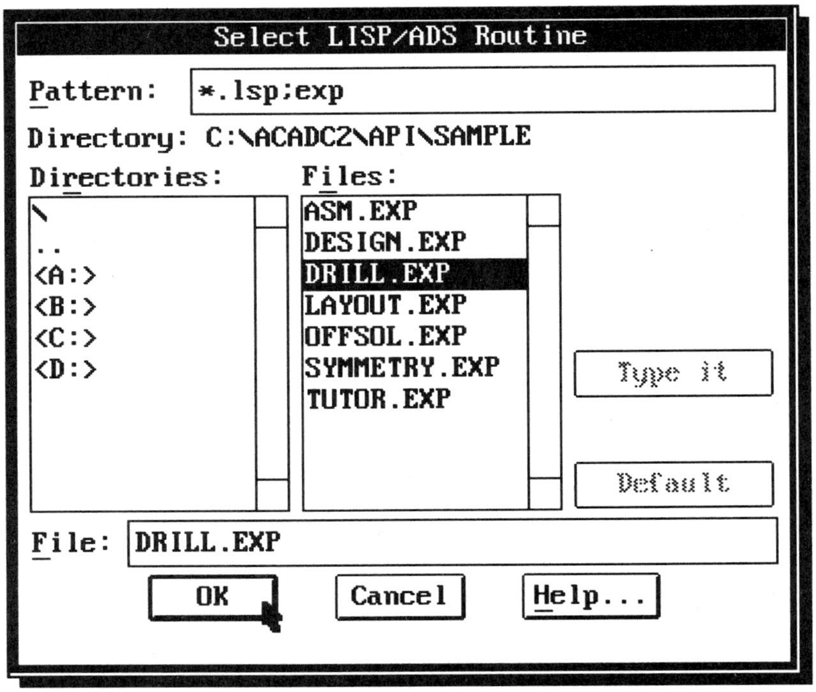

Figure B-2

LOAD, XLOAD

Another method for loading AutoLISP and ADS programs is to use the _Load_ and _Xload_ commands, respectively, at the command prompt. For example, if you wanted to load an AutoLISP program called SOLMAINT.LSP, the following command syntax is used.

Command: _(load "solmaint")_

The parentheses ( ) and the quotation marks " " must be used in the manner demonstrated above. This action would load the file so that it could be invoked like any other AutoCAD command. To start the program, type the following at the command prompt.

Command: _solmaint_

To load and start an <u>ADS</u> program, the format is the same, but you must use the *Xload* command. For example, to load the DRILL.EXP program, use the following command format.

Command: *(xload "drill")*

This action loads the file. Start the program by typing the name at the Command prompt.

Command: *drill*

The AutoLISP and ADS programs are listed by the file name with either the .LSP (AutoLISP) or the .EXP (ADS) extension (or .EXE for AutoCAD for Windows).

INSTALLING AutoCAD

There are several steps involved in installing AutoCAD Release 12 and preparing the software and hardware to run properly. The *AutoCAD Interface, Installation, and Performance Guide* should be used to guide you in the installation process. This guide is one of the many manuals Autodesk includes with the purchase of AutoCAD software. The general installation steps are:

1. Make sure your hardware is operational and complies with the "System Requirements" listed in Chapter 1 of the installation guide. AutoCAD Release 12 requires approximately 26 megabytes of disk space.

2. Install the software by following the instructions in Chapter 2, "Installing AutoCAD." AutoCAD has an automatic installation program which creates the necessary directories and copies the necessary files to your hard disk. A batch file is created that you can use to start AutoCAD. This batch file contains the required environment variables that are needed for AutoCAD to run properly.

3. Configure AutoCAD by following the steps given in Chapter 3 of the installation guide, "Configuring AutoCAD." This chapter leads you through the process of indicating the peripheral devices and related software drivers (plotter, printer, video display driver, etc.) that you want to use with your computer system.

4. Create a working directory to use as the default directory when drawing with AutoCAD. The working directory is usually where drawing files are saved and where AutoCAD creates the temporary files it needs to operate. For file management and security reasons, you should not use the same directory where the AutoCAD program files are located (usually C:\ACAD12). If you don't know how to make directories and change directories, consult your DOS manual for use of the MD and CD commands.

5. Maximize the speed and efficiency of AutoCAD performance on your computer system. Guidelines are given in Chapter 4 of the installation guide, "Performance." This chapter helps you make changes to the CONFIG.SYS, AUTOEXEC.BAT and start-up batch files for AutoCAD. Memory management and environment variables are also explained in this chapter.

Because each computer system is different and AutoCAD is a complex program that utilizes many aspects of a computer's capabilities, it is necessary to set up AutoCAD to run properly on your system. The *AutoCAD Interface, Installation, and Performance Guide* is fairly comprehensive and should encompass just about any installation situation. Be prepared, however, to read the suggested chapters and to spend the time needed to install, configure, and maximize the performance of AutoCAD for your system.

MECHANICAL TABLE OF LIMITS SETTINGS
(X axis x Y axis)

Paper Size (Inches)	Drawing Scale Factor 1 / Scale 1"=1" / Plot 1=1	1.33 / 3"=4" / 3/4=1	2 / 1"=2" / 1/2=1	2.67 / 3"=8" / 3/8=1	4 / 1"=4" / 1/4=1	5.33 / 3"=16" / 3/16=1	8 / 1"=8" / 1=8
A 11 x 8.5 In	11.0 x 8.5	14.4 x 11.3	22.0 x 17.0	29.3 x 22.7	44.0 x 34.0	58.7 x 45.3	88.0 x 68.0
B 17 x 11 In	17.0 x 11.0	22.7 x 14.7	34.0 x 22.0	45.3 x 29.3	68.0 x 44.0	90.7 x 58.7	136.0 x 88.0
C 22 x 17 In	22.0 x 17.0	29.3 x 22.7	44.0 x 34.0	58.7 x 45.3	88.0 x 68.0	117.0 x 90.7	176.0 x 136.0
D 34 x 22 In	34.0 x 22.0	45.3 x 29.3	68.0 x 44.0	90.7 x 58.7	136.0 x 88.0	181.0 x 117.0	272.0 x 176.0
E 44 x 34 In	44.0 x 34.0	58.7 x 45.3	88.0 x 68.0	117.0 x 90.7	176.0 x 136.0	235.0 x 181.0	352.0 x 272.0

ARCHITECTURAL TABLE OF LIMITS SETTINGS
(X axis x Y axis)

Paper Size (Inches)		Drawing Scale Factor 12 Scale 1" = 1' Plot 1 = 12	16 3/4" = 1' 1 = 16	24 1/2" = 1' 1 = 24	32 3/8" = 1' 1 = 32	48 1/4" = 1' 1 = 48	96 1/8" = 1' 1 = 96
A 12 x 9	Ft	12 x 9	16.3 x 12	24 x 18	32 x 24	48 x 36	96 x 72
	In	144 x 108	192 x 144	288 x 216	384 x 288	576 x 432	1152 x 864
B 18 x 12	Ft	18 x 12	24 x 16	36 x 24	48 x 32	72 x 48	144 x 96
	In	216 x 144	288 x 192	432 x 288	576 x 384	864 x 576	1728 x 1152
C 24 x 18	Ft	24 x 18	32 x 24	48 x 36	64 x 48	96 x 72	192 x 144
	In	288 x 216	384 x 288	576 x 432	768 x 576	1152 x 864	2304 x 1728
D 36 x 24	Ft	36 x 24	48 x 32	72 x 48	96 x 64	144 x 96	288 x 192
	In	432 x 288	576 x 384	864 x 576	1152 x 768	1728 x 1152	3456 x 2304
E 48 x 36	Ft	48 x 36	64 x 48	96 x 72	128 x 96	192 x 144	384 x 288
	In	576 x 432	768 x 576	1152 x 864	1536 x 1152	2304 x 1728	4608 x 3465

METRIC TABLE OF LIMITS SETTING
(X axis x Y axis)

Paper Size (mm)		Drawing Scale Factor 25.4 / Scale 1:1 / Plot 1 = 1	50.8 / 1:2 / 1 = 2	127 / 1:5 / 1 = 5	254 / 1:10 / 1 = 10	508 / 1:20 / 1 = 20	1270 / 1:50 / 1 = 50	2540 / 1:100 / 1 = 100
A4 297 x 210	mm	297 x 210	594 x 420	1485 x 1050	2970 x 2100	5940 x 4200	14,850 x 10,500	29,700 x 21,000
	m	.297 x .210	.594 x 420	1.485 x 1.050	2.97 x 2.10	5.94 x 4.20	14.85 x 10.50	29.70 x 21.00
A3 420 x 297	mm	420 x 297	840 x 594	2100 x 1485	4200 x 2970	8400 x 5940	21,000 x 14,850	42,000 x 29,700
	m	.420 x .297	.840 x .594	2.100 x 1.485	4.20 x 2.97	8.40 x 5.94	21.00 x 14.85	42.00 x 29.70
A2 594 x 420	mm	594 x 420	1188 x 840	2970 x 2100	5940 x 4200	11,880 x 8400	29,700 x 21,000	59,400 x 42,000
	m	.594 x .420	1.188 x .840	2.970 x 2.100	5.94 x 4.20	11.88 x 8.40	29.70 x 21.00	59.40 x 42.00
A1 841 x 594	mm	841 x 594	1682 x 1188	4205 x 2970	8410 x 5940	16,820 x 11,880	42,050 x 29,700	84,100 x 59,400
	m	.841 x .594	1.682 x 1.188	4.205 x 2.970	8.41 x 5.94	16.82 x 11.88	42.05 x 29.70	84.10 x 59.40
A0 1189 x 841	mm	1189 x 841	2378 x 1682	5945 x 4205	11,890 x 8410	23,780 x 16,820	59,450 x 42,050	118,900 x 84,100
	m	1.189 x .841	2.378 x 1.682	5.945 x 4.205	11.89 x 8.41	23.78 x 16.82	59.45 x 42.05	118.9 x 84.10

CIVIL TABLE OF LIMITS SETTINGS
(X axis x Y axis)

Paper Size (Inches)		Drawing Scale Factor 120 — Scale 1" = 10' — Plot 1 = 120	240 1" = 20' 1 = 240	360 1" = 30' 1 = 360	480 1" = 40' 1 = 480	600 1" = 50' 1 = 600
A. 11 x 8½	In	1320 x 1020	2640 x 2040	3960 x 3060	5280 x 4080	6600 x 5100
	Ft	110 x 85	170 x 110	330 x 255	440 x 340	550 x 425
B. 17 x 11	In	2040 x 1320	4080 x 2640	6120 x 3960	8160 x 5280	10,200 x 6600
	Ft	170 x 110	340 x 220	510 x 330	680 x 440	850 x 550
C. 22 x 17	In	2640 x 2040	5280 x 4080	7920 x 6120	10,560 x 8160	13,200 x 10,200
	Ft	220 x 170	440 x 340	660 x 510	880 x 680	1100 x 850
D. 34 x 22	In	4080 x 2640	8160 x 5280	12,240 x 7920	16,320 x 10,560	20,400 x 13,200
	Ft	340 x 220	680 x 440	1020 x 660	1360 x 880	1700 x 1100
E. 44 x 34	In	5280 x 4080	10,560 x 8160	15,840 x 12,240	21,120 x 16,320	26,400 x 20,400
	Ft	440 x 340	880 x 680	1320 x 1020	1760 x 1360	2200 x 1700

CAD References for *Engineering Graphics Communication*, Bertoline, et al.

NA=Not Applicable--capabilities not
provided in AutoCAD or not discussed.

INDEX